TEXT COVERAGE

Presented in the chart below are topics described by Educational Testing Services as being "Representative descriptions of topics covered in each category. The list, however, is not exhaustive." Also presented are chapters in the text in which the topics are discussed.

Praxis Language Arts Topics[1]

Topic	1	2	3	4	5	6	7	8	9	10	11	12	13
Teaching strategies and activities that will aid in the development, delivery, and evaluation of the following:													
Balanced reading, writing, speaking, and listening programs[2]	✔									✔	✔		✔
Integration into other content areas								✔	✔				
Scope and sequence of skills and materials		✔		✔	✔		✔				✔		
Learner objectives			✔	✔	✔	✔	✔	✔			✔		✔
Curricular materials–developmentally appropriate basal readers and anthologies; trade books; reference and nonfiction materials; children's literature; technology		✔	✔	✔	✔	✔	✔	✔	✔	✔			✔
Knowledge and understanding of topics, procedures, and methods (such as various teaching and learning strategies like guided instruction or modeling)			✔	✔	✔	✔	✔	✔	✔	✔	✔	✔	✔
Reading Instruction													
Determining individual reading levels		✔											
Language acquisition and readiness such as: knowing letter-sound correlations; concepts of print; spacing of words in reading and writing[2]	✔		✔										
Prereading instruction–for example, K-W-L chart; word recognition; structural analysis; semantics; syntactic; phonics; scanning				✔	✔	✔	✔	✔	✔	✔			
During reading–for example, vocabulary development; comprehension; reading aloud; word recognition; syllabication; decoding; graphic organizers				✔	✔	✔	✔	✔	✔	✔			
Post reading–for example, concept vocabulary; writing-journaling; reactions; comprehension and interpretations; rewriting information						✔	✔	✔	✔	✔	✔		
Writing, spelling, and listening[2]			✔								✔		
Writing process			✔								✔		
Stages of development—for example, invented spelling; use of words with prefixes and suffixes; proper punctuation; spacing and control in handwriting[2]			✔	✔							✔		
Memorization								✔					
Methods of adjusting instruction to meet students' needs–for example, what is appropriate and why; effective implementation, organization, and planning; reteaching, enrichment, and extensions			✔	✔	✔	✔	✔	✔	✔	✔	✔	✔	✔
Strategies for motivation and encouraging success–for example, feedback and follow-ups; cooperative groups; modeling; flexible skill groups	✔		✔	✔	✔	✔	✔	✔	✔	✔	✔	✔	✔
Assessment													
Analysis of student work		✔	✔	✔	✔	✔	✔	✔	✔	✔	✔		
Identifying strengths and weaknesses, misconceptions and errors, patterns		✔	✔	✔				✔	✔		✔		
Recognizing stages of development			✔	✔							✔		
Adjusting instruction			✔	✔	✔	✔	✔	✔	✔		✔		
Traditional and standardized forms of assessments			✔										
Basal reader assessments			✔							✔			
Fry Readability Index			✔										
Informal assessments			✔	✔	✔	✔	✔	✔	✔		✔	✔	✔
Informal reading inventory, miscue analysis, running record, cloze procedure			✔										
Anecdotal record			✔										
Conferencing			✔							✔	✔	✔	
Retellings			✔										
Portfolios			✔								✔		
Journals			✔								✔		

---

[1]Topics for this chart were taken from a description of the reading/language arts section of Praxis 0011 Elementary Education: Curriculum, Instruction, and Assessment. Available online at http://www.ets.org/media/tests/praxis/pdf/0011.pdf
[2]Handwriting, speaking, and listening are not covered in this text. Developmental spelling is discussed but not techniques for teaching spelling.

Where the classroom comes to life!

From watching actual classroom video footage of teachers and students interacting to building standards-based lessons and web-based portfolios . . . from a robust resource library of the "What Every Teacher Should Know About" series to complete instruction on writing an effective research paper . . . **MyLabSchool** brings together an amazing collection of resources for future teachers. This website gives you a wealth of videos, print and simulated cases, career advice, and much more.

Use **MyLabSchool** with this Allyn and Bacon Education text, and you will have everything you need to succeed in your course. Assignment IDs have also been incorporated into many Allyn and Bacon Education texts to link to the online material in **MyLabSchool** . . . connecting the teachers of tomorrow to the information they need today.

PEARSON **A/B**

VISIT www.mylabschool.com **to learn more about this invaluable resource and Take a Tour!**

Here's what you'll find in mylabschool
Where the classroom comes to life!

VideoLab ▶

Access hundreds of video clips of actual classroom situations from a variety of grade levels and school settings. These 3- to 5-minute closed-captioned video clips illustrate real teacher–student interaction, and are organized both topically *and* by discipline. Students can test their knowledge of classroom concepts with integrated observation questions.

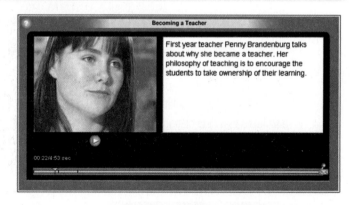

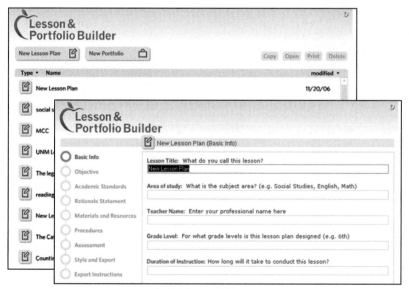

◀ Lesson & Portfolio Builder

This feature enables students to create, maintain, update, and share online portfolios and standards-based lesson plans. The Lesson Planner walks students, step-by-step, through the process of creating a complete lesson plan, including verifiable objectives, assessments, and related state standards. Upon completion, the lesson plan can be printed, saved, e-mailed, or uploaded to a website.

Here's what you'll find in ◖mylabschool™
Where the classroom comes to life!

Simulations ►

This area of MyLabSchool contains interactive tools designed to better prepare future teachers to provide an appropriate education to students with special needs. To achieve this goal, the IRIS (IDEA and Research for Inclusive Settings) Center at Vanderbilt University has created course enhancement materials. These resources include online interactive modules, case study units, information briefs, student activities, an online dictionary, and a searchable directory of disability-related web sites.

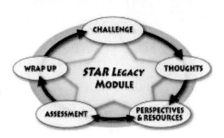

◄ Resource Library

MyLabSchool includes a collection of PDF files on crucial and timely topics within education. Each topic is applicable to any education class, and these documents are ideal resources to prepare students for the challenges they will face in the classroom. This resource can be used to reinforce a central topic of the course, or to enhance coverage of a topic you need to explore in more depth.

Research Navigator ►

This comprehensive research tool gives users access to four exclusive databases of authoritative and reliable source material. It offers a comprehensive, step-by-step walk-through of the research process. In addition, students can view sample research papers and consult guidelines on how to prepare endnotes and bibliographies. The latest release also features a new bibliography-maker program—AutoCite.

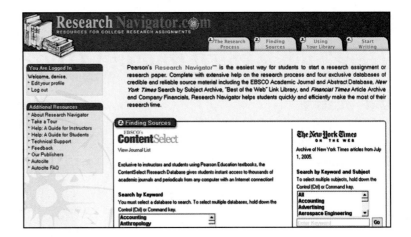

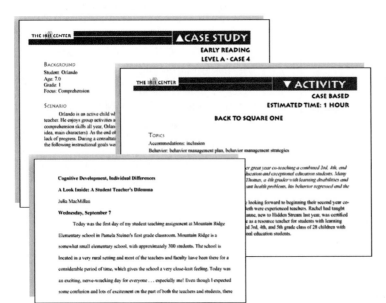

◄ Case Archive

This collection of print and simulated cases can be easily accessed by topic and subject area, and can be integrated into your course. The cases are drawn from Allyn & Bacon's best-selling books, and represent the complete range of disciplines and student ages. It's an ideal way to consider and react to real classroom scenarios. The possibilities for using these high-quality cases within the course are endless.

Creating Literacy Instruction for All Students

Sixth Edition

Creating Literacy Instruction for All Students

Thomas G. Gunning

Professor Emeritus, Southern Connecticut State University
Adjunct Professor, Central Connecticut State University

PEARSON
A&B

Boston   New York   San Francisco
Mexico City   Montreal   Toronto   London   Madrid   Munich   Paris
Hong Kong   Singapore   Tokyo   Cape Town   Sydney

Executive Editor: Aurora Martínez Ramos
Senior Development Editor: Mary Kriener
Series Editorial Assistant: Lynda Giles
Executive Marketing Manager: Krista Clark
Production Editor: Paula Carroll
Editorial Production Service: Lifland et al., Bookmakers
Composition Buyer: Linda Cox
Manufacturing Buyer: Megan Cochran
Electronic Composition: Modern Graphics, Inc.
Interior Design: Anne Flanagan
Photo Researcher: Helane Prottas
Cover Administrator: Linda Knowles

For related titles and support materials, visit our online catalog at www.ablongman.com.

Previous editions were published under the title *Creating Reading Instruction for All Children*, copyright © 2003, 2000, 1996, 1992 by Pearson Education, Inc.

Portions of this work are also published under the title *Creating Literacy for All Students in Grades 4 to 8, Second Edition*.

To obtain permission(s) to use material from this work, please submit a written request to Allyn and Bacon, Permissions Department, 75 Arlington Street, Boston, MA 02116 or fax your request to 617-848-7320.

Between the time website information is gathered and then published, it is not unusual for some sites to have closed. Also, the transcription of URLs can result in typographical errors. The publisher would appreciate notification where these errors occur so that they may be corrected in subsequent editions.

Library of Congress Cataloging-in-Publication Data

Gunning, Thomas G.
    Creating literacy instruction for all students / Thomas G. Gunning. — 6th ed.
        p. cm.
    Includes bibliographical references and index.
        ISBN 0-205-52366-8
        1. Reading (Elementary) 2. English language—Composition and exercises—Study and teaching (elementary) I. Title.

LB1573.G93 2007
372.4–dc22

                                                                                    2006048037

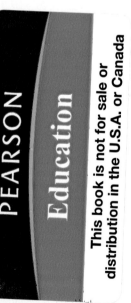

Printed in the United States of America
10 9 8 7 6 5 4 3   VHP 11 10 09 08

Credits appear on page 597, which constitutes an extension of the copyright page.

About the Author

Thomas G. Gunning has taught courses in methods of teaching reading and writing for more than 20 years and was director of the Reading Clinic at Southern Connecticut State University. Before that, as a secondary English teacher, a reading specialist, and an elementary school reading consultant, he worked extensively with achieving and struggling readers and writers. Dr. Gunning, who recently served as a Reading First consultant, is currently working with elementary school students to help them develop higher-level literacy skills, as well as serving as an adjunct professor in the Reading/Language Arts Department at Central Connecticut State University.

Over the years, Dr. Gunning's research has explored reading interests, informal reading inventories, decoding strategies, readability, higher-level literacy skills, and response to intervention. As a result of this research, he has created a number of informal assessments and programs for developing decoding and comprehension skills.

As a well-known and highly regarded textbook author, Dr. Gunning has written and revised such titles as *Developing Higher-Level Literacy in All Students: Building Reading, Reasoning, and Responding; Assessing and Correcting Reading and Writing Difficulties; Closing the Literacy Gap; Building Literacy in the Content Areas; Best Books for Building Literacy for Elementary School Children;* and *Building Words: A Resource Manual for Teaching Word Analysis and Spelling Strategies*—all published by Allyn & Bacon. Dr. Gunning is also the author of a number of children's books, including *Dream Cars* (Dillon Press) and *Amazing Escapes* (Dodd, Mead).

Brief Contents

Contents

2   Evaluation   24

3 Fostering Emergent/Early Literacy 86

4 Teaching Phonics, High-Frequency Words, and Syllabic Analysis 152

5   Building Vocabulary   224

6   Comprehension: Theory and Strategies   270

7 Comprehension: Text Structures and Teaching Procedures 318

8   Reading and Writing in the Content Areas
and Study Skills   356

9   Reading Literature   394

10 Approaches to Teaching Reading   430

11   Writing and Reading   464

12   Diversity in the Literacy Classroom: Adapting Instruction for English Language and At-Risk Learners   504

13 Creating and Managing a Literacy Program   532

Special Features

Reinforcement Activities

Student Strategies

Preface

This book will not tell you how to teach reading and writing. Teaching literacy is in large measure a matter of making choices: Should you use basal reader anthologies or children's books, or both? Should you teach children to read whole words or to sound out words letter by letter, or both? Should you have three reading groups or four, or no groups? There are no right answers to these questions. The answers depend on your personal philosophy, your interpretation of the research, the level at which you are teaching, the kinds of students you are teaching, community preferences, and the nature of your school's or school district's reading program.

What this book will do is help you discover approaches and techniques that fit your teaching style and your teaching situation. Its aim is to present as fairly, completely, and clearly as possible the major approaches and techniques shown by research and practice to be successful. This book also presents the theories behind the methods, so you will be free to choose, adapt, and/or construct approaches and techniques that best fit your style and teaching situation. You will be creating literacy instruction.

Although the text emphasizes approaches and techniques, methods are only a portion of the equation. Reading is not just a process; it is also very much a content area. What students read *does* matter, and, therefore, I have provided recommendations for specific children's books and other reading materials. The basic premise of this book is that the best reading programs result from a combination of effective techniques and plenty of worthwhile reading material.

Because children differ greatly in their backgrounds, needs, and interests, the book offers a variety of suggestions for both techniques and types of books to be used. The intent is to provide you with sufficient background knowledge of teaching methods, children's books, and other materials to enable you to create effective instruction for all the children you teach, whether they are rich or poor; bright, average, or slow; with disabilities or without; urban or suburban; or from any of the diverse cultural and ethnic groups found in today's classrooms.

This book also recognizes that reading is part of a larger language process; therefore, considerable attention is paid to writing and the other language arts, especially as these relate to reading instruction. Whether reading or writing is being addressed, emphasis is on making the students the center of instruction. For instance, activities are recommended that allow students to choose writing topics and reading materials. Approaches that foster a personal response to reading are also advocated. Just as you are encouraged by this text to create your own reading instruction, students must be encouraged to create their own literacy.

Changes to the Sixth Edition

During the three years that have elapsed since the fifth edition of this book, I have worked as a Reading First consultant and have also assisted intermediate students in an urban school. Most of that work was hands-on. I assessed students; taught phonics, syllabic analysis, vocabulary, and comprehension lessons; helped implement a new literacy program; examined data; attended grade-level meetings and study groups; obtained materials; created a leveling system and implemented it; monitored progress; and created an intervention program, including training tutors. I observed teachers in a variety of schools and talked to dozens of literacy specialists. Based on insights gained during this extensive first-hand experience, I have made a number of revisions in this sixth edition.

- Perhaps the most important insight gained from my recent work experience was the necessity of **building higher-level literacy skills**, a key element in NCLB's mandate to close the literacy gap. In focusing on the development of basic decoding skills and literal comprehension, teachers often end up neglecting both vocabulary and higher-level literacy skills. Therefore, the sixth edition has been infused with suggestions for fostering higher-level literacy. A special section called *Building Higher-Level Literacy* appears at the end of each chapter, and marginal annotations on higher-level literacy are found throughout the book. These include suggestions for developing the writing skills needed to answer higher-level questions.

HIGHER-LEVEL LITERACY

Use the language of thinking. Ask students to compare, contrast, analyze, infer, predict, or engage in whatever other thought process is appropriate (Gunning, 2007). Also, demonstrate the process: Show how you would compare, contrast, predict, etc. Think aloud as you demonstrate the process so that students gain insight into cognitive processes.

Tools for the Classroom

Building Higher-Level Literacy

Ironically, at-risk learners are typically presented with programs that foster basic skills but neglect higher-level thinking. Depending upon the factors causing them to be at risk, these students might have a more difficult time acquiring higher-level skills. For instance, they may have a more limited background of experience, or they might have attended a school that neglected higher-level skills. Consequently, at-risk learners need more instruction and experience aimed at building higher-level literacy, not less. When working with at-risk learners, purposely include activities designed to enrich their reading, writing, and responding.

Help for Struggling Readers and Writers

As you have undoubtedly noticed, most of the techniques presented in this chapter are the same as those discussed in previous chapters. In general, the techniques that work with achieving readers also work with students who are at risk. The chief difference in working with at-risk students is making appropriate adaptations and modifications. The following framework for planning a classroom intervention program is based on the major principles covered in this chapter and the exemplary intervention programs reviewed. The

- When instruction is aligned with and based on continuous monitoring of progress, results are dramatic. To foster this kind of assessment, the concept of **assessing for learning** has been amplified in this text, and marginal notes on this concept have been added throughout.

- Good teaching, parental interest, a well-stocked public library with caring librarians, and engaging texts set the stage for moving children from novice readers to fully engaged readers who internalize literacy as part of defining themselves. The power of engagement should be the core of a literacy program, and so **fostering engagement** is emphasized throughout this text.

ASSESSING FOR LEARNING

As the group reads silently, unobtrusively tap students on the shoulder as a signal to read orally to you (Fountas & Pinnell, 2006). Note needs and supply assistance. For word recognition needs, use the prompts presented on pp. 265.

FOSTERING ENGAGEMENT

Being involved in selecting words for study can be highly motivating to all students, but especially struggling readers. To limit the number of words chosen for class study, you might have students meet in small groups to discuss their words and select one for class study. Each group then presents its word to the class.

- Seeing firsthand the challenges that teachers face as they attempt to leave no child behind, I have tried to make the text **even more practical and as helpful to literacy teachers** as ever. Thus, this edition includes
  - several ways to make teaching phonics more effective;
  - more information on the use of data, including an expanded exploration of continuous progress monitoring;
  - a new leveling measure for beginning reading materials that grades books in terms of the phonics skills needed to read them;

- emphasis on enriched discussion and use of discussion groups, including exploration of accountable talk, which is important for developing higher-level thinking skills;

- a voluntary reading program that is more focused and more effective;

- a more organized, systematic approach to the use of graphic organizers;

- additional accounts of classroom practices;

- additional information about study groups and grade-level meetings;

- information on response to intervention (RTI), the newly adopted approach for identifying students who might be learning disabled, and coverage of the implications this has for classroom instruction; and

- exploration of some problematical practices.

Within each chapter of the sixth edition various discussions have been enhanced and new topics have been introduced to reflect the latest trends and research in literacy education:

Chapter 1

- Engaged Reading: Explains how engaged reading can lead to higher achievement.

- Impact of No Child Left Behind: Provides statistical data and a description of a school that was transformed by the impetus of NCLB.

- Response to Intervention (RTI): Providing instruction and seeing how students do may be used to identify students with learning disabilities. RTI results in obtaining timely assistance for struggling readers and writers. Suggestions for implementing RTI are provided.

- Building Higher-Level Literacy: Offers examples of the need for instruction in higher-level skills. Every chapter provides suggestions for building higher-level skills.

- Classroom Management for Learning: Students perform better when a classroom management system has been put in place.

Chapter 2

- Formative Assessment/Assessment for Learning: Formative assessment provides a basis for more effective instruction. Suggestions for assessment for learning are made throughout the text.

- Alignment of Assessment and Instruction: Alignment needs to be flexible.

- Instructionally Supportive Assessment: Identifies steps that can be followed so that information from tests can be used to improve instruction.

- Using Data to Improve Instruction: Successful schools use a variety of data to improve their programs.

- Rubrics for Constructed Responses: Rubrics can be used as a guide for students as they answer open-ended questions and for teachers as they help students improve their responses.

- Creating a Literacy Profile for English Learners: A literacy profile includes background information that can be used to better plan programs for ELLs.

- Measuring Growth: Explains why measuring the same students at the beginning of the year and then at the end of the year is better than comparing this year's students with last year's.

- Adaptive Tests: Describes computerized tests that adapt to the level of the student.

- Group Observation Sheet: Provides a device for obtaining observation data on students' grasp of key skills.

Chapter 3

- Using Prop Boxes: Props can be used to build vocabulary and background during read-alouds.

- Selecting Read-Aloud Books

- Dialogic Reading: In this form of shared book reading, questioning and prompts are used with a small group to develop deeper understanding in three successive readings.

- Exemplary Teaching: A new feature on "Writing with Corduroy"

- Exemplary Teaching: A new feature on "The Power of an Intriguing Book."

Chapter 4

- Differentiation of Phonics Instruction: Explains why grouping students for instruction according to their level of achievement is a better practice than whole-class instruction.

- New Approach to Teaching Clusters: Based on personal trials, the author offers an approach that eases the mastery of teaching clusters.

- Developmental Nature of Phonics Instruction: Explains why instruction should be geared to students' development and how this might be done.

- Balancing Decodable Text with Predictable Books: Explains the value of using both kinds of texts.

- Taking a Flexible Approach to Teaching Phonics: Explains the necessity of being able to adapt instruction.

- Monitoring Progress in Phonics: Explains and presents a method for periodically monitoring phonics. The system is based on the author's own work.
- Readability Based on Phonics Elements: Presents a leveling system based on the phonics elements needed to read a text.

Chapter 5

- Story Impressions: Based on previewing vocabulary from a story, students predict what the story might be.
- Word Experts: Students teach each other words.
- Deriving the Meaning of a Word from Context: This discussion has been revised based on recent research. This approach to teaching context clues emphasizes the use of the reader's background knowledge.

Chapter 6

- Surface Features of Text: Explains the importance of decoding skills, vocabulary, and fluency in comprehension.
- Status of Higher-Level Comprehension: A recent study shows which higher-level skills most students have learned and which pose problems.
- Strategy Instruction (Key Steps): Explains the six steps of strategy instruction.
- Prediction Chart: Helps students make predictions based upon evidence and also to change predictions.
- Making Inferences with It Says–I Say–And So: This chart provides the basic steps for drawing and supporting inferences.
- Macro-Cloze: Students use inferential skills to supply missing sentences.
- Difficulty Drawing Conclusions: Describes techniques used to help students draw conclusions.

Chapter 7

- Accountable Talk: This approach helps raise the quality and value of classroom discussions.
- Think-Pair-Share: Students share their thoughts and responses with each other.

Chapter 8

- Key Graphic Organizers: Provides a plan for systematically using eight carefully selected graphic organizers to represent key thinking and text patterns.
- Effective Test Preparation: Provides research-based suggestions for building overall achievement as well as preparation for high-stakes tests.
- Locate and Recall: An Essential Test-Taking Skill: Suggests steps for teaching this skill, which is based on an

analysis of students' responses, and is essential in answering open-ended questions. Failure to go back to selections and locate needed information or support is the number one reason why students have difficulty with constructed responses.

Chapter 9

- Exemplary Teaching: A new feature on "Developing Discussion Skills."
- Procedures for Literature Discussion Groups: A new chart lists the key steps in implementing and conducting discussions.
- Strategic Literature Discussions: Provides research-based suggestions for building strategies during literature discussions.
- Discussion Moves: Explains moves that can be used to make discussions more effective.
- Responding in Writing: Explains that in addition to responding orally, students should respond in writing, since that is how they will be assessed.
- Theme Analysis: Explores the importance of themes and techniques for helping students discover themes.
- Character Chart: Helps students make inferences about characters' traits.
- Revised Program for Fostering Self-Selected Reading: Identifies steps that can be taken to increase the benefit that students derive from self-selected reading.

Chapter 11

- Quickwrites: Explains the value of quickwrites and provides suggestions for introducing and fostering them.

Chapter 12

- Stages of Second-Language Acquisition: Discusses how instruction for English learners might be geared to their stage of English acquisition.

Chapter 13

- Study Groups and Grade-Level Meetings: Explains the role that study groups and grade-level meetings play in continued professional development.
- Using Reading to Close the Gap: Has suggestions for determining how much reading students are doing and suggestions for increasing that amount.

Appendix B

- Phonics Progress Monitoring Assessment: This assessment device, which is based on the author's work in schools, incorporates the sequence of skills presented in most programs and can be used to track students' progress.

Features of the Text

Throughout the sixth edition of *Creating Literacy Instruction for All Students*, special pedagogical features draw the reader's attention to issues of recurring importance in literacy instruction as well as aid with review and understanding of key concepts.

- **Case Studies** offer perspectives of teachers at work improving their programs.

Case Study

Teaching Vocabulary to
English Language Learners

Edguardo, a sixth-grader, is a conscientious, highly motivated student. Having attended a dual-language school since kindergarten, he is reading on grade level in Spanish and is fluent in English. Although his decoding skills in English reading are on grade level, Edguardo has difficulty with comprehension. He feels overwhelmed when he meets a number of words that he doesn't know. As might be expected of an ELL, Edguardo's English vocabulary is somewhat below grade level. Because he has had less opportunity to develop English vocabulary, Edguardo could benefit from a program of intensive vocabulary instruction. A general program of vocabulary development would be helpful. But even more effective would be a program designed to teach Edguardo, or any other student in similar circumstances, the words that he is most likely to meet in texts.

For Edguardo and other ELLs, much of their word learning will involve learning the English equivalent of words already known in their first language. When Edguardo learns the word *moon*, he need only associate it with the known Spanish word for moon, *luna*. In addition, there are thousands of cognates, words such as *artista, autor, contento*. See Table 12.3 (on p. 513) for a listing of high-frequency cognates.

- **IRA Position Statement** features sum up key issues, such as high-stakes testing and teaching English language learners, on which the International Reading Association has published position papers.

The IRA recognizes that the teaching of phonics is an essential part of beginning reading instruction. "However, effective phonics instruction must be embedded in the context of a total reading/language arts program. . . . Classroom teachers in the primary grades do value and do teach phonics as part of their reading programs. . . . Effective teachers of reading and writing ask when, how, how much, and under what circumstances phonics should be taught" (International Reading Association, 1999c). The IRA is against "curricular mandates that require teachers to blindly follow highly prescriptive plans for phonics instruction" but supports "curriculum development that effectively integrates phonics into the total reading program."

IRA Position Statement

on Key Issue

The Teaching of Phonics

- Model **Lessons** cover nearly every area of literacy instruction.

Lesson 4.3

Vowel Correspondence

Step 1. Phonemic awareness
Read a selection, such as *Cat Traps* (Coxe, 1996) or *The Cat Sat on the Mat* (Cameron, 1994), in which there are a number of short *a* words. Call student's attention to *a* words from the book: *cat, trap, sat*. Stressing the vowel sound as you say each word, ask students to tell what is the same about the words: "caaat," "traaap," and "saaat." Lead students to see that they all have an /a/ sound as in *cat*.

- **Student Strategies** outline step-by-step strategies to help students become independent learners.

> ### *Student Strategies*
>
> ### Applying the Variability Strategy to Consonant Correspondences
>
>
>
> 1. Try the main pronunciation—the one the letter usually stands for.
> 2. If the main pronunciation gives a word that is not a real one or does not make sense in the sentence, try the other pronunciation.
> 3. If you still get a word that is not a real word or does not make sense in the sentence, ask for help.

- **Reinforcement Activities** provide practice and application, particularly in the area of reading and writing for real purposes.

> ### *Reinforcement Activities*
>
> ### Morphemic Analysis
>
> - Provide students with several long words composed of a number of morphemic units, for example:
>
> | | | |
> |---|---|---|
> | unbelievable | improperly | unimaginable |
> | prehistoric | photographer | disagreeable |
> | irregularly | unfavorable | uncomfortable |
> | unreturnable | misjudgment | oceanographer |
>
> Have them determine the morphemic boundaries and try to figure out what the words mean based on analysis of the units. Good sources of other words to analyze are the texts that students are encountering in class.
>
> - Ask students to create webs of roots and affixes in which the element is displayed in several words (Tompkins & Yaden, 1986). A web for the root *loc* might look like Figure 5.8.

- **Student Reading Lists** are provided in all chapters as a resource for titles that reinforce the particular literacy skills being discussed.
- **Exemplary Teaching** features help make the descriptions of teaching techniques come alive by offering examples of good teaching practices. All are true-life accounts; many

> *W*orking with a class composed primarily of ESL students, Laura Harper (1997) feared that her lessons on revising weren't having much impact. Students' revisions consisted of a few changes here and there and recopying the piece in neater handwriting. She decided to use the revising tools described by Barry Lane (1993) in *After the End.*
>
> After explaining Questions, Harper had pairs of students ask questions about pieces they had written. The students then selected the most appealing questions about their drafts and freewrote on them. As she revised, one student, Elena, rethought her draft and transformed it from a lifeless description of her aunt to a poignant account of her relationship with her aunt.
>
>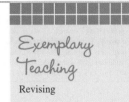
>
> *Exemplary Teaching*
>
> Revising

were drawn from the memoirs of gifted teachers, and others were garnered from newspaper reports or my own observations.

- **Various learning aids**, including Anticipation Guides, a page-by-page glossary, application suggestions, and Checkup questions, are included so that readers can review concepts and enhance understanding.

- **Marginal annotations** provide the reader with interesting, practical, and handy guidance for planning and adapting instruction. These notes are titled Adapting Instruction for Struggling Readers and Writers, Adapting Instruction for English Language Learners, Closing the Gap, Using Technology, Involving Parents, Fostering Engagement, Assessing for Learning, Building Language, Higher-Level Literacy, and FYI (which provide information on a variety of topics).

- The final section in each chapter—**Tools for the Classroom**—provides preservice and inservice teachers with valuable tips in subsections called Building Higher-Level Literacy, Help for Struggling Readers and Writers, Essential Standards, and Assessment. Action Plans in this section translate theory into practice by detailing steps that might be taken to put the major concepts of the chapter into practice.

Building Higher-Level Literacy

Regardless of which approach you use, chances are that it has not made sufficient provision for developing higher-level skills. Higher-level skills take lots of instruction and lots of practice, much more than most commercial programs provide. Supplement the program you are using with additional instruction and practice. Focus on a few key higher-level skills, rather than trying to cover all of them. It is better to teach a few skills in depth than to cover a dozen skills in shallow fashion.

Tools for the Classroom

Help for Struggling Readers and Writers

No single one of the approaches discussed in this chapter is necessarily best for struggling readers and writers. A program such as reading workshop that implements self-selected reading would be less likely to stigmatize poor readers, because students would be able to choose materials on their level. A basal program would offer the structure that struggling readers and writers need. However, it would be imperative that poor readers be given materials on the appropriate level of challenge, perhaps in a guided reading format. A literature-based program would work well, too, as long as students were given the skills instruction they needed and books on the appropriate level. The language-experience approach works well with struggling readers because it is based on their language. When obtaining suitable reading material is a problem because the struggling reader is older but is reading on a very low level, language-experience stories can be used as the student's reading material.

If you are using a basal, take advantage of the materials and techniques suggested for use with students who are struggling. Provide books that the students can handle successfully. Working with students who were struggling with literary selections, Cole (1998) used books from easy-to-read series, including *Step into Reading* (Random House), *Puffin Easy-to-Read* (Penguin), *All Aboard Reading* (Grosset & Dunlap), and *Bank Street Ready to Read* (Bantam). Books from these and other easy-to-read series can be found in Appendix A.

Regardless of the approach used, it is most helpful if struggling readers and writers are given extra instruction, perhaps in a small group. For younger students, there are a number of programs modeled on Reading Recovery. For students in grades 3 through 8, there is a program known as Project Success (Soar to Success) that features graphic organizers, discussion, and the reading of high-interest informational books. The program can be taught within the classroom by the classroom teacher or by a specialist (Cooper, 1996). Literacy programs for struggling readers are discussed in Chapter 13.

Action Plan

1. Become acquainted with the major approaches to teaching reading.
2. Whatever approach you use, incorporate principles of effective literacy instruction. Make sure that students are reading on their levels, are reading widely, are being taught skills in a functional fashion, and are being monitored for progress.

- Each chapter ends with a brief summary and activities designed to extend understanding of key concepts. Extending and Applying provides suggestions for practical applications. Developing a Professional Portfolio offers readers help in creating and maintaining a portfolio for professional development. **MyLabSchool** activities take students into live classrooms via video clips. Developing a Resource File gives practical suggestions for assembling assessment and instructional activities and materials.

Organization of the Text

The text's organization has been designed to reflect the order of the growth of literacy. Chapter 1 stresses the construction of a philosophy of teaching reading and writing. Chapter 2 presents techniques for evaluating individuals and programs so that assessment becomes an integral part of instruction. Chapters 3 and 4 discuss emergent literacy and basic decoding strategies, including phonics, syllabic analysis, and high-frequency words. Chapter 5 presents advanced word-recognition skills and strategies: morphemic analysis, dictionary skills, and techniques for building vocabulary. Chapters 6 through 8 are devoted to comprehension: Chapter 6 emphasizes comprehension strategies that children might use; Chapter 7 focuses on text structures and teaching procedures; Chapter 8 covers application of comprehension skills in the content areas and through studying. Chapter 9 takes a step beyond comprehension by focusing on responding to literature and fostering a love of reading.

Chapters 3 through 9, which emphasize essential reading strategies, constitute the core of the book. Chapters 10 through 13 provide information on creating a well-rounded literacy program. Chapter 10 describes approaches to teaching reading. Chapter 11 explains the process approach to writing and discusses how reading and writing are related. Chapter 12 suggests how previously presented strategies might be used with children from diverse cultures and those with special needs. Chapter 13 pulls all the topics together in a discussion of principles for organizing and implementing a literacy program. Also included in this final chapter is a section on technology and its place in a program of literacy instruction.

This text, designed to be practical, offers detailed explanations, and often examples of applications, for every major technique or strategy. Numerous suggestions for practice activities and reading materials are also included. I hope that this book will furnish you with an in-depth knowledge of literacy methods and materials so that you will be able to construct lively, effective reading and writing instruction for all the students you teach.

Supplements for Instructors and Students

Instructor's Manual with Test Bank and Transparency Masters For each chapter, the instructor's manual features a series of Learner Objectives, a Chapter Overview, suggestions for Before, After, and During Reading, a list of suggested Teaching Activities, Resource Masters (with study guide), and suggestions for Assessment. There is a Test Bank, which contains an assortment of multiple-choice, short essay, and long essay questions for each chapter. This supplement has been written completely by the text author, Tom Gunning.

Computerized Test Bank The printed Test Bank is also available electronically through Allyn & Bacon's computerized testing system, TestGen EQ. The fully networkable test-generating software is now available on multiplatform CD-ROM. The user-friendly interface enables instructors to view, edit, and add questions, transfer questions to tests, and print tests in a variety of fonts. Search and sort features allow instructors to locate questions quickly and arrange them in any preferred order.

PowerPoint™ Presentation Designed for teachers using the text, the PowerPoint™ Presentation consists of a series of slides (ten to twenty per chapter) that can be shown as is or used to make overhead transparencies. The presentation highlights key concepts and major topics for each chapter. It can be found online at the Instructor Resource Center: http://www.ablongman.com/irc.

Companion Web Site (http://www.ablongman.com/ab_gunning_creating_6)
Designed for students reading the text, the Web site includes the following sections: Chapter Overview, Learning Objectives, Practice Tests, and Weblinks.

In addition to the supplements available with *Creating Literacy Instruction for All Students,* Sixth Edition, Allyn & Bacon offers an array of student and instructor supplements on the overall topic of literacy. All are available with this textbook.

Allyn & Bacon Digital Media Archive CD-ROM for Literacy, 2002 This CD-ROM offers still images, video clips, audio clips, Web links, and assorted lecture resources that can be incorporated into multimedia presentations in the classroom.

Professionals in Action: Literacy Video This 90-minute video consists of 10- to 20-minute segments called Developing Phonemic Awareness, Teaching Phonics, Helping Students Become Strategic Readers, Organizing for Teaching with Literature, and Reading Intervention, plus discussions of literacy and brain research. The first four sections of each segment consist of actual classroom teaching footage accompanied by narrative. The final section presents, in question-and-answer format, discussion by leading experts in the field of literacy.

Allyn & Bacon Literacy Video Library Featuring renowned reading scholars Richard Allington, Donna Ogle, Dorothy Strickland, and Evelyn English, this six-video library addresses core topics for teaching literacy in the classroom: reading strategies, developing literacy in multiple intelligence classrooms, thoughtful literacy, and much more.

VideoWorkshop for Reading Methods, Version 2.0 An easy way to bring video into your course for maximized learning! This total teaching and learning system includes quality video footage on an easy-to-use CD-ROM plus a Student Learning Guide and an Instructor's Teaching Guide—both with questions and activity suggestions. The result? A program that brings textbook concepts to life and that helps students understand, analyze, and apply the objectives of the course. VideoWorkshop is available for students as a value-package option with this textbook.

MyLabSchool Available as a value-package item with student copies of *Creating Literacy Instruction for All Students,* MyLabSchool is a collection of online tools for student success in the course, in licensure exams, and the teaching career. Visit www.mylabschool.com to access the following: **video clips** from real classrooms, with opportunities for students to reflect on the videos and offer their own thoughts and suggestions for applying theory to practice; an extensive archive of **text and multimedia cases** that provide valuable perspectives on real classrooms and real teaching challenges; Allyn & Bacon's **Lesson and Portfolio Builder** application, which includes an integrated state standards correlation tool; help with research papers using **Research Navigator™**, which provides access to three exclusive databases of credible and reliable source material including EBSCO's ContentSelect Academic Journal Database, *New York Times* Search by Subject Archive, and "Best of the Web" Link Library. MyLabSchool also includes a **Careers Center** with resources for Praxis exams and licensure preparation, professional portfolio development, job search, and interview techniques.

Course Management Powered by Blackboard and hosted nationally, Allyn & Bacon's own course management system, CourseCompass, helps you manage all aspects of teaching your course. For colleges and universities with WebCT™ and Blackboard™ licenses, special course management packages can be requested in these formats as well. Allyn & Bacon is proud to offer premium testing content in these platforms. (Your sales representative can give you additional information.)

Research Navigator™ Accessible through MyLabSchool, and designed to help students select and evaluate research from the Web to find the best and most credible information available, Research Navigator™ is the easiest way for students to start a research assignment or research paper. It offers extensive help with the research process and includes three exclusive databases of credible and reliable source material: EBSCO's ContentSelect Academic Journal Database, *New York Times* Search by Subject Archive, and "Best of the Web" Link Library. Research Navigator™ helps students make the most of their research time quickly and efficiently. (Requires an access code for separate access.)

Themes of the Times for Literacy   Available in a value-package with the textbook, this collection of 50 *New York Times* articles provides students with real-world information about literacy.

Speak with your Allyn & Bacon sales representative about obtaining these supplements for your class!

Acknowledgments

I am indebted to Aurora Martínez Ramos, executive editor at Allyn and Bacon, who, once again, provided insightful suggestions as well as support and encouragement, and to Mary Kriener, senior development editor, whose competent guidance helped me reorganize the text so that it incorporates the latest in research and practice. I am also grateful to Lynda Giles, editorial assistant at Allyn and Bacon, for her conscientious, competent, and gracious assistance.

The following reviewers provided many perceptive comments and valuable suggestions. They challenged me to write the best book I could, and for this I am grateful.

For the sixth edition: Elaine Byrd, Utah Valley State College
Ward Cockrum, Northern Arizona University
Jo Ann Daly, Marymount University
Anita Iaquinta, Robert Morris University
Laura King, Mary Hogan School, VT (in-service)
Margaret Malenka, Michigan State University
Melinda Miller, Sam Houston State University
Sherrie Pardieck, Bradley University
Pamela Petty, Western KY University
Gail Singleton Taylor, Old Dominion University

For previous editions: Jack Bagford, University of Iowa; Suzanne Barchers, University of Colorado at Denver; John Beach, University of Nevada, Reno; Marian Beckman, Edinboro University of Pennsylvania; Barbara J. Chesler, Longwood University; Sharon Y. Cowan, East Central University; Donna Croll, Valdosta State University; Audrey DíAigneault, Pleasant Valley Elementary School; Lauren Freedman, Western Michigan University; Cynthia Gettys, University of Tennessee at Chattanooga; Maudine Jefferson, Kennesaw State University; H. Jon Jones, Oklahoma State University; Joanna Jones, Grand Canyon University; Betty Lou Land, Winthrop University; Janet W. Lerner, Northeastern Illinois University; Barbara Lyman, Southwest Texas University; Karl Matz, Mankato State University; Lea McGee, Boston College; Jean A. McWilliams, Rosemont College; John M. Ponder, Arkansas State University; Laurence Stewart Rice III, Humboldt State University; Judith Scheu, Kamehama Schools, Honolulu, Hawaii; Patricia Shaw, University of Wisconsin, Whitewater; Gail Silkebakken, East Central Oklahoma University; Shela D. Snyder, Central Missouri State University; Steven Stahl, University of Georgia; Donna Topping, Millersville University; Doris J. Walker-Dalhouse, Moorhead State University; Judith Wenrich, Millersville University; Joyce Feist-Willis, Youngstown State University; Shelley Hong Xu, California State University, Long Beach.

My wife, Joan, offered both thoughtful comments and continuous encouragement. I deeply appreciate her loving understanding, especially when deadlines approached.

T. G.

Creating Literacy Instruction for All Students

1 The Nature of Literacy and Today's Students

Complete the anticipation guide below. It will help to activate your prior knowledge so that you interact more fully with the chapter. It is designed to probe your attitudes and beliefs about important and sometimes controversial topics. There are often no right or wrong answers; the statements will alert you to your attitudes about reading instruction and encourage you to become aware of areas where you might require additional information. After completing the chapter, you might respond to the anticipation guide again to see if your answers have changed in light of what you have read. For each of the following statements, put a check under "Agree" or "Disagree" to show how you feel. Discuss your responses with classmates before you read the chapter.

	Agree	Disagree
1. Before children learn to read, they should know the sounds of most letters.	_____	_____
2. Reading should not be fragmented into a series of subskills.	_____	_____
3. Oral reading should be accurate.	_____	_____
4. Phonics should be taught after children have learned to read about 100 words.	_____	_____
5. Reading short passages and answering questions about them provide excellent practice.	_____	_____
6. Mistakes in oral reading should be ignored unless they change the sense of the passage.	_____	_____

This chapter provides a general introduction to literacy instruction in preschool and grades K–8. Before reading the chapter, examine your personal knowledge of the topic so that you will be better prepared to interact with the information. Sometimes, you may not realize what you know until you stop and think about it. Think over what you know about the nature of reading. What do you think reading is? What do you do when you read? What do you think the reader's role is? Is it simply to receive the author's message, or should it include some personal input? How about writing? What processes do you use when you write?

How would you go about teaching reading and writing to today's students? What do you think the basic principles of a literacy program should be? What elements have worked especially well in programs with which you are familiar?

■ The Nature of Reading

"Awake! Awake!" These are the first words I remember reading. But the words were as magical as any I have read since. Even after all these years, I still have vivid memories of that day long ago in first grade when reading came alive for me, and, indeed, awakened a lifetime of reading and a career as a reading teacher.

Reading is, first and foremost, magical, as those who recall learning to read or have witnessed their students discover the process will attest. It opens the door to a vast world of information, fulfillment, and enjoyment. After having learned to read, a person is never quite the same.

Importance of Language

As magical as it may be, reading is our second major intellectual accomplishment. Our first, and by far, most important, intellectual accomplishment is our acquisition of language. Without language, of course, there would be no reading. Reading is very much a language activity, and, ultimately, our ability to read is limited by our language skills. We can't read what we can't understand. Even if we can pronounce words we don't understand because of superior phonics skills, we are not reading. **Reading** is a process in which we construct meaning from print. Without meaning, there is no reading.

Developing Language

Language has a number of interacting components: **phonology** (speech sounds known as phonemes), **morphology** (word formation), **syntax** (sentence formation), **semantics** (word and sentence meaning), **prosody** (intonation and rhythm of speech), and **pragmatics** (effective use of language: knowing how to take turns in a conversation, using proper tone, using terms of politeness, etc.) (National Institute on Deafness and Other Communication Disorders, 2003). Key ingredients for language learning are an environment that fosters language and an apparent inborn ability to develop language—children seem born to talk. Although young children learn many words through imitation, language is also a constructive process. If children were mere imitators, they would be able to repeat only what they hear. But they construct sentences such as "Mommy goed work," which is something that adults do not say. Creating a hypothesis about how language works, young children note that *-ed* is used to express past action and then overapply this generalization. With feedback and experience, they revise the hypothesis and ultimately learn that some action words have special past-tense forms.

There are critical periods for language development. The most intensive period of speech and language development for humans is during the first three years of life (National Institute on Deafness and Other Communication Disorders, 2003). By age three, most of what the child says can be understood by adults. Children are talking in sentences and have a speaking vocabulary of 1,000 or more words. By the time they enter kindergarten, they may know as many as 5,000 words.

The major influence on the size of children's vocabularies is the quantity and quality of the kind of talk they are exposed to. According to language expert Todd Risley (2003), the most important thing parents and other caregivers can do for their children is to talk to them. The amount of talk directed toward infants and toddlers is powerfully related to their verbal abilities and their success in school. Hart and Risley (1995) collected data on the quantity and quality of parent talk. They collected enough data on a sufficient number of families that they could reliably estimate the average amount of parent talk. They found that the sheer volume of talk that infants and toddlers hear varies greatly. Some children hear fewer than 500 words in an hour of family life. Others are exposed to 3,000 words in an hour. Some parents express approval or affirmation forty times an hour, whereas others, fewer than four times an hour. These differences add up. By age four, some children have heard more than 50 million words, while others have heard just 10 million words. By age four, some children have had 800,000 affirmations, while others have heard just

■ **Reading** is a process in which we construct meaning from print.

■ **Phonology** is the language component that consists of producing and understanding speech sounds.

■ **Morphology** is the component of language that has to do with meaningful word parts, such as roots and affixes.

■ **Syntax** is the language component that has to do with the way in which words are arranged in a sentence.

■ **Semantics** is the component of language that has to do with word and sentence meaning.

■ **Prosody** is the component of language that has to do with the intonation and rhythm of speech: pitch, stress, and juncture.

■ **Pragmatics** is the component of language that has to do with engaging in effective communication.

80,000. But there is more than just a quantitative difference between the most talkative and the least talkative families. The least talkative families use talk primarily to control and guide children. The most talkative families also use talk in this way, but they go beyond giving directions. Much of their extra talk consists of descriptions and explanations and contains a more complex vocabulary and structure and added positive reinforcement. The amount of talk to which children are exposed is correlated with the size of their vocabularies and their later language and cognitive development.

Although studies show that the amount of talk is not strictly related to socioeconomic status, professionals talk the most, and parents on welfare talk the least. However, there is a great variability among the working class. Many of the most talkative parents, along with the quietest, are in the working class. And it is parental talkativeness rather than socioeconomic status that relates to later verbal ability. In other words, it isn't how much money parents have or how much education they have or whether they are members of a minority group that counts; it is how much and how well they talk to their children. As Risley (2003) hypothesized, "The accumulation of language experience is the major determiner of vocabulary growth and verbal intellectual development" (p. 2).

In a longitudinal study of children in Bristol, England, Wells (1986) found that children's language was best developed in one-to-one situations in which an adult discussed matters that were of interest and concern to the child or the two talked over a shared activity. It is also essential that the adult adjust his or her language so as to take into consideration and to compensate for the child's limited linguistic ability, something parents seem to do intuitively.

In his extensive study, Wells (1986) found that some parents intuitively provided maximum development for their children's language. Far from being directors of what their children said, these parents were collaborative constructors of meaning. Careful listeners, they made genuine attempts to use both nonverbal and verbal clues to understand what their children were saying. Through careful listening and active involvement in the conversation, parents were able to help the children extend their responses so that both knowledge of the world and linguistic abilities were fostered.

As a teacher, you can't change the quality or quantity of language to which children have been exposed, but you can increase the quantity and quality of talk in your classroom and encourage parents and other caregivers to do the same. This book emphasizes high-quality, language-rich social interactions of the type conducted by the parents who best foster their children's language development.

■ ■ ■ Checkup ■ ■ ■

1. How does language develop?
2. What impact do parents have on children's language development?
3. What might you as the teacher do to develop language?

■ ■ ■

Role of Cognitive Development

Many of the practices advocated in literacy education are based on the work of Jean Piaget and L. S. Vygotsky, the two leading developmental theorists of modern times. Vygotsky, a Russian psychologist, stressed the social nature of language and learning and the important role that adults play in both. Piaget, a Swiss psychologist, stressed stages of cognitive development and the unique nature of children's thinking.

Jean Piaget

Piaget concluded that children's thinking is qualitatively different from adults' thinking and that it evolves through a series of hierarchical stages. He believed that children's thinking develops through direct experience with their environment. Through adaptation, or

Children learn to read by reading.

interaction with the environment, the child builds psychological structures, or schemes, which are ways of making sense of the world. Adaptation includes two complementary processes: **assimilation** and **accommodation**. Through assimilation, the child interprets the world in terms of his schemes. Seeing a very small dog, he calls it "doggie" and assimilates this in his dog scheme. Seeing a goat for the first time, the child might relate it to his dog scheme and call it "doggie." Later, realizing that there is something different about this creature, he may accommodate his "doggie" scheme and exclude the goat and all creatures with horns. Thus, he has refined his dog scheme. To Piaget, direct experience rather than language was the key determiner of cognitive development.

L. S. Vygotsky

Although both Piaget and Vygotsky believed that children need to interact with the world around them, Vygotsky stressed the importance of social factors in cognitive development (1962). In a theory that has become a keystone for instruction, Vygotsky distinguished between actual and potential development. Actual development is a measure of the level at which a child is developing. In a sense, it is a measure of what the child has learned up to that point. Potential development is a measure of what the child might be capable of achieving. The difference between the two is known as the **zone of proximal development**. As explained by Vygotsky (1978), the zone of proximal development is "the distance between the actual developmental level as determined by independent problem solving and the level of potential development as determined through problem solving under adult guidance or in collaboration with more capable peers" (p. 84). In other words, the zone of proximal development is the difference between what a child can do on his or her own and what the child can do with help.

Focusing on the importance of interaction with adults or knowledgeable peers, Vygotsky's theory is that children learn through expert guidance. In time, they internalize the concepts and strategies employed by their mentors and so, ultimately, are able to perform on a higher level. The support and guidance provided by an adult or more capable peer is known as **scaffolding** (Bruner, 1975, 1986).

Ideally, instruction should be pitched somewhat above a child's current level of functioning. Instruction and collaboration with an adult or more capable peers will enable the child to reach the higher level and ultimately function on that level. Instruction and interaction are key elements. The overall theories of evaluation and instruction presented in this book are grounded in the concepts of actual and potential development and the zone of proximal development.

FYI

Vygotsky neglected the importance of other ways of learning. Children can and do learn through nonverbal imitation and self-discovery (Berk, 1997).

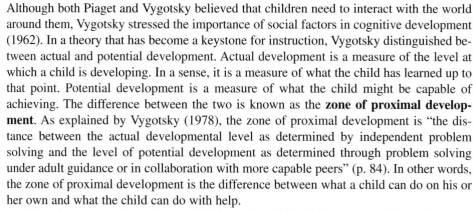

■ **Assimilation** is the process of incorporating new ideas into existing ones.

■ **Accommodation** is the process by which concepts or schemes are modified or new ones created to accommodate new knowledge.

■ The **zone of proximal development** is the difference between independent performance and potential performance as determined through problem solving under guidance of an adult or more capable peer.

■ **Scaffolding** refers to the support and guidance provided by an adult or more capable peer that helps a student function on a higher level.

■ **Transaction** refers to the relationship between the reader and the text in which meaning is created as the text is conditioned by the reader and the reader is conditioned by the text.

Implications based on an integration of the theories of Piaget and Vygotsky are listed below:

- Provide students with hands-on experiences and opportunities to make discoveries.
- Be aware of and plan for individual differences. Because children have different experiences and come from different backgrounds, they develop at different rates.
- Children learn best when activities are developmentally appropriate. Careful observation of processes the child is using provides insight into the child's level of development.
- Classrooms should be rich in verbal guidance. Interactions with the teacher and peers foster learning.

Importance of Experience

Although based on language, reading is also experiential. One second-grade class was reading a story that took place in a laundromat. None of the children had ever been to a laundromat or even heard of one, so they found the story confusing. Reading is not so much getting meaning from a story as it is bringing meaning to it. The more the reader brings to a story, the more she or he will be able to take away. For example, the child who can't seem to sit still will readily empathize with the boy in *Sit Still* (Carlson, 1996). In this instance, reading evokes an emotional response as well as an intellectual one.

Importance of the Students' Culture

Living as we do in a multicultural, pluralistic society, it is important for us to explore and understand the literacy histories of our pupils. We have to ask such questions as these: In students' culture(s), how are reading and writing used? What values are placed on them? What are the ways in which the students have observed and participated in reading and writing? Is literacy in their environment primarily a group or an individual activity? Given this information, the school should build on the children's experiences and develop and reinforce the skills and values important to their culture(s) as well as those important to the school.

■ ■ ■ Checkup ■ ■ ■

1. What are the main similarities and differences in Piaget's and Vygotsky's theories of cognitive development?
2. What are the implications of Piaget's and Vygotsky's theories for instruction?   ■ ■ ■

■ The Reader's Role in the Reading Process

What is the reader's role in the reading process? In the past, it was defined as being passive, getting the author's meaning. Today, reading requires a more active role—the reader must construct meaning from text. The model of transmission of information in which the reader was merely a recipient has given way to transactional theory, a two-way process involving a reader and a text:

> Every reading act is an event, or a **transaction**, involving a particular reader and a particular pattern of signs, a text, and occurring at a particular time in a particular context. Instead of two fixed entities acting on one another, the reader and the text are two aspects of a total dynamic situation. The "meaning" does not reside ready-made "in" the text or "in" the reader but happens or comes into being during the transaction between reader and text. (Rosenblatt, 1994, p. 1063)

In her study of how students read a poem, Rosenblatt (1978) noted that each reader was active:

> He was not a blank tape registering a ready-made message. He was actively involved in building up a poem for himself out of his responses to text. He had to draw on his past experiences with the verbal symbols. . . . The reader was not only paying attention to what the words pointed to in the external world, to their referents; he was also paying attention to the images, feelings, attitudes, associations, and ideas that the words and their referents evoked in him. (p. 10)

The type of reading, of course, has an effect on the transaction. The reader can take an efferent or an aesthetic **stance**. When reading a set of directions, a science text, or a math problem, the reader takes an **efferent** stance, the focus being on obtaining information that can be carried away (*efferent* is taken from the Latin verb *efferre*, "to carry away"). In the **aesthetic** stance, the reader pays attention to the associations, feelings, attitudes, and ideas that the words evoke.

Does it make any difference whether reading is viewed as being transmissional, transactional, or somewhere in between? Absolutely. If reading is viewed as transmissional, students are expected to stick close to the author's message. If reading is viewed as transactional, students are expected to put their personal selves into their reading, especially when encountering literature. From a transactional perspective, building background becomes especially important because it enriches the transaction between reader and text. Personal response and interpretation are at the center of the reading process. The reader's role is enhanced when a transactional view prevails.

■ ■ ■ Checkup ■ ■ ■

1. What is the reader's role in the reading process?

■ ■ ■

■ Approaches to Reading Instruction: Whole versus Part Learning

Just as there are philosophical differences about the role of the reader, there are differences in approaches to teaching reading. On one end of the continuum are those who espouse a subskills, or bottom-up, approach, and on the other end are those who advocate a **holistic**, or top-down, approach. In between are the interactionists. Where do you fit on the continuum? Go back to the anticipation guide at the beginning of the chapter. Take a look at how

---

■ **Stance** refers to the position or attitude that the reader takes. The two stances are aesthetic and efferent.

■ **Efferent** refers to a kind of reading in which the focus is on obtaining or carrying away information from the reading.

■ **Aesthetic** refers to a type of reading in which the reader focuses on experiencing the piece: the rhythm of the words, the past experiences the words call up (Rosenblatt, 1978, p. 10).

■ **Holistic** refers to the practice of learning through the completion of whole tasks rather than fragmented subskills and fragments of reading and writing.

■ **Bottom-up approach** refers to a kind of processing in which meaning is derived from the accurate, sequential processing of words. The emphasis is on the text rather than the reader's background knowledge or language ability.

■ **Top-down approach** refers to deriving meaning by using one's background knowledge, language ability, and expectations. The emphasis is on the reader rather than the text.

■ **Interactionists** hold the theoretical position that reading involves processing text and using one's background knowledge and language ability.

you answered the six statements. If you agreed with only the odd-numbered ones, you are a bottom-up advocate. If you agreed with only the even-numbered statements, you are a top-downer. If your answers were mixed, you are probably an interactionist.

Bottom-Uppers

In the **bottom-up approach**, children literally start at the bottom and work their way up. First, they learn the names and shapes of the letters of the alphabet. Next, they learn consonant sounds, followed by simple and then more complex vowel correspondences. As Carnine, Silbert, and Kame'enui (1990) explain, "Our position is that many students will not become successful readers unless teachers identify the essential reading skills, find out what skills students lack, and teach those skills directly" (p. 3).

Bottom-up procedures are intended to make learning to read easier by breaking complex tasks into their component skills. Instruction proceeds from the simple to the complex. In essence, there are probably no 100-percent bottom-uppers among reading teachers. Even those who strongly favor phonics recognize the importance of higher-level strategies.

USING TECHNOLOGY

The Association for Direct Instruction provides information about Direct Instruction, which is a bottom-up approach. The site has film clips showing Direct Instruction lessons.
http://www.adihome.org/phpshop

Top-Downers

A **top-down approach**, as its name indicates, starts at the top and works downward. Learning to read is seen as being similar to learning to speak; it is holistic and progresses naturally through immersion. Subskills are not taught because it is felt that they fragment the process and make learning to read more abstract and difficult (Goodman, 1986). One of the most influential models of reading is that proposed by Ken Goodman (1994b). According to Goodman, readers use their background knowledge and knowledge of language to predict and infer the content of print. Readers "use their selection strategies to choose only the most useful information from all that is available" (Goodman, 1994b, p. 1125). When reading the sentence "The moon is full tonight," the reader can use his or her knowledge of the moon, context clues, and perhaps the initial consonants *f* and *t* to reconstruct *full* and *tonight*. According to Goodman's theory, it is not necessary for the reader to process all the letters of *full* and *tonight*. However, in order to make use of background knowledge, context clues, and initial consonant cues, the reader must consider the whole text. If the words *full* and *tonight* were read in isolation, the reader would have to depend more heavily on processing all or most of the letters of each word. As far as comprehension is concerned, the top-down view is that students build their understanding through discussions of high-quality literature or informational texts. There is generally no direct, explicit instruction of comprehension strategies.

FYI

In Goodman's model, students use three cueing systems: semantic, syntactic, and graphophonic. Semantic cues derive from past experiences, so students construct meaning by bringing their background of knowledge to a story. Syntactic cues derive from knowledge of how the structure of language works. Graphophonic cues refer to the ability to sound out words or recognize them holistically. Based on their use of these cues, students predict the content of the text, confirm or revise their predictions, and reread if necessary.

Interactionists

Most practitioners tend to be more pragmatic than either strict top-downers or dyed-in-the-wool bottom-uppers and borrow practices from both ends of the continuum. These **interactionists** teach skills directly and systematically—especially in the beginning—but they avoid overdoing it, as they do not want to fragment the process. They also provide plenty of opportunities for students to experience the holistic nature of reading and writing by having them read whole books and write for real purposes. In his study of highly effective teachers, Pressley (2006) found that most were interactionists: "There is a great deal of skills instruction, with as many as 20 skills an hour covered, often in response to the needs of a reader or writer. Skills instruction is strongly balanced with holistic reading and writing, with students reading and experiencing substantial authentic literature and other texts that make sense for them to be reading given their needs" (p. 3).

FYI

■ To clarify your philosophy of teaching, ask: "What are my instructional practices, and why am I doing what I'm doing?" Examining your practices should help you uncover your beliefs.

■ This book takes the position that all sources of information—semantic, syntactic, background knowledge, and letter–sound relationships—are essential when processing text and emphasizes the use of both context and phonics. However, the book also agrees with the view that even in mature reading, nearly all words are processed.

USING TECHNOLOGY

Controversies such as "Is reading top-down or bottom-up?" are often explored on the Web sites of professional organizations, such as the International Reading Association's Web site:

http://www.reading.org/positions.html

■ Importance of Literacy Models

Why is it important to be aware of different models of teaching reading? For one thing, it is important that you formulate your own personal beliefs about reading and writing instruction. These beliefs will then be the foundation for your instruction. They will determine the goals you set, the instructional techniques you use, the materials you choose, the organization of your classroom, the reading and writing behaviors you expect students to exhibit, and the criteria you use to evaluate students. For instance, whether you use children's books or a basal, how you teach phonics, and whether you expect flawless oral reading or are satisfied if the student's rendition is faithful to the sense of the selection will depend upon your theoretical orientation (DeFord, 1985).

■ Approach Taken by this Text

This book draws heavily on research in cognitive psychology, combines an interactionist point of view with a holistic orientation, and takes an integrated approach. Both the bottom-up and top-down approaches are step by step (Kamhi & Catts, 1999). In the bottom-up model, the reader progresses from letter to sound to word. In the top-down process, the reader proceeds from sampling of language cues to prediction and to confirmation. However, in an integrated approach, the processes occur in parallel fashion. For instance, when students decode words, four processors are at work: orthographic, phonological, meaning, and context (Adams, 1990, 1994). The orthographic processor is responsible for perceiving the sequences of letters in text. The phonological processor is responsible for mapping the letters into their spoken equivalents. The meaning processor contains one's knowledge of word meanings, and the context processor is in charge of constructing a continuing understanding of the text (Stahl, Osborne, & Lehr, 1990). The processors work simultaneously, and they both receive information and send it to the other processors; however, the orthographic and phonological processors are always essential participants. Context may speed and/or assist the interpretation of orthographic and phonological information but does not take its place (see Figure 1.1). When information from one processor is weak, another may be called on to give assistance. With a word such as *lead*, the context processor provides extra help to the meaning and phonological processors in assigning the correct meaning and pronunciation.

In an integrated model, both top-down and bottom-up processes are used. However, depending on circumstances, either bottom-up or top-down processes are emphasized. If one is reading a handwritten note in which some words are illegible, top-down processes are stressed as knowledge of language and knowledge of the world are used to fill in what is missing. If one is reading unfamiliar proper names or words in isolation, bottom-up processes are emphasized.

In an integrated approach, reading is considered an active, constructive process, with the focus on the reader, whose experiences, cultural background, and point of view will play a part in her or his comprehension of a written piece. The focus is on cognitive processes or strategies used to decode words and understand and remember text: using phonics and context to decipher unknown words, activating one's knowledge of a topic, predicting meaning, summarizing, and visualizing.

Stress is also placed on teaching strategies in context and holistically applying them to children's books, periodicals, ads and other real-world materials, and content area textbooks. The integrated approach is a balanced approach in which systematic instruction and immersion in reading and writing play complementary roles.

■ ■ ■ Checkup ■ ■ ■

1. What are the bottom-up, top-down, and interactionist approaches?
2. What are the instructional implications of an integrated approach?

■ ■ ■

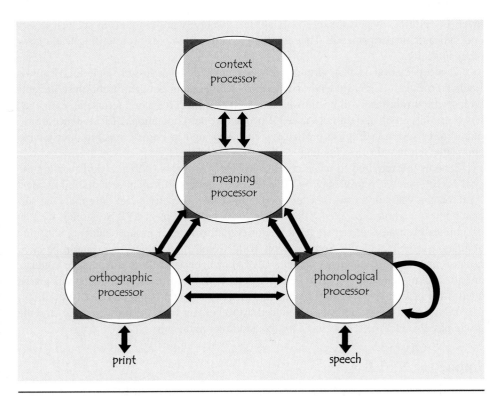

■■■ **FIGURE 1.1**

**Modeling the Reading
Systems: Four Processors**

Source: Adams, M. J. (1990). *Beginning to read: Thinking and learning about print: A summary.* Prepared by S. A. Stahl, J. Osborne, & F. Lehr. Urbana-Champaign, IL: Center for the Study of Reading, University of Illinois.

■ The Status of Literacy

According to national testing results, some 64 percent of fourth-graders and 73 percent of eighth-graders can read at least on a basic level (Perie, Grigg, & Donahue, 2005). The results of the National Assessment of Educational Progress (NAEP) suggest that U.S. fourth-graders are doing poorly in reading. You might be surprised to learn that when the overall reading of fourth-graders in the United States was tested and compared with the reading proficiency of fourth-graders from 34 other countries, only students from Sweden, the Netherlands, England, and Bulgaria outperformed those from the United States (Mullis, Martin, Gonzalez, & Kennedy, 2003). U.S. fourth-graders read as well as or better than the students from the other 30 countries. On the literacy subscale, only Sweden outperformed the United States. On the informational scale, five countries did better than the United States.

■ No Child Left Behind: Closing the Gap

To raise the achievement of all students but especially those who are struggling with reading, landmark legislation known as the No Child Left Behind Act of 2001 (NCLB) has been implemented. The purpose of NCLB is "to ensure that all children have a fair, equal and significant opportunity to obtain a high-quality education and reach, at a minimum, proficiency on challenging state academic achievement standards and state academic assessments." More specifically, the goal requires that 100 percent of all students reach the proficient level in math and reading/language arts by school year 2013–2014. Effective in 2007–2008, an assessment in science is also required in one of the grades in each of the following ranges: grades 3–5, 6–9, and 10–12.

The key indicator of progress is performance on state achievement tests. Each state is allowed to choose the test that it wishes to use, and each state also sets a proficiency

FYI

NAEP proficiency levels might be set too high. Only 31 percent of fourth-graders reached the proficient-or-above level on the NAEP; however, on the PIRLS, an international test, 68 percent of fourth-graders scored above the median (Mullis, Martin, Gonzalez, & Kennedy, 2003).

USING TECHNOLOGY   ■ ■ ■

To find the results of the latest NAEP in reading, consult the National Center for Educational Statistics:
http://nces.ed.gov/nationsreportcard

The Read • Write • Think Web site features a listing of IRA/NCTE standards and lessons geared to those standards.
http://www.readwritethink.org/standards/index.html

The best source of information about standards is Standards for Education:
http://edstandards.org/Standards.html

FYI

■ Meeting the standards will be especially difficult for the lowest performing schools (Linn, Baker, & Betebenner, 2002). For instance, some schools in Hartford, Connecticut, one of the poorest cites in the nation, have only 20 percent of students achieving proficiency. In addition, they have more subgroups than the higher-achieving schools in more affluent areas. Therefore, they will need to make dramatic gains.

■ In the 2004–2005 school year, the latest year for which there are figures, about 16 percent of schools failed to make adequate progress. A disproportionate percentage of these schools are in urban districts.

■ NCLB does have some drawbacks. There is an overemphasis on testing and lower-level skills. Because of the requirement that instruction and materials be scientifically based, there has also been an overuse of basal anthologies, as opposed to other approaches. There is also concern about testing requirements for English language learners and disabled readers.

USING TECHNOLOGY

Issued by a number of professional organizations, the Joint Organizational Statement on the No Child Left Behind (NCLB) Act offers suggestions for improving NCLB:

http://www.reading.org/resources/issues/focus_nclb.html

Adapting Instruction for Struggling Readers and Writers

Students with disabilities may be provided accommodations. Accommodations alter the testing conditions but not the test itself. For instance, accommodations may allow the student to be given extra time or to take the test in a quiet spot away from other students. Students with severe disabilities may be given an out-of-level test or alternate assessment.

level. In addition to performance on state tests, schools are required to include a second indicator of performance. This could be attendance, scores on a writing test, or another indicator.

The expectation is that virtually all students will be assessed, including Limited English Proficient (LEP) students and students with learning or other disabilities. Students with severe disabilities will be allowed to take out-of-level tests or alternate assessments; however, this group should not exceed 2 percent of the population. LEP students are required to be tested in English proficiency each year and in English reading after having completed ten months of schooling.

Schools are required to make acceptable yearly progress (AYP) toward meeting the goal of 100-percent proficiency by 2013–2014. If underperforming schools fail to meet AYP for two years in a row, they are subject to corrective action. Not only must the student body as a whole meet the AYP, but each subgroup must meet AYP. Subgroups include economically disadvantaged students, major ethnic and racial groups, students with disabilities, and LEP students. Some schools with overall high achievement might be cited because their English language learners (ELLs) or economically disadvantaged students are not making adequate progress. There is a safe harbor provision. Schools will not be cited if the percentage of nonproficient students in the group (subgroup or entire school) that did not meet the goal has been reduced by 10 percent from the previous year, and the group has also met the requirement for the additional indicator.

Impact of NCLB

NCLB is changing the way literacy is being taught. Because of NCLB, there is a greater emphasis on aligning curriculum and instruction with assessment, as well as on collecting assessment data and using it. As one educator commented, "Building by building, I see teachers sitting down and discussing low-performing students" (Center for Education Policy, 2006, p. 22). Because the progress of subgroups is assessed and reported, greater attention is being paid to struggling readers, students who previously were neglected. As one superintendent confessed, "We are being held accountable for all students, so we are looking at everyone! We can't just give them busywork in the back of the room anymore" (p. 27). The amount of professional development has also increased, with many schools hiring coaches to assist teachers.

Overall, scores on the NAEP since the implementation of NCLB are unchanged. However, on another national test of more than 300,000 students, scores in reading did improve in grades 3 through 8 between 2003 and 2005. However, the rate of improvement so far is not great enough to reach the goal of having all students reach the proficient level by 2013–2014 (Cronin, Kingsbury, McCall, & Bowe, 2005). Results on state tests are more encouraging. The Education Trust (Hall & Ken, 2006) found that elementary school reading achievement increased in 27 of 31 states. Middle schools do not do as well; reading achievement increased in just 20 of the 31 states examined. In one survey, nearly 80 percent of school districts reported increased scores (Center for Education Policy, 2006).

Having worked for a year in a Reading First school, I was able to see first-hand the impact of NCLB. With Reading First funds, the school was able to assemble a library, replace an outdated basal reader with high-quality materials, hire literacy specialists and tutors, put together an accountability system that included monitoring, and provide badly needed professional development. Given those resources, the vast majority of students were reading on grade level by the end of the year. Every student who wasn't reading on or close to grade level was provided with extra instruction. Results were especially dramatic in first grade. At year's end, 90 percent of those students were reading on grade level. The 10 percent of students not reading on grade level had mastered short-vowel patterns and were reading at least on a mid–first-grade level. Given continued extra assistance, there was a high probability that they would catch up by the end of second grade.

Watching struggling students make accelerated progress because they have been provided with extra help by a well-trained tutor who is using a highly effective program and carefully monitoring their progress and knowing that this progress wouldn't have happened without a push from NCLB, you can more clearly see the value of this act and of programs such as Reading First.

The goal of having all students achieve proficiency is a lofty one. Whether it is possible to reach that goal, only time will tell. However, it is possible to make dramatic improvements in students' literacy achievement. Reading Recovery (Reading Recovery North American Trainers Group, 2006) and other high-quality programs (Hiebert & Taylor, 2000; Reeves, 2003) have shown that most students will become proficient readers when properly taught. A substantial number of schools have beaten the odds. These are schools that have high achievement despite being in high-poverty areas (Education Trust, 2003; Reeves, 2003; Taylor, Pearson, Clark, & Walpole, 1999). However, achieving the goal will take not just an all-school effort; it will require the involvement of all of society. Well-stocked neighborhood and school libraries, adequate health care, parenting programs, contributions from business, and the support of all citizens will be needed to foster the high level of literacy achievement being called for. More than ever, parents will need to become partners in their children's education.

Implications of NCLB for Instruction

For you, as a classroom teacher, NCLB means that you will need to be able to help all of your students, including students who are struggling because of poverty, learning disabilities, uninvolved parents, or English-learning challenges. It means that you will need to monitor the progress of each student and change programs, supply special help, or get assistance if students fail to make progress. It means that your program will need to be carefully planned and implemented so as to be as effective as possible.

Closing the gap also requires taking a long-term view of literacy. As literacy professionals, we need to ask ourselves, "What kind of program will result in proficiency for the largest number of students?" The temptation is to drill students on the kinds of items they will be tested on. The drill-skill approach hasn't worked in the past and won't work now. It is too shallow. What is needed is an in-depth approach that builds students' background knowledge, fosters language development, and develops the kinds of skills needed to cope with the literacy demands of the school and the larger society.

As a teacher, you should become acquainted with the major findings of literacy research so that you can construct a literacy program that is based on research and you can assess whether new techniques or materials that you are thinking about trying are supported by research. You should also assess the research base to see if it is applicable to your students and your situation. A technique that works well on a one-to-one basis may not be effective with small groups. Of course, research doesn't answer all the instructional questions that arise. You need to become a teacher-researcher so that you can test out methods

Closing the Gap

"What Do We Know About Raising Minority Academic Achievement?" describes twenty programs that have successfully raised the achievement of struggling minority students:

http://www.aypf.org/publications/index.htm

Adapting Instruction for English Language Learners

States may exempt students who are new to this country and to the English language from the reading/language arts content assessment for 1 year.

FYI

Up to 2 percent of students with severe cognitive disabilities may be given an alternate assessment. Modified assessments may be given to 2 percent of students with learning disabilities who, despite high-quality instruction, are not likely to achieve grade-level proficiency in the school year covered by their Individualized Education Programs (IEPs). Modified standards and assessments must be more rigorous than alternate ones and must provide access to grade-level content.

---

*A*s part of NCLB, there has been a call for programs that are scientifically based. Key elements shown to be a part of successful scientifically based reading programs include phonological awareness, phonics, fluency, vocabulary, and comprehension. Scientific evidence of success has been interpreted as meaning studies in which Method A is compared with Method B and/or a control group and found to be statistically superior.

The International Reading Association (2002b) uses the term *evidence-based* rather than *scientifically based. Evidence-based* is a broader term and includes qualitative studies as well as the more scientifically based studies that include comparison of experimental and control groups. In addition to the areas specified in NCLB provisions, Thames and York (2003) identified four areas in which literacy experts from diverse backgrounds and differing philosophies agree. These include "motivating students to read; linking reading, writing, listening, and speaking; using a wide range of proven methods to create the right balance for each child (this emphasizes using silent reading when possible); and using a wide variety of printed materials and literature" (p. 607).

IRA Position Statement

on Key Issue

Scientifically Based Literacy Instruction

USING TECHNOLOGY

What is evidence-based reading instruction? The following site provides a summary of a position statement of the International Reading Association (2002b):

http://www.reading.org/resources/issues/positions_evidence_based.html

Research reported by the National Reading Panel (2000) has been judged to be scientifically based. The report contains many of the basic principles of teaching reading. The report is free and may be ordered at

http://www.nationalreadingpanel.org/Publications/publications.htm

This site contains information on the Reading First program for children in grades K–3:

http://www.ed.gov/programs/readingfirst/index.html

The Web site Focus on Response to Intervention provides added information about RTI:

http://www.reading.org/resources/issues/focus_rti.html

FYI

■ Reading First, a component of NCLB, has as its goal that students will be proficient readers by the end of third grade. To accomplish that goal, some $5 billion has been allocated for programs for struggling readers.

■ The three-tier model is the most popular approach to RTI. However, other approaches are possible. RTI is a flexible program and may be applied in different ways in different locations.

and materials and have a better basis for selecting those that are most effective in your situation. You also need to assess all aspects of your program with a view to replacing or improving elements that aren't working and adding elements that are missing.

Insofar as possible, the suggestions made in this text are evidence-based. However, in some instances they are based on personal experience or the experience of others. Teaching literacy is an art as well as a science.

■■■ Checkup ■■■

1. What impact is NCLB having on reading instruction?
2. What areas of instruction are said to be scientifically based?
3. What is the difference between scientifically based and evidence-based instruction?
4. What areas of instruction might be added because they are evidence-based but not scientifically based?

■■■

■ Response to Intervention (RTI)

Along with NCLB, RTI is having a major impact on classroom instruction. The reauthorized Individuals with Disabilities Education Improvement Act (IDEA) of 2004 (P.L. 108-446) has specified a change in the way students are identified as having a learning disability. In the past, students have been identified for special education on the basis of a gap between their ability and their achievement. Now they may be identified through a procedure known as **response to intervention (RTI)**. RTI is a commonsense approach in which struggling students are offered increasingly intensive instruction. Most students respond favorably when provided with added instruction (Vellutino et al., 1996). Failure to make adequate progress is an indicator of a learning difficulty.

RTI begins with the identification of at-risk students (Fuchs & Fuchs, 2006). A high-stakes test, a screening test, informal measures, or teacher observation might be used to identify at-risk students. Additional measures and observations might be used to support the identification. However, the screening should be universal, that is, including all students (Office of Special Education and Rehabilitation, 2005). Progress monitoring should be a part of the process, so students who are failing to make progress can be identified. Once identified, students are provided with intervention.

The intervention process typically has three tiers. In the first tier, the student is provided with high-quality instruction in the general education program. Instruction is differentiated as needed. Progress is monitored at least three times a year (Vaughn, 2003). Students who fail to make adequate progress enter tier 2, in which they are given more intensive instruction and more support from the classroom teacher, a specialist, a tutor, or a special education teacher. The intervention process supports the classroom program and lasts approximately 8 to 12 weeks. Tier 2 instruction lasts for 30 minutes each day and is in addition to classroom instruction. Again, progress is monitored. If students continue to fail to make progress, they enter tier 3, where they are given more intensive specialized instruction. This is in addition to regular classroom instruction. Tier 3 students may be assessed for possible placement in a special education program.

RTI should result in more accurate placement of students, earlier assistance being given to students who need it, and greater involvement of classroom teachers. Up to 15 percent of special education funds may be used in the general education program to beef

■ **Response to intervention** is an assessment approach in which students' ability to learn is evaluated by noting how well they respond to instruction of varying degrees of intensity.

up general instruction and pre-placement intervention. A major aim of RTI is to improve the instruction of the general education program.

As a classroom teacher, you will have primary responsibility for implementing tier 1 and also much of tier 2. You will be doing more assessing, monitoring, and differentiating of instruction. You will need to be knowledgeable about assessment and the instruction of struggling learners.

USING TECHNOLOGY

See also Star Legacy Modules on RTI from Vanderbilt University: http://iris.peabody.vanderbilt.edu/ onlinemodules.html

▪▪▪ Checkup ▪▪▪

1. What impact might RTI have on classroom teachers?

▪▪▪

▪ A Reading and Writing Program for Today's Students

The world is growing ever more complex, and so the demands for literacy are increasing. Functioning in today's global society requires a higher degree of literacy than did functioning in yesterday's pre–information-superhighway society. Requirements for tomorrow's citizens will be higher yet. Today's and tomorrow's readers need to be selective and efficient. Bombarded with information, students must be able to select the information that is important to them.

What kind of program will help meet the literacy needs of today's students? That is a question that the remainder of this book will attempt to answer. However, when all is said and done, the twelve principles discussed below, if followed faithfully, should make a difference in determining such a program.

1. *Children learn to read by reading.* Learning to read is a little like learning to drive a car—instruction and guidance are required. In addition to instruction and guidance, novice readers, like novice motorists, require practice. They must read a variety of fiction and nonfiction books, newspapers, and magazines to become truly skilled. In a way, each book or article makes a child a better reader. As Hirsch (1987) pointed out, children must

The teacher is the key to effective reading instruction.

have a broad background in a variety of areas in order to be able to understand much of what is being written and said in today's world. For example, a child who has read the fable "The Boy Who Cried Wolf" will have the background necessary to understand a story that includes the sentence "Frank cried wolf once too often." Reading is not simply a matter of acquiring and perfecting skills, it also requires accumulating vocabulary, concepts, experiences, and background knowledge.

To provide the necessary practice and background, children's books are an essential component of a reading program. Unfortunately, large numbers of students are aliterate: They *can* read, but they *do* not, at least not on a regular basis. In a recent study, only 35 percent of a large sample of fourth-graders reported reading daily or almost daily (Mullis, Martin, Gonzalez, & Kennedy, 2003). Responding to a reading attitude questionnaire, the Motivation to Read Profile (Gambrell, Codling, & Palmer, 1996), 17 percent of the students reported that they would rather clean their rooms than read, 10 percent said that people who read are boring, and 14 percent stated that they would spend little time reading when they grew up.

It is not surprising that those who do the most reading on their own are the most proficient readers (Anderson, Wilson, & Fielding, 1988; Applebee, Langer, & Mullis, 1988; Mullis, Martin, Gonzalez, & Kennedy, 2003). While it is true that better readers read more partly because reading is easier for them, Anderson, Wilson, and Fielding's (1988) analysis of data suggests a cause–effect relationship. Students are better readers because they read more.

The case for including children's books in a reading program is a compelling one. First, as just noted, those who read more, read better. Second, research suggests that students who read widely and are given some choice in what they read have a more favorable attitude toward reading (Cline & Kretke, 1980). In addition, all types of students—able readers, at-risk children, bilingual students—benefit from an approach that incorporates children's books. Based on their review of research, Tunnell and Jacobs (1989) concluded that programs using children's books achieve dramatic levels of success and are particularly effective with disabled and uninterested readers.

Using children's books in the reading program not only leads to an opportunity for a greater enjoyment of reading but also builds skill in reading. In addition, allowing some self-selection should produce students who can and do read. To assist you in choosing or recommending books for your students, lists of appropriate books are presented throughout the text along with a description of several extensive lists of leveled books (see Chapter 2). Chapter 2 also describes a number of devices for leveling or assessing the difficulty level of books. Appendix A presents high-quality books listed by suggested grade level.

2. *Reading should be easy—but not too easy.* Think about it this way: If children find reading difficult, they will acquire a distaste for it and will simply stop reading except when they have to. Because of inadequate practice, they will fall further behind, and their distaste for reading will grow. In addition, students will be unable to apply the strategies they have been taught, and learning will be hampered if the text is too difficult (Clay, 1993a). As Fry (1977a) put it years ago, make the match: Give students a book that they can handle with ease. Research by Berliner (1981) and Gambrell, Wilson, and Gantt (1981) suggested that students do best with reading materials in which no more than 2 to 5 percent of the words are difficult for them.

3. *Instruction should be functional and contextual.* Do not teach skills or strategies in isolation—teach a word-attack skill because students must have it to decipher words. For example, teach the prefix *pre-* just before the class reads a selection about prehistoric dinosaurs. Students learn better when what they are being taught has immediate value. Suggestions for lessons that are both functional and contextual are presented throughout this book.

4. *Teachers should make connections.* Build a bridge between children's experiences and what they are about to read. Help them see how what they know is related to the story or article. Students in Arizona reading about an ice hockey game may have no experience either playing or watching the sport. However, you could help create a bridge of understanding by discussing how hockey is similar to soccer, a sport with which they probably are familiar. You should also help students connect new concepts to old concepts. Relate reading, writing, listening, and speaking—they all build on each other. Reading and talking about humorous stories can expand students' concept of humor and remind them of funny things that have happened to them. They might then write about these events. Also build on what students know. This will make your teaching easier, since you will be starting at the students' level. It will also help students make a connection between what they know and what they are learning.

5. *Teachers should promote independence.* Whenever you teach a skill or strategy, ask yourself: How can I teach this so that students will eventually use it on their own? How will students be called upon to use this skill or strategy in school and in the outside world? When you teach students how to summarize, make predictions, or use context, phonics, or another skill or strategy, teach so that there is a gradual release of responsibility (Pearson & Gallagher, 1983). Gradually fade your instruction and guidance so that students are applying the skill or strategy on their own. Do the same with the selection of reading materials. Although you may discuss ways of choosing books with the class, you ultimately want students to reach a point where they select their own books.

6. *Teachers should believe that all children can learn to read and write.* Given the right kind of instruction, virtually all children can learn to read. There is increasing evidence that the vast majority of children can learn to read at least on a basic level. Over the past two decades, research (Reading Recovery Council of North America, 2006) has shown that Reading Recovery, an intensive 12- to 20-week early intervention program, can raise the reading levels of about 76 percent of the lowest achievers to that of average achievers in a class. Reading Recovery uses an inclusive model:

> It has been one of the surprises of Reading Recovery that all kinds of children with all kinds of difficulties can be included, can learn, and can reach average-band performance for their class in both reading and writing achievement. Exceptions are not made for children of lower intelligence, for second-language children, for children with low language skills, for children with poor motor coordination, for children who seem immature, for children who score poorly on readiness measures, or for children who have already been categorized by someone else as learning disabled. (Clay, 1991, p. 60)

A number of intervention programs have succeeded with struggling readers (Hiebert & Taylor, 2000). An important aspect of these efforts is that supplementary assistance is complemented by a strong classroom program. These results demonstrate the power of effective instruction and the belief that all children can learn to read. Actually, a quality program will prevent most problems. A national committee charged with making recommendations to help prevent reading difficulties concluded, "Excellent instruction is the best intervention for children who demonstrate problems learning to read" (Snow, Burns, & Griffin, 1998, p. 33).

In virtually every elementary and middle school classroom, there are a number of struggling readers and writers. Classroom teachers estimate that as many as one student out of four is reading more than one year below grade level (Baumann, Hoffman, Duffy-Hester, & Ro, 2000). Teachers also report that their greatest challenge is working with struggling readers. Fortunately, today's teachers have a strong commitment to helping struggling readers. Given the large number of struggling readers and writers in today's schools and the impact of NCLB and RTI, this text has numerous suggestions for helping these students and concludes each instructional chapter with a section entitled "Help for Struggling Readers and Writers," which discusses steps classroom teachers might take to help underachieving students.

7. *The literacy program should be goal-oriented and systematic.* In keeping with the current concern for articulating and teaching to high standards, this text provides suggested grade-by-grade content standards for each of the major instructional areas: emergent literacy, phonics and other word analysis skills and strategies, vocabulary,

Adapting Instruction for Struggling Readers and Writers

Classroom teachers are taking increased responsibility for helping struggling readers and writers. Suggestions for working with struggling readers and writers are made throughout this book.

comprehension, reading in the content areas, study skills, and writing. These objectives are presented at the end of each appropriate chapter in a feature entitled "Essential Standards."

8. *Teachers should build students' motivation and sense of competence.* Students perform at their best when they feel competent, view a task as being challenging but doable, understand why they are undertaking a task, are given choices, feel a part of the process, and have interesting materials and activities. For many students, working in a group fosters effort and persistence. Students also respond to knowledge of progress. They work harder when they see that they are improving, and they are also energized by praise from teachers, parents, and peers, especially when that praise is honest and specific (Schunk & Zimmerman, 1997; Sweet, 1997; Wigfield, 1997).

The aim of a literacy program is to produce engaged readers and writers. Engaged readers and writers are motivated, are knowledgeable, and have mastered key strategies. They also do well when working with others (Guthrie & Wigfield, 1997). From a purely practical point of view, engagement is the key to meeting the challenge of NCLB. Engagement incorporates the depth and breadth of the reading and writing skills required to achieve today's high levels of literacy, including those needed for high-stakes tests.

Engaged reading is powerful. As Guthrie (2004), an expert on engaged reading, concludes:

> Engaged reading can overcome traditional barriers to reading achievement, including gender, parental education, and income. . . . Young students who gain a modicum of skill in reading are enabled to read more stories and books, assuming they are available. With increased amounts of reading, students' fluency and knowledge expand, increasing basic word recognition. Contributing to this spiral is sense of identity and selfhood; improving readers see themselves as capable, which is gratifying. Beyond self-confidence, however, students on the upward spiral see themselves as readers who are learners and thinkers; these students internalize literacy as part of who they are. (pp. 5, 6).

Engagement will be explored in depth in this book and will be highlighted in annotations located in the margins.

9. *Teachers should build students' language proficiency.* Reading and writing are language based. Students' reading levels are ultimately limited by their language development. Students can't understand what they are reading if they don't know what the words mean or get tangled up in the syntax of the piece. One of the best ways to build reading and writing potential is to foster language development. In study after study, knowledge of vocabulary has been found to be the key element in comprehension. Students' listening level has also been found to be closely related to their reading level. The level of material that a student can understand orally is a good gauge of the level at which the student can read with understanding. While fostering language development is important for all students, it is absolutely essential for students who are learning English as a second language.

10. *Teachers should build higher-level literacy skills.* While working as a Reading First consultant in an urban school, I experienced what I would term an epiphany. I was observing a class during a test-taking session. Students were taking an end-of-theme test that was part of a newly purchased basal anthology reading program. The test assessed skills taught during the unit. One of the students began crying. She was one of the last to finish her end-of-theme test. When I asked her what was wrong, she replied, "I don't know how to do this." The question that puzzled her was a constructed query, "Could this story have happened in real life the way it is told here?" (Valencia, 2001, p. 10). I asked her to read the question so that I could judge whether she could do so. She read it smoothly. Thinking that maybe she didn't understand the story or the story was written on too high a level for her, I asked her to read a few lines. She read those smoothly. I then talked to her about the story. The story, *Who Took the Farmer's Hat* (Nodset, 1963), was about a farmer whose hat blew off. I asked her if that could happen in real life. She replied that it could. We then discussed the part in which the farmer asks the squirrel if he had seen his hat. The student said that that couldn't happen because animals can't talk. She said that the story was a fantasy. I suggested that she write down what she had just explained. However, her answer stated, "The story couldn't happen in real life. It is a fantasy" (Gunning, 2007).

My discussion with the student suggested that her comprehension of the story was adequate, as was her reasoning about it. However, she apparently didn't understand the ques-

HIGHER-LEVEL LITERACY

The first step in developing higher-level skills is to create a culture of understanding (Collins, 2005). In a culture of understanding, teachers make sure that everyone understands everything that is going on in the classroom. Teachers also make sure that directions and instructions are clear, and they teach students to seek understanding. Students are taught that if they don't understand directions or lessons, they should seek help.

tion or didn't realize that she knew the answer. Even after stating the answer, she was not successful in formulating it. She failed to tell why the story couldn't have happened in real life. In retrospect, I should have asked her to explain why it was a fantasy so that she might realize that she needed to show that it could not have happened in real life.

Observations and discussions with the students in this and other classes revealed that although some students were having difficulty because their higher-level thinking skills needed developing, there were a large number of students who comprehended on a high level but were unable to demonstrate that knowledge in writing. Meanwhile, teachers were reporting that although their students did well in oral discussions, they were doing poorly on the end-of-theme tests. Working with older students, Calder and Carlson (2002) found that the students in the middle ability level could talk better than they could write. The researchers concluded that "deep understandings seemed to evaporate when [the students] tried to wrestle their thoughts to paper. This told us that we had work to do if we wanted to distinguish between assessing understanding and assessing students' ability to communicate their understanding" (p. 2). Based on extensive work with struggling learners, Gaskins (2005) reported a similar problem.

Sadly, it appears that many students aren't getting credit for what they know because they lack the necessary writing skills. In subsequent chapters, this book will emphasize developing higher-level thinking skills and will also stress teaching the speaking and writing skills needed to answer higher-level discussion and test questions. Along with lessons in these higher-level skills, there will be suggestions for teaching students how to demonstrate their knowledge. Being able to demonstrate what one knows and can do is a key literacy skill, but one that has apparently been neglected. Given the importance of higher-level skills, two new features have been added to the text: marginal annotations entitled "Higher-Level Literacy" and an-end-of-chapter feature entitled "Building Higher-Level Literacy."

11. *Classroom management for learning should be an essential part of the literacy program.* The best-planned lessons are ineffective if students aren't paying attention or aren't actively engaged in the learning process. Indeed, the most effective teachers operate at the 90–90 level: Ninety percent of the students are on task 90 percent of the time. Actually, behavior improves when students are given the right level of challenge. They are more likely to participate. However, it is also essential to have a classroom management system. Such a system works best if the whole school has adopted it and if it is proactive. However, even if the school hasn't set up a system, you should create one for your classroom. One such system is known as the Responsive Classroom.

The Responsive Classroom combines academic and social learning and is based on the idea that positive learning behavior can be taught (Charney, 2002). It uses class discussions and the concept of natural consequences: A student who fails to complete work because of wasting time must use free time to finish it; a student who comes to literature circle unprepared must sit out the session. The Responsive Classroom system is also based on student choice: Students have a choice between obeying the class's rules and going to time-out, between talking in soft voices during center time and not being able to talk at all. The Responsive Classroom conveys a positive message: I care about you; it's not that I am correcting you as a person—it's your behavior. There is no use of sarcasm, personal attacks, or threats (Gunning, 2006).

A key element of the Responsive Classroom system is the teaching of routines. Routines are demonstrated and practiced until they become automatic. Routines are established for classroom discussion groups, reporting to the guided reading table, going to centers, selecting voluntary reading books, passing out materials, and all other key activities. As appropriate, routines will be suggested in this book for activities that require them.

12. *Ongoing assessment is an essential element in an effective literacy program.* Teachers need to know how students are progressing so that they can give extra help or change the program, if necessary. Assessment need not be formal. Observation can be a powerful assessment tool. However, assessment should be tied to the program's standards and should result in improvement in students' learning. In each chapter in which instructional objectives are stated, suggestions are made for assessing those objectives. Suggestions for assessment can also be found in annotations in the margins and in Chapter 2. In addition, there are several assessment instruments in Appendix B.

FYI

Students in schools using Responsive Classroom did better in reading than students in control schools (Rimm-Kaufman, Fan, Chiu, & You, April, 2006). As Elliott (1999) concluded "social skills function as academic enablers for students and thus appear to have a causal relationship to achievement test results" (p. 5).

USING TECHNOLOGY

An excellent source of information about the Responsive Classroom system is this Web site:
http://www.responsiveclassroom.org

■ ■ ■ **Checkup** ■ ■ ■

1. What are the twelve principles underlying an effective reading program?

■ ■ ■

■ Highly Effective Teachers

FYI

Based on a study of traditional and high-tech approaches to teaching literacy in sixteen kindergarten and first-grade classes, Paterson, Henry, O'Quin, Ceprano, & Blue (2003) found that it was the teacher who made the difference. Students achieved the most in classes in which most of the time was spent on instruction rather than management, in which varying grouping patterns were used, and in which students put more of themselves into their work—for instance, composing original pieces rather than simply completing stories by filling in blanks.

In the 1960s, the U.S. Department of Education spent millions of dollars in an attempt to find out which method of teaching reading was the best (Bond & Dykstra, 1967; Graves & Dykstra, 1997). More than a dozen approaches were studied. There was no clear winner. No one method was superior in all circumstances. What the researchers did find was that the teacher was key. Teachers using the same methods got differing results. Some teachers were simply more effective than others.

What are the characteristics of effective teachers? Over the past decade, a number of top researchers have visited the classes of teachers judged to be highly effective. Their students read more books and wrote more stories. Virtually all read on or above grade level. Their writing skills were surprisingly advanced. They also enjoyed school. On many occasions, observers watched in surprise as students skipped recess so that they could continue working on an activity. Their work was more appealing to them than play.

Caring and High Expectations

Perhaps the most outstanding characteristic of highly effective teachers is that they cared for their students and believed in them (Pressley, Allington, Wharton-McDonald, Block, & Morrow, 2001). They were genuinely convinced that their students could and would learn, and they acted accordingly. In writing, for instance, typical first-grade teachers believed that writing was difficult for young students and expected their students would only be able to produce pieces of writing composed of a sentence or two by year's end (Wharton-McDonald, 2001). Their expectations were discouragingly accurate. By year's end, most students in their classes were producing narratives that consisted of one to three loosely connected sentences with little attention to punctuation or capitalization.

Highly effective teachers had higher expectations. They believed that first-graders were capable of sustained writing. By year's end they expected a coherent paragraph that consisted of five or even more sentences, each of which started with a capital letter and ended with a period. And that's the kind of writing their students produced. Students have a way of living up to or down to teachers' expectations.

However, the highly effective teachers realized that high expectations are in the same category as good intentions; they need to be acted upon. High expectations were accompanied by the kind of instruction that allowed students to live up to those expectations. Highly effective teachers were also superior motivators. The teachers created a feeling of excitement about the subject matter or skill areas they taught (Ruddell, 1995).

Balanced Instruction

As students evidenced a need for instruction, effective teachers were quick to conduct a mini-lesson. A student attempting to spell *boat*, for instance, would be given an on-the-spot lesson on the *oa* spelling of long *o*. However, essential skills were not relegated to opportunistic teaching. Key skills were taught directly and thoroughly but were related to the reading and writing that students were doing.

Extensive Instruction

Effective teachers used every opportunity to reinforce skills. Wherever possible, connections were made between reading and writing and between reading and writing and content area concepts. Often, students would develop or apply science and social studies concepts in their writing.

Scaffolding

Exemplary teachers scaffolded students' responses. Instead of simply telling students answers, these teachers used prompts and other devices to help students reason their way to the correct response.

Classroom Management

Highly effective teachers were well organized. Routines were well established and highly effective. The core of their classroom management was building in students a sense of responsibility. Students learned to regulate their own behavior. One of the things that stood out in the rooms of highly effective teachers was the sense of purpose and orderliness. The greatest proportion of time was spent with high-payoff activities. When students composed illustrated booklets, for instance, the bulk of their time was spent researching and composing the booklets. Only a minimum of time was spent illustrating them.

Students learned how to work together. The classroom atmosphere was one of cooperation rather than competition. Effort was emphasized. Praise and reinforcement were used as appropriate. Students were also taught to be competent, independent learners. They were taught strategies for selecting appropriate-level books, for decoding unfamiliar words, and for understanding difficult text. Their efforts were affirmed so that they would be encouraged to continue using strategies. "Jonathan, I liked the way you previewed that book before selecting it to read. Now you have a better idea of what it is about and whether it is a just-right book for you."

High-Quality Materials

The best teachers used the best materials. Students listened to and read classics as well as outstanding contemporary works from children's literature. There was a decided emphasis on reading. Classrooms were well stocked with materials, and time was set aside for various kinds of reading: shared, partner, and individual.

Matching of Materials and Tasks to Student Competence

Highly effective teachers gave students materials and tasks that were somewhat challenging but not overwhelming. Teachers carefully monitored students and made assignments on the basis of students' performance. If the book students were reading seemed to have too many difficult words and concepts, students were given an easier book. If they mastered writing a brief paragraph, they were encouraged to write a more fully developed piece. However, they were provided with the assistance and instruction needed to cope with more challenging tasks.

Becoming a Highly Effective Teacher

How did highly effective teachers get that way? They worked at it (Day, 2001). They were always seeking better techniques and better materials. To sustain their desire for improvement, they kept up with developments in the field through taking courses, attending workshops and inservices, and reading the professional literature. They also reflected on their teaching and sought the advice of colleagues. When a technique failed to work or materials seemed too hard, they were quick to recognize this and quick to seek a better approach or more effective materials. They looked at new methods and materials in the light of students' needs:

> Exemplary teachers believe that excellent teaching consists of observing and understanding student perspectives on what they are learning, and examining materials in light of how well they fit with a particular child's needs. Rather than promote a method or program for its own sake, they look at it in the light of the specific children in front of them and whether it would be better or worse in meeting a need. (Day, 2001, p. 217)

Although a great variety of topics will be covered in later chapters, the twelve primary principles discussed above are emphasized throughout. Teaching suggestions and activities are included for fostering wide reading, keeping reading reasonably easy, keeping reading and writing functional, making connections, setting goals and assessing progress, and, above all, building a sense of competence and promoting independence. This book is based on the premise that virtually all children can learn to read and write.

■ ■ ■ Checkup ■ ■ ■

1. What are the characteristics of an effective teacher?
2. How might you go about becoming an effective teacher?

■ ■ ■

Tools for the Classroom

Building Higher-Level Literacy

Faced with basic literal questions, students do well. Some 64 percent of fourth-graders can read on a basic level but do poorly when required to respond to test items that assess higher-level thinking skills. Only about one-third of students are reading at the proficient level or above (Perie, Grigg, & Donahue, 2005). However, today's major reading programs present a number of basic and higher-level skills. Students are expected to summarize, make inferences, draw conclusions, compare texts, and identify and explain the impact of techniques used by writers as well as assess the credibility of the piece. In addition to being able to use higher-level thinking skills to comprehend challenging texts, students must be able to demonstrate such skills on both end-of-unit and high-stakes tests.

Today's world, both in and out of school, demands higher-level literacy skills. With the implementation of NCLB, there has been an emphasis on basic skills. While basic skills are essential, they aren't sufficient to allow students to prosper in an information-rich world or even to pass high-stakes tests. Higher-level skills must be built from the beginning. Developing vocabulary, language proficiency, and background knowledge, as recommended in this chapter, fosters the development of higher-level skills. The more background knowledge we have, the better we are able to think. The more developed our vocabulary and overall language, the better able we are to express abstract ideas.

Action Plan

1. Construct a personal philosophy of teaching literacy. Note the effects that your philosophy of teaching literacy would have on your approach to teaching, your assessment methods, grouping practices, and choice of learning activities and materials.
2. Create a plan for becoming an effective teacher. What steps will you take to create a high-quality program and to continue to develop your ability to teach literacy?

Summary

Reading is an active process in which the reader constructs meaning from text. Key elements in learning to read are language development, cognitive development, and background of experience. Reading development is also affected by one's culture. Reading can be viewed as being bottom-up, top-down, or interactive or integrated. Because little progress has been made in reading over the past three decades, legislation known as No Child Left Behind requires that all students reach proficiency on state assessments by 2013–2014. This legislation stresses the use of scientifically based instruction.

Widespread reading and functional instruction commensurate with children's abilities are essentials of an effective reading program. Also necessary is instruction that helps students make connections and fosters independence. Believing that virtually every child can learn to read and building students' motivation and sense of competence are important factors in an effective literacy program, as are set-ting goals; systematic, direct instruction; managing class-room behavior; building language proficiency; building higher-level literacy; and ongoing assessment. The ultimate key to a successful program is a highly effective teacher.

Extending and Applying

1. Analyze your beliefs about teaching reading. Make a list of your major beliefs. Are you a top-downer, a bottom-upper, or an interactionist? Now make a list of your major teaching and reinforcement activities. Do they fit your philosophy? If not, what changes might you make?

2. RTI is in the early stages of implementation. What provisions has your state made for implementing RTI?

3. Find out what your state's literacy goals or standards are. Most state departments of education list this information on their Web sites.

4. Analyze the instruction activities as you teach a reading lesson or observe a class being taught. Classify the activities as being top-down, bottom-up, or interactive. Also, note the reactions of the students to the activities. Do they find them interesting? Do they seem to be learning from them?

Developing a Professional Portfolio

Many school systems require applicants to submit a portfolio. Some require new teachers to complete portfolios as part of the evaluation process. Even if a portfolio is not required in your situation, creating and maintaining one provides you with the opportunity to reflect on your ideas about teaching and your teaching practices. It will help you get to know yourself better as a teacher and so provide a basis for im-provement. To assist you in creating a portfolio, each chapter will offer suggestions for developing it.

Set up a professional portfolio. The portfolio should highlight your professional preparation, relevant experience, and mastery of key teaching skills. Using the list compiled in item 1 of Extending and Applying, draw up a statement of your philosophy of teaching reading and writing.

Go to Allyn & Bacon's MyLabSchool: www.mylabschool.com

- Enter Assignment ID **GMV5** into **Assignment Finder,** and select the video titled "Strategies for Teaching Diverse Learners." In this video, two teachers discuss the importance of planning instruction to accommodate children's diverse needs. The teachers demonstrate how they provide multiple opportunities for students to access in-structional material and to show what they know.

- As you watch the video, identify the various strategies the teachers use to address the needs of students with different learning styles. Are the strategies effective?

- Explore MyLabSchool further to find the course areas for Reading Methods, Language Arts, and Content Area Reading and identify other assets that support concepts introduced in this chapter.

Developing a Resource File

As you read about various teaching and assessment procedures in the text, collect resources that will help you implement the procedures and assessments. The resources might be a list of books for reading out loud or a list of Web sites for developing vocabulary. For this chapter, you might collect articles that have helpful suggestions for setting up a literacy program.

To access chapter objectives, practice tests, weblinks, and flashcards, go to the companion website at www.ablongman.com/gunning6e.

2 Evaluation

For each of the following statements related to the chapter you are about to read, put a check under "Agree" or "Disagree" to show how you feel. Discuss your responses with classmates before you read the chapter.

	Agree	Disagree
1. Nationwide achievement tests are essential for the assessment of literacy.	_____	_____
2. Setting high standards and assessing student achievement on those standards is a good way to improve the quality of reading and writing instruction.	_____	_____
3. Most writing assessments are too subjective.	_____	_____
4. Today's students take too many tests.	_____	_____
5. A community has a right to know how its schools are doing.	_____	_____
6. Observation yields more information about a student's progress in reading and writing than a standardized test does.	_____	_____

Evaluation is an essential part of literacy learning. It is a judgment by teachers, children, parents, administrators, and the wider community as to whether instructional goals have been met. Evaluation also helps teachers determine what is and what is not working so that they can plan better programs. Self-evaluation gives students more control over their own learning.

What kinds of experiences have you had with evaluation? How has your schoolwork been assessed? Do you agree with the assessments, or do you think they were off the mark? Keeping in mind the current emphasis on balanced reading and writing processes and integration of language arts, what might be some appropriate ways to evaluate the literacy development of today's students?

■ The Nature of Evaluation

In evaluation, we ask, "How am I doing?" so that we can do better. **Evaluation** is a value judgment. We can also ask, "How is the education program doing?" and base our evaluation on tests, quizzes, records, work samples, observations, anecdotal records, portfolios, and similar information. The evaluation could be made by a student while reviewing her or his writing folder or by parents as they look over a report card. The evaluator could be a teacher, who, after examining a portfolio or collection of a student's work and thinking over recent observations of that student, concludes that the student has done well but could do better.

Evaluation should result in some kind of action. The evaluator must determine what that action should be, based on his or her judgment. The student may decide that he or she has been writing the same type of pieces and needs to branch out, the parents might decide that their child must study more, and the teacher might choose to add more silent reading time to the program.

FYI

■ A composite set of standards is available from the Mid-Central Regional Educational Laboratory, available online at http://www.mcrel.org/standards-benchmarks/

Composite goals are also available from New Standards (National Center on Education and the Economy & University of Pittsburgh, 1997).

■ Assessment data is used as the basis for evaluation.

■ Being able to read at Level 16 is the standard for Reading Recovery. This is similar to being able to read a first-grade selection on an informal reading inventory. Being able to read 40 words per minute on a first-grade selection is a rate standard. The most lenient standard requires scoring at the 30th percentile or higher on a norm-referenced reading test (Denton, Fletcher, & Ciancio, 2006).

The Starting Point

Evaluation starts with a set of goals. You cannot tell if you have reached your destination if you do not know where you were headed. For example, a teacher may decide that one of her goals will be to instill in children a love of reading. This is a worthy goal, but it is lacking in many programs. How will the teacher decide whether the goal has been reached, and what will the teacher use as evidence? The goal has to be stated in terms of a specific objective that includes, if possible, observable behavior—for example, students will voluntarily read at least twenty minutes a day or at least one book a month. The objective then becomes measurable, and the teacher can collect information that will provide evidence as to whether it has been met.

The Standards Movement

The centerpiece of the standards movement is the statement of goals or objectives. The standards movement grew out of concern for the quality of education in the United States. A National Educational Goals Panel was convened in the late 1980s. A set of broad goals was established. These have been translated into **standards** for every discipline, including reading and writing.

Currently all states are required to have standards in reading and assessment devices that measure progress toward reaching those standards. Because these assessments are used to rate schools, they are high-stakes tests.

The idea behind the standards is that clearly stated objectives should lead to improved instruction, especially if assessment is closely tied to the standards and if there are adequate instructional resources for helping students meet standards. Standards apparently work. In a recent study, researchers concluded that states that did the best job of implementing standards and that aligned assessment with those standards had the greatest gains in reading (*Education Week*, 2006). State standards are available at state departments of education. Ultimately, national and state standards have to be translated, adapted, and revised so that they fit the needs of your students.

Authentic Assessment

Through tests, observations, and other means, **assessment** provides the data necessary for effective instruction. One of the best sources of data to inform instruction is **authentic assessment**. The word *authentic* is used because these assessment procedures "reflect the actual learning and instructional activities of the classroom and out-of-school worlds" (Hiebert, Valencia, & Afflerbach, 1994, p. 11). In authentic assessment, students retell or summarize whole texts, as opposed to the kind of objective testing in which students respond to multiple-choice questions about short paragraphs. Observations, think-alouds, holistic scoring of writing, anecdotal records, and assembling and evaluating a portfolio are also examples of authentic assessment. Even large-scale assessments are becoming more authentic. Many state and national assessments now use longer passages and ask for constructed responses in which students respond in writing.

■ **Evaluation** is the process of using the results of tests, observations, work samples, and other devices to judge the effectiveness of a program. A program is evaluated in terms of its objectives. The ultimate purpose of evaluation is to improve the program.

■ **Standards** are statements of what students should know and be able to do.

■ **Assessment** is the process of gathering data about an area of learning through tests, observations, work samples, and other means.

■ **Authentic assessment** involves using tasks that are typical of the kinds of reading or writing that students perform in school and out.

■ A **high-stakes test** is one whose results are used to make an important decision such as passing students, graduating students, or rating a school.

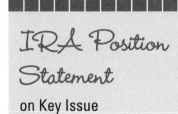

I R A Position Statement

on Key Issue

High-Stakes Testing

As its name suggests, a **high-stakes test** is one for which an important decision will be based on the outcome. Because of the role they play in decision making, high-stakes tests have the potential to dictate curriculum. Instead of teaching what their community has judged to be important, educators might teach what is tested. This has the effect of narrowing the curriculum. Knowing, for instance, that students will be tested on narrative writing in the fourth grade, teachers in the early grades overemphasize story writing and neglect expository writing. A great deal of time is also spent writing to a prompt because that is the way students will be assessed on the state tests. To combat the misuse of tests, the International Reading Association (1999a) has made the following recommendations:

Teachers should

- construct rigorous classroom assessments to help outside observers gain confidence in teacher techniques.
- educate parents, community members, and policy makers about classroom-based assessment.
- teach students how tests are structured, but not teach to the test.

■ ■ ■ Checkup ■ ■ ■

1. What effect do standards and high-stakes assessment have on assessment and instruction?
2. What are the components of assessment?

■ ■ ■

Assessing for Learning: Summative and Formative Assessment

Assessment can be characterized as being summative or formative. Summative assessment summarizes students' progress at the end of a unit or a semester or at some other point in time. Standardized and high-stakes tests are summative. Formative assessment is ongoing and is used to inform instruction. "Teachers need to know about their pupils' progress and difficulties with learning so that they can adapt their own work to meet pupils' needs— needs that are often unpredictable and that vary from one pupil to another" (Black & Wiliam, 1998). Teachers can find out what they need to know in a variety of ways: observing, using think-alouds, analyzing students' work, consulting anecdotal records, listening to discussions, and probing students' responses.

Formative assessment can be powerful. In an extensive study of this type of assessment, Black & Wiliam (1998) found that its use increased average student performance by as much as 24 percentile points. Formative assessment was especially helpful for struggling learners: "While formative assessment can help all pupils, it yields particularly good results with low achievers by concentrating on specific problems with their work and giving them a clear understanding of what is wrong and how to put it right."

Formative assessment is ongoing and focuses on tasks, not students. It is concerned with process as well as product. Process measures seek to answer such questions as these: How do students prepare to read an assignment? Do they reread or use some other strategy when the material they are reading doesn't make sense? Do students select, organize, and elaborate information as they read? As Black and Wiliam (1998) note, it is "important to look at or listen carefully to the talk, the writing, and the actions through which pupils develop and display the state of their understanding. Thus we maintain that *opportunities for pupils to express their understanding should be designed into any piece of teaching, for this will initiate the interaction through which formative assessment aids learning.* . . .

FYI

High-stakes assessment is especially controversial at the early levels. The National Educational Goals Panel (NEGP) advises against using standardized tests to make high-stakes accountability decisions before grades 3 or 4. Some children may have had minimal exposure to reading and writing activities. It would be erroneous to assume that these children have difficulty learning (Johnston & Rogers, 2001). A better course of action is to give them the opportunity to learn and see how they do.

USING TECHNOLOGY

A listing of standards compiled by the International Reading Association and National Council of Teachers of English is available at the IRA Web site: http://www.reading.org/publications/bbv/books/bk889

Most states have sample test items on their Web sites. Analyze the test items, and take the test to get a sense of what students must cope with.

Discussions in which pupils are led to talk about their understanding in their own ways are important aids to increasing knowledge and improving understanding. Dialogue with the teacher provides the opportunity for the teacher to respond to and reorient a pupil's thinking." The basic idea behind formative assessment is to obtain enough information about students so that you can give them the help they need.

Clear feedback is an essential part of formative assessment. Feedback should be such that students fully understand what they need to do to improve. Self-assessment is also an essential component of formative assessment. For students to carry out self-assessment, they need to know what it is they are supposed to know or be able to do (the objective), how they are doing (status), and what they need to do to be able to reach the goal (corrective action). Students can't work toward a goal if they don't know what it is, don't know what their current capabilities are, or don't know how to take corrective action. As Stiggins (2004) recommends, "We must build classroom environments in which students use assessments to understand what success looks like and how to do better the next time. In effect, we must help students use ongoing classroom assessment to take responsibility for their own academic success" (pp. 25–26).

Because of the importance of formative assessment, suggestions for its use appear throughout this book in the form of marginal notes titled "Assessing for Learning."

Product versus Process Measures

Authentic assessment emphasizes process rather than product. Product assessment is concerned with what the student has learned. Product measures include the number of correct answers on a quiz, the score on a norm-referenced test, the final copy of a composition, and the number of books read. Such measures help teachers assess students' current and past levels of achievement. They provide information on students' reading and writing levels and abilities, the kinds of materials they can read, the kinds of writing they can do, and how well they can spell. Knowing where each student is, the teacher can plan instruction and activities that build on what students have already accomplished.

Process assessment seeks to find out how the student learns. Process measures include observing students to see what strategies they use to arrive at a particular answer, to compose a piece of writing, or to study for a test. Having this kind of insight, the teacher is able to redirect errant thought processes, correct poorly applied strategies, or teach needed strategies. Actually, both process and product measures provide useful information. Knowing where a child is and how he or she got there, the teacher is better prepared to map out a successful journey toward improvement.

■ Judging Assessment Measures

Reliability

To be useful, tests and other assessment instruments must be both reliable and valid. **Reliability** is a measure of consistency, which means that if the same test were given to the same students a number of times, the results would be approximately the same.

FYI

Many process measures are said to be authentic.

■ **Reliability** is the degree to which a test yields consistent results. In other words, if students took a reliable test again, their scores would be approximately the same.

■ **Validity** is the degree to which a test measures what it is supposed to measure, or the extent to which a test will provide information needed to make a decision. Validity should be considered in terms of the consequences of the test results and the use to which the results will be put.

■ **Content validity** means that the tasks of an assessment device are representative of the subject or area being assessed.

Reliability is usually reported as a coefficient of correlation and ranges from 0.00 to 0.99 or −0.01 to −0.99. The higher the positive correlation, the more reliable the test. For tests on which individual decisions are being based, reliability should be in the 0.90s.

Reliability can also be thought of as generalizability. For observations and other informal approaches to assessment, it means that similar findings have been found by different judges and at different times (Johnston & Rogers, 2001). One way of increasing reliability is by training observers. Another is to have several observations.

A test that is not reliable is of no value. It is the equivalent of an elastic yardstick—the results of measurement would be different each time.

Validity

In general, **validity** means that a test measures what it says it measures: vocabulary knowledge or speed of reading, for instance. Ultimately, it means that a particular test will provide the information needed to make a decision, such as placing a student with an appropriate level book or indicating specific strengths and weaknesses in comprehension (Farr & Carey, 1986). Johnston and Rogers (2001) contend that unless an assessment practice helps to improve students' learning, it should not occur. Reading tests need content validity, meaning that the skills and strategies tested must be the same as those taught. Calfee and Hiebert (1991) define validity with the following question: "Does assessment match what I have taught and the way I have taught it?" (p. 282).

To check for **content validity**, list the objectives of the program and note how closely a particular test's objectives match them. The test selections should be examined, too, to see whether they reflect the type of material that the students read. Also, determine how reading is tested. If a test assesses skills or strategies that you do not cover or assesses them in a way that is not suitable, the test is not valid for your class.

Reading First and some other government programs require assessment measures that have concurrent and predictive validity. *Concurrent validity* means that an assessment measure correlates with a similar test or other form of assessment occurring at about the same time. *Predictive validity* means that there is a correlation between the assessment measure and some future behavior. This could be a correlation between phonological awareness in kindergarten and reading comprehension in third grade.

However, a number of assessment measures that have high statistical (concurrent and predictive) validity may be lacking in content validity. For instance, phonics tests that use nonsense words might correlate well with measures of current and future performance but distort the reading process and so have limited content validity and thus limited usefulness for teachers. If an assessment measure doesn't assess what you teach or assesses a skill in a way that differs from the way that students actually apply it, then the measure is lacking in content validity.

Closely tied to validity are the consequences or uses to which the assessment will be put. If the test assesses only a narrow part of the curriculum, it will be detrimental and thus invalid (Joint Task Force on Assessment, 1994). Assessment measures should also be fair to all who take them. There should be no biased items, and the content should be such that all students have had an equal opportunity to learn it.

FYI

■ Whether assessment is formal or informal, done through observation or paper-and-pencil testing, reliability is essential. As Farr (1991) observes, "If a test or other means of assessment is not reliable, it's no good. . . . If you stand on the bathroom scale and it registers 132 lbs. one morning, but it's 147 the next morning, and 85 the morning after that, you conclude it's time for a new set of bathroom scales." (p. 4).

■ One danger in evaluation is the temptation to gather too much information. Be economical. Do not waste time gathering information you are not going to use.

■ ■ ■ Checkup ■ ■ ■

1. How should assessment measures be judged?
2. Why is content validity more important for teachers than statistical validity?

■ ■ ■

General Questions for Evaluation

Essentially, evaluation is the process of asking a series of questions. Specific questions depend on a program's particular goals and objectives. However, some general questions that should be asked about every literacy program include the following:

- Where are students in their literacy development?
- At what level are they reading?
- Are they reading up to their ability level?
- Are they making adequate, ongoing progress?
- How well do they comprehend what they read?
- How adequate are students' reading vocabularies?
- What comprehension and word-analysis strategies do students use?
- What is the level of students' language development?
- What are their attitudes toward reading?
- Do they enjoy a variety of genres?
- Do they read on their own?
- How well do they write?
- What kinds of writing tasks have they attempted?
- Are students' reading and writing improving?
- Which students seem to have special needs in reading and writing?
- Are these special needs being met?

Answers to these essential questions help teachers plan, revise, and improve their reading and writing programs. The rest of this chapter explores a number of techniques for gathering the assessment information necessary to answer them. Both traditional and alternative means will be discussed.

■ Placement Information

FYI

If students are not yet reading, they can be given an emergent literacy assessment, as explained in Chapter 3.

The first question the classroom teacher of reading has to have answered is "Where are the students in their literacy development?" If they are reading, assessment begins with determining the levels at which they are reading. One of the best placement devices is an informal reading inventory (IRI). In fact, if properly given, it will provide just about everything a teacher needs to know about a student's reading. It will also supply useful information about language development, work habits, interests, and personal development.

■ An **informal reading inventory (IRI)** is an assessment device in which a student reads a series of selections that gradually increase in difficulty. The teacher records errors and assesses comprehension in order to determine levels of materials that a student can read.

■ The **independent level** is the level at which a student can read without any assistance. Comprehension is 90 percent or higher, and word recognition is 99 percent or higher.

■ The **instructional level** is the level at which a student needs a teacher's help. Comprehension is 75 percent or higher, and word recognition is 95 percent or higher.

■ The **frustration level** is the level at which reading material is so difficult that the student can't read it even with help. Frustration is reached when either word recognition is 90 percent or lower or comprehension is 50 percent or lower.

■ **Listening capacity** is the highest level of reading material that students can understand with 75 percent comprehension when it is read to them.

Informal Reading Inventory

An **informal reading inventory (IRI)** is a series of graded selections beginning at the very easiest level—preprimer—and extending up to eighth grade or beyond. Each level has two selections; one is silent and the other oral. Starting at an easy level, the student continues to read until it is obvious that the material has become too difficult.

An IRI yields information about four reading levels: independent, instructional, frustration, and listening capacity. The **independent level**, or the free-reading level, is the point at which students can read on their own without teacher assistance. The **instructional level** refers to the point at which students need assistance because the material contains too many unknown words or concepts or their background of experience is insufficient. This is also the level of materials used for teaching. Material at the **frustration level** is so difficult that students cannot read it even with teacher assistance. The fourth level is listening capacity, the highest level at which students can understand what has been read to them. **Listening capacity** is an informal measure of ability to comprehend spoken language. Theoretically, it is the level at which students should be able to read if they had all the necessary decoding skills. In practice, a small percentage of students have listening deficiencies, so a listening test might underestimate their true capacity. Younger students also tend to read below capacity because they are still acquiring basic reading skills. As students progress through the grades, listening and reading levels grow closer together (Sticht & James, 1984).

The first IRIs were constructed by teachers and were created using passages from basal readers. This was a good idea because it meant that there was an exact match between the material the student was tested on and the material the student would be reading. Because constructing IRIs is time consuming, most teachers now use commercially produced ones. (See Table 2.1.) However, IRIs are available for basal reading programs.

IRIs can also be based on children's books. If, for instance, your program emphasizes the reading of children's books, you might designate certain titles as benchmark books and construct questions or retelling activities based on these books. Benchmark books can be used to place students and check their progress. Sets of benchmark books and accompanying questions are also available from basal reader publishers. Or you can construct your

■■■ TABLE 2.1 Commercial Reading Inventories

Name	Publisher	Grades	Added Skill Areas
Analytical Reading Inventory	Merrill	1–9	
Bader Reading and Language Inventory	Merrill	1–12	phonics, language, emergent literacy
Basic Reading Inventory	Kendall/Hunt	1–8	emergent literacy
Burns and Roe Informal Inventory	Houghton Mifflin	1–12	
Classroom Reading Inventory	McGraw-Hill	1–8	spelling
Critical Reading Inventory: Assessing Students' Reading and Thinking	Prentice Hall	1–12	critical thinking
Ekwall/Shanker Reading Inventory	Allyn & Bacon	1–12	emergent literacy, word analysis
English-Español Reading Inventory for the Classroom	Prentice Hall	1–12	emergent literacy (has an English-only version)
Flynt-Cooter Reading Inventory for the Classroom	Merrill	1–12	emergent literacy
Informal Reading Thinking Inventory	Harcourt	1–11	
Phonological Awareness Literacy Screening (PALS)	University of Virginia	K–3	emergent literacy, spelling
Qualitative Reading Inventory III	Allyn & Bacon	1–12	
Stieglitz Informal Reading Inventory	Allyn & Bacon	1–8	emergent literacy
Texas Primary Reading Inventory	Texas Education Agency	K–3	emergent literacy, phonics (has a Spanish version)

▪▪▪ TABLE 2.2 Quantitative Criteria for IRI Placement Levels

Level	Word Recognition in Context (%)	Average Comprehension (%)
Independent	99–100	90–100
Instructional	95–98	75–89
Frustration	≤90	≤50
Listening capacity		75

own. This chapter lists benchmark books that can be used to judge the difficulty level of children's books. You might use these books as the basis for an informal reading inventory.

Determining Placement Levels

Placement levels are determined by having students read two selections, one orally and one silently, at appropriate grade levels. The percentages of oral-reading errors and comprehension questions answered correctly at each level are calculated. This information is then used to determine placement levels. Quantitative criteria for determining levels are presented in Table 2.2.

To be at the independent level, a reader must have, at minimum, both 99 percent word recognition and 90 percent comprehension. At the instructional level, the reader must have at least 95 percent word recognition and at least 75 percent comprehension. The frustration level is reached when word recognition drops to 90 percent or below or comprehension falls to 50 percent or below. Even with 80 percent comprehension and 90 percent word recognition, readers are at the frustration level because they are encountering too many words that they cannot decode. Listening capacity is the level at which students can understand 75 percent of the material that is read to them.

Running records and some other placement devices use lower standards, such as 90 to 95 percent word recognition. It is strongly advised that you stick to the 95 to 98 percent word recognition standard. Research indicates that students do best when they can read at least 95 to 98 percent of the words (Berliner, 1981; Biemiller, 1994; Gambrell, Wilson, & Gantt, 1981). It is also important that the examiner adhere to strict standards when marking word reading errors. Enz (1989) found that relaxing IRI standards resulted in a drop in both achievement and attitude. Students placed according to higher standards spent a greater proportion of time on task, had a higher success rate, and had a more positive attitude toward reading.

Administering the Word-List Test

Rather than guessing the grade level at which to begin the IRI, a teacher can administer a word-list test to locate an approximate starting point. This test consists of a series of ten to twenty words at each grade level. Students read the words in isolation, starting with the easiest and continuing until they reach a level where they get half or more of the words wrong. In a simplified administration of the test, students read the words from their copy of the list, and the teacher marks each response on her or his copy as being right or wrong.

In a diagnostic administration, the teacher uses three-by-five cards to flash the words for one second each. When students respond correctly, the teacher moves on to the next word. If the answer is incorrect or if students fail to respond, the teacher stops and lets them look at the word for as long as they wish (within reason). While students examine the missed word, the teacher writes down their response or marks

▪▪▪ TABLE 2.3 Word-List Marking Symbols

Word	Teacher Mark	Meaning
the	✓	Correct
was	✓	Incorrect response or repeated error
have	o	No response
dog	boy	Mispronunciation
are	dk	Don't know

a symbol in the flash (timed) column. If students make a second erroneous response, it is written in the second, or untimed, column. Symbols used to mark word-list tests are presented in Table 2.3. A corrected word-list test is shown in Figure 2.1.

Besides indicating the starting level for the IRI, a word-list test can yield valuable information about students' reading, especially if a diagnostic administration has been used. By comparing flash and untimed scores, teachers can assess the adequacy of students' sight vocabulary (their ability to recognize words immediately) and their proficiency with decoding. Teachers can note which decoding skills students are able to use and which must be taught. Looking at the performance depicted in Figure 2.1, it is clear that the student has a very limited sight vocabulary. The flash column shows that the student recognized few of the words immediately; the untimed column gives an overall picture of the student's ability to apply decoding skills. The student was able to use initial and final consonants and short vowels to decode words; for example, the student was able to read *wet, king, let,* and *bit* when given time to decode them. However, the student had difficulty with initial clusters; note how the student read *sick* for *stick, sell* for *smell,* and *for* for *floor.*

Administering the Inventory

The IRI is started at the level below the student's last perfect performance on the flash portion of the word-list test. If that perfect performance was at the fourth-grade level, the inventory is started at the third-grade level.

An IRI is like a directed reading lesson, except that its main purpose is to assess a student's reading. To administer an IRI, first explain to the student that she or he will be reading some stories and answering some questions so that you

■ ■ ■ **FIGURE 2.1 A Corrected Word-List Test**

		Flash	Untimed
1.	their	the	✓
2.	wet	o	✓
3.	king	o	✓
4.	off	o	dk
5.	alone	uh	along
6.	hurt	✓	
7.	near	✓	
8.	tiger	tie	✓
9.	stick	sick	✓
10.	move	moo	more
11.	let	o	✓
12.	men	✓	
13.	shoe	o	✓
14.	wish	✓	
15.	apple	o	dk
16.	on	o	✓
17.	sign	o	o
18.	bit	o	✓
19.	smell	sell	✓
20.	floor	for	✓
Percent correct		20%	60%

After reading an IRI selection, the student answers questions.

■■■ **TABLE 2.4** **Oral-Reading Symbols**

	Marking	Meaning
Quantitative errors	the b͞ig dog (bad)	Mispronounced
	the b͟ig dog	Omitted word
	the (ferocious) dog	Asked for word
	the big ∧ dog (bad)	Inserted word
Self-correction	the big dog (bad✓)	Self-corrected
Qualitative errors	I hit the ball⊗ and George ran.	Omitted punctuation
	The ‖ ferocious dog	Hesitation
	<u>the ferocious dog</u>	Repetition
	Good morning! ↑	Rising inflection
	Are you reading? ↓	Falling inflection
	W x W	Word-by-word reading
	HM	Head movement
	FP	Finger pointing
	PC	Use of picture clue

■ Increasingly, classroom teachers are administering IRIs. The *Classroom Reading Inventory* (Silvaroli & Wheelock, 2001), which is a streamlined inventory, was specifically designed to be given by classroom teachers and takes approximately twelve minutes to administer.

■ There is a modest (.4) correlation between accurate oral reading and comprehension when testing younger students using text that is easy and questions that are literal or easy inference (Paris & Carpenter, 2003). There is less of a correlation after grade 2. Oral reading is not as good an indicator of comprehension after grade 3.

HIGHER-LEVEL LITERACY

When selecting an IRI, check the kinds of questions being asked. IRIs vary in the quality and level of questions (Applegate, Quinn, & Applegate, 2002). Most IRI questions consist of recall or low-level inference questions. Since IRIs are informal, you can change questions or add your own. However, don't ask more than one or two higher-level questions. The basic purpose of an IRI is to establish reasonable reading levels. If you ask too many higher-level questions, you might underestimate students' basic reading levels.

can get some information about her or his reading. Before each selection is read, have the student read its title and predict what it will be about (Johns, 1997). Doing this will help the student set a purpose for reading, and it will give you a sense of the student's prediction ability and background of experience.

The student reads the first selection orally. This is one of the few times in which reading orally without having first read the selection silently is valid. As the student reads, use the symbols shown in Table 2.4 to record her or his performance. Although many different kinds of misreadings are noted, only the following are counted as errors or **miscues**: mispronunciations, omissions, insertions, and words supplied by the examiner because the student asked the examiner to read them or apparently could not read them on her or his own. Self-corrected errors are not counted. Hesitations, repetitions, and other qualitative misreadings are noted but not counted as errors. A corrected inventory selection is shown in Figure 2.2.

After the student finishes reading aloud, ask the series of comprehension questions that accompany the selection or ask for an oral retelling (see pp. 51–52 for information on retelling). Then, introduce a silent selection on the same level. Just as with the oral selection, allow a very brief preparation phase and have the student make a prediction. During the silent reading, note finger pointing, head movement, lip movement, and subvocalizing. Symbols for these behaviors are given in Table 2.5. Ask comprehension questions when the student finishes reading. Proceeding level by level, continue to test until the student

■ A **miscue** is an oral reading response that differs from the expected (correct) response. The term *miscue* is used because miscue theory holds that errors are not random but are the attempts of the reader to make sense of the text.

First Reader Selection: Oral   63 words

Spots That Talk

How do mother fish call their (children?)

One mother fish uses color. The mother
                    big   boo✓
fish has |bright| |blue| |spots| on her
           wents✓   little
|tail. When she w~~ants~~ her children to

come to her, she <u>moves her</u> tail up and
                        ↑
down! The baby fish see the blue   *W x W*
            move
|spots m~~oving~~. This tells them to go
   the   *sim✓*
to their mother⊗ They |swim t<u>o her</u> as
fat
~~fast~~ as they can.

$$\begin{array}{r} 0.89 \\ 63\overline{)56} \end{array}$$

89% accuracy rate

hesitant,
oral reading

choppy,
poor expression

difficulty with
clusters

---

reaches a frustration level—that is, misreads 10 percent or more of the words or misses at least half the comprehension questions.

When the frustration level has been reached, read to the student the oral and silent selections at each level beyond the frustration level until the student reaches the highest level at which she or he can answer 75 percent of the comprehension questions. This is the student's listening capacity, and it indicates how well the student would be able to read if she or he had the necessary word-recognition skills and related print-processing skills. For children who have limited language skills, limited background of experience, or deficient listening skills, you may have to backtrack and read selections at the frustration level and below. Because students will already have been exposed to the lower-level selections, you will have to use alternative selections to test listening comprehension.

After administering the inventory, enter the scores from each level on the inventory's summary sheet (see Figure 2.3). Word-recognition scores are determined by calculating the percentage of words read correctly on each oral selection (number of words read correctly divided by number of words in the selection). If the student made 5 miscues in a 103-word selection, the word-recognition score would be 98/103 = 95.1 percent.

Comprehension is calculated by averaging comprehension scores for the oral and silent selections at each level. Using the numbers on the summary sheet, determine the placement levels. Refer to the criteria in Table 2.2.

■■■ Checkup ■■■

1. What are the four levels yielded by an IRI? What is the significance of each level?
2. How are IRIs administered?

■■■

Interpreting the Inventory

After determining the student's levels, examine her or his performance on the inventory to determine word-recognition and comprehension strengths and weaknesses. What kinds of phonics skills can the student use? Is the student able to decode multisyllabic words? Could the student read words that have prefixes or suffixes? Did the student use context?

■■ ■■ **TABLE 2.5**

Silent-Reading Symbols

Symbol	Meaning
HM	Head movement
FP	Finger pointing
LM	Lip movement
SV	Subvocalizing

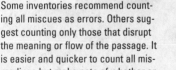

FYI

Some inventories recommend counting all miscues as errors. Others suggest counting only those that disrupt the meaning or flow of the passage. It is easier and quicker to count all misreadings but make note of whether or not they fit the sense of the passage. Deciding whether a miscue is significant is subjective. If standards are too lenient, the student being assessed may end up being placed with a text that is too difficult.

	Word-List Scores		Inventory Scores				
			Word recognition	Comprehension			Listening capacity
Level	Flash	Untimed	(in context)	(oral)	(silent)	(avg.)	
PP	80	95	100	100	90	95	
P	70	80	96	100	80	90	
1	30	55	89	60	60	60	
2							90
3							80
4							50
5							
6							
7							
8							

Levels		Strengths and weaknesses
Independent	PP	*Strong language development*
Instructional	P	*Difficulty with high-frequency*
Frustration	1	*words and clusters*
Listening capacity	3	

Did the student integrate the use of decoding skills with context? How did the student's word recognition compare with her or his comprehension? How did the student handle literal and inferential questions? How did comprehension on oral passages compare with comprehension on silent passages? You can also note the quality of the student's responses as she or he answered questions and the way the student approached the tasks. What level of language did the student use to answer questions? What was the student's level of confidence and effort as she or he undertook each task? Through careful observation, you can gain insight into the student's reading processes. For example, you may observe the student decoding unfamiliar words sound by sound or using a combination of context and phonics to handle difficult words. Strengths and weaknesses as well as immediate needs can be noted on the IRI summary sheet.

Probing Comprehension Problems

Most students have difficulty comprehending because there are too many words in a selection that they don't know. However, occasionally there are students who are good decoders but poor comprehenders (see the Case Study on p. 37). They sail through the word lists and read the oral passages flawlessly and with good expression. But they have difficulty answering the comprehension questions. To assess comprehension difficulties, probe responses so that you can gain some insight into the causes, which often have to do with

■ **Miscue analysis** is the process of analyzing miscues in order to determine which cueing systems or combination of cueing systems the student is using: semantic, syntactic, and/or phonic (graphophonic).

the students' thinking processes. Some possible causes of poor comprehension are listed below, along with questions that might be asked to determine causes of difficulties (Dewitz & Dewitz, 2003).

- *Inadequate background knowledge.* Ask questions about items that you believe the students might not know: "What can you tell me about planets? What is an asteroid? Have you ever seen a telescope?"
- *Difficulty with vocabulary.* Go back to the passage, point to a key word that you believe may be unfamiliar to the student, and ask, "What does this word mean?"
- *Difficulty with syntax.* Go back to the target sentence, and ask questions about it.
- *Overuse of background knowledge.* Ask, "What makes you think that the sun is closer to Earth in the summertime? How did you know that? Is that in the article?"
- *Failure to recall or comprehend directly stated information.* Ask, "Can you find the answer to that in the article?"
- *Failure to link ideas in a passage.* Ask, "What happened because it rained? What else could have made Lee sad? Who else caused the team to lose?"
- *Failure to make inferences.* Ask, "Why do you think the family decided to head west? What do you think the long, dry summer will cause to happen?"

Miscue Analysis of IRIs

Students use three cueing systems to decode printed words: syntactic, semantic, and phonic (graphophonic). In other words, they use their sense of how language sounds (syntax), the meaning of the sentence or passage (semantics), and phonics to read. To determine how they are using these systems, analyze their word-recognition errors, or miscues, with a modified **miscue analysis**. On a sheet similar to the one in Figure 2.4 (on p. 38), list the students' miscues. Try to list at least ten miscues, but do not analyze any that are at or beyond the frustration level. Miscues can be chosen from the independent and instructional levels and from the buffer zone between the instructional and frustration levels

Case Study
Good Decoding, Poor Comprehending

Although he has excellent decoding skills and reads orally with fluency and expression, Mark has problems understanding what he reads. He also has difficulty answering questions about selections that have been read to him. On a reading inventory known as the QRI-3, Mark was able to read the sixth-grade word list with no difficulty. He was also able to read the words on the sixth-grade oral passage with no errors. However, his comprehension was below 50 percent on the sixth-grade passage and also on the fourth- and fifth-grade passages. Puzzled by Mark's performance, the reading consultant analyzed Mark's responses (Dewitz & Dewitz, 2003). The consultant wanted to get some insight into Mark's thinking processes. The correct responses didn't reveal much about Mark's thinking. They simply restated what was in the text. When erroneous responses were analyzed, patterns appeared. Mark could answer questions that required comprehending only a single sentence. However, he had difficulty with questions that required linking ideas across sentences or passages. Putting ideas together posed problems for him. Mark could pick up information from one segment but couldn't integrate that with information from another segment.

Mark also overrelied on background knowledge. He made up answers. This happened when he was unable to recall a fact or put pieces of information together. Mark also had some minor difficulty with complex syntactical structures and vocabulary.

Based on an analysis of Mark's responses, the consultant created a program for Mark and other students who had similar difficulties. After instruction, Mark was able to comprehend sixth-grade material. He was no longer overrelying on background knowledge, and he was connecting and integrating ideas.

■■■ **FIGURE 2.4**

Miscue Analysis

Name: _____   Date: _____

Miscue	Text	Syntactic similarity	Semantic similarity	Graphic similarity	Beginning	Middle	End	Nonword	Self-correction
gots	gets	✓	✓	✓	✓	—	✓		
will	with	—	—	✓	✓	✓	—		
ran ✓	runs	✓	✓	✓	✓	—	✓		✓
balt	ball	—	—	✓	✓	✓	—	✓	
tricks	kicks	✓	—	✓	—	✓	✓		
my	me	—	✓	✓	✓		—		
trick	trust	✓	—	—	✓	—	—		
bell	ball	✓	—	✓	✓	—	✓		
frain	five	—	—	—	✓	—	—	✓	
grain	gray	—	—	✓	✓	✓			
there	that	—	—	—	✓	—	—		
eak	each	—	—	✓	✓		—	✓	
Totals		5	3	9	11	4	4	3	1
Numbers of miscues analyzed		12	12	12				12	12
Percentage		42	25	75				25	8

(91 to 94 percent word recognition). Also list the correct version of each error. Put a check in the syntactic column if the miscue is syntactically correct—that is, if it is the same part of speech as the word in the text or could be used in that context. Put a check in the semantic column if the miscue makes sense in the sentence. In the graphic column, use a check to show whether the miscue is graphically and/or phonically similar to the text word. It is similar if it contains at least half the sounds in the text word. Also use a check to show whether the beginning, middle, and end of the miscue are similar to the text word. Put a check in the nonword column if the miscue is not a real word. Also indicate corrected miscues with a check in the self-correction column.

Tally each column (as shown in Figure 2.4), and convert tallies to percentages. After tallying the columns, examine the numbers to see whether the student is reading for meaning. Miscues that make sense in the context of the selection, self-corrections, and absence of nonwords are positive signs. They show that the student is reading for meaning. Conversely, the presence of nonwords is a negative sign, as are miscues that do not fit the sense of the passage or the syntax.

Also compare the tallies to see whether the cueing systems are being used in balanced fashion or whether one is being overused or underused. The student could be overusing phonics and underusing semantic context, or vice versa. Draw tentative conclusions about the strategies that the student uses in his or her word recognition. Double-check those conclusions as you observe the student read in the classroom.

FYI

Generally, IRIs are given at the beginning of the school year to obtain placement information, when a new student enters the class, or whenever a student's placement is in doubt. They may also be given as pretests and posttests and are often more sensitive indicators of progress than norm-referenced tests.

An informal inventory yields a wealth of information.

As you can see from Figure 2.4, fewer than half of this student's miscues fit the context either syntactically or semantically. Moreover, three of them are nonwords, and the student had only one self-correction. All indications are that the student is failing to use context clues and is not reading for meaning. The student makes heavy use of phonics, especially at the beginning of words, but must better integrate the use of phonics with syntactic and semantic cues. The student also needs to improve the use of phonics skills with middle and ending elements.

IRIs require training and practice to administer and interpret. In the past, they were generally administered by the school's reading specialist. However, increasingly, classroom teachers are administering IRIs. To make the best possible use of time, classroom teachers might give a streamlined version of an IRI in which they give the full word-list test but administer only the oral passages of the inventory, without the listening portion. It will also save time if the inventory contains brief passages. Giving a shortened inventory reduces its reliability, so results should be regarded as tentative and should be verified by observation of the student's performance when reading books at the estimated instructional level.

Even if you, as a classroom teacher, never formally administer an IRI, it is still essential that you be familiar with the concept. Knowing the IRI standards for instructional and other levels, you have a basis for evaluating your students' reading performance. If students have difficulty orally reading more than five words out of a hundred, or if their oral and written comprehension seem closer to 50 percent than 75 percent, you may have to check the material they are reading to see whether it is too difficult. On the other hand, if both word recognition and comprehension in everyday reading tasks are close to perfect, you may want to try more challenging materials.

As children struggle with difficult words, you may also want to conduct a mental miscue analysis. By closely observing miscues, you can sense whether students might need added instruction in using context or phonics or in integrating the two.

■ ■ ■ Checkup ■ ■ ■

1. How are IRIs interpreted?

■ ■ ■

Running Records

Similar to the IRI and based on K. S. Goodman's (1974) theory of analyzing students' miscues to determine what strategies they are using to decode words, the **running record** has become a popular device for assessing students' progress. Like the IRI, the running record is administered individually. However, only an oral-reading sample is obtained. The running record has two major purposes: to determine whether students' reading materials are on the proper level and to obtain information about the word-recognition processes students are using. To get a fuller assessment of comprehension, some teachers supplement the administration of a running record by having students retell the selection. Teachers often take running records during guided reading, while other students are reading silently.

Although running records may be obtained from older readers, they are most often used to assess the performance of novice readers and are administered daily to Reading Recovery students. As used in Reading Recovery and recommended in *An Observation Survey of Early Literacy Achievement* (Clay, 1993a), running records are administered according to a standardized format in which students' errors and corrections are recorded on a separate sheet. As adapted for use by classroom teachers, running records may be recorded (as long as the fair-use provision of the copyright laws is adhered to or permission is obtained from the publisher) on a photocopy of the text that the student is using (Learning Media, 1991). To assess whether materials are on a suitable level of difficulty and to determine how well the child makes use of previously presented strategies, take a running record on a text that the student has recently read. To assess the student's ability to handle challenging materials and apply strategies independently, take a running record on material that the student has not previously read. If the book or article is very brief, take a running record of the whole piece. If the text is lengthy, select a sample of 100 to 200 words. As the student reads orally, record her or his performance with symbols such as those presented in Table 2.6. However, you may use the IRI symbols if you are more familiar with them. After taking a running record, record the number of words in the selection, number of errors made, error rate, number of self-corrections made, and the accuracy rate.

Clay (1993a) accepts 90 percent as an adequate accuracy rate; however, 95 percent seems more realistic. Word recognition is emphasized in a running record, so comprehension is not directly checked. However, you may ask the child to retell the story if you wish to obtain information about comprehension.

It is essential that you analyze a student's miscues in order to determine what strategies she or he is using. As you examine the student's miscues, ask the following questions:

■ Is the student reading for meaning? Do the student's miscues make sense?

■ Is the student self-correcting miscues, especially those that do not fit the meaning of the sentence? Is the student using meaning cues?

■ Is the student using visual or sound-symbol cues (phonics)? Are the student's miscues similar in appearance and sound to the target word?

■ Is the student using picture cues?

Running records are most often used to assess novice readers.

■ The **running record** is an assessment device in which a student's oral reading errors are noted and classified in order to determine whether the material is on the appropriate level of difficulty and to see which reading strategies the student is using.

■■■ **TABLE 2.6 Running Record Symbols**

Symbol	Text	Example
Words read correctly are marked with a check.	Janice kicked the ball.	✓ ✓ ✓ ✓
Substitutions are written above the line.	A barn owl hooted.	✓ big ✓ ✓ barn
Self-corrections are marked *SC*.	A barn owl hooted.	✓ big | SC ✓ ✓ barn
A dash is used to indicate no response.	I saw her yesterday.	✓ ✓ ✓ – yesterday
A dash is used to indicate an insertion of a word. The dash is placed beneath the inserted word.	We saw a big dog.	✓ ✓ ✓ bad ✓ —
A *T* is used to indicate that a child has been told a word.	Her cat ran away yesterday.	✓ ✓ ✓ ✓ T yesterday
The letter *A* indicates that the child has asked for help.	A large moose appeared.	✓ ✓ ✓ A appeared
At times, the student becomes so confused by a misreading that it is suggested that she or he "try that again" (coded *TTA*). Brackets are put around the section that has been misread, the whole misreading is counted as one error, and the student reads it again for a new score.	The deer leaped over the fence.	[✓ ✓ landed ✓ ✓ field] TTA leaped fence]
A repetition is indicated with an *R*. Although not counted as errors, repetitions are often part of an attempt to puzzle out a difficult item. The point to which the student returns in the repetition is indicated with an arrow.	The deer leaped over the fence.	✓ ✓ landed\SC ✓ ✓ field\SC. R leaped fence.

- Is the student integrating cues? Is the student balancing the use of meaning and sound-symbol cues?
- Based on the student's performance, what strategies does she or he need to work on?

For younger readers in the very early stages, note whether they read from left to right or top to bottom and whether there is a voice-print match (the word the child says matches the one she or he is looking at). For detailed information on analyzing and interpreting running records, see Clay (1993a, 2000) or Johnston (2000).

Developmental Reading Assessment (DRA)

The Developmental Reading Assessment (DRA) (2nd ed.) functions as an informal reading inventory or running record for students in grades 1–3. It also assesses fluency and decoding skills. DRA 4–8 (2nd ed.) is designed for grades 4–8. The DRA is a mandated test

USING TECHNOLOGY

For additional information about the DRA, go to the Web site for the Seattle Public Schools:

https://www.seattleschools.org/area/literacy/dra/dra-home.htm

in Washington state, in priority schools in Connecticut, in elementary schools in Louisiana, and in a number of other localities.

■ ■ ■ Checkup ■ ■ ■

1. How are running records similar to but different from IRIs?
2. How are running records administered and interpreted?

■ ■ ■

Group Inventories

Because of the time involved, it may be impractical to administer individual IRIs. However, you may choose to administer a group reading inventory. Information about constructing and administering group reading inventories can be found in *Informal Reading Inventories* (2nd ed.) by Johnson, Kress, & Pikulski (1987). Some reading series contain group reading inventories. There are also three tests that function as group inventories: Degrees of Reading Power, the Scholastic Reading Inventory, and STAR.

Degrees of Reading Power (DRP)

Composed of a series of passages that gradually increase in difficulty, Degrees of Reading Power (DRP) assesses overall reading ability by having students choose from among five options the one that best completes a portion of the passage from which words have been omitted. Each passage has nine deletions.

As in a traditional IRI, the passages gradually increase in difficulty and encompass a wide range of difficulty so that slow, average, and superior readers' ability may be appropriately assessed. Instead of yielding a grade-level score, the assessment provides a DRP score, which indicates what level of material the student should be able to read. A complementary readability formula is used to indicate the difficulty level of books in DRP units. Approximate grade equivalents of DRP units are presented in Table 2.7. The main purpose of DRP is to match students with books that are on their levels.

The Scholastic Reading Inventory

The Scholastic Reading Inventory, which also uses a modified cloze procedure and can be administered and scored manually or by computer, yields lexile scores. Lexile scores range from about 70 to 1700+. A score of 70 to 200 indicates a reading level of about mid-first grade. A score of 1700 represents the level at which difficult scientific journals are written. Approximate grade equivalents of lexile scores are presented in Table 2.7.

STAR

STAR (Advantage Learning Systems), which is administered and scored by computer and so doesn't require valuable teacher time, has a branching component: If students give correct answers, they are given higher-level passages, but if they respond incorrectly, they are given lower-level passages. STAR uses a modified cloze procedure and also assesses vocabulary. Students need a reading vocabulary of one hundred words in order to be able to take STAR. Testing time is ten minutes or less.

Word-List Tests

To save time, teachers sometimes administer word-list tests instead of IRIs. Because they require only the ability to pronounce words, these tests neglect comprehension and may yield misleading levels for students who are superior decoders but poor comprehenders, or vice versa. One of the most popular word-list tests is the Slosson Oral

■ **Norm-referenced tests** are those in which students' performance is compared with a norm group, which is a representative sampling of students.

comprehension might be assessed as in norm-referenced tests, with brief passages and multiple-choice questions. Despite these limitations, criterion-referenced tests are generally more useful to teachers than are norm-referenced tests. They indicate whether students have mastered particular skills and so are useful for making instructional decisions.

■ ■ ■ Checkup ■ ■ ■

1. How do norm-referenced and criterion-referenced tests differ?
2. What are the strengths and weaknesses of each?   ■ ■ ■

■ Reporting Performance

There are two primary ways of reporting scores: norm-referenced and criterion-referenced. In norm-referenced reporting, a student's performance is compared with that of other students. In criterion-referenced reporting, a student's performance might be described in terms of a standard or expected performance or in terms of the student's goals.

Norm-Referenced Reporting

Tests and other assessment measures yield a number of possible scores. To interpret results correctly, it is important to know the significance of each score. Here are commonly used types of scores:

- A **raw score** represents the total number of correct answers. It has no meaning until it is changed into a percentile rank or other score.

- A **percentile rank** tells where a student's raw score falls on a scale of 1 to 99. A score at the first percentile means that the student did better than 1 percent of those who took the test. A score at the 50th percentile indicates that the student did better than half of those who took the test. A top score is the 99th percentile. Most norm-referenced test results are reported in percentiles; however, the ranks are not equal units and should not be added, subtracted, divided, or used for subtest comparison.

- The **grade equivalent score** characterizes a student's performance as being equivalent to that of other students in a particular grade. A grade equivalent score of 5.2 indicates that the student correctly answered the same number of items as the average fifth-grader in the second month of that grade. Note that the grade equivalent score does not tell on what level the student is operating; that is, a score of 5.2 does not mean that a student is reading on a fifth-grade level. Grade equivalent scores are more meaningful when the test students have taken is at the right level and when the score is not more than a year above or a year below average. Because grade equivalent scores are misleading and easily misunderstood, they should be used with great care or not at all.

FYI

Grade equivalent scores, which have been opposed by the International Reading Association, are relatively valid when pupils are tested on their instructional level and when extrapolations are limited to a year or two beyond the target grade level.

- **Normal curve equivalents** (NCEs) rank scores on a scale of 1 through 99. The main difference between NCEs and percentile ranks is that NCEs represent equal units and so can be added and subtracted and used for comparing performance on subtests.

- **Stanine** is a combination of the words *standard* and *nine*. The stanines 4, 5, and 6 are average points, with 1, 2, and 3 being below average, and 7, 8, and 9 above average. Stanines are useful when making comparisons among the subtests of a norm-referenced test.

- **Scaled scores** are a continuous ranking of scores from the lowest levels of a series of norm-referenced tests—first grade, for example—through the highest levels—high school. They start at 000 and end at 999. They are useful for tracking long-term reading development through the grades. Lexiles, DRP units, and grade equivalents are also examples of scaled scores.

Grade equivalents and other scaled scores rise over time. However, percentiles, stanines, and normal curve equivalents may stay the same from year to year. If they do, this means that the student is making average progress in comparison with others. For instance, if a student is at the 35th percentile in third grade and then tests again at the 35th percentile in fourth grade, that means that his or her relative standing is the same; the student continues to do better than 35 percent of the students who took the test. However, if the student moves to a higher percentile, this means that he or she outperformed students who started off with similar scores. If the student scores at the 40th percentile in fourth grade, it means that he or she is moving up in the relative standings. Now the student is doing better than 40 percent of those who took the test.

Criterion-Referenced Reporting

Criterion-referenced results are reported in terms of a standard, or criterion. For example, the student answered 80 percent of the comprehension questions correctly. Two types of standards now being used in authentic assessment are the benchmark and the rubric, which are descriptive forms of criterion-referenced reporting.

Benchmarks

A **benchmark** is a written description of a key task that students are expected to perform. For instance, a benchmark for word recognition might be "Uses both context and phonics to identify words unknown in print." Benchmarks are useful because they provide a concrete description of what students are expected to do. They provide students, teachers, parents, and administrators with an observable framework for assessing accomplishments and needs. Using benchmarks, the teacher can assess whether the student has mastered key skills and strategies and is ready to move on. Opportunities for assessing benchmark behaviors include observing during shared reading, story discussions, drama, writing activities, and student conferences. Parent conferences during which parents provide information about the child's reading and writing at home offer additional sources of data.

Rubrics

A **rubric** is a written description of what is expected from students in order for them to meet a certain level of performance. It is usually accompanied by samples of several levels of performance. For assessing a piece of writing, such samples show the characteristics of an excellent, average, fair, and poor paper. A writing rubric is presented in Table 2.8. Although rubrics are typically used in the assessment of writing tasks, they can also be used to assess combined reading and writing tasks, portfolios, presentations, and projects.

In addition to their use as scoring guides, rubrics can be powerful teaching tools (Popham, 2000). Carefully constructed rubrics describe the key tasks that students must complete or the main elements that must be included in order to produce an excellent piece of work. This helps both the teacher and the student focus on key skills. To be effective, rubrics should contain only three to six evaluative criteria so that students and teachers do not get sidetracked by minor details. More important, each evaluative criterion must encompass a teachable skill. For instance, evaluative criteria for writing a story might call for an exciting plot, believable characters, an interesting setting, and the use of vivid language.

■ A **benchmark** is a written description of task performance against which a student's achievement might be assessed.

■ A **rubric** is a written description of the traits or characteristics of standards used to judge a process or product.

■■■ **TABLE 2.8   Rubric for Assessing Writing**

	Level 4 Most Successful	Level 3 Upper Half	Level 2 Lower Half (Basic)	Level 1 Least Successful (Skill Failure)
Content	Shows clear under-standing of content. Develops the topic with appropriate de-tail in each para-graph.	Generally understands content. At least two para-graphs used. Details relate clearly to topic sentence.	Appears to understand the topic. If using more than one paragraph, relation to overall topic may be weak.	Some misunderstand-ing of topic. Usually only one para-graph. Includes material not related to topic.
Organization	Organization and se-quence of ideas are clear and relate to one another in de-velopment of the overall topic.	Clear organization and sequences of detail. Relationship of para-graphs to major topic not fully devel-oped.	Basically sequential. Some weakness in re-lating paragraph de-tails to topic sentences.	Lacks coherence. Sequencing of ideas may be incorrect.
Sentence structure	Uses correct sentence structure, descrip-tive words, and phrases. Expands sentence patterns. Makes few grammati-cal errors.	Basic sentence pat-terns correct. Some difficulty with expanded sentence patterns and gram-mar.	Uses simple sen-tences. Errors in grammar when more complex structure is at-tempted. Some run-on and sen-tence fragments.	Uses basic simple sen-tences. Errors in noun–verb agreement. Infrequent use of mod-ifiers.
Mechanics	Capitalization, punctu-ation, and spelling are generally cor-rect.	Few problems with capitalization, punc-tuation, and spelling.	Errors in capitalization, punctuation, and spelling.	Frequent errors in cap-italization, punctua-tion, and spelling of words.
Word choice	Vocabulary includes some words usually used at a higher level.	Average for grade level. Vocabulary words used correctly.	Simple vocabulary words used, some incorrectly.	Poor word choice.

From *The Writing Handbook* (p. 19) by the Reading and Communications Arts Department, 1983, Hartford, CT: Hartford Public Schools. Reprinted by permis-sion of the Hartford Board of Education.

Creating a Rubric.   To develop a rubric, first identify the key characteristics or traits of the performance or piece of work to be assessed. For a rubric for a friendly letter, the key traits might include interesting content, chatty style, correct letter format, and correct me-chanics. If available, examine finished products to see what their major traits are. Write a definition of each trait. What exactly is meant by "interesting content," "chatty style," "correct letter format," and "correct mechanics"? Develop a scale for the characteristics. It is usually easiest to start with the top performance. If you have examples of students' work, sort them into piles: best, worst, and middle. Look over the best pieces and decide what makes them the best. Look at the poorest and decide where they are deficient. Write a description of the best and poorest performances. Then fill in the middle levels. For the middle levels, divide the remaining papers into two or more piles from best to worst, de-pending on how many levels you wish to have. However, the more levels you create, the more difficult it becomes to discriminate between adjoining levels. You may find that four suffice. Evaluate your rubric, using the following checklist:

- Does the rubric measure the key traits in the student performance?
- Are differences in the levels clearly specified?

FYI

Students should participate in the creation of rubrics. Through helping with the creation of rubrics, students form a clearer idea of what is ex-pected in their writing. In one study, students used a rubric they helped create to assess their own writing. They also took part in peer evaluation sessions in which the rubric was used to judge their writing. As a result of creating and using the rubric, stu-dents' writing of persuasive pieces showed a significant improvement (Boyle, 1996).

- Does the rubric clearly specify what students are required to do?
- Can the rubric be used as a learning guide by students?
- Can the rubric be used as an instructional guide by the teacher (Chicago Public Schools, 2000)?

Discuss the rubric with students, and invite feedback. Through helping with the creation of the rubric, students form a better idea of what is expected in the task being assessed and also feel more willing to use the rubric because they had a hand in its construction. When fourth-graders used cooperatively created rubrics to assess their writing (Boyle, 1996), their persuasive pieces showed a significant improvement.

Try out the rubric, revise it, and then use it. As you use the rubric with actual pieces of students' work, continue to revise it.

One source of rubrics might be the key standards for a grade. Teachers can align their rubrics with key state or local standards. To ease her students into using rubrics, Ferrell (Skillings & Ferrell, 2000) modeled the process. She also had students create rubrics for everyday activities such as picking the best restaurant. After students caught on to the idea of creating rubrics, she involved them in creating rubrics for basic writing tasks. To keep the rubrics simple, the class had just three levels: best, okay, not so good. Later, the class created rubrics for more complex tasks. Sample rubrics can be found at the following Web sites:

> Discovery School Kathy Schrock's Guide for Educators lists sources for sample rubrics and information about rubrics.
> http://school.discovery.com/schrockguide/assess.html

> Chicago Public Schools (2000) maintain an extensive electronic list of analytic and holistic scoring rubrics that span the broad array of subjects represented from kindergarten through high school.
> http://intranet.cps.k12.il.us/Assessments/Ideas_and_Rubrics/ideas_and_rubrics.html

Rubrics for Constructed Responses.   Along with rubrics for assessing stories and essays, create rubrics for assessing responses to open-ended questions of the type that your students will be asked to answer, if these are not already available (see Figure 2.5). These could be tests that you make up, tests from the reading program you are using, or state tests. Provide students with practice using the rubrics so that they understand what they are being asked to do. NAEP tests and some state tests supply rubrics and sample (or anchor) answers. Distribute sample answers and rubrics, and have students mark them. Begin with correct answers so that students have some guidance, and then have them assess answers that receive no credit or partial credit. As a shared whole-group activity, compose responses to open-ended questions, and then assess the responses with a rubric. Once students have some sense of how to respond to open-ended questions, have them compose individual responses and check them.

USING TECHNOLOGY

Rubistar contains hundreds of rubrics that might be used as is or adapted:
http://rubistar.4teachers.org/index.php

■■■■ FIGURE 2.5　Sample Scoring Rubric

Score	3	2	1	0
Criterion	Names an important lesson. Gives evidence from the story to support answers.	Names an important lesson. Fails to give evidence from the story to support answer.	Names an unimportant lesson.	Does not state a lesson that could be learned from the story. No response.

Instructionally Supportive Assessment. Most high-stakes tests assess so many items that they fail to provide information that the teacher can use to plan instruction (Popham, 2004). What would be helpful is classroom assessment that tests a limited number of objectives—about six over the course of a year—and that can be used to plan instruction. To make assessment data instructionally useful, select or create a rubric that will help you and your students determine responses' strengths and weaknesses.

Farr (2003) recommends that instructionally supportive tests be based on a framework of purposeful reading. Students can be taught to set a purpose for reading and then determine whether that purpose has been met. Using criteria for judging purposeful reading, the teacher can plan instruction that meets the needs of students. Three general evaluative criteria can be used as a basis for building a rubric to assess test responses:

- Accuracy—how *accurate* is the reader's grasp and use of the text?
- Relevance—how *relevant* is the textual detail or understanding the reader uses to fulfill the purpose?
- Sufficiency—does the reader demonstrate and use a *sufficient* amount of the text to fulfill the task?

These general criteria are spelled out on a text-by-purpose basis. For example, purposes for reading informational text include the following:

- Understanding the main points and supporting details,
- Recognizing expositional organization and its use, and
- Relating the text's content to broader issues or topics.

Teachers can use the evaluative criteria to teach the skill, and students can use them to better understand what is required of them and to judge their own responses. Tests then become an instrument for improving instruction. Realizing that a main purpose of reading informational text is to understand main ideas and supporting details, teachers and students can assess whether this has been done with accuracy, relevance, and sufficiency.

Using Data to Improve Instruction. As McKenna & Walpole (2005) comment, "There is compelling evidence that schools successful in meeting the needs of struggling readers gather and use data in structured and systematic ways" (p. 86). Besides being used to monitor students' progress and identify students who need intervention, assessment data can be used in other essential ways. It can indicate what skills are needed and what skills have been mastered. At one urban public school where I worked as a literacy consultant, periodic assessment revealed the need for a strong program covering syllabic analysis, vocabulary instruction, and higher-level literacy skills—areas that were being neglected. However, it also revealed what didn't need to be taught. Most students had mastered phonological awareness and basic phonics, although teachers continued to teach these skills. The assessment data showed that instructional time could be more profitably spent in other areas.

■■■ Checkup ■■■

> 1. How might rubrics be used to improve instruction and achievement?
> 2. How might rubrics be constructed so that they support instruction?
> ■■■

■ Measuring Growth

Measuring growth means that you need to make a comparison between where students were at the point of initial assessment and where they are at the end of assessment. You need to compare the same students at the beginning and end of the instructional period, not this year's students with last year's students, as most states do. The problem with this common comparison is that there might be significant differences between this year's students and last year's students. A better assessment uses a growth measure, in which you assess students at the beginning and at the end of the year and calculate how much progress they have made. The key point is that you are assessing the same students before and after instruction.

Threshold Measures

Threshold testing may mask growth. The NAEP and most state proficiency tests are threshold measures (Lee, 2006). Their results tell what percentage of students have met a certain standard, but not how much students' scores have changed. For instance, students' scores might be increasing, bringing them closer to meeting the standard, but this is not indicated in the results. The percentage of students who pass stays the same, although there has been marked improvement. Schools should be judged not just on the percentage of students that meet the standard, but on how much students improve. Unless growth is measured, schools that have large numbers of struggling students might be misjudged. For instance, many urban schools show below-level achievement and might be classified as low-performing or in need of improvement. However, their students might be making better-than-average gains, just not enough to take them over the threshold.

▪ ▪ ▪ Checkup ▪ ▪ ▪

1. Why is it important to measure growth as well as the percentage of students who have met a standard?
2. How might threshold measures mask improvement?

▪ ▪ ▪

▪ Functional Level Assessment

The typical elementary or middle school class will exhibit a wide range of reading ability. Just as students need appropriate levels of materials for instruction, they should have appropriate levels of materials for testing. Most literacy tests cover a limited range. For instance, a general reading test designed for fourth-graders will mostly have selections on a fourth-grade level, a selection or two on a third-grade level, and a few selections beyond the fourth-grade level. A fourth-grader reading on a second-grade level should not be given a fourth-grade reading test. It would be frustrating to the student and would yield misleading results. The student should take a test that includes material on her or his level of reading ability. This might mean giving the student a test designed for third grade but which includes second-grade material. Similarly, a second-grade-level test would probably not be appropriate for a second-grader reading on a fifth-grade level. It would probably lack an adequate ceiling and so would underestimate the student's true reading ability. Students should be tested at their **functional level**, which is not necessarily their grade level. Students reading significantly above or below grade level should be given out-of-level tests unless the tests they are taking cover a wide range of levels. As a rule of thumb, if a student answers more than 90 percent of the items on a test correctly, the student should be tested at a more difficult level (Touchstone Applied Science Associates, 2006). If a student answers less than 10 percent of the items correctly, she or he should be tested

---

▪ **Functional level testing** is the practice of assigning students to a test level on the basis of their reading ability rather than their grade level.

▪ **Retelling** is the process of summarizing or describing a story that one has read. The purpose of retelling is to assess comprehension.

at an easier level. Giving students a test at the wrong level results in erroneous, invalid information. This is true whether norm-referenced, criterion-referenced, or other type of assessment is being used.

Adaptive Tests

One way of providing students with the correct-level test is to use adaptive testing. Adaptive tests are usually taken on a computer. Based on the student's responses, the computer adapts to the student's level. If a student is getting all the questions correct, the computer presents higher-level questions. If the student is getting all or most of the items wrong, the computer switches to lower-level questions. Currently, there are two widely used adaptive tests: Measures of Academic Progress (MAP) and STAR. MAP tests consist of sentences or brief paragraphs and have a multiple-choice format. They can be given in grades 2 through 10 and can be given four times a year to monitor progress. MAP tests, which are used as Idaho's high-stakes tests, can also be used to indicate students' reading level. STAR uses multiple choice and modified cloze.

■ ■ ■ Checkup ■ ■ ■

1. What is functional level assessment?
2. How and why should functional level assessment be implemented?

■ ■ ■

■ Other Methods of Assessment

Retelling

Retelling has the potential for supplying more information about a student's comprehension than simply asking questions does. In a **retelling**, a student is asked to do what the name suggests: The student may retell a selection that has been read to her or him or one that the student has read. The student may do this orally or in writing. In addition to showing what the reader comprehended, retelling shows what she or he added to and inferred from the text (Irwin & Mitchell, 1983). Free from the influence of probes or questions, retelling demonstrates the student's construction of text and provides insight into her or his language and thought processes. It shows how the student organizes and shapes a response. The teacher can also assess the quality of language used by the student in the retelling.

To administer a retelling, explain to the student what she or he is supposed to do: Read a selection orally or silently, or listen to one read aloud. It may be a narrative or expository piece. Tell the student that she or he will be asked to retell the story in her or his own words. Use neutral phrasing, such as "Tell me about the story that you read." For a young child, say, "Pretend I haven't read the story. Tell it to me in your own words." A shy child can use props—such as a puppet—to facilitate the retelling. If a student stops before retelling the whole selection, encourage her or him to continue or elaborate. When the student is finished, ask questions about any key elements that were not included in the retelling.

Evaluating Retellings

As the student retells the selection, record it on audiocassette and/or jot down brief notes on the major events or ideas in the order in which the child relates them. Note any recalls that were not spontaneous but were elicited by your questions. Tape recording provides a full and accurate rendition of the retelling but is time-consuming.

Retellings can be scored numerically by giving students credit for each major unit that they retell. However, this is a laborious process. Far less time-consuming but still useful

FYI

■ Being less time-consuming, informal retellings are more practical for the classroom teacher. Of course, shy children may not perform up to their ability.

■ Because the person assessing them obviously knows the story, students might provide a contextualized retelling. They may not give the characters' names, referring to them as *he* or *she* because they assume that the examiner is familiar with the characters. Knowing that the examiner is familiar with the story, they might omit or abbreviate crucial details (Benson & Cummins, 2000). When using a retelling as an assessment, stress that the students should pretend that they are telling the story to someone who has not read it or heard it.

Name of student: _Jamie S._

	Retelling	Comments	Summary and recommendations
Elves and the shoemaker	Shoemaker said had only one piece of leather left. Elves made shoes.	Drew inference. Started with story problem.	Good grasp of story.
	Man in hat came in. Woman came in. Many people bought shoes. Shoemaker and wife waited up to see elves.	Told story in sequence.	Used structure of story to retell it.
	Elves had ragged clothes. Wife made new clothes. Elves thought new clothes looked funny. Elves said would no longer be cobras. Never came back.	Used picture to get information about elves. Misinterpreted passage. Missed _cobblers_.	Didn't go beyond story to suggest why elves started or stopped helping. Failed to use context to help with _cobblers_. Good average performance. Work on context and drawing conclusions.

is noting the major units in the retelling in one column, comments about it in a second column, and a summary and recommendations in a third. Because the main purpose of the retelling is to gain insight into students' reading processes, draw inferences about students' overall understanding of the selection and their ability to use strategies to construct the meaning of the piece. A sample retelling is presented in Figure 2.6.

Written Retellings

Written retellings allow the teacher to assess the class as a group. Using holistic scoring, the teacher can also assess the quality of the responses. It is important to keep in mind that, whether oral or written, the mode of expression will affect the information students convey. Students may have good knowledge of a selection but find it difficult to express their ideas orally and/or in writing. To obtain a better picture of that knowledge, the teacher might have a class discussion after students have completed their written retellings and compare impressions garnered from the discussion with those from the written versions.

Structured written retellings. In a structured written retelling, the teacher might ask students to read a whole selection and write answers to a series of broad questions. The questions are constructed to assess students' ability to understand major aspects of the text, such as characters, plot, and setting. The questions can also be framed to provide some insight into the strategies students are using. They are scored and analyzed by the teacher.

■　**Think-alouds** are procedures in which students are asked to describe the processes they are using as they engage in reading or another cognitive activity.

Think-Aloud Protocols

Think-alouds are used to show the thought processes students use as they attempt to construct meaning. During a think-aloud, the reader explains his or her thought processes while reading a text. These explanations might come after each sentence, at the end of each paragraph, or at the end of the whole selection. Students' thoughts might be expressed as "news bulletins or play-by-play accounts" of what students do mentally as they read (Brown & Lytle, 1988, p. 96).

Informal Think-Alouds

Whereas formal think-aloud procedures might be too time-consuming, informal think-alouds can be incorporated into individual and small-group reading conferences and classroom activities. For example, the teacher might simply ask students to share their thoughts on a difficult passage or question or to tell what strategies they used. Think-aloud questions can include the following:

- Tell me how you figured out that hard word.
- Tell me how you got the answer to that question.
- What were you thinking about when you read that selection?
- Pretend that you are an announcer at a sports game. Tell me play by play what was going on in your mind as you read that sentence (or paragraph) (Brown & Lytle, 1988).
- What do you think will happen next in the selection? What makes you think that?
- How did you feel when you read that passage? What thoughts or pictures were going through your mind?

Think-alouds may also be expressed in writing. In their learning logs, students can note the difficulties they encountered in hard passages and describe the processes they used to comprehend the selections. In follow-up class discussions, they can compare their thought processes and strategies with those of other students (Brown & Lytle, 1988). A simple way for students to keep track of perplexing passages is to record comprehension problems on sticky notes and place them next to the passages.

Observation

Teachers learn about children "by watching how they learn" (Goodman, 1985, p. 9). As "kidwatchers," teachers are better able to supply the necessary support or ask the kinds of questions that help students build on their evolving knowledge.

Opportunities for Observations

Observations can be made any time students are involved in reading and writing. Some especially fruitful opportunities for observation include shared reading (What emergent literacy behaviors are students evidencing?), reading and writing conferences (What are the students' strengths and weaknesses in these areas? What is their level of development? How might their progress in these areas be characterized?), and sustained silent reading (Do students enjoy reading? Are they able to select appropriate materials? What kinds of materials do they like to read?). Other valuable observation opportunities include author's circle, literature circle, and sharing periods in general (Australian Ministry of Education, 1990).

Teachers using a program known as Bookshop (Mondo) structure their observations. First, the teachers list from one to three focus areas for a lesson. Then they note whether students in the reading group master the focus area(s) or require added instruction. Each student in the group is listed, as shown in Figure 2.7 (on p. 54).

Focuses	Alison	Matt	Stacey	Jesse	Emma
Uses headings to hypothesize main idea					
Locates supporting details					
Summarizes main idea and key details					

Key: S—satisfactory; N—needs additional instruction

Notes for future instruction: _____

_____

_____

Anecdotal Records

An **anecdotal record** is a field note or description of a significant bit of student behavior. It is an observational technique long used by both anthropologists and teachers. Almost any observation that can shed light on a student's literacy endeavors is a suitable entry for an anecdotal record, including notes on strategies, miscues, interests, interactions with others, and work habits (Rhodes, 1990). The anecdotal record should be "recordings of what the child said or did—not interpretations" (Bush & Huebner, 1979, p. 355). Interpretation comes later and is based on several records and other sources of information. It is important to keep in mind that when recording observations of strategy use, the way in which strategies are used may vary according to the nature of the task—the type of story being read, its relative difficulty, and the purpose for reading it. Therefore, it would be helpful to record several observations before coming to a conclusion (Tierney, Readence, & Dishner, 1995). In going over anecdotal records, the teacher should ask what this information reveals about the student and how it can be used to plan her or his instructional program.

To keep track of observations and anecdotal records, you might keep a notebook that has a separate section for each student. Or you might use a handheld computer to record observations, which then can be downloaded into a database, classroom management system, or assessment management software, such as Learner Profile (Sunburst), which allows you to record and organize observations and other data in terms of standards or objectives. Sum up the anecdotal records periodically, and decide on the steps

Anecdotal records help teachers assess students' progress in literacy endeavors.

needed to assist each student (Boyd-Batstone, 2004). Observe five or six students a day. Have one sheet for each student.

Ratings

A structured and efficient way to collect data is through the use of **ratings**. Ratings generally indicate the "degree to which the child possesses a given trait or skill" (Bush & Huebner, 1979, p. 353). The three kinds of ratings are checklists, questionnaires, and interviews.

Checklists

Checklists can use a present–absent scale (a student either has the trait or does not have it) or one that shows degrees of involvement. The present–absent scale might be used for traits for which there is no degree of possession, such as knowing one's home address and telephone number. The degree scale is appropriate for traits that vary in the extent to which they are manifested, such as joining in class discussions. Figure 2.8 shows a sample observation checklist designed to assess voluntary reading.

Questionnaires

A good example of a reading attitude **questionnaire** is the Elementary Reading Attitude Survey (ERAS) (McKenna & Kerr, 1990). It includes twenty items designed to measure how students feel about recreational and school reading. ERAS can be read to younger, less-skilled readers; older, more-skilled students can read it themselves. The questionnaire addresses such areas as how children feel when they read a book on a rainy Saturday and how they feel about reading in school. Students respond by circling one of four illustrations of the cartoon cat Garfield, which range from very happy to very sad. Another questionnaire that might be used is the Reading Survey section of the Motivation to Read Profile (MRP), which can be found in the March 1996 issue of *The Reading Teacher*. The survey probes two aspects of reading motivation: self-concept as a reader and value of reading.

Questionnaires can provide information about reading interests, study habits, strategy use, and other areas in reading and writing. They can be forced-choice like ERAS or open-ended and requiring a written response. Questionnaires assessing study habits and skills might cover such topics as how students go about studying for a test, where they study, and how much time they spend doing homework each night.

FYI

Thanks to the generosity of the authors and the creator of the cartoon strip *Garfield*, Jim Davis, ERAS has not been copyrighted and was presented, ready to duplicate, in the May 1990 issue of *The Reading Teacher*.

■■■ **FIGURE 2.8**

Observation Checklist for Voluntary Reading

Name of student: _____	Date: _____		
	Never	Seldom	Occasionally	Frequently
Reads during free time	_____	_____	_____	_____
Visits the library	_____	_____	_____	_____
Reads books on a variety of topics	_____	_____	_____	_____
Recommends books to others in the class	_____	_____	_____	_____
Talks with others about books	_____	_____	_____	_____
Checks out books from the library	_____	_____	_____	_____

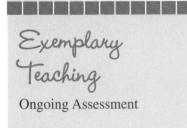

Exemplary Teaching

Ongoing Assessment

To make her instruction as fruitful as possible, Pat Loden, a first-grade teacher, bases it on ongoing assessment of students (Morrow & Asbury, 2001). Each day, she focuses on two students to assess. During the day, she carefully observes these students and records her observations. She keeps running records of their reading, assesses their story retellings, and notes their use of reading strategies. She also has a conference with them and goes over their reading logs. In their reading logs, they record titles and authors of books read and their reading goals for the week. During whole-class activities, Loden makes sure to direct questions to them and notes their responses. She also observes the two students as they work independently. She keeps a file on each student and uses the files when planning instruction, making decisions about placing students in guided reading groups, and before holding conferences with students. Loden also keeps records of conferences she holds during writing workshop. During the conferences, she asks questions that help reveal students' thought processes as they write and the strategies they use. Emphasis throughout the assessment is on obtaining a deeper understanding of where students are and what processes and strategies they are using so that individual and group instructional activities can be planned to further foster their development.

Interviews

Interviews are simply oral questionnaires. Their advantage is that the teacher can probe a student's replies, rephrase questions, and encourage extended answers, thereby obtaining a wide range of information. An interview can focus on such topics as a student's likes and dislikes about a reading group, preferences with respect to reading materials, and reasons for these attitudes. A good example of an interview is the Conversational Interview section of the Motivation to Read Profile (Gambrell, Codling, & Palmer, 1996). The Conversational Interview, which complements the Reading Survey, consists of a series of questions about a student's reading interests and habits and possible influences on those habits.

One kind of interview, the process interview, provides insight about the strategies students are using and also helps students become aware of their processes (Jett-Simpson, 1990). The process interview is best conducted informally on a one-to-one basis, but if time is limited, you might ask for written responses to your questions or hold sessions with small groups. Possible process interview questions include the following, which are adapted from Jett-Simpson (1990). Only one or two of these questions should be asked at one sitting.

1. If a young child asked you how to read, what would you tell him or her to do?
2. When you come to a word you don't know, what do you do?
3. How do you choose something to read?
4. How do you get ready for reading?
5. Where do you read or study at home?
6. When a paragraph is confusing, what do you do?
7. How do you check your reading?
8. What do you do to help you remember what you've read?

■ An **interview** is the process of asking a subject a series of questions on a topic.

Conferences

Like interviews, conferences can be an excellent source of assessment information. During writing conferences, you might ask such questions as, "What do you like best about writing? What kind of writing do you like to do? What is easy for you when you are writing? What is hard for you? What are some things that you might do to become an even better writer than you are now? What do you like best about reading? Do you have any favorite authors? Who are they? What is easy for you in reading? What is hard for you? What might you do to become a better reader?"

Checklists, questionnaires, interviews, and conferences, have a common weakness. Their usefulness depends on students' ability and willingness to supply accurate information. Students may give answers that they think the teacher wants to hear. Information gathered from these sources, therefore, should be verified with other data.

▪▪▪ Checkup ▪▪▪

1. What are the strengths and weaknesses of retellings, think-alouds, observations, anecdotal records, ratings, and conferences?
2. What role do these devices play in a literacy program?

▪ Self-Evaluation

The ultimate evaluation is, of course, self-evaluation. Students should be involved in all phases of the evaluation process and, insofar as possible, take responsibility for assessing their own work. Questionnaires and self-report checklists are especially useful for this. Figure 2.9 (on p. 58) shows a self-report checklist with which students in grade 3 and beyond can assess their use of strategies in learning from text.

Self-assessment should begin early. Ahlmann (1992) noted that by October, her first-graders are already evaluating their own work and that of authors they read. To self-assess, students reflect on their learning, assemble portfolios of their work, list their achievements, and, with the guidance of the teacher, put together a plan for what they hope to achieve.

In some classes, students complete exit slips on which they talk about what they have learned that day or raise questions that they did not have time to raise in class or were reluctant to raise. Learning logs and journals might perform a similar function. As an alternative, the teacher and the class might design a form on which students tell what they learned in a certain class and list questions that they still have. In reading and writing conferences, part of the discussion should center on skills mastered and goals for the future, and how those goals might be met. These conferences, of course, should be genuinely collaborative efforts so that students' input is shown to be valued.

As students engage in a literacy task, they should assess their performance. After reading a selection, they might ask themselves: How well did I understand this selection? Do I need to reread or take other steps to improve my comprehension? After completing a piece of writing, they should also evaluate their performance. If a rubric has been constructed for the piece of writing, they should assess their work in terms of the rubric.

Logs and Journals for Self-Evaluation

Reading logs and response journals can also be a part of students' self-evaluation, as well as a source of information for the teacher. Reading logs contain a list of books read and, perhaps, a brief summary or assessment. Response journals provide students with opportunities to record personal reactions to their reading. Both reading logs and response journals offer unique insights into students' growing ability to handle increasingly difficult books, their changing interests, and personal involvement with reading.

USING TECHNOLOGY

The National Center for Research on Evaluation, Standards, and Student Testing provides information on assessment.
http://cse.ucla.edu

The National Center on Educational Outcomes provides information on assessing students who have disabilities.
http://education.umn.edu/nceo

■■■■ **FIGURE 2.9** **Student's Self-Report Checklist on Strategies for Learning from Text**

	Usually	Often	Sometimes	Never
Before reading, do I				
1. Read the title, introductory paragraph, headings, and summary?	_____	_____	_____	_____
2. Look at photos, maps, charts, and graphs?	_____	_____	_____	_____
3. Think about what I know about the topic?	_____	_____	_____	_____
4. Predict what the text will be about or make up questions that the text might answer?	_____	_____	_____	_____
During reading, do I				
5. Read to answer questions that the teacher or I have made up?	_____	_____	_____	_____
6. Stop after each section and try to answer my questions?	_____	_____	_____	_____
7. Use headings, maps, charts, and graphs to help me understand the text?	_____	_____	_____	_____
8. Try to make pictures in my mind as I read?	_____	_____	_____	_____
9. Reread a sentence or get help if I don't understand what I am reading?	_____	_____	_____	_____
10. Use context or the glossary if I don't understand what I am reading?	_____	_____	_____	_____
After reading, do I				
11. Review the section to make sure that I know the most important information?	_____	_____	_____	_____
12. Try to organize the information in the text by creating a map, chart, time line, or summary?	_____	_____	_____	_____

■■■ **Checkup** ■■■

1. What is the importance of self-evaluation?
2. What are some devices for fostering self-evaluation?

■■■

■ Evaluating Writing

Students' writing can be evaluated by holistic scoring, analytic scoring, or a combination of the two.

Holistic Scoring

What captures the essence of a piece of writing—its style, its theme, its development, its adherence to conventions, its originality? The answer is all of these elements and more. Because of the way the parts of the piece work together, it must be viewed as a whole. In

■ **Holistic scoring** is a process for sorting or ranking students' written pieces on the basis of an overall impression of each piece. Sample pieces (anchors) or a description of standards (rubric) for rating the pieces might be used as guides.

■ **Analytic scoring** is a process for scoring that uses a description of major features to be considered when assessing a written piece.

holistic scoring, instead of noting specific strengths and weaknesses, a teacher evaluates a composition in terms of a limited number of general criteria. The criteria are used "only as a general guide . . . in reaching a holistic judgment" (Cooper & Odell, 1977, p. 4). The teacher does not stop to check the piece to see whether it meets each of the criteria but simply forms a general impression. The teacher can score a piece according to the presence or absence of key elements. There may be a scoring guide, which can be a checklist or a rubric. (A holistic scoring guide in the form of a rubric is shown in Table 2.8.) The teacher should also use anchor pieces along with the rubric to assess compositions. Anchor pieces, which may be drawn from the work of past classes or from the compositions that are currently being assessed, are writing samples that provide examples of deficient, fair, good, and superior pieces. The teacher decides which of the anchor pieces a student's composition most closely resembles.

Before scoring the pieces, the teacher should quickly read them all to get a sense of how well the class did overall. This prevents setting criteria that are too high or too low. After sorting the papers into four groups—beginning, developing, proficient, and advanced—the teacher rereads each work more carefully before confirming its placement. If possible, a second teacher should also evaluate the papers. This is especially important if the works are to be graded.

Analytic Scoring

Analytic scoring involves analyzing pieces and noting specific strengths and weaknesses. It requires the teacher to create a set of specific scoring criteria. (An analytic scoring guide for a friendly letter is presented in Figure 2.10.) Instead of overwhelming students with corrections, it is best to decide on a limited number of key features, such as those that have

FYI

When reviewing students' papers, teachers tend to note all errors. However, students do their best when comments are positive and when there is emphasis on one or two areas, such as providing more detail or using more vivid language. This is especially effective when instruction is geared to the areas highlighted and students revise targeted areas in their compositions (Dahl & Farnan, 1998).

■ ■ ■ **FIGURE 2.10**

Analytic Scoring Guide for a Friendly Letter

Name of student: _____   Date: _____

	Beginning	Developing	Proficient	Advanced
Content				
Has a natural but interesting beginning.	_____	_____	_____	_____
Includes several topics of interest.	_____	_____	_____	_____
Develops each topic in sufficient detail.	_____	_____	_____	_____
Shows an interest in what's happening to the reader.	_____	_____	_____	_____
Has a friendly way of ending the letter.	_____	_____	_____	_____
Style				
Has a friendly, natural tone.	_____	_____	_____	_____
Form				
Follows friendly letter form.	_____	_____	_____	_____
Indents paragraphs.	_____	_____	_____	_____
Is neat and legible.	_____	_____	_____	_____
Mechanics				
Begins each sentence with a capital.	_____	_____	_____	_____
Uses correct end punctuation.	_____	_____	_____	_____
Spells words correctly.	_____	_____	_____	_____

been emphasized for a particular writing activity. Spandel and Stiggins (1997) suggest the following six characteristics: ideas, organization, voice, word choice, sentence fluency, and conventions. Although more time-consuming than holistic scoring, analytic scoring allows the teacher to make constructive suggestions about students' writing.

Using a Combination of Techniques

In some cases, a combination of holistic and analytic scoring works best. Holistic scoring guards against the teacher's becoming overly caught up in mechanics or stylistics and neglecting the substance of the piece. Analytic scoring provides students with necessary direction for improving their work and becoming more proficient writers. Whichever approach is used, it is important that criteria for assessment be clearly understood. As Dahl and Farnan (1998) note, "When writers lack specific standards and intentions, their ability to reflect on and evaluate their writing is severely compromised. It is not surprising that if writers do not know what they want to accomplish with a particular writing, it will be difficult for them to judge whether they have created an effective composition" (p. 121).

■ ■ ■ Checkup ■ ■ ■

1. How should writing be evaluated?

■ ■ ■

■ Portfolios

Artists, photographers, designers, and others assemble their work in **portfolios** for assessment. Portfolios are now being used in a somewhat modified fashion to assess the literacy growth of elementary and middle school students. Portfolios have a number of advantages. First, they facilitate the assessment of growth over time. Because they provide the teacher with an opportunity to take a broad look at a student's literacy development, they are an appropriate method for assessing holistic approaches. Portfolio assessment can also lead to changes in the curriculum and teaching practices. In Au's (1994) study, for instance, teachers began emphasizing the revision phase of writing when portfolio assessment helped them see that they were neglecting that area. Teachers in Kentucky reported that portfolios were the key element in a program designed to improve writing (Stecher, Barron, Kaganoff, & Goodwin, 1998).

Types of Portfolios

There are five kinds of portfolios, each performing different functions and containing different kinds of materials: showcase, evaluation, documentation, process, and composite (Valencia & Place, 1994). Like the traditional portfolio used by artists to display their best works, the showcase portfolio is composed of works that students have selected as being their best. The focus in the evaluation portfolio is on collecting representative works from key areas. The samples included might be standardized—that is, based on a common text or a common topic—so that results are comparable across students. A documentation portfolio is designed to provide evidence of students' growth and so might contain the greatest number and variety of work samples. The process portfolio is designed to show how students work, so it includes samples from various stages of a project along with students'

■ A **portfolio** is a collection of work samples, test results, checklists, and other data used to assess a student's performance.

comments about how the project is progressing. A composite portfolio contains elements from two or more types of portfolios. For instance, a portfolio designed for district evaluation might contain showcase and process items.

Writing Samples

Collecting representative pieces from several types of writing assignments gives the teacher a broad view of a student's development. Including pieces written at different times of the year allows the teacher to trace the student's growth. Rough drafts as well as final copies illustrate the student's writing progress and indicate how well the student handles the various processes. Each student might include in her or his portfolio lists of pieces written, major writing skills learned, and current goals. Both student and teacher should have access to the portfolio and should agree on which pieces should be included. Teacher and student should also agree on how to choose what goes into the portfolio.

To help students reflect on their learning and make wise choices about the pieces they include, you might have them explain their choices by completing a self-evaluative statement. The statement can be a brief explanation with the heading "Why I Chose This Piece." Initially, reasons for inclusion and comments tend to be vague (Tierney, Carter, & Desai, 1991). However, through classroom discussions and conferences, you can help students explore criteria for including certain pieces rather than others—it tells a good story, it has a beginning that grabs the reader, it has many interesting examples, it seems to flow, and so on.

A portfolio can demonstrate the power of a reader and a writer. Unbeknownst to the teacher, a student may read dozens or hundreds of books or be a budding author. A reading log or sampling of written pieces should reveal this (Tierney, Carter, & Desai, 1991). However, you might invite students to include in their portfolios pieces they have written on their own as nonschool literacy endeavors.

Reading Samples

Some teachers use portfolios primarily to assess writing. If you wish to use portfolios to assess reading, include samples of reading. Samples to be included depend on the goals of the program. Valencia (1990) cautioned, "If the goals of instruction are not specified, portfolios have the potential to become reinforced holding files for odds and ends" (p. 339). If a goal of reading instruction is to teach students to visualize, drawings of reading selections might be included. If you have been working on summaries, you may want to see sample summaries. A list of books read might be appropriate for a goal of wide reading. Running records or informal reading inventories might be included to demonstrate fluency, word recognition in context, comprehension, or overall reading development.

At certain points, reading and writing will converge—written summaries of selections and research reports using several sources might count toward both reading and writing goals. Other items that might be placed in the portfolio are checklists, quizzes, standardized and informal test results, learning logs, written reactions to selections, and graphic organizers.

Reviewing Portfolios

To check on students' progress, periodically review their portfolios. Farr and Farr (1990) suggested that this be done a minimum of four times a year. In order to make the best use of your time and to help students organize their work, you might have them prepare a list of the items included in the portfolio. The portfolio should also contain a list of students' learning objectives. Students might write a cover letter or fill out a form summarizing work they have done, explaining which goals they feel they have met, which areas might need improvement, and what their plans for the future are. A sample portfolio evaluation form is presented in Figure 2.11 (on p. 62).

FOSTERING ENGAGEMENT

When students know why they are being assessed and when you share results with them and use results to plan reachable goals, they become more engaged in the learning process. Portfolio conferences are especially effective for engaging students, especially when they can compare current with past work samples and see progress.

FYI

Portfolios have the potential for demonstrating students' growth. As you assess folders, note the areas in which students have done especially well. Also note areas of weakness. In addition, portfolios provide information that shows class as well as individual needs. If the class as a whole is evidencing difficulty with the mechanics of writing, that might be an area in your curriculum that needs special attention.

■■■ **FIGURE 2.11**

Portfolio Evaluation by Student

Name: _____ Date: _____

Portfolio Evaluation

What were my goals in reading for this period?

What progress toward meeting these goals does my portfolio show?

What are my strengths?

What are my weaknesses?

What are my goals for improving as a reader?

How do I plan to meet those goals?

What were my goals in writing for this period?

What progress toward meeting these goals does my portfolio show?

What are my strengths as a writer?

What are my weaknesses?

What are my goals for improving as a writer?

How do I plan to meet these goals?

What questions do I have about my writing or my reading?

FYI

■ Giving students a say in portfolio decisions helps them maintain a sense of ownership (Simmons, 1990). It also fosters a more positive attitude and encourages students to take risks in their writing (Johnson, 1995).

■ Portfolios can mean the difference between passing and failing. In Florida, third-graders who fail the state's test are retained. However, they are promoted if they can demonstrate through a portfolio that their performance is equal to that demanded by the state test.

■ Portfolios are most useful when goals are clearly stated and specific criteria are listed for their assessment. It is essential, of course, that goals and criteria be understood by students (Snider, Lima, & DeVito, 1994).

■ In Kentucky, teachers reported that the portfolio system was the most influential factor in determining their instructional practice (Stecher, Barron, Kaganoff, & Goodwin, 1998). They also credited the portfolio system with helping them become better teachers and their students better writers.

INVOLVING PARENTS

Parents may feel uncomfortable or even threatened by portfolios. When portfolios are explained, parents prefer them to standardized tests (Tierney, Carter, & Desai, 1991). Tierney, Carter, and Desai (1991) suggested sitting down with parents and explaining the portfolio process to them. This not only helps parents understand the process, it also helps them see what their role might be.

Before you start to review a portfolio, decide what you want to focus on. It could be number of books read, changes in writing, or effort put into revisions. Your evaluation should, of course, consider the student's stated goals; it is also important to emphasize the student's strengths. As you assess the portfolio, consider a variety of pieces and look at the work in terms of its changes over time. Ask yourself: What does the student's work show about her or his progress over the time span covered? What might she or he do to make continued progress?

To save time and help you organize your assessment of the portfolio, you may want to use a checklist or rubric that is supplemented with personal comments. A sample portfolio review checklist is presented in Figure 2.12. Because the objective of evaluation is to improve instruction, students should be active partners in the process. "It follows that . . . assessment activities in which students are engaged in evaluating their own learning help them reflect on and understand their own strengths and needs, and it instills responsibility for their own learning" (Tierney, Carter, & Desai, 1991, p. 7).

■■■ **Checkup** ■■■

1. What are the essential components of a portfolio program?
2. What are the advantages and disadvantages of a portfolio program?

■■■

Name of student: _____   Date: _____

Voluntary Reading
  Number of books read   _____
  Variety of books read   _____
  Strengths   _____
  Needs   _____

Reading Comprehension
  Construction of meaning   _____
  Extension of meaning   _____
  Use of strategies   _____
  Quality of responses   _____
  Strengths   _____
  Needs   _____

Writing
  Amount of writing   _____
  Variety of writing   _____
  Planning   _____
  Revising   _____
  Self-editing   _____
  Content   _____
  Organization   _____
  Style   _____
  Mechanics   _____
  Strengths   _____
  Needs   _____

Comments: _____
_____
_____

■ Basal Reader Assessment Devices

Today's basal readers and literature anthologies offer a variety of assessment devices. Tests that accompany each selection or skills checks that are contained in workbooks can be used as part of a paper-and-pencil formative assessment. There are also numerous suggestions for ongoing, informal assessment through observation or use of checklists. In some instances, these suggestions are accompanied by corrective techniques: For instance, if students have difficulty making inferences, the teacher is provided with a reteaching lesson (Cooper & Pikulski, 2005). There are also numerous suggestions for self-assessment by students: "What parts of the selection were difficult for me? Why?" (Cooper & Pikulski, 2005). End-of-theme tests are also available, as are benchmark tests designed to be given quarterly. Portfolio systems are also part of the assessment package.

One especially valuable assessment device is the theme-level test or unit test. These tests assess the strategies and skills taught in a theme or unit. Presenting open-ended as well as multiple-choice items, theme-level or unit tests provide an excellent opportunity to assess students' ability to cope with high-stakes tests. In a sense, there is a bit of a disconnection between assessment and evaluation. Students demonstrate a skill taught during a unit or theme primarily through discussion with the whole class or in small groups. However, the skill is assessed through open-ended questions. Students might do well when answering such questions orally, but have difficulty getting their thoughts down on paper. In discussion, you can provide prompts and ask additional questions to draw out students' responses. However, on written assessments, students are not given these aids. As with any other skill, students need to be taught how to deal with open-ended questions, especially if they have not previously been exposed to such questions.

■ Screening and Diagnostic Instruments and Classroom-Based Assessment

FYI

■ Some programs, such as Reading First, have fairly strict requirements for screening, diagnostic, and ongoing monitoring or classroom-based assessment. Reading First also requires an outcomes measure to assess whether students are making adequate progress.

■ If students have serious reading problems, diagnostic testing might be conducted by the school's reading or learning disabilities specialist.

An assessment program should include screening and diagnostic instruments as well as classroom-based assessment. Screening instruments are assessment measures that indicate a possible problem and the need for a more thorough assessment. Group tests of reading can function as screening devices. Low scores indicate possible difficulty. A quick test of the ability to read lists of words can also function as a screening device. A carefully administered IRI is diagnostic because it yields a depth of information about a student's reading.

Classroom-based instructional assessments, which are also known as formative assessments, indicate whether students are making adequate progress or need more support. In classroom-based assessments, teachers use a variety of techniques for obtaining information about students' performance. Techniques include many of the informal devices presented in this chapter: running records, work samples such as pieces of writing, observations, checklists, anecdotal records, interviews, conferences, questionnaires, and portfolios. Classroom quizzes, basal reader assessments, and tests might also be included. The advantage of classroom-based assessment is that it provides information for planning instruction and making needed changes in a literacy program.

It is important to involve students in the classroom-based assessment process. As Stiggins (2004) recommends, "We must build classroom environments in which students use assessments to understand what success looks like and how to do better the next time. In effect, we must help students use ongoing classroom assessment to take responsibility for their own academic success" (pp. 25–26). Low-performing students benefit most from the use of formative assessment and accompanying corrective instruction.

Classroom-based assessment works best when a school system or school and its teachers decide what its standards or objectives are and then decide how to gather information in order to judge whether these standards are being reached. By discussing objectives, teachers clarify the schools' goals. In discussing assessment devices, they can address the issues of reliability and validity. What is the most valid way to judge that students are writing in a variety of genres? If a system of scoring written pieces is selected, how will it ensure that teachers' judgments are consistent so that the pieces judged to be proficient by one teacher would be judged proficient by other teachers?

Assessment systems that align teaching and assessment with objectives are available commercially. First Steps (Education Department of Western Australia, 1994) is one such system. In addition, a number of school systems have devised classroom-based assessment systems. Check to see if your state or your school district has created an assessment system.

Different assessment systems have differing visions of reading. Some espouse a strong phonics approach. Others favor use of context and a more holistic approach. You might use an existing system as a starting point but modify it to meet your vision of reading and the objectives that you emphasize. The list of standards and suggestions for assessment at the end of Chapters 4–9, 11, and 13 of this text could provide a starting point for the construction of a classroom-based assessment system.

Alignment of Assessment

A critical feature of assessment measures is alignment. Alignment means that the curriculum and instruction are based on agreed-upon objectives and the tests are assessing what is being taught (Webb, 1999). This is especially important in view of the demands of making adequate yearly progress. Classroom and other assessments should be aligned with standards (objectives) and instruction. Alignment needs to be flexible. Based on a study of fourth-graders' performance on the comprehension section of a state proficiency test, Riddle Buly and Valencia (2002) warn:

> Alignment is certainly a centerpiece of standards-based reform and, most of the time, it makes good sense. However, sometimes it can be oversimplified and inadvertently lead to inappropriate instruction. More specifically, aligning instruction with state assessments may help teachers focus on what is tested. . . . It will not address the skills and strategies that underlie such competence. . . . A focus on comprehension would miss those who have difficulty in word identification or fluency, or those with specific second language issues. Similarly, requiring teachers to align their instruction with grade level content standards may also fall short. Assuring, for example, that 4th-grade teachers are teaching the 4th-grade content standards does not assure they are providing appropriate instruction for all students. To be sure, some students would benefit from instruction and practice reading material that is at a lower grade level and some would benefit from more advanced curriculum. It is not that grade level standards or expectations are unimportant or that aligning instruction, assessment, and standards is wrong. However, for many struggling students, grade level standards are goals rather than immediate needs. The teacher's challenge is to bring the students to the point where those grade level goals are within reach. (p. 234)

If you are using a commercial program, chances are that it is aligned. However, examine it closely to see if any revisions are needed. In addition, you might need to make some adjustment to ensure that the program aligns with state, district, and other outside assessments. If you are using a program that you or your school has created, you will need to construct or adopt an assessment system that aligns with your objectives and instruction.

■ Evaluation and Closing the Gap

Evaluation is an essential element in closing the literacy gap (Good et al., 2003). The first step is to set challenging but realistic objectives for all students. These might be based on goals set by your school or school district, or you can use the Essential Standards listed in the Alignment Charts at the end of Chapters 4–9 and 11 and 13 in this text. Set end-of-grade benchmarks for key literacy skills. A realistic objective for kindergarten might be the ability to identify the twenty-six letters of the alphabet, to provide sounds for twenty consonants, to read 100 high-frequency words, and to read easy short-vowel patterns. For first grade, it might be the ability to use knowledge of basic vowel patterns to decode single-syllable words. For third grade, it might be the ability to read third-grade passages with 75 percent comprehension and to read at a rate of 100 words per minute. Also note entry-level benchmarks for your grade. Entry level for first grade might be the end-of-kindergarten benchmark. You might expect entering second-graders to be able to read most single-syllable words.

Once goals and benchmarks are established, conduct an initial assessment to find out where students are. Based on students' current status, plan a program. Make provisions for students who might need additional support or even intensive help. Students entering first grade who lack awareness of beginning sounds will need more help than those who have mastered initial consonant correspondences. Continue to monitor students' progress toward the objective. Some systems recommend monitoring progress three times a year. These are typically formal checks. Using classroom-based assessment measures, you

FYI

Benchmarks indicate the performance expected of the majority of students. Some students will exceed benchmarks; others will fall behind. Failure to reach a benchmark indicates a need for intervention. It is not an indication that the student should be retained.

Closing the Gap

More frequent monitoring helps you to note which students aren't making adequate progress and so to intervene earlier with more intensive instruction or different materials. DIBELS provides materials for benchmark monitoring, designed to be administered three times a year, and also materials for progress monitoring, which may be given more frequently.

Adapting Instruction for English Language Learners

A Spanish version of DIBELS is available: Indicadores dinámicos del éxito en la lectura™.

FYI

The DIBELS oral reading fluency passages for grade 1 are written on a level that the average first-grader will not reach until spring or the end of the year. Easier passages should be used for monitoring reading in early or mid–first grade.

might informally monitor students' progress weekly. More formal checks might be conducted monthly. With frequent monitoring, you are quicker to note when students are lagging behind and so need additional instruction, more review, or better materials.

Simply monitoring progress improves performance by a month or two. When teachers gear instruction based on the results of monitoring, gains can be quite dramatic and may improve by a year or more (Black & Wiliam, 1998). Results are magnified if the whole school is engaged in the monitoring process and grade-level meetings are held to discuss students' progress and ways of improving the program.

Continuous Progress Monitoring

As part of your monitoring, you might use a continuous progress monitoring system. Continuous progress monitoring systems are devices that increase in difficulty and thus track growth over time. They might consist of word lists or passages that become increasingly more difficult. You can create your own progress monitor or use one that has already been constructed.

One of the best known of the continuous progress monitoring systems is the Dynamic Indicators of Basic Early Literacy Skills (DIBELS), which is available on the Web at http:dibels.uoregon.edu and can be used for no charge. Designed for grades K–6, DIBELS measures phonological awareness, phonics, and oral reading fluency. Tasks are timed. Students are given 1 minute on each of the tasks so that slow-but-sure processors are penalized. The emphasis is on lower-level processes such as speed of pronouncing printed words. Higher-level comprehension and vocabulary skills are neglected. However, in the oral reading fluency assessment, the system does offer a number of passages at each level, beginning with mid–first grade, that might be used to track growth. These passages might be given as directed or modified and administered in the same fashion as an IRI or running record. If given in both standard and modified fashion, the passages yield reading rate scores, reading levels, and retelling scores. If a miscue analysis is administered, they also yield qualitative data about students' use of word analysis skills and strategies. When given in modified fashion, the DIBELS are more time-consuming to administer but yield more information.

AIMSWeb, which is similar to DIBELS but charges fees, features periodic assessment probes for reading fluency, comprehension, spelling, and early literacy (phonological awareness and phonics). Assessments cover grades K–8. Comprehension is assessed through **mazes**. Ed Checkup, at http://www.edcheckup.com, sells assessment probes for oral reading, maze passages, letter sounds, and isolated words, along with several writing probes.

Creating Your Own Continuous Monitoring System

Because of the overemphasis on speed of responding and a possible lack of correspondence between what current continuous progress monitoring systems assess and what you teach, you might choose to construct your own system. First, decide what your key objectives are. Then create or adapt measures that assess those objectives. For instance, for phonics, you might use the Phonics Progress Monitoring Assessment, explained in Chapter 4. For recognition of words in isolation, you might use the word lists from an IRI. For reading rate, you could use the DIBELS oral fluency passages. For comprehension, you might use the maze passages from *AIMSWeb*, IRI passages, or DIBELS passages with retellings or questions added.

■ A **maze** is a task in which students select from three or four options the one that correctly completes a sentence.

The phonics and word-recognition tests can be administered rapidly since they only involve reading lists of words. Oral reading rate can also be assessed quickly since it entails reading a passage for just 1 minute. These measures could be given frequently. However, if given individually, comprehension passages are more time-consuming to administer. Because growth in comprehension is generally slower than growth in skills such as phonics and reading lists of words, comprehension tests might be given just three or four times a year. Other measures might be given monthly or even weekly. Graph performance so that you can see whether students are on track. Older students might graph their own progress.

Data Analysis

Assessment data are playing an increasingly important role in education. Regardless of which tests or which assessment systems you use, keep a record of students' performance. Use that data to make instructional decisions. After an assessment has been administered, organize the results. Note especially students who did not perform adequately. What are some possible reasons for their poor performance? What might be done to assist them? If you have scores from the same or comparable assessments, note whether there has been an improvement and whether the improvement is such that the students are on track to reach the target benchmark by the school year's end. Also analyze items that students responded to. On a phonics test, for instance, note the items that students got correct. Perhaps the students got most of the short-vowel items correct but had difficulty with clusters (blends). This is the kind of information that you can use to plan instruction. Consider other sources of data. You might have information from an IRI, running record, or personal observation that sheds additional light on students' skill levels and cognitive processes.

FYI

Tests, observations, work samples, and other assessment devices can be used to verify and complement each other. A student's performance in phonics, for instance, might be assessed through a written quiz, an observation of oral reading, and an examination of his or her spelling. This triangulation of data might reveal that the student can read simple, short-vowel words (*top, pet*) but has difficulty with clusters (*stop, step*).

▪▪▪ Checkup ▪▪▪

1. What roles do screening, diagnostic, and classroom-based assessment—including continuous progress monitoring—play in a literacy program?
2. How might evaluation be used to close the literacy gap?

▪▪▪

▪ Assessing English Language Learners

Under the No Child Left Behind Act of 2001, the academic progress of every child in grades 3 through 8, including those learning English who have been enrolled in a U.S. school for at least a year, is tested in reading and math. English language learners (ELLs) are tested annually to measure how well they are learning English.

Apart from state and federal regulations, it is essential that you have information about ELLs' proficiency in literacy in their first language. Students who can read in another language will have learned basic concepts of reading. They will have developed phonological awareness, alphabetical knowledge, and knowledge of phonics. You can build on this knowledge. It is also essential that you have information about the students' proficiency in oral and written English. If students are weak in understanding English, you can plan a literacy program that develops oral language.

Key questions include:

- What is the student's proficiency in speaking her or his first language?
- What is the student's proficiency in speaking English?
- What is the student's proficiency in reading in the first language?
- What is the student's proficiency in reading in English?
- What is the educational background of the student?

Adapting Instruction for English Language Learners

Obtaining a valid assessment of the ability and performance of English language learners is a problem. ELLs can obtain conversational proficiency in two years or less. However, it may take five years or more for ELLs to learn enough academic English that they can do as well on tests of academic proficiency as native speakers of English do (Cummins, 2001).

Case Study

Lessons from 90/90/90 Schools

Assessment works best when it is tied into instruction and the attitude that all students can learn if given adequate instruction and whatever assistance they need. Assessment becomes a blueprint for instruction rather than a judgment. In 90/90/90 schools, there was frequent assessment of student progress with multiple opportunities for improvement. A 90/90/90 school was one in which 90 percent of the students are members of minority groups and live in poverty but attain the proficient level on high-stakes tests. In many instances, assessments in these schools were weekly and were constructed by classroom teachers. Since many of the students in these schools were struggling readers and writers, they often did poorly on assessments. However, the consequence of a poor performance was not a low grade or a sense of failure but additional instruction and practice.

Another characteristic of assessment in 90/90/90 schools was an emphasis on written responses in performance assessments. Because the responses were written rather than oral, students were better able to elaborate on their thinking, and teachers were better able to judge the quality of the students' responses. Being better able to examine and analyze students' responses, teachers had the information they needed to plan effective instructional activities. "By assessing student writing, teachers can discern whether the challenges faced by a student are the result of vocabulary issues, misunderstood directions, reasoning errors, or a host of other causes that are rarely revealed by typical tests" (Reeves, 2003, p. 5).

In 90/90/90 schools, teachers used a common rubric so that there were clear standards for writing and clear standards for assessing (Reeves, 2003). In addition, in many instances teachers would meet to assess papers or would exchange papers, so assessment was the result of applying the rubric rather than simply using highly subjective judgment. Disagreements about scoring generally arise when teachers use implicit criteria rather than stated criteria or when the criteria are not specific enough. For instance, a teacher might judge a paper partly on neatness, which isn't one of the stated criteria. Or a criterion such as "fully develops ideas," which lacks specificity, is interpreted in different ways by different teachers. By talking over standards and disagreements, teachers can clarify the criteria and refrain from adding criteria that are not stated.

The ESL or bilingual specialist should be able to provide information about the students' proficiency in literacy in their first language and also their knowledge of English. If this information is not available, use informal techniques to assess the students' proficiency in reading and writing their first language. Ask students to bring in books in their native tongue and read them to you and then retell the selection in English. Also ask them to bring in a piece of writing that they have done in their native language and read it to you and then retell it in English. Based on the ease with which they read, you can judge whether they are literate in their first language, even if you don't know the language. You might also obtain or construct a list of common words in their language and ask students to read them. Figure 2.13 contains a list of twenty common Spanish words, phonetically respelled and with their English translations. You might use a list such as this to get a very rough idea of the students' reading proficiency. If students can read all or most of these words, they can read at least at a basic level in Spanish. If you are fluent in Spanish, you might administer the Spanish Reading Inventory (Kendall/Hunt) or the English-Español Reading Inventory for the Classroom (Merrill).

To assess students' ability to understand language, request that they point to various objects: Point to the book. Point to the red dot. Point to the square. Point to your knee, your foot, your ear (Law & Eckes, 2002). Start with common objects, and progress to less com-

■ **Readability level** indicates the difficulty of a selection. A formula may be used to estimate readability by measuring quantitative factors such as sentence length and number of difficult words in the selection. A leveling system may use a number of qualitative factors to estimate the difficulty of the text. Best results are obtained by assessing both qualitative and quantitative factors.

mon ones: Point to the magnet. Point to the picture of the jet. Real objects work better, but you might also use magazine or other photos to assess students' receptive vocabulary. Also request that students follow a series of commands: Stand. Sit. Open the book. Raise your hand. Write your name. To assess expressive vocabulary, have the students identify objects that you point to. Also ask students a series of questions, and note how they respond: What is your name? How old are you? Where do you live? Count to ten. Name the colors that I point to. Name the letters that I point to. For a copy of informal language tests for English language learners and additional suggestions for assessment, refer to the text by Law and Eckes (2002), which is listed in the References section.

Creating a Literacy Profile

Jiménez (2004) recommends that a literacy profile be created for English language learners. The profile provides information about the language the students speak at home. It is also important to determine whether there have been gaps in ELLs' schooling. Their schooling may have been fragmented, or they may have been moved from a regular class to an ESL class or to a special education class.

When looking at scores from an ELL student, compare them to the scores of other ELLs. Also consider such factors as when the student began learning English and how many years of exposure to English the student has had. Also find out if the student can read in his or her native language. If so, skills can be transferred. Get information, too, on the students' literacy activities. Some students act as translators for their parents, an activity known as language brokering (Lalas, Solomon, & Johannessen, 2006). Language brokering apparently strengthens students' academic achievement. These students might be translating medical forms, advertisements, and even income tax forms. Affirm students' native language, and help them see that their native language can be a source of help in understanding English.

■ ■ ■ Checkup ■ ■ ■

1. What assessment information do you need to know to plan a program for ELLs?
2. How might you go about assessing ELLs?

■ ■ ■

■ Assessing Materials

Just about the most important instructional decision you will make is selecting the appropriate level of materials for your students. Choose a level that is too easy and students will be bored and unchallenged. Select material that is too difficult and they will be discouraged, have their academic self-concepts demolished, and fail to make progress. Perhaps, worst of all, they will learn to hate reading (Juel, 1994). As noted earlier, students should know at least 95 percent of the words in the materials they are asked to read and should have about 75 percent comprehension.

Publishers of school materials generally provide reading levels for their texts. Using a formula or subjective leveling scale, they estimate that the material is at, for example, a second-, third-, or fourth-grade level, which means that the average second-, third-, or fourth-grader should be able to read it. Or they may use letters or numbers to indicate a level rather than a grade. Some publishers of children's books also supply **readability levels**. If no

■■■■ FIGURE 2.13   Spanish Word List

Spanish Word	Pronunciation	Meaning
no	no	no
mi	me	my
uno	OO-no	one
esta	ES-tah	this
ella	AY-yah	she
señor	sen-YOR	mister
leer	lay-AIR	read
libro	LEE-bro	book
amigo	ah-ME-go	friend
pelota	peh-LOH-tah	ball
vaca	BAH-kah	cow
musica	MYEW-see-kah	music
sorpressa	sor-PRES-ah	surprise
leopardo	lay-oh-PAR-doh	leopard
abuela	ah-BWEH-lah	grandmother
bicicleta	bee-see-KLAY-tah	bicycle
mañana	mon-YAH-nah	tomorrow
primavera	pre-mah-BEAR-ah	spring
zapatos	sah-PAH-toes	shoes
zoológico	soh-oh-LOH-hee-koh	zoo

readability level is indicated for a book that you wish to use, you might check Appendix A, which lists high-quality leveled titles, or you can consult one of the following sources.

ATOS (Advantage-TASA Open Standard)

ATOS is a computerized formula that uses number of words per sentence, characters per word, and average grade level of words and analyzes the entire text to estimate the readability of a book and provide a grade-level equivalent. ATOS scores for more than 50,000 trade books are available from Renaissance Learning, the creators of Accelerated Reading, at http://www.renlearn.com. Click on Quizzes, and enter the title of the book for which you would like to have an ATOS score. ATOS scores are expressed in grade equivalents. First grade is subdivided into a series of levels that are equated with Reading Recovery levels. If the text for which you want a readability estimate is not available, contact Renaissance Learning. They may have the ATOS score. If not, if you provide sample passages from the book, the company will provide an ATOS score for you.

Lexile Scale

The lexile scale is a two-factor computerized formula that consists of a measurement of sentence length and word frequency. The lexile scale ranges from about 70 to 1700+, with 70 being very easy beginning reading material and 1700 being very difficult reading material of the type found in scientific journals. Table 2.7 (on p. 43) provides approximate grade equivalents for lexile scores. A software program for obtaining readability estimates, the *Lexile Analyzer*, is available from MetaMetrics. However, lexile scores for about 40,000 books are available online at http://www.lexile.com.

Degrees of Reading Power

The Degrees of Reading Power test measures sentence length, number of words not on the Dale List of words known by fourth-graders, and average number of letters per word (Touchstone Applied Science Associates, 1994). Compilations of readability levels expressed in DRP units for content area textbooks can be found on the following Web site: http://www.tasaliteracy.com. DRP readabilities for trade books are available on easy-to-use software called *BookLink*. DRP units range from 15 for the easiest materials to 85 for the most difficult reading material. Table 2.7 provides approximate grade equivalents for DRP scores.

Other Readability Formulas

If you are unable to get a readability level from one of these sources, or if you prefer to assess the readability of the text yourself, there are a number of formulas you can apply. One of the easiest to use is the Fry Readability Graph, which bases its estimate on two factors: sentence length and number of syllables in a word. Number of syllables in a word is a measure of vocabulary difficulty. In general, the more syllables a word has, the harder it tends to be. The Fry Readability Graph (Fry, 1977b) is presented in Figure 2.14. A formula that counts the number of hard words but is relatively easy to use is the Primary Readability Formula (Gunning, 2002); it can be used to assess the difficulty level of materials in grades 1 to 4. *The New Dale-Chall Readability Formula* (Chall & Dale, 1995), which also counts the number of hard words, is recommended for grades 3 and up.

One problem with readability formulas is that they are mechanical and so do not consider subjective factors, such as the density of concepts, use of illustrations, or background required to construct meaning from the text. Readability formulas should be complemented by the use of the subjective factors incorporated in a leveling system (Gunning, 2000b). A leveling system uses subjective or qualitative factors to estimate the difficulty level of materials.

■■■ ■ **FIGURE 2.14** Fry's Graph for Estimating Readability

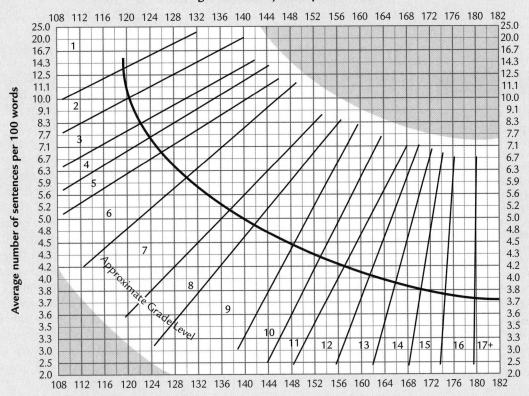

Expanded Directions for Working Readability Graph

1. Randomly select three (3) sample passages and count out exactly 100 words each, beginning with the beginning of a sentence. Do not count proper nouns, initializations, and numerals.

2. Count the number of sentences in the 100 words, estimating length of the fraction of the last sentence to the nearest one-tenth.

3. Count the total number of syllables in the 100-word passage. If you don't have a hand counter available, an easy way is to simply put a mark above every syllable over one in each word, then when you get to the end of the passage, count the number of marks and add 100. Small calculators can also be used by pushing numeral 1, then the + sign for each word or syllable when counting.

4. Enter graph with *average* sentence length and *average* number of syllables; plot dot where the two lines intersect. Area where dot is plotted will give you the approximate grade level.

5. If a great deal of variability is found in syllable count or sentence count, putting more samples into the average is desirable.

6. A word is defined as a group of symbols with space on either side; thus, *Joe, IRA, 1945,* and & are each one word.

7. A syllable is defined as a phonetic syllable. Generally, there are as many syllables as vowel sounds. For example, *stopped* is one syllable and *wanted* is two syllables. When counting syllables for numerals and initializations, count one syllable for each symbol. For example, *1945* is four syllables, *IRA* is three syllables, and & is one syllable.

■ ■ ■ **Checkup** ■ ■ ■

1. What are some key formulas for assessing readability?
2. What are the key components of each of these formulas?

■ ■ ■

Leveling Systems

In addition to failing to consider qualitative factors, traditional formulas do not work well at the very beginning levels. Formulas don't consider such factors as usefulness of illustrations and number of lines per page, which are major determinants of the difficulty level of beginning materials. Formulas do indicate with reasonable accuracy that materials are on a first-grade level. However, first-grade reading encompasses a wide range of material that includes counting or color books that have just one or two easy words per page as well as books, such as the Little Bear series, that contain brief chapters and may contain several hundred words. To make fine discriminations among the range of first-grade books, it is necessary to use a leveling system.

Although materials for beginning readers may look similar—large print and lots of illustrations—they incorporate different theories of teaching reading and have different uses (Hiebert, 1999). Early reading materials can be classified as being predictable, high frequency, or decodable. Predictable texts are written in such a way that the student can use illustrations or their knowledge of language to "read" the text. A predictable book might have the sentences "I can run. I can jump. I can sing. I can read," each on a separate page accompanied by an illustration showing the action. The reader gets heavy support from the illustrations and the repeated pattern. Predictable books are excellent for reinforcing concepts of print and giving students the feel of reading, and they can also help English language learners learn the patterns of English. Predictable books do a good job of introducing students to reading. Most students will pick up an initial reading vocabulary by repeatedly meeting words in print. However, some will continue to use picture and language clues, and the use of predictable text may actually hinder their progress.

Some texts emphasize high-frequency words. Words such as *of, and, the, was*, and *where* occur so often in print that they are said to be high-frequency. Most predictable books are composed primarily of high-frequency words.

Decodable texts contain phonics elements that have been taught. A story about a *bug* who lived in a *rug* would be decodable to students who have learned the *-ug* pattern. No text is totally decodable. High-frequency words such as *is, are*, and *the* need to be included, as do content words such as *bear* and *hungry* if the story is about a hungry bear.

The most widely used leveling system is based on the predictability of text. Adapting a system that was originally devised for Reading Recovery, Fountas and Pinnell (1996, 1999, 2006; Pinnell and Fountas, 2002) have compiled a list of 18,000 leveled books for students in kindergarten through grade 8. Books are leveled from A through Z, with A being very beginning reading and Z being eighth-grade reading. Table 2.7 provides approximate grade equivalents. Books in Appendix A have been leveled according to both predictability and decodability, based on quantitative as well as qualitative factors.

However, you may wish to use books that have not been leveled, or you may not have access to a listing of leveled books. In that case, you need to be able to level books on your own. To level books, consider key subjective factors and compare passages from the book you are leveling to passages from benchmark books. *The Qualitative Assessment of Text Difficulty* (Chall, Bissex, Conard, & Harris-Sharples, 1996) provides benchmark passages and directions for leveling both fictional and informational books. Or you might use the Basic Leveling Index, which is explained below.

The Basic Leveling Index

The Basic Leveling Index uses both quantitative and qualitative factors to level books. Subjected to extensive tryouts, it has been used to level several thousand books and compares favorably with other leveling systems (Gunning, 1998b, 2000b). Tryouts suggest that it is more accurate than readability formulas or subjective leveling systems used alone.

Using the Basic Leveling System with Beginning Reading Books.   Beginning reading books are more difficult to level than are upper-grade books because they encompass a very wide range of difficulty. The Basic Leveling System has seven beginning-reader through first-grade levels: picture, caption or frame (early preprimer), preprimer one, preprimer two, preprimer three, primer, and first. To determine the difficulty of an early reading text, compare the text being assessed with a benchmark book or benchmark passage. Ask: Which benchmark book or passage is this text most like? Also consider qualitative factors. Note especially the difficulty level of the words. Would your students be able to read them? Remember that they should be able to read about 95 percent of the words. At this level, most of the words will be in their listening vocabulary. Their major task is to pronounce or recognize the printed words. Words such as *the* and *are* appear with high frequency and so are easier to read. Some words such as *cat* and *hat* will be easy to decode. Consider, too, how helpful the illustrations are. Some of the words may be depicted by illustrations, which might also provide an overview of the text or portray significant portions of it. Be attentive to the overall interest of the selection, familiarity of the topic and language, repetition of elements, use of rhyme, and such format factors as number of lines per page. Also consider the length of the text; short pieces are easier to read than longer ones. Above all, note whether the average beginning reader would have the background information necessary to read the text. A book about the Vietnam War, no matter how simply written, would be beyond most beginning readers. Watch out, too, for the use of figurative language and allusions that are beyond beginning readers. When estimating difficulty level, be conservative. If you are undecided whether a book is on a primer or first level, place it at the higher level. It's better to give a student a book that is on the easy side rather than one that is too difficult.

Leveling books works best when those doing the leveling are carefully trained. Otherwise, the process is prone to error. To get a more reliable and more accurate estimate, use a quantitative measure along with the qualitative ones. The key objective factor that determines the difficulty level of early reading materials is vocabulary, or the difficulty the novice reader will experience pronouncing the words in a book. Stories that use a few common words should prove easier to read than those that use a variety of words, including some that do not occur with high frequency. Vocabulary difficulty is measured by counting the number of words that do not appear on the alphabetical listing of 500 high-frequency words, presented in Figure 2.15 (on p. 74). This compilation of the 500 words that occur with the highest frequency in first-grade textbooks and children's books that are on a first-grade level is based on *The Educator's Word Frequency Guide* (Zeno, Ivens, Millard, & Duvvuri, 1995). In tryouts, teachers who used the number of hard words as an aid in determining difficulty level were much more accurate than those who used only subjective factors (Gunning, 1996).

To determine the number of hard words, count the number of words in a selection that do not appear on the high-frequency list. Words that appear on the list but to which *-s, -es, -d, -ed,* or *-ing* has been added are considered *not* to be hard words. If the book being analyzed has fewer than 100 words, check all the words. For brief books, those with 300 or fewer words, analyze the entire work in 100-word segments. For longer texts, analyze as many samples as you can, but at least three. Select samples from the beginning, middle, and end of the book. The more samples you analyze, the more valid and reliable the estimate of difficulty. Many children's books increase in difficulty so that the latter part of the book has many more hard words than the beginning portions. Average the hard words scores of the passages sampled. Table 2.9 (on p. 75) provides estimated readability levels based on the proportion of hard words per 100 words.

However, a hard words score should *never* be used as the sole determining factor in estimating difficulty level. Qualitative factors should be carefully considered. In tryouts, when subjective factors were considered, changes were made in estimated difficulty levels

■■■ **FIGURE 2.15 Alphabetical Listing of 500 High-Frequency Words**

a	book	drop	gave	hurt	made	over	see	table	voice
about	both	duck	get	I	make	own	seed	take	wait
across	box	each	girl	I'll	man	paint	seem	talk	walk
afraid	boy	ear	give	I'm	many	paper	seen	tall	want
after	bring	earth	go	I've	mark	park	set	tell	warm
again	brother	eat	gone	if	may	part	she	ten	was
air	brown	egg	good	in	maybe	party	sheep	than	wasn't
all	bus	end	got	inside	me	people	ship	thank	watch
alone	but	enough	grandfather	into	mean	pet	shoe	that	water
along	by	even	grandma	is	men	pick	shop	that's	way
always	cake	ever	grandmother	isn't	might	picture	short	the	we
am	call	every	grandpa	it	minute	piece	should	their	we'll
an	came	everyone	grass	it's	mom	pig	shout	them	week
and	can	everything	great	its	money	place	show	then	well
animal	can't	eye	green	jeep	moon	plant	sick	there	went
another	cannot	face	ground	job	more	play	side	these	were
answer	car	fall	grow	jump	morning	please	sign	they	wet
any	care	family	guess	just	mother	pond	sing	thing	what
anybody	cat	far	had	keep	mouse	pretty	sister	think	what's
anything	catch	farm	hair	kept	move	pull	sit	this	wheel
are	change	farmer	hand	kid	much	push	sky	those	when
arm	children	fast	happen	kind	must	put	sleep	thought	where
around	city	father	happy	king	my	quick	slow	three	which
as	clean	feel	hard	kitten	name	quiet	small	through	while
ask	climb	feet	has	knew	near	rabbit	smile	time	white
at	close	fell	hat	know	need	race	snow	tired	who
away	cloud	felt	have	lake	never	rain	so	to	why
baby	cold	few	he	last	new	ran	some	toad	wife
back	come	find	head	late	next	reach	someone	today	will
bad	cook	fine	hear	laugh	nice	read	something	together	wind
bag	could	fire	heard	learn	night	ready	sometime	told	window
ball	couldn't	first	held	leave	no	real	soon	too	wish
be	cow	fish	hello	left	noise	really	sound	took	with
bear	cried	fix	help	leg	not	red	spot	top	without
because	cry	floor	hen	let	nothing	rest	stand	town	wolf
bed	cut	flower	her	let's	now	ride	star	train	woman
been	dad	fly	here	letter	of	right	start	tree	won't
before	dark	follow	high	light	off	river	stay	tried	wood
began	day	food	hill	like	oh	road	step	truck	word
behind	did	for	him	line	old	rock	stick	try	work
bell	didn't	found	himself	lion	on	room	still	turn	would
best	different	four	his	listen	once	run	stood	turtle	write
better	do	fox	hit	little	one	sad	stop	two	year
big	doctor	friend	hold	live	only	said	store	uncle	yell
bike	does	frog	hole	long	open	same	story	under	yellow
bird	dog	from	home	look	or	sat	street	until	yes
birthday	don't	front	horse	lost	other	saw	sun	up	you
black	door	fun	hot	lot	our	say	sure	us	you'll
blue	down	funny	house	love	out	school	surprise	use	your
boat	drink	game	how	lunch	outside	sea	swim	very	you're

■■■ TABLE 2.9 Estimate of Readability Level Based on Number of Hard Words

Level	Number of Hard Words
Picture	All words depicted by illustrations
Caption/Frame	Most words depicted by illustrations
High frequency PP1	1–3
Preprimer 2	4–6
Preprimer 3	7–8
Primer	9–10
First	11–12

Objective difficulty level _____

Estimated difficulty level of text (quantitative and qualitative factors) _____

about one third of the time. For the most accurate results, obtain an objective readability estimate based on the number of words not on the high-frequency list. Using that estimate as an anchor, consider the benchmark passages and qualitative factors. Then use both objective and subjective information to decide on a difficulty level. Use the worksheet in Figure 2.16 to note quantitative and qualitative factors. As you become familiar with using benchmark passages and subjective factors to level books, your estimates will become more accurate and there will be less need to rely on objective measures. However, objective measures provide a helpful check.

The next few pages provide a description of each level and a sample benchmark passage. Words that do not appear on the high-frequency list are boldfaced.

Picture Level.   In books at the picture level, a single word or phrase is depicted with an illustration (see Figure 2.17). The word *lion*, for instance, is accompanied by a drawing of a lion; the word *three* is accompanied by the numeral three and three dots. The text is so fully and clearly depicted that no reading is required. In some books, the student might need to use the initial consonant to help identify the picture. For instance, the student might not know whether a wolf or dog is being depicted. Seeing that the label for the pic-

■■■ FIGURE 2.16

Worksheet for Estimating Difficulty of Grade-1 Materials

Number of hard words depicted by illustrations:
None _____ Some _____ Most _____ All _____

Number of words that would be easy to decode:
None _____ Some _____ Most _____ All _____

Difficulty of vocabulary and concepts
_____ Familiar vocabulary and concepts
_____ One or two unfamiliar words or concepts
_____ Several unfamiliar words or concepts

Familiarity of topic or story line
High _____ Medium _____ Low _____

When compared with benchmark passages or books, what level(s) do the sample passages from the text seem to be most like?
Passage 1 _____
Passage 2 _____
Passage 3 _____
Average _____

■■■ **FIGURE 2.17**

ture starts with a *w*, the student uses knowledge of initial consonants to reason that a wolf is being depicted.

Benchmark books:

Colors by John Burningham

Numbers by Guy Smalley

Caption or Frame Level.   The text of caption level books is illustrated so that the reader can use pictures to identify most but not all of the words (see Figure 2.18). These books feature frame sentences, which are easy sentences, such as: "I can _____," I am _____," or "_____ can swim," that are repeated throughout the text. The name of the object, animal, or person that completes the frame is depicted. The student would need to know initial consonants and the few high-frequency words that make up the frame.

Benchmark books:

Have You Seen My Cat? by Eric Carle

My Barn by Craig Brown

Cat on the Mat by Brian Wildsmith

Benchmark passage: I see _____.

Preprimer 1 (Easy, High-Frequency Words).   Preprimer 1 books are similar to caption level books but there are a greater number of different words used and more reading is required. Illustrations usually depict some or much of the text. A preprimer 1 book requires increased knowledge of high-frequency words and some beginning familiarity with short-vowel patterns, such as *-at* and *-am*. As many as 1–3 words out of 100 might not be on the high-frequency list.

Benchmark books:

Brown Bear, Brown Bear, What Do You See? by Bill Martin

Bugs by Patricia and Fredrick McKissack

Benchmark passage: "The Bad Cat"

Matt is sad.
Matt had a hat.
Now **Pat** has **Matt's** hat.

Pat is a cat.
Matt ran after Pat.
But Pat ran away.
Pat ran away with Matt's hat.
Pat is a bad cat.

■■■ **FIGURE 2.18**

Preprimer 2.   Preprimer 2 books are similar to preprimer 1 books, but there are a greater number of different words used and more reading is required. Illustrations usually depict some of the text. This level requires increased knowledge of high-frequency words and some familiarity with most of the short-vowel patterns, such as *-at, -op,* and *-et*. As many as 4–6 words out of 100 might not appear on the high-frequency list.

Benchmark books:

Cat Traps by Molly Coxe

The Carrot Seed by Ruth Krauss

Benchmark passage: "The Red Kangaroo"

Hop! Hop! Hop!
Kangaroos like to hop.
The red kangaroo can **hop** the best.
The red kangaroo can hop over you.
The red kangaroo can hop over the top of a **van**.
The red kangaroo is big.
The red kangaroo has big back legs.
Its back legs are very **strong**.
And it has a long **tail**.
The red kangaroo is bigger than a man.
The red kangaroo is the biggest kangaroo of all.

Preprimer 3.   The preprimer 3 level is similar to preprimer 2 but requires increased knowledge of high-frequency words and increased familiarity with short-vowel patterns that make use of consonant combinations such as *tr, st,* and *sch*. There could be as many as 7–8 words out of 100 not on the high-frequency list.

Benchmark books:

The Foot Book by Dr. Seuss

Sleepy Dog by Harriet Ziefert

Benchmark passage: "Best Pet"

"I have the best pet," said **Ted**.
"My dog **barks** and **wags** his **tail** when I come home from school."
"No, I have the best pet," said **Robin**. "I have a cat. My cat **wakes** me up so that
I can go to school."
"I have the best pet," said Will. "I have a pet pig.
My pig can do many **tricks**."
Then Ted said, "We all have the best pet.
I have the pet that is best for me.
Robin has the pet that is best for her.
And Will has the pet that is best for him."

Primer.   At the primer level, vocabulary becomes more diverse, and illustrations are less helpful. Students need to know high-frequency words and short-vowel and long-vowel patterns (*-ake, -ike, -ope*). There could be approximately 9–10 words per 100 not on the high-frequency list. A primer-level book might also require some knowledge of *r*-vowel (*-ar, -er*) and other-vowel (*-our, -ought*) patterns.

Benchmark books:

And I Mean It Stanley by Crosby Bonsall

Jason's Bus Ride by Harriet Ziefert

Benchmark passage: The Little Red Hen

A little red hen lived on a farm with her **chickens**. One day she found a **grain** of **wheat** in the **barnyard**.
"Who will plant this wheat?" she said.
"Not I," said the Cat.
"Not I," said the Duck.
"I will do it **myself**," said the little Red Hen. And she planted the grain of wheat.
When the wheat was **ripe** she said, "Who will take this wheat to the **mill**?"
"Not I," said the Cat.
"Not I," said the Duck.
"I will, then," said the little Red Hen, and she took the wheat to the mill.

When she **brought** the **flour** home, she said, "Who will bake some bread with this flour?" (Only hard words in first 100 words were counted.)

First Grade.   At the first-grade level, selections are becoming longer and more complex. Books may be divided into very brief chapters. Students need to know short-vowel, long-vowel, and some of the easier other-vowel (*-ow, -oy, -oo, -aw*), and *r*-vowel patterns (*-ear, -or*). There may also be some easy two-syllable words. Illustrations support text and may depict a hard word or two. There could be 11–12 words out of 100 not on the high-frequency list.

Benchmark books:

The Cat in the Hat by Dr. Seuss

Little Bear's Visit by Else Minark

Benchmark passage: Johnny Appleseed

John Chapman wore a **tin pan** for a hat. And he was **dressed** in **rags**. But people liked John. He was kind to others, and he was kind to animals.

John loved **apples**. He left his home and headed **west** about 200 years ago. He wanted everyone to have apples. On his back he carried a **pack** of apple seeds. Walking from place to place, John planted his apple seeds. As the years **passed** the seeds **grew** into trees. After planting **hundreds** and hundreds of apple trees, John Chapman came to be called "**Johnny Appleseed**."

■■■ **Checkup** ■■■

1. What are the steps for implementing the Basic Leveling System for first-grade materials?

■■■

Leveling Books Beyond the First Grade.   If possible, use the Fry Readability Graph (shown in Figure 2.14) or one of the other formulas discussed, or obtain a readability score from one of the sources mentioned earlier in the chapter. Use the objective readability as an estimate. Compare 100-word passages from the book you are assessing with benchmark books or passages. Find the passage that is most like the one you are assessing. Pay particular attention to difficulty level of vocabulary, complexity of ideas, and sentence complexity. Be conservative. If undecided between the second- and third-grade level, go with the more difficult level. It does not hurt students to read a book that is on the easy side; it can be very frustrating for them to cope with a book that is too hard. If the book is very brief and has 100 words or fewer, assess the entire book. If the book is longer, assess three sample passages chosen from near the beginning, middle, and end of the book, but avoid using the first page as a sample. Average the three readability levels that you obtain. Also consider the qualitative factors listed in Figure 2.19. In the light of the comparison with the benchmark passages and qualitative factors, you might decide that the objective readability estimate is accurate, or you might move it up or down a level.

The next few pages provide descriptions of levels and benchmark passages. The Primary Readability Formula (Gunning, 2002), the *New Dale-Chall Readability Formula* (Chall & Dale, 1995), and qualitative factors were used to estimate readability. Words not on the high-frequency word list are boldfaced in benchmark passages for grade 2. Words not on the Dale list of words known by fourth-graders are boldfaced in passages for grades 3 and above.

Grade 2A.   At the grade 2A level, selections are longer, with more involved plots or more detailed explanations. Books are usually divided into chapters. Students need a grasp of basic vowel patterns. Texts have a number of multisyllabic words.

FYI

Grade 2A is a transition level between the end of first and the beginning of second grade. Some leveling systems and basal reading programs place the Frog and Toad and Henry and Mudge books in first grade; others place them in second grade.

■■■ **FIGURE 2.19**

Estimating Difficulty of Materials for Grades 2 through 8

Objective level (estimate yielded by formula) _____

Background required to read text	familiar	limited amount	considerable
Difficulty and density of concepts	easy	average	challenging
Difficulty of vocabulary	easy	average	challenging
Complexity of language	easy	average	challenging
Degree of interest of content	high	average	low
Use of graphics and other aids	high	average	low

When compared with benchmark passages or books, what level(s) do the sample passages from the text seem to be most like?

Passage 1 _____
Passage 2 _____
Passage 3 _____
Average   _____

Estimated difficulty level of text (objective and subjective factors) _____

Benchmark books:

Frog and Toad Together by Arnold Lobel

Henry and Mudge, the First Book by Cynthia Rylant

Arthur's Funny Money by Lillian Hoban

Benchmark passage: *Arthur's Funny Money* by Lillian Hoban

It was **Saturday** morning.
Violet was **counting numbers** on her **fingers**.
Arthur was counting the money in his **piggy bank**.
He counted three **dollars** and **seventy-eight cents**.
"Arthur," said Violet, "do you know numbers?"
"Yes I do," said Arthur. "I am working with numbers right now."
"Well," said Violet, "If I have five **peas** and you take three and give me back two, how many peas will I have?"
"All of them," said Arthur. "I don't like peas, so I **wouldn't** take any."
"I know you don't like peas," said Violet. "But I am trying to do a number **problem**."

Grade 2B. At the grade 2B level, sentences are becoming longer and more complex. There is an increase in multisyllabic words. Notice the high proportion of multisyllabic words in the benchmark passage.

Examples:

Bread and Jam for Frances by Russell Hoban

Thank You, Amelia Bedelia by Peggy Parish

Stone Soup by Anne McGovern

Benchmark passage: *Stone Soup* by Anne McGovern

"**Soup** from a **stone**," said the little old **lady**. "**Fancy** that."
The pot **bubbled** and bubbled.

After a **while**, the little old lady said, "This soup **tastes** good."

"It tastes good now," said the **hungry young** man. "But it would taste better with **beef bones**."

So the little old lady went to get some **juicy** beef bones.

Into the **pot** went the juicy beef bones, and the long, **thin carrots**, and the yellow **onions**, and the **round**, **gray** stone.

"Soup from a stone," said the little old lady. "Fancy that."

The pot bubbled and bubbled.

Grade 3.   In grade 3 books, sentences continue to increase in length, as does the number of multisyllabic words.

Benchmark books:

The Magic School Bus and the Electric Field Trip by Joanna Cole

Molly's Pilgrim by Barbara Cohen

The Courage of Sarah Noble by Alice Dalgliesh

Benchmark passage: *The Courage of Sarah Noble* by Alice Dalgliesh

Now they had come to the last day of the journey. The Indian trail had been narrow, the hills went up and down. **Sarah** and her father were tired, and even **Thomas** walked **wearily**.

By late afternoon they would be going home. Home? No, it wasn't really home, just a place out in the **wilderness**. But after a while it would be home. **John Noble** told Sarah it would be. His voice kept leading her on.

"Now we must be about two miles away."

"Now it is surely a mile . . . only a mile."

Grade 4.   In grade 4 books, sentences are somewhat longer. Vocabulary is somewhat more advanced and includes words such as *glistened, delicate,* and *veil* that might not be in some fourth-graders' listening vocabulary. There is also increased use of figurative language.

Benchmark books:

Help! I'm a Prisoner in the Library! by Eth Clifford

Little House in the Big Woods by Laura Ingalls Wilder

Charlotte's Web by E. B. White

Benchmark passage: *Charlotte's Web* by E. B. White

The next day was foggy. Everything on the farm was dripping wet. The grass looked like a magic carpet. The **asparagus** patch looked like a silver forest.

On foggy mornings, **Charlotte's** web was truly a thing of beauty. This morning each thin **strand** was **decorated** with dozens of tiny beads of water. The web **glistened** in the light and made a pattern of **loveliness** and mystery, like a **delicate veil**. **Lurvy**, who wasn't **particularly** interested in beauty, noticed the web when he came with the pig's breakfast. He noted how clearly it showed up and he noted how big and carefully built it was. And then he took another look and saw something that made him set his pail down. There, in the center of the web, neatly **woven** in block letters, was a message.

Grade 5.   At the grade 5 level, vocabulary becomes more advanced with the use of a greater number of words that may not be in readers' listening vocabularies. These books introduce experiences that readers may not be familiar with.

Benchmark books:

The Great Brain by John D. Fitzgerald

My Side of the Mountain by Jean C. George

Fear Place by Phyllis Naylor

Benchmark passage: Fear Place by Phyllis Naylor

Doug didn't know why he felt a **vague** sense of **discomfort**, like some **unpleasant** memory tapping at the side of his head. No, he thought **fiercely**. He was doing too well. No unpleasant thoughts now, thank you.

The **muscles** in Doug's legs carried him easily with each **stride**. He forced himself to think **positively**, **concentrating** on his **strength**. He didn't even bother to rest at the next place the ground leveled out, but moved on around the curve of the mountain, inching down steep, rocky **troughs chiseled** out by water, then making his way through a long **maze** of rocky outcrops.

Grade 6.   In grade-6 books, sentences are longer and more complex. Vocabulary is definitely more advanced. Concepts are becoming more abstract, and density of concepts has increased. Selections require increased ability to comprehend complex characters and situations.

Benchmark books:

Caddie Woodlawn by Carol Ryrie Brink

The Phantom Tollbooth by Norton Juster

Wolves of Willoughby Chase by Joan Aiken

Benchmark passage: Wolves of Willoughby Chase by Joan Aiken

Sylvia was an **orphan**, both her parents having been carried off by a fever when she was only an **infant**. She lived with her Aunt **Jane**, who was now becoming very aged and **frail** and had written to Sir **Willoughby** to **suggest** that he take on the care of the little girl. He had agreed at once to this **proposal**, for Sylvia, he knew, was **delicate**, and the country air would do her good. Besides, he welcomed the idea of her gentle **companionship** for his rather **harum scarum Bonnie**. Aunt Jane and Sylvia shared a room at the top of a house.

Grade 7.   At the grade 7 level, sentences are longer and more complex. These books include a greater proportion of advanced vocabulary. Plots are more complicated. Selections require increased ability to comprehend complex characters and situations.

Benchmark books:

Alice's Adventures in Wonderland by Lewis Carroll

The Jungle Book by Rudyard Kipling

Incredible Journey by Sheila Burnford

Benchmark passage: Incredible Journey by Sheila Burnford

This journey took place in a part of **Canada** which lies in the northwestern part of the great **sprawling province** of **Ontario**. It is a **vast** area of **deeply** wooded **wilderness**—of endless chains of lonely lakes and rushing rivers. Thousands of miles of country roads, rough timber lanes and **unmapped** trails snake across its length and **breadth**. It is a country of **far-flung**, lonely farms and a few widely scattered small towns and villages, of lonely **trappers' shacks** and logging camps. Most of its industry comes from the great **pulp** and paper companies who work their timber **concessions** deep in the very heart of the forests; and from the mines, for it is rich in **minerals**.

Grade 8.   At the grade 8 level, language is becoming increasingly literary and includes an increased number of difficult words.

Benchmark books:

The Hobbit by J. R. R. Tolkien

The Planet of Junior Brown by Virginia Hamilton

Treasure Island by Robert L. Stevenson

Benchmark passage: Treasure Island by Robert L. Stevenson

The red glare of the **torch**, lighting up the **interior** of the blockhouse, showed me the worst of my **apprehensions realized**. The **pirates** were in **possession** of the house and stores; there was the **cask** of **cognac**, there were the pork and bread, as before; and, what tenfold **increased** my **horror**, not a sign of any **prisoner**. I could only judge that all had **perished**, and my heart **smote** me sorely that I had not been there to **perish** with them. There were six of the **buccaneers**, all told; not another man was left alive. Five of them were on their feet. . . .

Verifying Readability Levels

The true measure of the difficulty level of a book is the proficiency with which students can read it. Note how well students are able to read books that have been leveled. Based on your observation of students' performance, be prepared to change the estimated difficulty level.

■ ■ ■ Checkup ■ ■ ■

1. What procedures might you use to estimate the readability of materials on a second-grade level or higher?

2. How do the characteristics of materials change as the materials become more advanced?

■ ■ ■

Tools for the Classroom

Building Higher-Level Literacy

Carefully planned assessment will help you incorporate the development of higher-level literacy into your program. The first step is to determine your students' level of literacy development. First, use an informal reading inventory, running records, or other placement measure to find out what students' general reading level is. Then analyze responses to determine how students do with such higher-level skills as drawing conclusions, making inferences, and evaluating what they read. Also take a look at students' performance on your state's high-stakes test. Note, too, how well students do during class discussions that require higher-level responses. Are they able to answer higher-level questions? Does prompting help? (Students may have a deep understanding of a selection but have difficulty expressing themselves.) Evaluate students' performance on end-of-unit tests or tests that you compose that assess higher-level literacy. Analyze these written responses, but also discuss them with students.

Some students may have difficulty because they didn't understand the selection or the questions. Others will have a good understanding of the selection but will experience difficulty responding to questions in writing. It's important to be able to differentiate between the two groups. The first group needs to work on thinking and comprehension strategies. The second group needs instruction in composing written responses to higher-level questions. Above all, as you assess students' level of literacy development, ask yourself,

"Why?" Asking why students are responding in a certain way will provide insights into their thinking processes that will allow you to provide needed guidance.

Action Plan

1. Become acquainted with national, state, and local standards and expectations.
2. Set standards or goals for your program. Translate goals or standards into measurable objectives.
3. Align materials and instructional activities with your objectives.
4. Align assessment with objectives and instruction. For each objective, you need formal and/or informal assessment devices so that you can tell whether objectives are being achieved.
5. Begin assessment by finding out where students are and what their strengths and needs are. This can be done with an IRI, emergent literacy measure, or other devices.
6. Screen students for special needs. Students identified as struggling should be given diagnostic tests that can be used to plan intervention programs.
7. Monitor students' progress on an ongoing basis. Set up a continuous progress monitoring program. Maintain a portfolio of students' work. On a quarterly basis, assess students in more depth. Involve students in the assessment process. Guide them so that they can self-assess. Involve them in setting standards and creating rubrics. Make adjustments in the program as required.
8. At year's end, administer an outcomes measure. This could be another form of the IRI or other measure that you administered at the beginning of the year. As part of your assessment, use information yielded by district-required or state or national tests.
9. Do not overtest. Don't give a test if it is not going to provide useful information or if you are not going to use the information. Make sure that students are tested at the appropriate level.
10. Make sure that there is a match between students' reading levels and the materials that they read. Obtain readability information from appropriate sources, and put a leveling system into place. In determining difficulty levels, be sure to use subjective judgment as well as objective data.

Summary

Evaluation entails making a subjective judgment about the effectiveness of instruction; it is based on data from tests, work samples, and observations. An evaluation is made in terms of standards or objectives and should result in the improvement of instruction.

The standards movement is an attempt to improve the quality of education by setting high but clear standards for all. As part of the standards movement, a goal has been set that 100 percent of students will reach proficiency in reading by the 2013–2014 school year. High-stakes tests are being used to assess progress. A concern with high-stakes testing is that it may result in a narrowing of the curriculum.

Placement information is necessary to indicate where students are on the road to literacy. Continuous progress monitoring is used to track students' progress. Norm-referenced tests and criterion-referenced tests, as well as a variety of informal measures, are used to assess students' progress. Norm-referenced tests compare students with a norm group. Criterion-referenced assessments indicate whether students have reached a standard or objective. Benchmarks and rubrics are criterion-referenced assessment devices that offer ways of holistically indicating performance. Holistic evaluation of writing, observations, anecdotal records, checklists, and portfolios provide authentic information that complement data yielded by more formal measures. Formative assessment makes use of a variety of measures in order to improve instruction.

Students should be given tests designed for the level on which they are reading. Tests that are too easy or too hard are invalid and yield erroneous information.

A number of objective readability formulas and several subjective leveling systems can be used to assess the difficulty level of materials. Difficulty level is best assessed by using both objective and subjective measures.

Extending and Applying

1. Examine the assessment devices in a basal or anthology series. Evaluate their content validity and format. Note whether all major areas of reading have been covered, whether guessing is a factor, and whether the devices have been tested and give information on validity and reliability.

2. Create a portfolio system for evaluation. Decide what kinds of items might be included in the portfolio. Also devise a checklist or summary sheet that can be used to keep track of and summarize the items.

3. Find out what the standards are for your state, how they are assessed, and how test results are used.

4. Administer an informal reading inventory or running record to at least one student. Based on the results of the assessment, draw up a list of the student's apparent strengths and needs.

Developing a Professional Portfolio

Place in your portfolio any checklists, rubrics, or other assessment devices that you have devised and used. Reflect on the effectiveness of these devices.

Go to Allyn & Bacon's MyLabSchool: www.mylabschool.com

- Enter Assignment ID **LAV1** into **Assignment Finder,** and select the video titled "Running Record." In this video, a reading specialist conducts a running record with an elementary school student, as a means of documenting the student's reading level and reading behaviors.

- As you watch the video, identify two skills that the teacher is attempting to assess while completing the run-

ning record. Why is the running record an effective assessment tool?

- Explore MyLabSchool further to find the course areas for Reading Methods, Language Arts, and Content Area Reading and identify other assets that support concepts introduced in this chapter.

Developing a Resource File

Keep a file of observation guides, checklists, sample tests, think-aloud protocols, questionnaires, sample tests, rubrics, and other assessment devices that might be useful. For a wealth of information about literacy assessments, go to the Southwest Educational Development Laboratory Web site: http://www.sedl.org/reading/rad

To access chapter objectives, practice tests, weblinks, and flashcards, go to the companion website at www.ablongman.com/gunning6e.

3 Fostering Emergent/ Early Literacy

or each of the following statements, put a check under "Agree" or "Disagree" to show how you feel. Discuss your responses with classmates before you read the chapter.

	Agree	Disagree
1. An informal, unstructured program works best in kindergarten.	_____	_____
2. Reading books to young children is a better use of instructional time than working on skills.	_____	_____
3. Allowing children to spell any way they can is harmful.	_____	_____
4. Children at risk should have their literacy development accelerated so that they can catch up.	_____	_____
5. The best way for young children to learn reading is through writing.	_____	_____
6. Kindergartners should be taught a full program of beginning phonics.	_____	_____

hapter 1 explored the nature of reading, discussed the reading status of children today, and presented twelve basic principles for teaching reading. This chapter on emergent literacy is based on those twelve principles. The word *literacy* encompasses both writing and reading; *emergent* indicates that the child has been engaged in reading and writing activities long before coming to school. Putting the two concepts together, Sulzby (1989b) defined emergent literacy as "the reading and writing behaviors that precede and develop into conventional literacy" (p. 84).

Before reading this chapter, reflect on your personal knowledge of emergent literacy. Have you observed young children as they explored reading and writing? How did they do this? What did their writing look like? What did they learn about reading and writing from their homes and the larger environment? How would you go about fostering emergent literacy?

■ Understanding Emergent Literacy

Children begin developing literacy long before they enter school. Unless they are disabled, all school-age children have acquired a fairly extensive oral language vocabulary and a sophisticated syntactic system. They have seen traffic signs and billboard advertising, printed messages on television, and printing on cereal boxes. They can tell the McDonald's logo from that of Burger King and distinguish a box of Fruit Loops from one of Captain Crunch. They have seen their parents read books, magazines, newspapers, letters, and bills and have observed them writing notes or letters, filling out forms, and making lists. They may also have imitated some of these activities. Their parents may have read books to them and provided them with crayons, pencils, and other tools of literacy. All children, no matter how impoverished their environment may be, have begun the journey along the path that begins with language acquisition and ends in formal literacy. The teacher must find out where each child is on the path and lead him or her on the way. "The issue," explains Purcell-Gates (1997), "is not getting children ready to learn, but rather creating

FYI

■ The term *early literacy* is sometimes used instead of *emergent literacy*. *Early literacy* suggests that the
child already has some knowledge of
reading and writing, whereas
emergent literacy might suggest that
the child is on the verge of acquiring
this knowledge.

■ Different cultures might value different literacy activities. Therefore, it
is important for the teacher to know
what kinds of writing and reading activities are stressed in the children's
homes and communities so that these
can be built on in the classroom.

■ For a time, children's concept of
letter-sound relationships may be
very specific. At age four, my granddaughter Paige told me that she had a
friend named *Paul* in school, and
commented, "He has my letter." She
had noticed that Paul's name began
with a *P*, as did hers. She regarded
the letters of her name as being personal and specific. The *P* in *Paige*
identified her. She did not realize that
P represents /p/ and can be used in
any word containing a /p/ sound (see
Ferreiro, 1986).

literacy environments within which the learning they already do on an ongoing basis includes the different emergent literacy concepts needed for school success" (p. 427).

The concept of **emergent literacy** is rooted in research conducted a number of years
ago. Read (1971) reported on a study of early spellers who had learned to spell in an informal manner. The early spellers were preschoolers who were given help in spelling when
they asked for it but were otherwise allowed to spell however they wanted. What surprised
Read was that these young children, who had no contact with each other, created spelling
systems that were remarkably similar and that, although not correct, made sense phonetically. For instance, *er* at the end of a word such as *tiger* was typically spelled with just an
r, as *tigr*. In this instance, *r* is syllabic; it functions as a vowel and so does not need to be
preceded by an *e*. For long vowels, children generally used the letter name, as in *sop* for
soap, where the name of the letter *o* contains the sound of the vowel. Commenting on his
findings, Read stated, "We can no longer assume that children must approach reading with
no discernible prior conception of its structure" (p. 34). Landmark studies by researchers
in several countries echoed and amplified Read's findings in both reading and writing
(Clay, 1972; Ferreiro & Teberosky, 1982; Teale & Sulzby, 1986).

These revelations about children's literacy abilities have a number of implications.
First and foremost, we must build on what children already know. In their five or six years
before coming to us, they have acquired a great deal of insight into the reading and writing processes. Instead of asking whether they are ready, we have to find out where they are
and take it from there. We must value and make use of their knowledge.

As children observe parents and peers reading and writing and as they themselves experiment with reading and writing, they construct theories about how these processes
work. For instance, based on their experience with picture books, children may believe that
pictures rather than words are read. Initially, children may believe that letters operate as
pictures. They may believe that letters represent objects in much the same way that pictures represent objects. Using this hypothesis, they may reason that *snake* would be a long
word because a snake is a long animal. *Mouse* would be a short word because a mouse is
a short animal. As children notice long words for little creatures (*hummingbird, mosquito*)
and little words for large creatures (*whale, tiger*), they assimilate this and make an accommodation by giving up their hypothesis of a physical relationship between size of
words and size of objects or creatures represented. They may then theorize that although
letters do not represent physical characteristics, letters do somehow identify the person or
thing named. They may theorize that the first letters of their names belong uniquely to
them (Ferreiro, 1986). Children need to see that other people's names may start with the
same letters as theirs but that some or all of the other letters are different. When Paige comments that Paul has her letter, Paige might be told that yes, she and Paul have the same letter at the beginning of their names and even the same second letter, but the other letters are
different. She might also be told that both their names begin with a *P* because they both
begin with the same sound /p/.

Before children discover the alphabet principle, they may refine their theories of the
purpose of letters and conclude that it is the arrangement of letters that matters. Through exposure to print, they will have noticed that words form patterns, and they begin to string letters together in what seem to be reasonable patterns. Usually, the words are between three
and seven characters long and only repeat the same letter twice (Schickedanz, 1999).
Known as mock words, these creations look like real words. After creating mock words,
children frequently ask adults what the words say. The adults may attempt sounding out the
words and realize that they don't say anything and inform the child of that fact. Realizing

■ **Emergent literacy** consists of the reading
and writing behaviors that evolve from children's earliest experiences with reading and
writing and that gradually grow into conventional literacy.

■ **Concepts of print** are understandings
about how print works—that printed words
represent spoken words, have boundaries,
are read from left to right, and so on.

that they can't simply string a series of letters together, children may begin asking adults how to spell words or copy words from signs or books. As adults write multisyllabic words for children, they might sound them out as they write each syllable and also say the letters: "An-dy . . . A-N-D-Y spells Andy." Hearing words sounded out, children catch on to the idea that letters represent speech sounds. Since the words they hear have been spoken in syllables as they were written, the children may use one letter to represent each syllable and one letter for the final sound and produce spellings such as *jrf* for *giraffe*.

If you have some insight into students' current schema for the writing system, you can provide the kind of explanation that will help them to move to a higher level of understanding. For children who are moving from a visual or physical hypothesis about how the alphabetical system operates to a phonological one, sounding out words as you spell them provides helpful information. Providing many opportunities to write also helps students to explore the writing system.

Essential Skills and Understandings for Emergent Literacy

Understanding how print works and the many roles it plays in people's lives is known as seeing the "big picture" (Purcell-Gates, 1997). The big picture is the foundation upon which all other information about reading and writing is built. Children also need to become more familiar with the types of language used in books and to acquire a deeper sense of how stories develop. On a more formal level, they need to construct basic **concepts of print**, if they have not already learned them. These concepts of print include the following:

■ What we say and what others say can be written down and read.

■ Words, not pictures, are read.

■ Sentences are made up of words, and words are made up of letters.

■ Reading goes from left to right and from top to bottom.

■ A book is read from front to back.

■ What we say is divided into words. (Some young students may believe that "How are you?" is a single word, for example.) Students must also grasp the concept of what a word is. Of course, they use words in their oral language, but understanding what a word is occurs on a higher level of abstraction, involving a metalinguistic or metacognitive awareness. This means that they must be able to think about language as well as use it.

■ Space separates written words. Students must be able to match words being read orally with their written counterparts. Hearing the sentence "The little dog ran," the student must focus on *the, little, dog,* and *ran* as each word is read.

■ Sentences begin with capital letters.

■ Sentences end with periods, question marks, or exclamation marks.

■ A book has a title, an author, and sometimes an illustrator.

■ Students must also develop phonological awareness and arrive at an understanding of the alphabetic principle. Phonological awareness involves being able to detect rhyming words, to segment words into their separate sounds, and to perceive beginning sounds. Understanding the alphabetic principle means grasping the concept that letters represent sounds.

The rate of children's literacy development varies, as does the richness of home environments. A few children will be able to read words or even whole sentences when they enter kindergarten. However, most will still be developing emergent literacy in kindergarten and possibly into first grade; a few may make very slow progress and may still be developing emergent literacy beyond first grade. The activities and procedures explored in this chapter apply to any students who might benefit from them, whether they are in kindergarten, first grade, or beyond. These activities and procedures may even be used with preschool children who are making very rapid progress.

FYI

■ Having reading and writing materials in the home, being read to, and talking to their caregivers about reading and writing foster children's formation of the "big picture." The more reading and writing they are exposed to, the more complete and detailed their big pictures become (Purcell-Gates, 1997).

■ Reinforce the concepts of print and print conventions whenever the opportunity presents itself. When writing on the board, emphasize that you are writing from left to right. If you are writing information that students are giving you, tell them that you are writing their words.

■ In a typical kindergarten, the levels of literacy development may span as much as five years between the lowest- and highest-functioning children; so some children will have the skill level of three-year-olds, while the most advanced will function like eight-year-olds (Riley, 1996).

■ ■ ■ **Checkup** ■ ■ ■

1. What is the concept of emergent, or early, literacy?
2. What are the essential skills and understandings for emergent literacy?

■ ■ ■

■ Fostering Emergent Literacy

Regardless of where children are in terms of literacy, an essential step in further development is to create an environment that promotes active reading, writing, listening, and speaking. Getting children to engage in literacy activities is partly a matter of providing an appealing environment. One means of encouragement is simply to have readily available writing instruments, paper of various kinds, and books and periodicals. In a classroom environment that fosters literacy, print is everywhere. Bulletin boards include words as well as pictures. There is a calendar of students' birthdays and other important upcoming events. Aquariums and terrariums are labeled with the names of their inhabitants. Most important of all, students' stories and booklets are displayed prominently. The classroom might have a student-run post office so that children can correspond with each other. If computer equipment is available, students might even make use of e-mail. Label mailboxes with children's names but also include their pictures so that students who cannot read can find the mailboxes they are looking for. Be sure to include a mailbox for yourself and anyone who regularly visits the class. To encourage the use of the mailboxes and to model the process of writing a letter, let students observe you as you write notes to parents, to the principal, and to the students. Also, encourage adults to write to your class. Read and post their letters (Jurek, 1995).

Although a classroom can be arranged in many ways to induce children to take part in literacy activities, Morrow (1997) recommended that a variety of centers be set up, including areas for writing, math, social studies, science, music, blocks and other manipulatives, **dramatic play**, and a library. A listening/viewing center and a computing center are also possibilities. If the classroom is small, some of these centers could be combined.

The writing center should contain the upper- and lowercase alphabets in manuscript form. Letters, stories, lists, and other models of writing can also be displayed. The materials should be posted at students' eye level for ease of use. A selection of writing instruments and paper should be available. Paper should come in various colors and should be unlined so that students are not unduly concerned with spacing. Small memo pads of paper are also recommended. Writing instruments should include crayons and magic markers, the latter being the choice of most children (Bauman, 1990). If pencils are provided, students should be instructed in using them safely. Other useful items for the writing center are chalkboards, magnetic letters, printing sets, a typewriter, and a computer with an easy-to-use word-processing program. Paste, tape, safety scissors, and staplers are also useful. Reference materials are important. For kindergarten children, such materials could consist primarily of picture dictionaries, both commercially produced and constructed by students.

The library or book corner should feature a wide selection of reading materials attractively displayed, including both commercial and student-written books. Extra copies of a book currently being read by the teacher or other books by the same author or on the same theme should be given a place of prominence. Rockers, cushions, bean-bag chairs, and pieces of rug will give students comfortable places to read. The listening/viewing center should have a wide variety of audio books and videotapes or, if available, CD-ROM

■ ■ ■ **USING TECHNOLOGY**

Between the Lions is an award-winning PBS TV series for children four to seven, designed to foster a love of reading and literacy skills. The programs are complemented by a Web site that features a host of supplementary activities, including reading stories and playing games. A number of the activities are designed for parents to engage in with their children. Kindergartners who watched the program made impressive gains in essential early literacy skills (Linebarger, 2000). A teaching guide for kindergarten teachers is available.
http://pbskids.org/lions

■ **Dramatic play** refers to a type of activity in which students play at being someone else: a doctor, a teacher, a firefighter.

versions that display favorite stories so that students can follow the text as the story is being read. Multiple copies of audio recordings of favorite books will allow small groups of students to listen to a book together. The dramatic play and housekeeping centers should be stocked with order blanks, note pads, signs, bills, and other realia of literacy. A technology center might include software, such as *Dr. Seuss Kindergarten* (Learning Company), *Reader Rabbit Kindergarten* (Learning Company), or *Learn about ABCs and Letter Sounds* (Sunburst), that reinforce key themes or skills. In a classroom that fosters literacy, the tools and products of writing and reading abound. A sample floor plan of a literacy-rich environment is presented in Figure 3.1.

An environment that fosters literacy is both physical and attitudinal. Attitudinally, the teacher believes that literacy is a broad-based, naturally occurring process that takes place over a long period of time. Although it can and should be taught, literacy can also be fostered by "setting the scene" and through subtle encouragement. The teacher should lose no opportunity to reinforce literacy concepts. For example, after the class's pet gerbil has been named George, a label containing his name is attached to the cage. While preparing the label, the teacher explains what is being done and shows the class that the letters *G-e-o-r-g-e* spell "George." When students are running software on the computer, the teacher points to the RETURN key and explains what the printing on it means. After turning a page on the calendar, the teacher points to the name of the new month and asks the class to guess what the word is. When a notice is being sent home, the

FYI

Physical surroundings impact learning. Rooms partitioned into small spaces lead to more talk and cooperation (Morrow, 2002).

USING TECHNOLOGY

Create a floor plan for your classroom by using the Classroom Architect tool:
http://4teachers.org

■ ■ ■ **FIGURE 3.1 Floor Plan for Early Childhood Classroom**

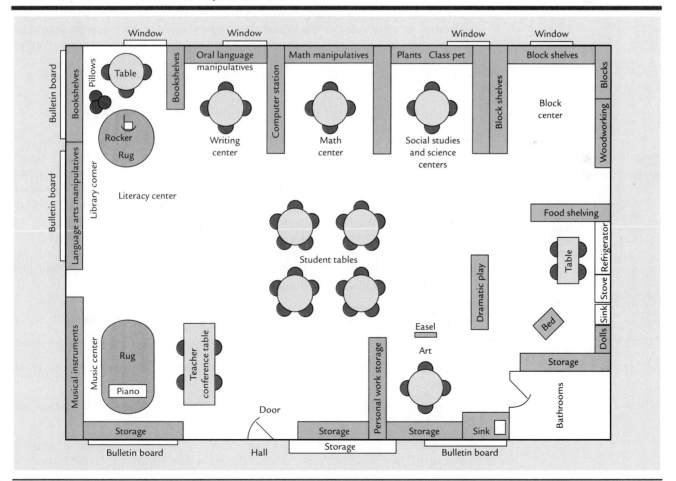

teacher reads it aloud to the class first. If students see any familiar words in the notice, they are encouraged to read them.

Classroom routines are placed on charts. For instance, procedures for using the computer, turning on the tape recorder, and signing out books are posted. Simple words and illustrations that help convey the meaning of the procedures are used (Jurek, 1995).

Labels and signs should be used generously. Cubbies and coat hooks should be labeled with children's names. Places where supplies are stored should be labeled: paper, paints, crayons. Signs should be used to designate learning centers and key locations in the classroom. Signs should also direct students to wash hands, to put away paints when finished, to walk rather than run, and so forth. The room might also have an attendance chart and a helper chart. Students can show that they are present by putting their names in the pockets of the attendance chart. Calendar charts and schedule charts also provide opportunities for discussing print as you talk over the fact that *Monday* and *May* both begin with the same letter, which makes an /m/ sound. Special days such as birthdays and holidays can be marked. On the weather chart, students can place in a pocket cards containing the words *sunny, cloudy, rainy,* or *snowy; cold, warm,* or *hot; windy* or *calm.* Cards might be illustrated with pictures of the sun, clouds, rain, and snow to help students identify them. Lists, recipes, and schedules for centers also provide opportunities for reading and writing.

The key is to make use of whatever opportunities are available to foster reading and writing concepts and skills. At snack time, point out the writing on the milk cartons and note that *m-i-l-k* spells "milk." On subsequent days, you might read the name of the dairy or have students tell you which word says "milk," tell what letter *milk* begins with, or tell what letters *milk* has. Talk about the letters and the words on the packaging of apple juice and crackers or whatever snack foods children are eating.

Students are also encouraged to write or draw, and the emphasis is on expression and exploration rather than on conventional spelling or handwriting. There is plenty of time for that later. The class library is an active place. Students read books in school and are allowed to take them home. The inevitable torn pages and jelly-stained covers and the occasional lost books are a small price to pay for the development of literacy skills.

Making Reading and Writing a Part of Classroom Activities

Closing the Gap

When working with difficult students who seemed to be doing everything wrong, kindergarten teacher Edwards (2000) discovered that it was better to accept what students could do and shape their behavior rather than criticize everything they did wrong.

Fostering literacy growth among young children is a matter of making reading and writing a natural part of their classroom activities. One way to increase early literacy experiences is to stock centers with the tools of writing and reading that might naturally appear there. In dramatic play centers, children can make use of these as they take on the roles of adults whom they see in their everyday lives. They also are more likely to role-play literacy tasks if the appropriate materials are available. Christie (1990) recommended that dramatic play centers be supplied with pens, pencils, note pads, diaries, cookbooks, telephone books, picture books, magazines, catalogs, and newspapers—in other words, the kinds of materials that might be found in the typical home. Opportunities for dramatic play that can stimulate reading and writing include the following:

1. Grocery store—creating signs, writing checks or food lists
2. Bank—writing deposit and withdrawal slips and checks
3. Doctor's office—writing prescriptions, making appointments, making bills
4. Restaurant—writing and reading menus, taking food orders, creating signs (Christie, 1990)
5. Post office—writing letters, addressing letters, mailing packages, selling stamps, delivering mail

In planning dramatic play centers, find out what kinds of experiences the children have had and how they have seen literacy function in their environments. For instance, if they are more familiar with fast-food eating places than with restaurants that have servers and individual menus, create wall-type menus characteristic of fast-food establishments.

To make dramatic play as valuable as possible, provide an introduction. Discuss the activity, or read students a book about it. Show props and talk about some of the ways they might be used (Bunce, 1995). Provide prompts or model interchanges in the initial stages or when students seem to be foundering.

For dramatic play at a railroad station, the best preparation would be to actually visit a station and take a short trip on a train. Other possibilities include having a conductor visit the class and talk about the things that a conductor does. Viewing videos and listening to informational books about trains would also extend students' knowledge of the topic. You might model some of the oral language that the children would be using: "Where are you going? A ticket to _____ will cost $100. How will you pay for that? Will you pay in cash? Or will you use a credit card? Train Number 5 to Washington will be leaving from track 5. Train Number 5 will be leaving in 10 minutes" (Bunce, 1995).

Change the dramatic play center frequently. Possible settings for dramatic play activities include an airport, bus terminal, train station, dock, grocery store, clothing store, toy store, doctor's office, dentist's office, firehouse, police station, recycling station, zoo, circus, movie theater, car wash, campground, beach, fast-food restaurant, pizza parlor, delivery truck, warehouse, beauty parlor, barber shop, hospital, post office, office, hotel, library, apartment, aquarium, vet. Possibilities are many and varied. Select the ones that interest and benefit your students the most.

Playing with print is an important part of literacy development through which children can explore the uses of the medium. After scrawling letterlike figures on a piece of paper, one child pretended he was reading a weather report (McLane & McNamee, 1990). Others have been police officers writing tickets, restaurant owners creating menus, store owners writing receipts, parents writing shopping lists, and authors writing books. Children have also pretended to read books to dolls, teddy bears, friends, and younger siblings. "Through play, children may come to feel that they are writers and readers before they actually have the necessary skills to write and read" (McLane & McNamee, 1990, p. 19).

As children learn about literacy skills through playing and observing how members of their families and communities use these skills, they become motivated to learn more about reading and writing so that they can make fuller use of these skills. In learning literacy, function fosters form. Students learn the what and the why of reading and writing as a prelude to learning the details of how to read and write.

■ ■ ■ Checkup ■ ■ ■

1. How might a literacy-rich environment be created?
2. What are some naturalistic ways in which emergent literacy might be fostered?

■ ■ ■

Reading to Students

What are your favorite memories of literacy instruction and activities when you were in elementary or middle school? All these years later, I still recall Sister Irene reading *Mr. Popper's Penguins* (Atwater & Atwater, 1938) to my first-grade class. I was absolutely enchanted with the tale and, to this day, am fascinated by penguins. Surveys of teachers reveal that I am not alone in citing being read to as a favorite school activity (Fisher, Flood, Lapp, & Frey, 2004).

Why is being read to so important? Being read to develops children's vocabulary, expands their experiential background, makes them aware of the language of books, introduces them to basic concepts of print and how books are read, and provides them with many pleasant associations with books. Perhaps most important is the power of books to help children create worlds based on words and story structures (Wells, 1986).

In conversation, the child can use context to help construct the meaning of a situation. For instance, if someone is pointing to a ball and making a throwing motion while saying "Throw me the ball," then the context of the statement—the pointing, the ball, and the

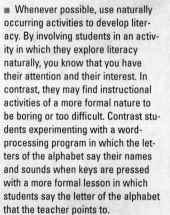

One of the best ways to develop students' emergent literacy is to read to them.

throwing motion—aids understanding. However, in a story, there is no context except for, possibly, illustrations. The child must therefore use language to construct meaning. As parents read storybooks to their children, they provide a bridge between conversation with all its support and the more abstract, noninteractive experience of hearing a story read. Intuitively, parents use the illustrations as well as explanations, gestures, and discussion to help children understand the storybook.

Initial readings are highly interactive. Over time, as the child becomes a more sophisticated listener and assimilates the format of storybook reading into her or his own schema or conceptual background, less support is offered by the reader. In the process, however, the child learns invaluable lessons about the language and structure of written text. As they read to their children, parents explain new words and expressions that crop up in storybooks. They also discuss unfamiliar concepts, intuitively relating new concepts to the child's background. Parents do not deliberately set out to teach their children new concepts and words; this happens as a natural part of reading to children. As a result of these interactions, children who are read to the most have the most highly developed language skills. They have larger vocabularies and are better able to narrate an event, describe a scene, and understand the teacher (Strickland & Taylor, 1989).

What kinds of books should be read to children? Books such as *The Very Hungry Caterpillar* (Carle, 1969), *Waiting for Wings* (Ehlert, 2001), and *What Do Animals Do in Winter?* (Berger & Berger, 1995) that have a richness of content are excellent choices. They build background. Nursery rhymes and books with repetitive patterns, such as *Are You My Mother?* (Eastman, 1960) and *I Swapped My Dog* (Ziefert, 1998), are also excellent choices. Be sure to include informational books as read-alouds. Reading informational text sparks intriguing discussions and raises interesting questions that help foster curiosity and background building. If possible, select books that relate to themes or topics that the class is studying. However, choose books that are on students' level of comprehension and background. A book on ancient Egypt, for instance, would be well beyond the comprehension and background level of most kindergarten or first-grade students. If students seem bored or restless while you are reading a book, make sure that the book is of interest to them, is on the proper level, and is not too long and complex. If students have little experience being read to, you may want to start out with brief, easy-to-understand texts and gradually move into longer, more complex books.

Before reading a selection aloud, preview it. Make sure that it is appropriate for your class and that your students will enjoy it. Note places where you might like to stop for a brief discussion. Also practice reading it aloud so that you get the flow of it.

Schedule read-alouds regularly. Don't withhold read-alouds as a punishment. They are too important a part of the curriculum (Campbell, 2001). Set the mood for read-aloud time. To signal the start of a read-aloud, you might play a little tune, ring a bell, or initiate a chant. Or have a puppet make the announcement.

Also establish a routine for the read-aloud itself. For most read-alouds, students are seated on large rugs. They should be seated far enough apart so that they aren't pushing against each other but can turn and talk to each other when you want them to discuss some aspect of the story with their partners (Fountas & Pinnell, 2006). If students are seated at desks, you might have them form a semicircle. Establish a routine for the students to follow as you read aloud. It is generally best if students don't respond or call out until you somehow signal or explicitly invite them to do so.

Before starting to read aloud, set the stage. You might set the stage in a number of ways, such as by asking students questions that enable them to make connections between their personal backgrounds and the story. For instance, before reading *All the Way Home* (Segal, 1973), which is a humorous tale about a little girl who falls and hurts herself and then cries all the way home, ask students to tell about a time when they fell and hurt themselves. You might also use your own experiences to introduce a read-aloud selection. In preparation for reading Eric Carle's (1973) *Have You Seen My Cat?*, you could tell about an experience you have had with a lost pet. You also might begin with a general discussion of the topic of the book or with a description that relates the book to one that you read to the class previously. Such discussions build essential concepts and background.

Hold up the book that is to be read. Point to and discuss the title. If it lends itself to it, use the title as a predictive device. Have students think about the title and guess what the story might be about. For example, before reading *Ducks Disappearing* (Naylor, 1997), ask them to tell why ducks might disappear.

Point to the author's name. Show a picture of the author, if there is one on the book jacket, and read the author's biography. Before reading *Have You Seen My Cat?*, you can show Carle's picture with his two cats and discuss how the pets may have given him the idea for the book and may also have been models for the drawings. Talk about the methods the author may have used to write the book—for example, did he write it in pen on pads of paper or type it? Emphasize the fact that stories can be written down and then read by others.

As you read a book, stop periodically to review what has happened, and encourage children to discuss the book with you and to make some predictions. Younger children will need more frequent stops, and their story conversations may be less focused. After you have finished reading, talk over whether their predictions came true. For example, when reading *Too Many Books* (Bauer, 1984), a story of a girl who accumulated a houseful of books, you might ask, "What do you think Marylou will do with all those books?" Encourage students to modify predictions, if necessary, and make new ones.

Hold the book so that students can see the illustrations as you read the selection. Discuss and ask questions about them. Looking at a picture in *Too Many Books*, you might ask, "What is different about Marylou's house?" Point to pictures as you read a book in order to illustrate words and concepts that might be unfamiliar to students. By pointing to the illustration of an unfamiliar word rather than stopping and defining it, you maintain the flow of the story. Another way of handling difficult words is to simply supply a brief meaning. When reading the book *The Relatives Came* (Rylant, 1985), you might explain that relatives are people in the family: mother, father, sisters, brothers, uncles, aunts, cousins, and grandparents. Dramatizing and highlighting onomatopoeia can also help provide meanings for words. For instance, when reading *The Cat in the Hat* (Geisel, 1957), emphasize the sounds of *bump* and *thump* as you read these words. You might even make bumping and thumping sounds (Schickedanz, 1999).

Developing Story Structure

Reading to children develops a sense of story as they become familiar with plot development and the interaction of plot, characters, and setting. This familiarity bolsters comprehension, the ability to discuss stories, and the ability to compose stories.

To develop a sense of story structure, discuss with the class literary language, or words and phrases that are frequently used in stories: "once upon a time," "lived happily ever after," "many years ago," and so on. Point out that most stories have a main character, who may be an older person, a young person, or even an animal who talks and acts like a human. Have students identify the main characters in stories they know. Discuss how setting, too, may be an important element.

After students have grasped the concepts of story language and characters, point out that the main characters usually have problems to solve. Give examples from familiar stories. Discuss how Marylou's problem with having too many books and the old man's problem in Wanda Gág's (1928) *Millions of Cats* are similar. Discuss the fact that problems are

ASSESSING FOR LEARNING

When choosing informational books, use children's interest and curiosity as your guide. What kinds of questions do they have? Do they want to know where fog comes from or where dinosaurs lived? Are they curious about rainbows or clouds or cows?

FYI

Books with subtle character development may be difficult for children who have not had much experience being read to. They may do better with tales in which action is emphasized.

■ ■ ■ ■ **BUILDING LANGUAGE**

Although predictable books allow students to think of themselves as readers, they aren't the best texts for developing language (Dickinson & Smith, 1994). Books that have more complex plots and better developed characters or that delve more deeply into topics offer a richer vocabulary and more opportunities for language development.

Adapting Instruction for Struggling Readers and Writers

Dramatizing a story after reading it helps students internalize the story's sequence (Edwards, 2000).

■ ■ ■ ■ **BUILDING LANGUAGE**

While listening to stories, children can sometimes use context to derive the meaning of an unfamiliar word, especially if the word is repeated. A brief explanation helps with any word that might lack adequate context. Explaining the word also calls attention to it and gives students a chance to think about it. Students will find it hard to think about the meaning of a new word and follow along with the story at the same time (Wasik, Bond, & Hindman, 2006).

usually solved in some way. Talk over how that occurred for Marylou and the old man. These kinds of questions not only build comprehension, discussion, and composing skills, they also develop and lay the groundwork for an understanding of literary techniques.

Building Comprehension

In your discussions about books, ask students a variety of questions, including those that involve important details, sequence, and drawing conclusions or making inferences and that provide a foundation for reading comprehension (Feitelson, Kita, & Goldstein, 1986). Do not use the questions primarily as a technique for gauging depth of understanding but as means for drawing attention to important details or relating details so that a conclusion can be reached or a main idea constructed. For example, after you have read *The Snowy Day* (Keats, 1962), ask students how Peter felt about the snow. Then ask them how they know that Peter liked the snow. Go back over the story if children have difficulty supplying details that back up the conclusion. Think of your discussions as a way of sharing so that books can be more fully understood and enjoyed.

Making Personal Connections

Students will not fully appreciate reading unless the stories touch their lives. Ask questions that involve personal reactions, such as how a story made them feel, what they liked best, whether they have ever met anyone like the main character, or whether they would like to hear a similar book. After reading *Whistle for Willie*, by Ezra Jack Keats (1964), have students describe how Willie felt at the end, and ask them about a time when they may have been proud themselves.

After discussing a story, you may want to provide follow-up or extension activities. The book could become the focus of learning center activities. Students might listen to a taped version or pretend to read the story to a partner. Pretend reading provides them with the opportunity to use book language. Follow-up activities also include illustrating a portion of the story; watching a videotape, CD-ROM, filmstrip, or videocassette version; or carrying out some activity suggested by the book. After reading *The Gingerbread Boy* (Galdone, 1975), students might have a hunt for a gingerbread man; reading *The Carrot Seed* (Krauss, 1945) might lead to the planting of seeds. Another excellent follow-up is reading another book by the same author.

Mason, Peterman, and Kerr (1988, Fig. 1) suggested using the following general plan when presenting narrative materials:

Before reading the narrative

Show the cover of the book to the children. Encourage discussion about the book's content.

Discuss the author and illustrator of the book.

Allow children to discuss their own experiences that are related to those raised in the book.

Discuss the type of text the children will be hearing (folk tale, repetitive story, fables, fantasies, etc.).

Introduce children to the story's main characters and to the time and place in which the story occurs.

Set a purpose for the children to listen to the story, usually what happens to the main character.

During the reading of the narrative

Encourage children to react to and comment on the story.

Elaborate on the text, when appropriate, in order to help children understand the written language used in the story and story components, such as the main character's problem, attempts to resolve the problem, and its resolution.

Ask occasional questions to monitor children's comprehension of the story or relevant vocabulary.

Rephrase the text when it is apparent that children are having difficulty with the words or phrases.

At appropriate points in the story, ask children to predict what will happen next.

Allow children to share their own interpretation of a story.

After reading the narrative

Review the story components (the setting, problem, goal, and resolution).

Help children make connections between the events in the story and similar events in their own lives.

Engage children in some kind of follow-up activity, such as a discussion of other books by the same author or illustrator, an art activity (perhaps as simple as drawing a picture about the story), or some other means of active involvement with the story.

For informational books, Mason, Peterman, and Kerr (1988, Fig. 2) recommended the following general plan:

Before reading the text

Determine children's level of understanding of the topic presented in the text. Do this by discussing the pictures in the text and having the children describe their experiences with the topic. You might also bring in relevant artifacts, such as model trucks when reading a book about trucks. Build background as necessary.

Provide demonstrations and in-context explanations of difficult concepts.

Discuss the relationship between the title and the topic to be addressed.

Set a purpose for listening. This might include finding the answers to questions the children raised in their discussion of the topic.

Provide a link between their experiences with the topic and what they will be learning from the text.

During the reading of the text

Ask open-ended questions, for example: "What did you learn about trucks? Do you think you would like to be a long-distance truck driver? Why or why not? What kind of truck would you most like to drive or ride in?"

Ask questions periodically to check their understanding of the text. Questions that actually appear in the text might provide excellent opportunities for discussion and demonstration of the topic.

Through comments about the pictures and through carefully selected questions, help children identify pictures that might represent unfamiliar concepts.

Provide suggestions about activities children might engage in later that will encourage them to further explore the topic.

After reading the text

Allow children to ask questions about the text.

Help them see how informational texts can be used to learn more about their own world.

Offer activities that will tie text concepts to children's experiences.

Book reading is particularly effective for developing language when the books are carefully chosen and when there is interaction before, during, and after the book has been read. This is especially true when the reader uses cognitively challenging talk. Cognitively challenging talk includes analyzing characters and events, predicting upcoming events, making connections between the text and real-life experiences, discussing or explaining vocabulary words, summarizing portions of the text, eliciting evaluative responses about the text by asking students to tell whether they liked the story or tell who the favorite character was and why (Dickinson & Smith, 1994). Although discussions are important, they shouldn't interrupt the flow of the story. Delay extended discussions until after the story has been read. Otherwise, children are likely to lose interest and become restless.

Developing Language and Thinking Skills

Being read to and discussing books also builds thinking skills. For instance, one group of kindergartners who were listening to *The Very Hungry Caterpillar* (Carle, 1969) were led through well-planned questions to make inferences about the caterpillar, learned what a cocoon is, and compared the caterpillar's home to that of other animals (Campbell, 2001). The quality of the children's thinking was determined by the quality of the questions and support provided by the teacher.

Because the children liked the book so much, it was read repeatedly. These repeated readings familiarized the children with the book and encouraged them to try the book on their own.

The teacher created a word wall for some key words from the story. With the help of the word wall and their invented spelling, students created stories of their own. Some simply retold a portion of the text. Others wrote about the eating habits of other animals.

Students also learned the days of the week and the numbers 1 through 5, which were highlighted in the story. And, through discussion and other read-alouds, they learned the life cycle of the caterpillar.

Typically, the questions teachers ask about read-alouds produce only brief responses, often just a single word (Beck & McKeown, 2001). To encourage students to provide elaborated responses, ask open-ended questions. Open-ended questions for *Harry the Dirty Dog* (Zion, 1956) might include "What do we know about Harry? How does what Harry did fit in with what we know about him? Why did the family call Harry a strange dog when they saw him in their backyard?" Since students often have a difficult time providing elaborated responses, the teacher might follow up these queries with prompts. Some of the prompts are general: "What does that mean? What is that all about? Can you tell me more about that? Would you explain what you mean?" Others are specific: "What else do we know about Harry? What else did Harry do?" Repeating what students said also helps. When students are unable to respond, rereading the portion of the story being queried helps them formulate a response. The key to developing language and thinking skills is to pose questions that elicit more elaborated responses and to provide support through prompts or reading that help students formulate a response. By evaluating children's responses, you can help build their language (Zevenbergen & Whitehurst, 2003). For instance, you might help a child use more precise vocabulary or expand a response. If a child identifies a moose as a deer, you might say, "That animal looks like a deer, but we call it a moose." If the child says, "Bad dog!" you might prompt an elaborated response: "Why is that dog bad? Can you tell me what the dog does that is bad?"

To make read-alouds more concrete and to develop language, try creating prop boxes (Wasik, Bond, & Hindman, 2006). Prop boxes contain books to be read and concrete objects that depict vocabulary words to be covered. A prop box for gardens might contain *The Carrot Seed* (Krauss, 1989) and *Jack's Garden* (Cole, 1995). The box might also contain the following props: seeds, a shovel, a rake, a small version of a garden hose, a watering can, plastic insects, plastic flowers, a stalk of corn, and a carrot. The props can be used to create interest and also to develop vocabulary. To develop vocabulary, decide which words you plan to present. Use the props as an aid. Also read the books twice. Discuss or point out vocabulary words as you encounter them. Use the target vocabulary throughout the day.

Selecting Read-Aloud Books

To make your read-alouds as valuable as possible, plan the texts that you intend to read to your students. Most important of all, choose books that students will enjoy and will be able

HIGHER-LEVEL LITERACY

How much children benefit from being read to depends on the quality of the book and the way it is read (Zevenbergen & Whitehurst, 2003). Children show greater gains when the reading is interactive—when they are asked questions or are involved in discussing the story.

FYI

Students who have been read to will pick up many concepts of print through observing and interacting with the person reading. Children may notice how print functions, ask questions about words and letters, or try to match print with the words being read.

to understand and relate to. If possible, the books should relate to a theme being explored, re-inforce skills that you are working on, and develop students' language. Most published programs offer lengthy lists of suggested read-alouds. By planning ahead for read-alouds, you can build on past read-alouds while reinforcing your curriculum. You might want to form a study group with other teachers and decide which books to read aloud at each grade level so that students in later grades aren't listening to books that were read to them in earlier grades. You can also share suggestions for good read-alouds and discuss how read-alouds can strengthen the school's literacy program (Fountas & Pinnell, 2006). Enlist the help of your school media specialist, and consult Titlewave and/or Trelease-on-Reading. See the Student Reading List for a number of books that are recommended for reading aloud.

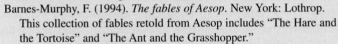

Student Reading List

Recommended Books for Read-Alouds

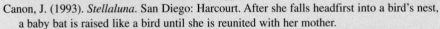

Angelou, M. (1994). *My painted house, my friendly chicken, and me.* New York: Clarkson N. Potter. An eight-year-old Ndebele girl tells about life in her village in South Africa.

Barnes-Murphy, F. (1994). *The fables of Aesop.* New York: Lothrop. This collection of fables retold from Aesop includes "The Hare and the Tortoise" and "The Ant and the Grasshopper."

Canon, J. (1993). *Stellaluna.* San Diego: Harcourt. After she falls headfirst into a bird's nest, a baby bat is raised like a bird until she is reunited with her mother.

Cowley, J. (2005). *Chameleon, chameleon.* New York: Scholastic. Full-color photos show the chameleon as it tracks down and eats a caterpillar.

Dorros, A. (1991). *Abuela.* New York: Dutton. While riding on a bus with her grandmother, a little girl imagines that they are carried up into the sky and fly over the sights of New York City.

Eastman, P. D. (1960). *Are you my mother?* New York: Random House. After falling out of its nest, a small bird searches for its mother.

Gershator, D., & Gershator, P. (1995). *Bread is for eating.* New York: Holt. When her son leaves bread on his plate, his mother explains why bread is for eating. And she sings him a song in Spanish.

Greenfield, E. *Honey, I love.* (1978, 1995). New York: HarperCollins. A young girl tells about the many things in her life that she loves.

Keats, E. J. (1962). *The snowy day.* New York: Viking. A small boy has fun in the snow.

Maitland, B. (2000). *Moo in the morning.* New York: Farrar Straus Giroux. A boy and his mother visit an uncle in the country because the city is noisy, but they find that the country has its own noises.

Martin, B., Jr. (1983). *Brown Bear, Brown Bear, what do you see?* New York: Holt. A brown bear, a blue horse, a purple cat, and other creatures are asked to tell what they see.

McCloskey, R. (1941). *Make way for ducklings.* New York: Viking. With the assistance of a kindly police officer, a mother duck and her brood waddle from the Charles River to the pond in Boston's Public Garden.

Parr, T. (2005). *Otto goes to school.* New York: Little, Brown. Otto, the dog, goes to school for the first time.

Reiser, L. (2006). *Hardworking puppies.* Orlando, FL: Harcourt. Ten puppies find jobs.

Stevens, J. (2005). *The great fuzz frenzy.* San Diego, CA: Harcourt. The frenzy starts when a dog drops a tennis ball down a prairie dog hole, and the prairie dogs start making fuzz and fighting over it. The frenzy finally subsides, but then the dog drops a second ball into the prairie dogs' home.

Literally thousands of books make enjoyable, worthwhile read-alouds. An excellent source of both titles and techniques for reading aloud is Trelease's (2006) *The New Read-Aloud Handbook*, 6th ed. Other sources of read-aloud titles include the following:

Children's Book Committee at the Bank Street College of Education. (2003). *Books to read aloud.* New York: Author.

USING TECHNOLOGY

Titlewave provides extensive information about books and other media, including interest level, readability level, book reviews, and awards that books have won. You can search by author, title, topic, grade level, subject area, or curriculum standard.
http://www.flr.follett.com

Trelease-on-Reading.com provides extensive information on read-alouds:
http://www.trelease-on-reading.com

FYI

Wells (1986) found book reading to be one of the most productive situations for developing language.

Adapting Instruction for Struggling Readers and Writers

In an urban prekindergarten, Maxie Perry enlisted the services of volunteers and aides to read to individual children. Because some of the volunteers had limited reading skills themselves and lacked confidence, she supplied sensitive guidance and suggestions (Strickland & Taylor, 1989).

Children's Book Committee at the Bank Street College of Education. (2006). *The best children's books of the year.* New York: Author.

Freeman, J. (1995). *More books kids will sit still for, a read-aloud guide.* New Providence, NJ: Bowker.

Hansen-Krening, N., Aoki, E. M., & Mizokawa, D. T. (Eds.). (2003). *Kaleidoscope: A multicultural booklist for grades K–8* (4th ed.). Urbana, IL: NCTE.

Indiana Library Federation. (2006). *Read-aloud books too good to miss.* Available at http://www.ilfonline.org/AIME/ReadAloud/readaloud.htm

Lipson, E. R. (2000). *The New York Times parent's guide to the best books for children* (3rd ed.). New York: Three Rivers Press.

If students have not been read to on a regular basis, schedule extra read-aloud sessions. When read to systematically on a one-to-one basis, economically disadvantaged preschoolers demonstrate a greater involvement with stories and increase the number and complexity of their questions and comments. Together with fostering a sense of story, the sessions apparently develop oral language and social skills (Morrow, 1988). Working with groups of five, Klesius and Griffith (1996) implemented interactive storybook reading with kindergarten children whose language development was below that of the other students in the class and who were not responsive to whole-class read-aloud sessions. In addition to developing overall literacy skills, the children "discovered that books are a source of enchantment and wonder" (p. 560).

■ ■ ■ Checkup ■ ■ ■

1. Why is reading aloud such an important part of an emergent literacy program?

2. What are some steps that might be taken to derive maximum benefit from a read-aloud program?

■ ■ ■

A Theme Approach

USING TECHNOLOGY

The Virtual Vine features a number of activities to accompany the song "Wheels on the Bus" and suggests a number of ways in which students might use the song as a model for composing similar songs.
http://www.thevirtualvine.com/WheelsOnTheBus.html

Instruction is most beneficial when connections are made. Creating units helps to build connections. A unit topic might be transportation, and the theme might be: "We travel in different ways." Activities revolve around the theme. In dramatic play, students manage bus stations, airports, docks, railroad stations, and a taxi company. Read-alouds include books about the various kinds of transportation: *Cars, Boats, Planes* (Emberley, 1987), *Cars* (Rockwell, 1984), *Boats and Ships from A to Z* (Alexander, 1961), *School Bus* (Crews, 1984), *The Adventures of Taxi Dog* (Barracca, 1990), *Jamie Goes on an Airplane* (Kremetz, 1986), *Airport* (Barton, 1982). Students also sing songs and recite rhymes related to the unit theme: "Row, Row, Row Your Boat," "Wheels on the Bus."

Instruction is also most beneficial when you have specific objectives. If you want to foster language and literacy skills, you need to specify these. You might note vocabulary words and structures that you would like students to learn. Vocabulary words might include *transportation, highway, airport, luggage, tickets, boarding pass, passengers, fuel, pilot, cabin attendants, driver, captain, port, dock, railroad, train station, engineer, conductor, platform, reservation, track,* and *coach.* Also note literacy objectives and activities. Objectives might be to have students read environmental print such as signs and logos, to become aware of the uses of print, and engage in writing. Activities such as reading signs at the railroad station or advertisements for recognizable products, an illustrated menu in a food car, or illustrated schedules and writing tickets and credit card slips would help achieve these objectives.

■   **Emergent storybook reading** is the evolving ability of a child to read storybooks, which progresses from simply telling a story suggested by the book's illustrations or having heard the book read aloud to reading the book conventionally.

Emergent Storybook Reading

On one visit with my four-year-old granddaughter Paige, she took me aside and whispered, "I can read." Sitting on the sofa, she "read" *Are You My Mother?* (Eastman, 1960) as she leafed through the pages. Although she was not actually reading the words on the pages—her retelling was guided by the pictures—her voice had the tone and expression of one who is reading aloud rather than of one who is telling a story. Paige was engaged in **emergent storybook reading**, a widespread phenomenon in homes and classrooms where children are read to frequently.

Children who have been read to imitate the process and engage in readinglike behaviors. As a result of being read to, children play with books, often for long periods of time, and gradually learn to reconstruct the stories conveyed in the books that have been read to them. For their pretend reading, or emergent storybook reading, children typically select a favorite storybook, one that has been read to them many times. Children's storybook reading can be placed in any of five broad categories beginning with talking about the illustrations in a storybook (but not creating a story) to actually reading a storybook in conventional fashion. The five categories are presented in Table 3.1.

Encourage students to "read" to themselves, to you, and to each other, even though that reading may be a simple retelling of the story. By providing them with opportunities to interact with books in this way, you will be setting the scene for their construction of more advanced understandings about the reading process. You might provide 10 minutes a day for reading time. Schedule it to follow your read-aloud segment so that students can choose to read or retell a book that you have just read. Students can read alone, to you, or to a classmate. Explain to them that they do not have to read like

Pretend reading helps develop emergent literacy.

■■■ **TABLE 3.1 Emergent Reading of Storybooks**

Category	Description
Attends to pictures but does not create a story	The child simply talks about the illustrations and does not attempt to make connections among the pictures so as to tell a story.
Uses pictures to create an oral story	Using the storybook's illustrations, the child creates a story. However, the child's expression and intonation are those of telling rather than reading a story.
Uses pictures to create a combined oral/reading story	Using the storybook's illustrations, the child retells a story. Portions of the retelling sound like oral storybook reading; however, other portions sound like an oral retelling of the story or are conversational.
Uses pictures to create a literary retelling	Using the storybook's illustrations, the child creates a literary rendition of a story. In wording, expression, and intonation, it sounds like the reading of a storybook. The reading may be verbatim but is not just memorized. The verbatim rendition is conceptual. The child uses knowledge of the specific events in the story to help recall the wording of the story (Sulzby, 1985).
Uses print to read	Ironically, the first subcategory here may be a refusal to read. As a child attempts to use print rather than pictures, the child may realize that she or he cannot decipher the print and therefore might say, "I don't know the words." In the second subcategory, the child pays attention to known aspects of print, such as a few known words or a repeated phrase.

Based on Classification Scheme for Children's Emergent Reading of Favorite Storybooks (simplified version) (pp. 137–138) by E. Sulzby (1992). In J. W. Irwin & M. A. Doyle (Eds.), *Reading/Writing Connections, Learning from Research*. Newark, DE: International Reading Association.

Adapting Instruction for Struggling Readers and Writers

Share-read books that are shorter and easier so that students will be better able to follow along. After a shared reading (as compared to a traditional oral reading of a storybook), students, in general, had richer re-tellings and were more enthusiastic; however, the average and below-average youngsters benefited most (Combs, 1987).

grownups; they can read in their own way (Sulzby & Barnhart, 1992). You might also provide a read-aloud center where students can read to a doll or stuffed animal or read along with a taped or CD-ROM version of a story.

Observe children as they read to themselves (young children's "silent" reading is generally audible), to a stuffed animal, to a friend, or to you. Observing children's storybook reading will provide insight into their understanding of the reading process, which has implications for instruction. If children do not use storybook intonation, for example, they may not have a grasp of the language of books and so may need to be read to more often (Sulzby & Barnhart, 1992). Until they have a sense of literary language, children may have difficulty grasping the concept that the printed words on a page convey the story and can be read aloud.

■■■ **Checkup** ■■■

1. What are the key stages in emergent storybook reading?

■■■

Using Shared Book Experiences

An excellent way to help students construct concepts of print (words are made up of letters, sentences are made up of words, reading goes from left to right and top to bottom, etc.) and other essential understandings is the **shared book experience**. Shared book experience is modeled on the bedtime story situation in which a parent or grandparent reads to a child, and, through observation and interaction, the child discovers the purpose of and satisfaction provided by books and begins to construct basic concepts of print (Holdaway, 1979). In order to make the print visible to a group, enlarged text or multiple copies are used. There are several ways of providing enlarged text. Holdaway (1979) suggested using a **big book**, an oversized book, measuring approximately 15 by 19 inches, in which the text is large enough so that students can follow the print as the teacher reads. Alternatives to a big book include using an opaque projector or an overhead projector and transparencies or carefully printing parts of the text on story paper or the chalkboard.

Before reading a big book, introduce the selection by discussing the title and cover illustration. Invite students to predict what the story might be about, build background and interest, and set a purpose for reading it. If it is a story that has already been shared with the class, the purpose can grow out of the original reading and discussion. Perhaps some details were not clear, and so children need to listen carefully to those parts. Or they may simply enjoy hearing a certain tale over and over again. The purpose also could lead to deeper involvement with the characters. Say, for example, that you have made a big book out of *Good as New* (Douglas, 1982), the story of a badly damaged teddy bear that was refurbished by its owner's grandfather. Students might imagine being the child who owns the bear. Have them read along with you and describe how they feel when K. C. cries for the bear. As the story progresses, ask them what they think when K. C. plays with the bear and treats it very roughly. What do they feel when the bear is just about ruined?

As you read, point to the words so that students have a sense of going from left to right and also begin to realize that printed words have spoken equivalents. Also discuss key happenings, clarify confusing elements, and have students revise or make new predictions. However, do not interrupt the flow of the reading. The focus should be on having students

■ **Shared book experience,** which is also known as shared reading, is the practice of reading repetitive stories, chants, poems, or songs, often in enlarged text, while the class follows along or joins in.

■ A **big book** is a book large enough so that all the words can be seen by all the members of the group or class. A typical size is 15 by 19 inches.

Having seen the effectiveness of the traditional bedtime story, Don Holdaway (1979), a primary teacher, reading clinician, and consultant in Auckland, New Zealand, decided to duplicate this experience in a kindergarten classroom. Here is his account of trying out a big book—which he calls an "enlarged book"—for the first time:

> Now we bring out our first enlarged book—a version of *The Three Billy Goats Gruff*. We choose this partly because of the strongly emotional language of the repetitive section which may draw the children into prediction and participation even on the first reading. The children are delighted with the enormous book and many keep their eyes glued on it as we use a pointer to follow the story as we read. Sure enough, on the second occasion of the "Trip, trap!" and the "Who's that tripping over my bridge?" some of the children chime in, encouraged by the invitational cues we give off. They are delighted in the closing couplet, "Snip, snap, snout, This tale's told out," and want to say it for themselves. (p. 66)

> The big book was a smashing success. After a period of experimentation and revision of the program, Holdaway concluded that the results seemed "more hopeful than we might at first have supposed" (p. 79). The shared experience apparently began a cycle of success in which the reading of high-quality literature led to more positive and enjoyable teaching, which led to a greater degree of attention and higher level of personal satisfaction among pupils, which, in turn, led to higher levels of achievement.

Exemplary Teaching

Shared Reading with Big Books

enjoy the experience. After you have shared a book, discuss it with the class, just as you would after reading a book orally to them.

Successive Readings

One goal of shared reading is to involve the students more deeply in the reading. If the book you have shared with students is one they would like to read again, conduct a second shared reading. During this second reading, encourage students to join in by reading refrains, or repeated phrases, sentences, or words that are readily predictable from context or illustrations. They can do this chorally as a group or as individual volunteers. In these subsequent shared readings, continue to point to each word as you read it so that students

Shared reading is an excellent way to construct and reinforce concepts of print.

can see that you are reading individual words. During a second reading of the book *Are You My Mother?* (Eastman, 1960), read the repeated sentence "Are you my mother?" pointing to each word as you read it. Have volunteers read the sentence. Again, point to each word as the sentence is being read. Then read the story once more. Tell students that you are going to read the story, but they are going to help. As you come to "Are you my mother?" pause and have the class read the sentence in unison as you point to each word. Schedule the book for additional readings with choral reading of the repeated sentence. From time to time, have individual volunteers read the line. During follow-up reading of *Rosie's Walk* (Hutchins, 1987), one teacher began introducing students to concepts of words and letters. Pointing to the first page, she asked the students what the page said. Because the story had been read to them previously, they were able to say that it told that Rosie the hen went for a walk. The teacher asked them to find the word *hen* and point to it with a pointer and to tell what letters were in *hen* (Campbell, 2001). Students might also talk about names of classmates that begin with *h* or about other *h* words in the story.

Concept of word is a key skill in shared reading. Concept of word means that students can point to separate words in a sentence when that sentence is being read either by the student or by someone else. Concept of word is facilitated by awareness of beginning sounds. Using beginning sounds, the students can mark the first sound of a word and use that as an anchor point. Once students have a concept of word, they are better able to build their knowledge of letter-sound relationships. Because they are able to follow along during shared reading, they begin to match sounds with letters and to learn whole words and additional letter-sound relationships, such as ending consonant correspondences. This process is aided if the teacher points to words as a big book is read and if the big book contains just one line on a page so that students can match spoken and printed words (Morris, Bloodgood, Lomax, & Perney, 2003). You can also start a word wall that contains words that have been introduced to the class. On the word wall, place words that have been repeated in the shared reading. Review these words, and encourage students to use them in their writing.

Once a big book has been shared, have students engage in follow-up activities. Some may choose to listen to a taped version of the book while reading a regular-size edition of the big book. A small group may want to read the big book once more, with one of their members assuming the role of teacher. Some may want to read to partners, while still others may want to listen to a new story in the listening center or draw an illustration related to the big book. Some may want to look at Komori's (1983) *Animal Mothers*, which uses realistic paintings to show how animal mothers get their babies to travel with them. Viewing a filmstrip, videotape, CD-ROM, or Web site on animal mothers and their young may be another option. Later, the class might compose a group-experience story based on observations of how the class's mother gerbil cares for her young. Some students may want to dictate an individual story telling how their cats or dogs cared for their young. Some students may want to compose their own stories, using drawings and **invented spellings**. Invented spellings, such as "I KN RT" for "I can write," reflect the evolving concept of how letter-sound relationships should be represented.

To help students get started, you might put three or four key words from the story on the classroom word wall or bulletin board. After sharing *Rosie's Walk* (Hutchins, 1987),

■ **Invented spelling** is the intuitive spelling that novices create before learning or while learning the conventional writing system. Invented spelling is also known as temporary, developmental, or transitional spelling (Strickland, 1998). These terms indicate that this spelling marks a passing stage in the child's development.

■ **Print conventions** refer to generally accepted ways of putting words on a page, such as arranging words from left to right and using capital letters and end punctuation.

■ **Language experience stories** can foster emergent literacy. One or a group of students dictate a story, which is then used as a basis for reading and writing instruction.

one class took a walk around the school grounds to see what they could see. Students then wrote a story about their walk (Campbell, 2001). Words from this story that might be put on a word wall include *walk, saw,* and *for.* The students' individual stories were collected in a book. Each student was given two pages. The student's version was pasted on the right-hand page and a correctly spelled rewritten version appeared on the left-hand page, so that other students could read the book.

Periodically, introduce other repetitive selections. They need not be stories—poems, rhymes, songs, and even jump-rope chants are suitable. Some of these selections may be in big books; others can be written on the chalkboard or on chart paper. As students' understanding of print develops, introduce additional concepts: Point out that words are composed of letters, talk about the sounds in words, discuss words that rhyme or begin with the same sound, and help students see that some words begin with the same letter and the same sound. Also discuss **print conventions**, such as punctuation marks, capital letters, and quotation marks. And, whenever introducing a new selection, point out the title and author's name.

Dialogic Reading

Dialogic reading is a form of shared book reading in which the questioning and prompts are used with a small group to develop deeper understanding (Doyle & Bramwell, 2006). Vocabulary is also developed through discussion of key ideas in a selection. For instance, a classroom discussion in one dialogic reading session became an extended discussion of why the character in the story was feeling *frustrated* (a new vocabulary word), about times at which the children had felt *frustrated*, and about some things they might do when they feel *frustrated*. Through this and similar discussions, dialogic reading is used to develop social and emotional skills as students read about and discuss challenging situations.

■ ■ ■ Checkup ■ ■ ■

1. How might shared reading be used to foster emergent literacy?

■ ■ ■

Using Language Experience Stories

Language experience stories can also be used to introduce the visual aspects of reading. They may be used instead of or in conjunction with big books and may be created by students working in groups or by individuals. As the name suggests, a language experience story is based on a real-life experience. For instance, the story in Figure 3.2 began with a class trip to a nearby apple orchard. When they returned to school, the students discussed the orchard and drew pictures to illustrate their trip. Pictures often result in more focused, coherent stories because they encapsulate the child's experience (Platt, 1978). The teacher (or an aide) discusses each child's picture, after which the child dictates a story about it. As the teacher writes the child's dictated story, the teacher tells the student what he or she is doing. Then the teacher reads the story back and asks if that is what the child wanted to say. The teacher invites the child to add to the story or make other changes. Once any requested changes have been made, the teacher again reads the story. Then the teacher and the child read the story together. After this shared reading, the child is invited to read his or her story to the teacher. Aided by the drawing and the familiarity of the experience, children usually are able to read their stories.

Individual stories are gathered into books, which children are encouraged to take home and read to their families. During the school year, students may create anywhere from one to a dozen books, depending on their interest in the activity and their emerging skills.

Adapting Instruction for English Language Learners

For individual stories, write the story just as the student says it, even if the grammar is not correct or the student uses both English and his native language. For group stories, use correct grammar or students may be confused.

■ ■ ■ **FIGURE 3.2 Language Experience Story**

The Apple Orchard

We went to the apple orchard.
I saw apples on the trees.
I saw a big red apple on the ground.

Miguel

ASSESSING FOR LEARNING

As students participate in shared writing, note what they can do. Can they supply initial or final consonants? Do they seem to know most of the consonant correspondences? Or do they just know the consonants that their names begin with? Can they read some words? What do your observations suggest about the type of instruction they might need?

Shared (Interactive) Writing

In **shared (interactive) writing**, which is modeled on experience stories and shared reading, both teacher and student compose a story (Martin, 1995). Just as in traditional language experience stories, the class writes about experiences they have had or books that have been read to them. Often, a shared reading of a favorite book sets the stage for the class's writing. After share reading Sarah Albee's *I Can Do It* (1997), in which the Muppets tell about some of the things they can do, one class composed a story about things they can do. In addition to suggesting content, students also participated in the actual writing. The teacher encouraged students to spell or write initial consonants, parts of words, or even whole words. One strategy that these novice writers are encouraged to use is knowledge of the spellings of their names. For instance, Carl was able to supply the first letter of *can* because *can* begins like *Carl*, and Roberto was able to supply the first letter of *ride*.

In shared writing, the teacher emphasizes reading for meaning and basic concepts of print. For instance, after adding a word to a story, the teacher goes back and reads the portion of the sentence that has been written so far. Focused on the details of the writing of a word, students may have lost the sense of the sentence. Going back over what has been written helps the students keep the story in mind and also helps them make a one-to-one match between written and spoken words. After, for example, adding "ride" to "Roberto can," the teacher rereads all that has been written of the sentence: "Roberto can ride." As part of the scaffolding, the teacher also asks such questions as the following:

Where do we begin writing?

How many words are there in our sentence?

Say the word slowly. What sounds do you hear?

Can you write the letter that stands for that sound?

Here is sample dialog to show how shared writing might be implemented:

Teacher: "What are some things that you can do?"

Maria: "I can ride a bike."

Teacher: "How shall we write that in our story?"

Felicia: "Maria can ride a bike."

Teacher: "How many words are in that sentence?"

Reginald: "Five."

Teacher: "What is the first word?"

Jason: "Maria."

Teacher: (pointing to spot on chalkboard) "Maria, will you write your name here?"

Teacher: (pointing to and reading "Maria") "What goes next?"

Thomas: "Can."

Teacher: "How many sounds does *can* (teacher stretches out word) have?"

James: "Three."

Teacher: "How does *can* (emphasizes first sound) begin? Who has a name that begins like *can*?"

Carl: "I do."

Teacher: "How does your name begin?"

Carl: "With a *c*."

■ In **shared (interactive) writing**, students may tell the teacher what letters to write or may actually write them in the piece.

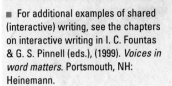

Teacher: "Would you write a *c* here?" (Judging that the students would not be able to spell the short *a* sound, the teacher adds an *a* and says,) "What should we add to /ca/ to make *can*?"

Class: "N."

Teacher: "Whose name has an *n*?"

Nan: Mine does.

Teacher: (After *n* has been added, she says, pointing to each word) "Maria can. What can Maria do?"

Class: "Ride a bike."

Teacher: "How many sounds does *ride* (teacher stretches out word) have?"

Cynthia: "Three."

Teacher: "How does *ride* (emphasizes first sound) begin? Whose name begins like *ride*?"

Roberto: "My name. *Roberto* begins like *ride*."

Teacher: "What other sounds do you hear in *ride*? What comes after *rrr*?"

Carl: "I–duh."

Teacher: "What letter spells /ī/?"

Carl: "That's easy. *I* spells /ī/."

Teacher: "What letter spells /d/?"

Carl: "D."

Teacher: "Can you write *i-d* for us?"

Carl: "I can write *i*, but I forget how *d* goes."

Teacher: "Can you find *d* on the alphabet chart?"

Teacher: (After adding an *e* to the *d* on the end of the word, she asks,) "Who will point to and read what we have written so far?"

The teacher continues until the story is completed.

FYI

■ For additional examples of shared (interactive) writing, see the chapters on interactive writing in I. C. Fountas & G. S. Pinnell (eds.), (1999). *Voices in word matters*. Portsmouth, NH: Heinemann.

■ Students are asked to point to the words they read to make sure that they are processing individual words and not just reciting a portion of the text that they have memorized.

Exemplary Teaching

Shared Writing in Kindergarten

Using a series of informal assessment devices, Paige Ferguson determined that only half of her kindergarten students could write their names and only two knew the letters of the alphabet. Given the children's low level of literacy development, she decided to use shared writing with them. As part of their literature unit, she read Paul Galdone's (1975) *The Gingerbread Boy* to the class. The class then took a walking tour of the school to find hidden gingerbread boys. After returning to the classroom, the class began creating a shared story. The story consisted of listing the places where they found the gingerbread boys.

Building on the students' knowledge of the sounds and letters in their names, the teacher introduced other sounds and letters as the class created additional shared stories. To reinforce the children's awareness of separate words, she had one student point to each word in the story while the other children read it. As the year progressed, the children learned to hear the separate sounds in words and represent these sounds with letters. They also learned to write in a variety of formats. They wrote shared letters to pen pals, retold stories, made lists, and summarized scientific observations that they had made.

In addition to writing interactively, the children wrote independently each day. Shared writing provided a foundation for their independent writing. They also reread the shared stories that had been hung up around the room. When assessed in the spring, the students demonstrated dramatic progress. They showed growth in phonemic awareness, knowledge of letter-sound relationships, alphabet knowledge, concepts of print, and writing. Most could also read some beginning first-grade-level books (Button, Johnson, & Ferguson, 1996).

Finished pieces are placed on the walls. The teacher share-reads the pieces. As students become familiar with the pieces, they are encouraged to read them. Lists of color, number, and other common words and students' names are also placed on the wall in alphabetical order. Students are encouraged to use these lists and the stories placed on the wall to help them with pieces that they write independently. Because shared writing is a group project, stories are written in standard spelling. When students write independently, they use invented spelling but are encouraged to use words from the wall. Their writing typically contains conventional spellings drawn from lists and stories on the walls.

■ ■ ■ Checkup ■ ■ ■

1. What are the steps in teaching students to create traditional language experience stories?
2. What are the steps in teaching shared writing?
3. What are the key benefits of language experience stories and shared writing?

■ ■ ■

A New Concept of Writing

Traditionally, writing was not taught until after students started reading. Often, it was equated with handwriting, copying, and spelling instruction. However, writing is not simply a matter of forming letters (Holdaway, 1979); it is a way of representing the world, progressing from apparently random scribbles to meaningful marks to increasingly more conventional letters and spellings. From their first day in school, children should be encouraged to write as best they can, in whatever way they can, whether by drawings, letterlike forms, or invented spellings.

Teachers should encourage students to write and draw, should accept and support their efforts, and should resist correcting "errors." Teachers should model the process, allowing students to see them writing on the chalkboard, chart paper, word processor, notepaper, and so on. Attempts at writing lead to discoveries about the alphabetic system that help students gain essential insights into both writing and reading.

Formation of Speech Sounds

Knowing how speech sounds are formed will help you to do a better job teaching phonological awareness, phonics, and spelling. It will help you to understand why *train* is frequently spelled CHRAN and why *girl* is often spelled GRIL and why clusters such as the *st* in *stop* and the *sp* in *spot* are often misread.

Consonant Formation

Consonants are formed by obstructing or interfering in some way with the flow of breath. In English, there are twenty-five consonant sounds (see Table 3.2). Consonants can be distinguished by place and manner of articulation and voice. Say the consonant sounds in Table 3.2. As you do so, focus on the formation of each one. Notice that you are using your tongue, lips, and teeth and that the consonants are formed in various parts of your mouth, nose, and throat. In addition, consonants are either voiced or voiceless. A voiced consonant is one that is accompanied by a vibration of the vocal cords. Thus /b/ is voiced, but /p/ is voiceless. If you say /b/ and /p/, you will notice that both have the same manner and place of articulation. The only difference between them is that one is voiced and the other is not.

Vowel Formation

Vowels are articulated with tongue, lips, and teeth. Vowels are classified according to where they are articulated. Say each of the vowel sounds in Table 3.3. What do you notice

■■■ **TABLE 3.2 Consonants: Place and Manner of Articulation**

	Lips (Labials)	Lips & Teeth (Labio-dentals)	Tongue between Teeth (Dentals)	Tongue behind Teeth (Aveolars)	Roof of Mouth (Palatal-velars)	Back of Mouth (Velars)	Throat (Glottal)
Stops							
Voiced	b (barn)			d (deer)		g (gate)	
Voiceless	p (pot)			t (time)		k (kite)	
Nasals	m (me)			n (now)		ng (sing)	
Fricatives							
Voiced		v (van)	th (thin)	z (zipper)	zh (azure)		
Voiceless		f (fan)	th (this)	s (sight)	sh (ship)		h (horse)
Affricatives							
Voiced					j (jug)		
Voiceless					ch (chip)		
Semivowels (glides)	w (we) hw (whale)				y (yacht)		
Liquids		r (ride)			l (lion)		

about their articulation? What happens to your tongue as you say the various vowels? Notice that your tongue moves from the very front of your mouth to the back. Your tongue also moves lower in your mouth as you say /ē/, /i/, /ā/, /e/, /a/, /ī/, /o/ and then begins to move up. Starting with /ē/, your lips are parted as though you were smiling. Gradually, your lips become rounded. The sounds /oy/ and /ow/ include two sounds.

Effect of Environment on Speech Sounds

Except for words like *I* and *oh*, most speech sounds don't appear in isolation; they have other speech sounds coming before or after them. Often, speech sounds are altered by the sounds surrounding them (Moats, 2000; 2004).

Nasalization. Nasal consonant sounds such as /m/, /n/, and /ŋ/ are partially absorbed by the preceding vowel and sometimes by the following consonant, so a word like *ant* may sound like /at/, and *sand* may sound like /sad/. Because of nasalization, it is difficult to segment the sounds in *ant*, *sand*, and similar words. There is also an increased possibility that words like *ant* and *sand* will be spelled without the nasal consonant—that is, will be spelled *at* and *sad*. Patterns that end in the nasal consonants /n/ and /m/ may need special handling. Contrast the sound of /a/ in *at* and *an*. When introducing *an* and *am* patterns,

■■■ **TABLE 3.3 American English Vowels**

	Front	Central	Back
High	ē (beat) i (bit)		ōō (boot) oo (book)
Mid	ā (bait) e (bet)	u (but) schwa	ō (boat)
Low	a (bat) ī (bite)	o (bottle) oy ow (combinations of vowel sounds)	aw (bought)

present them as a unit. Do not ask students to say the sound of *a* and then the sound of *n* and blend them together, and do not use words with such patterns for segmentation exercises.

Syllabic Consonants.   The sound /l/, /r/, /m/, or /n/ at the end of a word can represent a syllable. Therefore, it is logical for novice writers to spell *letter* and *little* as LETR and LITL. *Him* and *Dan* might be spelled HM and DN.

Affrication.   The phonemes /ch/ and /j/ are known as affricatives. In an affricative, a stop of breath is followed by a fricative. A fricative is a consonant sound that is produced through friction as in /v/ or /f/. The phonemes /t/ and /d/ are affricated when they appear before the sound /r/, so that /t/ sounds like /ch/ and /d/ sounds like /j/ as in *train* and *drum*. In the process of articulating an /r/, the mouth naturally forms a /ch/ or a /j/. Because of affrication, *train* is often spelled CHRAN and *drum* JUM or JM by children who are focusing on the sounds they hear.

Aspiration.   Holding a piece of paper a few inches from your mouth, say *pit* out loud. Now say *tip*. When you said *pit*, the paper moved but not when you said *tip*. The pronunciation of *pit* was accompanied by aspiration. Aspiration is a puff of air as when you articulate /h/. The voiceless stop consonants /p/, /t/, and /k/ are usually aspirated when they come at the beginning of a word or syllable. Voiceless stops are not aspirated when they come at the end of a word or syllable or as the second sound in a cluster as in *spot, stop*, or *scare*. Being unaspirated, they are harder to detect, so children have more difficulty identifying final sounds and the second sound in a cluster. Students might have a more difficult time segmenting the sounds in words that have unaspirated stops. Because the unaspirated forms may sound like their voiced counterparts, /p/ is often spelled as *b*, /t/ as *d*, and /k/ as *g* as in *pig* for *pick, cub* for *cup, sgar* for *scare*, and *sbot* for *spot* (Moats, 2000).

Vowel Blending.   Some vowels are difficult to detect because they blend in with the consonant that follows them. This is especially true of /l/ and /r/, as in *will* and *girl*. Children may spell *bird* as *brid*, not because they are confusing the sequence of sounds but because the /i/ and /r/ are blended and the /r/ sound dominates. This also explains the GRIL spelling of *girl*, where the /l/ sound dominates. Segmenting the sounds in these words can be difficult. When students have difficulty spelling these words, encouraging them to sound them out may be counterproductive. If they spell what they hear, chances are they will misspell the words (Moats, 2000). This is also true of words like *train, drum*, and *dress*. These elements need to be taught as onset-rime patterns. When taught such a rime as a unit, students aren't asked to separate the sounds in a word like *third* or *fort*.

■ ■ ■ Checkup ■ ■ ■

1. How are consonants formed? How are vowels formed?
2. What impact does the formation of speech sounds have on spelling and reading?

■ ■ ■

■ In the **prealphabetic (or prephonemic) stage**, students use letters but don't realize that the letters represent sounds.

■ The **alphabetic stage** is also known as the letter name stage because students use the names of the letters to figure out the sounds they represent. The name of *b*, for instance, contains its sound.

■ The **consolidated alphabetic stage** is sometimes known as the within word pattern or orthographic stage because students are beginning to see patterns such as final *e* and double vowel.

Development of Spelling

When does writing start? At the age of eighteen months, average toddlers will make marks on paper (Gibson & Levin, 1974). By age three, scribbling is no longer random or unorganized (Harste, Woodward, & Burke, 1984). Because it proceeds in a straight line across the page and may be composed of up-and-down or curved marks, it resembles genuine writing. In time, children may create letterlike figures, use a combination of numbers and letters, and eventually use only letters. Along the way, they discover the concept of sign (Clay, 1972)—that is, they arbitrarily use a graphic element to represent an idea or a word, a syllable, or a sound. For example, the child may use the letter *b* or *x* or a self-created letterlike form to represent the word *ball*.

The earliest spelling stage is the **prealphabetic (prephonemic) stage**. At this stage, children realize that letters are used to create words but have not caught on to the alphabetic principle—that is, that letters represent sounds. At age four, Paul Bissex used strings of letters to cheer his mother up. The letters were a random selection and were designed to convey the messages "Welcome home" in one instance and "Cheer up" in another (Bissex, 1980).

The next stage of spelling is the **alphabetic (letter name) stage**. In the early part of this stage, children start putting the alphabetic principle to work. Single letters may at first represent whole words but later may stand for syllables and then represent single sounds (Ferreiro, 1986). For instance, the letter *k* may be used to represent the word *car*. In later phases of this stage, a child may add the final consonant, spelling car as KR. Some consonant combination spellings may at first seem to have no connection to their sounds: *tr* is frequently spelled CH, and *dr* may be spelled JR. Try saying "train." Listen very carefully to the initial sound. The beginning sound is actually /ch/. Likewise, the *d* in *dr* combinations has a /j/ sound. The child is spelling what she or he hears (Read, 1971).

As the alphabetic (letter name) stage proceeds, children begin representing vowel sounds. Students continue to employ a strategy in which a letter is used to represent the sound heard in the letter's name, so *late* is spelled LAT and *feet* is spelled FET. This works for most consonants and long vowels but not for short ones, as the names of short vowels do not contain their pronunciations. To spell short vowels, children employ the "close to" tactic, in which they use the long-vowel name that is closest to the point in the mouth where the short vowel to be spelled is articulated. For instance, short *e* is formed very close to the point where long *a* is articulated, so the child spells short *e* with an A, as in BAD for *bed*. Based on the "close to" tactic, short *i* is spelled with an E (SET for *sit*), short *o* with an I (HIP for *hop*), and short *u* with an O (BOT for *but*) (Read, 1971).

As they are exposed to standard spellings in books and environmental print, children begin to notice that spelling incorporates certain conventions—that final *e* is used to mark long vowels, for instance. They enter the **consolidated alphabetic stage** (also known as the within word pattern or orthographic stage), in which they begin to consolidate visual or orthographic elements along with sound elements in their spelling (Henderson, 1990). Their spelling is no longer strictly guided by sound. Although their spelling may not always be accurate, they begin to use final *e* markers and double vowel letters to spell long vowel sounds. They may spell *mean* as MEEN or MENE. However, they begin to spell short vowels accurately. As children progress through this stage, their spelling becomes conventional, and ultimately they move into the stages of syllable juncture and derivational constancy, which are advanced stages of conventional spelling involving multisyllabic words (Henderson, 1990). See Table 3.4 for examples of the major stages of spelling.

As can be seen from the description of the stages of spelling, spelling is not merely a matter of memorizing words. Spelling is conceptual and involves three levels of understanding: alphabetic, pattern, and meaning. At the alphabetic level, students understand that letters represent sounds. At the pattern level, they realize that letters often form patterns, as in the spelling of *load* and *rope*, where long *o* is spelled with an *oa* and *o-e*. At the meaning level, students conclude that meaning may govern a word's spelling; that is, words that have a similar meaning have a similar spelling even though their pronunciations may differ: *sign/signature* (Bear & Templeton, 1998).

■■■ **TABLE 3.4 Stages of Spelling**

Age	Stage	Example
18 months	Random scribbling	*(handwritten scribble)*
3 years	Wordlike scribbling	*(handwritten scribble)*
4–5 years	Prealphabetic writing (prephonemic)	LWЭꞓ
4–6+ years	Early alphabetic (early letter name)	WL
5–7+ years	Alphabetic (letter name)	WAL
6–7+ years	Consolidated alphabetic (within word pattern)	whale
8–10+ years	Syllable juncture	whaling
10–20+ years	Derivational constancy	aquatic

As they have more experience with writing, children develop a deeper understanding of the spelling system. They begin to use visual and meaning features to spell words instead of just relying on sound characteristics. Instruction is most effective when it matches the student's stage of development. For instance, a student in the early letter name (early alphabetic) stage would have difficulty with final *e* words. She or he might be able to

■■■ **TABLE 3.5 The Elementary Spelling Inventory (with error guide)**

Stages		Early Letter Name	Letter Name	Within Word Pattern
1.	bed	b bd	bad	bed
2.	ship	s sp shp	sep shep	sip ship
3.	drive	jrv drv	griv driv	drieve draive drive
4.	bump	h bp bmp	bop bomp bup	bump
5.	when	w yn wn	wan whan	wen when
6.	train	j t trn	jran chran tan tran	teran traen trane train
7.	closet	k cs kt clst	clast clost clozt	clozit closit
8.	chase	j jass cs	tas cas chas chass	case chais chase
9.	float	f vt ft flt	fot flot flott	flowt floaut flote float
10.	beaches	b bs bcs	bechs becis behis	bechise beches beeches beaches
11.	preparing			preparng preypering
12.	popping			popin poping
13.	cattle			catl cadol
14.	caught			cot cote cout cought caught
15.	inspection			inspshn inspechin
16.	puncture			pucshr pungchr puncker
17.	cellar			salr selr celr seler
18.	pleasure			plasr plager plejer pleser plesher
19.	squirrel			scrl skwel skwerl
20.	fortunate			forhnat frehnit foohinit
21.	confident			
22.	civilize			
23.	flexible			
24.	opposition			opasiun opasishan opozcison opishien opasitian
25.	emphasize			

Note: The Preliterate Stage is not presented here.

memorize the spelling of *note* but would not understand the principle of final *e* and so would not apply it to other words.

To determine students' spelling stage, analyze samples of their writing. You might also use the Elementary Spelling Inventory (Bear & Barone, 1989), presented in Table 3.5. The inventory presents twenty-five words that increase in difficulty and embody key elements of the stages. Start with the first word and continue testing until the words become too difficult. Ask students to spell as best they can because even partially spelled words reveal important information about spelling stage. Before administering the inventory, explain to students that you want to see how they spell words. Tell them that some of the words may be hard, but they should do the best they can. Say each word, use it in a sentence, and say the word once more.

Using the error guide, carefully analyze the students' performance. Most novice readers will be in the early alphabetic (early letter name) stage. However, a few might be in a more advanced stage, and some may be in the prephonemic stage. Often, students move back and forth between adjacent stages. Figure 3.3 (on p. 114) shows examples of a child's use of invented spelling in kindergarten and in first grade.

ASSESSING FOR LEARNING

Invented spelling provides insight into the child's knowledge of letter-sound relationships. By analyzing the child's spelling and noting what the child seems to understand about letter-sound relationships, you can gear your instruction to the child's level of understanding.

INVOLVING PARENTS

Be sure to explain the nature of invented spelling to parents. Let them know that invented spelling is transitional and does not lead to poor spelling. Explain what you will be doing to teach conventional spelling.

■■■ Checkup ■■■

1. How does spelling ability develop? What are the stages of spelling development?
2. What are the three levels of students' understanding of spelling?

■■■ TABLE 3.5 (*continued*)

Syllable Juncture	Derivational Constancy
11. preparing prepairing preparing	
12. popping	
13. catel catle cattel cattle	
15. inspecshum inspecsion inspection	
16. punksher punture puncture	
17. seller sellar celler cellar	
18. plesour plesure	pleasure
19. scqoril sqrarel squirle squirrel	
20. forchenut fochininte fortunet	fortunate
21. confadent confedint confedent confadent conphident confiadent confeddent confendent confodent confident	
22. sivils sevelies sivilicse cifillazas sivelize sivalize civalise civilise civilize	
23. flecksibl flexobil fleckuble flecible flexeble flexibel flaxable flexibal flexable	flexible
24. opasition oppaashion oppisition	oposision oposition opposition
25. infaside infacize emfesize emfisize imfasize ephacise empasize emphasise	emphisize emphasize

■■■ **FIGURE 3.3**

A Student's Invented Spelling in Kindergarten and First Grade

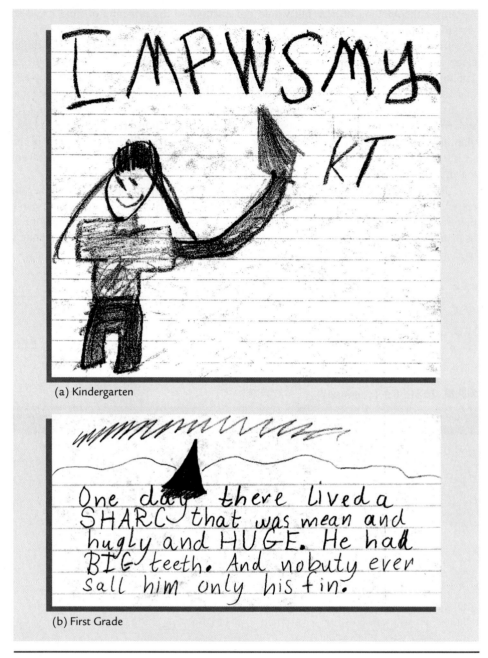

(a) Kindergarten

(b) First Grade

From stories written by Anne Lincoln. Used by permission.

Forms of Emergent Writing

Children's writing develops through seven forms, beginning with drawing and ending with conventional spelling. These forms include the spelling stages depicted in Table 3.4 but go beyond spelling to include the writer's intentions. The major forms of emergent writing described in Table 3.6 are based on research completed with kindergarten students (Sulzby, Barnhart, & Hieshima, 1989).

At the beginning of the kindergarten year, many children are operating on a scribbling level. Some continue to use that form throughout the year. However, even though some students cling to a scribble form of writing, the scribbles at the end of the year are more advanced than those created at the beginning of the year. How can one scribbled story be more advanced than another? Although, on the surface, two scribbled stories may seem

■■ ■ **ASSESSING FOR LEARNING**

Through observation and discreet probing, find out where children are in their writing development. Some may be drawing or scribble-writing. Others may have advanced to invented or even conventional spelling. Also note how children approach the task of writing. Do they jump right in, or are they hesitant and unsure?

■■■ **TABLE 3.6   Forms of Emergent Writing**

Form	Description
Drawing	The drawing is not an illustration for a story but is the story itself. The child reads the drawing as though it were text.
Scribbling	The scribbling resembles a line of writing. It may have the appearance of a series of waves or, in a more advanced representation, may resemble a series of letterlike forms.
Letterlike forms	Letterlike forms resemble manuscript or cursive letters and are generally written as separate forms rather than the continuous forms seen in scribbling. They are not real letters, and care needs to be taken that poorly formed real letters are not placed in this category.
Prephonemic spelling	The child writes with real letters, but the letters are a random collection or a meaningless pattern, such as repeating the same letter. Although the letters are real, they do not represent sounds.
Copying	The child copies from print found in his or her environment: signs, labels, etc. One child copied from a crayon box but, when asked to read his piece, told a story that had nothing to do with crayons (Sulzby, 1989).
Invented spelling	Students make use of the alphabetic principle. The letters they write represent sounds. Initially, one letter may represent a whole word. Over time, there is a gradual movement to conventional spelling. See Table 3.4 for a chart of spelling stages, including the several stages of invented spelling.
Conventional spelling	Student's spelling is conventional.

Based on Appendix 2.1, Forms of Writing and Rereading from Writing, Example List (pp. 51–63) by E. Sulzby (1989). In J. M. Mason (Ed.), *Reading and Writing Connections*. Boston: Allyn & Bacon.

very similar, they may have very different meanings for their creators. In children's writing, there may be more on the page than meets the eye. Sulzby (1989a) cautions, "One can only judge the quality of the form of writing by comparing it with the rereading a child uses with it" (p. 51).

After students write stories in whatever form or forms they choose, they are asked to read them. Just as in emergent storybook readings, described in Table 3.1, students read their written pieces on a variety of levels of sophistication. A child asked to read a scribbled story may simply retell a story that apparently has no connection with the scribbles. Another child may read the scribbles as though he or she is reading conventional writing. The child's voice may incorporate the intonation of a story, and he or she may even point to the scribbles as they are read as though pointing to a line of words. When the child comes to the end of the scribbles, his or her reading ceases. When asked to reread the scribbles, the child may use exactly the same words to retell the tale. In a sense, the child is reading the scribbles. Categories of reading from emergent writing are presented in Table 3.7 (on p. 116).

FYI

As Dierking (2006) notes, writing can be used to foster reading, and vice versa, even at the earliest stages. Writing slows down the processing of letters and sounds and so highlights individual sounds.

■■■ **Checkup** ■■■

1. How does writing develop?
2. What are the forms of emergent writing? What are the key characteristics of each form?

■■■

Encouraging Children to Write

Whether they are drawing, scribbling, copying, creating invented spellings, or entering into a transitional phase, children should be encouraged to write. This writing program should be informal but functional. The first prerequisite is that each student should realize that she or he has something to say. Whatever a student produces should be accepted and valued.

The teacher's role should be an active one, modeling the writing process at every opportunity. When the teacher is writing a note to parents explaining a field trip, the children

ASSESSING FOR LEARNING ■ ■ ■

Children use different forms of writing for different tasks. When writing brief pieces, kindergarten children tend to use conventional spelling. When writing a long story, they may scribble.

■■■■ **TABLE 3.7 Reading from Emergent Writing**

Category	Description
Null	The child refuses to read the story he or she has written, says that he or she cannot read it, or comments that nothing was written or the story does not say anything.
Labeling/describing	The child supplies labels or a description instead of reading. The child says, "Cat" or "This is a cat." A one-word response is a label; a sentence response is a description.
Dialogue	The child only responds if you ask questions, so the interchange takes on a question–answer format. The question–answer interchange may be initiated by the child.
Oral monologue	The child tells a story in the style of an oral retelling. It does not have the characteristics of the reading of a piece of writing.
Written monologue	The reading sounds as though the child is reading from a written piece. It has the sound and flow of oral reading of written text, but the child is not actually reading from the written piece.
Naming letters	The child names the letters that have been written.
Aspectual/strategic reading	The child is beginning to attend to the writing and may attempt to sound out some words and phrases while skipping others. The child may read the written piece while looking at the written words, but the written words may not completely match up with what the child is reading.
Conventional	The child uses the written words to read. The rendition may sound like written monologue, but the main difference is that the child is deciphering the written words while reading.

Based on Appendix 2.1, Forms of Writing and Rereading from Writing, Example List (pp. 51–63) by E. Sulzby (1989). In J. M. Mason (Ed.), *Reading and Writing Connections*. Boston: Allyn & Bacon.

FYI

■ Invented spelling contributed to the progress made by at-risk first-graders in acquiring phonological awareness and phonics (Santa & Høien, 1999).

■ Modeling is an important part of children's early writing attempts. In writing letters and notes, they imitate what they have seen parents, teachers, and older siblings do.

Adapting Instruction for Struggling Readers and Writers

Kindergarten teacher Linda Edwards (2000) divides her class into five groups for writing so that she is teaching students who are on similar levels and share common needs. She doesn't set up guided writing groups until children can remember tomorrow what they wrote today.

should be shown what the teacher is doing. They should see the teacher create signs for the room, draw up a list of supplies, complete a book order, and write messages on the board. Seeing real writing done for real purposes is especially important for students who may not have seen their parents do much writing.

Invitations to write should be extended to the children. The teacher might ask them to write about things they like to do. The teacher should model the process by writing a piece that tells what he or she likes to do. Students should then be encouraged to write as best they can or in any way they can. If they wish, they can draw pictures showing what they like to do, or they may both draw and write. The teacher should show samples of the various ways children can write—including scribbling, random letter strings, drawings, and invented spellings—and explain that each student is to write in her or his own way.

During the year, the students should engage in several writing projects, such as letters or invitations to family members and friends, stories, accounts of personal experiences, and lists. After writing a piece, a child should read it to an adult, who might want to transcribe it on another sheet of paper if the original is not readable. Transcriptions should be kept with the written pieces in a writing folder, which becomes a file of the child's writing development. As Sulzby and Barnhart (1992) commented,

> Many people are still shocked at the ease with which children at kindergarten age (or younger) write, when we invite them and if we accept the forms of writing they prefer. From working with and observing hundreds of classrooms, we can say confidently that all kindergartners reared in a literate culture like our own can and will write. (pp. 125–126)

Real Writing for Real Purposes

Emphasis in a writing program for young children is on writing a variety of pieces for a variety of reasons. Young children adopt different strategies for different tasks. They might use invented spelling when compiling a list but use scribbling for a lengthy tale (Martinez & Teale, 1987). Real-life activities have the effect of motivating them to use more sophisticated techniques. When writing invitations for the class's Thanksgiving feast, many kindergarten children in an experimental writing program, who until that time had used

Emphasis in a writing program for young children is on writing for a variety of purposes.

scribble writing, chose to use random strings of letters or even to attempt to spell words (Martinez & Teale, 1987).

Making Lists. One writing activity on which young children thrive is making lists. Clay (1975) called the motivation for this activity the inventory principle. Novice writers enjoy creating an inventory of letters or words that they can write. Suggested assignments include making lists of friends, family members, favorite foods, places visited, favorite toys, and so on.

Writing Names. One of the first words that a child learns to spell is his or her name. Special attention should be given to this task, because once children learn their names, they frequently use the letters to spell other words. Thus, each name becomes a source of known letters that can be used in various sequences and combinations (Temple, Nathan, Temple, & Burris, 1993).

Take full advantage of children's interest in their names. Put name tags on their cubbyholes, coat hooks, and/or shelf spaces. Ask the children to sign all their written work. When scheduling individuals for activities or assignments, write their names on the chalkboard so that they become used to seeing and reading their own names, as well as those of the other children.

Using Routines. Whenever possible, use routines to demonstrate literacy lessons. The Kamehameha School in Honolulu, Hawaii, uses a device known as the morning message to impart literacy skills (Kawakami-Arakaki, Oshiro, & Farran, 1989). Written by the teacher, the morning message gives the date and important information about the day's activities. Messages in the beginning of the year are relatively simple, but they become increasingly complex to match the growth in children's skills. A November message might be "Today is Monday, November 12. We will go to the firehouse this morning." The teacher reads it

 Adapting Instruction for Struggling Readers and Writers

Encouraging students to spell a word the way it sounds helps them to make discoveries about the spelling system. If they don't know how to begin, help them go through a word by sound and talk about the letters that spell those sounds. For words like *train, drum, girl,* and *bird,* which are not spelled the way they sound, explain to children that these are "tricky" spellings.

Exemplary Teaching

Writing with Corduroy

Taking Corduroy home served as a motivation for kindergartners to write journal entries. After teacher Marilyn Cook (2006) read *Corduroy* to her students, she explained that she was taking Corduroy (a stuffed version) home with her. They would have an adventure, and she would write about it. The next day, she brought Corduroy back and shared with her students what she had written. She then invited them to take turns taking Corduroy home and telling about their experiences in their journals. She prompted responses with such questions as "What would you like to do if you were Corduroy?" Students drew an illustration of their experience and composed a journal entry themselves or dictated it to someone.

Corduroy's hosts shared their adventures with the rest of the class, reporting that Corduroy played games, watched TV, and even went swimming. Each day, Cook used the journal entries to prompt a writing skill, such as beginning each sentence with a capital letter or allowing spaces between words. The teacher also modeled such writing skills as adding details and composing dialogue. Students composed a rubric for their journal entries: "I drew a picture of Corduroy's adventure at my house. I wrote two or more sentences about what Corduroy did at my house."

FYI

■ Students need lots of practice with sounding out. When using sounding out, first-graders failed to represent all the sounds in half the words. Second-graders did somewhat better, but failed to represent all the sounds in one-third of the words (Rittle-Johnson & Siegler, 1999).

■ The best teachers encourage invented spelling in the beginning stages of literacy development. However, as the teachers introduce students to phonological elements and high-frequency words in reading and spelling, they begin holding students responsible for the correct spelling of words that incorporate those items (Wharton-McDonald, 2001).

USING TECHNOLOGY

Read • Write • Think offers a complete description of Marilyn Cook's lesson "A Journal for Corduroy: Responding to Literature," as well as other high-quality literacy lessons.
http://www.readwritethink.org/lessons/lesson_view.asp?id=30

aloud and encourages the students to read along with her. At this juncture, the teacher wants the children to see that writing is functional (it conveys important information), that one reads writing from left to right and top to bottom, and that written messages are made up of individual words and letters. Later, longer messages are written, and more sophisticated skills—such as the concepts that words are made up of sounds and that certain sounds are represented by certain letters—are stressed. As students learn letter-sound relationships, the writing can be more interactive. Students can be asked to tell what letter each word begins with or even spell out high-frequency words they may have learned.

Students can also be encouraged to add to the morning message. This assures them that what they have to say is important. These additions also help students and the teacher get to know each other better, as the students' contributions might include major family events such as the birth of siblings or the death of grandparents and other news of personal importance.

Help with Spelling

Children should be encouraged to use their knowledge of letter-sound relationships to create spellings, even if the spellings are not accurate. You can foster this process by showing students how to elongate sounds as they spell them. One question that arises in a program emphasizing invented spelling is what to do when children ask how to spell a word. The advice offered most often is to encourage them to spell it as best they can or to say the word very slowly—to stretch it out—and work out the spelling. You might ask, "With what sound does the word start? What letter makes that sound? What sound comes next? What letter spells that sound?" The idea is to have students develop their own sense of the spelling system. If you spell words for students, they will begin to rely on your help instead of constructing their own spellings. Keep in mind that students' invented spellings reflect their understanding of the spelling system. Words that they create belong to them in a way that words that are spelled for them do not (Wilde, 1995).

Providing access to standard spelling could take the form of having picture dictionaries available; placing some frequently requested words on the board; posting word lists of animals, families, colors, foods, or other related items; labeling items; or creating a word wall (see Chapter 4). It could also mean providing assistance when students are unable to work out the spelling of a word and you believe that providing help will further their development.

■ **Dictation** is the process of recounting an experience orally and having someone else write down the words.

Case Study

An Exemplary Writing Program

In the Teachers College Reading and Writing Project, which has been implemented by thousands of teachers over nearly three decades, the ultimate goal is to have kindergarten children write stories that are five or six pages long (Calkins, 2003). Each page has a picture and one or two sentences. The project features a curriculum calendar, in which there is a focus of instruction for each month. Kindergartners start off by drawing pictures and then writing about the pictures, if they can. After three or four weeks, when the children have learned some or all of the letters of the alphabet, the children who at first only drew pictures begin labeling their drawings. The goal is that by the end of September, each kindergartner will be writing his or her name and labeling a drawing. As they label their drawings, children are encouraged to stretch out the words and write the letters for the sounds they hear. At this point, some of the more advanced children will be writing sentences. The goal is that by the end of October or November, most kindergartners will be writing sentences.

Units of study are blocked out for each month. In November, the focus is on writing about small moments, instead of writing stories that begin with waking up and end with going to bed. Recording sounds and leaving spaces between words are emphasized. In December, the focus is on writing for readers. Emphasis is on beginning sentences with capital letters, recording sounds, and using end punctuation so that readers will find it easier to read the story. The goal is to have most children using letter-sound correspondences by January. Teachers encourage students to spell as best they can. If students are having difficulty, teachers provide support by having them say the sounds in a word; if students cannot think of the letters that spell the sounds, the teachers supply them. In subsequent units, children write information pieces. They write a procedural text by using pictures and words to explain a process: feeding a dog, kicking a soccer ball, shooting a basket in basketball. Students also write an "All About" book, in which they write about T-ball, taking care of a puppy, or another topic with which they have personal experience.

The program is carefully managed. Students keep their work in writing folders and work at assigned tables. The folders have colored dots that correspond to the table color. A table monitor brings materials to the table. There is a toolbox for each table that contains pencils, markers, paper, staplers, glue sticks, and any other supplies that might be needed.

Occasionally, you might have students attempt to spell the word as best they can and then write the conventional spelling above their attempt, saying, "Here's how we usually spell ____. Look how close you came" (Ruddell & Ruddell, 1995, p. 103). Any help that you supply should take into account the student's understanding of the spelling system. If, for instance, the child spells *truck* with CH, you should say, "Truck sounds like it begins with a *ch* as in *Charles*, but it begins with a *t* as in *Tim* and an *r* as in *Raymond*" (Wilde, 1995).

Although students are encouraged to explore the writing system through invented spellings, they should be held accountable for any letter relationships they have been taught. If students have been taught initial *m* or *s*, they should be held accountable for spelling these sounds, although you might provide some prompting such as modeling the process of sounding out the first sound so as to be better able to perceive it (Invernizzi, Meier, Swank, & Juel, 2001).

Whatever you do, have a clear policy—one based on your beliefs about invented spelling. Be sure to explain your policy to both students and their parents. Parents should understand that one reason for encouraging children to write before they can spell conventionally is that it gives them a reason to learn the real system, the "code."

Dictation in the Writing Program

Although students should be encouraged to write as best they can, they may choose to dictate on occasion, such as when they are expressing heartfelt feelings or recounting events that touch them deeply. The content may be so intense that they cannot handle both it and the form. For example, one young student, who usually wrote on her own, chose to dictate when she told the story of how her mother had been involved in a serious auto accident. Both teacher-initiated and child-initiated writing and **dictation** are vital elements of a

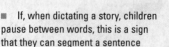

FYI

■ If, when dictating a story, children pause between words, this is a sign that they can segment a sentence into words (Oken-Wright, 1998).

■ With the acceptance of invented spelling, dictation of experience stories has been deemphasized. However, children's dictated pieces are more fully developed than those that they compose themselves. When content is essential, dictation is the better approach.

literacy program, as "they provide process as well as content for beginning reading" (Fields, Spangler, & Lee, 1991, p. 52).

Dictation helps children see the relationship between speaking and writing. They can see that if they speak too fast, the scribe has a difficult time keeping up. Over time, they learn to pace their dictation so that it matches the scribe's ability to record it. Of course, the scribe can also point out letters, words, and sentences while writing so that the child is better able to see the relationship between written and spoken language. One thing that should be made clear is the role of dictation. The teacher does not want to create the impression that he or she is writing because the student cannot. The teacher should explain that dictating is another way of writing. In addition to being used to capture emotional stories that individuals have to tell, dictated writing can also be used to record a group experience (Sulzby, Teale, & Kamberelis, 1989).

■ ■ ■ Checkup ■ ■ ■

1. What are some ways in which writing might be developed?

■ ■ ■

Planned Instruction of Essential Understandings

Setting the stage for developing reading and writing is important and arranging for many opportunities to read and write is vital, but explicit instruction should also be a key element in the literacy program. This is especially true when students are struggling.

Direct instruction should take place within the context of the kinds of reading and writing activities that are being explored in this chapter. Two areas in which students are most likely to need direct instruction are **phonological awareness** (ability to detect rhyme and beginning sounds and to hear separate sounds in words) and the alphabetic principle (the system by which speech sounds are represented by letters). In fact, the major cause of difficulty in learning to read is a deficiency in these areas (Adams, 1990).

Children vary greatly in knowledge of the alphabet and phonological awareness. In the fall of 1998, trained assessors conducted standardized, one-on-one assessments with a representative sample of about 22,000 kindergartners (West, Denton, & Germino-Hausken, 2000). A majority of entering kindergartners (66 percent) could recognize letters of the alphabet by name, whether they were upper- or lowercase. However, most kindergartners could not point to letters representing sounds at the beginning or end of simple words, read basic words in isolation, or read more complex words in the context of a sentence. Only about two children out of a hundred could read high-frequency words. And only about one in a hundred could read sentences (see Table 3.8). However, children raised in poverty are less proficient. Only 41 percent of children whose caregivers were receiving welfare benefits could identify the letters of the alphabet.

Learning the Letters of the Alphabet

Although it seems logical that students would learn letters by memorizing their shapes, that is not the way it happens. They learn to tell one letter from another and to identify particular letters by noting distinctive features such as whether lines are curved or slanted, open or closed (Gibson, Gibson, Pick, & Osser, 1962). To perceive distinctive features, students must be given many experiences comparing and contrasting letters. When introducing letters, teachers should present at least two at a time so that students can contrast them. It is also a good idea to present letters that have dissimilar appearances—*s* and *b*, for

FYI

■ The two best predictors of future success in reading are phonemic awareness and letter knowledge.

■ Children generally know more uppercase letters than lowercase ones. Uppercase letters are easier to learn, and adults generally write in uppercase when writing for children.

■ When should the alphabet be introduced? "As soon as the child is encouraged to write his name, his attention is being directed to letters. Often, the first two or three letters that occur in his name become distinctive because of these efforts" (Clay, 1991, pp. 266–267).

■ **Phonological awareness** is the consciousness of the sounds in words. It includes the ability to detect rhyme and separate the sounds in words. It is a broad term and includes the concept of phonemic awareness.

■■■ **TABLE 3.8** **Percentage of Kindergartners Passing Each Reading Proficiency Level**

Letter Recognition	Beginning Sounds	Ending Sounds	High-Frequency Words	Words in Context
66%	29%	17%	2%	1%

instance. Presenting similar letters such as *b* and *d* together can cause confusion. It is recommended, too, that upper- and lowercase forms of the letters be introduced at the same time, because students will see both in their reading.

Using names is a good way to introduce the alphabet. Discuss the fact that names are made up of letters. Write your name on the board, and talk about the letters in it. Explain that your first and last names begin with capital letters and that the other letters are lowercase. Write the names of some students, perhaps those that begin with the first three or four letters of the alphabet, and then move to other letters on succeeding days.

To emphasize a letter, ask students to raise their hands if their name has that letter—*m*, for example. Ask them to spell out their names; give assistance if they need it. Write the names on the board—*Manuel, Marcella,* and *Tom,* for example—and have students tell where the *m* is in each name.

Create signs for the class: "Writing Center," "In," "Out," and so on. Let students see you make the signs, and talk about the letters you used. Bring in familiar objects, such as cereal boxes, signs, and posters, and discuss the words printed on them and the letters that make up the words.

Obtain a computer or a typewriter or both. Keyboards invite exploration of the alphabet. If you are using *Dr. Peet's Talk/Writer* (Interest-Driven Learning), which has speech capability, the name of the letter will be pronounced when the child presses the key. Whole words are spoken when the space bar is pressed. *Dr. Peet's Talk/Writer* also has an ABC Discovery module that introduces the alphabet. In one activity, students are prompted to find the letter *P*. When they press the *P* key, they are shown the letter *P* in upper- and lowercase and a picture of two polar bears, and they hear a song that says, "*P* is for polar bear." Stamp printing sets, magnetic letters, and felt letters also encourage working with the alphabet.

Use games such as Alphabet Walk to teach the names of the letters of the alphabet. Place large alphabet cards on the floor. Begin playing music. As the music plays, students walk. When the music stops, they stop. Hold up an alphabet card. Ask the student who is standing on that card to identify it. If students are working on letter sounds, ask the student to tell what sound the letter makes and to name some word that begins with that sound (Invernizzi, Meier, Swank, & Juel, 2001).

As with all learning activities, proceed from the concrete to the abstract. Letters by their very nature are abstract; when they are in the contexts of names, signs, and labels, they are more concrete than letters in isolation.

Display a model alphabet so that students can see how letters are formed. Provide each child with his or her own alphabet to refer to as needed. At this point, do not emphasize letter formation. Students who are overly conscious of forming their letters perfectly will have a difficult time moving beyond that task to writing.

Read to the class some of the many alphabet books that are available. *A to Zoo: Subject Access to Children's Picture Books,* 7th ed. (Lima & Lima, 2006), lists more than 300 alphabet books. Some of these are included in the following Student Reading List. Look for books that present the letters clearly. Overly ornate letters may be aesthetically pleasing, but they can be distracting and confusing. Many of these books show words containing the beginning sound that a particular letter frequently represents. Do not emphasize these letter-sound relationships, as they require advanced skill. Focus instead on the appearance of each letter and how it differs from a similarly formed letter—for example,

Adapting Instruction for English Language Learners

Rafael, a kindergartner, whose family had recently moved from Colombia, was struggling to learn the alphabet and other essential literacy skills. Rafael was adept at learning from others. He spent long periods of time with partners going over books introduced during reading. With help from his friends, he was able to acquire enough skills so that he was successful in first grade.

FYI

The two kinds of typeface are serif and sans serif. A serif is a small line used to complete a stroke in a letter. Sans serif type lacks these strokes. Serif type is more distinctive and easier to read. However, the *a*'s and *g*'s in sans serif type are similar to the *a*'s and *g*'s in manuscript and so may be easier for emergent readers to identify.

USING TECHNOLOGY

For practical suggestions for teaching handwriting, see "How to Teach Letter Recognition" at
http://www.auburn.edu/~murraba

Literacy Center features a number of imaginative, interactive activities for building letter recognition and other emergent literacy skills.
http://www.literacycenter.net

how *y* is different from *t*. Point out that letters have two forms—capital and lowercase. Avoid the words *little* and *big* so that children do not use size to determine whether a letter is upper- or lowercase. When possible, choose alphabet books that present both forms.

Student Reading List

Alphabet Books

Aylesworth, J. (1991). *Old black fly*. New York: Holt. Rhyming text follows a mischievous black fly through the alphabet as he has a very busy day.

Ehlert, L. (1989). *Eating the alphabet*. New York: Harcourt. Drawings of foods beginning with the letter being presented are labeled with their names in both upper- and lowercase letters.

Hoban, T. (1982). *A, B, see!* New York: Greenwillow. Uppercase letters are accompanied by objects in silhouette that begin with the letter shown.

Howland, N. (2000). *ABC drive!* Boston: Clarion. While going for a drive with his mother, a boy encounters an ambulance, a bus, and other ABC items.

Musgrove, M. (1976). *Ashanti to Zulu*. New York: Dial. This Caldecott winner gives information about African tribes as it presents the alphabet.

Onyefulu, I. (1993). *A is for Africa*. New York: Dutton. Color photos and a brief paragraph using the target letter show everyday life in Africa.

Scarry, R. (1973). *Richard Scarry's find your ABC*. New York: Random. Each letter is illustrated with numerous objects and creatures whose names contain the letter.

Wood, A. (2003). *Alphabet mystery*. New York: Blue Sky Press. When the letter *x* is missing, the other 25 letters search for him.

Wood, J. (1993). *Animal parade*. New York: Bradbury. A parade starts with an aardvark, an antelope, and other animals whose names begin with *A* and proceeds through the rest of the letters of the alphabet.

Ziefert, H. (2006). *Me! Me! ABC*. Maplewood, NJ: Blue Apple Books. Dolls make a series of requests.

Reinforcement Activities

Alphabet Knowledge

- Have children create their own alphabet books.
- Help children create name cards. Explain that names begin with uppercase letters but that the other letters in a name are lowercase.
- Make a big book of the alphabet song, and point to the letters and words as children sing along.
- If children are using classroom computers, teach the letters of the alphabet as you teach them keyboarding skills.

■ **A phoneme** is the smallest unit of sound that distinguishes one word from another. *Pit* is different from *pat* because of the difference in the phonemes /i/ and /a/.

■ **Phonemic awareness** is the consciousness of individual sounds in words. It is the realization that a spoken word is composed of a sequence of speech sounds.

■ **Coarticulation** is the process of articulating a sound while still articulating the previous sound—for instance, saying /oy/ while still articulating /t/ in *toy*.

- Encourage students to write as best they can. This will foster learning of the alphabet as they move from using pictures and letterlike forms to actual letters to express themselves.

- As you write messages, announcements, or stories on the board, spell out the words so that students will hear the names of the letters in a very natural way.

- Sing songs, such as "Bingo," that spell out words or use letters as part of their lyrics.

- Read books such as *Chicka Chicka Boom Boom* (Martin & Archambault, 1989), in which letters play a prominent role.

- Most important, provide an environment in which children are surrounded by print. Encourage students to engage in reading and writing activities. These might include "reading" a wordless picture book, using a combination of drawings and letterlike figures to compose a story, creating some sort of list, using invented spelling to write a letter to a friend, exploring a computer keyboard, or listening to a taped account of a story. Interaction with print leads to knowledge of print. The ability to form letters improves without direct instruction (Hildreth, 1936). However, systematic instruction should complement the provision of opportunities to learn. Learning the alphabet is too important to be left to chance.

■ ■ ■ Checkup ■ ■ ■

1. How are the letters of the alphabet learned?
2. What are some ways to teach and reinforce letter knowledge?

■ ■ ■

Building Phonological Awareness

For children, the sounds in words blend so that words seem like the continuation of a single sound. In their natural environment, children do not have to deal with individual sounds; however, the ability to detect speech sounds in words is absolutely crucial for literacy development. Without the ability to abstract separate sounds, they will not be able to understand, for example, that the letter *b* stands for the sound /b/ heard at the beginning of *ball*. They will not even be able to consider a beginning sound because they will not be able to abstract it from the word itself. These children will also have difficulty with rhyme because of their inability to abstract the ending sounds. They may be able to write a few letters, but their writing will not evolve beyond the early alphabetic stage because they will be unable to isolate the sounds of words.

Savin (1972) stated, "In the present author's experience everyone who has failed to learn to read even the simplest prose by the end of first grade has been unable to analyze syllables into phonemes" (p. 321). (**Phonemes** are individual speech sounds. The word *cake* has four letters but three phonemes: /k/, /ā/, /k/.) Savin's assertion was echoed by Elkonin (1973), a Russian psychologist, who maintained that being able to analyze the sounds of words "is the most important prerequisite for the successful learning of reading and writing" (p. 571).

For many children, acquiring **phonemic awareness** is difficult (Snow, Burns, & Griffin, 1998). What makes detecting sounds in words difficult? Two elements: metalinguistic awareness and **coarticulation**. Metalinguistic awareness requires students to reflect on language on an abstract level, to treat language as an object of thought. Coarticulation is a feature of language that makes listening and speaking easy but makes reading difficult. For instance, when saying the word *cat*, you do not say /k/, /a/, /t/; you coarticulate the phonemes: As you form the /k/, you also form the /a/, and as the /a/ is being formed, you coarticulate the final sound /t/. Because of coarticulation, *cat* is a blend of

FYI

Phonemic awareness is not the same as speech discrimination. Speech discrimination is the ability to discriminate the sounds of language, such as being able to tell the difference between *bat* and *hat*. Students having adequate speech discrimination may have difficulty with phonemic awareness. Speech discrimination does not require abstracting sounds, whereas phonemic awareness does (Snow, Burns, & Griffin, 1998).

sounds, rather than three separate sounds. Coarticulation makes it easier to form and perceive words. However, because the sounds in the words are coarticulated, they seem to be one continuous sound and so are difficult for young children to pry apart (Liberman & Shankweiler, 1991).

Language is the foundation for phonological awareness. The larger children's vocabularies are and the better their articulation of speech sounds, the easier it is for them to acquire phonological awareness. Initially, children learn words as wholes. The ability to segment individual sounds in words apparently develops as children's vocabularies grow and they acquire larger numbers of words that have similar pronunciations, such as *cat, can, cap*, and *cab* (Metsala, 1999). For children to be able to distinguish among these words, they must be able to segment words into smaller units of pronunciation. It is theorized that children segment words by syllables and segment syllables by onset and rime and, later, sound by sound. Children with large vocabularies have segmented more words in this way (Metsala, 1999). Because they have elements that occur more frequently, some words will be easier to rhyme or segment than others. Children are better at rhyming *at* words than *ud* words. In other words, they are more likely to be able to say that *cat* and *rat* rhyme than that *bud* and *mud* rhyme. There are more *at* words than *ud* words, so children know more *at* words and thus have had more experience noting differences among them. Words that children learn early and word elements such as *at* that have a large number of examples are easier for students to learn (Metsala, 1999). For novice readers, begin instruction in phonemic awareness with patterns that appear in very basic words that students have learned early and also patterns that encompass many words. These are more likely to have segmented representations in children's memory (Goswami, 2001).

If students' vocabularies are limited, they may have difficulty with phonemic awareness. Students may also have difficulty with phonemic awareness if their pronunciation of sounds lacks accuracy and distinctiveness (Elbro, Bornstrom, & Petersen, 1998). Fostering language development lays a foundation for phonological awareness.

■ ■ ■ Checkup ■ ■ ■

1. What is phonological awareness?
2. Why is phonological awareness so essential but so difficult to learn? ■ ■ ■

Word Play. One of the best ways to develop phonological awareness is to have fun with words. As students play and experiment with language, they become aware of it on a more abstract level. They begin to think of words as words and become aware of the sounds of language on an abstract level. In addition to playing games with words in the classroom, read books that have fun with words, especially those that call attention to the parts of words.

An excellent book for developing phonological awareness is *Jamberry* (Degen, 1983), in which both real and nonsense words are formed by adding *berry* to a variety of words. After reading the tale to students, have them create *berry* words. *Don't Forget the Bacon!* (Hutchins, 1976) is another good choice for developing phonological awareness. Afraid that he will forget an item on his shopping list (six farm eggs, a cake for tea, and a pound of pears), the child rehearses the list as he heads for the store. Unfortunately, as he rehearses it, he makes substitutions in some of the words so that "a cake for tea" becomes "a cake for me" and later "a rake for leaves." Read the story to students, and discuss how the boy kept changing the sounds. This will build their awareness of sounds in words. Also have them role-play the rehearsing of the shopping list so that they can see firsthand how the sounds in the words are changed (Griffith & Olson, 1992). In *The Hungry Thing Goes to a Restaurant* (Slepian & Seidler, 1992), initial sounds are substituted. When the Hungry Thing orders a meal, the staff can't understand what he wants when he orders things such as bapple moose and spoonadish. As you read the story, have students guess what the

Hungry Thing was ordering (apple juice and tuna fish). Other books that play with sounds include most of the Dr. Seuss books and the sheep series by Shaw (including *Sheep in a Jeep*, *Sheep on a Ship*, and *Sheep in a Shop*).

Developing the Concept of Rhyme. Because longer units are easier to perceive than individual speech sounds, a good place to begin to develop phonological awareness is through rhymes, which are the easiest of the phonological awareness tasks for most students (Yopp, 1988). Read nursery rhymes and other rhyming tales to the students to help them develop the ability to detect rhyme. In a study conducted in Great Britain, children who knew nursery rhymes were better at detecting rhyme and also did better in early reading than those who had no such knowledge (Maclean, Bryant, & Bradley, 1987). At first, just read the nursery rhymes and rhyming tales so that the children enjoy the stories and the sounds. They may memorize some of the rhymes if they wish. Books that might be used to introduce and reinforce the concept of rhyme are listed in the Student Reading List.

Adapting Instruction for English Language Learners

ELLs may find detecting beginning sounds easier than detecting rhymes.

Student Reading List

Rhyming Books

Barrett, J. (2000). *I knew two who said moo.* New York: Atheneum. Humorous sentences contain words that rhyme with the number words *one* to *twenty*.

Cameron, P. (1961). *"I can't," said the ant.* New York: Coward. With the help of an army of ants and some spiders, an ant helps repair a broken teapot amid the encouragement of the kitchen's inhabitants.

dePaola, T. (1985). *Tomie dePaola's Mother Goose.* New York: Putnam. Traditional verses are accompanied by dePaola's lighthearted illustrations.

Fisher, J. (2000). *Pass the celery, Ellery.* New York: Stewart, Tabori & Chang. People pass a food that rhymes with their names: "Pass the egg, Meg."

Franton, D. (2002). *My beastie book of ABC rhymes and woodcuts.* New York: HarperCollins. Humorous animal rhymes.

Hague, M. (1993). *Teddy Bear Teddy Bear.* New York: Morrow. In this action rhyme, Teddy Bear is asked to do such things as turn around, touch the ground, and show his shoes.

Hale, G. (Ed.) (2003). *An illustrated treasury of read-aloud poems for young people: More than 100 of the world's best-loved poems for parent and child to share.* New York: Black Dog & Leventhal. This collection of new and classic poems was selected for young people.

Harwayne, S. (1995). *Jewels, children's play rhymes.* Greenvale, NY: Mondo. Twenty play rhymes from around the world include brief poems, as well as action, game, jump rope, and song rhymes.

Lobel, A. (1986). *The Random House book of Mother Goose.* New York: Random House. More than 300 nursery rhymes are presented.

Marzollo, J. (1990). *Pretend you're a cat.* New York: Dial. Rhyming verses ask the reader to purr like a cat, scratch like a dog, leap like a squirrel, and so on.

Raffi. (1987). *Down by the bay.* New York: Crown. This song celebrates silly rhymes: "Did you ever see a whale with a polka-dot tail, down by the bay?"

Samuells, J. (2003). *A nose like a hose.* New York: Scholastic. A little elephant has a very long nose.

Tafuri, N. (2006). *Five little chicks.* New York: Simon & Schuster. A mother hen helps her chicks find food.

Wong, E. Y. (1992). *Eek! There's a mouse in the house.* Boston: Houghton Mifflin. After the discovery of a mouse in the house, larger and larger animals are sent in, one after another, with increasingly chaotic results.

Wong, J. S. (2005). *Hide & seek.* San Diego, CA: Harcourt. A boy, his dad, and the family dog play hide and seek.

INVOLVING PARENTS

Parents can help their children develop phonological awareness by playing word games with them, reading rhyming stories to them, reciting traditional nursery rhymes, and singing songs.

Adapting Instruction for English Language Learners

When working with ELLs, focus on speech sounds that are common to both languages. Avoid sounds that might be unfamiliar to students until they have had a chance to learn them. Spanish has no short *a*, *i*, or *u*, but does have the long vowels. Start phonemic awareness with words containing long vowels. See Table 12.2 for an overview of differences between English and Spanish.

FYI

Being able to detect beginning sounds is a more important skill than being able to detect rhymes. Students are ready for instruction in phonics when they can detect beginning sounds; they are not yet ready when they can detect rhyme but not beginning sounds. Focus instruction on beginning sounds.

Discuss any rhyming stories that you read to the children, thereby building a background of literacy. In time, discuss the concept of rhyme itself. Lead students to see that the last word in one line has the same ending sound as the last word in another line. Reread some of the nursery rhymes aloud, emphasizing the rhyming words. Explain what rhyming words are, using examples such as *rake/cake, bell/well, ice/mice*, and so on. Also build rhymes with students. Using the element *an*, here is how a rhyme might be built: Say "an." Have students say "an." Explain to students that you are going to make words that have *an* in them. Say "c-an," emphasizing the *an* portion of the word. Ask students if they can hear the *an* in *c-an*. Holding up a picture of a can, have them say *can* and listen to the *an* in *c-an*. (By using pictures, you are reducing the burden on students' memories.) Hold up a picture of a pan. Have students tell what it is. Tell students that *p-an* has *an* in it. Ask them if they can hear the *an* in *f-an* as you hold up a picture of a fan. Introduce *man* and *van* in the same way. Ask students if they can tell what sound is the same in *can, pan, man, fan*, and *van*. Stress the *an* in each of these words. Explain that *can, pan, man, fan* and *van* rhyme because they all have *an* at the end. Invite students to suggest other words that rhyme with *can: tan, Dan, Jan, plan, ran* (Gunning, 2000c). Build other rhymes in similar fashion.

Reinforcement Activities

The Concept of Rhyme

■ Have students supply the final rhyming word of a couplet:

There was an old lady who lived in a shoe. She had so many children she didn't know what to _____.

I like to run. It's so much _____.

■ Students can compose a rhyming pictionary in which they paste on each page illustrations of words that rhyme. A typical page might include pictures of a man, a can, a fan, and a pan. Pictures might come from old magazines, workbooks, or computer clip art, or they can be drawn.

■ Read a rhyming story or verse to students. Pause before the rhyming word and have them predict what the word might be.

■ Have students sort cards containing illustrations of objects whose names rhyme. Begin by providing a model card (cat) and having students arrange rhyming cards under it (*bat, rat, hat*). Provide students with cards that do not rhyme with *cat*, as well as those that do. Later, have students sort two or three rhyming patterns at the same time. Discuss students' sorting.

■ Play the game I Spy using rhyming clues. "I spy something that rhymes with *walk* and *talk*" (chalk) (Ericson & Juliebo, 1998).

■ Sing traditional songs that have a strong rhyming element. After singing a song once, have students listen to a second singing to detect rhyming words. Also sing all of two rhyming lines except the last word, and let students say or sing the missing word.

Blending

Through blending, students create words by combining word parts. Blending builds on students' ability to rhyme and prepares them for segmenting or noting the beginning sounds in words. In the activities below, students blend onsets and rimes. The onset is the consonant or consonant cluster preceding the rime: *f-, pl-, scr-*. The rime is the part of the word following the onset, consisting of a vowel or vowels and any consonants that follow: *-at,*

-ot, -een. Using a hand puppet, tell students that the puppet says its words in parts. Instead of saying *moon* the way we do, it says *m-oon*; so we have to help the puppet by putting the parts of the word together. Have students help put the following words together: *m-an, s-and, h-at, r-at, r-an.* Present the words in groups of four. In order to actively involve all students, provide each student with a set of pictures showing the four words. When you say the word to be blended, students choose the picture that shows the word and hold it up. By observing students, you can tell who is catching on and who is struggling. Discuss the names of the pictures before beginning the activity so that students know them:

cat, hat, bat, rat

can, man, pan, fan

king, ring, wing, ball

lock, rock, sock, mop

pie, tie, tire, bus

After students have held up the picture for the word being blended, have them say the word. Affirm students' efforts but correct wrong responses. For a correct response, you might say, "Hat. That is correct. When you put /h/ and /at/ together, you get *hat.*" For an incorrect response, you might say, "That was a good try. But when I put /f/ and /an/ together, I get *fan.* You say it: *f-an—fan.*" After students have completed a group, go through it again. Encourage them to put the words together faster. If students have difficulty with the activity, provide assistance or go back to rhyming activities.

Have students solve riddles that incorporate both rhyming and blending:

I'm thinking of a word that begins with /m/ and rhymes with *pan.*

. . . begins with /h/ and rhymes with *pot.*

. . . begins with /s/ and rhymes with *wing.*

. . . begins with /r/ and rhymes with *king.*

Perceiving Beginning Consonant Sounds

Students will have difficulty learning phonics if they are unable to perceive the sounds of beginning consonants. For example, if a child confuses the sound /p/ with the sound /d/, when he or she is taught the letter that represents /p/, the child may actually associate it with the sound /d/, or vice versa.

To introduce the concept of beginning sounds, read and discuss *The Story of Z* (Modesitt, 1990), if possible. Tired of being last, *Z* leaves the alphabet so that children say things such as, "Can we go to the oo and see the ebras?" Have students supply the missing beginning sound and tell what the sound is. Using the same technique employed in *The Story of Z,* hold up objects or pictures of objects or creatures and ask such questions as "Is this an ee? (while holding up a picture of a bee). What is it? What sound did I leave off?" While holding up a pen, ask, "Is this an en?" Do the same with other objects and pictures. Another easy way to convey the concept of beginning sound is to ask questions such as "Do you hear /s/ in *sock* or *rock*?" (Murray, 2006b). (It's helpful if you are holding a sock and a rock.) Build on the student's response. Say, if the answer is correct, "Yes, you are right: *sssock* begins with an /s/ sound." If the answer is incorrect, say, "That's a good try. But *sock* begins with an /s/ sound."

Also, or as an alternative introduction, read aloud alliterative stories or alphabet books such as *Emma's Elephant & Other Favorite Animal Friends* (Ellwand, 1996), which features alliterative captions, or *Flatfoot Fox and the Case of the Bashful Beaver* (Clifford, 1995), which has a character who speaks in alliterative sentences. Some other alliterative books that might be used to reinforce the idea of beginning consonant sounds are listed in the following Student Reading List. At first, simply read such a book as you would any other picture book, showing pictures and discussing content. Then, lead students to see that

FYI

■ Rhyming and detecting beginning sounds are close in difficulty. Some students may actually find that noting that two words begin with the same sound is easier than detecting rhyme (Gough, Larson & Yopp, 2001).

■ Most major basal series introduce initial consonant correspondences and short-vowel patterns at the kindergarten level.

■ Books such as *Hoot and Holler* (Brown, 2001), in which two owl friends learn to overcome their shyness, can be used to develop a foundation for phonological awareness as children hear the alliterative names of the main characters and the drawn out *hoo-oot* as Hoot searches for Holler and as friends call out the words *yoo-hoo* and *too-hoo.*

many of the words begin with the same sound, and let them read some selections along with you. For instance, read the following from *Nedobeck's Alphabet Book* (Nedobeck, 1981):

Little Leonard Lion climbs a
Ladder to mail a Love Letter to Lori.

Also read the *L* page from Judith Gwyn Brown's (1976) *Alphabet Dreams*:

My name is Lucy,
And my husband's name is Lee.
We live in a log,
And we sell lamps.

Student Reading List

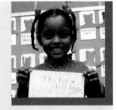

Alliterative Books for Reinforcing Beginning Consonants

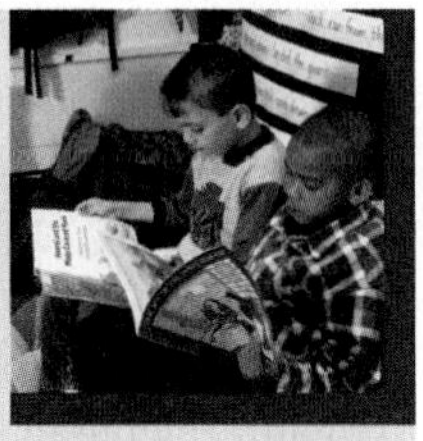

Bandes, H. (1993). *Sleepy river*. New York: Philomel. During a canoe ride at nightfall, a Native American mother and child glimpse ducks, fireflies, bats, and other wonders of nature.

Base, G. (1987). *Animalia*. New York: Harry N. Abrams. Each letter is illustrated and accompanied by an alliterative phrase, such as "Lazy lions lounging in the local library."

Bayer, J. (1984). *A, my name is Alice*. New York: Dial. The well-known jump rope rhyme that is built on letters of the alphabet is illustrated with animals from all over the world.

Cole, J., & Calmenson, S. (1993). *Six sick sheep*. New York: Morrow. This is a collection of all kinds of tongue twisters.

Geisel, T. S. (1973). *Dr. Seuss's ABC*. New York: Random. Letters of the alphabet are accompanied by an alliterative story and humorous illustrations.

Kellogg, S. (1987). *Aster Aardvark's alphabet adventures*. New York: Morrow. A highly alliterative story accompanies each letter.

Knutson, K. (1993). *Ska-tat*. New York: Macmillan. Children describe playing in the colorful, crunchy autumn leaves as the leaves fall to the ground.

Schwartz, A. (1972). *Busy buzzing bumblebees and other tongue twisters*. New York: HarperCollins. This is another fun collection of tongue twisters.

Steig, J. (1992). *Alpha beta chowder*. New York: HarperCollins. An alliterative, humorous verse for each letter of the alphabet is presented.

Stevenson, J. (1983). *Grandpa's great city tour*. New York: Greenwillow. Letters in upper- and lowercase are accompanied by numerous unlabeled objects whose names begin with the sound commonly associated with the letter being presented.

Adapting Instruction for Struggling Readers and Writers

Read, Write & Type! (Talking Fingers) is a research-based program that reinforces phonological awareness, decoding, writing, and comprehension. Because it uses a talking keyboard that says the sound of the letter being typed, this program is especially effective at building phonemic awareness and beginning consonant correspondences.

Reinforcement Activities

The Concept of Beginning Sounds

- Recite traditional alliterative pieces such as "Peter Piper picked a peck of pickled peppers," and have students attempt to repeat them. See *The Little Book of Big Tongue Twisters* by Foley Curtis (1977) or *Six Sick Sheep: 101 Tongue Twisters* by Cole and Calmenson (1993) for examples of alliterative pieces

USING TECHNOLOGY

Tongue twisters tested with students can be found at Wallach and Wallach's Tongue Twisters:
http://www.auburn.edu/~murraba/twisters.html

■ **Segmenting** is dividing a word into its separate sounds—cat is segmented as /k/, /a/, /t/.

■ **Continuants** are consonant sounds that are articulated with a continuous stream of breath: /s/, /f/, /h/, /w/, /m/, /r/, /l/, /sh/, /th/, /th/, /v/, /z/, /zh/, and /n/.

to accompany nearly every beginning sound. After reading each piece, give students examples of what is meant by "begin with the same sound," and then have them tell which words begin with the same sound.

- Say a word, and have students supply other words that begin with the same sound. Discuss students' names that begin with the same sound, such as *Benjamin, Barbara,* and *Billy.*

- Play the game I Spy with students. Tell them that you spy something whose name begins like the word *boat.* Encourage them to say the names of objects in the classroom that begin like *boat.* If necessary, give added clues: "It has covers. It can be read."

- Using a troll doll or puppet, have it say that only people whose names begin like the name *Sandy* (or whatever name you choose) may cross the bridge. Supply names, and have students tell which persons are allowed to cross (Stahl, 1990).

- Have students sort cards containing illustrations of objects whose names begin with the same sound (*ball, boy, banana, baby*). Sorts can be closed or open. In a closed sort, you provide a model (illustration of a ball). In an open sort, you provide the items (illustrations of /b/ words and /s/ words), and children decide how to sort them. Be sure to model sorting.

- Encourage students to stretch out the sounds of words as they write them, saying *soap* as "sss-ooo-ppp." This helps build awareness of separate sounds in words as well as perception of beginning sounds. It also helps students determine how to spell words.

Segmenting Words

After students have developed some sense of rhyme, blending, and initial sounds, introduce the concept of **segmenting**, or separating words into sounds. This can be done as you lead the class in reading a big book, an experience story, or the morning message. Choose two-phoneme words whose sounds are easily discriminated, and then elongate the words and discuss their sounds. For instance, after reading "Goldilocks and the Three Bears," stretch out the words *he, me, see,* and *she,* and help students abstract the separate sounds. After students can segment two-phoneme words, move on to words that have three phonemes. Focus on words that have **continuants** such as /s/ or /m/, because these are easier to say and detect than stops such as /b/ and /d/, which distort following vowels more than continuants do. Also teach the sounds that students will need to know to read and spell words. If the first words they are going to learn are *see* and *me,* teach /s/ and /m/.

As students try their hand at spelling, encourage them to stretch out words so that they can hear the sounds. As you write on the board, say the separate sounds that correspond to the letters so that students can hear them. As you write *Bob has a new pet,* say, "B-o-b h-a-z uh n-oo p-e-t." After students have begun to catch on to the concept of sounds, say words slowly and ask students to tell how many sounds are in them.

If students experience difficulty learning to segment words, you might try a technique designed by Blachman and colleagues (1994) known as Say It and Move It. As students say a sound in a word, they move a blank tile down the page. Looking at a picture of a man, the student would say /m/ while moving a first tile, /a/ while moving a second tile, and /n/ while moving a third tile. Later, the students might use a procedure suggested by Elkonin (1973) and widely used in intervention programs. Elkonin attempted to make the abstract skill of segmenting more concrete by using drawings and markers. The student is given a drawing of a short word, below which are blocks that correspond to the number of sounds in the word. Below a drawing of the word *sun,* for instance, there are three blocks, as in Figure 3.4. Markers are placed in the blocks to represent the three sounds in *sun.* To introduce the technique, carry out the steps outlined in Lesson 3.1. As students learn letter-sound relationships, they might fill in the blocks with the letters that represent the sounds.

 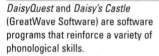

■■ ■ FIGURE 3.4
Elkonin Boxes

Source: *Word Building: Beginnings* by
T. Gunning, 1994. New York: Phoenix
Learning Resources. Reprinted by per-
mission of Galvin Publications.

FYI

According to Elkonin (1973), five- and
six-year-olds who used his technique
were able to learn to segment words.

**Adapting Instruction for
Struggling Readers
and Writers**

Elkonin blocks can be used informally. If a student is struggling with
the spelling of a word, draw one
box for each sound so that the student can see how many sounds the
word has. Encourage the student
to spell any sounds that he or she
can, and give help with the rest.

Lesson 3.1

Elkonin Phonemic Segmentation Technique

Step 1.
  Explain the task, model it, and guide the child through it.

Step 2.
  Give the child a drawing of the sun. Remind the child to say the
word that names the picture and to stretch the word out so that she
or he can hear the separate sounds. If the child has difficulty noting the sounds, very
carefully and deliberately pronounce the word. Emphasize each sound, but do not distort the word.

Step 3.
  Have the child put a marker in each block while saying each sound. The number of
blocks tells the child how many separate sounds there are in a word. The child says
/s/ and puts a marker in the first block, then says /u/ and puts a marker in the second
block, and finally puts a marker in the third block while saying /n/.

Step 4.
  As the child becomes more proficient, eliminate the blocks and markers, and have
her or him simply tell how many sounds are in a word.

  Once a child begins to catch on to the concept of segmenting, you might record a
word's letters in the appropriate blocks. The child then puts markers on the letters that represent the segmented sounds.

■ ■ ■ Checkup ■ ■ ■

  1. What are the key phonological awareness skills?
  2. How might they be introduced and reinforced?

■ ■ ■

Forming Sounds

Being aware of articulation fosters phonological awareness. Skjelfjord (1976) found that students did better when they were trained to prolong continuant sounds such as /s/ and /f/ and to stress plosives such as /p/, /b/, and /t/. In segmentation tests, students often said the word silently before responding. The harder a word was to segment, the more they repeated the word.

The easiest sounds to perceive are continuants because they are articulated with a continuous stream of breath: /f/, /h/, /l/, /m/, /n/, /w/, /r/, /s/, /sh/, /th/, /<u>th</u>/, /v/, /z/, /zh/, and /sh/. Other consonant sounds cannot be continued: /b/, /d/, /p/, /ch/, /j/, /k/, /t/, and /y/. To emphasize continuants such as /s/ or /m/, students can simply elongate the sound as in "ssssun" and "mmman." For sounds that cannot be elongated, students may use a process known as iteration, in which they repeat the sound as in "g-g-g-goat."

Sounds differ according to where they are formed, how they are formed, and whether they are voiced or unvoiced (see Tables 3.2 and 3.3 on p. 109). Demonstrating how and where sounds are formed helps students become aware of separate sounds. For instance, for the sounds /b/ and /p/, have them note how their lips make a popping sound. For /t/ or /d/, have them notice how they use their tongues to make the sound. For /f/ or /v/, they might note the use of teeth and lips. For /th/, they might note the use of teeth and tongue. For /n/, they might note the use of tongue and nose. For /m/, they might note how their lips come and stay together to make the sound and how the nose is used. Students could see what happens when they hold their noses and try to articulate one of the nasals: /m/, /n/, or /ŋ/. They might note, too, that some sounds—the stops, /b/, /d/, /k/, /g/, /p/, /t/—pop out, but the continuants are articulated with a continuous stream of breath. Students might note that /p/ and /b/ are both produced in the same way and in the same part of the mouth. However, /b/ is voiced—the larynx vibrates when it is articulated—and /p/ is not. Most consonants occur in pairs of voiced and unvoiced sounds (the first sound in each pair here is the voiced one): /d/–/t/, /g/–/k/, /z/–/s/, /v/–/f/, /zh/ (pleasure)–/sh/, /j/–/ch/, /<u>th</u>/ (that)–/th/ (think). The sound /h/ is formed by forcing air through an opening in the larynx, the glottis (Gunning, 2000c).

In the LIPS (Lindamood Phoneme Sequencing) Program (Lindamood & Lindamood, 1998), students are taught to become aware of the speech articulation movements involved in creating sounds by analyzing the way in which they form sounds. For instance, students can tell that there are three phonemes in the word *meat* because three movements are needed to articulate the word: lips closing for /m/, lips opening in a smile for /ee/, and tongue tapping the roof of the mouth for the final /t/. Sounds are given names based on the way they are formed. Sounds such as /p/ and /b/, for instance, are known as lip poppers. In the NewPhonics program (Birnbaum, 1999), which is designed for kindergartners, students are shown photos of faces of children articulating speech sounds. Each photograph has a descriptive label, such as the "itchy nose card" for the short-*i* sound, and a description of facial characteristics involved in the production of that phoneme. Helping children

Adapting Instruction for English Language Learners

ELLs have a difficult time segmenting English words because they are still learning the language. Blending sounds is easier because the separate sounds are pronounced for them. Use blending as a way of building an awareness of separate sounds in words.

FYI

■ If children cannot abstract the separate sounds in *hat* or the beginning sound of *ball*, they may learn to read a few words by sheer rote memory but will not be able to sound out words.

■ Having phonemic awareness means that the student must be able to abstract the sound from a real word and use it to read that word. Seeing the letter *m*, one struggling student could say /m/, but he could not say and blend /m/ and /ē/ when he saw the word *me*. Though he could say /m/ for the letter *m*, he could not apply this to a real word. He was unable to manipulate phonemes and so lacked genuine phonemic awareness.

The IRA recognizes the importance of phonological awareness. It recommends combining fun activities such as reading nursery rhymes and playing with language with direct instruction as needed. However, the IRA has some concern that research findings on phonemic awareness might be misused. "For example, mandates that require teachers to dedicate specific amounts of time to phonemic awareness instruction could compromise other important aspects of the literacy curriculum. The Association strongly supports a balanced approach to teaching reading—one that recognizes the importance of comprehension and enjoyment as much as discrete language skills" (International Reading Association, 1998a).

IRA Position Statement

on Key Issue

Phonological Awareness

■ How much phonemic awareness is needed before students are able to grasp phonics? Stahl (1998) asserts that the ability to segment or perceive initial consonants is sufficient.

■ Integrating phonemic awareness and instruction in phonics and spelling is the most effective way to foster early literacy. After learning to identify and/or segment initial sounds, students should use this knowledge to read and spell words that begin with the sound taught.

become aware of how sounds are formed may help them better perceive and then separate sounds in words, especially if they are struggling with this concept. However, this instruction can be informal and need not involve intensive study of how sounds are formed. Learning how sounds are articulated is a means to an end and not an end in itself.

Phonemic awareness may be learned through interaction with print, through specific training in segmenting and other skills, or through some combination of the two. Watson (1984) concluded that an underlying cognitive factor may be necessary for the development of phonemic awareness that is above and beyond what is required to develop listening and speaking skills. Thus, students who are skilled users of language may not acquire phonemic awareness, even when working with print, without some sort of intervention.

Integrating Phonological Awareness and Phonics

Although phonological awareness is an essential skill, it should be taught in functional fashion. Because it is so important, there is a tendency in some programs to teach phonological awareness in isolation and to teach more phonological awareness than is necessary. Phonological awareness is most effective when students learn to segment and identify phonemes as part of learning to read and write rather than as an isolated skill (Bus & van Ijzendoorn, 1999; Vandervelden & Siegel, 1997). Because the letters in a word represent the word's sounds, working with letters is a way of marking sounds. "Learning to attend to letters in words and relating these to how words sound appeared to make explicit the underlying phonemic structure" (Vandervelden & Siegel, 1997, p. 78). In a series of studies, students taught by an integrated approach outperformed those who were taught either phonemic awareness or phonics in isolation. "Letters may draw the child's attention to the sounds in spoken words, and a distinct visual symbol for each phoneme may anchor the phonemes perceptually" (Bus & van IJzendoorn, 1999, p. 412).

Instruction should also be geared to the students' level of understanding and need to know. Apparently, students do not need a high level of phonemic awareness before being able to tackle phonics. Being able to perceive and segment beginning sounds should be enough to get them started on learning initial consonant correspondences (Stahl, 1998). As they study initial consonant correspondences, they can do so in such a way that their phonemic awareness is enhanced. Stretching out sounds as they spell words ("mm-maaannn"), making new words by changing the initial consonant (making *hat* from *cat* by substituting *h* for *c*), and similar activities build phonemic awareness.

If students are about to be instructed in final consonants, that is the time to teach them to segment or isolate final sounds. If they are about to learn vowel sounds, they need to be able to segment all the sounds in a word (Stahl & McKenna, 2002). Some skills, such as deleting a sound from a word (say *sting* without the /t/) may be beyond what is necessary. On the other hand, phonological awareness should be an integral part of phonics and spelling lessons. Students can't learn to decode or spell sounds if they cannot detect them. Apparently, each phoneme needs to be understood individually. It is possible for a child to be able to abstract initial /s/ from a word but not initial /m/. When teaching a new phonics element such as *m* = /m/, be sure to teach students how to detect the sound /m/ at the beginning of *m* words (Stahl & McKenna, 2002). One reason students struggle with consonant clusters such as *st* or *bl* is that they may have difficulty segmenting the separate sounds in the clusters. Part of teaching students how to decode clusters is teaching them how to segment the sounds in a cluster. Students also do better when they are taught in small groups and when only key skills are emphasized (Ehri et al., 2001). Placing students in small groups means that that they can be taught according to their needs and that they get more individualized attention.

Speech-to-Print Phonics

One highly successful integrated program used speech-to-print recognition. Students were required only to recognize the printed form of a word spoken by the teacher. This is a relatively easy task and is highly recommended for use with students who are struggling with other approaches. The teacher presents a letter-sound correspondence, such as *m* = /m/, and shows students two cards—one of which contains a word that incorporates the correspondence. The teacher then asks students to point to the word that contains that correspondence. After two correspondences have been presented, the students are shown two words, one of which contains the correspondence just taught and one of which contains a correspondence previously taught. For instance, having taught the correspondences *s* = /s/ and *m* = /m/, the teacher presents the words *man* and *sun* and asks students to point to the word that says *man*. After a third correspondence has been taught, students choose from all three. However, as additional correspondences are introduced, drop one so that students are not required to choose from more than three correspondences. Choose correspondences whose letter names are known by students. An adapted lesson is presented in Lesson 3.2.

Lesson 3.2

Sample Lesson: Speech-to-Print—Introducing the Correspondence *m* = /m/

Step 1. Phonemic awareness
Teach the correspondence *m* = /m/. You might do this with a storybook such as *Moo in the Morning* (Maitland, 2000). Read the book aloud, and discuss it. Talk about the words *moo* and *morning* and how they begin with the same sound. Emphasize the sound of /m/ as you say *moo* and *morning*. Stress the way that the lips are pressed together to form the sound /m/. Show pictures of a man, moon, mouse, monkey, mirror, and mop. Have students say the name of each item. Repeat the names of the items, emphasizing the beginning sound as you do so. Ask students to tell what is the same about *man, moon, mouse, monkey, mirror*, and *mop*. Help students to see that they all begin with the same sound. Explain that *man, moon, mouse, monkey, mirror*, and *mop* begin with /m/. Have students say the words.

Step 2. Letter-sound integration
Write the words *man* and *moon* on the board. Stress the sounds as you write the letters that represent them. Explain that the letter *m* stands for the sound /m/ heard at the beginning of "mmman" and "mmmoon." If any of your students' names begin with /m/, also write their names—*Maria, Martin, Marisol*—on the board, again emphasizing the beginning sound as you do so.

Step 3. Guided practice
Assuming that the correspondences *s* = /s/ and *f* = /f/ have been introduced, present a group of three word cards containing the words *man, fish*, and *sun*. Ask: "Which word says *man*?"

After each correct response, ask questions similar to the following: "How do you know this word says *man*?" If the student says, "Because it begins with the letter *m*," ask, "What sound does *m* stand for?" If the student says he or she chose the word because it begins with an /m/ sound, ask what letter stands for /m/. In that way, students will make connections between the letters and the sounds they represent. If a student has given an incorrect response, read the word that was mistakenly pointed to and then point to the correct word and read it: "No, this word is *sun*. It begins with the letter *s*. *S* makes a /s/ sound. This is the word *man*. It begins with the letter *m*. *M* makes the /m/ sound that you hear at the beginning of *man*." Proceed to additional word groups similar to the following:

Which word says *sun*?   man sun fish

Which word says *fish*?   man sun fish   *(continued)*

FYI

At-risk students who took part in speech-to-print recognition activities of this type improved in phonemic awareness, letter-sound recognition, and the ability to learn new words (Vandervelden & Siegel, 1997).

Closing the Gap

Another integrated program is *Road to the Code* (Brookes Publishing). A variety of activities integrate phonemic awareness and phonics by having students learn the short vowels *a* and *i* and the consonants *m, t, s, r, b, f* and build a series of words using them. This program should be especially helpful to struggling learners.

FYI

■ For additional lessons see Building Literacy at:
http://www.thomasgunning.org

■ Encourage students to attempt to spell words. As students attempt to spell words, they focus on the sounds of words and make discoveries about the spelling system (Clarke, 1988).

Which word says *me*?	me see five
Which word says *five*?	me see five
Which word says *see*?	me see five
Which word says *mat*?	mat sat fat
Which word says *fat*?	mat sat fat
Which word says *sat*?	mat sat fat
Which word says *fad*?	mad sad fad
Which word says *mad*?	mad sad fad
Which word says *sad*?	mad sad fad

Go through the words in groups of three several times or until students seem to have some fluency with the words. To make the activity more concrete, you might have the students place a plastic letter on the word they have identified—placing an *m* on *man*, for example.

Step 4. Guided spelling
In guided spelling, the teacher carefully articulates the word, and the student spells it with a set of plastic letters. Initially, the student might simply select from three plastic letters the one that spells the beginning sound. Later, the student might be asked to spell two- or three-letter words and be given the letters in mixed-up order.

Step 5. Practice and application
Have students read and write stories that contain the phonic elements that have been taught.

An informal way to use speech-to-print phonics is to say a sound and have students choose from three letters the one that represents that sound. To make the task more challenging, have students write the letter that represents the sound.

FYI

In a study of more than 22,000 kindergartners, it was found that by the end of kindergarten, nearly all the children knew their letters (Denton, West, & Walston, 2003). About 70 percent knew beginning letter sounds. About one in four could read some high-frequency words. About one in ten could read brief stories.

Introducing Other Consonant Correspondences
After students have mastered the first set of consonants, gradually introduce additional correspondences. Taking distinctiveness and overall utility into consideration, the following correspondences are recommended: $r = /r/$, $h = /h/$, $b = /b/$, $n = /n/$, $p = /p/$, $c = /k/$, $d = /d/$, $t = /t/$, $w = /w/$, $g = /g/$, $k = /k/$. After students have learned initial consonants, they are introduced to final consonants and make matches based on both the initial and final consonants. For instance, presenting the students with the word cards *cat, can*, and *cap*, the teacher says, "Which word spells *can*? Which word spells *cat*? Which word spells *cap*?"

Later, vowel correspondences are introduced. After vowels have been introduced, choices are made on the basis of vowels. Given the word cards *bit, bet*, and *but*, the students are asked, "Which word spells *but*? Which word spells *bet*? Which word spells *bit*?"

Using Systematic Instruction to Close the Gap

High-readiness kindergartners make dramatically more progress than children with low readiness. In one study, the high-readiness group was able to spell beginning and ending consonants by the middle of kindergarten (Morris, Bloodgood, Lomax & Perney, 2003). The low-readiness groups did not acquire this ability until the second month of first grade. As a result, in first grade, the high-readiness group was able to read more than twice as many words as the low-readiness group. For the most part, students were taught with a holistic program in which the teacher conducted shared reading lessons and children were encouraged to write using invented spelling. However, except for being instructed in the alphabet and beginning consonant sounds, they were not provided with systematic instruction in letter-sound relationships. The high-readiness children picked up these skills

Closing the Gap

Struggling students may lack confidence. They may need more support or just a vote of confidence. They may need one more explanation or another walk-through. Or they may need to work with a partner (Edwards, 2000).

through shared reading. The low-readiness students needed a more systematic program. The message is clear. If students are not responding to a holistic, informal approach, they may do better with one that is more systematic and explicit.

■■■ Checkup ■■■

1. Why is it important to integrate phonological awareness and phonics?
2. What are some ways in which phonological awareness and phonics might be integrated?

    ■■■

Fostering Language Development

Although both home and school play key roles in developing a child's language and literacy skills, they do so in somewhat different ways.

The school is by necessity more formal and structured than the home; however, there should be continuity between home and school. The school should build on the language and literacy skills and understandings that children have learned at home. It should make use of the learning strategies that children are accustomed to using. As Wells (1986) states,

> As far as learning is concerned, therefore, entry into school should not be thought of as a beginning, but as a transition to a more broadly based community and to a wider range of opportunities for meaning making and mastery. Every child has competencies, and these provide a positive base from which to start. The teacher's responsibility is to discover what they are and to help each child extend and develop them. (pp. 68–69)

To ease the transition from home to school and to make full use of the knowledge and skills that children bring to school, it is important that the school resemble a rich, warm home environment, using techniques employed by the parents in such homes. In his comparison of home and school conversations, Wells (1986) concluded that home conversations were far richer. At school, the teacher dominates conversations, saying approximately three times as much as the children do. Teachers ask more questions—often of a quizlike nature—make more requests, initiate conversations more often, and choose the topic to be talked about more frequently. Because the teacher dominates conversations and discussions, both the amount and the complexity of students' contributions are drastically reduced. Syntax is less complex, vocabulary is more restricted, and utterances are briefer. Busy answering the teacher's many questions and requests, the students have limited opportunities to make a genuine contribution. Teachers are also only half as likely as parents to help children extend their statements (Wells, 1986).

To foster children's language development, try the following (Wells, 1986):

- Listen very carefully to what the student has to say. Try to see the world from the child's point of view. Do not run away with the topic. For instance, if a child mentions a trip to the zoo, find out what it was about the trip that intrigued her or him. Do not launch into a detailed description of your last trip to the zoo.

- Be open to what children want to talk about. Do not follow a preconceived plan for the direction you want the discussion to take. When discussing a story that you have read to the children, let them tell you what they liked best about it. Do not tell them what they should like best, and, of course, give them the freedom not to like it at all.

- Help students extend their responses by making encouraging comments. If a child says, "I have a new puppy," ask the child to tell you more about the puppy—how old the puppy is, what it looks like, what it eats, where it sleeps, and so forth.

- Provide students with opportunities to initiate conversations and ask questions.

- Arrange for small-group and one-on-one discussions as often as possible. Although whole-class discussions are valuable, they do not allow for much interaction.

- Use language that is on or slightly above their level when you respond to students.

Adapting Instruction for English Language Learners

Understanding a new language is easier than speaking it. To help ELLs bridge the gap between understanding words and speaking them, use prompts to help them formulate what they would like to say. Also focus on the meaning of what they say and not the form.

Closing the Gap

In one study, teachers used many of the techniques listed here to expand children's language. When the study began, children were fourteen months below average. At the study's end, they were just six months behind. Teachers did more defining, recasting, demonstrating, pointing, and using of props (Wasik, Bond, & Hindman, 2006).

- Use students' comments and questions to help them construct meaning. Students are active learners who are using what they know to try to make sense of their world.

- Give the children something to talk about. Take trips to zoos and museums. Plant seeds, and raise fish or hamsters. Have lots of experiences so that children have lots to talk about. But don't make the mistake of having the experience and not talking about it. It is through talk that students form concepts about what makes plants grow or why hippos at the zoo spend just about all their time in the water. Children develop language and concepts when they talk about what they have experienced.

- Foster conversations among children. One way children learn that talking is satisfying is by having enjoyable interchanges with other children. Fostering conversations can build language as well as social skills. Sometimes, teachers see themselves as the molders or builders of language. While this is so, teachers should also see themselves as the facilitators of language and encourage conversations and discussions among children whenever possible.

- Build upon children's talk. Whenever possible, have one-on-one conversations with children. Make certain that children have equal access. Often, the quiet children, those who need one-on-one conversation the most, are given the least. In conversations, ask questions that require extended answers. Also ask real questions, ones you don't already know the answers to. When replying to young children's statements or questions, elaborate. In answer to the statement, "The dog is barking," you might reply, "Yes, the dog is barking. Perhaps it is hungry or maybe it is lonely. It wants its owner to come home and play with it" (Bunce, 1995).

- By listening carefully to children, teach them how to listen to you and to converse with and listen to each other. Also establish routines, such as taking turns and raising hands.

- Model the use of expanded language. Instead of simply saying "Good story!" explain why the story a child has written is good: "I like the way you used what you know about letters and sounds to write your story." Instead of saying "Put the crayons away," say, "Put the crayons on the shelf next to the red box of magic markers."

- Use informational talk, or talk that makes use of vocabulary that students are learning or reinforces concepts: "Make the pirate's hat in the shape of a triangle, so that it has three sides. Make the treasure chest in the shape of rectangle. Two of its sides will be longer than the other two sides" (Wasik, Bond, & Hindman, 2006).

■ ■ ■ **Checkup** ■ ■ ■

1. How is the language of school different from the language of the home?

■ ■ ■

Assisting English Language Learners

Children vary in the rate at which they learn a second language. Aptitude for learning language varies. Some children have an easier time learning a second language. In addition, there are social and psychological factors. More outgoing children will learn a second language more rapidly, as will children who are highly motivated (Tabors, 1997). Children face a double bind when learning a second language. In order to do so, they must be socially accepted by their peers so that they can learn language from them. But to be socially accepted, they need to be able to speak to the other children. Age also has an impact on children's language development. Young children have less language to learn. However, they also have less cognitive capacity than older children, so they may take longer to learn a second language.

When they first enter a school environment in which English is spoken, English language learners (ELLs) may continue to use their native tongue. When they find that this isn't working, many of these students enter a nonverbal period, which may last a few weeks, a few months, or even an entire year. They use gestures and other nonverbal strate-

Sharing stories in a small group is helpful to English language learners.

gies in order to communicate. Gradually, the children use increasingly complex English to communicate. At first, ELLs learn object names: *blocks, water, paint, books*. They might also use commands or comments such as *stop, OK, uh-oh, please, yes, no, hi, bye-bye*. They also pick up a series of useful expressions or routine statements, such as "Good morning. What's happening? How did you do this?" They progress to useful sentence structures, such as "I want ___" or "I like ___," which they complete using a variety of words.

In order to cope with the demands of the school setting, ELLs use any of a number of strategies:

- Join a group and act as though they know what is going on. This might mean joining a group that is playing with toy cars or building with blocks. ELLs participate by watching the activities of the others.

- Connect what they see with what people are saying. If the teacher holds up a round object and says *ball* several times, they assume that the name of the round object is *ball*.

- Learn some words and expressions, and use them. Even though ELLs know very little of the language, they become part of a social group by making the most of what they do know and so will have the opportunity to expand their language.

- Find and use sources of help. Finding an adult or a friend who will teach them new words or expressions and help resolve confusions will foster language development (Tabors, 1997).

- Use a copying strategy. Not fully understanding directions or the complexity of an assignment, ELLs often imitate their English-speaking classmates. They look to see how they are doing a workbook page or might even copy a sentence composed as part of a writing assignment. This may be viewed by the teacher and classmates as a coping strategy and, thus, tolerated (Weber & Longhi-Chirlin, 2001). When not copying from others, students often copied words that were written around the room or copied words from stories they had read. Expression of their own ideas was very limited.

ELLs should be encouraged to ask questions or seek help when they don't understand what they are being taught or what they are supposed to do. These students are often confused by assignments or explanations or don't know what question the teacher is asking

FYI

Collins (2005) built the vocabulary of four- and five-year-old ELLs by inserting between five and nine challenging words into storybooks that were then read to the students three times. Students learned more words when the repeated readings were accompanied by explanations of the words and the use of the words in new sentences.

FYI

Children's acquisition of emergent literacy is determined in part by their social skills and work habits (Ritchey, 2004). Students who were rated higher on following directions and completing tasks did better on measures of emergent literacy at the end of kindergarten than students who were rated lower on these items.

because they don't understand enough of the language (Weber & Longhi-Chirlin, 2001). ELLs can do better in small groups because they are in a less intimidating environment and have the opportunity to ask peers for help.

The good news is that ELLs placed in an English-speaking classroom can and do make progress. They develop speaking, listening, reading, and writing skills when their teachers believe that they can learn and present them with meaningful instruction and activities, even though the teachers do not have any training teaching ELLs. Although these students have some success, they would more than likely do even better if teachers were trained or took special steps to assist them (Weber & Longhi-Chirlin, 2001). Some techniques for helping students learn English include modeling, running commentary, expansions, and redirects.

Modeling

Modeling consists of demonstrating some language element that the student is having difficulty with or needs to learn. For instance, to model the use of *this* and *is* and *these* and *are*, you might say, "This is my pencil. These are my pencils. This is my book. These are my books." The student is offered the opportunity to use the constructions but is not required to do so. He or she may need more time to assimilate the structures.

Running Commentary

In a running commentary, you take the role of a sports announcer and describe a process that you are carrying out (Bunce, 1995): "To make a paper bag puppet, first I ___, then I ___, and then I ___." The running commentary helps acquaint students with vocabulary and sentence structure. Since it accompanies an activity, it is concrete. It also provides insight into the teacher's thought processes and problem-solving strategies. Running commentary should be used selectively. If overused, running commentary could be overwhelming to students. It is best used when a process or activity is being demonstrated.

Expansion

In an expansion, you repeat the student's statement but supply a missing part. For example, if a student says, "Car red," you say, "Yes, the car is red." This affirms the student's comment but also gives the student a model of a more advanced form (Bunce, 1995).

Adapting Instruction for English Language Learners

For additional suggestions for working with ELLs, see Chapter 12.

Redirect

In a redirect, you encourage a student who has asked you a question or made a request to direct it to another student. If a student says that he wants to play with the blocks, but Martin is playing with them, you direct him to ask Martin. If necessary, you provide a prompt, "Say to Martin, 'May I play with the blocks?' " This prompting fosters both social and language growth.

▪ ▪ ▪ Checkup ▪ ▪ ▪

1. What are some techniques for fostering language development?
2. What are some barriers to learning that ELLs face?
3. What are some techniques for helping ELLs?

▪ ▪ ▪

▪ Core Activities for Building Emergent Literacy

This chapter has presented a number of techniques for building emergent literacy. Listed below are activities that are so highly effective that they should form the core of a literacy program for kindergarten children or other students on an emergent level. These core activities can be supplemented with other activities chosen by the teacher.

- Reading to children
- Shared reading
- Reading by children (could consist of reading along with a taped book or CD-ROM, reading a wordless or highly predictable book, pretend reading, or reading with a partner)
- Language experience/shared writing
- Independent writing
- Other language/literacy building activities

Once students have a sense of story, understand the purpose and the basic concepts of print, can identify most of the letters of the alphabet, and can detect beginning sounds in words, they are prepared for a higher level of instruction. Upcoming chapters contain suggestions for a more intensive and structured approach to reading that fosters children's growth in literacy areas such as phonics, knowledge of high-frequency words, and other word analysis skills. The next sections are devoted to reading in preschool, working with parents, and monitoring emergent literacy.

■ ■ ■ Checkup ■ ■ ■

1. What are core activities for a kindergarten literacy program?

■ ■ ■

■ Reading in Preschool

A joint committee of the International Reading Association (IRA) and the NAEYC (National Association for the Education of Young Children) (1998) recommended that preschool children build the foundations for learning to read and write. "Failing to give children literacy experiences until they are school-age can severely limit the reading and writing levels they ultimately obtain" (p. 197). The concept of ready to read has been replaced by the concept of preparing to read (Texas Instruments Foundation, Head Start of Greater Dallas, Southern Methodist University, 1996). Essential literacy standards for the preschool can be found at the end of this chapter. A prudent course would be to avoid formal instruction in literacy. Reading aloud regularly, shared reading, setting up areas for dramatic play and reading and writing and a classroom library, developing oral language skills, modeling reading and writing, and providing opportunities for children to write, draw, and explore language will naturally develop emergent literacy (Campbell, 1998).

Preschool programs have grown in popularity. Although most state-funded preschool programs are designed for poor children, a number of states have universal programs, open to all four-years-olds. With universal programs, parents choose whether or not to send their children. In a well-planned preschool program, students make gains of six to eight months in essential prereading skills (Gormley, Gayer, Phillips, & Dawson, 2005).

The National Early Reading Panel (Strickland & Shanahan, 2004) recommended activities to foster development in the following areas: language, alphabetical and phonological knowledge, and print knowledge.

Language

- Listening to and discussing stories, rhymes, and songs
- Engaging in small-group and one-on-one conversations with adults, especially conversations that elicit elaborated talk
- Retelling stories and events
- Listening in order to follow directions and gain information

Alphabetical and Phonological Knowledge

- Engaging in drawing and writing
- Listening to rhymes and tongue twisters and playing word games

- Exploring alphabet books
- Exploring letter names and sounds

Print Knowledge

- Exploring environmental signs
- Observing as adults read and write
- Dictating stories for adults to write down
- Exploring picture books

FYI

The highest-scoring 25 percent of Head Start students perform at about the same level as the average kindergarten student. The lowest 25 percent perform like the lowest 2 percent of the larger kindergarten population. However, by the end of kindergarten, Head Start graduates have made substantial gains (Zill et al., 2006).

USING TECHNOLOGY

Focus on Beginning Readers offers more suggestions for preschool literacy programs.
http://www.reading.org/resources/issues/focus_beginning.html

For details on literacy development and other outcomes for Head Start, visit
http://headstartinfo.org/publications/hsbulletin76/hsb76_09.htm

For information on the Early Reading First program, go to
http://www.ed.gov/programs/earlyreading/index.html

Federal Initiatives

Although there is much agreement on the curriculum for students in K–12, ideas for preschool education range from programs that are play-based and child-centered to those that embody direct instruction. The current trend is toward adding academics to early childhood education. Indeed, Head Start has performance standards that require children to:

1. Develop print and numeracy awareness,
2. Understand and use an increasingly complex vocabulary, and
3. Develop and demonstrate an appreciation of books.

Head Start standards also require that "children know that letters of the alphabet are a special category of visual graphics that can be individually named, recognize a word as a unit of print, identify at least 10 letters of the alphabet, and associate sounds with written words" (Taylor, 2001, p. 2).

Early Reading First

Early Reading First, which can be implemented in a Head Start setting, is a federal initiative designed to prepare children, especially those at risk, for reading instruction. Its overall purpose is to prepare young children to enter kindergarten with the necessary language, cognitive, and early reading skills to prevent reading difficulties. Key skill areas include the following:

- Learning the letters of the alphabet
- Learning to hear the individual sounds in words and to break words apart into their separate sounds (segmenting) and put sounds together to make words (blending)
- Learning new words and how to use them
- Learning early writing skills
- Learning to use language by asking and answering questions and by participating in discussions and engaging in conversations
- Learning about written language by looking at books and by listening to stories and other books that are read to them every day (U.S. Department of Education, 2002a)

Effective Preschool Programs

Low-income four-year-olds showed encouraging gains when stories were read to them on a regular basis and the teacher engaged them in discussions in which they made predictions, reflected on the story, and talked about words (Dickinson & Smith, 1994). When book reading and literacy interactions were enhanced by training the teachers and adding a library of children's books in child care centers for three- and four-year-olds, children outperformed a comparison group on vocabulary, concepts of print, concepts of writing, letter names, and phonemic awareness when assessed in kindergarten (Neuman, 1997).

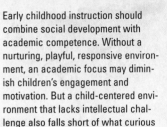

Para Los Niños

In Para Los Niños, a child care center in a part of Los Angeles known as Skid Row, a morning language and literacy program was instituted for approximately fifty four-year-old Spanish-speaking preschool children. The program included big-book shared reading, writing and reading centers, and a take-home library for parents. Workshops for parents were held on book-handling and home reading and writing activities. Students demonstrated encouraging gains in concepts of print, letter knowledge, and recognition of some phonics elements. Many of the families also established read-aloud routines at home (Yaden et al., 2001).

The outcomes of this program included successful transfer of early language awareness in Spanish to English. Although they were taught literacy skills in Spanish, these skills transferred to English. In fact, the students outscored native speakers of English who had participated in other preschool programs despite the fact that the emergent literacy tests were administered in English.

LEAP

For students at risk, a well-planned preschool program can mean the difference between success and failure in later schooling. Otherwise, children who start off behind tend to stay behind. As Hehir notes, the gap between potential and achievement widens as children progress through the grades (Language Enrichment Activities Program, 2004).

To give a boost to poor students in Head Start at the Cone Center (located in a poor section of Dallas, Texas), supplemental health, nutrition, and social services were added. Teachers and staff provided extended hours each day as well as operating the program year-round. Despite these additions, the children continued to enter kindergarten performing well behind their chronological age. To develop skills to promote success in kindergartern, the center initiated the Language Enrichment Activities Program (LEAP), which emphasizes language development, phonological awareness, knowledge of the letters of the alphabet, basic concepts, and prewriting fine motor skills. The program also included teacher training, workshops for volunteers, and a parent component.

Before the introduction of LEAP, students were scoring at the 30th percentile. Today, average scores exceed the 50th percentile. Key elements in the instructional program include the following:

- **Language with stories.** Teachers read aloud at least five books a day selected from a thematically organized bibliography of books appropriate for children whose language development is from two to four years. The book is introduced and discussed. Vocabulary and concepts are developed. Connections are made between the book's themes and other classroom activities.

- **Language with words.** Posters of objects and activities are used as stimuli for developing language. Students listen to, repeat, and produce responses in complete sentences. Teachers develop concepts and vocabulary throughout the day.

- **Language with sounds.** Beginning with their names, children learn to recognize individual words in phrases and sentences. Children also learn to identify the separate words in compound words and the syllables in two- and three-syllable words. The theory is that before students can learn to identify phonemes, they must learn to identify sentences, clauses, words, and syllables.

- **Language with letters.** Children learn the sounds of beginning consonants and the names of the letters that represent those sounds. They also learn the uppercase letters of the alphabet and how to sing the alphabet song. Children manipulate objects whose names have the same beginning sound.

- **Language with ideas.** Children learn shapes, sizes, colors, numbers, plurals, rhymes, opposites, and other concepts.

- **Language with prewriting motor skills.** Children learn the fine motor skills needed for writing.

USING TECHNOLOGY

From the U.S. Department of Education, *Teaching our youngest: A guide for preschool teachers and child care and family providers* contains helpful information for preschool instruction.
http://www.ed.gov/teachers/how/early/teachingouryoungest.pdf

The position statement of the International Reading Association on literacy development in the preschool years notes that preschools make a difference in children's lives; therefore, every three- and four-year-old child should have access to free, high-quality public preschool.
http://www.reading.org/resources/issues/positions_preschool.html

Personal/social skills are also fostered. Children begin school prepared to learn as opposed to ready to learn (Texas Instruments Foundation, Head Start of Greater Dallas, Southern Methodist University, 1996). Suggestions for setting up such a preschool program can be found at the Texas Instruments Foundation's Web site at: http://www.ti.com/corp/docs/company/citizen/foundation/leapsbounds/history.shtml

Webbing into Literacy

Webbing into Literacy (http://curry.edschool.virginia.edu/go/wil/home.html) also offers a wealth of resources for developing preschool literacy skills. Webbing into Literacy is a downloadable program designed to provide Head Start teachers with materials and instruction that will foster language development, phonological awareness, alphabet knowledge, and concepts of print. Because the site is designed for preschool students, the goal is exposure and awareness rather than mastery. Activities include shared reading and singing of nursery rhymes, sorting of word patterns, and using rhymes to complete riddles. Downloadable materials include cards and booklets containing nursery rhymes, picture card sets containing illustrated rhyming words, riddle rhymes, and covers for students' alphabet booklets.

■ ■ ■ Checkup ■ ■ ■

1. What is the role of the preschool in developing literacy?
2. What are some examples of effective preschool programs? What do these programs have in common?

■ ■ ■

■ Working with Parents

Because today's emergent literacy practices are different from those parents experienced when they attended school and there was a readiness orientation, it is important that the emergent literacy program be explained to them. Trace the roots of reading and writing, and explain to parents the essential role that they have played and continue to play. Be sensitive to different styles of parenting. Some parents, not having been read to themselves, may not realize the value of reading aloud to their children or, because of limited skills, may not feel able to do it well.

Affirm what parents have done, and encourage them to support their children's efforts as best they can. Also, explain each element of the program. Pay special attention to invented spelling and process writing, as these are areas that lend themselves to misunderstanding. Trace the development of children's writing from drawing and scribbling through invented spelling to conventional writing. Show examples of students' writing. Stress the benefits of early writing, and assure parents that invented spelling is transitory and will not harm their children's acquisition of conventional spelling.

The joint position statement of the International Reading Association and the National Association for the Education of Young Children (1998) suggests that parents can help emergent readers in the following ways:

- Read and reread narrative and informational stories to children daily.
- Encourage children's attempts at reading and writing.

FYI

Parents' ways of interacting with their children are determined by cultural factors. Some parents may read in an authoritative style and fail to interact with the child (Leseman & deJong, 1998). Sessions or video recordings that demonstrate effective read-aloud techniques can be helpful to these parents.

Adapting Instruction for English Language Learners

Parents of ELLs should be encouraged to use the language that they feel most comfortable with. Advising them to speak only English may hinder communication between parents and children.

■ A **family literacy program** has as its overall goal the sharing of reading and writing by family members. Although concerned with helping children become proficient readers and writers, another goal is the transmission of the family's culture. In one such program, parents wrote stories about their experiences that they then shared with their children (Akroyd, 1995).

- Allow children to participate in activities that involve writing and reading (for example, making grocery lists).
- Play games that involve specific directions (such as Simon Says).
- Have conversations with children during mealtimes and throughout the day.

Family Literacy Programs

One highly effective way of assisting children, especially those at risk, to fully develop literacy is to help their parents overcome their own literacy difficulties so that they can then help their children. A **family literacy program** can take several forms. Parents and children may attend sessions held after school or during the summer. The parents and children may be given separate sessions, or the program may be coordinated in such a way that the parents spend some of the time working directly with their children. In another form, just the parents attend sessions, where they are taught reading and writing skills, which they pass on to the children. Parents are then prepared to read storybooks to their children or to assist with homework. In a third version, parents are taught ways to enhance their children's reading and writing skills by reading to them, talking with them, or supervising homework. As they learn ways to help their children, parents' literacy skills improve. Parents may also meet in discussion groups to talk over difficulties they are having and ways in which they might help their children.

Parents may need ongoing, specific guidance in the use of techniques to build their children's literacy. Paratore (1995) found that it wasn't enough to provide parents with storybooks and demonstrations on how to read to children. The parents needed many opportunities to observe read-aloud sessions as well as opportunities to practice reading aloud. Discussing their read-aloud sessions and obtaining practical feedback also helped.

INVOLVING PARENTS

Children who are read to at least three times a week are twice as likely to be in the top 25th percentile of readers at the end of first grade (Denton & West, 2002).

Parents need specific suggestions for helping their children. Don't just suggest that they read books to their children. Provide a list of possible books and tips for reading aloud.

Exemplary Teaching

The Power of an Intriguing Book

During kindergarten, Anthony struggled with both reading and writing. He had particular difficulty with phonemic awareness. By midyear, he had caught on to rhyme but was having difficulty with beginning sounds. Gradually, he developed an awareness of beginning sounds, and his ability to learn new words improved. Still, by year's end, he was lagging behind his classmates and the school's kindergarten benchmarks. The kindergarten teacher warned Anthony's mother about summer slump and recommended that she take him to the town's library and check out beginners' books. (Fortunately, the school and the library communicated, so librarians had set aside books for novice readers.)

The first trip to the library went well. The library was holding a summer reading contest, which intrigued Anthony. He was also intrigued by the books his mother chose for him, especially Eastman's (1962) classic, *Go, Dog, Go!* On the ride home from the library, Anthony began reading *Go, Dog, Go!* When he came across a word he didn't know, he spelled it out and his mother told him what it was. Fortunately, *Go, Dog Go!* starts off with very easy words. Most of the words that might have posed problems were depicted with illustrations. Because the story was so intriguing, Anthony was motivated to use picture-context clues and his limited decoding skills. Anthony read the book several times. Each time, he learned a few new words. Some of the words that he initially had to figure out he began to read with ease.

Anthony read his book to all who would listen. The next day, he was up at 6 a.m. reading *Go, Dog, Go!* to himself. After breakfast, he read it to his parents before they went to work, and later, he read it to his grandparents. Previously, most of Anthony's reading fare had consisted of predictable books or decodable books, books that were lacking in intrinsic interest. Motivated by the humor in *Go, Dog, Go!* and the satisfaction of reading, Anthony read a number of beginning books during the summer months. Because of the power of an intriguing book, a concerned parent, a knowledgeable teacher, and cooperative librarians, he was well on his way to becoming a reader.

1. How might teachers help parents more effectively develop their children's language and literacy?

2. What is a family literacy program? What is its role in developing children's literacy?

■ ■ ■

■ Monitoring Emergent Literacy

ASSESSING FOR LEARNING

Based on your observations of a student's reading, plan instruction. For instance, if a student is using initial consonants but not vowels, probe further to see if the student knows common vowels. If not, introduce them. If the student does know common vowels, show him or her how to use vowels to help read words. Present a sentence such as *The (cap, cat) ran*, where the student must use the vowel as well as the initial consonant to choose the right word.

Emergent literacy can best be monitored through careful observation. As students read and write, try to get beyond the product to the process. As a student is reading, try to determine what he or she is reading. Is the student reading the pictures? Has the student simply memorized the text? Is it some sort of combination? What is the child attending to? Possibilities include pictures, overall memory of the selection, memorized words or phrases, context, beginning letters, beginning letters and ending letters, all the letters in the word, or a combination of elements. Knowing where the student is, you can build on his or her knowledge and, through scaffolding, lift the student to a higher level. For instance, if the student is simply using picture clues, you can help him or her use highly predictable text along with pictures. A checklist for evaluating a child's use of early reading strategies is presented in Table 3.9.

Note the level of the student's writing. Does the student have a sense of what writing is? Is the student attempting to convey a message? Is the student using invented spelling? Use the observation guide in Figure 3.5 (on pp. 146–147) to monitor writing, stages of storybook reading, oral language, concepts about reading, interest in reading and writing, and work habits. The observation guide is generic; use only those parts that fit in with your program.

Observation should be broad-based. Dahl (1992) suggests observing strategies that children use in reading and writing, the routines that students engage in every day, and the products of their efforts and the comments that they make about them.

■ **Strategies.** Note what strategies students use as they attempt to read or write a word. Do they elongate the sounds? Ask a teacher?

■ **Routines.** How do students choose books? What do they do when they write? Do they typically use a book as a model? Do they use a drawing as a story starter?

■ ■ ■ ■ TABLE 3.9 Checklist for Evaluating Early Reading Strategies

Strategy	Never	Seldom	Often
Uses pictures exclusively to retell story.	_____	_____	_____
Uses pictures and text to retell story.	_____	_____	_____
Uses pictures to help with difficult words.	_____	_____	_____
Uses memory of entire piece to read story.	_____	_____	_____
Uses memory of repeated phrases.	_____	_____	_____
Uses context to decipher words.	_____	_____	_____
Uses initial consonants and context to decipher words.	_____	_____	_____
Uses initial and final consonants and context to decipher words.	_____	_____	_____
Uses all or most of each word's parts to decipher words.	_____	_____	_____
Uses a variety of cues to decipher words.	_____	_____	_____

Based on Appendix 2.1, Forms of Writing and Rereading, Example List (pp. 51–63) by E. Sulzby (1989). In J. M. Mason (Ed.), *Reading and Writing Connections*. Boston: Allyn & Bacon.

■ **Products.** What do the illustrations children have made of their reading look like? What do their written pieces look like? Are they scribbling or using a combination of scribbles and invented spelling? How are the products changing over time?

■ **Comments.** What are children saying about their work? For instance, when Maurice tossed his piece of scribble writing into the wastebasket, his teacher asked him about it. Maurice replied, "My writing doesn't say anything." Maurice realized that he needed another form of writing in order to express meaning. His rejection of his scribble writing was a sign of development (Dahl, 1992). This is the kind of incident of which perceptive anecdotal records are made.

Observations should focus on what the child can do. For instance, the focus of the observation made about Maurice was his new understanding of what is required to represent spoken words in writing.

Notes taken after a discussion has been completed or a reading or writing conference has been held can also offer valuable insights. If the notes are put on gummed labels or sticky notes, they can be entered into a handheld computer or pasted into a looseleaf notebook that contains separate pages for each child.

Because young children's literacy behavior changes rapidly, observations should be ongoing. However, progress should be checked on a more formal basis approximately once a month. In addition to filling out checklists, keep anecdotal records. Note the emergence of significant behaviors, such as the appearance of finger pointing, word-by-word reading, and the use of invented spelling. Briefly describe the behavior and note the date. See Chapter 2 for more information on using checklists and anecdotal records.

Informal Assessment Measures

Emergent literacy measures need not be purchased. Teachers can put together a measure that is geared to their own concept of literacy and that meshes with their literacy program. Although it can be a paper-and-pencil test to allow for group administration, an informal type of one-to-one assessment often works better. A sample informal assessment, which is administered individually, follows.

■ **Letter Knowledge.** Print or type the twenty-six letters of the alphabet on cards. Make a set for uppercase letters and a set for lowercase ones. (Assess knowledge of uppercase letters first.)

■ **Writing Sample.** Ask the child to write his or her name as best he or she can. If the child can write his or her name, ask the child to write any other words that he or she knows. Ask the child to write a story as best he or she can. In the story, the child might tell about himself or herself and his or her family. This may be done with letterlike forms or drawings or real letters. Note the level of the child's writing and the number of words that he or she can write, if any.

■ **Print Familiarity.** Give *Have You Seen My Cat?* (Carle, 1973) or a similar book to the child. Discuss the book informally to find out how familiar the child is with print conventions. You might ask, "Have you ever seen this book? What do you think this book is about? How can you tell what the book is about? What do you do with a book?" Open to the first page of the story and say, "I'm going to read this page to you. Show me where I should start reading." (Note whether the child points to the illustration or the first word.) Ask the child if he or she can read any words on the page. Then tell the child that you are going to read the first sentence. Ask him or her to point to each word as you read it. (Note whether the child can do this.) Read the sentence again. Then ask the child to read it. Ask him or her to point to each word as he or she reads it. (Pointing to each word shows whether the child has a concept of separate words.) Point to a line of print and ask, "How many words are in this line?" Point to a word and ask, "How many letters are in this word?"

■■■ **FIGURE 3.5**
Emergent Literacy Observation Guide

Student's name: _____   Age: _____

Date: _____

Oral language	Below average	Average	Advanced
Uses a vocabulary appropriate for age level	1	2 3 4	5
Uses a sentence structure appropriate for age level	1	2 3 4	5
Can make himself/herself understood	1	2 3 4	5
Listens attentively to directions and stories	1	2 3 4	5
Can retell a story in own words	1	2 3 4	5
Understands oral directions	1	2 3 4	5
Asks questions when doesn't understand something	1	2 3 4	5

Concepts about reading	Below average	Average	Advanced
Knows the parts of a book	1	2 3 4	5
Understands that the print is read	1	2 3 4	5
Can follow a line of print as it is being read	1	2 3 4	5
Can point to words as each is being read	1	2 3 4	5
Can name letters of the alphabet	1	2 3 4	5
Can perceive beginning sounds	1	2 3 4	5
Can detect rhyming words	1	2 3 4	5
Can tell how many sounds are in a word	1	2 3 4	5
Can discriminate between words that have a similar appearance	1	2 3 4	5
Recognizes environmental print signs and labels	1	2 3 4	5
Can read own name	1	2 3 4	5

Interest in reading and writing	Below average	Average	Advanced
Enjoys being read to	1	2 3 4	5
Browses among books in class	1	2 3 4	5
"Reads" picture books	1	2 3 4	5
Asks questions about words, sentences, or other elements in books	1	2 3 4	5

Writing	Below average	Average	Advanced
Shows interest in writing	1	2 3 4	5
Writes or draws stories or letters	1	2 3 4	5
Understands the purpose of writing	1	2 3 4	5
Writes to communicate with others	1	2 3 4	5

For the most part his/her writing is best described as being at the following level:

Unorganized scribbles	_____	(The scribbles have no perceptible pattern.)
Drawings	_____	(Drawing is the child's primary mode of written expression.)
Organized scribbles	_____	(The scribbles show a pattern. They may be linear.)
Letterlike figures	_____	(The characters aren't real letters, but have some of the features of letters.)
Prephonemic spelling	_____	(The child uses real letters, but the letters have no apparent relationship to the sounds of the words he or she is writing.)
Early alphabetic spelling	_____	(Consonant sounds are spelled; *kitten* may be spelled *KTN*.)
Alphabetic spelling	_____	(Vowels are spelled with letter names; *RAN* for *rain*.)
Consolidated alphabetic spelling	_____	(Vowel markers are used; *RANE* for *rain*.)
Standard spelling	_____	

Work habits	Below average	Average	Advanced
Is able to work on own	1	2 3 4	5
Works at task until it is finished	1	2 3 4	5
Works well with others	1	2 3 4	5
Is able to share materials	1	2 3 4	5
Is able to take turns	1	2 3 4	5

Other Measures of Emergent Literacy

One of the best-known measures of print concepts is CAP, or Concepts about Print (Clay, 1982). CAP has twenty-four items and takes only 5 to 10 minutes to administer. The test has two forms: Sand and Stones. The tests are equivalent and consist of a storybook and a series of questions. Clay (2006) also assembled a battery of reading and writing measures known as the Observation Survey, which has recently been updated and can be used to assess emergent reading and early reading behaviors. The Bader Reading and Language Inventory (Bader, 2002) also includes a number of assessment devices for emergent literacy: Concepts about Print, Blending, Segmentation, Letter Knowledge, Hearing Letter Names in Words, and Syntax Matching (being able to match printed with spoken words).

Both the Bader inventory and CAPS are individually administered. The Phonological Literacy Screening (PALS) is a group or individual test and includes measures of rhyme, beginning sounds, alphabet recognition, letter sounds, spelling, concept of word, and word recognition (Invernizzi, Meir, Swank, & Juel, 2001). Measures of emergent literacy are also included in the teacher's manual of a basal reading series or as a separate item. One advantage of basal tests is that they are geared to the program for which they have been constructed. They are also generally accompanied by suggestions for working with students who do poorly on them.

USING TECHNOLOGY ■ ■ ■

Phonological awareness can be measured through the DIBELS subtests Initial Sounds Fluency and Phoneme Segmentation Fluency. Alphabet knowledge is assessed through Letter Name Fluency. All three subtests are 1-minute speed tests that have many versions so that students can be retested many times. This enables teachers to track progress continuously. After administering the timed tests, a teacher can give students untimed versions to see how well they do when speed is not a factor.
http://dibels.uoregon.edu

FYI

Tests of phonological awareness may not work well with children younger than five (Muter and Snowling, 1998). When given at age 5, such tests were relatively good predictors of later reading achievement, but when given at age 4, the tests failed to provide adequate predictions.

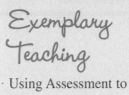

Exemplary Teaching

· Using Assessment to Reduce Potential Reading Problems

The purpose of the Early Intervention Reading Initiative in Virginia is to reduce the number of students in grades kindergarten through 3 with reading problems by using early diagnosis and acceleration of early reading skills. The initiative provides teachers with a screening tool that helps them determine which students would benefit from additional instruction. Schools are also given incentive funds to obtain additional instruction for students in need.

Students are administered the Phonological Literacy Screening (PALS) instrument. PALS-K (kindergarten) includes measures of rhyme, beginning sounds, alphabet recognition, letter sounds, spelling, concept of word, and word recognition. According to PALS scores, approximately 25 percent of students need additional instruction.

The PALS project makes heavy use of the Internet. When teachers report their scores, they get an immediate summary report. Principals can also get reports for their schools. The site contains instructional suggestions and a listing of materials. Instruction provided to students must be in addition to their regular classroom instruction. When retested in the spring, approximately 80 percent of kindergartners identified as needing added help were making satisfactory progress. Retention is not considered a means of providing additional assistance and is not the purpose of the Early Intervention Reading Initiative.

After screening ninety-two children with PALS, the four kindergarten teachers at the McGuffey School in Virginia found that twenty-three children needed an intervention program. The students worked with a PALS tutor for 30 minutes a day. The focus was on developing phonemic awareness, alphabet skills, and beginning consonants. The lessons also included shared reading of nursery rhymes and simple pattern books. This approach was designed to develop awareness of sounds, letter recognition, concept of word, and writing skills. Although all of the students had low overall scores on emergent literacy skills, some were especially weak in rhyming. Others had difficulty with letter recognition or matching beginning sounds. Students were placed in groups of four according to common needs so that instruction would be focused. Skills were introduced in integrated fashion. If the lesson's focus was on beginning sounds, the teacher read aloud a selection that contained the target sounds and discussed them. Students also sorted objects and pictures that shared the target sounds and then attempted to write the name of each object or picture. The lesson ended with a rhyme that contained the target sounds (Invernizzi, Meier, Swank, & Juel, 2001). For more information go to http://www.pen.k12.va.us/VDOE/Instruction/Reading/readinginitiative.html

FYI

We have no direct measure of phonemic awareness. Each of the assessment tasks has its own cognitive requirements. To blend a string of isolated phonemes, the child must first perceive those phonemes, then hold them in memory while trying to connect them into a word. To detect a rhyme, the child must identify both of the words' rimes, keep them in memory, and then decide if both end with the same rime.

Using the Assessment Results

The results of an emergent literacy assessment should help you plan instruction. Generally, an acceptable standard for letter knowledge and phonological awareness is 80 percent. Students falling below that level require additional help. Those who are lacking in print familiarity need more experience with concepts with which they had difficulty. Writing samples are also indicators of emergent literacy concepts. Based on the samples, note where children are on the path to literacy and, according to their level of development, what experiences will be most beneficial.

As indicated earlier, not every ability important to reading can be measured formally or informally. Learning to read requires hard work, perseverance, and a certain degree of maturity. It also demands reasonably good health, sufficient social skills to allow one to work with others, and adequate language skills so that the teacher's instructions and the material to be read can be understood.

■ ■ ■ Checkup ■ ■ ■

1. What emergent literacy knowledge, skills, and behaviors need to be monitored?
2. What are some effective techniques for monitoring emergent literacy?

Building Higher-Level Literacy

Although much of your preschool or kindergarten instruction will be devoted to developing phonological awareness, alphabet knowledge, and other emergent literacy skills, set aside time to build vocabulary, background knowledge, and thinking skills. As you read books to and with students, introduce new words and ask questions that lead them to think more deeply about the reading selections. Help them see similarities and differences, as well as causes and effects. Help them make connections between the ideas they hear and talk about in class and their own lives.

Help for Struggling Readers and Writers

Struggling readers and writers should be carefully assessed to determine their strengths and weaknesses. They should then be taught on a level that is comfortable for them. If students have had limited experience with print, spend extra time reading to them. If possible, have volunteers read to them individually or in small groups and discuss the selections much as a parent would. If students are hesitant to write, encourage them to write as best they can. Model the ways in which young children write, including drawing, and encourage them to pick the kind of writing that they feel they can do. Provide experiences with phonological awareness that are on the appropriate level. If children are having difficulty detecting rhyme or initial sounds, read rhyming or alliterative tales to them and engage in word-play activities to build their awareness of the sounds of language. Connect with the home and find out what kinds of literacy activities the children's families engage in. Build on these activities, and provide suggestions to the families for working with the children.

Also, take a preventive approach. As noted earlier, some impoverished families don't spend much time reading to their children or talking with them about letters and words until the children start engaging in these activities at school (Purcell-Gates, 1997). A family literacy or similar program that helps parents engage in these activities before their children enter school should provide children with a much richer foundation for reading and writing.

Essential Standards

Preschool: Awareness and exploration

Children explore their environments and develop a foundation for learning to read and write (IRA & NAEYC, 1998).
Students will

- listen to and talk about storybooks.
- develop language skills by talking a lot, talking to themselves to guide actions, telling stories, explaining and seeking information, and engaging in word-play (New Standards Speaking and Listening Committee, 2001).
- attempt to read and write.
- understand that print can be read.
- recognize labels and signs in the environment.
- engage in rhyming and other word-play games.
- recognize some letters and letter sounds.
- use letters or letterlike forms to write names and messages.

Kindergarten: Experimental reading and writing

Students develop oral language and listening skills, learn basic concepts of print, and explore the form and function of reading and writing.
Students will

- recognize and write the letters of the alphabet.
- develop phonological awareness: rhyming, beginning sounds, blending, segmentation of words.
- understand basic print concepts: left to right, top to bottom, front to back, spaces between words.

Tools for the Classroom

- match spoken words with printed ones.
- learn consonant-sound correspondences.
- learn some short-vowel word families: *-at, -am, -an*, etc.
- read some high-frequency words and simple stories.
- write their names and use their knowledge of letter-sound relationships to write words, lists, captions for drawings, messages, and stories.
- develop language skills by talking a lot, talking to themselves to guide actions, telling stories, explaining and seeking information, and engaging in word play (New Standards Speaking and Listening Committee, 2001).
- listen to, retell, answer questions about, and respond to stories.

Action Plan

1. Assess students to see where they are in terms of their literacy development. Assess concepts of print, alphabet knowledge, and phonological awareness. Also note language development and work habits. Plan a program that develops all these areas.
2. Establish a literacy-rich environment.
3. Use oral reading and shared reading to develop background, language and thinking skills, and literacy concepts.
4. Use word games and other activities to develop letter knowledge and phonemic awareness. Once students are aware of beginning sounds, tie letters into instruction.
5. Develop emerging writing skills.
6. Involve parents in their children's learning.
7. Make certain that the program is developmentally appropriate. Make sure that preschool, kindergarten, and grade 1 programs are articulated so that one builds on the other.
8. For English language learners, develop phonological awareness and beginning literacy skills in the students' native language, if possible. Make extra efforts to build language skills.
9. Monitor children's progress and make any necessary adjustments.

Assessment

Many of the early literacy objectives, especially in the preschool, can be assessed through careful observation. To make the observations more valid, observe each child in different settings and on more than one occasion. It's also helpful to have a checklist or some sort of observation guide, such as the one presented in Figure 3.5. Assessment is also more valid when you use more than one source of information. Suggestions for assessing letter knowledge and phonological awareness are presented on p. 145.

Summary

Emergent literacy instruction attempts to capitalize on the literacy skills that the child brings to school. To foster literacy, the teacher immerses the class in reading and writing activities. By reading to children, the teacher builds knowledge of story structure and story language, vocabulary, and background of experience. To build language, the school should use techniques to make the child an active partner in conversations and discussions. Through shared reading and language-experience stories, including shared writing, basic literacy concepts and skills are built.

Once primarily a matter of copying and learning letter formation, writing in kindergarten is now seen as a valid means of expression. Children are invited to write and spell as best they can.

Progress in literacy is closely tied to knowledge of the alphabet, phonological awareness, and students' persistence.

Increasingly, kindergarten and preschool programs are including instruction in literacy and preliteracy skills. Several preschool programs have been shown to be highly beneficial to at-risk learners. Parent involvement is an essential ingredient in fostering emergent literacy. A number of formal and informal measures can be used to assess emergent literacy.

Extending and Applying

1. Examine stories written by a kindergarten class. What are some characteristics of children's writing at this age? How do the pieces vary?

2. Read the description of Webbing into Literacy at http://curry.edschool.virginia.edu/go/wil/home.html. Examine the many resources offered. How might these be used in a preparatory literacy program for preschool children?

3. Search out alphabet books, rhyming tales, song books, and other materials that you might use to enhance alphabet knowledge, rhyming, and perception of beginning sounds. Keep an annotated bibliography of these materials.

4. Using the procedures described in this chapter, plan a lesson teaching alphabet letters, rhyming, or beginning sounds. Teach the lesson, and rate its effectiveness.

Developing a Professional Portfolio

Reflect on your beliefs about teaching literacy skills in preschool and kindergarten classes. Compose a statement in which you highlight your beliefs and how you might implement them. Teach a lesson as suggested in item 4 of Extending and Applying, and, if possible, make a video recording of it. On a paper copy of the lesson plan, reflect on the effectiveness of the lesson.

Go to Allyn & Bacon's MyLabSchool: www.mylabschool.com

- Enter Assignment ID **RMCS** into **Assignment Finder,** and select the case titled "Early Reading."

- Read through Level A, Case 1 on phonemic awareness. What strategies are identified for use in this case? What types of activities can you implement to reinforce phonemic awareness?

- Explore MyLabSchool further to find the course areas for Early Childhood Education, Reading Methods, and Language Arts and identify other assets that support concepts introduced in this chapter.

Developing a Resource File

Start and maintain a list of books and other materials that you might use to teach literacy in preschool or kindergarten.

Start a file of illustrations and nursery rhymes that you might use to develop phonological awareness.

To access chapter objectives, practice tests, weblinks, and flashcards, go to the companion website at www.ablongman.com/gunning6e.

4 Teaching Phonics,
   High-Frequency Words,
   and Syllabic Analysis

or each of the following statements, put a check under "Agree" or "Disagree" to show how you feel. Discuss your responses with classmates before you read the chapter.

	Agree	Disagree
1. Before they start to read, students should be taught most of the consonant letters and their sounds.	_____	_____
2. Phonics rules have so many exceptions that they are not worth teaching.	_____	_____
3. Phonics is hard to learn because English is so irregular.	_____	_____
4. The natural way to decode a word is sound by sound or letter by letter.	_____	_____
5. Memorizing is an inefficient way to learn new words.	_____	_____
6. Syllabication is not a very useful skill because you have to know how to decode a word before you can put it into syllables.	_____	_____

he writing system for the English language is alphabetic. Because a series of twenty-six letters has been created to represent the speech sounds of the language, our thoughts and ideas can be written down. To become literate, we must learn the relationship between letters and speech sounds. Chapter 3 presented techniques for teaching the nature and purpose of writing and reading, concepts of print, the alphabet, and awareness of speech sounds and for presenting initial consonants. These techniques form a foundation for learning phonics, which is the relationship between spelling and speech sounds as applied to reading. This chapter covers high-frequency words, some of which may not lend themselves to phonic analysis. In addition, the chapter explores syllabic analysis, which is the application of phonics to multisyllabic words, and fluency, which is freedom from word identification problems. This chapter will be more meaningful if you first reflect on what you already know about phonics, syllabic analysis, and fluency.

Think about how you use phonics and syllabic analysis to sound out strange names and other unfamiliar words. Think about how you might teach phonics, and ask yourself what role phonics should play in a reading program.

■ Rationale and Approaches for Phonics Instruction

As you read the following sentence out loud, think about the processes you are using.

> In *Palampam Day*, by David and Phyllis Gershator (1997), Papa Tata Wanga offers sage advice to Turn, who refuses to eat because on this day, the food talks back, as do the animals.

In addition to thinking about what the sentence is saying, did you find that you had to use **phonics** and syllabication skills to read *Palampam*, *Gershator*, and *Tata Wanga*? Phonics skills are absolutely essential for all readers. Most of the words we read are sight words. We've encountered them so many times that we don't need to take time to sound them out. They are in our mental storehouse of words that we recognize automatically. However, we need phonics for names of people or places or events that we have never met in print. Without phonics, we would not be able to read new words.

FYI

As adept readers, we apply our skills with lightning speed and process words by patterns of sound. Having read words such as *papa* and *tango*, you may have grouped the letters in *Tata* as "ta-ta" and those in *Wanga* as "Wang-(g)a" and pronounced the *a*'s in *Tata* just like the *a*'s in *papa* and the *ang* in *Wanga* just like the *ang* in *tango*.

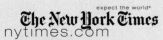

As adept readers, we use phonics occasionally. Because of our extensive experience in reading, we have met virtually all of the word patterns in the language. Although you may have never seen the word *Palampam* before, you have seen the word patterns *pal* and *am*. Chances are you used these patterns to decode *Palampam*. You probably decoded the word so rapidly that you may not even be conscious of applying your skills. For novice readers, phonics is a key skill. For a period in their development, novice readers may be using phonics in a conscious, deliberate fashion to decode many of the words that they read. In time, after they've had sufficient experience with a word, that word becomes part of their instant recognition vocabulary.

■ How Words Are Read

Words are read in one of five, often overlapping, ways. They are predicted, sounded out, chunked, read by analogy, or recognized immediately. Predicting means using context by itself or context plus some decoding to read a word. Seeing the letter *w* and using the context "Sam was pulling a red w _____," the student predicts that the word missing is *wagon*. Sounding out entails pronouncing words letter by letter or sound by sound (/h/ + /a/ + /t/) and then blending them into a word. As readers become more advanced, they group or chunk sounds into pronounceable units (/h/ + /at/). Readers may also decode a word because it is analogous to a known word. They can read the new word *net* because it is like the known word *pet*. In the fifth process, the words are recognized with virtually no mental effort. Adept readers have met some words so often that they recognize them just about as soon as they see them. These are called sight words because they are apparently recognized at sight (Ehri & McCormick, 1998).

How High-Frequency Words Are Learned

According to Ehri (1998), learning words at sight entails forging links that connect the written form of the word and its pronunciation and meaning. Looking at the spelling of a word, the experienced reader retrieves its pronunciation and meaning from her or his mental dictionary or storehouse of words instantaneously. Beginners might look at a word, analyze it into its component sounds, blend the sounds, and say the word. At the same time, they note how the word's letters symbolize single or groups of sounds. Over time, the connections that the reader makes between letters and sounds enable the reader to retrieve the spoken form and meaning of the word just about instantaneously. The reader makes adjustments for irregular words so that certain letters are flagged as being silent or having an unusual pronunciation. "Knowledge of letter-sound relations provides a powerful mnemonic system that bonds the written forms of specific words to their pronunciations in memory" (Ehri & McCormick, 1998, p. 140).

■ Stages in Reading Words

Prealphabetic Stage

Students go through stages or phases in their use of word analysis skills. Young children surprise their elders by reading McDonald's signs, soda can and milk carton labels, and the names of cereals. However, for the most part, these children are not translating letters into sounds as more mature readers would do; instead, they are associating "nonphonemic visual characteristics" with spoken words (Ehri, 1994). For instance, a child remembers the

■ **Phonics** is the study of speech sounds related to reading.

word *McDonald's* by associating it with the golden arches and the word *Pepsi* by associating it with its logo. At times, teachers take advantage of the nonphonemic characteristics of words. They tell students that the word *tall* might be remembered because it has three tall letters and that *camel* is easy to recall because the *m* in the middle of the word has two humps.

In the prealphabetic (prephonemic) stage, students learn a word by selective association, by selecting some nonphonemic feature that distinguishes it from other words (Gough, Juel, & Griffith, 1992). For the word *elephant*, it could be the length of the word; for the word *look*, it could be the two *o*'s that are like eyes. The problem with selective association is that students run out of distinctive clues, and the clues that they use do not help them decode new words. Students can learn only about forty words using nonphonemic clues (Gough & Hillinger, 1980). In addition, students don't begin to advance in their understanding of the alphabetic nature of the language until they begin to use letter-sound relationships to read words.

Students' invented or spontaneous spelling provides clues to the stage they are in. They may use random letters to represent a word. Or they may even be able to spell their names because they have memorized the letters. As students become aware of individual sounds in words and the fact that letters represent sounds, they move into the second stage of reading, the partial alphabetic stage (Byrne, 1992).

Partial Alphabetic Stage

In the alphabetic (letter name) stage, learners use letter-sound relationships to read words. In the partial alphabetic stage, they may use just a letter or two. They may use only the first letter of a word and combine the sound of that letter with context. For instance, in the sentence "The cat meowed," students may process only the initial *m* and then use context and their experience with cats to guess that the word is *meowed*. Or they may use the first and last letter to decode the word *cat* in "I lost my cat," so they read the word *cat* as opposed to *cap* or *car*. Students at this stage cannot use full decoding because they haven't yet learned vowel correspondences. Because they are using partial cues, these students store incomplete representations of words and so confuse words like *where, when*, and *were* (Pikulski, 2006).

In their spontaneous spelling, students at this stage may represent a word by using just the first letter, such as K for *car*, or by using the letters that represent the most distinctive sounds, as in KR for *car*. At the end of this stage, they begin using vowels but may not spell the words correctly.

Full Alphabetic Stage

In the full alphabetic stage, students begin to process all the letters in words. As they learn to apply their growing knowledge of letter-sound relationships, their reading may be slow and effortful. Focusing on using their newly learned decoding skills, students cautiously read word by word. Students are "glued to print" (Chall, 1996). The danger at this stage is that too much emphasis will be put on accuracy and sounding out. This could impede students' development. "Too analytical an approach . . . may hold up silent reading comprehension" (Chall, 1996, p. 47). With students glued to print, this is a bottom-up stage. As students build their store of known words, they are better able to see commonalities in words. They note that both *cat* and *hat* have *at*. Encountering the word *mat*, which they have never seen in print, they can decode it by noting the pronounceable part *at* and blending it with *m*. Or they may use an analogy strategy. Seeing that *mat* is similar to *cat* enables them to read the word.

Students spell vowel sounds in this stage but may not spell them correctly. Because they may not perceive patterns until the end of this stage, they may fail to use final *e* (*hope*) and double vowel letters (*coat*) to represent long-vowel sounds.

BUILDING LANGUAGE

As you develop students' phonics skills, be sure to continue to foster language development through discussions and read-alouds. It doesn't do students much good to sound out words whose meanings they don't know.

ASSESSING FOR LEARNING

To determine what stages students are in, note what phonics cues they use to read words and also their spelling. If they are using picture clues primarily, they may be in a prealphabetic stage. If they are using initial consonants primarily, they may be in an early alphabetic stage. Gear instruction to their stage of reading.

Consolidated Alphabetic Stage

In the consolidated alphabetic (within-word pattern) stage, students consolidate and process longer and more sophisticated units. For instance, instead of processing *hen* as *h-e-n*, they may divide it into two units: *h + en*. They process *light* as *l + ight* and make use of such elements as a final *e* (as in *cape*) to help them determine the pronunciation of a word. In spelling, they begin using final *e* or use two vowel letters to show that a vowel is long.

As students process the same words over and over again, connections are made, and they do not have to read *cat* as /k/ /a/ /t/, or even /k/ /at/. Rather, the printed representation of the word as a whole elicits its spoken equivalent. The printed representation becomes bonded with the spoken equivalent (Perfetti, 1992). As Ehri (1998) explains, "Sight word learning is at root an alphabetic process in which spellings of specific words are secured to their pronunciations in memory" (p. 105). Gough, Juel, and Griffith (1992) explain the process somewhat differently. They believe that just about all the letters in a word are analyzed. Through practice, access speed increases so that even though words are analyzed element by element, this is done so rapidly as to be almost instantaneous. Perfetti (1985) suggests that even when words are recognized immediately, the decoding processes are still at work but are on a subconscious level. This underlying processing verifies our word recognition so that we are alerted when we misread a word. This system also enables us to read very rapidly words we have never seen before.

Regardless of how the process is explained, the end result is the same. In time, nearly all the words expert readers encounter in print are read as sight words. They are recognized virtually instantaneously. What makes the instantaneous recognition possible are the connections that have been created between each word's spelling or phonics elements and its pronunciation and meaning. To create this bond between a word's written appearance and its pronunciation and meaning, students must have many opportunities to encounter the word in print. It is also important that students process the whole word rather than simply look at the initial consonant and guess what the rest of the word is. By processing the whole word, students are creating a stronger, clearer bond between the word and its pronunciation. However, the rate at which individuals create these bonds may vary. Research suggests that there is a processing ability that determines the rate at which these associations are formed (Torgeson et al., 1997). This means that some students will need more practice than others, and, in some instances, special help.

Having a firmer command of basic phonics skills, students at this stage begin to incorporate top-down strategies. They begin to rely more on "knowledge of language, of ideas, and of facts to anticipate meanings as well as new words" (Chall, 1996, p. 47). Students begin using an integrated approach. Their decoding also becomes fluent and virtually automatic so that they can devote full attention to comprehension.

In the beginning of this stage, students begin using final *e* and double letters to represent long-vowel sounds but may do so incorrectly. By the end of this stage, their spelling has become conventional.

Implications of Stage Theory

This theory of the stages of reading has two very important implications for the teaching of reading. First, it suggests that nearly all the words we acquire are learned through phonics. Therefore, words to be learned (except for a few highly irregular ones, such as *of* and *one*, and perhaps a few learned in the very beginning) should be taught through a phonics approach rather than through an approach based on visual memory. Most words that have been classified as having irregular spellings are at least partly predictable. For instance, the first and last letters of *was* are regular, as are the first and last letters of *been*. In fact, except for *of*, it is hard to find any word that does not have some degree of spelling-sound predictability. In teaching words, take advantage of that regularity. It will make the words easier to learn and to recognize. And establishing links between letters and sounds helps fix words in memory so that they are eventually recognized instantaneously, or at sight.

The stage theory also implies that instruction should be geared to the stage that a student is in. Students lacking in phonemic awareness may have difficulty with letter-sound instruction unless it incorporates practice with phonemic awareness. Whereas using picture clues and memorizing predictable stories is appropriate for building emergent literacy, students in the alphabetic stage should be focusing on letters and sounds. This helps foster their decoding ability. Moreover, a student in the partial alphabetic stage is not ready for the final-*e* pattern, as in *pipe* and *late*.

Differentiation of Phonics Instruction

In her study of the first-grade level of five basal anthology programs, Maslin (2003) noted that most of the programs recommended whole-class instruction and moving all students through phonics lessons at the same pace. Even through the programs recommended differentiating instruction on the basis of assessment, none of them suggested placing students at a lower-grade level if they were significantly behind in reading skills. As Invernizzi and Hayes (2004) comment, classes in which grouping is used to differentiate phonics instruction "seem to be slim to nil" (p. 223). They add, "Because of the ease of implementation, many teachers will want their students to continue through their grade-level program regardless of their instructional level. . . . Contrary to what commercial programs would have us believe, systematic, explicit instruction is not synonymous with everyone [being] on the same page at the same time in the same workbook" (pp. 224, 226).

■■■ Checkup ■■■

1. What are the key stages in learning to read?
2. How might knowledge of stages be used to guide instruction?

■■■

■ Basic Principles of Phonics Instruction

Phonics instruction is of no value unless it fulfills some specific conditions. First, it must teach skills necessary for decoding words. Being able to read the short *a* in *hat* is an important skill, but knowing whether the *a* is long or short is not important; students can guess that the *a* is short without being able to read the word. Noting so-called silent letters is another useless skill. Knowing that the *k* in *knight* is silent does not ensure that a student can read the word.

Second, the skill should be one that students do not already know. One second-grader who was reading a fourth-grade book was put through a second-grade phonics workbook to make sure she had the necessary skills. If students can read material on a third-grade level or above, they obviously have just about all the phonics skills they will ever need.

The IRA recognizes that the teaching of phonics is an essential part of beginning reading instruction. "However, effective phonics instruction must be embedded in the context of a total reading/language arts program. . . . Classroom teachers in the primary grades do value and do teach phonics as part of their reading programs. . . . Effective teachers of reading and writing ask when, how, how much, and under what circumstances phonics should be taught" (International Reading Association, 1999c). The IRA is against "curricular mandates that require teachers to blindly follow highly prescriptive plans for phonics instruction" but supports "curriculum development that effectively integrates phonics into the total reading program."

IRA Position Statement

on Key Issue

The Teaching of Phonics

Finally, the skills being taught should be related to reading tasks in which students are currently engaged or will soon be engaged. For instance, the time to teach that *ee* = /ē/ in words such as *jeep* and *sheep* is when students are about to read a book like *Sheep in a Jeep* (Shaw, 1986). All too often, they are taught skills far in advance of the time they will use them, or well after the relevant selection has been read, with no opportunity to apply the skills within a reasonable amount of time. This is ineffective instruction. Research indicates that children do not use or internalize information unless the skills they have been taught are applicable in their day-to-day reading (Adams, 1990).

In summary, phonics instruction must be functional, useful, and contextual to be of value. It also should be planned, systematic, and explicit (Fielding-Barnsley, 1997; Foorman et al., 1998).

■ Phonics Elements

Before considering how to teach phonics, you need to know the content of phonics. Knowing the content, you are in a better position to decide how to teach phonics elements and in what order these elements might be taught.

The content of phonics is fairly substantial. Depending on the dialect, English has forty or more sounds; however, many of them, especially vowels, may be spelled in more than one way. As a result, children have to learn more than a hundred spellings. The number would be even greater if relatively infrequent spellings were included, such as the *eigh* spelling of /ā/ in *neighbor* or the *o* spelling of /i/ in *women*.

Consonants

There are twenty-five consonant sounds in English (see Table 4.1). Some of the sounds are spelled with two letters (*church* and *ship*), and two letters that represent just one sound are known as **digraphs**. The most frequently occurring digraphs are *sh* (*shop*), *ch* (*child*), *ng* (*sing*), *wh* (*whip*), *th* (*thumb*), and *th* (*that*). Common digraphs are listed in Table 4.2.

Some groups of consonants represent two or even three sounds (*stop*, *strike*). These are known as **clusters,** or blends, and are listed in Table 4.3 (on p. 160). Most clusters are composed of *l, r,* or *s* and another consonant or two. Because they are composed of two or more sounds, clusters pose special problems for students. Novice readers have a difficult time discriminating separate sounds in a cluster and often decode just the first sound, the /s/ in *st*, for example.

Vowels

English has about sixteen vowel sounds. (The number varies somewhat because some dialects have more than others.) Each vowel sound has a variety of spellings. For example, /ā/, which is commonly referred to as long *a*, is usually spelled *a_e*, as in *late; a* at the end of a syllable, as in *favor*; or *ai* or *ay*, as in *train* and *tray*. So, the vowel sound /ā/ has four main spellings, two of which are closely related: *ay* appears in the final position, and *ai* is found in initial and medial positions.

■ **Digraphs** (*di,* "two"; *graphs,* "written symbols") are two letters used to spell a single sound. If you look at the consonant chart in Table 4.1, you will notice that some of the sounds are spelled with two letters. The sound /f/ is usually spelled with *f* as in *fox* but may also be spelled with *ph* or *gh,* as in *photograph.*

■ A **cluster** is composed of two or more letters that represent two or more sounds, such as the *br* in *broom.* Clusters are sometimes called blends. Because it is difficult to hear the separate sounds in a cluster, this element poses a special difficulty for many students.

■■■ TABLE 4.1   Consonant Spellings

Sound	Initial	Final	Model Word
/b/	*b*arn	ca*b*, ro*b*e	ball
/d/	*d*eer	ba*d*	dog
/f/	*f*un, *ph*oto	lau*gh*	fish
/g/	*g*ate, *gh*ost, *gu*ide	ra*g*	goat
/h/	*h*ouse, w*h*o		hat
/hw/	*wh*ale		whale
/j/	*j*ug, *g*ym, sol*d*ier	a*ge*, ju*dge*	jar
/k/	*c*an, *k*ite, *qu*ick, *ch*aos	ba*ck*, a*ch*e	cat, key
/l/	*l*ion	mai*l*	leaf
/m/	*m*e	hi*m*, co*mb*, autu*mn*	man
/n/	*n*ow, *kn*ow, *gn*u, *pn*eumonia	pa*n*	nail
/p/	*p*ot	to*p*	pen
/r/	*r*ide, *wr*ite		ring
/s/	*s*ight, *c*ity	bu*s*, mi*ss*, fa*ce*	sun
/t/	*t*ime	ra*t*, jump*ed*	table
/v/	*v*ase	lo*ve*	vest
/w/	*w*e, *wh*eel		wagon
/y/	*y*acht, on*i*on		yo-yo
/z/	*z*ipper	ha*s*, bu*zz*	zebra
/ch/	*ch*ip, *c*ello, ques*ti*on	ma*tch*	chair
/sh/	*sh*ip, *s*ure, *ch*ef, a*cti*on	pu*sh*, spe*ci*al, mi*ssi*on	sheep
/th/	*th*in	brea*th*	thumb
/<u>th</u>/	*th*is	brea*the*	the
/zh/	a*z*ure, ver*si*on	bei*ge*, gara*ge*	garage
/ŋ/		si*ng*	ring

All the other vowel sounds are similar to /ā/ in having two to four major spellings. Considering correspondences in this way makes vowel spellings seem fairly regular. It is true that /ā/ and other vowel sounds can each be spelled in a dozen or more ways, but many of these spellings are oddities. For instance, the *Random House Dictionary* (Flexner & Hauck, 1994) lists nineteen spellings of /ā/, in the words *ate, Gael, champagne, rain, arraign, gaol, gauge, ray, exposé, suede, steak, matinee, eh, veil, feign, Marseilles, demesne, beret,* and *obey*. Many of these are in words borrowed from other languages.

A chart of vowels and their major spellings is presented in Table 4.4 (on p. 161). Note that the chart lists twenty-two vowel sounds and includes *r* vowels, which are combinations of *r* and a vowel and so, technically, are not distinct vowels.

FYI

■ Go back to Table 3.3 on p. 109 to review the formation of vowel sounds.

■ Short vowels are the vowel sounds heard in *cat, pet, sit, hot,* and *cut.*

■ Long vowels are the vowel sounds heard in *cake, sleep, pie, boat,* and *use.*

■■■ TABLE 4.2   Common Consonant Digraphs

Correspondence	Examples	Correspondence	Examples
ch = /ch/	chair, church	*sh* = /sh/	shoe, shop
ck = /k/	tack, pick	(*s*)*si* = /sh/	mission
gh = /f/	rough, tough	*th* = /<u>th</u>/	there, them
kn = /n/	knot, knob	*th* = /th/	thumb, thunder
ng = /ŋ/	thing, sing	*ti* = /sh/	station, action
ph = /f/	phone, photograph	*wh* = /w/	wheel, where
sc = /s/	scissors, scientist	*wr* = /r/	wrench, wrestle

■■■■   **TABLE 4.3**   **Common Consonant Clusters**

Initial Clusters							
With *l*	Example Words	With *r*	Example Words	With *s*	Example Words	Other	Example Words
bl	blanket, black	*br*	broom, bread	*sc*	score, scale	*tw*	twelve, twin
cl	clock, clothes	*cr*	crow, crash	*sch*	school, schedule	*qu*	queen, quick
fl	flag, fly	*dr*	dress, drink	*scr*	scream, scrub		
gl	glove, glue	*fr*	frog, from	*sk*	sky, skin		
pl	plum, place	*gr*	green, ground	*sl*	sled, sleep		
sl	slide, slow	*pr*	prince, prepare	*sm*	smoke, smile		
				sn	snake, sneakers		
				sp	spider, spot		
				st	star, stop		
				sw	sweater, swim		

Final Clusters					
With *l*	Example Words	With *n*	Example Words	Other	Example Words
ld	field, old	*nce*	prince, chance	*ct*	fact, effect
lf	wolf, self	*nch*	lunch, bunch	*mp*	jump, camp
lk	milk, silk	*nd*	hand, wind	*sp*	wasp, grasp
lm	film	*nk*	tank, wink	*st*	nest, best
lp	help	*nt*	tent, sent		
lt	salt, belt				
lve	twelve, solve				

FYI

Although onsets and rimes seem to be natural units of language, some students may have to process individual sounds before being able to group them into rimes. They may need to learn *a* = /a/ and *t* = /t/ before learning the rime *-at.*

Onsets and Rimes

The **onset** is the consonant or consonant cluster preceding the rime: *b-, st-, scr-*. The **rime** is a vowel or vowels and any consonants that follow: *-at, -op, -een*. Rimes, which are also known as phonograms and word families, are highly predictable. When considered by itself, *a* can represent several sounds. However, when followed by a consonant, it is almost always short (*-at, -an, -am*).

■■■ Checkup ■■■

1. What are the key phonics elements?

■■■

■ Approaches to Teaching Phonics

There are two main approaches to teaching phonics: analytic and synthetic. In the **analytic approach**, consonants are generally not isolated but are taught within the context of a whole word. For example, the sound /b/ would be referred to as the one heard in the beginning of *ball* and *boy*. The sound /b/ is not pronounced in isolation because that would

■ The **onset** is the initial part of a word, the part that precedes the first vowel. The onset could be a single consonant (*c+at*), a digraph (*sh+eep*), or a cluster (*tr+ip*). A word that begins with a vowel, such as *owl* or *and,* does not have an onset.

■ The **rime** is the part of a word that rhymes, such as *-ook* in *look* or *-ow* in *cow.*

■ The **analytic approach** involves studying sounds within the context of the whole word; for example, /w/ is referred to as

the sound heard at the beginning of *wagon.*

■ The **synthetic approach** involves decoding words sound by sound and then synthesizing the sounds into words.

■■■ **TABLE 4.4   Vowel Spellings**

	Vowel Sound	Major Spellings	Model Word
Short Vowels	/a/	rag, happen, have	cat
	/e/	get, letter, thread	bed
	/i/	wig, middle, event	fish
	/o/	fox, problem, father	mop
	/u/	bus	cup
Long Vowels	/ā/	name, favor, say, sail	rake
	/ē/	he, even, eat, seed, bean, key, these, either, funny, serious	wheel
	/ī/	hide, tiny, high, lie, sky	nine
	/ō/	vote, open, coat, bowl, old, though	nose
	/ū/	use, human	cube
Other Vowels	/aw/	daughter, law, walk, off, bought	saw
	/oi/	noise, toy	boy
	/o͝o/	wood, should, push	foot
	/o͞o/	soon, new, prove, group, two, fruit, truth	school
	/ow/	tower, south	cow
	/ə/	above, operation, similar, opinion, suppose	banana
r Vowels	/ar/	far, large, heart	car
	/air/	hair, care, where, stair, bear	chair
	/i(ə)r/	dear, steer, here	deer
	/ər/	her, sir, fur, earth	bird
	/īər/	fire, wire	tire
	/or/	horse, door, tour, more	four

distort it to "buh." Although somewhat roundabout, the analytic approach does not distort the sound /b/.

In the **synthetic approach**, words are decoded sound by sound, and both consonant and vowel sounds are pronounced in isolation. A child decoding *cat* would say, "Kuh-ah-tuh." This approach is very direct, but it distorts consonant sounds, which cannot be pronounced accurately without a vowel. However, Ehri (1991) maintained that artificial procedures, such as saying the sound represented by each letter in a word, may be necessary to help beginning readers decipher words.

For most of the twentieth century, the major basals advocated an analytic approach in which letter sounds were never isolated and there was heavy reliance on the use of the initial consonant of a word and context. Selections were chosen on the basis of topic or literary quality, so they didn't reinforce the phonics elements that had been taught. Today, all of the basals use a systematic, synthetic approach to phonics, in which students are taught to say individual sounds and blend them. However, this book recommends a combination of the analytic and synthetic approaches. Novice readers need to have the target sound highlighted by hearing it in isolation, which is what the synthetic approach does. And they need to hear it in the context of a real word, which is what the analytic approach does.

Phonics instruction can also be part to whole or whole to part. In a whole-to-part approach, students listen to or share-read a selection. From the selection, the teacher draws the element to be presented. After share-reading "Star Light, Star Bright," the teacher might lead students to see that *bright*, *might*, and *light* contain the *ight* pattern. After discussing the pattern, students then read a selection such as *Sleepy Dog* (Ziefert, 1984) that contains the element. In a part-to-whole approach, the teacher presents the *ight* pattern in preparation for reading *Sleepy Dog*. Both approaches prepare students for an upcoming selection. However, the whole-to-part approach also helps students to relate the element to a familiar selection and words that they have seen in print (Moustafa & Maldonado-Colon, 1999).

Phonics instruction can be embedded or systematic. In systematic instruction, students are taught all the key elements in a logical sequence. With embedded instruction, students are taught phonics as a need arises and in the context of reading a selection in which the target element occurs. For instance, after share-reading the nursery rhyme "Little Boy Blue," students discuss the fact that *horn* and *corn* rhyme and are spelled with the rime -*orn*. Later, they discover that in the weather rhyme "Red sky at night, Sailor's delight; Red sky in the morning, Sailor's warning," the /orn/ sound is spelled *arn* in *warning*. Noting that the word *war* has an /or/ sound, they come to the conclusion that *w* sometimes has an effect on the vowel that follows it. There is a need for both embedded and systematic phonics instruction. While making discoveries is a highly effective way to learn, students may not make all the discoveries they need to make about phonics.

▪▪▪ Checkup ▪▪▪

1. What are the major approaches to teaching phonics?
2. What are the advantages and disadvantages of each?

▪▪▪

Teaching Initial Consonants

Phonics instruction typically begins with initial consonants. Being the first sound in a word, initial consonants are easier to hear. Initial consonants are typically the first element to appear in children's invented spelling. Students may pick up some knowledge of initial consonants through shared reading and through writing activities, but letter-sound relationships should also be taught explicitly to make sure that students have learned these important elements, to clarify any misconceptions that may have arisen, and to provide additional reinforcement. A phonics lesson starts with phonemic awareness to make sure students can perceive the sound of the element and then proceeds to the visual level, where the children integrate sound and letter knowledge. A six-step lesson for teaching initial consonants is detailed in Lesson 4.1. It assumes that the students can segment a word into its separate sounds, have a concept of beginning sounds, and realize that sounds are represented by letters; these skills were explained in Chapter 3. The lesson is synthetic and analytic: The consonant sound is presented both in isolation and in the context of a whole word. If possible, relate your instruction to a story, song, or rhyme or to a language experience story that you have share-read. This whole-to-part approach helps students relate the phonics they are learning to real reading (Moustafa & Maldonado-Colon, 1999).

ASSESSING FOR LEARNING

Observe students as they work with beginning sounds. If students are having difficulty perceiving initial *m*, ask questions that help them focus on the beginning sound. Pointing to a picture of the moon, ask, "Is this an 'oon'? No? What is it? What sound did I leave off?" Use this same procedure with other *m* words: *monkey, man, milk.*

Lesson 4.1

Analytic-Synthetic Introduction of Initial Consonant Correspondence

Step 1. Phonemic awareness

Teach the letter-sound relationship in the initial position of words. In teaching the correspondence (letter-sound relationship) *m* = /m/, read a story such as *Papa, Please Get the Moon for Me* (Carle, 1987) that contains a number of *m* words. Call students' attention to the *m* words from the book: *moon, me, man.* Explain how the lips are pressed together to form /m/. Stressing the initial sound as you say each word, ask students to tell what is the same about the words: "mmmoon," "mmme," and "mmman." Lead students to see that all the words begin in the same way. Ask them to supply other words that begin like *moon, me*, and *man*. Give hints, if necessary—an animal that can climb trees (monkey), something that we drink (milk).

Step 2. Letter-sound integration

Write the *m* words on the board, and ask what is the same about the way *moon, me*, and *man* are written. Lead students to see that the words all begin with the letter *m* and that the letter *m* stands for the sound /m/ heard at the beginning of *moon*. At this point, *moon* becomes a model word. This is a simple word that can be depicted and that contains the target letter and sound. When referring to the sound represented by *m*, say that it is /m/, the sound heard at the beginning of *moon*, so that students can hear the sound both in isolation and in the context of a word. You might ask if there is anyone in the class whose name begins like /m/ in *moon*. List the names of students whose names begin like /m/ in *moon*. Explain to students why you are using a capital letter for the names.

Step 3. Guided practice

Provide immediate practice. Help students read food labels that contain /m/ words: *milk, mayonnaise, margarine, mustard, marshmallows*. Read a story together about monkeys or masks, or sing a song or read a rhyme that has a generous share of /m/ words. Try to choose some items in which students integrate knowledge of the correspondence with context. Compose sentences such as "I will drink a glass of milk" and "At the zoo, we saw a monkey," and write them on the chalkboard. Read each sentence, stopping at the word beginning with /m/. Have students use context and their knowledge of the correspondence *m* = /m/ to predict the word.

Step 4. Application

As share reading or on their own, have students read selections that contain /m/ words. Students might read the *M* pages in alphabet books.

Step 5. Writing and spelling

If necessary, review the formation of the letter *m*. Dictate some easy *m* words (*me, man*), and have students spell them as best they can. Encourage students to use the letter *m* in their writing.

Step 6. Assessment and reteaching

Note whether students are able to read at least the initial consonant of *m* words and are using *m* in their writing. Review and reteach as necessary. Throughout the day, call attention to initial consonants that have been recently taught. As you prepare to write the word *Monday*, for instance, ask students to tell what sound *Monday* begins with and what letter makes that sound. Also label items in your class that begin with the letter *m: mirror, magnets*.

FYI

■ If students struggle with this approach to teaching initial consonants, try the speech-to-print approach on pp. 132–134.

■ Continuants like /m/, /f/, and /s/ are less distorted because they are articulated with a continuous stream of breath.

Using Children's Books to Reinforce Initial Consonants

A good children's book can be a powerful medium for presenting or providing practice with phonics. A book such as *Easy as Pie* (Folsom & Folsom, 1986) is excellent for integrating knowledge of initial consonants and context (see Figure 4.1). Common similes, except for the last word, are shown on the right-hand page, as is the letter of the missing word. The answer appears when the child turns the page. For instance, the *S* page contains the letter *S* and the words "Deep as the." Read the first part of the simile aloud, and tell the students that the next word begins with the letter *s*. Ask students to guess what they think the word is. Remind them that the word must begin with /s/, the sound heard at the beginning of *sun*. Write their responses on the board. If any word supplied does not begin with /s/, discuss why this could not be the right answer. Turn the page to uncover the word that completes the riddle, and let students read the answer. Discuss why the answer is correct.

■■■ **FIGURE 4.1**

S Pages from *Easy as Pie*

Deep as the Sea

From *Easy as Pie* by Marcia Folsom and Michael Folsom, 1986, Boston: Houghton Mifflin. Copyright © 1986 by Marcia Folsom and Michael Folsom. Reprinted by permission of Marcia Folsom.

FYI

■ Using context to verify decoding is known as cross-checking. The student checks to see whether the decoded word makes sense in the selection.

■ When using alphabet books, be on the lookout for confusing presentations. In one book, the words *tiger, thin,* and *the* are used to demonstrate the sound usually represented by the letter *t.* However, *th* in *thin* represents a different sound than that heard at the beginning of *tiger,* and *th* in *the* represents the voiced counterpart of *th* in *thin.*

Emphasize that it makes sense in the phrase and begins with /s/, the same sound heard at the beginning of *sun.*

Another book that combines context and knowledge of beginning consonant correspondences is *The Alphabet Tale,* by Jan Garten (1964). Shown on the *S* page is a large red *S,* a seal's tail, and a riddle:

His home is the Arctic
Raw fish is his meal.
This is the tale of a whiskered . . .

The next page shows the rest of the seal and the word *Seal.* The Student Reading List identifies more titles that may be used to reinforce initial consonants.

Student Reading List

Books for Reinforcing Initial Consonants

Amery, H. (1997). *Usborne farmyard tales, alphabet book.* London: Usborne. An alliterative sentence and question reinforce each target letter.

Calmenson, S. (1993). *It begins with an A.* New York: Hyperion. Rhyming riddles challenge the reader to guess objects whose names begin with letters *A* to *Z.*

Cohen, N. (1993). *From apple to zipper.* New York: Macmillan. Rhyming text is accompanied by illustrations that form the letters they represent.

Ellwand, D. (1996). *Emma's elephant & other favorite animal friends.* New York: Dutton. Black-and-white photos and brief alliterative captions depict children with animals.

Hindley, J. *Crazy ABC.* (1994). Cambridge, MA: Candlewick. Target letters are reinforced with zany alliterative sentences.

Hofbauer, M. (1993). *All the letters*. Bridgeport, CT: Greene Barke Press. Each letter is accompanied by an alliterative story.

Inches, A. (2003). *An ABC adventure*. New York: Simon & Schuster. By lifting flaps, readers find objects that begin with the target letter.

Joyce, S. (1999). *ABC animal riddles*. Columbus, NC: Peel Productions. Readers are asked to guess the identity of animals based on verbal and picture clues.

Laidlaw, K. (1996). *The amazing I spy ABC*. New York: Dial. Readers spy objects whose names begin with the target letter.

Moxley, S. (2001). *ABCD: An alphabet book of cats and dogs*. Boston: Little, Brown. An alliterative tale accompanies each letter.

Adapting Instruction for English Language Learners

Before teaching elements that are not present in Spanish—*sh*, for instance—make sure that these elements have been introduced in the ESL class. For easily confused auditory items—*sh* and *ch*, for example—provide added auditory-discrimination exercises in which students tell whether pairs of easily confused words such as *choose–shoes* or *shine–shine* are the same or different. Also, use the words in sentence context, or use real objects or pictures to illustrate them. When discussing *sheep*, for example, hold up a picture of sheep.

One problem with using alphabet books is that children might not be familiar with the objects being presented or may call the objects by different names. Children might mistake a wolf for a dog. A cap might be identified as a hat. A piece of software that avoids these difficulties but presents excellent reinforcement is *Kidspiration* (Inspiration). *Kidspiration* has a library of 1,200 illustrations and a speech component that can be used to create excellent phonics reinforcement activities. When working with initial consonant correspondences, students can search through illustrations and select those that begin with a target letter. Figure 4.2 shows a finished exercise in which items whose names begin with *b* have been selected. Because *Kidspiration* has speech capability, children using it can have the name of the item spoken and also spelled out.

After an alphabet or other book has been discussed, place it in the class library so that students may "read" it. Encourage children to check out books for home use.

Be sure to make use of students' emerging knowledge of letter-sound relationships when reading big books. After reading Paul Galdone's (1975) *The Gingerbread Boy*, for instance, turn to the page on which the gingerbread boy meets the cow. Read the words *cow, can*, and *catch*. Discuss how the words sound alike and begin with the letter *c*. Encourage the use of context. Reread the story, stopping when you come to a word that begins with *c*. Encourage students to read the word. Using *cow* as a key word, remind students that the word should begin with /k/ as in *cow*. Also remind them of the context of the sentence to help them learn to integrate letter-sound relationships with context. To further reinforce the *c* = /k/ correspondence, have students draw a picture of something they *can* do and write a short piece about it. Individual stories could be the basis for a group story or booklet that tells about the talents and abilities of all class members.

■ ■ ■ ■ **FIGURE 4.2**

Exercise Created with *Kidspiration*

Sorting

One activity that is especially useful in deepening students' understanding about phonics elements is sorting (Bear, 1995). Sorting forces children to analyze the elements in a word or picture and select critical features as they place the words or pictures in piles. Through sorting, students classify words and pictures on the basis of sound and spelling and construct an understanding of the spelling system. They also enjoy this active, hands-on, nonthreatening activity.

Students should sort only elements and words that they know. This allows them to construct basic understandings of the spelling system. Although they may be able to read *cat, hat*, and *bat*, they may not realize that the words all rhyme and follow a CVC (consonant-vowel-consonant) pattern. Sorting helps students come to these understandings.

Students' sorting activities are determined by their stage of spelling development. Students in the early alphabetic stage may sort pictures and, later, words according to their beginning sounds. In the consolidated alphabetic stage, students sort words according to whether they have long or short vowels, have an *e* marker, or have a double-vowel pattern, and then according to the specific long-vowel or other vowel pattern they illustrate. Words can also be sorted according to initial digraphs or consonant clusters or any other element that students need to study.

Lesson 4.2 shows how students in the early alphabetic stage might be taught to sort initial consonant sounds. The lesson is adapted from Bear (1995).

Lesson 4.2

Sorting by Beginning Consonant Sounds

Step 1. Set up the sort
Set up two columns. At the top of each column, place an illustration of the sound to be sorted. If you plan to have students sort /s/ and /r/ words, use an illustration of the sun and an illustration of a ring. A pocket chart works well for this activity.

Step 2. Explain sorting
Tell students that you will be giving them cards that have pictures on them. Explain that they will be placing the cards under the picture of the sun if the words begin with /s/, the sound heard at the beginning of *sun*, or under the picture of the ring if the words begin with /r/, the sound heard at the beginning of *ring*.

Step 3. Model the sorting procedure
Shuffle the cards. Tell the students, "Say the name of the picture. Listen carefully to see whether the name of the picture begins like /s/ as in *sun* or /r/ as in *ring*." Model the process with two or three cards: "This is a picture of a saw. *Saw* has an /s/ sound and begins like *sun*, so I will put it under *sun*. *Sun* and *saw* both begin with /s/."

Step 4. Children sort the cards
Distribute the cards. Have the students take turns placing a card in the /s/ or /r/ column. When students place their cards, have them say the picture's name and the sound it begins with. Correct errors quickly and simply. For instance, if a student puts a picture of a rat in the /s/ column, say, "*Rat* begins with /r/ and goes under *ring*," or ask why *rat* was put under *sun* and discuss its correct placement. A sample sort can be found in Figure 4.3. Have students sort cards a second and third time to solidify their perception of beginning sounds.

Step 5. Application
Have students find objects or pictures of objects whose names begin with /s/ or /r/. Proceed to other initial consonants, or sort known words that begin with /s/ or /r/.

Students might conduct sorts in pairs or small groups. A simple way to sort is to place a target word or illustration in the center of a table and then distribute cards, some of which contain the target element. Have students read or name the target element, and then have them take turns placing cards containing the target element. As students place cards, they should read the words or name the illustrations on them (Temple, Nathan, Temple, & Burris, 1993). For illustrations that can be used for sorting, go to the Webbing into Literacy Web site: http://curry.edschool.virginia.edu/go/wil/home.html. Although this site was designed for preschool students, the illustrations and word cards can be used with students of any age.

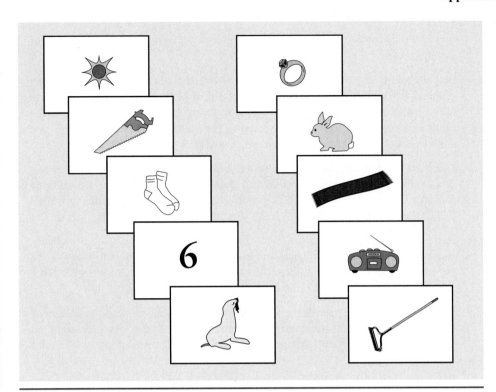

Sorts can be open or closed. In a closed sort, the teacher provides the basis for sorting the cards, as in Lesson 4.2. In an open sort, students decide the basis for sorting the cards.

Sometimes, students sort words visually. For example, after one -*at* word has been sorted, they simply put all the other -*at* words under it without actually thinking about the sound that the words have in common. To overcome this practice, use a blind sort. Draw a word from the pile to be sorted, and say it without showing it to the students. Then have them tell in which column it should be placed. After putting the word in the correct column, have a volunteer read it. For instance, picking up the word *rat*, you read it without showing it to students and they tell you whether it goes in the *cat, ran,* or *dad* column. A volunteer then reads all the words in that column (Johnston, 1999).

Reinforcement Activities

Consonant Letter-Sound Relationships

- Have students encounter initial consonants they know in books.
- Creating a language experience story also affords students the opportunity to meet phonics elements in print. While reading the story with an individual or group, the teacher can call attention to any consonants that have already been introduced. The teacher might pause before a word that begins with a known consonant and have a student attempt to read it.
- Play the game Going to Paris (Brewster, 1952). Players recite this:

  I'm going to Paris.
  I'm going to pack my bag with _____.

  The first player says an object whose name begins with the first letter of the alphabet. Subsequent players then say the names of all the objects mentioned by

FYI

The first word that most children learn is their name. To take advantage of this natural learning, create a chart of children's first names. When studying words that begin with a certain sound, refer to names on the chart that also begin with that sound. Attach photos of the students to the chart so that students may learn to associate printed names and faces.

■ ■ ■ **ASSESSING FOR LEARNING**

Some students need only a few repetitions in order to learn a correspondence. Others need numerous opportunities to practice skills. Note the degree of practice students need and be prepared to move on or to provide added reinforcement, depending on students' performance.

FYI

■ Have students create their own alphabet books. After a letter-sound relationship has been presented, direct students to create a page showing the upper- and lowercase forms of the letter along with a key word and an illustration of the word. As students learn to read words beginning with the letter and sound, they may add them to the page.

■ A good source of jump-rope chants and other rhymes is *A Rocket in My Pocket* (Withers, 1948), which is still available in paperback.

■ ■ ■ **USING TECHNOLOGY**

For additional sources for rhymes, see Building Literacy:
www.thomasgunning.org

previous players and identify an object whose name begins with the next letter of the alphabet.

■ Play the game Alphabet It. In this counting-out game, one child recites the letters of the alphabet. As the child says each letter, she or he points to the other members of the class whose names begin with the letter being recited. Each child pointed to removes himself or herself from the game. The alphabet is recited until just one child is left. That child is "it" for the next round or next game.

■ Use software that helps students discover letter-sound relationships, for instance, *Dr. Peet's Talk/Writer* (Interest-Driven Learning) or *Write Out Loud* (Don Johnston). These programs will say words that have been typed in. *Dr. Peet's Talk/Writer* also has an ABC Discovery module that introduces the alphabet.

■ Use CD-ROM software such as *Letter Sounds* (Sunburst). The student matches, sorts, and manipulates consonants and composes tongue twisters and songs based on initial sounds. *Curious George's ABC Adventure* (Sunburst) reinforces letter names and letter sounds.

■ As a review of initial consonant spelling-sound relationships, read the following jump-rope chant with students. Help students extend the chant through all the letters of the alphabet. Adapt the chant for boys by substituting *wife's* for *husband's*.

A—my name is Alice,
My husband's name is Andy,
We live in Alabama,
And we sell apples.

■ Traditional rhymes can also be used to reinforce initial consonant sounds. Do a shared reading of the rhyme first. Stress the target consonant letter-sound correspondence as you read the selection. During subsequent shared readings of the selection, encourage the class to read the words beginning with the target letter.

Deedle, deedle, dumpling, my son John,
Went to bed with his stockings on;
One shoe off, and one shoe on,
Deedle, deedle, dumpling, my son John.

Teaching Final Consonants

Final consonants are handled in much the same way as initial consonants. Relate them to their initial counterparts. And do not neglect them. According to a classic research study by Gibson, Osser, and Pick (1963), final consonants are a significant aid in the decoding of printed words. You might teach final consonants as you teach the word patterns that use them. For instance, teach final /t/ before or as you are teaching the *-at* pattern and final /d/ before or as you are teaching the *-ad* pattern. Be sure to develop phonemic awareness of final consonants. Use activities suggested in the lesson for initial consonants.

■ ■ ■ **Checkup** ■ ■ ■

1. How might consonant correspondences be taught?
2. What are some effective ways to reinforce initial consonants?

■ ■ ■

Teaching Consonant Clusters

Although consonants, consonant clusters, and vowel patterns are presented separately, their introduction should be integrated. As discussed earlier, clusters, which are sometimes known as blends, are combinations of consonants, as in *spot* or *straw*, that represent two (/s/ and /t/) or three (/s/ and /t/ and /r/) sounds clustered together. Many children have a great deal of difficulty learning the combination of sounds heard in clusters, such as *st* in *stop* and *fl* in *flag*. The problem is probably rooted in phonemic awareness. Children have difficulty separating the second sound in the cluster from the first. This is especially true of *l* and *r* clusters because they tend to merge with the preceding consonant. When teaching clusters, it is best to start with *s* clusters because they are more distinctive. When presenting a cluster, stress the separate sounds and also emphasize the second sound. To develop students' phonemic awareness, slowly say a word containing the cluster and have students count out the sounds, holding up a finger for each sound. For example, as you say "stick," hold up a finger as you say /s/, a second finger as you say /t/, a third as you say /i/, a fourth as you say /k/. Build on what students already know. In presenting the spelling of the cluster *st*, relate it to known words that begin with *s*. Place the word *sick* on the board, and have students read it. Carefully stretch out and count each sound: /s/, /i/, /k/. Ask them what needs to be added to *sick* to make the word *stick*. As you say "stick," emphasize the /t/. Present *sack–stack, sand–stand, sill–still*, and *sink–stink*. If students have had long-vowel words, you might also present *say–stay, sore–store*, and *seal–steal*. Once students have caught on to the *st* cluster, present other *st* words: *stop, stamp, step*.

Reinforcement Activities

Consonant Clusters

To help students distinguish between single consonants and clusters, have them sort stacks of word or picture cards representing single consonants and clusters containing that consonant. For instance, have students sort *s* and *st* words. Because students might have difficulty discriminating between the sound of /s/ and the sound of /st/, begin with picture sorts so that students can focus on sounds. Students might sort cards with the following pictures: sun, saw, sandwich, socks, six, seal, star, stick, step, and store. Pointing to the stack of cards portraying objects whose names begin with /s/ or /st/, tell students, "We're going to sort these picture cards. If the name of the picture begins with /s/ as in *sun*, we're going to put it in the sun column. If the name of the picture begins with /st/ as in *star*, we'll put it in the star column. Holding up a stamp, ask, "What is this? What sounds does it begin with? What column should we put it in?" Affirm or correct students' responses: "Yes, *stamp* begins with the sound /st/ that we hear in the beginning of *ssstttar*, so we'll put it in the star column." Go through the rest of the cards in this fashion. Once all the cards have been categorized, have volunteers say the names of all the cards in a column and note that they all begin with /s/ or /st/. Encourage students to suggest other words that might fit in the columns. Also have students sort the picture cards on their own to promote speed of response. You might then have them sort /s/ and /sp/ pictures (or words) and then /s/, /sp/, and /st/ pictures (or words).

Also try a spelling sort. For a spelling sort, set up two or three columns, and write the target element at the head of each column. For example, when presenting *s* and *st* words, write *s* above one column and *st* above the second, and dictate *s* and *st* words.

You can also use the following reinforcement activities:

- Use real-world materials to reinforce clusters. When introducing *sp*, for example, have students read food labels for spaghetti and spinach and brand names such as Spam and Spaghetti-Os.

■ Have students create words by adding newly learned clusters to previously presented word patterns. After being introduced to *st*, for instance, students might add it to short-vowel patterns that they have been taught: *-and, -ill, -ick,* and *-ing*.

■ The best reinforcement is to have students meet clusters in their reading. Clusters occur naturally in most books, so it's simply a matter of looking over texts and deciding which clusters you wish to emphasize. The following books have a high proportion of clusters:

O'Brien, J. (1995). *Sam and Spot: A silly story*. Boca Raton, FL: Cool Kids. A good alliterative read-aloud that emphasizes *s* clusters.

Ehlert, L. (1990). *Fish eyes: A book you can count on*. San Diego, CA: Harcourt. The text reinforces several major clusters.

Emberley, Ed. (1992). *Go away, Big Green Monster*. Boston: Little, Brown. This book reinforces *s* clusters.

Rohman, C. (1996). *Stories*. Live Oaks, CA: Outside the Box. Part of a series, this book reinforces the *st* cluster.

Troublesome Correspondences

The most difficult consonant letters are *c* and *g*. Both regularly represent two sounds: The letter *c* stands for /k/ and /s/, as in *cake* and *city*; the letter *g* represents /g/ and /j/, as in *go* and *giant*. The letter *c* represents /k/ far more often than it stands for /s/ (Gunning, 1975), and this is the sound students usually attach to it (Venezky, 1965); the letter *g* more often represents /g/. In teaching the consonant letters *c* and *g*, the more frequent sounds (*c* = /k/, *g* = /g/) should be presented first. The other sound represented by each letter (*c* = /s/, *g* = /j/) should be taught sometime later. At that point, it would also be helpful to teach the following generalizations:

■ The letter *g* usually stands for /j/ when followed by *e, i,* or *y*, as in *gem, giant,* or *gym*. (There are a number of exceptions: *geese, get, girl, give*.)

■ The letter *c* usually stands for /k/ when it is followed by *a, o,* or *u*, as in *cab, cob,* or *cub*.

■ The letter *c* usually stands for /s/ when followed by *e, i,* or *y*, as in *cereal, circle,* or *cycle*.

■ The letter *g* usually stands for /g/ when followed by *a, o,* or *u*, as in *gave, go,* or *gum*.

When teaching the *c* and *g* generalizations, do so inductively. For instance, list examples of the *c* spelling of /k/ in one column and the *c* spelling of /s/ in another. Have students read each word in the first column and note the sound that *c* represents and the vowel letter that follows *c*. Do the same with the second column. Then help students draw generalizations based on their observations. Better yet, have students sort *c* = /k/ and *c* = /s/ words and discover the generalization for themselves.

Variability Strategy.   An alternative to presenting the *c* and *g* generalizations is to teach students to be prepared to deal with the variability of the spelling of certain sounds. Students need to learn that, in English, letters can often stand for more than one sound. After learning the two sounds for *c* and *g*, students should be taught to use the following **variability strategy** when they are unsure how to read a word that begins with *c* or *g*.

FYI

■ The *g* generalizations help explain the *gu* spelling of /g/, as in *guide* and *guilt*. Without the *u* following the *g*, there would be a tendency to pronounce those words with the /j/ sound (Venezky, 1965). Determining the sound of *c* and *g* at the end of a word is relatively easy. If a word ends in *e*, *c* represents /s/ and *g* stands for /j/: *lace, page*. The letter *e* serves as a marker to indicate that *c* and *g* have their soft sounds.

■ Students need to see that the aim of phonics is to help them construct meaning from print. If they use phonics to decipher a word but end up with a nonword, they should try again. Even when they construct a real word, they should cross-check it by seeing if it makes sense in the sentence they are reading.

■ The **variability strategy** is a simpler procedure than the application of rules. Rather than trying to remember a rule, all the student has to do is try the major pronunciation, and, if that pronunciation does not work out, try another.

Student Strategies

Applying the Variability Strategy to Consonant Correspondences

1. Try the main pronunciation—the one the letter usually stands for.

2. If the main pronunciation gives a word that is not a real one or does not make sense in the sentence, try the other pronunciation.

3. If you still get a word that is not a real word or does not make sense in the sentence, ask for help.

Just as you post a chart to remind students of correct letter formation, display a chart showing all the major consonant correspondences and a key word for each. Students experiencing difficulty sounding out a word can refer to the chart. A child feeling puzzled when pronouncing *cider* as "kider" can look at the chart and note that *c* has two pronunciations: /k/ as in *cat* and /s/ as in *circle*. Since the /k/ pronunciation did not produce a word that made sense, the child tries the /s/ pronunciation. Table 4.1 could be used as a basis for constructing a consonant chart; a sample of such a chart is shown in Figure 4.4. Drawings, photos, or pictures may be used to illustrate each of the sounds. As new correspondences are learned, they can be added to the chart. The chart can also be used as a spelling aid.

▪ ▪ ▪ Checkup ▪ ▪ ▪

1. What makes consonant clusters hard to learn?
2. What special steps should be taken to teach consonant clusters?
3. Why is the variability strategy such a valuable tool for students?

▪ ▪ ▪

Teaching Vowel Correspondences

Vowels are taught in the same way as consonants. The main difference is that vowels can be spoken in isolation without distortion, so teaching vowels synthetically should not be confusing to students. Lesson 4.3 outlines how short *a* might be taught.

Lesson 4.3

Vowel Correspondence

Step 1. Phonemic awareness

Read a selection, such as *Cat Traps* (Coxe, 1996) or *The Cat Sat on the Mat* (Cameron, 1994), in which there are a number of short *a* words. Call student's attention to *a* words from the book: *cat, trap, sat*. Stressing the vowel sound as you say each word, ask students to tell what is the same about the words: "caaat," "traaap," and "saaat." Lead students to see that they all have an /a/ sound as in *cat*.

Step 2. Letter-sound integration

Write the words *cat, trap,* and *sat* on the board, saying each word as you do so. Ask students whether they can see what is the same about the words. Show them that all three words have an *a*, which stands for the sound /a/, as pronounced in *cat*. Have students read the words. Discuss other words, such as *man, bag,* and *dad,* that have the sound /a/. Have students read the words chorally and individually.

FYI

Vowels can be taught in isolation or as part of patterns. In this lesson, they are taught in isolation. Teaching vowels in isolation is helpful for students who are still learning to detect individual sounds in words.

Adapting Instruction for Struggling Readers and Writers

Struggling readers may have been taught a variety of decoding strategies, some of which may conflict with each other (Stahl, 1998). Focus on the teaching of a few strategies and meet with other professionals in the school to discuss and implement the use of a consistent set of strategies.

■■■ **FIGURE 4.4** **Beginning Consonant Chart**

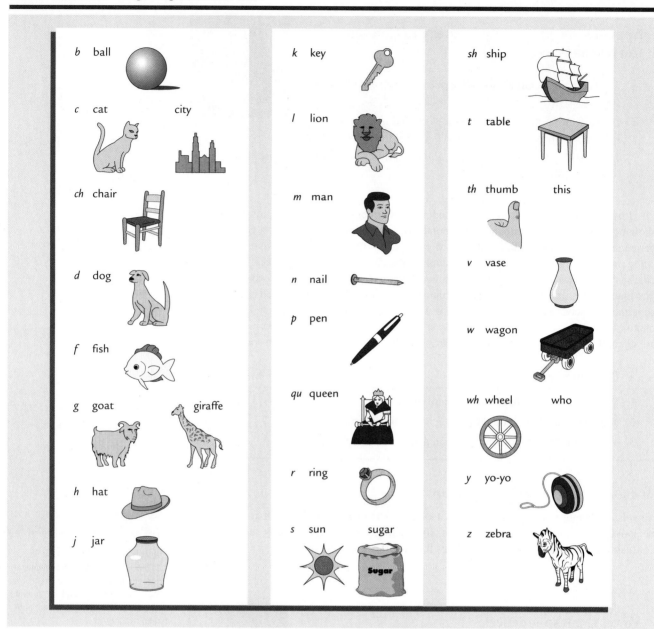

Step 3. Guided practice

Share-read a story that contains a number of short *a* words. Pause before the short *a* words, and invite students to read them. Also share-read songs, rhymes, announcements, and signs that contain short *a* words.

Step 4. Application

Have students read selections or create language experience stories that contain short *a*.

Step 5. Assessment and reteaching

Note students' ability to read and write short *a* words. Review and extend the pattern.

Teaching the Word-Building Approach

One convenient, economical way of introducing vowels is in rimes or patterns: for example, *-at* in *hat, pat,* and *cat,* or *-et* in *bet, wet,* and *set.* Patterns can be presented in a number of ways. A word-building approach helps children note the onset and the rime in each word (Gunning, 1995). Students are presented with a rime and then add onsets to create words. Next, students are provided with onsets and add rimes. Because some students have difficulty with rimes (Bruck, 1992; Juel & Minden-Cupp, 2000), rimes are broken down into their individual sounds after being presented as wholes. After introducing the rime *-et* as a whole, the teacher would highlight its individual sounds: /e/ and /t/. This fosters phonemic awareness. In a study involving high-risk students in four first grades, only the two groups of students taught with an onset–rime approach were reading close to grade level by year's end (Juel & Minden-Cupp, 2000). The students who did the best were those whose teachers broke the rimes into their individual sounds. Students also did their best when given differentiated instruction in word analysis that met their needs. The more time the at-risk students spent working at their level, the better their progress. This suggests that lessons provided to small groups of students who have approximately the same level of development in phonics is more effective than phonics instruction provided to the whole class. Small-group instruction benefits achieving readers as well, because they will not have to be subjected to instruction in skills that they have already mastered. Lesson 4.4 describes how the rime *-et* might be presented.

Adapting Instruction for Struggling Readers and Writers

Struggling readers often fail to process all the letters in a word and so misread it. To help students match all the sounds and letters in a word, try this activity. Say a word such as *snack*, stretching out its sounds as you do so: "sssnnnaaakkk." Have students repeat the word and *explain* how many sounds they hear. Show a card that has the word written on it. Match up the sounds and their spellings. Put the word in Elkonin boxes (see Figure 3.4 on p. 130). Have students tell why there are five letters but only four sounds. (Gaskins, 2005).

Lesson 4.4

Word-Building Pattern

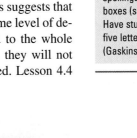

Step 1. Building words by adding onsets

To introduce the *-et* pattern, share-read a story or rhyme that contains *-et* words. Then write *et* on the board, and ask the class what letter would have to be added to *et* to make the word *pet*, as in the story that you just read. (This reviews initial consonants and helps students see how words are formed.) As you add *p* to *et*, carefully enunciate the /p/ and the /et/ and then the whole word. Have several volunteers read the word. Then write *et* underneath *pet*, and ask the class what letter should be added to *et* to make the word *wet*. As you add *w* to *et*, carefully enunciate /w/ and /et/ and then the whole word. Have the word *wet* read by volunteers. The word *pet* is then read, and the two words are contrasted. Ask students how the two are different. Other high-frequency *-et* words are formed in the same way: *get, let, jet,* and *net*. After the words have been formed, have students tell what is the same about all the words. Have students note that all the words end in the letters *e* and *t*, which make the sounds heard in *et*. Then have them tell which letter makes the /e/ sound and which makes the /t/, or ending, sound in *et*. Calling attention to the individual sounds in *et* will help students discriminate between *-et* and other short *e* patterns. It should also help students improve perception of individual sounds in words and so help improve their reading and spelling.

In a sense, word building takes a spelling approach. The teacher says a sound, and students supply the letter that would spell that sound. By slightly altering the directions, you can change to a reading approach when building words: Add the target letter, and then have students read the word. For instance, adding *p* to *et*, ask, "If I add *p* to *et*, what word do I make?" If students don't respond to a spelling approach, using a reading approach to building words provides another way of considering the elements in words.

Step 2. Building words by adding rimes to onsets

To make sure that students have a thorough grasp of both key parts of the word—the onset and the rime—present the onset, and have students supply the rime. Write *p* on

USING TECHNOLOGY

Between the Lions features a number of brief film clips of songs and stories that reinforce vowel patterns. The clips are fairly sophisticated, so they can be used with older as well as younger students.
http://pbskids.org/lions

FYI

▪ A children's book that may be used to introduce the concept of building words is dePaola's (1973) *Andy: That's My Name*, in which Andy watches as older kids use his name to construct a number of words: *and, sand, handy, sandy*, and so on.

▪ For a fuller discussion of word building, see Gunning (1995).

▪ Students who are unable to conserve or pay attention to two aspects of an object or a situation at the same time may have difficulty dealing with word patterns (Moustafa, 1995). Although they may know the words *hat* and *sat*, they may be unable to use their knowledge of these two words to read *bat* or *mat* because they fail to see the *-at* pattern. These children may still be processing words sound by sound. As their cognitive skills mature, they should be able to grasp patterns.

the board, and have students tell what sound it stands for. Then ask them to tell what should be added to *p* to make the word *pet*. After adding *et* to *p*, say the word in parts—/p/ /e/ /t/—and then as a whole. Pointing to *p*, say the sound /p/. Pointing to *e* and then *t*, say /e/ and then /t/. Running your hand under the whole word, say, "pet." Show *wet, get, let, jet*, and *net* being formed in the same way. After all words have been formed, have students read them.

Step 3. Providing mixed practice

Realizing that they are learning words that all end in the same way, students may focus on the initial letter and fail to take careful note of the rest of the word, the rime. After presenting a pattern, mix in words from previously presented patterns and have students read these. For example, after presenting the *-et* pattern, you might have students read the following words: *wet, when, pet, pen, net*, and *Ned* (assuming that *-en* and *-ed* have been previously taught). This gives students practice in processing all the letters in the words and also reviews patterns that have already been introduced.

Step 4. Creating a model word

Create a model word. This should be a word that is easy and can be depicted. Construct a chart on which model words are printed and depicted with a photo or illustration. (A sample chart of model words for short-vowel patterns is presented in Figure 4.5.) For the *-et* pattern, the word *net* might be used. Students can use the chart to help them decipher difficult words that incorporate patterns that have already been taught. Place the chart where all can see it. Explain to students that if they come across a word that ends in *-et* and forget how to say it, they can use the chart of model words to help them figure it out. Explain that the model word *net* has a picture that shows the word. In case they forget how to say the model word, the picture will help them.

Step 5. Guided practice

Under the teacher's direction, the class might read sentences or rhymes about a pet that got wet and was caught in a net, or they might create group or individual experience stories about pets they have or wish they had.

Step 6. Application

Students read stories and/or create pieces using *-et* words. Two very easy books that might be used to reinforce the *-et* pattern are *Let's Get a Pet* (Greydanus, 1988) and *A Pet for Pat* (Snow, 1984). Also have students read words such as *vet* and *yet*, which incorporate the pattern but which were not presented. As students encounter words such as *letter, better*, and *settle*, encourage them to use the known *et* element in each word to help them decode the whole word.

Step 7. Writing and spelling

If necessary, review the formation of the letters *e* and *t*. Dictate some easy but useful *-et* words (*get, let, wet*), and have students spell them. When dictating the words, stretch out their pronunciations (/g/–/e/–/t/) and encourage students to do the same so that they can better perceive the individual sounds. After students have attempted to spell the words, have them check their attempts against correct spellings placed on the board or overhead. Students should correct any misspellings. Encourage students to use *-et* words in their writing.

Step 8. Extension

Students learn other short *e* patterns: *-en, -ep, -ell*, and so on.

Step 9. Assessment and review

Note whether students are able to read words containing *-et*. Note, in particular, whether they are able to decode *-et* words that have not been taught. Note, too, whether students are spelling *-et* words in their writing.

■ ■ ■ **FIGURE 4.5** **Model Words**

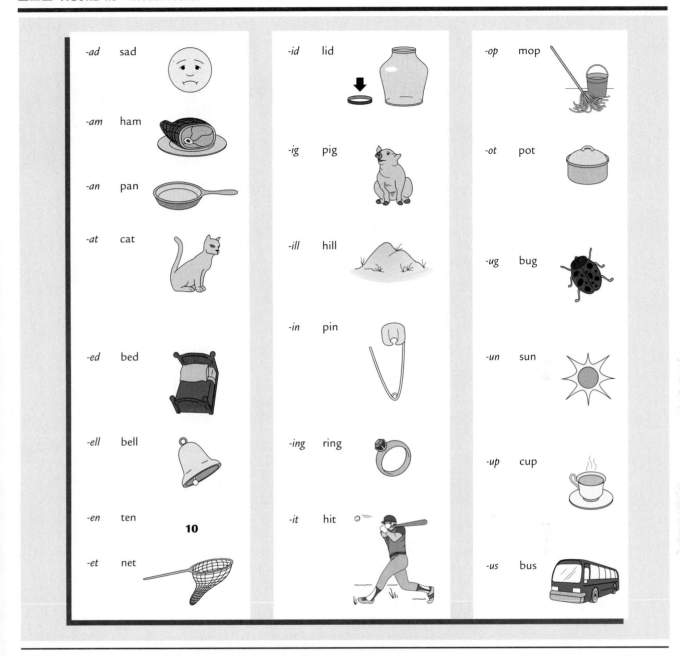

-ad	sad	*-id*	lid	*-op*	mop
-am	ham	*-ig*	pig	*-ot*	pot
-an	pan	*-ill*	hill	*-ug*	bug
-at	cat	*-in*	pin	*-un*	sun
-ed	bed	*-ing*	ring	*-up*	cup
-ell	bell	*-it*	hit	*-us*	bus
-en	ten				
-et	net				

From *Word Building, Book A* by T. Gunning (1994). New York, NY: Phoenix Learning Resources.

■ Application through Reading

As students begin to learn decoding strategies that combine context and knowledge of letter-sound correspondences, it is important that they have opportunities to apply these strategies to whole selections. If they read materials that contain elements they have been taught, they will learn the elements better and also be better at applying them to new words (Juel & Roper-Schneider, 1985). For instance, students who have been introduced to short *u* correspondences might read *Bugs* (McKissack & McKissack, 1988) and *Joshua James Likes Trucks* (Petrie, 1983), both of which are very easy to read; a somewhat more challenging text is *Buzz Said the Bee* (Lewison, 1992).

Books that might be used to reinforce vowel letter-sound relationships are listed in the following Student Reading List.

Student Reading List

Books that Reinforce Vowel Patterns

Short-Vowel Patterns

Level 1

Short a

Antee, N. (1985). *The good bad cat*. Grand Haven, MI: School Zone.
Cameron, A. (1994). *The cat sat on the mat*. Boston: Houghton Mifflin.
Carle, E. (1987). *Have you seen my cat?* New York: Scholastic.
Flanagan, A. K. (2000). *Cats: The sound of short a*. Elgin, IL: Child's World.
Maccarone, G. (1995). *"What is THAT?" said the cat*. New York: Scholastic.
Wildsmith, B. (1982). *Cat on the mat*. New York: Oxford.

Short i

Coxe, M. (1997). *Big egg*. New York: Random.
Greydanus, R. (1988). *Let's get a pet*. New York: Troll.
Meister, C. (1999). *When Tiny was tiny*. New York: Puffin.

Level 2

Short o

Flanagan, A. K. (2000). *Hot pot: The sound of short o*. Elgin, IL: Child's World.
McKissack, P. C. (1983). *Who is who?* Chicago: Children's Press.
Moncure, J. B. (1981). *No! no! Word Bird*. Elgin, IL: Child's World.
Worth, B. (2003). *Cooking with the cat*. New York: Random House.

Short e

Flanagan, A. K. (2000). *Ben's pens: The sound of short e*. Elgin, IL: Child's World.
Gregorich, B. (1984). *Nine men chase a hen*. Grand Haven, MI: School Zone.
Snow, P. (1984). *A pet for Pat*. Chicago: Children's Press.

Short u

Capucilli, A. S. (1996). *Biscuit*. New York: HarperCollins.
McKissack, P., & McKissack, F. (1988). *Bugs*. Chicago: Children's Press.
Petrie, C. (1983). *Joshua James likes trucks*. Chicago: Children's Press.
Rylant, C. (2002). *Puppy Mudge takes a bath*. New York: Simon & Schuster.

Levels 3 and 4

Review of Short Vowels

Boegehold, B. D. (1990). *You are much too small*. New York: Bantam.
Kraus, R. (1971). *Leo, the late bloomer*. New York: Simon & Schuster.
Lewison, W. C. (1992). *Buzz said the bee*. New York: Scholastic.

Long-Vowel Patterns

Level 5

Long a

Cohen, C. L. (1998). *How many fish?* New York: HarperCollins.
Flanagan, A. K. (2000). *Play day: The sound of long a*. Elgin, IL: Child's World.
Oppenheim, J. (1990). *Wake up, baby!* New York: Bantam.
Raffi. (1987). *Shake my sillies out*. New York: Crown.
Robart, R. (1986). *The cake that Mack ate*. Toronto: Kids Can Press.
Stadler, J. (1984). *Hooray for Snail!* New York: HarperTrophy.

Long i

Gelman, R. G. (1977). *More spaghetti I say*. New York: Scholastic.

Hoff, S. (1988). *Mrs. Brice's mice*. New York: HarperTrophy.

Ziefert, H. (1984). *Sleepy dog*. New York: Random House.

Ziefert, H. (1987). *Jason's bus ride*. New York: Random House.

Level 6

Long o

Armstrong, J. (1996). *The snowball*. New York: Random House.

Buller, J., & Schade, S. A. (1998). *Pig at play*. New York: Troll.

Cobb, A. (1996). *Wheels*. New York: Random House.

Hamsa, B. (1985). *Animal babies*. Chicago: Children's Press.

Kueffner, S. (1999). *Lucky duck*. Pleasantville, NY: Reader's Digest Children's Books.

McDermott, G. (1999). *Fox and the stork*. San Diego, CA: Harcourt.

Oppenheim, J. (1992). *The show-and-tell frog*. New York: Bantam.

Rader, L. (2005). *Silly pig*. New York: Sterling.

Schade, S. (1992). *Toad on the road*. New York: Random House.

Long e

Bonsall, C. (1974). *And I mean it, Stanley*. New York: Harper.

Milgrim, D. (2003). *See Pip point*. New York: Atheneum.

Shaw, N. (1986). *Sheep in a jeep*. Boston: Houghton Mifflin.

Ziefert, H. (1988). *Dark night, sleepy night*. New York: Puffin.

Ziefert, H. (1995). *The little red hen*. New York: Puffin.

Review of Long Vowels

Heling, K., & Hembrook, D. (2003). *Mouse's hide-and-seek words*. New York: Random House.

Matthias, C. (1983). *I love cats*. Chicago: Children's Press.

Parish, P. (1974). *Dinosaur time*. New York: Harper.

Phillips, J. (1986). *My new boy*. New York: Random House.

Ziefert, H. (1985). *A dozen dogs*. New York: Random House.

Level 7

/o͞o/ Vowels

Blocksma, M. (1992). *Yoo hoo, Moon!* New York: Bantam.

Phillips, M. (2000). *And the cow said "moo."* New York: Greenwillow.

Silverman, M. (1991). *My tooth is loose*. New York: Viking.

Wiseman, B. (1959). *Morris the moose*. New York: Harper.

Ziefert, H. (1997). *The ugly duckling*. New York: Puffin.

/o͝o/ Vowels

Brenner, B. (1989). *Lion and lamb*. New York: Bantam.

Platt, K. (1965). *Big Max*. New York: Harper.

Level 8

/ow/ Vowels

Lobel, A. (1975). *Owl at home*. New York: Harper.

Oppenheim, J. (1989). *"Not now!" said the cow*. New York: Bantam.

Siracusa, C. (1991). *Bingo, the best dog in the world*. New York: HarperCollins.

Level 9

/oy/ Vowels

Marshall, J. (1990). *Fox be nimble*. New York: Puffin.

Witty, B. (1991). *Noises in the night*. Grand Haven, MI: School Zone.

/aw/ Vowels

Crowley, N, (2006). *Ugh! A bug*. Minneapolis, MN: Millbrook Press.

Mann, P. Z. (1999). *Meet my monster*. Pleasantville, NY: Reader's Digest Children's Books.

USING TECHNOLOGY

Reading A–Z offers extensive reading materials and lesson plans for a small subscription fee. Most are in emergent literacy and phonics. Included are more than 50 decodable books and nearly 300 leveled books.

http://www.readinga-z.com

FYI

■ *Mouse's Hide-and-Seek Words* (Heling & Hembrook, 2003) can be used to reinforce finding pronounceable word parts. The book shows readers how to find little words in a big word. (Asking students to find a part they can say works better than finding little words in big words. Not all big words have little words.)

■ Display real-world materials that contain the phonics element you are working on. If working on *ch*, for example, bring in a box of Cheerios, chocolate chip cookies, and a menu that features cheeseburgers or chicken. Help students read the items, and encourage them to bring in some of their own.

Adapting Instruction for Struggling Readers and Writers

Struggling youngsters are often given too much phonics. What they need is lots of opportunities to practice their skills by reading easy books. Instruction in phonics should be balanced with application.

Oppenheim, J. (1991). *The donkey's tale.* New York: Bantam.
Oppenheim, J. (1993). *"Uh-oh!" said the crow.* New York: Bantam.
Rylant, C. (1989). *Henry and Mudge get the cold shivers.* New York: Bradbury.

Level 10

r *Vowels*
Arnold, M. (1996). *Quick, quack, quick!* New York: Random House.
Hooks, W. H. (1992). *Feed me!* New York: Bantam.
Penner, R. (1991). *Dinosaur babies.* New York: Random House.
Wynne, P. (1986). *Hungry, hungry sharks.* New York: Random House.
Ziefert, H. (1997). *The magic porridge pot.* New York: Puffin.

Review of r *Vowels and Other Vowel Patterns*
Brenner, B. (1989). *Annie's pet.* New York: Bantam.
Hays, A. J. (2003). *The pup speaks up.* New York: Random House.
Holub, J. (2001). *Scat, cats.* New York: Viking.
Hopkins, L. B. (1986). *Surprises.* New York: Harper.
Marshall, E. (1985). *Fox on wheels.* New York: Dutton.
Milton, J. (1985). *Dinosaur days.* New York: Random House.
Rylant, C. (1987). *Henry and Mudge: The first book.* New York: Bradbury.
Stambler, J. (1988). *Cat at bat.* New York: Dutton.

USING TECHNOLOGY

A number of illustrated rhymes can be found at the Web site for Webbing into Literacy:

http://curry.edschool.virginia.edu/go/wil/home.html

For other sources of rhymes, see the Building Literacy Web site:

http://www.thomasgunning.org

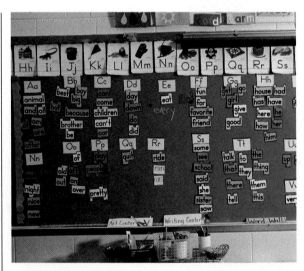

Words on the wall will help students with their reading and spelling.

Rhymes

Have students read nursery rhymes that contain the target pattern. Most nursery rhymes contain some unfamiliar words along with the target words. Share-read these rhymes with students until they are able to read them on their own. This builds fluency, automaticity, and confidence.

Word Wall

An excellent device to use for reinforcing both patterns and high-frequency words is a word wall. Words are placed on the wall in alphabetic order. About five new words are added each week (Cunningham & Allington, 1999). They are drawn from basals, trade books, experience stories, and real-world materials that students are reading. You might encourage students to suggest words for the wall from stories they have read or words that they would like to learn.

Kindergarten teachers might start their word wall by placing children's first names on it in alphabetical order. Placing the names in alphabetical order helps reinforce the alphabet (Campbell, 2001).

Before adding a word to the wall, discuss it with the children. Emphasize its spelling, pronunciation, and any distinguishing characteristics. Also talk over how it might relate to other words—for instance, it begins with the same sound, it rhymes, or it is an action word. To reinforce beginning consonants, highlight the first letter of the words containing the consonant you wish to spotlight: the *p* in *pumpkin* and *pull*. To reinforce rimes, highlight the rime you are reinforcing, such as *-at* in *hat* and *cat*.

Because the words are on the wall, they can be used as a kind of dictionary. If students want to know how to spell *there* or *ball*, they can find it on the wall. Being on the wall, the words are readily available for quick review. Troublesome words can be reviewed on a daily basis.

After a pattern has been introduced, place the new pattern words on a separate part of the wall, and arrange model words alphabetically by pattern. The *-ab* pattern would be placed first, followed by the *-ack* and *-ad* patterns, and so on. The model word should be placed first and should be accompanied by an illustration so that students can refer to the illustration if they forget how to read the model word. When students have difficulty with a pattern word and are unable to use a pronounceable word part to unlock the word's pronunciation, refer them to the word wall. Help them read the model word, and then use an analogy strategy to help them read the word they had difficulty with.

Review the words on the wall periodically, using the following or similar activities:

- Find as many animal names, color names, and number names as you can.

- Pantomime an action (sit, run) or use gestures to indicate an object or other item (pan, hat, cat, pen), and have students write the appropriate pattern word and then hold it up so that you can quickly check everyone's response. Have a volunteer read the word and point to it on the word wall. Before pantomiming the word, tell students what the model word of the pattern is—for example, *cat* or *pan*.

- Have students sort words by pattern. Students might sort a series of short *a* pattern words into *-at, -am,* and *-an* patterns or sort long *a* words according to their spellings: *a-e, -ay, -ai.*

Secret Messages

Have students create secret messages by substituting onsets in familiar words and then putting the newly formed words together to create a secret message (QuanSing, 1995). Besides being motivational, secret messages help students focus on the onsets and rimes of words and also foster sentence comprehension. Once students become familiar with the procedure, invite them to create secret messages. Here is a sample secret message.

> Take *H* from *He* and put in *W. We*
> Take *l* from *lot* and put in *g. got*
> Take *p* from *pen* and put in *t. ten*
> Take *st* from *stew* and put in *n. new*
> Take *l* from *looks* and put in *b. books*
> Secret message: *We got ten new books.*

Secret Word

Try "The Secret Word" (Cunningham & Allington, 1999). Select a word from a pattern, and jot it down on a sheet of paper, but do not reveal its identity. Have students number a paper from 1 to 5. Give a series of five clues as to the identity of the word. After each clue, students should write down their guess. The object of the activity is to guess the word on the basis of the fewest clues. The clues might be as follows:

1. The secret word is in the *-at* pattern.
2. It has three letters.
3. It is an animal.
4. It can fly.
5. The _____ flew into the cave.

After supplying the five clues, show the secret word (*bat*), and discuss students' responses. See who guessed the secret word first.

Making Words

Students put letters together to create words. Students assemble up to a dozen words, beginning with two-letter words and extending to five-letter or even longer ones (Cunningham & Cunningham, 1992). The last word that the students assemble contains all

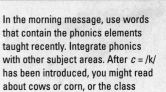

FYI

In the morning message, use words that contain the phonics elements taught recently. Integrate phonics with other subject areas. After *c* = /k/ has been introduced, you might read about cows or corn, or the class might follow a printed recipe for a custard cake.

USING TECHNOLOGY

Wordmaker (Don Johnston) is a computer program that students can use to make words. The program provides letters, says the word to be made, and allows students to check their responses.

Making words reinforces word patterns and is an enjoyable activity.

FOSTERING ENGAGEMENT

Creating secret messages, playing Secret Word, and making words foster engagement, along with providing reinforcement.

the letters they were given. For example, students are given the letters *a, d, n, s,* and *t* and are asked to do the following:

- Use two letters to make *at.*
- Add a letter to make *sat.*
- Take away a letter to make *at.*
- Change a letter to make *an.*
- Add a letter to make *Dan.*
- Change a letter to make *tan.*
- Take away a letter to make *an.*
- Add a letter to make *and.*
- Add a letter to make *sand.*
- Now break up your word, and see what word you can make with all the letters (*stand*).

Lesson 4.5

A Making Words Lesson

Step 1.
Distribute the letters. You may have one child distribute an *a* to each student, a second child distribute a *t*, and so on. Lowercase letters are written on one side of the card and uppercase on the other. The uppercase letters are used for the spelling of names.

Step 2.
Give the directions for each word: "Use two letters to make *at.*" Students form the word.

FYI

Scrabble letter holders can be used to hold students' letters, or letter holders can be constructed from cut-up file folders.

Step 3.
Have a volunteer assemble the correct response, the word *at*, on the chalkboard ledge (or pocket chart or letter holder). Have the volunteer read the word. Students should check and correct their responses.

Step 4.
Give the directions for the next word. Use the word in a sentence so that students hear it in context. If you have students who are struggling with phonological awareness and letter-sound relationships, slowly articulate each of the target words, and encourage them to stretch out the sounds as they spell them with their letters. If a target word is a proper name, make note of that.

Step 5.
On the chalkboard ledge, line up in order enlarged versions of the words the students were asked to make. Have volunteers read each of the words. Also have volunteers help sort the words according to patterns or beginning or ending sounds. For instance, holding up the word *at*, the teacher might ask a student to come up to the ledge and find the words that rhyme with *at*.

To plan a making words lesson, decide which patterns you wish to reinforce and how many letters you wish students to assemble. The letters chosen must form the word, so you may want to select the final word right after you have chosen the pattern. As students grow more adept, they can be given more challenging patterns and asked to make longer words using a greater variety of patterns. You might also include two or more vowels so that students become involved in vowel substitution.

■■■ Checkup ■■■

1. What are the steps in teaching a word-building lesson?
2. How might vowel patterns be applied and reinforced?

■■■

Using Technology to Create Reinforcement Activities

MatchWord.   *MatchWord* (Wright Group) is an outstanding piece of tool software that can be used to create a variety of phonics and related activities. *MatchWord* contains more than 19,000 words, 500 pictures, and 175 activities.

LeapPad.   LeapPad books incorporate an electronic device that "speaks" individual sounds or whole words when a special pen is passed over them. Because of this capability, students can have difficult words pronounced or have a sound or word spoken or a whole story read. Using a LeapPad phonics book (see Figure 4.6, on p. 182), students can select Say It to have a word said as a whole, Sound It to have a word spoken sound by sound, or Spell It to have a word spelled out. By touching the pen to Sound It, the student can have the word *it* read as /i/-/t/—*it*. *Leap* is read as /l/-/ee/-/p/—*leap*. This is an excellent device for helping students perceive the individual sounds in words. Note the labeled items (box, fan, leg) on the page in Figure 4.6. These are excellent for building vocabulary and would be especially helpful to ELLs.

Starfall.   Starfall (http://www.starfall.com/) features activities, stories, and short movies designed to introduce single-syllable patterns. Starfall has a speech component so that words can be read. It also has booklets and activities that can be downloaded or ordered. Materials are inexpensive.

 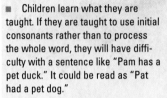

■■■ **FIGURE 4.6**

Page from LeapPad Text

From *LeapPad Interactive Book, A Collection from the LeapPad Library*, p. 6. © 2001 by LeapFrog Enterprises, Inc. Used with permission.

■ Scope and Sequence

A well-planned program of phonics instruction features a flexible but carefully planned scope and sequence. Although vowels could be introduced first in a reading program, it is recommended that consonants be presented initially, as their sounds have fewer spelling options. The consonant sound /b/, for example, is spelled *b* most of the time. In addition, initial letters, which are usually consonants, yield better clues to the pronunciation of a word than do medial or final letters.

When teaching initial consonants, present consonants that are easiest to say and that appear with the highest frequency first. The sounds /s/, /m/, and /r/ are recommended for early presentation because they are easy to distinguish and are among the most frequently occurring sounds in the English language. After introducing about ten high-frequency initial consonants (*s, m, f, t, d, r, l, g = /g/, n, h*), introduce a vowel or two so that students will be able to form some words using the correspondences they have learned. Usually, short *a* is introduced first. Short *i*, which is the most frequently occurring vowel, is generally introduced next, followed by short *o, e,* and *u*. Long vowels, other vowels, and *r* vowels are presented next.

Table 4.5 is a phonics scope-and-sequence chart that shows the approximate grade levels where key skills are taught in today's reading programs. Skills taught in one grade are often retaught or reviewed in the next grade.

Correspondences within each level are listed in order of approximate frequency of occurrence. The levels are rough approximations and must be adjusted to suit the needs and abilities of your students and the structure of your specific program. Some advanced kindergartners might be taught correspondences at the grade 1 level and even some at the grade 2 level. On the other hand, a fourth-grader with a reading disability may have difficulty with short vowels and would need to work at the grade 1 level.

First-grade basal programs typically start off with a review of consonants and short-vowel patterns. These basic elements are taught in kindergarten programs. The review moves quickly and is usually finished within three weeks. This isn't enough time for students to learn elements that they have forgotten or didn't learn, and much of the review is unnecessary for students who did learn the basic elements. A better plan would be to use kindergarten records to estimate where students are and to assess them to determine what

■■■ **TABLE 4.5   Scope-and-Sequence Chart for Phonics**

Level	Categories	Correspondence	Model Word	Correspondence	Model Word
K–1	Letter names, phonemic awareness, rhyming, segmentation, perception of initial consonants				
K–1	High-frequency initial consonants	s = /s/	sea	r = /r/	rug
		f = /f/	fish	l = /l/	lamp
		m = /m/	men	g = /g/	game
		t = /t/	toy	n = /n/	nine
		d = /d/	dog	h = /h/	hit

■■■ TABLE 4.5   Scope-and-Sequence Chart for Phonics *(continued)*

Level	Categories	Correspondence	Model Word	Correspondence	Model Word
K–1	Lower-frequency initial consonants and *x*	*c* = /k/	can	*c* = /s/	city
		b = /b/	boy	*g* = /j/	gym
		v = /v/	vase	*y* = /y/	yo-yo
		j = /j/	jacket	*z* = /z/	zebra
		p = /p/	pot	*x* = /ks/	box
		w = /w/	wagon	*x* = /gs/	example
		k = /k/	kite		
1	High-frequency initial consonant digraphs	*ch* = /ch/	church	*th* = /th/	thumb
		sh = /sh/	ship	*wh* = /wh/	wheel
		th = /th̲/	this		
K–1	Short vowels	*a* = /a/	hat	*e* = /e/	net
		i = /i/	fish	*u* = /u/	pup
		o = /o/	pot		
1–2	Initial consonant clusters	*st* = /st/	stop	*fr* = /fr/	free
		pl = /pl/	play	*fl* = /fl/	flood
		pr = /pr/	print	*str* = /str/	street
		gr = /gr/	green	*cr* = /kr/	cry
		tr = /tr/	tree	*sm* = /sm/	small
		cl = /kl/	clean	*sp* = /sp/	speak
		br = /br/	bring	*bl* = /bl/	blur
		dr = /dr/	drive		
1–2	Final consonant clusters	*ld* = /ld/	cold	*mp* = /mp/	lamp
		lf = /lf/	shelf	*nd* = /nd/	hand
		sk = /sk/	mask	*nt* = /nt/	ant
		st = /st/	best	*nk* = /ŋk/	think
2	Less frequent digraphs and other consonant elements	*ck* = /k/	lock		
		dge = /j/	bridge		
1–2	Long vowels: final *e* marker	*a-e* = /ā/	save	*e-e* = /ē/	these
		i-e = /ī/	five	*u-e* = /ū/	use
		o-e = /ō/	hope		
1–2	Long vowels: digraphs	*ee* = /ē/	green	*ow* = /ō/	show
		ai/ay = /ā/	aim, play	*igh* = /ī/	light
		oa = /ō/	boat		
		ea = /ē/	bean		
1–2	Other vowels	*ou/ow* = /ow/	out, owl	*oo* = /o͝o/	book
		oi/oy = /oi/	oil, toy	*oo* = /o͞o/	tool
		au/aw = /aw/	author, paw		
1–2	r vowels	*ar* = /ar/	car	*are* = /air/	care
		er = /ər/	her	*air* = /air/	hair
		ir = /ər/	sir	*ear* = /i(ə)r/	fear
		ur = /ər/	burn	*eer* = /i(ə)r/	steer
		or = /or/	for		
2–3	Consonants	*ti* = /sh/	action		
		ssi = /sh/	mission		
		t, ti = /ch/	future, question		
2–3	Consonant digraphs	*ch* = /k/	choir	*kn* = /n/	knee
		ch = /sh/	chef	*wr* = /r/	wrap
		gh = /g/	ghost	*ph* = /f/	photo
2–3	Vowels	*y* = /ē/	city	*o* = /aw/	off
		y = /ī/	why	*al* = /aw/	ball
		y = /i/	gym	*ew* = /ū/	few
		a = /o/	father	*a* = /ə/	alike
		e = /i/	remain		

elements they have learned and which need to be taught. This would be especially beneficial for struggling students who need more than a quick review.

Based on records and your assessment, start instruction where students show needs. Don't reteach skills that students have mastered; it's a waste of time teaching them what they already know. Some programs recommend reviewing basic phonics patterns, such as the *ai* or *ay* spelling of long *a* and the *ee* or *ea* spelling of long *e*, in grades 2 and 3. Being able to read second- or third-grade material is usually proof enough that students know these patterns. Use your own judgment and your knowledge of students' abilities when deciding what to teach.

Major Word Patterns

If you use word building or another pattern approach, you can think of scope and sequence in terms of word patterns. A listing of major word patterns is presented in Table 4.6. The sequence of presentation is similar to the order in which the elements are listed: short-vowel patterns, followed by long-vowel patterns, followed by other vowel and *r*-vowel patterns. However, within each grouping, patterns are presented in alphabetical order. Do not present the patterns in alphabetical order. Start with the easiest and most useful patterns. When teaching short *a* patterns, begin with the *-at* pattern, for instance. When introducing patterns, do not present every word that fits the pattern. Present only words that students know or that they will be likely to meet in the near future. It's better for them to attain a good grasp of a few high-frequency pattern words rather than have an uncertain knowledge of a large number of pattern words. It also saves time to introduce just the important words. It is not necessary to teach every pattern. For instance, after five or six short *a* patterns have been introduced, help students to generalize that all the patterns contain a short *a* sound and to apply this to short *a* words from patterns that have not been introduced. Words from low-frequency patterns such as *-ab, -ag, -aft,* and *-ax* might be presented in this way.

■ ■ ■ Checkup ■ ■ ■

1. What are the major phonics elements?
2. In what sequence are they typically taught?

■ ■ ■

Teaching Vowel Generalizations

"When two vowels go walking, the first one does the talking." Recited by millions of students, this generalization is one of the best known of the vowel rules. It refers to the tendency for the first letter in a digraph to represent the long sound typically associated with that letter: For example, *ea* in *team* represents long *e*, and *ai* in *paid* represents long *a*. Although heavily criticized because, as expressed, it applies only about 50 percent of the time, it can be helpful (Gunning, 1975; Johnston, 2001).

About one word out of every five has a digraph; however, the generalization does not apply equally to each situation. For some spellings—*ee*, for example—it applies nearly 100 percent of the time. The letters *ea*, however, represent at least four different sounds (as in *bean, bread, earth,* and *steak*). Moreover, the generalization does not apply to such vowel-letter combinations as *au, aw, oi, oy,* and *ou.*

This generalization about digraphs should not be taught as a blanket rule because it has too many exceptions. Instead, it should be broken down into a series of minigeneralizations in which the most useful and most consistent correspondences are emphasized. These minigeneralizations include the following:

Instances where digraphs usually represent a long sound

■ The letters *ai* and *ay* usually represent long *a*, as in *way* and *wait.*

■ The letters *ee* usually represent long *e*, as in *see* and *feet.*

TABLE 4.6   Major Word Patterns

Short Vowels

-ab	-ack	-ad	-ag	-am	-amp	-an	-and	-ang	-ank
cab	back	bad	bag	*ham	camp	an	and	bang	*bank
tab	jack	dad	rag	jam	damp	can	band	gang	sank
*crab	pack	had	tag	slam	*lamp	fan	*hand	hang	tank
	sack	mad	wag	swam	stamp	man	land	*rang	blank
	*tack	*sad	drag			*pan	sand	sang	thank
	black	glad	*flag			tan	stand		
	crack					plan			
	stack					than			

-ap	-at		-ed	-ell	-en	-end	-ent	-ess	-est
cap	at		*bed	*bell	den	end	bent	guess	best
lap	bat		fed	fell	hen	bend	dent	less	nest
*map	*cat		led	tell	men	lend	rent	mess	pest
tap	fat		red	well	pen	mend	sent	bless	rest
clap	hat		shed	yell	*ten	*send	*tent	*dress	test
slap	pat		sled	shell	then	tend	went	press	*vest
snap	rat			smell	when	spend	spent		west
trap	sat			spell					chest
wrap	that								guest

-et	-ead	-ick	-id	-ig	-ill	-im	-in	-ing	
bet	dead	kick	did	big	bill	dim	in	king	
get	head	lick	hid	dig	fill	him	fin	*ring	
jet	lead	pick	kid	*pig	*hill	skim	*pin	sing	
let	read	sick	rid	wig	kill	slim	sin	wing	
met	*bread	click	skid	twig	pill	*swim	tin	bring	
*net	spread	*stick	slid		will		win	sting	
pet	thread	thick			chill		chin	thing	
set		trick			skill		grin		
wet		quick			spill		skin		
							spin		
							thin		
							twin		

-ink	-ip	-it	-ob	-ock	-op	-ot			
link	dip	it	job	dock	cop	dot			
pink	lip	bit	mob	*lock	hop	got			
*sink	rip	fit	rob	rock	*mop	hot			
wink	tip	*hit	sob	sock	pop	lot			
blink	zip	kit	*knob	block	top	not			
clink	chip	sit		clock	chop	*pot			
drink	flip	knit		flock	drop	shot			
stink	*ship	quit		knock	shop	spot			
think	skip	split			stop				
	trip								
	whip								

-ub	-uck	-ug	-um	-ump	-un	-unk	-us(s)	-ust	-ut
cub	*duck	bug	bum	bump	bun	bunk	*bus	bust	but
rub	luck	dug	hum	dump	fun	hunk	plus	dust	cut
sub	cluck	hug	yum	hump	gun	junk	us	just	hut
tub	stuck	mug	*drum	*jump	run	sunk	fuss	*must	*nut
*club	struck	*rug	plum	lump	*sun	shrunk	muss	rust	shut
scrub	truck	tug		pump	spun	*skunk		trust	
		chug		thump		stunk			
				stump					

continued

■■■ **TABLE 4.6**   **Major Word Patterns** *(continued)*

Long Vowels

-ace	-ade	-age	-ake	-ale	-ame	-ape	-ate	-ave	-ail
*face	fade	age	bake	pale	came	ape	ate	*cave	fail
race	made	*cage	*cake	sale	game	*cape	date	gave	jail
place	grade	page	lake	tale	*name	tape	*gate	save	mail
space	*shade	rage	make	*scale	same	scrape	hate	wave	*nail
	trade	stage	rake		tame	grape	late	brave	pail
			take		blame	shape	mate		sail
			wake		shame		plate		tail
			flake				skate		snail
			shake				state		trail
			snake						

-ain	-ay		-ea	-each	-eak	-eal	-eam	-ean	-eat
main	bay		pea	each	*beak	deal	team	*bean	eat
pain	day		sea	beach	leak	heal	*dream	lean	beat
rain	*hay		*tea	*peach	peak	meal	scream	mean	neat
brain	lay		flea	reach	weak	real	stream	clean	*seat
chain	may			teach	creak	*seal			cheat
grain	pay			bleach	sneak	squeal			treat
*train	say				speak	steal			wheat
	way				squeak				
	gray								
	play								

-ee	-eed	-eel	-eep	-eet		-ice	-ide	-ile	-ime
*bee	deed	feel	beep	*feet		*mice	hide	mile	*dime
see	feed	heel	deep	meet		nice	ride	pile	lime
free	*seed	kneel	*jeep	sheet		rice	side	*smile	time
knee	weed	steel	keep	sleet		slice	wide	while	chime
tree	bleed	*wheel	peep	sweet		twice	*bride		
	freed		weep				slide		
	speed		creep						
			sleep						
			steep						
			sweep						

-ine	-ite	-ive	-ie	-ind	-y		-o, -oe	-oke	-ole
fine	bite	dive	die	find	by		go	joke	hole
line	*kite	*five	lie	kind	guy		*no	poke	mole
mine	quite	hive	pie	*mind	my		so	woke	*pole
*nine	white	live	*tie	blind	dry		doe	broke	stole
pine		drive			fly		hoe	*smoke	whole
					*sky		toe	spoke	
					try				
					why				

-one	-ope	-ose	-ote	-oad	-oat	-ow	-old		u-e
bone	hope	hose	*note	load	boat	bow	old		use
cone	nope	*nose	vote	*road	coat	low	cold		fuse
*phone	*rope	rose	quote	toad	*goat	tow	fold		*mule
shone	slope	chose	wrote		float	blow	hold		huge
		close				glow	*gold		
		those				grow	sold		
						slow	told		
						*snow			

■■■ **TABLE 4.6** **Major Word Patterns** *(continued)*

Other Vowels

-all	-aw	-au	-oss	-ost	-ought	-oil	-oy
*ball	caw	fault	boss	cost	ought	*boil	*boy
call	jaw	*caught	loss	*lost	*bought	soil	joy
fall	paw	taught	toss	frost	fought		toy
hall	*saw		*cross		brought		
wall	claw						
small	draw						
	straw						

-oud	-our	-out	-ound	-ow	-own	-ood	-ook	-ould
loud	our	out	bound	ow	down	good	*book	*could
*cloud	*hour	*shout	found	bow	gown	hood	cook	would
proud	sour	scout	hound	*cow	town	*wood	hook	should
	flour	spout	mound	how	brown	stood	look	
			pound	now	clown		took	
			*round	plow	*crown		shook	
			sound					
			wound					
			ground					

r Vowels

-air	-are	-ear, ere	-ar	-ard	-ark	-art	-ear
fair	care	*bear	*car	*card	bark	art	*ear
*hair	hare	pear	far	guard	dark	part	dear
pair	share	there	jar	hard	mark	*chart	fear
chair	scare	where	star		park	smart	hear
	spare				*shark		year
	*square				spark		clear

-eer	-or	-ore	-orn	-ort
*deer	*or	more	born	*fort
cheer	for	*sore	*corn	port
steer	nor	tore	torn	sort
		wore	worn	short
				sport

*May be used as model words.

From *Assessing and Correcting Reading and Writing Difficulties* (2nd ed.) by T. Gunning, 2002. Boston: Allyn & Bacon. Reprinted by permission of Allyn & Bacon.

■ The letters *ey* usually represent long *e*, as in *key*.

■ The letters *oa* usually represent long *o*, as in *boat* and *toad*.

Instances where digraphs regularly represent a long sound or another sound

■ Except when followed by *r*, the letters *ea* usually stand for long *e* (*bean*) or short *e* (*bread*).

■ The letters *ie* usually stand for long *e* (*piece*) or long *i* (*tie*).

■ The letters *ow* usually stand for a long *o* sound (*snow*) or an /ow/ sound (*cow*).

The minigeneralizations could also be taught as patterns, such as *seat, heat, neat*, and *beat* or *boat, goat*, and *float*. Whichever way they are taught, the emphasis should be on providing ample opportunities to meet the double vowels in print. Providing exposure is the key to learning phonics. Generalizations and patterns draw attention to regularities in

FYI

■ A number of vowel combinations are not used to spell long vowels:

au or *aw* = /aw/ *fault, saw*

oi or *oy* = /oy/ *toil, toy*

oo = /o͞o/ *moon*

oo = /o͝o/ *book*

ou or *ow* = /ow/ *pout, power*

■ One of the few generalizations that students make use of in their reading is the final *e* generalization. When they reach the consolidated alphabetic stage of reading, students make use of final *e* as part of a larger pattern: *-age, -ate, -ive*.

■ The best way to "learn" generalizations is to have plenty of practice reading open and closed syllable words, final *e* words, and other words covered by generalizations.

■ Because there is no way to predict on the basis of spelling whether *ow* will represent /ow/ (*cow*) or /ō/ (*snow*) or *oo* will represent a short vowel sound (*book*) or long one (*boot*), you need to teach students to check whether the sounds they construct create a real word. If not, have them try the other major pronunciation of *ow* or *oo*. Model this process for your students.

English spelling, but actually meeting the elements in print is the way students' decoding skills become automatic; they can then direct fuller attention to comprehension.

Most vowel rules are not worth teaching because they have limited utility, have too many exceptions, or are too difficult to apply. However, the following generalizations are relatively useful (Gunning, 1975):

■ *Closed syllable generalization.* A vowel is short when followed by a consonant: *wet, but–ter.* This is known as the closed syllable rule because it applies when a consonant "closes," or ends, a word or syllable.

■ *Open syllable generalization.* A vowel is usually long when it is found at the end of a word or syllable: *so, mo–ment.* This generalization is known as the open syllable rule because the word or syllable ends with a vowel and so is not closed by a consonant.

■ *Final* e *generalization.* A vowel is usually long when it is followed by a consonant and a final *e: pine, note.* Final *e* words are a major stumbling block for many learners. They represent a higher level of cognitive processing (Bear, personal communication, December, 2003). In short-vowel words, each letter represents a sound, and so such words may be processed in linear fashion: h-a-t. In contrast, final *e* words require the reader to note the final *e* as the word is being processed and use that as a sign that the vowel is probably long. Students need to use orthographic awareness as well as phonics skills when they decode final *e* words.

Vowel generalizations should be taught inductively. After experiencing many words that end in *e* preceded by a consonant, for example, students should conclude that words ending in a consonant plus *e* often have long vowels. Students might also discover this by sorting words that end in *e* and words that don't.

The real payoff from learning generalizations comes when students group elements within a word in such a way that they automatically map out the correct pronunciation most of the time. For example, when processing the words *vocal, token,* and *hotel* so that the first syllable is noted as being open (*vo–cal, to–ken, ho–tel*) and the vowel is noted as being long, students are able to decode the words quickly and accurately. This is a result of many hours of actual reading. However, it is also a process that can be taught (Glass, 1976).

Because none of the vowel generalizations applies 100 percent of the time, students should be introduced to the variability principle. They need to learn that digraphs and single vowels can represent a variety of sounds. If they try one pronunciation and it is not a real word or does not make sense in context, then they must try another. A child who read "heevy" for *heavy* would have to try another pronunciation, because *heevy* is not a real word. A child who read "dccd" for *dead* would need to check to see whether that pronunciation fits the context of the sentence in which the word was used. Although *deed* is a real word, it does not make sense in the sentence "Jill's cat was dead"; so, the student needs to try another pronunciation. This strategy needs to be taught explicitly, and students must have plenty of opportunity for practice. To sound out a word, they should be taught the general steps outlined in the following Student Strategy.

Student Strategies

Applying the Variability Strategy to Vowel Correspondences

1. Sound out the word as best you can.
2. After sounding out the word, ask yourself, "Is this a real word?" If not, try sounding out the word again. (Applying the variability principle to a word containing *ow*, a student might try the long-vowel pronunciation first. If that did not work out, he or she would try the /ow/,

Developmental Nature of Phonics Instruction   189

3. Read the word in the sentence. Ask yourself, "Does this word make sense in the sentence?" If not, try sounding it out again.

4. If you still cannot sound out a word so that it makes sense in the sentence, try context, skip it, or get help.

■■■ Checkup ■■■

1. What are the major vowel generalizations?
2. What role might they play in a phonics program?

■■■

Introducing Syllabic Analysis Early

Long words pose problems for students. Although students might know the words *car, pen*, and *her*, they have difficulty reading the word *carpenter*. Most multisyllabic words are composed of known word parts or patterns. After teaching several short-vowel patterns, present two-syllable words composed of those patterns. For instance, after students have studied the short *a* and short *i* patterns, present words such as *rabbit, napkin, distant*, and *instant*. When students encounter multisyllabic words, prompt them to use their knowledge of word parts to figure out the words. Also build words. After students have learned a word such as *swim*, have them make words that contain *swim*, including *swims, swimming*, and *swimmer*, so that they get used to reading words that contain suffixes.

■ Developmental Nature of Phonics Instruction

Often, teachers doing intervention note that students are weak in phonics and decide to begin from the beginning. This is a poor practice. It fails to give students credit for what they know and undermines them by giving them material that is too easy. Phonics instruction should be developmental (Gunning, 2006). Assess students to find out where they are, and begin instruction there, making adjustments as necessary.

Similarly, whole-class instruction in phonics is a poor practice. In virtually all classes, there is a range of phonics knowledge. Students have different levels of understanding of the alphabetic principle. Some are just beginning to grasp that letters represent sounds. Others have a concept that each sound in a word is represented by a letter—as with /h/, /a/, /t/ for *hat*—and are learning short-vowel patterns that, for the most part, show a one-to-one correspondence between letters and sounds. More advanced students realize that not all words can be processed sound by sound. They have come to the understanding that some words have a final-*e* marker that indicates that the preceding vowel is long, as in *hate*, or a vowel digraph that performs a similar function, as in *wait*. Instruction should be geared to students' developmental level. Students who are just beginning to grasp that each sound in a word is represented by a letter and have not mastered short-vowel patterns are not ready for instruction in final-*e* or digraph patterns. Research clearly indicates that students make the most progress when they are grouped according to their developmental level (Juel & Minden-Cupp, 2000). Some reading programs recommend whole-class instruction in phonics. However, the research clearly favors small-group, targeted instruction (National Reading Panel, 2000).

As a Reading First consultant, I observed the unfortunate consequences of whole-class phonics instruction in a first-grade classroom. Despite the fact that a number of the students were still struggling with short-vowel patterns, the lesson was on long vowels, as recommended by the basal anthology. After the lesson, students were assigned a workbook activity for reinforcement. The exercise was well beyond the capabilities of the students

ASSESSING FOR LEARNING   ■■■ ■

Riddle Buly and Valencia (2002) found a tendency to prescribe wholesale instruction in phonics to help the large numbers of fourth-graders who were failing the state reading test. However, when they assessed 107 students who failed the test, they found that the students had a variety of needs. While some did need phonics instruction, probably on advanced levels (perhaps syllabic analysis), others needed work in fluency, comprehension, vocabulary, or a combination of areas.

who were still learning short vowels. In addition to wasting their time by attempting to teach them a skill that they weren't ready to learn, the lesson chipped away at their academic self-concepts by presenting them with work that they couldn't do. It would have been much better to have used the instructional time to give them a lesson on short vowels so that their lagging skills would have been advanced and they could have experienced success.

■ Using Word Analysis References

From the very beginning, students should have references that they can use to help them read and spell unfamiliar words (Pinnell & Fountas, 1998). These references might include picture dictionaries, real dictionaries (for older students), illustrated charts of model words, lists of patterns and other words, a chart listing the steps in decoding a difficult word, and a talking word processor or talking electronic dictionary so that students could type in an unknown word and have it pronounced.

■ Using an Integrated Approach

Although phonics, context clues, and vocabulary are treated as separate topics in this book, students make use of all three when they face an unknown word. In fact, they make use of their total language system. As noted earlier, when students decode words, four processors are at work: orthographic, phonological, meaning, and context (Adams, 1990; 1994). The processors work simultaneously and both receive information and send it to the other processors. Therefore, phonics instruction must be viewed as being part of a larger language process. Phonics is easier to apply when context clues are used, and, in turn, it makes those clues easier to use. Students who are adept decoders will be able to recognize more words and so will have more context to use. Moreover, greater knowledge of the world, larger vocabularies, and better command of language increase students' ability to use phonics. If a student has a rich vocabulary, there is a better chance that the word he or she is decoding will be recognized by his or her meaning processor. Even if the word is not known, the student will have a better chance of deriving its meaning from context if most of the other words in the passage are known and if his or her background knowledge of the concepts in the passage is adequate.

To be most effective, therefore, phonics instruction should be presented in context and practiced and applied through extensive reading, which enables students to connect phonics with functioning as part of a total language system. Extensive reading also provides practice for phonics skills so that students' decoding becomes so effortless and automatic that they can devote full attention to comprehension, which is what reading is all about.

■ Dialect Variation

Note whether the words in each row have the same pronunciation or different pronunciations:

balm	bomb	
merry	Mary	marry
pin	pen	
root	route	

In some dialects, each word in a row has the same pronunciation. In other dialects, each word is pronounced differently. American English encompasses a variety of regional dialects. No one dialect is superior to another. However, if you teach a pronunciation that is

---

Adapting Instruction for Struggling Readers and Writers

Word analysis skills are interdependent. For instance, sight words are easier to learn if students know basic phonics. Analogies can only be used on a limited basis if there are few comparison words in the student's store of known words. Therefore, struggling readers often have difficulty in several areas of word analysis and so need broad-based instruction (Ehri & McCormick, 1998).

FYI

Good evidence for the integration of context and phonics cues comes from reading sentences containing a word whose pronunciation depends on its meaning. Good readers can read the following sentences without difficulty: "The does have no antlers, but the bull does." "He wound the bandage around the wound" (McCracken, 1991, p. 91).

different from that spoken by your students, it can be confusing. When teaching phonics, use the dialect that your students use. You might also give a brief lesson in dialects. If your dialect differs from that of your students, you might explain why this is so—because you came from a different part of the country, for instance. When you come to an element that you pronounce differently, explain that to students and let them pronounce the words in their own dialect. Some of the major dialect variations include the following:

/aw/ and /o/. Words such as *dog, frog,* and *hog* have an *aw* or short *o* pronunciation.

/o͞o/ and /o͝o/. Words such as *room* and *roof* have either a long double-*o* pronunciation or a short double-*o* pronunciation.

/i/ and /e/. In some dialects, short *e* is pronounced as a short *i,* so *pen* and *pin* and *tin* and *ten* are homophones.

/e/ and /ā/. In some dialects, words such as *egg* and *beg* are pronounced with a long *a* instead of the more typical short *e.*

/o͞o/ and /ow/. In some dialects, *route* rhymes with *boot*; in others, it rhymes with *bout.*

■ Phonics and Spelling

Recent research suggests that children who are encouraged to write early and allowed to spell as best they can develop insights that carry over into their ability to read words (Burns & Richgels, 1989). Although invented spellings and spelling instruction can help children gain insights into the alphabetic principle, a systematic program of teaching phonics is still necessary. Neither invented spelling nor regular spelling instruction provides all the skills necessary to decode printed words. Spelling is best seen as a useful adjunct to phonics instruction, especially in the beginning stages of reading, rather than as a major method of teaching students to crack the code.

■ Strategy Instruction

The ultimate value of phonics instruction is that it provides students with the keys for unlocking the pronunciations of unknown words encountered in print. For instance, a child who has studied both the *-at* and the *-et* patterns but has difficulty with the words *flat* and *yet* needs strategies for decoding those words. In addition to context, there are two powerful decoding strategies that the student might use: pronounceable word part and analogy (Gunning, 1995).

To apply the pronounceable word part strategy, a student who is having difficulty with a word seeks out familiar parts of the word. You might prompt the student by pointing to a word such as *yet* and asking, "Is there any part of the word that you can say?" If the student fails to see a pronounceable word part, cover up all but that part of the word (*et*), and ask the student if she or he can read it. Once the student reads the pronounceable part, she or he adds the onset (*y*) and says the word *yet.* (This assumes that the student knows the *y* = /y/ correspondence.) In most instances, the student will be able to say the pronounceable word part and use it to decode the whole word.

If a student is unable to use the pronounceable word part strategy, try the analogy strategy. With the analogy strategy, the student compares an unknown word to a known one. For instance, the student might compare the unknown word *yet* to the known word *net.* The teacher prompts the strategy by asking, "Is the word like any word that you know?" If the student is unable to respond, the teacher writes the model word *net,* has the student read it, and then compares *yet* to *net.* Or the teacher might refer the child to a model words chart.

When students reconstruct a word using the pronounceable word part or analogy strategy, they must always make sure that the word they have constructed is a real word. They

ASSESSING FOR LEARNING

With the help of the ESL or bilingual teacher, find out what literacy skills students possess in their native language. Then build on these skills. For instance, students may have a good command of phonics. Show the students how they might use this in English.

USING TECHNOLOGY

For a discussion of the research on phonics, see the National Reading Panel's report:

http://www.nationalreadingpanel.org

FYI

■ Although both spelling and phonics deal with sounds and letters, they are different processes. Reading requires that students translate letters into sounds. Spelling requires that sounds be translated into letters. Since sounds can be spelled in different ways, spelling tends to be more difficult than decoding. However, in the beginning stages, spelling might outstrip decoding. Using invented spelling, novice learners can spell almost any word but can read very few words.

■ Stretching out the sounds as you say a word out loud ("sssuuunnn") and encouraging students to think of the sounds they hear helps students spell words and builds their knowledge of phonics. It helps even more if students also say the word out loud and stretch out the sounds.

■ Do not ask students to "look for the little word in the big word." This may work sometimes but would result in a misleading pronunciation in a word like *mother.* Besides, there are many words that don't have "little words" in them.

FYI

■ The pronounceable word part strategy takes advantage of students' natural tendency to group sounds into pronounceable parts.

■ Prompting for clues should be closely related to the text (White, 2005). Asking a student to recall and apply a phonics generalization is getting away from the immediate text. Routine prompts, such as "Sound it out," aren't helpful either. The prompt should match the nature of the word. Don't ask a student to sound out a word such as *were*.

■ Students' strategies and teachers' prompts depend on the instructional approach and the students' stage of development (Brown, 2003). Teachers espousing a holistic approach might prompt a context cue: "What word would fit here?" Teachers using a phonics-based approach might prompt a phonics cue: "What is the first sound?" In the early stages of reading, students might be cued to decode a word sound by sound; later, they might be cued to read the rime and the onset.

■ To provide practice in applying strategies, give students a slip of paper, and have them record on the paper a word they have figured out in the text they are reading. During discussion of the text, have them tell what their word is and how they figured it out (White, 2005).

■ The prompt "Is there any word part that you can say?" allows students to select the word element they can best handle, which might be a single sound, a cluster, or a rime. For the word *blurt*, the student might recognize *b, bl, ur,* or *urt.*

■ The intervention program Responsive Reading advocates using a pronounceable word part strategy similar to that recommended in this text: "(a) Look for parts you know; (b) say the word slowly and blend the sounds; and (c) reread the sentence with the word in it and decide whether it makes sense" (Mathes et al., 2005, p. 159). It also advocates using an analogy strategy.

must also make sure it fits the context of the sentence. The pronounceable word part strategy should be tried before the analogy strategy because it is easier to apply and is more direct. Although students may have to be prompted to use these strategies, they should ultimately apply them on their own.

Incorporating Phonics Strategies with Context

Pronounceable word part and analogy strategies should be integrated with the use of context clues. There are some situations in which context simply does not work. There are others in which neither pronounceable word part nor analogy will work. For instance, the pronounceable word part and analogy strategies would not work with *have* in the following sentence, but context clues probably would: "I have three pets." However, in the sentence "I like trains," context probably would not be of much help in decoding the word *trains*, but the pronounceable word part or analogy strategy would work if the student knows the *-ain* pattern or the word *rain*. Based on their own studies and others, New Zealand researchers Chapman, Tunmer, and Prochnow (2001) concluded that in most instances, students will be more successful if they use the pronounceable word part strategy first: "Children . . . should be encouraged to look for familiar spelling patterns first and use context to confirm what unfamiliar words might be" (pp. 171–172).

To help students who rush through their oral reading and produce a host of "careless" errors, stress meaning. Have them focus on accurately reading short segments of text. For a while, they might read one sentence at a time. Initial reading should be silent so that they have time to work out difficult words. Encourage students to request help as needed. After their silent reading, have them read the sentences orally. Prompt the use of integrated clues. Students pay more attention to meaning and make fewer errors because they have spent more time carefully reading the segments. Where they request help, they are provided with prompts that lead them to use effective strategies (Buettner, 2002). Gradually, they incorporate these strategies and become meaning-based readers.

Student Strategies

Word Recognition

To cue the use of word recognition strategies, ask one or more of the following questions when encountering an unknown word in print:

1. Is there any part of this word that I can say?
2. Is this word like any word I know?
3. What word would make sense here?

Building Independence

When a student has difficulty with a printed word, you may be tempted to supply the word or give some unhelpful admonition, such as "You know that word. We had it yesterday." Size up the word. Think of the skills the student has, the nature of the word, and the context in which it appears. Then ask the question from the Student Strategy (changing "I" to "you") that will prompt the use of the cue that seems most likely to work. (Of course, if you feel the child has no chance of working out the word, supply two options by asking, "Would *pony* or *cow* fit here?" By giving students a choice of two words, one of which is the answer, you provide students with the opportunity to apply a skill and you also preserve their self-confidence.) Helping students apply decoding strategies provides them with a powerful tool that empowers them as readers. Encouraging them to work out words also affirms your faith in them and builds their confidence.

If a student is reading orally in a group situation, do not allow another student to correct her or him. This robs the student of her or his academic self-concept and also of the opportunity to apply strategies. If a student misreads a word and does not notice the error, do not immediately supply a correction or even stop the reading. Let the student continue to the end of the sentence or paragraph; there is a good chance that she or he will notice the misreading and correct it. If the student does correct the misreading, make sure that you affirm this behavior: "I like the way you went back and corrected your misreading. You must have seen that the word _____ didn't make sense in the sentence."

If the student does not self-correct a misreading, you have two choices. If the error is a minor one, such as *this* for *that* or *the* for *these*, which does not change the meaning of the sentence, ignore it. If the misreading does not fit the sense of the sentence, use a prompt that will help the student correct the misreading:

- If the misreading does not make sense, ask, "Does _____ make sense in that sentence?"
- If the misreading is not a real word, ask, "Does that sound right?"
- If the misreading makes sense but does not fit phonically, say, "*Dog* makes sense in the sentence, but the word in the sentence begins with a *w*. What letter does *dog* begin with? What word that begins with *w* would fit here?" (Clay, 1993b). (Prompt for a pronounceable word part or analogy if you think the student can work out the pronunciation of the word).

Periodically, model the process of using strategies to figure out a word. Using a think-aloud, show how you go about seeking a pronounceable word part or using an analogy strategy.

Children also use combinations of strategies. Over time, their ability to use strategies to decode an unfamiliar word or to spell a difficult word becomes faster and more accurate. Improvement is brought about by introducing and providing practice with more advanced strategies. But progress can also be obtained by fostering more effective use and more effective selection of existing strategies. As Rittle-Johnson and Siegler (1999) explain,

> When a new strategy is discovered, it typically is used only occasionally at first. Many changes occur not through introduction of new strategies but instead through increasingly efficient execution of existing strategies, increasing use of the more accurate strategies, and more adaptive choice among strategies. (p. 335)

▪▪▪ Checkup ▪▪▪

1. What is the developmental nature of phonics?
2. What are the key word analysis strategies?
3. How might those strategies be introduced and reinforced?

▪ Decodable Texts

Ardith Cole (1998) noticed that some of her first-graders who had apparently done well in the first half of the grade began to struggle in the second half. In fact, their progress came to a grinding halt. Heidi Mesmer (1999) observed a similar phenomenon. Both discovered a mismatch between their students and the materials they were reading. Their students did well with texts in which most of the words could be predicted by using illustrations as cues or with the help of repeated, highly predictable language. As students encountered more complex text, they floundered. Cole and Mesmer came to a similar conclusion. Choose texts that provide support to students.

Decodable texts are selections that contain only phonics elements that have been taught. Figure 4.7 shows a page from a well-written decodable text. Note that except for

FYI

- If other prompts don't work and you believe that a student can't decode a word, give the student a choice between two responses: "Is the word (incorrect response) or (correct response)?" This helps students think about what strategies might be used.

- Stopping occasionally to decode a hard word or because something does not sound right to the reader does not mean that the reader lacks fluency. It means that the reader is monitoring for meaning, which is something good readers do.

- A coverup can be a prompt: "Without saying anything, cover the word with your finger, and then slowly uncover the letters to help the reader sound out and blend. Some teachers use a small card, a bookmark, or a 'coverup stick' (a decorated popsicle stick). With children just beginning to decode, uncover single letters or digraphs (e.g., *s-a-ck*). With more advanced beginners, uncover syllable chunks (e.g., *news-pa-per*)" (Murray, 2006a).

ASSESSING FOR LEARNING   ▪ ▪ ▪

As students read, watch their eyes. A glance upward at an illustration generally signals that they have encountered a difficult word and are attempting to use picture clues.

INVOLVING PARENTS   ▪ ▪ ▪

Parents have different styles when helping children with their miscues (Mansell, Evans, & Hamilton-Hulak, 2005). Some supply the words; others encourage sounding out. Provide parents with guidance that fits your program. The safest approach is to have parents pause briefly and then supply the word. This prevents struggles between child and parent.

▪▪▪ **FIGURE 4.7** **Decodable Text**

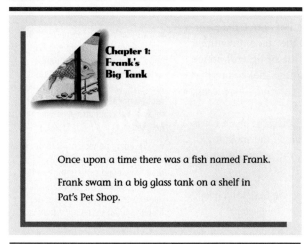

From *Frank the Fish Gets His Wish* by Laura Appleton-Smith, 1998. Lyme, NH: Flyleaf Publishing. Copyright © Laura Appleton-Smith. Reprinted by permission of Laura Appleton-Smith.

the familiar "Once upon a time" and a few high-frequency words, all of the words can be decoded by the application of short-vowel patterns.

No text is totally decodable. High-frequency words such as *is, are*, and *the* need to be included, as do content words such as *angry* and *animal* if the story is about an angry animal. Two factors have to be considered in order to determine the decodability of a text: the skills the student has learned and the skills demanded by the text. In Texas, the state purchases approved texts and then distributes them free to public schools. Texas will not approve or purchase series that do not have first-grade texts that are at least 80 percent decodable. Other states also require decodable texts. As a result, all of the early reading texts in today's basal reading programs are at least 80 percent decodable.

Some materials emphasize high-frequency words. Most predictable books are composed primarily of high-frequency words. However, as these books become more complex, they become less predictable. If students have not learned basic decoding skills, they will have difficulty coping with them.

Transitional Nature of Decodable Texts

Decodable texts are transitional. As students progress in phonics, there is less need for the support of decodable texts. The texts they use can be written in a more natural fashion and include easy children's books such as the *Little Bear* or *Frog and Toad* series. One well-known reading program (Houghton Mifflin) phases out decodable texts written specifically for the program halfway through the first-year program and switches over to selections from easy children's books that contain many of the patterns that have been taught.

As explained in Chapter 1, there are four processors at work when students read: orthographic, phonological, meaning, and context. The processors operate simultaneously. Rich context facilitates the use of phonics. For most students, a word in context is easier to read than a word in a list. In their attempt to provide students with decodable text, authors have sometimes included words that incorporate the phonic element that has been taught but the words are difficult or unusual and the language lacks a natural flow. Because one processor has been overemphasized and the others neglected, the reading is made more difficult. For instance, in their attempt to include as many decodable words as possible, authors might include unfamiliar words such as *vat* and *drat* while reinforcing the *-at* pattern. Because of the way students process written language, familiar *-at* pattern words are easier to decode than unfamiliar ones.

Because the inclusion of high-frequency words makes for more natural sounding text, because text that is partly predictable is easier to read, and because students should have the opportunity to apply decoding skills, the best texts are those that have a balanced mix of decodable elements, high-frequency words, and predictability. The focus should match students' stage of development. For students in the prealphabetic and early alphabetic stage, highly predictable texts work best. As students move into the alphabetic stage, they need decodable texts that will allow them to apply what they have learned. Over time, an increasing number of high-frequency words should be introduced so that texts have a more natural sound and more complex topics can be covered. Most of the texts contained in the Student Reading List on pp. 176–178 incorporate a balanced blend of decodability and predictability.

Balancing Decodable Texts with Predictable Books

A general principle of teaching phonics is that the books students read should reinforce the words or patterns they have been taught. In general, this means that students should be given decodable rather than predictable books. However, predictable books, with their picture support, are easy to read and so give students a sense of the fun of reading and also build confidence. They are especially important when working with struggling readers who have to work hard to apply their newly learned skills. I realized this when working with short-vowel patterns with a struggling first-grader. After working hard to read a brief, decodable text, she told me that she wasn't a very good reader. After that, I made sure that she spent some of her time with predictable text so that she could see that reading wasn't always a struggle.

■ ■ ■ Checkup ■ ■ ■

1. What are decodable texts?
2. What are their advantages and disadvantages?

Taking a Flexible Approach

As an elementary school reading consultant, I quickly discovered that no method of instruction works for all children. Working with struggling readers, I was having encouraging success with a systematic, structured reading program. Then, unexpectedly, it totally failed with one of the brightest of these struggling readers. He responded to a more holistic approach that included phonics, but emphasized meaning and context clues. Research by Connor, Morrison, & Katch (2006) confirmed my observations. They found

ASSESSING FOR LEARNING

■ Using whole-class instruction in phonics is justified by the assertion that the struggling readers will pick up the more advanced elements. This did not happen with the struggling first-graders I observed, who were still learning short vowels. When assessed after more than two months of whole-class exposure to long vowels, the students were unable to read any long-vowel words. Asked to read the test words *hat* and *hate*, one first-grader reported that they both said *hat* but one had an *e* on the end of it.

■ If something isn't working, figure out why and try another approach. Note how Heidi Mesmer (see Case Study) reassessed her instructional program when she saw that Cametera wasn't making adequate progress. She analyzed the program and changed it so that it became effective.

Case Study

Adjusting Instruction to Meet the Needs of a Struggling Reader

Despite having been given extra help, Cametera, who was in second grade, was in the beginning stages of reading. Based on an analysis of her miscues, Heidi Mesmer, who was instructing her, found that Cametera was making heavy use of context clues but was using phonic clues only 15 percent of the time (Mesmer, 1999). Careful observations revealed that Cametera was making heavy use of picture clues present in the highly predictable books that she was reading. Her miscues made sense but didn't make use of the alphabetic principle. For *pig*, she read *hog*. For *only*, she read *just*. For *plant*, she read *leaf*. Mesmer began teaching Cametera basic phonics skills, including consonant sounds and word patterns. Sorting was a key activity. Provision was also made for including newly introduced elements in Cametera's writing. Mesmer continued to use the predictable books that Cametera had been reading. This turned out to be a mistake. Cametera did well with the phonics activities but did not apply these skills to her reading. Instead of using her newly learned skills to sound out unfamiliar words, Cametera continued to rely too much on picture and other context clues.

Taking a step back, Mesmer analyzed her instruction and her materials. She realized that there was a mismatch between materials and instruction. The books included a variety of patterns, including many that had not yet been introduced. In addition, there was a lack of continuity. The next book in the series didn't reinforce patterns found in the previous book. Besides not providing sufficient practice with newly learned patterns, the books presented too many new words. Mesmer realized that Cametera needed materials in which patterns were introduced in some sort of controlled fashion. However, she didn't want to use books that were so highly controlled that they made little sense and sounded like tongue twisters. After some searching, Mesmer discovered a series known as the Ready Readers (Modern Curriculum Press) that provided a reasonable balance between controlled introduction of patterns and use of high-frequency words. The books were decodable but not so much so that they sounded unnatural. Texts that are approximately 70 percent decodable would seem to be adequate for helping novice readers learn to apply phonics skills (Beck & Juel, 1995). As a result of careful instruction and matching of materials to instruction, Cametera made encouraging progress. Miscue analysis showed that she made heavier use of phonics skills and also made a greater number of self-corrections. Once Cametera had a firm grasp of basic decoding skills, Mesmer planned to provide her with high-quality children's books. As she explained, "Decodable text is like a set of training wheels on a bicycle; it offers temporary support and is designed to facilitate future independence" (p. 140).

Adapting Instruction for Struggling Readers and Writers

As Pressley (2006) advises, "Excellent primary teachers adjust instruction to the needs of individual children, balancing skills instruction and holistic experiences within their classrooms so that some children receive a greater dose of skills and others are more completely immersed in holistic reading and writing" (p. 12).

Adapting Instruction for English Language Learners

In Spanish, the natural word unit is the syllable rather than the onset or the rime (Moustafa & Maldonado-Colon, 1999). When teaching students who can read in Spanish how to read in English, capitalize on their ability to recognize syllables in words by using word building and stressing pronounceable syllables. However, also spend time helping them recognize onsets and rimes.

that first-graders who had limited phonics knowledge did better when provided with systematic instruction, but students with solid phonics knowledge did better with a more holistic approach. Juel and Minden-Cupp (2000) reached a similar conclusion. Commenting on the success of the Benchmark School, which was established to instruct struggling readers, Pressley, Gaskins, and Fingeret (2006) stated, "A centerpiece of Benchmark School's instruction is that the teachers are always monitoring whether what they are trying is working, and if it is not, they try something else" (p. 48).

■ Teaching Phonics to English Language Learners

In teaching English language learners to read, determine the extent of their literacy in their first language and build upon that. Also, be aware of the similarities and differences between the two languages so that you can provide explanations or extra help where it is needed. There are some differences between Spanish and English that require some adjustments in an English phonics program for Spanish speakers.

Spanish has a simpler phonology and orthography than English. For one thing it has fewer speech sounds. In addition, there is a near one-to-one correspondence between Spanish sounds and the letters that represent them. However, Spanish has more multisyllabic words than English does.

There are significant differences between consonant sounds in English and Spanish (see Table 4.7). The following consonant sounds are not present in Spanish: /j/, /v/, /sh/, and /ŋ/. In addition, some consonant sounds that are the same in an initial position in English and Spanish do not occur in a final position in Spanish: final /b/ (*cab*), /f/ (*if*), /g/ (*bag*), and /ch/ (*match*). Just as in English, many Spanish words have clusters: There

■■■■ TABLE 4.7   Comparison of English and Spanish Consonants and Their Spellings

Phoneme	English	Spanish
b	b: *ball*	b, v: *bebé, vaca*
d	d: *dog*	d: *dentista*
f	f: *fish*	f: *familia*
g	g: *goat*	g: *gallina*
h	h: *hat*	j: *jardín*
j	j: *jar*	does not occur in Spanish
k	c, k: *cat, key*	c, k, qu: *caimán, kilo, qué*
l	l: *lion*	l: *lobo*
m	m: *man*	m: *mucho*
n	n: *nail*	n: *no*
ñ	like ni in *onion*	ñ: *niña*
p	p: *pen*	p: *papá*
r	r: *ring*	r: *rojo*
rr	does not occur in English	rr: *perro*
s	s: *sun*	s, z: *seis, zapatos*
t	t: *table*	t: *taxi*
v	v: *vest*	does not occur in Spanish
w	w, qu: *wagon, quiz*	u, hu: *cuarto, huerta*
y	y: *yo-yo*	y, i: *yo, fiambre*
z	z: *zebra*	does not occur in Spanish
ch	ch: *chair*	ch: *chapeo*
sh	sh: *shoe*	does not occur in Spanish
th	th: *thin*	does not occur in some Spanish dialects
th	th: *that*	does not occur in some Spanish dialects
ŋ	ng: *ring*	does not occur in Spanish
zh	age: *garage*	does not occur in Spanish

■■■ **TABLE 4.8   Comparison of English and Spanish Vowels and Their Spellings**

Phoneme	English	Spanish
a	a: *cat*	does not occur in Spanish
e	e: *bed*	e: *es*
i	i: *fish*	does not occur in Spanish
o	o: *mop*	a: *gato*
u	u: *cup*	does not occur in Spanish
ā	a-e, ai, ay: *rake*	ei, ey: *rey, seis*
ē	ee, e, ea, e-e: *wheel*	i, y: *misa, y*
ī	i-e, igh, ie, -y: *nine*	ai, ay: *baile, hay*
ō	o-e, o, ow, oa: *nose*	o: *oso*
ū	u-e, -u: *cube*	yu: *ayuda*
o͞o	oo, ew, ou, ui: *school*	u: *uno*
o͝o	oo, ou, u: *book*	does not occur in Spanish
aw	aw, au: *saw*	does not occur in Spanish
ow	ow, ou: *cow*	au: *causa*
oy	oi, oy: *boy*	oi, oy: *estoi, soy*
schwa	a, e, i, o, u: *banana*	does not occur in Spanish
ar	ar: *car*	ar: *carpa*
or	or, oor, our: *four*	or: *hora*
air	air, are, ere: *chair*	does not occur in Spanish
eer	ear, eer: *deer*	does not occur in Spanish
ier	ire: *fire*	does not occur in Spanish

are *l* clusters (*blusa, playa*) and *r* clusters (*fryoles, gratia*) but no *s* clusters in Spanish (*stop, spot*).

Most English reading programs start with short vowels. However, Spanish has no short *a* (*hat*), short *i* (*hit*), short *u* (*cut*), short *oo* (*book*), or schwa (*banana*) vowels (see Table 4.8). Most *r* vowels will also be unfamiliar to Spanish speakers. The sound /r/ has a different pronunciation in Spanish. However, *ar* (*cart, carne*) and *or* (*horn, horno*) have similar pronunciations in Spanish and English. The *r* sounds in *sir, fear, hair*, and *were* will be unfamiliar to Spanish speakers. Both English and Spanish have the /oy/ (*boy, soy*) and /ow/ (*cow*) sounds, but /ow/ is spelled *au* in Spanish (*causa*).

Because of differences in the sound systems of the two languages, Spanish speakers may experience confusion with the following:

final /b/ pronounced as /p/: *cab* becomes *cap*

/j/ pronounced as /y/: *jet* becomes *yet*

/ŋ/ pronounced as /n/: *thing* becomes *thin*

/ch/ pronounced as /sh/: *chin* becomes *shin*

/v/ pronounced as /b/: *vote* becomes *boat*

/y/ pronounced as /j/: *yes* becomes *jes*

s clusters pronounced with an *e: speak* becomes *espeak*

/a/ pronounced as /e/: *bat* becomes *bet*

/i/ pronounced as /e/: *hit* becomes *heat*

/ē/ pronounced as /i/: *heal* becomes *hill*

/u/ pronounced as /o/: *hut* becomes *hot*

/o͝o/ pronounced as /o͞o/: *look* becomes *Luke*

When learning English phonics, Spanish-speaking students need exercises that help them to perceive sounds not present in Spanish. When presenting a new phonics

■■■ **TABLE 4.9** Phonics Elements with the Same Sounds in Spanish and English But Different Spellings

Phoneme	English Spelling	Spanish Spelling
ē	e: *me* (i: *spaghetti*)	i: *mi*
ō	o: *top* (a: *father*)	a: *gato*
ā	a-e, ai, ay: *rake, rain, ray* (ei, ey: *reign, they*)	ei, ey: *rey, seis*
ī	i-e, igh, ie: *nine, high, tie*	ai, ay: *baile, haya*
ow	ou, ow: *out, owl*	au: *causa*

element that might be confusing, spend extra time introducing the sound of the element. Have students complete oral exercises such as the following, in which they discriminate between easily confused elements. Students tell which word correctly completes the spoken sentence:

Maria is wearing her new (choose, shoes).

The explorers sailed away on a large (chip, ship).

Little Bo Peep lost her (cheap, sheep).

Which book did you (choose, shoes) to read?

You may not (chew, shoe) gum in class.

You might enlist the help of the ESL or bilingual specialist to help students perceive unfamiliar speech sounds. However, focus on the purpose of phonics instruction. The purpose of instruction in phonics is to provide students with a tool for decoding difficult words. It isn't necessary that they be able to pronounce the words without any trace of an accent. Don't turn phonics lessons into speech lessons.

Teaching Students Who Are Literate in Spanish

When teaching students who are literate in Spanish to read in English, explain to them that they already know much of the phonics that they will meet in English (Thonis, 1983). You might create a chart showing them skills in Spanish that will transfer to English.

Unfortunately, some of the sounds that are the same in both languages have different spellings. For instance, long *e* is spelled with an *i* in Spanish as in *si*, and long *a* is typically spelled with an *ei* or *ey* as in *rey, seis*. (See Table 4.9 for a listing of divergent spellings.) In addition, Spanish does not have a final silent *e* that marks vowels as being long. Spanish readers seeing the word *came* might read it as *cahmay*. Such miscues tell you that the student is applying Spanish phonics to English spelling and needs instruction in English phonics. When introducing elements in which there are possible confusions, explain the potentially confusing part.

■■■ Checkup ■■■

1. What adjustments might be made when teaching phonics to Spanish speakers?

■■■

■ Monitoring Progress in Phonics

Students' progress in phonics should be monitored on a continuing basis to ensure that they are mastering the elements that are being taught. Phonics skills build upon each other. Students shouldn't progress to the next level until they have mastered the current level. They need not achieve perfection before moving on, but they should be able to get 80 percent or more of the items correct. If students are struggling, it is essential that they

Name _Joseph_   Grade _1_   School Year _2008–09_

	Sept.	Oct.	Nov.	Dec.	Jan.	Feb.	Mar.	Apr.	May	June
50										
49										
48										
47										
46										
45										
44										
43										
42										
41									✓	
40										
39										
38										
37										
36										
35										
34								✓		
33										
32										
31										
30										
29										
28							✓			
27										
26										
25										
24										
23										
22										
21										
20										
19										
18										
17										
16										
15										
14										
13						✓				
12										
11					✓					
10										
9				✓						
8										
7										
6			✓							
5										
4										
3		✓								
2										
1										

■■■ FIGURE 4.8

Monitoring Chart for Phonics Progress Monitoring Assessment

be monitored frequently so that the program can be intensified or changed to produce adequate progress.

Phonics Progress Monitoring Assessment

The Phonics Progress Monitoring Assessment, which is presented in Appendix B, can be used to monitor students' progress. It can also be used to determine students' knowledge of single-syllable phonics and to place the students in the appropriate level of instruction. The first ten words of the fifty-word set assess short-vowel patterns; the next ten words assess short-vowel patterns with clusters; the next ten assess long-vowel patterns; the fourth group assesses other-vowel patterns; and the last group of ten tests *r*-vowel patterns. Students who get at least eight out of ten of the first ten words but have difficulty with the second group should be instructed in short-vowel patterns that contain clusters.

The Progress Monitoring Chart (Figure 4.8, on p. 199) shows the actual performance of a struggling first-grader on the Phonics Progress Monitoring Assessment from October through May. The assessment is constructed so that phonics instruction is divided into ten units, with each unit being represented by five words. The goal for first-graders is that they will be able to read forty to forty-five of the fifty words by year's end, meaning that they will have mastered basic single-syllable phonics. It is expected that students will be able to read an additional four or five words each month. Because he was making slow progress in his regular program, the student in Figure 4.8 was provided with more intensive instruction and more instructional time, beginning at the end of January. Because he had completed five months of school, his expected performance was between twenty and twenty-five (four to five words a month). However, his score was 13. The goal for him was to be able to read forty to forty-five words by the end of the year. By the end of February, even with intervention, he was able to read only two additional test words. But then his progress accelerated. Notice the considerable jump he made from February to March and his substantial progress through May. Progress monitoring is a valuable tool for spurring changes in a program when students aren't advancing adequately.

Readability Based on Phonics Elements

As noted in Chapter 2, matching students with an appropriate-level text is absolutely essential. If you are using a program that presents phonics in systematic fashion, it's a good idea to level your books according to the skills needed to read them. In most basal reading programs, beginning reading (first grade) is divided into ten levels, with each student text covering two levels. Figure 4.9 lists the key phonics elements and the approximate levels in a first-grade reading program. To determine the level of a text, examine the book to see what key elements are needed to read it. For instance, if a book requires all the short vowels but doesn't have words with clusters, it is assigned at the end of level 2. The chart is based on an examination of basal reader programs and the levels at which most of them present skills. In a tryout with hundreds of books in a number of classrooms, the chart proved to be an excellent way to level books for students who were learning basic phonics. To make the chart fit your program, you might need to make a few adjustments. See pp. 176–178 for books listed by phonics level.

The Phonics Readability Chart is designed to be used with the Phonics Progress Monitoring Assessment in Appendix B. Each of the ten levels is represented by five words. For instance, if a student is able to read short-*a* and short-*i* words, but has difficulty with

> **Adapting Instruction for Struggling Readers and Writers**
>
> The student's intervention program included word building, sorting, making words, and reassembling cut-up sentences. He read poems, songs, selections from the lower levels of the classroom basal anthology, and many of the books listed on pp.176–178. Above all, he had a caring, well-prepared tutor.

▪ A **sight word** is one that is recognized immediately. Many sight words occur with high-frequency, and some are learned through visual memorization. However, the vast majority of words are learned through phonics.

▪ **High-frequency words** are words such as *the, of,* and *them* that appear in printed material with a high rate of occurrence.

Book	Level	Key Elements
1	1	Short-*a*, short-*i* patterns
	2	Short-*o*, short-*e*, short-*u* patterns; all short-vowel patterns
2	3	Short vowels with *r* clusters
	4	Short vowels with *s* and *l* clusters
3	5	Long vowels: *a* and *i*
	6	Long vowels: *o, e, u*
4	7	Other vowel digraphs: *oo, ew, ue*
	8	Other vowel digraphs: *ou, ow*; compound words
5	9	Other vowel digraphs: *oi, oy, au, aw*
	10	*r* vowels

short-*o*, short-*e*, and short-*u* words, the student should be given level 2 books. If a student can read words containing long-vowel patterns but has difficulty with other-vowel patterns, the student should be ready for level 7 books. Placement should be verified by observing the student as he or she attempts to read a book at the level in which the student has been placed.

■ ■ ■ **Checkup** ■ ■ ■

1. How might progress in phonics be monitored?

2. How do the systems for monitoring progress in phonics and assessing the phonics readability of texts complement each other?

          ■ ■ ■

■ High-Frequency Words

Close your book and on a separate piece of paper spell the word *once*. As you write the word, try to be aware of the processes you are using. Did your lips move? As you wrote the word, did you sound it out? A small number of words, such as *of* and *once*, and, to a lesser extent, *were* and *some*, are said to be irregular. Their spellings don't do a good job of representing their sounds. Because these words are irregular, at one time it was thought that the best way to learn them was to memorize them visually. They were put on cards and studied. Because it is believed that they were memorized visually, they became known as **sight words**. However, more recent research indicates that even irregular words are learned phonologically. That's why when you wrote the word *once*, chances are you said the word, at least subvocally, and then said the sounds of the word as you spelled each sound. There is also an element of visual memory involved. Otherwise, you may have spelled *once* as *wuns*.

    A list of **high-frequency words** is presented in Table 4.10. Note that these are all common words. Ironically, the words that appear most frequently tend to have the most irregular spellings, mainly because they are some of the oldest words in the language. Over

FYI

■ Introducing high-frequency words makes it possible to provide students with more natural-sounding text.

■ Knowing how to spell and/or sound out a word partially or fully helps students learn and remember new words (Ehri, 1991), but time spent discussing known definitions may be wasted (Kibby, 1989). However, hearing and seeing function words such as *the* and *are* is helpful.

■■■ **TABLE 4.10** **High-Frequency Words**

1. the	30. had	59. would	88. find	117. same	146. different	175. am
2. of	31. but	60. other	89. use	118. right	147. number	176. us
3. and	32. what	61. into	90. water	119. look	148. away	177. left
4. a	33. all	62. has	91. little	120. think	149. again	178. end
5. to	34. were	63. more	92. long	121. also	150. off	179. along
6. in	35. when	64. two	93. very	122. around	151. went	180. while
7. is	36. we	65. her	94. after	123. another	152. tell	181. sound
8. you	37. there	66. like	95. word	124. came	153. men	182. house
9. that	38. can	67. him	96. called	125. three	154. say	183. might
10. it	39. an	68. time	97. just	126. high	155. small	184. next
11. he	40. your	69. see	98. new	127. come	156. every	185. below
12. for	41. which	70. no	99. where	128. work	157. found	186. saw
13. was	42. their	71. could	100. most	129. must	158. still	187. something
14. on	43. said	72. make	101. know	130. part	159. big	188. thought
15. are	44. if	73. than	102. get	131. because	160. between	189. both
16. as	45. will	74. first	103. through	132. does	161. name	190. few
17. with	46. do	75. been	104. back	133. even	162. should	191. those
18. his	47. each	76. its	105. much	134. place	163. home	192. school
19. they	48. about	77. who	106. good	135. old	164. give	193. show
20. at	49. how	78. now	107. before	136. well	165. air	194. always
21. be	50. up	79. people	108. go	137. such	166. line	195. until
22. this	51. out	80. my	109. man	138. here	167. mother	196. large
23. from	52. then	81. made	110. our	139. take	168. set	197. often
24. I	53. them	82. over	111. want	140. why	169. world	198. together
25. have	54. she	83. did	112. sat	141. things	170. own	199. ask
26. not	55. many	84. down	113. me	142. great	171. under	200. write
27. or	56. some	85. way	114. day	143. help	172. last	
28. by	57. so	86. only	115. too	144. put	173. read	
29. one	58. these	87. may	116. any	145. years	174. never	

Adapted from *The Educator's Word Frequency Guide* by S. M. Zeno, S. H. Ivens, R. T. Millard, & R. Duvvuri, 1995. Brewster, NY: Touchstone Applied Science Associates.

the years, English evolved so that, in many instances, spellings no longer do a very good job of representing pronunciations.

Table 4.10 gives 200 high-frequency words in order of their frequency of appearance. The list is drawn from a compilation of words that appear in books and other materials read by school children (Zeno, Ivens, Millard, & Duvvuri, 1995). These 200 words make up about 60 percent of the words in continuous text. For example, the most frequently occurring word, *the*, comprises about 2 percent of text.

Many students pick up a number of high-frequency words through reading signs and other print to which they are exposed in class and through shared reading of big books and other materials. However, direct teaching is also necessary. When teaching high-frequency words, limit the number being taught to three or four. Choose words that students will soon be meeting in print. If they are about to read Dr. Seuss's *The Cat in the Hat Comes Back* (Geisel, 1961), you might present *this, off, done,* and *know,* irregular words that figure prominently in the story. Select words that are different in appearance. Presenting *put* and *but* or *where, when,* and *were* together is asking for trouble, as students are almost sure to confuse them.

When teaching high-frequency words, take full advantage of phonic regularities, such as initial and final consonant correspondences. Also, seek out commonalities of words. For instance, when teaching *at* as a high-frequency word, also teach *that* and show how the two are related; have students note that *that* contains the pronounceable word part *at*. Except for dramatically irregular words like *of* and *one*, help students match up spellings and sounds. For *were*, help students see that *w* represents /w/ and *ere* represents /er/ as in *her*. For the word *some*, match *s* with /s/, note that *o* is a very unusual way of spelling /u/, and match *m* with /m/. Encourage students to spell out the words and provide opportunities for them to meet the words in many contexts so that they form visual images of the words in addition to making phonological connections. As students are learning exception words such as *know* or *sure*, they also need to be taught specific distinguishing features of these words.

Because high-frequency words are such a prominent part of just about everything that students read, it is important that they learn to recognize them rapidly. The idea behind rapid recognition of words is that the human mind has only so much mental-processing ability and time. If students get caught up trying to sound out words, they lose the memory of what they are attempting to read. They need automaticity, the ability to process words effortlessly and automatically (Laberge & Samuels, 1974). Students who are able to recognize words rapidly have ample attention and mental energy left to comprehend what they are reading. Ultimately, because of lots of practice, most of the words that skilled readers meet in print, although learned through phonics, are processed as rapid-recognition words. Only when skilled readers meet strange names or unfamiliar words do they resort to decoding.

Teaching High-Frequency Words

When presenting high-frequency words, emphasize activities that reflect this purpose. Use phonics to help students accurately decode words—accuracy must come first. As Samuels (1994) notes, accuracy precedes automaticity, or rapid recognition. Use of knowledge of patterns and correspondences facilitates accurate recognition. Once accuracy has been achieved, stress rapid recognition.

As you gradually introduce added phonics skills, include high-frequency words as part of your instruction. For instance, when teaching the consonant cluster *bl*, use the high-frequency words *black* and *blue* as examples. When students are studying short *a*, present the high-frequency words *am*, *an*, and *at*. Being able to relate the printed versions of these words with their sounds gives students another way to process them, which aids memory and speed of processing. Use the steps listed in Lesson 4.6 as a framework for presenting high-frequency words.

Lesson 4.6

High-Frequency Words

Step 1. Develop understanding of the words
This step is only necessary if students do not have an adequate understanding of the words being presented. Since high-frequency words are among the most common in the language, they will be in the listening vocabularies of the majority of students. However, some high-frequency words may be unknown to English language learners.

Step 2. Present printed words in isolation
Write each word to be learned on the chalkboard, or present each one on a large card. Although students may not be able to read the words, they may know parts of them. Build on any part they know. This will make the task of learning the word easier, as students will be faced with learning only a portion of the word rather than the whole word; it also helps them connect new knowledge with old knowledge. If students know only initial consonant correspondences, build on that knowledge: Emphasize

FYI

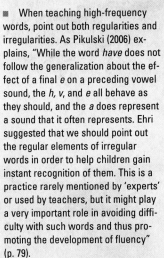

■ When teaching high-frequency words, point out both regularities and irregularities. As Pikulski (2006) explains, "While the word *have* does not follow the generalization about the effect of a final *e* on a preceding vowel sound, the *h, v,* and *e* all behave as they should, and the *a* does represent a sound that it often represents. Ehri suggested that we should point out the regular elements of irregular words in order to help children gain instant recognition of them. This is a practice rarely mentioned by 'experts' or used by teachers, but it might play a very important role in avoiding difficulty with such words and thus promoting the development of fluency" (p. 79).

■ Two factors are involved in rapid recognition of words: accuracy and automaticity (Samuels, 1994). To reach an effective level of accuracy, students must actively process words and process virtually every letter. Students need varying amounts of time to reach a high level of accuracy. Once they have reached an acceptable level of accuracy, they seem to gain automaticity at similar rates (Samuels, 1994). Children who seem to take longer to become fluent readers may not have achieved accuracy.

■ There are few words for which phonics cannot be used at least partially.

■ "Contrary to past beliefs, sight-word learning does not depend on rote association. Children learn sight words in just a few *quality* encounters. Quality encounters connect letters in a spelling to phonemes in the pronunciation, usually by sounding out and blending. In other words, we typically learn sight words through careful decoding. Though decoding demands great attention in young readers, it sets up reliable access routes to retrieve the word" (Murray, 2006c).

the *y* = /y/ in *you* and the *f* = /f/ in *for*. If they know initial and final consonants, talk about the *c* = /k/ and *n* = /n/ in *can*. If they know word patterns, make use of those: Help them use their knowledge of -*an* to read *man* and their knowledge of -*op* to read *stop*. Present these elements as ways of perceiving and remembering sight words, but do not turn the sight-word lesson into a phonics lesson. For words that are highly irregular, such as *of, one*, and *once*, stress the spellings. But note that the *n* in *one* represents /n/ and *nce* in *once* represents /ns/.

After all the words have been introduced, have students read them chorally and individually. Distribute cards containing the words so that each student has a set. The reverse side of each card might contain the word used in a sentence.

Step 3. Present printed words in context

On the chalkboard, story paper, or overhead transparency, present the high-frequency words in context. Underline the target words so that they stand out. Take care to use each word in the same sense in which students will most likely see it. For instance, if the high-frequency word *water* is going to be a verb in an upcoming story, show it as a verb. In composing sample sentences, except for the target high-frequency words, use words already taught so that students can concentrate their efforts on the new ones. Actually, using high-frequency words that have already been taught is a good way to review them. Read the sentences to the students, and then have them read in unison as you sweep your hand under the words. Later, individual volunteers can read the sentences.

Step 4. Practice

Provide ample practice for high-frequency words. Practice could be in the form of maze worksheets on which students choose from three words the one that correctly completes the sentence:

> take
> I am new years old.
> five

Practice might also use a brief story, a game, or a piece of computer software such as *Richard Scarry's Busytown* (Paramount Interactive) or *Bailey's Book House* (Edmark), in which a few high-frequency words are featured.

Step 5. Application

Have students create experience stories or read easy stories that contain target high-frequency words. Experience stories naturally contain a high proportion of sight words. Easy books also provide an opportunity for students to meet sight words in context. In one study, students who read easy books learned more sight words than those who used a basal series (Bridge, Winograd, & Haley, 1983). They also expressed more positive feelings about reading, and, because their books were written about a variety of topics, they had an opportunity to learn more about their world.

Step 6. Assessment and review

Observe students as they read to see how well they do when they encounter high-frequency words.

Using Children's Books to Build a High-Frequency Vocabulary

Several types of children's books, including predictable books, caption books, and label books, can be used to build high-frequency vocabulary. Predictable books are those that follow a set pattern, making it easy for the child to predict what the sentences are going to say. Caption books feature a single sentence per page that describes or relates to the illustration in much the same way that a caption goes with a photo. Label books, as their name suggests, depict a number of objects, actions, or people and provide printed labels for them. These kinds of books may be read over and over again.

There are literally thousands of children's books that can be used to foster instant recognition of words. However, it is important that the books be on the right level. Students should know most of the words, so that their focus is on moving just-introduced or barely known words to the category of words that are well known and rapidly recognized. Although it is helpful for students to build fluency by rereading the same book or story, it is also important that they read many different books to see the same words in a variety of contexts.

Appendix A presents a list of children's books that can be used to reinforce high-frequency words. Select books from the Picture, Caption/Frame, and Easy High-Frequency (Primer 1) levels. All the books at these levels are brief and well illustrated. They increase in difficulty from those that require a minimum of reading to those that contain three lines of text on a page. In addition to the children's books listed in Appendix A, several series of books are designed to reinforce sight words. These include the following:

Reading Corners. San Diego, CA: Dominie Press. This series reinforces a number of basic patterns: I like _____; I have _____; I do _____. Consisting of just eight to twelve pages of text, these books are very easy to read.

Read More Books. San Diego, CA: Dominie Press. This series presents a number of basic sentence patterns. The text is brief and explicitly illustrated with color photos and so is very easy to read.

Seedlings. Elizabethtown, PA: Continental Press. This series includes texts at levels from beginning reading to second grade.

Using Word Banks

A word bank is a collection of known words and consists primarily of high-frequency words. As students learn new words, these are added to their word banks. Students might also include words that they are working on or want to learn. A good source of words would be the high-frequency words in the books they are reading. After reading *Cat on the Mat* (Wildsmith, 1982), students might add *cat, on, the,* and *sat* to their word banks. Word banks should be limited to about a hundred words. Beyond that limit, the bank becomes too extensive to handle, and students' decoding skills should have developed to a point where word banks have lost their usefulness (Graves, Juel, & Graves, 2001).

Adapting Instruction for Struggling Readers and Writers

Poor readers may require extra practice to learn high-frequency words. Good readers apparently learn four times as many new words as poor readers (Adams & Higgins, 1985).

Reading children's books is a good way to reinforce high-frequency words.

So that the words in the banks are recognized automatically, students might work with them for brief periods each day. Working in pairs, students can quiz each other on words from their word banks. Using word-bank cards, they might make a list of things they can do. They can sort words by placing color words in one pile, action words in another, and animal words in a third. They can search out opposites or write stories about individual words. For concrete nouns or some action words, students might draw an illustration of the word on the reverse side of the paper or card. They might then quiz themselves by attempting to read the word, turning the card or paper over to see if they got it right. Creating sentences with words from their banks is another possible activity.

Using items from word banks is also one way of introducing or reinforcing phonics elements. After learning *see, so,* and *say,* students might be taught that *s* represents /s/. After learning *cat, hat,* and *sat,* they might be introduced to the *-at* pattern.

After students have accumulated a number of words in their word banks, they can keep them in alphabetical order by first letter. This will reinforce the use of the alphabet

INVOLVING PARENTS

Parents or grandparents can provide struggling readers and writers with the additional practice they need. One grandfather, following the advice of his grandson's teacher, taught his grandson 100 high-frequency words. Although the child was still far behind, the grandfather stopped helping his grandson because he didn't know what else he could do. A little time spent showing the grandfather what he might do would have had an invaluable payoff.

and also help them locate words. In time, the word bank becomes a kind of dictionary as well as a source of motivation: Word banks that are growing signal to the children that they are learning.

■ ■ ■ Checkup ■ ■ ■

1. How might high-frequency words be taught and reinforced?

■ ■ ■

■ Building Fluency

Adapting Instruction for English Language Learners

Reading along with a recorded version of a story is especially helpful for students whose reading speed is extremely slow and for students who are still learning English (Blum et al., 1995; Dowhower, 1987).

FYI

■ Fluency is sometimes equated with phrasing, smoothness, and expressiveness as well as rate, accuracy, and automaticity (Worthy & Broaddus, 2001).

■ Except when working with very beginning readers, the initial reading of a selection should almost always be silent. While discussing a selection read silently, students might read a favorite part orally, dramatize dialogue, or read a passage out loud to provide support for a point they are making.

In the beginning stages of learning to read, students may read in slow, halting fashion. This is understandable since students are still learning the code. However, if it persists, comprehension will suffer. Students will expend so much effort decoding that they won't be able to devote mental energy to understanding what they read. Students need to become fluent as well as accurate readers. Although often equated with smoothness of oral reading, **fluency** has been defined as "freedom from word identification problems that might hinder comprehension in silent reading or the expression of ideas in oral reading" (Harris & Hodges, 1995, p. 85). Fluency has two components: **accuracy** and **automaticity**. Students are accurate readers if they can recognize the words. They have automaticity if they recognize the words rapidly. Students can be accurate but slow decoders. As Samuels (2006) explains, fluency is based on automaticity, which is

> . . . the ability to perform two difficult tasks at the same time as the result of extended practice, whereas prior to practice only one task could be performed at a time. If two complex tasks can be performed simultaneously, then at least one of them is automatic. For example, at the beginning stage of reading, only one skill could be done at a time; first decoding, followed by comprehension. However, at the skilled stage, both decoding and comprehension can be performed together. Thus, the critical test of fluency is the ability to decode a text and understand it simultaneously. (pp. 39–41)

One way of judging fluency is by noting students' rate of silent reading and their comprehension. If they can read at a reasonable pace, then they probably are able to recognize the words rapidly. If they can answer questions about what they read, their word recognition is probably accurate. Another way of assessing fluency is by having students read a selection orally. If they misread a number of words, this indicates that accuracy is a problem. It also may be an indication that the material is beyond their instructional level. If they read word by word and seem to need to sound out an excessive number of words, then automaticity is an issue.

Comprehension is also an element in fluency. Students' phrasing and expressiveness should be noted. Does their reading indicate an understanding of what they are reading? Understanding what one reads is important for proper expression. Of course, it is essential that students be given material that is on the appropriate level. Given material that is too difficult, even the best readers become dysfluent.

Accuracy and speed of reading have to be balanced. An overemphasis on accuracy will lead to a decrease in reading speed. Do not insist on 100 percent accuracy (Samuels,

■ **Fluency** is freedom from word identification problems that might hinder comprehension in silent reading or the expression of ideas in oral reading. Fluency has levels of complexity. *Surface fluency* refers to rate of reading and reading with expression. *Deep fluency* means that the reader controls rate of reading and reading with expression to maximize comprehension (Topping, 2006). "The critical test of fluency is the ability to decode a text and understand it simultaneously" (Samuels, 2006, p. 41).

■ **Accuracy** means being able to pronounce or sound out a word and also knowing the word's meaning.

■ **Automaticity** refers to tasks that can be performed without attention or conscious effort.

1994). An overemphasis on oral reading will decrease reading speed. Students will also get the wrong idea about reading. They will begin to see reading as an oral performance activity in which they are expected to pronounce each word correctly. This could carry over into students' silent reading and so hinder comprehension. When students read orally, their purpose should be to convey the meaning of the passage rather than to render accurate pronunciation of each word.

Less fluent readers comprehend less. In a study of oral fluency among fourth-graders, the more fluent readers had better comprehension (Pinnell et al., 1995). Although they had 94 percent accuracy, the least fluent readers read much more slowly. Their average reading speed was just 65 words per minute. Fluent readers in fourth grade read between 126 and 162 words a minute.

The foundation for fluency is to build solid word analysis skills (Wolf & Katzir-Cohen, 2001) and to monitor for meaning. Beginning readers need to check themselves as they read by asking: "Do the words that I am reading match the letters? Do the words make sense?" Monitoring links the use of decoding and context (New Standards Primary Literacy Committee, 1999). Older readers also need to have well-developed decoding skills. While assessing the fluency of two classes of third-graders, I noticed that slowness in decoding multisyllabic words hampered the reading speed of about one student in ten. Stumbling over multisyllabic words or taking time to put a word into syllables slowed the students' reading and interfered with comprehension. The best way to boost the fluency of these students would have been to provide instruction in decoding multisyllabic words and also lots of practice and opportunities to read texts containing multisyllabic words so that their skills would have become more automatic.

In addition to prompting students to monitor for meaning, activities that foster rapid recognition of high-frequency words will foster fluency, as will wide reading of books at the students' independent level. This reading need not be oral. In fact, silent reading provides more realistic practice. At all levels, silent reading is recommended for building fluency. As they read books in which nearly all the words are known, students' ability to recognize the words faster should increase. Like any other complex behavior, reading requires substantial practice before it becomes automatic and seemingly effortless. If students persist in reading in a labored, halting fashion, the material is probably too difficult. Try material that is easy, and gradually move up to more difficult selections. Students, especially if they are younger, might also be encouraged to read the same selections a second, a third, or even a fourth time.

The ability to read orally with expression is, in part, a public speaking skill. Its goal is to convey meaning to others rather than to construct meaning. Oral reading should be preceded by silent reading. Readers need to construct a good understanding of the text so that they can then read it orally in such a way as to covey their interpretation. If you wish to promote oral reading skills, use drama and poetry to provide practice. Students don't mind reading a script over and over again if they are going to dramatize it. Students are also motivated to read accurately and expressively if they are reading to others. Having older children read to young children—first-graders reading to kindergartners, fourth-graders reading to second-graders—provides students with a reason to read a selection over and over again.

Choral Reading

Choral reading of selections also fosters fluency (McMaster, 1998). Choral reading involves two or more people but can take many forms. In unison reading, the whole group reads together. In refrain reading, the leader reads most of the text and the group reads the refrain. In antiphonal reading, two or more groups alternate. The boys may read one portion, the girls another. Or one side of the room might read a portion, and the other side read the other portion. Or one child or group reads a couplet or line, and another reads the next line or couplet (Bromley, 1998). One group might read designated lines in a loud voice; a second group, in a soft voice. Variations are endless.

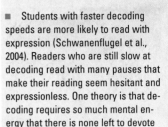

■■■ **TABLE 4.11** End-of-Year Reading Rate in Words per Minute

Instructional Reading level	Oral Reading	Silent Reading
Grade 1	55	55
Grade 2	85	85
Grade 3	115	130
Grade 4	135	155
Grade 5	145	185
Grade 6	150	205
Grades 7–8	150	225

Adapted from Powell (1980); cited in Lipson and Wixson (1997) and Harris and Sipay (1990).

USING TECHNOLOGY

TRW Resources provides a wealth of resources for paired reading. www.dundee.ac.uk/fedsoc/research/projects/trwresources/reading

FYI

■ Pausing for four seconds before supplying a word that a student is having difficulty with gives the student the chance to self-correct. Tutors have a tendency to provide a correction too quickly (Topping, 2006).

■ For beginning, middle, and end-of-year oral reading norms at various levels, see: Hasbrouck, J., & Tindal, G. A. (2006). Oral reading fluency norms: A valuable assessment tool for reading teachers. *The Reading Teacher, 59*, 636–644.

Adapting Instruction for Struggling Readers and Writers

In an adaptation of paired reading, children are given high-interest books that they would not be able to read on their own but that explore topics that develop background knowledge and vocabulary. Words that fit patterns that students have been taught are highlighted. The parent or volunteer reads the selection but pauses before highlighted words, which the student then reads.

Choral reading can be a whole-class or small-group activity. Choral reading is an excellent way to foster fluency and expression in reading. In a choral reading lesson, you might emphasize any of a number of oral reading skills: reading with expression, interpreting punctuation, phrasing of words, varying speed of reading. Poems, speeches, and tales with repeated parts lend themselves to choral reading. Choral reading lends itself to repeated reading as the class rereads in order to improve timing or expression or smoothness. It is a nonthreatening way for English language learners and struggling readers to practice their skills.

Because oral reading is used to measure fluency, there is a tendency to overemphasize oral reading as a way of fostering fluency. However, silent and oral reading are different tasks. Oral reading focuses the reader's attention on pronouncing words correctly. Silent reading stresses constructing meaning, which is the essence of reading. Silent reading also provides students the opportunity to work out troublesome words on their own without feeling rushed or embarrassed because people are listening to them struggle.

Silent reading is faster and more efficient. Readers can skip unnecessary words or sections. Beyond second grade, silent reading speed should exceed oral reading speed (see Table 4.11). If students are reading at a very slow pace, try to determine why and take corrective action. If the material is too difficult—if they miss more than five words out of one hundred—obtain materials on the appropriate level. If they are having difficulty decoding words, work on decoding skills. If they have mastered decoding skills but are reading in a slow or labored fashion, work on fluency. They may also be very anxious readers who feel they have to read each word carefully.

Modeled Techniques for Building Fluency

A first step in building fluency is to model the process. As you read orally, you are modeling the process of smooth, expressive reading. As you read orally to students, explain the techniques that you use: how you read in phrases, how you use your voice to express the author's meaning, how you read at a pace that listeners can keep up with but that isn't too fast.

Reading along with a taped or CD-ROM version of a selection can build oral fluency. Paired reading, which is also known as Duolog Reading (Topping, 1998), can be effective in building oral fluency. The teacher, a parent, or a child who is a more proficient reader teams up with a student. The student chooses the book to be read. The book selected is one that would be a little too difficult for the student to read on her or his own. After a brief discussion of the title and cover illustration, the helper and student simultaneously read the book out loud. During this dual reading, the helper adjusts his or her reading rate so it matches that of the student. When the student feels that she or he can read a portion of the text on her or his own, the student signals the helper by raising her or his left hand. When she or he wants the helper to resume reading with her or him, the student raises her or his right hand. The helper automatically provides assistance when the student stumbles over a word or is unable to read the word within four seconds (Topping, 1987; 1989). As an alternative to paired reading, the teacher, parent, or tutor may take turns reading the selection. At first, the teacher might do most of the reading. The student would read any words that she or he could. As the student becomes more proficient, she or he can read larger segments. All of these techniques provide a model of phrasing and expression that students might then incorporate into their silent reading.

Repeated Reading

A popular technique for fostering fluency is repeated reading (Samuels, 1979). Repeated reading helps students achieve accuracy and rapid recognition of high-frequency words. In one study, slow-reading second-graders doubled their reading speed after just seven weeks of repeated reading training (Dowhower, 1987). In another study, students enjoyed the fluency exercises so much that after the experiments were concluded, they asked for additional repeated reading sessions (Rashotte & Torgesen, 1985).

Rereadings are effective because students meet high-frequency words over and over, and these become part of their automatic recognition vocabulary (Dowhower, 1987). However, this means that the chosen selections should be on the same approximate level and should be on the students' instructional level. Lesson 4.7 lists suggested steps for a repeated reading lesson.

Lesson 4.7

Repeated Reading

Step 1. Introducing repeated reading

Explain the reasons behind repeated reading. Discuss how we get better when we practice. Explain to students that they will be practicing by reading the same story over and over. Tell students that this will help them read faster and better.

Step 2. Selecting a passage

Select or have the students choose a short, interesting selection of approximately 100 words. They might you or you might choose books, such as *The Cat in the Hat* (Geisel, 1957) or *Are You My Mother?* (Eastman, 1960), that are rhythmic and fun to read. Make sure that books are on the students' instructional level.

Step 3. Obtaining an initial timing

Obtain a baseline reading and accuracy rate. Have students read a selection orally. Time the reading, and record the number of words read correctly. If students take more than two minutes to read the selection and make more than five errors out of 100 words (not counting missed endings), the selection is too hard. If students make only one or two errors and read the selection at 85 words per minute or faster, the selection is too easy. If students can read 100 words a minute or close to it, repeated reading is probably a waste of instructional time (Dowhower, 1987). They would be better off with self-selected reading.

Step 4. Rereading

Go over the students' miscues with them. Help them read these words correctly. Also help them with phrasing problems or any other difficulties they may have had. Then direct them to reread the selection until they feel they can read it faster and more smoothly. Practice can take one of three forms: (1) reading the selection to oneself; (2) listening to an audiotape or viewing the selection on a CD-ROM while reading the selection silently, and then reading the selection without the aid of the tape or CD; (3) reading the selection to a partner. If students' reading speed is very slow, below 50 words per minute, they will do better reading along with a person or taped or CD version (Dowhower, 1987). After they reach speeds of 60 words per minute, they can practice without the tape or CD. Initially, students with very low reading rates will need lots of practice to reach 80 words per minute. But as reading rate increases, they won't need as many practice readings. Once they get used to the procedure, four or five rereadings should provide optimal returns for time spent. Additional rereadings would provide diminishing returns.

Step 5. Evaluating the reading

Students read the selection to you or to a partner. The number of word recognition errors and reading speed are recorded. Students are informed of their progress. A chart

Adapting Instruction for Struggling Readers and Writers

Repeated reading can be used to help struggling readers experience what it is like to read smoothly and with few or no mistakes (Allington, 2006).

ASSESSING FOR LEARNING

Tests that measure only reading rate might give a false impression. Samuels (2006) found that a number of English learners had good decoding skills and a good reading rate, but their comprehension was poor because of their difficulty in understanding the language.

might be constructed to show the degree of improvement. The goal is to have students in grade 3 and beyond read at least 80 to 100 words per minute. Students should practice until they reach that standard. Errors in word recognition should also decrease. However, do not insist upon perfect word recognition. Setting a standard of 100 percent accuracy leads students to conclude that reading is a word-pronouncing rather than a meaning-constructing activity. It also slows the reading rate. Afraid of making a mistake, students will read at a slow-but-sure pace (Samuels, 1988b).

Variations on Repeated Reading

Instead of working with a teacher, students may work in pairs. However, explain and model the procedure first. One student reads while the other charts his or her progress. Then they switch roles. Show students how to time the reading and count errors. To make the charting easier, have students check 100-word samples only. Students might read a selection that contains more than 100 words but only 100 words are used for charting reading rate. Students may hurry through a selection to obtain a fast time. Explain to students that they should read at a normal rate. On occasion, have students read a song or a poem instead of the usual reading selections. Because of their rhythm, narrative poems and songs lend themselves to a rapid reading.

Recorded-Book Method

To build students' ability to recognize words automatically and to improve their phrasing, have them read along as a selection is read. You or an aide can read selections to students, or you can have them read along with taped stories. Because taped stories are read at the pace of normal speech, this may be too rapid for the listener to match printed and spoken words. When a student reads along with a tape, the pace should be at about the same rate as the student can read orally or slightly faster. If the pace is too rapid, the student may not be able to keep up and may become frustrated (Carbo, 1997). In deciding which books to record, select those that are interesting and that students will be able to understand when they hear them read aloud. When recording selections, read with expression but read slowly enough so that students can follow along. Pace your reading at about 80 to 100 words per minute. Also obtain a tape recorder that has a speed regulator. Have students set the speed at a comfortable pace (Shany & Biemiller, 1995). As you encounter words or expressions that might be unfamiliar to students, pause before and after reading them so that students will have time to process them (Carbo, Dunn, & Dunn, 1986).

Recordings should be brief. Record from five to ten minutes of text on each side of a tape. Obtain short stories and brief articles that lend themselves to being recorded. Begin the recording by announcing title and author. Provide an overview of the selection to give students an orientation. Also provide a purpose for listening. Signal when it is time to turn a page and announce when the reading has been completed (Carbo, Dunn, & Dunn, 1986).

Encourage students to read along with the taped selection several times, until they judge that they can read it on their own. When they feel ready to read on their own, students should try reading the selection without the tape and note difficult parts. They should then listen to the tape once more and reread the text to practice the parts that proved to be difficult. Students can work alone or with partners. Partners can read to each other after practicing with the tape.

Listening to recorded stories is one way to build automatic word recognition.

CD-ROM Fluency Read-Alongs

Many reading software programs, such as *Reading Blasters* (Knowledge Adventure) have a feature that allows students to read stories out loud and then hear the read-aloud. After students have heard a story read and have read along with it, they can then record their reading of it and compare their reading with that of the professional reader. Students can practice reading a small segment and move on to the next segment once they have mastered it. They can have as many practice read-alouds as they want and can read along with the correct version as many times as they want. This could be especially helpful for English language learners who are struggling with correct pronunciation and expression.

Insights Reading Fluency uses sophisticated speech recognition software to measure and assist students' oral reading. The software tracks a student as she or he reads, corrects errors, and keeps a record of the student's performance. By using the mouse, the student can request that the program pronounce a word and provide a definition or even read portions of the selections. The program also checks comprehension. Although labeled a device for increasing fluency, it could also be used to build background, vocabulary, and comprehension. One of the best features of the program is that it presents high-quality selections.

Alternate Reading

In alternate reading, the teacher (or parent or tutor) and the student take turns reading the selection. Initially, the teacher reads most of the selection. The student reads any words or phrases that he or she can. For some students, this might be a few high-frequency and short-vowel words or a repeated sentence. As the student improves, he or she reads larger portions. The teacher reads the first page, and the student reads the second page. Or the teacher might read the difficult parts, and the pupil reads the easy parts. The teacher also provides whatever help the student needs. If the student encounters a difficult word, the teacher tells the student the word or provides prompts that help the student figure out the word.

Increasing the Amount of Reading

Fluency is most effectively fostered by increasing the amount of reading that students do. In one study, second-graders engaged in partner and echo reading of the basal text and silent reading in school and at home of self-selected books. Although the program was only a year long, students gained nearly two years (Stahl, Heubach, & Crammond, 1997). The students who gained the most were reading at least on a late preprimer level. Apparently, students need some foundational reading skill before they can profit from fluency instruction (Kuhn & Stahl, 2000).

Phrasing of Text

Fluency is more than just accuracy and speed in reading; it also includes proper phrasing. Word-by-word reading is frequently caused by giving students material that is too difficult so that they literally have to figure out just about every word. It also can be caused by a lack of automaticity. Students have to stop and decode a large proportion of words because they don't recognize them immediately. Word-by-word reading should fade as students improve their decoding skills and as their skills become automatic. If word-by-word reading persists even though word recognition is adequate and automatic, model reading orally in logical phrases, and have students read selections in which phrases are marked so that they have practice reading in meaningful chunks.

Why Fluency Instruction Works

Why does fluency instruction work? It seems to work because it increases the amount of reading that students do. Repeated reading and assisted reading may enable children to read more difficult material than they might otherwise be able to read or may provide a

USING TECHNOLOGY

Charlesbridge provides a demo of Insights Reading Fluency:
http://www.charlesbridge-fluency.com

FYI

■ Series books are especially effective for developing fluency. Because they have the same characters and often the same setting, series books are easier to read. If they like the first book they read in a series, chances are students will be motivated to read the other books. Often, students will read all the books in a twenty-book series. Because the reading is easy and highly motivating, this fosters automaticity of word recognition and speed of processing, which are key components in fluency. For kindergartners and first-graders, *Clifford, Curious George,* and *Arthur* are popular series. For students in grades 2 to 4, *Kids of Polk Street, Nate the Great, Cam Jansen,* and *Magic Tree House* are popular.

■ Students made fluency gains when engaged in repeated reading and when engaged in wide reading (Kuhn, 2004). However, the wide-reading group made greater gains in comprehension. The repeated-reading group might have been focused on expressive and accurate rendition. Comprehension might also have improved more in the wide-reading group because that group read eighteen texts and the repeated-reading group read just six.

manageable structure to enable increased amounts of reading (Kuhn & Stahl, 2003, p. 17). In a study comparing repeated reading of a selected number of texts and wider reading of a variety of texts, Van Bon, Bokesbeld, Font Freide, and Van den Hurk (1991) found that reading a variety of texts worked just as well as reading one text over and over.

■ ■ ■ Checkup ■ ■ ■

1. What is fluency?
2. What are some ways of fostering fluency?

■ ■ ■

■ Syllabic Analysis

Adapting Instruction for Struggling Readers and Writers

Some students have difficulty decoding multisyllabic words even though they are able to decode single-syllable words. These students may not realize that they can apply their single-syllable skills to the decoding of multisyllabic words. Having them seek out known parts in multisyllabic words helps them make use of what they know.

FYI

The term *structural analysis* is sometimes used to refer to syllabic analysis and morphemic analysis (study of affixes and roots).

Fortunately, many of the most frequently used words in English have just one syllable. The Harris-Jacobson list of words (Harris & Jacobson, 1982) that appears in at least half of basal readers has no multisyllabic words on the preprimer level. On the primer level, however, 15 percent are polysyllabic; on the first-grade level, the figure rises to more than 25 percent. By second grade, more than 30 percent are multisyllabic; by fourth grade, the figure is more than 60 percent. The implications are clear. Students have to know early on how to deal with multisyllabic words. That need grows rapidly as students progress to higher levels. **Syllabication**, or structural analysis as it is sometimes called, may be introduced informally in the latter half of first grade and should be taught formally in second grade and beyond.

Syllabic analysis is deceptively difficult. Surprisingly, in one study of thirty-seven second-graders who were proficient readers and could easily read *let* and *her*, several students read *letter* as *later*, *weeding* as *wedding*, *cabbage* as *cab bag*, and *ribbon* as *rib bahn*, the last two errors being nonwords (Gunning, 2001). For 20 percent of the multisyllabic words, students omitted at least one syllable. An analysis of students' errors has a number of implications for instruction, including the following:

- Students should be taught and prompted to process all the syllables in a word.
- Students need to be taught to see patterns in words. Students who can read *let* and *her* but read *letter* as *later* are not seeing the familiar *-et* pattern.
- Students need to be flexible in their decoding of words. If one pronunciation doesn't work out, they should be prepared to try another. This ties in with reading for meaning. Pronouncing *even* as *ev-en*, the student should note that this is not a word and so should try a long pronunciation: *e-ven*.
- Students should integrate context and syllabic analysis. A number of students read *wedding* for *weeding* in the sentence: "Amy was weeding her garden," which indicates failure to use context. A number of other students read the sentence as "Amy was watering her garden," which suggests that although they used context they failed to process the whole word.
- Students need to be reminded to use the orthographic aspects of phonics. Many students had difficulty with words containing final-*e* markers and digraphs. Students did not make use of the final-*e* marker that indicates a soft *g* in *cabbage* or the digraph *ai* in *contain* that indicates a long *a*. When presenting syllable patterns, you may find it helpful to review the single-syllable elements that make up those patterns.

■ **Syllabication** is the division of words into syllables. In reading, words are broken down into syllables phonemically, according to their sound (*gen e rous, butt er*), rather than orthographically, according to the rules governing end-of-line word division (*gen er ous, but ter*).

- Students should also be taught that sometimes an element in a multisyllabic word is not read in the same way as when it appears in a single-syllable word. For instance, many students read the *car* in *carrots* as though it were the word *car*. Students also need to know that often the pronunciation of an element changes when it is in a multisyllabic word. Because of reduced stress, the *on* in *ribbon* has a schwa rather than a short *o* pronunciation. Many students pronounced it as though it had a short *o* pronunciation and ended up with the nonword *ribbahn*. Students need to be flexible in their pronunciation of the syllables in multisyllabic words and should also be using context as an aid.

- Elements such as *tion* and *ture* as in *mention* and *future*, which occur only in multisyllabic words, need a careful introduction, frequent review, and a great deal of practice.

Generalization Approach to Teaching Syllabic Analysis

Sort the following words. You can have a question mark category for words that don't seem to fit a pattern.

spider	super	magnet	clever
secret	flavor	bitter	custom
rabbit	hotel	tiger	over
supper	music	fever	elbow
pepper	pupil	wagon	future

How did you sort the words? One way of sorting them is by sounds. All the words with long vowels are in one column; all the words with short vowels are in a second column. You can also sort them by sound and spelling. Notice that the words that end in a consonant seem to be short and those that end in a vowel seem to be long. You might also note that the long vowels were followed by one consonant and short vowels were followed by two consonants. However, there were two exception words: *wagon* and *clever*. Sorting is a way of helping students make discoveries about words. Through sorts of this type, students discover two of the most sweeping generalizations in phonics: the open syllable generalization states that syllables that end in a vowel are generally long, and the closed syllable generalization states that syllables that end in a consonant are generally short.

The two approaches to teaching syllabication are generalization and pattern. The generalization approach is more widespread but probably less effective. It can be combined with a pattern approach.

In the generalization approach, students learn general rules for dividing words into syllables. The generalizations listed below seem to be particularly useful (Gunning, 1975). These should be presented in the following order, which reflects both frequency of occurrence and approximate order of difficulty:

1. *Easy affixes: -ing, -er, -ly.* Most prefixes and suffixes form separate syllables: *un-safe, re-build, help-ful, quick-ly.* Except for *s* as a plural marker, affixes generally are composed of a vowel and consonant(s). Thus, they are syllables in themselves: *play-ing, re-play.*

2. *Compound words.* The words that make up a compound word usually form separate syllables: *sun-set, night-fall.*

3. *Two consonants between two vowels.* When two consonants appear between two vowels, the word generally divides between them: *win-ter, con-cept.* The place of division is often an indication of the pronunciation of the vowel. The *i* in *winter*, the *o* in the first syllable of *concept*, and the *e* in the second syllable of *concept* are short. Note that all three vowels are in closed syllables—that is, syllables that end in consonants: *win, con, cept.* Closed syllables often contain a short vowel. (The *e* in winter is not short because it is followed by *r.*) Note, too, that digraphs are not split: *broth-er, with-er.*

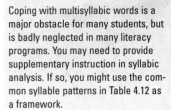

Adapting Instruction for Struggling Readers and Writers

Shefelbine and Newman (2000) found that average and poor decoders were two to four times more likely than good decoders to omit syllables when reading multisyllabic words. The researchers suggested a great deal of reading at the independent level. Direct instruction in using multisyllabic words should also be implemented.

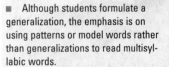

FYI

- Although students formulate a generalization, the emphasis is on using patterns or model words rather than generalizations to read multisyllabic words.

- Students often confuse open and closed syllables. They tend to read open syllables such as those occurring in *even* and *noticed* as closed syllables: *ev-en, not-iced.*

- Putting words into syllables can be a challenging task because it's sometimes difficult to tell where one syllable ends and another begins. Even the experts disagree. If you look up the word *vocational*, for instance, you will see that Merriam-Webster dictionaries divide it into syllables in one way and Thorndike-Barnhart dictionaries syllabicate it in another way.

FYI

Have students sort multisyllabic words. This enables them to discover generalizations and patterns. Words to be sorted should be words they can read.

4. *One consonant between two vowels.* When one consonant appears between two vowels, it often becomes a part of the syllable on the right: *ma-jor, e-vil*. When the single consonant moves to the right, the syllable to the left is said to be open because it ends in a vowel. If a syllable ends in a vowel, the vowel is generally long. In a number of exception words, however, the consonant becomes a part of the syllable on the left: *sev-en, wag-on*.

5. *The ending le.* The letters *le* at the end of a word are usually combined with a preceding consonant to create a separate syllable: *cra-dle, ma-ple*.

6. *Two vowels together.* A limited number of words split between two vowels: *i-de-a, di-al*.

It is important to keep in mind that syllabication is designed to help students decode an unfamiliar word by separating it into its syllabic parts and then recombining the parts into a whole. It is not necessary for students to divide the word exactly right, which is a highly technical process. All that matters is whether students are able to arrive at the approximate pronunciation.

Pattern Approach to Teaching Syllabic Analysis

Knowing syllabic generalizations is one thing; applying them is quite another. Research (Gunning, 1975) and experience suggest that many students apparently do not apply syllabic generalizations. When faced with unfamiliar, multisyllabic words, they attempt to search out pronounceable elements or simply skip the words. These students might fare better with an approach that presents syllables in patterns (Cunningham, 1978).

In a pattern approach, students examine a number of words that contain a syllable that has a high frequency. For example, dozens of words that begin with a consonant and are followed by a long *o* could be presented in pattern form. The advantage of this approach is that students learn to recognize pronounceable units in multisyllabic words and also to apply the open syllable generalization in a specific situation. The pattern could be introduced with a one-syllable word contrasted with multisyllabic words to make it easier for students to grasp, for example:

Adapting Instruction for Struggling Readers and Writers

When working with struggling readers, especially those who have been unsuccessful with a particular program or approach, try using a new approach and also new materials. Struggling readers don't want to work with a program or text that they associate with failure (Stahl, 1998).

so

soda

total

local

vocal

motel

hotel

notice

The steps to follow in teaching a syllabication lesson using the pattern approach are presented in Lesson 4.8.

Lesson 4.8

Syllabication Using the Pattern Approach

Step 1. Introducing the syllabic pattern(s)
To introduce a syllabic pattern, explain the importance of syllabic analysis, and then contrast the pattern with single-syllable words. This helps students to spot familiar parts in what might appear to be unfamiliar polysyllabic words.

Step 2. Presenting the *-us, -ut, uzz* pattern(s) and selecting a model word

Write the word *muss* on the board, and have students read it. Then write *muscle* under it, and have students read it. Note that the *c* in *muscle* has an /s/ sound. Contrast *muss* and *muscle* by pointing to the sound that each syllable makes. To help students perceive the separate syllables in *muscle*, write them in contrasting colors or underline them. Then have students read *muscle*. Present the words *mustache, mustang, custom, customer,* and *discuss* in the same way. Then have students read all the words. Tell students that *bus* is the model word for this pattern. If they forget the pattern or have difficulty with a word containing the syllable *us*, they can use the model word to help them. If you have a model words chart, add *bus* to it. If you do not have such a chart, you may wish to start one. To present the *ut* pattern, use *but, button, butter, clutter, flutter,* and *gutter.* The model word is *nut.* To present the *uzz* pattern, use *fuzz, fuzzy, puzzle, muzzle, buzzer,* and *buzzard. Fuzz* is the model word.

Step 3. Formulating a generalization

Lead students to see that *u* often has the short *u* sound when it is followed by two or more consonants or appears in a closed syllable.

Step 4. Guided practice

For guided practice, have students read a second set of short-*u* multisyllabic words: *custard, bonus, cactus, Celsius.* Also have students search out multisyllabic *-us, -ut,* and *-uzz* words in a reading selection so that they can see this pattern in context. Have students complete exercises similar to the following:

Make a word by putting together two of the three syllables in each row. Write the word on the lines.

ug	tom	cus	_____
ty	dus	is	_____
ton	ent	but	_____
ter	but	eat	_____
zle	op	puz	_____

Underline the word that better fits the sense of each sentence.

The turkey vulture is also known as the turkey (*buzzard, buzzer*).

Some people think vultures are (*disguising, disgusting*) because they eat dead animals.

Vultures are not (*further, fussy*) eaters.

With their strong wing (*muscles, muskets*), vultures can fly high in the sky.

With their (*butter, button*)-shaped eyes, vultures can spot food from hundreds of feet in the air. (Gunning, 1994)

Step 5. Application

Have students read selections—stories, informational pieces, and/or real-world materials—that contain short-*u* multisyllabic words.

Step 6. Assessment and review

Note students' ability to read multisyllabic words that follow the patterns introduced. Also note what they do when they encounter multisyllabic words. Are they able to use strategies to decode the words? Review and reteach as necessary.

Step 7. Extension

Present other short-*u* patterns. After presenting a number of short-vowel patterns, review them. Also review long-vowel, other-vowel, and *r*-vowel patterns.

FYI

■ Why might students who can read elements in single-syllable words have difficulty with those same elements in multisyllabic words? The students may have difficulty locating the known element in a longer word. For instance, *par* is a single-syllable word that appears as an element in *partial, parcel,* and *particle* but has a different identity in *parade* and *paradise.* As Shefelbine (1990) notes, "Identifying patterns of syllables requires more developed and complex knowledge of letter and spelling patterns than the knowledge needed for reading single syllable words" (p. 225).

■ After presenting a number of short-vowel syllabic patterns, review those patterns and help students to see that closed syllables usually contain a short vowel. Do the same with long-vowel syllabic patterns. Help students to contrast a number of closed and open syllables. Help them to see that open syllables usually have long vowels.

■ When students decode multisyllabic words, do not insist upon exact syllable division. All that should be expected is that the student break such a word into smaller units so that she or he can pronounce each one and then put the units back together again to form a whole word.

Additional Practice Activities for Multisyllabic Words

■ Have students read or sing song lyrics in which the separate syllables of multisyllabic words are indicated.

■ Make available books in which difficult words are put into syllables and phonetically respelled.

■ Have students read by syllables (Shefelbine & Newman, 2000). Write a syllable on the board, and have students read it. Then write another syllable on the board, and have students read it. Then have them read the word formed by putting the two syllables together. For example, students read *ab* and then *sent* and then *absent*. Emphasize the need to adjust the pronunciation of a syllable so as to say a real word. When occurring in unaccented syllables, vowels have a reduced pronunciation; for example, the second syllable in *velvet* is pronounced *vit* instead of *vet*.

■ Encourage students to bring in multisyllabic words that they have noticed in their reading and which they were able to pronounce. They might write their words on the board and have the other students read them.

■ When introducing new words that have more than one syllable, write the words on the board and encourage students to read them. Provide help as needed.

■ Use software, such as *Tenth Planet: Word Parts* (Sunburst), that challenges students to build words by combining syllables and to use multisyllabic words to compose poems, riddles, and stories.

■ To help students differentiate between open and closed syllables, have them read contrasting word pairs (*super, supper; biter, bitter*) or complete sentences by selecting one of two contrasting words: Although the dog looked mean, it was not a (*biter, bitter*). We had chicken and mashed potatoes for (*super, supper*).

Multisyllabic Patterns

In approximate order of difficulty, the major multisyllabic patterns are as follows:

■ Easy affixes: *play-ing, quick-ly*
■ Compound words: *base-ball, any-one*
■ Closed-syllable words: *rab-bit, let-ter*
■ Open-syllable words: *ba-by, ti-ny*
■ Final-*e* markers: *es-cape, do-nate*
■ Vowel digraphs: *a-gree, sea-son*
■ Other patterns: *cir-cle, sir-loin*

Major syllable patterns and example words for the patterns are presented in Table 4.12.

Combining the Generalization and Pattern Approaches

Although the pattern approach is highly effective and builds on what students know, students sometimes are unable to see patterns in words. In these instances, they should try applying generalizations. In his research, Shefelbine (1990) found that instruction in open (*mo-, ta-, fi-*) and closed (*-at, -em, -in*) syllables and affixes (*un-, pre-, -less, -ful*) was especially helpful. After teaching a number of open-syllable patterns, you might have students construct a generalization about the pattern, such as "Syllables that end in a vowel are often long (*ta ble*)." After teaching a number of closed-syllable patterns, you might have students construct a generalization about the pattern, such as "Syllables that end in a consonant are often short (*hap py*)."

To apply generalizations in words that don't have affixes, students should identify the first syllable by locating the first vowel and note whether the syllable is open (ending in a vowel) or closed (ending in a consonant). Students should say the first syllable and then

■■■ TABLE 4.12 Common Syllable Patterns

Compound-Word Pattern

some	day	out	sun
someone	daylight	outside	sunup
sometime	daytime	outdoor	sundown
something	daybreak	outline	sunfish
somehow	daydream	outgrow	sunlight
somewhere		outfield	sunbeam

Schwa *a* Pattern

a	a
ago	around
away	along
alone	alive
awake	apart
among	across
asleep	about

High-Frequency Patterns

en	o	er
pen	go	her
open	ago	under
happen	over	ever
enter	broken	never
twenty	spoken	other
plenty	frozen	farmer

ar	at	it
car	mat	sit
garden	matter	sitter
sharpen	batter	bitter
farmer	chatter	kitten
marker	clatter	kitchen
partner	scatter	pitcher

in	is(s)	un
win	miss	under
winter	mister	until
window	mistake	hunter
dinner	sister	thunder
finish	whisper	hundred

be	re	or
became	remind	order
beside	report	morning
below	reward	corner
begin	refuse	forty
belong	receive	before

a	y = /ē/	ey	ble
pay	sunny	turkey	able
paper	funny	monkey	table
baby	dusty	money	cable
famous	shady	honey	bubble
favorite			mumble

i	ur	um
tie	fur	sum
tiger	furry	summer
spider	hurry	number
tiny	turkey	pumpkin
title	turtle	stumble
Friday	purple	trumpet

ic(k)	et	et	im
pick	let	ticket	swim
picnic	letter	pocket	swimmer
attic	better	rocket	chimney
nickel	lettuce	bucket	limit
pickle	settle	magnet	improve
chicken	metal	jacket	simple

Short-Vowel Patterns

ab	ad	ag
cab	sad	bag
cabin	saddle	baggy
cabbage	paddle	dragon
rabbit	shadow	wagon
habit	ladder	magazine
absent	address	magnet

an	ap
can	nap
candy	napkin
handy	happy
handle	happen
giant	captain
distant	chapter

ent	el
went	yell
event	yellow
prevent	elbow
cement	elephant
invent	jelly
experiment	welcome

ep	es(s)	ev
pep	less	seven
pepper	lesson	several
peppermint	address	never
September	success	clever
shepherd	yesterday	every
separate	restaurant	level

ea	ea
sweat	treasure
sweater	measure
weather	pleasure
feather	pleasant
leather	threaten
meadow	wealthy

(continued)

■■■ TABLE 4.12 Common Syllable Patterns *(continued)*

id	ig	il
rid	wig	pill
riddle	wiggle	pillow
middle	giggle	silver
hidden	signal	silly
midnight	figure	building

ob	oc	od
rob	doc	cod
robber	doctor	body
problem	pocket	model
probably	chocolate	modern
hobby	rocket	product
gobble	hockey	somebody

ol	om	on
doll	mom	monster
dollar	momma	monument
volcano	comma	honest
follow	common	honor
holiday	comment	concrete
jolly	promise	responsible

op	ot	age
shop	rot	cabbage
shopper	rotten	bandage
chopper	gotten	damage
popular	bottom	message
opposite	bottle	baggage
copy	robot	garbage

ub	uc(k)	ud
rub	luck	mud
rubber	lucky	buddy
bubble	bucket	study
stubborn	chuckle	puddle
subject	success	huddle
public	product	sudden

uf	ug	up
stuff	bug	pup
stuffy	buggy	puppy
muffin	ugly	supper
suffer	suggest	upper
buffalo	struggle	puppet

us	ut	uz
muss	but	fuzz
mustard	button	fuzzy
muscle	butter	puzzle
custom	clutter	muzzle
customer	flutter	buzzer
discuss	gutter	buzzard

Long-Vowel Patterns

ade	ail/ale
parade	detail
invade	female
lemonade	airmail
centigrade	trailer

ain	ate
obtain	hesitate
explain	hibernate
complain	appreciate

ea	ea	ee	e
sea	eat	bee	see
season	eaten	beetle	secret
reason	beaten	needle	fever
beaver	repeat	indeed	female
eagle	leader	succeed	even
easily	reader		equal

ide	ire	ize	ise	ive
side	tire	prize	wise	drive
beside	entire	realize	surprise	arrive
divide	require	recognize	exercise	alive
decide	admire	memorize	advise	survive
provide	umpire	apologize	disguise	beehive

ope	one	u	ture
hope	phone	use	future
antelope	telephone	music	nature
envelope	microphone	human	adventure
telescope	xylophone	museum	creature

Other Vowel Patterns

al	au	au	aw
also	cause	caution	draw
always	saucer	faucet	drawing
already	author	sausage	crawling
altogether	August	daughter	strawberry
although	autumn	auditorium	awful
walrus	audience		awesome

oi	oy
point	joy
poison	enjoy
disappointment	destroy
noisy	royal
avoid	loyal
moisture	voyage

ou	ou	ow
round	mountain	power
around	fountain	tower
about	surround	flower
announce	compound	allow
amount	thousand	allowance

■■■ TABLE 4.12 Common Syllable Patterns (continued)

oo	ove	u	tion	tion	sion	y = /ī/
too	prove	Sue	action	question	conclusion	try
bamboo	proven	super	addition	mention	confusion	reply
shampoo	improve	student	station	suggestion	occasion	supply
cartoon	approve	studio	invention	exhaustion	explosion	deny
raccoon	remove	truly	information	indigestion	persuasion	magnify
balloon	movements	tuna				

From *Assessing and Correcting Reading and Writing Difficulties* (2nd ed.) by T. Gunning, 2002. Boston: Allyn & Bacon. Reprinted by permission of Allyn & Bacon.

proceed in this same way, syllable by syllable. After they have pronounced all the syllables, they should attempt to say the word, making any adjustments necessary. Prompt students as needed. If students misread an open syllable as a closed one—for instance, reading *no-tice* as *not-ice*—ask them to tell where the vowel is so they can see that the vowel should be ending the syllable and should be long. Often, vowel sounds are reduced when they appear in multisyllabic words, as in *educate*, where the *u* has a schwa pronunciation. Explain to students that they should not just pronounce syllables but should change pronunciations if they have to so that they can "read the real word" (Shefelbine & Newman, 2000).

Whether you teach using generalizations, patterns, or, as this book recommends, a combination of approaches, students must have a plan of attack or strategy when facing an unfamiliar multisyllabic word. Students can use the steps in the following Student Strategy on their own.

Student Strategies

Attacking Multisyllabic Words

1. See whether the word has any prefixes or suffixes. If so, pronounce the prefix, then the suffix, and then the remaining part(s) of the word. If the word has no prefix or suffix, start with the beginning of the word and divide it into syllables. Say each syllable.

2. Put the syllables together. If the word does not sound like a real word, try other pronunciations until you get a real word.

3. See if the word makes sense in the sentence in which it appears. If it does not, try other pronunciations.

4. If nothing works, use a dictionary or ask the teacher.

To help them apply this strategy, you might show students how to use *Spot and Dot*. When using *Spot and Dot* (Fast Track Reading, 2002), students spot the vowel and then place a dot over the place where the syllable ends. If a vowel is followed by one consonant (*bi ter*), the consonant most often goes with the second syllable and the vowel is long. If the vowel is followed by two consonants (*bit ter*), the consonants are usually split. The first syllable ends with a consonant (is closed) and usually has a short vowel. There are exceptions, so students need to be flexible.

Tools for the Classroom

Using the Pronounceable Word Part and Analogy Strategies

The pronounceable word part and analogy strategies recommended for decoding single-syllable words may also be used to decode multisyllabic words. For instance, if students are having difficulty with the word *silver*, they might look for a pronounceable word part such as *il* and add /s/ to make *sil*. They would then say *er*, add /v/ to make *ver* and reconstruct the whole word. In many instances, saying a part of the word—the *sil* in *silver*, for example— is enough of a clue to enable students to say the whole word. If the pronounceable word part strategy does not work, students may use an analogy strategy, in which they employ common words to help them sound out the syllables in a multisyllabic word that is in their listening but not their reading vocabulary. For instance, faced with the word *thunder*, the student works it out by making a series of comparisons. The first syllable is *thun*, which is similar to the known word *sun*, and the second syllable is *der*, which is similar to the known word *her*. Putting them together, the student synthesizes the word *thunder*.

As students read increasingly complex materials and meet a higher proportion of polysyllabic words, their ability to perceive the visual forms of syllables should develop naturally. As with phonics skills, the best way to practice dealing with polysyllabic words is through a combination of instruction and wide reading.

■ ■ ■ Checkup ■ ■ ■

1. What are the major syllable patterns?
2. What are the main approaches for teaching syllabication?

■ ■ ■

Building Higher-Level Literacy

Although it is important for students to have materials to which they can apply the decoding skills they have just been taught, decodable texts don't offer much in the way of stories or ideas. Insofar as possible, select decodable materials of relatively high quality. Also, don't get so caught up in teaching decoding skills that higher-level skills are neglected. From the very first, develop higher-level skills by reading aloud or share-reading high-quality materials. Make vocabulary and higher-level skills an ongoing focus of the curriculum, not elements to be implemented only after students learn basic skills.

Help for Struggling Readers and Writers

Struggling readers and writers do best with a systematic program in word analysis skills (Foorman et al., 1998). Although most students will grasp word analysis skills regardless of the approach used to teach them, at-risk learners need direct, clear instruction (Snow, Burns, & Griffin, 1998). For students who are struggling, this text recommends word building, with one important adaptation. When presenting a pattern, emphasize the components of the pattern. As explained in the sample lesson, say the parts of a pattern word. When adding *p* to *et* to form *pet*, say, "When I add /p/ to /et/, I get the word *pet*." Then point out each letter and the sound it represents. Pointing to *p* say /p/, pointing to *e* say /e/, pointing to *t* say /t/. Then say the word as a whole. Later, after adding *et* to *p* to form *pet*, again say the word in parts and then as a whole. Pointing to *p*, say the sound /p/. Pointing to *e*, say the sound /e/. Pointing to /t/, say the sound /t/. Then say the word as a whole. Have students say the word in parts and as a whole. Saying the individual sounds in a word helps the students to note all the sounds in the word and the letters that represent them. It also fosters phonemic awareness, which develops slowly in many struggling readers. In addition, some struggling readers may find it easier to deal with individual sounds.

Also, use spelling to reinforce phonics. Dictating and having students spell pattern words helps them to focus on the individual sounds and letters in the pattern words and provides another avenue of learning. Most important of all, encourage students to read widely. Struggling readers often need much more practice than do achieving readers. Reading books on their level that apply patterns they have been taught is the best possible practice.

For syllabic analysis, use the pattern approach. One advantage of this approach is that it reviews basic phonics as new elements are being introduced. For instance, when introducing the syllabic pattern *aw*, the teacher automatically reviews the *aw* element, as in *law*. This is helpful to struggling readers, who often have gaps in their skills. Shefelbine (1990) found that 15 to 20 percent of the students in the fourth- and eighth-grade classes that he tested had difficulty with multisyllabic words, and some students were still experiencing problems with single-syllable phonics, especially vowel elements.

Using Assessment to Close the Gap

As noted in Chapter 2, monitoring students' progress is important for all students but is absolutely essential for struggling readers. Set realistic word recognition and fluency goals for the class and for each student. Monitor students on a regular basis, at least three or four times a year. Students who are having difficulty should be monitored more frequently, at least once a month. If students are not making adequate progress, analyze the results and the teaching situation, as in the Case Study on p. 195, and make adjustments to improve performance. For phonics or syllabic analysis, you can use the Phonics Progress Monitoring Assessment or Syllable Survey in Appendix B. A reasonable goal would be that students achieve a score of 10 in the beginning of first grade, 20 in the middle of first grade, and 45 by the end of first grade. For the Syllable Survey, reasonable goals would be 10, 15, and 25 in the beginning, middle, and end of second grade and 25, 35, and 45 in the beginning, middle, and end of third grade. You might also use a test such as the Beginning Phonics Skills Test (BPST) (Shefelbine, 1997). Students who are not meeting benchmark goals should be provided with additional, perhaps intensive, instruction. Approximately 15 percent of students in a typical classroom may need intensive help to meet goals (Good et al., 2003). However, in some classes, as many as one-fourth of the students will need intensive help.

Essential Standards

Kindergarten

See Essential Standards at the end of Chapter 3.

Grade 1

Students will

- continue to develop phonemic awareness.
- learn consonant, consonant digraph, and consonant cluster correspondences, as well as short vowels, long vowels, other vowels, *r* vowels, and vowel patterns.
- recognize high-frequency, irregular words, such as *of, was,* and *what*.
- use pronounceable word part, analogy, picture clue, and contextual strategies.
- read words with inflectional endings such as *-s, -ed, -ing*.
- integrate the use of contextual and word analysis strategies.
- begin to read both regularly and irregularly spelled words automatically.
- begin to use common word patterns to read multisyllabic words.
- read with accuracy, fluency, and expression at about 50 to 60 wpm.

Grade 2

Students will

- learn advanced and less frequent consonant digraph and consonant cluster correspondences and advanced and less frequent short vowels, long vowels, other vowels, *r* vowels, and vowel patterns.
- use high-frequency syllabication patterns to decode words.
- use pronounceable word part, analogy, and contextual strategies to decode words.
- integrate the use of contextual and word analysis strategies.
- read with accuracy, fluency, and expression at about 70 to 90 wpm.

INVOLVING PARENTS

Parents might want to know what to do if their children ask for help with a word. Having them simply tell their children unknown words is the safest, least frustrating approach (Topping, 1989). But in some situations, you may want to have them encourage their children in the use of specific strategies.

FYI

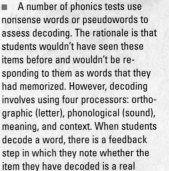

■ A number of phonics tests use nonsense words or pseudowords to assess decoding. The rationale is that students wouldn't have seen these items before and wouldn't be responding to them as words that they had memorized. However, decoding involves using four processors: orthographic (letter), phonological (sound), meaning, and context. When students decode a word, there is a feedback step in which they note whether the item they have decoded is a real word. If the item being decoded is a nonword, then the semantic process cannot be brought into play. Because of this missing feedback step, decoding nonsense words is apparently more difficult than decoding real words (Cunningham, Yoder, & McKenna, 1999).

■ As Invernizzi & Hayes (2004) note, a student's performance on a nonsense word task is not "instructionally transparent" to most teachers. It doesn't give teachers clear guidance in terms of what elements the student has mastered and what elements need to be taught or reviewed.

Grades 3 and 4 and beyond

Students will

- use a full range of phonics skills to decode words.
- use a full range of syllabic analysis skills and patterns to decode words.
- use pronounceable word part, analogy, and contextual strategies to decode words.
- integrate the use of contextual and word analysis strategies.
- read with accuracy, fluency, and expression at an appropriate rate (see Table 4.11).

Action Plan

1. Assess students' knowledge of word analysis skills and strategies.
2. Construct or adapt a program for development of word analysis skills and strategies based upon students' needs.
3. Introduce needed phonics and syllabication skills and strategies in a functional fashion.
4. Provide ample practice and application opportunities.
5. Develop fluency through modeling, instruction, wide reading, and rereading.
6. Plan a systematic program. However, provide on-the-spot instruction when the need arises.
7. For English language learners, plan a program that takes into consideration word analysis knowledge that they already possess in their native language, as well as areas that might pose problems.
8. Monitor students' progress, and make necessary adjustments.

Assessment

Assessment should be ongoing. Through observation, note whether students are learning the skills and strategies they have been taught. Watch to see what they do when they come across an unfamiliar word. Do they attempt to apply pronounceable word part, analogy, or context strategies? When they read, what phonics elements are they able to handle? What phonics elements pose problems for them? In addition to observation, you might use the Phonics Progress Monitoring Assessment to assess students' knowledge of major phonics patterns and the Syllable Survey in Appendix B to get a sense of students' ability to handle multisyllabic words. Chapter 2 contains additional assessment suggestions, including use of running records.

Summary

The ultimate goal of phonics, syllabic analysis, and other word recognition skills is to enable students to become independent readers. Functional practice and extensive reading are recommended to help them reach that goal. Instruction should be developmental and differentiated so that it matches students' understanding of the writing system. Progress should be monitored, and added instruction should be provided as needed. Students should be taught how to use two powerful word identification strategies: pronounceable word part and analogy. Because they occur so frequently, students should be given extra practice with high-frequency words in order to recognize them rapidly. Although virtually all words are learned by creating a bond between sounds and spellings, most words are ultimately recognized just about instantaneously. Fluency is fostered by providing a solid foundation in word analysis and rapid recognition of high-frequency words. Numerous opportunities to read materials on the appropriate level of challenge also builds fluency.

Extending and Applying

1. Read over the pronunciation key of a dictionary. Notice the spellings given for the consonant sounds and the vowel sounds. Check each of the sounds. Are there any that are not in your dialect? The following words have at least two pronunciations: dog ("dawg" or "dog"), roof ("roof" or "roof"), route ("root" or "rowt"). How do you pronounce them?

2. Examine the word analysis component of a basal series. What is its approach to teaching phonics and syllabic analysis? Are the lessons and activities functional and contextual? Is adequate practice provided? What is your overall evaluation of the word analysis program in this series?

3. Using the word-building (pattern) approach described in this chapter, plan a lesson in which a phonics or a syllabic analysis element is introduced. State your objectives, and describe each of the steps of the lesson. List the titles of children's books or other materials that might be used to reinforce or apply the element taught. Teach the lesson, and evaluate its effectiveness.

4. Working with a small group of students, note which strategies they use when they encounter difficult words. Providing the necessary instruction and prompts, encourage them to use the pronounceable word part, analogy, and context strategies.

Developing a Professional Portfolio

Document your knowledge of and ability to teach word analysis skills. Include a sample word analysis lesson that you have taught and your reflection on it. Keep a record of any inservice sessions or workshop sessions on word analysis that you have attended.

Go to Allyn & Bacon's MyLabSchool: www.mylabschool.com

- Enter Assignment ID **RMV2** into **Assignment Finder,** and select the video titled "Word Chunking." This video demonstrates a teacher working with an individual child on the use of chunking as a word identification strategy.

- As you watch the video, recall the differences between *explicit* and *implicit* teaching of phonics. How does the teacher make the transition from explicit teaching to meaningful teaching within a context?

- Explore MyLabSchool further to find the course areas for Reading Methods, Language Arts, and Content Area Reading and identify other assets that support concepts introduced in this chapter.

Developing a Resource File

Maintain a list of books that you might use to provide students with opportunities to apply their word analysis skills.

Seek out books with natural sounding text.

To access chapter objectives, practice tests, weblinks, and flashcards, go to the companion website at www.ablongman.com/gunning6e.

5 Building Vocabulary

F or each of the following statements, put a check under "Agree" or "Disagree" to show how you feel. Discuss your responses with classmates before you read the chapter.

	Agree	Disagree
1. Vocabulary words should be taught only when students have a need to learn them.	_____	_____
2. All or most of the difficult words in a selection should be taught before the selection is read.	_____	_____
3. Building vocabulary leads to improved comprehension.	_____	_____
4. The best way to build vocabulary is to study a set number of words each week.	_____	_____
5. Using context is the easiest way to get the meaning of an unfamiliar word.	_____	_____
6. The best way to learn about roots, prefixes, and suffixes is to have a lot of experience with these word parts.	_____	_____
7. Using the dictionary as a strategy to get the meanings of unfamiliar words is inefficient.	_____	_____

C hapter 4 explained techniques for teaching children how to decode words that were in their listening vocabularies but might not be recognizable to them in print. This chapter is also concerned with reading words. However, the focus in this chapter is on dealing with words whose meanings are unknown. In preparation for reading this chapter, explore your knowledge of this topic.

Using What You Know

How many words would you estimate are in your vocabulary? Where and how did you learn them? Have you ever read a book or taken a course designed to increase your vocabulary? If so, how well did the book or the course work? What strategies do you use when you encounter an unknown word? How would you go about teaching vocabulary to an elementary or middle school class?

■ The Need for Vocabulary Instruction

Read the following paragraph, which is excerpted from Beverly Cleary's *Ramona Quimby, Age 8* (1981), a book typically read in grade 3. What challenges does the passage present for the typical third-grader?

> Rainy Sunday afternoons in November were always dismal, but Ramona felt this Sunday was the most dismal of all. She pressed her nose against the living-room window, watching the ceaseless rain pelting down as bare black branches clawed at the electric wires in front of the house. Even lunch, leftovers Mrs. Quimby had wanted to clear out of the refrigerator, had been dreary, with her parents, who seemed tired or discouraged or both, having little to say and Beezus mysteriously moody. Ramona longed for sunshine, sidewalks dry enough for roller skating, a smiling happy family. (p. 33)

Although meant for third-graders, the passage has surprisingly advanced vocabulary. Students might have difficulty with *dismal, ceaseless, pelting*, and *longed*. In the initial stages of reading, virtually all the words are known by readers. They are in the readers'

FYI

Estimates of the number of words known by average first-graders vary widely from 2,500 to 24,000. However, 5,000 to 6,000 seems a reasonable figure.

225

The New York Times
expect the world®
nytimes.com

Themes of the Times

Expand your knowledge of the concepts discussed in this chapter by reading current and historical articles from *The New York Times* by visiting the "Themes of the Times" section of the Companion Website.

FYI

It is difficult to say when a word is learned. Some concrete words may be learned instantaneously; others may be learned slowly, after repeated encounters. In time, words take on a greater depth of meaning as they conjure up more associations.

Closing the Gap

By the end of grade 2, children in the lowest quartile know about 4,000 root word meanings. Average children know about 6,000 root word meanings, and children in the highest quartile know about 8,000 (Biemiller, 2005). Adding 10 root word meanings per week could add almost 400 over a year. If implemented from kindergarten through grade 2, this technique could add 1,200 new root words to a child's vocabulary (Boote, 2006).

listening vocabularies. But as students advance into higher-level texts, vocabulary becomes more challenging. To be proficient readers and writers, students must build their vocabularies and learn strategies for coping with difficult words. As students progress through the grades, a key element in their growth as readers and writers is vocabulary development.

■ Stages of Word Knowledge

Knowing a word's meaning is not an either/or proposition. Graves (1987) posited six tasks in word knowledge:

Task 1: Learning to read known words. Learning to read known words involves sounding out words that students understand but do not recognize in print. It includes learning a sight vocabulary and using phonics and syllabication to sound out words.

Task 2: Learning new meanings for known words. Even a cursory examination of a dictionary reveals that most words have more than one meaning. A large part of expanding a student's vocabulary is adding new shades of meaning to known words.

Task 3: Learning new words that represent known concepts. Because the concept is already known, this really is little more than learning a new label.

Task 4: Learning new words that represent new concepts. As Graves (1987) observed, "Learning new words that represent new concepts is the most difficult word-learning task students face" (p. 169).

Task 5: Clarifying and enriching the meanings of known words. Although this task is accomplished when students meet known words in diverse contexts, Graves (1987) felt that more systematic, more direct involvement is called for. Teachers have to help students forge connections among known words and provide a variety of enrichment exercises to ensure greater depth of understanding.

Task 6: Moving words from receptive to expressive vocabulary. It is necessary to teach words in such a way that they appear in students' speaking and writing vocabularies. The ultimate test is whether students actually use newly learned words correctly. As Nagy and Scott (2000) comment, "Knowing a word means being able to do things with it. . . . Knowing a word is more like being able to use a tool than it is like being able to state a fact" (p. 273).

As can be seen from the six tasks just described, word knowledge is often a question of degree. The person who uses a CD burner on a regular basis has a better knowledge of the words *CD burner* than does one who has simply seen the device advertised. Instruction needs to be devoted to refining as well as to introducing vocabulary and concepts.

■ ■ ■ Checkup ■ ■ ■

1. What are the stages of word knowledge?

■ ■ ■

■ Seven Principles of Developing Vocabulary

Developing vocabulary is not simply a matter of listing ten or twenty words and their definitions on the board each Monday morning and administering a vocabulary quiz every Friday. In a sense, it is a part of living. Children learn their initial 5,000 to 6,000 words by

■ A **label** is simply a name for a concept. Students may use labels without really understanding the meanings behind them.

interacting with parents and peers, gradually learning labels for the people, objects, and ideas in their environment. As children grow and have additional experiences, their vocabularies continue to develop. They learn *pitcher, batter, shortstop*, and *home run* by playing or watching softball or baseball. They learn *gear shift, brake cable, kick stand*, and *reflector* when they begin riding a bicycle.

Depending upon the nature of the words to be learned and the students' background knowledge, vocabulary development represents two related but somewhat different cognitive tasks: establishing associations and developing conceptual knowledge (Baumann, Kame'enui, & Ash, 2003). To learn an association between a known concept and a new label for that concept, students don't have to do much more than hear and/or use the label several times or use mnemonic devices to help them remember the word. Intensive instruction is not required.

However, depending on its complexity, a concept might require considerable instruction. Conceptual learning is a far more demanding cognitive task. Such words as *democracy, photosynthesis, personality, state, government, emigration, fossils*, and *poverty* require experience and/or extensive explanation and discussion before understanding is achieved. The new word becomes a label for the concept. Of course, having the label does not guarantee understanding the concept behind the label. Students can tell what state they live in without knowing what a state is.

Concepts are organized into networks. For instance, if I say "cake," chances are you will say something like "ice cream" or "chocolate" or "party." These don't define what a cake is but present associations or experiences that you have with cake. Of course, the more experiences you have with cake, the more associations you can construct. Because our concepts are stored in networks, conceptual words are best presented in frameworks that show how they are related to other concepts and also how they are related to students' background of knowledge. Unfamiliar concepts are best learned when they are presented within the context of known concepts or words. That way they become part of a network. That's one reason why simply presenting words in unrelated lists is the least effective way to present new vocabulary.

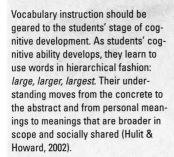

FYI

Vocabulary instruction should be geared to the students' stage of cognitive development. As students' cognitive ability develops, they learn to use words in hierarchical fashion: *large, larger, largest.* Their understanding moves from the concrete to the abstract and from personal meanings to meanings that are broader in scope and socially shared (Hulit & Howard, 2002).

Building Experiential Background

The first and most effective step that a teacher can take to build vocabulary is to provide students with a variety of rich experiences. These experiences might involve taking children to an apple orchard, supermarket, zoo, museum, or office. Working on projects, conducting experiments, handling artifacts, and other hands-on activities also build a background of experience.

Not all activities can be direct. Viewing computer simulations and demonstrations, films, videotapes, filmstrips, and special TV shows helps build experience, as do discussing, listening, and reading. The key is to make the activity as concrete as possible.

Talking Over Experiences

Although experiences form the foundation of vocabulary, they are not enough; labels or series of labels must be attached to them. A presurvey and postsurvey of visitors to a large zoo found that people did not know much more about the animals after leaving the park than they did before they arrived. Apparently, simply looking at the animals was not enough; visitors needed words to define their experiences. This is especially true for young children.

Learning Concepts versus Learning Labels

For maximum benefit, it is important that experiences be discussed. It is also important to distinguish between learning **labels** and building concepts. For example, the words *petrol* and *lorry* would probably be unfamiliar to American students preparing to read a story set in England. The students would readily understand them if the teacher explained that to the British *petrol* means "gasoline" and *lorry* means "truck." Since the concepts of gasoline and truck are already known, it would simply be a matter of learning two new labels.

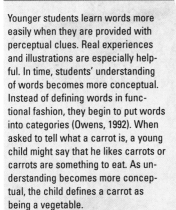

FYI

Younger students learn words more easily when they are provided with perceptual clues. Real experiences and illustrations are especially helpful. In time, students' understanding of words becomes more conceptual. Instead of defining words in functional fashion, they begin to put words into categories (Owens, 1992). When asked to tell what a carrot is, a young child might say that he likes carrots or carrots are something to eat. As understanding becomes more conceptual, the child defines a carrot as being a vegetable.

If the word *fossil* appeared in the selection, however, and the students had no idea what a fossil was, the concept would have to be developed. To provide a concrete experience, the teacher might borrow a fossil from the science department and show it to the class while explaining what it is and relating it to the children's experiences. Building the **concept** of fossil would take quite a bit more teaching than would learning the labels *petrol* and *lorry*.

Relating Vocabulary to Background

The second principle of vocabulary development is relating vocabulary to students' background. It is essential to relate new words to experiences that students may have had. To teach the word *compliment*, the teacher might mention some nice things that were said that were complimentary. Working in pairs, students might compose compliments for each other.

Gipe (1980) devised a background-relating technique in which students are asked to respond to new words that require some sort of personal judgment or observation. For example, after studying the word *beacon*, students might be asked, "Where have you seen a beacon that is a warning sign?" (p. 400). In a similar vein, Beck and McKeown (1983) asked students to "tell about someone you might want to eavesdrop on," or "describe the most melodious sound you can think of" (p. 624). Carr (1983) required students to note a personal clue for each new word. It could be an experience, object, or person. One student associated a local creek with *murky*; another related *numbed* to how one's hands feel when shoveling snow.

Building Relationships

The third principle of developing vocabulary is showing how new words are related to each other. For example, students may be about to read a selection on autobiographies and biographies that includes the unfamiliar words *accomplishment, obstacles*, and *nonfiction*, as well as *autobiography* and *biography*. Instead of simply presenting these words separately, demonstrate how they are related to each other. Discuss how autobiography and biography are two similar types of nonfiction, and they often describe the subject's accomplishments and some of the obstacles that he or she had to overcome.

Other techniques for establishing relationships include noting synonyms and antonyms, classifying words, and completing graphic organizers. (These devices are covered later in this chapter.)

Developing Depth of Meaning

The fourth vocabulary-building principle is developing depth of meaning. The most frequent method of teaching new words is to define them. Definitions, however, may provide only a superficial level of knowledge (Nagy, 1988). They may be adequate when new labels are being learned for familiar concepts, but they are not sufficient for new concepts. Definitions also may fail to indicate how a word should be used. The following sentences were created by students who had only definitional knowledge. Obviously, they had some understanding of the words, but it was inadequate.

The *vague* windshield needed cleaning.
At noon we *receded* to camp for lunch.

■   A **concept** is a general idea, an abstraction derived from particular experiences with a phenomenon. In the rush to cover content, teachers may not take the time necessary to develop concepts thoroughly; thus, students may simply learn empty labels for complex concepts such as democracy or gravity.

It takes time to learn a word well enough to use it appropriately in a sentence. Instead of having students write sentences using newly learned words, have them complete sentence stems, which prompt them to use the word appropriately and show that they know the meaning of the word: The farmers had to irrigate their fields because _____. In order to complete the sentence, students will have to know what *irrigate* means and why farmers might have to irrigate their fields (Beck, McKeown, & Kucan, 2002).

Words may have subtle shades of meanings that dictionary definitions may not quite capture. Most students have difficulty composing sentences using new words when their knowledge of the words is based solely on definitions (McKeown, 1993). Placing words in context (Gipe, 1980) seems to work better, as it illustrates use of the words and thereby helps to define them. However, in order for vocabulary development to aid in the comprehension of a selection, both the definition and the context should reflect the way the word is used in the selection the students are about to read.

Obviously, word knowledge is a necessary part of comprehension. Ideas couched in unfamiliar terms will not be understood. However, preteaching difficult vocabulary has not always resulted in improved comprehension. In their review of the research on teaching vocabulary, Stahl and Fairbanks (1986) found that methods that provided only definitional information about each word to be learned did not produce a significant effect on comprehension; nor did methods that gave only one or two exposures to meaningful information about each word. For vocabulary instruction to have an impact on comprehension, students must acquire knowledge of new words that is both accurate and enriched (Beck, McKeown, & Omanson, 1987). Experiencing a newly learned word in several contexts broadens and deepens understanding of it. For instance, the contexts *persistent detective, persistent salesperson, persistent pain*, and *persistent rain* provide a more expanded sense of the word *persistent* than might be conveyed by a dictionary or glossary definition.

Presenting Several Exposures

Frequency of exposure is the fifth principle of vocabulary building. Beck, McKeown, and Omanson (1987) suggested that students meet new words at least ten times; however, Stahl and Fairbanks (1986) found that as few as two exposures were effective. It also helps if words appear in different contexts so that students experience their shades of meaning. Frequent exposure to or repetition of vocabulary is essential to comprehension because of limitations of attention and memory. Third-graders reading a selection about the brain that uses the new words *lobe* and *hemisphere* may not recall the words if the teacher has discussed them only once. Although the students may have understood the meanings of the words at the time of the original discussion, when they meet the words in print, they are vague about their definitions and must try to recall what they mean. Because they give so much attention to trying to remember the meanings of the new words, they lose the gist of the fairly complex passage. Preteaching the vocabulary did not improve their comprehension because their reading was interrupted when they failed to recall the words' meanings immediately or because their knowledge of the words was too vague.

Creating an Interest in Words

Generating interest in words can have a significant impact on vocabulary development. In their experimental program, Beck and McKeown (1983) awarded the title "Word Wizard" to any student who noted an example of a taught word outside of class and reported it to the group. Children virtually swamped their teachers with instances of seeing, hearing, or using the words as they worked toward gaining points on the Word Wizard Chart. On some days, every child in the class came in with a Word Wizard contribution. Teachers also reported that the children would occasionally cause a minor disruption—for example, at an assembly when a speaker used one of the taught words and "the entire class buzzed with recognition" (p. 625).

FYI

■ When concerned about comprehension, choose a few key terms for intensive teaching. The words should be taught so well that students don't have to pause when they encounter them.

■ Although students may derive only a vague idea of a word's meaning after a single exposure, additional incidental exposures help clarify the meaning. Over a period of time, many words are acquired in this way.

■ Vocabulary knowledge is the most important predictor of reading comprehension (Davis, 1968; Thorndike, 1973).

FOSTERING ENGAGEMENT

Word Wizard motivates students to notice newly learned words and to share their discoveries.

FYI

A useful resource for word play activities is *Wordworks: Exploring Language Play* by Bonnie von Hoff Johnson. Golden, CO: Fulcrum Publishing.

Teaching Students How to Learn New Words

The seventh and last principle of vocabulary development is promoting independent word-learning skills. Teaching vocabulary thoroughly enough to make a difference takes time. If carefully taught, only about 400 words a year can be introduced (Beck, McKeown, & Omanson, 1987). However, students have to learn thousands of words, so teachers also have to show them how to use such tools of vocabulary acquisition as context clues, morphemic analysis, and dictionary skills. Vocabulary instruction must move beyond the teaching of words directly as a primary activity. Because students derive the meanings of many words incidentally, without instruction, another possible role of instruction is to enhance the strategies readers use when they do learn words incidentally. Directly teaching such strategies holds the promise of helping children become better independent word learners (Kame'enui, Dixon, & Carnine, 1987).

■■■ Checkup ■■■

1. What are the seven principles of developing vocabulary?

■■■

■ Techniques for Teaching Words

Dozens of techniques are available for introducing and reinforcing new vocabulary. Those discussed here follow all or some of the seven principles just presented.

Graphic Organizers

FYI

Inspiration (Inspiration Software) or similar software can be used to create graphic organizers.

Graphic organizers are semantic maps, pictorial maps, webs, and other devices that allow students to view and construct relationships among words. Because they are visual displays, they allow students to picture and remember word relationships.

Semantic Maps

Suppose that your students are about to read an informational piece on snakes that introduces a number of new concepts and words. For example, it states that snakes are reptiles, a concept that you believe will be new to the class. You have scheduled an article about alligators and crocodiles for future reading. Wouldn't it be efficient if you could clarify students' concept of snakes and also prepare them to relate it to the upcoming article? There is a device for getting a sense of what your students know about snakes, helping them organize their knowledge, and preparing them for related concepts: semantic mapping, or, simply, mapping.

A **semantic map** is a device for organizing information graphically according to categories. It can be used for concepts, vocabulary, topics, and background. It may also be used as a study device to track the plot and character development of a story or as a prewriting exercise. Mapping may be presented in a variety of ways but is generally introduced through the following steps (Heimlich & Pittelman, 1986; Johnson & Pearson, 1984):

1. *Introduce the concept, term, or topic to be mapped.* Write the key word for it on the chalkboard, overhead transparency, or chart paper.

2. *Brainstorm.* Ask students to tell what other words come to mind when they think of the key word. Encourage them to volunteer as many words as they can. This may be

---

■ A **graphic organizer** is a diagram used to show the interrelationships among words or ideas.

■ A **semantic map** is a graphic organizer that uses lines and circles to organize information according to categories.

done orally, or students may write their lists and share them. If the new words that you plan to teach are not suggested, present them and discuss them.

3. *Group the words by category, discussing why certain words go together.* Encourage students to supply category names.

4. *Create the class map, putting it on a large sheet of paper so that the class can refer to it and add to it.*

5. *Discuss the finished map.* Encourage students to add items to already established categories or to suggest new categories.

6. *Extend the map.* As students discover, through further reading, additional new words related to the topic or key word, add these to the map.

Lesson 5.1 shows, in abbreviated form, how a map on *snakes* was produced by a class of third-graders.

Semantic Mapping

Step 1.
The teacher writes the word *snakes* on the board and asks the class to tell what words come to mind when they think of snakes.

Step 2.
Students suggest the following words, which are written on the chalkboard: *poisonous, rattlesnakes, nonpoisonous, garter snakes, sneaky, king snakes, dangerous, frightening, deserts, rocky places,* and *forests*. No one mentions *reptiles*, which is a key word in the article students are about to read. The teacher says that he would like to add that word and asks students if they know what a reptile is. One student says reptiles are cold-blooded. This word is also added to the list.

Step 3.
Words are grouped, and category names are elicited. Students have difficulty with the task, so the teacher helps. He points to the words *forests* and *deserts* and asks what these tell about snakes. The class decides that they tell where snakes live. The teacher then asks the class to find another word that tells where snakes live. Other words are categorized in this same way, and category labels are composed.

Step 4.
The map, shown in Figure 5.1 (on p. 232), is created.

Step 5.
Students discuss the map. Two of them think of other kinds of snakes—water moccasins and boa constrictors—which are added. During the discussion, the teacher clarifies concepts that seem fuzzy and clears up misconceptions. One student, for instance, thinks that all snakes are poisonous.

Step 6.
Students read to find out more information about snakes. They refer to the map, which is displayed in the front of the room, to help them with vocabulary and concepts. After reading and discussing the selection, students are invited to add words or concepts they learned. The following are added: *dry, smooth skin; scales; vertebrae;* and *flexible jaws*.

A few weeks later, the class reads a selection about helpful snakes. The map is reviewed before reading the story and then expanded to include new concepts and vocabulary.

FYI

Actively involving students aids both their understanding of concepts and their retention. In one project in which maps were used to help portray complex concepts, students failed to show improvement. Analysis revealed that the instructors were doing much of the map making. Having minimal involvement in the process, students received minimal benefit (Santa, 1989).

■■■ **FIGURE 5.1   Semantic Map on Snakes**

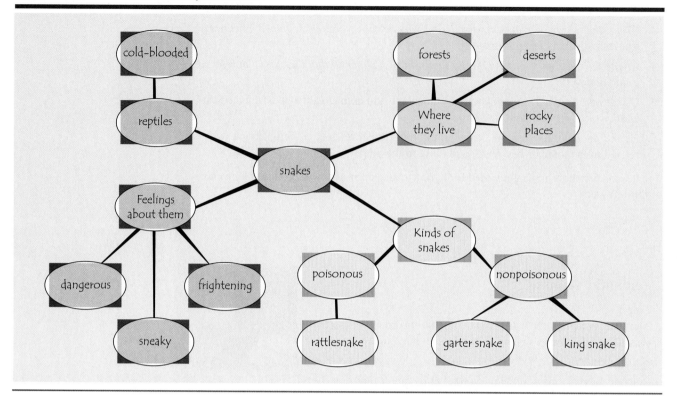

After students have grasped the idea of mapping, they can take a greater share of responsibility for creating maps. The sequence listed below gradually gives children ownership of the technique (Johnson & Pearson, 1984).

1. Students cooperatively create a map under the teacher's direction.

2. Students begin assuming some responsibility for creating maps. After a series of items has been grouped, they might suggest a category name.

3. Students are given partially completed maps and asked to finish them. They can work in groups or individually.

4. The teacher supplies the class with a list of vocabulary words. Working in groups, students use the list to create maps.

5. Working in groups or individually, students create their own maps.

Pictorial Maps and Webs

Pictorial and mixed pictorial–verbal maps work as well as, and sometimes better than, purely verbal maps. A **pictorial map** uses pictures along with words. For some words or concepts, teachers may want to use a more directed approach to constructing semantic maps. After introducing the topic of the planet Mars, the teacher might discuss the characteristics in a **web**, which is a simplified semantic map (see Figure 5.2). A web does not

---

▪ A **pictorial map** uses drawings, with or without labels, to show interrelationships among words or concepts.

▪ A **web** is another name for a semantic map, especially a simplified one.

▪ A **semantic feature analysis** is a graphic organizer that uses a grid to compare a series of words or other items on a number of characteristics.

▪ A **Venn diagram** is a graphic organizer that uses overlapping circles to show relationships between words or other items.

have a hierarchical organization, and it is especially useful for displaying concrete concepts (Marzano & Marzano, 1988).

Semantic Feature Analysis

Semantic feature analysis uses a grid to compare words that fall in a single category. For example, it could be used to compare different mammals, means of transportation, tools, sports, and so on. In constructing a semantic feature analysis, complete the steps outlined in Lesson 5.2, which are adapted from Johnson and Pearson (1984).

Eventually, students should compose their own grids. Through actively creating categories of qualities and comparing items on the basis of a number of features, students sharpen their sense of the meaning of each word and establish relationships among them.

■■■ **FIGURE 5.2 Web for Mars**

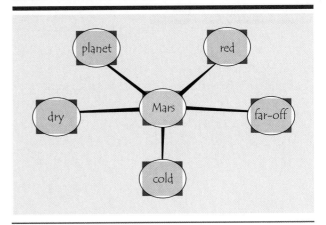

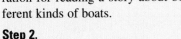 *Lesson 5.2*

Semantic Feature Analysis

Step 1.
Announce the topic, and ask students to give examples. In preparation for reading a story about boats, ask students to name different kinds of boats.

Step 2.
List the types of boats in the grid's left-hand column.

Step 3.
Ask students to suggest characteristics that boats have. List these in a row above the grid.

Step 4.
Look over the grid to see if it is complete. Have students add other types of boats and their characteristics. At this point, you might suggest additional kinds of boats or other features of boats.

Step 5.
Complete the grid with the class. A completed grid is shown in Figure 5.3 (on p. 234). Put a plus or minus in each square to indicate whether a particular kind of boat usually has the specific characteristic being considered. If unsure, put a question mark in the square. Encourage students to discuss items about which they may have a question—for example, whether hydrofoils sail above or through the water. As students become proficient with grids, they may complete them independently.

Step 6.
Discuss the grid. Help students get an overview of how boats are alike as well as of how specific types differ.

Step 7.
Extend the grid. As students acquire more information, they may want to add other kinds of boats and characteristics.

Venn Diagram

Somewhat similar in intent to the semantic feature analysis grid is the **Venn diagram** (Nagy, 1988), in which two or three concepts or subjects are compared. The main characteristics of each are placed in overlapping circles. Those traits that are shared are entered in the overlapping area, and individual traits are entered in the portions that do not over-

■■■ **FIGURE 5.3**
Semantic Feature Analysis

BOATS	On water	Under water	Above water	Paddles, oars	Sails	Engines
Canoe	+	–	–	+	–	–
Rowboat	+	–	–	+	–	–
Motorboat	+	–	–	?	–	+
Sailboat	+	–	–	?	+	?
Submarine	–	+	–	–	–	+
Hydrofoil	–	–	+	–	–	+
Hovercraft	–	–	+	–	–	+

FYI

Although Venn diagrams are popular, compare/contrast frames (frame matrixes) work better when a number of elements are being compared or a number of categories are being considered (see Table 8.2, p. 368).

lap. In discussing crocodiles and alligators, the teacher might encourage students to list the major characteristics of each, noting which belong only to the alligator and which belong only to the crocodile. A Venn diagram like that in Figure 5.4 could then be constructed. After they grasp the technique, students should be encouraged to construct their own diagrams. Because this activity requires active comparing and contrasting, it aids both understanding and memory.

■■■ **Checkup** ■■■

1. What are the major graphic organizers?
2. How does each of these organizers foster vocabulary development?

■■■

Dramatizing

Although direct experience is the best teacher of vocabulary, it is not possible to provide it for all the words that have to be learned. Dramatization can be a reasonable substitute. Putting words in the context of simple skits adds interest and reality.

Dramatizations can be excerpted from a book or created by teachers or students. They need not be elaborate; a simple skit will work in most instances. Here is one dramatizing the word *irate*.

Student 1: Hey, Brian, what's wrong? You seem really mad.

Student 2: Someone's eaten my lunch. They must have known my dad packed my favorite sandwich, peanut butter and banana with raisins. I'm boiling inside. I'm really irate.

■■■ **FIGURE 5.4**
A Venn Diagram

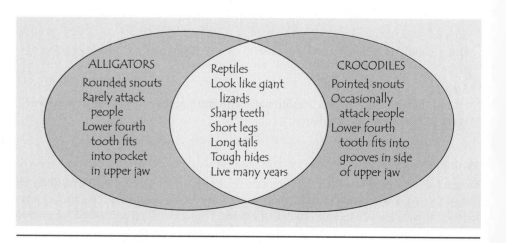

Student 1: I'd be irate, too, if someone took my lunch. But before you blow your lid, calm down. Maybe you misplaced it. Say, isn't that your dad coming down the hall? And what's that in his hand? It looks like a lunch bag.

Another way of dramatizing words is to use a hinting strategy (Jiganti & Tindall, 1986). After a series of new words has been introduced and discussed, the teacher distributes cards to individuals or pairs of students; on each card is one of the new words. Each student or pair creates a series of sentences that contain hints to the identity of the target word. Hints for *exaggerate* can be found in the following paragraph:

> I like being around Fred, but he tends to stretch the truth a little. The other day, he caught a fairly large fish. But to hear him tell it, it sounded like a whale. When Fred catches five fish, he pretends that he really caught twenty. And when it's a little chilly, Fred says it's the coldest day of the year. I like Fred, but I wish he'd stick a little closer to the facts.

The new words are written on the chalkboard. Students read their hints, and the class then tries to figure out which of the new words they describe.

Exploring Word Histories

Knowing the histories of words helps students in three ways: It sheds light on their meanings and helps students remember them better and longer; it "can function as a memory device by providing additional context" (Dale & O'Rourke, 1971, p. 70); and it can spark an interest in words.

Large numbers of words and expressions are drawn from Greek and Roman mythology. Read Greek and Roman myths to students, or, if they are able, have them read some on their own. As a follow-up, discuss words that have been derived from them. After reading about one of Hercules' adventures, discuss what a herculean task might be. After reading about Mars, the god of war, ask what martial music is. Discuss, too, expressions that are drawn from Greek and Roman mythology: Achilles heel, Midas touch, Gordian knot, Pandora's box, and laconic reply. The books in the following Student Reading List provide word histories.

FYI

Find the origins of *boycott, pasteurized,* and *iridescent.* How would knowing the origins help your students understand the words?

Student Reading List

Word Histories

Baker, R. F. (2003). *In a word: 750 words and their fascinating stories and origins.* Peterborough, NH: Cobblestone.

Houghton Mifflin. (2004). *Word histories and mysteries: From abracadabra to Zeus.* Boston: Author.

Houghton Mifflin. (2006). *More word histories and mysteries: From aardvark to zombie.* Boston: Author.

Metcalf, A. A. (1999). *The world in so many words: A country-by-country tour of words that have shaped our language.* Boston: Houghton Mifflin.

Umstatter, J. (2002). *Where words come from.* New York: Franklin Watts.

Enjoying Words

In school, words are used to instruct, correct, and direct. They should also be used to have fun, as one of the functions of language is to create enjoyment. Recite appropriate puns, limericks, and jokes to the children, and encourage them to share their favorites. Include word-play collections, such as those listed in the following Student Reading List, in the classroom library.

USING TECHNOLOGY

Funbrain.com features a variety of intriguing activities, including several word games.

http://www.funbrain.com/vocab/index.html

Student Reading List

Word Play

Cerf, B. (1960). *Bennett Cerf's book of riddles*. New York: Random House. This collection features a variety of easy-to-read riddles.

Christopher, M. (1996). *Baseball jokes and riddles*. Boston: Little, Brown. This book presents more than fifty jokes and riddles.

Clark, E. C. (1991). *I never saw a purple cow and other nonsense rhymes*. Boston: Little, Brown. The collector has illustrated her collection of more than 120 nonsense rhymes about animals.

Hall, K., & Eisenberg, L. (1998). *Puppy riddles*. New York: Dial. Presents a series of forty-two easy-to-read riddles about puppies.

Joyce, S. (1999). *ABC animal riddles*. Gilsum, NH: Peel Productions. Readers use the alphabet to help guess the answers to riddles.

Kitchen, B. (1990). *Gorilla/chinchilla and other animal rhymes*. New York: Dial. Rhymed text describes a variety of animals whose names rhyme but who have very different habits and appearances.

Lederer, R. (1996). *Pun and games: Jokes, riddles, daffynitions, tairy fales, rhymes, and more word play for kids*. Chicago: Chicago Review Press. This book features a variety of word-play activities for older students.

Mathews, J., & Robinson, F. (1993). *Oh, how waffle! Riddles you can eat*. Morton Grove, IL: Whitman, 1993. This book features riddles related to food.

Meddaugh, S. (1992). *Martha speaks*. Boston: Houghton Mifflin. Problems arise when Martha, the family dog, learns to speak after eating alphabet soup.

Rattigan, J. (1994). *Truman's aunt farm*. Boston: Houghton Mifflin. When Truman sends in the coupon for an ant farm, a birthday present from his Aunt Fran, he gets more than he bargains for when aunts instead of ants show up.

Rosen, M. (1995). *Walking the bridge of your nose: Wordplay poems and rhymes*. London: Kingfisher. This collection features a variety of poems and rhymes that play with words.

Terban, M. (1992). *Funny you should ask: How to make up jokes and riddles with wordplay*. Boston: Houghton Mifflin.

Terban, M. (2007). *Eight ate: A feast of homonym riddles*. Boston: Houghton Mifflin. This collection features clever riddles based on homonyms.

HIGHER-LEVEL LITERACY

Riddles and other word plays help students notice how words are used and also encourage them to think outside the box as they answer tricky questions and understand puns.

USING TECHNOLOGY

Worksheet Magic Plus (Teacher Support Software) or a similar piece of software can be used to create crossword puzzle grids. Crossword and other puzzles can also be created at Web sites such as Puzzlemaker. All you have to do is supply the words and definitions.

http://puzzlemaker.school.discovery.com/

Puzzles and word games provide excellent reinforcement for newly learned words.

Crossword Puzzles

Crossword puzzles are excellent for reinforcing students' vocabulary. When creating them, also use previously introduced words. Puzzles are more valuable if they revolve around a theme—such as farm implements, the parts of the eye, or words that describe moods. For younger readers, start out with limited puzzles that have only five to ten words and expand puzzles as students gain in proficiency.

Riddles

Riddles are inherently interesting to youngsters, and they provide an enjoyable context for developing vocabulary. They can be used to expand knowledge of homonyms, multiple meanings, figurative versus literal language, and intonation as a determiner of word meaning (Tyson & Mountain, 1982). Homonyms can be presented through riddles such as the following:

Why is Sunday the strongest day?
Because the other days are weak days. (p.171)

Multiple meanings might be reinforced through riddles of the following type:

> Why couldn't anyone play cards on the boat?
> Because the captain was standing on the deck. (p. 171)

Riddles containing figurative language can be used to provide practice with common figures of speech:

> Why were the mice afraid to be out in the storm?
> Because it was raining cats and dogs. (p. 172)

Some of the riddle books listed in the Student Reading List might be used to implement these suggestions. Also, plan activities in which riddles and puzzles are not tied to a lesson, so that students can experience them just for the fun of it.

Discovering Sesquipedalian Words

Students enjoy the challenge of sesquipedalian words (Dale & O'Rourke, 1971). Composed of the Latin form *sesqui* ("one and one-half") and *ped* ("foot"), *sesquipedalian* means "foot and a half," or very long words. Long or obviously difficult words tend to be easier to learn than short ones because they are distinctive. Given the prestige and pride involved in learning them, students are also willing to put in more effort. Set up a sesquipedalian bulletin board. Encourage students to contribute to it. They can write the words, including the sentence context in which the words were used, on three-by-five cards, which can then be placed on the bulletin board. Other students should be encouraged to read each word and see whether they can use context to determine its meaning. Then they can use the dictionary to check whether their guess is correct and learn how to pronounce the word. The ultimate aim is to have students become lifetime collectors of long and interesting words.

Word of the Day

A good way to begin the day is with a new word. The word might tie in with the day, the time of year, or some special local or national event. Or choose a word related to a topic the students are studying. Select interesting, useful words. Write the word on the chalkboard, or put it on a special bulletin board. Read or write the context in which the word is

---

Borrowing from Sylvia Ashton-Warner, Mrs. Warren, a resource room teacher at P.S. 94 in the Bronx, New York, invites her remedial readers each day to choose a word that they would like to learn. A second-grader chose *discrimination*; a third-grader asked to learn *suede*. The words chosen were as varied as the children.

Warren's students are operating well below grade level. Having a history of failure, they feel discouraged, frustrated, and incompetent. Learning long words builds their confidence and their self-esteem. As they learn words such as *discombobulate, spectacular,* and *advise,* they begin to see themselves as competent learners.

As Warren explains, "You have to prove to these children that they can learn. Telling them is not enough. You have to get them to be successful at something. The words convince them they're smart." Learning new words also builds an interest that snowballs. "If you can get children to love words, for whatever reason, you've got it made," Warren comments (Rimer, 1990, p. B5).

The students draw their words from many sources. Some come from their reading, others from discussions or television. A favorite source is a 365-new-words-a-year calendar. Students record their words on three-by-five index cards and keep them in a file box. The growing number of cards becomes a testament to their success in building their vocabularies and their overall competence as learners.

Exemplary Teaching

Developing Vocabulary and Confidence

BUILDING LANGUAGE

Students enjoy the challenge of learning long words. Actually, long words are easier to learn because their length makes them more distinctive.

FYI

Labeling helps students visualize words. Information may be coded in words or images (Sadowski & Paivio, 1994), and if it can be coded into both, memory is enhanced.

USING TECHNOLOGY

The Way Things Work (Dorling Kindersley), a CD-ROM program, uses explanations, labeled illustrations, and animations to show how dozens of technical devices work. Excellent for building background and vocabulary.

used. Have students try to guess the meaning of the word. Provide a history of the word, and discuss why it's an important word. Encourage students to collect examples of the word's use. Working alone or in pairs, older students might present their own words of the day.

Labeling

Labeling provides greater depth of meaning to words by offering at least second-hand experience and, in some instances, helps illustrate relationships. The parts of plants, of the human body, of an airplane, or of many other items lend themselves to labeling. For instance, when students are about to read a true-life adventure about a pilot whose life was endangered when the flaps and ailerons froze, present a labeled diagram showing these and other airplane parts, such as fuselage, landing gear, stabilator, fin, rudder, and trim tab. A sample of such a labeled drawing is presented in Figure 5.5. Discuss each part and its function. Relate the parts to each other and show how they work together to make the plane fly. Ask students to picture the parts in operation during takeoff, level flight, turns, and landing. After the story has been read, give them drawings of a plane. Have them label the parts. Better yet, let them label their own drawings of a plane.

Feature Comparison

Through questions that contain two newly learned words, students can compare major meanings (Beck & McKeown, 1983). For example, ask such questions as "Could a virtuoso be a rival?" and "Could a philanthropist be a miser?" (p. 624). Answering correctly is not the crucial point of this kind of activity. What is important is that students have the opportunity to discuss their responses so as to clarify their reasoning processes and their grasp of the meanings of the words.

Using Word-Building Reference Books

Dictionaries give definitions, illustrative sentences, and sometimes drawings of words. However, this is often not enough, especially for words that apply to concepts that are unknown or vague. For example, a dictionary definition of *laser* is not sufficient for a

FIGURE 5.5
Labeled Drawing of an Airplane

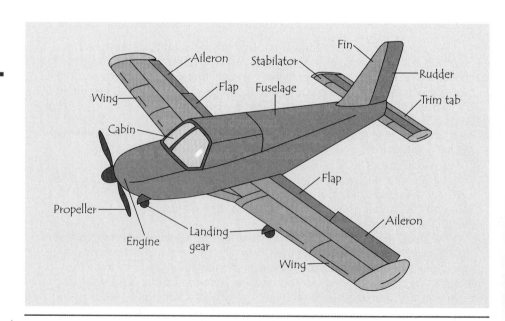

student who is reading a selection that assumes knowledge of both the operation and the uses of lasers. In contrast, an encyclopedia entry on lasers explains how they work, what their major uses are, and how they were invented. Encourage the use of the encyclopedia so that students eventually refer to it or other suitable references to clarify difficult words on their own.

Predicting Vocabulary Words

The main purpose of studying vocabulary words before reading a selection is to improve comprehension. Two techniques that relate new vocabulary to the selection to be read are the predict-o-gram, which works only with fictional pieces, and possible sentences, which works best with informational text.

Predict-o-Gram

In a predict-o-gram, students organize vocabulary in terms of the story grammar of a selection (Blachowicz, 1977). Students predict which words would be used to describe the setting, the characters, the story problem, the plot, or the resolution. Here's how the technique works: First, the teacher selects key words from the story. The words are written on the board and discussed to make sure students have some grasp of the meanings of the words. Students are then asked to predict which words the author would use to tell about the main parts of a story: the setting, the characters, the story problem, the plot, the resolution. The teacher asks the class to predict which words might fit in each part of the story grammar: "Which words tell about the setting? Which tell about the characters?" and so on. Once all the words have been placed, students might predict what the story is about. A completed predict-o-gram based on *Make Way for Ducklings* (McCloskey, 1941) is presented in Figure 5.6.

The predict-o-gram forces students to think about new vocabulary words in terms of a story that is to be read. It also helps students relate the words to each other. After the story has been read, students should discuss their predictions in terms of the actual content and structure of the story. They should also revise their predict-o-grams, which provides them with additional experience with the new words.

Possible Sentences

Possible sentences is a technique by which students use new vocabulary words to predict sentences that might appear in the selection to be read. Possible sentences has five steps (Moore & Moore, 1986):

1. *List key vocabulary.* The teacher analyzes the selection to be read and selects two or three concepts that are the most important. Vocabulary words from the selection that are essential to understanding those concepts are chosen. These words are listed on the board, pronounced by the teacher, and briefly discussed with the class.

■■■ **FIGURE 5.6**   Predict-o-Gram for *Make Way for Ducklings*

Setting	Characters	Story Problem	Plot	Resolution
Boston	Mr. and Mrs. Mallard	nest	hatched	Michael
Public Garden	Michael	pond	responsibility	police
Charles River		island		
		ducklings		
		eggs		

2. *Elicit sentences.* Students use the words listed to compose sentences. They must use at least two words in each sentence and create sentences they feel might occur in the selection. It is suggested that the teacher model the creation of a sample sentence and the thinking processes involved. Students' sentences are written on the board even if not correct. Words may be used more than once. This step ends when all the words have been used in sentences or after a specified time.

3. *Read to verify sentences.* Students read the text to verify the accuracy of their possible sentences.

4. *Evaluate sentences.* After reading the selection, students evaluate their sentences. They discuss each sentence in terms of whether or not it could appear in the selection. Sentences are modified as needed.

5. *Create new sentences.* Students use the words to create new sentences. These sentences are also discussed and checked for accuracy of usage.

The value of the possible sentences technique is that, in addition to being motivational, it helps students use informational text to refine their knowledge of new words. Because students write the words, it also helps them put new words into their active vocabularies. Putting new words in sentences is difficult, so the teacher should provide whatever guidance is necessary.

Story Impressions

Story impressions is an activity that uses vocabulary from a story to activate students' story schema and build word knowledge. Students use vocabulary from a selection to reconstruct the story. Although students are encouraged to create a story that is as close as possible to the original one, faithfulness to the original is not as important as the ability to use the clues to create a logical, coherent story. To present story impressions, adapt the steps described in Lesson 5.3.

Lesson 5.3

Story Impressions

Step 1. Developing a set of story impression clues
Read the story to get an overview. Then go back over the story and select words that highlight characters, setting, and key elements of the plot. Use single words or two- or three-word phrases. Select ten to fifteen words or phrases, and list them vertically on the chalkboard or overhead in chronological order under the title of the story. Select words that are easy as well as some that might be challenging to students. Use arrows to show that one word or phrase leads to another. See Figure 5.7, which presents a list of story impression clues based on Gary Soto's (1998) *Big, Bushy Mustache.*

Step 2. Explaining story impressions
Explain the purpose of story impressions and how it works. Point out the title and the list of words and phrases. Explain to students that they will use the words and phrases to create a story and then will read the actual story to compare it with theirs. Explain that the words and phrases are listed in the order in which they appear in the selection.

Step 3. Reading the story's words and phrases
Read the words and phrases with students. Discuss any words that may be unfamiliar. Encourage students to think about the kind of story that might be created, based on the words listed.

FYI

After completing a group story impression, students might work in pairs or individually to create their own story. As Richek (2005) notes, creating a story impression "has benefits beyond learning vocabulary. The strategy improves students' abilities to write and revise sensible narratives. They develop pride of authorship in a story that contains 'their' words" (p. 415).

Step 4. Creating a story impression

After discussing the words and phrases, you and the class create a story impression based on the clues. All listed words must be used. Students may add words and phrases not presented, may add endings to words, and may use the words more than once. Focus on creating a story that is interesting and logical. Provide help as needed so that a sensible story is formulated. After the story has been written on the board, discuss it, and encourage students to evaluate it and make revisions, if needed.

Step 5. Reading of the author's story

Invite students to read the author's story and then compare their version with it.

Step 6. Discussing the story

Discuss the author's story. Compare the author's and the class's versions. As students grow in proficiency, they might create and discuss story impressions in small cooperative learning groups. Story impressions can also be used as part of the writing program (McGinley & Denner, 1987; Richek, 2005). This activity provides excellent practice in constructing narrative pieces.

Word Experts

This activity works well when there are many words to be learned (Richek, 2005). The teacher compiles a list of words from materials that will soon be read. Page numbers on which the words appear are included. After words have been selected, the list is distributed to students. Students are directed to begin constructing their expert cards. Each student is assigned two words and writes each on a three-by-five card. The students locate the words in the reading selection and copy the sentences in which they were used. Students then obtain dictionary definitions for the words. The process of locating appropriate definitions is reviewed. Next, students write the definitions, which must be approved by the teacher, on the cards; they can also include a personal connection to the word and an illustration, if appropriate. The illustration need not be a drawing but can be an image from the Web or a magazine. Students can also dramatize their words.

After completing the expert cards, students pair up and teach their words to a partner. The student shows the first word to the partner and asks the partner if he or she knows what the word means. If not, the first student begins to give clues. The student has the partner read the sentence to see if he or she can get the meaning from context. The student then shows the illustration. If that doesn't work, the student may dramatize the word. Finally, the student reveals the dictionary definition and gives any other information about the word that might make it more memorable: its history or etymology, its part of speech, and any other uses that it has. Once a student has taught both words, the other student teaches his or her words. The process is repeated on successive days until all the words have been learned. When taught in this way, 92 to 97 percent of the listed words were learned (Richek, 2005).

Word Sorts

Word sorts is a useful activity when dealing with groups of related words. Sorting forces students to think about each word and to see similarities and differences among words. Students might sort the following words: *melancholy, weary, tired, sorrowful, exhausted, glad, contented, cheerful, delighted, unhappy, gloomy, overworked, dejected*. The sort could be open, which means that students would decide on categories, or it could be closed. In a closed sort, the teacher decides the categories: happy, sad, tired. After sorting the words, students would discuss why they sorted them the way they did.

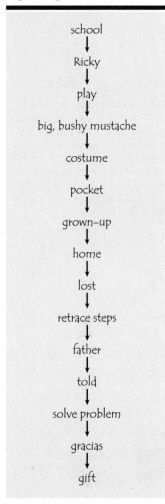

■■■ **FIGURE 5.7**
Story Impression Clues for ***Big, Bushy Mustache***

school
↓
Ricky
↓
play
↓
big, bushy mustache
↓
costume
↓
pocket
↓
grown-up
↓
home
↓
lost
↓
retrace steps
↓
father
↓
told
↓
solve problem
↓
gracias
↓
gift

■ ■ ■ Checkup ■ ■ ■

> **1.** In addition to graphic organizers, what are some other techniques and activities that might be used to develop word knowledge?
>
> ■ ■ ■

Vocabulary Self-Collection Strategy (VSS)

When given the opportunity to personalize their learning, students become more involved. (Blachowicz & Fisher, 2000). A device that helps students personalize their learning is the vocabulary self-collection strategy (VSS) (Ruddell, 1992). In VSS, after reading a new selection, each student chooses one word to learn. The word selected should be one that the student believes is important enough for the whole class to learn. VSS is initiated after the text has been read because being familiar with the text helps students select words that are important. The teacher also selects a word. Students record the printed sentence in which they discovered the word. Students also tell what they think the word means in the context in which it was found and explain why they think the class should learn the word.

Words are discussed, and dictionaries and glossaries may be checked to make sure that the correct pronunciation and definition have been obtained. As the words and their possible meanings are discussed, the teacher might model the use of context clues and the dictionary. The teacher adds his or her word, and the class list is reviewed. Words selected are recorded in vocabulary notebooks or study sheets. Realizing that they are responsible for selecting a word for the whole class to study, students suddenly become word-conscious and begin noticing words as possible candidates for selection. As students become more conscious of words, they begin acquiring new vocabulary words at an increased rate (Shearer, 1999). VSS can be extended by encouraging students to bring in new words they hear in oral contexts—television, radio, or conversations.

Wide Reading

The most productive method for building vocabulary—wide reading—requires no special planning or extra effort (Nagy & Herman, 1987). Research (Herman, Anderson, Pearson, & Nagy, 1987) indicates that average students have between a one in twenty and a one in five chance of learning an unfamiliar word they meet in context. Those who read for twenty-five minutes a day at the rate of 200 words per minute for 200 days of the year will encounter a million words (Nagy & Herman, 1987). About 15,000 to 30,000 of these words will be unfamiliar. Assuming a one in twenty chance of learning an unfamiliar word from context, students should pick up between 750 and 1,500 new words. Of course, if they read more, they have even greater opportunity for vocabulary growth. If they read 2 million rather than 1 million words a year, they theoretically would double the number of new words they learn.

Many of today's informational books for young people contain glossaries or phonetic spellings of difficult words and provide definitions in context. Some also contain labeled diagrams of technical terms. Note how the following excerpt from a reader-friendly informational book entitled *Fish That Play Tricks* (Souza, 1998) provides both phonetic respelling and contextual definitions:

> The grouper is only one of more than 20,000 different species (SPEE-sheez), or kinds, of fish that live in waters around the world. All fish are cold-blooded, meaning they cannot make themselves much warmer than the temperature around them. Like you, fish are vertebrates (VUHR-tuh-brits), or animals with skeletons inside their bodies. The skeletons of some fish, such as sharks and rays, are made of cartilage, a flexible tissue. (p. 4)

In addition to encouraging wide reading of varied materials, teachers can also provide students with strategies for using context clues, morphemic analysis, and the dictionary to decipher unknown words. Sternberg (1987) found that average adults trained to use context clues were able to decipher seven times as many words as those who spent the same amount of time memorizing words and definitions. If elementary school students are taught to use such clues with greater efficiency, it should boost their vocabulary development as well. For instance, students reading the book *Fish That Play Tricks*, from which the excerpt above was taken, would benefit if they were helped to discover that many of the terms in the book are explained in context, and the explanatory context often begins with the word *or*. Modeling the use of context clues and guided practice should also prove to be helpful.

Some books that are especially effective at building vocabulary are listed below.

Student Reading List

Building Vocabulary

DuTemple, L. A. (1998). *Moose*. Minneapolis: Lerner.
Frasier, D. (2000). *Miss Alaineus: A vocabulary disaster*. San Diego: Harcourt Brace.
Gibbons, G. (1990). *Weather words and what they mean*. New York: Holiday House.
Juster, N. (1961). *The phantom toll booth*. New York: Random House.
Parson, A. (1997). *Electricity*. Chicago: World Book.
Souza, D. M. (1998). *Fish that play tricks*. Minneapolis: Carolrhoda.
Tarsky, S. (1997). *The busy building book*. New York: Putnam.

Reading to Students

Read-aloud books are better sources of new words for students in the early grades than are the books they read silently. Up until about grade 3 or 4, the books that students read are composed primarily of known words. At these levels, teachers frequently read books to students that would be too hard for them to read on their own. Therefore, carefully chosen read-alouds can be effective for building word knowledge. Whereas it is best to introduce words beforehand when students are reading on their own, it is better to discuss vocabulary words after a selection has been read aloud to students. If words are needed for an understanding of a selection, then they can be explained briefly as the selection is being read. That way, students can immediately use their knowledge of the new words to comprehend the selection.

Beck and McKeown (2001) devised an approach in which a portion of the read-aloud was devoted to developing vocabulary. From each book, two to four words were selected. Words were selected that were probably unknown to students but that labeled concepts or experiences that would be familiar. These included words such as *reluctant, immense, miserable*, and *searched*. The words were presented in the context of the story, discussed, and later used by students. After reading *A Pocket for Corduroy* (Freeman, 1978) to students, the teacher stated, "In the story, Lisa was reluctant to leave the laundromat without Corduroy. *Reluctant* means you are not sure you want to do something. Say the word for me" (Beck, McKeown, & Kucan, 2002, p. 51). Students say the word so that they gain a phonological representation of it. The teacher then gives examples of *reluctant*, such as foods that they might be reluctant to eat or amusement park rides that they might be reluctant to go on. Students are then asked to tell about some things that they might be reluctant to do. "Tell about something that you might be reluctant to do. Try to use *reluctant* when you tell about it. You could start by saying something like 'I would be reluctant to _____.' " (p. 51).

Notice how the teacher provided a prompt to help students formulate a sentence using *reluctant*. This would be especially helpful to English language learners. Note, too, the steps in the presentation:

1. Presenting the word in story context.

2. Providing an understandable definition of the word.

3. Providing examples of the use of the word in other contexts, so that the word generalizes. Otherwise, students might form the impression that *reluctant* means "to leave something behind that you don't want to leave behind" as in "leaving the laundromat without Corduroy."

4. Having children relate the word to their own lives. They did this by talking about things that they were reluctant to do. They might also make a list of things that they are reluctant to do or write about a time when they felt reluctant.

5. Reviewing the word. The word is related to other words that are being introduced and to other words that students have learned. For instance, students might discuss how *reluctant* and *eager* are opposites. As occasions arise, the teacher uses newly taught words. She or he might talk about being reluctant to go outside because it is cold and rainy or reluctant to take down the Thanksgiving decorations because they look so nice. She might also read aloud *The Reluctant Dragon* (Grahame, 1966).

6. Encouraging students to use the word in their speaking and writing and also to note examples of hearing or seeing the word. As Dale and O'Rourke (1971) explain, learning a new word is serendipitous. Newly learned words have a way of cropping up in our reading and listening.

Some books are better than others for developing vocabulary. The frequency with which a new word appears in the text, whether the word is illustrated, and the helpfulness of the context in which the word appears are factors that promote the learning of a new word (Elley, 1989). Having students retell a story in which a word appears also seems to foster vocabulary growth. Words are used with more precision and in more elaborated fashion during students' second and third retellings (Leung, 1992).

To be more effective at building vocabulary, the story being read to students should be within their listening comprehension. If the words are too abstract for the students' level, gains may be minimal. In one study in which a fairly difficult text was read to students aged eight to ten, only the best readers made significant gains (Nicholson & Whyte, 1992). An inspection of the target words in the text suggested that they may have been too far above the level of the average and below-average readers. The study also suggested that while bright students might pick up words from a single reading, average and below-average students may require multiple encounters with the words.

Speaking and Writing

The ultimate aim of vocabulary development is to have students use new words in their speaking and writing. In-depth study of words and multiple exposures will help students attain sufficient understanding of words and how they are used so that they will be able to employ them in their speech and writing. Students should be encouraged to use new words in the classroom so that they become comfortable with them and so feel confident in using them in other situations. Students should also be encouraged to use new words in their written reports and presentations. As part of preparing students for a writing assignment, teachers might highlight words that lend themselves to inclusion in the written pieces.

Using a Thesaurus

Students tend to use familiar, everyday words to express their thoughts. A thesaurus is an excellent tool to help them use a greater range of vocabulary by seeking out and using synonyms. In addition to helping students use a more varied vocabulary, a thesaurus can help students become aware of the shades of meanings of words and can acquaint them with new words for old meanings. By providing synonyms, a thesaurus can also clarify the meaning of the word being looked up. Many thesauruses also provide antonyms. Being provided with a word's opposites also clarifies the meaning of the word. Because most word-processing programs have a thesaurus, using a thesaurus is convenient and easy.

To introduce a thesaurus, you may have students brainstorm synonyms for an overused word such as *said*. After listing the synonyms, show students how they can use a thesaurus to accomplish the same purpose. A good practice activity would be to provide students with a paragraph in which overused words are underlined and have them select synonyms for them. Stress the importance of finding the appropriate synonym. The synonym must match the meaning of the word according to the way it is being used. Initially, underline only those words that are relatively easy to find synonyms for. Once students have a basic grasp of how to use a thesaurus, show how it can be used to improve the wording of a written piece. Encourage them to use a thesaurus to provide a more varied vocabulary in their writing.

Introducing New Words

At a minimum, introduction of new words should include a definition of the word, the use of the word in sentence or story context, an activity that relates the word to other words being introduced, and an activity that relates the word to the students' background. In the sixth-grade level of one basal series (Flood et al., 2001), the words *participate, ordeals, grimaced, spat, encounter,* and *victorious* are introduced with definitions in preparation for reading the selection *Ta-Na-E-Ka* (Whitebird, 2001). The words are also used in context and discussed. To help students relate the words to their backgrounds of experience, the following types of questions are asked:

- What school activities do you like to participate in?
- Have you ever had to go through something that you consider an ordeal?
- In what contest would you most like to be victorious? (p. 140D)

■ ■ ■ Checkup ■ ■ ■

1. How might reading, speaking, and writing be used to develop vocabulary?
2. Of all the techniques discussed, which seem to be the most effective? Why?

■ ■ ■

Developing the Vocabulary of English Language Learners

English language learners know fewer English words than their native speaking peers, and they also possess fewer meanings for these words (Verhallen & Schoonen, 1993). Ironically, when reading, ELLs rely more on their vocabulary knowledge than do native speakers of English. Intensive instruction in vocabulary can make a difference. After two years of systematic instruction, ELLs closed the gap in vocabulary and comprehension that existed between their performance and that of native speakers by about 50 percent (McLaughlin et al., 2000). Taking part in a similar program that lasted for four years, language minority elementary school students in Holland made gains of one or two years beyond that made by a control group (Appel & Vermeer, 1996, as cited in McLaughlin et al., 2000). There were also encouraging gains in reading comprehension. The researchers concluded that language minority students can catch up to native speakers in vocabulary knowledge if they receive targeted vocabulary instruction for about four hours a week throughout the school year and if the instruction is carried out for all eight grades of elementary and middle school.

Knowing how words are stored in bilingual students' minds will help you plan ways to develop their vocabularies. Unfortunately, there is no agreement on how words are

Adapting Instruction for English Language Learners

A key task for ELLs is learning the English labels for concepts that they possess in their native language.

Adapting Instruction for English Language Learners

Television, radio, lessons, lectures, discussions, and conversations are rich sources of new words. Set aside a few minutes each day to discuss new words that your pupils have heard. This could be especially helpful to students still learning English. They may have questions about pronunciation and shades of meaning.

stored. Some experts believe that the words are stored separately. Words learned in Spanish are not stored in the same place as words stored in English, so *amigo* and *friend* would not share a storage location. Others believe that there is a single store, so *amigo* and *friend* are stored in the same location. A third possibility is that the English words are linked to the Spanish words. When the student hears *friend*, he or she thinks first of the equivalent in his or her language: *amigo*. The fourth theory is that there are overlapping stores: Some words are linked; some are not. The most reasonable theory seems to be that there is overlap between the two stores (Cook, 2001). With some words, students might have to access the meaning in their native language first. With other words, they can access the meaning without going through a translation process. It is easier for young students to learn a word through translation than it is through an explanation, definition, or even illustration. A young Spanish-speaking student will learn the word *cat* faster if you say it means "el gato" than if you show her or him a picture of a cat or point to a cat (Durgunoglu & Oney, 2000).

To promote full understanding, provide translations of new vocabulary words. If you are unable to translate the words, enlist the services of an older student, a parent, or a bilingual teacher. You might post key vocabulary words in both languages in a prominent spot. Also explore **cognates**. Some cognates have identical spellings, such as as *color* (KOH-lor) and *chocolate* (choh-koh-LAH-teh) but, as you can see, do not have the same pronunciations. Others have similar spellings: *calendario, excelente, lista*. Still others have spellings that are similar but might not be similar enough to be recognized: *carro* (*car*), *crema* (*cream*), *difícil* (*difficult*).

Spanish-speaking students may know some advanced English words without realizing it. For instance, the word *luna* (*moon*) would be known by very young Spanish-speaking children. However, *lunar*, as in *lunar landing*, is an advanced word for native speakers of English. Spanish developed from Latin; *luna*, for instance, is a Latin word. Although English has thousands of words borrowed from Latin, English developed primarily from Anglo-Saxon. Its most basic words are derived from Anglo-Saxon. Words derived from Latin tend to be a more advanced way of expressing common concepts encapsulated by the most basic English words. Although Spanish-speaking students have to learn most common English words from scratch, they have a running start on learning many of the more advanced words because a large proportion of these words are derived from Latin. Explain to Spanish-speaking students that they know some of the harder words in English; you might use *lunar* as an example. This will affirm the value of the students' first language but will also provide them with a most valuable tool for learning English. Make use of this principle when introducing new vocabulary. For instance, when introducing *annual*, ask Spanish-speaking students to tell you the Spanish word for *year* (*año*). Help them to see that the word *annual* is related to *año*. Follow a similar approach for words like *arbor* (*árbol–tree*), *ascend* (*ascensor*), *grand* (*grande–big*), *primary* (*primero–first*), *rapidly* (*rapidamente–quickly*), and *tardy* (*tarde–late*).

Not having had the same opportunity to learn English as native speakers have, ELLs understandably have a more limited store of English words. Experts agree that this is their main stumbling block on the road to literacy in English. They need a long-term, well-planned program of vocabulary development, which builds on their growing knowledge of English and their command of another language. In many instances, vocabulary development for them will simply consist of learning the English label for a familiar concept. In other instances, they might be able to use cognates to help them develop their English vocabulary.

▪ **Cognates** are words that are similar in both languages, have a common derivation, and share a common meaning, although the pronunciation may differ.

▪ A **planned program** is one in which a certain amount of time is set aside each week for vocabulary instruction. Vocabulary may be preselected from materials students are about to read or from words they may need to understand content-area concepts.

Case Study

Teaching Vocabulary to English Language Learners

Edguardo, a sixth-grader, is a conscientious, highly motivated student. Having attended a dual-language school since kindergarten, he is reading on grade level in Spanish and is fluent in English. Although his decoding skills in English reading are on grade level, Edguardo has difficulty with comprehension. He feels overwhelmed when he meets a number of words that he doesn't know. As might be expected of an ELL, Edguardo's English vocabulary is somewhat below grade level. Because he has had less opportunity to develop English vocabulary, Edguardo could benefit from a program of intensive vocabulary instruction. A general program of vocabulary development would be helpful. But even more effective would be a program designed to teach Edguardo, or any other student in similar circumstances, the words that he is most likely to meet in texts.

For Edguardo and other ELLs, much of their word learning will involve learning the English equivalent of words already known in their first language. When Edguardo learns the word *moon*, he need only associate it with the known Spanish word for moon, *luna*. In addition, there are thousands of cognates, words such as *artista, autor, contento*. See Table 12.3 (on p. 513) for a listing of high-frequency cognates.

■■■ Checkup ■■■

1. What are some special steps that you might take to foster word knowledge in ELLs?
2. What are some ways in which you might build on students' knowledge of their first language to build word knowledge in English?

■■■

■ A Planned Program

Although young people apparently learn an amazing number of words incidentally, a **planned program** of vocabulary development is highly advisable. Research from as far back as the 1930s (Gray & Holmes, 1938, cited in Curtis, 1987) suggested that direct teaching is more effective than a program that relies solely on incidental learning. A more recent review of a number of research studies confirmed these results (Petty, Herold, & Stoll, 1968).

Based on their extensive investigations, Beck, McKeown, and Omanson (1987) opted for a program that includes both direct teaching and incidental learning of words and also differentiates among words. Words especially important to the curriculum are given "rich instruction." These words are chosen from basals, content-area texts, or trade books that are to be read by students, and they are selected on the basis of their importance in understanding the text, frequency of appearance in students' reading, and general usefulness. Rich instruction goes beyond simple definition to include discussion, application, and further activities. Words selected for rich instruction might be presented five to ten times or more. Less important words are simply defined and used in context. This process introduces words that become more familiar as students meet them in new contexts. Any remaining new words are left to incidental learning. Perhaps the most important feature of this program is that words are taught within the context of reading, as opposed to being presented in isolated lists.

Science is an excellent source of new words.

Another important component of a planned vocabulary program is motivation. Students will try harder and presumably do better if they encounter intriguing words in interesting stories and if they can relate learning vocabulary to their personal lives. As Sternberg (1987) commented, "In most of one's life, one learns because one wants to or because one truly has to, or both" (p. 96).

A Balanced Blend

Vocabulary instruction should be a balanced blend of the planned and the incidental. The **incidental approach** capitalizes on students' immediate need to know words. It gives the program spontaneity and vitality. A planned approach ensures that vocabulary instruction is given the attention it deserves. Important words and techniques for learning words are taught systematically and in depth. Combining these two types of approaches should provide the best possible program.

■ ■ ■ Checkup ■ ■ ■

1. What are some characteristics of a balanced program of vocabulary development?
2. Why is a balanced program thought to be more effective than an incidental or planned approach?

■ ■ ■

■ Teaching Special Features of Words

Many words have special characteristics that have to be learned if the words are to be understood fully. Among such important features are homophones, homographs, figurative language, multiple meanings, connotation, and denotation.

Homophones

Homophones are words that are pronounced the same but differ in spelling and meaning and often have different origins as well: for example, *cheap* and *cheep* or *knew, gnu,* and *new*. In reality, homophones are more of a problem for spelling than for reading because context usually clarifies their meaning. In some instances, however, it is important to note spelling to interpret the meaning of a sentence correctly—for example:

He complements his wife.
The shed is dun.
To avoid being tackled, you must feint.

To build awareness of homophones, discuss riddles. Write a riddle on the chalkboard, and have students identify the word that has a homophone—for example, "What is black

FYI

To convey the concept of homophones, you might have students translate sentences that have been written in homophones, like these: Aye gnu Gym wood bee hear. Dew ewe no hymn?

■ The **incidental approach** to vocabulary instruction involves the study of vocabulary words as they occur in the natural course of reading and writing. A balanced vocabulary program is a blend of the incidental and planned approaches.

■ The combining form *phon* means "sound," so **homophones** are words that have the same sound but differ in meaning and often have different origins. They usually do not have the same spelling: *be, bee; him, hymn.*

■ *Graph* is a combining form meaning "written element," so **homographs** are two or more words that have the same spelling but different meanings and different word origins. Homographs may have the same or different pronunciations: *bark* (dog), *bark* (tree); *bow* (ribbon), *bow* (front of a boat).

■ An **idiomatic expression** is one that is peculiar to a language and cannot be understood from the individual words making up the expression: for example, *call up* a friend.

and white and read all over?" (the newspaper). Additional riddles may be found in the books presented in the Student Reading List for Word Play (p. 236). Students might enjoy reading Fred Gwynne's books on homophones, such as *The King Who Rained* (1987), *A Chocolate Moose for Dinner* (1988a), and *A Little Pigeon Toad* (1988b), or one of Peggy Parrish's *Amelia Bedelia* books.

Homographs

Homographs are words that have the same spelling but different meanings and possibly different pronunciations—for example, *palm* (part of the hand or a tree) and *bat* (a club or a mammal). They make spelling easier but reading more difficult. For instance, on seeing the word *page*, the reader must use context to decide whether the word means "a piece of paper" or "someone who attends a knight or runs errands for lawmakers." Homographs may share a single pronunciation or have different pronunciations. Homographs such as the following, which have two distinct pronunciations, can be particularly troublesome for students: *bass, bow, desert, dove, lead, minute, sewer,* and *sow.*

As students learn that a word may have two, three, or even more entirely separate meanings, stress the importance of matching meaning with context. Students may also need to learn an entirely new meaning, and perhaps a pronunciation, for a word that looks familiar. Reading the sentence "The neighbors had a terrible row," students will see that neither of the familiar meanings "paddle a boat" or "in a line" fits this sense of *row*. They must learn from context, a dictionary, or another source that the word's third meaning is "a noisy fight or quarrel." They will also need to learn that *row* in this context is pronounced /rau/.

Figurative Language

Young students tend to interpret language literally and may have difficulty with figurative language. This is especially true for children who have a profound hearing loss and those whose native language is not English. It is important to make young children aware that language is not always to be taken literally. As they grow in their ability to handle figurative expressions, they should be led to appreciate phrases that are especially apt and colorful. The *Amelia Bedelia* books, in which Amelia takes language very literally, can serve as a good introduction. Children might also keep a dictionary of figurative and **idiomatic expressions**. Some books of idioms are included in the following Student Reading List.

Student Reading List

Figurative Language

Arnold, T. (2001). *More parts*. New York: Dial.
Christopher, M. (1996). *Baseball jokes and riddles*. Boston: Little, Brown.
Rosen, M. (1995). *Walking the bridge of your nose: Wordplay poems and rhymes*. London: Kingfisher.
Terban, M. (1990). *Punching the clock: Funny action idioms*. Boston: Clarion.
Terban, M. (1993). *It figures! Fun figures of speech*. New York: Scholastic.
Terban, M. (1998). *Scholastic dictionary of idioms*. New York: Scholastic.

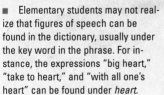

Multiple Meanings

One study found that 72 percent of the words that appear frequently in elementary school materials have more than one meaning (Johnson, Moe, & Baumann, 1983). When teaching new meanings for old words, stress the fact that words may have a number of

FYI

■ Elementary students may not realize that figures of speech can be found in the dictionary, usually under the key word in the phrase. For instance, the expressions "big heart," "take to heart," and "with all one's heart" can be found under *heart.*

■ When learning words that have multiple meanings, students learn concrete and functional meanings first ("The dog barked at me"), followed by more abstract meanings ("The coach barked out instructions for the team") (Asch & Nerlove, 1967).

different meanings and that the context is the final determinant of meaning. Some words with apparently multiple meanings are actually homographs. For instance, *bark* means "a noise made by a dog," "the covering of a tree," and "a type of sailing ship." These are really three different words and have separate dictionary entries. Other examples for which there are diverse meanings associated with one word are *elevator* ("platform that moves people up and down," "place for storing grain," "part of airplane") and *magazine* ("periodical" and "building where arms and/or ammunition are stored"). Provide exercises that highlight the new meaning of an old word by asking questions specific to a definition: "What does a plane's elevator do? Why would a fort have a magazine?"

▪ ▪ ▪ Checkup ▪ ▪ ▪

1. What are some special features of words that need to be taught?
2. How would you go about teaching these special features?

▪ ▪ ▪

▪ Learning How to Learn Words

A key objective for a vocabulary-building program is to teach students how to learn words on their own. Three major skills for learning the meanings of unknown words are morphemic analysis, contextual clues, and dictionary usage.

Morphemic Analysis

One of the most powerful word-attack skills is **morphemic analysis**, determining a word's meaning through examination of its prefix, root, and/or suffix. A **morpheme** is the smallest unit of meaning. It may be a word, a prefix, a suffix, or a root. The word *believe* has a single morpheme; however, *unbelievable* has three: *un-believ(e)-able*. *Telegraph* has two morphemes: *tele-graph*. Whereas syllabic analysis involves chunks of sounds, morphemic analysis is concerned with chunks of meaning.

Instruction must be generative and conceptual rather than mechanical and isolated. For example, students can use their knowledge of the familiar word *microscope* to figure out what *micro* means and to apply that knowledge to *microsecond, microwave, micrometer,* and *microbe*. By considering known words, they can generate a concept of *micro* and apply it to unknown words, which, in turn, enriches that concept (Dale & O'Rourke, 1971). The key to teaching morphemic analysis is to help students note prefixes, suffixes, and roots and discover their meanings. It is also essential that elements having a high transfer value be taught and that students be trained in transferring knowledge (Dale & O'Rourke, 1971).

Frequency of occurrence, number of words in the word family, and transparency also determine whether morphemic units are utilized to learn meaning. There are two kinds of transparency: phonological and orthographical. To be phonologically transparent, the base of a derived word must retain its original pronunciation. Hence, *growth* is phonologically transparent, but *health* is not (Carlisle & Stone, 2005). *Grow* keeps its pronunciation in *growth*, but *heal* changes its pronunciation in *health*. A word is orthographically transparent when the spelling of the base stays the same with the addition of affixes. Both *growth*

Adapting Instruction for Struggling Readers and Writers

Learning-disabled students' knowledge of morphemic elements is especially poor. However, given systematic instruction, they make encouraging gains (Henry, 1990).

▪ **Morphemic analysis** is the examination of a word in order to locate and derive the meanings of the morphemes.

▪ A **morpheme** is the smallest unit of meaning. The word *nervously* has three morphemes: *nerv(e)-ous-ly*.

▪ A **prefix** is an affix placed at the beginning of a word or root in order to form a new word: for example, *prepay*.

▪ An **affix** is a morphemic element added to the beginning or ending of a word or root in order to add to the meaning of the word or change its function. Prefixes and suffixes are affixes: for example, *prepayment*.

and *health* are orthographically transparent, but *opportune* (*op* + *port* = "carry towards") is not. If words are not phonologically transparent, orthographical transparency can be helpful, especially to older readers.

Prefixes

In general, **prefixes** are easier to learn than suffixes (Dale & O'Rourke, 1964, cited in O'Rourke, 1974). According to Graves and Hammond (1980), there are relatively few prefixes, and they tend to have constant, concrete meanings and relatively consistent spellings. When learning prefixes and other morphemic elements, students should have the opportunity to observe each one in a number of words so that they have a solid basis for constructing an understanding of the element. Lesson 5.4 describes how the prefix *pre-* might be taught.

Lesson 5.4

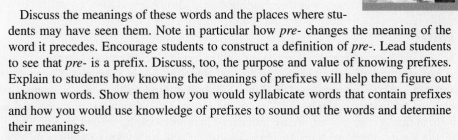

Prefixes

Step 1. Constructing the meaning of the prefix
Place the following words on the board:

pregame   prepay   preview   pretest   predawn

Discuss the meanings of these words and the places where students may have seen them. Note in particular how *pre-* changes the meaning of the word it precedes. Encourage students to construct a definition of *pre-*. Lead students to see that *pre-* is a prefix. Discuss, too, the purpose and value of knowing prefixes. Explain to students how knowing the meanings of prefixes will help them figure out unknown words. Show them how you would syllabicate words that contain prefixes and how you would use knowledge of prefixes to sound out the words and determine their meanings.

Step 2. Guided practice
Have students complete practice exercises similar to the following:

Fill in the blanks with these words containing prefixes: *preview, pregame, prepay, predawn, pretest.*

To make sure they had enough money to buy the food, the party's planners asked everyone to _____.

The _____ show starts thirty minutes before the kickoff.

The _____ of the movie made it seem more exciting than it really was.

Everyone got low marks on the spelling _____ because they had not been taught the words yet.

In the _____ quiet, only the far-off barking of a dog could be heard.

Step 3. Application
Have students read selections that contain the prefix *pre-* and note its use in real-world materials.

Step 4. Extension
Present the prefix *post-*, and contrast it with *pre-*. Since *post-* is an opposite, this will help clarify the meaning of *pre-*.

Step 5. Assessment and reteaching
Through observation, note whether students are able to use their knowledge of **affixes** to help them pronounce and figure out the meanings of unfamiliar words. Review common affixes from time to time. Discuss affixes that appear in selections that students are reading.

FYI

■ Prefixes are easier to learn than suffixes and are more useful in decoding words. When applying morphemic analysis, readers remove the prefix and the suffix and then note if there is a root. However, in many instances they might not need to remove the suffix to identify the root word (White, Power, & White, 1989).

■ The most frequently occurring prefixes are *un-, re-, in-, im-, ir-, il-, dis-, en-, em-, non-, in-, im-* (meaning "into"), *over-, mis-, sub-, pre-, inter-, fore-, de-, trans-, super-, semi-, anti-, mid-,* and *under-* (White, Sowell, & Yanagihara, 1989).

■ Prefixes are most useful when they contribute to the meaning of a word and can be added to other words. The prefix *un-* is both productive and easy to detect (*unafraid, unable, unhappy*), but the prefix *con-* in *condition* is unproductive and difficult to detect (McArthur, 1992).

■■■ **TABLE 5.1**   **Scope-and-Sequence Chart for Common Prefixes**

Grade	Prefix	Meaning	Example	Grade	Prefix	Meaning	Example
2–3	*un-*	not	unhappy	5–6	*ex-*	out, out of	exhaust
	un-	opposite	undo		*ex-*	former	explayer
	under-	under	underground		*inter-*	between	international
3–4	*dis-*	not	dishonest		*mis-*	not	misunderstanding
	dis-	opposite	disappear		*mis-*	bad	misfortune
	re-	again	reappear	6–7	*en-*	forms verb	enrage
	re-	back	replace		*ir-*	not	irresponsible
4–5	*im-*	not	impossible		*trans-*	across	transatlantic
	in-	not	invisible	8	*anti-*	against	antiwar
	pre-	before	pregame		*pro-*	in favor of	prowar
	sub-	under	submarine		*sub-*	under	submarine
					super-	above	supersonic

Scope-and-Sequence Chart.   Since some prefixes appear in reading materials as early as second grade, this seems to be the appropriate level at which to initiate instruction. A scope-and-sequence chart based on an analysis of current reading programs is presented in Table 5.1. At each level, elements from earlier grades should be reviewed. Additional prefixes that students encounter in their reading should also be introduced.

Suffixes

The two kinds of **suffixes** are derivational and inflectional. **Derivational suffixes** change the part of speech of a word or change the function of a word in some way. Common derivational suffixes are presented in Table 5.2. **Inflectional suffixes** mark grammatical items and are learned early. In fact, *-s, -ed,* and *-ing* occur in the easiest materials and are taught in first grade; *-er, -est, -ly* are introduced in most basals by second grade.

For the most part, students are already using inflectional suffixes widely in their oral language by the time they meet them in their reading. They simply have to become used to translating the letters into sounds. If they are reading for meaning and using syntactic as well as semantic cues, translating the letters into sounds should happen almost automatically. For example, children's grammatical sense will tell them that a /z/ sound is used in the italicized word in the following sentence: The two *boys* were fighting. Also, it is not necessary to teach students that *s* represents /z/ at the end of some words: *friends, cars,* and so on. The sound is automatically translated. In the same way, students automatically pronounce *-ed* correctly in the following words, even though three different pronunciations are represented: *called, planted,* and *jumped.* Exercises designed to have children identify which pronunciation each *-ed* represents—/d/, /id/, or /t/—are time wasters.

Suffixes are taught in the same way as prefixes. As can be seen from Tables 5.1 and 5.2, the definitions of prefixes and suffixes are sometimes vague. Although only one or two definitions are given in the tables, in reality, some affixes have four or five. To give students a sense of the meaning of each affix, provide experience with several examples. Experience is a better teacher than mere definition.

FYI

The most frequently occurring derivational suffixes are *-er, -tion* (*-ion*), *-ible* (*-able*), *-al* (*-ial*), *-y, -ness, -ity* (*-ty*), *-ment, -ic, -ous* (*-ious*), *-en, -ive, -ful,* and *-less* (White, Sowell, & Yanagihara, 1989).

▪ A **suffix** is an affix added to the end of a word or a root in order to form a new word: for example, *helpless.*

▪ A **derivational suffix** produces a new word by changing a word's part of speech or meaning: *happy, happiness.*

▪ An **inflectional suffix** changes the inflected ending of a word by adding an ending such as *-s* or *-ed* that shows number or tense: *girls, helped.*

▪ The **root** of a word is the part of the word that is left after all the affixes have been removed. A root is also defined as the source of present-day words. The Latin verb *decidere* is the root of the English verb *decide* (McArthur, 1992).

The words *base, combining form, root,* and *stem* are sometimes used interchangeably but actually have different meanings. To keep matters simple, this text uses the word *root.*

■■■ **TABLE 5.2 Scope-and-Sequence Chart for Common Derivational Suffixes**

Grade	Suffix	Meaning	Example	Grade	Suffix	Meaning	Example
1–2	-en	made of	wooden	4–5	-ian	one who is in a certain field	musician
	-er	one who	painter		-ic	of; having the form of	gigantic
	-or	one who	actor		-ish	having the quality of	foolish
2–3	-able	is; can be	comfortable		-ive	being	creative
	-ible	is; can be	visible	5–6	-ian	one who	guardian
	-ful	full of; having	joyful		-ist	a person who	scientist
	-ness	having	sadness		-ity	state of	reality
	-(t)ion	act of	construction		-ize	make	apologize
	-y	being; having	dirty	6–7	-ar	forms adjectives	muscular
3–4	-al	having	magical		-age	forms nouns	postage
	-ance	state of	allowance		-ess	female	hostess
	-ence	state of; quality of	patience	7–8	-ary	forms adjectives	budgetary
	-ify	make	magnify		-ette	small	dinette
	-less	without	fearless		-some	forms adjectives	troublesome
	-ment	state of	advertisement				
	-ous	having	curious				

Root Words

As students move through the grades, knowledge of morphemic elements becomes more important for handling increasingly complex reading material. As the reading becomes more abstract and therefore more difficult in every subject area, the number of words made up of **roots** and affixes becomes greater. Science, for instance, often uses Greek and Latin words and compounds (O'Rourke, 1974). As with prefixes and suffixes, roots that should be taught are those that appear with high frequency, transfer to other words, and are on the appropriate level of difficulty. For example, the root *cil* (*council*), meaning "call," should probably not be taught because it is difficult to distinguish in a word. Roots such as *graph* (*autograph*) and *phon* (*telephone*) are easy to spot and appear in words likely to be read by elementary and middle school students. Table 5.3 shows roots that are good candidates

■■■ **TABLE 5.3 Scope-and-Sequence Chart for Common Roots**

Grade	Root	Meaning	Example	Grade	Root	Meaning	Example
3	graph	writing	autograph	7	mid	middle	midday
	tele	distance	telescope		ped	foot	pedestrian
4	port	carry	import		chrono	time	chronometer
	saur	lizard	dinosaur		dict	say	dictate
	phon	sound	telephone		hemi	half	hemisphere
	vid, vis	see	visible		manu	hand	manuscript
5	astro	star	astronaut	8	bio	life	biology
	cred	believe	incredible		geo	earth	geology
	duct	lead	conductor		micro	small	microscope
	tri	three	triangle		mono	one	monotone
6	aud	hearing	auditorium		semi	half, part	semisweet
	auto	self	autobiography		some	group	foursome
	bi	two	bicycle				
	ology	study of	geology				
	scrib, script	writing	inscription				
	therm	heat	thermometer				

FYI

Included among the list of roots are combining forms. A combining form is a base designed to combine with another combining form (*tri + pod*) or a word (*tri + angle*). Combining forms differ from affixes because two combining forms can be put together to make a word but two affixes cannot. Although combining forms are not roots, they are included with the roots because that is where they are presented in most texts (McArthur, 1992).

for inclusion in a literacy program. The sequence is based on O'Rourke's research (1974) and an analysis of the roots found in current reading programs.

Teaching Root Words.   Teach root words inductively, and take advantage of every opportunity to develop students' knowledge of them. For example, if students wonder what a thermal wind is, discuss known words such as *thermos, thermostat,* and *thermometer.* Lead them to see that in all three words, *therm* has to do with heat; thus, thermal winds are warm winds. Choose elements to be taught from students' reading. If students read about dinosaurs, use the opportunity to introduce *tri, saurus, pod, ornitho,* and other roots. This often helps students use the name to identify the distinguishing characteristics of the creature. For example, *triceratops* uses three word parts to describe a dinosaur that has three horns, two of which are over the eyes: *tri,* "three"; *cerat,* "horn"; and *ops,* "eyes." Two of the parts also transfer to a number of other words: *tri* to *triangle, tripod,* etc., and *op* to *optical, optician, optometrist,* etc.

Scope-and-sequence charts for affixes and roots have been provided to give you a sense of when certain ones are usually presented. The real determinants, however, are the needs of the students and the demands of their reading tasks.

Morphemic Analysis for English Language Learners

Just as in English, Spanish has roots, prefixes, and suffixes. In fact, Spanish has more affixes than English does because Spanish nouns and adjectives have endings that show agreement in gender and number. However, there are many similarities between Spanish and English. A number of elements are identical in both languages or altered slightly. For instance, the prefixes *re-* and *sub-* are the same in both languages; so are the suffixes *-able* and *-ion.* The suffix *-tion* is slightly different in Spanish: It is often spelled *-cion* but may also be spelled *-sion* or *-xion.* If students know prefixes, suffixes, and roots in Spanish, they can transfer some of this knowledge to English.

Reinforcement Activities

Morphemic Analysis

- Provide students with several long words composed of a number of morphemic units, for example:

unbelievable	improperly	unimaginable
prehistoric	photographer	disagreeable
irregularly	unfavorable	uncomfortable
unreturnable	misjudgment	oceanographer

  Have them determine the morphemic boundaries and try to figure out what the words mean based on analysis of the units. Good sources of other words to analyze are the texts that students are encountering in class.

- Ask students to create webs of roots and affixes in which the element is displayed in several words (Tompkins & Yaden, 1986). A web for the root *loc* might look like Figure 5.8.

- **Contextual analysis** is an attempt to derive the meaning of a word by examining the context in which the unknown word appears.

■■■ **FIGURE 5.8   Web for the Root** *Loc*

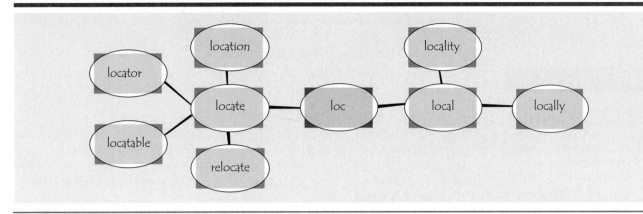

- Students can incorporate roots and affixes into their everyday lives by constructing personal experiences. Have them tell or write about times when they were helpful or helpless, careful or careless.

- Using root words, prefixes, and suffixes, let students create words that label a new creature, invention, or discovery. For example, a *quintocycle* would be a cycle with five wheels. A *monovideopod* would be a single walking eye.

- Ask students to bring in examples of roots and affixes from periodicals, children's books, textbooks, signs, and labels or from spoken language. For example, a child who has recently been on an airplane may have noted the word *preboard*. Let the class determine the word's root and/or affix and discuss the word's meaning.

■■■ **Checkup** ■■■

1. What are the major components of morphemic analysis?
2. How would you go about teaching and reinforcing morphemic analysis?

■■■

Contextual Analysis

Imagine that you are a fourth-grader who has never seen or heard the word *salutations*. What does the following passage indicate about its meaning?

"Salutations!" repeated the voice.

"What are they, and where are you?" screamed Wilbur. "Please, please, tell me where you are. And what are salutations?"

"Salutations are greetings," said the voice. "When I say 'salutations' it's just my fancy way of saying hello or good morning." (White, 1952, p. 35)

Not only does E. B. White define the word *salutations* in context in *Charlotte's Web*, but he also implies that its use is somewhat pompous. Of course, not all difficult words are explained with such care; in fact, in many instances, **contextual analysis** is not at all helpful (Schatz & Baldwin, 1986). Context determines the particular meaning of a word, but it may not reveal it (Deighton, 1959).

However, it is estimated that the average reader is able to use context successfully only between 5 and 20 percent of the time (Jenkins, Matlock, & Slocum, 1989; Nagy, Anderson, & Herman, 1987). Even when context clues are fairly obvious, students may fail to take advantage of them. Fortunately, children do become more proficient at using context clues as they progress through the grades. They also do significantly better with practice. Simply directing students to use context to get the meaning of an unfamiliar word is not effective. The directive has to be accompanied by practice and feedback to let them know whether their contextual guesses are correct (Carnine, Kame'enui, & Coyle, 1984).

Deriving the Meaning of a Word from Context

Deriving the meaning of an unfamiliar word generally involves the following steps (Gunning, 2006):

■ Recognizing that the word is unknown (Nation, 2001).

■ Deciding to use context to derive the meaning of the unknown word. Many readers simply skip unknown words. Even if they do not, most of their use of context is incidental (Rapaport, 2004). The typical reader doesn't make deliberate use of context until she or he notes a disruption in meaning and makes the decision to use context (Kibby, Rapaport, & Wieland, 2004).

■ Applying experience to the word. The reader notes whether she or he has ever seen or heard this word before.

■ Noting morphemic units. The student notes prefixes, suffixes, and roots that might provide helpful clues to the word's meaning.

■ Selecting clues to the word's meaning. From the passage as a whole, the reader seeks information that might shed light on the word's meaning. These clues constrain the meaning of the word but might not fully reveal it (Kibby, Rapaport, & Wieland, 2004). For instance, they might indicate that the target word is a noun or verb or suggest a negative rather than a positive meaning.

■ Using context clues, background, and reasoning to compose a general meaning of the word. The reader uses clues from the text, her or his background of experience, and reasoning to create a hypothesis about the word's meaning. Although the text is used to provide context clues, the reader's background knowledge is often a more important factor. Context leads the reader to use her or his background of experience to make inferences. The reader revises her or his hypothesis based on subsequent encounters with the word (Rapaport, 2004). Subsequent encounters may provide additional clues to the word's meaning. In a sense, context is in the reader's head rather than on the page. One way to increase the effectiveness of students' use of context clues is to show students how to make inferences based on background knowledge. In one experiment, although all the students had the necessary background knowledge to infer that a brachet is a small hound, only half were able to use their knowledge to make this inference. The other half could not guess the word's meaning until given additional clues (Rapaport, 2004).

■ Testing the meaning of the word and changing or refining it, if necessary. The reader tries out the hypothesized meaning to see if it fits. If it doesn't fit, the reader repeats the process. Good readers revise when they find the hypothesized definition is not working out. Poor readers start all over again with a new hypothesis. In one study, readers required five or six encounters with a word before they could derive an accurate meaning (Kibby, Rapaport, & Wieland, 2004).

Encourage students to follow these key steps for using context:

1. *Reread and gather clues.* Reread the sentence and see how the target word is used. Look for clues to the meaning of the word. If there are no clues or the clues don't help, read the sentence before and after the target sentence.

2. *Identify part of speech.* Determine the word's part of speech.

3. *Summarize.* In your mind, summarize what the text has said so far. Combine that with all the clues that the text has offered.

4. *Use background knowledge.* Use what you know, the sense of the passage, and the clues you have gathered. Make a careful guess (hypothesis) as to the word's meaning.

5. *Check your careful guess.* See if your guess fits the context.

6. *Revise.* If your careful guess doesn't fit, try again. If the word is used in other places in the selection, get clues from those uses.

Instruction in the use of context clues should make explicit the thinking processes involved. Here is how the key steps would be put to use to figure out the meaning of *dismal* in this passage from Cleary's (1981) *Ramona Quimby, Age 8*:

> Rainy Sunday afternoons in November were always dismal, but Ramona felt this Sunday was the most dismal of all. She pressed her nose against the living-room window, watching the ceaseless rain pelting down as bare black branches clawed at the electric wires in front of the house. Even lunch, leftovers Mrs. Quimby had wanted to clear out of the refrigerator, had been dreary, with her parents, who seemed tired or discouraged or both, having little to say and Beezus mysteriously moody. Ramona longed for sunshine, sidewalks dry enough for roller skating, a smiling happy family. (p. 33)

1. *Reread and gather clues.* What information in the sentence containing the unknown word will help me figure out what this word means? Is there any information in earlier sentences that will help? Is there any information in later sentences that will help?

   Helpful clues include the rain, Ramona's obvious boredom, the moods of the other family members, and Ramona's longing for sunshine, sidewalks dry enough for roller skating, and a smiling happy family.

2. *Identify part of speech.* How is the word being used?

   Dismal is identified as being an adjective. The readers infer that *dismal* is being used to describe.

3. *Summarize.* When I think about all the information given about this unknown word, what does the word seem to mean?

   When readers put all the clues together, they can see that the scene that is being described is a gloomy or unhappy one.

4. *Use background knowledge.* What do I know that will help me figure out the meaning of this word?

   Using past experience, students can think about days on which it was raining and they couldn't go out and everyone seemed crabby. This will help them decide that *dismal* means "gloomy" or "unhappy."

5. *Check your careful guess.* Does my meaning seem to fit the context?

   Once readers have used context to construct a tentative meaning for the unknown word, they should try substituting the tentative meaning into the text.

6. *Revise.* What do I need to do to make a better guess?

   If the meaning does not fit the sense of the text's sentence, students should revise their guess, use the dictionary, or get help.

Types of Context Clues

Listed below, in approximate order of difficulty, are seven main types of context clues. They have been drawn from a variety of materials that elementary or middle school students might read.

   1. *Explicit explanation or definition.* The easiest clue to use is a definition in context. For instance, the following passage from *The Wright Brothers at Kitty Hawk* (Sobol, 1961) gives a detailed, conceptual explanation of warping:

> "Why the wings are twisting!" exclaimed Bill Tate.
>   "We call it warping," said Orville. "See the wings on the side? Their ends are turned upward and forward."

FYI

■ Context clues should be used to complement phonics strategies and help students predict the pronunciations of words that are in their listening vocabularies but not in their reading vocabularies. However, context clues in this section are designed to help students derive the meanings of words that are not in the students' listening or reading vocabularies.

■ Oral context is probably more helpful than written context. As Beck, McKeown, and Kucan (2002) explain, "Written context lacks many of the features of oral language that support learning new words, such as intonation, body language, and shared physical surroundings. As such, the text is a far less effective vehicle for learning new words than oral language" (p. 3).

■ Emphasize the need to comprehend a passage in order to use context. Often, the general sense of the passage will provide a clue as to the meaning of a word. However, students won't be able to use the overall sense of the passage if they don't comprehend it (Beck, McKeown, & Kucan, 2002). Ask students what's going on in the passage, and then discuss what the target word might mean.

"And the wings on the left side are pulled downwards and rearward," said Bill Tate.

Orville let go of the rope. "Now, in front—"

"Hold on," said Bill Tate. "I'm not sure I understand what I saw."

"The warping is our idea for keeping the glider level," said Orville. Carefully he explained how it changed the way the wind pushed against the wings. (p. 24)

Explicit definitions are usually more concise, as in this excerpt from *Brown Bears* (Stone, 1998): "Brownies are omnivores (AHM-nih-vorz). Omnivores eat both plants and animals" (p. 14).

2. *Appositives.* Definitions are sometimes supplied in the form of appositives immediately after the difficult word: "On a clear summer morning, a pod, or group, of close to fifty dusky dolphins moves toward deeper water" (Souza, 1998, p. 27).

3. *Synonyms.* Finding a synonym sometimes takes some searching. It often appears in a sentence after the one that used the target word. In the following passage from *Little House on the Prairie* (Wilder, 1941), the synonym for *ague* is given in a preceding sentence: "Next day he had a little chill and a little fever. Ma blamed the watermelon. But next she had a chill and a little fever. So they did not know what could have caused their fever 'n' ague" (p. 198).

4. *Function indicators.* Sometimes, context provides clues to meaning because it gives the purpose or function of the difficult word (Sternberg, 1987). In the following sentence, the reader gets an excellent clue to the meaning of *derrick* in a sentence that indicates what a derrick does: "The derrick lifted the glider into the sky" (Sobol, 1961, p. 27).

5. *Examples.* The example—lions—in the following passage gives the reader a sense of the meaning of *predators*: "Only 5 percent of cheetah cubs live to become adults. The remainder die from disease, starvation, or attacks from other predators, such as lions" (Thompson, 1998, p. 7).

6. *Comparison–contrast.* By contrasting the unknown word *foreigners* with the known word *nationals* in the following passage, readers can gain an understanding of the unknown word: "Halmoni walked Yunni over to the long line that said 'Foreigners.' The line moved slowly as the officer checked each passport. Halmoni got to stand in the fast-moving line that said 'Nationals.' Yunni looked like all the Koreans in the nationals line, but she had to stand in the foreigners line" (Choi, 2001, p. 146). Students must be able to reason that the word *foreigners* is the opposite of *nationals*, however. Being able to use *nationals* as a context clue also requires that students know the meaning of *nationals*.

7. *Experience.* A main clue to the meaning of an unfamiliar word is students' background of experience. In the following passage, readers can use their own experience of being cut or injured to help them to make an informed guess as to what the unfamiliar word *excruciating* means: "Suddenly, the hedge clippers caught a branch, and my left middle finger was pulled into the blades. I felt an excruciating pain. The tip of my finger was hanging by a thread" (Rolfer, 1990, p. 25).

Presenting Context Clues

Use of context should permeate the reading program from its very beginning. When emerging readers use phonics skills to try to decode words that are in their listening but not in their reading vocabulary, they should use context as well, both as an aid to sounding out and as a check to make sure they have decoded the words correctly. Context clues presented in this chapter are designed to help readers derive the meanings of unknown words—words that are not in the students' listening vocabularies. Although the use of context clues ideally becomes automatic over the years, it should be taught explicitly. Using a direct teaching model, the teacher should explain what the clues are, why it is important to use context, and how they can be applied. Modeling the use of clues, guided practice, and application are important elements in the process. Lesson 5.5 describes how context clues might be presented.

Lesson 5.5

Context Clues

Step 1. Explain context

Explain the usefulness of context clues. Select five or six difficult words from a book the class is reading, and show how context could be used to derive their meanings.

Step 2. Demonstrate the process of using context

Ask the following questions:

What information in the selection will help me figure out what the unknown word means?

How is the unknown word being used? (What is its part of speech?)

From all the information given about the unknown word, what does it seem to mean?

What do I know from my own experience that will help me figure out the meaning of the word?

Step 3. Try out the tentative meaning of the unknown word

Show students how to try out the tentative meaning of the unknown word by substituting the meaning for the word and reading the sentence to see whether the substitution fits. Explain that if the tentative meaning does not fit the sense of the sentence, they should revise it.

Step 4. Model the process

Model the process of using context with a variety of words. Explain the thinking processes that you go through as you attempt to figure out their meanings and then try out these tentative meanings. Show, for example, how you might interpret examples, use a comparison, search out synonyms, look for appositives, use your background of experience, or try a combination of strategies. Show, too, how you would use context and experience to construct a tentative meaning for the unknown word and then try out the meaning by substituting it in the sentence.

Step 5. Guided practice

Have students use context clues to figure out unfamiliar words in selected passages that provide substantial clues. Do one or two cooperatively; then have students try the process on their own. Discuss the meanings of the unfamiliar words and the types of clues they used.

Step 6. Application

Encourage students to try using context clues for an unknown word in a reading selection. After the reading, talk over the meanings that they derived and the strategies they used. Ask how they went about determining what the unknown word meant, what clues they used, and how they decided on their definition of the unknown word.

Step 7. Assessment and review

Note how often and how well students apply context clues on their own. From time to time, check on their use of context. Provide additional instruction as needed.

Subsequent Lessons in the Use of Context Clues

In a series of lessons, present other major context clues, emphasizing the thinking processes involved in using each one. After introducing all the types of clues appropriate for students' level, review them. However, instruction should be focused on using context

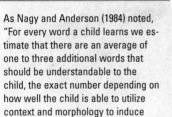

FYI

As Nagy and Anderson (1984) noted, "For every word a child learns we estimate that there are an average of one to three additional words that should be understandable to the child, the exact number depending on how well the child is able to utilize context and morphology to induce meaning" (p. 304).

USING TECHNOLOGY

Vocabulary Drill for Kids presents words in context. Students select from three options the one they think is the correct response.
http://www.edu4kids.com/index.php

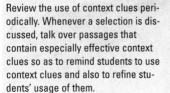

FYI

Review the use of context clues periodically. Whenever a selection is discussed, talk over passages that contain especially effective context clues so as to remind students to use context clues and also to refine students' usage of them.

FYI

Students can help each other learn new words. If they get stuck on a word while reading and neither context clues nor morphemic analysis or other strategies work, students can place a stick-on note next to the challenging word (Lubliner and Smetana, 2005). Later, working in small groups or during discussion of the selection, they can seek help from their fellow students.

clues effectively rather than on identification of types of clues. Draw sample sentences from children's periodicals, trade books, content-area texts, and the Internet, so that students can see that the skills have relevance and that context clues will help them analyze words. Most important, encourage students to get in the habit of using context to figure out the meanings of unfamiliar words. Instead of merely suggesting that they use clues, model the process from time to time to remind them about it. Also, encourage students to use the dictionary as a means of checking definitions derived by using context clues.

Also integrate the use of context with morphemic and syllabic analysis. Note how morphemic analysis and context clues might be used to derive the meanings of *microbats* and *megabats*.

> Bats are the masters of the ultrasonic world. They are divided into two groups, the microbats and the megabats. Most microbats are insect eaters. All microbats rely on ultrasound to guide them when they fly and to help them find food and communicate with each other. The large, fruiteating megabats can make ultrasounds, too, but they do not use them when flying or searching for food. (Arnold, 2001)

■ ■ ■ Checkup ■ ■ ■

1. How do students begin processing context clues?
2. What are the major types of context clues?
3. How might you teach and reinforce the use of context clues?

■ ■ ■

Dictionary Usage

Context, especially when combined with phonics and morphemic and syllabic analysis, is a powerful word-attack strategy, but some words defy even these four strategies. When all else fails, it is time for the student to consult the world's greatest expert on words, the dictionary. Although students might not use a real dictionary in first and second grades, preparation begins early. In first grade and, in some cases, kindergarten, students compile word books and picture dictionaries. They also learn alphabetical order, a prerequisite skill for locating words, and phonics, which is necessary for using the pronunciation key.

Using Predictionaries

Most students are not able to use dictionaries until the third grade. However, predictionaries, which can be used by first- and second-graders, have been compiled by several publishers. **Predictionaries** are books in which limited numbers of words are defined through illustrations. A more advanced predictionary, which is usually called the first dictionary, uses sentences and pictures to define words but does not supply syllabications or pronunciation. Predictionaries are available on CD-ROM; the advantage of this format is that the selected words are pronounced orally and their definitions spoken. A predictionary is a useful tool but must be used with care. Because it includes only a limited number of words, students may find that many words they want to look up are not there. Locating entry words may also be fairly time-consuming, unless an electronic version is used.

> ■ A **predictionary** is an easy dictionary that has fewer entries than a regular dictionary, simplifies definitions, but does not contain a pronunciation key.

A glossary is a valuable word-learning tool.

Using Glossaries

Glossaries are included in the anthologies of major reading programs and content-area texts. In some programs, glossaries can be found as early as first grade. Easier to use than dictionaries because they have only a limited number of words and definitions, glossaries are helpful and prepare students for the dictionary.

Using Dictionaries

By third grade, students with average reading achievement are ready to use real dictionaries. They should, of course, use beginning dictionaries that are simplified so that the definitions are readable. For reading, students must have three major skills: locating the target word, finding the proper definition, and learning the pronunciation. For writing, determining correct spelling and usage is also important.

Locating the Words to Be Looked Up. The first thing that students must realize is that words are arranged in alphabetical order—*a* to *z*—by first letter and then by second letter, and, if necessary, by third letter, and so on. From the beginning, train students to use guide words so that they do not adopt the time-wasting habit of simply thumbing through the *s*'s or the *w*'s page by page until they find the appropriate location. Even after they have mastered alphabetical order, students may be confused as they search for some entry words. Entry words often exclude inflected forms. A student looking up *rallies* or *exporter*, for example, will have to look under *rally* or *export*.

Locating and Understanding Meanings. Definitions are not the only way words are explained. Many dictionaries also include synonyms, illustrations, and phrases or sentences in which the word is used. Some give a word history for selected words and explain how words that are synonyms differ in meaning. For instance, *Webster's New World Dictionary* supplies a definition for *kiosk*, gives a history of the term, and includes a photo of a kiosk. For the word *model*, it presents a brief explanatory paragraph that contrasts *model* and *pattern*.

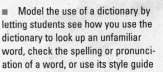

Adapting Instruction for English Language Learners

For ELLs, a translation dictionary that contains English and their first language could be an invaluable aid. Students might use one of the many language translators found on the Web, such as Web-a-dex Language Translator: http://www.web-a-dex.com/translate.htm

FYI

■ Build your pupils' skill in using dictionary phonetic respellings to get the correct pronunciations along with the meanings of unknown words. Just as it's easier to remember a person's name if you can pronounce it, so, too, it's easier to remember a new word if you can say it correctly.

■ Merriam-Webster presents a number of vocabulary-building exercises. The site also provides pronunciations for words. http://www.m-w.com

Demonstrate the various ways a dictionary explains words. Direct students to look up words that are accompanied by illustrations. Discuss the definition, illustration, synonym, and example, if given, for each one. Words likely to have illustrations include the following (this will vary from dictionary to dictionary): *manatee, lattice, isobar, ibex, hoe, heart,* and *funnel.* Choose examples that are at the appropriate level for your students and that would be helpful for them to know.

Once students have a good grasp of how to locate words and how to use the several kinds of defining and explanatory information, have them look up words. Choose words that students have a genuine need to know, such as hard words from a content-area text or children's book that they are reading. In the beginning, stress words that have just one or two meanings, like *edifice, egret,* or *cellist.*

As students grow in skill in using the dictionary, tell them that some words may have many meanings. Have them look up the following words and count the number of meanings given: *ace, bit, bowl, comb,* and *free.* Emphasize that context can help them choose the correct meaning for a word that has several definitions. Have them practice finding the correct meaning for each of several words that have just two or three distinct meanings:

Because I moved the camera, the photo was a bit *fuzzy.*

The blanket was warm and *fuzzy.*

The explorers packed up their *gear* and left.

Use second *gear* when going up a steep hill.

Homographs.   Have students note how homographs are handled in their dictionaries. Usually, they are listed as separate entries and numbered, as in Figure 5.9. For practice, students can use context to help them determine which definition is correct in sentences such as the following:

The doctor gave me medicine for my *sty.*

The king signed the paper and put his *seal* on it.

We landed on a small sandy *key.*

Constructing the Correct Pronunciation.   After students have acquired some skill in locating words and choosing appropriate meanings, introduce the concept of phonetic respellings. Display and discuss the pronunciation key contained in the dictionary your class is using. To avoid confusion, have all students use the same dictionary series, if possible, because different publishers use different keys. Help students discover what they already know about the key. Almost all the phonetic respellings of consonants will be familiar, except for, perhaps, *ng* in words like *sung,* which is signified by /ŋ/ in some systems. Short vowels, indicated by *a, e, i, o* (sometimes symbolized as /ä/), and *u,* will also be familiar. Inform the students that long vowels are indicated by a symbol known as a macron, as in

■■■ **FIGURE 5.9**
Homographs in a Dictionary

bay¹ (bā), a part of a sea or lake extending into the land. A bay is usually smaller than a gulf and larger than a cove. *noun.*
bay² (bā), **1** a long, deep barking, especially by a large dog: *We heard the distant bay of the hounds.* **2** to bark with long, deep sounds: *Dogs sometimes bay at the moon.* 1 *noun,* 2 *verb.*
bay³ (bā), **1** reddish-brown. **2** a reddish-brown horse with black mane and tail. 1 *adjective,* 2 *noun.*

Scott, Foresman Beginning Dictionary (p. 51) by E. L. Thorndike & C. L. Barnhart, 1988, Glenview, IL: Scott, Foresman and Company. Copyright © 1988 by Scott, Foresman & Company. Reprinted by permission of Scott, Foresman and Company.

/gōt/. Explain that the macron is a diacritical mark and that such marks are used to show pronunciation. Show how diacritical marks are used to indicate the pronunciation of *r* vowels, short and long double *o*, schwa, the vowel sounds heard in *paw, toy,* and *out,* and short *o*.

After providing an overview of the pronunciation key, concentrate on its segments so that students acquire a working knowledge of the system. In order of difficulty, these segments might include consonants and short vowels, long vowels, *r* vowels, short and long double *o*, other vowels, and schwa. After introducing each segment, have students read words using the elements discussed. Encourage the active use of the pronunciation key.

Once students have mastered phonetic respelling, introduce the concept of accent. One way to do this would be to say a series of words whose meaning changes according to whether the first or second syllable is accented: *record, present, desert, minute, object.* As you say the words, stress the accented syllable. Have students listen to hear which syllable is said with more stress. After the class decides which syllable is stressed, write the words on the board and put in the accent marks while explaining what they mean. Discuss how the change in stress changes the pronunciation, meaning, or use of each word. To provide guided practice, select unknown words from materials students are about to read and have students reconstruct their pronunciation. Discuss these reconstructions, and provide ample opportunity for independent application. Later, introduce the concept of secondary stress.

Electronic Dictionaries.   Electronic dictionaries are far easier to use than book versions. Words are easier to look up. All the student has to do is to type in the target word. Some electronic dictionaries accept misspelled words, so students looking up the spelling of a word can find it even if they can't spell it accurately. Speaking dictionaries also pronounce the word being looked up and read the definition, so students don't have to be able to use the pronunciation key before they can use the dictionary. Electronic dictionaries are also motivational: They're more fun to use than a traditional dictionary. Electronic dictionaries come in CD-ROM and handheld versions and are available on the Web and with some computer programs. Handheld versions have the advantage of being small and portable. And some of the simpler models are not much more expensive than book versions.

The Dictionary as a Tool.   Many school dictionaries include generous instructions for use, along with practice exercises. Use these selectively. Avoid isolated drill on dictionary skills. Concentrate on building dictionary skills through functional use—that is, show students how to use the dictionary, and encourage them to incorporate it as a tool for understanding language. For instance, when they have questions about word meaning, pronunciation, spelling, or usage, encourage them to seek help in the dictionary.

One word of caution is in order: For word recognition, the dictionary should generally be used as a last resort. Looking up a word while reading a story interrupts the flow of the story and disturbs comprehension. Students should try context, phonics, and morphemic or syllabic analysis before going to the dictionary. Moreover, unless the word is crucial to understanding the story, they should wait until they have read the selection to look up the word. The dictionary is also a good check on definitions derived from context clues. After reading a story in which they used context clues, students should check their educated guesses against the dictionary's definitions.

■ ■ ■ Checkup ■ ■ ■

1. What are the key skills involved in using the dictionary?
2. How might these skills be presented and reinforced?

■ ■ ■

USING TECHNOLOGY

KidsClick provides a list of online dictionaries that range from regular to rhyming.
http://kidsclick.org

If possible, acquire a CD-ROM or other electronic dictionary. The advantages of an electronic dictionary are that it locates the word faster and is motivational. An electronic dictionary may also read the word and its definition. This is a help for students whose reading skills are limited.

My First Incredible Amazing Dictionary (Dorling Kindersley) is an excellent example of a talking predictionary.

Handheld electronic dictionaries are available from Franklin Learning Resources, One Franklin Plaza, Burlington, NJ, 08016-4907, 800-266-5626.

■ Supplying Corrective Feedback

A student is reading and is suddenly stopped cold by an unknown word. What should the teacher do? If the student does not self-correct and the error is not substantive—the student says *this* for *that*—you may choose to do nothing. Sometimes, an error is substantive and disturbs the sense of the sentence, but it is obvious that the student will not be able to work out the word using phonics, syllabication, context, or morphemic analysis. In such a case, you might supply the word as one of two options so that the student is involved in the process: "Would *chat* or *champ* fit here?" If there is a chance that the student can use strategies to decode the word, pause briefly—about five seconds or so—to provide an opportunity for the student to work out the word (Harris & Sipay, 1990). If the student fails to work out the word but might be able to with a little help, try a **corrective cues hierarchy** (McCoy & Pany, 1986).

Applying a Corrective Cues Hierarchy

The following corrective cues hierarchy is adapted from McCoy and Pany (1986).

For words in the students' listening but not reading vocabulary:

■ *Strategy 1.* Seeking out a pronounceable word part and using it to reconstruct a word is often the simplest, most direct strategy and, in most instances, should be attempted first. When encountering an unknown word, the student should ask, "Is there any part of this word that I can say?" If that does not work, the student should try an analogy strategy, asking, "Is this word like any word I know?" If the word is a multisyllabic one, the student might need to reconstruct the word part by part. Once the word has been reconstructed, the student should verify the reconstruction by checking whether the word is real and fits the context of the sentence.

■ *Strategy 2.* If the student is unable to use the pronounceable word part or analogy strategy to work out the pronunciation of the difficult word rapidly, encourage the use of context. The student should say "blank" for the unknown word and read to the end of the sentence and ask, "What would make sense here?"

For words not in the students' listening or reading vocabulary:

■ *Strategy 1.* The student should use context clues designed to help derive the meaning of an unknown word. The student should determine what information in the sentence containing the unknown word—and additional sentences, if necessary—helps in figuring out the word. The student should think about all the information given and about what she or he knows that might help in determining the meaning of the word. The student should then check to make sure that the meaning fits the context of the sentence.

■ *Strategy 2.* If the meaning of the word is unknown and context does not help, the student should use morphemic analysis. The student should look for parts of the word whose meaning he or she knows and use those parts to construct the meaning of the word. The student should then reread the sentence, substituting the constructed meaning to see whether it fits the sense of the sentence. If neither contextual analysis nor morphemic analysis works, students should use a glossary or the dictionary.

Although the strategies are presented here in consecutive order, they may be applied in tandem. For instance, a student may use both morphemic analysis and context to derive

■ A **corrective cues hierarchy** is a series of corrective feedback statements arranged in order of utility and ease of application.

■ **Think-alouds** are procedures in which students are asked to describe the processes they are using as they engage in reading or another cognitive activity.

the meaning of a word or may use context and pronounceable word parts or phonics and syllabication to reconstruct the pronunciation of a word.

Using Prompts

When students are having difficulty with a word, use a prompt to encourage the use of word analysis. Listed below are prompting questions that you might ask students in order to cue the use of a particular strategy. Some of the prompts have been adapted from the highly successful early intervention program Reading Recovery.

- *Pronounceable word part.* Is there any part of the word that you can say?
- *Analogy.* Is the word like any that you know?
- *Context.* What would make sense here? What would fit? Say "blank" for the word, and read to the end of the sentence. Then ask yourself, "What word would make sense here?"
- *Syllabic analysis.* How would you say the first syllable? The second syllable? The next syllable? What does the word seem to be?
- *Morphemic analysis.* Is there any part of the word that you know?
- *Dictionary or glossary usage.* Would the dictionary or glossary help?
- *Affirmation.* I like the way you used context (or another strategy) to help you figure out that word.
- *Probing.* What could you do to help you figure out that word?

How you prompt a student determines what the student learns (Schwartz, 2005). For instance, if a student misreads *top* as *toy*, you might have the student sound the word out. But if you want to foster monitoring and self-correction, let the student finish the sentence to see if he or she self-corrects. If not, provide a prompt that leads the student to see the need to correct: "That makes sense, but does the word say *toy*?" If students look to you for help instead of attempting to work out the words themselves, you might ask, "What could you try?" (Schwartz, 2005).

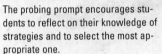

FYI

The probing prompt encourages students to reflect on their knowledge of strategies and to select the most appropriate one.

Using Think-Alouds

To assess students' use of word analysis skills and to provide guidance in their use, conduct a **think-aloud** (Harmon, 1998). In a think-aloud, students stop when they come to a difficult word and then give a description of what is going on in their minds as they try to figure out the word. Instead of providing direct instruction, the teacher offers neutral prompts that encourage students to explain their thinking: "Can you tell me what you are thinking? Can you tell me more?" Once you know what strategies students are using, you can then use the think-aloud as an instructional tool. You might use prompts like these: "Can you find clues to the word's meaning in other sentences or other parts of the article? What might help you to get the word's meaning? Would the glossary help?"

Guidance provided in a think-aloud is designed to help students apply and integrate strategies. It also helps build students' confidence in their word analysis skills and their sense of competence. If individual think-alouds are too time-consuming, group think-alouds might be used instead. That way students learn from each other.

■ ■ ■ Checkup ■ ■ ■

1. What are some steps that you might take if students have difficulty with words as they are reading?
2. What are the key prompts that you might use?
3. How might think-alouds be used to improve use of word analysis strategies?

■ ■ ■

Tools for the Classroom

Building Higher-Level Literacy

As students acquire vocabulary, help them to develop a deep understanding of the new words. Also help them to see the connotations that words have and the power of words. If students' vocabulary is below average, spend extra time on building vocabulary. Foster an interest in words so that students become active word learners.

Help for Struggling Readers and Writers

As struggling readers and writers make their way through the grades, they may master phonics only to find that they are having difficulty in reading because their background knowledge and vocabularies are limited. Having struggled with reading, poor readers generally read less and so meet and learn fewer new words and acquire less background information. With these students, it is essential to build background and related vocabulary. Spend more time building essential concepts and vocabulary before they read a selection. Also, after the selection has been read, spend time clarifying and deepening concepts. Try to help students see how new concepts are related to concepts they already know.

Encourage students to read widely, but be sure that they have lots of materials on their level. Also seek out reader-friendly informational books, such as those from the *Early Bird Nature Books* series, that do a particularly good job of building background and vocabulary.

Struggling readers often have poor concepts of themselves as learners. To build their self-concepts and vocabulary, plan a program of vocabulary development that introduces challenging words to them. They will appreciate learning "big" words. Also provide instruction in morphemic analysis, context clues, and dictionary skills to help them become independent word learners. A handheld speaking electronic dictionary can be a big help for struggling readers and writers. It allows them to obtain the pronunciations of words in their listening but not their reading vocabularies as well as the meanings of words not in their listening vocabularies. It also helps them with their spelling.

Essential Standards

Kindergarten

- Students will expand their vocabularies.

Grade 1

Students will

- expand their vocabularies.
- use context to derive the pronunciations of words that are in their listening vocabularies but not in their reading vocabularies.
- identify simple homophones.
- identify the meanings of simple words that have multiple meanings.
- use picture dictionaries, predictionaries, and simplified glossaries.
- use simple morphemic analysis with such elements as *-s, -ed,* and *-ing*.

Grade 2

Students will

- use context to derive the pronunciations of words that are in their listening vocabularies but not in their reading vocabularies.
- expand their vocabularies.
- use picture dictionaries, predictionaries, and simplified glossaries.
- use simple morphemic analysis with such elements as *-ly, -en, -er, over-,* and *un-*.

- use knowledge of simple homophones, synonyms, and antonyms to determine the meanings of words.
- identify the meanings of simple words that have multiple meanings.

Grades 3 through 8

Students will

- use context to derive the meanings of unknown words.
- use knowledge of homophones, homographs, synonyms, antonyms, and idioms to determine the meanings of words.
- use knowledge of word origins and derivations to determine the meanings of words.
- expand their vocabularies.
- use dictionaries, including electronic ones, and glossaries.
- use morphemic analysis to derive the meanings of words.
- identify the specific meanings of words that have multiple meanings.

Action plan

1. Assess students' word knowledge.
2. Construct or adapt a program for vocabulary development based upon students' needs.
3. Gear instruction to the students' level of knowledge. Words that convey new concepts need a greater degree of teaching than words that are simply labels for known concepts.
4. Develop depth of meaning for a core set of essential words rather than trying to cover a wide range of words.
5. Use graphic organizers, wide reading, games, sorting, self-collection of words, and other activities to provide practice and application.
6. Introduce morphemic analysis, context clues, and dictionary usage in functional fashion. Integrate use of skills.
7. Provide ample practice and application opportunities.
8. Help students to develop an interest in words.
9. Help English language learners recognize and take advantage of cognates. Be aware that these students have many concepts developed in their native language and may only be lacking English labels for the concepts.
10. Monitor students' progress, and make necessary adjustments.

Assessment

Through observation, note whether students are learning the skills and strategies they have been taught. Watch to see what they do when they come across an unfamiliar word. Do they attempt to use context? Do they attempt to apply morphemic analysis? Do they have a working knowledge of the morphemic elements that have been introduced? When all else fails, do they use a dictionary or glossary as an aid? Do they know when to use which strategy? Are they able to integrate strategies?

Also, note the quality of students' word knowledge. Is their vocabulary adequate for the materials they must read and the concepts they must learn? Are they acquiring new words at an adequate rate? Do they have an interest in words? Standardized tests often have a vocabulary section. If so, use these results as a possible indicator of the students' word knowledge. Note, however, whether the test required students to read the words or whether the words and definitions were read to students. Poor readers' vocabularies are underestimated if they have to read the vocabulary words. (See Chapter 2 for limitations of standardized test results.)

Summary

Average first-graders know between 5,000 and 6,000 root words and learn about 3,000 new ones each year. Having rich experiences and talking about them are important factors in learning new words. Also important are relating vocabulary to background knowledge, building relationships, developing depth of meaning, presenting numerous exposures, creating an interest in words, and promoting transfer. A variety of activities, such as using graphic organizers and playing word games, can be used to develop word knowledge. The most powerful word learning activity is wide reading.

A balanced program of vocabulary development that includes planned and incidental instruction is advisable. Words chosen for intensive instruction should be key words that will be encountered again and again. A balanced program of vocabulary development should include provisions for teaching students how to learn words on their own through the use of morphemic analysis, contextual analysis, and the dictionary.

Extending and Applying

1. Try using graphic devices, such as semantic feature analysis, a Venn diagram, or a semantic map, to organize words that you are studying or in which you are interested. Which of these devices works best for you? Why?

2. Plan a program of vocabulary development. Include a description of the class, your objectives, the source of words, the activities that you will use to reinforce words, and the techniques you will use. Also tell how you will evaluate the program.

3. Choose four to six words from a chapter in a children's book. Then, using the steps detailed in this chapter, create a vocabulary lesson. Teach the lesson to a group of students, and critique it. What worked well? What might be changed?

4. Investigate one of the vocabulary-building Web sites mentioned or one that you have discovered. How might you use this site?

5. Using procedures explained in this chapter, create a semantic map with a class. Evaluate the map's effectiveness. In what ways did it help students? Did the activity engage their attention?

Developing a Professional Portfolio

Teach and record a lesson on morphemic analysis. Select elements that appear in students' texts and have a high degree of utility. Summarize the lesson, and reflect on its effectiveness.

Go to Allyn & Bacon's MyLabSchool: www.mylabschool.com

- Enter Assignment ID **RMCS** into **Assignment Finder,** and select the case titled "Comprehension and Vocabulary."

- Read through Level A, Case 1, on vocabulary development. What strategies are identified for use in this case? What activities can you use to reinforce vocabulary development?

- Explore MyLabSchool further to find the course areas for Reading Methods, Content Area Reading, and Language Arts and identify other assets that support concepts introduced in this chapter.

Developing a Resource File

Keep a list of children's books and Web sites that do a particularly good job of developing vocabulary. Also collect riddles, jokes, and games that make learning words fun.

To access chapter objectives, practice tests, weblinks, and flashcards, go to the companion website at www.ablongman.com/gunning6e.

6 Comprehension
Theory and Strategies

For each of the following statements related to the chapter you are about to read, put a check under "Agree" or "Disagree" to show how you feel. Discuss your responses with classmates before you read the chapter.

	Agree	Disagree
1. Reading comprehension is understanding the author's meaning.	_____	_____
2. The less one knows about a topic, the more one will learn by reading about it.	_____	_____
3. Comprehension is a social activity.	_____	_____
4. Knowledge of words is the most important ingredient in comprehension.	_____	_____
5. As students read, they should be aware of whether they are comprehending what they're reading.	_____	_____
6. Before learning to draw inferences, the reader must master comprehension of literal details.	_____	_____
7. In comprehension instruction, the teacher should focus on the processes students use rather than on whether they obtain the right answers.	_____	_____

In a sense, all the previous chapters have provided a foundation for this one, which is about comprehension. This chapter begins with a discussion of the nature of comprehension and goes on to describe and suggest how to teach strategies for obtaining meaning from reading. Comprehension is very much a matter of bringing your knowledge to the task. What do you know about comprehension? What strategies do you use as you try to understand what you read? What do you do when you fail to comprehend something you read? What tips for comprehension might you share with a younger reader?

■ The Process of Comprehending

Comprehension is the main purpose of reading. In fact, without it, there is no reading, since reading is the process of constructing meaning from print. A recent assessment of nearly 20,000 fifth-graders showed that, overall, 97 percent of the fifth-graders tested were proficient in understanding words in context (sentence comprehension); 87 percent, in making literal inferences; 70 percent, in deriving meaning (making and supporting inferences); 44 percent, in making interpretations beyond the text (author's craft, making connections); and 7 percent, in evaluating nonfiction (tone, author's purpose, and evidence for and against a position) (Princiotta, Flanagan, & Germino Hausken, 2006). Fifth-graders do well with literal comprehension, but their performance falls when they are faced with higher-level comprehension. Results from the NAEP reading assessment show a similar pattern for fourth- and eighth-graders (Perie, Grigg, & Donahue, 2005).

Comprehension is a constructive, interactive process involving three factors—the reader, the text, and the context in which the text is read. For comprehension to improve, the interaction among all three factors must be taken into consideration. Readers vary in the amount and type of prior knowledge they possess, the strategies they use, their attitudes toward reading, and their work habits. Texts vary in genre, theme or topic, style, difficulty level, and appeal. The context includes when, where, and why a text is being read.

HIGHER-LEVEL LITERACY

Because comprehension is dependent on schemata, building background knowledge lays the foundation for higher-level comprehension. Students who read more, and so have more background knowledge, actually boost their IQ scores. "Those who read a lot will enhance their verbal intelligence; that is, reading will make them smarter" (Cunningham & Stanovich, 1998, p. 7).

FYI

Because comprehension is dependent on what we know, one way to foster comprehension is to build background.

Is it being read at home in preparation for a test the next day? Is it an antidote description printed on a can of pesticide, being read by a frantic parent whose child has sprayed himself with the substance? Or is it a novel being read for pleasure in an easy chair on a lazy weekend? Although the bulk of this chapter will discuss comprehension strategies, the use of these strategies will be affected by reader, text, and context.

Schema Theory

To gain some insight into the process of comprehension, read the following paragraph, which has been divided into a series of sentences. Stop after reading each sentence and ask yourself, "What did the sentence say? How did I go about comprehending it? What does this paragraph seem to be about?"

> A hoatzin has a clever way of escaping from its enemies.
>
> It generally builds its home in a branch that extends over a swamp or stream.
>
> If an enemy approaches, the hoatzin plunges into the water below.
>
> Once the coast is clear, it uses its fingerlike claws to climb back up the tree.
>
> Hoatzin are born with claws on their wings but lose the claws as they get older.

To make sense of the selection, you have to rely heavily on the knowledge you bring to the text. One definition of comprehension is that it is the process of building a connection between what we know and what we do not know, or the new and the old (Searfoss & Readence, 1994). It is currently theorized that our knowledge is packaged into units known as schemata. A **schema** is the organized knowledge that one has about people, places, things, or events (Rumelhart, 1984). A schema may be very broad and general (for example, a schema for animals) or it may be fairly narrow (for example, a schema for Siamese cats).

In Anderson's (1984) view, comprehension primarily involves activating or constructing a schema that accounts for the elements in a text, similar to constructing an outline of a script. For example, a script outline for buying and selling includes the following categories, which are known as slots: buyer, seller, merchandise, money, and bargaining (Rumelhart, 1980). Comprehending a story involves filling these slots with particular examples or instances. As a student reads about a character in a story who is purchasing a bicycle, her or his buying-and-selling schema is activated. The student fills in the buyer and seller slots with the characters' names. The bicycle is placed in the merchandise slot. The story says that the buyer got a good deal, so that is placed in the bargaining slot. The story may not say how the character paid for the bike—cash, check, credit card, or an IOU—but the reader may infer that it was with cash because in her or his buying-and-selling schema, goods are purchased with cash. A schema thus provides a framework for comprehending a story and making inferences that flesh it out. A schema also aids retention, as students use it to organize their reconstruction of the events.

In constructing the meaning of the selection on the hoatzin, you used various processes to activate the appropriate schema and fill the slots. In reading the first sentence, assuming that you did not know what a hoatzin is, you may have made a reasoned prediction that it was some kind of animal. The information in the first sentence was probably enough to activate your animal-survival-from-enemies schema. The slots might include type of animal, enemies, ability to flee, and ability to fight; guided by your schema, you

---

■ A **schema** is a unit of organized knowledge. (The plural of *schema* is *schemata*.)

■ A **situation model**, also known as a mental model, views comprehension as a

"process of building and maintaining a model of situations and events described in text" (McNamara, Miller, & Bransford, 1991, p. 491). Schema theory describes

how familiar situations are understood; situation model theory describes how new situations are comprehended.

may have been on the lookout for information to fill the slots. Integrating or summarizing the first three sentences made it possible for you to place "plunges into the water" into the ability-to-flee slot. You also did quite a bit of inferencing. When you read about the wings in the last sentence, you probably inferred that the hoatzin is a bird, even though it dives into the water. Thus, you were able to fill in the type of animal slot. You probably also inferred that the hoatzin's enemies could not reach it in the water. You may have inferred, too, that the creature is not fierce, since it seems to prefer fleeing to fighting. These inferences enabled you to fill in the enemies and ability-to-fight slots. As you can probably see, comprehending the selection about the hoatzin was not so much a question of getting meaning from the text as it was of bringing meaning to it or constructing meaning by transacting with the text.

Not only do readers have schemata for ideas and events, they also have schemata for text structures, which help them organize information. For instance, a selection might be organized in terms of a main idea and details. A reader who realizes this can use the structure of the text to organize the information in his or her memory.

Although activating schemata is essential in reading, reading is more complex than simply filling slots. As they transact with text, proficient, active readers are constantly relating what they are reading to other experiences they have had, other information in the text they have read, and texts previously read. Their interest in the text plays a powerful role in the web of linkages that they construct (Hartman, 1994). A student captivated by the idea that a bird has claws on its wings might relate this text to passages that he or she has read or a TV show about unusual animals.

Situation Model Theory

Comprehension can also be thought of as the construction of a mental or **situation model**. Comprehension requires that readers create a mental model or representation of textual information and its interpretation (van den Broek & Kremer, 2000). In expository text, the mental model reflects the organization of the content. The situation model for a science article might include a representation or mental sketch of the physical parts of the system, the steps in the system's process, relationships among the parts of the system and the steps in its operation, and the ways in which people might use the system.

As they read, adept readers ask themselves "why" questions about processes. They want to know why an event occurred or why the author decided to include a certain piece of information in the text. In reading about the formations on the ceilings of underground caves, the reader might wonder why crystals form on the cave's ceilings. The cause, which is often answered in the next sentence, is then connected to the effect. Causal connections are made in rapid-fire fashion. These causal connections are the glue that holds the information together. They provide a bridge from one sentence or thought to the next (Graesser & Bertus, 1998). The process is especially fast when the reader's expectation of the cause is confirmed. However, if the topic of the text is unfamiliar and the reader has little background knowledge to bring to it, making causal connections is more difficult. Making connections is also impeded if the reader is not committed to active comprehension. Situation models emphasize the active, constructivist nature of comprehension and the importance of prior knowledge.

Role of Reasoning

Reasoning is a key component in comprehension. Students may be called upon to infer character traits, judge a solution, analyze a situation, compare settings, draw conclusions, form concepts, apply a principle, or evaluate the credibility of information. Reasoning and background knowledge interact. Comprehension relies heavily on the reader's ability to use background knowledge to make inferences. Students who have a richer background and can make more connections between what they know and what they are reading have better comprehension and retention.

FYI

- Activating schemata is part of a situation model. As Zwaan and Graesser (1998) noted, "To construct situation models, readers must integrate information from the text with prior knowledge" (p. 197).

- A mental model might go beyond what is explicitly stated and include inferences the reader has made and background knowledge the reader has (Glenberg, Gutierrez, Levin, Japuntich, & Kaschak, 2004).

- Making inferences about consequences is more difficult than inferring causes. Making inferences about consequences, because it entails predicting future events, requires a deliberate approach, one that makes use of specific strategies (Graesser & Bertus, 1998).

- Based on a situation model, you could take at least three steps to improve comprehension: build background, give students material on the appropriate level, and teach strategies, such as generating questions as they read, that will help them make connections.

- Following written directions is an example of the use of a situation model of reading. It requires that students go beyond merely remembering information. They must also put the information to use.

Role of Attention

Attention is also a factor in comprehension. Constructing meaning is hindered if the student is not reading actively and purposely: "Successful comprehension depends in part on readers' ability to allocate their limited attention efficiently and effectively to the most relevant pieces of information within the text and within memory" (van den Broek & Kremer, 2000, p. 7).

As McKeown (2006) explains, "The core of comprehension is a reader building a coherent representation of a text. Within this process, readers move through text—attending to information, making decisions about which information is important, connecting information to related text information or to what they already know, and eventually putting it all together to develop meaning. In shorthand we might think of the process of comprehension as focused attention, connection, and integration, and the outcome of comprehension as a coherent mental representation of the ideas in a text" (p. 1).

Role of Surface Features

Compare the following two excerpts (Touchstone Applied Science Associates, 2006, p. 2):

> Ford saw all this. But he didn't like it. The workers had to keep going back and forth to get parts. Again and again. Too many minutes and even hours were wasted. Ford was concerned. Such a great waste of _____ was disturbing. "There must be a better way," he thought. (DRP = 43)

> Henry Ford was the trailblazer of mass production in the automotive industry. When Ford began manufacturing, automobiles were usually assembled like houses, with the chassis fabricated at stationary locations where mechanics gathered around, attaching various parts. Assistants were constantly required to fetch materials, a practice that consumed numerous man-hours. Ford studied these production methods and was concerned. Such a great waste of _____ was disturbing. (DRP = 73)

Although both excerpts cover the same content, the second is written in a more complex style. In the second excerpt, vocabulary is more advanced, and sentences are longer and more complex. As might be expected, when presented with the full version of the more complex text, students' scores fell. Students were able to fill in 70 percent of the missing words in the less complex version but only 48 percent in the more complex one. As the sample passages suggest, surface features impede comprehension (Touchstone Applied Science Associates, 2006). Although background knowledge is an essential element in comprehension, decoding and related skills are also important. Students who lack adequate vocabulary or have difficulty with syntax will experience difficulty understanding the more complex passage. The performance on the sample passages underscores the importance of automaticity in decoding and of adequate language skills, including vocabulary. The research also dramatizes the importance of providing students with materials that are on their level.

Developmental Nature of Comprehension

As children's background knowledge increases and their reasoning ability matures, their ability to comprehend improves. Until they reach Piaget's stage of concrete operations, children might have difficulty comprehending tales in which things are not what they

■ A **strategy** is a deliberate, planned activity or procedure designed to achieve a certain goal.

seem. They take their reading very literally. For instance, one second-grader had a great deal of difficulty with a trickster tale in which a fox disguised itself as a tree to make a meal of the hens. Despite the fact that the story described the tree's feet and teeth, she believed that it was still a tree. Between the ages of five and seven, children tend to think in one dimension (Donovan & Smolkin, 2001). By about age eight, children are able to think in more than one dimension and so can learn comprehension strategies more readily. Young children also experience difficulty with metacognitive tasks. They have difficulty both explaining their cognitive processes and planning cognitive strategies. Comprehension instruction for young children should be explicit and concrete and in keeping with where they are developmentally. This does not mean that they should not be taught comprehension skills; what it does mean is that they need to be taught skills that coincide with their level of understanding. In discussions, it is important to probe to see how students are understanding what they read and to build on their understanding. Open-ended questions work best at revealing children's thinking: "What is happening here? What is the author telling us? Is there anything that is puzzling you?" Also ask questions that guide children's thinking as they read: "What is different about this tree? Do you know any trees that have feet and teeth? Why do you think this tree has feet and teeth?"

> ### Closing the Gap
>
> Students do well in early grades but lose momentum as they advance in the grades (Pearson, 2003). To close this gap, it is recommended that more attention be paid to developing comprehension and high-level thinking skills, applying skills in the content areas, making connections, and integrating instruction (Pearson, 2003).

■ ■ ■ Checkup ■ ■ ■

1. What are the schema and situation (mental) models of comprehension?
2. What role do reasoning, attention, and surface features play in comprehension?

■ ■ ■

■ Comprehension Strategies

Before you began reading this chapter, what did you do? Did you read the title? Did you ask yourself what you know about comprehension? As you read, did you question what the text was saying? Did you try to relate information in the text to your experience? Did you reread sections because you didn't quite understand what was being said or were momentarily distracted? If you did any of these things, you were using reading strategies.

To help you understand strategies, think about the processes you use as you read. Because you are an experienced reader, your strategies have become relatively automatic. Stop your reading from time to time, and think about the processes you are using to comprehend what you are reading. Do this especially when you are reading difficult material. Strategies tend to become more conscious when the material is difficult because we have to take deliberate steps to comprehend it. One group of highly effective staff developers and classroom teachers tried out each strategy on their own reading before teaching it. They discovered that their comprehension as well as their understanding of strategies and ability to teach them to students improved.

> We test the strategies on our reading. We became more conscious of our own thinking processes as readers. We realized that we could concentrate simultaneously on the text and our ways of thinking about it. What seems most extraordinary, however, was that by thinking about our own thinking—by being metacognitive (literally, to think about one's thinking)—we could actually deepen and enhance our comprehension of the text. (Keene & Zimmermann, 1997, p. 21)

According to schema and situation models of comprehension, the reader plays a very active role in constructing an understanding of text. One way the active reader constructs meaning is by using **strategies**, which are deliberate, planned procedures designed to help the reader reach a goal. Comprehension strategies include preparing, organizing, elaborating, rehearsing, and monitoring. There are also affective strategies (Weinstein & Mayer, 1986), in which motivation and interest play a role in the construction of meaning.

Preparational strategies are processes that readers use to prepare themselves to construct meaning, such as surveying a text and predicting what it will be about. Using

INVOLVING PARENTS ■ ■ ■

Designed for both parents and teachers, *7 Keys to Comprehension* (Zimmermann & Hutchins, 2003) provides an excellent overview on comprehension instruction. It has many helpful suggestions of ways parents can help their children better understand what they read.

FYI

When second- through sixth-graders were surveyed to determine what teachers could do to help them comprehend, the students wanted teachers to (a) describe what they did to understand the "things that occurred in books," (b) show how they knew which meanings went with which words, and (c) explain "just about everything that they did in their minds to comprehend" (Block & Israel, 2004).

organizational strategies, readers construct relationships among ideas in the text, specifically between the main idea and supporting details. Paraphrasing, summarizing, clustering related words, noting and using the structure of a text, and creating semantic maps are also ways of organizing.

Elaborating involves building associations between information being read and prior knowledge or integrating information by manipulating or transforming it. Elaboration strategies include drawing inferences, creating analogies, visualizing, and evaluating, or reading critically. (Evaluating is discussed in Chapter 7.)

Rehearsing involves taking basic steps to remember material. Outlining, taking notes, underlining, testing oneself, and rereading are rehearsal strategies. Organizing, elaborating, and rehearsing are often used in combination to learn complex material.

Monitoring consists of being aware of one's comprehension and regulating it. Monitoring strategies include setting goals for reading, adjusting reading speed to difficulty of material, checking comprehension, and taking corrective steps when comprehension fails. (Some preparational strategies are actually a special set of monitoring strategies that are employed prior to reading.) See Table 6.1 for a listing of comprehension strategies.

Strategy Instruction

Whatever the strategy (whether inferring, summarizing, or predicting), strategy instruction has six key steps: introducing the strategy, demonstrating and modeling the strategy, guided practice, independent practice and application, assessment and reteaching, and ongoing reinforcement and implementation.

1. *Introducing the strategy.* Explain what the strategy is, why it is being taught, how it will benefit students, and when and where it might be used.

2. *Demonstrating and modeling the strategy.* Show how the strategy is put to use. Model the process, and do a think-aloud as you demonstrate activation of the strategy. If possible, select a text that genuinely puzzled you so that the think-aloud seems real to the students. Have students note the difficulty you are having and the steps you are taking to resolve the difficulty. Provide examples of situations in which you or others have used the strategy effectively. Sum up by providing students with clear, specific directions for applying the strategy. If possible, incorporate a mnemonic into the steps. Post a list of the steps in the classroom.

3. *Guided practice.* Guidance might be tightly structured initially. Gradually turn over more responsibility to students. Initially, the teacher does most of the talking, but students help out. Later, students do most of the work, and the teacher provides assistance. Although strategies might be taught to the whole class, Boyles (2004) recommends that guided practice be completed in small groups of from four to six in the earlier grades and up to eight in the upper grades. With this arrangement, students can be grouped according to reading ability, and instruction can be geared to their level of development. As part of guided practice, have students work in pairs in which one student implements the strategy and the other student checks the implementation, and then they switch roles. (They might use a checklist of the steps involved in applying a strategy, as in the explanation of applying the details strategy found in Lesson 6.2, under "How do we use this strategy?" on p. 288.) In the initial stages of guided practice, it is a good idea to use materials that are brief and relatively easy. That way, students can focus their full mental energies on applying the strategy.

■ **Rehearsing** is studying or repeating something so as to remember it.

■ **Monitoring** is being aware of or checking one's cognitive processes. In reading comprehension, the reader monitors his or her understanding of the text.

■■■ TABLE 6.1   Major Comprehension Strategies

Preparational Strategies	Organizational Strategies	Elaboration Strategies	Metacognitive Strategies
Previewing Activating prior knowledge Setting purpose and goals Predicting	Comprehending the main idea Determining important details Organizing details Sequencing Following directions Summarizing	Making inferences Imaging Generating questions Evaluating (critical reading)	Regulating Checking Repairing

4. *Independent practice and application.* Strategy learning is contextual. Its application tends to be limited to the context or subject in which it was learned. To promote transfer, have the students apply the strategy to a variety of materials and to other content areas.

5. *Assessment and reteaching.* Observe students to see if they apply the strategy and apply it effectively. Also conduct a written assessment. Reteach and review as necessary.

6. *Ongoing reinforcement and implementation.* After a month or so of practice and application, students should have an initial grasp of the strategy. They can add it to their repertoire and move on to the next strategy. However, continue to review the strategy from time to time and also remind students to use it, perhaps by using cues. Cues differ from scaffolds because they provide brief reminders but do not "tell us all that we are to do or say" (Beyer, 2001, p. 421). To cue students, simply mention the name of a strategy to be used, or you might provide a brief description of it; you might also ask students to tell what strategy they might use in a particular situation, point out a chart containing the strategy, or refer to a mnemonic that reminds students of the main steps of a strategy. (For example, a mnemonic for one summarizing strategy is WITS: Write the main idea. Include only the key details. Take out unimportant details and unnecessary words. Smooth out the summary.) Mnemonics or other cues might be placed on charts or bookmarks.

Boyles (2004, p. 15) explains the changing roles of teacher (I) and students (you) as students take on more responsibility for strategy application:

Explain/model	I do; you watch.
Initial guided practice	I do; you help.
Later guided practice	You do; I help.
Independence	You do; I watch.

To reinforce strategy use in your post-reading discussion of a selection, talk over the strategies that were used. You might ask, "What strategies did you use?" If there is no response, use more specific questions: "Did you ask questions as you read? Did pictures pop into your mind as you were reading?" Ask students to support their responses by reading portions of the text. "What part of the text caused that picture to pop into your mind? Could you read it for us? What part of the text led you to ask questions?" Also discuss how the strategies helped students understand the text: "How did using that strategy help you to understand what you were reading?"

ASSESSING FOR LEARNING   ■■ ■ ■

Observing students as they apply strategies and asking questions about their use of strategies will provide feedback that will allow you to give them the guidance they need.

■ ■ ■ Checkup ■ ■ ■

1. What are comprehension strategies? What role do they play in comprehension?

2. How should comprehension strategies be taught?

■ ■ ■

Teaching Preparational Strategies

Preparational strategies include previewing, activating prior knowledge about a topic before reading, and predicting what a piece is about or what will happen in a story. Setting purposes and goals are also preparational strategies.

Activating Prior Knowledge

Because comprehension involves relating the unknown to the known, it is important that students become aware of what they know about a subject. The teacher should model the process. In preparation for reading an article, the teacher should show the class how she or he previews, asks what she or he already knows about the subject, and then decides what she or he would like to find out.

Before students read a selection, the teacher activates students' **prior knowledge** through questioning. This works best when both subject knowledge (school-type knowledge) and personal knowledge are activated. For instance, before reading a story about poisonous snakes, the teacher asks students to tell what they know about poisonous snakes and also relate any personal knowledge they have about snakes. In one study, students who activated both subject knowledge and personal knowledge prior to reading were better able to apply their knowledge and also had a more positive attitude (Spires & Donley, 1998). In time, students should be led to activate both subject and personal knowledge on their own, because much of their reading will be done without benefit of preparatory discussion or teacher assistance.

Setting Purpose and Goals

Although the teacher often sets the **purpose** for reading a piece by giving students a question to answer, students must be able to set their own purpose. This could fit in with activating prior knowledge. As readers activate knowledge about computers, they may wonder how the machines work, which could be a purpose for reading. Readers also have to decide on their overall **goal** for reading—for pleasure, to gain information, or to study for a test—as each goal requires a different style of reading. Again, these are processes that the teacher should model and discuss. However, students should gradually take responsibility for setting purposes and goals.

Previewing

A strategy that helps readers set a purpose for reading is **previewing**. In previewing, also known as surveying, students read a selection's title, headings, introduction, and summary and look at illustrations to get an overview of the selection. This preview orients them to the piece so that they have some sense of what it will be about. A preview can function as a kind of blueprint for constructing a mental model of the text and also activates readers' schemata. As readers preview, they ask themselves what they know about the subject. Previewing is often used with predicting: Information gathered from previewing can be used to make predictions.

Predicting

Powerful, but relatively easy to use, predicting activates readers' schemata because predictions are made on the basis of prior knowledge. Predicting also gives readers a purpose

Adapting Instruction for Struggling Readers and Writers

Stress that the goal of reading is to construct meaning. Poor readers may be more concerned with pronouncing words correctly than with making meaning. If students realize that the goal of reading is comprehension, they are more likely to be "actively involved in achieving this goal by monitoring their effectiveness toward it" (Westby, 1999, p. 154).

■ **Prior knowledge** is the background information that a reader brings to the text.

■ The **purpose** for reading is the question that the reader wants to answer or the information the reader is seeking.

■ The **goal** of reading is the outcome the reader is seeking: to gain information, to prepare for a test, to learn how to put a toy together, to relax, etc.

■ **Previewing** can also be applied during reading. A reader may complete a section and then activate prior knowledge and make predictions for the upcoming section.

USING TECHNOLOGY

Technology can foster active reading. In *Alex's Scribbles*, Max the koala has a series of adventures. To continue each story, the reader must point and click in response to a question. This site also lends itself to writing. Alex, the coauthor, and Max invite readers to e-mail them.
http://www.scribbles.com.au/max/bookmain.html

for reading and turns reading into an active search to see whether a prediction is correct. However, one danger of predicting is that students' predictions run the risk of simply being guesses, with little thought backing them up. To improve predictions, stress the importance of having a solid basis for them. To encourage students to base their predictions on experience and textual clues, ask two questions: one that asks what the prediction is ("What do you think will happen in the story?" or "How do you think the main character will resolve her problem?") and one that asks for support of the prediction ("What makes you predict that?" or "What have you experienced and what clues from the story lead you to make that prediction?") (Nessel, 1987). For nonfiction, have students predict what they might learn about the topic.

If students look at both the title of a selection and the cover illustration, they are likely to rely primarily on the illustration, and this might limit their predictions (Benson-Castagna, 2005). Write the title of a selection that students are about to read on the chalkboard. Have them use just the title to make predictions, if it lends itself to it. Model the process of making predictions. For a story such as *A Bad, Bad Day*, explain what you think a bad day would be and how you use your background knowledge to predict what might happen in the story. After making a prediction based on the title, explain how the cover illustration helps you to add to your prediction. You can predict some of the things that might happen because the boy is shown missing the school bus. Also, discuss how the illustration relates to the title.

For nonfiction, students also preview the title and cover illustration, but in addition, they look at headings, additional illustrations, and the table of contents, if there is one. Before students read informational text, it is especially important to activate their prior knowledge. Oczkus (2005) prompts students to activate prior knowledge by first discussing the title and having students tell what they already know about pets, ants, rockets, germs, or whatever the topic happens to be. Once they have discussed what they know about the topic, students are in a better position to make predictions. For informational text, they predict what the author will tell them about the topic or what they will learn about the topic.

As with fiction, model the process of making predictions about informational text. In previewing the title of a selection entitled "Robots at Work," start by telling what you know about robots: "I know that robots help put cars together, but I don't know how they do that. Maybe the article will explain how they assemble cars. A friend of mine has a robot that vacuums his home. I wonder if there are robots that scrub floors. I predict that the article will tell what kinds of jobs robot do beside putting cars together and vacuuming floors. I predict that the author will also explain how robots are able to do certain jobs."

Some students have difficulty making predictions. Possible reasons include limited background of experience, failure to activate prior knowledge, difficulty inferring, or reluctance to take a risk. To get students accustomed to making predictions, have them make predictions about everyday events: "What do you predict will be on the lunch menu today? What do you predict tomorrow's weather will be?" To build confidence and skill in making predictions, provide students with brief fictional selections that lend themselves to making predictions. Do lots of modeling and coaching. For younger children, lift-the-tab books, such as *Where's Spot?* (Hill, 1980), are especially good for making predictions. Another book for young readers that lends itself to making predictions is *Where's the Bear?* (Pomerantz, 1984). For older students, detective stories, such as the *Sebastian Super Sleuth* series, provide opportunities for making continuous predictions. You might also have students make predictions based on illustrations. They can describe what is happening in an illustration and predict what might happen next.

Some students are so reluctant to take a risk and make predictions that they read ahead so that their predictions aren't predictions at all. Emphasize that predictions are just careful guesses; the important thing is that predictions will help them think about their reading. The key element is the thinking that goes along with the prediction rather than the accuracy of the prediction. Emphasize the importance of well-thought-out predictions. Deemphasize the rightness or wrongness of predictions. Stress plausibility and flexibility.

◼◼◼ **FIGURE 6.1**
Prediction Chart

Prediction	Clues What led me to make this prediction?	Changes in Predictions As I read the text, what changes did I have to make in my predictions?

The focus is on building thinking skills. When students are practicing predicting, have them cover up the portions of the text that they haven't read yet. That way, they aren't tempted to read ahead and find out what happens so that their predictions can be "accurate." The prediction chart in Figure 6.1 helps students make reasoned predictions.

Gradually, students can create their own predictions as they read. Predicting becomes an excellent device for enhancing comprehension when students are reading independently—ideally, it will become automatic. Predicting should also be a lifelong strategy. As they move into higher grades, students should use predicting as part of a study technique as well as for other sustained reading.

Part of being an effective user of comprehension strategies is knowing when and where to use a particular strategy. Making predictions requires prior knowledge. Students who are beginning to read about a topic on which they have little background information will have difficulty making reasonable predictions and so should use another strategy.

▪▪▪ **Checkup** ▪▪▪

1. What is the role of preparational strategies?
2. What are some key preparational strategies?
3. How might they be taught?

▪▪▪

Teaching Organizational Strategies

Organizational strategies are at the heart of constructing meaning. In contrast to preparational strategies, they are employed during reading as well as after reading. As students read, they form a situation model. Organizational strategies involve selecting important details and building relationships among them. For reading, this entails identifying the main idea of a passage and its supporting details and summarizing.

Comprehending the Main Idea

Deriving the main idea is at the core of constructing meaning from text, as the main idea provides a framework for organizing, understanding, and remembering the essential details. Without it, students wander aimlessly among details. Being able to identify or compose main ideas is essential for summarizing, note taking, and outlining. (Although

▪ The **main idea** is the overall meaning or gist of a passage. It is what the passage is all about, a summary statement of its meaning.

suggestions for teaching comprehension of main ideas and important details are presented separately in this chapter for the sake of clarity, these should be taught together.)

Although it has been defined in a variety of ways (Cunningham & Moore, 1986), in this book, the **main idea** is a summary statement that includes the other details in a paragraph or longer piece; it is what all the sentences are about. Despite the importance of main ideas, little is known about how elementary and middle school students generate them.

Adept readers tend to use either a whole-to-part strategy, in which they draft or hypothesize the whole and confirm it by reading the parts, or a part-to-whole strategy, in which they note important parts, construct relationships among them, and compose a main idea statement (Afflerbach, 1990; Afflerbach & Johnston, 1986). The whole-to-part strategy fits best with a schema theory of comprehension; the part-to-whole strategy exemplifies the construction of a situation model.

Because of its complexity and importance, main idea comprehension has to be taught step by step. Instruction should include presenting underlying processes, one of which is classifying.

Classifying. Determining the main idea is partly a classification skill. The main idea statement is a category label for all or most of the details in the piece. The best way to convey the concept of a main idea and to provide instruction in its underlying cognitive process is to have students classify a series of objects or words (Baumann, 1986; Johnson & Kress, 1965; Williams, 1986b).

To demonstrate classifying to younger students, bring in a variety of objects and indicate how they might be sorted. For example, display an apple, orange, pear, banana, and book, and ask students to tell which go together. Discuss why the book does not belong. Put the objects in a box. Tell students you want to label the box so that you know what is in it and ask them what word you might use. Students can name other objects that might be put in the box, with a discussion of why they belong there. Follow a similar procedure with tools, toys, and other objects.

Once students have grasped the idea of classifying objects, have them classify words. First, give them lists of words that include labels. Model how you would go about choosing the category label. Tell students that you are looking for a word that tells about all the others. Read a series of related words that have been written on the board: *cats, fish, pets, dogs*. Model how you would choose *pets* as the label because it includes the other three words. After working through several sample series of words, have students complete exercises similar to the following, which contains words that are easy enough for first-graders. For older students, select more challenging items.

ball	toys	blocks	doll
oak	trees	maple	pine
fruit	apple	peach	banana

To vary the activity, include an item in the series that does not belong (*train, bus, car, ball*) and have students identify it. Also, list a series of related items (*three, nine, four, two*) and let students supply a category label.

After students are able to categorize words with ease, have them categorize groups of sentences by identifying the one that tells about all the others. Call this the main idea sentence. To construct exercises of this type, locate brief paragraphs that have an explicitly stated main idea. Write the sentences in list form, and have students point out which sentence tells about all the others. Groups of sentences similar to the following can be used:

The car door locks were frozen.

Small children refused to venture from their warm homes.

It was the coldest day that anyone could remember.

The temperature was twenty below zero.

The lake was frozen solid.

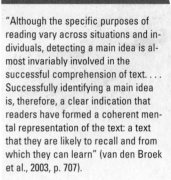

HIGHER-LEVEL LITERACY

"Although the specific purposes of reading vary across situations and individuals, detecting a main idea is almost invariably involved in the successful comprehension of text. . . . Successfully identifying a main idea is, therefore, a clear indication that readers have formed a coherent mental representation of the text: a text that they are likely to recall and from which they can learn" (van den Broek et al., 2003, p. 707).

Model the process of choosing the most inclusive sentence, thinking aloud as you choose it. Let students see that the process involves checking each sentence to determine which one includes all the others and then examining the other sentences to make sure that each one can be included under the main sentence. In your explanation, you might use the analogy of a roof. Explain that the main idea sentence is like a roof. The other sentences contain details that hold up the roof. They are like the walls that support a roof. As part of the process, explain how pointing out the inclusive sentence will help them find main ideas in their reading. After students have acquired a concept of an inclusive sentence, have students complete a series of similar exercises under your guidance.

Recognizing Topic Sentences.   Once students have a sense of what a main idea is, begin working with brief paragraphs that contain an explicitly stated main idea, a sentence that tells about all the others. Explain that the main idea sentence is called a topic sentence because it contains the topic of the paragraph. It is often the first sentence of a paragraph, but may be last or in the middle. Move the topic sentence in a sample paragraph around to show students how it could make sense in a number of positions. Also point out how the details in the paragraph support the main idea.

Provide students with guided practice in locating topic sentences and supporting details in paragraphs. Locating supporting details is like proving a problem in math: If the details do not support the sentence chosen as the topic sentence, the student has probably not located the real topic sentence. Take practice paragraphs from children's periodicals, books, and textbooks. At first, select paragraphs in which the main idea sentence comes first, as this is the easiest organizational pattern to understand. Students have more difficulty with paragraphs in which the topic sentence occurs last (Kimmel & MacGinitie, 1984). Make sure to choose paragraphs that are interesting and well written. Students will then enjoy the activity more and will pick up incidental information. Using real books and periodicals also demonstrates that recognizing topic sentences is a practical activity, one students can use in their everyday reading. It also makes the practice more realistic because students will be working with the kinds of material they actually read rather than with paragraphs contrived for teaching the main idea. The following is an example of a paragraph that might be used:

> The largest members of the cat family are truly large. They range in size from about 6 feet to 12 feet long, measured from the tips of their noses to the tips of their tails. They weigh from 50 to 500 pounds, and are 22 to 44 inches tall at the shoulder. (Thompson, 1998, p. 26)

Presenting paragraphs that contain topic sentences makes sense in the beginning stages of instruction, as it simplifies identifying the main idea, but you must emphasize that not all paragraphs contain topic sentences. In fact, most do not. Baumann and Serra (1984) found that only 44 percent of the paragraphs in elementary social studies textbooks had explicitly stated main ideas, and only 27 percent of the main ideas occurred in the opening sentence.

Even when the main idea is explicitly stated and is in the opening sentence, readers must still infer that the first sentence tells what the rest of the paragraph is about. Young readers and poor readers tend to select the first sentence as the topic sentence almost automatically (Gold & Fleisher, 1986). To prevent this, ask them to check by specifying the supporting details in this paragraph and to see whether all the other sentences support the first one (Duffelmeyer, 1985). If that is the case, the first sentence is the topic sentence. If not, the students should search for a sentence that does serve that function.

Selecting or Constructing the Main Idea

Most passages do not have an explicitly stated main idea, so it must be constructed. Students might use the following steps (which should be posted in the classroom, as given here or in adapted form) to select a stated main idea or construct a main idea if it is not stated:

HIGHER-LEVEL LITERACY

Young students find it easier to select titles than to identify main idea statements. Titles are more familiar and more concrete. Students' ability to identify main ideas improves with age (van den Broek et al., 2003).

FYI

▪ Although well-formed paragraphs might be used for initial instruction in main ideas, students should apply their strategies to informational trade books and texts. Authors do not begin each paragraph with a main idea. Often, the main idea is implied, and some paragraphs simply provide an introduction or additional information and lack a clear-cut main idea.

▪ In addition to modeling strategy use and providing practice, develop with students a series of steps to be followed in order to carry out the strategy, such as those listed for determining the main idea.

1. Use the heading, title, or first sentence to make a hypothesis (careful guess) as to what the main idea is.

2. Read each sentence and see whether it supports the hypothesis. If not, revise the hypothesis.

3. If you can't make a hypothesis about what the main idea is, see what all or most of the sentences have in common or are talking about.

4. Select a sentence or make a sentence that tells what all the sentences are about.

One problem that students have in recognizing or generating main ideas is a tendency to focus on a narrow statement of a single detail instead of on a broad statement that includes all the essential information in a paragraph (Williams, 1986a). As students work with paragraphs, you might use a series of prompts to help them identify what the paragraph is about. Start off by asking them what the general topic of the paragraph is, and then ask them to identify the specific topic and check whether all the details support it. For instance, using the following simple paragraph about robots, you might ask, "What is the general topic of the paragraph? What is the specific topic? What does the paragraph tell us about robots?"

> Robots help us in many ways. Robots work in factories. They help put cars and TVs together. In some offices, robots deliver the mail. And in some hospitals, robots bring food to sick people. A new kind of robot can mow lawns. And some day there may even be robots that can take out the trash and take the dog for a walk.

If students provide the correct specific topic, ask them to verify their response. The class should go over each sentence to determine whether it tells how robots help out. If, on the other hand, students supply a supporting detail rather than a statement of the specific topic, have the class examine the detail to see if it encompassed all the other details in the paragraph. Lesson 6.1 presents suggestions for teaching how to determine the main idea.

Lesson 6.1

Determining the Main Idea and Its Supporting Details

Step 1. Introducing the strategy
Explain what main ideas and supporting details are and why it is important to locate and understand them in reading. Give a clear definition of what a main idea is—it tells what the paragraph or section is all about. Provide examples of main ideas.

Step 2. Modeling the process
Show how you would go about determining a main idea and its supporting details. Starting off with well-constructed paragraphs, demonstrate the hypothesis strategy, because this is the strategy most frequently used by adept readers. Show students how you would use a title, heading, graphic clues, and the apparent topic sentence to predict the main idea. Then confirm or revise your hypothesis as you read and see whether the details support your hypothesized main idea. (Even if the main idea is directly stated, it is still necessary to use a hypothesis or other strategy, because readers cannot be sure that the sentence is indeed a topic sentence until they read the rest of the paragraph.)

In subsequent lessons that tackle paragraphs with implied main ideas and no titles or headings that could be clues to the main idea, you may have to use a part-to-whole

FYI

Comprehension instruction requires scaffolding. Teachers provide examples, modeling, explicit instruction, prompts, and discussions in helping students learn strategies (Dole, Duffy, Roehler, & Pearson, 1991). In time, the scaffolding is reduced, and the students apply the strategies independently.

strategy. Note the details in such a paragraph and then construct a main idea statement after seeing how the details are related or what they have in common. A part-to-whole strategy is best taught after students have a firm grasp of the hypothesis-confirmation strategy. Model the process with a variety of paragraphs.

Step 3. Guided practice

Have students derive main ideas from brief, well-constructed paragraphs. If possible, choose paragraphs that cover familiar topics, as it is easier to construct main ideas when the content and vocabulary are known. Students face a double burden when they must grapple with difficult concepts and vocabulary while trying to construct a main idea. Although shorter paragraphs should be used in the beginning stages, have students gradually apply this skill to longer pieces, such as selections from content-area textbooks.

Step 4. Independent practice and application

Have students derive main ideas and supporting details in children's books, textbooks, periodicals, and other materials that they read on their own. From well-written, well-organized science or social studies textbooks or children's books, choose sections that convey an overall main idea or theme and develop it in several paragraphs. At first, choose pieces that have an explicitly stated main idea. Show students how you would use a hypothesis strategy to derive the main idea. Using a selection similar to that illustrated in Figure 6.2, demonstrate how you would use the heading ("Eggs-traordinary" Eggs!), the subheadings, and the illustrations to guess what the main idea of the section is. Lead students to see that the main idea seems to be stated in the heading and that the main idea of each paragraph is found in the first one or two sentences.

Step 5. Assessment and reteaching

Observe students as they obtain main ideas from a variety of passages in texts and trade books. Note how well they can do the following:

Identify the main idea and supporting details in a brief, well constructed paragraph in which the main idea is directly stated in the first sentence.

Identify the main idea and supporting details in a brief, well-constructed paragraph in which the main idea is directly stated in the middle or end of the paragraph.

Infer the main idea in a well-constructed paragraph in which the main idea is not directly stated.

Identify or infer the main idea in general reading.

Based on the results of your assessment, review and reteach.

Student Strategies

Determining the Main Idea

In a discussion with students, create a series of steps that they might use to locate or construct the main idea. Make a chart containing the steps, and put it in a prominent place so that students can refer to it while reading. (Use the steps listed on p. 283 or an adaptation of them.)

■■■ **FIGURE 6.2   Main Ideas in a Science Text**

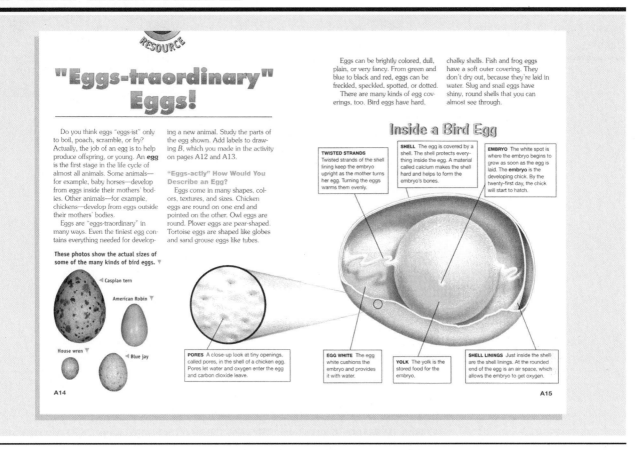

From *Science Discovery Works Grade 3* by Carolyn Sumners, et al. © by Silver Burdett Ginn, Simon & Schuster Education Group. Used by permission.

Extending the Ability to Construct the Main Idea.   Take advantage of discussions of selections that students have read and other naturally occurring opportunities to apply and extend the skill of constructing main ideas. Note how important details are related to the main idea of a selection. Also apply the concept to writing. Have students create and develop topic sentences on nonfiction subjects of their own choosing.

Graphic displays can help students identify the topic sentence and its supporting details. Use a simplified semantic map, which is sometimes called a *spider web* when the supporting details are of equal importance, as shown in Figure 6.3. Use a linear display like that in Figure 6.4 when the piece has a sequential order, that is, when the ideas are listed in order of occurrence.

Main idea instruction is more appropriate for nonfiction than for fiction. Fiction has a theme rather than a main idea. Identifying a theme can be subtler and more complex than noting a main idea. Most children's fiction also has a central problem that gives coherence to the story (Moldofsky, 1983).

Reviewing the Strategy

Learning a strategy may take a month or more. In subsequent lessons, review and extend the strategy. To review the strategy, ask the following kinds of questions:

- What strategy are we learning to use? (main idea)
- How does this strategy help us? (helps us understand and remember what we read; helps us organize important details)

FYI

Like teaching other strategies, teaching students to identify main ideas involves a gradual release of responsibility. As students grow in skill, they gradually take responsibility for their own learning.

■■■ **FIGURE 6.3**
Spider Web for Main Idea and Equally Important Supporting Details

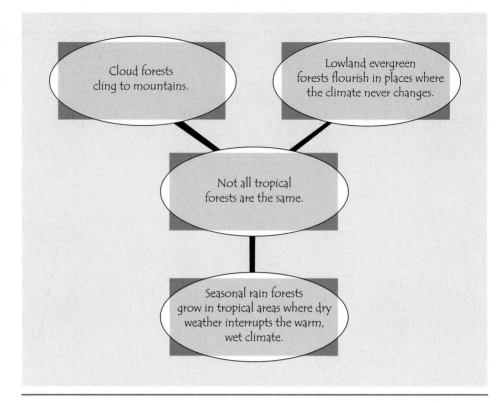

- When do we use this strategy? (with nonfiction)
- How do we use this strategy? (Review the steps presented on p. 283.) Also ask students to tell about instances when they used the strategy on their own (Scott, 1998).

Reinforcement Activities

Main Idea Construction

- Cut out newspaper headlines and titles of articles, and have students match them with the articles.
- Have students classify lists of items.
- When discussing selections that students have read, include questions that require them to identify and/or construct a main idea.

■■■ **FIGURE 6.4**
Main Idea and Details in Sequential Display

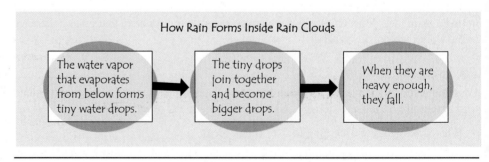

How Rain Forms Inside Rain Clouds

The water vapor that evaporates from below forms tiny water drops. → The tiny drops join together and become bigger drops. → When they are heavy enough, they fall.

Text from *Weather Words,* by G. Gibbons, 1990, New York: Holiday House.

▪▪▪ Checkup ▪▪▪

1. What is the role of organizational strategies?
2. What are the steps in teaching students to select or construct the main idea?
3. How might the main idea strategy be reviewed and extended?

▪▪▪

Determining the Relative Importance of Information

The ability to determine what is important in a selection is a key factor in comprehension, as it keeps readers from drowning in a sea of details or having to cull out trivial information. Identifying main ideas and determining the relative importance of information should be taught together. Determination of what is important in a selection is often dependent on the derivation of the main idea. Once they know the main idea, readers are in a better position to identify the relative importance of information and to construct a situation model of the text. For instance, once readers know that the main idea of an article is how to use a video camera, they can assume that the steps in the process will be the important details. Readers have to ask themselves which details support or explain a selection's main idea or, if the article is especially rich in details, which are the most important. If an article cites twenty capabilities of lasers, readers might decide which five are most essential or group similar capabilities.

Semantic maps and other graphic organizers can help students organize information.

Adept readers will use textual clues to help determine which details are most important. A carefully written text might state which details are essential. Or the reader might note those details that are discussed first and given the most print. Minor details might be signaled by words such as *also*, as in the sentence "Laser readers are also used to check out books in many libraries and to check times in many competitive sports."

Expert readers also use text structure, relational terms, and repetition of words or concepts to determine importance. Relational terms and expressions such as "most important of all" and "three main causes" help readers determine important ideas. A repeated word or concept is an especially useful clue. The structure of the piece also gives clues as to which details are most essential (Afflerbach & Johnston, 1986). With a problem–solution organization, an adept reader will seek out the problem and solution and ignore extraneous descriptions or examples.

In addition to using textual clues, readers can use their schemata or background knowledge to determine what is important. A student who raises tropical fish would seek out certain kinds of information when reading about a new species, such as a description of the species, its habits, and where it is found. The purpose for reading is also a factor. A student who is contemplating buying a new tropical fish will realize that details on cost and care are significant.

Expert readers also use their beliefs about the author's intention to determine which details are essential and which are not (Afflerbach & Johnston, 1986). Expert readers are able to step back from the text and consider the author's purpose. If, for instance, the author is trying to establish that a certain point is true, the reader will seek out the details or examples the author provides as proof of the contention. Lesson 6.2 includes some steps that might be used to help students determine important information.

Lesson 6.2

Determining Important Details

Step 1. Introduction of strategy

Explain what is meant by "important details" and why being able to identify them is an essential skill. Display and discuss several short selections that contain both important and unimportant information, and help students discriminate between the two.

Step 2. Model the process

Determine important information in a sample paragraph. Show how you would use contextual clues: topic sentences, placement of ideas, and graphic aids. In another session, demonstrate how you might use knowledge of the topic or your purpose for reading.

Step 3. Guided practice

Provide guidance as students determine important information in a selection. Start with well-structured texts that supply plenty of clues and gradually work up to selections from their basal readers, content-area textbooks, library books, or periodicals. Ask students to justify their choice of important details, because this skill is somewhat subjective.

Step 4. Application

Have students note important ideas in materials that they read independently. The more experience students have with varied reading materials and the broader and deeper their knowledge base, the better prepared they will be to determine the relative importance of information. Set purposes that lead students to grasp essential information. Ask questions that focus on important information. By asking such questions, you will be modeling the kinds of questions that students should be asking themselves before they read and as they read.

Step 5. Assessment and reteaching

During discussions of selections that have been read, ask questions that require selecting important details. Take note of students' performance. Ask the kinds of questions that provide insight into students' reasoning processes. Supply on-the-spot help if students need it. Also, plan reteaching lessons if needed.

Reviewing the Strategy

In subsequent lessons, review and extend the strategy. To review the strategy, ask the following kinds of questions:

- What strategy are we learning to use? (understanding important ideas)
- How does this strategy help us? (helps us understand and remember important details; keeps us from getting lost in too many details)
- When do we use this strategy? (with nonfiction)
- How do we use this strategy? (The following steps should be posted in the classroom)
  1. Use the title, heading, and first sentence to make a hypothesis (careful guess) about what the main idea will be.
  2. Read the selection to see whether you have chosen the right main idea. If not, change it.
  3. Choose the most important details. These will be details that support the main idea. The author might signal the most important details by using phrases such as "most important of all" (Scott, 1998).

BUILDING LANGUAGE

Having students talk about strategies they are using, especially when they describe specific instances of strategy use, develops academic language.

Reinforcement Activities

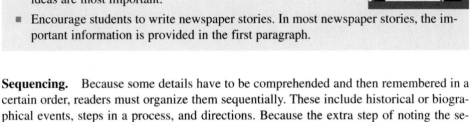

Determining Importance of Information

- Have students predict the important ideas in a selection they are about to read.

- After they have read a selection, ask students to tell which ideas are most important.

- Encourage students to write newspaper stories. In most newspaper stories, the important information is provided in the first paragraph.

Sequencing.   Because some details have to be comprehended and then remembered in a certain order, readers must organize them sequentially. These include historical or biographical events, steps in a process, and directions. Because the extra step of noting the sequence is involved, organizing sequential details often poses special problems, especially for younger readers. To introduce sequence, have students tell about some simple sequential activities in which they engage, such as washing dishes, playing a favorite game, or assembling a puzzle. Discuss the order of the activities, and place them on the chalkboard using cue words such as *first, second, next, then, before, last,* and *after.*

Place lists of other events on the chalkboard, and ask students to put them in order. Start with a series of three or four events for younger students and work up to six or seven items for more advanced readers. Encourage students to use their sense of the situation or the process to put the events in order. Show how cue words help indicate sequence.

After students have become adept at this activity, let them apply their skill to stories and articles. To help them become aware of the sequence of a story, have them map out the main events, showing how the story progresses to its climax and the resolution of a problem. Help students create causal links between events in a story, as this aids retention (McNamara, Miller, & Bransford, 1991).

For biographies and historical accounts, show students how to use dates to keep events in order. Show students books like *The Ancient Greeks* (Shuter, 1997) and *Leonardo da Vinci* (Malam, 1998), in which the authors use time lines or chronologies to help readers keep track of key events. When time lines have not been included in a selection, encourage students to create them to help keep a sequence of events in order. As students read about the steps in a process (e.g., a caterpillar becoming a butterfly), have them note the sequence and visualize it if possible. Show them how they might use a graphic organizer to display a process or chain of events. Figure 6.5 presents a chain map showing how radar works.

Following Directions.   Following directions is a natural outgrowth of sequencing. As students read directions, remind them to make use of cue words such as *first, next,* and *last.* Also introduce words such as *list, match,* and *underline,* which are frequently found in directions and with which young children often have difficulty (Boehm, 1971). Students can

FYI

To provide practice with the sequence of steps in a process, you might encourage students to read such books as *Howling Hurricanes* (Richards, 2002) or *Recycle! A Handbook for Kids* (Gibbons, 1992).

USING TECHNOLOGY

HyperHistory Online presents a variety of time lines for famous people and key events.
http://www.hyperhistory.com/online_n2/History_n2/a.html

■■■ **FIGURE 6.5**   **A Chain Map**

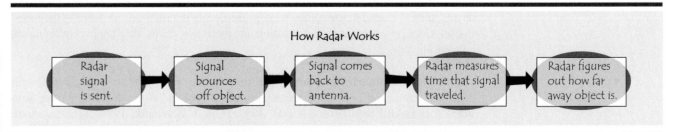

How Radar Works

Radar signal is sent. → Signal bounces off object. → Signal comes back to antenna. → Radar measures time that signal traveled. → Radar figures out how far away object is.

FYI

■ Being able to comprehend and follow directions is more important than ever. Many items that we purchase come unassembled. And many appliances have to be programmed. Downloading a file from the Internet or using a new program requires being able to follow sophisticated directions.

■ Use writing to support reading. Encourage students to write a series of directions for a favorite game or other activity. Have students work in pairs. The partners can check the clarity of each other's directions by trying them out and seeing whether they can follow them.

Adapting Instruction for Struggling Readers and Writers

Have students practice following directions by reading and responding to books such as those published by Klutz Press that involve making and doing things.

BUILDING LANGUAGE

Demonstrate how you would explain a series of directions. Emphasize the use of signal words such as *first, second, last,* and phrases such as "gather all materials" and "next step" that occur frequently in directions. Have students give directions orally and in writing.

create mental models of directions by visually depicting the process, using an accompanying diagram or other illustration, or by describing the steps. If possible, have students carry out the procedures outlined in the directions.

Student Strategies

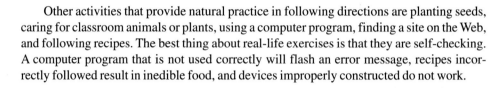

Following Directions

Students can use these steps (which should be posted for them to refer to) to follow directions:

■ Read the directions to get an overview.

■ Look at any pictures or diagrams that go along with the directions.

■ Make sure all parts have been included.

■ Get all necessary tools, materials, or ingredients.

■ Read and follow each step. Use any pictures or diagrams as an aid.

Other activities that provide natural practice in following directions are planting seeds, caring for classroom animals or plants, using a computer program, finding a site on the Web, and following recipes. The best thing about real-life exercises is that they are self-checking. A computer program that is not used correctly will flash an error message, recipes incorrectly followed result in inedible food, and devices improperly constructed do not work.

Summarizing

What is the most effective comprehension strategy of all? When five experts in learning examined the research on comprehension in order to discover which strategies seemed to have the greatest payoff and were the most solidly grounded in research, they listed summarization first (Pressley, Johnson, Symons, McGoldrick, & Kurita, 1989). Summarization, which builds on the organizational strategy of determining main ideas and supporting details, improves comprehension and increases retention. It is also a metacognitive means of monitoring, through which students can evaluate their understanding of a passage that they have just read. If a student has not comprehended a selection, she or he is almost certain to have difficulty summarizing it. Summarizing also helps students understand the structure of text. In writing a summary, students are brought face-to-face with the organization of a piece of writing. This should help them detect the underlying structure of the text, which is a key to understanding text and writing effective summaries (Touchstone Applied Science Associates, 1997).

Summarizing is a complex skill that takes years to develop. Even college students may have difficulty summarizing. Young children realize that a summary is a retelling of material; however, they have difficulty determining what points should be included in a summary. The view of young students seems to be egocentric: They choose details that are personally interesting rather than selecting details that seem important from the author's point of view. Young students also have difficulty with the procedures necessary to summarize (Hidi & Anderson, 1986). They delete information but do not combine or condense details; they also tend to use a copy strategy, recording details word for word in their summaries. Once they learn to put information into their own words, they begin combining and condensing.

Introducing Summarizing. Summaries need not be written. All of us make oral summaries of movie and book plots, events, conversations, and so on. Because writing summaries can be difficult (Brown & Day, 1983; Hare & Borchardt, 1984), teachers should first develop students' ability to summarize orally.

Retelling is a natural way to lead into summarizing. Young children tend to recount every incident in a story and give every detail about a topic. Help them structure their retellings so as to emphasize major events and main ideas. Ask questions like these: "What were the two most important things that the main character did? What were the three main things that happened in the story? What are the main things you learned about robots? What are the main ways in which robots are used?" (See Chapter 7 for a fuller discussion of retelling.)

From kindergarten on, teachers can model the process of summarizing by providing summaries of selections read, especially nonfiction, and of discussions and directions. As students get into content-area material, they can be directed to pay special attention to chapter summaries. Although they may not be capable of writing well-formed summaries until the upper elementary or middle school grades, they can begin learning the skill in developmentally appropriate ways from their very first years of school. With younger and less able students, emphasize inclusion of the most important information in a summary. As students become proficient in extracting the most essential information, teach techniques for condensing information.

Certain activities can build summarizing or its underlying skills. Encourage students to use titles, illustrations, topic sentences, headings, and other textual clues. In Taylor's (1986) study, many students failed to use the title and topic sentence when composing their summaries, although both contained the main idea of the selection. Teach students how to read expository text. Ineffectual summarizers read such works as though they are fiction and so fail to note textual cues that could help them create better summaries (Taylor, 1986). Have students compose oral summaries of stories, articles, and class discussions. Also compose group summaries.

To create a group summary, read an informational article aloud and ask students what the most important points are. After listing the points on the board, have the class summarize them. Group summaries provide preparation for the creation of independent summaries (Moore, Moore, Cunningham, & Cunningham, 1986).

Summarizing can be an excellent device for checking comprehension. Encourage students to stop after reading key sections of expository text and mentally summarize the materials. Once they have some ability to identify relevant details, make use of structural cues, and identify and construct main ideas, they are ready for a more formal type of instruction in summarizing.

Presenting Summarizing Skills.   When teaching summarizing, begin with shorter, easier text. Texts that are shorter and easier to comprehend are easier to summarize. Also, start with narrative text, which is easier than expository text to summarize (Hidi & Anderson, 1986). Focus on the content rather than the form of the summaries. After students become accustomed to summarizing essential details, stress the need for well-formed, polished summaries. Because many students have great difficulty determining which details are important, have them list important details. Discuss these lists before they compose their summaries. Also have students create semantic maps before writing summaries. In addition to helping students select important information, such maps may help them detect important relationships among key ideas. One study found that students who constructed maps before summarizing used a greater number of cohesive ties than those who did not (Ruddell & Boyle, 1989).

■ ■ ■ Checkup ■ ■ ■

1. In addition to identifying the main idea, what are the other key organizational strategies?

2. How might these strategies be taught?

3. What is the most effective organizational strategy? Why is this strategy said to be most effective?

■ ■ ■

Teaching Elaboration Strategies

Elaboration is a generative activity in which the reader constructs connections between information from text and prior knowledge. Like organizational strategies, elaboration strategies are employed both during reading and after reading. The reader generates inferences, images, questions, judgments, and other elaborations. Use of elaboration strategies increased comprehension by 50 percent in a number of studies (Linden & Wittrock, 1981).

Making Inferences

Although children have the cognitive ability to draw inferences, some do not do so spontaneously. A probable cause of this deficiency is a lack of background information about the topic or the failure to process information in the text that would foster drawing inferences. Or students may not realize that inferences are necessary. They might believe that only literal comprehension is called for (Westby, 1999). Two approaches enhance the ability to make inferences: building background and teaching specific strategies for making inferences. However, sustained instruction is required. When students were taught processes for making inferences, no significant change was noted until after four weeks of teaching. The effects were long-lasting, and, as a side benefit, literal comprehension improved (Dewitz, Carr, & Patberg, 1987).

There are two kinds of inferences: schema-based and text-based (Winne, Graham, & Prock, 1993). Schema-based inferences depend on prior knowledge. For instance, inferring from the sentence "They rode into the sunset" that it was late in the day and the riders were heading west is schema-based. The reader uses her or his schema for the position of the sun to infer approximate time and direction. Schema-based inferences allow the reader to elaborate on the text by adding information that has been implied by the author. A text-based inference is one that requires putting together two or more pieces of information from the text. Reading that peanuts have more food energy than sugar and that a pound of peanut butter has more protein than thirty-two eggs but more fat than ice cream, the reader might put all this information together to infer that peanuts are nutritious but fattening.

Making inferences is the most important elaboration strategy. Much of the information in a piece, especially fiction, is implied. Authors show and dramatize rather than tell. Instead of directly stating that a main character is a liar, the author dramatizes situations in which the character lies. This is true even in the simplest of stories. For instance, in the third paragraph of *The Tale of Peter Rabbit*, Beatrix Potter (1908) wrote:

> "Now, my dears," said old Mrs. Rabbit one morning, "you may go into the field or down the lane, but don't go into Mr. McGregor's garden. Your Father had an accident there. He was put in a pie by Mrs. McGregor."

The reader must infer that Father was killed by Mr. McGregor and that Mr. McGregor will harm any rabbits that he catches in his garden. The reader might also infer that the reason Mr. McGregor does not like rabbits is that they eat the vegetables in his garden. None of this is stated, so the reader must use his schema for rabbits and gardens, together with his comprehension of the story, to produce a series of inferences. In a sense, the author erects the story's framework, and the reader must construct the full meaning by filling in the missing parts.

■ **Elaboration** refers to additional processing of text by a reader, which may result in improved comprehension and recall. Elaboration involves building connections between one's background knowledge and the text or integrating new information through manipulating or transforming it.

Activating prior knowledge helps students make inferences. For instance, if the teacher discusses the fact that rabbits anger gardeners by nibbling their vegetables before students read *The Tale of Peter Rabbit*, they will be much more likely to draw appropriate inferences from the passage previously cited. Asking questions that require students to make inferences also helps. It increases both their ability and their inclination to make inferences (Hansen, 1981).

Although above-average students make more inferences than average ones (Carr, 1983), below-average readers can be taught the skill. Hansen and Pearson (1982) combined activation of prior knowledge, direct instruction in an inference-making strategy, posing of inferential questions, and predicting to create a series of lessons in which poor readers improved to such an extent that their inferential comprehension became equal to that of good readers. Here is how Hansen and Pearson's prior knowledge–prediction strategy works:

1. The teacher reads the story and analyzes it for two or three important ideas.

2. For each important idea, the teacher creates a previous-experience question that elicits from students any similar experiences that they may have had. This is a have-you-ever question (Pearson, 1985).

3. For each previous-experience question, an accompanying prediction question is created. This is a what-do-you-think-will-happen question.

4. Students read the selection to check their predictions.

5. Students discuss their predictions. Inferential questions, especially those related to the key ideas, are discussed.

The following important ideas, previous-experience questions, and prediction questions were used in the study (Pearson, 1985, Appendix B):

Important idea number 1: Even adults can be afraid of things.

Previous-experience question: Tell something an adult you know is afraid of.

Prediction question: In the story, Cousin Alma is afraid of something even though she is an adult. What do you think it is?

Important idea number 2: People sometimes act more bravely than they feel.

Previous-experience question: Tell about how you acted some time when you were afraid and tried not to show it.

Prediction question: How do you think that Fats, the boy in the story, will act when he is afraid and tries not to show it?

Important idea number 3: Our experience sometimes convinces us that we are capable of doing things we thought we couldn't do.

Previous-experience question: Tell about a time when you were able to do something you thought you couldn't do.

Prediction question: In the story, what do you think Cousin Alma is able to do that she thought she couldn't do?

An important element of the technique is the discussion, with students' responses acting as a catalyst. One student's answer reminds others of similar experiences that they have had but do not think apply. For example, a girl mentioning that her uncle is afraid of snakes might trigger in another student the memory that his grandfather is afraid of dogs, even small ones. The teacher also emphasizes that students should compare their real-life experiences with events in the story.

In addition to having background activated and being asked inferential questions, students should be taught a strategy for making inferences. Gordon (1985) mapped out a five-step process, which is outlined in Lesson 6.3.

 Adapting Instruction for Struggling Readers and Writers

As Hansen and Pearson (1982) noted, poor readers are typically asked literal questions, so their inferential skills are underdeveloped. If carefully taught, lower-achieving readers can make inferences.

Lesson 6.3

Making Inferences

Step 1. Explaining the skill

The teacher explains what the skill is, why it is important, and when and how it is used. This explanation might be illustrated with examples.

Step 2. Modeling the process

While modeling how inferences are made with a brief piece of text written on the chalkboard, the teacher reveals her or his thinking processes: "It says here that Jim thought Fred would make a great center when he first saw him walk into the classroom. The center is usually the tallest person on a basketball team, so I inferred that Fred is tall." The teacher also models the process with several other selections, so students see that inferences can be drawn from a variety of materials.

Step 3. Sharing the task

Students are asked to take part in making inferences. The teacher asks an inferential question about a brief sample paragraph or excerpt and then answers it. The students supply supporting evidence for the inference from the selection itself and from their background knowledge. The reasoning processes involved in making the inference are discussed. The teacher stresses the need to substantiate inferences with details from the story.

Step 4. Reversing the process

The teacher asks an inferential question and the students supply the inference. The teacher provides the evidence. As an alternative, the teacher might supply the evidence and have the students draw an inference based on it. Either way, a discussion of reasoning processes follows.

Step 5. Integrating the process

The teacher just asks the inferential question. The students both make the inference and supply the evidence. As a final step, students might create their own inferential questions and then supply the answers and evidence. Basically, the procedure turns responsibility for the strategy over to students.

Step 6. Application

The students apply the process to texts and trade books.

Step 7. Assessment

Observe students as they make inferences while reading texts and trade books. Note how well they can do the following:

Make an inference based on two or more pieces of information in the text.

Make an inference based on information in the text and their own background knowledge.

Find support for an inference.

Make increasingly sophisticated inferences.

FYI

Although making inferences is more difficult than understanding the literal content of a text, it isn't necessary for students to master literal comprehension before they are instructed in making inferences. Both can and should be taught simultaneously.

Reviewing the Strategy.   In subsequent lessons, review and extend the strategy. To review the strategy, ask the following kinds of questions:

- What strategy are we learning to use? (making inferences)
- How does this strategy help us? (helps us to read between the lines, to fill in details that the author has hinted at but has not directly stated)

■ When do we use this strategy? (when we have to put together two or more pieces of information in a story or when the author has hinted at but not directly stated information)

■ How do we use this strategy? (Post these steps for students to refer to.)

1. As you read, think, "What is the author suggesting here?"
2. Put together pieces of information from the story or put together information from the story with what you know.
3. Make an inference or come to a conclusion.

Using QAR

Some students are text-bound and may not realize that answers to some questions require putting together several pieces of information from the reading or using their background of experience plus that information to draw inferences. Teachers frequently hear students lament that the answer is not in the book; those students do not know how to construct the answer from prior knowledge and textual content (Carr, Dewitz, & Patberg, 1989). Such readers may benefit from using QAR (question–answer relationship), in which questions are described as having the following four levels, based on where the answers are found (International Reading Association, 1988):

Students learn to locate evidence for inferences they have made.

1. *Right there.* The answer is found within a single sentence in the text.

2. *Put together.* The answer is found in several sentences in the text.

3. *On my own.* The answer is in the student's background of knowledge.

4. *Writer and me.* A combination of information from the text and the reader's background is required to answer the question.

In a series of studies, Raphael (1984) observed that students' comprehension improved when they were introduced to the concept of QAR and given extensive training in locating the source of the answer. Initially, they worked with sentences and very short paragraphs, but they progressed to 400-word selections. Raphael (1986) recommended starting with two categories of answers: "in the book" and "in my head." This would be especially helpful when working with elementary students. "In the book" includes answers that are "right there" or require "putting together." "In my head" items are "on my own" and "writer and me" answers. Based on Raphael's (1986) suggestions, QAR might be presented in the manner described in Lesson 6.4.

 6.4

Presenting QAR

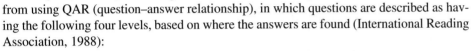

Step 1. Introducing the concept of QAR

Introduce the concept by writing on the board a paragraph similar to the following:

> Andy let the first pitch go by. It was too low. The second pitch was too high. But the third toss was letter high. Andy lined it over the left fielder's outstretched glove.

Ask a series of literal questions: "Which pitch did Andy hit? Where did the ball go? Why didn't Andy swing at the first pitch? The second pitch?" Lead students to see that the answers to these questions are "in the book."

Next, ask a series of questions that depend on the readers' background: "What game was Andy playing? What do you think Andy did after he hit the ball? Do you think he

FYI

■ As Alvermann and Phelps (1994) explain, the QAR progression is oversimplified. Readers do not begin by comprehending information that is right there, then move on to putting it together, and end up with on-my-own or writer-and-me responses. These processes operate simultaneously and interact with each other. However, QAR is a useful way of viewing the process of question answering.

■ To provide practice with making inferences at all levels, have students infer character traits based on the character's actions, because authors typically let a character's actions show what kind of a person the character is. In addition, even kindergartners make inferences about people based on their actions.

USING TECHNOLOGY

eThemes is an extensive database of reading and writing and other educational resources organized around themes. It lists a number of excellent sites for building comprehension.
http://www.emints.org/ethemes

scored a run? Why or why not?" Show students that the answers to these questions depend on their knowledge of baseball. Discuss the fact that these answers are "in my head."

Step 2. Extending the concept of QAR

After students have mastered the concept of "in the book" and "in my head," extend the in-the-book category to include both "right there" and "put together." Once students have a solid working knowledge of these, expand the in-my-head category to include both "on my own" and "writer and me." The major difference between these two is whether the student has to read the text for the question to make sense. For instance, the question "Do you think Andy's hit was a home run?" requires knowledge of baseball and information from the story. The question "How do you feel when you get a hit?" involves only experience in hitting a baseball.

Step 3. Providing practice

Provide ample opportunity for guided and independent practice. Also refine and extend students' awareness of sources for answers and methods for constructing responses.

Difficulties in Making Inferences

Some students' responses to inference questions are too specific. In addition to knowing that they can use both text and background knowledge as sources of information, students need to learn to gather all the information that is pertinent (McCormick, 1992). They need to base their inferences on several pieces of textual or background information. Some students choose the wrong information on which to base their inferences, and others do not use the text at all. They overrely on prior knowledge or do not recall or use sufficient pertinent text to make valid inferences (McCormick, 1992). This is especially true of poor readers.

Case Study

Making Comprehension Connections

Mark had difficulty integrating information from different parts of an article and had problems connecting ideas. He often used his background knowledge to answer questions rather than referring to the text. Mark had to learn how to use the text to construct meaning. Mark also had difficulty making inferences. As a starting point, Mark's teacher introduced QAR. QAR might help Mark understand where the answers to questions could be found and highlight the importance of the text and also the importance of combining information from text with background knowledge. His teacher hoped that QAR would help Mark see that "comprehension involves the search for and construction of meaning" (Dewitz & Dewitz, 2003, p. 432). Direct instruction in making text-based inferences was accompanied by modeling and think-alouds. The teacher chose texts that required the kinds of strategies and thinking processes that were being taught.

Content-area texts were chosen because they embody the kinds of reading that Mark would be required to do. When planning a lesson, the teacher read each text twice, once to get an overview of the text and once to determine the kinds of strategies and cognitive process that would be required to comprehend the text. The teacher read the text as though he were Mark.

To help Mark with the difficulty he had making connections, the teacher physically marked where he made connections as he modeled reading the text. The teacher also noted what kinds of connections he was making: connections to other sentences or paragraphs, connections to background knowledge, connections to other texts, and so on. As Mark read, he used sticky notes to indicate connections that he was making. After reading passages, Mark discussed the kinds of connections that he made as he read. As Mark grew proficient at making connections, marking them with sticky notes was phased out. Through discussions and probes, the teacher continued to gain insight into Mark's reasoning process. By year's end, Mark was making text-based responses and was able to comprehend both narrative and expository text at a high level.

Applying the Skill

Comprehension relies heavily on the reader's ability to use background knowledge to make inferences. Inferencing is a cognitive skill that can be used in all areas of learning. Have students apply it in class discussions and when reading in the content areas. Emphasize the need to go beyond facts and details in order to make inferences.

Making Inferences with It Says–I Say–And So

It Says–I Say–And So is a series of prompts that guide students as they make inferences about a story (Beers, 2003). Students fill in four columns of a chart like the one in Figure 6.6. In the *Question* column, students record the question they are answering. Under *It Says*, they answer the question with information from the text. Under *I Say*, students use their background knowledge to write what they know about the text information recorded in the *It Says* column. In the *And So* column, they use both text and their background knowledge to make an inference.

Macro-Cloze

After students have mastered traditional cloze activities, introduce macro-cloze. In macro-cloze, students use their background of experience and inferential reasoning to supply a missing sentence (Yuill and Oakhill, 1991).

The team had hoped to play a game of baseball.

_____

They played basketball instead.

Jeff thought he would finish his chores in less than an hour.

_____

He didn't finish until three hours later.

FYI

■ Although poor decoding skills are the main cause of poor comprehension, a number of struggling readers are good decoders but poor comprehenders (Shankweiler et al., 1999). As many as 20 percent of struggling readers are good decoders but poor comprehenders (Duke, 2003). See the Case Study on the preceding page.

■ Students who are good decoders but poor comprehenders have problems with all kinds of comprehension, but they have the most difficulty making inferences (Oakhill & Yuill, 1996).

■■■ **FIGURE 6.6   It Says–I Say–And So Chart**

Question Read the question.	It Says Find information from the text that will help you answer the question.	I Say Think about what you know about the information from the text.	And So Put together what the text says and what you know.
How did Jason feel as the lunch period approached?	Jason's stomach was growling. He had skipped breakfast. He didn't want to be late for his first day at the new school. Even so, he wasn't looking forward to lunch. He wondered where he would sit and if anyone would talk to him.	I remember my first day at a new school after we moved. The worst part of the day was lunchtime. Even though I was hungry, I wished they would just skip lunch.	And so that's why I think Jason was nervous and maybe a little bit afraid. He didn't know if anyone would invite him to sit with them or if he would have to sit all by himself or maybe someone would make fun of him.

Tanya thought she had scored 100 on the spelling test.

_____

She made up her mind to study harder for the next spelling test.

Explain to students that the macro-cloze activities can be completed in a number of ways. The key element is that the sentences make sense together after the missing sentence is inserted. Help students see that the inferences we make are based on our backgrounds and that each of us has a different background and sees life in a unique way (Paul & Elder, 2001). Challenge students to create their own macro-cloze activities and share them with classmates.

Difficulty Drawing Conclusions

Working with students who were having difficulty drawing conclusions, McMackin and Witherell (2005) observed that the students failed to consider information provided in the text. Students were urged to think about the passage they had just read, to note what they knew for sure because it was contained in the passage, and then to stop and think about this information so they could draw a conclusion: "I must combine what I know for sure from the text with what I think about it and then determine what else I can figure out from the information provided." Students were asked, "What were you able to figure out from the passage you read?" They were also asked to cite support for their conclusions. McMackin and Witherell also used graphic organizers to scaffold students' efforts. They differentiated instruction by providing different levels of organizers.

■ ■ ■ Checkup ■ ■ ■

1. What is the role of elaboration strategies?
2. What are some ways in which making inferences might be taught?

■ ■ ■

Imaging

Although readers rely heavily on verbal abilities to comprehend text, they also use imaging. According to a **dual coding** theory of cognitive processing, information can be coded verbally or nonverbally. The word *robot*, for instance, can be encoded verbally. It can also be encoded visually as a mental picture of a robot. Because it can be encoded as a word or mental picture, it can be retrieved from memory either verbally or visually, so it is twice as memorable. In one research study, participants who encoded words visually remembered twice as many words as those who encoded the words just verbally (Schnorr & Atkinson, 1969).

Imaging is relatively easy to teach. In one study, students' comprehension increased after just thirty minutes of instruction (Gambrell & Bales, 1986). The increase was not large, but it was significant. When teaching students to create images, start with single sentences and then move on to short paragraphs and, later, longer pieces. Have students read the sentence or paragraph first, and then ask them to form a picture of it.

Creating images serves three functions: fostering understanding, retaining information, and monitoring for meaning. If students are unable to form an image, or if their image is incomplete or inaccurate, encourage them to reread the section and then add to the pic-

---

■ **Dual coding** is the concept that text can be processed verbally and nonverbally. Nonverbal coding focuses on imaging.

■ **Imaging** refers to creating sensory representations of items in text.

Exemplary Teaching

Using Imaging

reating images is a powerful strategy for enhancing both comprehension and memory of text. Maria (1990) encouraged fourth-graders to construct images to foster their understanding of a social studies passage that described an Iroquois village. Maria started the lesson by having students study a detailed drawing of an Iroquois village. After shutting their eyes and visualizing the scene, students discussed what they had seen. Their images varied.

Students were then directed to close their eyes as Maria described a scene laden with sensory images and asked image-evoking questions:

> You are at an Iroquois village in New York State about the year 1650. It is winter. Feel how cold you are. Feel the snow crunch under your feet. The wind is blowing. You can hear it and feel it right through your clothes. See yourself walk through the gate into the village. See the tall fence all around the village. . . . (p. 198)

After discussing what they saw, heard, and felt, the students read a passage in their social studies textbook about life in an Iroquois longhouse. After each paragraph, they stopped and created images of what they had read and discussed the images. In the discussion, Maria asked questions that focused on the important details so that when students later created images on their own, they, too, would focus on these elements. The images that students created demonstrated that their comprehension was indeed enriched. Best of all, many of the students who responded were those who usually had little to say in class discussions.

ture in their minds or create a new one. As a comprehension strategy, imaging can help students who are having difficulty understanding a high-imagery passage such as the following visual description:

> A comet is like a dirty snowcone. A comet has three parts: a head, coma, and tail. The head is made of ice, gases, and particles of rocks. The heads of most comets are only a few kilometers wide. As a comet nears the sun, gases escape from the head. A large, fuzzy, ball-shaped cloud is formed. This ball-shaped cloud is the coma. The tail is present only when the coma is heated by the sun. The tail is made of fine dust and gas. A comet's tail always points away from the sun. The tail can be millions of kilometers long. (Hackett, Moyer, & Adams, 1989, p. 108)

Imaging can also be used as a pictorial summary. After reading a paragraph similar to the one about comets, students can review what they have read by trying to picture a comet and all its parts. A next step might be to draw a comet based on their visual summary. They might then compare their drawing with an illustration in the text or an encyclopedia and also with the text itself to make sure that they have included all the major components.

Like other elaboration strategies, imaging should be taught directly. The teacher should explain and model the strategy; discuss when, where, and under what conditions it might be used; and provide guided practice and application. From time to time, the teacher should review the strategy and encourage students to apply it.

Questions that ask students to create visual images should become a natural part of postreading discussions. Auditory and kinesthetic or tactile imaging should also be fostered. Students might be asked to tell how the hurricane in a story sounded or what the velvet seats in the limousine they read about felt like. In discussing images that children have formed, remind them that each of us makes our own individual picture in our mind. Ask a variety of students to tell what pictures they formed.

Whether used with fiction or nonfiction, imaging should follow these guidelines (Fredericks, 1986):

- Students create images based on their backgrounds. Images will differ.
- Teachers should not alter students' images but might suggest that students reread a selection and then decide whether they want to change their images.

 Adapting Instruction for English Language Learners

Have students draw pictures of concepts or topics rather than use words to describe or talk about them. This works especially well with students who are still learning English or other students who might have difficulty expressing their ideas through words alone.

FYI

Younger students might need demonstrations of how to create mental images, whereas older readers might just need timely reminders and encouragement. However, even older readers may need instruction to transfer imaging from one subject to another.

▪ Students should be given sufficient time to form images.

▪ Teachers should encourage students to elaborate on or expand their images through careful questioning: "What did the truck look like? Was it old or new? What model was it? What color? Did it have any special features?"

▪▪▪ Checkup ▪▪▪

1. What are some of the advantages of imaging?
2. How might imaging be taught and reinforced?

▪▪▪

Question Generation

Accustomed to answering questions posed by teachers and texts, students enjoy composing questions of their own. In addition to being a novel and interesting activity, **question generation** is also an effective strategy for fostering comprehension. It transforms the reader from passive observer to active participant. It also encourages the reader to set purposes for reading and to note important segments of text so that questions can be asked about them and possible answers considered. Creating questions also fosters active awareness of the comprehension process. Students who create questions are likely to be more aware of whether they are understanding the text and are more likely to take corrective action if their comprehension is inadequate (Andre & Anderson, 1978–1979).

ReQuest.   One of the simplest and most effective devices for getting children to create questions is **ReQuest**, or reciprocal questioning (Manzo, 1969; Manzo & Manzo, 1993; Manzo, Manzo, & Albee, 2004). Although originally designed for one-on-one instruction of remedial pupils, ReQuest has been adapted for use with groups of students and whole classes. In ReQuest, the teacher and students take turns asking questions. ReQuest can be implemented by following the steps outlined in Lesson 6.5.

Lesson 6.5

ReQuest Procedure

Step 1.
Choose a text that is on the students' level but is fairly dense so that it is possible to ask a number of questions about it.

Step 2.
Explain the ReQuest procedure to students. Tell them that they will be using a technique that will help them better understand what they read. Explain that in ReQuest, they get a chance to be the teacher because they and you take turns asking questions.

Step 3.
Survey the text. Read the title, examine any illustrations that are part of the introduction, and discuss what the selection might be about.

▪ **Question generation** is a powerful elaboration strategy. Through creating questions, students' comprehension jumped from the 50th percentile to the 66th percentile and in some instances to the 86th percentile (Rosenshine, Meister, & Chapman, 1996).

▪ **ReQuest** is a procedure in which the teacher and student(s) take turns asking and answering questions.

Step 4.
Direct students to read the first significant segment of text. This could be the first sentence or the first paragraph but should not be any longer than a paragraph. Explain that as they read, they are to think up questions to ask you. Students can make up as many questions as they wish. Tell them to ask the kinds of questions that a teacher might ask (Manzo & Manzo, 1993). Model how they might go about composing questions. Read the segment with the students.

Step 5.
Students ask their questions. Your book is placed face down. However, students may refer to their texts. If necessary, questions are restated or clarified. Answers can be checked by referring back to the text.

Step 6.
After students have asked questions, ask your questions. Pupils' books are face down. You might model higher-level questioning by asking for responses that require integrating several details in the text. If difficult concepts or vocabulary words are encountered, they should be discussed.

Step 7.
Go to the next sentence or paragraph. The questioning proceeds until enough information has been gathered to set a purpose for reading the remainder of the text. This could be in the form of a prediction: "What do you think the rest of the article will be about?" Manzo and Manzo (1993) recommended that the questioning be concluded as soon as a logical purpose can be set but no longer than ten minutes after beginning.

Step 8.
After students have read the rest of the selection silently, the purpose question and any related questions are discussed. The discussion might start off with the question "Did we read for the right purpose?" (Manzo, Manzo, & Albee, 2004, p. 303).

FYI

ReQuest can be combined with QAR to guide students to ask questions whose answers involve "putting together" and "writer and me," as well as being "right there."

Students enjoy reversing roles and asking questions. Initially, they may ask lower-level questions, but with coaching and modeling will soon ask higher-level ones. ReQuest is especially effective with lower-achieving readers.

Other elaboration strategies include applying information that has been obtained from reading, creating analogies to explain it, and evaluating text (covered in Chapter 7). A general principle underlying elaboration is that the more readers do with or to text, the better they will understand and retain it.

■ ■ ■ Checkup ■ ■ ■

1. Why is question generation an effective strategy?
2. What are the steps in teaching ReQuest?   ■ ■ ■

Teaching Monitoring (Metacognitive) Strategies

As you were reading this chapter, did you reread a section because you didn't quite understand it? Did you go back and reread any sentences? Were you aware of whether the text was making sense? Did you decide to use a particular strategy such as summarizing or questioning or imaging? If so, you were engaged in metacognition. Summarizing, inferring, creating images, predicting, and other strategies are valuable tools for enhancing comprehension. Knowing how to use them is not enough, however; it is also essential to know when and where to use them. For example, visualizing works best with materials that are concrete and lend themselves to being pictured in the imagination (Prawat, 1989). Predictions work best when the reader has a good background of knowledge about the topic. Knowing when and where to use these and other strategies is part of monitoring, which is also known as **metacognition**, or metacognitive awareness.

Monitoring also means recognizing what one does and does not know, which is a valuable asset in reading. If a reader mouths the words of a passage without comprehending their meaning and does not recognize his or her lack of comprehension, the reader will not reread the passage or take other steps to understand it; the reader is not even aware that there is a problem. "Metacognitive awareness is the ability to reflect on one's own cognitive processes, to be aware of one's own activities while reading, solving problems, and so on" (Baker & Brown, 1984, p. 353). A key feature of metacognitive awareness is knowing what one is expected to be able to do as a result of reading a selection. All of the other activities are examined in light of the desired outcome. Students will read a book one way if they are reading it as part of voluntary reading, another way if they are to evaluate it, and still another way if they are taking a test on it. Their criteria for success will depend on their specific goal for reading the text. A critical factor is the level of comprehension that students demand. Proficient readers generally demand a higher level of comprehension than do struggling readers.

The four major aspects of metacognition in reading are knowing oneself as a learner, regulating, checking, and repairing (Baker & Brown, 1984; McNeil, 1987).

Knowing Oneself as a Learner

The student is aware of what he or she knows, his or her reading abilities, what is easy and what is hard, what he or she likes and dislikes. The student is able to activate his or her prior knowledge in preparation for reading a selection:

> I know that Theodore Roosevelt was a president a long time ago. Was it during the late 1800s or early 1900s? I'm not sure. I remember reading a story about how he was weak as a child and had bad eyesight. I'll read about him in the encyclopedia. I'll try *World Book* instead of *Encyclopedia Britannica*. *Encyclopedia Britannica* is too hard, but I can handle *World Book*.

Regulating

In **regulating**, the student knows what to read and how to read it and is able to put that knowledge to use. The student is aware of the structure of the text and how this might be used to aid comprehension. The student also understands the task he or she will be expected to do as a result of reading this selection: retelling, writing a story, taking a test. He or she surveys the material, gets a sense of organization, sets a purpose, and then chooses and implements an effective strategy:

> Wow! This is a long article about Roosevelt. But I don't have to read all of it. I just need information about his boyhood. These headings will tell me which section I should read. Here's one that says "Early Life." I'll read it to find out what his childhood was like. After I read it, I'll make notes on the important points.

Checking

The student is able to evaluate his or her performance. He or she is aware when comprehension suffers because an unknown term is interfering with meaning or an idea is confusing. Checking also involves noting whether one is focusing on important, relevant

---

■ **Metacognition**, or metacognitive awareness, means being conscious of one's mental processes.

■ **Regulating** is a metacognitive process in which the reader guides his or her reading processes.

■ **Repairing** refers to taking steps to correct faulty comprehension.

information and engaging in self-questioning to determine whether goals are being achieved (Baker & Brown, 1984):

> The part about Roosevelt's great-grandparents isn't important. I'll skim over it. I wonder what *puny* and *asthma* mean. I've heard of asthma, but I don't know what it is. This is confusing, too. It says, "He studied under tutors." What does that mean? Let's see if I have all this straight. Roosevelt's family was wealthy. He was sickly, but then he worked out in the gym until he became strong. He liked studying nature and he was determined. I don't know about his early schooling, though, and I ought to know what *asthma* and *puny* mean.

Repairing

In **repairing**, the student takes corrective action when comprehension falters. Not only is the student aware that there is a problem in understanding the text, he or she does something about it:

> I'll look up *asthma, puny,* and *tutor* in the dictionary. Okay, I see that *tutor* means "a private teacher." Oh, yeah, it's like when my brother Bill had trouble with math and Mom got a college student to help him. Did Roosevelt have trouble in school? Is that why he had tutors? I'm still confused about his early schooling. I think I'll ask the teacher about it.

Failure to comprehend might be caused by a problem at any level of reading (Collins & Smith, 1980):

- Words may be unknown or may be known but used in an unfamiliar way.

- Concepts are unknown.

- Punctuation is misread.

- Words or phrases are given the wrong emphasis.

- Paragraph organization is difficult to follow.

- Pronouns and antecedent relationships are confused. Relationships among ideas are unclear.

- Relationships among paragraphs and sections are not established.

- The reader becomes lost in details. Key ideas are misinterpreted.

- The reader has inadequate prior knowledge, or a conflict exists between that knowledge and the text.

Repair strategies (Baker & Brown, 1984; Harris & Sipay, 1990) include the following:

- Rereading a sentence or paragraph may clear up a confusing point or provide context for a difficult word.

- Reading to the end of the page or section might provide clarification.

- Having failed to grasp the gist of a section, the student might reread the preceding section.

- If a student cannot remember specific details, she or he should skim back through the material to find them.

- The text may be difficult or may require closer reading, so the student may have to slow down, adjusting his or her rate of reading.

- Consulting a map, diagram, photo, chart, or illustration may provide clarification of a puzzling passage.

- Using a glossary or dictionary will provide the meaning of an unknown word.

- Consulting an encyclopedia or similar reference may clarify a confusing concept.

Adapting Instruction for Struggling Readers and Writers

Research on metacognitive processes suggests that poor readers find it especially difficult to monitor or repair their reading. They often read materials that are far beyond their instructional levels. Because poor readers are overwhelmed with difficult words and concepts, comprehension is literally beyond them.

■■■ **FIGURE 6.7**   **Repair Strategies**

What to Do When I Don't Understand

What is keeping me from understanding?

Should I read the sentence or paragraph again?

Will looking at maps, charts, photos, or drawings help?

Should I look up key words?

Should I keep on reading and see whether my problem is cleared up?

Should I slow down?

Should I ask for help?

FYI

Although teachers agree that monitoring strategies are important, they may not spend enough time teaching them. In one study, the teachers assessed and provided opportunities for students to practice using these strategies but spent little time teaching students how to use them (Pressley, Wharton-McDonald, Mistretta-Hampston, & Echevarria, 1998).

Figure 6.7 shows a series of questions that students might ask themselves if they encounter difficulties as they read. The questions provide prompts for the major repair strategies and should be posted in a prominent spot in the classroom.

Lookback.   Students may not realize that they can look back at a text when they cannot recall a specific bit of information or do not understand a passage (Garner, Hare, Alexander, Haynes & Winograd, 1984). If students' overall comprehension of a passage is faulty, they need to reread the entire passage. If, however, they have simply forgotten or misunderstood a detail, they may use **lookback**, a strategy that involves skimming back over the text and locating the portion that contains the information they need.

To present this strategy, the teacher should explain that it is not possible to remember everything (Garner, MacCready, & Wagoner, 1984). Therefore, it is often necessary to go back over a story. The teacher should then model the strategy by showing what he or she does when unable to respond to a question. The teacher should demonstrate how to skim through an article to find pertinent information and then use that information to answer a difficult question. Guided practice and application opportunities should be provided. When students are unable to respond to questions during class discussions or on study sheets or similar projects, they can be reminded to use lookbacks. As they learn how to use lookbacks, students should discover when to use them. Lookbacks are useful only when the information needed to answer the question is present in the text.

Instruction in Metacognitive Strategies

For most students, metacognitive awareness develops automatically over time; however, instruction is also helpful (Anthony, Pearson, & Raphael, 1989). In fact, it should be a part of every reading strategy lesson.

During each part of the lesson, the teacher should make explicit the cognitive processes involved. For instance, the teacher might model how he or she recalls prior knowledge, sets a purpose, decides on a reading strategy, executes the strategy, monitors for meaning, organizes information, takes corrective action when necessary, and applies knowledge gained from reading. The teacher should also discuss these processes with students, asking them what they know about a topic, how they plan to read a selection, and what they might do if they do not understand what they are reading. The ultimate aim is to have metacognitive processes become automatic. In the past, teachers have not made their thinking processes explicit. The teaching of reading now follows the novice–expert or master craftsperson–apprentice model. The student learns from the teacher's modeling and guidance as she or he progresses from novice reader to expert.

One way of reminding students of metacognitive strategies is to make a list of those that have been introduced and place them in a prominent spot in the classroom. A sample list of metacognitive strategies appears in Figure 6.8. You may want to adapt the list so that it fits the needs of your class. You may also want to have two lists: one for fiction and one for nonfiction.

To reinforce the use of metacognition, ask process, as well as product, questions. Product questions get at the content of a story: You might ask who the main character is, what problem he or she had in the story, and how he felt. A process question attempts to

■ **Lookback** is the strategy of skimming back over a selection that has already been   read in order to locate missed, forgotten, or misunderstood information.

uncover how a student arrived at an answer. After a student responds that the main character was angry, ask, "How do you know that?" Other process questions are "How did you figure out that word? How did you find the answer? What did you do when you realized that you had forgotten some main facts?"

Metacognitive awareness has to be built into virtually all reading instruction; "any attempt to comprehend must involve comprehension monitoring" (Baker & Brown, 1984, p. 385). This monitoring need not be on a conscious level. The skilled reader operates on automatic pilot until some sort of triggering event signals that comprehension is not taking place. At that point, the reader slows down, focuses on the problem, and decides how to deal with it (Baker & Brown, 1984).

Click and Clunk

To reinforce monitoring for meaning, use the click-and-clunk analogy, in which reading is compared to driving a car: When everything is going smoothly, the car is clicking along. When the car hits a pothole, there is a clunk. Clicks are portions of the text that are easy to understand. Clunks are problem portions. When students hit clunks, which are generally hard words or confusing sentences, they attempt to clarify them. Strategies for dealing with clunks might be listed on a chart or a bookmark. If students are unable to resolve a clunk, they can place a sticky note next to the confusing element and get help later (Vaughn, Klinger, & Schumm, n. d.).

As might be expected, younger readers and poorer readers are less aware of the purpose of reading and the most effective reading strategies. They may see reading primarily as a decoding task and fail to search for meaning. They may not notice when the text fails to make sense (Bransford, Stein, Shelton, & Owings, 1981). In other words, they don't know when they don't know. Therefore, metacognitive skills have to be taught early. Children should be informed early in their schooling that the purpose of reading is to construct meaning and not just to sound out words.

In addition to scheduling lessons devoted to teaching monitoring and repair strategies, be alert for opportunities to do on-the-spot teaching or reinforcement. When a student is reading orally and makes an error, do not immediately correct her or him. Give the student the opportunity to monitor her or his own reading and correct any errors. In fact, if the miscue makes sense in the sentence, you might ignore it. If it changes the meaning of the sentence and the student does not correct it, ask questions like these: "Did that sentence make sense? What might you do to read the sentence correctly?" If the student cannot make the correction after a reasonable effort, supply the correct word by asking, "Would (unknown word) fit here?" or "Does it look like (unknown word)?" However, it is important that students be given a chance to correct their errors. To develop monitoring and repair strategies, students need ample opportunity to apply them. They also need an environment in which they are not afraid to make mistakes.

To promote the use of monitoring and repair strategies during silent reading, review these strategies from time to time. At times when it is not possible for students to get help with comprehension difficulties, have them make a note of problems they encounter. For example, a student might put a sticky note by the word or passage that poses a problem. As part of every postreading discussion, talk over any difficulties that students may have had while reading the text. Also make sure that the text is not too difficult for students. They will have difficulty monitoring for meaning if they are unable to construct a coherent situation model of the text (Paris, Wasik, & Turner, 1991).

To understand metacognition and to become aware of the strategies that you use when reading becomes difficult and comprehension breaks down, reflect on the repair strategies that you use.

■ ■ ■ **FIGURE 6.8** **Metacognitive Strategies**

> **Thinking and Reading**
>
> **Before reading**
>
> What does this selection seem to be about?
> What do I already know about this subject?
> What do I want to learn or find out?
> Why am I reading this?
>
> **While reading**
>
> What am I learning or finding out?
> Is the selection making sense?
> If I'm having trouble understanding the selection, what can I do?
>
> **After reading**
>
> What have I learned or found out?
> How does what I read fit in with what I know?
> What questions do I still have?

FOSTERING ENGAGEMENT

Click and clunk is a useful way to motivate students to become involved in monitoring for meaning.

 Adapting Instruction for Struggling Readers and Writers

Good readers have good monitoring skills, and poor readers don't. Poor readers are less likely to detect lapses in comprehension and, when they do detect them, are less able to repair them. However, when instructed, poor readers can and do learn to become effective monitors (Palincsar et al., 1993).

■ ■ ■ **Checkup** ■ ■ ■

1. Why is monitoring a key reading strategy?
2. What are the components of monitoring?
3. What steps might students take to repair comprehension?

■ ■ ■

■ Closing the Gap by Making Connections

Students who have a richer background and can make more connections between what they know and what they are reading have better comprehension and retention. For instance, students reading about germs might relate what they read to a time when they had strep throat and took medicine to get rid of the germs. Comprehension can be thought of as a network of ideas connected largely by causal–logical relationships. Good readers use higher-level thought processes to establish relationships and store information in network form so that the concept of germs, for example, has a number of connections in their schemata.

One way of helping students, especially below-level readers, improve their comprehension is to use causal questioning. In causal questioning, students are asked why and how questions to help them make inferences. These questions can be asked during discussions or can be added to the text at locations where comprehension is likely to falter. This might be at points where important cause–effect relationships are being established (van den Broek & Kremer, 2000).

Special Comprehension Strategies for Bilingual Readers

Bilingual students find reading and comprehending in their weaker or nondominant language more difficult. One of the major obstacles is vocabulary. If bilingual students have recently learned to speak English, chances are they will encounter a greater number of unknown words than will their same-age English-speaking counterparts. Fortunately, successful bilingual readers do use a repertoire of strategies to aid themselves. For one thing, they seem to be more metacognitively aware. Apparently, the process of learning a second language has provided them with insights into language on an abstract level, as an object of study. They are more likely to notice problems in word recognition or comprehension. While using the same kinds of strategies (predicting, inferencing, monitoring, etc.) as their monolingual counterparts, they also use additional strategies: translating from one language to another and transferring information learned in one language to another.

Achieving bilingual readers see similarities between their native language and their new language. They use their native language as a source of help by activating prior knowledge in both languages and by translating when encountering a difficult passage, especially when they are in the earlier stages of learning English. Transferring, translating, and reflecting on text in their native or stronger language has the potential for improving comprehension (Jiménez, 1997).

■ ■ ■ **Checkup** ■ ■ ■

1. Why is making connections important?
2. How might you help students make connections?
3. What special strategies do bilingual readers use?

■ ■ ■

■ **Reciprocal teaching** is a form of cooperative learning in which students learn to use four key reading strategies in order to achieve improved comprehension: predicting, question generating, clarifying, and summarizing.

■ Social-Constructivist Nature of Comprehension

According to Vygotsky (1978), learning is a social process. Directions and explanations provided by a more knowledgeable other are internalized by the learner and become part of his or her thinking. When a teacher and students or a group of students discuss a reading selection, they help each other construct meaning. Comprehension is still an individual task. Participants discuss their personal understandings of the text, but as they engage in an interchange of ideas, they may modify their understandings as they perceive the selection from other perspectives. This is especially true in reading literature, where understandings are enriched and broadened by discussion with others. However, even when reading informational texts, understandings are deepened and clarified through discussion. When students explain how they comprehended a particular passage or what they did when a passage was confusing, understanding of reading processes is enhanced (Kucan & Beck, 1996).

The degree to which comprehension is fostered depends on the quality of the thinking and the ideas exchanged. The talk must be accountable (New Standards Primary Literacy Committee, 1999). It must go beyond mere opinion. Students must be prepared to back up a judgment about a literary piece by using passages from the text, for instance. Or, if they draw a conclusion from a passage in a social studies text, they must cite supporting details. In this way, students learn to draw evidence from text, check facts, and reason with information. Teachers play a key role in modeling accountable talk and in shaping discussions so that student talk becomes accountable.

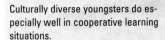

FYI

Culturally diverse youngsters do especially well in cooperative learning situations.

BUILDING LANGUAGE

Model accountable talk by showing how you use facts and details or passages from a selection to back up your judgments. Use probes and prompts to coach students as they do the same. Discuss the difference between opinions that have no backing and those that are supported by facts or examples.

Reciprocal Teaching

Reciprocal teaching is a form of social–constructivist learning and cognitive apprenticeship in which students gradually learn key comprehension strategies by imitating and working along with the teacher. Reciprocal teaching introduces group discussion techniques created to improve understanding and retention of the main points of a selection. Reciprocal teaching also has built-in monitoring devices that enable students to check their understanding of what they are reading and to take steps to improve their comprehension if necessary.

Reading and discussing a story in a small group help children learn key comprehension strategies.

In a reciprocal teaching situation, the group reads a story and then discusses it. Members of the group take turns leading the discussion. They use four tried-and-true techniques for building comprehension and for monitoring for meaning—predicting, question generating, clarifying, and summarizing (Palincsar & Brown, 1986):

1. *Predicting.* Students predict what information a section of text will present based on what they have read in a prior section. If they are just starting a selection, their prediction is based on illustrations, headings, or an introductory paragraph. They must activate their background knowledge to guess what the author is going to say next. Predicting makes them active readers and gives them a purpose for reading.

2. *Question generating.* Students must seek out the kinds of information in a text that provide a basis for well-formed questions. Not being able to formulate a question may be a sign that they have failed to understand the significant points in the text and so must reread or take other corrective action.

3. *Clarifying.* Students note words, concepts, expressions, or other items that hinder comprehension, and they ask for explanations during discussion.

4. *Summarizing.* The discussion leader, with or without the help of the group, retells the selection, highlighting the main points. This retelling reviews and integrates the information and is also a monitoring device. Inability to paraphrase is a sign that comprehension is poor and rereading is in order (Brown, 1985). Summarizing also becomes a springboard for making predictions about the content of the next section.

Using direct instruction, the teacher introduces reciprocal teaching over approximately a week's time but may take longer if necessary. Lesson 6.6 outlines the teacher's role in reciprocal teaching.

Lesson 6.6

Reciprocal Teaching

Step 1. Introduce reciprocal teaching
Ask students whether they have ever wanted to switch places with the teacher. Tell them that they will be using a new method to help them read with better understanding and that each student will have a chance to lead a discussion of a story that the class has read. Outline for the students the four parts of the method: predicting what will happen; making up questions; clarifying, or clearing up details that are hard to understand; and summarizing.

Step 2. Explain the four basic parts
(a) Explain that predicting helps readers think what a story might be about and that it gives them a purpose for reading. Students will want to see whether their predictions are correct, so they will read with greater interest and understanding. Model the process, and give students a chance to try it out.
(b) Explain to students that asking questions will help them read with better understanding. Model the process by reading a selection and constructing questions. Emphasize the need to ask questions about the important parts of the selection, and provide guided practice in constructing some questions.
(c) Explain what clarifying is. Tell students that it is important to notice words or ideas that make it hard to understand a selection. Explain that clarifying hard parts of a selection will help them get more meaning out of what they are reading. Have them locate which words, sentences, or ideas in a sample selection need clarifying. Explain that what is clear to one person may not be clear to another.

(d) Explain why summarizing is an important skill. Tell students that summarizing a paragraph helps them concentrate on important points while reading. Demonstrate creating a summary for a model paragraph. Explain that if students summarize, they will better understand what they read and remember it longer.

Depending on students' age, ability, and previous experience with the strategies, the teacher might introduce the strategies all at once, one a day, or even one a week. The teacher should not expect students to become proficient in using the strategies or even to fully understand them at this point. That will come when the strategies are applied in a reciprocal teaching lesson. At first, the teacher plays a major role in the application of reciprocal teaching, modeling the four strategies, making corrections, and providing guidance when necessary. Gradually, the students take more responsibility for leading discussions and applying the strategies.

The following is a sample reciprocal teaching lesson based on the reading of a selection about Daisy Low, the founder of the Girl Scouts of America.

(Lead-in question)

Carmen (student discussion leader): My question is, how did Daisy Low help people and animals?

Paula: She fed stray cats and dogs.

Frank: She got clothes for needy children.

(Clarification request)

Charles: I think we should clarify *needy*.

Ann: I think needy children need stuff, like clothes and maybe food.

Teacher: What would be another word for *needy*?

James: Poor. I think *poor* means the same thing as *needy*.

Teacher: Good answer. *Poor* and *needy* mean just about the same thing. I have another question. Why did Daisy put a blanket on the cow?

Paula: She was afraid it would get cold.

James: I think that should be clarified. Do cows get cold?

Teacher: Does anybody know? Did any of you ever live on a farm? How can we find out?

Paula: We could look in the encyclopedia.

John: My grandfather raised cows. He's visiting us. I could ask him.

Teacher: That's a great idea. You ask him and report back to us. Maybe your grandfather could come in and talk to the class about life on a farm. By the way, Carmen, do you feel that your question has been answered?

Carmen: I think the story tells about some more things that Daisy Low did to help people. Can anyone tell me what they were?

Ann: Yes, she started a children's group called Helping Hands.

Frank: And the first sentence says that she was the founder of the Girl Scouts in America.

Teacher: Those are good answers. Can you summarize this section of the story, Carmen?

(Summary)

Carmen: The paragraph tells about Daisy Low.

Teacher: That's right, Carmen. The paragraph tells us about Daisy Low. In a summary, you give the main idea and main details. What does the paragraph tell us about Daisy Low?

Carmen: She helped animals and children who were in need.

(Prediction)

Teacher: Very good, Carmen. What do you predict will happen next?

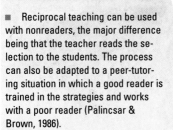

FYI

■ Reciprocal teaching can be used with nonreaders, the major difference being that the teacher reads the selection to the students. The process can also be adapted to a peer-tutoring situation in which a good reader is trained in the strategies and works with a poor reader (Palincsar & Brown, 1986).

■ Develop dialogue along with strategies (Benson-Castagna, 2005). The objective of reciprocal teaching is to develop students' self-awareness of their learning and to turn thinking into language. Thus, through discussions, students can become more aware of their thinking and share their thinking with each other.

FYI

The teacher might assign roles to students in implementing reciprocal teaching; for example, one student predicts, one creates questions, and one summarizes. Students might work in pairs or small groups to fulfill their roles and complete their preparation before the larger group meets.

■ ■ ■ ■   **USING TECHNOLOGY**

The video *Reciprocal Teaching Strategies at Work: Improving Reading Comprehension, Grades 2–6* (Oczkus, 2005), distributed by the International Reading Association, provides several examples of reciprocal teaching in the classroom.

Carmen: I think the story will tell how Daisy Low started the Girl Scouts.

Teacher: Does anyone have a different prediction? Okay. Let's read the next section to see how our prediction works out. Who would like to be the leader for this section?

During the session, the teacher provides guidance through prompts and probes, where needed, and also models the four strategies. For instance, creating questions is difficult for many students. The teacher might show how she or he would go about creating a question, supply question words—*who, what, why, when, where,* and *how*—or use prompts to help students reformulate awkward questions. Ultimately, students should be able to apply the strategy lessons they have learned. Research suggests that this does happen: Students who were trained in the use of the strategies were apparently able to apply them to their social studies and science reading; their rankings in content-area evaluations shot up from the 20th to the 50th percentile (Brown, 1985).

Reciprocal teaching can be used in literature circles and other book discussion groups (see Chapter 9 for information about literature discussion groups). Oczkus (2003) used reciprocal teaching with literature circles to bolster students' comprehension: "Reciprocal teaching adds a 'read and learn to comprehend' dimension to literature circles because it gives students the basics for comprehending well" (p. 134). Some teachers introduce reciprocal teaching in small groups or to the whole class early in the year and by spring have students use reciprocal teaching in their literature discussion groups.

An entire class can use reciprocal teaching if the technique is adapted in the following two ways. First, students use the headings in a selection to make two predictions about the content of the text they are about to read. Second, after reading a segment, they write two questions and a summary, as well as list any items that require clarification. The predictions, summaries, and clarification requests are discussed after the selection has been read. Even with these whole group adaptations, students' comprehension improved 20 percent after using the approach for just one month (Palincsar & Brown, 1986).

Why is reciprocal teaching so powerful? Reciprocal teaching leads students to a deeper processing of text. It may also change the way students read. It focuses their attention on trying to make sense of what they read, instead of just decoding words (Rosenshine & Meister, 1994).

■ ■ ■   **Checkup**   ■ ■ ■

1. How is reading comprehension partly a social process?
2. How does reciprocal teaching make use of social processes to foster comprehension?
3. How might reciprocal teaching be adapted?

■ ■ ■

Questioning the Author

FYI

In Questioning the Author, the teacher asks students to tell what an author is saying and builds on the students' responses (Beck & McKeown, 2006). The teacher follows up on responses and uses them to create a focused discussion. Questions should be carefully planned; if not, they may lead students away from the text. Questions focusing on personal connections, for instance, might lead into a discussion of experiences not closely related to key concepts.

Another highly effective technique that emphasizes collaboration and discussion is Questioning the Author. Based on their research, McKeown, Beck, and Sandora (1996) found that fifth-graders weren't learning very much from content-area texts. The researchers sought ways to help the students get more out of their reading. A program was set up in which students read brief segments of text and then responded to teacher queries so that they were cooperatively constructing meaning as they processed the text instead of reading the entire text and then answering questions. Students were told that sometimes the author's meaning wasn't clear, so they would have to ask themselves questions like "What is the author trying to say here?" Having students ask such questions made reading a more active process. Rather than simply extracting information from text, readers had to build a genuine understanding of the text. Beck, McKeown, Hamilton, and Kucan (1997) compared it to the difference between building a model ship and being given one. The student who has assembled a model ship knows a great deal more about its parts than the one who has simply looked at the model.

The teacher used general queries to get the discussion started and to keep it moving. Initiating queries included: "What is the author trying to say here? What is the author's message? What is the author trying to tells us?" Follow-up queries were designed to help the students construct meaning. If a passage didn't seem clear, the teacher might ask, "What did the author mean here? Did the author explain this clearly?" Questions could also be asked that helped students connect ideas that had been encountered previously: "How does this connect to what the author told us before? How do these two ideas fit together?" Other kinds of questions lead students to seek reasons: "Does the author tell us why? Why do you think the author included this information?" Questions might also help students see how what they are learning relates to what they know: "How does this fit in with what you know?"

To structure the discussion so that it helps students construct meaning, the teacher uses six Questioning the Author moves: marking, turning back, revoicing, modeling, annotating, and recapping.

Marking. The teacher highlights a student's comment or idea that is important to the meaning being built. The teacher might remark, "You are saying that immigration was a good thing. It helped the United States grow and develop." Or the teacher might simply say, "Good point!"

Turning back. The teacher turns students' attention back to the text so that they can get more information, fix a misreading, or clarify their thinking: "Yes, I agree that people should have been pleased to have so many newcomers to build railroads and work in factories. But what does the author tell us about how the newcomers were actually treated?"

Revoicing. The teacher helps students clearly express what they were attempting to say: "So what you're telling us is that the newcomers put up with hardships and worked long hours so that their children would have a better life."

Modeling. The teacher shows how he or she might go about creating meaning from text. The teacher may model how to clarify a difficult passage, draw a conclusion, visualize a complex process, or use context to derive the meaning of a difficult word. The teacher might say, "Here's what was going through my mind as I read that passage," or "Here's how I figured out what the author meant," or, "When an author explains how something works, I try to picture the steps in my mind."

Annotating. The teacher fills in information that is missing from a discussion but that is important for understanding key ideas. It might be information that the author failed to include: "The author tells us that factory goods were so cheap that people stopped making clothes and household items at home and bought them instead. What the author doesn't say is that more and more people became dependent on a job. Up to this time, they had raised their own food and made much of what they needed. Now they needed money to live."

Recapping. The teacher highlights key points and summarizes. "Now that we understand how immigrant parents sacrificed for their children, let's see whether the children benefited from all those sacrifices." Lesson 6.7 presents the steps in a Questioning the Author lesson.

Closing the Gap

Questioning the Author works with all students but has been especially successful with struggling readers and writers and students in urban schools.

FYI

■ In ten years of study, Beck and McKeown (2006) found that few students were able to build a coherent representation of what they had read. Many could only provide surface information. The researchers noted problems with decoding, fluency, vocabulary, and engagement.

■ For detailed information on how to conduct a Questioning the Author lesson, see *Questioning the Author, An Approach for Enhancing Student Engagement with Text* (Beck, McKeown, Hamilton, & Kucan, 1997).

FOSTERING ENGAGEMENT

Because they involve students in helping each other to construct meaning, techniques such as reciprocal teaching and Questioning the Author energize students' learning.

Lesson 6.7

Questioning the Author

Step 1.
Analyze the text and decide what you want students to know or understand as a result of reading the text. List two or three major understandings.

Step 2.
Note any potential difficulties in the text that might hamper students' comprehension. Problems might include difficult vocabulary or concepts or a lack of background knowledge.

Step 3.
Segment the text into readable blocks. A segment could be a single sentence or paragraph or several paragraphs. A block should generally encompass one major idea.

Step 4.
In light of the understandings you wish students to attain and the possible difficulties in the text, plan your queries. Plan queries for each segment.

Step 5.
Introduce the selection. Clarify difficult vocabulary and other hindrances to comprehension in a particular segment before students read that segment.

Step 6.
Students read the first segment silently.

Step 7.
Students and teacher discuss the first segment.

Step 8.
Students go on to the next segment.

Step 9.
At the conclusion, the class, with the teacher's help, sums up what they have read.

■ ■ ■ Checkup ■ ■ ■

1. What are the basic principles on which Questioning the Author is built?
2. What are the six moves that can be used to foster discussion?

■ ■ ■

■ Integration of Strategies

For the sake of clarity, the major comprehension strategies presented in this chapter have been discussed in isolation. However, it should be emphasized that reading is a holistic act. Often, several interacting strategies are being applied simultaneously. As Pressley, Borkowski, Forrest-Pressley, Gaskins, and Wiley (1993) explained,

> Strategies are rarely used in isolation. Rather, they are integrated into higher-order sequences that accomplish complex cognitive goals. For example, good reading may begin with previewing, activation of prior knowledge about the topic of a to-be-read text, and self-questioning about what might be presented in the text. These prereading activities are then followed by careful reading, reviewing, and rereading as necessary. General strategies (e.g., self-testing) are used to monitor whether subgoals have been accomplished, prompting the reader to move on when it is appropriate to do so or motivating reprocessing when subgoals have not been met. That is, good strategy users evaluate whether the strategies they are using are producing progress toward goals they have set for themselves. (p. 9)

Learning to use a strategy is a long process. Although researchers may get positive results after twenty lessons on predicting or summarizing, it may actually take students many months to master a particular strategy (Pressley, 1994). In addition, strategies learned at one level may have to be refined when used at higher levels with more complex materials.

■ Making Strategy Instruction Work

Strategy instruction works best when students evidence a need for a strategy, when the strategy taught is applied to a selection, when the teacher repeatedly models and explains the strategy, when the students have many opportunities to use the strategy, and when assessment is based on comprehension of the text and the use of the strategy (Duffy, 2002). The key element is the teacher's ability to adapt instruction to students' understanding and to provide sufficient instruction. In teaching how to identify the main idea, for instance, the most effective teachers provided extensive modeling and adjusted guided practice to help students overcome shortcomings in their thinking. If students identify a main idea that is too broad, teachers use prompts that help the students narrow their main idea. When students select details that are very interesting but do not encompass all the details in a selection, teachers use prompts to help students redirect their thinking.

■ Importance of Affective Factors

Being attentive, active, and reflective are key factors in strategy use. Provide students with a rationale for being attentive: the more attentive you are, the more you learn and remember. Attentiveness is enhanced by applying strategies covered here—predicting, inferring, and monitoring—all of which require active student involvement. Students are also more motivated and more involved when they are consulted and given choices and when they have the opportunity to collaborate with classmates. Reflection is also important. Taking time to think about what we have read improves comprehension and retention. Provide students with questions that require careful thinking about what they have read. And provide time for them to reflect (Gaskins, 1998).

■ ■ ■ Checkup ■ ■ ■

1. How are strategies integrated?
2. What role do affective strategies play in comprehension?   ■ ■ ■

■ Explicit versus Nonexplicit Instruction of Strategies

Strategy instruction varies in its explicitness. Guided reading, for instance, focuses on having students and the teacher mutually construct a representation of the text. Strategies might not be taught explicitly. The assumption is that after repeated encounters students will infer that they should use these strategies on their own. Explicit teaching grew out of concern for struggling readers who might not pick up strategies without direct instruction. As Duffy (2002) explains

> Explicit teaching is intentional and direct about teaching individual strategies on the assumption that clear and unambivalent information about how strategies work will put struggling readers in a better position to control their own comprehension; other approaches, on the other hand, emphasize quality interaction with text content but avoid explicit teacher talk designed to develop students' metacognitive awareness of when and how to use a particular strategy. . . . Many struggling readers cannot, by simply watching a teacher guide their reading, figure out what they are supposed to do on their own. Consequently, they remain mystified and do not achieve the desired "inner control." (pp. 30–31)

In other approaches, the goal is student comprehension of text. In explicit teaching, the goal is student mastery of strategies. Approaches in which the focus is on comprehension of text rather than mastery of strategies include the guided reading lesson, directed reading-thinking activity, and KWL, which are covered in Chapter 7.

Tools for the Classroom

Building Higher-Level Literacy

Except when a basic literal understanding is being constructed, comprehension requires higher-level thinking. When teaching strategies, emphasize the thinking involved. The major higher-level thinking skills are classifying/categorizing, comparing/contrasting, inferring/concluding, and judging. Provide opportunities for students to use these skills during discussions and read-alouds and in all subject areas. Pay particular attention to developing students' ability to use higher-level thinking skills in discussion groups.

Help for Struggling Readers and Writers

When they are taught strategies explicitly, poor readers typically do as well as average or even better-than-average readers. However, it is essential that struggling readers be given materials on their level. They should know at least 95 percent of the words and have 75 percent comprehension of materials used for instructional purposes. Material on a higher level than that is so overwhelming that the students are unable to apply strategies (Kletzien, 1991).

Intensive, step-by-step, explicit instruction is also part of the package. At the Benchmark School, which is a special school for struggling readers, students are taught one strategy at a time, with each strategy being taught for nearly two months. During that time, students have frequent reviews and use the strategy daily. A chart that reviews the steps of the strategy is displayed, and students discuss when, where, and how to use the strategy. Strategy instruction is also made an integral part of the reading lesson. Along with building background and introducing new vocabulary, the teacher introduces or reviews a strategy that students are expected to use in their reading. After reading, the students discuss the selection and also talk about how they used the strategy in their reading. After students have thoroughly learned one strategy, a new strategy is introduced. The new strategy is related to the previous one, and students are shown how to use both together.

Another key to success is to apply a strategy to a variety of materials and especially to the content areas, so that it generalizes (Gaskins, 1998). Two strategies that are especially helpful for struggling readers are self-questioning and summarizing. In addition to helping students become more active, these strategies also serve as a self-check on understanding. If students can't summarize or answer questions that they have posed, this is a sign that they haven't understood what they have read and should lead to rereading, using illustrations, or some other repair strategy.

To foster comprehension when students don't seem to be reading for meaning, when they are just saying the words, you might have them use manipulatives to show the action in a story (Glenberg, Gutierrez, Levin, Japuntich, & Kaschak, 2004). For instance, if the story says that the dog ran after the cat, the students pick up a toy dog and toy cat and show the dog running after the cat. After students have mastered this ability, you could move into imaging. Then, instead of manipulating the elements in the story, students imagine them, mentally picturing the dog running after the cat.

Essential Standards

Grades 1 through 3

Students will

- prepare for reading by previewing, activating prior knowledge, and setting a purpose for reading.
- seek out main ideas and essential details as they read and summarize by retelling a selection.
- make inferences, create images, generate questions, and make judgments about their reading.
- make connections between what they have read and their own experiences.
- monitor their reading to see that it makes sense and use basic fix-up strategies, such as using illustrations and rereading, if it doesn't.

- compare selections that they have read.
- follow increasingly complex written directions.
- apply information that they have gained through reading.

Grades 4 through 8

Students will

- prepare for reading by previewing, activating prior knowledge, setting a purpose for reading, and deciding how a selection should be read.
- adjust rate and style of reading to purpose for reading and nature of the material being read.
- seek out main ideas and essential details as they read and demonstrate comprehension by orally summarizing a selection and by using graphic organizers and/or creating written summaries.
- make inferences, create images, and generate questions about their reading.
- monitor their reading to see that it makes sense and use basic and advanced fix-up strategies if it doesn't.

Action Plan

1. Use test and quiz results, observations of students as they discuss selections, think-alouds, and samples of written responses to assess students' comprehension. Plan a program accordingly.
2. Use modeling, think-alouds, explanation, and explicit, direct instruction of strategies with lots of opportunities for practice, review, and application.
3. Provide activities that help students activate prior knowledge, set a purpose and goals, preview the selection, and predict based on their previews.
4. Develop strategies such as comprehending the main idea, determining important details, organizing details, and summarizing that help students organize information.
5. Develop strategies such as inferring, imaging, generating questions, and evaluating that help students make connections between what they have read and their prior knowledge.
6. Provide instruction and activities that help students become aware of their comprehension and to take corrective action when comprehension is inadequate.
7. Use approaches such as reciprocal teaching that make use of discussion and working together to construct meaning.
8. Model how you would integrate strategies. Also model how you select which strategies to use. Provide practice and application opportunities.
9. Adapt instruction for English language learners by spending extra time building background and vocabulary. Also use culturally relevant materials and draw on the students' background knowledge and strong metacognitive skills. Focus on the content of student responses rather than the way they express their answers.
10. Provide extra instruction for struggling readers. Make sure struggling readers are given materials on their level.
11. Monitor students' progress and revise the program as needed.

Assessment

Assessment should be ongoing. Through observation, note the strategies students use before, during, and after reading. Note in particular what they do when they are stumped by a passage. During discussions, note the overall quality of their comprehension and the kinds of strategies they seem to be using. Occasionally, ask them how they were able to comprehend a difficult passage. Ask them to describe the strategies they used. You might ask older students to submit a web of a selection or a written summary. Also, from time to time, have students mark confusing passages. Analyze the passages and discuss students' difficulties to get a sense of the kinds of things that are hindering their comprehension. Also note how students do with different types of texts being read for different purposes. How well do students do when reading on a literal level? How well do they read when they have to organize, infer, or evaluate information?

Summary

Comprehending involves activating a schema, which is a unit of organized knowledge. Comprehension can also be viewed as a process of constructing situation models. While processing text, the reader continually reconstructs or updates the situation model.

Major types of comprehension strategies include preparational, organizational, elaboration, and monitoring (metacognition). Preparational strategies are activities a reader engages in just before reading a selection. Organizational strategies involve selecting the most important details in a piece and constructing relationships among them. Elaboration strategies involve constructing relationships between prior knowledge and knowledge obtained from print. Monitoring strategies include being aware of oneself as a learner and of the learning task, regulating and planning comprehension activities, monitoring one's comprehension, and repairing it when it is faulty.

Reciprocal teaching integrates predicting, question generating, clarifying, and summarizing. Questioning the Author breaks a text into brief segments to allow for intensive, collaborative construction of meaning. Integrating strategies and establishing an environment conducive to learning foster comprehension. Students' motivation, willingness to pay attention, active involvement, and reflection also have an impact on comprehension.

Extending and Applying

1. Try out one of the strategies introduced in this chapter in your own reading for at least a week. Note its effectiveness. Did you encounter any difficulties implementing it?

2. To gain insight into the comprehension process, do a think-aloud with a partner as you read a challenging selection. What processes and strategies did you use? What difficulties, if any, did you experience? How did you cope with these difficulties?

3. Plan a direct instruction lesson for teaching one of the comprehension strategies. If possible, teach the lesson and evaluate its effectiveness.

4. Obtain information about a student's use of comprehension strategies. Ask the student what she or he does to prepare for reading. Then ask what the student does if she or he is reading a selection and discovers that she or he does not understand it.

5. Introduce ReQuest or reciprocal teaching to a group of students or try it out with a group of classmates. What seem to be the advantages and disadvantages of the approach? (If you choose to try out reciprocal teaching, be aware that it will take some time. This is a complex technique with many parts, but it is highly effective and so worth the effort.)

Developing a Professional Portfolio

Videotape a lesson in which you teach a comprehension strategy to a group of students. Describe the lesson and reflect on its effectiveness. Explain what you did in subsequent lessons to help the students apply the strategy. Document progress that the students made in comprehension. Documentation might include completed graphic organizers, written summaries, or pre- and post-test results.

Go to Allyn & Bacon's MyLabSchool: www.mylabschool.com

- Enter Assignment ID **RMV8** into **Assignment Finder,** and select the video titled "Reading for Comprehension." In this video, a teacher models how to teach comprehension skills through questioning and think-alouds.

- As you watch the video, observe how the students react to the think-aloud strategy. What did you observe? Explain the importance of the following concepts to reading comprehension: word accuracy, fluency, prior knowledge, and metacognition.

- Explore MyLabSchool further to find the course areas for Reading Methods, Language Arts, and Content Area Reading and identify other assets that support concepts introduced in this chapter.

Developing a Resource File

Keep a list of activities and techniques that foster comprehension. Also keep a list of books, periodicals, and Web sites that are especially effective for practicing comprehension strategies: books that lend themselves to imaging, books that lend themselves to creating questions, etc. Collect brief articles from periodicals, children's books, or other sources that might be used to provide practice with inferring, visualizing, or other strategies.

Companion Website

To access chapter objectives, practice tests, weblinks, and flashcards, go to the companion website at www.ablongman.com/gunning6e.

7 Comprehension

*Text Structures and
Teaching Procedures*

For each of the following statements related to the chapter you are about to read, put a check under "Agree" or "Disagree" to show how you feel. Discuss your responses with classmates before you read the chapter.

Anticipation Guide

	Agree	Disagree
1. The structure of a piece of writing influences its level of difficulty.	_____	_____
2. Talking about the structure of a story ruins the fun of reading it.	_____	_____
3. How you ask a question is more important than what you ask.	_____	_____
4. Struggling learners should be asked a greater proportion of lower-level questions.	_____	_____
5. Students should play the most important role in class discussions.	_____	_____
6. Structured reading lessons usually work better than unstructured ones.	_____	_____
7. Critical (evaluative) reading skills have never been more important or more neglected.	_____	_____

The emphasis in Chapter 6 was on learners and the strategies they might use to construct meaning. Of course, strategies have to be integrated with text, and that determines the types of strategies that can be applied. This chapter emphasizes the role of text, both narrative and expository, in comprehension. It also explores a number of teaching procedures, such as the use of questions and techniques for asking them, reading lessons, and the cloze procedure, which consists of supplying missing words. The chapter also includes a section on critical (evaluative) reading.

What do you already know about text structure? How might that knowledge improve your comprehension? What kinds of questions might foster comprehension? How should questions be asked? Think back on lessons that were used to introduce reading selections when you were in school. What procedures did the teacher use? What aspects of those procedures worked best?

Using What You Know

■ Nature of the Text

A text has both content and organization. Students are prepared for the content when the teacher activates a schema or builds background; however, they also have to interact with the structure. Therefore, they develop another schema for organizational patterns. Knowledge of structure provides a blueprint for constructing a situation model of a story or informational piece. As students read, they transform text into ideas or details known as **propositions**. Propositions are combined, deleted, and integrated to form a macrostructure. The **macrostructure** is a running summary of the text. The propositions are organized according to their relative importance in a hierarchy. A general statement is toward the top of the hierarchy. Details are lower. A reader who is able to detect the main idea of a text and its supporting details will better understand and retain information in the text than will a reader who fails to use the text's organization. Likewise, a reader who has a good sense of story structure can use the structure of a story as a framework for remembering it (Gordon, 1989).

FYI

Bartlett (1932), a British psychologist, asked subjects to read and retell an Indian folk tale, which contained an unfamiliar structure. In the retelling, aspects of the tale were changed so that the reconstructed tale was more like that of a traditional English tale. Bartlett concluded that we tend to reinterpret tales in terms of our own experience.

Narrative Text and Story Schema

Hearing the phrase "Once upon a time . . . " triggers an immediate expectation in both children and adults: They expect to hear a story, most likely a traditional tale that took place many years ago, in some far-off land. It will probably have a hero or heroine and some sort of evil character. A problem or conflict will most likely develop and be resolved, perhaps with the help of magic. The story might end with the phrase ". . . and they all lived happily ever after."

Having heard a variety of stories over a period of years, children as young as four develop a schema for them—that is, an internal representation or sense of story. This sense of story continues to grow, and students use it to guide them through a tale, remember the selection, and write stories of their own. They "use a sort of structural outline of the major story categories in their minds to make predictions and hypotheses about forthcoming information" (Fitzgerald, 1989, p. 19). To put it another way, the reader uses structure to construct a situation model of the story.

Various **story grammars**, or schemes, are available for analyzing a story into its parts. Although each may use different terminology, they all tend to concentrate on setting, characters, and plot. Plot is divided into the story problem and/or the main character's goal, the principal episodes, and the resolution of the problem. In most story grammars, characters are included in the setting; however, as *setting* is a literary word that has long been used to indicate only time and place, it is used in that sense in this book. Different types of stories have different types of structures, and, as students progress through the grades, both stories and structures become more complex. Goals and motivations of major characters become more important. Settings may be exotic and include mood as well as time and place.

Narratives progress primarily in terms of the main character's goals. The reader comprehends the story in terms of the main character's attempts to resolve a problem or conflict. For instance, readers comprehend *The Barn* (Avi, 1994) in terms of Ben's goal of building a barn so that his father will be inspired to recover.

Narratives differ in their overall orientation. Some are action-oriented. Mystery novels, such as the *Cam Jansen* or *Nate the Great* series, tend to fall in this category. They stress actions. Others emphasize characters' consciousness and explore thoughts and feelings and motivations. *The Pinballs* (Byars, 1977), a story of children in a foster home, and *Charlotte's Web* (White, 1952) delve into the characters' emotions. In action-oriented narratives, the tale is composed of a series of episodes arranged in the order in which they happened. Little space is devoted to the psychological states of the main characters. The story is usually told from the perspective of a third-person narrator (Westby, 1999). More complex are stories that embody the consciousness of the characters. These are often told from the perspectives of several characters and are more complex because they require an understanding of human motivation. This involves understanding the actions of others in terms of their goals and plans (Bruce, 1980). Most stories combine action and consciousness but emphasize one or the other.

What can be done to build a sense of story? The most effective strategy is to read aloud to students from a variety of materials, from pre-school right through high school. Most children gain a sense of story simply from this exposure, but it is also helpful to highlight major structural elements. This can be done by discussing the story's setting, characters, plot, and main problem. Discussions about story structure can be guided through questions such as the following (Sadow, 1982):

■ A **proposition** is a statement of information. "Janice hit the ball" is a proposition; "Janice hit the red ball" is two propositions because it contains two pieces of information: Janice hit the ball. The ball is red.

■ **Macrostructure** is the overall organization of a selection, including the main idea or overall meaning of the selection. Microstructure refers to the details of a selection.

■ A **story grammar** is a series of rules designed to show how the parts of a story are interrelated.

■ **Story maps** provide an overview of a story: characters, setting, problem, plot, and ending.

When and where does the story take place?

Who are the characters?

What problem does the main character face?

What does the main character do about the problem? Or what happens to the main character as a result of the problem?

How is the problem resolved?

These questions will help students create an understanding of action-oriented narratives. However, to promote understanding of consciousness-oriented narratives, it is necessary to ask questions about motives and feelings: "Why did Marty lie to his parents? How do you think he felt about it? How would you feel if you lied to your parents?" Consciousness-oriented narratives have a double level: the level of action and the level of thought and emotion. The student must be prepared to grasp both levels.

Asking what, how, and why questions fosters understanding. What questions generally assess literal understanding; why and how questions help the reader integrate aspects of the story and create causal or other relationships. Why questions also foster making inferences (Trabasso & Magliano, 1996).

Discussions should also include an opportunity for students to construct personal responses. The structure is the skeleton of a story. The reader's response is the heart of the piece.

Another technique for reinforcing story structure is having students fill out generic guide sheets. Students reading significantly below grade level found that guide sheets and maps based on story structure helped them better understand the selections they read (Cunningham & Foster, 1978; Idol & Croll, 1985). In their review of the research, Davis and McPherson (1989) concluded that **story maps** are effective because they require students to read actively to complete the maps and also require self-monitoring.

A generic story map based on McGee and Tompkins's (1981) simplified version of Thorndyke's (1977) story grammar is presented in Figure 7.1. As students meet increasingly complex stories, other elements can be added—for example, theme, conflict, and

 Adapting Instruction for English Language Learners

Some ESL students and even some native-speaking students may come from cultures that have different norms for storytelling. In some cultures, children only listen to stories. They don't tell them until they are teenagers (Westby, 1999).

Closing the Gap

If students have limited experience hearing stories, spend additional time reading to them, and encourage parents and grandparents to also spend time reading and telling stories. Provide specific suggestions for caregivers.

 **FIGURE 7.1**

A Generic Story Map

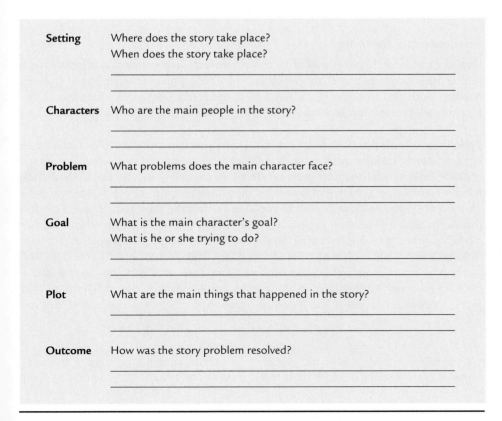

Setting	Where does the story take place? When does the story take place?
Characters	Who are the main people in the story?
Problem	What problems does the main character face?
Goal	What is the main character's goal? What is he or she trying to do?
Plot	What are the main things that happened in the story?
Outcome	How was the story problem resolved?

multiple episodes. Maps can be filled in by students working alone or in small groups, with each student having a different part to work on. They can also be used in the prereading portion of the lesson. The teacher might give students a partially completed map and ask them to finish it after reading.

Retelling

One of the best devices for developing both comprehension and awareness of text structure—**retelling**—has been around since the dawn of speech but is seldom used in classrooms. It has proved to be effective in improving comprehension and providing a sense of text structure for average learners and learning-disabled students (Koskinen, Gambrell, Kapinus, & Heathington, 1988; Rose, Cundick, & Higbee, 1983); it also develops language skills. According to research by Morrow (1985), children who retell stories use syntactically more complex sentences, gain a greater sense of story structure, and evidence better comprehension than those who simply draw pictures of the stories that are read to them. Combining questions with retelling enhances the effectiveness of the technique. This was especially true in Morrow's study, when the questions prompted students whose retelling was flagging or helped students elaborate. Kindergarten students who retold stories and answered questions did better than those who only retold stories or only answered questions. They also seemed to become more confident and were better at story-sequencing tasks.

Although all of us engage in retelling everyday, it is more complex than it might first seem. Retelling begins with meaning. If children fail to grasp the meaning of a selection, they will not be able to retell it. To be successful at retelling, students must not only comprehend the story, they must also understand the components of a story, be able to analyze the story, have the language required to retell the story, and have the cognitive tools to retell the selection in sequence (Benson & Cummins, 2000). Some children have formed a detailed representation of a story but lack the skill to relate that representation to others. Some students have difficulty with retelling because they have had few opportunities to hear and discuss stories. English language learners may be able to construct representations in their home language but might not have sufficient grasp of English to retell stories.

Developmental Retelling

Developmental retelling is a way of improving students' comprehension of selections as well as their language and cognitive skills by building prerequisite skills and fostering retelling skills that match students' level of development (Benson & Cummins, 2000). Major developmental levels consist of pretelling, guided retelling, and written retelling.

Pretelling.   At the pretelling level, students learn to explain everyday tasks, such as making a sandwich, taking a pet for a walk, playing a game, catching a baseball, covering a book, or using a new computer program. To retell, the child must be able to think backwards to reconstruct the steps of a task and then think forwards to put the steps in order. The best activities are those that can be conducted within the classroom. Students can take part in the activity and then identify the steps in the activity. As with other strategies, model the process. In demonstrating the steps in making a paper bag puppet, for instance, show each step while explaining what you are doing. Then in reconstructing the steps, hold up the puppet and show and explain what was done first, what was done second, and so forth. Then model putting the steps in order by writing them on the chalkboard or chart paper. Emphasize the use of the sequence-signaling words *first, second, third,* and *last.*

■ **Retelling** is telling a story that one has read or heard. Retelling is used to check comprehension or gain insight into a student's reading processes.

After more modeling, invite students to share in pretellings. When ready, students pretell with partners and then alone.

When students are able to retell the key steps in an activity, introduce guided retelling. Since guided retelling requires familiarity with story structure, read aloud and discuss books that have a strong story structure. Books with a clearly delineated plot should be introduced first, followed by books in which the setting is key, followed by books with characters that stand out. Continue to read aloud and discuss books until students have acquired a strong sense of story structure. At that point, introduce guided retelling.

Guided Retelling. In guided retelling, students are aided first by illustrations and then by artifacts. Read selections aloud, and show how you use the illustrations to help you retell the story. Select pieces that have illustrations that do a particularly good job of depicting a story. Once students catch on to the idea of using illustrations to retell a story, invite them to join in as you retell with illustrations. Then have them engage in illustration-supported retellings. Encourage students to use only the illustrations when retelling. In fact, it's probably best if you use correction tape or some other means of covering up the words. Once students have caught on to retelling with illustrations, have them use props. Props can be puppets; artifacts such as a ball, a bat, a glove, and a baseball cap for a baseball story; or pictures of objects or people. However, the props do not convey every element in the selection the way pictures do in an illustration-aided retelling. Props might consist of four or five pictures or artifacts that represent highlights of the selection. Felt boards or pocket charts might be used to hold the props.

After mastering retelling with props, students use story maps or graphic organizers to aid their retellings. Graphic organizers help students pick out key elements and note relationships among elements. The graphic organizer might be a story map as in Figure 7.1, a time line as in Figure 7.2 (which could be used for biographies as well as stories), or another type of graphic organizer. The type of graphic organizer will depend on the type of selection being retold and the purpose for retelling. Graphic organizers also provide good preparation for written retelling. At each stage, model the process of retelling but gradually turn the process over to students.

Writing Stories. Story structure can also be used as a framework for composing stories. Laura Pessah, a staff developer at P.S. 148 in New York City, introduced students to the fact that picture books have different patterns of development (Calkins & Harwayne, 1991). Students discovered that some are a series of snapshots; others are circular, as the ending returns to the beginning; still others embody contrasts. Studying these structures gave students ideas about how they might organize picture books they were creating. However, students should be encouraged to follow the dictates of their own imaginations. As Calkins and Harwayne noted, too strict an adherence to structure could

Adapting Instruction for English Language Learners

Because they are still learning English, retelling a story will be more difficult for ELLs but could be a valuable tool for developing language. Model the process and provide prompts. Also, start with simple stories and work up to more complex ones.

FYI

In five-finger retelling, students use their five fingers or a glove as an aid to retelling a story. Each finger represents a key element in the story: Who are the main characters? Where does the story take place? What happened in the beginning? What happened in the middle? What happened at the end?

 FIGURE 7.2

Lincoln Time Line

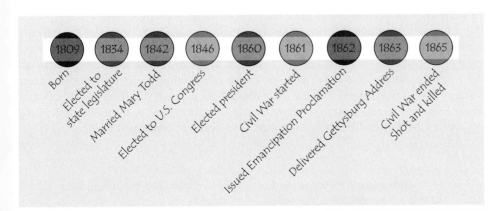

A story web can be created and then later used as an aid while a student is retelling the story.

limit individual visions. Fitzgerald (1989) cautioned, "Strict adherence to a particular story structure could have a detrimental effect, resulting in formulaic stories" (p. 20).

Comprehension of Narratives

Fostering the comprehension of narratives requires being aware of the students' level of knowledge of narratives. To assess students' understanding of narrative schema, ask them to retell a familiar story or to compose a story based on a wordless picture book. Also note students' understanding of a story that they have read. Ask questions that probe the students' understanding of a story: "How did Yvonne feel at the end of the game? Why do you think she felt that way? What might she do to make up for her error?" Students with poorly developed story schema will compose or retell stories as a string of unrelated episodes or will have difficulty composing or retelling a coherent story. Younger students and struggling learners will also have difficulty inferring goals, motivation, emotions, and characteristics. The ability to grasp what characters think, feel, and believe undergoes a fuller development between the ages of nine and eleven, as does the ability to view situations through the perspective of more than one character (Westby, 1999).

Fostering the comprehension of narratives also requires being aware of the students' culture. In European American culture, the best-known fairy tales follow a story grammar type of organization in which there is a problem and a sequential series of episodes that lead to a resolution of the problem. However, other cultures use different structures. African American children, who use more roundabout methods of telling a story, often include a series of events that might seem unrelated but which lead to the theme of the story. Japanese American children tend to recount their stories in condensed fashion.

■ **Expository text** is writing that is designed to explain or provide information.

■ **Text structure** is the way a piece of writing is organized: main idea and details, comparison–contrast, problem–solution, etc.

■ ■ ■ **Checkup** ■ ■ ■

1. What role does knowledge of text structure play in comprehension?
2. What can be done to build students' sense of story structure?

■ ■ ■

Expository Text

Generally speaking, stories are easier to read than science articles, how-to features, and descriptions of historical events (Graesser, Golding, & Long, 1991). Children's schema for **expository text** develops later than that for narration. Expository text has a greater variety of organizational patterns, and, typically, young students have limited experience hearing and reading it. Narrative text is linear; there is generally an initiating event and a series of following episodes that lead to a climax or high point, a resolution of the story problem, and the ending. Because of its structure and linear quality, narrative text is generally more predictable than expository text.

Narrative and expository text are also based on different ways of thinking. We think in narrative fashion. Narrative texts are based on this more straightforward style of thinking, whereas expository text is based on the more complex logical–scientific style (Bruner, 1986). If children are presented with narrative text only, they tend to focus on linear thinking (Trussell-Cullen, 1994). A mix of narrative and expository text is needed to promote a full range of thinking and comprehension skills.

One key to comprehension of expository text is understanding the **text structure**— that is, the way the author has organized her or his ideas. The author may develop an idea by listing a series of reasons, describing a location, supplying causes, or using some other technique. Often, content dictates structure. In science texts, students expect to see both descriptive passages that tell, for example, what a nerve cell is or what an anteater looks like and explanatory paragraphs that tell how a nerve cell passes on impulses or how an anteater obtains food.

Knowledge of structure has a three-fold payoff: It focuses attention on individual ideas, it provides a clearer view of the relationship among ideas, and it is a framework to aid retention of information (Slater & Graves, 1989). The reader can use text structure to organize information from the text and build a situation model.

Types of Expository Text Structure

Following are some of the most important types of expository text structure (Armbruster & Anderson, 1981; Meyer & Rice, 1984):

1. *Enumeration–description.* This type of structure lists details about a subject without giving any cause–effect or time relationship among them. Included in this category are structures that describe, give examples, and define concepts. This structure uses no specific signal words except in pieces that provide examples, where *for example* and *for instance* may be used as signals.

2. *Time sequence.* This type of structure is similar to enumeration; however, time order is specified. Signal words include the following:

after	first	and then
today	next	finally
afterward	second	earlier
tomorrow	then	dates
before	third	later

3. *Explanation–process.* An explanation tells how something works, such as how coal is formed, how a diesel engine works, or how a bill becomes law. Sequence may be involved, but steps in a process rather than time order are stressed. An explanation

Adapting Instruction for English Language Learners

Students who are still learning English can transfer their ability to use text structure in their native language to the ability to use it in English. However, students must be proficient readers in their native language and proficient in reading English (Hague, 1989). A lack of proficiency in English short-circuits the transfer process.

HIGHER-LEVEL LITERACY

Use the language of thinking. Ask students to compare, contrast, analyze, infer, predict, or engage in whatever other thought process is appropriate (Gunning, 2007). Also, demonstrate the process: Show how you would compare, contrast, predict, etc. Think aloud as you demonstrate the process so that students gain insight into cognitive processes.

structure may include some of the same signal words as those found in a time-sequence structure.

4. *Comparison–contrast.* This type of structure presents differences and/or similarities. Signal words and phrases include the following:

although	similar	on the one hand
but	different	on the other hand
however	different from	

5. *Problem–solution.* A statement of a problem is followed by a possible solution or series of solutions. Signal words are *problem* and *solution*.

6. *Cause–effect.* An effect is presented along with a single cause or a series of causes. Signal words and phrases include the following:

because	therefore	thus
cause	since	for this reason
effect	as a result	consequently

Some kinds of text structure can facilitate comprehension and retention. Readers understand more and retain information better from text having a cause–effect or comparison–contrast structure than they do when the text has an enumeration–description structure (Pearson & Camperell, 1994):

> These structures apparently provide readers with additional schemata to help them understand and remember the information. . . . [A comparison–contrast structure] indicates that the information will be about opposing views. . . . Cause–effect structures indicate that the information will be about problems and solutions. . . . Enumeration–description structures are more loosely organized, however, and do not provide additional information. (p. 460)

When reading, students need to activate two kinds of schemata: prior knowledge and text structure. The content of a text cannot be separated from the way that content is expressed. Teachers are "well advised to model for students how to figure out what the author's general framework or structure is and allow students to practice finding it on their own" (Pearson & Camperell, 1994, p. 463).

Teaching Expository Text Structure

Being aware of how a text is structured will help readers build a coherent representation of the text (Dymock, 2005). Dymock recommends using the CORE model (Connect, Organize, Reflect, Extend) when teaching expository text. In the Connect step, the teacher helps the students build on the known by connecting what they know to the topic the text will investigate. In the Organize step, the teacher helps the students to see how the information in the text is structured. Each major text structure is explicitly taught. Students learn to diagram the text, or display elements of its organization. In the Reflect step, students think over how the text is organized and how knowing the organization helps them better understand it. Then the teacher might ask, "What was the structure of the text that we read today? What would be a good way to diagram it?" In the Extend step, students extend their learning. If they used a web in the Organize step to diagram information from the expository text, they might gather additional information to add to the web.

Direct instruction in the recognition of text patterns is also helpful. Text patterns should be introduced one at a time. Start off with well-organized, single paragraphs that reflect the structure being taught. Present any signal words used in that structure. To provide practice in the recognition of signal words, use a cut-up paragraph or article and have students recreate the piece by using signal words and the sense of the piece as guides. For instance, students might use dates to help them rearrange a chronologically organized piece. Or they might use the signal words *first, second, next,* and *last* to arrange sentences or paragraphs explaining a step-by-step process. Gradually, work up to longer selections.

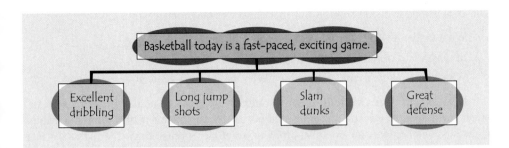

Graphic Organizer for Enumeration–Description Structure

Whole articles and chapters often use several text structures, and students should be aware of that. However, in many cases, a particular structure dominates.

Using Graphic Organizers.   As a postreading activity, students might fill in a time line, as in Figure 7.2, to capitalize on both content and structure. Or they may use a graphic organizer, in which concepts are written in circles, rectangles, or triangles, and interrelationships are shown with lines and arrows. Generally, the more important ideas are shown at the top of the display and subordinate concepts are shown at the bottom. The organizers can be constructed to reflect a variety of patterns (Sinatra, Stahl-Gemeke, & Berg, 1984; Sinatra, Stahl-Gemeke, & Morgan, 1986). After reading a selection, students complete an appropriate graphic organizer and, in so doing, organize the major concepts in a text and discover its underlying structural pattern. Graphic organizers for two major types of text structures, enumeration–description and time sequence, are presented in Figures 7.3 and 7.4.

Students might also use photos or drawings to help them grasp a selection's organizational pattern. For time sequence, they might sequentially arrange photos of a vacation trip they have taken with their family. For explanation–process, they might create a series of drawings showing how to plant tomato seeds. They might use a series of photos to compare or contrast two vehicles, two countries, or two animals. After arranging the graphics, students can add a title, headings, and captions.

Using Questions to Make Connections.   Identifying the structure of a text is only a first step. The reader must then make two kinds of connections: internal (how ideas in the text are related to each other) and external (how text ideas are related to the reader's background) (Muth, 1987). The right kinds of questions can help students detect relationships among ideas in a text. For instance, if the text has a cause–effect structure, you can ask questions that highlight that relationship among the ideas. Your questions can seek out causes or effects. Questions can also help the students relate ideas in the text to their own backgrounds. Here are some questions (adapted from Muth, 1987) that might be asked to help students make internal connections after reading a piece about the process of rusting:

What causes rusting?

What are some effects of rusting?

Under what conditions does rusting take place fastest? Why?

■■■ **FIGURE 7.4   Graphic Organizer for Time-Sequence Structure**

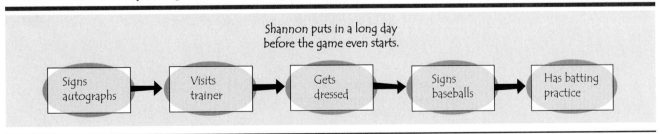

These questions focus on helping students make external connections:

What kinds of things rust in your house? Why?

In what areas of the house do things rust? Why?

What can be done to prevent rusting? Why would these preventive steps work?

Note that all these questions require students to establish internal or external cause–effect relationships. Questions can also be posed that facilitate establishing relationships in texts having comparison–contrast, problem–solution, or other kinds of structures. Once students have grasped the concept, have them create their own connection questions.

Writing for Organization.   Another way to teach expository text structure is to encourage students to compose pieces that employ comparison–contrast and other types of structures. After reading a text that has an explanation–process structure, students might write an explanation of a process they find intriguing. Over time, they should have the opportunity to practice with all the major types of structures.

Using Narrative and Expository Text for Mutual Support

If students are about to read expository text on a difficult topic, arrange for them to read an informative narrative piece on the subject first. Before students read about Pearl Harbor, they might build their background knowledge by reading *A Boy at War: A Novel of Pearl Harbor* (Mazer, 2001). Expository text can be used to support a narrative as well. Before reading the novel *Counting on Grace* (Winthrop, 2006), students might read an informational selection about child labor in the early 1900s.

■ ■ ■ Checkup ■ ■ ■

1. What are the major kinds of expository text structures?
2. What can be done to foster knowledge of text structure?

■ ■ ■

■ The Role of Questions in Comprehension

Questions play a central role in facilitating comprehension. They can be used to develop concepts, build background, clarify reasoning processes, and even lead students to higher levels of thinking. In one study, second-graders became more adept at making inferences simply by being asked inferential questions (Hansen & Pearson, 1980).

Questions foster understanding and retention. When students are asked questions about information in text, they remember that information longer. Asking higher-level questions is especially helpful. Questioning that demands integrating information in a text "will promote deeper processing, and therefore more learning and better remembering than questions that require recall of specific facts only" (Sundbye, 1987, p. 85). As Wixson (1983) put it, "What you ask about is what children learn" (p. 287). If you ask questions about trivial facts, then those facts are what children will focus on and remember. The questions we ask shape students' comprehension and also their concept of what is important in a text.

■   A **taxonomy** is a classification of objectives, types of questions, or other items, based on difficulty.

Planning Questions

Because of their importance, questions need to be planned carefully. They should be used to establish the main elements in a story or the main concepts in a nonfiction selection (Beck, Omanson, & McKeown, 1982). Poor readers benefit from questions that elicit the basic elements in a selection (Medley, 1977). Once the basic plot of a story or the main facts in an article are established, students can be led to a deeper understanding of the material. It is important to ask questions that help children see relationships among ideas, relate new information to their background of experience, and modify their schema. Students must also have opportunities to respond in a personal way to literary pieces—to judge the material and apply the information they gather to their own lives.

Placement of Questions

The placement of questions has an impact on their effect. Questions asked before reading help readers activate a schema and set a purpose (Harris & Sipay, 1990). They guide readers into the text and tell them what information to seek. Questions that are asked after reading help readers organize and summarize the text. Questions asked during reading help readers process text. During-reading questions are especially prevalent in the primary grades. Teachers may stop the reading of a selection halfway through or even at the end of each page and pose questions. Such questioning can clarify any confusing elements in text just read and prepare students to read the upcoming segment. Questions can also be embedded in text at key points. Embedded questions help readers to maintain an ongoing summary of what they have read, to reflect on their reading, and to monitor their reading. This book uses embedded questions. What impact have they had on your reading?

Types of Questions

One way of looking at questions is to examine the kinds of thinking processes involved in asking and answering them. An arrangement of skills from least demanding to those that require the highest mental powers is known as a **taxonomy**. The following taxonomy of types of questions is based on Weinstein and Mayer's (1986) system, which has also been used to classify the comprehension strategies described in this text. However, the lowest level, comprehending, is drawn from Bloom's (1957) taxonomy.

Comprehending. Students understand prose on a literal level. They can recite five facts stated in a selection, name the main characters, and indicate dates and places. This level also includes having students put information in their own words.

Organizing. Students select important details from the selection and construct relationships among them. This involves identifying or constructing main ideas, classifying, noting sequence, and summarizing.

Elaborating. Elaborating entails making connections between information from the text and prior knowledge and includes a wide range of activities: making inferences, creating images and analogies, and evaluating or judging.

Monitoring. Monitoring involves being aware of cognitive processes. It entails knowing whether a selection makes sense and knowing what steps might be taken to improve comprehension.

Listed below are examples of each type of question. They are drawn from *Supergiants: The Biggest Dinosaurs* (Lessem, 1997).

Comprehending

Which of the dinosaurs was the biggest? When was the biggest dinosaur discovered? Which of the dinosaurs was the longest?

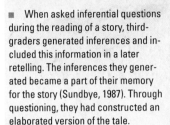

Organizing

In what ways were the biggest dinosaurs alike? In what ways were they different?

Elaborating

How do you know that Professor Rodolfo is determined and hard-working?

In your mind, picture Argentinosaurus. What does Argentinosaurus look like?

What is the area where Argentinosaurus lives like? What sounds do you hear?

Monitoring

Did you find any confusing parts?

Did you run into any words that you couldn't read or whose meanings you didn't know? If so, what did you do?

Can you summarize each dinosaur's main characteristics? If you forget some important details, what might you do?

Using Wait Time

One way of extending responses is to make use of **wait time**. Teachers often expect an immediate answer and, when none is forthcoming, call on another student. Waiting five seconds results in longer, more elaborative responses, higher-level thought processes, and fewer no-responses and I-don't-knows. Teachers who use wait time become more proficient at helping students clarify and expand their responses (Dillon, 1983; Gambrell, 1980). It would be difficult to find a better instructional use of five seconds of silence.

Silence after an answer is given also helps. Used to rapid-fire responding, teachers tend to call on another pupil the second the respondent stops talking. Often, however, students have more to say if given a few moments to catch their mental breath. Dillon (1983) suggested waiting from three to five seconds when a student pauses, seems to be unable to continue, or seems to be finished speaking. Often the student will resume talking and may even supply the most thoughtful part of the response at that point. The postresponse wait time must be a genuine grace period. Maintain eye contact and do not turn away. Failing to maintain eye contact and turning away are cues that your attention is being diverted and will shut down any additional response that the student is about to make (Christenbury & Kelly, 1983).

Classroom Atmosphere

Even more important than using wait time or asking thought-provoking questions is establishing the right classroom atmosphere. The spirit of inquiry and exploration should be obvious. The teacher must be warm and accepting, so students will feel free to speculate, go out on an intellectual limb, or take an unpopular stand without being criticized. Criticism by teachers or classmates actually leads to lowered

The teacher should establish a classroom atmosphere that is receptive to all responses from students.

■   **Wait time** is a period of silence between asking a question and repeating or rephrasing the question, calling on another student, or making some sort of comment.

performance. Less emphasis should be placed on the rightness or wrongness of an answer and more on the reasons supporting the response.

Questions should be democratic, with everyone's contribution valued. That means calling on slower students as often as brighter ones and giving introverts as much opportunity to respond as extroverts. Ironically, research suggests that bright students are not only asked more questions than slow students, they are also given more prompts (Brophy & Good, 1970). All too often, the teacher calls on another student as soon as a slower learner begins to falter. Thus, those who would profit the most from prompting receive the least.

Techniques for Asking Questions

Discussions should be considered opportunities to expand students' background and enhance their verbal and thinking skills. All too often, however, discussions become oral quizzes with a focus on correct answers; emphasis should instead be on helping the child. If a student is unable to provide an answer, it may be the fault of the question—rephrase it, or ask an easier one (Pearson & Johnson, 1978). Some students, because of shyness or because they come from an environment that does not prepare them for the types of questions asked in school, have difficulty answering higher-level questions (Heath, 1991). They may know the answers but must be prompted to help shape their responses. Questioning procedures that make effective use of prompts are described below.

FELS

A useful, research-based technique for using questions to evoke higher-level thinking processes was devised by Taba (1965). Known by the acronym FELS, it consists of asking questions and using prompts and probes that are Focusing, Extending, Lifting, and Substantiating.

Focusing questions, as the name implies, direct students' attention to a particular topic—for example, the peculiar behavior of Sam, a character in a story. The teacher asks literal questions designed to help students describe that behavior.

Extending questions are designed to elicit clarification and elaboration. By extending students' thoughts on the same level, the teacher can encourage them to seek additional information about a character or event and clear up points of confusion. Extending is important because it prepares students for the next step and provides slower students with an opportunity to become involved.

Lifting is the crucial stage. Through questioning or other means, the teacher lifts the discussion to a higher level. Through focusing and extending, the teacher has established that Sam refused to go into the reptile house on the class trip to the zoo, would not get out of the car when the family stopped for a picnic in the woods, and has not visited his friend Joe since Joe obtained a pet snake. The teacher asks, "What do all these actions tell us about Sam?" Now, instead of just giving factual responses, students are asked to draw the conclusion that Sam is afraid of snakes.

Substantiating questions ask students what evidence they found or what standards or criteria they used to draw a conclusion, make a judgment, or prove a point—for example, the evidence that allowed them to conclude that Sam is afraid of snakes.

The following example shows how FELS might be used to build higher-level comprehension. The questions are based on a selection about Andrea, a knowledgeable backpacker who is trekking through a forest.

Focusing

Teacher: Where was Andrea?

Student: In a forest.

Teacher: What did she watch out for?

Student: Snakes.

Teacher: What was she wearing?

Student: Shirt and jeans.

Extending

Teacher: What else did she watch out for besides snakes?

Student: I don't know.

Teacher: Let's look back over the story.

Student: Oh, I see. She was watching out for poison ivy.

Teacher: What kind of shirt was she wearing?

Student: Old.

Teacher: What kind of sleeves did it have?

Student: Long.

Lifting

Teacher: We usually judge people by their actions. Think over Andrea's actions. What do they tell us about her? What kind of person does she seem to be?

Student: Careful.

Substantiating

Teacher: Which actions led you to believe that Andrea is careful?

Student: She watched out for snakes and poison ivy. She wore a shirt with long sleeves so she wouldn't get poison ivy or insect bites.

Taba (1965) cautioned that FELS should be used with care. Frequent shifting from level to level may produce lack of sustained achievement at any level and result in a return to a more basic level. It is also important for teachers to encourage students to reason out and substantiate their answers. If teachers do the students' thinking for them, the strategy is ineffective. Timing and pacing are also important. The teacher has to know, for example, when to proceed to a higher level. Moving to lifting before building a solid understanding of the selection through focusing and extending hinders students' progress. It is also important that the FELS procedure be individualized, as some students require more time on a level than others (Taba, 1965).

Responsive Elaboration

Despite use of a carefully constructed questioning procedure such as FELS, students' thought processes sometimes go astray. They may have misinterpreted instructions or may be misapplying a strategy. A procedure that works well in these instances is **responsive elaboration** (Duffy & Roehler, 1987). Responsive elaboration is not an introduction to or a new explanation of a strategy or skill but an elaboration. It is responsive because it is based on students' answers, which are used as guides to students' thought processes.

To use responsive elaboration, teachers listen to answers to determine how students arrived at those responses. Instead of asking, "Is this answer right or wrong?" they ask, "What thought processes led the student to this response?" And, if the answer is wrong, "How can those thought processes be redirected?" Instead of calling on another student, telling where the answer might be found, or giving obvious hints, teachers ask questions or make statements that help put students' thinking back on the right track. The key to using responsive elaboration is asking yourself two questions: "What has gone wrong with the student's thinking?" and "What can I ask or state that would guide the student's thinking to the right thought processes and correct answer?"

■ **Responsive elaboration** is a procedure in which the teacher analyzes a student's thought processes in order to determine how to adjust or elaborate instruction so as to redirect the student's thinking.

The following is an example of how a teacher might use responsive elaboration with a student who has inferred a main idea that is too narrow in scope:

Student (giving incorrect main idea): Getting new words from Indians.

Teacher: Well, let's test it. Is the first sentence talking about new words from the Indians?

Student: Yes.

Teacher: Is the next?

Student: Yes.

Teacher: How about the next?

Student: No.

Teacher: No. It says that Indians also learned new words from the settlers, right? Can you fit that into your main idea?

Student: The Indians taught the settlers words and the settlers taught the Indians words.

Teacher: Good. You see, you have to think about all the ideas in the paragraph to decide on the main idea. (Duffy & Roehler, 1987, p. 517)

Other Probes and Prompts

In addition to the probes and prompts recommended for FELS and responsive elaboration, there are several additional ones that can be used to foster students' thinking. If students' answers are too brief, use an elaboration probe: "Would you please tell me more?" If a response is unclear, you might use a restating–crystallizing probe. You restate what you believe the student said and then ask whether your restatement is correct: "You seem to be saying that Gopher should have told someone about his problem. Is that right?" The purpose of a restating–crystallizing probe is to help the speaker clarify her or his thoughts. It can also be used to keep the speaker on track if she or he has gotten off the subject (Hyman, 1978).

Accountable Talk

Accountable talk, which makes extensive use of probes and prompts, has been specifically designed to foster higher-level thinking. Through accountable talk, students learn to think carefully about their responses and to base assertions on passages from a text or other sources of information (Resnick & Hall, 2001). Accountable talk respects and builds on what others say. It takes place throughout the day in small-group discussions, in whole-class discussions, in student presentations, and in teacher-student conferences. Students are accountable to the learning community, to knowledge, and to rigorous thinking.

USING TECHNOLOGY

The site of the Institute for Learning has additional information about accountable talk.
http://www.instituteforlearning.org

Accountability to the learning community. Students stick to the topic and have as their goal the development of a topic or an idea. Students listen to each other, acknowledge and build on others' contributions, and paraphrase or revoice the contributions of others. They invite the contributions of all students.

Accountability to knowledge. Students cite passages or examples to back up assertions. When using information from outside sources, they are careful to make sure that it is accurate. Students ask for clarification and explanation of terms and substantiation of claims. They may challenge statements but not persons. Students also note when more information is needed.

Accountability to rigorous thinking. Students draw logical conclusions and provide support for them. Students make connections among sources of information and use multiple sources. Students question, explain, and compare and contrast.

For talk to be an effective builder of higher-level skills, it must be substantive. It must include discussion of complex ideas of the type found in high-quality literary selections and texts with challenging content (Resnick, 1999). Because students might not be accustomed to responding to higher-level questions, they will probably need carefully scaffolded instruction. Teachers develop accountable talk by explaining, demonstrating, modeling, and coaching. They elicit accountable talk through questions and probes that

seek clarification and explanation when called for,

ask for proof or justification for positions or statements,

recognize and help clarify erroneous concepts, and

interpret and summarize students' statements (Resnick & Hall, 2001).

Following are examples of the kinds of prompts and probes a teacher might use.

Substantiating: What in the text leads you to say that the main character made a bad decision?

Clarifying: Could you explain what you mean by that? I'm not sure I understand.

Explaining: Can you tell us, step-by-step, how that process works?

Predicting: What do you think will happen next? Why?

Summarizing: So far this is what the author has told us. . . .

Affirming: I like the way you described the character's actions to prove your point.

Students also use specific kinds of statements to foster accountable talk.

Stating: Here is how she became an outstanding soccer player.

Supporting/substantiating: This is why I believe she was an outstanding soccer player.

Agreeing: I agree with you and here's why.

Disagreeing: I understand what you are saying, but I have a different opinion. (For additional discussion moves, see pp. 407 and 408.)

Think-Pair-Share

Think-Pair-Share is an easy to use but powerful technique for fostering discussing and thinking (Lyman, 1981). In the Think step, the teacher poses a question or idea and the students reflect on it. As an option, they can write a brief response. The purpose is to give them some time to gather their thoughts. In the Pair step, students share their thinking with a partner. This helps students develop and organize their thoughts and also allows them to hear another perspective. As an option, two pairs can then share their ideas. This further expands the students' thinking. In the Share step, the pairs or groups share with the whole class via a spokesperson, who shares not only his or her own thoughts but also those of his or her partner or group. The technique can be streamlined by simply having pairs of students share with each other. You might give them specific directions, such as "Share your prediction with your partner, and explain what led you to that prediction." Model the sharing technique. Show students what the speaker does and what the listener does, so that they have an understanding of both roles. Whole-class sharing is usually enriched when students have had some time to think and the opportunity to share with a partner.

FYI

Turn and talk is a simplified version of Think-Pair-Share. Students simply turn and talk to a partner. You might give students a specific direction, such as "Tell your partner what your favorite after-school activity is and why that is your favorite" (Calkins & Mermelstein, 2003).

▪▪▪ Checkup ▪▪▪

1. What role do questions play in comprehension?
2. What steps can be taken to improve the effectiveness of questioning in the classroom?
3. What are some techniques for asking questions?

▪▪▪

▪ **Guided reading** is an instructional framework within which the teacher supplies whatever help or guidance students need to read a story successfully. It is an updated version of a framework known as the directed reading activity.

■ Frameworks for Fostering Comprehension

Asking the right kinds of questions, building background, activating schema, learning to use strategies, and monitoring one's cognitive processes are all essential elements in fostering comprehension. Systematic but unified approaches that incorporate all these elements are required so that building background and vocabulary and prereading and postreading questions are all related to the selection's major concepts and the students' needs. Two such frameworks are guided reading and the directed reading–thinking activity.

Guided Reading

Guided reading is a framework within which the teacher supplies whatever assistance or guidance students need to read a selection successfully (Fountas & Pinnell, 1996, 2001a). Guided reading is used with individuals or with groups of students who are on approximately the same level of reading development. Selections are provided that match the students' level of development. Students should know most but not all of the words (at least 95 percent). Selections should contain some challenge so that students can apply strategies but should not contain so many new words or unfamiliar concepts as to be overwhelming. "The ultimate goal in guided reading is to help children learn how to use independent reading strategies successfully" (Fountas & Pinnell, 1996, p. 2). Independent reading strategies include both word recognition and comprehension strategies. Students read silently and, as they progress in skill, read increasingly more difficult selections or whole books.

Guided reading can be initiated as soon as students have a firm sense of what reading is, know some initial consonant correspondences, and have learned some high-frequency words. Students are able to take part in guided reading when they can read the kinds of books listed at the Caption/Frame level in Appendix A.

A guided reading lesson consists of five steps: introducing the text (preparation), reading the text, discussing the text, rereading or revisiting the text, and extending the text (follow-up) (Fountas & Pinnell, 1996, 2001c). Extending the text is optional.

Steps in a Guided Reading Lesson

A Guided Reading Lesson proceeds as follows.

Introducing the Text.   Although described as conversation about the text, the introductory phase might use discussion, demonstrations, video clips or other audiovisual aids, and/or simulations to give students guidance in the following areas:

■ *Experiential background or concepts.* Experiential gaps that impede understanding of the selection's major concepts are filled in. If students are about to read a piece about solar power but have no experience with the subject, the teacher might demonstrate the workings of a solar toy. Concepts or ideas crucial to understanding the selection are also developed. Batteries would be an important concept in this instance; however, in the discussion, students might indicate that they know that batteries are necessary to make certain devices run, but they do not know why. The battery's use as a device for storing energy would then be discussed.

■ *Critical vocabulary.* Vocabulary necessary for understanding the selection is presented. For a factual article about Australia's animals, the words *kangaroos, marsupials*, and *herbivores* are presented. Care is taken to show how these words are related to each other.

■ *Reading strategies.* Students have to know how a selection is to be read. Most selections require a mix of preparational, organizational, and elaboration strategies. However, some strategies work better than others with certain kinds of materials. An editorial, for example, requires evaluation. A fictional story might require students to visualize the setting. At times, the format of a selection might be unfamiliar. For example, before tackling a play, students should be given tips on reading stage directions and dialogue.

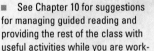

FYI

■ See Chapter 10 for suggestions for managing guided reading and providing the rest of the class with useful activities while you are working with groups.

■ Even if they have the necessary background knowledge, students don't automatically activate it. Plan questions or activities that will help students recall what they know.

■ The guided reading lesson is the model for basal reader lessons and the foundation for the informal reading inventory.

■ To establish the purpose for reading, students might complete a graphic organizer or a reading guide.

■ Very beginning readers typically read audibly even when asked to read silently. They move through five kinds of reading: oral, whisper, mumble (reading that is audible but not decipherable), lip movement, and silent (Wright, Sherman, & Jones, 2004). You might ask students who are reading out loud to whisper read instead.

■ By year's end, all but one of forty first-graders tested were reading silently or were in the lip movement phase, but regressed when given difficult material (Wright et al., 2004). An increase in audible reading is a sign that the selection is too difficult.

ASSESSING FOR LEARNING

As the group reads silently, unobtrusively tap students on the shoulder as a signal to read orally to you (Fountas & Pinnell, 2006). Note needs and supply assistance. For word recognition needs, use the prompts presented on pp. 265.

HIGHER-LEVEL LITERACY

To foster comprehension, use checkup questions placed at strategic points (as is done in this text). Encourage students to use sticky notes to identify puzzling passages. You might also break into the silent reading to remind students to use a particular strategy or to clarify a passage they are having difficulty with.

Adapting Instruction for English Language Learners

Discussions can take a number of forms. Students might discuss in pairs or in small groups. These discussions can be ends in themselves or preparation for discussions by the whole class. If ELLs discuss a selection in pairs or small groups, they will be better prepared for a large-group discussion (Neubert & Wilkins, 2004).

Because teaching a strategy is time-consuming, it is best if the needed strategy is taught beforehand and then briefly reviewed or cued during the introductory discussion.

■ *Purpose for reading.* Whether set by the teacher or by the class, the purpose for reading usually embraces the overall significance of the selection. It may grow out of the introductory discussion. Students discussing hearing-ear dogs might want to find out how they are chosen, and that would become the purpose for reading. On other occasions, the teacher might set the reading purpose.

■ *Interest.* Last but not least, the teacher tries to create interest in the selection. To do this for a piece about an explorer lost in a jungle, the teacher might read the portion of the selection that describes the imminent dangers the explorer faced.

For the purpose of clarity, the elements in the introductory step have been described separately, but in actual practice they are merged. For instance, background concepts and the vocabulary used to label them are presented at the same time. The purpose for reading flows from the overall discussion, and throughout the discussion, the teacher tries to create an interest in the selection. Reading strategies might become a part of the purpose: "Read the story straight through, but read it carefully, to find out how the Great Brain solved the mystery" (reading purpose). "Look for clues as you read the story and try to figure out what they mean" (reading strategy).

Reading the Text. The first reading is usually silent. Silent reading is preferred because reading is a meaning-obtaining process rather than a speech activity. What a student understands is more important than how the selection's words are pronounced. During silent reading, a student might reread a difficult portion of text, get help from an illustration, use context, look up a word in the glossary, or take other steps to foster comprehension. Normally, none of these steps would be taken during an oral reading (Hammond, 2001). During the silent reading, the teacher should be alert to any problems students might be having. If the class is listless, the piece may be too difficult or too boring. If it is humorous and no one is chuckling, perhaps the humor is too sophisticated or too childish. Finger pointing and lip movement are signs that individuals are having difficulty with the selection. The teacher should also be available to give assistance as needed, making note of who requested help and what kinds of help were supplied. Those students can then be scheduled for added instruction or practice in those areas. Reading speed should also be noted. Very fast reading with good comprehension might be a sign that materials are too easy. Very slow reading might be a sign that they are too difficult.

During the silent reading, students should monitor their comprehension to check whether they adequately understand what they are reading and, if necessary, take appropriate steps to correct any difficulties. The teacher should note these monitoring and repair strategies. In some classrooms, steps for attacking unfamiliar words or repairing comprehension failure are posted in prominent spots.

The teacher should be actively involved during the silent reading step. In addition to helping those who request assistance or who are obviously struggling, the teacher should unobtrusively interrupt readers to see how they are doing and ask them to tell about any difficulties they have experienced, passages that were puzzling, or words that were difficult. The teacher might also ask the student to read a brief passage orally. The student might select a favorite passage or might locate and read a passage that answers a question posed by the teacher. In this way, the teacher can provide individual assistance within a group approach.

Discussion. The discussion complements the purpose for reading. Students read a selection for a specific purpose; the discussion begins with the purpose question. If the students read about how hearing-ear dogs are trained, the purpose question is "How are hearing-ear dogs trained?" During the discussion, concepts are clarified and expanded, background is built, and relationships between known and unknown, new and old are reinforced.

Difficulties applying comprehension and word-attack strategies are corrected spontaneously, if possible. The teacher also evaluates students' performance, noting whether they were able to consider evidence carefully and draw conclusions and noting weaknesses in concepts, comprehension, word attack, and application. Any difficulties students are having provide direction not only for immediate help for problems that can be resolved on the spot, but also for future lessons for problems that require more work. Although the discussion is partly evaluative, it should not be regarded as an oral quiz. Its main purpose is to build understanding, not test it. Questioning techniques such as probes, prompts, FELS, and wait time should be used. Part of the discussion might also be devoted to asking students to describe their use of strategies, with a focus on the strategy being emphasized.

Revisiting. In most lessons, revisiting takes the form of reading selected passages and blends in naturally with the discussion. Revisiting may be done to correct misinformation, to obtain additional data, to enhance appreciation or deepen understanding, and to give students opportunities for purposeful oral reading. During the discussion of hearing-ear dogs, students might indicate that they believe the dogs are easy to train (a mistaken notion). Students can then be directed to locate and read aloud passages that describe how long training takes. If students disagree about the main character traits such dogs should possess, they can be asked to locate and read orally passages that support their assertions.

On occasion, revisiting may be an entirely separate step. For instance, students might dramatize a story that has a substantial amount of dialogue or reread a selection to gain a deeper appreciation of the author's style. A separate reading is generally undertaken for a new purpose, although it may be for a purpose that grows out of the discussion. Revisiting is not a necessary step. Some selections are not worth reading a second time, or students might grasp the essence in the first reading.

In the revisiting stage, oral reading should not be overemphasized. Unless a selection is being dramatized, it is generally a poor practice to have students reread an entire selection orally. Oral rereading should be for specific purposes: to clarify a point, to listen to a humorous passage or enjoy an especially vivid description, or to substantiate a conclusion or an answer to a question.

Extending. Extension activities offer opportunities to work on comprehension or word-attack weaknesses evidenced during the discussion phase, to provide additional practice, to extend concepts introduced in the selection, or to apply skills and strategies. These activities may involve any or all of the language arts or creative arts. Students might read a selection on the same topic or by the same author, draw illustrations for the selection, hold a panel discussion on a controversial idea, create an advertisement for the text, or write a letter to the author. The possibilities are virtually limitless, but the follow-up should grow out of the selection and should encompass worthwhile language or creative arts activities. As with revisiting, it is not necessary to have follow-up or extension activities for every reading. In fact, extension activities should be conducted sparingly. "Extending every book (brief books that can be read in a single sitting) through art, writing, or drama is impractical and could interfere with time needed to read widely" (Fountas & Pinnell, 1996, p. 3).

HIGHER-LEVEL LITERACY

In the series Junior Great Books, selections are always read at least twice. In the first reading, students get the general gist of the selection. In the second reading, students take directed notes. They mark passages that help them to engage in shared inquiry. Shared inquiry is the exploration and discussion of an open-ended, interpretive question (Great Books Foundation, 2006).

During a guided reading activity discussion, students may be asked to go back to the text to find support for a statement.

Guided Reading for Beginning Readers

The amount of guidance provided in a guided reading lesson varies depending on students' abilities and the complexity of the selection to be read. For beginning readers, the guidance might consist of going through the text page by page and discussing the selection and highlighting unfamiliar expressions, unknown concepts, and difficult words. The lesson that follows illustrates what a thorough introduction to a selection might look like. Because the teacher figuratively walks the students through the selection page by page and pictures are used to provide an overview of the selection, this type of heavily guided lesson is sometimes called a text walk or picture walk.

As part of an analysis of the book *Up the Ladder, Down the Slide* (Everitt, 1998), a book on a primer level, the teacher noted that readers would need to know what things you might do if you went to the park to have a picnic. The expressions "sun peeks out" and "blow a kiss" might be unfamiliar to some students. Students might also have difficulty decoding words such as *spread, peeks, shout, ladder, slide*, and *share*.

Lesson 7.1

Text Walk for Beginning Readers

Step 1. Introducing the text

Introduce the title, *Up the Ladder, Down the Slide*, to the students. Point to each word as you read the title. Ask students to tell where the children are. Invite them to predict what might happen in the story. Walk the students through the first twenty-four pages of the story page by page or picture by picture so that they get an overview of the tale. Knowing the gist of the selection and being familiar with the format, the students will be better able to use contextual and other clues to achieve a successful reading. As you walk the students through the story, preview words, concepts, and language structures that you think students might have difficulty understanding. Paraphrase key portions of the text that contain difficult items. Then help the students point out these items. For instance, after paraphrasing the second page, in which the unfamiliar word *spread* is used, ask students to point to the word *spread*. On the next page, discuss the expression "sun peeks out." Then have students point to the word *peeks*. After paraphrasing the following page, have students point to the word *shout*. Go through the rest of the book in this same fashion. Stop three or four pages from the end and have students predict what the rest of the story will tell. Then have students read the book on their own to find out about the rest of the story.

Step 2. Reading the text

Encourage the students to read the story on their own, but provide guidance and support as needed. Generally, stories are read silently first. However, selected portions might be read aloud during the discussion to back up or clarify responses or dramatize a portion of the text.

Step 3. Discussing the text

Discuss the story. Start with the students' purpose for reading, which was to find out the rest of the story. Discuss with students what the children did at the park. You might have them read aloud passages that tell what the children did. As children read selected portions aloud, note whether the selection seems to be on the appropriate level and also analyze the students' performance to see what strategies they are using and which strategies they might need to work on. Also take the opportunity to reinforce students' use of strategies. Begin by affirming students' efforts. Praise the students for their use of strategies: "I like the way you used the meaning of the story to help you read *with*." Call attention to strategies that might need introducing or refining: "You read this word (pointing to *fold*) as *hold*. The word *hold* makes sense in the story. But

FYI

■ For more information about the text walk technique, see the article "Introducing a New Storybook to Young Readers" (Clay, 1992).

■ As you walk students through the selection, summarize what is happening and highlight elements that might be difficult. "The children are going to the park to play. Now the sun peeks out. What does that mean? Can you find *peeks*?"

Adapting Instruction for Struggling Readers and Writers

Although originally used with young readers, the text walk technique can be used with older students who are struggling with reading.

what letter does *hold* begin with? What letter does this word begin with? What word that begins with *f* and rhymes with *hold* might make sense here?"

Step 4. Rereading

Encourage the students to dramatize the story. Each student might read one or two pages and pantomime the actions described.

Step 5. Extension

Students might draw pictures that show what they like to do at the park or playground and write captions for their pictures.

FYI

Fountas and Pinnell (2001c) suggest that students in the earliest stages of literacy whisper-read. As students whisper-read, the teacher can listen carefully and provide on-the-spot assistance to those who are struggling.

Guided Reading with More Advanced Students

More advanced students don't usually need to be walked through a text page by page. However, they do need the kind of thorough preparation detailed in the following section.

Preparing a Guided Reading Lesson

Creating a guided reading lesson starts with an analysis of the selection to be read. After reading the selection, the teacher decides what she or he wants the students to learn from it. Content analysis of fiction may result in statements about plot, theme, character, setting, or author's style. For nonfiction, the statements concern the main principles, ideas, concepts, rules, or whatever the children are expected to learn. After analyzing the selection, the teacher chooses two or three ideas or story elements that she or he feels are most important. The piece may be saturated with important concepts; however, more than two or three cannot be handled in any depth at one time and could diffuse the focus of the activity. Even if an accompanying teacher's guide lists important concepts or provides key story events, the teacher should still complete a content analysis. That way, the teacher, not the textbook author, decides what is important for the class to learn. For example, for a piece entitled "Dream Cars for Tomorrow," the teacher lists the following major learnings. These will provide the focus for prereading and postreading activities and determine key strategies for prereading, during reading, and postreading.

The T-X will be easier to care for, repair, and guide.

The T-X will be safer and more flexible.

The Express will be faster.

After selecting these major ideas, the teacher lists vocabulary necessary to understand them. As a rule of thumb, no more than five or six vocabulary words should be chosen. If the list contains a dozen terms, the teacher knows that is too many to attempt to cover. An excessive number of difficult words may be a sign that the selection is too difficult.

The teacher selects the words that will be difficult for the students. From the list of difficult words, those most essential to an understanding of the selection are chosen. For example, the following words are chosen as most essential to the three learnings listed for the dream cars selection and as being ones that students are likely to find difficult: *turbine engine, protective devices, sensors, communicate,* and *satellites*. Examining these words gives the teacher a sense of what prior knowledge or schema the passage requires. A mental assessment of the students helps the teacher decide whether additional background has to be built. For example, poor or urban children whose families do not own a car may have very limited experience with cars and so would require more background than middle-class children or children from the suburbs whose families own one or two cars.

Once the major understandings and difficult vocabulary words have been chosen, the teacher looks over the selection to decide what cognitive and reading strategies are necessary to understand it. For the dream cars selection, visualizing and using illustrations would be helpful strategies. Comprehension should be improved if students visualize the futuristic vehicles and their major capabilities and characteristics. In addition, the photos illustrating the cars being described should help students understand the text.

Building background and vocabulary, activating schema, piquing interest, setting purposes, and giving guidance in reading and cognitive strategies are all done in the preparatory segment of the lesson. Generally, this takes the form of a discussion. Key vocabulary words are written on the board. When discussing each word, the teacher points to it on the board so that students become familiar with it in print. Lesson 7.2 presents a sample guided reading lesson for "Dream Cars for Tomorrow."

Lesson 7.2

A Sample Guided Reading Lesson

Step 1. Introducing the text

During the introduction, the teacher presents vocabulary words and concepts that might be difficult for students. (These are italicized below.) As the teacher mentions the words, she or he points to each, which has already been written on the board. To start the discussion, the teacher asks, "What is your favorite car? What do you like best about that car? If you were a designer of cars for the future, what kind of a dream car would you build? What kind of an engine would you put in it? A *turbine engine*? Why or why not? (Explain that a turbine engine is used on jets.) How many passengers would your car hold? What kind of *protective devices* would it have? Protective devices are things like air bags and seat belts that help keep passengers safe in case of a crash. Would you have any devices that would help you *communicate*? What do we do when we communicate? Would your car make use of *satellites*? What are satellites, and how might they help car drivers? What kind of sensors might the car have? What do sensors do? (Although judged to be difficult for students, the key words *module* and *guidance system* are not introduced because it is felt that they are adequately explained in the selection.) Now that we have talked over some of the parts of a future car, put all your ideas together, close your eyes, and picture your dream car and its main parts. (Students are given a few minutes to picture their dream cars.) What do your dream cars look like? (Students discuss possible dream cars.) Read 'Dream Cars for Tomorrow.' Find out what two of tomorrow's dream cars, the T-X and the Express, are like. As you read, use the imaging strategy that we have been studying. (Teacher briefly goes over the steps of the strategy, which are posted in the front of the room.) Try to picture in your mind what the car or car part looks like or what's happening in the car. Also look at the pictures of the T-X and Express. They will help you to understand the selection."

Step 2. Reading

During silent reading, the teacher looks around to get a sense of the students' reactions to the story. Their silence suggests that they are intrigued. She notes that most of them are glancing at the photos as they read. One student raises his hand and asks for help with the word *ambulance*. The teacher suggests that he look for pronounceable word parts and put them together; when he is unable to do so or to decode the word through an analogy or a contextual strategy, she asks whether the word *ambulance* or *animal* would fit the sense of the selection. Another student has difficulty with *anniversary*, a third with *efficiently*, and a fourth with *kilometers*. The teacher makes a note to work with polysyllabic words in the future.

■ A **story elements map** lists the key components of a story: theme, problem, plot, and needed concepts. One way of creating a story elements map is to begin by noting the problem or the conflict. Then list the major events leading up to the resolution. At that point, use that information to compose the story's theme or moral. You might also list the key characters and identify and list any vocabulary or concepts needed to understand the key elements of the story. Then create questions that focus on the central elements of the story.

Step 3. Discussion

The teacher begins the discussion with the purpose question "What are the T-X and Express like?" Additional questions flow from the students' responses; however, the teacher keeps in mind the three major understandings that she wants students to learn and makes sure that they are explored: "Why might a variety of people buy the T-X? What could an owner who needed more passenger room do? How many passengers will the T-X hold?" There is some disagreement, and the teacher asks the class to go back over the story to find a passage that will answer the question. Then she asks, "How will the T-X use a satellite link?" The class seems confused. *Satellite link* is an important concept. The teacher decides that it is worth some in-depth teaching. She directs the class to go back over the part that tells about it. She reminds students to try to picture in their minds how the satellite link operates and suggests that after rereading the section, they make a drawing showing how it works. The drawings are discussed, demonstrating students' improved understanding. The teacher asks further questions: "How will the driver and the car use the satellite link? Why will the T-X be hard to steal? Why do you think there will be fewer accidents with a T-X? In case of an accident, would the passengers be safer than if they were in a regular car? What is the Express like? Which car do you like better? How do these cars compare with your dream car?" The teacher also asks about students' use of strategies: "What strategies did you use to help you read the story? How did the pictures help? How did imaging help? Which parts of the selection did you image? What did your image look like? Did it have sounds? What were the sounds like?"

Step 4. Revisiting the text

During the discussion, the teacher notes that the students had difficulty scanning through the selection to find facts that would justify their responses. The next day, she reviews the skill of scanning. She models the process and explains why it is important and when it is used. She gives the class a series of questions whose answers are numerals, alerting them to this fact so they know to look for numerals rather than words. The questions are "How fast does the T-X go? How fast does the Express go? When will cars like the Express be seen?"

   The teacher also reviews methods for attacking multisyllabic words and stresses the importance of both syllabication and context. Students scan to find the words *information, ambulance, notified, location, kilometers,* and *anniversary,* and then examine the words in context. Students use both syllabication and context clues to figure them out. As a review of vocabulary, students create and then discuss semantic maps for words they learned in "Dream Cars for Tomorrow."

Step 5. Extending the text

Some students design their own dream cars and create ads for them. Others read books about transportation in the future or other books about cars. Still others elect to read about satellites. A few write to auto manufacturers to obtain information about the newest experimental cars. One group checks the Internet for information about experimental cars. They look under the heading "Concept Cars." The class also makes plans to visit an auto show.

Guided Reading for Fiction

Lesson 7.2 was written for an informational text. A lesson for a piece of fiction would incorporate the same features; however, it might use a **story elements map** instead of a list of main concepts as the framework. Created by Beck, Omanson, and McKeown (1982), the story elements map results in better questions and improved comprehension. Basically the teacher asks himself or herself, "What is the core of this story?" and then focuses questions for students on the core. To reach the core, the teacher decides what the starting point of the story is and then lists "the major events and ideas that constitute the plot or gist of

■■■ **FIGURE 7.5**
A Story Elements Map

Title:	*Leo the Late Bloomer*
Author:	Robert Kraus
Theme:	Some people take longer than others to develop.
Problem:	Leo can't do the things that others his age can do.
Plot:	Leo can't do anything right.
	Leo's mom says he is a late bloomer.
	Leo's father watches for signs of blooming, but nothing happens.
	Leo's mother tells the father to stop watching, but nothing happens.
	At last, Leo can do things.
Ending:	Leo says, "I made it."
Needed Concepts or Ideas:	*Bloom* means "to grow and develop." Late bloomers are people who take longer to develop.

the story, being sure to include implied ideas that are part of the story though not part of the text, and the links between events and ideas that unify the story" (Beck, Omanson, & McKeown, 1982, p. 479). A sample story elements map is presented in Figure 7.5.

A story elements map provides a sense of the most important elements in a story, allowing the teacher to gear preparatory and postreading activities to understanding those elements. Preliminary questions lead up to the story; postreading questions enhance understanding of its main elements. Questions about style and questions that lead to appreciation of the author's craft are asked after the reader has a grasp of the essentials. However, some provision should be made for eliciting a personal response.

How do you get started with guided reading? Start off with reading aloud, shared reading, and other group activities. Also, introduce independent reading. As students are reading independently or working in centers, administer an abbreviated informal reading inventory if you don't know the students' reading levels. To save time, use only the oral selections. Based on inventory results and other data that you have, form groups. You may wish to start with just one small group and gradually form additional groups.

■■■ **Checkup** ■■■

1. What is guided reading?
2. What are the main features of guided reading?
3. What are the steps in a guided reading lesson?

■■■

Directed Reading–Thinking Activity

The guided reading lesson is primarily a teacher-directed lesson. The **DR–TA (directed reading–thinking activity)** has been designed to help students begin to take responsibility for their own learning. Although based on the guided reading lesson, the DR–TA puts the ball in the students' court. The teacher leads them to establish their own purposes for

USING TECHNOLOGY

Using Guided Reading to Strengthen Students' Reading Skills at the Developing Level Grades 1–3 is a video training program created by Fountas and Pinnell (2001c) that provides a number of examples of guided reading lessons.

■ **Directed reading–thinking activity (DR–TA)** is an adaptation of the guided reading lesson (or the directed reading activity) in which readers use preview and prediction strategies to set their own purposes for reading.

reading, to decide when these purposes have been fulfilled, and to attack unfamiliar words independently. The DR–TA works best when students have background knowledge to bring to the selection and can attack difficult words independently. If students lack background or have weak word analysis skills, then the guided reading lesson is a better choice.

Stauffer (1970), the creator of the DR–TA, based the approach on people's penchant for predicting and hypothesizing. By nature, we have an innate tendency to look ahead. We are also decision-making creatures who need opportunities as well as the freedom to make decisions. Building on these propensities, Stauffer structured a predict–read strategy that has the following facets:

- *Setting purposes.* Students have to know how to ask questions about text they are about to read.

- *Obtaining information.* Students have to know how to sift through reading material to get the information they need to answer a question.

- *Keeping goals in mind.* Students must be able to work within the constraints of their goals, noting information that fits in with these goals and not being led astray by information that does not.

- *Keeping personal feelings in bounds.* Students have to be able to suspend personal judgments when reading a piece that contains ideas with which they might not agree, at least until they have finished the piece and have a good grasp of what the author is trying to say.

- *Considering options.* Students must be able to consider a number of choices as they make their predictions and also be flexible enough to change or refine a prediction in the light of new information.

Like the guided reading lesson, the DR–TA has five steps, as outlined in Lesson 7.3. The major difference is that students are given a more active role in the DR–TA (Stauffer, 1969).

Lesson 7.3

A DR–TA

Step 1. Introducing the text

Students are led to create their own purposes for reading. The title of the selection, headings and subheads, illustrations, and/or the beginning paragraph are used to stimulate predictions about the content of the selection. For example, in preparation for reading "Live Cargo!" which is the first chapter of *Misty of Chincoteague* (Henry, 1947), the teacher might have the students examine the title of the chapter. After discussing it, the teacher would have the students examine the first illustration—a Spanish galleon—and then ask them what they think the chapter might be about. Responses, which might include slaves, prisoners, horses, and cattle, would be written on the board. Because the DR–TA is an active process, all students are encouraged to make a prediction or at least to indicate a preference for one of the predictions made by others. The teacher reads the predictions aloud and asks students to raise their hands to show which one they think is most likely.

Step 2. Reading the text

Students read silently until they are able to evaluate their predictions; this might entail reading a single page, several pages, or a whole chapter. Students are encouraged to modify their initial predictions if they find information that runs counter to them.

Adapting Instruction for Struggling Readers and Writers

One adaptation of the DR–TA involves reading the selection to students if it is too difficult for them to read on their own. In a directed listening–thinking activity (DL–TA), the prediction portion is the same. As you read, stop periodically to involve students in discussing predictions and modifying them, summarizing, asking questions about text, and clarifying key terms and confusing passages.

Step 3. Discussion

This stage is almost identical to Step 3 of the guided reading lesson, except that it begins with the consideration of the class's predictions. After reading a portion of "Live Cargo!" students evaluate their predictions and identify which ones were correct and which required rethinking. Additional questions flowing from the sense of the selection are then asked: "Where were the ponies being taken? Why was the captain headed for trouble? What is a stallion?" During the discussion, students offer proof of the adequacy of their predictions or clarify disputed points by reading passages orally. As in the guided reading lesson, the teacher develops comprehension, background, and concepts as the need arises and opportunities present themselves. The discussion also leads students into making further predictions, as the teacher asks, "Why do you think the captain is angry with the stallion? What do you think will happen next?" If students do not respond to these prediction-making questions, the questions should be rephrased or altered. For instance, after getting no response to the question "What do you think will happen next?" the teacher might ask, "What do you think will happen to the stallion and the ponies?" The teacher might also read a few paragraphs aloud to stimulate predictions. As in Step 1, predictions are written on the board and students select the ones they believe are best or most probable.

Step 4. Revisiting the text

This is the same as Step 4 of the guided reading lesson (see p. 341).

Step 5. Extending the text

This is the same as Step 5 of the guided reading lesson (see p. 341).

The DR–TA should be used with both fiction and nonfiction. If students apply the strategies of surveying, predicting, sifting, and verifying to fiction only, they may not develop the ability to transfer these to nonfiction. In time, the strategies practiced in the DR–TA should become automatic.

■ ■ ■ Checkup ■ ■ ■

1. How does a DR–TA differ from guided reading?
2. What are the advantages and disadvantages of a DR–TA?

■ ■ ■

■ The Cloze Procedure

Closing the Gap

For students who are overly focused on pronouncing words and who neglect comprehension, cloze can be an effective antidote. Because words are missing from the blanks, students are forced to think about what they are reading so that they can supply the missing words. Cloze also helps students who overuse phonics and neglect context.

Another approach used to foster comprehension is cloze; it is illustrated in the following exercise. As you read the paragraph, supply the missing words.

> If we see a part of a person or object, we tend to fill in the missing portions. If someone omits the final word of a sentence, we supply it _____ her or him. There is something about the human _____ that can't _____ incompleteness. This tendency to fill in what's _____ is the basis of cloze, a technique by which readers achieve closure by filling in the _____ words in a selection. Based on the concept of gestalt _____, cloze was first proposed as a _____ for measuring the difficulty _____ of reading material. Today it is also used to test reading ability and to build comprehension.

Cloze is an excellent device for building comprehension. Filling in missing words forces a reader to use semantic and syntactic clues together with symbol–sound information and to predict meaning. It also activates the reader's background knowledge. The reader's knowledge of the world must be used to figure out which words should be put in

> ■ **Cloze** is a procedure in which the reader demonstrates comprehension by supplying missing words. Cloze is short for "closure," which is the tendency to fill in missing or incomplete information.

the blanks. Cloze works especially well with students who are concentrating so hard on sounding out words that they fail to read for meaning.

Cloze has also has been used to build students' ability to make inferences (Carr, Dewitz, & Patberg, 1989). Dewitz, Carr, and Patberg (1987) theorized that completing cloze exercises is similar to drawing inferences. After learning to complete cloze exercises, students in the study applied the technique to intact social studies passages. After reading a passage, students used the same strategies they had used to complete the cloze exercises. They were shown how to use their prior knowledge and clues with the passage, just as they had done when completing the cloze exercises. "In both instances the reader becomes accustomed to looking at text carefully while monitoring knowledge and searching for additional information across text" (p. 102).

Classic Cloze

In classic cloze, the teacher deletes words at random from a narrative or expository passage. The first and last sentences are left intact, and no proper nouns are removed; otherwise, every fifth, sixth, seventh, eighth, ninth, or tenth word is deleted. (Generally, the interval for word deletion should be no fewer than every fifth and no more than every tenth.)

The teacher explains the purpose of cloze, gives tips such as the following for completing the exercise, and models the process of completing a cloze activity.

- Read the whole exercise first.
- Use all the clues given in a passage.
- Read past the blank to the end of the sentence. Sometimes the best clues come after a blank.
- If necessary, read a sentence or two ahead to get additional clues.
- Spell as best you can. You lose no points for misspelled words.
- Do your best, but do not worry if you cannot correctly complete each blank. Most readers will be able to fill in fewer than half the blanks correctly.
- After you have filled in as many blanks as you can, reread the selection. Make any changes that you think are necessary.

Scoring Cloze

Exact Replacement

There are two ways of scoring a cloze exercise. When it is used as a test, only exact replacements are counted as correct. Otherwise, marking becomes both time-consuming and subjective. Scores are noticeably lower on cloze exercises than they are on multiple-choice activities; a score of 50 percent is adequate. Criteria for scoring a cloze procedure using exact replacement are shown below:

Level	Percentage
Independent	> 57
Instructional	44–57
Frustration	< 44

Substitution Scoring

When cloze is used for instructional purposes, substitution scoring is generally used. A response is considered correct if it fits both semantically and syntactically. Thus, the following sentence would have a number of correct responses, such as *wagon, toy, ball, bike, coat,* and *dress*:

The child pointed to the red _____ and cried, "I want that!"

Adapting Instruction for English Language Learners

Cloze activities are more difficult for ELLs than they are for native speakers because ELLs are less familiar with the language and find it harder to retrieve or predict words that fit in the blanks.

Discussion for Comprehension

Discussion enhances the value of cloze as a comprehension building technique (Jongsma, 1980). Discussions can be led by the teacher or by students. During the discussion, participants talk over their responses and give reasons for their choices, thus justifying their responses and clarifying their thinking processes. They also compare their answers; in the process, they broaden vocabulary, concepts, and experience and learn to consider and value different perspectives.

Constructing Cloze Exercises

The first rule for constructing cloze exercises is to choose selections that are interesting so that students will be motivated to complete them. It is best to start with easier exercises and progress to more difficult ones. In general, the following items affect the difficulty of a cloze exercise (Rye, 1982):

■ *Number of deletions.* The fewer the deletions, the easier the task.

■ *Types of words deleted.* Content words such as nouns, verbs, adverbs, and, to a lesser degree, adjectives are more difficult to replace than structure words such as articles, prepositions, and conjunctions.

■ *Location of deletion.* Deletions in the beginning of a sentence are more difficult to replace than those in the middle or end.

In early exercises, the teacher may want to delete just one word out of ten—mainly structure words that occur in the second half of a sentence. In time, the number of deletions can be increased, more content words can be omitted, and a proportion of words can be taken out of the beginnings of sentences. The kinds of deletions will be dictated by instructional objectives. If the teacher wants students to work on seeing relationships, she may delete structure words such as *if, then, and, but, moreover,* and *however.* Deleting nouns and verbs and, to a lesser extent, adjectives and adverbs will place the focus on content. Deleting adjectives and adverbs could be a device for having students note how modifiers alter a selection.

Variations on Cloze

Traditional cloze exercises are not recommended until students are in fourth grade or have achieved a fourth-grade reading level. However, modified cloze activities can be introduced as early as kindergarten.

Oral Cloze

Very young students can complete cloze exercises orally. The teacher reads a story, hesitates before a word that students have a good chance of supplying because of its predictability, and asks them to tell what word comes next. For example, when reading *The Little House* (Burton, 1942) aloud, the teacher would pause on reaching the italicized words:

> Once upon a time there was a Little House way out in the *country.* She was a pretty Little *House* and she was strong and well built. The men who built her so well said, "This Little House shall never be sold for gold or *silver* and she will live to see our great-great-grandchildren's great-great-grandchildren living in *her.*" (p. 1)

Oral cloze is greeted enthusiastically by students and occasions lively discussion of alternatives (Blachowicz, 1977). It also introduces children to predicting.

Word Masking

As children begin to acquire some reading skills, word masking is used. A nursery rhyme, poem, or story is shared with students. Students follow along as the teacher reads the selection in a big book. During the second reading, some of the words are covered over. When the teacher gets to one of them, he or she pauses and the children predict what it might be. After they respond, the teacher uncovers the word and asks students whether they were correct (Hornsby, Sukarna, & Parry, 1986).

Modified Cloze

In modified cloze, which is also known as mazes, each blank is accompanied by answer choices so that students do not have to supply the word; they simply identify the best of three or four possible choices. This is a format employed by a number of commercial workbooks and some tests. Although they provide valuable practice, these exercises shift the focus from predicting a word to considering which alternative is best. The task is changed from constructing meaning to recognizing meaning, a subtle but significant alteration. However, modified cloze can be good preparation for completing classic cloze exercises.

FYI

Modified cloze is used in a number of tests: Degrees of Reading Power (DRP), Star (Renaissance Learning), Scholastic Reading Inventory, and Mazes (aimsweb.com).

■ ■ ■ **Checkup** ■ ■ ■

1. What is cloze?
2. For what kinds of students is cloze an especially valuable activity?
3. What are some variations of cloze?

■ ■ ■

■ Critical Reading

What is your reaction on reading the following excerpt from an Internet site titled "The Pacific Northwest Tree Octopus"?

> The Pacific Northwest tree octopus (*Octopus paxarbolis*) can be found in the temperate rainforests of the Olympic Peninsula on the west coast of North America. The habitat lies on the eastern side of the Olympic mountain range, adjacent to Hood Canal. These solitary cephalopods reach an average size (measured from arm-tip to mantle-tip) of 30–33 cm. Unlike most other cephalopods, tree octopuses are amphibious, spending only their early life and the period of their mating season in their ancestral aquatic environment. Because of the moistness of the rainforests and specialized skin adaptations, they are able to keep from becoming desiccated for prolonged periods of time, but given the chance they would prefer resting in pooled water.

Do you feel a bit skeptical about the existence of an octopus that lives in trees? When a class of seventh-graders visited the site and read the article, all but one were convinced that the information was accurate (New Literacies Research Team, 2006; Leu, 2006). Most continued to believe in the veracity of the site even after told that it was a hoax. The incident dramatizes the importance of teaching students to read critically. In a related study, researchers determined that only 4 percent of middle school students reported always checking the accuracy of the information they read online at school (New Literacies Research Team, 2006). Only 2 percent of students always check the accuracy of the information they read online outside of school. In general, students surveyed in five middle schools

Today's students should be taught how to read magazines critically.

did not think critically about the information they encountered on the Internet or about who composed the information.

Today's students are barraged with an overwhelming number of sophisticated, slick television and print ads. Even the youngest readers encounter slanted writing, illogical arguments, and persuasive techniques of all types. In addition, the Internet has become a major source of information. Virtually anyone can put information on the Internet. Unlike book and periodical publishers, Web site sponsors do not necessarily have any editors or reviewers to check the accuracy or fairness of the information. Many of the sites and services provided on the Internet are sponsored by commercial enterprises, so the information may be biased. The ability to evaluate what one hears and reads has never been more important.

Children who read critically judge what they read. This judgment is not a mere opinion but an evaluation based on either internal or external standards. In the process of learning to evaluate what they read, students deal critically with words, statements, and whole selections.

Critical reading is an affective as well as a cognitive skill. To read critically, students must be able to suspend judgment and consider other viewpoints. Generally, people tend to interpret what they read in light of their beliefs. Some readers (and this seems to be especially true of poor readers) reject information that contradicts their beliefs. On the other hand, some readers suffer from a malady that one educator called the "Gutenberg syndrome" (J. Rothermich, personal communication, January 1980): If a statement appears in print, it must be true. Students have to challenge what they read and realize that a printed or online statement might be erroneous or simply be someone else's opinion.

To encourage critical reading, a teacher must create a spirit of inquiry. Students must feel free to challenge statements, support controversial ideas, offer divergent viewpoints, and venture statements that conflict with the majority view. When they see that their own ideas are accepted, they are better able to accept the ideas of others. The program, of course, must be balanced. The idea is not to turn students into mistrustful young cynics but to create judicious thinkers.

There are dozens of critical reading skills. The suggested skills listed in Table 7.1 are based on examination of professional materials and analysis of critical reading tasks. There is no timetable for acquiring these skills.

Uses of Language

A good starting point for a study of critical reading is to examine how language is used. What do words do? What functions do statements fulfill? Words are used in four main ways: to describe, to evaluate, to point out, and to interject (Wilson, 1960). The words *car, take,* and *dog* describe bits of reality. The words *evil* and *stupid* evaluate, going beyond mere description to judgment. Some words both describe and evaluate: *jalopy, steal,* and *mutt* describe objects and actions, but they also incorporate unfavorable evaluations. A key strategy in critical reading is to note whether words offer neutral descriptions, evaluations, or both.

To introduce the concept of the uses of words, write a series of sentences similar to the following on the board:

The horse weighs 950 pounds.

The horse is black with white spots.

▪ **Critical reading** refers to a type of reading in which the reader evaluates or judges the accuracy and truthfulness of the content.

■■■ **TABLE 7.1 Critical Reading Skills**

Distinguishing between facts and opinions
Identifying words that signal opinions
Verifying factual statements
Identifying the uses of words (e.g., to describe, to judge)
Recognizing denotations and connotations
Identifying persuasive language
Identifying an author's purpose
Drawing logical conclusions
Supporting conclusions
Judging sources of information
Identifying slanted or biased writing
Identifying major propaganda techniques

The horse is lazy.

The horse is wonderful.

Discuss which words just tell about the horse and which judge it. Guide students as they locate words in their texts that describe, judge, or do both. While discussing selections that students have read, note words that are used to judge. To extend the concept of uses of words, introduce the concept of connotations; have students note words that have favorable connotations (*thrifty, slim*) and those that have unfavorable ones (*selfish, skinny*). For younger students, you may want to use phrases like "sounds better" and "sounds worse," instead of "favorable connotations" and "unfavorable connotations."

Introduce the concept of persuasive language by bringing in ads and package labels. Have students locate words that sell or persuade in television and print ads—*fresh, delicious, new*, and *improved*. They can even compose their own persuasive advertising.

Understanding Factual Statements and Opinions

Factual statement are those that can be verified through objective evidence or through analyzing language. The statement "It is raining" can be verified by looking outside. Even if the sun is shining, the statement is a factual one rather than an opinion because it can be verified. If the sun is shining, the statement is verified to be inaccurate. The statement "A hurricane is called a *typhoon* when it occurs over the Pacific Ocean" cannot be verified by observing hurricanes or typhoons. It is verified by analyzing the statement to see whether the language is being used accurately. Analytic statements of this type are frequently verified by using a reference. Because the word *fact* suggests something that is true, it is better to use the term *factual statement* rather than *fact*.

To introduce the concept of factual statement and opinions, place sentences similar to the following on the board:

We have twenty-five players on our soccer team.

We have won twelve games in a row.

Our uniforms are red.

Soccer is the best sport.

Show students that the first three sentences can be proved in some way, but the last one cannot. It is simply an opinion, a statement that tells how someone feels. Help students locate statements of fact and opinion in their texts. To reinforce and extend this concept, plan lessons and activities such as the following.

Reinforcement Activities

Extending the Concept of Facts and Opinions

■ Present words that signal opinions, such as *good, bad, worse, terrible, wonderful,* and *awful*. Ask students to use these and other signal words in differentiating between factual statements and opinions.

■ Introduce the concept of verifying factual statements. Explain to students that factual statements can be proved in some way—by measuring, weighing, observing, touching, hearing, counting, and so on. Bring in a kiwi or other unusual fruit, and encourage students to make factual statements about it—for example, "The kiwi is brown" and "It has fuzzy skin." Discuss how each statement might be proved. Bring in a scale and a measuring tape so that the kiwi can be weighed and measured. Have students make other factual statements and tell how they might prove them—that is, whether they would mainly count, measure, weigh, touch, listen, or observe to prove the statements.

■ Let students examine an object and make at least five factual statements about it based on counting, measuring, weighing, touching, listening, observing, or checking a reference book. Then ask them to write down their personal opinions about that object. This might be an opportunity for them to be especially imaginative and creative.

■ Ask students whether a particular statement in a reading selection is a fact or an opinion. Take special note of opinions that might be mistaken for facts.

Recognizing the Author's Purpose

The three main purposes for writing are to inform, to entertain, and to persuade. Recognizing which one applies to a particular selection enables students to match their reading strategy to the selection. For example, knowing that a writer is attempting to persuade, they will look at the piece with a critical eye. To introduce the concept of purpose, read aloud an ad or an editorial, an encyclopedia article, and a short story, and discuss each author's purpose. Help students suggest other writings that are designed to inform, entertain, and persuade.

To extend the concept, have students predict the author's purpose before reading a selection and then discuss their predictions after reading. For each book report that students complete, have them identify the author's purpose. Students can also decide what their own purpose is before writing a piece. Let them write editorials for the school newspaper or letters to the editor. Bring in persuasive pieces, and discuss them with the class. Help the class see what persuasive techniques are being used.

Drawing Logical Conclusions

A conclusion is a type of inference. Drawing a conclusion usually entails examining several facts or details and coming to some sort of reasoned judgment based on the information. In critical reading, stress is placed on drawing conclusions that are logical, have sufficient support, and consider all the evidence. In many instances, different conclusions can be applied to a set of facts. Students should be shown that they should reach the most likely conclusion while keeping an open mind because other conclusions are possible.

To introduce drawing logical conclusions, model the process and provide guided practice. Have students apply the skill to all content areas, drawing conclusions about the main character in a piece of fiction, about experiments in science, and about historical events and figures in social studies. Stress the need to consider the evidence very carefully.

Judging Sources

Because students tend to believe everything they read, whether in print or on a computer screen, they should understand that some sources are better than others. Three main criteria are used to judge a source: whether the source has expert knowledge about the subject, whether the information is up to date, and whether the source is unbiased.

Encourage students to examine their textbooks to see whether they are written by experts and are up to date. When students read nonfiction, have them note who wrote the information and then examine the book jacket or another source of information to see whether the author seems to be an expert. For a Web site, students should see whether the author's name is given and whether the author's credentials are provided. Students should also check the date of publication. When examining Web sites, students can note when the site was last updated. Also, discuss the issue of author bias. For instance, talk over why a book or Web site on coal mining written by someone who works for a coal company might be considered to be written by an expert but could be biased in favor of the coal industry.

When using the Internet, students might also determine what the URL tells them about a site. Students can tell whether the site is educational (edu), governmental (gov), organizational (org), or commercial (com) (Caruso, 1997). A tilde (~) in the Internet address indicates that the Web site is the work of an individual. One might have more trust in a site sponsored by a library, university, or government agency than in one sponsored by a commercial entity or an individual.

When using a Web site, students should evaluate the accuracy and fairness of information.

Slanted Writing

Slanted, or biased, writing uses emotionally charged words and specially chosen details to create an unfairly favorable or unfavorable impression about a person, place, object, or idea. It is found in political speeches, personal opinion columns in magazines and newspapers and Internet sites, sports articles, biographies and autobiographies, and history texts.

Show students how words and details can be selected so as to shape readers' opinions. Discuss why it is important to recognize slanted writing. Assign selections, some of which are slanted and some of which are neutral, and ask students to decide which are which. They should take note of techniques used to slant writing. Most important, they must be able to detect it as they are reading. To reinforce this skill, keep a file of examples of slanted writing, and from time to time, share and discuss some of them with the class. Encourage students to bring in examples of slanted writing, and discuss these also. Have students look for examples of slanted writing in what they themselves write.

Student Strategies

Judging Sources

Once students seem to grasp the concept of judging sources for fairness, help them develop a set of questions that they might use to assess printed sources and Web sites they consult:

Is the source up to date?

Who is the author?

Is the author unbiased? Is there any reason that the author would be in favor of one side or one position?

USING TECHNOLOGY

Checklists for evaluating Web sources can be found in the following:

Kathy Schrock's Guide for Educators: Critical Evaluation Information
http://school.discovery.com/schrockguide/eval.html

Evaluating Internet Resources: A Checklist
http://www.infopeople.org/resources/select.html

How to Critically Analyze Information Sources
http://www.library.cornell.edu/okuref/research/skill26.htm

FYI

Visual appeal is the main element most adults use when evaluating the credibility of a Web site (Fogg, Soohoo, Danielson, Marable, Stanford, & Tauber, 2003).

Is the writing fair, or does it seem to be slanted?

Does the author give enough proof for all conclusions?

You might post the questions as a reminder for students to use them when they are reading. The questions might also be adapted and used in evaluating speeches and informational TV programs.

■ ■ ■ Checkup ■ ■ ■

1. What is critical reading?
2. What are some key critical reading skills? How would you go about teaching them?

■ ■ ■

Tools for the Classroom

Building Higher-Level Literacy

Use prompts and probes to lift students' thinking to higher levels. Used in combination, FELS and responsive elaboration are especially valuable in lifting student thinking to higher levels. Both techniques are deceptive, in that they seem straightforward but are difficult to apply. They require a deliberate effort on your part to implement and lots of conscious practice until they become virtually automatic. Also foster in students the habit of reading and listening with a critical attitude. In all subject areas and in discussions, assess the reliability and credibility of claims and information. Call attention to biased passages or bring in biased materials from time to time and discuss whether they are fair.

Help for Struggling Readers and Writers

Achieving readers often pick up strategies on their own. Struggling readers and writers have a greater need for structure and explicit instruction. They also need to have materials of an appropriate level of difficulty. In an experiment with a class of thirty-two fourth-graders in an elementary school that was part of a public housing project, Mosenthal (1990) noted that all thirty-two youngsters received whole class instruction and read from a text that was on grade level, even though some children were reading below grade level. Selecting the seven lowest-achieving students, Mosenthal and the children's teacher, who was highly experienced, obtained materials on a second-grade level and provided the children with supplementary comprehension instruction that consisted of directed reading–thinking activities and written retellings. Retellings were chosen because they offered insights into the children's changing ability to comprehend narrative text.

Over a period of three months, the students' retellings improved dramatically. They became more complete and began to reflect the most important elements in the tales that had been read. Although instruction and practice were undoubtedly essential factors in the children's improvement, setting may have been even more important than the quality of instruction. As the children's teacher noted, "I know at times in the beginning that they (the students in the reading and writing group) were elated that they were part of a small group. I think the stories helped. They were stories they could read and they could enjoy" (Mosenthal, 1990, p. 282). Although reluctant to write at first, the children's attitude changed because they were praised for their efforts. Over time, they also felt better about themselves. As their teacher remarked, "They saw improvement and I think they felt better about what they were doing" (Mosenthal, 1990, p. 283).

As the researchers noted, improved learning environment interacted with direct instruction in reading and writing. Being given materials they could read, tasks they could perform, and a positive, can-do atmosphere, students were able to make the most of instruction.

Essential Standards

Kindergarten through grade 3

Students will

- use their knowledge of story grammar to help them understand narratives.
- recognize cause and effect and other relationships.
- grow in their ability to use retelling procedures to build and demonstrate comprehension.
- begin to use expository text structures to foster comprehension of informational text.
- distinguish between factual statements and opinions.
- identify persuasive and slanted language.
- identify an author's purpose.
- draw conclusions.
- judge sources of information.

Grades 4 through 8

Students will

- use their knowledge of story grammar to help them understand narratives.
- grow in their ability to use retelling procedures to build and demonstrate comprehension.
- use expository text structures to foster comprehension of informational text.
- distinguish between factual statements and opinions.
- identify persuasive and slanted language.
- identify an author's purpose.
- draw conclusions.
- judge sources of information.
- identify slanted or biased writing.

Action Plan

1. Gear instruction to students' level of cognitive development. With activities such as retelling, begin with supported retelling and gradually lead students to independent retelling.
2. Guide students in the use of text structure to help them comprehend narrative and expository selections.
3. Create a classroom atmosphere that values inquiry and discussion but in which the students feel safe to venture opinions and conjectures.
4. Ask questions on a variety of levels. Use wait time, prompts, and probes to build students' confidence and comprehension.
5. Use frameworks such as text walk, guided reading lessons, and DR–TA to foster comprehension. Adapt techniques to the needs of the students. Use a guided reading lesson for students who need maximum structure and DR–TA for those who need less structure.
6. Incorporate activities and ask questions that lead students to evaluate what they read.

Assessment

Through observation and discussion and oral or written retellings, note students' ability to use story grammar and knowledge of text structure to foster comprehension. Using these same assessment techniques, note students' ability to think, read, and write critically. Use techniques such as responsive elaboration to both assess and guide students' thinking and processing of text. Through assessment, obtain information that you can then use to improve instruction. See Chapter 2 for additional information on assessing comprehension.

Summary

Through hearing stories, reading, and writing, children develop a schema for narrative tales. Generally, expository works are harder to read than narratives, but knowledge of text structures can foster improved comprehension. Questions and an atmosphere conducive to open discussion also play a role in facilitating comprehension.

Guided reading is a highly useful framework for conducting reading lessons. The DR–TA (directed reading–thinking activity) gives students more responsibility for their learning. Cloze is valuable for building comprehension because it forces students to read for meaning, use context, and make predictions.

An affective as well as a cognitive skill, critical reading involves willingness to suspend judgment, consider another point of view, and think carefully about what one reads. Thoughtful reading and discussion promote critical thinking.

Extending and Applying

1. Collect samples of biased writing from children's periodicals and textbooks.

2. Examine a lesson from a basal series that is no more than three or four years old. Examine the questions for three selections, and classify them according to Weinstein and Mayer's taxonomy. What percentage are on a comprehending level? Organizing level? Elaborating level? Monitoring level?

3. Plan a guided reading lesson for a chapter of a children's book, a short story, an informational piece, or information from a Web site. Teach the lesson, and evaluate its effectiveness.

4. Create and teach a cloze lesson. Evaluate its effectiveness.

5. Try out the FELS technique for asking questions with a class. Also use wait time, and create an accepting atmosphere. Do this for a week. Have a colleague observe your performance and give you objective feedback.

Developing a Professional Portfolio

Look over the comprehension standards issued by the state or district where you are teaching or plan to teach. Also look at the tests or other devices used to assess comprehension. How well are the two aligned? In your portfolio, note any work you have done or plan to do to make your instructional program align with state or district standards and the assessment measures for comprehension.

Go to Allyn & Bacon's MyLabSchool: www.mylabschool.com

- Enter Assignment ID **RMV7** into the **Assignment Finder,** and select the case titled "Teaching with Literature."

- What did the teacher do to make the guided reading lesson effective and engaging? How did she differentiate instruction?

- Explore MyLabSchool further to find the course areas for Reading Methods, Language Arts, and Content Area Reading and identify other assets that support concepts introduced in this chapter.

Developing a Resource File

Maintain a file of different types of text structures that can be used to illustrate ways in which ideas can be presented. Also maintain a file of passages, selections, and Web sites that can be used to provide practice with distinguishing fact and opinion, drawing conclusions, and evaluating sources.

To access chapter objectives, practice tests, weblinks, and flashcards, go to the companion website at www.ablongman.com/gunning6e.

8 Reading and Writing
in the Content Areas
and Study Skills

For each of the following statements related to the chapter you are about to read, put a check under "Agree" or "Disagree" to show how you feel. Discuss your responses with classmates before you read the chapter.

	Agree	Disagree
1. Content-area textbooks should be simplified.	_____	_____
2. The strategies that are most effective in promoting comprehension of content-area material are those that are used after students have read the text.	_____	_____
3. When teaching reading of content-area material, a teacher should stress content rather than strategies.	_____	_____
4. Content-area teachers should be responsible for teaching the reading skills students need to use their subjects' texts.	_____	_____
5. Content-area information should be presented to poor readers through discussions, experiments, and audiovisual aids rather than through texts that might be too difficult for them.	_____	_____
6. Most students learn effective study techniques without any formal instruction.	_____	_____

Chapters 6 and 7 presented a variety of strategies for improving comprehension of narrative and expository text. This chapter focuses on applying those strategies to improve literacy in the content areas. Additional aids to comprehension are introduced, and some special difficulties inherent in reading in the content areas are explained. The chapter also explores study skills and techniques for remembering content-area information and other material.

Before reading this chapter, reflect on your knowledge of reading in science, history, and other content areas. Do you use any special strategies to comprehend what you read in the content areas? If so, what are they? How well do they work for you? Do you have any problems reading in the content areas? Do you have any problems studying? How might you improve your comprehension and retention of the material? How might you help students improve their reading in the content areas? How might you help them improve their studying?

■ The Challenge of Content-Area Reading

As students move up through the grades and spend more time learning social studies and science concepts, emphasis shifts to reading to learn.

Content-area textbooks account for an estimated 75 to 90 percent of the material presented in subject-matter classes. However, students may be poorly prepared to learn from content-area texts. Stories are emphasized in the early years, so students may have little experience with informational text. Often, the informational text they do read in their basals has a strong narrative thread. Content-area text has a different, more complex structure. Instead of following a narrative, readers must understand complex processes and identify causes and effects as well as problems and solutions.

Adapting Instruction for Struggling Readers and Writers

■ Today's textbooks have many suggestions for assisting struggling readers. Some offer key concepts rewritten at an easier reading level. Others offer graphic organizers, vocabulary exercises, visuals, recordings, and other devices designed to assist struggling readers.

■ The typical sequence for handling the reading of content-area texts is read-listen-discuss. Students read a chapter, perhaps for homework, which the teacher then explains. After the explanation, the class discusses the text. A more effective sequence might be listen-read-discuss, in which the teacher gives a five- to fifteen-minute explanation of the material, directs the students to read it, and then has the class discuss it. Because the explanation precedes the reading of the text, the students are better prepared to read it.

 FYI

■ Texts should be on the appropriate level of difficulty. There should be a match between students' reading levels and the texts they are required to read.

■ The teacher should decide on objectives and topics to be covered and then select the materials. The textbook should be supplemented with informational children's books, periodicals, primary sources, audiovisual aids, computer software, and, information from the Internet.

Readers must also cope with greater density of ideas and more technical vocabulary and concepts for which they may have a very limited background. However, what really sets content-area reading apart from other reading is its purpose, which is to allow children to learn about a subject area and, ultimately, to be able to apply what is learned.

Fortunately, the best of today's content-area texts provide a wealth of support for the reading and writing skills needed to comprehend and remember key concepts. They build background and vocabulary and provide previews, overviews, lots of helpful graphics, review questions, and activities. In one recently published social studies program, students are taught a target reading strategy that will assist them as they read the chapter (Boyd et al., 2003). In a chapter on the American Revolutionary War, students are taught to recognize cause-and-effect structure and to make use of this structure to comprehend the text. After being taught the skill in the context of an article on events leading up to the Revolutionary War, they apply the skill throughout the chapter (see Figure 8.1). Questions build on the skill and lead students to apply it. For instance, students are asked questions like these: "What effect did the Sons of Liberty have on the Stamp Act? What caused British leaders to pass the Townshend Acts?" Graphic organizers also reinforce skills as students fill in missing causes on a cause–effect organizer.

Writing is used to foster learning. Students are asked to imagine being a member of the Virginia House of Burgesses and write a speech opposing the Stamp Act.

Assessment is tied to instruction. For instance, if students are unable to tell how the Townshend Acts were similar to but different from the Stamp Act, it is suggested that the teacher guide students as they create a graphic organizer designed to show differences and similarities.

The best content-area texts are so carefully designed that they are potentially more effective for building literacy skills than many of literacy programs designed specifically to develop skills. This doesn't mean that the history teacher has become a teacher of reading and writing. It means that the teacher is helping students acquire skills needed to learn history. Through acquiring effective learning strategies, students learn more content.

■■■■ **FIGURE 8.1**   **Reading Aids in a Content-Area Textbook**

From Scott Foresman Social Studies, *The United States, Multimedia Teacher's Edition, Volume One* by Candy Dawson Boyd, et al. © 2003 by Pearson Education, Inc. Used by permission.

Textual Features That Foster Learning

From a reading standpoint, a number of features promote learning from a textbook. As noted in Chapter 6, the five major groups of strategies (excluding rehearsal) are preparing to read; selecting and organizing relevant information; elaborating on the information once it has been selected, which means integrating the new information with existing knowledge structures or schemata; monitoring for meaning; and implementing affective or motivational strategies. Table 8.1 presents textual features that foster these processes.

In many classrooms, the entire class reads the same textbook, generally one designed for the average student. In the average class, however, such a book will be too difficult for at least one child out of four. Singer and Donlan (1989) claimed that in the upper grades, as many as 50 percent of students may have difficulty with their textbooks. Other children will be able to use a more challenging book. Some provision has to be made for these varying reading abilities, especially for students reading significantly below the level of the textbook. Possibilities are providing extra help with the text, obtaining an audio version of the text, reading the text to students and then cooperatively composing a summary of key points, using trade books on an easier reading level (content-area teacher's manuals generally contain lists of recommended trade books on various levels), using easier texts, or some combination of these techniques. Among publishers that issue easy-to-read content-area texts are American Guidance Services, Globe Fearon, and Steck Vaughn. Whichever approach you choose, make sure that students do some content-area reading. Otherwise, they will never acquire needed skills.

Content-area texts have a more complex structure.

Adapting Instruction for Struggling Readers and Writers

In some content-area programs, the core text is accompanied by below-level, on-level, and advanced readers, all of which cover the same content or topic. These leveled readers are accompanied by a teacher's guide that contains graphic organizers.

■ ■ ■ TABLE 8.1   Textual Features That Foster Use of Learning Strategies

Benefit	Examples
Help students prepare	Chapter overview that lets students activate schemata Semantic maps or other graphic organizers Heading and illustrations that allow students to make predictions Key terms and explanations Glossary
Help students select relevant information and organize it	Introduction and summaries to highlight important information Headings and subheadings highlighting main ideas Details that clearly support main ideas Topics developed in sufficient detail but not so much as to overwhelm readers Clear, well-written text with connectives and transitions where needed Graphic aids Questions and activities at the end of each chapter Explanations to relate new knowledge to readers' background
Help students elaborate or integrate important information	Questions or activities that help readers relate what they have read to their prior knowledge or experience
Help students monitor reading	Questions at the end of each chapter or interspersed throughout chapters that ask students to check their understanding Illustrations and other graphic devices that give the text an appealing look
Foster students' motivation	Interesting style that engages the reader; use of anecdotes Relationships drawn between content and students' lives

Adapted from *Textual Features That Aid Learning from Text*, unpublished manuscript by B. Armbruster, 1987. Champaign, IL: Center for the Study of Reading.

■ ■ ■ **Checkup** ■ ■ ■

1. Why is reading in the content areas difficult?
2. Why should all students read content-area materials?
3. What can be done to make content-area materials accessible to struggling readers?

■ ■ ■

■ Instructional Techniques

The first principle of content-area reading instruction is to help students build conceptual understanding. In their study of upper elementary school students reading a U.S. history text, researchers McKeown, Beck, and Sandora (1996) found that students took "one swift pass through the words on a page, and then formed them into a shallow representation of the text" (p. 101). They didn't seek out key ideas or relate what they were reading to what they already knew. Conceptual understanding means going beyond the facts or the events and building a deeper understanding.

Building conceptual understanding requires that the teacher decide what major concepts she or he wishes her students to learn and then design learning activities that will help students construct those concepts. For instance, a teacher might want students studying World War II to understand that excessive national pride, economic needs, and conflicting ideologies lead to wars. Activities need to be designed that lead to these understandings. Simply answering factual end-of-chapter questions will promote only shallow understanding. Through careful reading, discussions, and questions that help students see the big picture, a conceptual understanding can be fostered.

It is also important that students make connections. Concepts are stored in networks. Students can understand and retain new information better if they relate it to already existing schemata. For instance, if students have a well-developed schema for World War I, they are better able to understand how economic hardship and the humiliation of the Treaty of Versailles set the stage for Germany's aggression and the beginning of World War II. Instead of being isolated bits of knowledge, information about the two wars becomes a part of a larger web of knowledge about wars. Going beyond dates of battles and names of countries and leaders, looking at the big picture, including the underlying causes and effects of the war, will also foster a deeper understanding. Questions and activities that involve students in making comparisons, connecting bits of information, and drawing conclusions help students construct a conceptual understanding. For instance, students might compare World War II with recent wars and current conflicts and draw conclusions about wars in general.

Because the text is a key source of information in the content areas, being able to use effective reading and learning strategies will help students acquire the information that forms a base for building a conceptual understanding. Specific techniques for helping students get more out of their content-area reading are used before reading, during reading, and after reading.

Before Reading

In preparing to read a text, strategic readers survey the text, activate appropriate prior knowledge, predict what the text will be about, set goals, and decide how to read the material. To help the reader learn and apply these strategies independently, the teacher uses

Closing the Gap

■ Responding to pressure to do well on state proficiency tests in reading, many schools have abbreviated or eliminated content-area reading, especially in the lower grades. Ironically, in so doing they are eliminating a potential solution to closing the gap. Content-area reading is an excellent means for building vocabulary, background, advanced comprehension strategies, and critical thinking.

■ Realizing that many of their students struggle with texts, some teachers instead use lectures, discussions, and other activities to present content. This deprives students of the opportunity to learn to read in the content areas.

■ An **anticipation guide** is an instructional technique designed to activate and have students reflect on background knowledge.

the DR–TA, ReQuest, reciprocal teaching, or Questioning-the-Author techniques, which were introduced in Chapters 6 and 7. Two other instructional procedures, anticipation guides and structured overviews, can also be used.

Anticipation Guides

There is nothing like a good old-fashioned debate to perk up a class. Everyone, young and old, enjoys expressing opinions on controversial subjects. One device that capitalizes on this predilection is the **anticipation guide**—a listing of three or more debatable statements about a topic on which students indicate whether they agree with each statement before they read about the topic. (An adapted anticipation guide introduces each chapter in this book.)

Besides building interest, the anticipation guide activates prior knowledge. Readers have to activate information that they possess to decide whether they agree or disagree with each statement. The guide also gives students a purpose for reading: to evaluate their responses. In addition, it opens the students' minds. Some students, especially those who are younger or who are poor readers, tend to reject statements in print that contradict concepts they might have (Lipson, 1984; Maria & MacGinitie, 1987). By comparing their responses with what the author said and by listening to the class discussion of the statements, they can correct and clarify these ideas.

The anticipation guide can be used with any age group and works best when students have some familiarity with the subject. If they do not know anything about it, they do not have much to agree or disagree with. The guide is also most effective when used with subjects about which students have misconceptions—for example, diet, pollution, legal rights, snakes, and insects. The recommended steps for constructing and using an anticipation guide are described in Lesson 8.1 (Head & Readence, 1986).

FYI

The anticipation guide should help students refine erroneous concepts because it involves confronting erroneous beliefs.

 Lesson 8.1

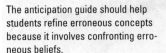

Using an Anticipation Guide

Step 1. Identification of major concepts
List two to four major concepts that you wish students to learn.

Step 2. Determination of students' background
Consider the experiential and cultural backgrounds of your students. Ask yourself how their backgrounds will affect their knowledge and beliefs about the topic under study. What misconceptions might they have?

Step 3. Creation of statements for the guide
Write three to five statements (or more) that are sufficiently open-ended or general to encourage a discussion. Do not choose simple, factual statements. Instead, think of those that might touch on students' misconceptions or involve areas in which students have partial knowledge. The statements can be arranged in the order in which the concepts they reflect appear in the selection or from simplest to most complex. They may be written on the chalkboard or on paper.

Step 4. Introduction of the guide
Introduce and explain the guide, and have students respond to the statements. Emphasize that they should think about their responses because they will be asked to defend them.

Step 5. Discussion of responses
Talk over each statement. You might begin by having students raise their hands if they agree with a statement. Ask volunteers to tell why they agreed or disagreed.

Step 6. Reading of the text
Sum up the main points of the discussion and have students read the text to compare their responses with what the material states. In some instances, the text may contain

information that proves or disproves a statement. However, if the statements have been constructed carefully, they will be sufficiently open-ended that students will find information that may support a position but will not prove it one way or another.

Step 7. Discussion of text and statements

Talk over each statement in light of the information in the text. Ask students whether they changed their responses because of information in the text. Ask what that information was and why it changed their minds. Responses can be discussed in small or large groups. If small groups are used, bring the whole class together for a summary after the groups have finished their discussions. At this point, you might want to go over at greater length any statements that seem especially controversial or confusing.

The anticipation guide can be extended. In an extended anticipation guide, students note next to each response whether they have found support for their responses. If the text contains information that runs counter to a response, they then write a summary statement of that information next to their response. This helps students to correct misconceptions.

Structured Overviews

Students learn new concepts more easily if they can relate them to old ones. It is also helpful if students have an overview of what is to be learned so that they can see this relationship and how the new concepts are related to each other. For example, it is easier to understand the new concepts *gavials* and *caimans* once one sees that these creatures are related to alligators and crocodiles and that they all belong to the group known as crocodilians.

Adapting a strategy devised by Ausubel (1960) known as the advanced organizer, Barron (1969) created the **structured overview**, which uses vocabulary words to relate new materials to old materials and to show interrelationships among both old and new concepts. The overview should provide a structure "so that it does not appear to students that they are being taught a series of unrelated or equally important words" (Estes, Mills, & Barron, 1969, p. 41). To construct an overview, follow the six steps listed below (Barron, 1969):

1. *Selection of concepts.* Analyze the selection to be read or the unit to be introduced, and select two to four concepts that you think are important.
2. *Analysis of vocabulary.* Analyze and list the vocabulary necessary to understand the concepts.
3. *Arrangement of words.* Arrange the list of words into a diagram that shows their interrelationships.
4. *Addition of known words.* Add vocabulary words that you think students already understand so that they can see how the new words relate to them.
5. *Evaluation of overview.* Evaluate the overview. Ask whether the major relationships are clearly shown. Can the overview be simplified and still do a good job?
6. *Introduction of overview.* Introduce students to the learning task. Display the structured overview, and explain why you arranged the words the way you did. Have students suggest any words they want to add. During the learning task, use the overview as a guide. As the new words are encountered, refer to their position on the overview and discuss how they are related to the other words.

■ The **structured overview** is a technique designed to help students relate new words and concepts to known words and concepts.

A fifth-grade class has just finished a unit on invertebrates and is now tackling a unit on vertebrates. The teacher examines the textbook chapter and thinks about what students already know about vertebrates and what is important for them to learn. The teacher decides to emphasize the following concepts:

1. Vertebrates have a skeleton.
2. There are seven main groups of vertebrates.

The teacher then lists the following words that seem necessary to understand the two concepts about vertebrates:

vertebrates	fish	reptiles	amphibians	warm-blooded
backbone	jawless fish	lizards	newts	cold-blooded
mammals	cartilage fish	turtles	metamorphosis	
birds	bony fish	crocodilians		

The teacher organizes the words in a structured overview and then, after examining the overview, adds *animals, invertebrates*, and *no backbones*, so that students can see how the information on vertebrates fits in with the information on invertebrates. Believing that students will not know the word *amphibian*, the teacher adds *frogs* to the list so that students will have an example of an amphibian. The teacher evaluates the overview. The words *metamorphosis* and *newts* are important; however, they seem to be making the display too complex, so they are removed. The revised structured overview is shown in Figure 8.2.

The teacher presents the overview. The class discusses the fact that there are two main types of animals: vertebrates and invertebrates. Various interrelationships are discussed. A question is raised about *cartilage*; its meaning is discussed.

■■■ FIGURE 8.2   A Sample Structured Overview

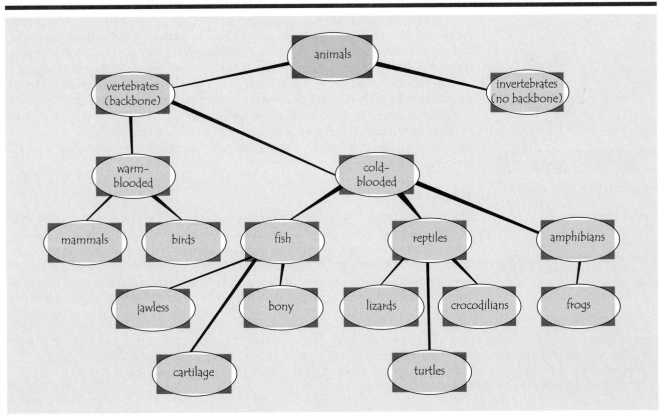

The overview becomes a unifying element for the unit. As each group of vertebrates is discussed, the class refers to the overview. It is expanded to include other examples of amphibians, reptiles, birds, mammals, and the three kinds of fish. Students are thus able to see how these new words relate to the ones already contained in the structured overview.

As students gain skill in seeing relationships, they take part in constructing the overviews. They might construct overviews in cooperative learning groups. Eventually, they should be guided to use overviews as study aids. Although designed to be used at the beginning of a unit or lesson, an overview can also be used as a summary at its conclusion.

■ ■ ■ Checkup ■ ■ ■

1. What are some prereading techniques for fostering understanding of content-area texts?
2. What are the steps in presenting these techniques?

■ ■ ■

During Reading

During reading, strategic readers construct meaning. They distinguish between important and unimportant details, organize information from the text, summarize sections, and generate questions. They also integrate information from the text with prior knowledge, make inferences, check predictions, seek clarification, and, perhaps, create images of scenes and events portrayed by the text. They use the structure of the text as an aid to comprehension. Strategic readers also regulate their rate of reading and monitor their understanding of the passage. They may reread or seek clarification if their comprehension breaks down. During-reading strategies include using chapter organization and text structure and think-alouds.

Chapter Organization and Text Structure

Numerous typographical aids are generally included in most content-area textbooks to assist the reader in determining organization and noting important points. These include the chapter title, heads and subheads, colored panels, sidebars, bullets, use of color type, and words printed in italics or boldface. Questions might also be posed in the margins. Figure 8.3 displays a page that uses a number of these devices. Although typographical aids are often used to preview a chapter, they should also be used as the reader interacts with the text. Personal observation and experience suggest that they are given only limited attention, however. Perhaps students do not realize their full value. With the help of a textbook that makes especially good use of these elements, explain the purpose and value of each one. Then model how you might use them to aid your understanding of the content.

Think-Alouds

Think-alouds are just what their name suggests. The teacher models a silent reading strategy by thinking aloud as she or he processes a text, thus making explicit skills that normally cannot be observed. Originally a research technique for studying reading processes, think-alouds are used to model comprehension processes, such as making predictions, creating images, linking information in text with prior knowledge, monitoring comprehension, and using a repair strategy when there is a problem with word recognition or

FYI

Note that some strategies, such as summarizing, question generating, and imaging, can be used during and after reading.

FYI

Think-alouds indicate the difficulty level of text. Think-alouds by several students on the same text may indicate that the text is hard to understand because the author didn't include enough information to enable the reader to make necessary inferences (Trabasso & Magliano, 1996).

■ **Think-alouds** follow the expert–apprentice model. As the expert, the teacher demonstrates how she or he reads text so the students (apprentices) can gain insight into the process. Cooperative learning is also involved as students work on their think-alouds with partners.

■■■ **FIGURE 8.3** **Use of Typographical Aids in a Science Textbook**

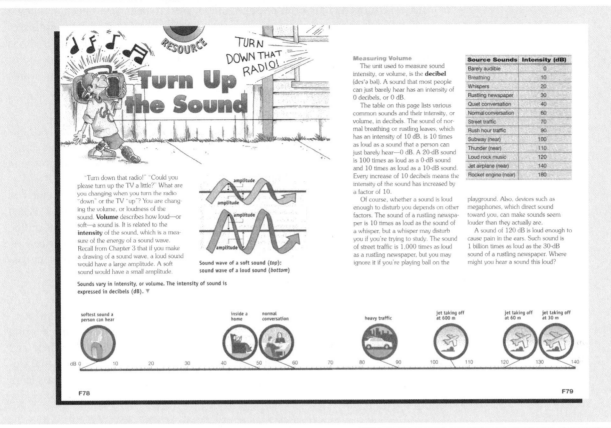

From *Science Discovery Works Grade 3* by Carolyn Sumners, et al. © by Silver Burdett Ginn, Simon & Schuster Education Group. Used by permission.

comprehension. In addition to being a demonstration technique, think-alouds can be used by students to become more aware of their reading processes and to make needed changes in the way they read.

Lesson 8.2 illustrates how the technique is put into operation to help students understand content-area materials.

Lesson 8.2

Think-Alouds

Step 1. Modeling

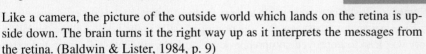

The teacher reads a brief passage aloud, showing what her or his thoughts are when the text does not make sense and what repair strategies she or he might implement:

> Like a camera, the picture of the outside world which lands on the retina is upside down. The brain turns it the right way up as it interprets the messages from the retina. (Baldwin & Lister, 1984, p. 9)

Then the teacher thinks aloud, "I don't get this. I don't know where the retina is. I'll take a look at the diagram. There it is; it's the lining at the back of the eyeball, and there's the optic nerve. The optic nerve goes from the retina to the brain. Now I understand."

FYI

In addition to yielding information about comprehension processes, think-alouds foster improved comprehension. Think-alouds demand more focused attention and deeper processing. Through talking about the text, the reader makes connections among ideas, constructs explanations, and makes more predictions. Thinking aloud also promotes monitoring. When students think aloud, they note difficult or confusing passages. This monitoring helps the teacher understand the reader's processes and shows the teacher where to provide assistance.

Step 2. Working with partners

Students take turns reading brief passages orally to each other. The selections should be fairly difficult or contain problems. The reader thinks aloud to show what processes he or she is using, what problems he or she is encountering, and how he or she is attempting to solve those problems. The partner is encouraged to ask questions: "Are you trying to picture the main character as you read? Do you see any words you don't know?"

Step 3. Practicing

Students practice thinking through materials as they read them silently. Self-questionnaires or checklists are used to encourage readers to use active processes and to monitor their reading. A sample self-questionnaire, to which students may respond orally or in writing, is shown in Figure 8.4.

As an alternative to a self-questionnaire, you might use a checklist such as the one in Figure 8.5. It assesses use of before-, during-, and after-reading strategies. When using a checklist, include only strategies that have been introduced. Also, model the use of the self-questionnaire or checklist before using it. An even simpler device is to have students place a sticky note next to passages that pose problems. Problem passages can be discussed later.

Step 4. Applying think-alouds

Students apply the strategy to everyday and content-area material. During postreading discussions, the teacher asks students to tell about their comprehension processes: "What pictures did you create in your mind as you read? Were there any confusing passages? How did you handle them?" Discussing strategies helps the student to clarify his or her use of strategies. It also helps the members of the class learn how others process text.

■ ■ ■ **Checkup** ■ ■ ■

1. What are some during-reading techniques for fostering understanding of content-area texts?
2. How does each of the techniques foster increased comprehension and learning?

■ ■ ■

After Reading

After completing reading, strategic readers reflect on what they have read, continue to integrate new information with old information, may evaluate the new information or use it in some way, and may seek additional information on the topic. To help students learn to use after-reading strategies, the teacher can apply several instructional procedures in addition to summarizing, retelling, and other postreading strategies covered in previous chapters. These additional procedures include constructing analogies, creating graphic organizers, and applying and extending.

Constructing Analogies

Analogies can foster comprehension and are frequently used in the content areas, especially in science. An analogy between the functioning of cells in the body and the operation of a factory will lead to improved comprehension. Similarly, students will better understand an article about the game of cricket when given analogies between cricket and baseball or other information from which they can construct their own analogies (Hayes & Tierney, 1982).

HIGHER-LEVEL LITERACY

Trade books and periodicals can expand students' knowledge and their ability to think deeply about key concepts and events. It is important that students see connections and grasp the big picture—and not just learn isolated facts.

■ ■ ■ **USING TECHNOLOGY**

News Resources for Kids lists high-quality news sources for young people, ranging from *National Geographic* and *Weekly Reader* to CNN Student News.
http://sp.askforkids.com/docs/askforkids/help/tours/newsresources.htm

■   **Graphic organizers** are visual devices designed to help the reader note relationships between key concepts, main points, basic steps, or major events in a selection.

Recognizing and constructing analogies is one way of helping students bridge the gap between the new and the old. Point out analogies when they appear. Traditional analogies include those between the eye and a camera, the heart and a pump, the brain and a computer, and memory and a file cabinet. The best analogies are those in which the items being compared share a number of features, which is why the analogy between the eye and a camera is especially effective. However, it is important that the item that is the basis for comparison (the camera) be familiar. If students don't know how a camera works, the analogy won't be very helpful (Glynn, 1994). Help students create their own analogies by comparing old information and new concepts. You might ask, for instance, "How is the eye like a camera? How is memory like a file cabinet?" Self-created analogies are generally more effective than those made up by others.

For best results in using analogies, discuss each analogy thoroughly. After introducing the target concept, explain the analogy, identifying both similarities and differences between the target concept and the analog. Clarify any confusions that students might have (Glynn, 1994).

Creating Graphic Organizers

One of the most effective ways to understand and retain complex content-area information is to use some sort of **graphic organizer** to represent key concepts, main points, or basic steps. In addition to highlighting essential information, graphic organizers show how ideas are interrelated. The content and structure of material and the teaching–learning purpose dictate the type of organizer used: tree diagram, time line, or an organizer that highlights the steps in a process, contrasts elements, or identifies causes. Hyerle (2001) recommends that schools adopt a common set of graphic organizers. He matched each of eight kinds of thinking with a graphic organizer that fosters that specific kind of cognitive processing (see Table 8.2). The key graphic organizers are an adaptation of Hyerle's Thinking Maps®. Whatever form it takes, the visual display should focus on the most essential information and do so vividly. Key concepts should "jump out at the students as soon as their eyes meet the page" (Robinson, 1998, p. 100).

■■■ **FIGURE 8.4   A Think-Aloud Self-Questionnaire**

A. Before reading
  1. How do I prepare for reading?
B. During reading
  1. What do I do to improve my understanding of what I am reading?
  2. What do I do if I come across a word I don't know?
  3. What do I do if the selection doesn't make sense?
C. After reading
  1. Do I do anything special with the information I just read? If so, what?

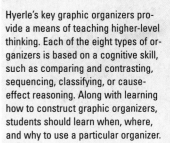

HIGHER-LEVEL LITERACY

Hyerle's key graphic organizers provide a means of teaching higher-level thinking. Each of the eight types of organizers is based on a cognitive skill, such as comparing and contrasting, sequencing, classifying, or cause-effect reasoning. Along with learning how to construct graphic organizers, students should learn when, where, and why to use a particular organizer.

USING TECHNOLOGY ■ ■ ■

Designs for Thinking presents more information on Thinking Maps®.
http://www.mapthemind.com

■■■ **FIGURE 8.5   Think-Aloud Checklist**

Put a check next to the things you did before, during, and after you read.

Before Reading	During Reading	After Reading
Surveyed title, headings, illustrations _____	Predicted what might happen next _____	Summarized what I had read _____
Thought about what I know about the topic _____	Inferred ideas not stated _____	Thought about what I had read _____
Predicted what the text might be about or what might happen _____	Got main idea of section _____	Connected what I had read to what I already knew _____
Made up a question to answer _____	Got important details _____	Applied what I had learned in the selection _____
Other (describe) _____ _____	Summarized each section _____	Other (describe) _____ _____
	Created images about parts of the selections _____	
	Thought about what I had read _____	
	Judged whether information was true or the story seemed real _____	
	Made up questions to be answered _____	
	Checked to make sure I was understanding what I read _____	
	Repaired by rereading puzzling parts, getting meaning of hard words, etc. _____	
	Other (describe) _____	

■■■ **TABLE 8.2**   **Key Graphic Organizers**

Organizer	Thinking Skill	Example
Descriptive map (web)	Locate and assemble main idea and details	
Classification map (semantic map)	Categorize and classify	
Sequence map	Arrange in chronological order	
Process map (chain or flow map)	Arrange in step-by-step fashion	
Cyclical map	Arrange in circular fashion to show a process	
Tree diagram	Categorize and classify in hierarchical fashion	
Frame matrix (or Venn diagram)	Compare and contrast	
Cause–effect map	Locate or infer causes and/or effects	

FYI

Graphic organizers may also lead to dual encoding. They may be encoded and stored in memory verbally and visually. This dual encoding would make the information easier to recall (Robinson, 1998).

HIGHER-LEVEL LITERACY

In order to construct graphic organizers, "students have to engage in powerful information processing and higher order thinking skills such as using cues to recognize important information, making decisions about what is important or essential, consolidating information and identifying main ideas and supporting details, [and] making decisions about the best way to structure the information" (Ellis, 2004).

The structured overview is one of the most useful graphic organizers because it shows subordinate relationships. Figure 8.6 shows a structured overview for the concept of galaxies. Earlier in this chapter, the structured overview was presented as a device for preparing students to read. It also can be created or added to as an after-reading activity. It then enhances understanding and retention of important concepts, especially if students play an active role in creating it. After the selection has been read, the overview's elements are discussed again. Information obtained from reading might be placed on lines beneath each element. For example, a brief definition of the word *galaxy* might be given, together with descriptions of irregular, spiral, and elliptical galaxies. If given their own copies of the overview, students can add information about the elements as they read. They can also use drawings to illustrate concepts, such as irregular, spiral, and elliptical galaxies.

Another kind of graphic organizer that can be used as a postreading aid was presented in Chapter 7—an organizer that reflects the actual structure of the text (enumeration–description, time-sequence, explanation–process, comparison–contrast, problem–solution, or cause–effect). Building as it does on structure, this kind of organizer enhances understanding of the interrelationships of the ideas covered in the text or the process being explained. For instance, an explanation–process organizer can be used to show how an engine operates, how solar cells turn sunlight into energy, how the water cycle operates, or how numerous other systems work (see Figure 8.7). Boxes or circles containing explanatory text show the steps in the process, with arrows indicating the flow of the process.

■■■ FIGURE 8.6

A Structured Overview (Tree Diagram) on Galaxies

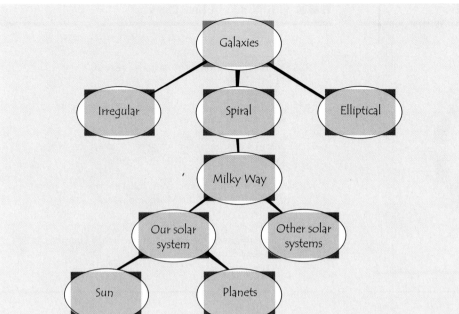

Text drawn from *Merrill Science 5* (pp. 98–99), by J. K. Hackett, R. H. Moyer, and D. K. Adams, 1989, Columbus, OH: Merrill.

■■■ FIGURE 8.7

An Explanation–Process Organizer (Cyclical Map)

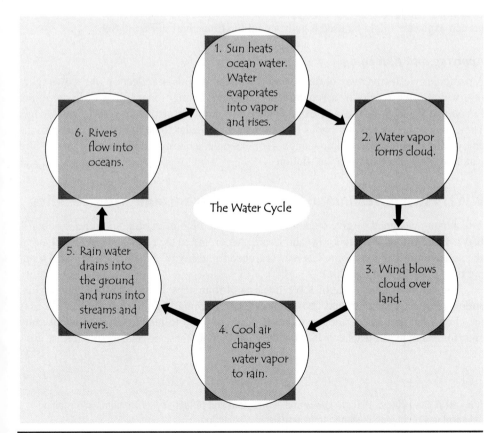

Based on text from *Fearon's United States Geography*, by W. Lefkowitz, 1990, Belmont, CA: Fearon Education.

■■■ **FIGURE 8.8** **Diagram of the Eye**

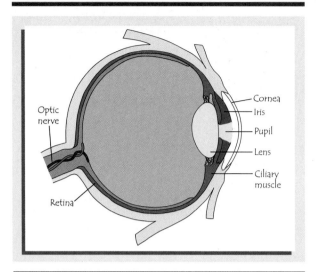

■■■ **FIGURE 8.9** **A Time Chart**

1524—Verrazano explored the eastern coast of North America.

1535—Jacques Cartier sailed up the Saint Lawrence River and claimed that area for France.

1608—Samuel de Champlain founded Quebec, the first permanent French colony in the Americas.

1673—Father Marquette and Louis Joliet set out on a journey that took them to the Mississippi River.

1682—Robert de La Salle reached the Gulf of Mexico after canoeing down the Mississippi River. He claimed the area for France.

For some elements, the best graphic organizer is a diagram. For example, a diagram is the best way to show the parts of the eye (see Figure 8.8). Initially, a diagram can be drawn or traced by the teacher. However, having students create their own diagrams makes reading an active process.

For reading material that has a chronological organization, a time chart is a useful way to highlight major events (see Figure 8.9 for an example). A time line or sequence map serves the same function and may be used instead of a time chart. Often, two or more kinds of graphic organizers can be combined. For instance, a map showing the voyages of the French explorers might be used together with the time chart in Figure 8.9.

Applying and Extending

A particularly effective way of deepening comprehension is to reflect on one's own reading, which often results in a sense of not knowing enough or wanting to know more. Encourage students to use and extend what they know by expanding their knowledge. They can do this by reading books that explore a particular topic in detail or that provide enjoyment while increasing knowledge—for example, a book of math puzzles, one on bird watching, or a piece of historical fiction.

KWL Plus: A Technique for Before, During, and After Reading

A technique designed to give students an active role before, during, and after reading is **KWL Plus**: Know, Want to know, and Learn. According to Ogle (1989), KWL evolved as she and a number of classroom teachers searched for a way to "build active personal reading of expository text" (p. 206).

The before-reading stage of KWL consists of four steps: brainstorming, categorizing, anticipating or predicting, and questioning. Brainstorming begins when the teacher asks the class what they know about a topic. If they are about to read a selection about army ants, for example, the teacher asks what they know about these insects. Responses are writ-

■ **KWL Plus** (Know, Want to know, and Learn) is a technique designed to help readers build and organize background and seek out and reflect on key elements in a reading selection.

ten on the board and discussed. If a disagreement occurs or students seem puzzled by a statement, this cognitive conflict can be used to create a what-we-want-to-find-out question. Brainstorming activates prior knowledge so that students become more aware of what they know. The students then write about their personal knowledge of army ants in the first column of a KWL worksheet.

Next, in a step similar to semantic mapping, students categorize their prior knowledge. The process of categorization is modeled. Brainstormed items already written on the board are placed in appropriate categories. Students then label the items in the "what we know" column with letters that indicate category names as shown in Figure 8.10: H = habitat, C = characteristics, and F = food. Students also anticipate what categories of information the author will provide. This helps them both anticipate the content of the text and organize the information as they read it. The process of anticipating categories is modeled. The teacher might ask, for example, what kinds of information an author might provide about army ants. Students then write these categories at the bottom of the KWL worksheet.

In the third step, questions are created. As a group, the class discusses what they want to know about army ants. Questions are written on the chalkboard. Each student then records in the second column of the worksheet her or his own questions.

With these questions in mind, the class reads the text. After reading, students discuss what they learned and the teacher writes their responses on the chalkboard. Information is organized, misconceptions are clarified, and emerging concepts are developed more fully. After the discussion, students enter what they learned on their own in the third column. In light of this information, they cross out any misconceptions they wrote in the first column. They may find that they still have questions about the topic, so a fourth column—with the heading "what we still want to know"—can be added to the worksheet. The teacher can discuss with the students how they might go about finding the answers to the questions they still have. A completed KWL worksheet is presented in Figure 8.10. Ogle (1989) presents a fuller description of KWL, including a sample lesson.

FYI

■ The categorizing and anticipating steps in KWL are frequently skipped and can be considered optional.

■ KWL is excellent preparation for writing a report. Each category of information can be written up as a separate paragraph.

A KWL worksheet helps students learn how to read for information.

■■■ **FIGURE 8.10**
KWL Plus Worksheet

Name: _____   Topic: _Army ants_   Date: _____

What we know	What we want to find out	What we learned	What we still want to know
H Live in the jungle	How large a	Tens of thousands	Do army ants
C Are fierce	group do army	form a group.	harm people?
H Live in the	ants form?	The queen lays	What are larvae
ground	Why are there so	100,000 to	and pupae?
F Eat plants	many army ants	300,000 eggs	
C Work together	in a group?	at a time.	
F Eat insects	Why do the ants	Form armies to	
	form armies?	get food for	
	What do army	larvae and pupae	
	ants eat?	Kill other insects	
		and small	
		animals and take	
		them back to	
		their home	
		Live in the ground	
		or in trees in the	
		jungles of South	
		America	

Categories of information we expect to see

Habitat
Food
Characteristics
Society
Travel
Appearance

FYI

Primary-grade teachers might use KWL strictly as a group technique until students have sufficient writing ability to fill out the worksheet individually. However, teachers have found that just discussing what we know, what we want to find out, and what we have learned is helpful. The ultimate purpose is to lead students to ask these questions automatically as they read.

■■■ **Checkup** ■■■

1. What are some after-reading techniques for fostering understanding of content-area texts and retention of key concepts?

2. How might each of these techniques be presented?

3. What makes KWL an effective technique?

■■■

■ Writing to Learn

Writing is a way of learning as well as a method of communication. Zinsser (1988), a professional writer and teacher of writing, observed:

> We write to find out what we know and want to say. I thought of how often as a writer I had made clear to myself some subject I had previously known nothing about by just putting one sentence after another—by reasoning my way in sequential steps to its meaning. (pp. viii–ix)

However, some kinds of writing are better than others for learning. Different kinds of writing lead students to think in different kinds of ways. Writing short answers aids recall over the short term. However, activities in which students manipulate information lead to

Exemplary
Teaching

CORI: A Motivational
Content-Area Theme Unit

All too often, students read to complete an assignment rather than to learn. Their goal is to get to the end of the chapter rather than to construct meaning. Students need to be engaged in the reading task. Using a framework known as CORI (Concept Oriented Reading Instruction) with fifth-grade students in a Title 1 program, Anderson and Guthrie (1996) established a teaching unit that builds strategies and intrinsic motivation. CORI incorporates four main elements.

1. *Observing and personalizing.* To initiate a unit of study, students observed some phenomenon. This ranged from crickets, the life cycle of caterpillars, and the phases of the moon to the social environment. Students' observations were discussed, and, in a KWL-type activity, they noted what they knew about the topic and what they wanted to learn. Topics of interest and questions to be answered were listed. Observations were recorded.

2. *Searching and retrieving.* Through brainstorming about sources of information, students learned where to go to get information to answer their questions and to search for subtopics related to their general area of interest. Students learned how to locate appropriate trade books, to make appropriate scientific observations, and to use globes and other sources of information. In addition to discussion, direct instruction was used to show students how to use a table of contents and an index to locate relevant information.

3. *Comprehending and integrating.* Students learned how to identify important ideas and how to take notes to summarize what they had read and synthesize information. They also learned how to combine information from several sources, including both informational and fiction books and real-life sources. Technical vocabulary was developed. During this and other stages, peer interaction was encouraged.

4. *Communicating to others.* Students learned to use the process approach to compose a report. Typical reporting activities included sketching and labeling the parts of the creature or element being studied, inventing an insect, creating habitat posters, creating fictional pieces based on facts they researched, and creating other types of reports (Guthrie & McCann, 1997).

Because the CORI program combined strategy instruction with other elements, such as building on student's choices, students who participated were intrinsically motivated and, as a result, read more, understood what they read better, and were better able to transfer both their knowledge and strategies to solve new problems.

increased recall over a longer period of time and to deeper understanding. Writing that involves comparing, contrasting, concluding, and evaluating has a greater impact than writing that requires only restating. Writing in which students have a sense of ownership and in which they see value because it fosters their learning and which they feel competent to undertake seems to work best (Langer & Applebee, 1987).

Writing activities such as the following can help clarify complex topics:

- Comparing, contrasting, or evaluating key points in a chapter

- Writing critical reports on famous people or events or taking on the role of the famous person or describing the key event as though one were there

- Interpreting the results of a science experiment conducted in class

- Writing an essay on a social studies or science topic

Students' writing in the content areas often consists of simply retelling information. One solution is to have them conduct firsthand investigations and report the results. They might undertake activities such as the following:

- Writing observations about a natural phenomenon (for example, changes in plants that are being grown from seed)

HIGHER-LEVEL LITERACY

Students should do the kinds of writing assignments, such as those involving comparing and contrasting, concluding, or judging, that foster the development of higher-level thinking skills.

Content-area texts have a more complex structure.

■ Describing birds that visit a bird feeder, changes in a tree from season to season, or changes in a puppy or kitten as it develops over a period of months

■ Summarizing and interpreting the results of a classroom poll

■ Interviewing older family members about life when they were growing up

A writing activity that can be used in any content-area class is having students explain a process to someone who has no knowledge of it. Processes include finding the area of a rectangle or describing how magnets work, how the president is elected, and how to find a particular state on a map. Students might include graphics to help explain a process.

Other writing-to-learn activities include the following (Noyce & Christie, 1989):

■ Writing letters to convey personal reactions or request information on a topic

■ Writing scripts to dramatize key events in history

■ Writing historical fiction

■ Writing a children's book on an interesting social studies or science topic

■ Writing an editorial or commentary about a social issue

■ Writing a glossary of key terms

■ Creating captions for photos of a scientific experiment

■ Creating a puzzle using key terms

Learning Logs

One easy device that combines personal reaction with exploration of content is the **learning log**. It consists of a notebook that is

> . . . informal, tentative, first draft, and brief, usually consisting of no more than ten minutes of focused free writing. The teacher poses questions and situations or sets themes that invite students to observe, speculate, list, chart, web, brainstorm, roleplay, ask questions, activate prior knowledge, collaborate, correspond, summarize, predict, or shift to a new perspective: in short, to participate in their own learning. (Atwell, 1990, p. xvii)

The class can discuss their learning logs, or the teacher can collect them and respond to them in writing. Following is a learning log from a third-grader who wrote a summary based on the teacher's reading of *Squirrels* (Wildsmith, 1988):

> Squirrels nests are called dreys. Squirrels tails are used for leaps, a parachute, change directions, swim, balance, blanket. Sometimes squirrels steal eggs. (Thompson, 1990, p. 48)

The main purpose of logs is to have students examine and express what they are learning, not to air personal matters (Atwell, 1990). Logs can also be used to ask questions. Calkins (1986) suggested that before viewing a film or reading a selection, students might record the questions they have about that topic. Later, they can evaluate how well their questions were answered. On other occasions, students might record what they know about a topic before reading a selection or undertaking a unit of study.

Whether students pose a question, jot down a reaction, or create a semantic map, the writing stimulus should help them think as scientists, historians, or mathematicians and think about what they are learning. At times, they can draft free responses in their learning logs; at other times, the teacher might want to provide a prompt. For a unit on weather, one of the following prompts might be provided for any one log-writing session:

- What do I know about weather forecasting?
- What questions do I have about weather?
- What is the worst kind of storm? Why?
- What kind of weather do I like best? Least? Why?
- How does weather affect my life?
- What kinds of people might be most affected by the weather?
- What causes fog?
- What are some of the ways in which people who are not scientists predict the weather?

Prompts that foster reflection, manipulation of information, evaluation, and relating information to one's personal life also foster higher-level thinking skills.

Students can also write prelearning and postlearning entries in their logs. Before reading a selection on snakes, they might write what they know about snakes and then share their knowledge with a partner. Talking to a partner helps them to elicit more information. Students then read the selection and make log entries indicating what they know now. Prelearning and postlearning entries help students become more metacognitive, more aware of what they know and are learning (Santa, 1994).

Log entries can be used to reflect on the use of newly learned strategies. For instance, after being taught imagery, students could be asked to apply this strategy to their reading and reflect on its effectiveness in their logs (K. Dayton, personal communication, November 25, 2003).

■■■ Checkup ■■■

1. What are some ways in which students might write to learn?
2. How might each of these approaches be presented?

■■■

■ Sheltered English for English Learners

Introduced in the 1980s by Krashen (1991), **sheltered English** is a way of fostering English through the study of content areas. As students learn science and social studies, they develop English language skills. Sheltered English is generally taught by content-area specialists who have training in teaching English, but some of the techniques employed in sheltered English can be adapted by classroom teachers.

Sheltered English is student-centered. It involves high levels of student interaction, with much of the work being done in cooperative learning groups. Hands-on activities are stressed. Making the input comprehensible to students is also emphasized. The following steps can be taken to make content understandable:

- The presentation should be as understandable as possible. Speak at a slower pace with deliberate enunciation. Use simple, straightforward language. Avoid figurative language, idioms, and cultural references that students might not recognize (Gunning, 2003).
- Use visuals to support the verbal presentation. Use audiovisual aids, gestures, facial expressions, and demonstrations to make the language more meaningful. When introducing a new word, show a picture of what it represents, if possible, and write it on the board. When mentioning a place, write its name on the board and show it on a map.

Pantomime actions and demonstrate processes. Use time lines, graphs, videos, and filmclips on CD-ROM. Use manipulatives such as globes.

- When giving directions, show students what to do in addition to telling them. If possible, model the process for them. Then ask students to carry out directions or apply a concept under your guidance. Provide additional help as needed.

- Plan lots of hands-on activities, drawings, webs, maps, and other graphic organizers so that students can use techniques that are less language dependent to extend their understanding and express their knowledge.

- Use brainstorming, quick write, and similar techniques to activate background knowledge. In a quick write, students are given two or three minutes to sum up what they have just learned.

- Modify use of text. Conduct text walks, or read and explain portions of the text. Make generous use of the text's illustrations. Also point out cognates. You might use Questioning the Author or reciprocal teaching to help students construct meaning.

- Obtain texts that use simpler language.

- Make use of the students' native language. Provide explanations of complex concepts in the students' native language. If you are unfamiliar with their native language, ask another student who knows the language to provide the explanation. Encourage students to discuss content in their native language as well as in English.

- Scaffold instruction. Provide prompts and other assistance as needed. Use prompts that encourage students to clarify or expand responses: "That's interesting. I'd like to hear more about that. Can you explain that? Can you tell us more? So what happened next?"

- Plan opportunities for students to talk over ideas. This could be in whole-class discussions, pairs, or small groups. This gives English language learners (ELLs) the opportunity to use academic language as they engage in activities and discuss procedures and findings. ELLs are more willing to engage in discussions in small groups than they are in larger groups.

- Use real-world materials such as signs, recycling and nutrition labels, menus, job applications, and bank deposit slips.

- Provide wait time. Instead of requiring students to answer as soon as you pose a question, wait a few seconds. This is helpful to all students (Lake, 1973; Rowe, 1969) but is especially beneficial to ELLs because, being less familiar with the language, they need extra time to formulate their responses.

- When assessing students' work, allow students to demonstrate their knowledge in multiple ways. If possible, include ways that don't rely so heavily on language. Students might conduct an experiment, draw a diagram, or complete a project.

In addition to teaching content-area vocabulary, it is also important to teach academic language, the language of instruction, so students understand what they are to do when they are asked to *compare, contrast, discuss, illustrate, predict, summarize,* or *give examples.* Here is how one teacher combined instruction in content vocabulary with instruction in academic language while introducing the concept of buoyancy (Echevarria, Vogt, & Short, 2000). Mr. Lew explained that the purpose of the unit was to find out why some objects float and others sink. As he said the word *float,* he pointed to an orange floating in a tank. As he said the word *sink,* he placed a peeled orange in the tank and the class watched as it sank. He also told the students that at the end of the unit, they would be able to calculate and predict whether an object would be buoyant enough to float. The words *float, sink, buoyant, calculate,* and *predict* were written on the board. Mr. Lew used the word *calculate* on purpose. He could have used the word *figure,* but he believed that students would recognize *calculate* more readily because it is a cognate of *calcular* in Spanish, and most of his students were native speakers of Spanish.

■■■ **Checkup** ■■■

1. What are the basic principles of sheltered English?

2. What are some things that you might do to make content more understandable to ELLs?

■■■

■ Reading to Remember

Marge, a fifth-grader, is feeling anxious. She has been told to study the chapter on the Revolutionary War for a unit test the next day. Marge is a good reader and usually does well in school, but she is having trouble with history. She understands what she reads, but she does not remember the dates and names that the tests ask for. She remembers most of the main ideas but not the details. Marge's problem is a common one. She knows how to read for understanding, but she has no strategies for reading for retention. Marge has another problem, too: She has read for main ideas, but the test will concentrate on details. Marge has to gear her studying for the type of test she will be given. Research suggests that knowing the type of test to be taken is an important factor in effective studying (Anderson & Armbruster, 1984).

Some students seem to learn on their own how to study for different types of tests, while others require instruction. Teachers should let students know what types of tests they intend to give and should explain how to study for each one. For example, essay tests require knowing the main ideas of the material; objective tests require more attention to details. Teachers should also discuss the difference between studying for multiple-choice tests, which require only that one recognize correct answers, and studying for fill-in-the-blank exams, which require recalling names, dates, or terms. Recognizing is, of course, far easier than recalling.

Studying also has an affective component. Up to 75 percent of academic failure is attributed to poor study habits or strategies. However, a number of studies conducted over the years indicate that when students are taught these skills, their performance improves significantly (Richardson & Morgan, 1994). A key element is motivation. When students are convinced of the value of study skills, they are more likely to use them (Schunk & Rice, 1987). Another crucial element in study strategy instruction is proving to students that these strategies work—they need to see that better studying leads to better grades.

Study habits develop early, and effective study skills take many years to learn. Locating, organizing, and taking steps to retain information should be an integral part of the elementary and middle school curriculum. From the very beginning, students should be taught how to preview a book to get an overview of its content and how to use the table of contents. Students should also be taught in the earliest grades how to preview a section of text, make predictions, create questions, summarize, and then apply what they read. Instruction in these strategies will help build a solid foundation for effective study skills. This instruction will pave the way for the teaching of more formal study strategies such as SQ3R.

■ Fostering Retention

Knowing how memory works is the key to devising techniques to improve retention. Memory has three stages: encoding, storing, and retrieving. Encoding should be clear and purposeful; text that is vaguely understood will be quickly forgotten. Storage works best when the material is meaningful. Students will remember a piece of information better if they concentrate on its meaning rather than on the exact words used, which is why it is best to respond to questions in one's own words. Retrieval, or remembering, works best when the material is carefully encoded.

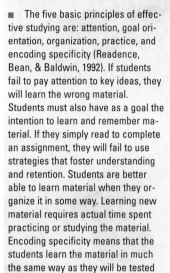

FYI

■ The five basic principles of effective studying are: attention, goal orientation, organization, practice, and encoding specificity (Readence, Bean, & Baldwin, 1992). If students fail to pay attention to key ideas, they will learn the wrong material. Students must also have as a goal the intention to learn and remember material. If they simply read to complete an assignment, they will fail to use strategies that foster understanding and retention. Students are better able to learn material when they organize it in some way. Learning new material requires actual time spent practicing or studying the material. Encoding specificity means that the students learn the material in much the same way as they will be tested on it.

■ Understanding content material isn't sufficient. Because students must also be able to retain and retrieve new information, study skills are an essential part of the elementary and middle school literacy curriculum.

Depth of processing also has an impact on memory (Craik & Lockhart, 1972). Some information is processed only on a shallow level, such as when we only half listen to a lecture. Other information is processed in depth, such as when we plan how we might apply information that we have just read. Repeating information, such as a date we wish to remember, requires only shallow processing. Organizing information, relating new information to old information, evaluating the validity of information, and applying information involve a deeper level of processing. More connections are made through deeper-level processing, so information that is processed more elaborately or more deeply is more easily retrieved. Deeper processing elaborates the representation of the information in memory (Ashcraft, 1994). Material that students read will become more memorable if, as they read, they seek out connections between ideas in the passage or between what they are reading and what they know.

To get a sense of how memory works, read the following paragraph and see how much of it you can remember.

With hocked gems financing him, our hero bravely defied all scornful laughter that tried to prevent his scheme. "Your eyes deceive," he had said. "An egg, not a table correctly typifies this unexplored planet." Now three sturdy sisters sought proof. Forging along, sometimes through calm vastness, yet more often over turbulent peaks and valleys, days became weeks as many doubters spread fearful rumors about the edge. At last, from nowhere a welcomed winged creature appeared, signifying momentous success. (Carlson & Buskist, 1997, p. 247)

How much of this paragraph do you remember? Most people don't remember very much because the paragraph is not very meaningful to them. Unable to make connections, they can process it only on a shallow level. But now give the paragraph a title, "Columbus Discovers America." Read the paragraph again. Now how much do you remember? In experiments, people who were told the title before reading remembered significantly more (Dooling & Lachman, 1971). Improving encoding by making the material more understandable improves memory just as activating schema improves students' understanding and memory of a selection to be read.

Elaborating information also aids memory. For example, suppose a student reads and wants to remember the following three facts from a selection about anteaters:

1. They have a long, thin snout.
2. They have sharp claws.
3. They have sticky tongues.

The student elaborates on the text by asking herself or himself why anteaters have a long, thin snout, sharp claws, and a sticky tongue, and determines that an anteater can use its long snout to poke into underground ant nests, its claws to rip open the nests, and its sticky tongue to pick up the ants. This elaboration aids long-term storage and retrieval.

The more connections that are constructed between items of information in memory, the greater the number of retrieval paths (Atkinson, Atkinson, Smith, & Hilgard, 1987). "Questions about the causes and consequences of an event are particularly effective elaborations because each question sets up a meaningful connection, or retrieval path, to the event" (p. 269).

■ **Overlearning** refers to the practice of continuing to study after material has been learned in order to foster increased retention.

■ **Rehearsal** refers to the process of memorizing information.

Principles for Improving Memory

The following principles are based on the way memory is believed to work and should aid retention:

- Get a clear, meaningful encoding of the material to be learned.

- Have a purposeful intention to learn. Activate strategies that will aid retention.

- Organize and elaborate information so that it will have a greater number of meaningful connections and thus will be easier to store and retrieve. Creating outlines, summaries, and maps; taking notes; reflecting; and applying information promote retention.

- Overlearning aids retention. **Overlearning** means that a person continues to study after material has been learned. This extra practice pays off in longer-lasting retention. Novice students often make the mistake of halting their study efforts as soon as they are able to recite the desired material. Added practice sessions should help maintain the level of performance.

- When it is not possible to structure meaningful connections between material to be learned and prior knowledge, use memory devices to create connections. Some popular memory devices are described in the following section.

- Give your mind a rest. After intensive studying, take a break, rest, and get enough sleep. Sleep, it is believed, gives the brain the opportunity to organize information.

Memory Devices

Conceptual Understanding

The best way to remember new material is to achieve conceptual understanding. Bransford (1994) gives an example of a student who is studying arteries and veins for a test: The student knows that one type of blood vessel is thick and elastic, and one is thin and nonelastic, but he is not sure which is which. He can use a number of strategies to help him remember. He could use simple rehearsal and just say, "artery, thick, elastic" over and over. But a far better approach would be to seek conceptual understanding and ask, "Why are arteries thick and elastic?" The student has read that blood is pumped from the heart through the arteries in spurts and reasons, therefore, that the arteries must be elastic so that they can contract and expand as the heart pumps. They have to be thick because they must withstand the pressure of the blood. If the explanation that enables the learner to see the significance of the information is not provided in the reading, the learner must seek it out.

Rehearsal

The simplest memory device of all is **rehearsal**. Rehearsal may be used when conceptual understanding is not feasible or possible. For instance, one has to memorize a list of dates. In its most basic form, rehearsal involves saying the item to be memorized over and over again. It is the way students learn the names of the letters of the alphabet, the names of the vowels, and their home addresses and telephone numbers. Rehearsal works because it focuses the learner's attention on the items to be learned and transfers material into long-term memory (Weinstein & Mayer, 1986).

     Young children use rehearsal strategies, but they may not do so spontaneously. They may have to be taught how to use such strategies, and then they may have to be reminded to apply them. Natural development is also a factor. Older children, even when not instructed to do so, tend to use rehearsal more frequently than younger children do. A program of study skills for elementary and middle school students would have to balance students' development with careful instruction. As students grow older, they can learn to use more complex rehearsal strategies, such as rereading text aloud or silently. They also learn how to test themselves.

Mnemonic Method

Rehearsal is an inefficient way to remember material. If at all possible, a more meaningful approach should be used. If conceptual understanding is not possible, learners might use a mnemonic method that constructs connections that are artificially meaningful. **Mnemonics** are artificial memory devices, such as the verse used to remember how many days there are in each month ("thirty days has September, April, June, and November"). Mnemonics are used when it is not possible to create more meaningful connections.

Mnemonic Rhymes.   Many traditional rhymes were written specifically to help school children with memory tasks:

> In fourteen hundred and ninety-two
> Columbus sailed the ocean blue. . . .

> Use *i* before *e* except after *c*
> or when sounded like *a* as in *neighbor* and *weigh*.

Acronyms.   Words made from the first letters of a series of words are often used to assist memory. Common **acronyms** include *roy g. biv* for the colors of visible light in the order in which they appear in the spectrum (red, orange, yellow, green, blue, indigo, violet); and *homes* for the Great Lakes (Huron, Ontario, Michigan, Erie, and Superior).

Acrostics.   In **acrostics**, a simple phrase is used to learn a series of words or letters. For instance, *Every Good Boy Does Fine* has long been used as an aid in memorizing the letters (E, G, B, D, and F) representing the tuning of guitar strings or the notes on the treble clef in written music. Similarly, *My Very Educated Mother Just Served Us Noodles* can help people remember the names of the eight planets (Mercury, Venus, Earth, Mars, Jupiter, Saturn, Uranus, Neptune). Acrostics and acronyms work because they provide a way to organize information that is essentially random.

The best mnemonic devices are those that students create for themselves. Help the class create rhymes or other devices for remembering important dates, names, rules, or other items that have to be memorized.

▪▪▪ Checkup ▪▪▪

1. What are some steps that might be taken to improve retention of information?
2. What are the basic principles for improving retention?
3. What are some helpful devices for enhancing memory?

▪ SQ3R: A Theory-Based Study Strategy

A five-step technique known as SQ3R—Survey, Question, Read, Recite, and Review—implements many of the principles presented in this chapter. Devised in the 1930s, it is the most thoroughly documented and widely used study technique in English-speaking countries. SQ3R, or a method based on it, appears in nearly every text that discusses studying. It is very effective when properly applied (Caverly & Orlando, 1991).

▪ **Mnemonics** are artificial devices (such as a rhyme) used to aid memory. Mnemonics represent a level of processing deeper than simply saying an item over and over.

▪ An **acronym** is a word made up of the first letter of each of a series of words.

▪ An **acrostic** is a device in which the first letters in a series of words spell out a word or phrase or correspond to the first letters in another series of words to be memorized.

Principles of SQ3R

SQ3R is based on the following principles, derived from F. P. Robinson's (1970) review of research on studying:

■ Surveying headings and summaries increases speed of reading, helps students remember the text and, perhaps most importantly, provides an overview of the text.

■ Asking a question before reading each section improves comprehension.

■ Reciting from memory immediately after reading slows down forgetting. If asked questions immediately after reading, students are able to answer only about half of them. After just one day, 50 percent of what was learned is forgotten. Students are then able to answer just 25 percent of questions asked about a text. However, those who review the material have a retention rate of more than 80 percent one day later. In another study, students who spent 20 percent of their time reading and 80 percent reciting were able to answer twice as many questions as those who simply read the material (Gates, 1917).

■ Understanding major ideas and seeing relationships among ideas helps comprehension and retention.

■ Having short review sessions, outlining, and relating information to students' personal needs and interests are helpful.

Applying any one of Robinson's (1970) principles should result in more effective studying. However, Robinson based SQ3R on all of them. Applied as described in the following Student Strategies box, SQ3R prepares students to read and helps them organize, elaborate, and rehearse information from text.

Student Strategies

Applying SQ3R

1. *Survey.* Survey the chapter that you are about to read to get an overall picture of what it is about. Glance over the title and headings. Quickly read the overview and summary. Note what main ideas are covered. This quick survey will help you organize the information in the chapter as you read it.

2. *Question.* Turn each heading into a question. The heading "Causes of the Great Depression" would become "What were the causes of the Great Depression?" Answering the question you created gives you a purpose for reading.

3. *Read.* Read to answer the question. Having a question to answer focuses your attention and makes you a more active reader.

4. *Recite.* When you come to the end of the section, stop and test yourself. Try to answer your question. If you cannot, go back over the section and then try once again to answer the question. The answer may be oral or written. Note, however, that a written answer is preferable because writing things down is more active than simply saying them; writing forces you to summarize what you have learned. The answer should also be brief; otherwise, SQ3R takes up too much time.

   Do not take notes until you have read the entire section. Taking notes before completing the section interrupts your reading and could interfere with your understanding of the section. Repeat steps 2, 3, and 4 until you have read the entire selection.

FYI

■ In addition to needing many opportunities to apply the technique, students using SQ3R require individual feedback so that they can make necessary adjustments in the way the technique is applied.

■ "SQ3R is hard to teach because it requires not only the development of component skills but the replacement of old habits. Consider that most students—even the best of them—turn to the first page of a chapter and begin at the first word. It's the student in a hurry, sometimes the less conscientious one, who is sensible enough to turn first to the questions at the end to see what the authors consider important. The survey step requires skimming and scanning, which many students, again the better ones, shun" (Early & Sawyer, 1984, p. 422).

■ Numerous adaptations have been made to SQ3R. A step that several practitioners advocate adding is reflecting (Pauk, 1989; Thomas & Robinson, 1972; Vacca & Vacca, 1986). After reading, students are encouraged to think about the material and how they might use it. Before reading, students reflect on what they already know about the topic.

5. *Review.* When you have finished the assignment, spend a few minutes reviewing what you read. If you took notes, cover them up. Then, asking yourself the questions you created from the headings, try to recall the major points that support the headings. The review helps you put information together and remember it longer.

In general, special elements should be treated the same way as text. The titles of graphs, tables, and maps are turned into questions and the information in the graph, table, or map is then used to answer the questions (Robinson, 1970). A diagram may be as important as the text and merit special effort. After examining the diagram carefully, students should try to draw it from memory and then compare their drawings with the diagram in the book (Robinson, 1970). Drawing becomes a form of recitation.

Teaching SQ3R

Although originally designed for college students, SQ3R works well with elementary and middle school students. In fact, if SQ3R or some of its elements are not taught in the early grades, college may be too late. By the upper elementary and middle school years, unless students have learned otherwise, they may have acquired inefficient study habits that are resistant to change (Walker, 1995). Very young readers can and should be taught to survey material, make predictions, and read to answer questions they have composed or to check how accurate their predictions were. Answering questions and reacting to predictions is a form of recitation. Once students are reading large amounts of text (in fourth grade or so) and are expected to remember information for tests, they should be introduced to all the principles of SQ3R. If students are to be tested, they must know how to prepare for tests.

Teaching SQ3R requires a commitment of time and effort. Each step must be taught carefully, with ample opportunity provided for practice and application. Early and Sawyer (1984) recommended spending at least a semester using it with older students. Slower students require additional instruction and practice time (Caverly & Orlando, 1991). Even after it has been taught carefully and practiced conscientiously, SQ3R requires periodic review and reteaching.

To use SQ3R fully, students should be able to generate main ideas. It also helps if they have some knowledge of text structures (Walker, 1995).

■■■ **Checkup** ■■■

1. What are the basic principles on which SQ3R is based?
2. What are the steps in SQ3R?
3. How might SQ3R be taught?

■■■

■ Test-Taking Strategies

As discussed in Chapter 2, as of 2005, students in grades 3 through 8 must be assessed in reading and math each year. Results of the tests are used to judge the proficiency of students and the effectiveness of school. States and local school districts may also decide to give additional tests. The best way to prepare students for high-stakes tests of this type is to have in place a high-quality literacy program and intervention programs for students who need them. In addition, students also need to know how to take tests. In their study of standardized test-taking among elementary school students, Calkins, Montgomery, and Santman (1998) found that a number of students had poor test-taking skills. They failed to follow directions, did not take guesses when it was to their benefit to do so, did not look back over a passage to find the right answer, did not check answers, and often used background rather than text knowledge to answer questions.

A program of test preparation should include:

- Teaching the language of tests and teaching students how to read and follow directions
- Teaching students how to use lookbacks, use their time well, and check answers
- Teaching students to read intensively and with full concentration as they take a test
- Teaching students to answer questions on the basis of information in the test passage rather than their personal experience or opinion

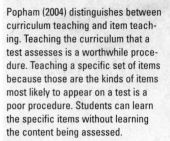

FYI

Popham (2004) distinguishes between curriculum teaching and item teaching. Teaching the curriculum that a test assesses is a worthwhile procedure. Teaching a specific set of items because those are the kinds of items most likely to appear on a test is a poor procedure. Students can learn the specific items without learning the content being assessed.

To gain insight into students' test-taking skills, observe them as they take a test. Note their test-taking strategies and how they use their time. Discuss their test-taking strategies with them. Model test-taking strategies. Show how you go about taking a test. Explain your thinking processes as you read and follow directions. Show how you answer the easiest items first and go about eliminating answer choices when you are not sure of an answer. Model the process of checking answers and pacing yourself. Provide extra coaching for students whose responding style lowers their scores: those who work too rapidly and fail to check answers as well as those who work too slowly and are overly concerned with making a mistake. Provide students with strategies for reading difficult passages and answering tough questions. Also explain the correction factor: On some tests, students lose a quarter of a point for wrong responses, and so are better off leaving an answer blank if they have no idea which of the answer options is correct. However, if they eliminate more than one of the options, the odds of getting the right answer are in their favor. If there is no penalty for guessing, students should make their best guess.

While students are taking a practice test, do a think-aloud. Have them tell you what's going on in their minds as they read the passage and answer questions. You might also interview students after they have taken a practice test. Scruggs, Bennion, and Lifson (1985) found that students who were able to describe specific test-taking strategies had higher scores. Two effective strategies were text referring ("I thought I had seen that in the story, so I checked back") and inferring ("I figured this must be the correct answer because of what the story said"). Struggling learners were far less strategic.

Adapted to test-taking, QAR should prove to be effective in helping students decide whether the answer is "right there" so that if they don't recall needed information, they can go back over the passage and find it, or whether it's "author and me" so that they have to make an inference based on information contained in the passage. Also question students as to how sure they are of the correctness of their answers. Higher-scoring students are better able to predict their performance. This is an advantage because they then know which items to recheck (Scruggs & Mastropieri, 1992).

Test preparation should be ethical. Providing students with items from the actual test is unethical. It is also unethical to raise students' scores without also increasing their underlying knowledge and skill (Popham, 2000). The goal of test preparation is to instruct students so that they have the test-taking skills to enable them to show what they know and can do. Test-taking preparation should not be so extensive that it displaces other valuable literacy activities.

Speaking of commercial test-preparation materials, Raphael and Au (2005) comment:

> Test preparation typically takes the form of having students complete workbook exercises with items of a form and content ostensibly similar to those on upcoming tests. In general, students practice by reading short passages and responding to multiple-choice items. Most test preparation packages involve little or no instruction by the teacher. The problem with practice-only activities is that students who have not already acquired reading comprehension strategies gain little or nothing from the large amounts of time spent on these activities. (p. 206)

Effective Test Preparation

Based on his analysis of the research on testing, Guthrie (2002) established estimates of the components of effective test performance. The three major components are reading ability (40 percent), content knowledge (20 percent), and motivation (15 percent). Instruction in test format or "test wiseness" accounted for just 10 percent of performance. The remaining 15 percent was due to errors in testing, such as imperfections in the testing process.

The first step in the process of preparing students for tests is to align instructional objectives with test objectives. For instance, if the test is assessing the ability to make inferences, this should be one of the instructional objectives. Strategies needed to accomplish objectives should be determined, assessed, and taught. Strategy instruction is a long-term venture. Strategies should be taught throughout the school year and, in fact, throughout students' school careers.

Certain strategies are especially effective in taking tests. Locating the information needed to answer a question is especially critical; unless a student has a photographic memory, it will be necessary to go back to the text to obtain information for answers. Using background knowledge is also a valuable strategy. Questions on reading tests can often be answered on the basis of background knowledge, and inferential questions typically require the use of background knowledge. Self-monitoring and checking also help improve test performance. Test-taking strategies should be taught as part of the regular curriculum: "Incorporating the comprehension strategies needed on a test into the mainstream curriculum planning is the most likely technique for building students' competence and self-confidence for successful test performance" (Guthrie, 2002, p. 381).

Wide reading, both in school and out, should be fostered. As Guthrie (2002) notes, the strongest predictor of achievement on standardized tests is the amount of reading students do:

> If a fifth grader is facing a high-stakes test in April, the best thing the student can do is to begin reading widely and frequently in October. If a teacher will encounter a high-stakes test for her classroom in April, her best preparation is to increase motivation of students for extended, learning-focused, independent reading as early as possible in the academic year. (p. 384)

Practice in test-taking skills does improve performance, especially if the format is unfamiliar. Students taking a test with an analogy, cloze, or other unfamiliar format should be provided with exercises that familiarize them with the format. However, instruction should be limited. Excessive time spent on test preparation is time taken away from an activity that might be more valuable.

Locate and Recall: An Essential Test-Taking Skill

Locate and recall is a technique for comprehending explicitly stated text, such as supporting details, and basic story elements, such as setting, characters, and plot. Locating and recalling have a natural working relationship. When we fail to recall information, we go back to the text to locate it. Recently, I served on a committee that was reviewing high-stakes tests. As part of the review process, we read the tests and answered the questions. This activity intensified my awareness of the importance of being able to locate information accurately and quickly. For most questions, I found myself going back to the passage to locate information so that I could select an answer or compose a response. Being able to locate information is an important everyday reading skill. For test-taking, it might be one of the most important skills of all. It is hard to see how any student who lacks lookback skills can pass a high-stakes test. Indeed, the number-one shortcoming of students' responses on high-stakes tests is the failure to support responses (Gunning, 2006). Supporting a response entails going back over the selection and locating supporting details. Students need to learn how to go back to a passage to locate details, to verify information, and to find support for a position. On the easiest level, students simply locate directly stated information. On a higher level, they make inferences and draw conclusions from information they have located.

Despite the absolute importance of being able to locate information, observations suggest that many students do not refer back to passages. In discussions with students, some expressed the belief that it was cheating to go back over the passage. Locating should be explained, modeled, and practiced so that it becomes virtually automatic. To introduce locating, explain to students that we can't remember everything we read, but we can go back to check facts or find details that we can't recall. Do a think-aloud with a sample multiple-choice test. Explain as you come to a challenging question that you are not sure which is the correct answer, so you go over the test passage and locate information that will help you. Show how you quickly skim over the passage to find the pertinent information. Provide students with a lengthy, fact-packed passage and lots of questions. As a class, read the passage and then respond to the questions. Help students as they go back over the passage to locate information. Provide practice with this skill.

Embed instruction in ongoing class activities. During discussions, encourage students to go back over a selection when they can't answer questions. Also, ask them to read from a selection to support a point they are making. Ask questions like these: "Can you read the sentence that tells us at what age the inventor thought up the idea for TV?" "Can you read the part that suggests that the old woman was kind?" When students are completing assignments or taking tests, remind them of the importance of looking back.

As students become accustomed to going back to a passage to verify information or locate a detail, introduce the skill of using information from a passage to construct a response. Along with reinforcing this skill in discussions, provide instruction and practice in applying this skill when writing.

■ ■ ■ Checkup ■ ■ ■

1. What is the role of test-taking preparation in a literacy program?
2. What steps might you take to foster students' test-taking skills?

■ ■ ■

■ Study Habits

Ideally, each student should have a quiet place to study that is free of distractions. The area should be well lit, contain a desk or other writing surface, and be supplied with paper, pens, pencils, and a few basic reference books, such as a dictionary and an almanac. Of course, not every child has the luxury of such a retreat, but children should be advised to find the best study spot they can. In even the most crowded homes, there is a time when quiet prevails. One member of a ten-person family did his studying early in the morning while everyone else was asleep.

Studying, however, is more a matter of attitude than place. Research and common practice suggest that students study best when they meet the following conditions:

- They know how to study.
- They know why they are studying. The assignment has value and the students understand what that value is.
- They know what type of test they are studying for and how to adjust their efforts to meet its demands.
- They have a routine. Studying requires discipline. Students should determine the best time for them to study and then study at that time every day. Generally, study should precede recreation.
- Studying is active and purposeful. An hour of concentrated study is better than two hours of studying in which the student takes many breaks and lets her or his attention wander.

Another condition that fosters effective studying is rewarding oneself. Suggest that students reward themselves for a job well done. For instance, they might treat themselves to a snack or to watching a favorite TV show after forty-five minutes of concentrated study. Having an interest in the material also makes it easier to study and learn. Some material is intrinsically interesting; in other cases, interest has to be built. Students should be encouraged to envision how a certain subject might fit in with their personal needs and

Taking notes is an essential study skill.

goals. If that fails, they can remember the extrinsic rewards—studying the material will result in a higher grade, for example.

Introducing Study Strategies and Habits

Discuss with students the importance of studying and the specific payoffs it has. Also, discuss the results of not studying. Talk over hindrances to studying and how these might be overcome. You might also model how you go about studying for a test and then provide guided practice. Observe students as they study and discuss the procedures that they use. Lead them to use efficient study strategies. Also, help students make a detailed study plan. This should include not only what they will study and why, but where, when, for how long, and under what circumstances. Study plans should be individualized, so encourage students to try different techniques. Part of learning to study is discovering how, when, and where one studies best.

■ Expressive Study Skills

A key part of studying is recording information in some way. This might be done by taking traditional or simplified notes or by using various kinds of graphic organizers.

Taking Notes

Taking notes is an essential study skill. It is also a very practical one. Writing telephone messages is a form of note taking, as is jotting down a series of complex details. Teaching students how to take phone messages provides them with a practical skill and can also be an effective introduction to note taking. Model the process of taking messages. Emphasize that it is necessary to obtain only the essential information: who called, whom the call was for, and the caller's message. Pretend that you are a caller and have students take notes. Discuss the clarity and conciseness of their notes. Have pairs of students role-play, with one student playing the part of the caller, the other the message taker. Also, discuss real-life cases in which students have taken notes.

As students begin writing expository reports, a natural need arises for note taking. They have to have some method for preserving information drawn from a variety of

FYI

■ Learning a new habit takes about three months or more (Prochaska, Norcross, & DiClemente, 1994). Provide ongoing instruction, practice, and encouragement.

■ Taking notes is better than highlighting. When taking notes we think more deeply about the information, so we understand it better and remember it longer (Carlson & Buskist, 1997).

sources. As they prepare to write reports, share with them experiences you have had taking notes. Model how you might take notes from an encyclopedia or other source. Teach students a tried-and-true procedure that might include the steps outlined in the following Student Strategy.

Student Strategies

Taking Notes

1. Write the topic on the top line of a note card: for example, "Camels—how they help people." Turn the topic into a question: "How do camels help people?"

2. Search for information that answers the question. You do not have to read every word of each article that you locate on your topic. You can skim through to find the relevant facts, and you can skip parts that do not contain what you are looking for.

3. Take notes on details that answer your question. Put the notes in your own words. The best way to do this is to read a brief section and write the important facts from memory. To save time and space, leave out words that are not important like *the, a*, and *an*. Write in phrases instead of sentences, and do not bother with punctuation except in quotations.

4. Check back over the section. Make sure that you have taken all the notes that answer your question and that you have put them in your own words. Sometimes, you may want to quote someone's exact words. Maybe a famous scientist said something interesting about camels. If you use exact words, make sure that you put quotation marks around them. Also make sure that you write exactly what the person said.

5. Fill in identifying information at the top of the card below the topic. Write the author's name, title of the article, title of the book or periodical, volume number if it has one, publisher's name, location of the publisher, date of publication, and page number(s) where you got your information. (Younger students may use a simplified bibliographic reference.) The finished notes might look like those in Figure 8.11.

■ ■ ■ **FIGURE 8.11**
Example of Note Taking

Camels—how they help people

Dagg, Ann Innis. Camel. *World Book Encyclopedia,*
Vol. 3, Chicago: World Book, 2000, pp. 75–78.

Pull plows
Turn water wheels to work pumps
Carry grain to market
Carry people and their goods
Meat of young camels is eaten—can be tough
Fat from hump used as butter
Can drink camel's milk and make cheese
Camel's milk is very rich
Hair made into cloth and blankets
Skin used to make tents
Skin used to make leather for shoes, saddles, saddlebags
Bones used for decorations and as cooking and eating utensils

A major problem with elementary and even middle school students' research reports is that often they are verbatim copies of encyclopedia articles. Having students take notes in their own words is one way to eliminate this. Another is to request that students obtain information from at least two sources. Actually, encyclopedias should be only a starting point. Their information is limited and often dated. Encourage students to find other sources from the large number of high-quality informational books published each year and high-quality Web sites. Students should also be encouraged to think over the information they have collected and to select only the most essential details for inclusion in their reports. The ultimate solution to the problem of verbatim copying is to have students explore topics in which they have a genuine interest. Calkins and Harwayne (1991) called this "writing with voice": "We will write with voice when we have read, questioned, dreamed, argued, worried, wept, gossiped, and laughed over a topic" (p. 201).

■■■ Checkup ■■■

1. What are the conditions that foster effective studying?
2. What steps might you take to build students' study skills?
3. How would you go about teaching note-taking skills?   ■ ■ ■

Using the Internet to Obtain Information

Searching for information on Web sites leads to what Leu (2006) refers to as an Internet bottleneck. Students have difficulty creating the question that will help them obtain the information they need. Once they have located potential sites, they fail to evaluate their effectiveness. One study found that 85 percent of students didn't read the search engine's descriptions of the sites to determine which ones might best answer their questions (New Literacies Research Team, 2006). They used a click-and-pick strategy: They simply clicked on the first site that appeared; then if it didn't appeal or seem relevant, they clicked on the next one.

In preparation for a search of the Internet, discuss students' topics and their key questions. After students have established their questions, they might decide what keywords or concept words will enable them to obtain pertinent answers. For instance, a student interested in how robots help manufacture cars might frame her questions as follows: "How are robots used to manufacture cars?" Possible keywords might include *robots, cars, manufacture*, and synonyms of these words. A sample worksheet for searching the Internet is presented in Figure 8.12.

Using Subject Directories and Indexes

Subject directories and indexes are often overlooked as sources of information. Indexes or directories arrange information by categories. They can be searched by examining and clicking on categories or entering keywords. Directories are arranged in hierarchical fashion. For instance, in Yahooligans, *alpaca* is listed under *farm animals*, which is listed under *animals*, which is listed under *science and nature*. Students can start with *science and nature* and work their way on to *alpacas* or simply type in the keyword *alpacas*. One advantage of directories is that students need have only a general idea of what they are looking for. They do not have to know precise terms.

Search Engines and Directories for Students

A number of search engines and directories have been specially designed for student use. Sites have been inspected by librarians or other professionals to make sure that they are appropriate for students. Here are some of the most widely used:

■ *Ask for Kids:* Uses questions rather than keywords to conduct a search. The student types in a question, and the search engine responds by listing that question and/or sim-

Internet Search Form

What question do you want answered? Be as specific as you can.

<u>How are robots used to manufacture cars?</u>

What are the keywords in your question? What are synonyms for your keywords?

Keywords	Synonyms
car	auto, vehicle
robot	
manufacture	assemble

Using only keywords, what will you ask the search engine to find?

(car* OR auto* OR vehicle) AND robot* AND (manufacture OR assemble)

Hints: Put parentheses around synonyms and join them with OR. Put AND between keywords. Use an asterisk to signal a search for different forms of the words: auto, autos, automobile, automobiles, automotive.

Adapted from Creighton University (2001). *Conducting an Internet Search.* Available online at http://www.creighton.edu.

ilar questions and sites that provide possible answers to the questions.
http://www.askforkids.com

- *KidsClick!* Web search for kids by librarians. Lists about 5,000 Web sites. Gives estimated readabilities of sites.
http://sunsite.berkeley.edu/KidsClick!

- *Yahooligans!* Launched in 1996 and designed for young people from seven to twelve, Yahooligans is the oldest major directory for students.
http://www.yahooligans.yahoo.com

After locating sources of information, students need to sift through and identify sources that are offering pertinent information. It is important that today's students, who are overloaded with information, learn how to select the best data. Model and discuss with students techniques for selecting material that provides answers to their questions. Demonstrate how you use titles or brief annotations or quickly skim articles to decide whether a source is pertinent. In addition to assessing a source to see whether it contains pertinent information, students must also evaluate the source to see whether the information is reliable, as was explained in Chapter 7.

■ ■ ■ Checkup ■ ■ ■

1. What are some skills that students need to learn in order to use the Internet to obtain information?
2. What might students do in order to prepare for an Internet search?   ■ ■ ■

■ Metacognitive Study Strategies

The key to teaching students how to direct their study is to present metacognitive study strategies within the context of material to be read or a project to be undertaken. Although presented in context, the strategies must be taught in such a way that they transfer to other texts and other situations. As with the comprehension strategies introduced in earlier chapters, it is essential that the metacognitive strategies be integrated with cognitive and affective factors.

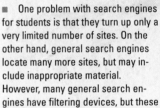

FYI

- One problem with search engines for students is that they turn up only a very limited number of sites. On the other hand, general search engines locate many more sites, but may include inappropriate material. However, many general search engines have filtering devices, but these may exclude sites that should be included and fail to block some that are objectionable.

- Also available on the Internet are computerized searches of periodicals and databases that include the text, so students can view the references and obtain the articles. One such service is InfoTrac, which has several versions designed specifically for students. Libraries subscribe to the service and then offer it to patrons. Patrons use their library bar codes or some sort of password to access the service from their home or school computer.

■■■ **TABLE 8.3** **Metacognitive Study Strategies**

Strategy	Description
Asking questions: What do I want to learn?	This includes setting up hypotheses, setting aims, defining boundaries of area to be explored, discovering audience, and relating task to previous work.
Planning: How will I go about the task?	This includes deciding on tactics and subdividing the overall task into sub-tasks.
Monitoring: Am I answering my questions?	This is a continuing attempt to see whether the results of one's efforts match the questions posed or purposes set.
Checking: How have I done so far?	This is a preliminary check to assess results and tactics.
Revising: What do I have to change?	Tactics, results, or goals may have to be changed.
Self-testing: How did I do? What did I learn?	In this final evaluation, both the results and the method of achieving them are assessed.

Metacognitive strategies that apply to virtually all study tasks are listed in Table 8.3 (Nisbet & Shucksmith, 1986). Students involved in writing reports and other long-term projects should learn to go through the six stages: asking questions, planning, monitoring, checking, revising, and self-testing, as shown in the table. These stages, in adapted, abbreviated form, can also be used in studying for tests and completing daily homework assignments. Initially, you should walk the students step by step through these stages. Gradually, they should assume responsibility for each stage on their own; ideally, the strategies will become automatic.

Along with applying these metacognitive strategies, students also need to use self-regulatory behaviors to complete academic tasks. They must use self-discipline and perseverance in order to overcome obstacles and forge ahead. Students work best when they understand why they are undertaking a project and what they are to do, feel that the task is doable, and have the necessary materials and strategies. Encourage students to tell you about any obstacles that they encounter. Discuss how they might overcome these obstacles. Provide guidance and encouragement as needed (Gensemer, 1998).

■■■ Checkup ■■■

1. What are the key metacognitive study strategies?
2. How might you foster students' self-regulatory behaviors?

■■■

Tools for the Classroom

Building Higher-Level Literacy

Informational text, especially in the major content areas, provides students with substantive material to think about and challenges them to apply comprehension strategies. Informational text also provides an excellent opportunity for students to apply critical thinking skills, such as noting bias, checking the reliability of sources, and drawing logical conclusions.

Knowing assorted facts about a content area is not sufficient. What students need to enhance comprehension is depth of knowledge about a topic (Pressley, 1994). It is not enough simply to tell students about the food pyramid; students must process that information. They must understand the significance of the food pyramid, why carbohydrates are at the bottom and fats are at the top. Of course, they should know what carbohydrates and fats are. Students should also be thinking about the foods they eat and whether their own diets reflect the food pyramid.

Higher-level thinking is fostered when students are guided so that they see the big picture, or the major ideas in subject matter areas. It is also fostered when students ask why questions and use understanding as the main means for studying and retaining information.

Help for Struggling Readers and Writers

Struggling readers and writers can be helped in a number of ways to cope with content-area materials. An attempt should be made to provide materials that are as close as possible to students' reading levels. This might entail obtaining easy-to-read texts or easy-to-read trade books that cover key content-area topics. Some of these trade books are listed in Appendix A. You might make the text more accessible by providing extra help with key words and concepts, reading all or parts of it with students, or making or obtaining tapes of it. You might also use a language experience approach. You read portions of the text to students or discuss key concepts and then discuss the information. After the discussion, students, aided by your prompts, dictate a summary, which you write on the chalkboard or overhead transparency. After the summary has been composed, you read it and then volunteers read it and discuss it. The summary is duplicated and given to students to read on their own. A collection of these summaries might be assembled and used as a content-area text.

Adapting Instruction for Struggling Readers and Writers

For students who have severe reading difficulties, obtain recorded versions of their texts and review ways of studying information from an oral source. Recordings for the Blind and Dyslexic (20 Roszel Road, Princeton, NJ 08540) provides taped versions of school textbooks for students with reading problems. Taped periodicals and children's books are available from Talking Books, National Library Service for the Blind and Physically Handicapped (includes dyslexia), Library of Congress, Washington, DC.

Essential Standards

Grades 1 through 3

Students will

- use a variety of strategies to learn from informational text.
- use text features such as headings, maps, charts, and graphs to foster understanding.
- use various types of writing to learn content-area information.
- use understanding, rehearsal, and mnemonics to remember information.
- select an appropriate place to study and develop appropriate study habits.
- take simple notes.
- identify questions to be explored, use a variety of sources to locate information, and present information gathered.
- use basic test-taking strategies.

Grades 4 through 8

Students will

- use a variety of strategies to learn from informational text.
- use various types of writing to learn content-area information.
- use text features such as headings, maps, charts, and graphs to foster understanding.
- use understanding, rehearsal, and mnemonics to remember information.
- take notes from text and interviews.
- identify questions to be explored, use multiple sources, including Internet sources, and present reports that use visuals to support the report.
- plan and complete short-term and long-term assignments.
- select an appropriate place to study and develop appropriate study habits.
- use effective test-taking strategies.

Action Plan

1. Decide what content you want to teach.
2. Select appropriate materials, including texts, trade books, periodicals, CD-ROMs, and Web sites.
3. Match materials to students' level of reading ability. Make adjustments in materials and approaches and provide additional help as needed.

4. Use anticipation guides, structured overviews, and other techniques to prepare students for their reading.

5. Guide students in the use of chapter organization, text structure, and think-alouds to foster comprehension during reading.

6. Use analogies, graphic organizers, and applying and extending to deepen students' understanding after they have finished reading.

7. Use KWL to foster understanding before, during, and after reading.

8. Use writing-to-learn activities such as learning logs to foster students' learning.

9. Use sheltered English or a similar approach to help ELLs learn English as they learn content.

10. Guide students in the use of mnemonic devices and study techniques such as SQ3R.

11. Teach students test-taking strategies but do not overemphasize them.

12. Build effective study habits and metacognitive awareness of study skills.

13. Teach note taking and other expressive study skills.

14. Guide students in the use of the Internet to obtain information.

15. Monitor students' progress and make adjustments as necessary.

Assessment

Using observations, quizzes, tests, samples of students' work, and discussions, note how well students are able to comprehend content-area materials. Assess, in particular, how effectively they use appropriate strategies. Assess, too, whether students are using study strategies and whether or not they have good study habits. One way of determining this is to analyze their test grades and the quality of their projects.

Summary

Content-area textbooks, which account for most of the material covered in subject-matter classes, pose special problems because they are more complex than narrative materials and may contain a high proportion of difficult concepts and technical vocabulary. Trade books, periodicals, Web sites, and other materials enliven content-area instruction and can be used along with or instead of textbooks.

Students can use numerous strategies to foster understanding before, during, and after reading. Teaching content and teaching strategies should be combined. Increased content knowledge makes strategies easier to apply. Writing is a powerful way to promote learning in the content areas. With sheltered English, students learn both content and English.

Studying requires remembering in addition to understanding material. Retention of important information is improved by understanding, organization, and elaboration. Rehearsal (including the use of mnemonics) is an appropriate strategy for learning materials that lack meaningful connections.

A study strategy that has been effective with a variety of students is SQ3R (Study, Question, Read, Recite, and Review). Learning to take notes is an important study skill, as is learning to take tests. Good study habits include finding an appropriate time and place to study and studying purposefully as part of a regular routine. Studying should be metacognitive. Help for struggling readers and writers includes making the content information accessible to students and providing hands-on experiences.

Extending and Applying

1. Examine an up-to-date content-area book. Using the Fry readability graph (Figure 2.11) or the Qualitative Assessment of Texts (Chall, Bissex, Conard, & Harris-Sharples, 1996) on at least three separate passages of 100 words or more, obtain an estimate of the readability of the book. Also note textual features such as those listed in Table 8.1. How readable is the book? What are its strengths and weaknesses?

2. Try out one of the strategies described in this chapter for at least a week. Use a learning log to keep a record of your experience. How well did the strategy work? How hard was it to use? How practical is it?

3. Create a lesson showing how you would introduce KWL or another technique to a class. If possible, teach the lesson and evaluate its effectiveness.

Developing a Professional Portfolio

Include items that demonstrate your ability to teach content area literacy skills or study skills. The items might be a taped lesson, lesson or unit plans, or examples of students' work, such as a learning log or completed KWL sheet. Be sure to describe and reflect on items included.

   Go to Allyn & Bacon's MyLabSchool: www.mylabschool.com

- Enter Assignment ID **CRV1** into **Assignment Finder,** and select the video titled "Promoting Literacy." In this video, strategies used to promote literacy in the content areas—including defining vocabulary, understanding facts, graphic literacy, and research—are discussed.

- As you watch the video, identify the techniques the teacher uses to promote literacy. Why is it important for students to "make connections" when reading nonfiction materials?

- Explore MyLabSchool further to find the course areas for Reading Methods, Language Arts, and Content Area Reading and identify other assets that support concepts introduced in this chapter.

Developing a Resource File

Collect and/or create mnemonic devices for learning key facts in a subject matter area that you teach. Start a collection of bibliography cards or database entries on books that might supplement or replace the textbook in the content area that you teach or plan to teach. Try to locate books on easy, average, and challenging levels.

To access chapter objectives, practice tests, weblinks, and flashcards, go to the companion website at www.ablongman.com/gunning6e.

9 Reading Literature

or each of the following statements related to the chapter you are about to read, put a check under "Agree" or "Disagree" to show how you feel. Discuss your responses with classmates before you read the chapter.

	Agree	Disagree
1. A literature program for the elementary and middle schools should emphasize the classics.	_____	_____
2. The main danger of a literature approach to reading is that selections will be overanalyzed.	_____	_____
3. Students need to rely on the teacher for an accurate interpretation of literature.	_____	_____
4. Students should have some say in choosing the literature they read.	_____	_____
5. It does not really matter what children read just as long as they read something.	_____	_____
6. Setting aside a period each day for voluntary reading is an excellent use of time.	_____	_____

ow do you go about reading a piece of literature? Do you read it in the same way that you read a popular novel? If your approach is different, how is it different? When reading literature, students use many of the same processes that they use when reading more mundane materials; word-attack skills and comprehension strategies are necessary. However, reading literature involves going beyond mere comprehension. The focus is on appreciation, enjoyment, and reader response. This chapter explores ideas for building understanding and appreciation of folklore, myths, poems, plays, and novels and ends with suggestions for promoting voluntary reading.

What are your favorite kinds of literature? What experiences have you had that created a love of literature? What experiences have you had that may have created negative feelings about literature? How might literature be taught so that students learn to understand and appreciate it without losing the fun of reading it? What might be done to make students lifelong readers of high-quality novels, poetry, plays, and biographies?

■ Experiencing Literature

Reading literature involves a dimension beyond reading ordinary material. If read properly, a classic tale draws out a feeling of wholeness or oneness, a carefully drawn character or situation evokes a feeling of recognition, and a poem that speaks to the heart engenders a feeling of tranquility. Louise Rosenblatt (1978) identified this response as characteristic of **aesthetic reading**: "In aesthetic reading, the reader's attention is centered directly on what he is living through during his relationship with that particular text" (p. 25).

In contrast to aesthetic reading is **efferent reading**, in which the reader's attention is directed to "concepts to be refined, ideas to be tested, actions to be performed after the reading" (Rosenblatt, 1978, p. 24). In efferent reading, the reader "carries away" meaning. In aesthetic reading, the reader is carried away by feelings evoked by the text. Text can be read efferently or aesthetically, depending on the reader's stance. For example, we could read an

FYI

■ Students interpret literature in terms of their own experience. For instance, in their discussions of *Maniac Magee* (Spinnelli, 1990), a tale of a homeless boy and race relations in a small town, students spoke of how characters in the book reminded them of family members (Lehr & Thompson, 2000). They made connections between events in their lives and what was happening to the characters in the book. One student, who had been shuffled between his mother's and grandmother's houses, identified with Maniac Magee's satisfaction at finally having an address.

■ "The signs of the aesthetic response [in students] may include: picturing and imagining while reading or viewing; imagining themselves in a character's place or in story events; questioning or hypothesizing about a story; making associations with other stories and their own life experiences; and mentioning feelings evoked" (Cox & Many, 1992, pp. 32–33).

■ Readers who make aesthetic responses enjoy a richer experience and produce more elaborated written responses. When students write from an aesthetic stance, their responses are more fully developed and more likely to show connections between the text and their lives. Efferent responses are more likely to consist of a barebones retelling of the tale and a brief evaluation of literary elements (Many, 1990, 1991).

essay efferently for ideas or information, but if we respond to its biting satire or subtle humor, our stance becomes aesthetic. Thus, reading is not an either/or proposition but falls on a continuum, with the reader moving closer to one stance or the other depending on her or his expectations and focus (Dias, 1990). As Rosenblatt (1991) explained, "We read for information, but we are conscious of emotions about it and feel pleasure when the words we call up arouse vivid images and are rhythmic to the inner ear" (p. 445).

Rosenblatt cautioned that it is important to have a clear sense of purpose when asking children to read a particular piece. The purpose should fit in with the nature of the piece and the objective for presenting it. By its nature, for instance, poetry generally demands an aesthetic reading. But if the focus of the reading is on literal comprehension, then the experience will be efferent. The reading is aesthetic if the focus is on experiencing the poem or story and savoring the sounds, sights, and emotions that the words conjure up.

Reading aesthetically results in a deeper level of involvement for students (Cox & Many, 1992). As they read aesthetically, children tend to picture the story in their minds. They imagine scenes, actions, and characters. As they become more deeply involved, they may enter the world they have constructed and try to understand events and characters "in terms of how people in their world would act in similar circumstances" (Cox & Many, 1992, p. 30). Aesthetic readers also extend and hypothesize. They might wonder what happens to the characters after the story is over and imagine possible scenarios or create alternative endings. Students might also identify with a particular character and wonder how they might act if they were that character and experienced the story events.

Reader Response

How does one go about eliciting reader response? Probst (1988) described the following general steps:

1. *Creating a reader response environment.* Establish a setting in which students feel free to respond and each response is valued so that students do not worry about rightness or wrongness.

2. *Preparing to read the literary piece.* Preparation for reading a literary piece is basically the same as that for reading any text: A guided reading framework might be used. In the preparatory stage, a schema is activated, new concepts and vocabulary words are taught, interest in reading the selection is engendered, and a purpose is set. The purpose generally is open-ended, to evoke a response. As an alternative, the teacher might read aloud and discuss the first portion, especially if it is a chapter book or novel.

3. *Reading the literary piece.* Students read the work silently. However, if it is a poem, the teacher may elect to read it aloud, as the sound of poetry is essential to its impact.

4. *Small-group discussion.* The literary piece is discussed by groups of four or five students. In small groups, each student has a better opportunity to express her or his response to the piece and compare it with those of others. Discussion is essential, because it leads to deeper exploration of a piece.

To foster a fuller discussion, students might be asked to jot down their responses before they discuss them. Writing facilitates careful consideration. Questions that might be used to evoke a response include the following, some of which were suggested by Probst (1988). Four or five questions should be sufficient to evoke a full discussion.

■ Which part of the selection stands out in your mind the most?

■ Picture a part of the piece in your mind. Which part did you picture? Why?

■ **Aesthetic reading** refers to emotions experienced or evoked while reading a piece of writing.

■ **Efferent reading** means reading to comprehend the information conveyed by a piece of writing.

- Was there anything in the selection that bothered you?
- Was there anything in it that surprised you?
- What main feeling did it stir up?
- What is the best line or paragraph in the piece?
- Does this selection make you think of anything that has happened in your life?
- As you read, did your feelings change? If so, how?
- Does this piece remind you of anything else that you have read?
- If the author were here, what would you say to her or him?
- What questions would you ask?
- If you were the editor, what changes might you suggest that the author make?
- What do you think the writer was trying to say?
- What special words, expressions, or writing devices did the author use? Which of these did you like best? Least?
- If you were grading the author, what mark would you give her or him? Why? What comments might you write on the author's paper?

5. *Class discussion.* After the small groups have discussed the piece for about ten minutes, extend the discussion to the whole class. The discussion should center on the responses, beginning with those made in the small groups. Ask each group, "How did your group respond to the piece? How were the responses the same? Is there anything about the work that we can agree on? How were the responses different? Did your response change as your group discussed the piece? If so, how?"

Throughout the discussion, you, as the teacher, must remain neutral and not intervene with your interpretation. Students have to be empowered to construct their own interpretations, and they need opportunities to develop their interpretive skills. Lesson 9.1 shows how a reader response lesson might be presented using the poem "The Land of Counterpane" (Stevenson, 1885).

Lesson 9.1

Reader Response

Step 1. Preparing to read the literary piece
Ask students to tell what they do when they aren't feeling well and have to spend the day in bed. Explain that the author of the poem they are about to read, Robert Louis Stevenson, was a sickly child and often spent time in bed. Also explain that *counterpane* is an old-fashioned word for *bedspread*.

Step 2. Reading the literary piece
Have students read "The Land of Counterpane" or listen as you read it. Their purpose should be to see what feelings, thoughts, or pictures the poem brings to mind.

The Land of Counterpane

When I was sick and lay a-bed,
I had two pillows at my head,
And all my toys beside me lay
To keep me happy all the day.
And sometimes for an hour or so
I watched my leaden soldiers go,
With different uniforms and drills,
Among the bed-clothes, through the hills;
And sometimes sent my ships in fleets
All up and down among the sheets;
Or brought my trees and houses out,

FYI

- Students need assistance in holding discussions. Set ground rules, and have a group role-play the process.

- This is a menu of questions. Choose ones that are most appropriate for your circumstances, but do not attempt to ask them all.

- Rosenblatt (1991) comments: Textbooks and teachers' questions too often hurry students away from the lived-through experience. After the reading, the experience should be recaptured, reflected on. It can be the subject of further aesthetic activities—drawing, dancing, miming, talking, writing, role-playing, or oral interpretation. It can be discussed and analyzed efferently. Or it can yield information. But first, if it is indeed to be literature for these students, it must be experienced" (p. 447).

- Refrain from asking "Why?" after a reader has described his response. "Why?" implies that the youngster must justify his or her reaction to a piece, which tends to make him or her defensive. Instead of asking why, request that the student "tell me more about how you're thinking" (McClure & Kristo, 1994, p. xvi).

- Choose literary works that touch students' lives and to which they identify and respond. "The Land of Counterpane" would probably work best with third-graders.

HIGHER-LEVEL LITERACY

Discussions are enlivened when students consider the ideas in a text and challenge each other and the text (Gambrell, 2004). These discussions help students "gain not only a deeper understanding and appreciation of text ideas, but also a deeper understanding of what it means to think about those ideas" (Kucan & Beck, 2003, p. 3).

And planted cities all about.
I am the giant great and still
That sits upon the pillow-hill,
And sees before him, dale and plain,
The pleasant land of counterpane.

Step 3. Responding to the piece

Have students write a brief response to each of the following questions:

■ What feelings, thoughts, or pictures come to mind as you read the poem?

■ After reading the poem, what stands out most in your mind?

■ Was there anything in the poem that bothered you or surprised you?

■ Does the poem remind you of anything that has ever happened to you?

■ Have you ever had a day like the boy had?

Step 4. Small-group discussion

Students talk over their responses in groups of four or five. Each question should be discussed. Students will have been taught previously to accept everyone's responses, but they can ask for explanations or justifications. Each group should have a discussion leader and a spokesperson. The leader keeps the discussion moving and on track. The spokesperson sums up the group's reactions.

Step 5. Whole-class discussion

Have the whole class discuss the responses. Being careful not to inject your own interpretation, guide the discussion to obtain a full range of responses, thereby making it possible for students to hear them all. You can first take a quick survey of reactions by calling on the spokesperson for each group. Probe and develop those responses by calling on other members of the class. Encourage students to justify their responses by reading phrases or lines from the poem. As the opportunity presents itself, discuss how the language of the poem helps create feelings, images, and thoughts. Also, talk about the mental pictures the poem evokes. Students might want to discuss mental pictures they have formed of the boy.

Step 6. Extension

Have students read other poems by Robert Louis Stevenson. Many of his poems for children can be found in his classic collection, *A Child's Garden of Verses*.

■ ■ ■ **Checkup** ■ ■ ■

1. How is reading literature different from reading other materials?
2. What steps can be followed to elicit reader response?

■ ■ ■

Using Journals to Elicit Responses

Response journals, or literary logs, can also be used to encourage responses to literature. After reading a chapter in a novel, students might write their thoughts and reactions in a literary log. These responses could be open-ended or could be the result of a prompt. Parsons (1990) suggested the following types of questions, some of which have been altered slightly:

- What surprised you about the section that you read today? How does it affect what might happen next in the story?

- As you read today, what feelings did you experience in response to events or characters; for example, did you feel anger, surprise, irritation, or disappointment? Why do you think you responded that way?

- What startling, unusual, or effective words, phrases, expressions, or images did you come across in your reading that you would like to have explained or clarified?

- What characters and situations in the story reminded you of people and situations in your own life? How are they similar, and how do they differ?

Two other response prompts that might be used are "What if . . . " and "If I were in the story. . . . " In response to the "What if . . . " prompt, readers speculate what might have happened if a character had taken a different course of action or if a key event in the story had been different. In responding to "If I were in the story . . . ," readers tell what they would have done if they had been a part of the story's action (Raphael & Boyd, 1997).

Generally, students would be provided with just one or two prompts but should feel free to respond to other concerns or situations. Gradually, the prompts should be faded so that students can come up with their own concerns. Responses in the journals become the basis for discussion of the next day's selection. In supplying prompts for journals, Meyers (1988) took a different tack. She supplied students with a list of twenty questions, similar to those listed above and earlier in this chapter. They were free to choose two or three questions from the list.

Three other kinds of journals are literary, double-entry, and dialogue journals. In the literary journal, the student assumes the role of one of the characters in a selection and writes as though he or she were that character. A student assuming the role of Carlie in *The Pinballs* (Byars, 1977) might tell how she felt when she saw how sick Harvey had become.

Double-entry journals have two columns. In the left column, the student records information or a quote from the text. In the right column, the student reflects on or questions the material in the left column. In a model lesson on using double-entry journals, Dennis-Shaw (2006) had students note in the left column specific passages that reminded them of something in their lives. In the right column, they described the personal connection that they were able to make.

In dialogue journals, students write to the teacher and the teacher responds, or pairs of students might write to each other. Dialogue journals help the teacher keep close contact

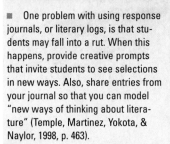

FYI

- One problem with using response journals, or literary logs, is that students may fall into a rut. When this happens, provide creative prompts that invite students to see selections in new ways. Also, share entries from your journal so that you can model "new ways of thinking about literature" (Temple, Martinez, Yokota, & Naylor, 1998, p. 463).

- Although students should be given choices concerning their written responses to literature, assigned writing can sometimes lead students to investigate themes and issues that they might not have considered (Lehr & Thompson, 2000). In one study of literature discussions, students were asked to write a letter from the point of view of the main character. The assignment gave the students the opportunity to role-play, see life from a character's perspective, and problem solve.

USING TECHNOLOGY

To see Dennis-Shaw's well-planned lesson on using double-entry journals, visit the Read•Write•Think site.
http://www.readwritethink.org/lessons/lesson_view.asp?id=228

During a discussion of a literary work, emphasis is placed on eliciting an aesthetic response.

with students and also extend their understanding of selections. The journal writing should be a genuine exchange between teacher and student and not simply a means for checking on students' reading. If viewed as a checking device, journals may lose their vitality. In a study by Bagge-Rynerson (1994), students' responses in their dialogue journals were more lively after the teacher modeled the kinds of responses that might be written and also made her own responses more personal and more affirming.

Journal entries can be used to foster the process of reading. For instance, to encourage students to make connections as they read, provide a prompt that includes making connections, such as "How did the events in this story remind you of something that has happened to you?" In your dialogue with the students, discuss the connections that they made. As appropriate, encourage them to make deeper connections or connections they might not have thought of (K. Dayton, personal communication, November 25, 2003).

Other Forms of Response

Having students respond in a variety of imaginative ways builds interest and motivation. It also gives students multiple ways of responding and so builds multiple skills. For instance, by responding both visually and verbally, students are building both areas. In addition, some selections lend themselves to one mode of response but not to another. Listed below are some creative but effective response activities. Most have been drawn from the California Literature Project (1992).

- *Open mind.* Open mind is a visualization activity in which an individual or small group analyzes a character in depth and, using an outline drawing of the back of a head, which signifies an open mind, represents what a character in a story is thinking and feeling, what the character's motivations might be, or how the character sees himself or others. The open mind might be divided into two halves to show a conflict the character is experiencing or the pros and cons of a decision the character is making. Students may draw pictures or paste in images or symbols in a collage format to show what the character is feeling and thinking or imagining. Happiness may be signified with bright sunshine, sadness with a gray cloud (Arciero, 1998). Words or phrases might also be used.

- *Postcard.* A character from a story writes a postcard to another character or to the reader. The front of the postcard is illustrated and the back has a stamp and a dated postmark.

- *Duologue.* Pairs of students select a scene from a story and then have a conversation of the type that two characters from the story might have had.

- *Press conference.* A character from a novel or the subject of a biography holds a press conference to announce a new discovery, invention, retirement, or other momentous news. Other students play the role of reporters.

- *Story rap.* Students summarize the whole selection or a portion of it in a rap.

Using Literature Discussion Groups to Elicit Responses

One effective technique for fostering a genuine response to literature is to form a literature discussion group, an interpretative community that shares a text much as a group of adults might do. This sharing can be both formal and informal. It can take place in whole-class discussions, small groups, or between partners. Students can complete their reading for discussion groups in various ways. They can read at home, in class, or in both places. Vicki Yousoofian, a first-grade teacher, sends books home over the weekend to be read with parents. Included with the books is a letter that explains literature circles and suggests ways that parents might discuss the books with their children (Noe, 2002). Sticky notes are provided so that students can use them to mark favorite passages. Realizing that not all children will receive the suggested help, the teacher schedules time for the children to read over their books on Monday before they gather in their circles.

FYI

■ Responses need not be written. Young children may respond by drawing their favorite character, favorite part of the story, funniest or scariest event, and so on. The drawings become a basis for response-oriented discussions.

■ To help students get a feeling for literary techniques, Elbow (2004) encourages students to try them out. Students might compose a story that contains flashbacks or try their hand at alliteration or onomatopoeia.

■ A natural way to begin discussions is to pose questions about aspects of a selection that are puzzling (Adler & Rougle, 2005). After listening to or reading a selection, students compose "wonder questions" on slips of paper. The wonder questions are placed in a hat. Students then take turns drawing a wonder question, which is read aloud and discussed.

■ Giving students some say in creating rules for discussion groups builds community and ownership. One way of eliciting rules is to have students describe a good conversation or discussion and then note what made it so (Adler & Rougle, 2005).

■ It takes time for students to learn how to conduct discussions. Almasi, O'Flahavan, and Arya (2001) found that it takes at least five meetings before students learn to function together.

Students can respond in a variety of ways to their reading (Noe, 2002). They can fill out role sheets, make notes on bookmarks, use sticky notes to record observations, and respond in logs or journals, with journals being more reflective than logs. They can respond to questions or prompts, or their responses can be more open-ended. You might use some of the reader response prompts listed on pages 396–397. Teachers have found it helpful to have students suggest prompts or to report on prompts that have worked especially well. A favorite prompt is "What if . . . ?" which leads students to reflect on what might have happened if the main character had taken a different course of action or if something else in the story had been changed.

Literature discussion groups can be organized in a variety of ways. Students may have roles. Or they might simply gather for discussion without having predetermined roles. In some instances, the teacher might appoint a starter who initiates the discussion. The teacher may be an active member, an occasional visitor, or an observer. Literature discussion groups can meet once a week or even every day. The teacher can have one group meet each day or can have all groups meeting simultaneously. Table 9.1 presents the general procedures to be used by literature discussion groups.

An essential part of the literature discussion group is a debriefing in which the teacher and students discuss the quality of the discussion, what went well, and what might need to be worked on. Debriefings should be short and focused and contain a tip or two for improving discussions (Noe, 2002). Students might also reflect on their discussions in their journals.

Literature discussion groups, which are also known as literature circles, literature study groups, conversational discussion groups, and book clubs, are an attempt to improve upon the quiz-type formats that are typical of many traditional classroom discussions. In traditional discussions, the teacher's questions follow an IRE (Initiate, Respond, Evaluate) format, in which the teacher initiates a question, the student responds, and the teacher evaluates the response. Literature discussion groups allow students to describe responses, compare impressions, contrast interpretations, and, in general, engage in the same type of talk that we might have with peers when we talk about books we have read. The discussions, which have been termed "grand conversations," feature a natural give-and-take and a freedom to offer one's interpretation with the expectation that it will be respected (Eeds & Wells, 1989). In preparation for meeting with their discussion group, students read the selection and might jot down a response in a log or journal. The ultimate intent of literature discussion groups is to lead students to engage in higher-level talk, not just more talk.

Students find literature discussion groups to be valuable in fostering deeper comprehension of material that they have read (Alvermann et al., 1996). However, groups need to

FYI

■ Questions designed to elicit a genuine response from a reader are much like those that might occur in a conversation between two adults discussing a book. Thus, a question about Patricia MacLachlan's *Sarah, Plain and Tall* (1985) might go like this: "Sarah made me think of the time I moved to the Midwest from New England. I missed the ocean and landscape, much as Sarah did. Have any of you had a similar kind of experience?" (McClure & Kristo, 1994, pp. xv–xvi).

■ When working with a group discussing a literary piece, the most difficult part might be refraining from taking over. "The real work of adults in the group is to LISTEN, LISTEN, LISTEN. The children are working at creating meaning for themselves. By listening carefully, our own reflections can be carefully phrased to stimulate higher levels of thinking or at least more informed reflections" (Borders & Naylor, 1993, p. 27).

HIGHER-LEVEL LITERACY

A Think-Pair-Share or quickwrite completed before a discussion can enrich the discussion, because students have had time to think about the topic and organize their thoughts.

■■■■ **TABLE 9.1 Procedures for Literature Discussion Groups**

Procedure	Description
Book selection	Students choose from among about five books; each student might list three choices.
Formation of groups	Teacher forms groups based on students' selections. Reading ability can be a factor.
Agreement on procedures	Class formulates basic procedures for completing assignments and discussing books.
Group discussions	Groups meet one or more times a week. Groups can be teacher- or student-led. Students can use role sheets, respond to teacher prompts, or use sticky notes to highlight passages for discussion.
Debriefing	Group talks about how discussions went and decides on ways to improve discussions.
Whole-class sharing	Groups periodically talk with the rest of the class about the books they are reading.

HIGHER-LEVEL LITERACY

Rearranging the furniture can cause a change in response patterns. Students are more likely to respond to each other when they are facing each other.

■ **Closing the Gap**

By having students read literature circle selections at home instead of at school, you can increase the amount of time they read.

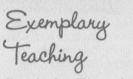

Developing Discussion Skills

be carefully prepared and monitored. Proficient discussion groups are especially effective at staying on task and sticking with a topic long enough to develop it fairly fully (Almasi, O'Flahavan, & Arya, 2001). They are effective at making connections between the current topic and points made earlier in the discussion or in previous discussions. The teacher's role is crucial. Although the teacher needs to provide direction, especially in the early stages, it is important that the teacher gradually turn over responsibility to students. Students need to learn how to manage group processes. If the teacher becomes the one who provides directives for staying on task, the students will not take ownership of the procedure. Deprived of the opportunity to think through problems, students fail to learn how to conduct discussions. Through scaffolded instruction, the teacher must lead students to recognize when procedural problems arise and to resolve them. However, over time, the teacher must assign this responsibility to students. As Almasi, O'Flahavan, and Arya (2001) noted, "By failing to give students the opportunity to monitor their own discussion, teachers may hinder students' ability to operate in the group independent of the teacher" (p. 118).

So that her third-graders would get the most out of literature discussion groups, Mrs. P. provided extensive preparation (Maloch, 2004). She stressed the need for a sense of caring and being responsible for each other. The class also participated in self-selected reading and teacher-led whole-class or guided reading discussions. These activities gave them experience selecting and discussing books. As more direct preparation, in whole-class discussions of *Charlotte's Web* (White, 1952), Mrs. P. posed the kinds of questions that she hoped students would ask each other in their discussion groups. After whole-group discussions, she arranged for students to work with partners. They were given a choice of two topics and were to write about one of them in their response journals and then discuss their responses with their partners. The topics stressed making personal connections: "Charlotte consoled Wilbur when he had gotten some bad news. Write about a time that you either helped someone out or a time when you needed help and someone helped you" (Maloch, 2004, p. 8). Gradually, Mrs. P. turned responsibility for the selection of the writing and discussion topics over to the students. Students were asked to select "something that was important to you in that chapter, something that the two of you think will be a good thing to write about" (p. 8). Students shared their written responses in the whole group. During this whole-group sharing, Mrs. P. was able to provide students with suggestions for improving topic selection and discussions.

After students developed some skill working in pairs, they began working in groups of four. As the groups of students discussed, Mrs. P. visited each one and provided assistance and instruction as needed. She addressed issues of behavior, emphasizing the need to respect each other and to learn to solve interpersonal issues. After discussions, students reflected on these questions: "What did I do/say in my group that was helpful? What did I do to make it work?" (p. 13). Mrs. P. also scaffolded students' discussion techniques, such as building on what others have said and providing support for one's positions. And she fostered students' ability to ask higher-level questions and to consider key issues, so that they would move beyond a retelling of the plot or a superficial comparison of characters. By observing and listening carefully to her students' responses, Mrs. P. was able to determine what kinds of guidance the students needed to solidify and expand their comprehension and discussion skills.

The building of interpersonal skills took most of their time, but as students learned how to work together, Mrs. P. could focus more on developing discussion and thinking skills. At the end of the preparatory period and before moving into literature discussion groups, students articulated the elements of an effective discussion group by brainstorming answers to this query: "What makes a good literature group?" (p. 14). Having had guided experience with whole-class, paired, and small-group discussions, the third-graders were ready to work responsibly and profitably in literature discussion groups.

Literature Discussion Groups as Cooperative Learning Groups

Some literature discussion groups incorporate the principles of cooperative learning to provide more structure (Bjorklund, Handler, Mitten, & Stockwell, 1998). The groups are composed of five or six students who have chosen to read the same book. Students choose from six books the three they would most like to read. Books could cover the same theme or topic, be in the same genre, or have the same author. They might all be biographies, or they might all have survival in the wilderness as a theme, for instance. The books should represent a range of interests and difficulty levels so that students have a genuine choice, and the list of choices should include books that are appropriate for average, below-average, and above-average readers.

The books are presented. The teacher provides an overview of each one, and students are invited to examine the books to see whether they are interesting and whether they are on the right level of challenge. Students are urged to read two or three pages at scattered intervals in order to judge the difficulty level of the book. Students then list their top three choices.

Based on the students' choices, the teacher forms four or five groups. The teacher tries to get a mix of students in each group so that a number of perspectives are represented and a number of personalities are included. The teacher also tries to match below-average readers with books that they can handle.

Once the groups have been formed, roles are assigned by the teacher, or the group decides who will fulfill which role. Key roles are the discussion leader, summarizer, literacy reporter, illustrator, word chief, and connector. The discussion leader develops questions for the group and leads the discussion. The summarizer summarizes the selection. The literacy reporter locates passages that stand out because they are funny, sad, contain key incidents, or feature memorable language. The reporter can read the passages out loud, ask the group to read them silently and discuss them, or, with other members of the group, dramatize them. An illustrator illustrates a key part of the selection with a drawing or graphic organizer. The word chief locates difficult words or expressions from the selection, looks them up in the dictionary, and writes down their definitions. At the circle meeting, the word chief points out and discusses the words with the group. The connector finds links between the book and other books the group has read or between the book and real events, problems, or situations. The connector describes the connection and discusses it with the group. Although each student has a certain role to fulfill in the circle, any student may bring up a question for discussion, a passage that stands out, a confusing word, a vivid figure of speech, or a possible connection.

The roles reflect the kinds of things that students should be doing as they read a text. They should be creating questions in their minds, making connections, visualizing, summarizing, noting key passages, coping with difficult words and confusing passages, and appreciating expressive language and literary techniques. Students switch roles periodically so that each student has the opportunity to carry out each of the roles.

To help students fulfill their roles, they are given job sheets. A sample job sheet for a discussion leader is shown in Figure 9.1. Each of the roles is also modeled and discussed. The class, as a whole, also practices each of the jobs by applying it to a brief, relatively easy selection. Creation of questions is given special attention. Questions that lead to in-depth sharing of responses are stressed. Discussions are modeled. The teacher might do this by training a group and then having them demonstrate before the class. Students are given two or three weeks to complete a book. After a group has been formed, the group meets and sets up a schedule for how much reading members will do each evening. A written schedule is created and pasted to the inside cover of the response journal. If students are doing most or all of their work in school, they meet every other day. Days they don't meet are used to complete their reading and related tasks.

The teacher visits each group and, in the early stages, might model asking questions or responding to a selection. As students become more adept, the teacher takes on the role of participant. Students also rely less on their job sheets. Job sheets are a temporary scaffold designed to show students how to analyze and respond to text and discuss it (Daniels,

Adapting Instruction for Struggling Readers and Writers

Although similar to book clubs, literature discussion groups provide students with choice and also can be organized according to cooperative learning principles, with each student having a well-defined role. Because students have a choice of materials, struggling readers can select books that are closer to their level. Struggling ELLs and many members of minority groups do better in cooperative learning groups.

FYI

■ Literature discussion groups meet for about twenty minutes. Discussions might be student-led, teacher-led, or a combination of the two (Temple, Martinez, Yokota, & Naylor, 1998). Students feel freer to express themselves when the teacher isn't present, but the teacher can provide expert assistance. Even if the discussion is student-led, in the beginning the teacher can assist the group in getting started and might model the kinds of literary questions that students are learning to ask. The teacher should also monitor each group to make sure it is on task and everyone is participating. From time to time, the teacher might drop in to model higher-level questioning or to perk up a flagging group.

■ If there are more roles than students, some students may fulfill more than one role, or roles may be combined.

Closing the Gap

Encourage parents to discuss books with their children. Book discussions foster both reading and language development. It is important, however, that you give parents sufficient guidance and encouragement.

◼◼◼ USING TECHNOLOGY

The video *Looking into Literature Circles* (Stenhouse) portrays three real literature circles.

Literature Circles.com features book recommendations, management ideas, and tips from veteran teachers. http://www.literaturecircles.com

Literature Circles Resource Center provides information and resources on literature circles. http://www.litcircles.org

2002). As students learn basic skills involved in reading, responding, and discussing, the job sheets can be phased out or used only to prepare for the discussion. If students hold onto the job sheets too long, they may limit their discussions to what's written on the sheets rather than having a fuller, more spontaneous discussion of the text. However, job sheets might also be used to shore up flagging discussions if students haven't used them previously.

Whole-class sessions are held each day so that groups can share with each other. This is also a good time to present minilessons or perhaps read aloud a selection that pertains to the theme or topic of the books being read.

After the books have been completely read and discussed, students meet in groups according to the roles they fulfilled. All the discussion leaders meet, as do all the sumarizers, connectors, illustrators, word chiefs, and literary reporters. In these groups, students give an overview of the book they read and their opinion of the book. They also discuss the books they read from the point of view of their roles. In this way, all of the students become acquainted with the books read in other groups.

Each group also makes a brief presentation of its book to the whole class. This might be in the form of an ad, a skit based on the book, a panel discussion, an interview of the main character, or a dramatization of a key passage.

Literature discussion groups can be less structured so that students don't have specific roles. However, teachers who have used a structured approach find that in time, students automatically carry out the various roles as they read.

Although student discussions about literary works can be fruitful, teacher guidance is essential in some situations. When students are reading fiction in which historical events play an important role, as in Mildred Taylor's (1987) *The Friendship*, it is important that the teacher play an active role. In their study of fifth-graders, Lehr and Thompson (2000) found that many of the students were misinformed about key historical events. Because of a lack of knowledge of history, they had difficulty interpreting the novel, which deals with civil rights in the 1930s. Students needed teacher guidance to help them correct their misconceptions. Students also needed the teacher to guide them to a higher level of understanding. Students' initial responses were on a literal level. They seemed to need to know who did what before they could begin to interpret the characters' actions.

After observing videotaped literature discussion groups in which urban fourth graders were participating, Long and Gove (2003–2004) concluded that although the students

◼◼◼ FIGURE 9.1
Discussion Leader Job Sheet

The discussion leader's job is to ask a series of questions about the part of the book that your group will be discussing. Ask questions that will make the other students in your group think carefully about what they read and walk in the shoes of the main characters. Some possible questions are:

How do you feel about this part of the story?

Was there anything that bothered or surprised you?

What would you have done if you had been the main character?

What do you think will happen in the next part of the story?

Write your questions on the lines below.

1. _____

2. _____

3. _____

4. _____

Adapted from Daniels, H. (1994). *Literature Circles, Voice and Choice in the Student-Centered Classroom.* York, ME: Stenhouse.

Students can eventually conduct literature discussion groups on their own, without much teacher involvement.

were displaying an enjoyment of their reading, their discussions consisted mainly of retellings of surface events. However, when Long and Gove read the text aloud to students and invited them to "make connections with, reflect upon, and question the text with us as we read to them" (p. 351), the students' responses became more critical.

To foster a deeper engagement and understanding, help students build envisionments. An envisionment is "the understanding a reader has about a text—what the reader understands at a particular point in time, the questions she has, as well as her hunches about how the piece will unfold" (Langer, 1990, p. 817). The students progress from forming an initial understanding to developing interpretations to reflecting on personal experience and proceed to evaluating the reading. Careful questioning can help students develop their envisionments. Initially, you might pose the kinds of questions that lead to deeper understanding, but, over time, with your guidance, students should take more responsibility for asking these kinds of questions in their literature circle discussions. Langer (1990) suggests that teachers pose four levels of questions.

1. *Initial understandings.* Ask typical reader response questions, which enable students to share their reactions to the piece: "Which part of the work stands out in your mind? Was there anything in the work that bothered you? Was there anything in it that surprised you? Do you have any questions about the work?"

2. *Developing interpretations.* Ask questions that encourage students to think more deeply about the story. These questions can help students think about motivations, character development, theme, or setting: "Do you think the main character acted responsibly? What do you think made the main character confess, even though he was innocent? What is the author trying to say here?" Helping students develop interpretations of character is especially important. As Westby (1999) notes, "Understanding of characters' emotions, thoughts, and beliefs [is] the glue that ties the action of stories together" (p. 172). Students may experience difficulty drawing inferences about characters because they focus on action rather than on inner states; they misinterpret the character's emotions and motivations because they mistakenly believe the character is just like them, because they fail to consider the whole story, or because they focus on the perspective of just one of the characters (Westby, 1999).

3. *Reflecting on personal experience.* Ask questions that help students relate what they have read to personal knowledge or experience. These questions can help them re-

FYI

Literature circles can embrace nonfiction. Stien and Beed (2004) made the transition from fiction to nonfiction circles by using biographies. Roles were altered slightly. The Fantastic Fact Finder collected important facts; the Timeline Traveler kept track of key dates; and the Vital Statistics Collector assembled basic information about the subject. After growing in proficiency, instead of using role sheets, students used sticky notes to mark passages they wanted to discuss.

HIGHER-LEVEL LITERACY

Envisionment questions can be a guide for discussing literature. You can use general questions from each of the four levels. Or use the levels to compose your own more specific questions. Some teachers create a list of envisionment questions for students to use as a guide as they read (Adler & Rougle, 2005).

■ When using envisionment questions, it isn't necessary to begin at the lowest level and work your way up. You might start a discussion with an evaluative question but use a lower-level question to provide support.

■ In addition to instruction in strategies, "Students need to be taught how to engage in dialogue.... They need to be taught to actively listen to group members' ideas and questions and to thoughtfully respond to those ideas and questions before moving on to other topics" (Berne & Clark, 2006).

ASSESSING FOR LEARNING

To keep track of students' responses, create a seating chart and record students' responses (Great Books Foundation, 1999). This will help you to see who is responding, who needs encouraging, and who is having difficulty as well as to gauge the overall quality of the discussion.

Adapting Instruction for Struggling Readers and Writers

On occasions when you wish to involve all students in discussion, including those who cannot read the book on their own, read aloud to the class and have students follow along. However, make sure that struggling readers have ample opportunities at other times to read texts on their level.

consider current or previous understandings or feelings. Some of the reader response questions will work well here: "Does the main character remind you of anyone you know? Have you ever been in a situation similar to the one he was in? How would you have handled it? Does this story make you think of anything that has happened in your life?"

4. Evaluating. Once students have responded to the work, refined their interpretations, and looked at the work in terms of their own background knowledge and experiences, help them step back and take a critical look at the piece as a work of art. They might compare it with other pieces they have read and evaluate it in terms of character development, originality, and plausibility of the plot, development of the theme, suitability of setting, style, and overall impact. Students should consider the author's craft so they might come to a better understanding of the creative process and perhaps apply some of the techniques they experienced to their own writing. The following are questions that might be asked: "Does this piece remind you of anything else that you read? What was the best line or paragraph in the piece? Did the characters seem real? What made them seem real? Was the plot believable? What special words, expressions, or writing devices did the author use? Which of these did you like best? Least? If you were the author's editor, what would you say to the author? What changes might you ask the author to make?"

Strategic Literature Discussions

While observing students involved in a literature discussion group, researchers Clark and Berne (2005; Berne & Clark, 2006) noticed that students were using comprehension strategies to construct meaning, but they were not using a full range of strategies and were not using the strategies very effectively. As Berne and Clark (2006) comment, "Students need to be taught how to employ comprehension strategies to assist themselves and group members as they collaboratively puzzle through ideas in the text." To deepen comprehension, teach key strategies explicitly and prompt the use of the strategies during discussions. For instance, the following prompts, some of which are taken directly from Clark and Berne (2005, 2006) and some of which have been adapted from Clark and Berne (2005, 2006), might be used for the strategies noted:

Summarizing

■ There were so many details here. What were the main things that happened?

■ If you had to tell me what this was about very briefly, what would you say?

Analyzing the author's craft

■ What did the author do to help us understand the text?

■ What special techniques did the author use?

Questioning

■ Are there parts that were hard to understand?

■ As you read, what did you wonder?

■ As you read, what questions came to mind?

Making connections

■ This makes me think of another story that we read that had a mystery in it. How was the mystery in that story like the mystery in this one?

■ How did the main character feel? Have you ever felt the way the main character did? (Clark & Berne, 2006).

Looking back

■ What in the story makes you say that?

■ What makes you think the girl was clever?

■ Can you read the line that explains why the boy wasn't prepared for the test?

Exemplary Teaching

Literature Circles

t the Sandy Hook School in Connecticut, the fourth- and fifth-grade teachers fostered appreciation through the use of literature circles. Students were given a choice of six books to read. The books might explore a common question or topic (survival, for instance), or they constituted an author study (all being written by the same author). Students listed three books they would most like to read, and based on their choices, groups were formed. The groups were heterogeneous, so all the poorest readers or all the best readers didn't end up in the same group. However, the teacher matched up books and students so that all students, including below-level readers, had books they could handle.

After the groups were formed and jobs were assigned (jobs included discussion leader, summarizer, literacy reporter, illustrator, word chief, and connector), students were given a calendar and asked to make up a schedule for reading their book and completing their jobs. Students were required to complete the book in two weeks, but they decided how many pages they would read each night. They could choose to do the most reading on days when they had few afternoon activities. After the schedule was created, students were given two copies of it, one for home and one to be kept at school.

Students seldom missed their assignments. Having been able to choose their reading and set up their schedules, they were committed to completing their assignments. Besides, there was considerable peer pressure. If they didn't complete an assignment, they were letting the group down. If students did not complete their assignments, they were not allowed to take part in the circle. Instead, they worked by themselves to complete the missed work.

Each day, just two of the four groups met for discussion. The other two groups worked on their assignments. By having just two groups meet each day, each teacher was better able to oversee their discussions and provide any needed help. But mostly, the teacher took on the role of participant. To be a realistic participant, the teacher responded to the story in her journal and then brought her journal to the circle. Thus, she was a genuine participant and not just someone who came to direct or assess.

Students were enthusiastic about their circles, and they also improved their ability to appreciate and respond to literature. By year's end, they incorporated the six roles into their reading; as they read, they were asking themselves questions, summarizing, visualizing, appreciating the author's craft, making connections, and noting difficult words and confusing passages.

What was the secret of the teachers' success? Through careful planning and implementation, they let the students know what was expected and set them up for success. The teachers also were caring and enthusiastic (Bjorklund, Handler, Mitten, & Stockwell, 1998).

A key strategy in discussions is going back to the text for clarification or to locate support for a position.

With proper preparation and supervision, literature discussion groups have the potential to develop students' comprehension strategies as well as their understanding of a selection.

■ Discussion Moves

Approaches that attempt to foster students' discussion of literature vary in their effectiveness. All increase the amount of talk. However, their impact on comprehension varies from minimal to quite significant (Murphy & Edwards, 2004). Overall, two of the most effective approaches are Junior Great Books and Questioning the Author. Both approaches provide extensive training and have a well-planned, systematic implementation plan. A key feature of both is that discussion moves are spelled out. Discussion moves are statements that students can make to maintain a discussion or that the teacher may make to

USING TECHNOLOGY

Great Books Foundation offers extensive information about Junior Great Books and features film clips of discussion techniques.

http://www.greatbooks.org

foster effective discussion. For example, instead of saying, "You're wrong," a student would say something like this: "I understand what you are saying about the father, but I think the father was wrong to get rid of the dog."

Table 9.2 lists discussion moves from a number of approaches, including Junior Great Books and Questioning the Author. The moves marked with an asterisk are typically used by the teacher but might sometimes be used by students. Conversely, the teacher might use some of the moves that students typically use.

■ Responding in Writing

In addition to responding to literary works during discussions, students need to learn to respond in writing. Writing affords the opportunity to think more deeply about a selection and to take the time to organize one's thoughts. As a practical matter, many high-stakes tests assess students' ability to construct a written response to a passage.

■ ■ ■ Checkup ■ ■ ■

1. How might literature discussion groups be used to foster reader response?
2. What steps would you take to set up an effective discussion group?
3. What kinds of questions or prompts might be used to foster understanding and involvement?

■ ■ ■

USING TECHNOLOGY

Cooperative Children's Book Center features a number of lists of recommended books including *Thirty Multicultural Books That Every Child Should Know*.

http://www.education.wisc.edu/ccbc/books/multicultural.asp

The Children's Literature Web Guides page provides a wealth of information about children's literature and has many links to other sites.

http://www.ucalgary.ca/~dkbrown

Making Multicultural Connections through Trade Books offers many resources for using multicultural books. The site provides an extensive listing of multicultural books and suggestions for content and technology connections.

http://www.mcps.k12.md.us/curriculum/socialstd/MBD/Books_Begin.html

FYI

To find varied versions of folktales, consult *The Storyteller's Sourcebook: A Subject, Title, and Motif Index to Folklore Collections for Children 1983–1989* (MacDonald & Sturm, 2001).

■ Types of Literature

Folklore

A good place to start the study of literature is with folklore, which includes folktales, myths, rituals, superstitions, songs, and jokes. **Folklore** follows an oral tradition. As Taylor (1990) put it, "The tales of the tongue are a good introduction to the tales of the pen." Having stood the test of time, folklore has universal appeal.

Every culture has produced its own **folktales**. Students can investigate those drawn from the culture of their ancestors. African American students might look into one of Verna Aardema's works, such as *Why Mosquitoes Buzz in People's Ears: A West African Folk Tale* (1975), or one of Harold Courlander's collections of African folktales. Closer to home is Virginia Hamilton's (1985) *The People Could Fly: American Black Folktales*. Latino students might enjoy one of Alma Flor Ada's tales. Other outstanding sources of materials about diverse cultures are *Kaleidoscope: A Multicultural Booklist for Grades K–8*, Fourth Edition (Hansen-Krening, Aoki, & Mizokawa, 2003), and *Multicultural Teaching* (Tiedt & Tiedt, 2006). To provide follow-up after students have read and discussed a piece of folklore, have them dramatize the tale or compare it to other tales.

Poetry

Students like poetry that has humor and a narrative element and that rhymes. Include both light verse and more thoughtful pieces. Before reading a poem to the class, practice it so that your reading is strong and dramatic. Briefly discuss vocabulary words or concepts that

---

■ **Folklore** refers to the tales, rituals, superstitions, nursery rhymes, and other oral works created by people.

■ **Folktales** are stories handed down orally from generation to generation.

Folktales include fairy tales, myths, legends, and tall tales.

■■■ **TABLE 9.2** **Major Discussion Moves**

Discussion Move	Description	Example(s)
Stating	Stating an idea or opinion	This is what I think happened that day.
Explaining	Explaining a statement	Here is what I meant when I said that Alex made a mistake.
Supporting/ Substantiating	Providing details or examples to prove or back up an assertion	This is why I believe the main character was a genius.
Agreeing	Expressing agreement with a position and often explaining why	I agree with you, Anna, because . . .
Disagreeing	Expressing disagreement with a position and often explaining why	I understand what you are saying about the father, but I think the father was wrong to get rid of the dog.
Building	Building on what others say	I'd like to add to what Monique said about Amelia Earhart's courage.
Extending/Following/ Expanding	Seeking elaboration	Tell me more about that.
Clarifying	Asking to have a confusing point clarified	I'm not sure what you mean here. (If a response is not clear, the teacher might restate what he or she believes the student said and then ask if the restatement is correct: "You seem to be saying that having a pet gave Tyrique a sense of responsibility, which carried over to his school work.")
Initiating/Opening*	Opening discussion	What is the author trying to say here?
Inviting*	Inviting others to respond	Josh, what do you have to say about Franklin. Do you think he acted responsibly?
Connecting*	Inviting others to make connections with another part of the text, another text, or the world	What is the connection between getting a pet in the first party of the story and Manuel's attitude at the end of the story? What story that we read does this one remind you of? Has anything like this ever happened to you?
Monitoring*	Facilitating discussion	Let's hold our responses until we hear what Milano has to say.
Summarizing*	Highlighting main points	From what we have discussed, what seem to be the main causes of the problem?
Including*	Inviting students who have not responded to participate	We haven't heard from James yet. James, what is your opinion of the main character?
Modeling*	Demonstrating a discussion technique, reasoning, or reading strategy	Sometimes I find myself thinking about what I want to say rather than listening to the person speaking. Here is what I do . . .
Prompting Strategy Use*	Prompting the use of questioning, comparing, connecting, imaging, appreciating, evaluating, or another strategy	What questions came to mind as you read? How would you compare Chuck and Lisa? Does this remind you of another story that we have read? Something that has happened to you? Did you make any pictures in your mind as you read about the fierceness of the dog? What did the author do to build suspense? Did the characters seem true to life?
Debriefing/ Reflecting*	Assessing quality and impact of a discussion	Did the discussion change your views? We seemed to be getting off topic. What might we do to stay on topic?

*These moves are typically used by the teacher but can be used by students.

Reading poetry aloud can enhance the enjoyment for students.

FYI

■ Reactions to poetry are very personal. One student's favorite could be another student's least liked. For example, in Terry's (1974) study of preferences, a sixth-grade boy had a special feeling for Edwin Hoey's "Foul Shot" because it reminded him of something that happened in a game in which he had played. A fourth-grade girl, however, disliked the poem because she had difficulty making shots.

■ For additional ideas for poetry activities, see *The poetry break* (Bauer, 1995).

might interfere with students' understanding or enjoyment. Give students a purpose for listening, such as creating images in their minds, awaiting a surprise ending, or hearing unusual words.

You might emphasize questions that evoke a personal response: "What about the poem stands out most in your mind? What pictures came to mind as you listened? Which line do you like best? How does the poem make you feel? Is there anything in the poem that you do not like? Is there anything in it that surprises you?" Better yet, invite students to ask questions about anything in the poem that may have confused them. Gear discussions toward personal responses and interpretations. The emphasis should be "upon delight rather than dissection" (Sloan, 1984, p. 86). The following Student Reading List presents a sampling of some of the many fine poetry anthologies available for young people.

Student Reading List

Poetry

Ciardi, J. (1962). *You read to me, I'll read to you*. New York: HarperCollins. Features thirty-five lighthearted poems.

Dyer, G. L., Jr. (2001). *40 Poems for "T": The fun of writing poetry*. Catskill, NY: Tige. Letters to a young boy explains what poetry is, how to collect ideas for poems, and how to write them.

Greenfield, E. (1991). *Night on neighborhood street*. New York: Dial. A collection of seventeen poems that focuses on life in an African American neighborhood.

Hopkins, L. B. (Ed.). (1986). *Surprises*. New York: Harper. Thirty-eight easy-to-read poems on a variety of subjects ranging from pets to flying.

Hopkins, L. B. (Ed.). (2001). *My America: A poetry atlas of the United States*. Fifty-one poems celebrate different sections of the United States.

Hudson, W. (1993). *Pass it on: African-American poetry for children*. New York: Scholastic. An illustrated collection of poetry by such African American poets as Langston Hughes, Nikki Giovanni, Eloise Greenfield, and Lucille Clifton.

Hughes, L. (1993). *The dream keeper and other poems*. New York: Knopf. A collection of sixty-six poems selected by the author for young readers, including lyrical poems and songs, many of which explore the African American tradition.

Kennedy, C. (2005). *A family of poems, My favorite poetry for children*. New York: Hyperion. Collection of a variety of poems organized around the themes of self, humor, animals, seasons, seashore, adventure, and bedtime.

Kennedy, X. J., & Kennedy, D. M. (1999). *Knock at a star: A child's introduction to poetry*. Boston: Little, Brown. Praised by a *Horn Book* review as one of the best introductions to poetry.

Knudson, R. R., & Swenson, M. (1988). *American sports poems*. New York: Orchard. A collection that should be welcomed by sports fans.

Kuskin, K. (1992). *Soap soup and other verses*. New York: HarperCollins. Features a variety of easy-to-read poems.

Kuskin, K. (2003). *Moon, have you met my mother?* New York: Harper Collins. Comprehensive collection of poems on animals, insects, food, the seasons, and many other topics.

Prelutsky, J. (1997). *The beauty of the beast*. New York: Knopf. Features a variety of poems about ants, cats, birds, dogs, fish, sharks, lizards, toads, and other creatures; could tie in with a study of animals.

▪▪▪ Checkup ▪▪▪

1. How might folklore and poetry be presented?

▪▪▪

Chapter Books and Novels

In a literature-based program, chapter books or novels are often set aside as a separate unit of study. Before embarking on a chapter book or novel, students should receive some guidance to build the background essential for understanding the text. Their interest in the book should also be piqued. Place particular emphasis on understanding the first chapter. If students, especially poorer readers, have a thorough understanding of the first chapter, they will have a solid foundation for comprehending the rest of the text. It will also build their confidence in their ability to read the rest of the book (Ford, 1994).

Generally, students are asked to read a chapter or more each day. The teacher may provide questions to be considered during reading, or students might make predictions and read to evaluate them. Students might also keep a response journal for their reading. Responses might be open-ended, with students jotting down their general reactions to the segment being read, or students might respond to questions posed by the teacher.

After a segment has been read, it is discussed. Students might also do some rereading to clarify confusing points or might dramatize exciting parts. A cumulative plot outline or story map could be constructed to keep track of the main events. If the story involves a long journey, the characters' progress might be charted on a map. Extension activities can be undertaken once the book has been completed. The novel might be presented within the framework of an extended guided reading lesson or directed reading–thinking activity, or it might be discussed as a grand conversation in a literature discussion group. Emphasis is on building appreciation and evoking a response; skills are secondary.

Both content and form should be discussed. Design questions to help students understand what is happening in the story and to see how the setting, plot, characters,

FYI

Through prompts, teachers can lead students to practice a variety of literacy and comprehension strategies. Prompts might ask students to predict what will happen next or make inferences about a character based on the character's actions, for instance. Or prompts might ask students to create character webs or note examples of figurative language.

■■■ **TABLE 9.3   Possible Questions for Novels**

Setting	Where does the story take place? When does the story take place? How important is the setting to the story? Could the story have happened in a different place at a different time? Why or why not? When you close your eyes and imagine the setting, what do you see? How does the author give you a "you-are-there" feeling?
Characters	Who are the main characters? What kinds of people are they? Do they seem like real people? Why or why not? How does the author let you know what the main characters are like? Did the characters change? If so, how? Were these changes unexpected? Did they surprise you? Why or why not? Can you picture the characters in your mind? What do they look like? What do they do? What do they say? Do you know anyone like them? Would you like to meet them? Why or why not?
Plot	What event started the story? What is the main problem? What is making the problem better? What is making the problem worse? What has been the most exciting part of the story so far? Could you guess what was going to happen, or did the author surprise you? How? How is the problem resolved? How does the story end?
Point of view	How is the story told? Is it told by a narrator who is a part of the story and who calls himself "I"? Is it told in the second person, using the pronoun "you"? Is the story told by someone outside, a person who can see all and tell all? How does the author seem to feel about the characters? Who seems to be the author's favorite?
Theme	What seems to be the main or most important idea in the story? What main idea do you take away from the story?
Style	What are some especially well-written passages? What are some examples of colorful words that the author uses? Does the author use figures of speech or images? If so, give some examples. What special writing techniques does the author use? Give some examples. Does this story remind you of any other stories that you have read? If so, which one(s)? In what ways are they similar? Does this author remind you of any other authors you have read? If so, who? How are they similar? Would you like to read another book by this same author or about this same subject? Why or why not? Would you recommend this book to a friend? Why or why not? If you could, would you make changes in this book? Why or why not? Give some changes you would make. Do you think this book would make a good movie or a good television show? Why or why not?

theme, point of view, and author's style work together. However, take care that you do not overanalyze a piece or ask too many questions at any one time. Balance analysis with eliciting personal responses. Response should precede analysis and general discussion. Once the reader has responded, she or he is in a better position to analyze the piece. Part of the analysis might involve discovering what elements in the piece caused the student to respond (see the earlier section on reader response for some questions). Some general questions for novels are outlined in Table 9.3. Do not attempt to ask all the questions listed; choose only those that seem most appropriate for your students.

The following Student Reading List identifies some outstanding chapter books and novels (in the list, C indicates challenging books, and E indicates easy ones).

Student Reading List

Chapter Books and Novels

Grade 1
Bridwell, N. (1972). *Clifford the small red puppy*. New York: Scholastic.
Keats, E. J. (1964). *Whistle for Willie*. New York: Puffin.
Minarik, E. H. (1968). *A Kiss for little bear*. New York: HarperCollins.
Rylant, C. (1990). *Henry and Mudge, the first book*. New York: Simon & Schuster.

Grade 2
Byars, B. (1996). *My brother, Ant*. New York: Viking.
Henkes, K. (1996). *Lilly's purple plastic purse*. New York: Greenwillow.
Hoban, R. (1964). *Bread and jam for Frances*. New York: HarperCollins.
Keats, E. J. (1962). *The snowy day*. New York: Viking.
Krensky, S. (1996). *Lionel and his friends*. New York: Dial.
Lobel, A. (1979). *Days with Frog and Toad*. New York: HarperCollins.
Look, L. (2004). *Ruby Lu, brave and true*. New York: Atheneum.
Lowry, L. (2002). *Gooney Bird Greene*. Boston: Houghton Mifflin.
Marshall, J. (1992). *Fox be nimble*. New York: Penguin.
Zion, G. (1956). *Harry the dirty dog*. New York: HarperCollins.

Grade 3
Ada, A. F. (1993). *My name is Maria Isabel*. New York: Simon & Schuster.
Bulla, C. R. (1987). *The chalk box kid*. New York: Random House.
Cleary, B. (1981). *Ramona Quimby, age 8*. New York: Dell. C
Cohen, B. Z. (1983). *Molly's pilgrim*. New York: Bantam Doubleday Dell.
Dahl, R. (1961). *James and the giant peach*. New York: Puffin.
Dalgliesh, A. (1954). *Courage of Sarah Noble*. New York: Scribner's.
Surat, M. M. (1983). *Angel child, dragon child*. New York: Scholastic.

Grade 4
Bulla, C. R. (1975). *Shoeshine girl*. New York: Crowell. E
Butterworth, O. (1956). *The enormous egg*. Boston: Little, Brown.
Gardiner, J. R. (1980). *Stone fox*. New York: HarperCollins. E
Krumgold, J. (1953). *And now Miguel*. New York: Crowell.
MacLachlan, P. (1985). *Sarah, plain and tall*. New York: HarperCollins.
Taylor, M. (1976). *Roll of thunder, hear my cry*. New York: Puffin.
White, E. B. (1952). *Charlotte's web*. New York: HarperCollins.
Wilder, L. I. (1932). *Little house in the big woods*. New York: HarperCollins.

Grade 5
Burnett, F. H. (1912). *The secret garden*. New York: HarperCollins.
Byars, B. (1977). *The pinballs*. New York: HarperCollins.
Choldenko, C. (2004). *Al Capone does my shirts*. New York: Putnam.
Cleary, B. (1983). *Dear Mr. Henshaw*. New York: Morrow.
Codell, E. R. (2003). *Sarah special*. New York: Hyperion.
Dahl, R. (1964). *Charlie and the chocolate factory*. New York: Penguin.
Giff, P. R. (1997). *Lily's crossing*. New York: Delacorte.
Kadohata, C. (2004). *Kira-kira*. New York: Aladdin.
Konigsburg, E. L. (1967). *From the mixed-up files of Mrs. Basil E. Frankweiler*. New York: Atheneum.
Lewis, C. S. (1950). *The lion, the witch, and the wardrobe*. New York: HarperCollins.
Lowry, L. (1989). *Number the stars*. Boston: Houghton Mifflin.
Naylor, P. R. (1991). *Shiloh*. New York: Dell. E
O'Dell, S. (1960). *Island of the blue dolphins*. Boston: Houghton Mifflin. E
Spinelli, J. (1997). *Wringer*. New York: HarperCollins. E

FYI

Chapter books and novels sometimes deal with mature or controversial issues. Before recommending a book to students, make sure that its content is suitable for them.

Grade 6

Armstrong, A. (2005). *Whittington*. New York: Random House.
Blos, J. W. (1979). *A gathering of days*. New York: Aladdin. C
Byars, B. (1970). *Summer of the swans*. New York: Viking. E
DiCamillo, K. (2000). *Because of Winn-Dixie*. Cambridge, MA: Candlewick Press.
Fox, P. (1984). *One-eyed cat*. New York: Bantam Doubleday Dell.
Gutman, D. (2006). *Satch and me*. New York: HarperCollins. E
Juster, N. (1961). *The phantom toll booth*. New York: Knopf.
Konigsburg, E. L. (1996). *The view from Saturday*. New York: Atheneum. C
L'Engle, M. (1962). *A wrinkle in time*. New York: Bantam Doubleday Dell.
Lowry, L. (1993). *The giver*. New York: Bantam Doubleday Dell. C
O'Brien, R. C. (1971). *Mrs. Frisby and the rats of NIMH*. New York: Aladdin.
Paterson, K. (1977). *Bridge to Terabithia*. New York: HarperCollins.
Paulsen, G. (1987). *Hatchet*. New York: Simon & Schuster. E
Sachar, L. (1998). *Holes*. New York: Farrar, Straus & Giroux.
Sperry, A. (1940). *Call it courage*. New York: Macmillan.
Spinelli, J. (1996). *Crash*. New York: Knopf. E
Taylor, T. (1969). *The cay*. New York: Avon. E

Grades 7 and 8

Collier, J. L. (1974). *My brother Sam is dead*. New York: Scholastic. E
Craighead, J. G. (1959). *My side of the mountain*. New York: Puffin.
Curtis, C. P. (1999). *Bud, not Buddy*. New York: Delacorte Press.
Forbes, E. (1943). *Johnny Tremain*. New York: Dell.
Hunt, I. (1986). *Across five Aprils*. New York: Berkeley.
Jones, R. (1976). *Acorn people*. New York: Bantam.
London, J. (1903/1996). *The call of the wild*. New York: Viking. C
Perkins, L. R. (2005). *Criss Cross*. New York: Greenwillow.
Stevenson, R. L. (1883/2006). *Treasure Island*. New York: Scribner's.
Twain, M. (1876/2002). *Adventures of Tom Sawyer*. New York: Penguin.
Yep, L. (1990). *Child of the owl*. New York: HarperCollins. E

Story Element Activities

Several activities help students gain a deeper understanding and appreciation of story elements.

▪ Children aged ten and younger have a more difficult time comprehending the internal states of characters than they do the more concrete elements in a story, such as characters' specific actions (van den Broek et al., 2003).

▪ A character continuum can be used to show how characters change (Barton & Sawyer, 2003). For example, a continuum for the prince in *The Whipping Boy* (Fleschman, 1986) might show how the prince started out being selfish and self-centered but gradually became self-reliant and caring.

Character Analysis. A number of devices can be used to analyze characters in a story. One such device is the Character Chart (see Figure 9.2). Students list the facts that an author uses to create a character and note what these facts reveal about the character. The facts are listed in the chart under "What the story says." The facts are interpreted in the adjoining column, headed "What the reader can infer." When introducing the Character Chart, think aloud as you fill it in.

Another device for character analysis is an opinion–proof, in which readers write an opinion about a character and cite proof to back it up. The proof could be the character's actions or comments made about the character by other characters or the author (Santa, 1988). Figure 9.3 presents an opinion–proof for Chibi from *Crow Boy* (Yashima, 1955).

Plot Analysis. Understanding the structure of a story aids comprehension and gives students a framework for composing their own stories. A plot chart shows the story problem, the main actions or events leading up to the climax, the climax, the resolution of the problem, and the ending. It could be a series of rectangles, a diagram, or a picture. Figure 9.4 (on p. 416) provides an example of a plot chart.

Students might also draw pictures of major events of a story or put the events on a time line. Acting out key scenes or putting on a puppet show could highlight the action. To help them choose the most exciting parts, have students pretend that they are making a

Name of character _____		
	What the story says	**What the reader can infer**
Character's actions		
Character's thoughts		
Character's conversations		
What others say about the character		
What the author says about the character		

■■■ **FIGURE 9.2**
Character Chart

movie of the story and must decide which scenes to depict in a preview of coming attractions and which scene to show on a poster advertising the movie.

Theme Analysis.   Theme is the underlying meaning of a story; it can be a universal truth or a significant statement about society, human nature, or the human condition (Stauffer, 1999). The theme is not the same as a lesson or moral. In children's books, the theme often "reflects those developmental values inherent in the process of growing up. The theme may be concerned with overcoming jealousy or fear, adjusting to a physical handicap, or accepting a stepparent" (Sutherland, 1997, p. 31). Thus, analysis of changes that major characters undergo can provide insight into a particular theme.

Developing the concept of theme is a two-part process. In the first part, students draw generalizations or themes from the text; in the second part, they seek support for these generalizations or themes (Norton, 1989). Readers are seeking the answers to two questions: "What is the author trying to tell us that would make a difference in our lives? How do we know the author is telling us _____?" (Norton, 1989, p. 431).

Identifying themes can be a difficult task. When asked to identify the theme, students might retell the story. Remind them to think about what the author is trying to say in the story. To help them understand the concept of theme, read a short story or picture book to students. Read a selection that is brief but has a well-developed theme. Before reading the selection, set a purpose. Have students listen to discover what important thing the author is trying to tell readers about life. Discuss possible themes with students. List the possible themes on the chalkboard or overhead projector. Read the selection again. This time have students listen to the story in order to find support for the themes. List the evidence under each theme.

Most chapter books and novels lend themselves to a variety of follow-up activities. Plan activities such as the following to deepen students' understanding and appreciation of a book and to promote the development of language arts skills.

FYI

■ Remember that the goal of having students read a book is for them to understand, enjoy, and appreciate it. Do not assign so many activities that the life is squeezed out of the book. Some teachers report spending a month or more with a novel. For most books, two weeks should be adequate.

■ Encourage students to obtain library cards. Pave the way by acquainting them with the locations of public libraries and their regulations.

■ To help children build personal libraries, use books as prizes in school contests.

Opinion	Proof
Chibi knew the ways of nature.	He could hold insects in his hand.
	He knew where wild grapes and wild potatoes grew.
	He knew about flowers.
	He could imitate the voices of crows.

■■■ **FIGURE 9.3**
Opinion–Proof for Chibi from *Crow Boy*

■■ ■■ **FIGURE 9.4**
Illustrated Plot Chart for
Crow Boy

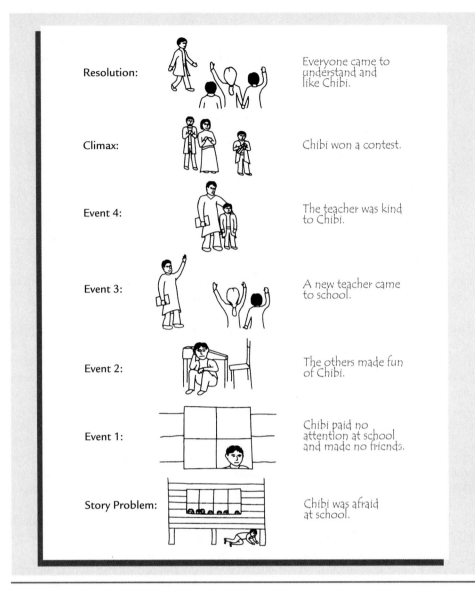

Resolution:	Everyone came to understand and like Chibi.
Climax:	Chibi won a contest.
Event 4:	The teacher was kind to Chibi.
Event 3:	A new teacher came to school.
Event 2:	The others made fun of Chibi.
Event 1:	Chibi paid no attention at school and made no friends.
Story Problem:	Chibi was afraid at school.

Reinforcement Activities

Chapter Books and Novels

- Read a sequel or another book by the same author or a book that develops the same theme or can be contrasted with the book just completed.
- Dramatize portions of the book.
- Create a print or TV ad for the book.
- Create a dust cover for the book, complete with blurbs that highlight the story and that tell about the author.
- View a movie based on the book, and then compare the two.
- Create a montage, diorama, or other piece of art related to the book.
- Write a review of the book for the school newspaper.
- Have a Characters' Day, during which students dress up and act the parts of characters in the book.

Case Study

Using Literature to Assist a Struggling Reader

Despite being a virtual nonreader, fourth-grader Kent refused to consider any book that was not at least on a fourth-grade level and declared that he was going to read *The Prisoner of Zenda* (Hope, 1894), a book that the teacher didn't read until he was 15 (Bertrand, 2000).

Using a modified paired reading strategy, Kent was able to read portions of *The Prisoner of Zenda* with a lot of help and encouragement from his teacher. For three months, Kent's teacher helped him with that novel and other books. Through these one-on-one sessions, Kent began picking up some basic decoding skills. He had previously been hostile and uncooperative, but gradually he began to be more cooperative and calmer. However, one day he complained bitterly that there was nothing that he could read on his own. The teacher obtained some beginning reading books and persuaded Kent to read three easy books a day. In return, the teacher would spend extra time helping Kent with more difficult books that he was interested in. With the extra instruction and on-level application, Kent made encouraging progress. By year's end, he was able to read on a second-grade level.

- Arrange for a panel discussion of the book. The panel might be composed of the book's characters.
- Describe books on the school's or class's homepage. Include links to the author's site, if there is one.

■ ■ ■ Checkup ■ ■ ■

1. What are the steps in presenting a chapter book or novel?
2. What are some activities that might be undertaken to foster a better understanding of a chapter book or novel?

■ ■ ■

Drama

Plays are a welcome change of pace but require some special reading skills. Although designed to be acted out or at least read orally, plays should first be read silently so that students get the gist of the work. Students need to be taught to read stage directions so that they can picture the setting. They also require practice in reading dialogue, which does not contain the familiar transitions and descriptive passages of their usual reading. If possible, students should see plays put on by local professional or amateur groups to give them firsthand experience with theater.

Plays are found in many basal readers. Scripts from TV shows and movies are often included in children's magazines. The magazine *Plays* is, of course, an excellent source. The following Student Reading List identifies a number of anthologies of children's plays.

FYI

Acting out plays provides a legitimate opportunity for students to read orally. Give them ample time to rehearse their parts, however. A drama could be presented as a radio play. Sound effects and background music might be used, but no costumes would be required. If students tape-record the play, other classes might enjoy their efforts.

Student Reading List

Drama

Barchers, S. I. (1993). *Reader's theatre for beginning readers*. Englewood, CO: Teachers Ideas Press.

Barchers, S. I. (2001). *From Atlanta to Zeus: Reader's theatre from Greek mythology*. Littleton, CO: Libraries Unlimited.

Blau, T. (2000). *The best of reader's theatre*. Bellevue, WA: One From the Heart Publications.

Braun, W., & Braun, C. (2000). *A reader's theatre treasury of stories*. Winnipeg, Manitoba, CAN: Portage & Main Press.

Friedman, L. (2001). *Break a leg! The kid's guide to acting and stagecraft*. New York: Workman. A thorough introduction to acting.

Kamerman, S. E. (Ed.). (1996). *Great American events on stage*. Boston: Plays. Fifteen plays celebrate America's past.

Kamerman, S. E. (Ed.). (2001). *Plays of great achievers: One-act plays about inventors, scientists, statesmen, humanitarians, and explorers*. Boston: Plays. Plays that celebrate achievement.

McBride-Smith, B. (2001). *Tell it together: Foolproof scripts for story theatre*. Little Rock, AR: August House.

Dramatizations

To dramatize a story, actors must understand the action and must think carefully about the characters they are portraying. Instead of settling for passive comprehension, readers as actors must put themselves into the piece. They must make the characters come alive by giving them voice, expression, and motivation. This requires that readers think carefully and creatively about what they have read.

Story Theater.   In **story theater**, students pantomime a selection—a folktale, a realistic story, or a poem—while a narrator reads it aloud. Actions need not be limited to those performed by human characters. For example, the sun, the wind, trees swaying in the breeze, and a babbling brook can all be pantomimed. The teacher will probably have to help students organize the production, at least in the beginning. As students become familiar with the technique, they should be able to work out production details for themselves. Working out the details encourages cooperative learning and also involves all the language arts.

Reader's Theater.   In **reader's theater**, participants dramatize a selection by reading it aloud. A whole selection or just one portion of it can be dramatized. Selections that contain a generous amount of dialogue work best. A narrator reads the portions not spoken by characters. Parts are not memorized but are read from the text. Even though they do not have to memorize their parts, readers should spend time developing their interpretation of the dialogue and rehearsing. A reader's theater production might be implemented in the following way (Pike, Compain, & Mumper, 1994):

  1. *Select or write the script.* When starting out, it might be helpful to use scripts that have already been prepared for reader's theater. Any script used should include extensive dialogue, be interesting to your students, and be on the appropriate level of difficulty. A script should have from three to eight parts for students to read. Scripts can also be written by the students, but this takes more time and effort. Composing a script could be a fruitful cooperative learning project. However, students will need some guidance.

  2. *Assign parts.* The parts can be either assigned by the teacher or decided on by students.

  3. *Rehearse the script.* Although the scripts are read aloud, they should be rehearsed. Before students rehearse a script, they should have read and discussed the selection. As a group, students should decide how each part is to be read. Focus should be on interpreting the character's mood and feelings. Should a character sound angry, sad, or frightened? How are these emotions to be portrayed? Students then rehearse individually and as a group.

FYI

■ Although fostering enjoyment of literature is paramount, it is also important to develop children's understanding of literary techniques: personification, figurative language, and, at higher levels, theme and symbols. For poetry, discuss rhyme, rhythm, and poetic language.

■ Students might also like to try role-playing, improvisation, and use of puppets. Role-playing works well with all ages, but seems to work best with younger children; improvisation seems to suit older children better. Using improvisation, students spontaneously dramatize a story or situation. Improvisation might be used to portray a character in a tale or extend a story. It might also be used to dramatize a concept in science or social studies.

■ Introduce students to a variety of types of reading: short stories, novels, biographies, poems, plays, and informational pieces. Students may have a favored genre or may exclude informational texts. They need to experience a full range of literary genres.

USING TECHNOLOGY

Aaron Shepard's RT Page gives an overview of reader's theater and provides a number of scripts for students in grades three and up.
http://www.aaronshep.com/rt

■ **Story theater** is a form of dramatization in which participants pantomime a selection while a narrator reads it aloud.

■ **Reader's theater** is a form of dramatization in which the participants read aloud a selection as though it were a play.

acters in the story like anyone you know? Does this book remind you of any book that you have read? Why do you think this book is so popular with young people? Do you think the characters were realistic? What was the saddest part of the story? What message is the author trying to get across? On a scale of 1 to 10, how would you rate this book? Why?" The questions that you ask will depend upon your main purpose for reading aloud. If you are reading books aloud to try to motivate students to read on their own, ask questions that focus on the enjoyment or personal satisfaction of reading. If you are trying to build thinking skills, ask questions that have them make comparisons, see similarities, draw conclusions, and make judgments.

It's important, too, to set routines for reading aloud, so that you do it at a certain time and for a designated period of time. That way read-alouds aren't relegated to an activity that is undertaken when everything else is done. Read-alouds are valuable enough that they should be regularly scheduled.

Read-alouds should be previewed. You want to prepare your read-aloud. You also want to make sure that there is nothing in the text that would embarrass students or that is not appropriate for them.

■ Voluntary (Self-Selected) Reading

The key to improved reading achievement is very simple: Encourage students to read on their own for ten minutes a day. According to carefully conducted research, these extra ten minutes result in significant improvements in reading (Fielding, Wilson, & Anderson, 1986). Unfortunately, a nationally administered questionnaire revealed that fewer than half the nation's fourth-graders read for fun every day, and 13 percent never or hardly ever read for fun on their own time (Mullis, Campbell, & Farstrup, 1993). A study of fifth-graders had an even gloomier finding: Only 30 percent of the students read for ten minutes or more a day (Anderson, Wilson, & Fielding, 1988). Responding to the Motivation to Read Profile (Gambrell, Codling, & Palmer, 1996), 17 percent of students reported that they would rather clean their rooms than read, 10 percent said that people who read are boring, and 14 percent stated that they would spend little time reading when they grew up.

What can be done to motivate children to read? First, demonstrate that reading is both personally fulfilling and fun, and put children in contact with books that they will enjoy. Attractive classroom libraries attract readers. In a large-scale study of children's reading, the classroom library was the major source of books for most of the children. Children also like to choose their books, and they like to talk about them with other students and the teacher. Students frequently selected a book to read because a friend or a teacher had recommended it (Gambrell, Codling, & Palmer, 1996).

Step 1: Determining Interests and Attitudes

A good starting point for creating a voluntary (or self-selected) reading program is to determine students' reading interests and their attitudes toward reading. Close observation of your students yields useful information about these factors. In addition, you probably have a good sense of who likes to read and who does not. Through observation, classroom discussions, and conversations with individual children, you probably also know who likes sports, who prefers mysteries, and who is interested in animals. An easy way to obtain an overview of the kinds of books your students might enjoy reading voluntarily is to duplicate several pages listing books at their grade level from the catalog of a distributor of children's books. Ask students to circle the titles that interest them. One experienced librarian recommended indirect questioning when exploring children's interests:

> The best way to learn what any child likes to read is to ask, but a direct question may not elicit clear information. A bit of probing may be necessary. What does he do with leisure time? What are his favorite television programs? The last good book he read? (Halstead, 1988, p. 35)

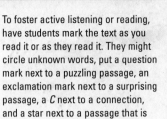

HIGHER-LEVEL LITERACY

To foster active listening or reading, have students mark the text as you read it or as they read it. They might circle unknown words, put a question mark next to a puzzling passage, an exclamation mark next to a surprising passage, a *C* next to a connection, and a star next to a passage that is memorable (Adler & Rougle, 2005).

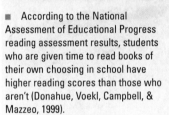

FYI

■ According to the National Assessment of Educational Progress reading assessment results, students who are given time to read books of their own choosing in school have higher reading scores than those who aren't (Donahue, Voekl, Campbell, & Mazzeo, 1999).

■ Students like to read about characters who are their own age or who are facing problems that are similar to theirs (Harris & Sipay, 1990). Children of all ages also enjoy humor (Greenlaw, 1983). Animals and make-believe are ranked high by primary-grade students; upper-grade students, on the other hand, have a distinct preference for mystery, adventure, or sports.

■ When it comes to reading for enjoyment, U.S. fourth graders are below the international average (Ogle et al., 2003). Only 35 percent of U.S. fourth-graders report reading for fun every day or almost every day; the international average is 40 percent.

■ The quality of the book being read is a key determinant of the effectiveness of voluntary reading.

■ Surveys and questionnaires might be used to complement data from observations. Two copyright-free, useful surveys of reading attitudes are the Motivation to Read Profile (MRP) (Gambrell, Codling, & Palmer, 1996) and the Elementary Reading Attitude Survey (ERAS) (McKenna & Kerr, 1990).

IRA Position Statement

on Key Issue

Providing Books and Other Print Materials for Classroom and School Libraries

"Children who are allowed to self-select and who have access to varied sources of print materials in their classrooms, school libraries, town libraries, and at home, read more and read more widely, both for pleasure and for information" (International Reading Association, 1999b, p. 2). Frequent reading develops language and improves comprehension, word analysis skills, and fluency. It also builds background and vocabulary. "Given that there are approximately 180 days in the school year, a child should be able to select within the classroom a new book to read each day. This averages to about seven books per student in each classroom library. . . ." (International Reading Association, 1999b, p. 3). School libraries should have a minimum of twenty books per child. In addition, it is recommended that each year one new book per student should be added to every classroom library and two new books per child should be added to the school library collection.

FYI

■ Many libraries make special provision for teachers and will loan them a hundred or more books.

■ See *Guiding Readers and Writers, Grades 3–6* (Fountas & Pinnell, 2001a) for a thorough step-by-step explanation of setting up a program of voluntary reading.

Closing the Gap

Voluntary reading is a key means for extending reading skills. If you can't get parents to take their children to the library, maybe you can get children to take their parents. In one school in San José, California, the children enjoyed the books that they were reading in school so much that they persuaded their parents to take them to the library so that they could read more books by the same authors (Maldonado-Colon, 2003).

USING TECHNOLOGY

For information on the latest and best-selling children's books, consult the Web sites of online book stores, such as these:
Amazon.com
http://www.amazon.com

Barnes and Noble
http://www.bn.com

Step 2: Building the Classroom Library

Once you have a sense of what your class might like to read, start building a classroom library and involve students in the process. Propinquity is a primary principle in promoting voluntary reading. When books are close by and easy to check out, students will read more. The goal is to build a community of readers (Fielding, Wilson, & Anderson, 1986). If students feel they have a stake in the classroom library, they will be more highly motivated to read.

Invite students, their parents, and the community at large to contribute books to your classroom library. You might also be able to obtain some volumes from the school librarian and other local librarians. Students, as they get older, find paperbacks especially appealing. Paperbacks are also cheaper to buy and to replace if lost or damaged.

Obtaining Books on a Variety of Levels

Students need reading material they can handle. They are most likely to read on their own when they have books (or periodicals) that are interesting and when they feel competent enough to read the materials (Gambrell, Codling, & Palmer, 1996). Although students will read books that are beyond their level if they have a special interest in the subject, a steady diet of such books can be discouraging. A study of sixth-graders found that both good and poor readers chose books on the same level; however, a higher percentage of good readers finished their books (Anderson, Higgins, & Wurster, 1985). If the less-able readers had selected books closer to their ability, perhaps they would have completed them.

Young children may require special provisions during self-selected reading. Kaissen (1987) observed that voluntary reading works well with first-graders if several books are available to them, including those that have been read to them previously. In addition, books on the easiest levels and taped books should be available (see Appendix A). Kindergartners showed a preference for books that had been read to them that morning or earlier in the week (Gutkin, 1990).

The reading levels of books in classroom and school libraries should be determined and marked on the books. This is especially important at the lower levels. However, don't overemphasize levels. Focus on choosing books that students can read smoothly or that will help them grow as readers (Calkins, 2001). Instead of saying, "You need to read books that have a blue dot," say, "You might be able to read a blue dot book faster and more smoothly" or "Why don't you try a blue dot book for now and try the green dot books after you read some blue dot ones?" Or you might ask, "Is this a stop-and-go book—are you stopping a lot to try to figure out hard words? Try a blue dot book. You won't have so many stops" (Calkins, 2001). At the upper levels, instead of marking books with dots, you might have a section of "fast reads" intended for below-level readers. However, encourage all students to select from these fast reads; otherwise, the books become stigmatized.

Setting Up the Classroom Library

Make the classroom library as appealing as possible. Display books with their covers showing. You might also have special displays of books on high-interest topics. Update the collection periodically—at least once a month, add new titles to keep children interested.

Managing the Classroom Library

Wilson (1992) suggested that the teacher involve the poorest readers in helping with the management of the classroom collection. By helping display, advertise, and keep track of the collection, poor readers become familiar with its contents.

Involve students in setting up check-out procedures and rules. Keep the rules simple; if they are complicated and punitive, they will discourage borrowing (Wilson, 1986). Inevitably, some books will be lost or damaged. Consider this part of the cost of "doing business." Do not charge late fines or fees for lost or damaged books; these could be a genuine hardship for poor children. Instead, have a talk with students about being more responsible. If it is not a hardship, students could contribute replacement books, which do not necessarily have to have the same titles as the lost books. Put students in charge of keeping track of books; they can handle checking in, checking out, and putting books away.

Step 3: Setting Up a Management System

Discuss with the class the purpose of self-selected reading and explain how the books are organized. Set aside a time each day for self-selected reading. A typical session might last 20 to 30 minutes. However, it might be necessary to start with shorter sessions, in order to build stamina, especially for younger children. It is generally a good idea to have students select and check out their books before the session begins so that they are ready to read as soon as it starts. Also, have books available to read during transitional times or during spare moments of the day. Encourage students to check out more than one book. If they don't like their first selection, they have a backup. You might have students check out several books at the beginning of the week; these become the basis for the week's voluntary reading. Calkins (2001) advocates creating "book shelves," which are magazine boxes or other suitable containers. One school has students keep their books in cloth bags, which are hung on the backs of their chairs. The box or bag holds the student's books, bookmarks, conference record sheets, and log of books read.

Step 4: Teaching Students How to Select Books

Model book selection techniques. Show how you judge a book by examining the cover, seeing who the author is, reading the blurb on the jacket, glancing through the book, and reading brief parts. Discuss with students how they choose books. Post book selection suggestions such as those noted in Figure 9.5. Guide students, especially those who are reading below grade level, as they select books. Have them read a passage or two. If the passage seems too hard, suggest an easier book. Set aside time for students to recommend books they think others in the class might enjoy.

- Does the book look interesting?
- Is the book about as hard as other books I have read?
- Can I read most of the words?
- Can I understand what the book is saying?

FYI

■ Gear activities to the level of the students' reading development. Students whose reading is very limited will not benefit from self-selected reading or reading with a partner. Have them read along with a recorded selection or CD or try echo reading. Novice and struggling readers need lots of experience with contextual reading (Carbo, 1997).

■ Read Jodi Crum Marshall's (2002) account of how she set up a voluntary reading program for middle school students.

ASSESSING FOR LEARNING

Book selection is an essential skill. By observing students as they select books and discussing with them how they go about selecting a book, you can decide whether they need help choosing books and what form that help might take.

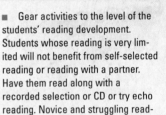

**FIGURE 9.5
Choosing Books**

You might also hold a brainstorming session to see what children know about selecting books. Based on their observation with six, seven, and eight-year-olds, Wutz and Wedwick (2005) discovered that students selected books on the basis of the title and length. Not surprisingly, only eight of twenty-two students reported that they usually finished books they had selected. The students cited word difficulty, length, and lack of interest as the main reasons they didn't finish reading books. In discussions with students, Wutz created a list of criteria for selecting books and posted these. She also modeled each of the criteria—for example, how to select a book that doesn't have too many hard words or that isn't too long. After students had a chance to try out a criterion, they discussed how they were able to use it to choose books.

Step 5: Teaching Students How to Talk About Books

Students read more and get more out of their reading if they have a chance to talk about books. You might have students gather in groups of three or four to discuss their books—to engage in buddy buzz (Fountas & Pinnell, 2001a). So that buddy buzz may be profitable, students are given a prompt beforehand. They might be asked, for instance, to attach sticky notes to two passages that they would like to share. During the buzz, they read the passages they marked and explain why they chose them. They also ask each other questions. Before engaging in buddy buzz, students are taught to be respectful of each other, listen attentively, ask questions after each presentation, and take turns. They also learn how to provide support for their statements and how to politely voice opposing opinions.

Possible prompts for buddy buzz sessions are as follows:

- Mark two passages that you would like to share.
- Mark two passages that are interesting.
- Mark two passages that are funny, exciting, or sad.
- Mark two passages that tell you things you didn't know.
- Mark two passages that you think the others in the group would like to hear.
- Mark two passages that contain interesting language.
- Mark two passages that give you information you can use.
- Mark two passages that tell about a place that you would like to visit.

Students should have time during the day when they can read books of their own choosing.

Step 6: Teaching Students How to Work Together

Elicit from students guidelines for working together: reading silently, holding questions or concerns until the teacher is available (unless it's an emergency), and so forth.

Step 7: Teaching Students to Recommend Books

Display books that students have recommended on a special shelf or rack. Discuss with students how they might decide whether to recommend a book and how they might compose a recommendation.

Case Study
Creating a Better Self-Selected Reading Program

Realizing the importance of extensive reading, Jodi Crum Marshall (2002) initiated a self-selected reading program. At first, she thought the program was working well. The room was quiet. There were no complaints. But then she noticed that the room was too quiet. There was no expression of excitement or enjoyment. And while there were no complaints, there were no positive comments either. After discussing the self-selected reading program with her students, Marshall concluded that she had made a series of blunders. She had failed to set expectations or goals for the program with students. They saw the session as a free period. If they didn't raise a fuss, they could quietly do whatever they wanted. She had not included them in setting up the program or acquiring books. Although her classes were made up of sixth-, seventh-, and eighth-grade struggling readers, she had failed to acquire books on the appropriate levels. Most were too difficult. And she hadn't really done anything to spark an interest in reading. Because the books were difficult and lacking in appeal, many of the students weren't really reading. Some would begin to read a book but quit when they found that it was too difficult. As one student put it, none of the books "make sense."

Marshall reformed the program. First, she had conversations with students about the program. The students wanted more books and more time to read. They also wanted to discuss their books, but they didn't want the discussions to seem like quizzes. Responding to the issues that students raised, Marshall changed discussions so that they were more like conversations than oral quizzes. She also held individual conversations with students. And she encouraged students to keep logs of their reading. This served a practical purpose, because often they forgot where they had left off reading the day before. She also began reading aloud to the class. This motivated students to read the books that she was reading to them. She also passed out book catalogs to students and had them mark the books they would like to read. These and other titles were added to the class library. But perhaps the most important thing she did was to get to know her students, their reading strengths and weaknesses, and their interests. Using this knowledge, she was able to match them up with books that they could read and wanted to read. Not surprisingly, students' attitudes changed. And their gains on tests of reading comprehension and language were better than expected.

Activities for Motivating Voluntary Reading

To motivate voluntary reading, be enthusiastic, accepting, and flexible. Present reading as an interesting, vital activity. Include a wide range of material from comics to classics. Do not present books as vitamins, saying, "Read them. They're good for you." Share reading with students in the same way that you might share with friends. By doing so, you are accepting students as serious readers. Above all, be a reader yourself. Some activities for motivating voluntary reading follow:

- *Match books with interests.* Make personal recommendations. For a Gary Paulsen fan, you might say, "Joe, I know you enjoy Gary Paulsen's books. The school library has a new book by him. I read it, and it's very interesting."

- *Use the indirect approach.* Choose a book that would be appropriate for your students and that you would enjoy reading. Carry the book to class with you. Mention that the book is interesting, and tell students that they can borrow it when you're finished. Or you may just want to carry the book around and see how many inquiries you get.

- *Pique students' interest.* Read a portion of a book and stop at a cliff-hanging moment; then tell students that they can read the rest themselves if they want to find out what happened.

- *Use videotapes to preview books.* Show a portion of a movie based on a book; then encourage students to find out what happened by reading the book. (First, be sure that the book is available to students.)

- *Substitute voluntary reading for workbook or other seatwork assignments.* The Center for the Study of Reading (1990) made the following statement: "Independent, silent reading can fulfill many of the same functions as workbook activities—it permits students to practice what they are learning, and it keeps the rest of the class occupied while you meet with a small group of students" (p. 5).

FYI

- Sometimes known as sustained silent reading, self-selected reading (SSR) is a time when all the students in a class, or even in a school, read materials of their own choosing.

- We want children to read the best that has been written. However, students must be allowed to choose what they wish to read. Once students experience the joy of reading, then, through skillful guidance, they might be led to experience high-quality literature.

USING TECHNOLOGY

Authors and Illustrators on the Web lists author sites.

http://www.acs.ucalgary.ca/~dkbrown/authors.html

INVOLVING PARENTS

Richgels and Wold (1998) involved parents of first-graders in their children's reading by sending home "Three for the Road" backpacks. Each backpack contained three books; three sock puppets, which students could use to talk about their reading; a response notebook; markers and pencils; a letter to parents; and suggestions for using the backpack.

Adapting Instruction for Struggling Readers and Writers

Some struggling readers select books that are beyond their capability because they want to read the same books that their friends are reading. Have available books that are interesting but easy. From time to time, highlight these books and allow everyone to read them so that they don't become stigmatized as "baby books."

■ *Have students visit author sites on the Web to learn of the latest books by their favorite authors.*

■ *Have students keep records of books they read voluntarily.* Recording books read gives students a sense of accountability and accomplishment.

■ *Encourage partner reading.* Young and less able readers might be willing to attempt a challenging book if they get some help and support from a partner. Such readers might also be more willing to read on their own if given a "running start" that gets them solidly into the book (Castle, 1994).

■ *Recommend books by a popular series author.* Students who have enjoyed one of Beverly Cleary's books about Ramona Quimby or Henry Huggins might not be aware that other equally funny books feature these same characters.

■ *Introduce students to book clubs that cater to school-age populations.* Book clubs offer a variety of interesting books at bargain prices. When students choose and pay money for a book, it is highly likely that they will read it. Make alternative provisions for economically disadvantaged children.

■ *Do not overlooked community resources.* Invite the public librarian and a representative from a local bookstore to visit the class and tell students what is "hot" in children's books. Inform speakers beforehand about the reading levels and interests of students so that they can suggest suitable titles.

■ *Encourage students to build personal libraries with a few inexpensive paperbacks.* They can add to their collection by requesting books as gifts.

■ *Once a month, give students the opportunity to trade books they have read.* Before the trading session, students might want to post a list or announce titles that they will swap. You might also have a trading shelf in the classroom from which students may take any book they wish, as long as they put one in its place.

■ *Suggest and have on hand books that relate to people or subjects being taught in the content areas.* Reading a brief biography of John F. Kennedy, for instance, could help shed light on his presidency and the early 1960s.

■ *Use the Web.* On the class or school homepage, list books that parents might obtain for their children at either the local library or a bookstore.

Incentives seem to work best when the nature of the reward fits with the nature of the activity and when the incentive is tied to meeting a specific goal rather than simply engaging in the activity. In Running Start, a reading incentive program, the goal was reading twenty brief books within ten weeks. As an incentive, students could select a book to keep (Gambrell, Codling, & Palmer, 1996).

■ ■ ■ **Checkup** ■ ■ ■

1. What steps might be taken to foster increased voluntary reading?
2. What are the elements of an effective voluntary reading program?

■ ■ ■

Exemplary Teaching

Motivating Reading

On the first day of school, third-grade teacher Cathy Clarkson (2000) gathers her students in a circle on the rug. Piled in front of Clarkson are her favorite books from childhood. During that first session and in subsequent sessions, she shares some of her favorites with her students. She also invites students to bring in their favorite books. If students don't have favorite books to bring in, they can select books from a collection of favorite books. Included in that collection are books that previous teachers read to Clarkson's students. Throughout the year, students share past and current favorites.

Building Higher-Level Literacy

When discussing literary selections, pose interpretive questions, those for which there is no definite answer. Instead, students take positions and support their positions through their reasoning and by citing passages. For examples of discussions that use interpretive questions, refer to the Junior Great Books site at http://www.greatbooks.org.

Help for Struggling Readers and Writers

Because they are reading below grade level, struggling readers may experience difficulty handling literary selections. If they are reading only slightly below the level of the selection, providing them with additional help with difficult vocabulary and concepts might make it possible for them to read the text successfully. Reading all or part of the selection to them or obtaining an audiotape or CD-ROM version of the text is another possibility. However, one reason struggling readers are behind is because they typically read less. They should be given access to quality selections on their reading level to give them the experience of reading on their own.

For voluntary reading, make sure you have a variety of high-interest materials on levels that are appropriate for your struggling readers. Because some students would rather clean their rooms than read, have available intriguing, highly motivating materials: joke and riddle books; sports biographies and animal books that are heavily illustrated but have limited text; high-interest periodicals, such as *Sports Illustrated for Kids*; books on CD-ROM; and books that incorporate activities, such as a book about magnets that is accompanied by magnets.

Tools for the Classroom

Essential Standards

Kindergarten

Students will

- listen and respond to a variety of classic and current literary works.
- identify characters, setting, and important plot events.
- listen, speak, and read to gain knowledge of their own culture, the culture of others, and the common elements of cultures.
- listen to one or two books read aloud at school and one or two books read at home or in an after-school daycare program.
- "read" alone, with a partner, or with an adult two to four familiar books a day.

Grades 1 and 2

Students will

- listen to or read and understand and appreciate a variety of types of literary selections.
- describe key elements in a selection, such as characters, setting, story problem, and plot.
- respond to literary selections in writing, art, movement, or drama, and in discussion groups.
- compare and contrast different versions of the same tale and works by different authors and connect ideas and themes across texts.
- identify and appreciate literary techniques, such as rhythm, rhyme, alliteration, and imaginative use of language.
- learn basic literary techniques such as using dialogue and action to develop characters.
- recite, read aloud with expression, or dramatize poems, stories, and plays.
- listen, speak, and read to gain knowledge of their own culture, the culture of others, and the common elements of cultures.
- read and enjoy a variety of books and periodicals.

- read to acquire information that is important to them.
- read two to four short books or other texts such as poems or songs each day, alone or with assistance, or read one or two brief chapter books each day.

Grades 3 through 8

Students will

- understand and appreciate a variety of types of literary selections.
- respond to literary selections through writing, art, movement, or drama, and in discussion groups.
- support responses and conclusions by referring back to the text.
- determine the underlying theme of a selection and connect ideas and themes across texts.
- learn advanced literary techniques, such as using metaphors, similes, and symbols.
- use a set of increasingly sophisticated standards to evaluate literary works.
- read and discuss to gain knowledge of their own culture, the culture of others, and the common elements of cultures.
- read and enjoy a variety of books and periodicals.
- read to acquire information that is important to them.
- read the equivalent of thirty chapter books a year (third-graders) or the equivalent of twenty-five full-length books (fourth- through eighth-graders).

(Some of the above standards have been adapted from the Texas, California, and New Standards.)

Action Plan

1. Use a reader response approach to literature. Through focusing on personal response, foster in students enjoyment of and appreciation for literature.
2. Introduce students to a variety of genres and authors.
3. Use class discussions, literature discussion groups, journals, dramatizations, and art to foster responses to literature.
4. Use a unit or theme approach so that students explore themes in depth and make connections among major ideas.
5. Involve students in the establishment and management of a classroom library. Encourage students to read widely and frequently. Encourage them to share their responses to reading with friends, classmates, and family.
6. Obtain materials on a variety of levels and topics so that all students have a choice of appealing and readable materials.

Assessment

Based on your observations and students' written and oral responses, assess whether they appreciate and respond on a personal and aesthetic level to works of literature. Through their responses, also determine whether they are becoming knowledgeable about techniques used in creating literature and whether they are acquiring standards for judging literary selections. Note whether students choose to read books on their own and talk about books. Note whether they have a favorite book or a favorite author. Look over students' reading logs or journals to see how much students are reading, what they are reading, and how they are responding to their reading. You might also use the Motivation to Read Profile (Gambrell, Codling, & Palmer, 1996) or the Elementary Reading Attitude Survey (McKenna & Kerr, 1990) to obtain additional information about students' reading attitudes and habits.

Summary

Until recently, reading was looked upon as being primarily a skills subject. Today, the emphasis is on reading quality materials. Reading literature involves fostering appreciation and enjoyment as well as understanding. The focus is on eliciting personal responses and valuing students' interpretations. Students should read a variety of types of literature.

Just ten minutes a day of voluntary reading results in significant gains in reading achievement. To promote voluntary reading, demonstrate that it is enjoyable and personally fulfilling.

For struggling readers, make adaptations so that they have access to literary selections that the class is reading. To foster voluntary reading, provide for students' interests and reading levels. Have available joke, riddle, and other appealing but easy-to-read books.

Extending and Applying

1. Read at least three current anthologies of children's poetry. Which poems did you like best? Which do you think would appeal to your students?
2. With a group of classmates, start a literature discussion group in which you discuss children's books.
3. Create a lesson in which you introduce a poem, play, or other literary piece. In your lesson, stress appreciation, enjoyment, and personal response. Teach the lesson and evaluate it.
4. Try out one of the suggestions listed in this chapter or an idea of your own for increasing voluntary reading. Implement the idea and evaluate its effectiveness.

Developing a Professional Portfolio

Document your ability to develop an understanding and appreciation of literary works by composing a written description of a literature unit. If possible, illustrate the description with photos of students in discussion groups or photos of presentations. Also include samples of students' literature logs or response journals or other responses to literature.

mylabschool
Where the classroom comes to life!

Go to Allyn & Bacon's MyLabSchool: **www.mylabschool.com**

- Enter Assignment ID **CRV3** into **Assignment Finder,** and select the video titled "Using Literature." In this video, Dorothy Grier explains types of literature that can bring a subject alive for students, enhance their interest, and give them a variety of perspectives to enhance their learning.
- As you watch the video, identify the various types of literature that teachers use in the classroom. Can you think of other types that were not identified in the video? What are some ways in which literature can aid learning in a content area?
- Explore MyLabSchool further to find the course areas for Reading Methods, Language Arts, and Content Area Reading and identify other assets that support concepts introduced in this chapter.

Developing a Resource File

1. Keep a card or computer database file of high-quality chapter books and novels that you believe would appeal to students you are teaching or plan to teach. Include bibliographic information, summaries of the selections, some questions you might ask about each work, and some ideas for extension activities.
2. Keep a file of activities that might be used to motivate students to read.

Companion Website

To access chapter objectives, practice tests, weblinks, and flashcards, go to the companion website at **www.ablongman.com/gunning6e.**

10 Approaches to Teaching Reading

or each of the following statements related to the chapter you are about to read, put a check under "Agree" or "Disagree" to show how you feel. Discuss your responses with classmates before you read the chapter.

	Agree	Disagree
1. A structured approach to reading is most effective.	_____	_____
2. Extensive reading of children's books should be a part of every elementary and middle school reading program.	_____	_____
3. Teacher and method are equally important.	_____	_____
4. A writing approach to reading works best with young children.	_____	_____
5. An individualized reading program is hard to manage.	_____	_____
6. A commercial reading program, such as a basal series or literature anthology, is best for new teachers because it shows them step by step how to teach reading.	_____	_____
7. Teachers should combine the best parts of each reading approach.	_____	_____
8. Teachers should be free to choose the approach to reading that they feel works best.	_____	_____

here are really just two main ways of learning to read: by reading and by writing, or some combination of the two. The approach that uses writing is known as language experience. Reading approaches use textbooks (including basal anthologies and linguistic reading series) and children's books. Children's books are used in the individualized and literature-based approaches. Of course, these approaches can also be combined in various ways. Teachers who use basals or literature anthologies often supplement their programs with language-experience stories and children's books.

Which of these approaches are you familiar with? What are the characteristics of the approaches? What are their advantages? Their disadvantages?

■ Changing Approaches to Teaching Reading

In a little more than a decade, there have been two dramatic changes in reading instruction in the United States. Up until the mid-1980s, most American children were taught through basal readers. However, a holistic movement espousing the use of children's books to teach reading took hold. There was a switch from basals to children's literature and from structured teaching to a more naturalistic approach to literacy. Now, after more than a decade in which skills were downplayed in many areas, there is a movement to use a balanced approach that integrates skills instruction and reading of good literature. Basal readers have also made a comeback. They are more skills oriented than ever. However, they also advocate use of high-quality literary selections and feature extensive libraries of children's literature.

The New York Times
expect the world®
nytimes.com
Themes of the Times

Expand your knowledge of the concepts discussed in this chapter by reading current and historical articles from *The New York Times* by visiting the "Themes of the Times" section of the Companion Website.

FYI

▪ Until recently, reading was considered a skills subject; it did not really matter what students read. Today, content is paramount, the idea being that students' minds and lives will be enriched if they read the best that has been written.

▪ Producing a basal program is a three-year undertaking involving fifteen to twenty program authors, consultants, editors, writers, teacher advisors, student advisors, designers, artists, and publishers' representatives and consultants (Singleton, 1997).

USING TECHNOLOGY

Information about the major basal series is available on the following sites:

Harcourt School Publishers
http://www.harcourtschool.com

Houghton Mifflin
http://www.eduplace.com

McGraw Hill
http://www.mhschool.com/reading/index.html

Open Court
http://www.sra-4kids.com

Scott Foresman
http://www.sfreading.com

Regardless of whether they are holistic or balanced, effective approaches incorporate the basic principles of teaching literacy that have been emphasized throughout this book:

▪ Children become readers and writers by reading and writing.

▪ Reading programs should include a rich variety of interesting, appropriate material and should stress a great deal of reading and writing.

▪ Strategies that promote independence in word recognition and comprehension should be taught.

▪ Reading programs should be language-based. Provision should be made for developing speaking and listening as well as reading and writing skills.

▪ Because reading fosters writing development and writing fosters reading development, literacy programs should develop both.

▪ Provision should be made for individual differences. Because students differ in terms of interests, abilities, learning rate, experiential background, and culture, the approach used should take into consideration the needs of all students.

▪ Students' progress should be monitored, and provision should be made for helping students fully develop their potential.

This chapter examines the major approaches to teaching reading and writing. Each approach has its strengths and weaknesses. Suggestions are made for adapting each approach to take advantage of its strengths and compensate for its weaknesses. For instance, ways to make the basal approach more holistic are suggested. Thus, if it has been mandated that you use a basal series but you prefer a holistic approach, you can adapt your instruction to make the program more holistic and still keep within the guidelines of the school or school district that employs you.

▪ Basal/Anthology Approach

How were you taught to read? Chances are you were taught through a **basal reading program**. Basal readers are the main approach to teaching reading in the United States. A complex package based on a relatively simple concept, the basal program includes a series of readers or anthologies and supplementary materials that gradually increase in difficulty, thus serving as stepping stones along a path that begins with emergent literacy and extends through sixth-grade reading. Accompanying teacher's manuals provide guidance so that the classroom teacher can lead students upward.

Basal reading programs have changed from the time when you were in elementary school. For most of the twentieth century, the major basals advocated an analytic approach in which letter sounds were never isolated and there was heavy reliance on the use of the initial consonant of a word and context. Selections were chosen on the basis of topic or literary quality, so they didn't reinforce the phonics elements that had been taught. Today, all basals use a systematic approach to phonics in which students are taught to say individual sounds and blend them, and all apply skills in selections that incorporate the elements that have been presented.

Basals have also became more language-based. Today's basals generally include writing and spelling along with reading and are known as literacy, rather than reading, series. In fact, basal systems offer an embarrassment of riches. In addition to anthologies, related workbooks, and detailed teacher's manuals packed with teaching suggestions, basals offer

▪ A **basal reading program** is a comprehensive program for teaching reading that includes readers or anthologies that gradually increase in difficulty, teacher's manuals, workbooks, and assessment measures. In grades 7 and 8 and sometimes in grade 6, teachers use literature texts instead of basals.

big books, supplementary libraries of the best in children's books, read-aloud books, a wide array of games and manipulatives, audiotapes, computer software, videodiscs, inservice programs, posters, charts, supplementary spelling and language books, a wide variety of unit and end-of-book tests, placement tests, observation guides, portfolio systems, Web sites, and more.

Clearly, today's basals are bigger and better than ever. But the real question is "Are today's basals good enough?" The answer is yes and no. Basals have many advantages, but they also have some shortcomings.

Advantages of Basals

Basals offer teachers a convenient package of materials, techniques, and assessment devices, as well as a plan for orchestrating the various components of a total literacy program. In their anthologies, which, for the most part, gradually increase in difficulty, basals offer students a steady progression from emergent literacy through a sixth-grade reading level. They also offer varied reading selections, an abundance of practice material, carefully planned units and lessons, and a wealth of follow-up and enrichment activities.

Disadvantages of Basals

Despite a major overhaul, basals are still driven by the same engine. The core of the basal reading program is the trio of anthology, workbook, and manual. Although the contents of the anthology are much improved, its function remains the same—to provide a base of materials for all students to move through. However, students have diverse interests and abilities and progress at different rates. Although basal selections are meant to be of high quality, they will not all be of interest to all students. The sports biography that delights one child is a total bore to another.

A second shortcoming has to do with the way basal readers are assembled: They are anthologies and often contain excerpts from whole books. For example, the fourth-grade reader from a typical series contains "The Diary of Leigh Botts," a delightful tale of a budding young writer that is excerpted from Beverly Cleary's 1983 Newbury Award winner, *Dear Mr. Henshaw*. If reading the excerpt is worthwhile, reading the whole book should be even better.

There is also the question of pacing and time spent with a selection. Students often move through basals in lockstep fashion. Part of the problem is the nature of the teacher's manuals; they offer too much of a good thing. Stories and even poems are overtaught. There are too many questions asked before a selection is read, too many asked after the piece has been read, and too many follow-up activities. A class might spend three to five days on a thousand-word story. To be fair, the manuals do present activities as choices. Teachers can choose those they wish to undertake and omit the others. Teachers may even be provided a choice of ways of presenting a story: interactively, with the teacher modeling strategies; independently, with the teacher providing a minimum of assistance; or with support, which means that students follow along as the teacher reads the story. All in all, the typical basal lesson has many fine suggestions, but the ideas are "canned," that is, created by someone in an editorial office far from the classroom. Designed to be all things to all teachers, the activities are not designed for a specific class of students with specific needs and interests.

Perhaps the biggest disadvantage of basals is the organizational pattern they suggest. Basal reading series have core selections in anthologies and also supplementary reading in libraries of leveled

Today's basal/anthology systems include anthologies, charts, big books, and a host of other materials.

FYI

In her comparison of students who were read *to* and students who read *with* her, Kuhn (2004) found that students showed more growth when they read rather than being read to.

readers. The core basal selections are presented to the whole class. The selections are generally appropriate for average students but may not be challenging enough for the best readers and are too hard for as many as the one student out of four in the typical classroom who is reading below grade level. Suggestions are made for adapting instruction for all learners. This may mean reading selections to the poorest readers or providing them with an audio version of the selection so that they can read along. Or, the teacher might simply read the selection to the whole class. Whatever your approach, you need to provide access for all students. If you do read the selection to students, have them follow along in their text. This provides them with exposure to print. To keep them involved, from time to time, call on the whole group to read a portion with you in choral reading style.

In addition to reading or listening to the core selection, students also read in guided reading groups. All basal series have sets of books on three levels—easy, average, and challenging—giving all students the opportunity to read books on their level. However, a key question remains: Which students do the least reading? Since the average and above-average students read the core selection and the least advanced group listens to the selection, those students most in need of reading practice do the least amount of reading. If you are using a basal, you need to make adjustments so that struggling readers are reading more, not less, than the other students. Some basals offer an alternative selection for struggling readers, which is related to the theme in the core selection but is easier to read. If available, you might use this option.

Unfortunately, even the use of both interactive read-alouds and guided reading groups does not quite solve the problem of meeting the needs of below-level readers. All of a theme's (or unit's) activities revolve around the core selection, including phonics or other decoding lessons and workbook exercises. However, these activities are on the same level as the core selection and so are too difficult and/or inappropriate for below-level readers. For instance, consider a basal core selection that is on a mid–first-grade level. The phonics lesson introduces the final-*e* long-*i* pattern, but the below-level readers haven't yet mastered short-vowel patterns. Long-vowel patterns are beyond their grasp. Workbook exercises reinforce the pattern. The core selection, *The Kite* by Alma Flor Ada, also provides practice with the pattern. Listening to the core selection would be useful for below-level readers, but taking part in the phonics lesson or attempting the workbook exercises would not be appropriate and, in fact, could undermine the confidence of the below-level readers, as noted in Chapter 4. What's the solution?

Above all, struggling readers need materials and instruction on their level. The "trickle-down" approach does not meet the needs of these readers. They need decoding instruction and selections that reinforce the decoding skills they have been taught. The teacher might use texts and activities from the program that are on these students' level. For example, first-grade struggling readers might be placed in theme 2 (out of ten themes covered in a year's time) rather than theme 5, which is where the achieving readers are working. Second-graders who are below level might work in first-grade readers, perhaps starting with theme 6 or 7, depending upon their reading level and the skills they have mastered. Using lower-level materials that match struggling readers' reading levels is generally the best solution, since it allows them to develop the skills needed to make progress in the program and provides coordination between the skills taught, the practice activities, and the key selections being read.

Another solution is to use the resources provided in the basal reading program. All basals include below-level books and phonics readers created for the series, as well as a listing of below-level trade books. These materials can be used with struggling readers, as long as they match those students' reading levels. Although these materials can provide much needed practice and application, they are not accompanied by essential decoding instruction. You will need to supply this.

A third solution is to use an intervention program. Most basal programs include an intervention program, or you can obtain a stand-alone program. Of course, you can combine these solutions. A good combination is to use the lower-level reader or anthology of the basal program that matches struggling readers' needs and an intervention program that provides added instruction and practice so that the struggling readers can catch up.

Adapting Basals

Despite the criticisms voiced here and elsewhere, there is nothing intrinsically wrong with basals. Over the years, thousands of teachers have successfully used basals to teach millions of children. However, in keeping with today's research and promising practices, basals should be adapted in the following ways.

Although basal manuals have been criticized as being too didactic (Goodman, 1994a), the fault may be with the professionals who use them. Manuals and, in fact, the entire basal program should be viewed as a resource. The manual is a treasure chest of ideas, and the anthologies are good, representative collections of children's literature. As professionals, we should feel free to use those selections that seem appropriate and to use the manual as a resource rather than a guide. Select only those suggestions and activities that seem appropriate and effective.

As a new teacher in a large urban school system, I had the good fortune to work for administrators who encouraged the integration of language arts and the use of themed units but frowned on the use of teacher's manuals and workbooks. In fact, a manual was not available for the basal that I used. Not having a teacher's manual, I planned my own units and my own lessons. In retrospect, I realize that some of my lessons fell flat. However, others worked extremely well. I still recall with pride being asked to present a model lesson for other new teachers at one of our monthly meetings. Good, bad, or indifferent, the lessons were my own, and so I had made a commitment to them. When I planned my lessons, I kept in mind the needs and interests of my students. I especially enjoyed building interest in a story so that they really wanted to read it. And I did not present any stories I disliked or thought the students would not like.

Other adaptations that might be made to make basals more effective include the following:

■ *Emphasize real writing and real reading.* Many of the activities promoted in basals are practice exercises. According to Edelsky (1994), language is learned by using it for some real purpose. Because reading and writing are forms of language, they too should be learned through real use. Thus, for example, students should read directions to find out how to operate a new computer, read a story for pleasure, make a shopping list, or write a letter to a friend. Basal activities in which children write a letter to a storybook character or reread a story to practice reading in phrases or to reinforce new vocabulary words are exercises (Edelsky, 1994). They do not constitute reading and writing for real purposes. Where feasible, students should write letters that get mailed and respond openly to stories and poems. They should also be encouraged to set their own purposes for reading and writing.

■ *Use workbooks judiciously.* Workbooks have both management and instructional roles. Students can work in them independently while the teacher meets with a small group or individual children. Some workbook exercises provide valuable reinforcement. However, as Pincus (2005) comments, "Many workbook tasks are not interesting, do not provide rich instructional possibilities, lack clear objectives, allow false-positive feedback, consume teachers' time in scoring them, and, most importantly, occupy time that can be otherwise spent teaching students what they do not already know" (p. 79). Before using a workbook exercise, ask yourself these questions: Is the exercise worth doing? Does it reinforce a skill in which students need added practice? How should the exercise be completed? Should it be done independently, or does it require instruction? Also make sure that the exercise is on the appropriate level for your students. Especially valuable are workbook exercises that provide additional reading of paragraphs or other text, added experience with vocabulary words, or practice with graphic organizers. If a workbook exercise fails to measure up, it should be skipped. The teacher should provide alternative activities, such as having students read children's books or work in learning centers. Reading builds background and gives students an opportunity to integrate and apply skills. Instead of just practicing for the main event, they are taking part in it. In fact, students get far better practice reading children's books than they do completing

FYI

■ Reading easy books independently provides students with much needed practice. "Clocking up reading mileage on easy materials is one of the most important aspects of independent reading" (Learning Media, 1991, p. 76).

■ As Murray (2006d) notes, today's basal anthologies have high-quality selections and abundant resources. However, they differ in the quality and effectiveness of their lessons and the amount of reinforcement provided. Comprehension strategies—especially strategies as complex as summarizing—require extensive teaching and practice, probably more than a commercial reading program can offer. If you are using a commercial program, you will probably need to supplement it with comprehension instruction.

workbook exercises. Writing, drawing, discussing, and preparing a presentation also provide superior alternatives to workbook exercises.

■ *Emphasize wide reading of a variety of materials.* No matter how well the basal program has been put together, students need to read a broader range of fiction and nonfiction materials, including books, magazines, newspapers, sets of directions, brochures, ads, menus, schedules, and other real-world materials. Make use of the extensive libraries of children's books offered by basal publishers to supplement the basal materials; excellent suggestions for additional reading are also provided in basal manuals.

■ *Focus on a few key skills or strategies.* Teach and use key skills and strategies in context. Today's basal series offer instruction in a wide variety of skills or strategies. In trying to cover so many areas, they typically spread themselves too thin and so fail to present crucial skills in sufficient depth. It may take twenty lessons or more before students are able to draw inferences or identify main ideas, but a basal program might present just two or three lessons on such skills.

■ *Provide opportunities for struggling readers to read appropriate-level material every day.* Make use of the supplementary programs or leveled libraries designed for struggling readers.

■ *Gradually take control of your literacy program.* Decide what your philosophy of teaching literacy is. List the objectives you see as most important, aligning them, of course, with the standards set by your school and school district. If possible, work with other professionals to create a literacy program that makes sense for your situation. Consider basals as only one source of materials and teaching ideas. Basals are neither a method nor an approach to teaching reading. They are simply carefully crafted sets of materials. The core of any reading program is the teacher. It is the teacher who should decide how and when to use basals and whether to choose alternative materials.

Basal readers extend only to grade 6. In grade 7 and beyond, students use literature anthologies or sets of texts that have literary value instead of basal readers. The main difference between basal readers and literature anthologies is the focus on literature. Literature anthologies also place emphasis on appreciation. However, the anthologies often provide some coverage of reading skills. Today's literature anthologies are very comprehensive. They typically feature a mix of contemporary works and classics. A full-length novel may accompany the anthology. The best of these anthologies provide a host of materials that teachers can use to prepare students to read the selections and to extend their appreciation and understanding. Well-designed literature anthologies also feature a program of skill development for struggling readers. In general, literature anthologies have the same advantages and disadvantages as basal series.

Phonic–Linguistic Basals

Several minor basal series, such as *Reading Mastery* (also known as *Distar*) (SRA) and *Merrill Linguistic Readers* (SRA), have been written specifically to reinforce phonic elements or **linguistic patterns**. *Reading Mastery* is a highly scripted program with a strict behaviorist approach, in which teachers use hand signals to prompt responses. However, it has been used successfully with at-risk learners. *Merrill Linguistic Readers* is based on having students contrast word patterns and does not use phonics or sound-

USING TECHNOLOGY

The National Institute for Direct Instruction provides more information on the theory behind Reading Mastery, which is a Direct Instruction program.
http://nifdi.org

■ **Linguistic patterns** are regularities in the spelling of English words. A linguistic patterns approach presents patterns by comparing and contrasting words that have minimal differences (*pat–pan*) so that students can see how they differ. Although such an approach isn't used by many classroom teachers, it is frequently employed by remedial specialists.

ing out. Programs such as these feature tightly controlled vocabulary and are used primarily with struggling readers. As a result of the tightly controlled vocabulary, the selections are highly contrived and stilted. Because the selections are contrived, it is difficult for students to use context clues.

Minibook Series

A number of beginning-reading programs consist of kits of minibooks of increasing difficulty. The kits ease children into reading and move them from emergent to fluent reading. Books at the emergent stage are designed so that students can enjoy them before they can actually read them. Illustrations help children predict what the text might say. The text itself is brief, often consisting of a single sentence that contains a repetitive phrase. Each page of the book might contain the same repeated phrase. The books are read through shared reading, and eventually students can, with the help of illustrations, read the books on their own. At this point, students are primarily "reading" pictures rather than text. The intent is to emphasize reading for enjoyment and meaning. Of course, students are also picking up concepts about print.

After students have enjoyed a number of books and shown an interest in reading print, text-reading strategies are introduced. Difficulty and length of text are carefully controlled so that students gradually grow into reading. As students gain in skill, they move into more challenging stages. Some of the best-known kits include *Story Box*® (The Wright Group), *Sunshine™ Series* (The Wright Group), and *Rigby Literacy* (Harcourt Achieve). One drawback of these kits is that the texts at the early levels do not adequately reinforce decoding patterns. They are not decodable. A minibook series that provides reinforcement for phonics patterns without resorting to tongue-twisting tales is *Ready Readers* (Modern Curriculum Press). Minibook series enjoy widespread use, especially in grade 1, and are often used as supplements to a basal or other approach. In fact, all of today's basal series have supplementary kits of easy-to-read booklets, which feature decodable texts at the early levels.

Closing the Gap: Providing Better Reinforcement

With the right kind of intervention, it is possible for struggling readers to catch up. In one study of first-graders, struggling readers caught up to average readers in just fifteen weeks (Menon & Hiebert, 2003). The control group had a typical basal. The intervention group was given a series of 150 minibooks that were designed to reinforce the phonics patterns they had been taught but were not written in the sing-song fashion characteristic of some decodable texts. The minibooks were carefully sequenced so that in all instances easier books were presented before more difficult books. The books gradually became more challenging. In addition to reading books that were more carefully sequenced and did a better job of reinforcing patterns that had been taught, the intervention group read a greater variety of words. They read between 500 and 1,000 words a week. The basal group read an average of 250 words. The basal group, which devoted a full week to a selection, reread the same story several times, so they may have read as many words as the intervention group, but they did this by reading the same words over and over again. Reading several books seems to be more effective than reading the same book over and over again.

FYI

Programs such as Breakthrough to Literacy and Lightspan make heavy use of technology. In addition to computerized lessons, Breakthrough to Literacy includes big books, pupil books, and take-home books. Lightspan uses the Internet as well as traditional methods to provide ongoing assessment, professional development, and additional learning activities.

USING TECHNOLOGY

Titlewave offers lists of books to be used in conjunction with popular textbook programs (including basal anthologies), books for guided and leveled reading, and award-winning books.
http://www.flr.follett.com

■ ■ ■   Checkup   ■ ■ ■

1. What is a basal/anthology approach?
2. What are some of the advantages and disadvantages of a basal/anthology approach?
3. How might a basal/anthology approach be adapted?

  ■ ■ ■

■ Literature-Based Approach

More and more teachers are using literature as the core of their programs. Today's basal anthologies feature high-quality selections drawn from children's literature. Increasingly, basals are including children's books in their entirety as an integral part of the program or as a recommended component. Although there is some overlap between a basal program and a literature-based approach, the term **literature-based approach** is used here to describe a program that uses sets of children's books as a basis for providing instruction in literacy. A major advantage of this approach is that teachers, independently or in committees, choose the books they wish to use with their students; thus, the reading material is tailored to students' interests and needs.

A literature-based program may be organized in a variety of ways. Three popular models are core literature, text sets, and thematic units.

Core Literature

Core literature is literature that has been selected for a careful, intensive reading. Core selections are often read by the whole class, but may be read by selected groups. Core literature pieces might include such children's classics as *The Little House* (Burton, 1942) and *Aesop's Fables* or more recent works, such as *Shiloh* (Naylor, 1991) and *Number the Stars* (Lowry, 1989).

In addition to providing students with a rich foundation in the best of children's literature, the use of core selections also builds community (Ford, 1994). It gives students a shared experience, thereby providing the class with common ground for conversations about selections and also a point of reference for comparing and contrasting a number of selections. The use of core literature should help boost the self-esteem of the poorer readers, who are often given less mature or less significant reading material. As Cox and Zarillo (1993) noted, in the core literature model, "no child is denied access to the best of children's literature" (p. 109).

However, there are some obvious problems with the core literature approach. Children have diverse interests and abilities. What is exciting to one child may be boring to another. An easy read for one child may be an overwhelming task for another. Careful selection of core books with universal appeal should take care of the interest factor. It is difficult, for instance, to imagine any child not being intrigued by Wilder's *Little House in the Big Woods* (1932). Selections can also be presented in such a way as to be accessible to all. Suggestions for presenting texts to students of varying abilities can be found in Chapter 12.

Core selections might also be overanalyzed. Move at a lively pace when working with a core book. Do not move so slowly that the book becomes boring—but do not rush through the book so that slower readers cannot keep up. Do allow students to read ahead if they want to. If they finish the text early, they might read related books or books of their own choosing. Also, avoid assigning too many activities. Activities should build reading and writing skills or background knowledge and should deepen or extend students' understanding of the text. In addition, if you do use core books, make sure that students are provided with some opportunities to select books, so that teacher-selected texts are balanced by student-selected ones. Also provide for individual differences in reading ability. If core

FOSTERING ENGAGEMENT

Provide students with choices in their reading. They might choose from a selection of three to five novels, for instance.

■ The **literature-based approach** is a way of teaching reading by using literary selections as the primary instructional materials.

■ **Core literature** is literature selected to be read and analyzed by a group or an en-

tire class. In a core literature approach, students read the same book.

■ A **text set** is a group of related books. Because the books are related, reading and comparing them deepen readers' understanding of the unifying theme or topic.

■ A **unit** is a way of organizing instruction around a central idea, topic, or focus.

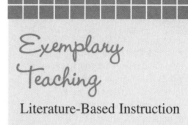

Exemplary Teaching

Literature-Based Instruction

oming to a second-grade classroom composed primarily of poor children, many of whom were reading on a beginning reading level, researcher James Baumann set up a balanced literature-based program that was based on three principles: reading of high-quality children's books, explicit instruction in skills and strategies, and engaging in a significant amount of reading and writing each day.

The program was implemented through a series of routines that included reading aloud to students; intensive instruction in skills and strategies; providing students opportunities to read and discuss high-quality literature selections; providing time for self-selected, independent reading; and conducting writer's workshops. In addition, Baumann related reading and writing, used a variety of grouping patterns so that individual needs were met, and conducted a study buddies program with the fifth-grade class next door. In the study buddies program, half of Baumann's class went next door to meet their study buddies. The other half stayed where they were, and the study buddies came to them. During the thirty-minute sessions, the second-graders worked on reading and writing with the help of their study buddies.

Baumann made use of a wide variety of techniques, including reading aloud, shared reading, choral reading, direct instruction, functional phonics lessons, and guided reading. Although explicit instruction was stressed, it was conducted within the context of real reading or writing. Baumann used an 80–20 rule, which meant that 80 percent of the time was spent reading and 20 percent was spent in skills/strategy instruction.

Working closely with parents, Baumann kept them informed about their children's progress and the work the class was doing. In notes sent home and in formal and informal conferences, parents were given suggestions for supporting their children's work. To foster reading at home, Baumann invited the children to take turns taking home Read-With-Lion or Molly, the Read-With-Me Monkey. Both stuffed animals had a pocket to hold a book and a parent card describing techniques that the parents might use to share the book with the child.

Assessment was conducted through observation, interviews, and examination of samples of the children's work. An abbreviated informal reading inventory was also administered. Inventory results showed that the children gained an average of two years. More importantly, they became avid readers. As Baumann commented, "They read up a storm" (Baumann & Duffy, 1997; Baumann & Ivey, 1997).

books are too difficult for some students, provide additional assistance, or, if necessary, read the books to them or obtain audiotapes of the texts. If audiotapes are available for all to use, there will be no stigma attached to using them. However, make sure that low-achieving readers have ample opportunity to read books on their level. This may entail scheduling sessions in which books on their level are introduced and discussed.

Text Sets

Text sets are groups of related books. Reading text sets fosters the making of connections. When students can make connections, their reading of all related texts is enriched (Harste, Short, & Burke, 1988). In addition to deepening readers' background, text sets broaden readers' framework for thinking about literature. Having read two or more related books, they can compare and contrast them. Discussions are also enlivened because students have more to talk about. If students read books on the same topic, understanding can be developed in greater depth.

Thematic Units

Another model of literature-based instruction is the **unit**, which has a theme or other unifying element. Its unifying element may be the study of a particular author, a genre—mystery or picture books, for example—or a theme. Possible themes include such diverse

Closing the Gap

Because they delve into a topic in depth and repeat the same key words, thematic units are recommended for building the background and vocabulary of struggling readers and ELLs.

FYI

■ For a unit on trees, the major ideas that teacher Elaine Weiner wanted to emphasize were "We cannot live on earth without trees" and "Trees provide shade, beauty, paper, homes for animals, and more" (Routman, 1991, p. 278).

■ As you plan a unit, focus on the theme rather than on activities. Given the unit's theme and major concepts, ask: "What activities will best help students acquire an understanding of the unit's theme and major concepts?" (Lipson, Valencia, Wixson, & Peters, 1993).

■ Core books, a text set, or books chosen by a literature discussion group could also be the focus of a unit. The unit would then consist of reading the books and completing related activities.

topics as heroes, distant places, sports and hobbies, animals, teddy bears, friendship, plants, or the Westward Movement. A unit's theme may involve only the language arts, or it may cut across the curriculum and include social studies, science, math, and the visual and performing arts.

Thematic organization has a number of advantages, the principal one being that it helps students make connections among reading, writing, listening, speaking, and viewing activities and among different pieces of literature. If the language arts are integrated with other subjects, even broader and more numerous connections can be constructed. However, Routman (1991) cautioned that before the language arts are integrated with content-area subjects, they should first be integrated with each other.

Routman (1991) also warned that some thematic units lack depth and "are nothing more than suggested activities clustered around a central focus or topic" (p. 277). In her judgment, this is correlation rather than integration. In order for true integration to occur, the unit must develop some overall concepts or understandings, and activities must be designed to support those concepts or understandings. For instance, a unit may revolve around famous people, with students reading and writing about such people, but the unit is not truly integrated unless the reading and related activities developed a genuine theme or core idea. "Famous people" is a topic rather than a theme because it does not express a unifying idea. A unifying idea for a unit might be expressed as "Successful people have had to overcome obstacles on their way to success" or "Successful people have many characteristics in common." An excellent way to integrate such a unit is to create broad questions to be answered by students: "What are the secrets of success?" or "What are successful people like?" Ideally, these are questions that students have had a hand in creating. As part of the unit's activities, students read about successful people, then interview and write about them in order to integrate information from the unit and answer broad questions. They might also look at successful people in science, social studies, and the arts.

A suggested procedure for creating and implementing a thematic unit follows:

1. *Select a topic or theme that you wish to explore.* When deciding upon a theme, select one that encompasses concepts that are an important part of the curriculum and that will facilitate the development of essential language arts goals. The theme should be significant and interesting to students. A unit called "Westward Wagons" was planned by the fifth-grade teacher, the librarian, and the reading consultant in an elementary school in North Scituate, Rhode Island (DiLuglio, Eaton, & de Tarnowsky, 1988). This unit on the Westward Movement is appropriate for fifth-graders because it has a topic typically presented in that grade and it lends itself to a wide variety of language arts, science, social studies, and art activities.

2. *Involve students in the planning.* Determine through a modified KWL or similar technique what they know about the topic and what they would like to learn.

3. *State the overall ideas that you wish the unit to emphasize.* Include questions that your students might have about the topic (Routman, 1991). The teachers who created "Westward Wagons" decided on four overall ideas: reasons for moving west, problems encountered during the move, transportation in the west, and life in a frontier settlement. Also, compose a list of language arts objectives. What literary appreciations and comprehension, study, and writing or other skills and strategies will the unit develop? These objectives should tie in with the unit's overall ideas. They should help students understand the nature of the Westward Movement. Included in the list of skill/strategy objectives are reading skills, such as summarizing, and writing skills, such as report writing, that students need in order to investigate the Westward Movement. Because the unit is interdisciplinary, objectives are listed for each content area.

4. *Decide on the reading materials and activities that will be included in the unit.* You may wish to focus on a core book that will become the center of the unit. Using a semantic map or web, show how you might integrate each of the language arts. Show, too, how you might integrate science, social studies, and other areas. Each activity should advance the theme of the unit. Activities should also promote skill/strategy development in the language arts and other areas. For instance, in the "Westward Wagons" unit, students simulated a journey west. As part of the simulation, they wrote journal entries and tracked their progress on a map.

5. *List and gather resources, including materials to be read, centers to be set up, audiovisual aids, and guest speakers or resource personnel.* Be sure to work closely with school and town librarians if students will be doing outside reading or research. The "Westward Wagons" unit listed *Sarah, Plain and Tall* (MacLachlan, 1985), *Caddie Woodlawn* (Brink, 1935), *A Gathering of Days* (Blos, 1979), and other high-quality selections. These texts varied in difficulty level from grade 3 to grade 7, so all the students might have materials on an appropriate level of difficulty.

6. *Plan a unit opener that will set the stage for the unit.* A unit opener might involve showing a film or video, reading a poem or the first chapter of the core book, or staging a simulation. The opener might involve brainstorming with students to decide which aspect of the topic they would like to explore. For the "Westward Wagons" unit, students were asked to imagine how it might feel if they were making a long, dangerous trip across the country.

7. *Evaluate.* Evaluation should be broad-based and keyed to the objectives that you have set for your students or that they have set for themselves in collaboration with you. It should include the unit's major concepts or ideas as well as skills and strategies that were emphasized. For example, if the ability to visualize was emphasized, it needs to be assessed. If you emphasized the ability to take notes or to write journals, that might be assessed through holistic evaluation of students' written pieces. As part of the evaluation, you must decide whether students learned the concepts and skills or strategies listed in the objectives. If not, reteaching is in order. In addition, you should evaluate the unit itself and

Case Study

Implementing a Thematic Approach

In a multi-year project with struggling readers and writers in grades 6 through 8, teachers in Memphis, Tennessee, implemented a thematic approach that involved cooperating across subject-matter boundaries. The idea behind the project was to "move curriculum from an unlinked catalog of texts, collection of superficially related works, or sequential or chronological structure to a more integrated whole of episodes echoing one another in support of ongoing curricular conversations" (Athanases, 2003, p. 110). In other words, teachers structured activities so as to make connections among key ideas to give students a broader perspective on major concepts and a deeper understanding of them. Ideas introduced in language arts class were reinforced and expanded in history and science classes. While the theme of community was being developed through reading literary works, the science teacher further developed the theme by exploring one of the theme's big ideas: interdependence. Family history was linked to science themes of nature versus nurture. Subthemes of discovery, motivation, and curiosity were developed through historical biographies of exploration and scientific experimentation.

As students were studying community, a tornado ripped through Memphis, causing enormous damage but also providing numerous opportunities for people of all economic, racial, and ethnic groups to come together and help each other out. Having studied interdependence in their community unit, students were able to arrive at a deeper understanding of what was happening in their city and do a better job writing about it.

At the outset, students' concepts of community were simplistic and tended to be limited to concepts of neighborhood. By year's end, students' concepts of community had grown considerably in breadth and depth. They were able to use analogies and metaphors in their discussions of community. They were also able to draw from the literature they had read. As their teacher commented:

That was exciting to me to see that all of a sudden literature wasn't just born in books that sit on the shelf. It was "literature and my life." There is some connection there and I think the themes do that. . . .
(Athanases, 2003, p. 116)

determine what might be done to improve it. You might eliminate activities or materials that proved boring or ineffective and revise other elements as necessary.

Self-Selection

Reading a chapter book, novel, or full-length biography is a major commitment of time. Students will be more willing to put forth the necessary effort if they enjoy the book and have some say in its selection. Even when working with groups, it is possible to allow some self-selection. Obtain several copies of a number of appropriate books. Give a brief overview of each, and have students list them in order of preference. Group students by their preferences into literature discussion groups or similar groups (see the discussion of literature discussion groups in Chapter 9). You can even allow some self-selection when using a core literature approach with the entire class. Give the students a choice of two or three core books from which to select. If it is necessary for the entire class to read a particular book, plan some activities in which students can select their own reading materials. You might also alternate teacher selection with self-selection: After teaching a unit that revolves around a teacher-selected book, plan a unit in which students select books.

Choosing Materials

One of the most important tasks in structuring a literature-based program is choosing the books. If the program is to be schoolwide or districtwide, teachers at each grade level should meet and decide which books might be offered at that level. Quality and appeal of the materials must be considered. Teachers also have to think about students' reading abilities, with easy, average, and challenging books provided for each grade. All genres should be included: novels, short stories, poems, plays, myths, and well-written informational books. And, of course, as noted above, students should have a voice in the selection of books to be read.

A wealth of children's books exists. More than 4,000 children's books are published each year (Homa, 2000). The latest edition of *Children's Books in Print* (2006) lists more than 385,000 titles. In addition, thousands of high-quality books have gone out of print but can be found in school and public libraries across the country or from Internet bookstores. It is almost too much of a good thing. How does a busy teacher keep up with the latest and the best in children's books? The following journals regularly provide information about children's books:

Book Links: Connecting Books, Libraries, and Classrooms. Published bimonthly. Features book reviews, discussions, and teaching suggestions.

Booklist. Published biweekly by the American Library Association. Includes reviews of books and other media on all levels.

Bulletin of the Center for Children's Books. Published monthly except August. Reviews children's books.

The Horn Book. Published six times a year. Includes articles about authors and illustrators, together with reviews.

Journal of Adolescent and Adult Literacy. Published monthly during the school year. Features articles on literacy and reviews of books for teens.

Language Arts. Published monthly during the school year. Features articles about teaching language arts in elementary school. Regularly reviews children's books.

The Reading Teacher. Published monthly during the school year. Features articles on teaching reading and reviews of children's books.

> ■ A **literature guide** is a teaching aid that may include questions and activities for a text and background information.

School Library Journal. Issued monthly except June and July. Reviews more than a hundred children's books in each issue.

Other sources of information about children's books include the following:

Gunning, T. (2000). *Best books for building literacy in the elementary school.* Boston: Allyn & Bacon. Features an annotated list of more than 1,000 books for grades 1 through 6.

Carol Hurst's Children's Literature Site at http://www.carolhurst.com. Provides reviews of children's books and links to related sites.

Lima, C. W. (2006). *A to zoo: Subject access to children's picture books* (7th ed.). Westport, CT: Libraries Unlimited. Categorizes thousands of picture books by subject, author, and title.

Freeman, E. B., Martinez, M., Yokota, J., & Temple, C. A. (2006). *Children's books in children's hands: An introduction to their literature* (3rd ed.). Boston: Allyn & Bacon. Provides descriptions of numerous literary works.

Kathy Schrock's Guide for Educators—Literature and Language Arts at http://school.discovery.com/schrockguide/arts/artlit.html. Features a number of links to high-quality literature sites.

Titlewave at http://www.flr.follett.com. Provides extensive information about a vast number of books and other media.

Literature Guides

One advantage of using basal or literature anthologies is that lessons and extension activities have already been planned. When teachers use children's books, they must obtain or create their own lessons. Commercially prepared **literature guides** are available from a number of publishers and range in size from a few pages to a small booklet. Apart from length, literary guides should be examined from the perspectives of format, assumptions about reading instruction, and usability (Helper, 1989). Buying a guide could mean buying into the author's philosophy of teaching literature and view of the relationship between reader and text. A key issue in selecting guides is therefore whether questions and activities foster students' construction of meaning and response or lean toward a single interpretation, with the teacher (or the guide) being the ultimate authority. The best guides, of course, are the ones teachers create themselves. The classroom teacher is in the best position to decide which approaches and activities are right for her or his students.

FYI

Inviting Children's Responses to Literature (McClure & Kristo, 1994) presents brief guides for fifty-seven notable books.

Advantages and Disadvantages of a Literature-Based Approach

The primary advantage of a literature-based approach is that books can be chosen to meet students' needs and interests. The major disadvantage of a literature-based program is that fine literature may be misused, by being made simply a means for developing reading skills rather than a basis for fostering personal response and an aesthetic sense. A second major disadvantage is that the books chosen may not be equally appealing to all students and may in some cases be too difficult for struggling readers.

Adapting a Literature-Based Approach

In a literature-based approach, selections can be read in one of three ways: whole-class, small-group, or individually. Whole-class reading creates a sense of community and builds a common background of knowledge but neglects individual differences in reading ability and interest. Working in small groups does not build a sense of larger commu-

In a literature-based approach, students read whole books by well-known authors.

USING TECHNOLOGY

Children's Publishers on the Internet lists a variety of sites maintained by publishers of children's books. Some of the sites include free teaching guides and other instructional resources. http://www.acs.ucalgary.ca/~dkbrown/publish.html

nity but can better provide for individual differences. Individualized reading, which is described in the next section, provides for individual differences and fosters self-selection but may be inefficient. If you do use whole-class reading, use it on a limited basis and complement it with small groups or an individualized approach and self-selection.

■ ■ ■ **Checkup** ■ ■ ■

1. What are the main features of a literature-based approach?
2. What are some of the advantages and disadvantages of a literature-based approach?
3. How might a literature-based approach be adapted?

■ ■ ■

■ Individualized Reading/Reading Workshop

The **individualized reading** approach is designed to create readers who can and do read. Each child chooses her or his own reading material and has periodic conferences with the teacher to discuss it. The most popular form of individualized reading is known as **reading workshop**. Reading workshop is similar to writing workshop, but the focus is on reading. Reading workshop has three major components: preparation time, self-selected reading and responding, and student sharing (Atwell, 1987; Cooper, 1997; Reutzel and Cooter, 1991).

Preparation Time

Reading workshop begins with preparation time, which includes a state-of-the-class conference and a minilesson. The state-of-the-class conference is a housekeeping procedure and can be as brief as a minute or two. During this time, the schedule for the workshop is set, and students note what they will be doing. In the minilesson, the teacher presents a skill or strategy lesson based on a need evidenced by the whole class. It could be a lesson on making inferences, predicting, using context clues, deciphering multisyllabic words, or interpreting metaphors. Or it could be a lesson on selecting a book, finding more time to read, or how to share a book with a partner (Calkins, 2001). The minilesson might be drawn from the basal series or a literature guide or might be created by the teacher (Cooper, 1997). It should be presented within the framework of a story or article that students have read or listened to, and it should be applicable to the reading that they will do that day. The minilesson should last approximately ten minutes, but could be longer.

Although brief, minilessons should be memorable and effective. Calkins (2001) has found a five-part format to be effective. The parts are connection, teaching, active involvement, link, and follow-up. The connection explains why a particular strategy or topic was chosen. For instance, the teacher might say, "When I'm reading a book about a new topic, I use the pictures to help me. Yesterday, I was reading about robots. I don't know much about robots, but the illustrations really helped." The teaching is the actual instruction. The teacher shows specifically how the illustrations and diagrams added to his or her

FYI

■ Pinnell and Fountas (2002) recommend that guided reading be a part of reading workshop for students in grades three and beyond.

■ Minilessons may not allow sufficient time for instruction in complex skills. When introducing a skill, especially a complex one, you may need to extend the lesson. A shorter lesson might suffice when you are reviewing a skill.

■ Literature discussion groups can be a part of a reading workshop.

■ **Individualized reading** is a system of teaching reading in which students select their own reading material, read at their own pace, and are instructed in individual conferences and whole-class or small-group lessons.

■ **Reading workshop** is a form of individualized reading in which students choose their own books and have individual or group conferences but may meet in groups to discuss books or work on projects. There may also be whole-class or small-group lessons.

understanding of robots and clarified some ideas that weren't clear. In the active involvement part of the minilesson, students try out the strategy or a portion of it for at least a few minutes. For example, the teacher gives students a handout that describes several unusual animals but contains no illustrations. The teacher then gives students the same handout with illustrations. The students briefly discuss how the second handout helped them better understand the selection. The link part connects the strategy with a story that the students are about to read. If students are reading informational books of their own choosing, the teacher could suggest that they use the illustrations to help them better understand the topics they are reading about. In the follow-up, students are asked to tell or demonstrate how they applied the strategy. The teacher asks students to tell how illustrations helped them better understand what they read.

Self-Selected Reading and Responding

At the heart of the reading workshop is the time when students read self-selected books, respond to their reading, or engage in group or individual conferences. Self-selected reading may last approximately thirty minutes; if time is available, this period can be extended. If children have difficulty reading alone for that period of time, a portion of the period might be set aside for reading with a partner or in a small group. Because students will be reading their self-selected books independently, they should be encouraged to use appropriate strategies. Before reading, they should survey, predict, and set a purpose for reading. As they read, they should use summarizing, inferencing, and imaging strategies—if appropriate—and should monitor for meaning. As they read, students can use sticky notes to indicate a difficult word or puzzling passage. Or, as suggested by Atwell (1987), they can record difficult words and the page numbers of puzzling passages on a bookmark. A full bookmark could be a sign that a book is too difficult. After reading, students should evaluate their original prediction and judge whether they can retell the selection and relate it to their own experiences.

Response time may last from fifteen to thirty minutes or longer. During response time, students may meet in a literature discussion group to discuss their reading, write in their journals, work on an extension activity, plan a reader's theater or other type of presentation, work at one of the classroom's centers, continue to read, or attend a conference. During response time, hold individual and/or group conferences. If time allows, circulate around the room, giving help and guidance as needed. Visiting literature discussion groups should be a priority.

Conferences

Just as for writing workshop, conferences are a key part of reading workshop. Both individual and group conferences are recommended, each having distinct advantages.

Individual Conferences. Although time-consuming, the individual conference allows each student to have the teacher's full attention and direct guidance and instruction for at least a brief period. It builds a warm relationship between teacher and student and provides the teacher with valuable insights into the needs of each child. While individual conferences are being held, other students are engaged in silent reading. No interruption of the conference is allowed, and those involved in silent reading are not to be disturbed.

An individual conference begins with some questions designed to put the student at ease and to get a general sense of the student's understanding of the book. Through questioning, the teacher also attempts to elicit the child's personal response to the text and encourages the child to relate the text to her or his own life. The teacher poses questions to clear up difficulties and to build comprehension—and concepts, if necessary—and reviews difficult vocabulary. If the teacher has taught a particular skill or strategy, such as analyzing characters, using context clues, or making personal connections, that might be the focus of a conference. In addition, the teacher assesses how well the student understood the book, whether she or he enjoyed it, and whether she or he is able to apply the

FYI

Instead of filling out a response sheet (or in addition to doing so), students might use sticky notes to mark interesting or puzzling passages, difficult words, or other items they would like to talk about in a conference.

strategies and skills that have been taught. The teacher notes any needs the student has and may provide spontaneous instruction or give help later.

To prepare for individual conferences, students choose a favorite part of the book to read to the teacher and also give a personal assessment of the book, telling why they did or did not like it or what they learned from it. Students also bring words, ideas, or items they want clarified or questions that they have about the text. In addition, students may be asked to complete a generic response sheet or a specific response sheet geared to the book they have read. Figures 10.1 and 10.2 present generic response forms designed to elicit a personal response from students. To avoid having students do an excessive amount of writing, you might focus on just a few of the personal response questions, or have students respond to the questions orally rather than in writing.

■■■ **FIGURE 10.1**
Response Sheet for Fiction

Name: _____ Date: _____

Title of book: _____ Publisher: _____

Author: _____ Date of publication: _____

Plot

       Problem: _____

       _____

Main happenings: _____

_____

_____

_____

_____

       Climax: _____

_____

       Outcome: _____

Answer any three of the following questions:

1. What did you like best about the book?

    _____

    _____

    _____

2. Is there anything in the book that you would like to change? If so, what? Also tell why you would like to make changes.

    _____

    _____

    _____

3. Is there anything in the book that puzzled you or bothered you?

    _____

    _____

    _____

4. Would you like to be friends with any of the characters in the book? Why or why not?

    _____

    _____

    _____

5. If other students your age asked whether you thought they might like to read this book, what would you tell them?

    _____

    _____

    _____

■■■ FIGURE 10.2
Response Sheet for
Informational Books

Name: _____ Date: _____

Title of book: _____ Publisher: _____

Author: _____ Date of publication: _____

Topic of book: _____

Main things I learned: _____

_____

_____

Most interesting thing I learned: _____

_____

Questions I still have about the topic: _____

_____

Recommendation to others: _____

_____

■■■ FIGURE 10.2
Response Sheet for
Informational Books

Another way that students can prepare for an individual conference is to keep track of their reading in journals. Students note the date, the title and author of the book, and their personal response to the piece, answering questions such as these: How does the selection make me feel? What will I most remember about it? Was there anything in it that bothered me (Gage, 1990)? Did it remind me of a person or event in my life? Do I have any questions about the piece (Parsons, 1990)? For an informational book, students answer such questions as these: What did I learn? Which details did I find most interesting? How might I use the information? What questions do I still have about the topic? Questions should not be so time-consuming or arduous to answer that children avoid reading so that they will not have to answer them. As an alternative, you might have students keep a dialogue journal, as described later in this chapter. Younger children may respond to a book by drawing a picture. Whatever form the response takes, it should be geared to the maturity level of the child and the nature of the text.

Students should keep a record of all books that they read. While helping the teacher keep track of students' reading, such records are also motivational. Students get a sense of accomplishment from seeing their list grow. A simple record such as that in Figure 10.3 is adequate.

FYI

Reading workshop can be time-consuming to plan and implement. Bookshop (Mondo) is a commercial program that includes a wide variety of children's books and other materials and extensive lesson plans. In several research studies, Bookshop has been shown to be an effective intervention program (Crévola & Vineis, 2004).

■■■ FIGURE 10.3
A Reading Log

Name: _____

Title of book: _____

Author: _____

Publisher: _____

Date of publication: _____

Number of pages: _____

Subject: _____

Date started: _____

Date completed: _____

Recommendations to others: _____

_____

_____

ASSESSING FOR LEARNING

After holding a conference, be sure to summarize it. Include date, selection read, and student's reaction to the text: Did the student enjoy it? Is she or he able to respond to it? Is the book too difficult or too easy? Does the student select books wisely? Did you note any needs? If so, how will these be provided for? Will she or he engage in an extension or enrichment activity? Will she or he read another book?

FYI

Teachers might hold conferences during silent reading and during response time.

USING TECHNOLOGY

Field Guides provides suggestions for introducing and discussing children's books in a workshop setting.
http://fieldguides.heinemann.com

BUILDING LANGUAGE

To develop students' use of language, you can ask them to expand on responses. If a student said that he liked *Heads or Tails* (Gantos, 1994) because it was funny, ask him to tell what made it funny or to tell what the funniest part was.

HIGHER-LEVEL LITERACY

Through the use of dialogue journals, you can prompt students to look more deeply at characters and theme and to think more critically about their reading.

Individual conferences can last anywhere from five to ten minutes. At least one individual or group conference should be held for each student each week. However, not every book needs a conference. A student who is reading two or three books a week should decide on one book to talk about. On the other hand, if the student is a slow reader, a conference may be held when she or he is halfway through the book. Conferences should be scheduled. A simple way to do this is to have students who are ready for conferences list their names on the chalkboard. The teacher can then fill in the times for the conferences.

After the conference is over, the teacher should make brief notes in the student's folder, including date, title of book read, assessment of student's understanding and satisfaction with the book, strategies or skills introduced or reinforced, student's present and future needs, and student's future plans. A sample conference report form is presented in Figure 10.4.

Group Conferences.   Group conferences are an efficient use of time and can be used along with or instead of individual conferences. The teacher has the opportunity to work with five or six students rather than just one. Conferences can be held to discuss books by the same author, those with a common theme, or those in the same genre. Group conferences work best when students have read the same book. If several copies of a book are available, they can be given to interested students, who then confer.

A group conference includes three types of questions: an opening question to get the discussion started, following questions to keep the discussion moving, and process questions to "help the children focus on particular elements of the text" (Hornsby, Sukarna, & Parry, 1986, p. 62). Process questions focus on comprehending and appreciating a piece and are similar to those asked in the discussion and rereading portions of a guided reading lesson. They are often related to reading strategies and might ask students to summarize a passage, compare characters, predict events, clarify difficult terms, or locate proof for an inference. Students should also have the opportunity to respond personally to the text. Process and response questions might be interwoven. The teacher should lead the discussion, although students eventually may take on that role. Just as in individual conferences, the teacher evaluates students' performance, notes needs, and plans future activities based on those needs. Along with or instead of a group conference, students might take part in a literature discussion group.

Using Dialogue Journals

If you are working with older students, you might try **dialogue journals** as an alternative or supplement to conferences. After Nancy Atwell (1987) instituted self-selection and time to read in her classroom, her students read an average of thirty-five books. She commented, "Last year's average of thirty-five books per student grew as much from students' power to choose as from the time I made for them to read. I heard again and again from students of every ability that freedom of choice had turned them into readers" (p. 161). Although providing students with time to read and freedom to choose started them reading, Atwell was not satisfied. She realized that response was needed to allow students to reflect on their reading and deepen their understanding and appreciation. Because individual conferences were so brief, they did not lend themselves to an in-depth discussion of the text. To provide the framework for response, Atwell used dialogue journals to initiate an exchange with the students.

▪   A **dialogue journal** is a journal in which the student reacts to or makes observations about reading selections and the teacher responds by writing in the journal.

Name: *Althea S.*   Date: *10/19*

Title: *Owl at Home*   Author: *Arnold Lobel*

Understanding of text and personal response:	*Discussion of Ch. 1 of text: Saw humor in story. Remembered time when furnace broke and apartment was cold but became cozy again.*
Oral reading:	*Fairly smooth. Good interpretation. Some difficulty reading dialogue. 97% accuracy.*
Needs:	*Read <u>behav</u> for <u>behave</u>. Needs to integrate context and phonics.*
Future plans:	*Plans to finish book by end of week. Will join Arnold Lobel Literature Circle and compare <u>Owl</u> books with <u>Frog and Toad</u> books. Will share funniest incident with whole class.*

■ ■ ■ **FIGURE 10.4**
An Individualized Reading Conference Report

Having the opportunity to write about their reading gave students time to reflect and led to deeper insights. The give and take of dialogue journals led them to develop their thoughts and reconsider interpretations. In addition to providing students with an opportunity to respond, dialogue journals yield insight into students' growth as readers. Thus, they offer the teacher a rich source of ideas for teaching lessons. Although, at first, the dialogue was between teacher and individual students, Atwell discovered students passing notes about poems they had read. She extended an invitation for students to dialogue with a partner, and students began exchanging their responses. Because responding to each student's journal on a daily basis could be overwhelming, you might want to have one-fifth of the class turn in their journals each day. That way you respond each day to just a few students, but you see each student's journal once a week.

Student Sharing

During the student-sharing portion of reading workshop, which should last from ten to twenty minutes, students share their reading with the entire class. They might give the highlights of a book they especially enjoyed, read an exciting passage, share a poem, make a recommendation, enact a reader's theater performance, or share in some other way. "Sharing time advertises and promotes the excitement of literacy learning and helps to promote the class as a community of readers" (Cooper, 1997, p. 491). As an alternative to whole-class sharing, the teacher might arrange for small-group sharing with about four students in each group. The teacher can then visit with the groups as a participant or observer (Cooper, 1997).

Organizing the Program

The classroom must be organized carefully. Just as in a library, it should have an inviting browsing area where students can choose books and settle down comfortably to read. Routines should be established for selecting books, keeping track of books circulated, taking part in conferences, and completing independent activities. The nature of the activity should determine the types of rules and routines. Because they are expected to follow these procedures, students should have a role in formulating them. The teacher might describe the situation and have students suggest ways to make it work.

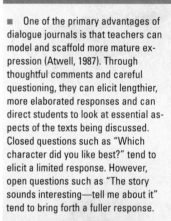

FYI

■ One of the primary advantages of dialogue journals is that teachers can model and scaffold more mature expression (Atwell, 1987). Through thoughtful comments and careful questioning, they can elicit lengthier, more elaborated responses and can direct students to look at essential aspects of the texts being discussed. Closed questions such as "Which character did you like best?" tend to elicit a limited response. However, open questions such as "The story sounds interesting—tell me about it" tend to bring forth a fuller response.

■ An approach that features self-selected reading requires a large collection of materials. As a general rule, there should be at least three times as many books as children in the class, with more books being added over time. School and local libraries might loan a classroom collection, children might bring in books from home, or the community might be asked to contribute. Old basals can be a part of the collection.

■ A main reason that teachers found individualized reading unmanageable in the past was the demand that conferences made on their time. However, with group conferences and the experience gained by holding writing conferences, this should no longer be a major hindrance.

During the sharing portion of reading workshop, students might present favorite books.

The following basic conditions must be met: (1) the teacher must be able to hold individual or group conferences with students without interruptions; (2) students must be able to work on their own without disturbing others; and (3) students must be responsible for choosing books on their own and reading them. Rules and routines might include the following:

■ *Book selection.* The number of students choosing books at one time is limited to five; students may select two books at one time; students may make one exchange. Some students, especially those who are struggling with their reading, may waste a great deal of time choosing books. Instead of having students select books during reading workshop, you might have students gather books from the school or classroom library prior to reading. Younger students might gather four or five books that they intend to read. Older students might gather two or three. These can be kept in book boxes or accordion folders or oversized envelopes along with students' reading logs and conference sheets and any other reading aids, such as a model words chart (Calkins, 2001).

■ *Circulation.* Students are responsible for the books they check out; a card, sign-out sheet, or computerized system is used to keep track of books; students are in charge of the circulation system; books may be taken home.

■ *Conference time.* No one may interrupt the teacher during conferences; students must come prepared to conferences; students (or the teacher) must arrange for periodic conferences.

■ The **language-experience approach** to teaching reading involves students dictating a story based on an experience they have had. The dictated story is written down by a teacher or aide and used to instruct the students in reading. Shared writing and interactive writing are language-experience activities.

Advantages and Disadvantages of Reading Workshop

Self-selection, moving at one's own pace, using group processes, and relating reading and writing are the major advantages of reading workshop. Disadvantages include potential neglect of skills and the possibility that the teacher might spread himself or herself too thin in an attempt to meet with a variety of groups and individuals and respond to students' journal entries. Also, reading workshop might be unsuitable for students who have a difficult time working independently or whose skills are so limited that there are few books they can read on their own.

Adapting Reading Workshop

Reading workshop can be used instead of a basal series or along with one. For instance, you might use a basal three days and reading workshop two days. Or you might use a basal for a part of the day and reading workshop for a portion. Use whole-class instruction as appropriate. For instance, teach book selection and strategies needed by all students to the whole class. Use small-group instruction for those children who evidence a specific need for additional help. Obtain multiple copies of selected titles, just as you might do for a literature-based approach, and periodically invite students to choose one of the titles and read it as part of a small-group guided reading lesson. Use efficient management techniques, and do not overextend yourself. If you use reading workshop with younger students whose writing skills are still rather limited, gradually lead them into the use of dialogue journals. They might begin by drawing pictures in response to selections they read.

■■■ Checkup ■■■

1. What are the main features of reading workshop?
2. What are some of the advantages and disadvantages of reading workshop?
3. How might reading workshop be adapted?

■■■

■ Language-Experience Approach

The **language-experience approach**, introduced in Chapter 3, is very personal. Children's experiences, expressed in their own language and written down by the teacher or an aide, become their reading material. Because both the language and the experience are familiar, this method presents fewer difficulties for children who are learning to read. It also integrates thinking, listening, speaking, reading, and writing. Through discussion, the teacher can lead students to organize and reflect on their experiences. If time order is garbled, the teacher can ask, "What happened first? What happened next?" If details are scant, the teacher can request that the children tell more or can ask open-ended questions, such as "How do you think the dinosaur tracks got there? What do the tracks tell us about dinosaurs?" Through comments that show an interest in the children and the topic, the teacher affirms them and encourages them to elaborate.

Whereas the teacher should affirm, support, encourage, and scaffold, she or he needs to be careful not to take over. The teacher should draw language from the children—not put words in their mouths. When recording students' stories, it is important to write their exact words. Rephrasing what they have dictated shows a lack of acceptance for the language used. In addition, if the story is expressed in words that the child does not normally use, the child may have difficulty reading it. For instance, if the child dictates, "I been over my grandma's house," and the teacher rewords it as "I have been to my grandma's house," the child might stumble over the unfamiliar syntax. As Cunningham and Allington (1999) have observed,

> If language experience is being used with an individual child to help the child understand
> what reading and writing are and that the child can write and read what he or she can say,

Adapting Instruction for Struggling Readers and Writers

Because students select their own books and read at their own pace, individualized reading or reading workshop works extremely well with students reading below grade. No longer are they stigmatized by being put in the low group or forced to read material that is too difficult for them.

FYI

When initiating the language-experience approach, start with group stories so that the class becomes familiar with procedures. As students share experiences and learn about each other, they build a sense of community.

Adapting Instruction for Struggling Readers and Writers

The language-experience approach is most often used in the beginning stages of reading and is usually combined with another approach. However, it can be very useful when working with older students reading on a very low level. Instead of using books that are "babyish," students can read their language-experience stories.

then the child's exact words must be written down. To do anything else will hopelessly confuse the child about the very things you are trying to clarify by using individual language experience. (p. 92)

However, when a group story is being written, the situation is somewhat different. The story and the way it is written reflect the language structures that the group typically uses. To record a nonstandard structure might confuse some members of the group and result in criticism for the child who volunteered the structure. Displaying group stories containing nonstandard structures might also result in protests from parents and administrators (Cunningham & Allington, 1999).

The language-experience approach can be used with individuals or groups. Lesson 10.1 describes the steps for a group activity that extends over three days.

Lesson 10.1

Group Language-Experience Chart

Day 1

Step 1. Building experiential background for the story
The students have an experience that they share as a group and that they can write about. It might be a field trip, the acquisition of a pet for the classroom, the baking of bread, or another experience.

Step 2. Discussing the experience
Students reflect on their experience and talk about it. During the discussion, the teacher helps them organize the experience. In discussing a visit to the circus, the teacher might ask them to tell what they liked best so that they do not get lost in details. If they baked bread, the teacher would pose questions in such a way that the children would list in order the steps involved.

Step 3. Dictating the story
The children dictate the story. The teacher or aide writes it on large lined paper, an overhead transparency, or on the chalkboard or might type it on a computer that has an attachment to magnify the input and project it on a screen. The teacher reads aloud what she or he is writing so that children can see the spoken words being written. The teacher reads each sentence to make sure it is what the child who volunteered the sentence wanted to say. The teacher sweeps her or his hand under the print being read so that students can see where each word begins and ends and that reading is done from left to right. For students just learning to read, each sentence is written on a separate line, when possible.

Step 4. Reviewing the story
After the whole story has been written, the teacher reads it aloud once more. Children listen to see that the story says what they want it to say. They are invited to make changes.

Step 5. Reading of story by teacher and students
The teacher reads the story, running her or his hand under each word as it is read. The children read along with the teacher.

Step 6. Reading of familiar parts by students
Volunteers are asked to read sentences or words that they know. The teacher notes those children who are learning words and phrases and those who are just getting a sense of what reading is all about.

Day 2

Step 1. Rereading of story

The story is reread by the teacher, who points to each word as it is read. The children read along. The story might then be read in unison by the teacher and students. The teacher continues to point to each word. Volunteers might be able to read some familiar words or phrases.

Step 2. Matching of story parts

The teacher has duplicated the story and cut it into strips. The teacher points to a line in the master story, and students find the duplicated strip that matches it. Individual words might also be matched. A volunteer reads the strip, with the teacher helping out as necessary.

For students who can go beyond matching, the teacher plans activities that involve reading, asking questions such as the following: "Which strip tells where we went? Which strip tells what we saw?" Students identify and read the strips. On a still more advanced level, students assemble the strips in correct order. This works best with stories that have no more than four or five sentences.

Individual sentences can also be cut up into words that students assemble into sentences. This can be done as a pocket chart activity. The scrambled words are displayed, and volunteers read each one. Then a volunteer reads the word that should come first, puts it in its place, and reads it once more. A second volunteer reads the word that should come next and places it after the first word. The teacher reads the two words that have been correctly placed or calls on a volunteer to do so. This continues until the sentence has been assembled correctly. Once the entire strip has been assembled, the teacher or a volunteer reads it. The class listens to see whether the sentence has been put together correctly. Once students agree that it has, they read it in unison. This technique works best with short sentences.

Day 3

Step 1. Rereading of story

A copy of the story is distributed to each student. The story is discussed and read in unison.

Step 2. Identification of familiar words

Students underline words that they know. Known words are placed in word banks or otherwise saved for further study and used in other activities (see sections on high-frequency words and phonics in Chapter 4).

FYI

Working with individual words helps both the least able and the most able readers. It helps poor readers see where words begin and end and more advanced readers learn to read words automatically. When words are looked at individually, students note their characteristics, such as which letter comes first and the length of the word.

Personalizing Group Stories

One way to personalize group language-experience stories is to identify the name of each contributor. After a volunteer has supplied a sentence, the teacher writes the student's name and the sentence, as shown in Figure 10.5 (on p. 454). When the story is reread, each student can read the sentence that she or he contributed originally. Seeing their names in print gives students a sense of ownership of the story. It also helps them remember the sentences that they supplied.

An Individual Approach

Individual language-experience stories are similar to group stories, except that they are more personalized. (Figure 3.2 in Chapter 3 is an individual language-experience story about a trip to an apple orchard.) Just as in the group approach, the child dictates a story

FYI

If your students are creating individual language-experience stories, it's helpful to have an aide or volunteers to assist with dictation. First, explain the process to your helpers, and let them observe you until they feel they can undertake it on their own.

■■■ FIGURE 10.5   Personalized Group Language-Experience Story

> OUR PETS
>
> Billy said, "I have a dog.
> My dog's name is Ralph."
> Amy said, "I have a cat.
> My cat's name is Sam."
> Julio said, "My pets are goldfish.
> They don't have names.
> They just swim and swim."

and the teacher, an aide, or a volunteer writes it down and uses it as the basis for teaching reading. Often, an individual language-experience story starts out as a drawing. The child then dictates a story that tells about the drawing. A photo can also be used to illustrate a story or as a stimulus for dictating one.

When dictating a language-experience story, a child may bring up experiences that are highly personal or that reveal private family matters. Affirm the child's feelings, but suggest a more appropriate way for the child to relate the experience: "I'm pleased that you trusted me enough to share that with me, but I think maybe you should tell your mom or dad about it." If the child uses language that is unsuitable for the classroom, have her or him use more appropriate language: "Can you think of another way to say it?" (Tierney, Readence, and Dishner, 1995). Maintaining the child's dignity and self-concept is of primary importance. Handle delicate situations with sensitivity and careful professional judgment.

■■ **Adapting Instruction for English Language Learners**

Because the language-experience approach is based on children's language, it is a very effective technique to use with students who are still learning English.

FYI

■ Because the language-experience approach is based on students' individual backgrounds, it allows each student to share her or his culture, experience, and mode of self-expression. The approach has the power to promote understanding and community among students whose backgrounds may differ.

■ How to handle dialect is a controversial issue. Shuy (1973) made the point that it is developmentally inappropriate to introduce another dialect to a young child. The child will be confused and will not pick up the second dialect. As students grow older, they may choose to use other dialects to be able to communicate more effectively with diverse groups. This does not mean that they will surrender their home dialect.

The Language-Experience Approach and English Language Learners

Because it uses a child's own language and can draw on aspects of the child's culture, the language-experience approach can be especially helpful for ELLs. However, even a bilingual child who has learned enough English to read a little may have difficulty with idiomatic expressions, many syntactical structures, and, of course, some words.

Teachers often wonder whether they should edit an ELL's dictation if it contains unconventional or nonstandard items. As with native speakers of English, the best advice is to accept the child's language and show that it is valued. If the teacher edits it, it becomes the teacher's language, not the child's. This is especially true when children are in the initial stages of learning to read. In general, students' words should be written exactly as they are dictated; however, even if mispronounced, they should be spelled correctly, for example:

Dictation: I happy. My dog do'an be sick.

Written: I happy. My dog don't be sick.

As children's language skills improve, they will have opportunities to develop fuller knowledge of verbs, contractions, and pronunciation. The teacher might work on these patterns at appropriate times or consult with the ESL teacher if the child is taking part in such a program. However, focus at this point should be on introducing reading in English. Because the child is demonstrating a basic grasp of English, waiting for further refinement is an unnecessary delay.

Variant Dialects

Some students may speak a **dialect** that is somewhat different from that typically expected by the school. It is important to accept children's dialects: They will be confused if they say one thing and you write another, and constant correction will turn them off. At this point, children are rapidly acquiring vocabulary and developing their understanding of increasingly complex constructions. The last thing a teacher wants to do is to cut off the flow

---

■ A **dialect** is a variant of a language that may differ somewhat in pronunciation, grammar, and vocabulary.

of language and risk interfering with their development. Introducing a standard dialect and correcting variant English should not be a part of early reading instruction.

The Language-Experience Approach in the Content Areas

Science and social studies topics are often covered in the primary grades without books. Group-experience stories can be used to summarize main concepts or events. After studying mammals, for example, the teacher can discuss the main ideas and have the class dictate an experience story that highlights them. Duplicated copies of the stories can be distributed and collected into a science booklet; students can then illustrate their booklets.

In the intermediate grades, science and social studies textbooks might be too difficult for some students. Discussion projects, filmstrips, and experiments can be used to present the subject matter. Language-experience stories can be used to summarize key topics so that students have a text—their own—to read.

Take a look at the sample experience story in Figure 10.6. It is part of a summary of a section of a sixth-grade science text, *Discovery Works* (Badders et al., 1999). The text was too difficult for one group of students to read on their own, so the teacher read it out loud instead. The group then composed an experience story summarizing the segment. The segment was revised and edited. Once the class had finished editing the selection and the teacher had reread it to them, they discussed it. They discussed what density is and why it could be used to predict whether something would sink or float. To make sure that students could read key words in the selection, the teacher asked them to read sentences orally. They were asked to read the sentence that tells what density is and also the sentence that tells what the density of water is. They also discussed what a gram is and what a milliliter is. To develop word analysis skills, the students worked on the prefix *milli-* and the suffix *-ity* and, later looked at other words that contain these elements.

Copies of the story were printed so that each student would have one. They were placed in binders that contained other summaries, so that students had material to review or to use to study for a test.

Other Uses for the Language-Experience Approach

The language-experience approach does not have to be confined to narratives or summaries of content-area textbooks. Thank-you notes to a visiting author, a letter to a classmate who is hospitalized, an invitation to a guest speaker, recipes, a set of directions for the computer, class rules, charts, lists, captions, diaries, booklets, plays, and similar items are suitable for the language-experience approach. When possible, the pieces should be written for real purposes.

FYI

Group language-experience stories can be used beyond the beginning or early reading level to demonstrate writing techniques. One way of showing students how to write a letter to the editor or a persuasive essay is to have the class compose the item as a group.

■■■ **FIGURE 10.6**
Group Language-Experience Story: Summary of Segment of Science Text

---

Density and Rotten Eggs

Knowing about density can keep you from eating a rotten egg. A fresh egg has a smaller density than a rotten egg. Density is the amount of matter in space. Pick up a piece of wood and a piece of iron that are the same size. The piece of iron is heavier. That is because iron has more matter in the same amount of space than a piece of wood.

Density can tell you whether something will sink or float. If an object has a greater density than water, it will sink. If it has a density that is less than that of water, it will float. Water has a density of 1.0 g/mL. That means it has one gram of matter for each milliliter of space. A fresh egg has a density of about 1.2 g/mL. A rotten egg has a density of about 0.9 g/m. That is why a rotten egg will float. So if you are going to boil an egg for breakfast and it floats, throw it away!

Shared writing is another way in which the language-experience approach might be used. Shared writing is a cooperative venture involving teacher and students. In a regular language-experience story, the teacher records students' exact words. In shared writing, the teacher draws from the children the substance of what they want to say but may rephrase it (Cunningham & Allington, 1999). For instance, at the end of the day, the teacher may ask the students what they learned that day. Summarizing the contributions of many children, the teacher records the day's highlights. In doing so, the teacher is modeling how spoken language is transformed into written language.

Advantages and Disadvantages of the Language-Experience Approach

The language-experience approach is most frequently used as a supplement to other programs and is especially useful with children who are in the beginning stages of learning to read. The major advantage of the approach is that it builds on children's language and experience. A major disadvantage of using it as the sole approach to teaching reading is that the child's reading will be limited to his or her own experiences.

Adapting the Language-Experience Approach

Because it neglects published reading materials and because it limits children's reading experiences, language experience should not be the sole approach to reading instruction. However, it makes an excellent supplement to any of the other approaches presented in this chapter, especially at the emergent and early stages of reading.

■ ■ ■ Checkup ■ ■ ■

1. How might the language-experience approach be implemented?
2. What are some ways in which the language-experience approach might be used?

■ ■ ■

■ Whole Language

Described as a philosophy of learning rather than a teaching approach, **whole language** incorporates a naturalistic, organic view of literacy learning. The basic premise is that children learn to read and write in much the same way as they learn to speak. Oral language is learned by being used for real purposes, not by completing artificial practice exercises that present it piecemeal—work on adjectives today, nouns tomorrow, verbs the day after. Because theorists see reading and writing as a part of a whole, they reason that these skills should be learned in the same way oral language is learned—through use and for real purposes. The basic belief underlying whole language is acquisition of all aspects of language, including reading and writing, "through use not exercise" (Altwerger, Edelsky, & Flores, 1987, p. 149).

Because whole language is not a prescribed program or method, its implementation varies from setting to setting and is expected to evolve and change as more is learned about how literacy is acquired. Basically, whole language embodies the following principles.

First, reading is best learned through actual use. Students learn by reading whole stories, articles, and real-world materials. Because of the richness of these materials, children

FYI

See the discussion of language-experience stories in Chapter 3.

FYI

■ In whole language classes, students take responsibility for their own learning. As Crafton (1991) explains, "When learners of any age initiate their own learning, the intent and purpose of the experience are clear. With self-initiation comes a greater degree of ownership, involvement, and commitment to the activity" (p. 16).

■ Whole-to-part learning, an important element in a holistic approach, is a form of instruction in which students experience the skill or strategy to be learned in the context of a reading or writing selection or other activity, then focus on the skill or strategy, and apply or encounter it in a new reading selection or other context.

■ **Whole language** is a naturalistic theory of literacy learning based on the premise that students learn to read and write by being actively involved in reading and writing for real purposes.

are able to use their sense of language and the three cueing systems of semantics, syntax, and letter–sound relationships to improve in reading.

In a whole language classroom, students read and write for real purposes. There are no letters written to aunts who do not exist, thanking them for gifts that were not sent, just so that students can practice the format of the friendly letter. They write letters to real people for real reasons and mail them. Nor are children given isolated skill exercises such as circling words that contain short *a*. Instead, they read a story that has short-*a* words.

According to the whole language philosophy, literacy is a social undertaking best learned in the context of a group. Therefore, in whole language classrooms, one sees writing workshops, group conferences, peer editing, and other examples of cooperative learning.

USING TECHNOLOGY

NCTE/Whole Language Umbrella provides information about whole language.
http://www.ncte.org/groups/wlu

To join a group discussing whole language, you can sign up with this listserv:
TAWL@Listserv.Arizona.Edu

▪▪▪ Checkup ▪▪▪

1. What are the basic principles of whole language?
2. How might whole language principles be implemented in the approaches discussed?

▪ Guided Reading

Guided reading is a way of organizing reading instruction that uses grouping. In guided reading, students are grouped and instructed according to their level of development (Fountas & Pinnell, 1996, 2001c). The groups meet daily for ten to thirty minutes or more. The teacher may organize as many groups as she believes are necessary, but the more groups assembled, the less time there is for each one. As a practical matter, three or four groups are the most that can be handled efficiently. Grouping, however, is flexible. When appropriate, students are moved into other groups.

What does the rest of the class do while the teacher is working with guided reading groups? Students can engage in a number of independent activities. These activities should provide students with the opportunity to apply and extend their skills. One of the best activities for developing reading skills is, of course, to read. Students can

- read independently in the reading corner,
- read with a buddy,

Case Study

Guided Reading

After whole-group shared reading and writing, students in Pat Loden's first-grade class assemble for guided reading. Loden has four groups of four or five students. Students are grouped according to their levels and needs. While Loden is meeting with a group, other students read independently for twenty minutes. They reread books that were read during guided reading or select new books. A record is kept of books read, and each student responds to at least one book each week. After twenty minutes of silent reading, students engage in journal writing. After completing journal writing, they work in learning centers that focus on Internet pen-pals, science, literacy, poetry, writing, letter and word work, and read-the-room exercises. Each center contains directions for completing the activity. Students also make a note of the work that they complete at a center.

Meanwhile, Loden conducts her guided reading lessons. Each lesson begins with a minilesson designed to teach a skill related to the reading of the day's text. Children read the text silently. While the group reads silently, Loden has each of the children in the group read a passage orally to her. After students finish reading the selection, they discuss it. Loden then signals another group to come to the guided reading table (Morrow & Asbury, 2001).

■ Not all teachers favor learning centers. Having students read independently or meet with a literature discussion group or a cooperative learning group can be more productive than working at learning centers, especially with students in grades 2 and above.

■ Centers should contain puzzles, magnets, word games, magazines, and manipulatives that are appealing to children and allow them to make discoveries on their own. The best centers are those that children would want to work at even if they weren't assigned to do so (Cunningham & Allington, 2003).

Adapting Instruction for Struggling Readers and Writers

Specialists in one elementary school helped teachers plan their learning centers and incorporate activities that would assist struggling learners (Guastello & Lenz, 2005). To check on the effectiveness of the centers, teachers had students take turns reporting what they learned.

- read along with an audiotape or CD-ROM,
- read charts and stories posted around the room,
- meet with a literature discussion group,
- meet with a cooperative learning group,
- work on a piece of writing,
- research a project in the library or on the Internet,
- work on a carefully chosen Web site that fosters literacy, or
- work at one of the classroom learning centers.

Learning Centers

Learning centers can provide practice for skills, provide enrichment, or allow students to explore interests. Many of the reinforcement activities suggested throughout this text can be made into learning centers. For instance, word-analysis centers can be set up that include sorting activities. The nature of the centers should be dictated by learning outcomes. What do you want students to know or be able to do as a result of using the centers? Centers offer an almost infinite number of possibilities. However, most classrooms feature a reading center or book corner in which students choose and read books or periodicals; a listening center in which students listen to taped stories or CD-ROMs; an Internet center in which students engage in Web-related activities; a writing center in which students compose messages, poems, or stories; a word-work center that might feature riddles, word games, or sorting activities; and a drama center that might feature books or scripts and puppets that can be used to dramatize selections or compose scripts. There might also be math, science, art, and social studies centers. For younger students, there might be a pretend play or role-playing center.

Connect the centers to the curriculum. The centers should extend skills and themes students are currently working on. Each center should have an objective. If your curriculum is standards-based, you might want to note the standard that it addresses. This prevents having centers that are fun and interesting but don't really further any educational

■■■■ **FIGURE 10.7**
Two Sample Learning Centers

Adapted from Ford, 1994.

Adapting Instruction for English Language Learners

Center activities should reinforce themes so that concepts are extended and vocabulary is reinforced. This added reinforcement is especially helpful to ELLs.

Type	Objective	Sequence of Activities
Listening post	Building fluency	1. Students listen to a brief taped play. 2. Students read along with the taped play. Each student reads his part. 3. Students listen to the taped play again. 4. Students dramatize the play once more.
CD-ROM center	Building understanding	1. Students examine the title and illustration on the first frame and predict what the story might be about. 2. Students read the story silently. 3. Students discuss the story in light of their predictions. 4. Students take turns reading their favorite part to each other. 5. Students fill out a response form, supplying their name, the title of the story, and a summarizing sentence that tells what the story is about.

objective. Also, have a means for tracking student's performance at the centers. After working at a center, students might record the title of a book and the number of pages they read, or they might produce a piece of writing or note a story that they dramatized. Also, have students discuss with the class the kinds of things they are doing at the centers. This helps keep the work at the centers related to the overall objectives of the classroom. Components of a learning center include title, activities, directions, materials, and assessment. See Figure 10.7 for a description of the activities in two typical centers.

Involve students in the creation of learning centers. Change the content of the centers frequently to keep them interesting. Although the nature of a center might stay the same, change the activities and materials periodically. Assess the centers. Which ones seem most popular? Which ones seem to result in the most learning?

Where possible, provide choices. Students might practice a phonics skill by reading a selection along with a CD-ROM, or they might complete a crossword puzzle or a sorting activity. The objective is the same in each case, but the means for getting there varies.

The Internet is an excellent resource for centers. The LiteracyCenter.net, for instance, offers a range of interactive alphabet-recognition, letter-formation, and word-creation activities for students in pre-K and kindergarten. The teacher needs to provide directions for logging on, select activities, and assess students' performance.

At a listening center, students can follow a story in print as they hear it read to them.

USING TECHNOLOGY

Apples for a Teacher offers a host of suggestions for literacy centers:
http://pages.cthome.net/jtburn/teacher.htm

Education Place provides a variety of links that could be used in learning centers. Click on Houghton Mifflin Reading to access links.
http://www.eduplace.com

Managing Learning Centers

To manage the use of learning centers, a magnetic schedule board or pocket chart can be helpful. On the board, list the possible activities, as in Figure 10.8.

Depending on the length of time students will be working independently, they may complete two or three activities. In Figure 10.8, students have each been assigned three activities. Students may be required to complete certain activities, or they might be given choices. Some teachers post a schedule so that students know exactly what they are to do. This allows visits to centers to be staggered so that the centers don't become too crowded.

■■■ **FIGURE 10.8**
Pocket Chart Schedule of Learning Centers

	Wednesday	November 15	
Edna, Ashley, Kayla, Michael, Dylan	ABC	🎧	✏️
Luis, Juan, Alyssa, William	💻	✏️	📖
Jacob, Aaron, Maria, Marisol	🎧	📖	ABC
Rachel, Edith, Latasha, Carlos	📖	💻	🎧
Raymond, Nicole, Michael, Angel	✏️	ABC	💻

Advantages and Disadvantages of Guided Reading

A key advantage of guided reading is that students are instructed on their level and are given the support and instruction they need. The approach works especially well if the grouping is flexible and if students not meeting in groups are provided with worthwhile activities. However, unless carefully planned, learning centers can deteriorate into busywork.

■ ■ ■ Checkup ■ ■ ■

1. What is guided reading?
2. How might guided reading be implemented?

■ ■ ■

USING TECHNOLOGY

The Position Statement of the International Reading Association, "Multiple Methods of Beginning Reading Instruction," discusses in more depth why teachers need to be able to use more than one method to teach reading.

http://www.reading.org/positions/begin_reading.html

Closing the Gap

Reading programs vary in the rate at which they introduce skills, the number of words they introduce, and the amount of practice they provide (Hiebert et al., 2005). If your program does not offer enough practice or introduces skills too rapidly, use supplementary materials or children's books for reinforcement.

■ An Integrated Approach

A large-scale comparison of approaches to teaching reading in the 1960s came up with no clear winner (Bond & Dykstra, 1967, 1997). All of the approaches evaluated were effective in some cases but ineffective in others. The study suggested that the teacher is more important than the method and that a method successful in one situation may not be successful in all. Combinations of approaches were recommended. Adding language experience to a basal program seemed to strengthen the program. A word-attack element also seemed to be an important component, a conclusion that was reached repeatedly in a number of studies and research reviews (Adams, 1990; Anderson, Hiebert, Scott, & Wilkinson, 1985; Chall, 1967, 1983a; Dykstra, 1974; Snow, Burns, & Griffin, 1998).

Another interpretation of the research strongly suggests that what is really most effective is using the best features of all approaches. Draw from holistic literature-based approaches the emphasis on functional–contextual instruction, the use of children's literature, and integration of language arts. From basal programs, adopt some of the structure built into the skills and strategies components. From individualized approaches, take the emphasis on self-selection of students' reading material. From the language-experience approach, adopt the practice of using writing to build and extend literacy skills.

Above all else, use your professional judgment. This book presents a core of essential skills and strategies in word recognition, comprehension, reading in the content areas, and study skills. Use this core of skills as a foundation when implementing your literacy program, regardless of which approach or approaches you use. If a skill or strategy is omitted

IRA Position Statement

on Key Issue

Multiple Methods of Beginning Reading Instruction

Several large-scale studies of reading methods have shown that no one method is better than any other method in all settings and situations (International Reading Association, 1998a). For every method studied, some children learned to read very well while others had great difficulty. Perhaps the most important reason for a search for the best method is that there are a significant number of children who do not read as well as they must to function in a society that has increasing demands for literacy. Reading is not being taught as well as it should be. "Because there is no clearly documented best way to teach beginning reading, professionals who are closest to the children must be the ones to make the decisions about what reading methods to use, and they must have the flexibility to modify those methods when they determine that particular children are not learning" (International Reading Association, 1999a, p. 5).

or neglected in one approach, then add it or strengthen it. For instance, not all basals recommend the use of pronounceable word parts or analogy strategies. If you are using a basal and these elements are missing, add them.

■ ■ ■ Checkup ■ ■ ■

> **1.** How might you integrate the best features of the approaches discussed in this chapter?
>
>   ■ ■ ■

Building Higher-Level Literacy

Regardless of which approach you use, chances are that it has not made sufficient provision for developing higher-level skills. Higher-level skills take lots of instruction and lots of practice, much more than most commercial programs provide. Supplement the program you are using with additional instruction and practice. Focus on a few key higher-level skills, rather than trying to cover all of them. It is better to teach a few skills in depth than to cover a dozen skills in shallow fashion.

Help for Struggling Readers and Writers

No single one of the approaches discussed in this chapter is necessarily best for struggling readers and writers. A program such as reading workshop that implements self-selected reading would be less likely to stigmatize poor readers, because students would be able to choose materials on their level. A basal program would offer the structure that struggling readers and writers need. However, it would be imperative that poor readers be given materials on the appropriate level of challenge, perhaps in a guided reading format. A literature-based program would work well, too, as long as students were given the skills instruction they needed and books on the appropriate level. The language-experience approach works well with struggling readers because it is based on their language. When obtaining suitable reading material is a problem because the struggling reader is older but is reading on a very low level, language-experience stories can be used as the student's reading material.

    If you are using a basal, take advantage of the materials and techniques suggested for use with students who are struggling. Provide books that the students can handle successfully. Working with students who were struggling with literary selections, Cole (1998) used books from easy-to-read series, including *Step into Reading* (Random House), *Puffin Easy-to-Read* (Penguin), *All Aboard Reading* (Grosset & Dunlap), and *Bank Street Ready to Read* (Bantam). Books from these and other easy-to-read series can be found in Appendix A.

    Regardless of the approach used, it is most helpful if struggling readers and writers are given extra instruction, perhaps in a small group. For younger students, there are a number of programs modeled on Reading Recovery. For students in grades 3 through 8, there is a program known as Project Success (Soar to Success) that features graphic organizers, discussion, and the reading of high-interest informational books. The program can be taught within the classroom by the classroom teacher or by a specialist (Cooper, 1996). Literacy programs for struggling readers are discussed in Chapter 13.

Action Plan

1. Become acquainted with the major approaches to teaching reading.
2. Whatever approach you use, incorporate principles of effective literacy instruction. Make sure that students are reading on their levels, are reading widely, are being taught skills in a functional fashion, and are being monitored for progress.

Tools for the Classroom

3. If students don't learn with one approach, try to find out why this is so and make adjustments. If the approach fails to work despite your best efforts, try another approach. Also, match approaches to students' needs. Most students will learn regardless of what approach you use. But some students will only be successful when certain approaches are used. That is why it is necessary for you to have command of several approaches. If you are mandated to use a particular approach, make modifications so that the program is as effective as it can be.

4. Set up learning centers that are appealing to students, but provide them with opportunities to apply skills independently.

5. Monitor the effectiveness of your program and make adjustments as necessary.

Summary

A number of approaches are used to teach reading. Approaches that use an anthology to teach reading include basal and linguistic. The literature-based approach and reading workshop use children's books, as does whole language, which is more a philosophy than a method. The language-experience approach uses writing to teach reading. Each approach has advantages and disadvantages and may be combined with other approaches and/or adapted to individual teaching goals.

Guided reading can be used along with most approaches to teaching reading. Guided reading is a way of grouping and instructing students according to their needs.

According to research, no single approach to teaching reading yields consistently superior results. A combination is probably best. Teachers should use their professional judgment and know-how to adapt programs to fit the needs of their students. Struggling readers need materials on their level and will benefit from additional instruction.

Extending and Applying

1. Examine your philosophy of teaching literacy. Make a list of your beliefs and your teaching practices. Also, note the approach that best fits in with your philosophy of teaching reading. Do your practices fit in with your beliefs? If not, what might you do to align the two?

2. Examine a current basal series. Look at a particular level and assess the interest of the selections, the kinds of strategies and teaching suggestions presented in the manual, and the usefulness of the workbook exercises. Summarize your findings.

3. Plan a series of language-experience lessons, either for an individual or for a group of students, in which an experience story is written and used to present or reinforce appropriate literacy understandings or skills and strategies. Evaluate the effectiveness of your lessons.

4. Adapt a lesson in a basal reader to fit the needs of a group of students you are teaching. Teach the lesson, and assess its appropriateness. In what ways was the manual a helpful resource? What adaptations did you have to make?

Developing a Professional Portfolio

If possible, videotape the adapted basal reader lesson you taught for item 4 of Extending and Applying. Place the videotape and/or a typed copy of the plan for the lesson in your portfolio. Summarize the plan, and note adaptations you made to the lesson as described in the basal reader manual. Explain why adaptations were made, and reflect on the effectiveness of the lesson.

Go to Allyn & Bacon's MyLabSchool: www.mylabschool.com

- Enter Assignment ID **ENV3** into **Assignment Finder,** and select the video titled "Writing Strategies." In this adapted version of the language-experience approach, the teacher emphasizes writing skills but is also developing reading skills.

- As you watch the video, identify techniques that you might use to teach students who are English language learners. If you were fluent in the children's native language, how might your choice of techniques be different?

- Explore MyLabSchool further to find the course areas for Reading Methods, Language Arts, and Content Area Reading and identify other assets that support concepts introduced in this chapter.

Developing a Resource File

Prepare conference cards or database entries for three children's books that you might use to teach reading. Include bibliographic information, a summary of the selection, a series of questions that you might ask about the book, and a description of some possible extension activities. Keep a list of possible learning centers that you might set up in your classroom.

To access chapter objectives, practice tests, weblinks, and flashcards, go to the companion website at www.ablongman.com/gunning6e.

11 Writing and Reading

For each of the following statements related to the chapter you are about to read, put a check under "Agree" or "Disagree" to show how you feel. Discuss your responses with classmates before you read the chapter.

	Agree	Disagree
1. Reading and writing are two sides of the same coin.	_____	_____
2. New writers should write short pieces to keep their mistakes to a minimum.	_____	_____
3. Students should be allowed to choose their own topics.	_____	_____
4. Completing endings for unfinished stories written by others is good practice for budding fiction writers.	_____	_____
5. The most time-consuming part of the writing process is revising.	_____	_____
6. Teachers should mark all uncorrected errors after a student has edited a piece.	_____	_____
7. Emphasis in a writing program for elementary and middle school students should be on content rather than form.	_____	_____

Writing and reading are related processes that are mutually supportive. Reading improves writing, and vice versa. The last two decades have witnessed a revolution in writing instruction, which today is based on the processes that expert student and professional writers use as they compose pieces.

What is your writing process? What steps do you take before you begin writing? What elements do you consider when you choose a topic? How do you plan your writing? How do you go about revising and editing your writing? How are your reading and writing related? What impact does your reading have on your writing? What impact does writing have on your reading?

■ **The Roots of Writing**

The roots of writing go deep and begin their growth early. Writing evolves from the prespeech gestures children make and from the language they hear and later use, as well as from the developing realization that the spoken word is not the only way to represent reality.

Children discover pictures and words in storybooks that are read aloud to them. They draw pictures of mommy and daddy and their house. They scribble for the fun of it. In time, these scribbles become invested with meaning. Ultimately, children discover that not only can they draw pictures of people and objects but they can also represent people and objects with words. Many children make this crucial discovery about writing before they reach kindergarten; for other kindergartners, the concept is still emerging.

It is important to determine where children are on the writing continuum to know how best to help them. Writing development generally follows the stages listed in Figure 11.1 (on p. 466). However, children can and do move back and forth between stages,

Themes of the Times

Expand your knowledge of the concepts discussed in this chapter by reading current and historical articles from *The New York Times* by visiting the "Themes of the Times" section of the Companion Website.

■■■ **FIGURE 11.1   Developmental Stages/Scoring Guidelines**

Stage 1: The Emerging Writer

- Little or no topic development, organization, and/or detail.
- Little awareness of audience or writing task.
- Errors in surface features prevent the reader from understanding the writer's message.

Stage 2: The Developing Writer

- Topic beginning to be developed. Response contains the beginning of an organization plan.
- Simple word choice and sentence patterns.
- Limited awareness of audience and/or task.
- Errors in surface features interfere with communication.

Stage 3: The Focusing Writer

- Topic clear even though development is incomplete. Plan apparent although ideas are loosely organized.
- Sense of audience and/or task.
- Minimal variety of vocabulary and sentence patterns.
- Errors in surface features interrupt the flow of communication.

Stage 4: The Experimenting Writer

- Topic clear and developed (development may be uneven). Clear plan with beginning, middle, and end (beginning and/or ending may be clumsy).

- Written for an audience.
- Experiments with language and sentence patterns. Word combinations and word choice may be novel.
- Errors in surface features may interrupt the flow of communication.

Stage 5: The Engaging Writer

- Topic well developed. Clear beginning, middle, and end. Organization sustains the writer's purpose.
- Engages the reader.
- Effective use of varied language and sentence patterns.
- Errors in surface features do not interfere with meaning.

Stage 6: The Extending Writer

- Topic fully elaborated with rich details. Organization sustains the writer's purpose and moves the reader through the piece.
- Engages and sustains the reader's interest.
- Creative and novel use of language and effective use of varied sentence patterns.
- Errors in surface features do not interfere with meaning.

From Georgia Department of Education, *Developmental Stages/Scoring Guidelines for Writing*, Atlanta, GA: 2000.

FYI

■ *Units of Study for Primary Writing: A Yearlong Curriculum (K–2)* (Calkins et al., 2003) and *Units of Study for Teaching Writing, Grades 3–5* (Calkins et al., 2006) provide step-by-step suggestions for teaching writing to young writers. Both contain numerous real-life examples.

■ Students in any one class can range from those who are having difficulty composing a basic message to those who are well on their way to becoming proficient writers.

■ Based on the results of the NAEP 2002 writing assessment, students in grades 4 and 8 are writing better than ever (Persky, Daane, & Jin, 2003). However, there is a large gap between students who qualify for free or reduced price lunch and those who don't. There is also a large gap between scores of boys and girls.

and the stages overlap. In addition, a student may be in one stage for narrative writing and another for expository.

Although the description of the stages of writing may not indicate it, all acts of writing are not the same. Writing a poem or essay relies on more complex processes than writing a friendly letter. Processes also develop and change with age and experience. Novice writers use a knowledge-telling process, in which writing is similar to telling a story orally or providing an oral explanation. It requires "no greater amount of planning or goal setting than ordinary conversation" (Bereiter & Scardamalia, 1982, p. 9). Novice writers also use a what-next strategy, in which they write from one sentence to the next without having an overall plan for the whole piece (Dahl & Farnan, 1998). The sentence currently being written provides a springboard for the next sentence.

Gradually, writers acquire a knowledge-transforming ability that allows them to alter their thoughts as they write. As they compose, their writing affects their thinking, and their thinking affects their writing. Instead of merely summarizing thoughts, writers are reconsidering and drawing conclusions, which are reflected in their writing. Thus, as students progress, some of the writing activities provided should go beyond having them merely list or summarize and should ask them to compare, contrast, conclude, and evaluate.

■ The **process approach** is an approach to teaching writing that is based on the way professionals and students actually write.

■ Guided Writing

Just as reading instruction should be geared to the students' level of reading development, writing instruction should be geared to students' level of writing development. Although some skills can be taught to the whole class, students' specific needs can be targeted more directly if students are members of small groups. To estimate where students are in their writing development, examine samples of their writing, using Figure 11.1 as a guide. The teacher meets with one or two groups each day and conducts a writing process or strategy lesson. Grouped by their level of development, students are given instruction geared to their stage. For the emergent writer, the focus of instruction might be on drawing to illustrate a recent field trip and then writing about the drawing. For the experimenting writer, the focus of instruction might be on using examples or details to develop a topic (Davis, Jackson, & Johnson, 2000). As part of guided writing, students need to be taught specific strategies for reading and writing. Teaching students writing strategies has four steps:

1. Identifying a strategy worth teaching.
2. Introducing the strategy by modeling it.
3. Helping students try the strategy out with teacher guidance.
4. Helping students work toward independent mastery of the strategy through repeated practice and reinforcement. (Collins, 1998, p. 65)

To identify a strategy that needs teaching, examine students' writing. You might also discuss their writing with them. Note areas that students are having difficulty with. Choose a strategy such as adding interesting examples that would seem to be of most benefit to them in terms of their level of development. The strategy can be introduced to a whole class, to a guided writing group, or to an individual. After the strategy has been introduced, students should have ample opportunity to apply it. As you work with students, help them adapt the strategy so that it becomes a part of their writing repertoire. Provide opportunities for students to use the strategy in a number of situations so that they attain independent mastery of it. Guided strategic writing is presented within the framework of a process writing approach.

■ ■ ■ Checkup ■ ■ ■

1. How does writing develop?
2. What are the stages of writing?

■ ■ ■

■ The Process Approach to Writing

In the **process approach**, writing instruction is based on writing processes that professional writers and students actually use. The research of Graves (1983), Emig (1971), and others describes a series of steps that reflect how writers write. The steps are prewriting, composing, revising, editing, and publishing. However, these steps are not linear; they are recursive. Writers may engage in prewriting activities after composing and may be revising while composing.

Implicit in the process approach is the role of writing in the writer's life. Each of us is a writer. We have written letters, essays, lists, notes, plans, goals, diary and journal entries, term papers, and stories and poems. Part of teaching the writing process is helping students see the power and importance of writing in their lives. As teachers, we need to set up an environment in which writing has meaning for students and thus they will want to write (Calkins, 1994). This is best done by showing rather than telling. We need to show students the part that writing plays in our lives and encourage them to share the role that writing plays in their lives. We might share how, through writing, we keep in touch with

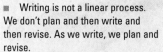

FYI

■ Writing is not a linear process. We don't plan and then write and then revise. As we write, we plan and revise.

■ The process approach to writing needs to be applied flexibly. Writing a friendly letter, for instance, requires a bare minimum of planning and doesn't usually involve revising and editing. A letter to the editor, however, might require very careful planning, revising, and editing.

friends, explore topics of interest, record the everyday events of our lives, or entertain or enlighten others, and invite our students to do the same.

Prewriting

Easily the most important step, prewriting encompasses all necessary preparation for writing, including topic selection, researching the topic, and gathering information.

Topic Selection

Topic selection is the hallmark of the process approach. In the past, students were supplied with topics and story starters. The intent was to help, but the result was writing that was wooden, contrived, and lacking in substance and feeling because the students had no interest in the topics. Letting students choose their own topics is one of the keys to good writing, because there is a greater chance that students will invest more of themselves in a piece that means something to them. When seven-year-olds were allowed to choose their topics, they wrote four times as much as a group of peers who were assigned subjects (Graves, 1975).

Murray (1989) suggested that teaching writing is mainly a matter of helping students discover what they have to say and how to say it. The teacher should model the process of selecting a topic and begin by discussing what he or she has done, seen, or knows that he or she would like to tell others. The teacher then jots down three or four topics on the chalkboard. They might be similar to the following:

I saw a real whale close up.

I saw the tallest building in the world.

I saw the longest baseball game ever played.

As the class listens, the teacher goes through the process of choosing a topic. The teacher rejects the first two because many people have seen whales and the tallest building, but only a handful of fans watched the longest game ever played. Most important, that is the topic that holds the greatest interest for the teacher.

Once the teacher has demonstrated the process, he or she asks the class to **brainstorm** topics and then lists them on the board. This helps others discover subjects of interest. After a discussion, each student lists three or four tentative topics and, later, chooses one to develop. In group discussions and one-on-one conversations or conferences with the teacher, children discover additional topics. With the teacher's questioning as a stimulus, they find subjects in which they have expertise, that they would like to explore, and that they would like to share.

Knowing that they will be writing nearly every day and so must have many subjects to write about, students search for topics continuously. They find them on television, in their reading, in their other classes, in their homes, in writing notebooks, and in outside activities. They can keep lists of topics in their folders or in special notebooks or journals (Calkins, 1994; Calkins & Harwayne, 1991). Students might also keep a list of questions. Questions to be answered are an excellent source of topics. The list could include personal questions, questions about sports or hobbies, or questions about a topic they are studying or an interesting fact that they heard (Spandel, 2001).

Journals are a favorite repository for writers' observations and ideas. In their writing journals, students can list topic ideas, outline observations they have made, or explore

FYI

▪ It isn't necessary for students to have a piece blocked out in their minds before they begin writing. In a way, writing is an exploration. Writers may not be sure what they want to say until they've said it.

▪ Canned topics have been repackaged as writing prompts. Pressured to prepare students for competency tests, teachers require students to write to test-type prompts. While it is important to prepare students for tests, practice should not be excessive. Students' abilities are best developed through a balanced program of writing instruction.

▪ Teachers in the Columbia Writing Project suggest that students record their topic ideas in a small spiral notepad (Calkins et al., 2003). To model the practice, the teacher jots down possible topics in full view of the students as ideas strike her.

▪ **Brainstorming** is a process in which members of a group attempt to accomplish a task by submitting ideas and writing spontaneously.

▪ **Clustering** is a form of brainstorming that involves creating a map of words and associations linked by lines and circles.

ideas. They can also record passages from their reading that were especially memorable or that contained distinctive language. Students might also use their journals to test out writing techniques or experiment with story ideas. Journals keep ideas germinating until they are ready to flower. When students keep writing journals or notebooks, prewriting might consist primarily of selecting an anecdote or question from the notebook to explore or elaborate.

With students, establish guidelines for journals. If you plan to read the journals, make that known to students so that the journals do not become private diaries. Reading students' writing journals has several advantages. It makes the journals part of the writing program and encourages students to make entries. It also provides you with the opportunity to gain insight into students' thoughts about writing and to respond. Students could highlight any items that they would like you to focus on, and they can mark as private or fold over a page containing any item that they do not want you to see. Journals are not graded, and corrections are not made, because doing so will shut off the flow of ideas. However, you should write a response.

One of the shortcomings of journals is that they can, over time, become a diary of mundane events. Encourage students to take a broader look at the world and also to dig beneath the surface. The student's journal entry "I struck out three times in the Little League game" might draw the following responses from the teacher: "What happened because you struck out? How did you feel? Why do you think you struck out? What might you do about it? Could this be the start of a story?" You might also encourage students to write for several days on a topic they care about (Routman, 2000). From time to time, model the process of composing journal entries. Show students how you develop topics or try out new techniques in your journal.

Planning

Research and preparation are also essential parts of prewriting. For older students, preparation might take the form of discussing, brainstorming, creating semantic maps or webs, reading, viewing films or filmstrips, or devising a plot outline or general outline. For younger students, it could be discussing topics or drawing a picture. Drawing is especially useful, as it provides a frame of reference. Drawing also helps older students who have difficulty expressing themselves verbally.

A particularly effective prewriting strategy is to have students brainstorm words that they think they might use to develop their topics. Brainstorming is a free-flowing, spontaneous activity. All ideas should be accepted and recorded but not critiqued. Everyone should contribute. After brainstorming, ideas generated can be discussed, elaborated on, and clarified. Related ideas can also be introduced.

Brainstorming helps students note details to include in their pieces (Bereiter & Scardamalia, 1982). D'Arcy (1989) recommended several different kinds of brainstorming. The simplest form involves writing down names—of birds, famous people, or mystery places, for example. Students jot down the results of their brainstorming rather than simply thinking aloud. This gives them a written record of their associations as well as concrete proof of the power of brainstorming to draw out items. Students then share their lists with partners, which may result in additional items. At this point, students might circle the name of a bird, famous person, or place that they know the most about and brainstorm that item. Later, they brainstorm questions about the item they have chosen: "Where do bald eagles live? What kinds of nests do they have? Are they in danger of becoming extinct? What do they eat? How fast do they fly?" The questions can be the basis for exploring and writing pieces about the topic.

Memories, feelings, images, and scenes can also be brainstormed. For instance, students might go down their lists of items and note the one that aroused the strongest feelings or created the sharpest image. Words to describe the feelings or details that describe the image could be brainstormed and listed.

Clustering and freewriting are versions of brainstorming. **Clustering** is a kind of mapping in which students jot down the associations evoked by a word. Lines and circles are

FYI

Frustrated that a number of her students typically produced brief paragraphs almost totally devoid of detail, J. L. Olson (1987) encouraged them to draw a picture of their subjects. After discussing the drawings with her, the students then wrote. The improvement was dramatic; the resulting pieces were rich in detail. Drawing helped students retrieve details about their subjects.

used to show relationships. In **freewriting**, students write freely for approximately ten minutes on an assigned or self-selected topic, about a real event or an imagined one. The idea is to have children catch the flow of their thoughts and feelings by writing nonstop. Ideas or themes generated can then become the basis for more focused work. In some instances, freewriting might be an end in itself—an exercise that promotes spontaneity in writing.

To help students flesh out their writing and determine what kinds of details they might include, model how you might brainstorm possible questions that the readers of your article might have. For instance, if students plan to write about flying snakes, they might brainstorm questions such as these:

How do the snakes fly?

Where do they live?

Are they poisonous?

How big are they?

What do they eat?

Why do they fly out of trees?

Orally sharing ideas is another form of preparing for writing. Discussing helps students "order their thoughts and generate many more ideas and angles for writing" (Muschla, 1993, p. 37). This technique is especially effective when students work in pairs. After students have generated ideas through brainstorming, clustering, or some other method, have them talk over their ideas with their partners. The listener should summarize what the speaker has said, ask the speaker to clarify any parts that are not clear, and answer questions that the speaker might have, thereby helping the speaker shape and clarify his or her ideas.

Role-playing can be an effective way to draw out ideas (Muschla, 1993). Students can role-play fictional or actual events, including historical events or events that they have personally experienced. Role-playing can also help students elaborate on and clarify what they want to say. For instance, if students are about to write a letter to a classmate who has moved away, they might work in pairs and role-play the writer of the letter and the intended receiver. Students might role-play situations that they intend to write about: persuading the town to fix up the park or requesting that the local health department get rid of rats in the neighborhood. Students might also role-play Washington's crossing of the Delaware, the landing of astronauts on the moon, or other historical occasions. Or they could role-play a Little League coach giving her team a pep talk, the principal confronting two students who have been arguing, or a zookeeper answering questions about the newly acquired giraffe.

Actually beginning to write is another way of getting started. "Writing is generative. The hardest line to write is the first one" (Spandel, 2001, p. 135). Often, after writers get that first sentence down, the ideas begin to flow.

Rehearsing

Experienced writers do a substantial amount of **rehearsing**, or writing in their heads, composing articles, stories, and even parts of books at odd moments during the day or before

---

■ **Freewriting** is a form of writing in which participants write for a brief period of time on an assigned or self-selected topic without prior planning and without stopping. Freewriting can be used as a warm-up activity or a way of freeing up the participant's writing ability. One danger of freewriting is that students might get the mistaken idea that writing is an unplanned, spontaneous activity.

■ **Rehearsing** is that part of the writing process in which the writer thinks over or mentally composes a piece of writing.

■ **Composing** is that part of the writing process in which the writer creates a piece.

going to sleep. Professional writers, if they can avoid it, do not write "cold." They are ready to write down ideas that they have been rehearsing in their minds when they finally sit down at their desks. How important is rehearsal? Donald Murray (1989), Pulitzer Prize–winning journalist, commented, "When the writing goes well, it usually means I have mulled over the idea and the material for quite a long time" (p. 250).

In a way, rehearsing is a way of looking at life. Throughout the day, the writer is aware of episodes or objects that might become a topic for writing or an element in a story. An item in a newspaper or an overheard conversation might trigger a story. A puzzling question might set off an exploration and result in an essay or informational book. Throughout the day, students should be alert to possible sources of writing topics and record these in their journal notebooks.

■ ■ ■ Checkup ■ ■ ■

1. What is the process approach to writing?
2. What steps might the teacher take to foster writing during the prewriting stage of the process approach?

■ ■ ■

Composing

Composing is the act of writing a piece. The idea is for the writer to put her or his thoughts down on paper without concern for neatness, spelling, or mechanics. A writer who is concerned about spelling is taking valuable time away from the more important job of creating. Reassure students that they will have time later to revise and edit. Model how you go about composing a piece. As you compose your piece, explain what is going on in your mind so that students can gain insight into the process.

Experienced writers generally have far more information than they can use, and discard much of it either before or after it is put on the page. However, elementary school students often do not seem to have enough to say. According to Scardamalia and Bereiter (1986), "For young writers finding enough content is frequently a problem and they cannot imagine discarding anything that would fit" (p. 785).

Finding enough to say may be essentially a problem of access (Scardamalia & Bereiter, 1986). Younger students are used to oral conversations in which the responses of the listener act as cues for retrieving knowledge. When the speaker fails to supply enough information, the listener's blank look or questions ferret out more talk:

> Written speech is more abstract than oral speech. . . . It is speech without an interlocutor. This creates a situation completely foreign to the conversation the child is accustomed to. In written speech, those to whom the speech is directed are either absent or out of contact with the writer. Written speech is speech with a white sheet of paper, with an imaginary or conceptualized interlocutor. Still, like oral speech, it is a conversational situation. Written speech requires a dual abstraction from the child. (Vygotsky, 1987, pp. 202–203)

This need to supply the missing listener when writing explains, perhaps, why prewriting activities are so important and why postdrafting conferences are so helpful in evoking a full written response from younger students. Scardamalia, Bereiter, and Goelman (1982) found that just encouraging young writers, who claimed to have written everything they knew, doubled their output. What the children had apparently done was extract their top-level memories, which are the main ideas, the generalities. They had not mined the lower-level memories, the examples, details, and explanations, that give body to the general ideas. With encouragement, they proceeded to do so.

Instruction for novice writers might begin with narrative writing. Narrative writing is easier and more natural for young writers than is expository writing. They are used to hearing and reading stories. Narratives by beginning writers might only be a sentence or two long (New Standards Primary Literacy Committee, 1999). Later, in about grade 2, young writers use a technique known as chaining, in which one event is linked to another but there is no central focus. In one early form of narrative, students write "bed to bed" stories, in which they simply recount the day's happenings. In a dialogue narrative, which is another form of early writing, the story is told through conversations between two people: The boy said, "I am scared." Then the girl said, "Why are you scared?" The boy said, "I am afraid that dog will bite me." Then the girl said, "I don't think that dog will bite you." In an event narrative, a third form of early writing, young writers simply recount one event after another with no attempt to show connections. By about third grade, students are able to write simple narratives that have a central focus.

A number of techniques foster the development of narrative writing. Shared reading can be used to present models of narrative writing. One easy type of writing is to use the structure of a familiar piece but substitute one's own ideas or words. For instance, using the structure of *Brown Bear, Brown Bear, What Do You See?* (Martin, 1983), students might write a story entitled "Gray Owl, Gray Owl, What Do You Spy?"

After students have acquired some experience writing narratives, wordless picture books, such as the *Carl* series, might be used to encourage young students to create a story that goes along with the illustrations. Also, have students use toys, puppets, a felt board, or other props to create a story (Education Department of Western Australia, 1994). This helps them structure their stories.

For older students, cut out a series of pictures and have students sequence the pictures and create a story to accompany the pictures. This could be a whole-class or small-group activity. Students might also create a storyboard. A storyboard is a series of drawings used by creators of ads, TV shows, and movies to show the plot of their work. The storyboard might show the main scenes, actions, or events.

For novice writers, the mechanical production of letters and words may take an extraordinary amount of effort. Place less emphasis on handwriting and mechanics so that students can focus on content and style.

Composing is not a smooth process. If a writer is primed and the ideas flow, he or she may produce page after page of text, in seemingly effortless, almost automatic fashion. Another writer may simply stare at the page for endless moments before finally producing a tortured paragraph. A third writer may write in fits and starts, with an initial burst of writing followed by intense reflection, which is then followed by another burst of writing.

Preparation can help the composing process, but perseverance is required. A writer must be prepared to overcome various obstacles and blocks. By using strategies that experienced writers employ, the writer can avoid certain pitfalls. A key pitfall for elementary school students is believing that the **first draft** is the last draft, which blocks their writing through an overconcern with correctness and neatness. As Calkins (1986) commented,

> By the time many unskilled writers have written three words . . . they already believe they have made an error. . . . They continually interrupt themselves to worry about spelling, to reread, and to fret. This "stuttering in writing" leads to tangled syntax and destroys fluency. (p. 16)

Students need to know that their first writing is just a draft and that the focus should be on getting thoughts down. There is plenty of time for revising and correcting later.

Beginnings are often the most difficult part of a piece to create. If students are blocked by an inability to create an interesting beginning, advise them to write down the best beginning they can think of and then return to it after they have completed their first draft. This same principle applies to other aspects of composing. If students cannot remember a fact, a name, or how to spell a word, they can leave a blank or insert a question mark and come back later. Nothing should interrupt the forward flow of the composing process.

■ A **first draft** is the writer's initial effort and is not intended to be a finished product.

■ **Revising** is that part of the writing process in which the author reconsiders and alters what she or he has written.

Some students freeze at the sight of a blank piece of paper. Discuss some possible opening sentences. If nothing else works, suggest to the students that they just start writing. Their first sentence might simply be a statement that they are having difficulty getting started. As they continue to write, it is very likely that other thoughts will come to them.

Focusing on Audience

Although we make lists or diary entries strictly for ourselves, most of our writing is geared toward an audience. A sense of audience helps shape our writing. As we write, we consider the backgrounds and interests of our readers. We try to think of ways of making our writing appealing as well as informative. Young writers typically lack a sense of audience and may assume that the readers already know whatever the writers know. A first step in writing is to define whom one is writing for. To help young students write for a particular audience, help them ponder the following questions (Learning Media, 1991):

What is my topic?

Why am I writing this piece?

Who will read my piece?

What might they already know about the topic?

What do they need to know?

The answers to these questions should help sharpen students' focus and provide them with a plan for gathering information. As they look over what they need to know and what they want to tell their audience, students can begin collecting information from books, family members, Web sites, computer databases, or experts. They might then use semantic webs or other diagrams to help them organize their information. Again, audience comes into play as students ask themselves, "How can I present this information so that my audience will understand it?" Teacher modeling, minilessons, and conferences with teacher and peers might be used to help students organize their material.

To help students gain a sense of audience, have them share what they have written. Students should focus on communicating with others rather than writing to meet a certain standard of performance or earn a certain grade. As they get feedback, they can clarify confusing details or add examples if that is what their audience seemed to need. The teacher can model sharing by reading pieces she has written and inviting students to respond.

■ ■ ■ Checkup ■ ■ ■

1. How do students' composing processes and the difficulties they face change as they become more experienced writers?
2. What might the teacher do to help students compose more effectively?

■ ■ ■

Revising

For many students, revising means making mechanical corrections—putting in missing periods and capital letters and checking suspicious spellings. Actually, **revising** goes to the heart of the piece and could involve adding or deleting material, changing the sequence, getting a better lead, adding details, or substituting more vivid words for overused expressions. Revising means rethinking a work and can, in fact, lead to a total reworking of the piece. Revision may be aided by a peer conference or a conference with the teacher.

Modeling the Revision Process

One way of conveying the concept of revision is for the teacher to model the process. The teacher puts an original draft that she or he has written on the chalkboard or overhead and poses pertinent questions: "Does this piece say what I want it to say? Have I fully explained what I want to say? Is it clear? Is it interesting? Is it well organized?" The teacher

FYI

If students are using word-processing programs, show them the mechanics of making revisions: how to check spelling, how to replace and delete items, how to use the thesaurus. Demonstrate how they might make major changes by adding ideas or shifting sentences or whole paragraphs around.

can then show how to add details, clarify a confusing passage, or switch sentences around. The teacher might also model some highly productive revising routines. Essential routines include rewriting for clarity, rewriting beginnings and endings to give them more impact, substituting more vivid or more appropriate words, rearranging sentences or paragraphs, and adding additional examples or details.

Another helpful approach is to use samples of published pieces and students' writing to demonstrate effective writing. When working on improving leads, for instance, show students a variety of pieces in which writers have composed especially effective openings. Also, encourage students to note particularly creative leads in their reading. Do the same with endings and middles. Summarize by looking at pieces that do all three well.

To dramatize the power of good leads, share a piece that has an especially good opening, but omit the opening. Instead, have students select from three leads the one they think the author wrote. Do the same with conclusions.

Over a series of lessons, the teacher shows students how to make revisions, focusing on the kinds of writing challenges that students are facing. One group might be grappling with lead sentences, whereas another group might not be fully developing ideas. In time, students can demonstrate to their peers how they successfully revised a piece. Having professional writers such as children's authors and newspaper reporters visit the class to demonstrate how they revise will emphasize the importance of revision and the fact that virtually everyone who writes must do it.

Have students practice by revising someone else's paper. The paper could be one that you have composed for this purpose, one from a published source, or one done by a student in a former class. The author, of course, should be anonymous. Start with papers that obviously need revising but aren't so hopelessly bad that they would overwhelm students. Revise some of the papers as a group exercise. Allow students to add or delete details or examples so that they aren't just rewording the piece. After students have caught on to the idea of revising, have them work in pairs and then individually. When working in pairs, they should discuss the reasons for any changes they made. As they work individually, they revise their own writing. However, after revising a paper, they might then confer with a partner.

▪▪▪ FIGURE 11.2   A Sample Revision Checklist

____ Does the piece say what I want it to say?
____ Will the audience understand it?
____ Is it interesting?
____ What might I do to make it more interesting?
____ Did I give enough details or examples?
____ Does it sound right?

Instruction should also include the mechanical techniques of revision. Students can cross out, cut and paste, and use carets to insert to their hearts' content. Long insertions may be indicated with an asterisk and placed on a separate sheet of paper. Students should be encouraged to revise as much as they feel they have to. To remind students of the kinds of things they should be doing when they revise, you might develop a revision checklist. Figure 11.2 presents a sample checklist.

Students have five areas of concern in writing: spelling, motor aesthetic (handwriting and appearance), conventions, topic information, and revision (Graves, 1983). Although they are thinking about all five areas from the very first stages of writing, early emphasis is on the lower-level processes: spelling, motor aesthetic, and conventions. New writers find it most difficult to revise content. However, what the teacher stresses in class also has an effect on what the child emphasizes. Given good teaching, children will put aside undue concern about spelling, handwriting, and appearance and concentrate on improving content and expression. Spelling, handwriting, and conventions must be taught, but in perspective. Mechanical issues usually recede into the background by the time a child is around seven years old, but if overemphasized, they could "last a lifetime" (Graves, 1983, p. 237). From an early concern with spelling and handwriting, children can be led to add information to their pieces and, later, to make more complex revisions, such as reordering sentences or clarifying confusing points. One of the last revision skills to develop is the ability—and willingness—to delete material that should be left out.

Conferences help children move beyond mechanical revisions. "Revisions that children make as a result of the conference can be at a much higher level than those made when the child is working and reading alone" (Graves, 1983, p. 153). This is an excellent manifestation of Vygotsky's (1987) concept of zone of proximal development, which states that with the support of adults, children can operate on a higher level and, ultimately, perform higher-level tasks on their own. In other words, what students ask for help with now they will be able to do on their own in the future.

As with other cognitive activities, younger students are less likely to monitor their writing. For example, they may fail to consider the background or interests of their intended audience (Maimon & Nodine, 1979). Through skillful questioning in conferences, the teacher can help students see their writing from the point of view of the audience. This helps them figure out what they want to say and how to say it so others will understand. The teacher provides an executive structure to help students revise effectively (Scardamalia & Bereiter, 1986). In time, students internalize such a structure, which allows them to monitor their writing, just as they learn with experience and instruction to monitor their reading.

During the revision process, focus on one element. Revision is more effective when the focus is on just one element at a time—the lead, details, word choices, or concluding sentence (Spandel, 2001).

Tools of Revision

In his publications *After the End* (Lane, 1993) and *The Reviser's Tool Box* (Lane, 1998), Barry Lane proposes the use of five tools for helping students revise the substance of their pieces: Questions, Snapshots, Thoughtshots, Exploding a Moment, and Building a Scene.

Questions.   Listeners jot down any questions they have as the author reads his or her piece. The author answers these questions and then decides whether to include any of the answers in the story. The answer to a key question may result in a substantial expansion of the piece or may help the writer redirect the piece.

Snapshots.   Like a photographer using a camera with a zoom lens, the writer uses details to bring a character or event into focus. This is more than just adding an adjective or two;

Exemplary Teaching

Revising

*W*orking with a class composed primarily of ESL students, Laura Harper (1997) feared that her lessons on revising weren't having much impact. Students' revisions consisted of a few changes here and there and recopying the piece in neater handwriting. She decided to use the revising tools described by Barry Lane (1993) in *After the End*.

After explaining Questions, Harper had pairs of students ask questions about pieces they had written. The students then selected the most appealing questions about their drafts and freewrote on them. As she revised, one student, Elena, rethought her draft and transformed it from a lifeless description of her aunt to a poignant account of her relationship with her aunt.

After discussing Snapshots, students created Snapshots of each other, writing a description of what they saw or drawing a picture. Working in pairs, students looked for places in each other's drafts that were difficult to visualize. Using the technique, Amber vividly described the experience of getting an unusual haircut.

Using Thoughtshots, Maria described the thought processes she went through and her actions as she decided whether she should face up to a scolding her parents were sure to deliver or hide with her little brother. Using Exploding a Moment, Felicia was able to recreate the terror she felt when she was locked inside the trunk of a car. Using Building a Scene, Monica added dialogue to make her description of a house robbery come alive.

As a result of their training, students became better writers and better conference partners. As one student, Tait, put it, "I used to think revision was just a waste of time. But now I see what revision can do to a story" (p. 199).

FYI

Revising should not be neglected, but there is some danger in overemphasizing it. Although all pieces should be reread carefully, they may not have to be revised or may require only minor changes. This is especially true if the writer is experienced and has prepared carefully before writing. Knowing when to revise and when not to revise is an important skill.

it's making a character or event come alive by showing what the character does or the particulars of the event.

Thoughtshots. In expository writing, the Thoughtshot is the main idea of the piece. The writer asks: "What point am I trying to get across here?" In fiction or biographical writing, the Thoughtshot is the thinking of the characters or subjects. To create Thoughtshots, students ask themselves, "What might the main character be thinking? If I were the main character, what would I be thinking?"

Exploding a Moment. Novice writers often finish off an exciting moment with a sentence or two. What should have been a climactic event lacks the necessary build-up. Read exciting passages from trade books to students and discuss how the author built suspense. Writers might use these prompts: "How can I show the reader what happened? How can I build excitement and suspense?" Exploding a moment might involve both Thoughtshots and Snapshots.

Building a Scene. The writer combines dialogue with Snapshots and Thoughtshots to build a scene.

Editing

In the **editing** stage, students check carefully for mechanical errors, adding commas and question marks and correcting misspelled words. Ideally, all mechanical errors should be corrected. Realistically, the teacher should stress certain major elements. For some students, correcting all errors could be a very discouraging process. The degree of editing depends on students' maturity and proficiency.

In the editing stage, students check carefully for mechanical errors.

Editing can begin as early as kindergarten, with children checking to make sure they put names, dates, and page numbers on their pieces (Calkins, 1986). As new skills are acquired, the items to be checked increase to include spelling, punctuation, capitalization, and so on.

Just as with revision, editing should be modeled. Children should also have access to editing tools: pencils, a dictionary, easy style guides, and editing checklists. Such checklists help support students' evolving executive function and encourage them to focus on the conventions of writing, which requires looking at writing objectively and abstractly. Such a checklist should be geared to the students' expertise and experience; a sample is presented in Figure 11.3. Peer editing can also be employed. However, this is just an additional check. Student writers need to realize that, ultimately, it is their own responsibility to correct errors.

As part of learning the editing process, students should be introduced to the use of a writer's indispensable tool—the dictionary. Although students may understand that the dictionary is used to look up the meanings and spellings of unfamiliar words, they may not realize that dictionaries can be used to check capitalization and usage and that most dictionaries contain sections on grammar, punctuation, forming endings, ways to address dignitaries, and correct forms for business and friendly letters and thank-you notes. Model the various ways in which the dictionary can be used in editing and, as the need arises, encourage and guide stu-

> ■ **Editing** is that part of the writing process in which the author searches for spelling, typographical, and other mechanical errors.

■■■ **FIGURE 11.3**
A Sample Editing Checklist

dents in their use of the dictionary. If possible, each student should have a copy of a dictionary on the appropriate level. Also, model and encourage the use of style guides and thesauruses. If these tools are available on word-processing programs used by the class, show how the computerized versions are used. A useful device, especially for struggling readers and writers, is a talking word-processing program.

When deciding which editing skills to introduce, examine students' current writing and see what is most needed. Sometimes, the nature of the writing will dictate the skill. If students are writing pieces in which they will be referring to titles of books, introduce italicizing and underlining. After you have taught a skill, have students add it to their editing checklists. Also, display a brief explanation or example of the skill's use on the bulletin board, as shown in Figure 11.4, so that students have a reminder of it (Muschla, 1993).

USING TECHNOLOGY ■ ■ ■

With talking word-processing programs, students can listen as the program recites their pieces. Hearing their pieces read, they are better able to note dropped *-ings* and *-eds*, omitted words, and awkward expressions.

Underline the titles of books, magazines, newspapers, and movies:
Charlotte's Web, Weekly Reader, Sports Illustrated for Kids, Jurassic Park.
(If you are using a word processor, italicize instead of underlining. Underlining is used to tell whoever is printing the piece to use italics.)

■■■ **FIGURE 11.4**
Editing Reminder

As a final editing check, the teacher should examine the piece before approving it to be copied on clean paper or typed. The teacher might decide to note all errors with an advanced student and to focus on only one or two with a less advanced student. If the piece is to be published, however, all errors should be corrected. Noting the corrections should be done gently; you want the child to continue to feel pride in her or his product. Making such corrections must be recognized for the lower-level, mechanical skill that it is.

The writing process has been described here step by step to make it more understandable; however, in reality, many steps may be operating at the same time, and the steps are not necessarily executed in order. For example, writers mentally plan and revise and edit as they compose (Scardamalia & Bereiter, 1986). Books designed to assist young writers are listed in the following Student Reading List.

Student Reading List

Books for Young Writers

Ashley, S. (2005). *I can write a letter*. Milwaukee, WI: Weekly Reader Early Learning Library. Explains to primary students how to write and mail a letter.

Bauer, M. D. (1992). *What's your story? A young person's guide to writing fiction*. New York: Clarion Books. Practical tips for writing fiction from a highly regarded writer.

Christopher, D. (2004). *Behind the desk with . . . Matt Christopher: The #1 sports writer for kids*. Boston: Little, Brown. Describes how Matt Christopher goes about his writing.

Fletcher, R. J. (2000). *How writers work: Finding a process that works for you.* New York: Harper. Has many practical suggestions for student writers.

Jacobs, P. D. (2005). *Putting on a play: Drama activities for kids.* Layton, UT: Gibbs Smith. Includes suggestions for writing a script as well as putting on a play.

Kehret, P. (2002). *Five pages a day: A writer's journey.* Morton Grove, IL: Whitman. Discusses how Kehret became a writer and why she writes.

Leedy, L. (2004). *Look at my book: How kids can write and illustrate terrific books.* New York: Holiday House. Explains to students how they can create a picture book.

Otfinoski, S. (2005). *Extraordinary short story writing.* New York: Franklin Watts. Gives step-by-step advice for writing stories.

▪▪▪ Checkup ▪▪▪

1. How do students change the way they revise their writing as they become more experienced?
2. What are some techniques the teacher might use to foster more effective revising?
3. How should editing be taught and reinforced?

▪▪▪

Publishing

According to Elbow (2002), writing should be treated as a way of communicating, just as oral language is. All too often it is treated as an academic exercise in which the students write and the teacher corrects. As Elbow explains:

> The biggest problem in writing comes from the heavily evaluative, school context for writing that I described at the start: students come to experience writing not as a human act of reaching out to say what's on their mind to others, rather, they tend to experience writing as an attempt to say what they don't understand very well to a teacher who already understands it much better than they do—and all for the sake of being graded on how well they did. (p. 4)

Elbow isn't calling for a casual, careless kind of writing replete with errors. He is suggesting that pieces be written to real people for real purposes. He sees publishing as the antidote for lifeless prose. As he put it, "I believe publication is the single strongest way to help encourage students to revise and copyedit" (2002, p. 5). Knowing that others will be reading their words, students work hard to produce the best writing possible.

Students' work can be published in varied ways. Poems are collected in anthologies. Stories are bound in books, which are placed in the library. Essays and reports are shared and placed on classroom and school bulletin boards or on the class or school Web site. Scripts are dramatized. Essays and stories are entered in contests and printed in class and school publications or submitted to Web sites and children's magazines that print young people's works. Other ways of **publishing** include creating charts, posters, ads, brochures, announcements, sets of directions, book reviews, and video- or audiotapes.

▪ **Publishing** is that part of the writing process in which an author makes a piece of writing public.

▪ **Author's chair** is the practice of having a student author share her work with the rest of the class.

▪ A **conference** is a conversation between teacher and student(s) or between students designed to foster the development of one or more aspects of the writing process.

Case Study

Getting Students Involved in Writing

One way to get students published is to produce a class newspaper. Wanting to put some excitement into his language arts program, fifth-grade teacher Mark Levin decided that a class newspaper would be just the thing. The students wrote the articles, but he translated their handwritten creations into finished products.

Realizing that the students would get more out of it if they put more into it, he turned the whole process over to them. And, of course, he provided needed guidance. One of the first things he did was to create a stylebook, so the students would know what was ex-pected when writing a newspaper. He then taught them how to follow the stylebook and how to use a desktop publishing computer program.

Before students were accepted as staff members on the newspaper, they had to earn their press badges. To do this, they had to learn the basics of putting a newspaper together. They could then apply for various jobs: editor, artist, reporter covering a special beat, photographer, business manager, and circulation manager. Levin made sure that training was provided for each of these positions. However, everybody was also a reporter. Each student contributed at least one piece.

Levin reports that running a class newspaper is challenging. But it is also rewarding. Students' attitudes toward writing change. As he comments, "You'll find your students asking, 'Can I have a whole page?' instead of 'How long does this have to be?' " (Levin, 2002, p. 37)

To emphasize the importance of the writer, the teacher might arrange to have a student share his or her writing orally through use of the **author's chair**. Seated in this special chair, the author reads her or his piece to the class and invites comments. Special assemblies can also honor authors. Professional writers are invited to share with the other writers in the class. With publication and celebration, children put their hearts into their writing.

Conferences

Wanting to improve her writing, Lucy McCormick Calkins (1986) wrote to Donald Murray, a well-known writing teacher, and asked if he could help her. Murray agreed to hold **conferences** with her once a month. For two years, Calkins made the five-hour round trip from Connecticut to the University of New Hampshire each month for a fifteen-minute conference, which was primarily a conversation about her writing. Was the drive worth it? According to Calkins, yes: "He taught me I had something to say" (p. 124).

Conference Questions

In a typical conference, three types of questions are asked: opening, following, and process. They are nonjudgmental and are intended to evoke an open and honest response. Opening questions might take one of the following forms: "How is it going? How is your piece coming? What are you working on today?" The student's response provides clues for following questions, which are asked to find out more about how the child's writing is progressing. Process questions such as "What will you do next?" prompt students to make plans or take action. However, do not be so concerned about asking questions that you forget to listen. Calkins (1986) cautioned, "Our first job in a conference, then, is to be a person, not just a teacher. It is to enjoy, to care, and to respond" (p. 119).

Sometimes, a human response is all that is necessary. At other times, the teacher reflects the child's line of thinking but gently nudges the child forward. The student might say, for example, "I'm not sure how to describe my dog. My dog isn't a purebred." The teacher reflects that concern by saying, "You're not sure how to describe your dog because he is just an ordinary dog?" The repetition is an expression of interest that encourages the

FYI

■ In helping young writers, teachers tend to stress content, which is as it should be. However, some attention has to be paid to form, especially when children are exploring new modes, such as their first informational piece or mystery.

■ When conferencing with a student, if a portion of the piece isn't fully developed or clear, you might read the piece to the student so that he or she can be helped to notice a part that might not be clear to the reader or a part where the reader might want more information (Calkins, 2003).

child to elaborate and continue the flow. If that does not work, more directed responses might include such questions as "You say your dog isn't a purebred, but is there anything special about him? What does your dog look like? Can you think of anything about the way your dog acts or looks that might set him apart from other dogs?" The teacher must take care not to make questions too directed, however, to avoid taking over the writing. The purpose of the questioning is to have writers explore ways in which they might develop their work.

If a piece is confusing, the teacher might say, "I liked the way you talked about the funny things your dog did, but I don't understand how you taught him to roll over." The child will then tell how she or he taught the dog to roll over and most likely realize that this is an element to be included in the piece.

If a child has not developed a piece adequately, the teacher might say, "You said your dog was always getting into trouble. Can you tell me what kind of trouble he gets into?" Often, the response will be an oral rehearsal of what to write in the next draft. "They tell me what they are going to write in the next draft, and they hear their own voices telling me. I listen and they learn" (Murray, 1979, p. 16).

Through questioning, the teacher comes to an understanding of the writer. Using this understanding, the teacher is better able to supply the guidance that will best help the writer develop. A teacher should wonder, "Of all that I could say to this student, what will help her most?" (Calkins, 1994). Questions are geared to the nature and needs of the student. In every conference, include something positive about the student's work. However, also make a teaching point (Calkins, 2003). You might ask a student to reread her piece to see if it has all the details that the readers need. If the student doesn't notice that essential details are missing, read the piece to her and have her listen to see if there is something missing. If necessary, point out the difficulty and help the student revise her piece. After the revision, review what has been done so that the student can apply this to future writing: "Good work, Sabrina. You have added a detail that tells why your dog had to be taken to the vet. A good piece of writing tells why things happened. Look over your story and see if there are any other things that need to be explained."

Table 11.1 presents some common writing difficulties that students encounter and teacher prompts that might be used to help them focus on these difficulties. At times, students will reject the teacher's hints or suggestions, preferring to take a piece in a different direction. That is their prerogative. After each conference, note the student's writing strengths, needs, plans, and other pertinent information. A sample writing conference summary sheet is shown in Figure 11.5.

Adapting Instruction for English Language Learners

If ELLs can write in their first language, they will be able to transfer many of these writing skills to English. However, in addition to learning English vocabulary and syntax, these students may also be faced with learning a new orthography. For some, it might mean learning the entire alphabet. For others, it might mean learning a few letters or punctuation marks that are formed differently.

Through discussing their writing with peers, students develop a sense of audience.

Peer Conferences

What all writers need is feedback from an audience. Published writers rely on colleagues, spouses, or friends to critique their writing before sending it off to an editor. Student partners might perform this function for each other. With instruction and practice, they can bounce ideas off each other and get feedback that will help them to make audience-friendly revisions. As appropriate, have pairs or small groups of students talk over topic ideas and read each other's drafts. Partners can affirm each other by telling what they like about a piece. They can promote improvement by raising questions about puzzling passages, asking for more information, or pointing out passages that might be made more interesting.

Effective peer conferencing is a learned behavior. Discuss the ingredients of a successful conference and then model and supervise the process. In addition to being effective and producing improved writing, conferences should

■■■ **TABLE 11.1**   **Teacher Prompts in Response to Common Writing Difficulties**

Writing Difficulty	Teacher Prompts
Topic is too broad or lacks focus	What is your purpose in writing this? What's the most important or most interesting idea here? How might you develop that?
Piece lacks details or examples	I like your piece about _____. But I don't know very much about _____. Can you tell more about it?
Needs a beginning sentence	How might you start this off? What might you say to pull your reader into this story?
Inadequate conclusion or lack of ending	How might you sum up what you've said? What thought or idea do you want your reader to take away from this?
Lack of coherence or unity	What is your main purpose here? Do all your ideas fit? Are your ideas in the best order?

Adapted from *Writing Workshop Survival Kit* by G. R. Muschla, 1993, West Nyack, NY: The Center for Applied Research in Education.

build a sense of community and respect. Some general principles of conferencing include the following:

- Students should learn to listen carefully.
- Students should lead off with a positive comment about the piece.
- Students should make concrete suggestions.
- Suggestions should be put in positive terms.

Highly effective teachers carefully instruct students in the art of conducting successful writing and reading conferences. They might even have a group of students from a previous year model a conference. Teachers also continue to monitor conferences to make sure that they are as productive as they can be (Wharton-McDonald, 2001). Working with a student, model a peer conference and show how suggestions can be used to make revisions.

■■■ **FIGURE 11.5**
Writing Conference Summary

Name	Date	Topic	Strengths	Needs	Plans
Angel	11/15	Football game	Exciting opening.	Key part not clear.	Tell how he caught pass.
Amy	11/15	Pet rabbit	Interesting subject.	Not developed enough.	Give examples of pet's tricks.
James		Little sister			
Keisha		Making friends			
Maria		Dream vacation			
Marsha		Recycling trash			
Robert		Letter to sports star			
Stephanie		New bicycle			

Adapted from *Writing Workshop Survival Kit* by G. R. Muschla, 1993, West Nyack, NY: The Center for Applied Research in Education.

Authors' Circle

One form of peer conference is the **authors' circle**. When students have pieces they wish to share, they gather at an authors' table and read their works to each other. The teacher may also join the circle. The only requirement is that everyone in the circle have a work he or she wishes to read (Harste, Short, & Burke, 1988).

The authors' circle is designed for rough drafts rather than edited pieces. By seeking and listening to the reactions of others, students can determine whether their works need clarification and which parts might have to be revised. Both authors and listeners benefit from the circle. Harste, Short, and Burke (1988) commented:

> As they shared their stories with others through informal interactions and authors' circles, the children shifted from taking the perspective of an author to taking the perspective of reader and critic. These shifts occurred as they read their pieces aloud and listened to the comments other authors made about their stories. As children became aware of their audience, they were able to see their writing in a different light. (p. 32)

The ultimate purpose of conferences is to help writers internalize the process so that they ask themselves questions like these: "How is my writing going? What will I do next? Do I like what I have written? Is there anything I would like to change?"

■ ■ ■ Checkup ■ ■ ■

1. What role do conferences play in the writing process?
2. What are the characteristics of an effective writing conference?

■ ■ ■

■ Writing Workshop

Just as students learn to read by reading, they learn to write by writing. The **writing workshop** is a way of providing students with the opportunity to try out newly introduced strategies under the teacher's guidance (Collins, 1998). Through individual or small-group conferences, the teacher can help students adapt and implement strategies that were taught in whole-class or guided writing sessions. Writing workshop consists of the following elements: minilessons, guided writing, writing time, conferences, and sharing. If possible, the workshop should be held every day.

Minilesson

Minilessons are generally presented to the whole group. The purpose of a **minilesson** is to present a needed writing skill. The minilesson lasts for only about ten minutes, so the skill should be one that is fairly easy to understand. The skill could be capitalizing titles, selecting topics, using correct letter form, or any one of a dozen fairly easy-to-teach skills. Minilessons can also be used to explain workshop procedures.

Guided Writing (or Strategic Writing)

During guided writing, students are taught writing strategies in small groups in which all members are at the same stage of writing development. To teach a writing strategy, pro-

---

■ An **authors' circle** is a form of peer conference in which several students meet to discuss their drafts and obtain suggestions for possible revision.

■ **Writing workshop** is a way of organizing writing instruction that includes a minilesson, time for students to write, individual and group conferences, and whole-class sharing.

■ The **minilesson** is a brief lesson on a needed writing skill. The skill is usually applied in the following writing workshop.

vide examples of the target strategy as it appears in selections that students are reading and also in pieces written by their peers and you. Just as in other sample lessons, discuss the strategy and how it will help their writing. Model the use of the strategy, showing, for instance, how you might write an interesting lead. Provide guided practice, and have students apply the skill by using it in their own writing. Revision and evaluation should focus on the element introduced. The skill should be reviewed and reintroduced in conferences and follow-up lessons until it becomes virtually automatic. Here is a sample writing strategy lesson. Notice that this lesson is more extensive than a minilesson and may take ten to twenty minutes to teach.

Lesson 11.1

Writing Strategy: Adding Specific Details

Step 1.

Show a paragraph, such as the following, that calls out for elaboration. Do not use a student's paragraph, as this will embarrass the writer.

The Strange Day

I turned on the radio. The announcer said to stay inside. She said that the streets were very dangerous. My father said that the announcement was a joke. But it wasn't.

Invite students to read the paragraph. Ask students whether they have questions that they might like to have answered. Write students' questions on the board. Discuss the author's failure to include needed details.

Step 2.

Show the students how the writer could make the piece come alive by adding details. Add needed details and compare the revised paragraph with the original.

The Strange Day

On my way to my place at the breakfast table, I switched on the radio. My favorite song was being played. Suddenly, the music stopped. "We have an important news flash for our listeners," the announcer said. "A monkey stole keys from the zoo keeper and opened all the cages. The streets are now full of dangerous, wild animals. The elephants have already smashed five cars. Stay in your homes. If you spot any wild animals, call the police immediately. But do not let the animals into your home."

"Hey, Mom and Dad," I shouted. "Come quick. There's trouble in the streets." When I told them what I had heard, they started laughing. Dad pointed to the calendar. "Don't you remember what day this is? It's April first. It's April Fool's Day. Somebody is playing a trick on the town."

Dad was still laughing when he headed out the door for work. But he wasn't laughing seconds later when he rushed back inside and slammed the door shut. "Call 911!" he shouted. "There's a tiger sitting on the roof of my car."

Step 3. Guided practice

Provide one or two practice paragraphs that lack details. Working with students, add needed details.

Step 4. Application

Encourage students to flesh out their stories by adding details. During the ensuing workshop session, provide any needed assistance.

Step 5. Extension

As a follow-up, have volunteers show how they added details to their stories. In subsequent lessons, discuss the many ways in which writing can be elaborated.

Step 6. Assessment and review

In conferences and while looking over various drafts of students' writing, evaluate whether they are fully developing their pieces. Provide additional instruction as needed.

There are a number of ways of introducing strategies. In addition to showing how a piece might be improved, as in the sample lesson, you might have students compare two pieces, one of which is more effective because it uses the target strategy. You might examine the works of published writers to see how they used strategies that you wish to present, give a demonstration of how you use a particular strategy, or introduce a strategy through individual coaching and prompting. Regardless of how a writing strategy is taught, be sure to name it and tell why it is used so that students will adopt it: "Writers use details to make their stories seem real to their readers." Post a chart of strategies with brief examples of their use (Calkins, 2006).

Writing Strategies

There are dozens of writing strategies. Listed below are those that seem most essential for students. The strategies are listed in approximate order of difficulty. However, some strategies are taught at every level. For instance, writing an interesting lead is important for writers throughout the elementary and middle school grades but is a more complex undertaking in the upper grades than in the lower ones.

Expository Writing

■ Writing clear, complete sentences.

■ Writing a lead or beginning sentence. The lead or beginning sentence often gives the main idea of a piece and should grab the reader's interest and entice her or him to read the piece.

■ Developing informational pieces. Informational pieces can be developed with details, including facts, opinions, examples, and descriptions. Failure to develop a topic is a major flaw in students' writing.

■ Writing an effective ending. An effective ending should provide a summary of the piece and/or restate the main point of the piece in such a way that it has an impact on the reader.

■ Using precise, varied, and vivid words—finding substitutes for *said* or *good*, for instance.

■ Using a thesaurus to help achieve a varied vocabulary.

■ Gathering appropriate and sufficient information for a piece. Writers do their best work when they are overflowing with information and can't wait to put it down on paper.

■ Using figurative language, including similes and metaphors.

■ Using advanced writing devices such as alliteration and rhetorical questions.

■ Using varied sentence patterns.

■ Combining short sentences into longer ones.

■ Writing in a variety of forms: poems, stories, plays, letters, advertisements, announcements, expository pieces, newspaper articles, essays.

■ Writing for a variety of purposes and audiences.

■ Providing transitions so that one thought leads into another and the writing flows.

■ Creating headings and subheadings for longer pieces.

■ Eliminating details that detract from a piece.

Narrative or Fiction Writing

- Writing a story that has a well-developed beginning, middle, and end.
- Developing believable characters by using description, action, and dialogue.
- Creating a setting.
- Developing an interesting plot.
- Creating an interesting ending or even a surprise ending.
- Writing dialogue that sounds natural.
- Creating a title that makes the reader want to read the piece.
- Building suspense.
- Using advanced fiction techniques, such as the flashback or starting in the middle of the story (*in media res*).

Writing Time

Writing time, which is the core of the writing workshop, lasts for thirty minutes or longer. During that time, students work on their individual pieces, have peer or teacher conferences, meet in small groups to discuss their writing, or meet in their guided writing groups. Before beginning this portion of the lesson, you may want to check with students to see what their plans are for this period.

As students write, hold one or two guided writing sessions. As time allows, circulate in the classroom and supply help or encouragement as needed. You might show one student how to use the spell checker, applaud another who has just finished a piece, encourage a third who is searching for just the right ending, and discuss topic possibilities with a student who cannot seem to decide what to write about. You might also have scheduled conferences with several students or sit in on a peer conference that students have convened.

In peer conferences, students can meet in pairs or in small groups of four or five. In these conferences, one or more students may read their drafts and seek the comments and suggestions of the others.

You should also plan for a mid-workshop teaching point (Calkins & Martinelli, 2006). About midway through the workshop or when students' efforts seem to be lagging, take about two minutes to remind students of the target skill from the minilesson or to provide a teaching tip based on your observations during the workshop. However, if students are doing well, you might skip the mid-workshop teaching point.

Group Sharing

At appropriate times, such as at the end of the day, students gather for group sharing. Volunteers read their pieces. The atmosphere is positive, and other students listen attentively and tell the author what they like about the piece. They also ask questions and make suggestions and might inquire about the author's future plans for writing. Group sharing builds a sense of community. Student writers are shown appreciation by their audience. They also have the opportunity to hear what their peers are writing about, what techniques their peers are using, and what struggles they are having.

Management of Writing Workshop

Active and multifaceted, writing workshop requires careful management. The room should be well organized. Professional writers have offices, studies, or at least desks at which to work. They also have access to the tools of writing. The classroom should be set up as a writer's workshop. Younger students need an assortment of soft lead pencils, crayons, magic markers, and sheets of unlined paper. Older students can get by with pencil and paper but should have some choices, too. At times, they might feel the need to write on a

---

ASSESSING FOR LEARNING

As you observe and talk with students during writing workshop, note what they might need to improve their progress. Perhaps they are struggling as they try to add dialogue. Hold a brief mid-workshop minilesson to give them needed guidance.

FYI

"Time is an important element in writing workshop. If students are going to become deeply invested in their writing . . . and if they are going to let their ideas grow and gather momentum, if they are going to draft and revise, sharing their texts with one another as they write, they need the luxury of time" (Calkins, 1994, p. 186).

In group sharing, students have the opportunity to hear what their peers are writing about and to give positive feedback.

BUILDING LANGUAGE

As students read and discuss their pieces, build the academic language needed to talk about writing: *writing an interesting lead, developing a topic, sticking to the topic, supplying interesting examples, using signal words,* and so on.

yellow legal pad or with a pink magic marker. You should have a round table or two for group meetings, a word-processing or editing corner, and a reference corner that contains a dictionary, style guide, almanac, and other references. Staplers, paper, and writing instruments of various kinds should be placed in the supply corner. Writing folders or portfolios should be arranged alphabetically in cartons. Involve students in helping with housekeeping chores. They can take turns seeing that materials are put away and that writing folders are in order.

Before starting the workshop, explain the setup of the room and show where supplies and materials are located. With the class, develop a series of rules and routines. Before students engage in peer conferences or small sharing groups, discuss and model these activities.

Be aware of students' productivity. Students should have specific plans for each day's workshop: revise a piece, confer with the teacher, obtain additional information about a topic, start a new piece. Make sure that peer conferences are devoted to writing and not last night's TV programs.

Writing is a social as well as a cognitive act. Writers are influenced by the teacher's expectations and by the expectations of peers. Students try to figure out what the teacher wants and write accordingly. Writers also want approval from their peers. They may hesitate to include certain details or write on certain topics if they fear their classmates will criticize them (Dahl & Farnan, 1998).

It is important to note the social dynamics of peer conferences. Lensmire (1994) found teasing in the peer groups in his third-grade classroom. And he found that students who were not socially accepted in general were mistreated in the peer conferences. Lensmire suggested that students work toward a common goal, such as investigating a particular genre. With a common goal to guide them, he hoped that the focus would be on working toward the goal rather than on peer relationships. He also recommended more teacher guidance in the workshop setting. Getting feedback from students on the impact of peer and teacher conferences and other aspects of the workshop on their development as writers is also helpful (Dahl & Farnan, 1998).

FIGURE 11.6
Daily Log: Students' Plans for Writing Workshop

Name	Topic	M	T	W	Th	F
Angel	Football game	D-1, TC	RE			
Amy	Pet rabbit	E, TC	PE			
James	Little sister	AC	R, TC			
Keisha	Making friends	AC	M			
Maria	Dream vacation	TC, D-2	E			
Marsha	Recycling trash	M	P, S			
Robert	Letter to sports star	AC	R			
Stephanie	New bicycle	R	D-3, TC			

Key
P: Planning   PE: Peer editing   PC: Peer conference
D: Drafting   PUB: Publishing   TC: Teacher conference
R: Revising   M: Making final copy   AC: Author's circle
E: Editing   RE: Researching   S: Sharing

Adapted from *Writing Workshop Survival Kit* by G. R. Muschla, 1993, West Nyack, NY: The Center for Applied Research in Education.

Note students who do more conferencing than writing, those who never seem to confer, and those who have been working on the same piece for weeks. You might keep a record of students' activities in a daily log. A sample daily log, adapted from Muschla (1993), is presented in Figure 11.6.

As you circulate in the room, note students' strengths and weaknesses. During the guided writing or sharing period, call attention to the positive things that you saw: Mary Lou's colorful use of language, Fred's title, Jamie's interesting topic. Needs that you note might be the basis for a future minilesson or guided writing lesson, a brief, one-on-one lesson, or—if several students display a common need—a small-group lesson.

Most of all, serious writing demands time. Even professionals need a warm-up period to get into their writing. Once the thoughts begin to flow on paper, however, writers have to keep on writing. If possible, at least thirty minutes to an hour a day, three to five days a week, should be set aside for writing.

■■■ Checkup ■■■

1. What are the major components of writing workshop?
2. How might each of these components be implemented?
■■■

■ Quickwrites

Quickwrites are brief first drafts written in response to reading a short piece of literature, a line from a poem or essay, or a prompt. Quickwrites can also be used to react to concepts learned in a content area, to summarize a lesson, or to react to an idea. The purpose of quickwrites is to get ideas down on paper and to write frequently. Because the task is brief

FYI

The strength of the quickwrite is also its weakness. It might take students a few minutes to get their mental wheels rolling—by then time is up. Slow starters might need help or a little added time for their quickwrites.

and limited, the quickwrite can be especially effective with struggling writers. As a bonus, quickwrites provide practice in writing on demand in a timed situation.

Students who have difficulty responding with words can use stick figures to represent their response. They might also use stick figures to describe an event or tell a story. After telling a story in stick figure format, students can then add words. For some struggling readers, drawing stick figures is a highly effective aid.

If writers wish, they can expand their quickwrites into more extended pieces. Rief (2003), a middle school teacher, has her students collect their quickwrites in a section of their response journals. From time to time, students reexamine their quickwrites and may decide to expand some of them. Rief checks the quickwrites regularly, and if she sees one that cries out for elaboration, she might suggest that to the writer.

▪▪▪ Checkup ▪▪▪

1. What are quickwrites, and how can they be used?

▪▪▪

▪ Interpersonal Writing

FYI

Duffy (1994) used written conversation with primary-grade students. When visiting a writing group, she would jot down an initiating sentence in each of their journals. As they wrote responses, Duffy would visit another group and then return to the first group to reply to their responses. Prompted by the teacher's writing, typical student responses might be as long as 100 words. Written conversations have also been used with older learning-disabled children. Both reading and writing fluency increased (Rhodes & Dudley-Marling, 1988).

A highly motivating method for eliciting writing from students is **interpersonal writing**, which is a dialogue or conversation conducted in writing. It can be conducted between teacher and student, two students, student and pen pal, or student and grandparent or other adult. Interpersonal writing most often takes the form of dialogue journals but can be embodied in letters, notes, e-mails, or written conversations.

In a **written conversation**, two students or a student and a teacher converse by writing to each other. Either party may initiate the conversation, which may be conducted at a table or other convenient spot. The teacher might start with a question such as "How is your new puppy?" The student responds, and then the teacher replies. As one student is responding, the teacher can initiate a written conversation with a second student, and then a third.

Written conversations provide practice in both reading and writing. The teacher's writing is geared to the student's reading level. If the student's reading level is very limited, the teacher can read her letter to the student. If a student's writing ability is so rudimentary that the teacher cannot understand it, the student is asked to read it.

The use of interpersonal writing does raise several issues. Students' privacy must be respected. Teacher responses need to be genuine, caring, and sensitive. If health or safety concerns are raised because of information revealed by students, consult with the school principal regarding your legal and ethical responsibilities.

▪▪▪ Checkup ▪▪▪

1. What are some of the major forms of interpersonal writing?

▪▪▪

▪ Improving Expository Writing

Although some students seem to have a natural bent for narrative and others prefer composing expository text, all students should become acquainted with all major writing structures, learning how each is developed. Part of that instruction simply involves hav-

---

▪ **Interpersonal writing** is writing that two participants exchange over a period of time.

▪ **Written conversation** is a type of writing in which teacher and student or two students carry on a conversation by writing a series of notes to each other.

▪ **Cognitive strategy instruction in writing** is an approach to writing that emphasizes instruction in text structure and writing process and uses think sheets as a scaffolding device. It has been especially useful for students with learning disabilities.

ing children read widely in order to acquire a rich background of comparison–contrast, problem–solution, and other expository and narrative structures. However, instruction should also include explaining each structure, modeling the writing of it, and having students compose similar structures.

Expository writing needs special attention. Students' early writing is primarily narrative, so that as students progress through the primary grades, there is a growing gap between narrative and expository writing. Whereas students can write fairly complex narrative structures in third grade, their expository writing typically contains a simple listing of the main idea and supporting details (Langer, 1986).

In a program known as **cognitive strategy instruction in writing**, Raphael, Englert, and Kirschner (1989) combined instruction in text structure and writing process to improve students' composing skills. Based on trials and experiments that spanned a number of years, these researchers devised strategies that help students make use of text structure to both understand and produce expository prose. In addition to instruction, scaffolding is provided through the use of a series of guides that students might use to plan, compose, and revise their pieces. These guides are dubbed "think sheets" and correspond to the major types of text organization; there are sheets for narrative pieces, compare–contrast structures, explanation, and other text forms. The think sheets are designed to be "concrete reminders of appropriate strategies to use and of the times when particular strategies might be relevant" (Raphael & Englert, 1990, p. 242).

The first think sheet, for planning (shown in Figure 11.7), prompts students to plan their writing by noting their audience and reason for writing and to list details that might be included in the piece. Students might also be asked to group ideas or show how they might be organized: steps in a process, comparison–contrast, or problem–solution, for instance. Having shown which ideas they will include and how they will organize their writing, students must then consider an interesting beginning and suitable closing. These can

FYI

- Personal narratives are a popular form of writing. If left to their own devices, children will write personal narratives to the exclusion of other kinds of writing (Hagerty, Hiebert, & Owens, 1989). Although it is important to give children choice in their writing, they need to be encouraged to try many different kinds of writing.
- How-to books provide models for children to follow. How-to pieces are particularly good assignments because they provide a one-step-at-a-time structure that aids children in composing and revising (Duthie, 1996).
- To foster expository writing, read informational pieces aloud so that students get a feel for the language of expository prose.

FIGURE 11.7
Planning Think Sheet

Author's Name: ____________ Date: ____________

Topic: Echolocation

Who: Who am I writing for?
The kids in my group.

Why: Why am I writing this?
Our group is making a book on dolphins.

What: What is being explained?
How dolphins find objects.

What are the steps?

First, Dolphin sends out clicks.

Next, Clicks bounce off object.

Third, Clicks return to dolphin.

Then, Dolphin senses how long it took click to return.

Finally, Dophin can tell how far away object is.

Adapted from *Cognitive Strategy Instruction in Writing Project* by C. S. Englert, T. E. Raphael, & L. M. Anderson, 1989, East Lansing, MI: Institute for Research on Teaching.

■■■ **FIGURE 11.8**
Self-Edit Think Sheet

Author's Name: _____ Date: _____

First, reread my paper. Then answer the following:

What do I like best about my paper? Gives a good explanation

Why? Has all the steps

What parts are not clear?

Why not?

Did I . . .

1. Tell what was being explained?	(Yes)	Sort of	No
2. Make the steps clear?	(Yes)	Sort of	No
3. Use keywords to make it clear?	(Yes)	Sort of	No
4. Make it interesting to my reader?	Yes	(Sort of)	No

What parts do I want to change?
Make a more interesting beginning
_____

What questions do I have for my editor?
Is the explanation clear?
Is the ending OK?

Adapted from *Cognitive Strategy Instruction in Writing Project* by C. S. Englert, T. E. Raphael, & L. M. Anderson, 1989, East Lansing, MI: Institute for Research on Teaching.

FYI

■ Composing nonfiction pieces may result in "dump truck" writing, in which the author simply dumps in facts and neglects style (Duthie, 1996). The resulting piece lacks voice and interest. Encourage students to put their unique stamp on nonfiction writing.

■ Encourage students to explore the use of visuals in their nonfiction writing.

be created as students compose a rough draft, or they can be noted at the bottom of the planning think sheet.

After composing their pieces, students use a self-edit think sheet (shown in Figure 11.8) to assess their pieces. This think sheet prompts them through the first stage of the revising process and asks them to note whether the piece is clear, interesting, and well organized. Because the think sheet will be used by a peer editor to examine the first draft, the student also notes changes that she or he plans to make or questions for the editor. The peer editor uses the sheet to make recommendations for changes. The editor lists changes that might be made and can also offer suggestions for making the paper more interesting.

After a conference with the peer editor, the student lists the editor's suggestions, decides which ones to use, lists ways of making the paper more interesting, completes a revision think sheet (as shown in Figure 11.9), and then revises the piece.

In real writing, some of the subprocesses presented separately are combined and some may be skipped. Others, such as revision, may be repeated several times. However, it is recommended that students go through all the steps of the process and use the suggested think sheets. Later, as students no longer need scaffolding to use appropriate writing strategies, they may adapt the process. Like other forms of scaffolding, think sheets are intended to be used only until students are able to use the strategies without being prompted to do so. Having incorporated the strategies prompted by the think sheets, the students will no longer need the think sheets.

■■■ **Checkup** ■■■

1. What are some ways in which expository writing should be taught?
2. How should think sheets be used?

■■■

■ ■ ■ **FIGURE 11.9**
Revision Think Sheet

Suggestions from My Editor

List all the suggestions your editor has given you:

X   1.   *Use a question as a beginning sentence.*

X   2.   *Use more key words.*

X   3.   *Write a good closing.*

    4.   _____

Put an X next to all the suggestions you would like to use in revising your paper. Also think of ideas of your own that might make your paper clearer or more interesting. Read your paper once more, and ask yourself:

Is my beginning interesting? Will it make people want to read my paper?   Not exactly

Are the steps in my explanation clear?   Yes

Did I write down all the steps?   Yes

Are the steps in the right order?   Yes

Do I have a good closing sentence?   No

Returning to My Draft

On your draft, make all the changes you think will help your paper. Use ideas from the list above, those from your self-edit think sheet, and any other ideas you may have for your paper. When you are ready, you can write your revised copy.

Adapted from *Cognitive Strategy Instruction in Writing Project* by C. S. Englert, T. E. Raphael, & L. M. Anderson, 1989, East Lansing, MI: Institute for Research on Teaching.

■ Guiding the Writing of Reports

For young students, writing a report poses problems. The earliest reports are lists of details about a topic (New Standards Primary Literacy Committee, 1999). They tell what the writer knows about the topic, but lack organization. By about third grade, students' reports have a clearly defined beginning, middle, and end.

In writing reports, students differ greatly in the degree of elaboration and in the organization. Writing an organized report involves analyzing the information and classifying it by category. Analyzing and classifying information is easier if students are writing about a familiar topic. If students are writing about an unfamiliar topic, they will have difficulty highlighting important information. Because the information is new to them, they won't be able to distinguish important ideas from trivial details. Organization will also be a problem. They will lack the understanding needed to create categories of information and will probably simply use the headings contained in their source material.

Even older students may not understand what is involved in writing a report. In a study of eleven- and twelve-year-olds assigned to research and write on a topic related to World War II, the students perceived the task in one of three ways: accumulating information, transferring information, or transforming information (Many, Fyfe, Lewis, & Mitchell, 1996). Those who interpreted the assignment in terms of accumulating or transferring information took a task-completion approach. Their goal was to fill up the twelve-page booklets they had been given. There was little thought given to considering the audience or even sticking to the topic.

Although they had created planning webs at the beginning of the project, the information accumulators paid little attention to them. They included in their reports any

HIGHER-LEVEL LITERACY

■ Part of students' difficulty in writing about an unfamiliar topic may be rooted in their reading. Because the material is new, their understanding may be so limited that they are forced to use the author's words. Chances are they will not understand the material well enough to put it into their own words. Writing in which students use a few phrases of their own to string together material taken directly from their source material is known as "patch" writing.

■ Building a deeper understanding of background material can foster more effective report writing. Students do best when they have a deep understanding of their material and when they are provided with the type of guidance that helps them select relevant information and organize it (New Standards Primary Literacy Committee, 1999).

Having appropriate materials available is a factor in the quality of students' reports.

information that was interesting, even if it did not support their specific topic. They chose resource materials on the basis of availability, even if they weren't appropriate. Their reports consisted primarily of paraphrased information.

Students who saw the task as a transferring process sought out pertinent materials and recorded that information in their own words. However, although they may have used multiple sources, they failed to synthesize information. Instead, they used one source for one subtopic and another source for a second subtopic, and so forth.

Information transformers saw their task as compiling information for a specific audience—in this case, students their own age. They reviewed and revised their work in light of their planning and their audience. They synthesized information from multiple sources and reflected on the information the sources presented. Instead of focusing on filling up the pages, their goal was to convey accurate information in an interesting, understandable fashion.

The availability of appropriate resources was a major factor in the nature and quality of the reports. When the references were difficult to read, even the most capable writers relied on paraphrasing or word-for-word copying. To help all students become information transformers, try the following:

■ Make sure that students understand the nature and purpose of the assignment. With as much student input as possible, compose a rubric so that students have a clear idea of what is expected.

■ If possible, students should be given a choice of topics so that they have a sense of ownership. They will then be willing to invest the time and energy needed to create a thoughtfully composed report. Before students make a final choice of a topic, encourage them to do some preliminary exploration so that they are better able to determine whether this is a topic that interests them and that there is enough information available for them to develop the topic. The information should not be so difficult or complex that students would not be able to understand it.

- With your help, students select sources of information. Make sure that you have materials on a variety of levels so that below-level readers have accessible sources. Finding relevant information is surprisingly complex (Gans, 1940). Model the process and provide guided practice. Pose questions or topics and have students search through indices and tables of contents to locate what seem to be relevant passages. Then have the class read the passages and decide whether the passages are relevant. You might also distribute copies of selected passages and have the class decide whether they pertain to a particular topic (Singer & Donlan, 1989).

- Students complete a planning guide that includes a brief description of the audience, the topic, key supporting subtopics, and a list of sources of information.

- Students compile relevant information. Because younger students and less-expert writers have a tendency to copy, they need instruction in taking notes. Students might be taught a paraphrasing strategy in which they read a relevant passage, recall what they have read, and summarize what they have read in their own words on physical or electronic note cards.

- Students organize their information by grouping physical or electronic cards that contain information on the same subtopic. Groups of cards are then placed in sequential or some other kind of logical order.

- Using information they have compiled, students compose their reports. When using multiple sources, students use a cut-and-paste synthesis or a discourse synthesis. In a cut-and-paste synthesis, students simply jot down information from one source and then information from a second source. In discourse synthesis, students integrate the information from two or more sources. To help students use a discourse synthesis, model the process and provide guided practice.

- Students review their reports to make sure they are accurate and contain sufficient information (Many, Fyfe, Lewis, & Mitchell, 1996). Students also examine their reports to make sure they are interesting and that the mechanics are correct.

Because report writing is complex, you might do a shared report involving the whole class or a guided writing group. The next step would be to have cooperative groups compose reports. If available, provide students with sample reports written by former students. To make the task of writing a report more manageable, you might also break it down into segments: The first segment might be topic selection, preliminary exploration, and completion of a planning guide. The second segment might be the first draft. The third segment could be revising and editing. The final segment might be the finished report.

■■■ Checkup ■■■

1. What are the three approaches that middle school students might take in writing reports?
2. What are some ways to guide students so that they write more effective reports?

Closing the Gap

Writing reports can be a powerful learning tool. In fact, well-planned student-created reports are a characteristic of 90/90/90 schools—schools in which 90 percent of the students are members of a minority group, 90 percent live in poverty, but 90 percent achieve at or above grade level. An important instructional element in 90/90/90 schools is a focus on informational writing (Parker, 2002). Students are required to produce an acceptable piece of writing each month (elementary schools) or quarter (secondary schools). After being provided with thorough guidance and instruction, students write an informative piece and then revise and edit their work as much as necessary in order to produce an acceptable piece.

In their informational pieces, students must include information that they do not already know so that the project becomes a genuine quest for new knowledge. The format can vary: a report, a persuasive editorial, a biography, or an explanation of a process in science. In writing their pieces, students not only increase content knowledge, they also develop thinking and writing skills (Knox, 2002).

Instruction is both whole class and small group. The whole class is instructed in procedures or skills that all need to learn. Small-group instruction is used to teach groups of students who have common needs.

Writing is a whole-school activity and is assessed using a common rubric. The rubric highlights key characteristics of effective writing. The principal and teachers regularly discuss and share students' writing to maintain a focus on key characteristics of students' writing.

■ Assessing and Improving Writing: The Key Traits Approach

Improving writing requires having a concept of what good writing is, being able to explain to and show students the traits of good writing, and having an assessment system that enables students and teachers to judge whether a piece of writing contains those characteristics. The final requirement is devising a plan for teaching students how to revise their writing so as to strengthen key characteristics (Spandel, 2001). In a sense, it's creating a rubric that students can use to plan their writing, assess their writing, and revise their writing. The teacher can use this same rubric, or perhaps a more elaborated form, to plan instruction and assess students' writing. Such a system enables a teacher to base instruction on assessment.

The main element in effective writing as determined by Profiles Network and Six Traits Plus, a popular writing assessment system, is content. These are the ideas or information that the piece conveys or, for narrative, the story that it tells. The remainder of the characteristics have to do with form, the way the content is presented. Form can be subdivided into organization, word choice, sentence construction, and mechanics. A final element is voice, which reflects the individual personality of the author.

To help students become aware of the components of good writing, invite them to tell what they think these components are. Write their responses on the board and create a web of the elements. Their responses will tell you what they think the important elements are and, by implication, where they put their efforts when they are writing. Share samples of good writing with students. Discuss with students what it is about these pieces that makes them effective. This will help students broaden their concept of what good writing is (Spandel, 2001). Provide an overview of the characteristics, but then focus on them one by one. You can start with any trait you want, but because content is key, most teachers start with that.

To help students become familiar with the traits and to provide practice for assessing writing, have students assess the writing of unknown writers. You might start with published writers who have written works on the students' level. One good source would be periodicals designed for young people. For third-graders, for instance, look at samples from *Weekly Reader, Scholastic Magazine,* and *Time for Kids* (*News Scoop*). If you don't subscribe to these and they are not available in your school library, sample articles are usually available on the publishers' Web sites. Collect pieces of writing that illustrate key elements in writing. Collect examples of both good and bad writing so that you can show how the two differ. After students have had some practice assessing the writing of others, have them assess their own writing (Spandel, 2001). The key characteristics should be translated into a rubric (see Figure 2.7 on p. 54). Although a generic rubric is helpful, rubrics geared to each major kind of writing would be more effective because they would offer more specific guidance. In addition, different types of writing have different demands. Focusing on key elements, the most effective rubrics are concise and contain only three to six evaluative criteria. Each evaluative criterion must encompass a teachable skill. For instance, evaluative criteria for a how-to piece might include clear description of steps;

he Profiles Network is an organization of teachers who ask students in kindergarten through twelfth grade to write to a common prompt. They seek out the best pieces and then analyze these pieces to extract attributes of effective writing. This helps teachers better understand the writing process, and it also provides them with a basis for instruction. Using feedback from their analysis and model pieces, they instruct their students.

Implementing the Profiles approach, teachers in Hamtramck, Michigan, had their students write to the prompt "What I do best." Teachers met and analyzed the papers in order to determine what kinds of things students could do well in their writing and what kinds of things they had difficulty with. On the basis of this analysis, the teachers set general goals and grade-level objectives. From the best papers, they were able to select strategies that the best students used, and they also used these as model pieces of writing.

Teachers also filled out a form for students that told them what was good about the writing and what they might do to improve. In order to help them focus their instruction, teachers also answered a series of questions about students' writing:

- What knowledge and skills are reflected in the student's writing?
- What challenges does the student face?
- What areas does she or he need to develop more fully?
- What interventions or supports would assist this student in meeting the challenges she or he faces? (What can the teacher do to help the student grow as a writer?) (Weber, Nelson, & Woods, 2000, p. 45)

Exemplary Teaching

The Profiles Network

list of needed materials; effective, sequential organization; and correct use of mechanics. All of these criteria are teachable.

Increasingly, high-stakes assessments are used to assess students' writing. As Baldwin (2004) notes, it is important that teachers understand how writing is assessed. Some states use such indirect measures as multiple-choice items covering grammar, usage, and punctuation (Maryland), whereas others rely more heavily on direct, or authentic, writing (New Jersey and Massachusetts). In Wisconsin, two rubrics are used to score students' papers: A composing rubric measures students' ability to write organized prose directed clearly and effectively to an audience; and a conventions rubric measures students' ability to apply the conventions of standard written English.

Use rubrics to help students understand how to respond to high-stakes writing assessments. In preparation for Pennsylvania's state-mandated tests, for example, students learn to evaluate their own and their peers' writing by applying the official rubrics for focus, content, organization, style, and conventions, which assess each aspect on a four-point scale: Advanced, Proficient, Basic, and Below Basic.

Develop rubrics with your students for the writing they do. You might ask them to use markers or highlighters to color-code evidence in their compositions that shows that their writing meets each criterion in the rubric (Saddler & Andrade, 2004). For instance, the rubric might ask for at least two examples that support the main idea. Students mark their examples, and if they can't find them, they make a note to add them.

So that they can more readily assess their progress over time, students should have a place to store and keep track of their completed works, works in progress, and future writing plans. File folders make convenient, inexpensive portfolios. Two for each student are recommended—one for completed works and one for works in progress. The works-in-progress folder should also contain a listing of the key characteristics of good writing, an editing checklist, a list of skills mastered, a list of topics attempted, and a list of possible future topics.

The works-completed folder, or portfolio, provides a means of examining the student's development. If all drafts of a piece are saved, the teacher can see how the student progressed through the writing steps. A comparison of current works with beginning

FYI

- A writing program should do more than just prepare students for writing assessments. Speaking of high-stakes writing tests, Thomas (2004) warns, "When assessment rubrics and sample essays become templates for students to follow, we lose any chance of achieving authentic or valuable writing instruction. When a test wields power like this, teachers abdicate their expertise as writing instructors."

- To help students understand rubrics, distribute examples of good, middling, and poor responses to a writing assignment—preferably ones written by students in the previous year's class (with names removed). Using a rubric, students rank the responses and then articulate what features of each response led to its ranking (Saddler & Andrade, 2004).

ASSESSING FOR LEARNING

The Writing Observation Framework (Henk et al., 2003) is a guide used to assess writing instruction. You might fill it out yourself or invite a colleague to observe your class and fill it out.

pieces will show how the writer has developed over the course of the year. Careful examination of the portfolio's contents should reveal strengths and weaknesses and provide insights into interests and abilities. While reading through the portfolio, the teacher might try to ascertain whether a student is finding his or her own voice, has a pattern of interests, is showing a bent for certain kinds of writing, is applying certain techniques, and is being challenged to grow and develop. The teacher then decides what will best help the student progress further.

Students should also examine their portfolios with a critical eye. What have they learned? What topics have they explored? What pieces do they like best? What kinds of writing do they enjoy most? What are some signs of growth? What questions do they have about their writing? What would help them become better writers? Are there some kinds of writing that they have not yet attempted but would like to try? Of course, teacher and student should confer about the portfolio, reviewing past accomplishments, discussing current concerns, and setting up future goals and projects. (For more information on portfolio assessment, see Chapter 2.)

■ ■ ■ **Checkup** ■ ■ ■

1. How does the key traits approach work?
2. How would you go about applying a key traits approach?

■ ■ ■

■ Technology and Writing

Computers are making significant changes in the ways in which we record our ideas. Using a computer results in better writing, especially for less accomplished writers (Bangert-Downs, 1993). Less adept writers seem to be motivated by the added engagement that a word-processing program offers.

Using a computer may also lead to more collaboration, because it makes the students' writing more visible. This seems to lead to discussions about writing between the teacher and student and among students (Dahl & Farnan, 1998). Word-processing programs have taken the drudgery out of revising. No longer is it necessary to recopy a piece just because a revision has been made. Editing features allow the user to move words, phrases, sentences, or whole passages; eliminate unwanted words and other elements; and revise elements with a minimum of effort. Many word-processing programs also contain spell checkers that alert students to possible spelling and typing errors. Some programs include a thesaurus, so student writers can seek substitutes for overworked words. The more sophisticated programs even check grammar, indicate average sentence length, and note certain characteristics of style that might require alteration, such as overusing certain words and writing mostly in simple sentences.

Desktop Publishing

As the last step in the writing process, publishing is often ignored. However, it is the step that gives purpose to writing. **Desktop publishing**, as its name suggests, provides publishing opportunities where none existed before. With it, students can produce high-quality posters, banners, signs, forms, brochures, résumés, classroom or school newspapers, reports, and newsletters for clubs. They can also illustrate stories or write stories

FYI

■ Word processing makes students' text readily visible, so it is easier for the teacher to take a quick look at the students' work. This visibility makes peer conferencing and collaboration easier (Zorfass, Corley, & Remy, 1994).

■ Generally, it is advisable for students to compose their first drafts with pencil and paper because they are faster at writing than they are at typing.

■ Text-to-speech word processing programs such as *Write: Outloud* (Don Johnston), *Dr. Peet's Talk/Writer* (Interest-Driven Learning), and *Special Writer Coach* (Tom Snyder) say the words that students type in. These programs are especially helpful for students with impaired vision and for very young students. They can also be used by students who have difficulty detecting errors in their writing. Students who reread a written piece without detecting a dropped *-ed* or *-ing*, missing words, or awkward phrases often notice these errors when they hear the computer read the piece aloud.

■ **Desktop publishing** is the combining of word processing with layout and other graphic design features that allow the user to place print and graphic elements on a page.

based on illustrations. With some programs, students can insert background music, sound effects, animation, and speech.

Perhaps desktop publishing's greatest advantage is that it leads to more polished writing. Without any coercion by the teacher, students take one last look at their pieces before having them printed out. Often, they discover a misspelled word, an awkward phrase, or erroneous punctuation that would have otherwise gone unnoticed.

Computer-Assisted Presentations

Computer-assisted presentations (CAPs) created with PowerPoint, Keynote, or other presentation software have become widespread, both in businesses and in schools. CAPs foster the blending of visual and verbal information. Illustrations can act as prompts to help students provide added information or a fuller explanation. CAPs can also be motivational, and they lend themselves to group work. CAPs are especially effective for students who have difficulty expressing themselves verbally. CAPs can be planned using the same steps used in creating reports, but with an emphasis on visuals.

E-Mail

One of the most popular features of the Internet is e-mail. E-mailing and instant messaging friends are favorite activities for young people. Being an immediate form of communication, e-mail is motivating to students. Being able to use it is also a critical skill, as more and more adults use it to keep in touch with friends and to communicate at work. When discussing e-mailing, compare it to the traditional postcard and letter. Share with students how you go about composing an e-mail. Note that e-mail is less formal, but that the correct use of mechanics and spelling is still important.

Discuss the use of a subject heading for e-mail, the importance of typing the address accurately, and the convenience of the address book. Discuss, too, including digital photos or illustrations and attachments. Emphasize the importance of courtesy and safety. With parental permission, you might have students e-mail you and each other. E-mail might be used for practical purposes, such as communicating with members of a literature discussion group or submitting a project or homework assignment. You might also arrange for students to have keypals in other schools. Sources of keypals are listed below.

IECC-Intercultural E-mail ClassroomConnections: http://www.iecc.org

ePALS Classroom Exchange: http://www.epals.com

Mighty Media Keypals Club: http://www.mightymedia.com/keypals

■■■ Checkup ■■■

1. What are some ways in which technology can be used to foster better writing?

■■■

■ Reading Helps Writing

Frequent reading is associated with superior writing. This fact was borne out by the results of several studies reviewed by Stotsky (1983). Students who were assigned additional reading improved in expository writing as much as or more than those who studied grammar or were assigned extra writing practice. It should be noted that the students who improved did engage in writing tasks. Improved writing resulted only for students who engaged in additional reading.

One of the most fundamental ways in which reading enhances writing is by providing a model of form. Children's writing reflects the forms with which they are familiar. Dahl and Freppon (1995) found that first-graders in an inner-city school used their reading

---

books as sources of structures and ideas for their writing. Reading trade books and hearing their teacher read enriched their writing. Calkins (1986) described how a group of sixth-graders moved from reading mysteries to writing their own. Through a discussion of the books they were reading, they came to understand and appreciate the components of a mystery and believed that the authors were showing them how to write in this genre.

Students can also learn stylistic features from their reading. After a trip to the zoo, one first-grade teacher read *The Day Jimmy's Boa Ate the Wash* (Noble, 1980) to the class. The book begins with the query "How was your trip to the zoo?" and goes on to recount a series of amazing and amusing incidents. A student also began his piece with "How was your trip to the zoo?" However, the rest of his work told how one class member became lost and was found watching the tigers. The boy used *The Day Jimmy's Boa Ate the Wash* to shape his piece but not to determine its content (Franklin, 1988). The stylistic device of using an opening question was borrowed, but the content was original.

In addition to being a source of ideas, books and articles can also provide model formats. For instance, *Cinderella's Rat* (Meddaugh, 1997) models telling a story from another point of view. Using this format, students might tell about themselves from the point of view of their dog, a neighbor, a peer, or a sibling. After reading *Spider Boy* (Fletcher, 1997), in which the main character keeps a journal, students might keep journals of their own. Reading can also help with topic selection. For instance, reading about some funny incidents that happened to Ramona Quimby, one of Beverly Cleary's characters, may remind students of humorous events in their lives.

Students have a better chance of learning about writing through reading if they "read like a writer," which means that as they read, they notice the techniques the author uses to create a story. This process is enhanced if students respond to their reading in journals. As they begin to look at characters' motives and other story elements, they might then begin to incorporate them in their own writing (Hiebert et al., 1998). It also helps if students take note of authors' techniques during discussions of books read. Teachers might make specific recommendations of pieces that students could use as models or sources of techniques. For example, one of Beverly Cleary's or Betsy Byars's works might help a student who is attempting to write conversational prose.

▪▪▪ Checkup ▪▪▪

1. How does reading help writing?

▪ A Full Menu

Students should engage in a full range of writing activities. With guidance, everyone can and should write poetry, plays, and stories. How can we tell what our limits are unless we try? Exploring a new genre helps students understand that particular form and provides them with a different kind of writing experience. Another advantage is that the skills learned in one mode often transfer to other modes. Writing poetry improves word choice and figurative language. Writing plays helps improve dialogue when writing fiction. Fictional techniques enliven expository writing.

Budding writers need a full menu of writing experiences. They should write everything from postcards and thank-you notes to poetry, the most demanding kind of writing. Table 11.2 lists some of the kinds of writing activities that might be introduced in an elementary or middle school. It is not a definitive list and offers only suggestions. It should be adapted to fit the needs of your students and your school district's curriculum.

▪▪▪ Checkup ▪▪▪

1. What kinds of writing should students be encouraged to do?

■■■ **TABLE 11.2**   **Suggested Writing Activities**

Academic
Book review/book report
Essay test
State competency test
Computer-assisted presentation
Web site

Business/Economic
Business letter
Consumer complaint
Correcting a mistake
Seeking information
Ordering a product

Civic/Personal Development Letters
Letter to the editor
Making a suggestion
Protesting a government decision
Requesting help
Seeking information

Everyday/Practical
Directions
List
Message (computer, telephone)
Notice

Social
E-mail
Friendly letter
Postcard
Thank-you note
Get-well card and note
Special occasion card and note
Invitation
Fan letter

General Communication
Announcement
Newsletter

Newspaper
Ad
Editorial
Feature
Letter to editor
News story
Photo essay/caption

Creative
Story
Poem/verse
Essay (humorous or serious)
Play/script

Personal
Diary
Journal

Writing to Learn
Descriptions of characters, persons, places, events, experiments
Comparisons of characters, places, events, issues, processes
Explanation of processes, events, movements, causes, and effects
Diary of events
Journal of observation
Summary of information
Synthesis of several sources of information
Critique of a story, play, movie, or TV program

Building Higher-Level Literacy

Research suggests that there are large numbers of students who can respond orally to higher-level questions but who have difficulty when asked to answer the same questions in writing (Gunning, 2005, 2006). Make sure that students have ample opportunity to answer higher-level questions in writing and that they are given instruction in how to do so. You might try presenting them with one challenging question each week. At first, respond to the question as a shared writing activity. Gradually turn over more responsibility to the students.

Help for Struggling Readers and Writers

Although word-processing programs offer assistance to all writers, they are particularly helpful to struggling readers and writers, especially if they have text-to-speech capability. Hearing their compositions read aloud helps students note errors or awkward portions of their pieces that they may not otherwise have detected. Text-to-speech programs can be used to create practice exercises for struggling readers. *Write: Outloud* (Don Johnston) has a large picture library. The names of the pictures, captions, or paragraphs can be typed under them so that students can practice reading words, sentences, or whole stories. Because of the software's speech capability, students could have difficult words read to them.

Struggling writers also benefit from suggestions provided in teacher and peer conferences. These serve as scaffolds directing them where and how to revise (Dahl & Farnan, 1998).

Think sheets, as explained earlier in the chapter, would also be of benefit to struggling writers, as would direct instruction in writing techniques and the use of frames. Frames are partly written paragraphs that students complete. A frame for comparison–contrast paragraphs is presented in Figure 11.10 (on p. 500). As struggling writers gain skill, frames can be faded.

Tools for the Classroom

■■■ **FIGURE 11.10**
Sample Comparison–Contrast
Frame Paragraphs

> African and Asian elephants have many similarities.
>
> Both African and Asian elephants are_____.
>
> Both_____.
>
> However, there are several differences between African and Asian elephants.
>
> African elephants_____,
>
> but Asian elephants_____.
>
> African elephants_____.
>
> However, Asian elephants_____.
>
> As you can see, African and Asian elephants differ in the way they look and how they act.

All too often, struggling writers judge that they have nothing worth putting down on paper. To show these writers that they have something to say, find out in which areas they are experts. Do they know a lot about raising a puppy, making cookies, or playing basketball? Encourage them to read to find out about favorite topics and to write in their areas of expertise (Hiebert et al., 1998).

Essential Standards

Kindergarten

Students will

- use drawings, letters, and phonetically spelled words to tell stories, respond to literature, recount experiences, and tell someone what to do.
- begin to use spacing between words, capitalization, punctuation, and other conventions.

Grade 1

Students will

- write letters, lists, captions, directions, explanations, simple narratives, and responses to literature.
- write narratives that have a beginning, middle, and end and show a sense of story.
- use invented spellings.
- write in sentences and use capital letters and end punctuation marks.
- begin to revise, edit, and proofread.

Grades 2 and 3

Students will

- write letters, directions, explanations, reports, opinions, narratives, and responses to literature.
- write narratives that have a beginning, middle, and end and show a sense of story.
- write in complete sentences and use correct end punctuation, commas in a series, quotation marks, and capitalization of proper nouns.
- use varied sentence patterns and conventional spelling.
- use stylistic devices such as dialogue.
- use one or two details and/or examples to develop an idea.
- show a sense of audience.
- revise, edit, and proofread.

Grades 4 through 8

Students will

- write letters, directions, explanations, reports, opinions, narratives, and responses to literature.
- write narratives that have more complex plots and more fully developed characters.
- use varied sentence patterns.
- use descriptive words and vivid verbs.
- follow basic rules of capitalization and punctuation.
- use story-telling techniques, such as building suspense and writing a surprise ending.
- use a number of details and/or examples to develop an idea.
- write multiparagraph pieces that contain an introduction, development, and conclusion.
- use dialogue, figurative language, and other stylistic devices.
- show increased sense of audience.
- revise text by adding, deleting, rearranging, and expanding text.
- use a rubric to evaluate and revise their writing.

Action Plan

1. Use writing samples, observations of students at work, and rubrics to assess students' current writing development and needs.
2. Based on students' needs, provide guided writing instruction to students.
3. Use discussion, brainstorming, clustering, freewriting, and other techniques to prepare students for writing. Also, encourage students to collect topic ideas in journals.
4. Model and discuss the process of composing. Use conferences, wordless books, drawings, models of stories, student research, reading, or other devices to aid students as they compose. If necessary, use frames or guides like those provided in cognitive strategy instruction in writing, but fade their use as students grow more proficient.
5. Model the process of revising and editing. Provide practice by having students analyze and revise sample pieces. Provide guidance for peer revising and self-revising. Stress revising to make pieces more interesting and more informative. Encourage the use of devices such as Questions, Snapshots, Thoughtshots, Exploding a Moment, and Building a Scene.
6. Provide opportunities to publish so that students are motivated to write and gain a sense of audience.
7. Model and explain the process of composing reports. Provide extensive guidance.
8. Guide students as they use word-processing programs and construct multimedia presentations.
9. Plan a full range of writing activities. Create a program that balances students' need to engage in a variety of writing tasks with their need to write on topics of personal interest.
10. Prepare students for local, state, and national assessments. However, don't spend an excessive amount of time practicing for the kinds of writing they will be tested on. Remember that a well-rounded writing program is the best preparation for any writing assessment.
11. Use portfolios and observations to monitor students' progress and make adjustments as called for. Involve students in the creation of rubrics to give them an understanding of writing assignments and a sense of participation in the assessment process.
12. Monitor the effectiveness of your program and make adjustments as necessary.

Assessment

In addition to the assessment measures discussed in this chapter, use the devices presented in Chapter 2. The portfolios and holistic and analytic devices described in that chapter should prove especially useful. Also, observe students in writing workshop. Note how they approach writing and carry out their writing activities. Do they have strategies for getting started and developing their pieces? Do they see themselves as competent writers? If not, what might be done to build their sense of competence?

Summary

Writing evolves from the prespeech gestures children make and from the language they hear and later use. Writing develops in stages. Instruction should be geared to students' stage of writing development. Needed writing strategies should be identified, presented, practiced, and applied.

Once viewed primarily as a product, writing today is viewed as both process and product. Major processes involved in writing include prewriting (topic selection, planning, and rehearsing), composing, revising, editing, and publishing.

Essential techniques for teaching writing include modeling, conferencing, sharing, and direct teaching of skills and strategies. Improving writing requires knowing what the characteristics of good writing are. These can be translated into rubrics or checklists that help students better understand the requirements of a piece of writing and that provide guidance for assessment and revision. Portfolios in the form of file folders are recommended for storing and keeping track of students' writing.

Although the emphasis in writing instruction is on content, form is also important. Good form improves content. A balanced writing program includes instruction and exploration of a variety of narrative and expository forms.

Instruction in composing and mechanical skills should be geared to students' current needs and should be continuing and systematic, including daily instruction as well as on-the-spot aid when problems arise.

Good readers tend to be good writers, and vice versa. Also, students who read more tend to be better at writing. Their writing reflects structures and stylistic elements learned through reading. Through reading, they also pick up ideas for topics.

Extending and Applying

1. Observe a group of students as they write. Note how they go about prewriting, composing, revising, and editing. What strategies do they use? How effectively do they employ them? What other strategies might they use?

2. Try writing for a short period of time three to five days a week to gain insight into the process. If possible, have conferences with a colleague. Note your strengths and areas that need work.

3. Examine a student's permanent writing folder. Track the student's growth. Note gains and needs as well as the types of topics the student has explored and the kinds of writing the student has done. With the student, make plans for future activities.

4. Plan a writing lesson. Using the process approach, focus on topic selection and planning. If possible, teach the lesson. Give an overview of the results of the lesson.

Developing a Professional Portfolio

Keep a portfolio of your writing, especially professional pieces such as articles that you have written and class newsletters or other student projects that you have guided. Also include a videotape and/or copy of a lesson plan completed for item 4 in Extending and Applying or for another writing lesson. Keep documents for any special writing projects that you conducted with your students.

- Enter Assignment ID **RMV4** into **Assignment Finder,** and select the video titled "Writing and Reading." This video provides an overview of strategies for helping students see the reading-writing connection. A kindergarten teacher uses writing as a means for helping students learn to read.

- How is the relationship between reading and writing demonstrated in this video? As a teacher, how might you use technology to facilitate students' appreciation of the reading-writing connection?

- Explore MyLabSchool further to find the course areas for Reading Methods, Language Arts, and Content Area Reading and identify other assets that support concepts introduced in this chapter.

Developing a Resource File

Maintain a collection of published and unpublished pieces that might be used to illustrate various writing techniques. Also collect pieces of writing that might be used by students to practice assessing or revising writing. Maintain a list of possible topics and rubrics.

To access chapter objectives, practice tests, weblinks, and flashcards, go to the companion website at www.ablongman.com/gunning6e.

12 Diversity in the Literacy Classroom

Adapting Instruction for English Language and At-Risk Learners

For each of the following statements related to the chapter you are about to read, put a check under "Agree" or "Disagree" to show how you feel. Discuss your responses with classmates before you read the chapter.

	Agree	Disagree
1. By and large, techniques used to teach average students also work with those who have special needs.	_____	_____
2. Labeling students as reading disabled, learning disabled, or at risk is harmful.	_____	_____
3. Economically disadvantaged children may have difficulty learning to read because their language is inadequate when they begin school.	_____	_____
4. Of all the special needs students, gifted children require the least help.	_____	_____
5. It is best to teach English language learners to read in their native language.	_____	_____
6. Even students with serious reading or other learning disabilities should be taught in the regular classroom.	_____	_____

The United States is the most culturally diverse nation in the world. Dozens of languages are spoken in U.S. schools, and dozens of cultures are represented. Adding to that diversity is the trend toward inclusion. Increasingly, students who have learning or reading disabilities, visual or hearing impairments, emotional or health problems, or other disabilities are being taught in regular classrooms. Because these children have special needs, their programs may have to be adjusted so that they can reach their full potential. Adjustments also need to be made for children who are economically disadvantaged or who are still learning English. The gifted and talented also have special needs and require assistance to reach their full potential.

What has been your experience teaching children from other cultures or children who are just learning to speak English? What has been your experience with students who have special needs? Think of some special needs students you have known. What provisions did the school make for these students? Could the school have done more? If so, what? What are some adjustments that you make now or might make in the future for such students?

■ English Language Learners

Children in today's schools come from more than a hundred language communities. Among the languages spoken, in order of number of speakers, are Spanish, Vietnamese, Hmong, Haitian Creole, Korean, Arabic, Chinese (Cantonese), Russian, Tagalog, Navajo, Khmer, Portuguese, Urd, Chinese (Mandarin), Serbo-Croatian, Lao, and Japanese. As a result of the large number of members in these language communities, there are currently more than 5 million school children in the United States who have been classified as Limited English Proficient (LEP) (Office of English Language Acquisition, Language Enhancement and Academic Achievement for Limited English Proficient Students, 2005). This is 10 percent of the school-age population. LEP is "the legal term for students who were not born in the United States or whose native language is not

FYI

■ The largest proportion of ELLs are Latinos. Latino students compose 8 percent of students in pre-K through high school (OELA, 2005).

■ English learners should be involved in reading and writing English as soon as possible. "Written language is fixed. It does not speed past the way oral language does. So when teachers read big books, students acquiring English can follow along and start to make connections between the print and the new language they are acquiring" (Freeman & Freeman, 1998, p. 412).

■ In California, which is home to more than 1.5 million ELLs, students are provided with one year of sheltered English immersion. Parents can request waivers to keep their children in bilingual programs. However, the school need not offer bilingual education unless at least twenty waivers have been granted at a particular grade level.

Adapting Instruction for English Language Learners

■ English language learners do fairly well on tests of basic skills up to fourth grade. In fourth grade and beyond, as greater demands are made on language proficiency, scores begin to decline (Bielenberg & Fillmore, 2004).

■ See p. 454 for suggestions for using the language-experience approach to teach ELLs.

English and who cannot participate effectively in the regular curriculum because they have difficulty speaking, understanding, reading, and writing English" (U.S. Department of Education, Office of Bilingual Education, 1998, p. 3). However, this text uses the term English language learner (ELL). About 75 percent of ELLs attend high-poverty schools. For many ELL students, schooling is a struggle.

■ Overview of a Program for English Language Learners

The question of how English language learners should be taught to read and write strikes at the core of what reading is—that is, a language activity. Using prior experience and knowledge of language, the reader constructs meaning. Common sense and research (Fillmore & Valdez, 1986) dictate that the best way to teach reading and writing to ELLs is to teach them in their native language. Learning to read and write are complex tasks that involve the total language system: semantic, syntactic, and phonological components. Until children have a basic grasp of the meaning of a language, they will be unable to read it. Even if they are able to sound out the words, they do not understand the meaning.

The prestigious Committee on the Prevention of Reading Difficulties in Young Children recommends teaching ELLs to read in their native language while, at the same time, teaching them to speak English as a second language (Snow, Burns, & Griffin, 1998). Once they have a sufficient grasp of English and of basic reading in their native language, they can then learn to read in English. This type of approach has several advantages. First of all, children build a solid foundation in their native tongue. With language development, thinking skills are enhanced, concepts are clarified and organized, and children learn to use language in an abstract way. Because they are also learning math, science, and social studies in their native language, background experience is being developed.

Thinking skills, background of knowledge, and reading skills learned in students' native language transfer to reading and writing in English. One objection to a bilingual approach is that it delays instruction in reading and writing in English, thereby causing children to lose ground. Research clearly indicates that this is not the case. In several studies, students taught to read in their native language and then later in a second language outperformed those taught to read in the second language (Modiano, 1968). Furthermore, as they progressed through the grades, the difference between the two groups increased (Rosier, 1977). Learning to read in their native language provides ELLs with a solid foundation for learning to read in another language (Constantino, 1999).

The key to a successful bilingual reading program may lie in knowing when to start instruction in the second language. Students should first read relatively proficiently in their native language. Thonis (cited in Fillmore & Valdez, 1986) cautioned that reading in a second language should not be attempted until students have reached a level where they can interpret the text and draw inferences. This indicates that they have developed higher-level comprehension skills, which can then be transferred to reading in the second language. A number of bilingual Spanish–English reading systems include one component in Spanish and one in English. Some also include a transitional component that eases the transfer from Spanish into English.

■ ■ ■ Checkup ■ ■ ■

1. What are the advantages of teaching ELLs to read in their native language?
2. What might be some disadvantages?

ESL Only.   Not all ELLs have access to a bilingual program. In California and several other states, for instance, most bilingual programs have been terminated and students are being provided one year of intensive English instead (Gandara, 2000). If the only program

If possible, English language learners should be taught to read in their native language.

offered is one that teaches the students English as a second language, it is best to delay formal reading instruction until the children have a reasonable command of English (Snow, Burns, & Griffin, 1998). However, students can engage in shared reading, complete language-experience stories, and read predictable books as they learn English. They should also be encouraged to write as best they can. As they gain proficiency in oral English, they can tackle increasingly complex reading and writing tasks. Their oral-language skills will support their reading and writing, and their reading and writing will reinforce and build oral-language skills.

The classroom teacher's role is to support the efforts of bilingual and/or ESL professionals by meeting regularly with them and working with them to plan activities that will enhance students' progress. Even after students have finished the ESL program, they still require special language-development activities. Some adjustments that might be made to adapt classroom instruction to ELLs' needs are described in the following subsections.

BUILDING LANGUAGE

Monitor the speech you use in your classroom. What you say should be understandable but rich enough that it fosters language growth. Deliberately introduce challenging vocabulary and advanced language structures.

Case Study

Teaching Literacy to English Language Learners

Two groups of Spanish-speaking students were instructed in literacy skills over a period of four years (August, Calderón, & Carlo, 2001). The approach used to teach both groups was a structured phonics program known as Success for All (SFA). One group was instructed in the Spanish version of SFA and later switched to English. The other group was instructed in English.

Despite being taught to read in Spanish initially, the Spanish-instructed students outperformed students taught the English version of SFA. Many of the skills taught in Spanish transferred to English. Students who did well in Spanish reading also did well in English reading. Students taught to read in Spanish also knew more cognates, so that they were better prepared to use their knowledge of Spanish to read English. Not having been exposed to a formal written Spanish program, students taught to read in English knew fewer cognates. Students taught to read in Spanish had a double benefit. Not only did they become more proficient readers in English, they also learned to read in their native language and, in so doing, strengthened their knowledge of Spanish.

Build Language

The greatest need of ELLs is to develop skills in understanding and using English. Special emphasis should be placed on academic language. As students learn English, they first acquire functional structures that allow them to greet others, make conversational statements, and ask questions. This type of everyday communication is heavily contextualized and is augmented by gestures, pointing at objects, and pantomiming. It takes approximately two years for students to become socially proficient in English (Cummins, 2001). However, schooling demands academic language, which is more varied and abstract and relatively decontextualized. This is the language in which math procedures and subject matter concepts are explained. Proficiency in academic English may take up to five years or more. Even though ELLs may seem proficient in oral English, they may have difficulty with academic language. Mastery of conversational English may mask deficiencies in important higher-level language skills (Sutton, 1989). Because of the time required to acquire academic language, ELLs may not demonstrate their true abilities on achievement and cognitive ability tests administered in English.

Increasing the amount of oral language in the classroom enhances English speaking. Structure conversations at the beginning of the school day and at other convenient times to talk about current events, weather, hobbies, sports, or other topics of interest. Encourage students to participate in discussions and provide opportunities for them to use "language for a broad variety of functions, both social and academic" (Allen, 1991, p. 362).

Also plan strategic use of the students' native language. Use that level of English that students are familiar with. However, for developing complex concepts, use the students' native language, if possible, or ask another student to provide a translation. That way the student doesn't have the burden of trying to understand difficult concepts expressed in terms that may be hard to understand.

A reading program for ELL students should include children's books. "Children's books can provide a rich input of cohesive language, made comprehensible by patterned language, predictable structure, and strong, supportive illustrations" (Allen, 1994, pp. 117–118). Children's books can be used as a stimulus for discussion, show objects that ELLs may not be familiar with, and build concepts. Books that are well illustrated and whose illustrations support the text are especially helpful. A predictable book such as *Cat on the Mat* (Wildsmith, 1982) repeats the simple pattern "The _____ sat on the mat." Eric Carle's *Have You Seen My Cat?* (1973) repeats the question pattern "Have you seen my _____?" Such books build knowledge of basic syntactical patterns as well as vocabulary. After reading texts of this type, students might use the patterns in their oral language and writing.

The speed with which students learn English will be determined in part by the quality of their English-learning experiences. Students learn English faster if there is ample comprehensible input, which means that the level of English is such that the students can make sense of it (Cummins, 1994; Krashen, 1993). Students learn more English when they have confidence in their ability to learn it. Instruction that accepts students' language and culture and builds on their knowledge fosters language development. Students also learn English faster in classes that are student centered.

To facilitate understanding of oral language, add illustrative elements to discussions. Use objects, models, and pictures to illustrate vocabulary words that might be difficult. Role-play situations and pantomime activities. When talking about rocks in a geology unit, bring some in and hold them up when mentioning their names. When discussing a story about a tiger, point to a picture of the tiger. When introducing a unit on magnets, hold up a magnet every time you use the word; point to the poles each time you mention them. Supplement oral directions with gestures and demonstrations. Think of yourself as an actor in a silent movie who must use body language to convey meaning.

Stages of Second-Language Acquisition

Although there is some overlap among stages, a second language develops in approximately five stages: preproduction, early production, speech emergence, intermediate, and advanced, as shown in Table 12.1. (Stages are adapted from Díaz-Rico, 2004; Guzman-

---

■■■ **TABLE 12.1   Stages of Second-Language Acquisition**

Level of Language	Characteristics of Learner	Teaching Suggestions	Building Literacy
Preproduction	Students know a few English words but primarily use gestures and pointing to communicate. This stage is known as the silent period, because students speak only a few words of English or none at all. This stage may last up to six months. Despite not speaking, students may acquire an understanding of up to 500 words.	Use concrete objects, gestures, and pointing; repeat and paraphrase; speak slowly; ask what, who where, and yes/no questions.	Can use books that label illustrations. Encourage drawing and writing of labels and captions.
Early production	Students can understand and use some common words and expressions such as "OK," "That mine," "Can I sharpen pencil?" This stage may last up to six months. Students may acquire a combined listening–speaking vocabulary of 1,000 words.	Use concrete objects, gestures, and pointing; speak slowly; simplify language; build English vocabulary; ask what, who, where, and either/or questions and questions that elicit a simple list of words.	Students can understand easy predictable text. Encourage writing of brief pieces that use basic sentence patterns. Use repeated sentences from predictable books as models.
Speech emergence	Students can use brief, everyday expressions and have greater receptive than expressive command of English. Students begin to participate in class discussions. This stage may last for up to a year. Most students acquire about 3,000 words by end of stage.	Use heavy visual support and gestures; develop English vocabulary; ask what, who, where, and when questions and questions that can be answered with a phrase or brief sentence.	Student can read more advanced predictable text; may benefit from interactive writing.
Intermediate	Students have a fairly good grasp of everyday English and begin to grasp and use academic English. Can work in groups. This stage may last for up to a year. Most students acquire about 6,000 words by end of stage.	Use visual supports, including graphic organizers, and gestures; use prompts to foster elaboration; ask what, who, where, when, and why questions and questions that required explanation or elaboration. Some students can benefit from sheltered instruction.	Students may need easier texts and/or assistance with texts; most benefit from language experience. Scaffold writing by introducing needed vocabulary and forms; use frame paragraphs.
Advanced	Language is comparable to that of a native speaker. Students may take up to five years or more to reach this stage.	Continue to provide visual support and build vocabulary.	Students can read grade-level texts. Develop higher-level thinking skills; develop full array of writing skills.

Johannessen, 2006; Northwest Regional Educational Laboratory, 2003.) Gear questions and other activities to students' language level (Lalas, Solomon, & Johannessen, 2006). For the earliest levels, for instance, ask what, who, and where questions. These can be answered with single words. Progress to when questions, which might demand a phrase, and then to how and why questions, which require more elaborated language.

In preparation for teaching ELLs, take note of the students' level of knowledge and language. Plan for the kinds of difficulties they might experience. Ask yourself, "What specifically am I going to do to increase comprehensibility? How will I differentiate for

Case Study

Encouraging ELLs to be Seekers of Words

$\mathcal{W}$hen Josephine Nobisso, a native speaker of Italian, struggled to find a word to express an idea, her parents encouraged her to seek an approximation. This led Josephine to become a seeker of words and a published writer. Based on her experiences as an ELL, she recommends that students pursue a word when they believe that they have heard one that expresses the meaning that they have in mind. She supplies this example:

> A child asks a teacher, "What's the word for a round thing, like 'circle' but not 'circle'?" Her response, "Do you mean a sphere?" helps the child to enter the word into his lifelong lexicon (Nobisso, 2002).

Adapting Instruction for English Language Learners

■ Teachers might underestimate the abilities of ELLs. Because they are speaking in broken English, ELLs might not seem as knowledgeable or as intelligent as native English speakers. However, teachers might have unrealistic expectations for ELLs at the intermediate stage. At this stage, students might seem to have more advanced language than they possess (Lalas, Solomon, & Johannessen, 2006).

■ Because of limited English, ELLs may have difficulty fully explaining what they know about a selection they have read. They may mispronounce words whose meanings they know. The key element is whether students are getting meaning from the words, not whether they are pronouncing them correctly. In one study, students who were good readers in Spanish and were becoming proficient readers in English were not given instruction in comprehension because the teachers wrongly believed that their mispronunciations were a sign of weak decoding skills (Moll, Estrada, Diaz, & Lopez, 1980, cited in García, Pearson, & Jiménez, 1994).

ELLs at different levels?" Develop knowledge of text structures and use graphic organizers. Go through each chapter in any text you plan to use and note features, such as illustrations, that will be of help to ELLs. After the lesson, reflect. Ask yourself, "Have I fostered language development? Was I able to make the text accessible?" (Lalas, Solomon, & Johannessen, 2006).

Use Cooperative Learning and Peer Tutoring Strategies

Working with peers provides excellent opportunities for ELLs to apply language skills. In a small group, they are less reluctant to speak. In addition, they are better able to make themselves understood and better able to understand others. Working with buddies and in small groups provides context and fosters language learning (Cummins, 1994).

Use Print

Use print to support and expand the oral-language learning of English learners. Label items in the room. Write directions, schedules, and similar information about routines on the chalkboard. As you write them, read them orally (Sutton, 1989). Also encourage students to write:

> Provide experiences in which language is greatly contextualized (as, for example, a field trip, a science experiment, role playing, planning a class party, solving a puzzle). Use print materials with these activities as a natural extension of the oral language generated: write a class language experience report about the field trip; record information on a science chart; write dialogues or captions for a set of pictures; make lists of party items needed; follow written directions to find a hidden treasure. (p. 686)

Adapt Instruction

Compare the child's native language with English and note features that might cause difficulty; then provide help in those areas. For example, some major phonological, morphological, and syntactical differences between Spanish and English are noted in Table 12.2 (O'Brien, 1973). Other differences between Spanish and English include a lack of contractions in Spanish; confusion is also caused by idiomatic expressions, such as "shout down the street" and "call up a friend." Another difference has to do with relationships between speakers and listeners. In Hispanic cultures, for example, it is customary to avert one's eyes when speaking to persons in authority. However, for many cultural groups, the opposite is true. Students learning English should learn the cultural expectations of the language along with vocabulary and syntax.

Adapt lessons to meet the needs of ELLs. For example, when teaching phonics, start with sound–symbol relationships that are the same in both languages. For Spanish-

■■■ **TABLE 12.2**   **Areas of Special Difficulty for Native Speakers of Spanish**

Phonological	Morphological	Syntactical
Fewer vowel sounds: no short *a* (*hat*), short *i* (*fish*), short *u* (*up*), short double *o* (*took*), or schwa (*sofa*) *Fewer consonant sounds:* no /j/ (*jump*), /v/ (*vase*), /z/ (*zipper*), /sh/ (*shoe*), /ŋ/ (*sing*), /hw/ (*when*), /zh/ (*beige*) *Some possible confusions:* /b/ pronounced /p/: *cab* becomes *cap* /j/ pronounced /y/: *jet* becomes *yet* /ŋ/ pronounced as /n/: *thing* becomes *thin* /ch/ pronounced as /sh/: *chin* becomes *shin* /v/ pronounced as /b/: *vote* becomes *boat* /y/ pronounced as /j/: *yes* becomes *jes* /sk/, /sp/, /st/ pronounced as /esk/, /esp/, /est/: *speak* becomes *espeak* /a/ pronounced as /e/: *bat* becomes *bet* /i/ pronounced as /ē/: *hit* becomes *heat* /ē/ pronounced as /i/: *heal* becomes *hill* /u/ pronounced as /o/: *hut* becomes *hot* /o͞o/ pronounced as /o͞o/: *look* becomes *Luke*	*de* (of) used to show possession: *Joe's pen* becomes *the pen of Joe* *mas* (more) used to show comparison: *faster* becomes *more fast*	Use of *no* for *not*: He no do his homework. No *s* for plural: my two friend No auxiliary verbs: She no play soccer. Adjectives after nouns: the car blue Agreement of adjectives: the elephants bigs No inversion of question: Anna is here? Articles with professional titles: I went to the Dr. Rodriguez.

Adapted from C. A. O'Brien, *Teaching the Language-Different Child to Read*, Columbus, OH: Merrill, 1973.

speaking children, you might start with long *o*, since that sound is common in both English and Spanish. Before teaching elements that are not present in Spanish—short *i*, for instance—make sure that these elements have been introduced in the ESL class. For easily confused auditory items—long *e* and short *i*, for example—provide added auditory-discrimination exercises. Also, use the items in context or use real objects or pictures to illustrate them. When discussing shoes, for example, point to them.

When teaching a reading lesson, examine the text for items that might cause special problems. Pay particular attention to the following:

■ *Vocabulary.* What vocabulary words might pose problems for ELLs? Unfamiliar vocabulary is a major stumbling block for ELLs. There may be a number of common English words that ELLs may not be familiar with. Expand and deepen their knowledge of English words. Words with multiple meanings, for example, can be particularly challenging. Students might understand one meaning of a word—for example, "a thin sheet of paper" for *tissue*—but be confused when they hear the same word while studying the human body in science class (Lalas, Solomon, & Johannessen, 2006).

■ *Background of experience.* What background is needed to understand the selection? Coming from diverse lands, ELLs may not have the experiences assumed by the author of the selection. Their background knowledge might be different from that taught in U.S. schools. This is especially true in the social studies: Students from other cultures might have different understandings of concepts such as democracy and the right to privacy. Or, they might be unfamiliar with Halloween and other holidays and celebrations (Lalas, Solomon, & Johannessen, 2006).

■ *Syntax.* Does the selection use sentence patterns that ELLs might have difficulty with? Does it use numerous contractions?

■ *Semantics.* Will certain figures of speech or idiomatic expressions cause confusion?

■ *Culture.* What cultural items might cause problems in understanding the selection? For instance, some ELLs from traditional cultures might have difficulty understanding the casual relationship that children in the mainstream culture have with authority figures.

 Adapting Instruction for English Language Learners

In your lesson plans for ELLs, include language objectives that focus on vocabulary, syntax, figurative language, and other elements that might pose problems for your students. In addition to making key concepts more accessible to ELLs, such lessons will build their language skills (Bielenberg & Fillmore, 2004).

USING TECHNOLOGY ■ ■ ■

National Clearinghouse for English Language Acquisition provides a wealth of information on bilingual education and includes excellent links to useful sites.
http://ncela.gwu.edu

Dr. Mora's Web Site is also an excellent source of information about bilingual education.
http://coe.sdsu.edu/people/jmora

The teacher does not have to attempt to present all potentially confusing items. Those most important to a basic understanding of the selection should be chosen. Some potentially difficult items might be discussed after the story has been read.

Of course, as with any group of students, care must be taken to explain to ELLs concepts and vocabulary that could hinder their understanding, as well as to build background and activate schemata. Before students read a piece, activate their prior knowledge.

The first reading of a selection should be silent. Because ELLs are still learning English, the temptation is to have them read orally. However, this turns the reading lesson into a speech lesson. Plan legitimate activities for purposeful oral rereading after the selection has been read silently and discussed.

Chances are that ELLs will read more slowly than native speakers of English. Because they are learning the language, it will take them longer to process what they read. Until their recognition of English words becomes automatic, they may have to translate words from English into their native tongue. Seeing the word *cow*, the student may have to search his lexicon for the Spanish equivalent of *cow, vaca*. The extra step slows down the reading.

Provide Emotional Support and Understanding

English language learners must deal with the trauma of leaving home and the cultural shock of living in an unfamiliar country (Lalas, Solomon, & Johannessen, 2006). Their experiences of home, family, and school may differ from those of native-born students. In addition, ELLs might have a different approach to learning—the school they attended might have stressed rote learning rather than understanding. For all these reasons, ELLs need emotional support and understanding.

Build on Students' Strengths

Use a language-experience approach. This avoids the problem of unfamiliar syntax and vocabulary, because children read selections that they dictate. Some students might dictate stories that contain words in both English and their native tongue. This should be allowed and could be an aid to ELLs.

Although students are learning to read in English, they should still be encouraged to read in their native tongue if they are literate in that language. In the classroom library, include books written in the various languages of your ELLs. Because Spanish is spoken by a large proportion of the U.S. population, a number of books are published in Spanish, including both translations and original works. Most of the major educational and children's book publishers offer translations of favorite books.

Fortunately, ELLs have several strategies they can use to foster comprehension. One strategy is the use of cognates. Cognates are words that are descended from the same language or form. The word for *electricity* in Spanish is *electricidad*. Seeing the word *electricity*, the Spanish-speaking reader realizes that it means the same thing as *electricidad*. Native speakers of Spanish may not realize how many Spanish words have English cognates. See Table 12.3. You might model the process by demonstrating how cognates help you read Spanish words.

Another strength that ELLs may possess is enhanced metacognitive awareness. Learning a second language has provided them with greater insights into language on an abstract level (García, Pearson, & Jiménez, 1994). ELLs can also use their native language to foster comprehension by activating prior knowledge in both languages. Another useful strategy is translating difficult passages, especially when students are in the earlier stages of learning English. Transferring prior knowledge, translating passages into their native language, and reflecting on text in their native or stronger language have the potential to improve comprehension (Jiménez, 1997).

When responding to questions or retelling a story, students should be encouraged to use their native language if they cannot respond in English. Being able to use their native language helps students to express ideas that they might not have the words for in English. If you don't speak a student's native language, you might ask the student to translate for you. If the student is unable to translate, perhaps another student in the class can do so (Kamil & Bernhardt, 2001). One way of building vocabulary is to create a word wall or charts of words in English and Spanish or other languages. If the class is about to read a selection about snakes, you might list key English words such as *snakes, poisonous, prey, fangs*, and *skin* with their counterparts in the native language of the ELLs. The ELLs can help you with the words in their native language (Kamil & Bernhardt, 2001).

Informational text may be easier for ELLs to read than narrative text. This is especially true if the informational text is developing topics with which ELLs are familiar. In addition, informational text tends to be more culture-free than narrative text, so ELLs are not puzzled by unfamiliar cultural references (Kamil & Bernhardt, 2001).

◼ ◼◼ **TABLE 12.3** **Frequently Used Spanish Cognates**

artista	famoso	música
autor	foto	necesita
bebé	favorito	nota
biografía	fruta	número
carácter	gigante	oficina
carro	gorila	página
causa	grado	papá
contento	hipopótamo	perfecta
describir	importante	rápido
diferente	insecto	teléfono
difícil	jirafa	tigre
elefante	mamá	tomate
enciclopedia	mágico	uniforme
eléctrica	mayo	vegetales
familia	minuto	zoológico

Use Technology to Assist English Language Learners

Software programs and Web sites that have a speech component can be helpful to ELLs. *Usborne's Animated First Thousand Words* is software that includes a dictionary that illustrates words and says them in both English and Spanish. Printed words also appear in English and Spanish. The program also offers a variety of challenging games and activities for reinforcing words. Students select any one of thirty-five scenes and have a choice of five games for each of the scenes. Children can hear words read aloud, see them depicted with illustrations, match words to pictures, sort words, and practice saying words by hearing a word read, recording the word, and comparing their recording to the original version. *Usborne's Animated First Thousand Words* provides excellent practice for both English speakers and ELLs.

Little Explorers Picture Dictionary (http://www.enchantedlearning.com/Dictionary. html) features nearly 2,000 illustrated dictionary entries. Each word is used in a meaningful example sentence. Most entries have links to a related Web site. There are English, English–Spanish, English–French, English–German, English–Italian, English–Japanese,

USING TECHNOLOGY ◼ ◼ ◼

The Barahona Center for the Study of Books in Spanish for Children and Adolescents features a list of more than 3,000 recommended books in Spanish. Books are listed by age, grade level, and country. Also includes books in English about Latinos.
http://www.csusm.edu/csb/english

More than 3,000 books in Spanish, ranging from beginning reading to secondary reading, with readability levels can be found at:
http://www.renlearn.com

Because she recently arrived from Southeast Asia, Nora's command of English is limited. Realizing that Nora and several other ELLs in the class will have difficulty with the concept of the water cycle if it is presented in the typical manner, the teacher uses a heavily illustrated big book to present the concept. In her lesson, she will build language as well as content knowledge. Her content objective is that students will be able to represent the water cycle in a series of drawings. Her language objective is that students will be able to explain the water cycle orally in simple sentences. As she reads the brief sentences in the big book, Nora's teacher tracks print. When she comes to key content words such as *clouds*, she points to the illustration of the clouds. After reading the book, she shows the students pictures of *clouds, rain*, and other content words. For guided practice, she has students say key words when she points to pictures that illustrate them. As an application, she gives students a booklet that has sentences that describe the four phases of the water cycle. Students are asked to draw illustrations for the sentences. To assess students, she notes at various points of the lesson whether students can identify key words or illustrate the sentences describing the water cycle. Students are also asked to retell the description of the water cycle (Echevarria, 1998).

Exemplary Teaching

Developing Content Knowledge and Language Skills

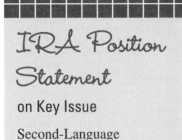

"Research has shown that literacy learning is easiest when schools provide initial instruction in the child's home language. Literacy skills developed in the home language can then be applied more easily to learning to read and write in the dominant language. At the same time, however, some parents may prefer initial instruction to be delivered in the school's dominant language. In addition, local, state or provincial, or national policies and resources may make home-language instruction impossible" (International Reading Association, 2001b, par. 2). However, the right of the child to choose to be bilingual, bicultural, and biliterate *or* monolingual, monocultural, and monoliterate must be honored and respected.

and English–Portuguese versions of the dictionary. This site also provides illustrations of hundreds of animals that can be colored. The animals' names are provided in both English and Spanish. In addition, the site features rebus rhymes, calendars, and numerous other learning aids.

▪ Closing the Gap

Because learning an academic language takes a considerable amount of time, it is the responsibility of every teacher to modify instruction to meet the needs of ELLs. Much of that modification will simply be good teaching, in which you do whatever it takes to convey concepts and strategies. In fact, programs designed to assist ELLs in mainstream classes incorporate the kinds of procedures that benefit all students.

If possible, team teach with an ESL or bilingual teacher, or at least confer with such a specialist so that you are able to structure an effective program for your ELLs. If you have grade-level or subject-matter meetings, invite the ESL teacher to attend, or at least act as a resource. Collaboration is the key to closing the gap.

▪ ▪ ▪ Checkup ▪ ▪ ▪

1. What are some basic features that should be part of a literacy program for ELLs?
2. What are some ways in which literacy instruction might be adapted for ELLs?
3. What might be done to close the achievement gap between ELLs and native speakers of English?

▪ Students at Risk

Although widely used, the term **at-risk** is avoided by some because it has a negative connotation.

> By focusing primarily on characteristics of the students, their families and their communities, the accompanying responsibility and blame for the at-risk condition is placed on the population themselves. . . . Instead . . . attention should be focused on the educational sit-

---

▪ **At risk** refers to students who have been judged likely to have difficulty at school because of poverty, low grades, retention in a grade, excessive absence, or other potentially limiting factors.

uation and on the sociocultural factors that have contributed to the at-risk condition. (García, Pearson, & Jiménez, 1994, p. 4)

Moreover, if educators blame the victims or their backgrounds, they may lower their expectations for these students. Slavin (1997–1998) suggests that we start looking at these students as having promise and give them the kinds of high-quality programs that foster success.

Economically Disadvantaged Students

The percentage of children living below the poverty level has increased recently: 17.8 percent of the nation's children live below the official poverty level (U.S. Census Bureau, 2005). About 800,000 school children are homeless. Poverty in and of itself does not mean that children cannot and will not be successful in school. For instance, even in the poorest neighborhoods, about one child out of a hundred enters kindergarten knowing letter–sound relationships and how to read words (West, Denton, & Germino-Hausken, 2000). (The proportion is two out of a hundred for middle-class children.) However, being poor does make getting an education more difficult, and many students who live in poverty experience lower achievement in literacy skills.

Principles for Teaching Economically Disadvantaged Children

Build Background.   It is important to develop background in reading in all children. For some economically disadvantaged children, this background will have to be extensive. Limited incomes generally mean limited travel and lack of opportunity for vacations, summer camps, and other expensive activities. However, the teacher should not assume that children do not have the necessary background for a particular selection they are about to read. One teacher was somewhat surprised to learn that a group of low-income sixth-graders with whom she was working had a fairly large amount of knowledge about the feudal system (Maria, 1990). Use a technique such as brainstorming or simple questioning to probe students' background to avoid making unwarranted assumptions about knowledge.

Create an Atmosphere of Success.   Teachers sometimes emphasize problems, not successes. MacArthur Award recipient L. D. Delpit (1990) said that teachers must maintain visions of success for students who are disadvantaged—to help them get *A*s, not just pass.

Make Instruction Explicit.   Middle-class children are more likely to be taught strategies at home that will help them achieve success in school and are more likely to receive help at home if they have difficulty or fail to understand implicit instruction at school. Low-income children need direct, explicit instruction. If children do not learn skills at school, family members will be less likely to supply or obtain remedial help for them. Disadvantaged students must have better teaching and more of it (Delpit, 1990).

Provide a Balanced Program.   Because the economically disadvantaged as a group do less well on skills tests, teachers may overemphasize basic skills (García, 1990). Economically disadvantaged students need higher-level as well as basic skills and strategies. These skills should be taught in context with plenty of opportunity to apply them to high-quality reading materials and real life.

Provide Access to Books and Magazines.   One of the most powerful determiners of how well children read is how much they read. Unfortunately, poor children often have few books in their homes. One study found that poor children, on average, had fewer than three books in their homes. What's more, their classrooms, schools, and public libraries had far fewer books than did those in more affluent areas (Krashen, 1997–1998). This is unfortunate, because the number of books a student reads is related to the number of books available and to having a quiet, comfortable place to read (Krashen, 1997–1998).

FYI

Middle-class children also need instruction to counteract the fourth-grade slump, but economically disadvantaged children must be given extra or more thorough instruction in this area because they are less likely to get help at home.

Counteract the Fourth-Grade Slump.   In their study of children of poverty, Chall, Jacobs, and Baldwin (1990) observed a phenomenon known as the fourth-grade slump. Students perform well in second and third grades on measures of reading and language, although form lags behind content in writing. However, beginning in fourth grade, many poor students slump in several areas. They have particular difficulty defining abstract, more academically oriented words. In addition to vocabulary, word recognition and spelling scores begin to slip. These are the skills that undergird achievement in reading and writing. They are also the skills for which the schools bear primary responsibility.

From fourth grade on, the school's role in the development of low-income children's literacy capabilities becomes especially important. The school must teach the vocabulary and concepts necessary to cope with subject matter texts. Chall, Jacobs, and Baldwin (1990) recommended systematic teaching of word-recognition skills in the primary grades and the use of children's books, both informational and fictional, in all grades. "Exposure to books on a variety of subjects and on a wide range of difficulty levels was particularly effective in the development of vocabulary" (p. 155).

Added opportunity for writing and reading in the content areas was also recommended. The researchers noted that children who wrote more comprehended better, and those who were in classes where the teachers taught content-area reading had higher vocabulary scores. It also helps to "overdetermine success." Overdetermining success "anticipates all the ways children might fail and then plans how each will be prevented or quickly and effectively dealt with" (Slavin, 1997–1998). This means making arrangements for tutoring, counseling, and family support.

■ ■ ■ Checkup ■ ■ ■

1. What are some basic principles for building the literacy skills of economically disadvantaged students?
2. What is the fourth-grade slump? How might it be overcome?

Culturally Diverse Students

It is important to value and build on every student's culture. Children from other cultures may not see the connection between their culture and school. First and foremost, it is essential that teachers become acquainted with the children's culture, especially if the teachers' backgrounds are different from those of the children they teach (Strickland, 1998). Reading, discussions with the children, visits to homes, and interaction with those who are knowledgeable about the various cultures represented in the classroom are some informal ways of obtaining information. The teacher should constantly make efforts to become familiar with the literary heritage of the cultures represented in his or her class, especially how literacy is used. For example, according to Taylor and Dorsey-Gaines (1988), African American families may read for a wide range of purposes, but the school often fails to reinforce the purposes for reading and writing taught in the home. According to Goldenberg (1994), parents of Hispanic students have high academic aspirations for their children, but the school may not realize this.

Understanding students' cultural background can lead to more effective teaching. Various cultural groups might have socialization practices and expectations that put children at a disadvantage when they attend school. For instance, children of Mexican immigrants are taught to be passive around adults. They are also discouraged from showing

FYI

Strickland (1998) recommends using talk to foster students' understanding: "Engage students in literature study groups, group discussion, partner activities, and research groups. Plan activities where talk is used along with reading and writing as a tool for learning" (p. 402).

■ The term **learning styles** refers to individual preferences in acquiring, remembering, and applying new information and skills. Learning styles include auditory, visual, or hands-on learning; learning in wholes or pieces; and learning alone or with others.

A single classroom may include children from a number of cultural groups.

off what they know (Valdes, 1996). However, in the typical public school classroom, students are expected to be assertive and demonstrate their knowledge. As a result of a lack of assertiveness and a failure to display what they know, children of Mexican immigrants may be judged to be lacking in skills and background knowledge and placed in lower reading groups.

In working with children and parents from other cultures, you need to be metacognitive: You need to realize that you perceive your students and their parents through your own cultural lens (Maldonado-Colon, 2003) and that the lives of your students are different in some ways from yours. You need to study the culture of your students and find out as much as you can about your students' everyday lives. If you do these things, there is a greater likelihood that your teaching will be more relevant and more effective.

In developing teaching techniques that are appropriate for diverse **learning styles**, you have to be aware of the ways in which students think and process information. Teaching needs to be more collaborative. You have to ask children how they construct meaning so that you can gain insight into their thinking processes. You need to try varied approaches to teaching and organizing classes to learn which ones work best. You also need to give students choices to determine the kinds of activities they prefer. Many suggestions for increasing the achievement of ethnic and linguistic minority children—such as cooperative learning and being sensitive to learning styles—should help all children learn better (Banks, 1994).

Accepting the Student's Language

A student's language is part of who she or he is. Rejecting it is interpreted as a personal rejection. Everyone speaks a dialect, which is determined by place of birth, socioeconomic status, and other factors. Some African American children speak a dialect known as Black English, which is very similar to standard English. The differences between the two dialects are minor and include features such as dropping the suffixes *-ing* and *-ed*, omitting

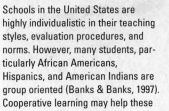

FYI

Schools in the United States are highly individualistic in their teaching styles, evaluation procedures, and norms. However, many students, particularly African Americans, Hispanics, and American Indians are group oriented (Banks & Banks, 1997). Cooperative learning may help these students learn more effectively.

FYI

As is true of a number of dialects, some African American English pronunciations can cause slight difficulty in phonics. Students might not perceive some final consonant clustering and may confuse word parts, as in *toll* and *told* or *coal* and *cold*. The use of context and added work on auditory discrimination will help take care of this minor interference.

the word *is* ("He busy"), and using some variations in pronunciation such as "pin" for *pen* (Shuy, 1973).

Dialect has no negative effect on reading achievement; it may, however, influence teacher attitude (Goodman & Goodman, 1978). Teachers who form unfavorable opinions on the basis of variant dialects can convey those feelings and associated lowered expectations to students. If they constantly correct language, teachers might also be hindering communication between themselves and their students.

Even when reading orally, a child who uses a variant dialect should not be corrected. In fact, translation of printed symbols into one's dialect is a positive sign (Goodman & Goodman, 1978). It indicates that the student is reading for meaning and not just making sounds.

Teachers should use standard English, thus providing a model for children who speak a variant dialect. Although all dialects are equally acceptable, the use of standard English can be a factor in vocational success. Rather than correcting or eradicating a variant dialect, Brown (1988) recommended that standard English be presented as a second dialect that students may use if they wish. The New Standards Speaking and Listening Committee (2001) suggests that students who have been in school a few years should be expected to use standard English for academic purposes but not necessarily in social situations. "All students should learn the shared rules of standard English—but not in ways that tread on their heritage" (p. 24).

▪▪▪ Checkup ▪▪▪

1. Why is it important to understand students' cultures?
2. What steps might you take to better understand your students' cultures?

▪▪▪

Students with Learning Disabilities

One of the largest categories of special needs students is the group identified as learning disabled. Nearly 5 percent of all U.S. students (almost 3 million students) have been determined to be learning disabled (U.S. Department of Education, 2003). About 80 percent of those diagnosed as having a learning disability have a serious reading problem. The term *learning disability* is controversial; experts disagree as to what constitutes a learning disability. The most widely followed definition is that used by the federal government and contained in the Individuals with Disabilities Education Act, or IDEA (PL 108–446):

> Specific **learning disability** means a disorder in one or more of the basic psychological processes involved in understanding or in using language, spoken or written, which may manifest itself in an imperfect ability to listen, think, speak, read, write, spell, or to do mathematical calculations. The term includes such conditions as perceptual handicaps, brain injury, minimal brain dysfunction, dyslexia, and developmental aphasia. The term does not include children who have learning problems which are primarily the result of visual, hearing, or motor handicaps, of mental retardation, or of environmental, cultural, or economic disadvantage. [PL 94–142, section 5(b)(4)]

In the past, a definition based on some measurable discrepancy between performance and ability was used to identify learning disabilities. However, this definition often delayed services, because a sufficient discrepancy didn't show up until students had been in school for several years. School systems now have the option of using response to instruction as an identification tool. The theory is that if students are offered effective, re-

---

▪ **Learning disability** is a general term used to refer to a group of disorders that are evidenced by difficulty learning to read, write, speak, listen, or do math. The speaking and listening difficulties are not caused by articulation disorders or impaired hearing.

search-based instruction and they fail to make progress, their lack of progress indicates a learning disability.

Characteristics of Students with Learning Disabilities

Because of the broad definition, the learning-disabled group is quite heterogeneous. It includes students who have visual- or auditory-perceptual dysfunction, difficulty paying attention, memory deficits, problems using language to learn, or all of these conditions. Students may have an underlying problem that manifests itself in all school subjects, or the problem may be restricted to a single area, such as reading, writing, or math. The most common reason for referral is a reading problem. About 80 percent of students classified as learning-disabled have a reading difficulty.

Literacy Program for Students with Learning Disabilities

Based on the major behavioral and academic characteristics noted, a literacy program for learning-disabled students should include several important features. These students should be provided with reading materials at their instructional level so that they can experience success and begin to see themselves as learners.

Students who have learning disabilities, especially those with reading difficulties, often experience problems with basic decoding skills. Having difficulty with phonemic awareness, these children might not absorb rudimentary phonics instruction when it is provided in primary grades. As they move through the grades, it might be assumed that they have mastered these skills. Through an IRI, a word-list test, or observation, find out where struggling readers are and provide instruction in basic decoding skills if necessary. Word building, discussed in Chapter 4, is a very thorough approach. Relate the skills taught to books and stories students are reading. Provide plenty of reinforcement in the form of books and materials that incorporate the phonics elements or patterns you have taught.

Some disabled readers have been taught a full range of decoding skills but at too rapid a pace, so the skills never became automatic. What these students need is ample opportunity to apply their skills with texts that are relatively easy for them to read. Some students need more practice time than others, perhaps because they never got sufficient opportunity to apply their skills. If students do not respond to your best efforts, seek help from the reading teacher or specialist in learning disabilities.

Materials for Students with Learning Disabilities

Because they frequently read below grade level, students with learning disabilities often need high-interest, easy-to-read books. There are also periodicals specifically designed for older disabled readers:

Know Your World Extra (Stamford, CT: Weekly Reader Corporation). Written on grade levels 2 to 4, this is designed for poor readers in grade 5 and up. It is a well-rounded periodical that includes news and science articles, recreational features, puzzles, and word games.

Scholastic Action (New York: Scholastic). Written on grade levels 4 to 5, this periodical is designed for poor readers in grade 7 and up. It features news and recreational and general interest features and often contains a TV script.

Writing and Students with Learning Disabilities

Writing is an area in which symptoms of a learning disability show up dramatically. Unlike silent reading, the end product of writing is there for all to see. Learning-disabled students often experience difficulty with the higher-level composing aspects of writing as well as with the lower-level mechanical processes. Some have more difficulty than average children with letter formation, spacing, letter orientation, and letter order. (Reversals are normal until about age 7. Research is not clear about what they signify beyond that age. Because reversing letters is normal for beginning readers, it is also normal for older stu-

USING TECHNOLOGY

For more information on learning disabilities, visit these sites:

Learning Disability Association of America
http://www.ldanatl.org

International Dyslexia Association
http://www.interdys.org

Council for Exceptional Children
http://www.cec.sped.org

dents who are still in the beginning stages of reading.) Other students with learning disabilities have difficulty organizing their thoughts when composing. For some, disorganized writing reflects disorganized speaking patterns. However, a number of learning-disabled writers have average or superior oral-language expression but still have difficulty putting their thoughts down on paper.

As with average students, writing instruction for students with learning disabilities should emphasize the expressive function. Graves (1985) described the strengths that Billy, a third-grader, displayed as he attempted to record his thoughts on paper. Billy's paper was smudged and blackened, showing evidence of many valiant efforts to spell correctly the few words he had managed to write. However, as Graves wisely observed, spelling and handwriting were the least of Billy's writing problems. Billy had diagnosed himself as a poor writer because of a perceived lack of worthwhile ideas and experiences; he was well versed in what he could not do. Billy had been drilled on handwriting and spelling in isolation. There was no question that he needed expert help in these areas; however, the mechanical skills should have been connected to the total writing process so that he could see the true function of handwriting and spelling. Most of all, Billy needed to know that he had something worthwhile to say so that he could see himself as a writer. Otherwise, he would not be able to make full use of the mechanical skills that he was being taught.

Struggling writers also benefit from structure. Cognitive strategy instruction in writing, which was explained in Chapter 11, works very well with learning-disabled writers.

▪▪▪ Checkup ▪▪▪

1. What are the key characteristics of students with learning disabilities?
2. What are some steps that might be taken to help students with learning disabilities to develop literacy skills?

Students with Attention Deficit Disorder

As many as 3 to 5 percent of the school population has **attention deficit disorder** (Children and Adults with Attention-Deficit/Hyperactivity Disorder, 2006). Attention deficit disorder (ADD) has as its primary symptom difficulty in focusing and sustaining attention. This may be due to a chemical imbalance and is frequently accompanied by **hyperactivity** or **impulsivity**.

ADD is not classified as a learning or reading disorder. A student can have ADD but demonstrate no difficulty learning. However, there is considerable overlap between the two categories. Many students diagnosed as having a learning disability also have difficulty with attention. ADD students do qualify for special services (U.S. Department of Education, 1991).

Assisting Students with ADD

The nature and extent of ADD are still being debated. However, it is clear that large numbers of students have difficulty learning because of a problem with attention. Literacy educator Constance Weaver (1994), whose son has been diagnosed as having ADHD (the *H* stands for hyperactivity), has a number of humane and practical suggestions for helping

USING TECHNOLOGY

The Web site of CHADD (Children and Adults with Attention-Deficit/Hyperactivity Disorder) provides a wealth of information on ADD.
http://www.chadd.org

▪ **Attention deficit disorder** refers to a difficulty focusing and maintaining attention.

▪ **Hyperactivity** refers to the tendency to be overly active, impulsive, or distractible.

▪ **Impulsivity** refers to the tendency to act on the spur of the moment without thinking of the consequences.

▪ **Mental retardation** refers to a low level of mental functioning accompanied by deficits in adaptive behavior.

these children. Her chief concern is that we not blame the victim. Instead, she suggests that we look at ways in which we can help the student perform better in school and in which the school can adjust to the student's characteristics. For instance, ADHD children, by definition, have difficulty sitting still. Why not allow them stretch breaks or the opportunity to participate in projects that involve movement? Instead of just focusing on trying to change the child, teachers need to work with him or her and modify the program.

Other suggestions include the following, many of which would be beneficial to all students:

- Provide students with tasks that are meaningful and interesting.
- Give students a choice of materials and activities.
- Allow mobility in the classroom; use writing, reading, and other learning centers.
- Allow students to confer with peers or work in cooperative groups.
- Minimize formal tests.
- Make sure students understand directions. Establish eye contact. Give directions one step at a time, writing them on the board as you do so. Make sure that the students have copied the directions accurately and understand them.
- When students have homework assignments, make sure they leave with all the necessary materials and directions.
- Help students keep a schedule for major assignments. Break the assignment down into a series of smaller steps. Check to see that each step is completed.
- Use visual aids, such as pictures, the overhead projector, and videos whenever possible.
- Schedule many brief periods of practice for rote material rather than a few long ones.
- Work closely with parents so that the home supports the school's efforts, and vice versa.
- Minimize distractions. Have ADD students sit near you and put away any books or tools they aren't using.
- Make sure classroom procedures are clear and everyone understands them (Smith, Polloway, Patton, & Dowdy, 1998; Weaver, 1994).
- Highlight important information. In one study, writing the difficult parts of spelling words in red resulted in improved performance for ADD students (Zutell, 1998).
- Use peer tutoring. In several studies, peer tutoring dramatically increased the on-task behavior and performance of both ADD students and non-ADD students (DuPaul & Eckert, 1996).
- Use computers. Computer programs increased the on-task behavior and academic achievement of ADD students. Programs with games and simulations worked better than programs without such incentives (DuPaul & Eckert, 1996).

■ ■ ■ Checkup ■ ■ ■

1. What are the main characteristics of students with attention deficit disorder?
2. What might you do to help students with attention deficit disorder learn more effectively?

           ■ ■ ■

Students with Mental Retardation

About 2 percent of the population is classified as having some degree of **mental retardation**. Mental retardation is determined by two criteria: low level of intellectual functioning and deficits in adaptive behavior. Low level of intellectual functioning translates into an IQ score of approximately 69 or less, or two standard deviations below the mean.

A primary problem for students with mental retardation is limited reasoning ability. Through modeling and other techniques, the teacher must make explicit the processes of

FYI

Currently, about half a million U.S. students are classified as mentally retarded.

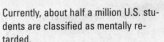

reading and writing that average students often pick up on their own. Book selection and the use of decoding, comprehension, study, and writing skills have to be modeled carefully and continually. The teacher must also model processes that underlie learning: paying attention, staying on task, listening, and determining relevant information.

For most children who have mental retardation, the major obstacles to reading achievement are vocabulary and conceptual development. Because of limited cognitive ability and, perhaps, lack of experiential background, they may have difficulty comprehending what they read. They need to have concepts and background built in functional, concrete ways. They also need appropriate materials. Students need materials that appeal to their age but that are on the appropriate reading level. A language-experience approach, because it is based on students' language, is especially effective.

Some students with mental retardation may never read beyond a second-grade level. Others will never be able to do any sustained reading. Because their literacy development is so limited, it is important that they be taught the literacy skills they need to function in society. These skills include reading traffic and warning signs, labels, simple cooking directions, and common forms. They also have to know how to write their names, addresses, telephone numbers, dates of birth, names of family members, and other information frequently requested on forms.

Students with mental retardation should also be taught how to read the newspaper, especially for functional items like weather forecasts, movie times, want ads, and grocery and other ads. They must know, too, how to use the white, blue, and yellow pages of the telephone book. Stress should be placed on locating emergency numbers.

Teaching students with disabilities to read and write may mean adapting techniques and using technology but is mostly a matter of acceptance and caring.

Slow Learners

Functioning generally on a higher level than students with mental retardation but on a lower level than average students are a large number of students known as **slow learners**. They make up approximately 14 percent of the school population. Because they have IQ scores between 70 and 85 (approximately), they function on too high a level to be classified as having mental retardation but are frequently excluded from learning-disabled and remedial reading programs because their IQ scores are too low. Although they have some special needs, slow learners are often denied special services.

Slow learners manifest some of the same characteristics that students with mental retardation display, but to a lesser degree. They tend to be concrete in their thinking, need help with strategies and organization, and are eager for success. They have difficulty with abstract concepts and so need a lot of concrete examples. They also need more practice and more repetition (Cooter & Cooter, 2004). Their executive functioning is on a higher level than that of children with mental retardation. They are better able to decide when and where to use strategies and are better able to classify and group information. They also are more aware of their mental processes and can take more responsibility for their learning.

In terms of instruction, these are "more so" students; they need the same instruction that regular students need, but more so. They must be given more guidance, more practice, and more time to complete learning tasks. One of their greatest needs is to have materials and instruction on their level. (Materials for learning-disabled students can also be used

---

■ **Slow learners** have below-average ability but are not retarded. In general, IQs of slow learners range between 70 and 85.

■ **Gifted and talented students** have mental abilities or other talents that are well above average. Approximately the top

2 percent of the population is classified as being gifted or talented.

with slow learners.) A slow learner in the fifth grade might be reading on a second- or third-grade level. All too often, slow learners are given a basal that is below grade level but still above their reading level or a content-area textbook that is on grade level and well above their reading level. This is frustrating and leads to lowered self-concept and lowered achievement.

▪▪▪ Checkup ▪▪▪

1. What are the main characteristics of students with mental retardation?
2. How are slow learners different from but similar to students who have mental retardation?
3. What might be done to help students with mental retardation?
4. What might be done to help slow learners acquire literacy skills?

▪▪▪

Students with Language and Speech Disorders

Speech impairments do not directly affect reading or writing. The teacher's role consists primarily of being sensitive to the difficulty and helping the child apply skills in the classroom that she or he learned while working with a speech therapist. The teacher should also be supportive and help the child build confidence, providing opportunities for the child to take part in discussions and purposeful oral reading. Consultation with the speech therapist and "promotion of a classroom atmosphere conducive to unpressured verbal interaction" (Cartwright, Cartwright, & Ward, 1989, p. 174) are also recommended.

Although articulation difficulties do not generally impair the acquisition of reading and writing skills, other less noticeable language difficulties may pose significant problems. Some children's language development follows a normal path but is slow. These children may experience a delay acquiring basic reading and writing skills.

Students who suffer from language disorders experience a disruption in the language development process (Hardman, Drew, Egan, & Wolf, 1993). The disruption may be expressive or receptive or a combination of the two. Receptive language disorders affect students' understanding of language. Expressive disorders hinder the ability to communicate. Students with an expressive disorder may possess information but have difficulty communicating it.

One expressive language disorder is difficulty finding the words to express what one wants to say. For instance, unable to retrieve the word *bat*, a student might say, "The thing that you hit a ball with." The speech of these students is marked by hesitations, roundabout expressions, and "you knows." They may have difficulty using picture and context clues because they cannot retrieve from memory the name of the object shown in the picture or think of the word that might fit the context. These students are helped by graphic organizers.

▪ Gifted and Talented Students

A reading and writing program for **gifted and talented students** should take into account the individual characteristics of the children. About 50 percent of the gifted come to school already reading (Terman, 1954). Provision should be made for them and for those reading above grade level. For example, gifted second-graders reading on a fifth- or sixth-grade level should not be restricted to second-grade material. The materials they read should be on their instructional and interest levels. (See Appendix A for challenging books at each grade level.)

Because they master basic reading skills early and may not be sufficiently challenged by the classroom collections of books, gifted students should learn how to select books from the school library. To enable them to investigate areas of special interest, provide early instruction in the use of dictionaries, encyclopedias, Internet, and other basic references, as well as in the use of research skills. These students may also need help with study skills as they progress through the grades. Some are able to get by in the lower grades because of their ability, but as they reach more advanced grades, they may not have acquired the study habits and skills that will enable them to work up to their abilities.

Reading and writing workshops work quite well for the gifted. Through self-selected reading in reading workshop, gifted students are free to pursue advanced work

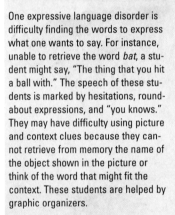

USING TECHNOLOGY

For additional information about giftedness, visit one of the following sites:

National Research Center on the Gifted and Talented
http://www.gifted.uconn.edu/NRCGT.html

Neag Center for Gifted and Talented Development
http://www.gifted.uconn.edu

FYI

■ Although the Junior Great Books shared inquiry program can be used with any student who has the skill to read the books, it is frequently used with gifted readers. It could be a part of the classroom routine or an after-school or out-of-class activity.

■ Although overrepresented in special needs groups, students still acquiring English, students who are members of a minority group, and students who are poor are underrepresented in programs for the gifted. Special attempts need to be made to identify students from these groups who have special abilities.

■ Junior Great Books has been successfully used with below-level readers as well as with average and gifted readers.

■ To provide students with disabilities with a high-quality education, federal law requires that these students be included in state- and districtwide assessments, with or without accommodations. Alternate assessments must be developed for students who cannot participate in regular assessments. The IEPs should ensure that students with disabilities have access to the regular education curriculum (Individuals with Disabilities Act Amendments of 1997).

Adapting Instruction for Struggling Readers and Writers

If a student will be taking an alternative form of a state test or will be provided with modifications, the IEP must explain why (Office of Special Education and Rehabilitation, 2005).

at an accelerated pace. Through writing workshop, gifted students can also explore a broad range of writing genres. In creating reports on subjects of interest, they can investigate topics in depth and apply a host of practical research skills. Gifted students might also attempt some of the more difficult kinds of writing, such as poetry, drama, and short pieces of fiction.

One program that works exceptionally well with the gifted is Junior Great Books, a program in which students read literary classics and discuss them using a technique known as shared inquiry. The group leader, who is trained by the Great Books Foundation, initiates and guides the discussion, but it is up to the group to interpret the reading and validate its interpretation with evidence from the text. In addition to developing skill in the careful reading of complex materials, shared inquiry is designed to develop discussion and thinking skills and "a deeper understanding of self and others, as well as the motivation and desire to be life-long learners" (Tierney & Readence, 2000, p. 301). In an independent study comparing major discussion approaches, Junior Great Books was superior, by far, to all the others in preparing students to obtain higher comprehension scores (Murphy & Edwards, 2005). The program features high-quality selections, excellent discussion guides and follow-up materials, and conscientious training of leaders. (Junior Great Books also works well with average and at-risk readers.)

■■■ Checkup ■■■

1. What special literacy needs do gifted students have?
2. What are some approaches to literacy instruction that should be effective with gifted students?

■■■

■ Inclusion

Inclusion means teaching students who have disabilities or special needs within the general education classroom. In order to accelerate the trend toward educating special education students within the regular classroom, the concept of inclusion has been widely adopted. Inclusion has come to mean providing support to classroom teachers as they, in turn, provide support for the education of disabled students. Supporting disabled students means creating and maintaining a warm, accepting atmosphere for all students and making whatever accommodations and modifications are required to develop their literacy abilities.

Modifications refers to altering the curriculum, changing the school attendance requirement, or making other changes in school policy designed to aid disabled students. **Accommodations** refers to changes in the way students are taught. These could include changes in instruction, assessment, or the assignment of homework (Smith, Polloway, Patton, & Dowdy, 1998). Allowing a test to be taken orally, for instance, would be an accommodation. In making accommodations, it is best if the accommodations benefit all students. Providing a talking software program, such as *Co: Writer* (Don Johnston) or *Doctor Peet's Talk Writer* (Edmark), would be an accommodation that would benefit all students.

■ **Inclusion** is the practice of educating within the classroom all students, including those with special needs. In full inclusion, all support services are provided within the classroom setting. In partial inclusion, the student may be pulled out of the classroom for special instruction.

■ A **modification** is a change in the content or structure of instruction—changing the curriculum, for instance.

■ An **accommodation** is a change in the process of instruction or assessment—allowing a student to listen to rather than read a story or take an exam orally, for example.

Effective teachers individualize instruction and seek support from the special education resource teacher (Schulz, 1993). Depending on the disability, they also use shortened assignments, study buddies, oral tests, easier materials, and preferential seating.

Inclusion fits in with current trends in teaching literacy. Recommended practices for inclusion include cooperative learning, self-management, strategy instruction, direct instruction, and goal setting (King-Sears & Cummings, 1996), all of which are emphasized in this text because they are effective practices for all students. Self-selected reading and the workshop approach to reading and writing, which are emphasized in this text, also lend themselves to inclusion. In addition, assistive technology has made it possible for students to compensate for a variety of handicapping conditions.

▪▪▪ Checkup ▪▪▪

1. What are some adaptations that might be made to make literacy classrooms more inclusive?

▪▪▪

▪ Intervention Programs

Over the last decade, a number of programs have been created that are designed to help those students who are most at risk of failing to learn to read and write. Because of its dramatic but well-documented success, one such program, Reading Recovery, is being implemented in every state. In the United States, 78 percent of Reading Recovery students, not including students who dropped out or did not complete a full set of lessons, were able to read at the average level of their classmates after twelve to twenty weeks of instruction (Reading Recovery Council of North America, 2006).

Reading Recovery

Devised by Marie Clay (1993b) and colleagues in New Zealand, Reading Recovery is based on a series of highly effective procedures developed through discussion and experimentation. The idea behind Reading Recovery is to intervene early, before students are discouraged by failure and before they pick up unproductive reading strategies. A program that ignores labels, Reading Recovery is designed for the lowest-achieving 20 percent of a class. In thirty-minute, one-on-one daily sessions, students read whole books, write, and are taught how to use a variety of decoding strategies and how to monitor their reading. Instructors are highly trained. A key element in Reading Recovery's success is the teacher's guidance, which is based on close observation of each student and a thorough knowledge of the reading process.

Table 12.4 (on p. 526) presents an overview of a Reading Recovery lesson. For a complete description of Reading Recovery, see *Reading Recovery: A Guidebook for Teachers in Training* (Clay, 1993b).

Other Intervention Programs

Although Reading Recovery is an outstanding program, it is costly to implement. However, there are a number of other highly successful early intervention programs that do not require extensive training and may be implemented with small groups of students by the classroom teacher, Title 1 instructor, or remedial specialist. These include Early Intervention in Reading, a program in which the first-grade teacher spends twenty minutes a day working with five to seven of the lowest-achieving students (Hiebert & Taylor, 2000; Taylor, Strait, & Medo, 1994), and the Boulder Project, in which Title 1 teachers work with small groups of low-achieving students (Hiebert, 1994; Hiebert & Taylor, 2000). In both programs, phonemic awareness and phonics are emphasized. In Early Intervention in

FYI

Consider how adaptations will be viewed by the whole class and by students receiving them. For homework assignments, students most favored adaptations that would make the homework shorter and easier to complete for all students. Students were opposed to any adaptations that would be unfair and would make the learning-disabled students feel inferior (Nelson et al., 1998, p. 115).

Adapting Instruction for Struggling Readers and Writers

Reading Recovery uses students' miscues to teach strategies. "We need to let students make an error and allow enough time for them to notice their error independently. Usually this means at least letting students finish reading the sentence in which the error occurs" (Schwartz, 2005, p. 439).

FYI

■ The Spanish version of Reading Recovery, Descubriendo La Lectura, has also been used successfully, but not as extensively. Reading Recovery has also been used successfully with ELLs who lacked instructional support in their native language (Kelly, Gomez-Valdez, Neal, & Klein, 1995).

■ In Early Steps, a one-to-one program that emphasizes direct, systematic instruction in phonemic awareness and phonics, the lowest achievers did particularly well. Through direct instruction in word patterns and sorting and encouragement of invented spelling, Early Steps may have been reaching some of the kinds of students who needed a more intensive, more explicit approach to phonics than that offered by Reading Recovery (Santa & Høien, 1999).

USING TECHNOLOGY

The Success for All site contains extensive information about the program.
http://www.successforall.net

The Florida Center for Reading Research provides information about Harcourt Trophies Intervention and other intervention programs.
http://www.fcrr.org/FCRRReports/index.htm

■■■ **TABLE 12.4   Overview of a Reading Recovery Lesson**

Reading familiar stories	Student reads one or more familiar books to build fluency.
Taking a running record using yesterday's book	The teacher analyzes the student's performance as she or he reads the book introduced in yesterday's lesson.
Working with letters	Magnetic letters are used at various points in the lesson to provide instruction in letter–sound relationships.
Writing a story	The student, under the teacher's guidance, composes a one-sentence or longer story related to an experience the student has had or a book read during the lesson. The story is taken home to be read for practice.
Reading a new book	Carefully chosen so as to present an appropriate level of challenge, the new book is introduced by the teacher before being read orally by the student.

Drawn from *Partners in Learning: Teachers and Children in Reading Recovery* by C. A. Lyons, G. S. Pinnell, & D. E. DeFord, New York: Teachers College Press, 1993.

Reading, skills are taught through a spelling approach. In the Boulder Project, phonics is taught through a pattern approach and applied through children's books that incorporate the patterns presented. The program has been adapted for use in second and third grades. Meeting in groups of no more than seven for twenty to thirty minutes, students study word patterns, read easy chapter books, and engage in writing activities.

Unlike other early intervention programs, Success for All was designed for an entire elementary school and now has a middle school component. Success for All stresses prevention of reading problems and teaching in such a way that children are successful. "Getting reading right the first time is a kind of a motto for the program, which is rooted in the research-based finding that a reading failure in the early grades is fundamentally preventable" (Slavin et al., 1994, p. 126). Results of Success for All are cumulative. By the end of first grade, Success for All students outperform students in control groups by three months. By the end of fifth grade, Success for All participants are a year ahead of the comparison group (Slavin & Madden, 1998; Success for All Foundation, 2006).

Intervention in Basal and Literature Anthology Programs

Today's basals and literature programs make provisions for struggling readers. One advantage of these programs is that they are closely tied to the core program. The core program and the intervention program are mutually reinforcing, giving struggling readers

IRA Position Statement

on Key Issue

Social Promotion and Grade Retention

he IRA opposes imposing standards for promotion without providing students the necessary instructional support they need to meet those standards. "Research has shown that simply retaining students in a grade is an expensive and ineffective approach to meeting the needs of struggling students. . . . Students who are retained generally never catch up with their non-retained peers and are more likely to drop out of school. . . . A number of studies have shown that, with high quality professional support, most children can attain high levels of literacy proficiency: Some just need more help" (International Reading Association, 1998b, pars. 1–2). Children who have difficulty learning to read should be provided with early intervention and ongoing support at every grade level as needed. Appropriate intensive, personalized intervention might include tutoring, small-group instruction, and access to after-school and summer school programs.

■■■ **TABLE 12.5** **Commercial Intervention Programs**

Title	Publisher	Interest Level	Grade Level	Main Areas
Bookshop	Mondo	K–3	K–3	Phonological awareness, decoding, comprehension, oral and written language
Corrective Reading	SRA	4–12	1–5+	Scripted decoding and comprehension
Fast Track	McGraw-Hill	4–8	1–5+	Decoding and comprehension
Foundations	Wright Group	K–2	K–2	Phonological awareness, decoding
High Noon	High Noon	3–12	1–4+	Decoding and comprehension
High Point	Hampton Brown	4–12	1–6	Decoding, comprehension, writing, and oral language
Lightspan Early Reading Program	Lightspan	K–3	K–3	Phonological awareness, decoding, comprehension, vocabulary, and background knowledge
Reading Mastery	SRA	K–6	K–6	Scripted decoding and comprehension
Reading Rescue	Literacy Trust	1–2	1–2	Phonological awareness, decoding, fluency, vocabulary, comprehension
Ready Readers	Modern Curriculum Press	K–3	K–3	Phonological awareness, decoding
Sidewalks	Scott Foresman	1–5	1–5	Phonological awareness, decoding, fluency, vocabulary, comprehension
Soar to Success	Houghton Mifflin	3–8	2–8	Comprehension
Success for All	Success for All Foundation	K–8	K–8	Phonological awareness, decoding, comprehension, and writing
Voyager Reading Intervention	Voyager	K–8	K–8	Phonological awareness, decoding, comprehension, and writing; has an extended-day and summer program.
Word Detectives	Benchmark School	1–5+	1–5	Phonological awareness, decoding

maximum assistance. For instance, Harcourt Trophies (Farr et al., 2006) provides a parallel intervention program that follows the same theme as the anthology and introduces some of the same vocabulary. However, the intervention reader is written on a lower level and is decodable. Selections in the intervention program reinforce high-frequency words and key phonics patterns. Each lesson is accompanied by instruction in a key skill and practice and application activities. Guided reading lessons are specially geared to struggling readers. The selection is read in short chunks with lots of guidance by the teacher. For a listing of commercial intervention programs see Table 12.5.

Lessons from Intervention Programs

What lessons can be learned from these intervention programs? Although they differ on specifics, all stress the importance of providing ample opportunity for students to read materials on the appropriate level, teaching students to be strategic readers, monitoring their progress, evaluating the program, providing inservice training, and having strong leadership. Programs at the early levels also have a strong decoding component. Successful programs are additive. They provide instruction that is in addition to the regular classroom program. Most important of all, the programs strongly affirm the ability of at-risk children to succeed, and have convincingly confirmed this.

■■■ **Checkup** ■■■

1. How would you summarize the intervention programs described in this section?
2. What are the key features of an effective intervention program?

■■■

Adapting Instruction for Struggling Readers and Writers

Interventions generally reduce the number of struggling readers to 4.5 percent or less of the school population (Mathes et al., 2005; Torgesen et al., 2003).

USING TECHNOLOGY ■ ■■ ■

RTI Partnership at UCR provides information about RTI (Response to Intervention) and helpful links.
http://rti.ucr.edu/rtidetails.htm

Neuhaus Center Handouts feature a number of teaching activities for struggling readers.
http://www.neuhaus.org/Handouts.htm

Intervention Central offers useful information and links for interventions and progress monitoring.
http://www.interventioncentral.org

Tools for the Classroom

Building Higher-Level Literacy

Ironically, at-risk learners are typically presented with programs that foster basic skills but neglect higher-level thinking. Depending upon the factors causing them to be at risk, these students might have a more difficult time acquiring higher-level skills. For instance, they may have a more limited background of experience, or they might have attended a school that neglected higher-level skills. Consequently, at-risk learners need more instruction and experience aimed at building higher-level literacy, not less. When working with at-risk learners, purposely include activities designed to enrich their reading, writing, and responding.

Help for Struggling Readers and Writers

As you have undoubtedly noticed, most of the techniques presented in this chapter are the same as those discussed in previous chapters. In general, the techniques that work with achieving readers also work with students who are at risk. The chief difference in working with at-risk students is making appropriate adaptations and modifications. The following framework for planning a classroom intervention program is based on the major principles covered in this chapter and the exemplary intervention programs reviewed. The framework is flexible and can be used with students who are experiencing difficulty with word recognition, comprehension, vocabulary, study skills, writing, or all five.

Building Literacy: A Classroom Intervention Program

Goals and Objectives

Objectives should be those that are most likely to result in maximum improvement in literacy.

Direct, Systematic Instruction

Struggling readers and writers need direct, systematic instruction gcarcd to their strengths. High-quality instructional techniques emphasized in this text feature word building; guided reading, including text walk; shared reading; language experience, including shared writing and interactive writing; and use of graphic organizers, ReQuest, reciprocal teaching, and Questioning the Author.

Selecting Students

Select students with the greatest needs in reading and writing. Depending on students' levels, use an informal reading inventory and/or assessment devices from Appendix B. Also use observation, samples of students' work, and portfolios, if available.

Size of Group

A group of six or seven is the maximum size that can be taught effectively. However, the more serious the difficulties, the smaller the group should be.

Scheduling Instruction

Intervention instruction is most beneficial when it's in addition to the instruction already provided. Students who are behind need more instructional time if they are expected to catch up. Before school, after school, Saturday, and summer programs are recommended. However, if this is not practical, arrange intervention sessions when they would best fit into the daily schedule. You might hold intervention sessions when the rest of the class is engaged in sustained reading, working at learning centers, or working on individual or group projects. Intervention groups should be scheduled every day, if possible, but not less than three times a week. Sessions can last from twenty to forty-five minutes, with forty minutes being the recommended duration.

Materials

Use high-interest materials. Select materials that are attractive, are well illustrated, and don't have a whole lot of print on a page. Make sure that materials are on the appropriate level of difficulty. Books listed in Appendix A, especially those listed in the Easy category, can be used as a starting point. Also, have students use technology, such as talking software, to help them overcome learning difficulties.

Evaluation
Continuously monitor students' progress. Keep records of books read and conduct a running record or modified informal reading inventory monthly or weekly, if possible. If decoding is a problem area, use the Phonics Progress Monitoring Assessment or a similar instrument (see pp. 198–199). Observe and make note of student's daily progress. Maintain a portfolio of work samples. Periodically, at least once a month, review each student's progress and make any necessary adjustments.

Parental Involvement
Let the parents know about the program. Keep them informed about the children's progress. Also, enlist their support. Students in the program should read twenty minutes a night at least four times a week. Discuss with parents how they might help their children fulfill this requirement. Parents might also volunteer to help out. They might work with the rest of the class while you are teaching the intervention group. Or they may work with individuals on experience stories or listen to them read.

Professional Support
Discuss your program with the principal and enlist her or his support. Also, talk it over with other professionals. They may have suggestions for improvement or may provide assistance should serious problems arise.

Parts of a Building Literacy Lesson
A Building Literacy lesson should include certain key elements. At a minimum, there should be a review of past material, an introduction or extension of a new skill or strategy, and an opportunity to apply that skill or strategy by reading a selection. If time allows, there should be a writing activity. Conclude the session with a brief activity chosen by the student: a game, computer time, or reading of a riddle or verse, for instance. Students should also have a take-home activity, such as a book or periodical to read or reread.

Action Plan
1. Plan and implement a program that provides for all students.
2. Modify assignments as necessary to meet any special needs that students have.
3. Provide extra instruction or alternative instruction for students who are not making progress.
4. For ELLs, build language as you build literacy. Build on background knowledge and skills that students bring to class. Make use of cognates, for instance. If possible, students should be taught to read in their first language. When they are taught to read in English, be aware of differences between English and the native language so you can pay special attention to elements that are likely to pose problems.
5. If students are struggling, intervene early. If intervention programs are not available, create your own. Set aside a period of the day when you can work with struggling readers.
6. Monitor the progress of students who are not achieving adequately and make adjustments as necessary.

Summary

More than 5 million school children in the United States are English language learners (ELLs). These students are at risk for having difficulty in school. Additional factors putting children at risk include poverty, attending a substandard school, retention in a grade, low marks, illness, excessive absence, membership in a special education class, and negative self-image.

Students at risk benefit from instruction that develops language, background, and literacy skills and that respects their language and culture. Increasingly, students with a range of learning and physical disabilities are taught within the regular classroom. Working closely with special education resource personnel, the classroom teacher should make adjustments in the physical environment and/or program so that these students learn to read and write to their full capacities. Gifted and talented students need to be given challenging material and programs.

Reading Recovery and other intervention programs have demonstrated that, given the right kind of instruction, children at risk for failure can be successful. Today's basals and literature anthologies have intervention components.

Extending and Applying

1. Interview the special education, Title 1, or remedial reading specialist at the school where you teach or at a nearby elementary or middle school. Find out what kinds of programs the school offers for special education, Title 1, and remedial students.

2. Observe a classroom in which remedial or special education instruction is offered according to the inclusion model. What arrangements have the specialist and the classroom teacher made for working together? What are the advantages of this type of arrangement? What are some of the disadvantages?

3. Investigate the culture of a minority group that is represented in a class you are now teaching or that you may be teaching in the future. Find out information about the group's literature, language, and customs. How might you use this information to plan more effective instruction for the class? Plan a lesson using this information. If possible, teach the lesson and evaluate its effectiveness.

4. Plan a reading lesson for a student with a reading disability. Obtain material that is of interest to the student but that is on his or her reading level. If possible, teach the lesson, and evaluate its effectiveness.

Developing a Professional Portfolio

Teach a lesson as suggested in item 4 of Extending and Applying and record it on a video or CD-ROM and/or keep a copy of the plan for the lesson. Reflect on the effectiveness of the lesson. Experiment with the language-experience approach, sheltered instruction, cooperative learning, or other techniques and approaches that have been shown to be effective with ELLs. Summarize and reflect on your use of the techniques.

- Enter Assignment ID **SPCS** into **Assignment Finder,** and select the case titled "He's Just a Goofy Guy."
- Read through the case on behavior management. Then answer the questions at the end of the case.

- Explore MyLabSchool further to find the course areas for Reading Methods, Language Arts, and Content Area Reading and identify other assets that support concepts introduced in this chapter.

Developing a Resource File

Maintain a bibliography of books and other materials that you might use to teach students who have special needs.

Also maintain a bibliography of multicultural literature that would be appropriate for the age level that you teach.

To access chapter objectives, practice tests, weblinks, and flashcards, go to the companion website at www.ablongman.com/gunning6e.

13 Creating and Managing
a Literacy Program

or each of the following statements related to the chapter you are about to read, put a check under "Agree" or "Disagree" to show how you feel. Discuss your responses with classmates before you read the chapter.

	Agree	Disagree
1. Students should be grouped heterogeneously rather than homogeneously for reading instruction.	_____	_____
2. Teaching small groups of students with common needs is just about the best way to provide for individual differences.	_____	_____
3. Ultimate responsibility for the progress of struggling readers rests with the classroom teacher.	_____	_____
4. Without parental support, literacy programs have a greatly diminished chance for success.	_____	_____
5. Instruction in the use of the Internet should be a part of the literacy program.	_____	_____
6. Educators have been oversold on the educational value of technology.	_____	_____

he best teachers are caring individuals who have solid knowledge of their field, broad knowledge of children and how they learn, and a firm grasp of effective teaching strategies. In addition, they must be skilled managers. They must have goals and objectives and the means to meet them. They must make wise and efficient use of their resources: time, materials, and professional assistance. They must also have positive interactions with students, administrative and supervising staff, resource personnel, parents, and the community at large. Clearly, a tall order.

Think of some teachers you have had who were excellent managers. What management strategies did they use? What routines did they devise to keep the class running smoothly? As you read this chapter, try to visualize how you might implement those strategies and routines. Also think about the components of a successful literacy program. What elements does such a program have?

■ Constructing a Literacy Program

Previous chapters provided the building blocks for a literacy program. Constructing a program means assembling the blocks in some logical way and then reassembling them when necessary. Effective programs have some common features, such as a philosophy that all children can learn to read, high expectations for students, objectives that are specific and clearly stated, varied and appropriate materials, effective teaching strategies, motivation, building a sense of community, efficient use of time and increased time on task, continuous monitoring of progress, involvement of parents, cooperation among staff, a consistent program that builds on past learnings, prevention and intervention as necessary, and a process for evaluating the program (Hiebert et al., 1998; Hoffman, 1991; Samuels, 1988a).

Construction of a literacy program starts with the students. The program should be based on their interests, their cultures, their abilities, and the nature of the community in

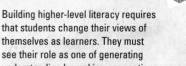

HIGHER-LEVEL LITERACY

Building higher-level literacy requires that students change their views of themselves as learners. They must see their role as one of generating understanding by making connections between new information and what they already know. Up to this point they may have thought that their role was to memorize and record (Wittrock, 1991).

HIGHER-LEVEL LITERACY

When setting goals, be sure to include higher-level literacy. This is especially important for struggling learners, whose higher-level skills tend to be neglected because of an emphasis on basic skills. A balanced program needs to make provision for both.

FYI

"A clear understanding of a school's shared goals is the cornerstone to successful reading programs" (Hiebert et al., 1998, p. 3).

USING TECHNOLOGY

Developing Educational Standards offers a wealth of information about curriculum frameworks and standards and provides links to each state's standards and to national standards in all subject fields.
http://edstandards.org/Standards.html

Adapting Instruction for Struggling Readers and Writers

When selecting materials, make sure that the readability of the materials is appropriate for your students. It is especially important to have plentiful material for below-level readers. See Chapter 2 for suggestions for assessing the difficulty of materials.

which they live. To build an effective program, you need to ask, "What are the children's needs? What are their interests? What aspirations do their parents have for them? What literacy skills do they need in order to survive and prosper now and in the future?"

After acquiring as much information as you can about your students and their community, you should consider your philosophy of teaching reading and writing. Do you prefer a top-down approach, a bottom-up approach, or an interactive approach? Will you use direct systematic instruction, an opportunistic approach, or a combination of approaches? Will you use a basal series, children's books, or some sort of combination? What role will technology play in your program?

Setting Goals

Once you have acquired some basic information about students and have clarified your philosophy of teaching reading and writing, you can start setting goals. In setting goals, you might consider the objectives set forth in this text, the school and school district's curriculum framework, and state and national standards. Setting goals should be a collaborative activity among the staff in a school. Teachers need to create a shared vision of what they want their literacy program to do and what shape it will take. Once they agree on common objectives, they can begin planning activities that help them meet those objectives and select the kinds of assessment devices that will keep them aware of how they are doing and flag problem areas.

Although research suggests that literacy programs should have specific objectives, teachers should take a broad view of literacy and also set broad goals (Au & Mason, 1989). These goals should include reading for enjoyment as well as building reading and writing skills to meet the demands of school and society. In addition, specific objectives should be established that lead to fulfilling the goals.

Ultimately, goals and objectives will be determined by the needs of the students. A goal for fourth-graders who will be reading a great deal of content-area material, for example, may be to have them learn and apply study strategies. A goal for second-graders who are struggling with phonics may be to have them improve their automatic application of skills. As a practical matter, you must consider the high-stakes tests that students will be required to take. Ideally, assessments should be aligned with standards and objectives, but sometimes this is not the case.

Choosing Materials

Goals and philosophy lead naturally into a choice of materials and activities. For instance, one teacher may elect to use children's books together with a holistic approach to phonics. A second might use a specialized basal, such as *Reading Mastery* (Distar), which focuses on phonic elements. Both approaches have the same goals but reflect different philosophies.

Regardless of philosophy, materials should be varied and should include children's books, both fiction and informational. Because children's interests and abilities are diverse, the selection should cover a wide variety of topics and include easy as well as challenging books. There should also be reference books, children's magazines and newspapers, pamphlets, menus, telephone books, and directions for activities as diverse as planting seeds and operating the classroom computer.

Supplementary materials, such as a VCR and videocassette library, tape recorders and audiocassettes, computers and software, and a DVD player and DVD library should also be available. There should also be access to the Web. (Additional information on the use of computers and today's technology in a literacy program is offered at the end of this chapter.) Basals and other commercial materials should be on hand if the teacher chooses to use them.

■■■ **TABLE 13.1**   **Essential Techniques for Teaching Literacy**

Technique	Appropriate Grade Level
Reading to students	All grades
Shared or assisted reading	Primary grades/remedial
Language experience	Primary grades/remedial
Inductive phonics lesson	Primary grades/remedial
Word building	Primary grades/remedial
Pattern approach to syllabication	Grade 2 and up
Morphemic analysis	Grade 3 and up
Direct instructional lesson for skills and strategies	All grades
Modeling	All grades
Think-aloud lesson	All grades
Guided reading (DRA)	All grades
DR–TA	All grades
Text walk	All grades
Cooperative learning	All grades
Literature discussion groups	All grades
ReQuest	Grade 3 and up
Reciprocal teaching	All grades
KWL Plus	All grades
Questioning the Author	Grade 3 and up
Responsive elaboration	All grades
Process approach to writing	All grades

Selecting Techniques and Strategies

The heart of the instructional program is the quality of the teaching. Effective teachers will have mastered a variety of techniques that they can adapt to fit the needs of their students. Some basic techniques for teaching literacy are listed in Table 13.1.

Teachers must also decide when it is time to substitute one technique or approach for another. For instance, if discussion techniques such as KWL or Questioning the Author aren't working, the teacher might try direct, explicit teaching of strategies. The important point is that the teacher chooses the techniques to be used and makes adjustments when necessary.

Some key student strategies are listed in Table 13.2 (on p. 536). It is important to teach students a variety of strategies: Research suggests that, because of the novelty factor, changing strategies enhances achievement.

■■■ Checkup ■■■

1. Why are goals so important in constructing a literacy program?
2. When choosing materials, techniques, and strategies, what factors do you need to consider?

■■■

Building Motivation

Strategy instruction should also take into account affective factors so that students become engaged learners. Engaged learners possess the necessary cognitive tools, but they are also excited about learning. Without motivation, "the difficult work of cognitive learning does not occur rapidly, if it occurs at all" (Guthrie & Wigfield, 1997, p. 3). To foster engagement and motivate students to apply strategies, the teacher involves students, helps them set goals, provides them with choices, and, in general, helps them understand what they are doing and why.

USING TECHNOLOGY ■ ■ ■ ■

The What Works Clearinghouse provides information about research on the best instructional practices.
www.w-w-c.org

FYI

Teachers' knowledge of techniques should be metacognitive. Not only should they know how to teach the techniques, they should also know where and when to use them. For example, a group of students who need a maximum of structure and assistance should be taught within a guided reading (DRA) framework. As their work habits improve, the DR–TA can be introduced to foster independence. Later, reciprocal teaching might be employed.

■■■ **TABLE 13.2**   **Learning Strategies and Related Instructional Techniques**

	Student's Learning Strategies	Teacher's Instructional Techniques
Preparational	Activating prior knowledge Previewing Predicting Setting purpose SQ3R	Brainstorming Discussion KWL DR–TA Guided reading Text walk Discussing misconceptions Modeling Direct instruction Questioning the Author Reciprocal teaching, ReQuest Think-alouds Responsive elaboration
Selecting/organizing	Selecting important or relevant details Identifying main idea Summarizing Questioning Using graphic organizers SQ3R	Think-alouds DR–TA Guided reading Modeling Direct instruction Reciprocal teaching KWL Discussing Questioning the Author Study guide Responsive elaboration
Elaborational	Inferring Evaluating Applying Imaging SQ3R	Direct instruction DR–TA Guided reading Modeling Think-alouds Reciprocal teaching Questioning the Author Discussing KWL Responsive elaboration
Monitoring/metacognitive	Monitoring for meaning SQ3R Using fix-up strategies	Think-alouds Modeling Reciprocal teaching Direct instruction Questioning the Author
Affective	Attending/concentrating Staying on task Using self-talk	Think-alouds Modeling Discussing Encouraging
Rehearsal/study	Using understanding Using mnemonic devices Rehearsing SQ3R	Modeling Think-alouds Direct instruction
Word recognition	Using pronounceable word parts Using analogies Sounding out words Using context Using morphemic analysis Using syllabic analysis Using the dictionary Integrating word-attack skills	Modeling Word building Direct instruction Think-alouds Responsive elaboration

Adapted from Jones, Palincsar, Ogle, & Carr, 1986.

In a series of studies on effective instruction, Pressley (2001) discovered that motivation had a significant impact on students' learning. Motivation, the researcher discovered, is mainly a matter of creating a positive and encouraging but challenging environment. Students get the feeling that they're valued and competent and that they are engaged in interesting, worthwhile learning activities. The following characteristics of the learning context are also important in fostering motivation (Boothroyd, 2001):

- Variety of techniques are used. Techniques are matched to students' needs.
- Routines and procedures are well established. The classroom is orderly.
- Effort is emphasized. Praise and reinforcement are used as appropriate.
- The teacher builds a sense of excitement and enthusiasm.
- Cooperation rather than competition is emphasized.
- Manipulatives and hands-on activities are prominent. However, the activities engage students' minds and have legitimate learning goals.

Building a Sense of Community

In an effective literacy program, the teacher focuses on building a community of learners. Traditionally, the focus in schools has been on the individual. As the importance of learning from others through scaffolding, discussion, cooperative learning, and consideration of multiple perspectives has become apparent, it is clear that the focus must be on group learning. In an ideal community of learners, all students' contributions are valued. Activities and discussions are genuine because students feel that they are a valuable part of the learning community.

■■■ Checkup ■■■

1. How would you go about building motivation and a sense of community in a literacy program?

■ Managing a Literacy Program

A teacher of literacy must be an efficient manager, determining how to handle physical setup, materials, time, paid classroom assistants, and volunteers. With the current emphasis on inclusion and collaboration, the teacher must also coordinate his or her efforts with a number of specialists: the special education teacher, Title 1 personnel, the reading

FOSTERING ENGAGEMENT

Based on observations of 827 first-grade classrooms, researchers in a federal study concluded that both behavior and engagement in academic activities were improved in classrooms that provided both emotional and academic support (NICHD Early Child Care Research Network, 2002). Observations of 780 third-grade classrooms resulted in similar findings (NICHD Early Child Care Research Network, 2005).

FYI

It is essential that teachers build communities of learning so that students learn from each other and about each other (Peterson, 1992).

Exemplary Teaching

Organizing for Self-Regulated Learning

In an intensive study of ten fourth- and fifth-grade literacy classes, Ms. Kurtz's students stood out. Although the atmosphere in her class was friendly, it was also purposeful. Students were actively engaged in their learning, were seldom seen to be wasting time, were highly motivated, and had excellent work habits.

What was the secret of Ms. Kurtz's success? Involvement and instruction. Whenever possible, she gave students choices, and she also actively involved them in planning activities. Ms. Kurtz's instruction was organized around thematic units, with theme topics including survival, mysteries, the Revolutionary War, and others. After a unit was planned, she provided students with a list of unit activities and let them decide when to complete the activities. Instead of leaving them to their own devices, she actively promoted self-regulated learning. She assisted students with decision making and helped them plan their assignments. Students were also encouraged to reflect on and evaluate their work.

She expected students to be independent, but she taught them how to work on their own. Having been given the tools to become independent and the motivation to use them, the students lived up to expectations (Pressley, Wharton-McDonald, Mistretta-Hampston, & Echevarria, 1998).

An effective literacy program is well-managed and fosters group learning and a sense of community.

FYI

■ One source of help for struggling readers, and the rest of the class, too, is tutors. Tutors should be screened, trained, supervised, and appreciated. See Wasik (1999) for excellent suggestions for using volunteers.

■ To make better use of time, avoid teaching students what they already know and stop having them practice skills they have mastered. When introducing new words for a selection, do not spend time on those that are already familiar. One study found that students already knew 80 percent of the words recommended for instruction in the basal materials (Stallman et al., 1990). If the unknown words are words that students recognize when they hear them but do not know in print, do not waste time teaching the meanings. Emphasize the phonic form of the words, which is the unknown element.

consultant, and the bilingual and ESL teachers. The teacher must consult with the school social worker, nurse, vice principal, principal, and supervisory personnel and must enlist the support of parents.

Using Time Efficiently

Research clearly indicates that the more time students spend engaged in learning activities and the more content they cover, the more they learn (Berliner, 1985; Brophy & Good, 1986; Rosenshine & Stevens, 1984). Although time on task is a major ingredient in learning, the nature of the task plays a key role. If the task is too easy, too difficult, or not educationally valid, the time is wasted. A better measure of time use is academic learning time. Academic learning time (ALT) is the amount of time a student spends attending to relevant academic tasks while performing those tasks with a high rate of success (Berliner, 1984; Caldwell, Huitt, and Graeber, 1982). "For engaged time to be really useful, the student must be participating in useful activities at a high rate of success. Neither succeeding at worthless activities nor failing at worthwhile tasks will lead to improved performance" (Peterson & Swing, 1992). The amount of time spent on reading varies greatly; states or local districts often specify a minimum. In one study, time set aside for reading ranged from 47 to 118 minutes in second grade and from 60 to 127 minutes in fifth grade (Guthrie, 1980). Thus, some students receive more than twice as much instruction as others. For primary grades, aim for a minimum of 90 minutes for literacy instruction, but 120 is more desirable. For the upper grades, aim for a minimum of 60 minutes, but 90 is more desirable.

Pacing

Proper pacing plays a key role in literacy achievement (Barr, 1974; Clay, 1993b). Teachers must eliminate those activities that have limited or no value. They should critically examine every activity, asking whether it results in effective learning or practice. Also, eliminate unnecessary seatwork. Use cooperative learning, have students read self-selected books, meet in literature discussion groups, and work at learning centers. Well-planned centers can provide excellent opportunities for exploration and skills application. To be effective, each center should have a specific objective. The key is to arrange a sequence of valuable activities that students can perform without teacher direction. If some of the planned activities involve partners or small groups, students can obtain feedback and elaboration from each other. Table 13.3 describes two sample learning centers.

Closing the Gap: Making Use of Summers

During the summer, students lose about 10 percent of what they learned the previous year in spelling and math (Cooper, 2003). The loss in reading is less pronounced, especially if students come from middle-class families, where they might have greater access to books or educational experiences. Poor children and struggling readers, on the other hand, are more likely to experience a loss in literacy skills over the summer. One way of preventing this loss is to offer summer school programs for students. The programs that work best are designed for small groups, provide individual attention, and last for a significant period of time. In her review of studies, Karweit (1985) suggested that an additional thirty-five days of instruction are needed in order to make a significant difference. However, a key factor is how that time is used. If summer school is not available for your students, provide take-home activities, such as booklists and reading records and journals, that might help them maintain and possibly improve their skills. You might be able to work with the local librarian to create a summer reading program.

Providing for Individual Differences

With inclusion, today's classrooms are more diverse than ever. In first grade, the range of achievement in a class can be expected to be two or more years; in fourth grade, four years or more; by sixth grade, six years or more (Kulik, 1992). One way of providing for individual differences is to use reading and writing workshops, which were explained in Chapters 10 and 11. A second technique is to give extra help to low-achieving students. They might be given one-on-one or small-group instruction before or after school, on Saturdays, or in special summer programs. A third technique is to adapt or modify the program to meet individual needs. Adaptations have been discussed throughout the text and include providing added instruction, easier materials, or specialized aids to learning and changing the learning environment or using assistive technology. A fourth technique is to

■■■ **TABLE 13.3   Two Sample Learning Centers**

Type	Objective	Sequence of Activities
Word study center	Building decoding skills	1. Students follow directions to make new words by substituting clusters for single consonants. 2. Students read the new words. 3. Students assemble the words and read the message they created (see Secret Messages, p. 179). 4. Students write the message in their learning center logs.
Making and doing center	Following directions	1. Students select an activity that requires following directions. 2. Students read the directions to get an overview. 3. Students check to see that they have needed materials. 4. Students follow the directions. 5. Students describe the finished activity in their logs.

Adapted from Ford, 1994.

FYI

■ Grouping is the practice of dividing students into classes or within classes by age, ability, achievement, interests, or some other criterion.

■ Ability groups tend to be inflexible. Once students have been placed in a group, they tend to stay there. This is especially true of slow learners. One group of students who were tracked into the below-average group in kindergarten stayed there throughout their elementary school years (Rist, 1970).

use varied, **flexible grouping**. Possible groups include whole-class groups, guided reading groups, temporary skills groups, cooperative learning groups, and interest groups.

Whole-Class Grouping

Whole-class instruction can be efficient and build a sense of community. Reading aloud to students, shared reading, and introducing new concepts and strategies lend themselves to whole-class instruction. Reading and writing workshops begin and end with whole-class activities. Preparation for reading a selection is provided to the whole class. Anticipating difficulties that students might have with the text, the teacher develops background knowledge, activates schema, builds vocabulary, sets a purpose, and creates interest in the selection.

Although the initial preparatory instruction may be the same for all students, students might read the text in different ways. Adapting instruction to students' varied reading approaches is known as **tiered instruction**. When using tiered instruction, teachers teach the same concept or skill but adjust the level of difficulty of materials, how the materials are to be presented, how much help is provided, or the difficulty level of the assignment. Higher-achieving students read independently. Others can receive varying degrees of assistance. The teacher might spend additional time reviewing vocabulary, reading a portion of the selection to get the students started, or guiding students through the selection section by section. For children who have more serious reading problems, the teacher might use shared or assisted reading or allow them to listen to a taped version of the selection or view it on CD-ROM.

After the selection has been read, the whole class discusses it. Having read and discussed a story together builds community among students. However, it should be emphasized that although the selection might have been easy or just slightly challenging for some students, it was probably very difficult for others. For this reason, whole-group reading of selections should be used sparingly, and some teachers might choose not to use it at all. If used, whole-group reading should be balanced by providing lower-achieving students with opportunities to read on their instructional or independent levels.

Guided Reading

In guided reading, students are grouped by reading proficiency (Fountas & Pinnell, 1996, 2001c). The groups meet daily for ten to thirty minutes or more. The teacher may organize as many groups as she or he believes are necessary, but the more groups assembled, the less time there is for each one. As a practical matter, three or four groups are the most that can be handled efficiently. Grouping, however, is flexible. When appropriate, students are moved into other groups.

Temporary Skills Groups

In **skills groups**, students are grouped based on the need for a particular skill. Once the skill has been mastered, the group is disbanded. For example, if a number of students are

■ Because **flexible grouping** allows students to be in a variety of groups, some based on need, some on interest, some on personal choices, students are not tracked into low, average, or above-average groups. Flexible grouping also makes it easier for specialists to work with small groups of students. While the specialist is working with one small group, the classroom teacher can be working with another (Ogle & Fogelberg, 2001).

■ **Whole-class instruction** is the practice of teaching the entire class at the same time. Although whole-class grouping is efficient and builds a sense of community, it does have disadvantages. Teaching tends to be teacher-centered, there is less opportunity to provide for individual differences, and students have less opportunity to contribute (Radencich, 1995).

■ **Tiered instruction** consists of differentiating instruction so that the same concept or skill is presented in appropriate ways to students of varying abilities.

■ A **skills group** is a temporary group, sometimes known as an ad hoc group, that is formed for the purpose of learning a skill.

■ An **interest group** is a group formed on the basis of students' mutual interest.

having difficulty monitoring their comprehension, you might group them for lessons and practice sessions on how to use strategies in this area. Make sure that skills groups provide for the special needs of high-achieving students so that the groups are not stigmatized as being remedial (Radencich, 1995).

Study Buddies

Pairs of students can work together in a variety of ways—for example, as reading partners who take turns reading to each other, as study buddies who work on an assignment together, or as peer editors who read and comment on each other's written pieces.

Interest Groups

Students who are interested in a particular topic, author, or genre can join together in **interest groups**. For example, groups can be set up to discuss particular categories of famous people, such as inventors, entertainers, athletes, or scientists. Students who select famous inventors form one group. Those electing to study scientists, a second group, and so on. Each student in the group decides on a particular person to study. The group creates questions to be answered and uses trade books and other sources to gather information. The students work together in cooperative-learning style. One advantage of this type of grouping is that it includes students with diverse abilities and acts as a counterbalance to ability or achievement grouping. It also provides students with choices.

Regrouping

Regrouping is the practice of assigning students from several classes who are reading on the same grade level to instructional groups. If the reading, special education, and other specialists agree to take groups, groups can be relatively small. A variation of regrouping is the Joplin plan, in which students from different grade levels are regrouped. Regrouping, when properly implemented, has been shown to increase achievement (Slavin, 1987a) and is growing in popularity. Regrouping on an informal basis can also be effective. Two fifth-grade teachers might agree that one will take the lowest-level and the other will take the highest-level students. This cuts down on the range of pupils and number of groups. Disadvantages of regrouping include time lost going from class to class and lack of flexibility in the schedule: Students must move into their groups at a certain time.

Balanced Grouping

Grouping patterns should be balanced and flexible. At times, it is best for the class to work as a whole; at other times, small groups or pairs work best, and students should also have some experience working individually. By employing several patterns, the teacher gives students the opportunity to mix with a greater variety of their peers, and there is less of a chance that lower-achieving students will brand themselves as "slow" learners. The foundation of balanced grouping lies in the building of a sense of community. Realizing that they are valued and have a common purpose, students are better able to work with each other.

Grouping can result in gains of an extra two or three months on reading achievement tests. However, grouping is only effective when instruction is tailored to the group (Kulik, 1992). There is no gain when students are placed in groups but all are taught essentially the same material in the same way. It is also essential that students be assessed frequently and that group placement be changed when called for. Limiting the number of groups so that each group gets as much teacher attention as possible is also helpful (Slavin, 1987a).

Advantages and Disadvantages of Grouping

Grouping reduces variability in achievement and so makes it easier for the teacher to target instruction to the students' needs. The teacher is able to move at a faster pace for achieving students and provide more review and practice for struggling readers. However,

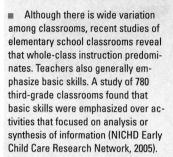

grouping can be harmful to the self-concepts of struggling readers, who may begin to see themselves as slow learners. Students in the lowest groups are also deprived of the opportunity to learn from the example and ideas of achieving readers. There is also a danger that low expectations will be set for struggling readers and that they will be given activities that are geared to lower-level skills so that they are deprived of opportunities to develop high-level thinking skills (Barr & Dreeben, 1991).

■ ■ ■ Checkup ■ ■ ■

1. What are some ways of providing for individual differences?
2. What some advantages and disadvantages of grouping?

Continuous Monitoring of Progress

A near universal finding of research on effective teaching is that it is essential to know where students are (Hoffman, 1991). **Monitoring** should be continuous. Continuous monitoring assumes that if something is lacking in the students' learning, the program will be modified. Skills and strategies that have been forgotten will be retaught; processes that have gone off on the wrong path will be rerouted. If materials prove to be too dull or too hard, substitutions will be made. If a child needs extra time to learn, it will be supplied. Such adjustments are especially important for slow learners (see pp. 522–523).

■ ■ ■ Checkup ■ ■ ■

1. How might you go about monitoring students' progress?

Importance of Parents

INVOLVING PARENTS

When parents are involved with their children's schools, their children do better and so does the school. Teachers feel more appreciated and are reaffirmed by the improved performance of their students. See the IRA position statement on family and school partnerships at:

http://www.reading.org/positions/family-school.html

Family Information Center provides a variety of information for parents.
http://www.indiana.edu/~reading/www/indexfr.html

In a landmark study, Hart and Risley (1995) found incredible differences in the amounts of language to which children were exposed. Although children from more privileged backgrounds are more likely to be provided with the language and skills necessary for success in school, it isn't social class that is the deciding factor. As Hart and Risley (1995) comment:

> Our data showed that the magnitude of children's accomplishments depend less on the material and educational advantages available in the home and more on the amount of experience children accumulate with parenting that provides language diversity, affirmative feedback, symbolic emphasis, gentle guidance, and responsiveness. (p. 210)

The implications for schooling are clear. While it is important for the school to stress language development and higher-level thinking skills and to set up an affirming and encouraging atmosphere, it is also important that the school work with parents. Parents can be shown how to listen to and talk with their children and to encourage them. Schools can emphasize students' positive achievements and encourage parents to build on them. In addition, programs that coach parents of infants and toddlers to talk to and encourage their children should result in children who have a richer vocabulary and more advanced language development, which is the foundation for literacy.

■ **Monitoring** refers to the assessment of students' progress to see whether they are performing adequately.

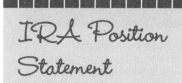

IRA Position Statement

on Key Issue

Family-School Partnerships

"Educators need to view partnerships with families as an integral part of good teaching and student success. . . . School programs and educator practices to organize family-school connections are equalizers to help families who would not become involved on their own" (Epstein & Dauber, 1991). "The benefits of developing collaborative relationships with all families are many, and they accrue to educators, families, and students. . . . Children from low-income and culturally and racially diverse families experience greater success when schools involve families, enlist them as allies, and build on their strengths. Family involvement in a child's education is a more important factor in student success than family income or education" (International Reading Association, 2002a, par. 3).

Involving Parents

Parents have a right to be kept informed about their child's literacy program. As a practical matter, keeping them up to date, especially if the program is a new one, will forestall complaints due to misunderstanding and will build support.

Study after study shows that even the most impoverished and least educated parents have high aspirations for their children (Wigfield & Asher, 1984). Prior to changes made to improve the effectiveness of the program in an impoverished elementary school in Southern California, teachers incorrectly assumed that parents lacked the time, ability, or motivation to help their children (Goldenberg, 1994). Although the parents were not well educated, they had high aspirations for their children. The school sent home reading materials and suggestions for ways in which the materials might be used. Even though parents were interested and supportive, merely making suggestions at the beginning of the year wasn't enough. The teachers found that it was important to use follow-up notes, phone calls, and regular homework assignments. With follow-through and monitoring, parents began providing assistance and students' achievement increased. The lesson is clear: The school must establish and maintain contact with parents. Quarterly report cards and PTA notices are a start, but more is necessary. Encourage students to take their papers home to show their parents and to read to their parents from their basals and/or trade books. This is especially important for novice readers. After students have finished a level in their basals or completed a trade book, help them prepare a passage to read to their parents.

A key step in communicating with parents is to keep them informed about your program when changes are made. Parents may expect instruction to be the way it was when they were in school. If they understand how a program works, they will be more inclined to support it, which helps ensure the program's success. The school might hold open houses and special meetings to explain the program. Letters in which the teacher describes what students are studying and why and how parents can help should be sent home periodically. Parents want to help their children but may not know what to do. Provide suggestions specific to the current unit, as well as more general ones with more far-reaching consequences. For example, reading to a child is a powerful technique for developing language and for developing a close relationship with the child. Parents can also provide a place and a time for the child to study, even if it is just a relatively quiet corner in a small apartment. Psychological support is more important than physical space.

USING TECHNOLOGY

Especially for Parents has resources that provide suggestions for ways in which parents can foster their children's literacy development.
http://www.ed.gov/parents/landing/jhtml?src=pn

To increase communication with parents and to provide help with homework, supply students and parents with an e-mail address where they can get in touch with you, or explain the homework assignment on the school's voice mail. You might also create a Web page that contains information valuable to parents.

FYI

Parents tend to have a bottom-up view of reading (Evans, Fox, Cremaso, & McKinnon, 2004)—that is, they favor systematic instruction in reading with lots of practice and accurate oral reading. If your approach is more holistic, you will need to clearly explain its benefits.

■ ■ ■ Checkup ■ ■ ■

1. Why is it important to involve parents?
2. What might be done to foster the involvement of parents?

■ In one elementary school in Connecticut, the writing strategies taught by the learning disabilities specialist were so effective that they were adopted by the whole school. Through collaboration, classroom teachers learned about effective strategies and learning disabilities teachers increased their knowledge of the curriculum.

■ Some study groups might prefer to meet without administrators present. They feel freer to discuss issues. The advantage of having administrators attend is that they can provide support and resources for recommendations.

Working with Other Professionals

Mirroring the trend toward cooperative and group learning activities, today's model of effective literacy instruction is one of cooperation and collaboration. The classroom teacher works closely with other school personnel, sharing expertise, experience, and resources. In many schools, teachers meet not only to plan programs but also to support each other and to explore new developments in the field.

Study Groups and Grade-Level Meetings

In many schools, teachers meet in study groups or grade-level or department meetings to discuss the latest children's book, techniques for teaching comprehension, or ways to help struggling learners. Study groups provide a forum in which teachers can share ideas and attack a common problem (Gunning, 2006). Participants can develop collaborative units, share lesson plans, develop materials, adapt programs, view videos, read and discuss a professional text, or investigate areas of concern (Murphy, 1992). As a result of their study, the group members may decide to make some change in the program. As members implement changes, they can advise and support each other.

To get started, meet with a group and decide some possible areas of study. Also decide on the mechanics: where, when, and how often you will meet and who will be the group leader. Decide on ground rules, such as starting on time, ending on time, and setting an agenda for each meeting. You might also want to draw up an action plan that implements the results of your meetings. See "Join the Club" (Roberts, 2006) at http://teacher.scholastic.com/products/instructor/jointheclub.htm for suggestions for starting a study group.

In grade-level or department meetings, teachers from the same grade or department meet regularly to share their expertise and learn from others. Possible topics of discussion include program implementation, students who are having difficulty, successful practices, analysis of screening data, consideration of possible improvements, and factors that are hindering progress in closing the gap. Grade-level meetings work best when they are frequent and follow an agreed-upon format and agenda. A permanent agenda item should be to determine whether the actions formulated at previous meetings have been carried out. Grade-level meetings are also more useful when administrators and literacy facilitators and other specialists attend and when the group has chosen a leader who monitors the discussions and takes care of meeting arrangements. Grade-level meetings should be complemented with cross–grade-level meetings. This provides an opportunity to discuss broader concerns and to plan a program that is articulated across grade levels. In addition, cross–grade-level meetings promote teamwork and a whole-school spirit (Gunning, 2006).

Working with Resource Personnel

With the emphasis on inclusion, classroom teachers are also working more closely with the special education teacher, the reading–language arts consultant, and other specialists.

Because of the emphasis on using children's books and technology in the literacy program, it is important for classroom teachers to work with the media specialist. A well-balanced reading program must have a continuous supply of children's books. Media specialists can hold story hours, teach library skills, conduct book talks, help students use computers that are housed in the library, arrange special displays, and help children find appropriate books. They may even be able to provide loans to the classroom library and can keep teachers informed about the latest children's books. Classroom teachers can assist by letting the media specialist know when they plan to ask students to obtain books on certain topics or suggest that students read books by a certain author so that these materials can be assembled.

Because students with special needs are being included in many classrooms, classroom teachers collaborate with special education teachers, reading teachers, and other learning specialists. Through collaboration, classroom teachers can obtain services and materials for special needs students and also learn teaching and management techniques that will help them more effectively instruct these students. Often, the techniques used and strategies taught work well with all students, so some of these might be used with the whole class.

Collaboration works best when the professionals involved meet regularly, establish common goals, and are flexible but work diligently to meet their common goals and make adjustments as necessary. Carefully planned and implemented collaboration can result in improved learning for both the special needs students and the rest of the class.

Using Reading to Close the Gap

In 90/90/90 schools, 90 percent or more of the students are eligible for free and reduced lunch, 90 percent are members of ethnic minority groups, but 90 percent of students meet academic standards in reading or another area (Reeves, 2003). These schools have the following features:

- Focus on academic achievement
- Clear curriculum choices
- Frequent assessment of student progress and multiple opportunities for improvement
- Emphasis on nonfiction writing
- Collaborative scoring of student work by teachers

To catch up, students who are behind must read more. Adding reading time to a crowded day can be a problem. However, one solution is to make better use of the time available. Having efficient management routines can save time. If the guided reading group gets started promptly, they might have 5 more minutes of reading time. If students have carefully chosen their books for voluntary or self-selected reading and are engaged in their reading, instead of leafing through the book or looking at pictures, that, too, can add valuable minutes to reading time. Any reading in content areas, of course, adds to reading time. And having books on the appropriate level provides below-level readers with added time (Guthrie, 2004).

Making significant progress in reading takes extended effort. A fourth-grader who is two years behind might need an extra hour of reading each school day for a period of two years to catch up. The key is not how many minutes the students have books in their hands. The key is how many minutes they are engrossed in reading text that is on the appropriate level of challenge.

Take a reading audit of your class. Count up the minutes of actual reading that your students do. How do your lowest-achieving readers compare with your highest-achieving readers? To help struggling readers, Allington (2006) advises, "The intervention that I would propose is straightforward. Provide these children with high-success reading experiences all day long. Fill their desks with books that they can read accurately, fluently, and with understanding" (p. 102).

■ Literacy and Technology: The New Literacies

New literacies are the new reading, writing, and communication skills that are required for successful use of information and communications technologies, especially the Internet. These are traditional reading skills adapted to technology and include identifying problems, searching for information, critically evaluating information, synthesizing it, and communicating it (Leu, 2006).

The Internet

The Internet is a vast reservoir of learning activities. The state of California, for instance, has produced a number of Cyberguides. Cyberguides use Web-based activities to help students extend and apply their understanding of literary selections at all grade levels. In one unit, students read *Caddie Woodlawn* (Brink, 1935) and then are asked to visit a number

USING TECHNOLOGY

"Using the Internet requires . . . that you identify a question that you want to answer. You then have to plan a search. You have to determine the best source of information and also when you have sufficient information. You must evaluate the information. You must also integrate and synthesize information" (Leu, 2006).

of sites that will provide them with information about the Westward Expansion so that they can create a brochure to convince others to join a wagon train. Students are provided with a rubric that spells out how their project will be graded (Martinez, 1998).

WebQuests (http://webquest.org) are similar to Cyberguides. A WebQuest is an inquiry-based learning task that makes use of Internet resources (Dodge, 2001). The best WebQuests engage students as active learners and foster higher-level learning skills. Tasks range from obtaining information and answering intriguing questions to solving mysteries, synthesizing data from several sources, creating a product or plan, persuading others, building self-knowledge, analyzing events or issues, or making reasoned judgments. Typical WebQuests might involve giving a PowerPoint presentation on the deserts of the world and offering solutions to the problem of desertification based on material found at several Web sites, comparing the biographies of two authors after visiting their sites, deciding what most likely happened to the Mayan people, creating a newspaper report of an historical event after visiting sites containing primary sources, designing an energy-efficient home after visiting pertinent sites, and persuading others of your viewpoint after visiting sites that contain information about controversial issues.

Because sites for a WebQuest are already chosen for students, students make efficient use of their time. Students don't spend a lot of time surfing the Net. Because the sites are chosen by the teacher, they are high quality and safe and geared to the teacher's instructional objectives. Listed below are suggested steps for creating a WebQuest.

Steps in Creating a WebQuest

Step 1: Stating Objectives.   What is it that you want students to know or be able to do as a result of the WebQuest? You might want them to be able to write a poem, compare contrasting opinions on a timely topic, or create a Web site by following directions.

Step 2: Finding Appropriate Sites.   Find sites that enable students to achieve their learning objective. For instance, if the goal is to have them write a poem, you might select sites that contain a variety of poems, explain how poems are created, and provide templates for the creation of easy-to-compose poems.

Step 3: Organize the WebQuest.   Create a guide that explains the purpose of the WebQuest and how to implement it. For each site they visit, students might be provided a brief overview as well as questions to be answered or a task to be completed. The questions or tasks should foster higher-level thinking as well as basic understanding. The WebQuest should go beyond merely having students retell information.

Step 4: Establish Outcome Activities.   Decide how you want students to use this knowledge or skill that they have gained through engaging in the WebQuest. Will they write a letter of protest? Will they create a modern-day fable? Will they share information with younger students?

Step 5: Assessing the WebQuest.   Using a rubric or other assessment device, evaluate the students' learning and also the effectiveness of the WebQuest. Did they attain the learning objectives? Did the WebQuest spark interest and higher-level thinking? How might it be improved?

Lists of Sites

There are thousands of sites designed for elementary and middle school students. Here is a list of recommended sites:

> ■   A **simulation** is a type of computer program that presents activities or gives the feel of the real experience.

- *Awesome Library* provides links to 22,000 carefully reviewed resources for students of all ages. The browser is available in a dozen languages and has a translation feature. http://www.awesomelibrary.org

- *Enchanted Learning* features a wealth of information about animals and other topics, and a variety of activities and illustrations that can be printed out. Materials are in English and Spanish, including a Little Explorer's Picture Dictionary. http://www.enchantedlearning.com

- A popular site for teachers, *Kathy Schrock's Guide for Educators* is compiled by a school librarian who has also created a collection for students http://school.discovery.com/schrockguide

- Billed as the best homework and reference resource, *Kid Info/School Subjects* is arranged by subject area and linked to many of the best educational sites online. http://www.kidinfo.com

- *PBS Teachersource* lists sites selected for curriculum content, arranged by subject areas. http://www.pbs.org/teachersource

- *Great Sites for Kids* is compiled by members of the American Library Association for students, teachers, librarians, and parents. http://www.ala.org/greatsites

Talking Web Sites

With the appropriate software, Web sites can be made to talk. AspireREADER (Tom Snyder) reads aloud text from the Internet or word-processing programs. Awesome Talking Library (http://www.awesomelibrary.org) also has software that reads Web sites. The software from Awesome Talking Library is free to download and is very easy to use. In addition, some computers have a built-in screen reader.

Issues of Safety

For all its potential value, the Internet can be a source of harm to young people. The Internet is essentially unregulated, so objectionable material is available. Filtering software can be used to restrict access to some objectionable sites. Software that keeps track of sites that have been visited is also available. There is also the issue of security. Unfortunately, some adults have used the Internet to prey on children. The best defense is to educate students and their parents about the dangers of the Internet and precautions that might be taken. In many schools, parents and students sign an agreement to use the Internet ethically and responsibly. Students also need to be supervised when using the Internet. As a practical matter, monitors should be set up so that teachers can readily see what students are viewing.

Other Uses of Computers

The power of computers and the quality of educational software are continually improving. In addition to providing a portal to the Internet, computers have four major educational uses, which sometimes overlap: They provide practice, tutorial instruction, and simulations, and they can be used as writing tools.

    Kidspiration (Inspiration Software) is a particularly useful tool for students. Designed for students in grades K–3, it provides illustrations that students can use to brainstorm ideas or illustrate their writing pieces. It also has templates for creating semantic webs and prompts for writing.

    Tutorial software, such as *Simon S.I.O.* (Don Johnston), walks the student through a lesson with a series of questions and answers or activities. Active participation is required. After a skill is explained, reinforcement exercises are provided. One of the best instructional uses of software is the presentation of **simulations**. Students can travel back in time, take journeys across country, and perform experiments without leaving their computers. For example, in *Message in a Bottle* (Brighter Child Interactive), students become paleontologists. They excavate a fossil, label its parts, and prepare a museum exhibit.

Adapting Instruction for Struggling Readers and Writers

Software known as AspireREADER (http://www.cast.org) reads aloud and highlights text from the Internet or word-processing programs. It provides access to materials poor readers might not be able to read on their own.

FYI

Teachers in 94 percent of public schools monitor Internet use, and 74 percent of schools have blocking or filtering software. Nearly two-thirds of schools also have an honor code relating to Internet use. Virtually all schools have an acceptable use policy (Cattagni & Westnat, 2001).

Using the Computer as a Tool

Computers are most powerful in literacy learning when they are used as a tool. They can help locate data, retrieve information, organize data, compose information, and present information.

Word Processing.   Computers are most frequently used as aids to composition. The major advantage of word-processing software is that students can revise without rewriting or retyping the whole piece. Some software can also help with planning, checking spelling, and checking grammar and usage. Bundling word-processing features with design and illustration capabilities, desktop publishing systems allow students to create newspapers, newsletters, brochures, and booklets. See Chapter 11 for additional information about word processing and desktop publishing.

Using the Computer as a Source of Information

The increased power of computers allows students to have access to dictionaries, encyclopedias, thesauri, picture libraries, atlases, and other databases of information available in inexpensive CD-ROM format. They often come with features that help students locate and organize information. Many of these are also available on the Web.

Selecting Software

The key to making effective use of the computer is to obtain high-quality software. Before selecting software, decide what you want it to do and how you might use it. Decide what education objective you wish to fulfill. In addition to being appealing and motivational, software should fulfill an educational purpose.

To assess software, ask the following questions, which are adapted from Cook (1986) and Bitter (1999):

- Does the software help attain an educationally valid objective?
- Are its activities consistent with the way I teach reading or writing?
- Does it make use of the special capabilities of the computer—providing immediate knowledge of results, learner participation, use of graphics, use of speech, keeping track of progress, and so on?
- Does the software include learning aids, such as pronouncing and/or defining difficult words on request and providing additional information or more practice if needed?
- Is the material presented accurately and on the proper level of readability?
- Is the software reasonably easy to use?
- Can it be modified to add customized examples or exercises?

Getting the Most Out of Computers

Computer software, like other educational materials, requires teacher guidance. Students have to be prepared to complete the activity offered by the software or site they are about to visit. They must have their background knowledge activated, have a purpose for completing the assignment, and know how to read the material. Should they read it fast or slow? Should they read it in parts or as a whole? They also have to know how to use any learning aids that might be built into the program. After students have completed the activity, give them the opportunity to discuss what they have learned; clarify misconceptions, integrate new and old information, and extend and apply their learning.

In dealing with electronic media, students use many of the same basic skills and strategies that they use when engaged in traditional reading and writing. However, computers and other electronic devices demand new skills and adaptations of old ones. Given the accessibility of information, students need to be able to quickly and accurately select information that is relevant.

"The Internet and other forms of information and communication technology (ICT) such as word processors, Web editors, presentation software, and e-mail are regularly redefining the nature of literacy. To become fully literate in today's world, students must become proficient in the new literacies of ICT. Therefore, literacy educators have a responsibility to effectively integrate these technologies into the literacy curriculum in order to prepare students for the literacy future they deserve" (International Reading Association, 2001a, par 1).

IRA Position Statement

on Key Issue

Integrating Literacy and Technology in the Curriculum

It is important that technology, no matter how promising or exciting or complex, be seen as a tool and not the focus of instruction. A long-term study of the effect of technology on students found that "students worked best when technology was not the topic itself but was integrated into the entire curriculum" (Bitter, 1999, p. 109).

Teacher Tools

Technology has also created a variety of valuable tools for the teacher. For instance, using *Wynn Reader* (Enable Mart), the teacher can make adaptations in electronic text. Text can be added, deleted, or simplified. Study aids, such as voice notes, and a built-in dictionary are available. *Worksheet Magic Plus* (Gamco Educational Software) makes it possible to create fifteen different kinds of practice activities, including crossword puzzles and word searches. *Inspiration* (Inspiration Software) can be used by both students and teachers to make graphic organizers. The software includes thirty-five graphic organizer templates and 1,250 pieces of clip art. Presentation software such as *PowerPoint* (Microsoft) or *Keynote* (Apple) can be used by both teachers and students to make slides, transparencies, and computer presentations. Software such as *Front Page* (Microsoft) can be used in the construction of Web pages.

Other Technologies

Audio and audiovisual technologies can be used to motivate children to read or to expand children's understanding and appreciation of a selection. For poor readers, audiovisual aids may provide access to a piece of literature that they would not be able to read on their own.

Audio Technologies

Audio versions of books have three advantages (Rickelman & Henk, 1990). Although warmth and interaction are missing in an electronic reading, it can be played over and over by the student. In addition, audio books often include sound effects, may be dramatized, and may even have been recorded by the author of the work. Because of their superior sound quality, CD versions are preferable to taped ones but may not be available for certain titles.

Audiovisual Technologies

Films and videos are available for a wide variety of children's books. There are hundreds of children's books on video cassettes, CDs, or DVDs, including *Frog and Toad Are Friends* (Clearvue & SVE), *Cinderella* (Playhouse Video), *Mufaro's Beautiful Daughters* (Clearvue & SVE), and *Follow the Drinking Gourd* (Clearvue & SVE).

USING TECHNOLOGY

4 Teachers provides easy-to-use tools. With QuizStar, a teacher can create online quizzes. With Web Worksheet Wizard, the teacher can create Web pages. Using Project Poster, students can create Web pages. TrackStar enables teachers to create Web site projects that are based on a series of links to other sites and to customize already existing Tracks. RubiStar allows teachers to customize any one of several dozen rubrics. NoteStar helps students take notes from online sources.
http://4teachers.org

Sites for Teachers features hundreds of sites that offer teaching suggestions, activities, and clip art.
http://www.sitesforteachers.com/index.html

USING TECHNOLOGY

Titlewave provides information on videos and sound recordings.
http://www.titlewave.com

■■■ **Checkup** ■■■

1. What are some ways that technology might be used to foster literacy?   ■■■

■ Literacy in Today's and Tomorrow's World

FYI

The December/January 2005 issue of *The Reading Teacher* (pp. 388–393) contains rubrics for assessing your performance on running records, guided reading, and graphic organizers.

Increasingly, literacy will include the ability to use computers and other technology. Students need to know how to use resources such as the Internet and how to construct multimedia reports. They also need to understand how to get the most out of interactive encyclopedias and other sophisticated sources of information. Computer literacy still requires traditional skills: the ability to read with understanding, to write coherently, and to think clearly. However, today's technology also requires a higher level of literacy. Internet searches allow students to obtain greater amounts of data on a particular topic, including data published that day. Students need the skills to skim and scan data so that they can quickly select information that is relevant and important. A key reading skill for the era of the information superhighway is the ability to decide quickly and efficiently whether an article, study, or other document merits reading. With so much more information available, it is essential that students not waste time reading texts that are not pertinent or worthwhile.

Having more data to work with means that students must be better at organizing information, evaluating it, drawing conclusions, and conveying the essence of the information to others. They also need cognitive flexibility to make use of the growing amounts of information in proposing diverse solutions to the increasingly complex problems sure to arise in the coming years.

Increasingly, literacy will include the ability to use computers and other high-technology devices.

■ Professional Development

To keep up with the latest developments in the fields of reading and writing instruction, it is necessary to be professionally active—to join professional organizations, attend meetings, take part in staff-development activities, and read in the field. The International Reading Association (100 Barksdale Road, Newark, DE 19714) and the National Council of Teachers of English (1111 Kenyon Road, Urbana, IL 61801) are devoted to professional improvement in reading and the language arts. The IRA publishes the widely read periodicals *The Reading Teacher* and *Journal of Adolescent and Adult Literacy.*

The NCTE publishes *Language Arts.* Both organizations have local and state chapters and sponsor regional and national conferences.

As with any other vital endeavor, teachers should set both long-term goals and short-term professional objectives, asking such questions as the following:

USING TECHNOLOGY

The web site of the National Council of Teachers of English provides teaching suggestions, sample lesson plans, and sample units, as well as a number of forums through which teachers can exchange ideas.
http://www.ncte.org

The International Reading Association site provides a wealth of information on the teaching of reading and writing.
http://www.reading.org

Kathy Schrock's Guide for Educators is an award-winning resource.
http://school.discovery.com/schrockguide

■ Where do I want to be professionally five years from now?

■ What steps do I have to take to get there?

■ What are my strengths and weaknesses as a teacher of reading and writing?

■ How can I build on my strengths and remediate my weaknesses?

■ What new professional techniques, skills, or areas of knowledge would I most like to learn?

The answers should result in a plan of professional development.

Filling out the checklist in Figure 13.1 will help you create a profile of your strengths and weaknesses as a reading and writing teacher. The checklist covers the entire literacy program and incorporates the major principles covered in the text. As such, it provides a review of the book as well as a means of self-assessment.

■■■ **FIGURE 13.1   Checklist for an Effective Literacy Program**

Directions: To read each question, insert the phrase "Do I" before it (e.g., "Do I read aloud regularly?"). Then circle the appropriate response. If you are not in the teaching situation described, respond as though you were. When finished, analyze your answers. What are your strengths? What are some areas in which you might need improvement?

Teaching Practices: General	Never	Seldom	Often	Usually
Read aloud regularly	1	2	3	4
Directly teach key strategies and skills	1	2	3	4
Model reading and writing processes	1	2	3	4
Use think-alouds to make reading and writing processes explicit	1	2	3	4
Provide adequate guided practice	1	2	3	4
Provide opportunities for application	1	2	3	4
Integrate reading, writing, listening, and speaking	1	2	3	4

Teaching Practices: Comprehension/Study Skills				
Build background and activate prior knowledge	1	2	3	4
Set or encourage the setting of purposes	1	2	3	4
Present a variety of comprehension strategies	1	2	3	4
Teach monitoring/strategic reading	1	2	3	4
Provide adequate practice/application	1	2	3	4

Teaching Practices: Word Recognition				
Provide systematic instruction in major skill areas: phonics, context clues, syllabication, morphemic analysis, dictionary skills	1	2	3	4
Provide systematic instruction in use of major cueing systems: phonological, syntactic, semantic	1	2	3	4
Encourage the use of a variety of decoding strategies	1	2	3	4
Provide opportunities for students to read widely so skills become automatic	1	2	3	4

Teaching Practices: Content Area				
Use high-quality content-area texts	1	2	3	4
Supplement content-area texts with informational books and nonprint materials	1	2	3	4
Provide texts on appropriate levels of difficulty or make adjustments	1	2	3	4
Present skills and strategies necessary to learn from informational texts	1	2	3	4

Teaching Practices: Writing				
Encourage self-selection of topics	1	2	3	4
Use a process approach	1	2	3	4
Provide guided instruction in writing strategies	1	2	3	4
Provide frequent opportunities for writing	1	2	3	4
Provide opportunities to compose in a variety of forms	1	2	3	4

(continued)

■ ▪ ■ **FIGURE 13.1**   **Checklist for an Effective Literacy Program,** *continued*

	Never	Seldom	Often	Usually
Materials				
Use a variety of print materials	1	2	3	4
Children's books, fiction and nonfiction	1	2	3	4
Supplementary materials	1	2	3	4
Basal series	1	2	3	4
Periodicals	1	2	3	4
Real-world materials	1	2	3	4
Pamphlets, brochures	1	2	3	4
Pupil-written works	1	2	3	4
Use a variety of nonprint materials	1	2	3	4
Tape recorder	1	2	3	4
VCR	1	2	3	4
Videodiscs/DVDs	1	2	3	4
Film/video clips	1	2	3	4
Computer software	1	2	3	4
Web sites	1	2	3	4
Games	1	2	3	4
Adapt materials to students' needs	1	2	3	4
Provide materials for slow as well as bright students	1	2	3	4
Evaluate materials before using them	1	2	3	4
Evaluation				
Set goals and objectives (standards) for the program	1	2	3	4
Align standards (objectives) and assessment	1	2	3	4
Collect formal and informal data to use as a basis for evaluating the program	1	2	3	4
Encourage self-assessment	1	2	3	4
Assess data-collection instruments in terms of validity and reliability	1	2	3	4
Assemble a portfolio for each student	1	2	3	4
Share assessment data with students and parents	1	2	3	4
Use assessment data to improve instruction for each student and to improve program	1	2	3	4
Organization/Management				
Provide for individual differences	1	2	3	4
Use a variety of grouping strategies	1	2	3	4
Use time and materials efficiently	1	2	3	4

Building Higher-Level Literacy

As part of your program planning, carefully consider the place of higher-level literacy. Start with your standards, goals, and objectives. How well do these align with outside assessment and your assessments? Note whether your assessments are providing you with the information you need for instruction. Look, too, at the data. What do the data tell you about your students' performance? How well are instruction, goals, and assessment aligned? Talk to teachers at your grade level and other grade levels. Teaching skills for higher-level literacy requires an intensive, long-term effort. As Gaskins (2005) explains, it takes several years before students begin to show a grasp of such skills.

Tools for the Classroom

Essential Standards

Kindergarten and grade 1

Students will

- operate a computer in order to run easy-to-use educational software.
- use a simple word-processing program and a simple desktop publishing system.
- use audio tape recorders to play and record information.

Grades 2 and 3

Students will

- operate a computer in order to run basic educational software.
- use a basic word-processing program and a basic desktop publishing system.
- compose e-mail and communicate with other students.
- use selected bookmarked sites to gather information.
- use audio tape recorders to play and record information.
- use technology ethically and responsibly.

Grades 4 through 8

Students will

- operate a computer in order to run advanced educational software.
- use an advanced word-processing program and an advanced desktop publishing system.
- use a database to organize information.
- compose e-mail and communicate with other students.
- use CD-ROM and online encyclopedias, databases, and other electronic reference sources.
- use a variety of Internet sites to gather information.
- use presentation software.
- use technology ethically and responsibly.

Action Plan

1. Obtain basic information about your students' culture, literacy strengths, and needs.
2. Construct a program based on the nature of students you will be teaching. Set goals and objectives.
3. Obtain materials and select teaching techniques and activities that will help you reach those goals.
4. Build motivation by helping students experience the joy of successful learning. Build a classroom community in which students help each other learn.
5. Use time efficiently and provide for individual differences. Use a variety of types of grouping. However, make sure that grouping is flexible; students move back and forth between groups and there is no stigma to being in certain groups.

6. Make sure that students, especially struggling readers, are given materials and instruction at their level each day.

7. Continuously monitor progress with both formal and informal instruments. Make sure that instruction is guided by assessment.

8. Involve parents in their children's learning. Use a variety of techniques to keep them informed about their children's progress. Provide specific suggestions of things they might do to help their children. Make use of their talents and knowledge in the classroom by having them give presentations and help out through tutoring, translating, or performing other tasks.

9. Work cooperatively with the media specialist, the learning disabilities teacher, the reading teacher, and other professionals. Coordinate efforts so that students receive maximum benefit.

10. Make use of technology to foster literacy and guide students so that they learn to use technology as a literacy tool.

11. Evaluate your program and make adjustments as needed.

12. Create a plan for professional development. Include long-term goals and short-term objectives. Keep up with the professional literature, take courses, attend workshops and conferences, observe highly effective teachers, and join a study group to further your professional development.

Summary

The construction of a literacy program starts with consideration of the needs and characteristics of students, the parents' wishes, and the nature of the community. General goals and specific objectives are based on these factors. Other elements in the construction of a literacy program include high-quality teaching, use of varied materials, continuous monitoring of students' progress, involvement of parents, efficient management of time and resources, provision for individual differences, and collaboration with other professionals.

Literacy includes the ability to use technology. Technology should be integrated into the literacy program. Effective use of the Internet requires instruction in efficient searching techniques and the ability to judge the relevance and reliability of information. Word-processing programs, desktop publishing systems, and presentation software can help students present information. Audio and audiovisual technologies can be used to motivate students.

Extending and Applying

1. Set up goals and objectives for a reading/language arts program that you are now teaching or plan to teach. Discuss your goals and objectives with a colleague or classmate.

2. Complete the checklist in Figure 13.1. If you are not teaching now, base your responses on how you believe you will conduct yourself when you are a teacher. What strengths and weaknesses do your responses reveal?

3. Respond to the questions about professional goals and objectives on page 550. Based on these responses and your responses to the checklist in Figure 13.1, plan a series of professional development activities.

4. For a week, keep a record of the activities in your reading/language arts class. Which seem to be especially valuable? Which, if any, seem to have limited value or take up excessive time? Based on your observations,

construct a plan for making better use of instructional time. If you are not teaching now, arrange to observe a teacher who has a reputation for having a well-managed classroom. Note the strategies that the teacher uses to keep the class running smoothly and to make efficient use of time.

5. Assess parental involvement in your literacy program. Based on your assessment and the suggestions made in this chapter, make any changes that seem to be needed.

Developing a Professional Portfolio

Keep a record of experiences that you have had with technology. This might include Web sites that you set up or helped set up, video productions that you have supervised, or audio tapes that you or your students have created. Note

any special training that you have had with technology. Also include lesson plans in which you made effective use of technology.

Go to Allyn & Bacon's MyLabSchool: www.mylabschool.com

- Enter Assignment ID **EPV7** into **Assignment Finder,** and select the video titled "Involving Parents." In this video, a teacher discusses how she communicates with parents and why she believes that it is important to involve them in the educational process. A parent volunteers to help with a lesson in vocabulary.

- As you watch the video, identify the various strategies the teacher uses to involve parents in the educational process.

How do the students, the teacher, and the parents benefit from this kind of classroom interaction?

- Explore MyLabSchool further to find the course areas for Reading Methods, Language Arts, and Content Area Reading and identify other assets that support concepts introduced in this chapter.

Developing a Resource File

Start and maintain a file of Internet sites or titles of software and other technology that seem to be especially valuable for the grade level that you teach or plan to teach.

To access chapter objectives, practice tests, weblinks, and flashcards, go to the companion website at www.ablongman.com/gunning6e.

APPENDIX A

Graded Listing of Outstanding Children's Books

N   Designates nonfiction

Reading Level: Caption/Frame

Beginning Preprimer 1

Arnosky, Jim. *Mouse Colors*. Houghton Mifflin, 2001, 46 pp.

Asch, Frank. *Little Fish, Big Fish*. Scholastic, 1992, 16 pp.

Brown, Craig. *My Barn*. Greenwillow, 1991, 20 pp.

Cameron, Alice. *The Cat Sat on the Mat*. Houghton Mifflin, 1994, 30 pp.

Carle, Eric. *Do You Want to Be My Friend?* Harper, 1971, 30 pp.

Carle, Eric. *Have You Seen My Cat?* Scholastic, 1987, 24 pp.

Gomi, Taro. *My Friends*. Chronicle Books, 1990, 32 pp.

Gomi, Taro. *Who Hid It?* Millbrook Press, 1991, 22 pp.

Grejniec, Michael. *What Do You Like?* North-South Books, 1992, 28 pp.

Grundy, Lynn N. *A Is for Apple*. Ladybird Books, 1980, 26 pp.

Hutchins, Pat. *1 Hunter*. Greenwillow, 1982, 22 pp.

Maris, Ron. *My Book*. Puffin, 1983, 30 pp.

McMillan, Bruce. *One, Two, One Pair*. Scholastic, 1991, 30 pp.

McMillan, Bruce. *Beach Ball-Left, Right*. Holiday House, 1992, 28 pp.

McMillan, Bruce. *Mouse Views: What the Class Pet Saw*. Holiday House, 1993, 30 pp.

Rathmann, Peggy. *Good Night, Gorilla*. Putnam, 1994, 34 pp.

Rotner, Shelley, & Kreisler, Ken. *Faces*. Simon & Schuster, 1994, 24 pp.

Rubinstein, Gillian. *Dog In, Cat Out*. Ticknor & Fields, 1993, 28 pp.

Tafuri, Nancy. *Have You Seen My Duckling?* Greenwillow, 1984, 24 pp.

Wildsmith, Brian. *Cat on the Mat*. Oxford, 1982, 16 pp.

Reading Level: Preprimer 1

Easy High-Frequency Words

Agee, John. *Flapstick*. Dutton, 1993, 20 pp.

Appelt, Kathy. *Elephants Aloft*. Harcourt, 1993, 28 pp.

Aruego, Jose, & Dewey, Ariane. *We Hide, You Seek*. Greenwillow, 1979, 30 pp.

Asch, Frank. *Moonbear's Books*. Simon & Schuster, 1993, 12 pp.

Barton, Byron. *Where's Al?* Houghton Mifflin, 1972, 30 pp.

Beck, Ian. *Five Little Ducks*. Holt, 1992, 24 pp.

Berenstain, Stan, & Berenstain, Jan. *Inside Outside Upside Down*. Random House, 1968, 27 pp.

Berenstain, Stan, & Berenstain, Jan. *Bears on Wheels*. Random House, 1969, 32 pp.

Bond, Michael. *Paddington's Opposites*. Viking, 1991, 32 pp.

Carle, Eric. *Do You Want to Be My Friend?* HarperCollins, 1976, 30 pp.

Carle, Eric, & Kazuo, Iwamura. *Where Are You Going? To See My Friend!* Orchard, 2001, 28 pp.

Christelow, Eileen. *Five Little Monkeys Jumping on the Bed*. Clarion, 1989, 32 pp.

Clarke, Gus. *EIEIO: The Story of Old MacDonald Who Had a Farm*. Lothrop, Lee & Shepard, 1992, 24 pp.

Cousins, Lucy. *What Can Rabbit See?* Tambourine, 1991, 16 pp.

Crews, Donald. *School Bus*. Greenwillow, 1984, 32 pp. N

de Regniers, Beatrice Schenk. *Going for a Walk*. HarperCollins, 1961, 1993, 24 pp.

Edwards, Frank B. *New at the Zoo*. Firefly, 1998, 24 pp.

Ellwand, David. *Emma's Elephant & Other Favorite Animal Friends*. Dutton, 1996, 32 pp. N

Fleming, Denise. *In the Tall, Tall Grass*. Holt, 1991, 30 pp.

Florian, Douglas. *A Winter Day*. Greenwillow, 1988, 22 pp.

Ginsburg, Mirra. *The Chick and the Duckling*. Simon & Schuster, 1972, 24 pp.

Ginsburg, Mirra. *Asleep, Asleep*. Greenwillow, 1992, 22 pp.

Gomi, Taro. *Where's the Fish?* Morrow, 1977, 24 pp.

Greene, Carol. *Snow Joe*. Children's Press, 1982, 30 pp.

Hague, Michael. *Teddy Bear, Teddy Bear*. Morrow, 1993, 16 pp.

Hall, Nancy. *The Mess*. Children's Press, 1990, 29 pp.

Henkes, Kevin. *SHHHH*. Greenwillow, 1989, 20 pp.

Hoban, Tana. *One Little Kitten*. Greenwillow, 1979, 22 pp.

Hutchins, Pat. *Rosie's Walk*. Simon & Schuster, 1968, 30 pp.

Hutchins, Pat. *What Game Shall We Play?* Greenwillow, 1990, 22 pp.

Jonas, Ann. *Now We Can Go*. Greenwillow, 1986, 23 pp.

Jonas, Ann. *Where Can It Be?* Greenwillow, 1986, 30 pp.

Keats, Ezra Jack. *Kitten for a Day*. Four Winds, 1974, 30 pp.

Kraus, Robert. *Whose Mouse Are You?* Simon & Schuster, 1970, 28 pp.

Lillegard, Dee. *Where Is It?* Children's Press, 1984, 30 pp.

Mansell, Dom. *My Old Teddy*. Candlewick Press, 1991, 24 pp.

Maris, Ron. *Is Anyone Home?* Greenwillow, 1985, 30 pp.

Martin, Bill, Jr. *Brown Bear, Brown Bear, What Do You See?* Holt, 1967, 24 pp.

Marzollo, Jean. *Ten Cats Have Hats*. Scholastic, 1994, 20 pp.

Matthias, Catherine. *Out the Door*. Children's Press, 1982, 31 pp.

Matthias, Catherine. *Over-Under*. Children's Press, 1984, 29 pp.

McKissack, Patricia. *Who Is Who?* Children's Press, 1983, 30 pp.

McKissack, Patricia. *Who Is Coming?* Children's Press, 1986, 31 pp.

McKissack, Patricia, & McKissack, Fredrick. *Bugs!* Children's Press, 1988, 30 pp. N

McMillan, Bruce. *One Sun*. Holiday House, 1990, 30 pp.

McMillan, Bruce. *Play Day, A Book of Terse Verse*. Holiday House, 1991, 30 pp.

Miller, Margaret. *Whose Hat?* Greenwillow, 1988, 36 pp.

Miller, Margaret. *Who Uses This?* Greenwillow, 1990, 37 pp. N

Miller, Margaret. *Whose Shoe?* Greenwillow, 1991, 36 pp. N

Morris, Ann. *Tools*. Lothrop, Lee & Shepard, 1992, 32 pp. N

Morris, Ann. *I Am Six*. Silver Press, 1995, 28 pp.

Namm, Diane. *Little Bear*. Children's Press, 1990, 24 pp.

Peek, Merle. *Roll Over! A Counting Song*. Clarion, 1980, 24 pp.

Perkins, Al. *The Ear Book*. Random House, 1968, 28 pp.

Petrie, Catherine. *Joshua James Likes Trucks*. Children's Press, 1982, 32 pp.

Pienkowski, Jan. *Weather*. Simon & Schuster, 1975, 22 pp. N

Pomerantz, Charlotte. *Where's the Bear?* Greenwillow, 1984, 32 pp.

Raffi. *Wheels on the Bus*. Crown, 1988, 28 pp.

Raffi. *Five Little Ducks*. Crown, 1989, 30 pp.

Raschka, Chris. *Yo! Yes!* Orchard, 1993, 24 pp.

Rees, Mary. *Ten in a Bed*. Little, Brown, 1988, 24 pp.

Ruane, Joanna. *Boats, Boats, Boats*. Children's Press, 1990, 28 pp. **N**

Shaw, Charles G. *It Looked Like Spilt Milk*. HarperCollins, 1947, 30 pp.

Snow, Pegree. *A Pet for Pat*. Children's Press, 1984, 32 pp.

Steptoe, John. *Baby Says*. Lothrop, Lee & Shepard, 1988, 24 pp.

Stobbs, William. *Gregory's Dog*. Oxford, 1987, 16 pp.

Tafuri, Nancy. *Early Morning in the Barn*. Greenwillow, 1983, 21 pp.

Tafuri, Nancy. *Rabbit's Morning*. Greenwillow, 1985, 24 pp.

Tafuri, Nancy. *Spots, Feathers, and Curly Tails*. Greenwillow, 1988, 28 pp.

Tafuri, Nancy. *The Ball Bounced*. Greenwillow, 1989, 22 pp.

Tafuri, Nancy. *This Is the Farmer*. Greenwillow, 1994, 24 pp.

Williams, Sue. *I Went Walking*. Harcourt, 1989, 30 pp.

Winter, Susan. *I Can*. Kindersley, 1993, 32 pp.

Wong, Olive. *From My Window*. Silver Burdett Press, 1995, 32 pp.

Wood, Leslie. *The Frog and the Fly*. Oxford University Press, 1997, 16 pp.

Ziefert, Harriet. *The Turnip*. Penguin, 1996, 30 pp.

Reading Level: Preprimer 2

Asch, Frank. *Just Like Daddy*. Simon & Schuster, 1981, 30 pp.

Auster, Benjamin. *I Like It When*. Raintree, 1990, 24 pp.

Barton, Byron. *Bones, Bones, Dinosaur Bones*. Crowell, 1990, 30 pp. **N**

Barton, Byron. *My Car*. Greenwillow, 2001, 32 pp. **N**

Bennett, David. *One Cow Moo Moo!* Holt, 1990, 28 pp.

Brown, Margaret. *Where Have You Been?* Scholastic, 1952, 32 pp.

Brown, Margaret Wise. *Four Fur Feet*. Hyperion, 1961, 1994, 21 pp.

Brown, Ruth. *A Dark, Dark Tale*. Dial Press, 1981, 28 pp.

Bullock, Kathleen. *She'll Be Comin' Round the Mountain*. Simon & Schuster, 1993, 32 pp.

Carle, Eric. *Papa, Please Get the Moon for Me*. Picture Book Studio, 1986, 26 pp.

Cebulash, Mel. *Willie's Wonderful Pet*. Scholastic, 1972, 28 pp.

Cohen, Caron Lee. *Where's the Fly?* Greenwillow, 1996, 28 pp.

Coxe, Molly. *Cat Traps*. Random House, 1996, 32 pp.

Coxe, Molly. *Big Egg*. Random House, 1997, 32 pp.

Crews, Donald. *Flying*. Greenwillow, 1986, 32 pp.

Dabcovich, Lydia. *Sleepy Bear*. Dutton, 1982, 22 pp.

dePaola, Tomie. *Andy, That's My Name*. Simon & Schuster, 1973, 30 pp.

dePaola, Tomie. *The Wind and the Sun*. Silver Press, 1995, 28 pp.

Dodds, Ann Dayle. *Wheel Away*. HarperCollins, 1989, 28 pp.

Ford, Miela. *Little Elephant*. Greenwillow, 1994, 20 pp. **N**

Ford, Miela. *Bear Play*. Greenwillow, 1995, 20 pp.

Geisel, Theodor (Dr. Seuss). *The Foot Book*. Random House, 1968, 28 pp.

Ginsburg, Mirra. *Across the Stream*. Greenwillow, 1982, 21 pp.

Ginsburg, Mirra. *Asleep, Asleep*. Greenwillow, 1992, 22 pp.

Gomi, Taro. *Coco Can't Wait*. Morrow, 1984, 30 pp.

Gregorich, Barbara. *Nine Men Chase a Hen*. School Zone, 1984, 16 pp.

Hamm, Diane Johnston. *How Many Feet in the Bed?* Simon & Schuster, 1991, 27 pp.

Hamsa, Bobbie. *Animal Babies*. Children's Press, 1985, 30 pp. **N**

Herman, Gail. *My Dog Talks*. Scholastic, 1995, 29 pp.

Herman, Gail. *Teddy Bear for Sale*. Scholastic, 1995, 29 pp.

Hill, Eric. *Where's Spot?* Putnam, 1980, 22 pp.

Hill, Eric. *Spot's First Walk*. Putnam, 1981, 22 pp.

Hindley, Judy. *The Big Red Bus*. Candlewick Press, 1995, 24 pp.

Hutchins, Pat. *Little Pink Pig*. Greenwillow, 1994, 28 pp.

Jonas, Ann. *Splash*. Greenwillow, 1995, 22 pp.

Jones, Carol. *This Old Man*. Houghton Mifflin, 1990, 48 pp.

Kalan, Robert. *Jump, Frog, Jump*. Greenwillow, 1981, 1995, 30 pp.

Krauss, Ruth. *The Carrot Seed*. HarperCollins, 1945, 24 pp.

Langstaff, John. *Oh, A-Hunting We Will Go*. Atheneum, 1974, 26 pp.

Lewison, Wendy Cheyette. *"Buzz" Said the Bee*. Scholastic, 1992, 30 pp.

Maccarone, Grace. *Cars, Cars, Cars*. Scholastic, 1995, 24 pp.

Maris, Ron. *Are You There, Bear?* Greenwillow, 1984, 32 pp.

Martin, Bill, Jr., & Archambault, John. *Here Are My Hands*. Holt, 1987, 24 pp.

Matthias, Catherine. *I Love Cats*. Children's Press, 1983, 32 pp.

Milgrim, David. *Why Benny Barks*. Random House, 1994, 30 pp.

Milios, Rita. *Bears, Bears, Everywhere*. Children's Press, 1988, 32 pp.

Mora, Pat. *Listen to the Desert*. Clarion, 1994, 22 pp.

Morris, Ann. *Shoes Shoes Shoes*. Lothrop, Lee & Shepard, 1995, 29 pp. **N**

Morris, Ann. *Work*. Lothrop, Lee & Shepard, 1998, 29 pp. **N**

Moss, Sally. *Peter's Painting*. Mondo, 1995, 24 pp.

Nodset, Joan L. *Who Took the Farmer's Hat?* HarperCollins, 1963, 28 pp.

Paxton, Tom. *Going to the Zoo*. Morrow, 1996, 29 pp.

Phillips, Mildred. *And the Cow Said "Moo."* Greenwillow, 2000, 32 pp.

Raffi. *Down by the Bay*. Crown, 1987, 32 pp.

Raffi. *Shake My Sillies Out*. Crown, 1987, 32 pp.

Rockwell, Anne. *Sweet Potato Pie*. Random House, 1996, 32 pp.

Serfozo, Mary. *Who Said Red?* Simon & Schuster, 1988, 28 pp.

Snow, Pegeen. *Eat Your Peas, Louise*. Children's Press, 1993, 30 pp.

Tolstoy, Alexei. *The Great Big Enormous Turnip*. Franklin Watts, 1968, 28 pp.

Walsh, Ellen Stoll. *Hop Jump*. Harcourt, 1993, 26 pp.

Walsh, Ellen Stoll. *Pip's Magic*. Harcourt, 1994, 29 pp.

West, Colin. *"I Don't Care!" Said the Bear*. Candlewick, 1996, 27 pp.

Yolen, Jane. *Hoptoad*. Harcourt, 2003, 30 pp.

Yoshi. *The Butterfly Hunt*. Picturebook Studio, 1990, 24 pp.

Reading Level: Preprimer 3

Alborough, Jez. *Duck in the Truck*. HarperCollins, 2000, 30 pp.

Anholt, Catherine. *Good Days, Bad Days*. Putnam, 1991, 24 pp.

Asch, Frank. *Water*. Harcourt, 1995, 25 pp.

Baker, Alan. *White Rabbit's Color Book*. Kingfisher Books, 1994, 22 pp.

Browne, Anthony. *I Like Books*. Knopf, 1989, 18 pp.

Browne, Anthony. *Things I Like*. Knopf, 1989, 18 pp.

Bullock, Kathleen. *She'll Be Comin' Round the Mountain*. Simon & Schuster, 1993, 32 pp.

Cobb, Annie. *Wheels*. Random House, 1996, 32 pp. **N**

Crews, Donald. *Freight Train*. Greenwillow, 1978, 22 pp. **N**

Donnelly, Liza. *Dinosaur Days*. Scholastic, 1987, 30 pp. **N**

Emberley, Ed. *Go Away, Big Green Monster*. Little, Brown, 1992, 30 pp.

Fleming, Denise. *Count*. Holt, 1992, 30 pp.

Florian, Douglas. *A Beach Day*. Greenwillow, 1990, 32 pp.

Geisel, Theodor (Dr. Seuss). *The Foot Book*. Random House, 1968, 28 pp.

Gomi, Taro. *Who Ate It?* Millbrook Press, 1991, 22 pp.

Gordon, Sharon. *What a Dog*. Troll, 1980, 32 pp.

Hamm, Diane Johnston. *Rockabye Farm*. Simon & Schuster, 1992, 24 pp.

Heling, Kathryn, & Hembrook, Deborah. *Mouse's Hide-and-Seek Words*. Random, 2003, 32 pp.

Hobsson, Sally. *Chicken Little*. Simon & Schuster, 2000, 26 pp.

Koch, Michelle. *Hoot Howl Hiss*. Greenwillow, 1991, 22 pp.

Kulman, Andrew. *Red Light Stop, Green Light Go*. Simon & Schuster, 1993, 24 pp.

Maccarone, Grace. *Oink! Moo! How Do You Do?* Scholastic, 1994, 20 pp.

Maris, Ron. *I Wish I Could Fly*. Greenwillow, 1986, 30 pp.

McMillan, Bruce. *Puffins Climb, Penguins Rhyme*. Harcourt, 1995, 30 pp.

Medearis, Angela Shelf. *Here Comes the Snow*. Scholastic, 1996, 29 pp.

Miller, Margaret. *Guess Who?* Greenwillow, 1994, 36 pp.

Miller, Margaret. *My Five Senses*. Simon & Schuster, 1994, 22 pp. **N**

Minarik, Else Holmelund. *It's Spring*. Greenwillow, 1989, 18 pp.

Modesitt, Jeanne. *Mama, If You Had a Wish*. Green Tiger Press, 1993, 26 pp.

Neasi, Barbara J. *Just Like Me*. Children's Press, 1984, 30 pp.

Peek, Merle. *Mary Wore Her Red Dress and Henry Wore His Green Sneakers*. Clarion, 1985, 22 pp.

Pomerantz, Charlotte. *Flap Your Wings and Try*. Greenwillow, 1989, 22 pp.

Raffi. *Everything Grows*. Crown, 1989, 28 pp.

Raffi. *Tingalayo*. Crown, 1989, 30 pp.

Raffi. *Spider on the Floor*. Crown, 1993, 28 pp.

Reiser, Lynn. *Any Kind of Dog*. Greenwillow, 1992, 20 pp.

Rockwell, Anne. *Boats*. Dutton, 1982, 22 pp. **N**

Rockwell, Anne. *Cars*. Dutton, 1984, 22 pp. **N**

Rockwell, Anne. *Sweet Potato Pie*. Random House, 1996, 32 pp.

Rohman, Eric. *My Friend Rabbit*. Roaring Brook Press, 2002, 30 pp.

Rotner, Shelley, & Kreisler, Ken. *Citybook*. Orchard, 1994, 29 pp.

Russo, Marisabina. *Time to Wake Up*. Greenwillow, 1994, 22 pp.

Sheppard, Jeff. *Splash, Splash*. Simon & Schuster, 1994, 40 pp.

Stobbs, William. *There's a Hole in My Bucket*. Oxford, 1982, 24 pp.

Testa, Fulvio. *If You Take a Paintbrush, A Book of Colors*. Dial, 1982, 24 pp.

Truus. *What Kouka Knows*. Lothrop, Lee & Shepard, 1993, 24 pp.

Walsh, Ellen Stoll. *Hop Jump*. Harcourt, 1993, 26 pp.

West, Colin. *"Pardon?" Said the Giraffe*. HarperCollins, 1986, 16 pp.

Wildsmith, Brian, & Wildsmith, Rebecca. *Wake Up, Wake Up*. Harcourt, 1993, 16 pp.

Wiseman, B. *Morris the Moose*. HarperCollins, 1959, 32 pp.

Ziefert, Harriet. *Sleepy Dog*. Random House, 1984, 32 pp.

Ziefert, Harriet. *Say Good Night*. Viking Kestrel, 1987, 30 pp.

Ziefert, Harriett. *Gingerbread Boy*. Viking, 1995, 29 pp.

Ziefert, Harriet. *I Swapped My Dog*. Houghton Mifflin, 1998, 22 pp.

Reading Level: Primer

Alborough, Jez. *Duck in the Truck*. HarperCollins, 2000, 30 pp.

Aldis, Dorothy. *Hiding*. Viking, 1993, 30 pp.

Alexander, Martha. *You're a Genius, Blackboard Bear*. Candlewick Press, 1995, 22 pp.

Aliki. *Hush Little Baby*. Simon & Schuster, 1986, 30 pp.

Aliki. *My Five Senses*. Crowell, 1962, 1989, 32 pp. **N**

Anholt, Catherine, & Anholt, Laurence. *All About You*. Viking, 1991, 26 pp.

Arnold, Kataya. *Knock, Knock, Teremok*. North-South, 1994, 24 pp.

Arnosky, Jim. *Deer at the Brook*. Lothrop, Lee & Shepard, 1986, 30 pp. **N**

Asch, Frank. *The Last Puppy*. Simon & Schuster, 1980, 24 pp.

Asch, Frank. *Moongame*. Simon & Schuster, 1984, 28 pp.

Averill, Esther. *Fire Cat*. HarperCollins, 1960, 64 pp.

Baker, Keith. *Who Is the Beast?* Harcourt, 1990, 32 pp.

Barton, Byron. *The Little Red Hen*. HarperCollins, 1993, 28 pp.

Berends, Polly Berrien. *"I Heard," Said the Bird*. Dial, 1995, 29 pp.

Bogacki, Tomek. *The Story of a Blue Bird*. Farrar, Straus & Giroux, 1998, 24 pp.

Bonsall, Crosby. *And I Mean It, Stanley*. HarperCollins, 1974, 32 pp.

Bornstein, Ruth. *Little Gorilla*. Clarion, 1976, 28 pp.

Bornstein, Ruth Lercher. *Rabbit's Good News*. Clarion, 1995, 28 pp.

Brenner, Barbara. *Annie's Pet*. Bantam, 1989, 32 pp.

Brenner, Barbara. *Too Many Mice*. Bantam, 1992, 32 pp.

Brisson, Pat. *Benny's Pennies*. Doubleday, 1993, 28 pp.

Brown, Margaret Wise. *Big Red Barn*. HarperCollins, 1956, 1989, 30 pp.

Burningham, John. *Aldo*. Crown, 1991, 30 pp.

Calmenson, Stephanie. *It Begins with an A*. Hyperion, 1993, 28 pp.

Capucilli, Alyssa. *Biscuit*. HarperCollins, 1997, 26 pp.

Carle, Eric. *Little Cloud*. Philomel, 1996, 24 pp.

Carle, Eric. *Hello, Red Fox*. Simon & Schuster, 1998, 27 pp.

Carlson, Judy. *Here Comes Kate!* Raintree, 1989, 31 pp.

Carter, Penny. *A New House for the Morrisons*. Viking, 1993, 32 pp.

Cousins, Lucy. *Za-Za's Baby Brother*. Candlewick, 1995, 24 pp.

Crebbin, June. *The Train Ride*. Candlewick Press, 1995, 24 pp.

de Brunhoff, Laurent. *Babar's Little Circus Story*. Random House, 1988, 32 pp.

Demi. *Find Demi's Sea Creatures*. Putnam, 1991, 36 pp. **N**

de Regniers, Beatrice Schenk. *How Joe the Bear and Sam the Mouse Got Together*. Lothrop, Lee & Shepard, 1990, 28 pp.

Dorros, Arthur. *Alligator Shoes*. Puffin, 1982, 22 pp.

Driscoll, Laura. *The Bravest Cat! The True Story of Scarlett*. Grosset & Dunlap, 1997, 32 pp. **N**

Dunbar, Joyce. *A Cake for Barney*. Orchard, 1987, 30 pp.

Dunbar, Joyce. *Seven Sillies*. Western, 1993, 30 pp.

Eastman, P. D. *Are You My Mother?* Random House, 1960, 64 pp.

Eastman, P. D. *Go, Dog, Go*. Random House, 1961, 64 pp.

Ehlert, Lois. *Growing Vegetable Soup*. Harcourt, 1987, 30 pp.

Ehlert, Lois. *Planting a Rainbow*. Harcourt, 1988, 28 pp.

Ehlert, Lois. *Color Zoo*. Lippincott, 1989, 28 pp.

Ehlert, Lois. *Feathers for Lunch*. Harcourt, 1990, 26 pp.

Ehlert, Lois. *Fish Eyes, A Book You Can Count On*. Harcourt, 1990, 32 pp.

Elting, Mary, & Folsom, Michael. *Q Is for Duck*. Houghton Mifflin, 1980, 60 pp.

Flack, Marjorie. *Ask Mr. Bear*. Simon & Schuster, 1932, 32 pp.

Fleming, Denise. *In the Tall, Tall Grass*. Holt, 1991, 30 pp.

Fleming, Denise. *Lunch*. Holt, 1992, 28 pp.

Florian, Douglas. *Nature Walk*. Greenwillow, 1989, 28 pp.

Florian, Douglas. *A Carpenter*. Greenwillow, 1991, 22 pp.

Fox, Mem. *Hattie and the Fox*. Bradbury Press, 1987, 30 pp.

Fox, Mem. *Time for Bed*. Harcourt, 1993, 28 pp.

Fox, Mem. *Zoo Looking*. Mondo, 1996, 27 pp.

Galdone, Paul. *Henny Penny*. Clarion, 1968, 30 pp.

Geisel, Theodor (Dr. Seuss). *Green Eggs and Ham*. Random House, 1960, 62 pp.

Geisel, Theodor (Dr. Seuss). *Ten Apples Up on Top*. Random House, 1961, 62 pp.

Geisel, Theodor (Dr. Seuss). *Hop on Pop*. Random House, 1963, 64 pp.

Gelman, Rita Golden. *More Spaghetti, I Say!* Scholastic, 1977, 30 pp.

Ginsburg, Mirra. *Good Morning, Chick*. Greenwillow, 1980, 32 pp.

Greenfield, Eloise. *Honey, I Love*. HarperCollins, 1978, 16 pp.

Gretz, Susanna. *Duck Takes Off*. Four Winds, 1991, 24 pp.

Hale, Sara Joseph. *Mary Had a Little Lamb*. Scholastic, 1990, 26 pp.

Hawkins, Colin, & Hawkins, Jacqui. *I Know an Old Lady Who Swallowed a Fly*. Putnam, 1987, 22 pp.

Hayes, Sarah. *This Is the Bear*. HarperCollins, 1986, 24 pp.

Hayes, Sarah. *Nine Ducks Nine*. Lothrop, Lee & Shepard, 1990, 24 pp.

Hayes, Sarah. *This Is the Bear and the Scary Night*. Walker, 1992, 24 pp.

Hays, Anna Jane. *The Pup Speaks Up*. Random House, 2003, 28 pp.

Herman, Gail. *What a Hungry Puppy!* Grosset & Dunlap, 1993, 32 pp.

Hill, Eric. *Spot Goes to the Circus*. Putnam, 1986, 22 pp.

Hillenbrand, Will. *Fiddle-I-Fee*. Harcourt, 2002, 32 pp.

Hines, Anna Grossnickle. *What Joe Saw*. Greenwillow, 1994, 30 pp.

Hoberman, Mary Ann. *Miss Mary Mack*. Little, Brown, 1998, 32 pp.

Holub, Joan. *Scat, Cats*. Viking, 2001, 30 pp.

Horse, Harry. *A Friend for Little Bear*. Candlewick, 1996, 30 pp.

Hutchins, Pat. *The Doorbell Rang*. Greenwillow, 1986, 24 pp.

Johnson, Crockett. *A Picture for Harold's Room*. HarperCollins, 1960, 64 pp.

Jones, Maurice. *I'm Going on a Dragon Hunt*. Simon & Schuster, 1987, 30 pp.

Joyce, William. *George Shrinks*. HarperCollins, 1985, 28 pp.

Kandoian, Ellen. *Maybe She Forgot*. Dutton, 1990, 28 pp.

Kasza, Keiko. *When the Elephant Walks*. Putnam, 1990, 26 pp.

Kennedy, Jimmy. *Teddy Bears' Picnic*. Holt, 1992, 28 pp.

Klingel, Cynthia, & Noyed, Robert B. *Pigs*. The Child's World, 2001, 24 pp. **N**

Kraus, Robert. *Leo the Late Bloomer*. Simon & Schuster, 1971, 28 pp.

Kraus, Robert. *Come Out and Play, Little Mouse*. Greenwillow, 1987, 28 pp.

Lee, Ho Baek. *While We Were Out*. Kane/Miller, 2003, 30 pp.

Lewison, Wendy Cheyette. *Going to Sleep on the Farm*. Dial, 1992, 22 pp.

Lionni, Leo. *Little Blue and Little Yellow*. Astor-Honor, 1959, 36 pp.

Lopshire, Robert. *Put Me in the Zoo*. Random, 1960, 61 pp.

Maccarone, Grace. *"What Is THAT?" Said the Cat*. Scholastic, 1995, 28 pp.

Manning, Maurie J. *The Aunts Go Marching*. Boyds Mill, 2003, 30 pp.

Martin, Bill, Jr. *Polar Bear, Polar Bear, What Do You Hear?* Holt, 1991, 24 pp.

Mayer, Mercer. *There's a Nightmare in My Closet*. Dial, 1968, 28 pp.

McGuire, Richard. *Night Becomes Day*. Viking, 1994, 32 pp.

McPhail, David. *Lost!* Little, Brown, 1990, 28 pp.

Medearis, Angela Shelf. *Here Comes the Snow*. Scholastic, 1996, 29 pp.

Merriam, Eve. *The Hole Story*. Simon & Schuster, 1995, 32 pp.

Most, Bernard. *Hippopotamus Fun*. Harcourt, 1994, 31 pp.

Noll, Sally. *That Bothered Kate*. Greenwillow, 1991, 30 pp.

Oppenheim, Joanne. *Wake Up, Baby*. Bantam, 1990, 32 pp.

Oppenheim, Joanne. *The Show and Tell Frog*. Bantam, 1992, 32 pp.

Phillips, Joan. *My New Boy*. Random House, 1986, 32 pp.

Philpot, Lorna, & Philpot, Graham. *Amazing Anthony Ant*. Random House, 1993, 22 pp.

Raschka, Chris. *Can't Sleep*. Orchard, 1995, 32 pp.

Rathmann, Peggy. *Ruby the Copycat*. Scholastic, 1991, 27 pp.

Reiser, Lynn. *Bedtime Cat*. Greenwillow, 1991, 20 pp.

Robart, Rose. *The Cake That Mack Ate*. Kids Can Press, 1991, 24 pp.

Rockwell, Anne. *What We Like*. Simon & Schuster, 1992, 24 pp.

Rotner, Shelley. *Pick a Pet*. Orchard Books, 1999, 28 pp.

Schade, Susan. *Toad on the Road*. Random House, 1992, 32 pp.

Schindel, John, & O'Malley, Kevin. *What's for Lunch?* Lothrop, Lee & Shepard, 1994, 21 pp.

Shaw, Nancy. *Sheep in a Jeep*. Houghton Mifflin, 1986, 32 pp.

Stadler, John. *Cat at Bat*. Dutton, 1979, 32 pp.

Stadler, John. *Hooray for Snail!* HarperCollins, 1984, 32 pp.

Stadler, John. *Snail Saves the Day*. Crowell, 1985, 32 pp.

Stadler, John. *Cat at Bat Is Back*. Dutton, 1991, 32 pp.

Stevenson, James. *If I Owned a Candy Factory*. Greenwillow, 1968, 1989, 28 pp.

Stoeke, Janet Morgan. *A Hat for Minerva Louise*. Dutton, 1994, 22 pp.

Sweeney, Jacqueline. *Lou Goes Too!* Marshall Cavendish, 2000, 32 pp.

Taylor, Barbara. *A Day at the Farm*. Dorling Kindersley, 1998, 32 pp. **N**

Tripp, Valerie. *Baby Koala Finds a Home*. Children's Press, 1987, 24 pp.

Waddell, Martin. *When the Teddy Bears Came*. Candlewick, 1994, 24 pp.

Wallace, Karen. *A Trip to the Zoo*. Dorling Kindersley, 2003, 32 pp. **N**

Walsh, Ellen Stoll. *Mouse Paint*. Harcourt, 1989, 30 pp.

Walsh, Ellen Stoll. *Mouse Count*. Harcourt, 1991, 28 pp.

Watson, John. *We're the Noisy Dinosaurs*. Candlewick Press, 1992, 26 pp.

Weiss, Nicki. *Where Does the Brown Bear Go?* Greenwillow, 1989, 22 pp.

Westcott, Nadine Bernard. *I Know an Old Lady Who Swallowed a Fly*. Little, Brown, 1980, 28 pp.

Westcott, Nadine Bernard. *The Lady with the Alligator Purse*. Little, Brown, 1988, 22 pp.

Yolen, Jane. *Mouse's Birthday*. Putnam, 1993, 26 pp.

Young, Ruth. *Who Says Moo?* Viking, 1994, 28 pp.

Ziefert, Harriet. *Jason's Bus Ride*. Puffin, 1987, 32 pp.

Ziefert, Harriet. *Strike Four*. Viking, 1989, 32 pp.

Ziefert, Harriet. *Dark Night, Sleepy Night*. Penguin, 1993, 32 pp.

Ziefert, Harriet. *The Little Red Hen*. Puffin, 1995, 32 pp.

Ziefert, Harriet. *Oh, What a Noisy Farm!* Tambourine, 1995, 27 pp.

Zimmermann, H. Werner. *Henny Penny*. Scholastic, 1989, 28 pp.

Reading Level: First Grade

Alborough, Jez. *Where's My Teddy?* Candlewick Press, 1992, 24 pp.

Aliki. *We Are Best Friends*. Greenwillow, 1982, 28 pp.

Allen, Jonathan. *My Dog*. Gareth Stevens, 1987, 30 pp.

Allen, Pamela. *Who Sank the Boat?* Coward-McCann, 1982, 28 pp.

Arnold, Marsha. *Quick, Quack, Quick!* Random House, 1996, 32 pp.

Arnold, Tedd. *Green Wilma*. Dial, 1993, 30 pp.

Arnosky, Jim. *Come Out, Muskrats*. Lothrop, Lee & Shepard, 1989, 22 pp. **N**

Asch, Frank. *Bear Shadow*. Simon & Schuster, 1985, 28 pp.

Asch, Frank. *Goodbye House*. Simon & Schuster, 1986, 28 pp.

Baker, Barbara. *Digby and Kate and the Beautiful Day*. Dutton, 1998, 48 pp.

Barton, Byron. *Airport*. HarperCollins, 1982, 32 pp.

Beaton, Clare. *How Big Is a Pig?* Barefoot Books, 2000, 24 pp.

Beck, Ian. *Home before Dark*. Scholastic, 1997, 30 pp.

Blocksma, Mary. *Yoo Hoo, Moon*. Bantam, 1992, 32 pp.

Borden, Louise. *Caps, Hats, Socks, and Mittens*. Scholastic, 1992, 24 pp.

Brandenberg, Franz. *Otto Is Different*. Greenwillow, 1985, 21 pp.

Brenner, Barbara. *The Plant That Kept on Growing*. Bantam, 1996, 29 pp.

Breslow, Susan, & Blakemore, Sally. *I Really Want a Dog*. Dutton, 1990, 37 pp.

Bridwell, Norman. *Clifford the Small Red Puppy*. Scholastic, 1972, 28 pp.

Brown, Marc. *Arthur's Reading Race*. Random House, 1995, 24 pp.

Brown, Margaret Wise. *Little Donkey, Close Your Eyes*. HarperCollins, 1957, 1985, 1995, 26 pp.

Burningham, John. *Mr. Gumpy's Outing*. Henry Holt, 1970, 32 pp.

Byars, Betsy. *My Brother Ant*. Viking, 1996, 32 pp.

Capucilli, Alyssa Satin. *Inside a Barn in the Country*. Scholastic, 1995, 27 pp.

Carle, Eric. *The Very Hungry Caterpillar*. Philomel, 1969, 22 pp.

Carle, Eric. *The Very Lonely Firefly*. Philomel, 1995, 26 pp.

Carlstom, Nancy White. *I'm Not Moving, Mama*. Simon & Schuster, 1990, 28 pp.

Cerf, Bennett. *Bennett Cerf's Book of Animal Riddles*. Random House, 1964, 62 pp.

Child, Lydia Maria. *Over the River and Through the Woods, A Song for Thanksgiving.* HarperCollins, 1993, 28 pp.

Cole, Joanna. *It's Too Noisy.* Crowell, 1989, 28 pp.

Cowen-Fletcher, Jane. *Mama Zooms.* Scholastic, 1993, 30 pp.

Crews, Donald. *Night at the Fair.* Greenwillow, 1998, 22 pp.

Dussling, Jennifer. *Stars.* Grosset & Dunlap, 1996, 32 pp. N

Ehlert, Lois. *Snowballs.* Harcourt, 1995, 32 pp.

Fowler, Allan. *Hearing Things.* Children's Press, 1991, 31 pp. N

Frith, Michael. *I'll Teach My Dog 100 Words.* Random, 1973, 26 pp.

Gackenbach, Dick. *Claude Has a Picnic.* Clarion, 1993, 30 pp.

Galdone, Paul. *The Gingerbread Boy.* Clarion, 1975, 40 pp.

Geisel, Theodor (Dr. Seuss). *The Cat in the Hat.* Random House, 1957, 62 pp.

Geisel, Theodor (Dr. Seuss). *The Cat in the Hat Comes Back.* Random House, 1957, 62 pp.

Geisel, Theodor (Dr. Seuss). *One Fish Two Fish Red Fish Blue Fish.* Random House, 1960, 62 pp.

Geisel, Theodor (Dr. Seuss). *Great Day for Up.* Random House, 1974, 64 pp.

Goennel, Heidi. *The Circus.* Tambourine, 1992, 26 pp.

Gretz, Susanna, & Sage, Alison. *Teddy Bears at the Seaside.* Simon & Schuster, 1972, 1989, 30 pp.

Guarino, Deborah. *Is Your Mama a Llama?* Scholastic, 1989, 27 pp.

Harrison, Joanna. *Dear Bear.* Carolrhoda, 1994, 29 pp.

Hazen, Barbara Shook. *Stay, Fang.* Atheneum, 1990, 28 pp.

Heller, Nicholas. *Happy Birthday, Moe Dog.* Greenwillow, 1988, 21 pp.

Hendrick, Mary Jean. *If Anything Ever Goes Wrong with the Zoo.* Harcourt, 1993, 27 pp.

Ho, Mingfong. *Hush! A Thai Lullaby.* Orchard, 1996, 30 pp.

Hoff, Syd. *Danny and the Dinosaur.* HarperCollins, 1958, 64 pp.

Hoff, Syd. *Oliver.* HarperCollins, 1960, 64 pp.

Hoff, Syd. *The Horse in Harry's Room.* HarperCollins, 1970, 32 pp.

Hoff, Syd. *Barkley.* HarperCollins, 1975, 32 pp.

Hoff, Syd. *Albert the Albatross.* HarperCollins, 1988, 32 pp.

Hoff, Syd. *Mrs. Brice's Mice.* HarperCollins, 1988, 32 pp.

Howe, James. *The Day the Teacher Went Bananas.* Dutton, 1984, 28 pp.

Hutchins, Pat. *Don't Forget the Bacon.* Greenwillow, 1976, 28 pp.

Johnson, Angela. *Do Like Kyla.* Orchard Books, 1990, 27 pp.

Johnson, Angela. *Shoes Like Miss Alice's.* Orchard Books, 1995, 26 pp.

Johnson, Suzanne C. *Fribbity Ribbit.* Knopf, 2001, 32 pp.

Keats, Ezra Jack. *Whistle for Willie.* Puffin, 1964, 29 pp.

Kessler, Leonard. *Old Turtle's Riddle and Joke Book.* Greenwillow, 1986, 48 pp.

Kimmel, Eric A. *The Gingerbread Man.* Holiday House, 1993, 28 pp.

Kuskin, Karla. *Which Horse Is William?* Greenwillow, 1959, 1987, 21 pp.

Lenski, Lois. *Sing a Song of People.* Little, Brown, 1965, 1987, 28 pp.

Lobel, Arnold. *Grasshopper on the Road.* HarperCollins, 1978, 62 pp.

Lowry, Lois. *Gooney Bird Greene.* Houghton Mifflin, 2002, 96 pp.

Mayer, Mercer. *There's Something in My Attic.* Dial, 1988, 29 pp.

McGovern, Ann. *Too Much Noise.* Houghton Mifflin, 1967, 40 pp.

Milios, Rita. *The Hungry Billy Goat.* Children's Press, 1989, 30 pp.

Minarik, Else Holmelund. *Little Bear's Visit.* HarperCollins, 1961, 64 pp.

Minarik, Else Holmelund. *A Kiss for Little Bear.* HarperCollins, 1968, 32 pp.

Most, Bernard. *If the Dinosaurs Came Back.* Harcourt, 1978, 25 pp.

Most, Bernard. *Pets in Trumpets and Other Word-Play Riddles.* Harcourt, 1991, 32 pp.

Munsch, Robert N. *The Dark.* Annick Press, 1989, 28 pp.

Nerlove, Miriam. *I Meant to Clean My Room Today.* Macmillan, 1988, 26 pp.

Nims, Bonnie Larkin. *Where Is the Bear?* Whitman, 1988, 20 pp.

Nims, Bonnie Larkin. *Where Is the Bear in the City?* Whitman, 1992, 20 pp.

Noble, Trinka Hakes. *The Day Jimmy's Boa Ate the Wash.* Dial, 1980, 26 pp.

Numeroff, Laura. *Dogs Don't Wear Sneakers.* Simon & Schuster, 1993, 27 pp.

Oppenheim, Joanne. *"Not Now!" Said the Cow.* Bantam, 1989, 32 pp.

Oppenheim, Joanne. *The Donkey's Tale.* Bantam, 1991, 32 pp.

Parish, Peggy. *Dinosaur Time.* HarperCollins, 1974, 32 pp. N

Rockwell, Anne. *Fire Engines.* Dutton, 1986, 22 pp. N

Rylant, Cynthia. *Mr. Putter and Tabby Walk the Dog.* Harcourt, 1994, 38 pp.

Simon, Norma. *Fire Fighters.* Simon & Schuster, 1995, 22 pp.

Siracusa, Catherine. *Bingo, the Best Dog in the World.* HarperCollins, 1991, 64 pp.

Slavin, Bill. *The Cat Came Back.* Whitman, 1992, 26 pp.

Slobodkina, Esphyr. *Caps for Sale.* HarperCollins, 1947, 42 pp.

Snyder, Carol. *One Up, One Down.* Atheneum, 1995, 26 pp.

Stevenson, James. *B, R, R, R, R!* Greenwillow, 1991, 30 pp.

Stevenson, Robert Louis. *The Moon.* HarperCollins, 1984, 27 pp.

Trapani, Iza. *The Itsy Bitsy Spider.* Whispering Coyote Press, 1993, 26 pp.

Weiss, Leatie. *My Teacher Sleeps in School.* Puffin, 1984, 28 pp.

Westcott, Nadine Bernard. *Skip to My Lou.* Little, Brown, 1989, 28 pp.

Westcott, Nadine Bernard. *I've Been Working on the Railroad.* Hyperion, 1996, 27 pp.

Williams, Sherley Anne. *Working Cotton.* Harcourt, 1992, 26 pp.

Wong, Herbert Yee. *Eek! There's a Mouse in the House.* Houghton Mifflin, 1992, 24 pp.

Wood, Audrey. *The Napping House.* Harcourt, 1984, 30 pp.

Ziefert, Harriet. *The Three Little Pigs.* Puffin, 1995, 30 pp.

Ziefert, Harriet. *The Cow in the House.* Viking, 1997, 30 pp.

Ziefert, Harriet. *A Dozen Ducklings Lost and Found.* Houghton Mifflin, 2003, 28 pp.

Reading Level: 2A
Transitional between End of First and Early Second Grade

Abercrombie, Barbara. *Michael and the Cats.* Simon & Schuster, 1993, 18 pp.

Alda, Arlene. *Sheep, Sheep, Sheep, Help Me Fall Asleep.* Doubleday, 1992, 28 pp.

Adler, David A. *Young Cam Jansen and the Double Beach Mystery.* Viking, 2002, 32 pp.

Aliki. *Best Friends Together Again.* Greenwillow, 1995, 28 pp.

Anholt, Laurence. *The New Puppy.* Western, 1994, 30 pp.

Babbitt, Natalie. *Bub or the Very Best Thing.* HarperCollins, 1994, 27 pp.

Baker, Barbara. *Digby and Kate.* Dutton, 1988, 48 pp.

Ballard, Robin. *Cat and Alex and the Magic Flying Carpet.* HarperCollins, 1991, 32 pp.

Bancroft, Henrietta, & Van Gelder, Richard G. *Animals in Winter.* HarperCollins, 1997, 32 pp. N

Barracca, Debra, & Barracca, Sal. *The Adventures of Taxi Dog.* Dial, 1990, 30 pp.

Bauman, A. F. *Guess Where You're Going, Guess What You'll Do.* Houghton Mifflin, 1989, 32 pp.

Bayer, Jane. *A My Name Is Alice.* Dial, 1984, 26 pp.

Benchley, Nathaniel. *Oscar Otter.* HarperCollins, 1966, 64 pp.

Brenner, Barbara, & Hooks, William H. *Ups and Downs of Lion and Lamb.* Bantam, 1991, 48 pp.

Bridwell, Norman. *Clifford's Puppy Days.* Scholastic, 1989, 30 pp.

Brown, Craig. *Tractor.* Greenwillow, 1995, 24 pp.

Brown, Marc. *Spooky Riddles.* Random House, 1983, 38 pp. N

Brown, Ruth. *Ladybug, Ladybug.* Dutton, 1988, 26 pp.

Burton, Virginia. *The Little House.* Houghton Mifflin, 1942, 40 pp.

Byars, Betsy. *Hooray for the Golly Sisters.* HarperCollins, 1990, 64 pp.

Camp, Lindsay. *Keeping up with Cheetah.* Lothrop, Lee & Shepard, 1993, 24 pp.

Carlson, Nancy. *Arnie and the New Kid.* Viking, 1990, 28 pp.

Celsi, Teresa. *The Fourth Little Pig.* Steck Vaughn, 1990, 23 pp.

Clifton, Lucille. *Everett Anderson's Friend.* Holt, 1976, 1992, 20 pp.

Clifton, Lucille. *Three Wishes.* Doubleday, 1992, 28 pp.

Coffelt, Nancy. *Tom's Fish.* Harcourt, 1994, 30 pp.

Cole, Joanna. *Hungry, Hungry Sharks.* Random House, 1986, 48 pp. **N**

Cosgrove, Stephen. *The Fine Family Farm.* Forest House, 1991, 22 pp.

Cowen-Fletcher, Jane. *It Takes a Village.* Scholastic, 1994, 28 pp.

Crews, Donald. *Bigmama's.* Greenwillow, 1991, 30 pp.

Deetlerfs, Renee. *Tabu and the Dancing Elephants.* Dutton, 1995, 27 pp.

Demarest, Chris L. *My Little Red Car.* Boyds Mill, 1992, 28 pp.

Demuth, Patrick. *Johnny Appleseed.* Grosset & Dunlap, 1996, 32 pp. **N**

de Regniers, Beatrice Schenk. *It Does Not Say Meow.* Seabury Press, 1972, 40 pp.

Dinardo, Jeffrey. *The Wolf Who Cried Boy.* Grossett & Dunlap, 1989, 30 pp.

Ehlert, Lois. *Mole's Hill: A Woodland Tale.* Harcourt, 1994, 30 pp.

Everitt, Betsy. *Frida the Wondercat.* Harcourt, 1990, 30 pp.

Faulkner, Matt. *Jack and the Beanstalk.* Scholastic, 1986, 48 pp.

Flack, Marjorie. *The Story about Ping.* Viking, 1933, 1961, 32 pp.

Fowler, Susi Gregg. *Fog.* Greenwillow, 1992, 30 pp.

Gackenbach, Dick. *Dog for a Day.* Houghton Mifflin, 1987, 30 pp.

Gág, Wanda. *Millions of Cats.* Putnam, 1928, 32 pp.

Galdone, Paul. *The Three Billy Goats Gruff.* Clarion, 1973, 30 pp.

Galdone, Paul. *The Three Little Kittens.* Clarion, 1986, 30 pp.

Gantos, Jack. *Rotten Ralph's Show and Tell.* Houghton Mifflin, 1989, 30 pp.

Garten, Jan. *Alphabet Tale.* Greenwillow, 1994, 52 pp.

Gibson, Betty. *The Story of Little Quack.* Little, Brown, 1990, 30 pp.

Ginsburg, Mirra. *Good Morning, Chick.* Greenwillow, 1980, 32 pp.

Goodman, Susan E. *Pilgrims of Plymouth.* National Geographic Society, 2001, 16 pp.

Greenfield, Eloise. *She Come Bringing Me That Little Baby Girl.* HarperCollins, 1974, 1990, 28 pp.

Hall, Katy, & Eisenberg, Lisa. *Buggy Riddles.* Puffin, 1986, 48 pp. **N**

Harwayne, Shelley. *Jewels, Children's Play Rhymes.* Mondo, 1995, 21 pp.

Havill, Juanita. *Jamaica's Find.* Scholastic, 1986, 31 pp.

Havill, Juanita. *Jamaica's Blue Marker.* Houghton Mifflin, 1995, 28 pp.

Hazen, Barbara. *Fang.* Atheneum, 1987, 28 pp.

Hoban, Lillian. *Arthur's Funny Money.* HarperCollins, 1981, 64 pp.

Hoff, Syd. *Sammy the Seal.* HarperCollins, 1959, 64 pp.

Hoff, Syd. *Duncan the Dancing Duck.* Clarion Books, 1994, 32 pp.

Hoff, Syd. *The Lighthouse Children.* HarperCollins, 1994, 32 pp.

Hurwitz, Johanna. *New Shoes for Silvia.* Morrow, 1993, 28 pp.

Ivimey, John W. *Three Blind Mice.* Clarion, 1987, 30 pp.

Johnson, Angela. *The Leaving Morning.* Orchard Books, 1992, 28 pp.

Johnson, Crockett. *Harold and the Purple Crayon.* HarperCollins, 1955, 1993, 61 pp.

Jordan, Helene J. *How a Seed Grows.* HarperCollins, 1960, 1992, 30 pp. **N**

Kasza, Keiko. *The Rat and the Tiger.* Putnam, 1993, 29 pp.

Keats, Ezra Jack. *The Snowy Day.* Viking, 1962, 32 pp.

Keats, Ezra Jack. *Louie.* Greenwillow, 1975, 32 pp.

Kessler, Leonard. *Here Comes the Strikeout.* HarperCollins, 1966, 64 pp.

Kessler, Leonard. *Kick, Pass, and Run.* HarperCollins, 1966, 64 pp.

Kessler, Leonard. *Super Bowl.* Greenwillow, 1980, 56 pp.

Kessler, Leonard. *The Big Mile Race.* Greenwillow, 1983, 47 pp.

Ketteman, Helen. *Not Yet, Yvette.* Whitman, 1992, 22 pp.

Kimmel, Eric A. *Anansi and the Moss-Covered Rock.* Holiday House, 1988, 28 pp.

Kimmel, Eric A. *I Took My Frog to the Library.* Viking, 1990, 24 pp.

Kimmel, Eric A. *The Old Woman and Her Pig.* Holiday, 1992, 30 pp.

Krensky, Stephen. *Lionel at Large.* Dial, 1986, 56 pp.

Lee, Huy Voun. *At the Beach.* Holt, 1994, 26 pp.

Ling, Mary. *See How They Grow, Butterfly.* Dorling Kindersley, 1992, 21 pp. **N**

Lobel, Arnold. *Frog and Toad Together.* HarperCollins, 1971, 64 pp.

Lobel, Arnold. *Owl at Home.* HarperCollins, 1975, 62 pp.

Lobel, Arnold. *Mouse Soup.* HarperCollins, 1977, 62 pp.

Lobel, Arnold. *Days with Frog and Toad.* HarperCollins, 1979, 64 pp.

Marshall, James. *Fox Be Nimble.* Penguin, 1992, 48 pp.

Martin, Bill, Jr., & Archambault, John. *Chicka Chicka Boom Boom.* Simon & Schuster, 1989, 30 pp.

Marx, David F. *Ramadan.* Children's Press, 2002, 32 pp. **N**

Marzollo, Jean. *Pretend You're a Cat.* Dial, 1990, 26 pp.

Marzollo, Jean. *Snow Angel.* Scholastic, 1995, 28 pp.

Mayer, Mercer. *There's an Alligator under My Bed.* Dial, 1987, 30 pp.

McCully, Emily Arnold. *The Grandma Mix-up.* HarperCollins, 1988, 64 pp.

McDermott, Gerald. *Anansi the Spider: A Tale from the Ashanti.* Holt, 1972, 34 pp.

McDermott, Gerald. *Zomo the Rabbit: A Trickster Tale from West Africa.* Harcourt, 1992, 30 pp.

McPhail, David. *The Day the Sheep Showed Up.* Scholastic, 1998, 32 pp.

Miles, Betty. *Tortoise and the Hare.* Simon & Schuster, 1998, 32 pp.

Moore, Inga. *Six-Dinner Sid.* Simon & Schuster, 1991, 28 pp.

Mozelle, Shirley. *Zack's Alligator.* HarperCollins, 1989, 64 pp.

Naylor, Phyllis Reynolds. *Ducks Disappearing.* Atheneum, 1997, 30 pp.

Neitzel, Shirley. *The Bag I'm Taking to Grandma's.* Greenwillow, 1995, 30 pp.

Numeroff, Laura Joffe. *If You Give a Mouse a Cookie.* HarperCollins, 1985, 30 pp.

Numeroff, Laura. *If You Give a Pig a Pancake.* HarperCollins, 1998, 30 pp.

Parish, Peggy. *Amelia Bedelia Helps Out.* Greenwillow, 1979, 64 pp.

Penner, Lucille. *Dinosaur Babies.* Random House, 1991, 32 pp. **N**

Raffi. *Baby Beluga.* Crown, 1990, 30 pp.

Reiser, Lynn. *The Surprise Family.* Greenwillow, 1994, 28 pp.

Rey, H. A. *Curious George.* Houghton Mifflin, 1941, 54 pp.

Rotner, Shelley, & Kreisler, Ken. *Nature Spy.* Simon & Schuster, 1992, 26 pp. **N**

Rounds, Glen. *The Three Billy Goats Gruff.* Holiday House, 1993, 29 pp.

Rylant, Cynthia. *Henry and Mudge, The First Book.* Scholastic, 1987, 40 pp.

Rylant, Cynthia. *Poppleton Everyday.* Scholastic, 1997, 48 pp.

Schwartz, Alvin. *All of Our Noses Are Here and Other Noodle Tales.* HarperCollins, 1985, 64 pp.

Sendak, Maurice. *Where the Wild Things Are.* HarperCollins, 1964, 36 pp.

Serfozo, Mary. *Who Wants One?* Simon & Schuster, 1989, 32 pp.

Sharmat, Marjorie. *Mitchell Is Moving.* Simon & Schuster, 1978, 46 pp.

Simon, Norma. *Cats Do, Dogs Don't.* Whitman, 1986, 29 pp. **N**

Siracusa, Catherine. *No Mail for Mitchell.* Random House, 1990, 32 pp.

Slepian, Jan, & Seidler, Ann. *The Hungry Thing.* Scholastic, 1967, 30 pp.

Slepian, Jan, & Seidler, Ann. *The Hungry Thing Returns.* Scholastic, 1990, 28 pp.

Stadler, John. *The Adventures of Snail at School.* HarperCollins, 1993, 64 pp.

Stevenson, James. *Will You Please Feed Our Cat?* Greenwillow, 1987, 30 pp.

Van Leeuwen, Jean. *Tales of Amanda Pig.* Dial, 1983, 56 pp.

Walsh, Ellen Stoll. *You Silly Goose.* Harcourt, 1992, 30 pp.

Wheeler, Cindy. *Bookstore Cat*. Random House, 1994, 32 pp.

Wilcox, Cathy. *Enzo the Wonderfish*. Ticknor & Fields, 1983, 30 pp.

Wormel, Mary. *Hilda Hen's Search*. Harcourt, 1994, 28 pp.

Wormell, Mary. *Hilda Hen's Happy Birthday*. Harcourt, 1995, 28 pp.

Yoshi. *Who's Hiding Here?* Picture Book Studio, 1987, 32 pp.

Ziefert, Harriet. *Pete's Chicken*. Tambourine, 1994, 32 pp.

Ziefert, Harriet. *The Magic Porridge Pot*. Puffin, 1997, 30 pp.

Ziefert, Harriet. *The Ugly Duckling*. Puffin, 1997, 30 pp.

Zimmerman, Andrea, & Clemesha, David. *The Cow Buzzed*. HarperCollins, 1993, 28 pp.

Zion, Gene. *Harry the Dirty Dog*. HarperCollins, 1956, 28 pp.

Zion, Gene. *No Roses for Harry*. HarperCollins, 1958, 28 pp.

Reading Level: 2B

Alcott, Susan. *Young Amelia Earhart: A Dream to Fly*. Troll, 1992, 32 pp. **N**

Allard, Harry, & Marshall, James. *Miss Nelson Is Missing*. Houghton Mifflin, 1985, 32 pp.

Arnosky, Jim. *Otters under Water*. Putnam, 1992, 24 pp. **N**

Arnosky, Jim. *Every Autumn Comes the Bear*. Putnam, 1993, 28 pp. **N**

Baehr, Patricia. *Mouse in the House*. Holiday, 1994, 29 pp.

Bang, Molly. *The Paper Crane*. Greenwillow, 1985, 29 pp.

Bemelmans, Ludwig. *Madeline*. Penguin, 1939, 44 pp.

Blume, Judy. *Freckle Juice*. Bantam Doubleday Dell, 1971, 47 pp.

Blume, Judy. *The One in the Middle Is the Green Kangaroo*. Bantam Doubleday Dell, 1981, 39 pp.

Boegehold, Betty D. *A Horse Called Starfire*. Bantam, 1991, 32 pp.

Brenner, Barbara. *Wagon Wheels*. HarperCollins, 1978, 64 pp.

Brown, Marc. *Arthur's Pet Business*. Little, Brown, 1990, 30 pp.

Coerr, Eleanor. *The Josephina Story Quilt*. HarperCollins, 1986, 64 pp.

Coerr, Eleanor. *Chang's Paper Pony*. HarperCollins, 1988, 64 pp.

Cole, Joanna, & Calmeson, Stephanie. *Why Did the Chicken Cross the Road? And Other Riddles Old and New*. Morrow, 1994, 64 pp. **N**

Cosby, Bill. *The Best Way to Play*. Scholastic, 1997, 33 pp.

Cosby, Bill. *The Meanest Thing to Say*. Scholastic, 1997, 33 pp.

Cristaldi, Kathryn. *Baseball Ballerina*. Random, 1992, 48 pp.

Demuth, Patricia Brennan. *Achoo!* Grosset & Dunlap, 1997, 30 pp. **N**

de Paola, Tomie. *Charlie Needs a Cloak*. Prentice-Hall, 1973, 27 pp.

Disalvo-Ryan, Dyanne. *City Green*. Morrow, 1994, 30 pp.

Dorros, Arthur. *Abuela*. Dutton, 1991, 36 pp.

Dorros, Arthur. *Radio Man*. HarperCollins, 1993, 32 pp.

Ehlert, Lois. *Red Leaf, Yellow Leaf*. Harcourt, 1992, 31 pp.

Fowler, Allan. *The Biggest Animal Ever*. Children's Press, 1992, 30 pp. **N**

Fowler, Allan. *Frogs and Toads and Tadpoles, Too*. Children's Press, 1992, 32 pp. **N**

Fowler, Allan. *What Magnets Can Do*. Children's Press, 1993, 32 pp. **N**

Fowler, Allan. *The Best Way to See a Shark*. Children's Press, 1995, 31 pp. **N**

Freeman, Don. *Corduroy*. Viking, 1968, 32 pp.

Galdone, Paul. *Little Red Riding Hood*. McGraw-Hill, 1974, 29 pp.

Gibbons, Gail. *Farming*. Holiday House, 1988, 30 pp. **N**

Giff, Patricia Reilly. *Today Was a Terrible Day*. Viking, 1985, 25 pp.

Giff, Patricia Reilly. *Watch Out, Ronald Morgan*. Viking, 1985, 25 pp.

Giff, Patricia Reilly. *The Secret at the Polk Street School*. Dell, 1987, 72 pp.

Hall, Katy, & Eisenberg, Lisa. *Sheepish Riddles*. Dial, 1996, 48 pp. **N**

Heo, Yumi. *Father's Rubber Shoes*. Orchard, 1995, 29 pp.

Hoban, Lillian. *Arthur's Pen Pal*. HarperCollins, 1976, 64 pp.

Hoban, Russell. *Bread and Jam for Frances*. HarperCollins, 1964, 31 pp.

Hoberman, Mary Ann. *One of Each*. Little, Brown, 1997, 30 pp.

Hopkins, Lee Bennett (Ed.). *Surprises*. HarperCollins, 1986, 64 pp.

Howard, Elizabeth Fitzgerald. *Aunt Flossie's Hats (and Crab Cakes Later)*. Houghton Mifflin, 1991, 31 pp.

Jaffe, Nina. *Sing, Little Sack!* Bantam, 1993, 48 pp.

Johnson, Angela. *Julius*. Orchard, 1993, 30 pp.

Johnson, Dolores. *What Kind of Baby-Sitter Is This?* Simon & Schuster, 1991, 32 pp.

Johnson, Doug. *Never Babysit the Hippopotamuses*. Holt, 1993, 28 pp.

Keats, Ezra Jack. *Pet Show!* Simon & Schuster, 1972, 32 pp.

Kramer, Sydelle. *Wagon Train*. Grosset & Dunlap, 1997, 48 pp. **N**

Kuskin, Karla. *Roar and More*. HarperCollins, 1956, 1990, 42 pp.

Kuskin, Karla. *Something Sleeping in the Hall*. HarperCollins, 1985, 64 pp.

Kuskin, Karla. *Soap Soup and Other Verses*. HarperCollins, 1992, 64 pp.

Kuskin, Karla. *City Dog*. Clarion, 1994, 27 pp.

Lionni, Leo. *Swimmy*. Knopf, 1963, 28 pp.

Maestro, Marco, & Maestro, Giulio. *What Do You Hear When Cows Sing? and Other Silly Riddles*. HarperCollins, 1996, 48 pp. **N**

Marshall, James. *George and Martha Rise and Shine*. Houghton Mifflin 1976, 44 pp.

Marzollo, Jean. *Soccer Sam*. Random, 1987, 48 pp.

McDonald, Megan. *Is This a House for Hermit Crab?* Orchard, 1990, 26 pp.

McGovern, Ann. *Stone Soup*. Scholastic, 1968, 32 pp.

Meddaugh, Susan. *Tree of Birds*. Houghton Mifflin, 1990, 30 pp.

Most, Bernard. *A Dinosaur Named after Me*. Harcourt, 1991, 32 pp.

Numeroff, Laura Joffe. *If You Give a Moose a Muffin*. HarperCollins, 1989, 30 pp.

Oechsli, Kelly. *Mice at Bat*. HarperCollins, 1986, 64 pp.

Oppenheim, Joanne. *"Uh-Oh!" Said the Crow*. Bantam, 1993, 32 pp.

Parish, Peggy. *Thank You, Amelia Bedelia*. HarperCollins, 1964, 30 pp.

Penner, Lucille Recht. *The True Story of Pocahontas*. Random House, 1994, 48 pp. **N**

Pilkey, Dav. *When Cats Dream*. Orchard, 1992, 29 pp.

Platt, Kin. *Big Max*. HarperCollins, 1965, 64 pp.

Rabe, Tish. *On Beyond Bugs! All about Insects*. Random House, 1999, 44 pp. **N**

Rotner, Shelley. *Wheels Around*. Houghton Mifflin, 1995, 29 pp. **N**

Rylant, Cynthia. *The Relatives Came*. Bradbury, 1985, 28 pp.

Sendak, Maurice. *Chicken Soup with Rice*. HarperCollins, 1962, 32 pp.

Sharmat, Marjorie W. *Nate the Great Saves the King of Sweden*. Delacorte, 1998, 48 pp.

Soto, Gary. *Too Many Tamales*. Putnam, 1993, 32 pp.

Stevenson, James. *Fun No Fun*. Greenwillow, 1994, 30 pp.

Teague, Mark. *The Field beyond the Outfield*. Scholastic, 1992, 30 pp.

Teague, Mark. *Pigsty*. Scholastic, 1994, 30 pp.

Viorst, Judith. *Alexander and the Terrible, Horrible, No Good, Very Bad Day*. Atheneum, 1972, 28 pp.

Waber, Ira. *Ira Sleeps Over*. Scholastic, 1972, 46 pp.

Waggoner, Karen. *The Lemonade Babysitter*. Little, Brown, 1992, 29 pp.

Wildsmith, Brian. *The Owl and the Woodpecker*. Oxford University Press, 1971, 30 pp.

Williams, Vera B. *A Chair for My Mother*. Greenwillow, 1982, 28 pp.

Wu, Norbert. *Fish Faces*. Holt, 1993, 28 pp. **N**

Yee, Wong Herbert. *Mrs. Brown Went to Town*. Houghton Mifflin, 1996, 28 pp.

Yolen, Jane. *Owl Moon*. Philomel, 1987, 32 pp.

Zoehfeld, Kathleen Weidner. *What Lives in a Shell?* HarperCollins, 1994, 26 pp. **N**

Challenging Reading Level: Grade 3 (Interest Level: Grade 2)

Choi, Sook Nyul. *The Best Older Sister*. Delacorte, 1997, 47 pp.

Kline, Suzy. *Song Lee and the Hamster Hunt*. Viking, 1994, 52 pp.

Kline, Suzy. *Marvin and the Mean Words*. Putnam, 1997, 81 pp.

Milne, A. A. *Winnie-The-Pooh*. Bantam Doubleday Dell, 1926, 161 pp.

Stevenson, James. *Sam the Zamboni Man*. Greenwillow, 1998, 29 pp.

Third-Grade Books

Easy Reading Level: Grade 2 (Interest Level: Grade 3)

Alphin, Elaine Marie. *A Bear for Miguel*. HarperCollins, 1996, 64 pp.

Bolognese, Don. *Little Hawk's New Name*. Scholastic, 1995, 48 pp.

Bulla, Clyde Robert. *The Chalk Box Kid*. Random House, 1987, 57 pp.

Bunting, Eve. *December*. Harcourt, 1997, 28 pp.

Dorros, Arthur. *Ant Cities*. HarperCollins, 1987, 32 pp. **N**

Hopkins, L. B. (Ed.). *Questions, Poems of Wonder*. HarperCollins, 1992, 64 pp. **N**

Lundell, Margo. *A Girl Named Helen Keller*. Scholastic, 1995, 48 pp. **N**

Penner, Lucille Recht. *Sitting Bull*. Grosset & Dunlap, 1995, 48 pp. **N**

Average Reading Level: Grade 3 (Interest Level: Grade 3)

Aardema, Verna. *Anansi Does the Impossible! An Ashanti Tale*. Atheneum, 1997, 28 pp.

Adler, David A. *A Picture Book of Benjamin Franklin*. Holiday House, 1990, 32 pp. **N**

Adler, David A. *A Picture Book of Harriett Tubman*. Holiday House, 1992, 32 pp. **N**

Adler, David A. *A Picture Book of Rosa Parks*. Holiday House, 1993, 32 pp. **N**

Angelou, Maya. *Kofi and His Magic*. Clarkson Potter, 1996, 38 pp. **N**

Arnosky, Jim. *Crinkleroot's Guide to Knowing Butterflies and Moths*. Simon & Schuster, 1996, 32 pp. **N**

Ball, Jacqueline. *Do Fish Drink? First Questions and Answers about Water*. Time Life, 1993, 48 pp. **N**

Barrett, Judi. *Cloudy with a Chance of Meatballs*. Atheneum, 1978, 30 pp.

Bloom, Valerie. *Fruits: A Caribbean Counting Poem*. Holt, 1992, 26 pp.

Bottner, Barbara. *Nana Hannah's Piano*. Putnam, 1996, 32 pp.

Calmenson, Stephanie. *The Frog Principal*. Scholastic, 2001, 28 pp.

Choi, Yangsook. *New Cat*. Farrar, Straus & Giroux, 1999, 28 pp.

Clifford, Eth. *Flatfoot Fox*. Houghton Mifflin, 1995, 47 pp.

Codell, Esmé Raji. *Sahara Special*. Hyperion, 2003, 192 pp.

Cohen, Barbara. *Molly's Pilgrim*. Bantam Doubleday Dell, 1983, 41 pp.

Cole, Joanna. *The Magic School Bus and the Electric Field Trip*. Scholastic, 1997, 48 pp. **N**

Dalgliesh, Alice. *Courage of Sarah Noble*. Scribner's, 1954, 54 pp.

Darling, Kathy. *Rain Forest Babies*. Walker, 1996, 32 pp. **N**

Demuth, Patricia Brennan. *In Trouble with Teacher*. Dutton, 1995, 73 pp.

Duffey, Betsy. *Hey, New Kid*. Viking, 1996, 89 pp.

Florian, Douglas. *Bow Wow Meow Meow, It's Rhyming Cats and Dogs*. Harcourt, 2003, 48 pp.

Garland, Sherry. *My Father's Boat*. Scholastic, 1998, 30 pp.

George, Jean Craighead. *Arctic Son*. Hyperion, 1997, 30 pp.

Gershator, David, & Gershator, Phillis. *Palampam Day*. Marshall Cavendish, 1997, 24 pp.

Gerstein, Mordicai. *Behind the Couch*. Hyperion, 1996, 57 pp.

Gibbons, Gail. *Weather Words and What They Mean*. Holiday House, 1990, 30 pp. **N**

Gibbons, Gail. *Marshes and Swamps*. Holiday House, 1998, 30 pp. **N**

Giff, Patricia Reilly. *A Glass Slipper for Rosie*. Viking, 1997, 73 pp.

Hautzig, Deborah. *Beauty and the Beast*. Random House, 1995, 32 pp.

Hodge, Deborah. *Whales, Killer Whales, Blue Whales and More*. Kids Can Press, 1997, 32 pp. **N**

Johnson, Dolores. *Grandma's Hands*. Marshall Cavendish, 1998, 30 pp.

Kimmel, Eric A. *Easy Work! An Old Tale!* Holiday House, 1998, 30 pp.

Look, Lenore. *Ruby Lu, Brave and True*. Atheneum, 2004, 176 pp.

MacDonald, Margaret Read. *Pickin' Peas*. HarperCollins, 1998, 28 pp.

Markle, Sandra. *Outside and Inside Bats*. Atheneum, 1997, 40 pp. **N**

McCourt, Lisa. *The Goodness Gorillas*. Health Communications, 1997, 29 pp.

Meddaugh, Susan. *Cinderella's Rat*. Houghton Mifflin, 1997, 32 pp.

Medina, Tony. *Deshawn Days*. Lee and Low, 2001, 30 pp.

Miller, Debbie E. *Are Trees Alive?* Walker, 2002, 30 pp. **N**

Mitchell, Rhonda. *The Talking Cloth*. Orchard, 1997, 26 pp.

Naylor, Phyllis Reynolds. *I Can't Take You Anywhere*. Atheneum, 1997, 32 pp.

Polacco, Patricia. *Aunt Chip and the Great Triple Creek Dam Affair*. Philomel, 1996, 36 pp.

Riggio, Anita. *Secret Signs along the Underground Railroad*. Boyds Mill Press, 1997, 28 pp.

Sanders, Scott Russell. *A Place Called Freedom*. Simon & Schuster, 1997, 28 pp.

Silverstein, Shel. *Where the Sidewalk Ends*. HarperCollins, 1974, 166 pp.

Slepian, Jan, & Seidler, Ann. *The Hungry Thing Goes to a Restaurant*. Scholastic, 1992, 30 pp.

Stolz, Mary. *King Emmett the Second*. Greenwillow, 1991, 56 pp.

Teague, Mark. *The Secret Shortcut*. Scholastic, 1996, 24 pp.

Warner, Gertrude C. *The Boxcar Children: Mystery Behind the Wall*. Albert Whitman, 1973, 127 pp.

Yolen, Jane. *Sleeping Ugly*. Coward, McCann & Geoghegan, 1981, 64 pp.

Challenging Reading Level: Grade 4 (Interest Level: Grade 3)

Ada, Alma Flor. *My Name Is Maria Isabel*. Simon & Schuster, 1993, 57 pp.

Adler, David A. *A Picture Book of Thurgood Marshall*. Holiday, 1997, 32 pp. **N**

Bond, Michael. *A Bear Called Paddington*. Houghton Mifflin, 1958, 128 pp.

Brown, Marc. *Arthur Makes the Team*. Little, Brown, 1998, 61 pp.

Cleary, Beverly. *Muggie Maggie*. Avon, 1990, 70 pp.

Gibbons, Gail. *Recycle! A Handbook for Kids*. Little, Brown, 1992, 28 pp. **N**

Gibbons, Gail. *Planet Earth/Inside Out*. Morrow, 1995, 26 pp. **N**

Harrison, Michael, & Stuart-Clark, Christopher. *The New Oxford Treasury of Children's Poems*. Oxford University Press, 1995, 174 pp.

Hickox, Rebecca. *The Golden Sandal: A Middle Eastern Cinderella Story*. Holiday House, 1998, 28 pp.

Lindberg, Becky Thoman. *Thomas Tuttle, Just in Time*. Whitman, 1994, 111 pp.

MacDonald, Betty. *Mrs. Piggle-Wiggle*. HarperCollins, 1947, 119 pp.

Penner, Lucille Recht. *Monster Bugs*. Random House, 1996, 48 pp. **N**

Steig, William. *Sylvester and the Magic Pebble*. Simon & Schuster, 1969, 30 pp.

Zoehfeld, Kathleen Weidner. *Terrible Tyrannosaurus*. HarperCollins, 2001, 30 pp. **N**

Fourth-Grade Books

Easy Reading Level: Grade 2 (Interest Level: Grade 4)

Bulla, Clyde Robert. *Shoeshine Girl*. Crowell, 1975, 84 pp.

Shea, George. *Amazing Rescues*. Random House, 1992, 48 pp. **N**

Easy Reading Level: Grade 3 (Interest Level: Grade 4)

Abbott, Tony. *Danger Guys*. HarperCollins, 1994, 69 pp.

Adler, David A. *Lou Gehrig, The Luckiest Man*. Harcourt Brace, 1997, 30 pp. **N**

Avi. *Man from the Sky*. Knopf, 1980, 117 pp.

Ballard, Robert. *Finding the* Titanic. Scholastic, 1993, 48 pp. **N**

Berends, Polly. *The Case of the Elevator Duck*. Random House, 1973, 60 pp.

Blume, Judy. *Blubber*. Dell, 1974, 153 pp.

Bunting, Eve. *Train to Somewhere*. Houghton Mifflin, 1996, 32 pp.

Clymer, Eleanor. *The Trolley Car Family*. Scholastic, 1947, 216 pp.

Danziger, Paula. *Amber Brown Goes Fourth.* Putnam, 1995, 101 pp.

DiCamillo, Kate. *Because of Winn-Dixie.* Candlewick Press, 2000, 182 pp.

Donnelly, Judy. *The Titanic Lost and Found.* Random House, 1987, 48 pp. **N**

Donnelly, Judy. *Tut's Mummy Lost . . . and Found.* Random House, 1988, 48 pp. **N**

Fritz, Jean. *Just a Few Words, Mr. Lincoln.* Grossett & Dunlap, 1993, 48 pp. **N**

Giff, Patricia Reilly. *Shark in School.* Delacorte, 1994, 103 pp.

Hall, Lynn. *Barry, The Bravest Saint Bernard.* Random House, 1973, 48 pp. **N**

Hirschman, Kris. *Oh Baby! Amazing Baby Animals.* Scholastic, 2002, 30 pp. **N**

Kunhardt, Edith. *Pompeii . . . Buried Alive.* Random House, 1987, 48 pp. **N**

Lears, Laurie. *Ian's Walk, A Story about Autism.* Whitman, 1998, 28 pp.

Louie, Ai-Ling. *Yeh-Shen: A Cinderella Story from China.* Philomel, 1982, 28 pp.

Milton, Joyce. *Mummies.* Grossett & Dunlap, 1996, 48 pp. **N**

Mora, Pat. *Tomás and the Library Lady.* Random House, 1997, 28 pp.

O'Connor, Jim. *Comeback! Four True Stories.* Random House, 1992, 48 pp. **N**

Penner, Lucille Recht. *Twisters.* Random House, 1996, 46 pp. **N**

Pinkwater, Daniel. *Mush: A Dog from Space.* Atheneum, 1995, 40 pp.

Prelutsky, Jack. *The Beauty of the Beast.* Knopf, 1997, 100 pp. **N**

Sachar, Louis. *Wayside School Is Falling Down.* Avon, 1989, 179 pp.

Sachar, Louis. *Wayside School Gets a Little Stranger.* Avon, 1995, 168 pp.

Sobol, Donald J. *Encyclopedia Brown Saves the Day.* Bantam, 1970, 114 pp.

Steptoe, John. *Creativity.* Houghton Mifflin, 1997, 28 pp.

Terhune, Albert Payson. *Lad, a Dog* (retold by Margo Lundell). Scholastic, 1997, 44 pp.

Wells, Robert E. *What's Faster than a Speeding Cheetah?* Whitman, 1997, 29 pp. **N**

Average Reading Level: Grade 4 (Interest Level: Grade 4)

Aardema, Verna. *Why Mosquitoes Buzz in People's Ears.* Dial, 1975, 21 pp.

Ada, Alma Flor. *The Gold Coin.* Atheneum, 1991, 32 pp.

Arnold, Eric. *Volcanoes! Mountains of Fire.* Random House, 1997, 64 pp. **N**

Atwater, Richard, & Atwater, Florence. *Mr. Popper's Penguins.* Little, Brown, 1938, 139 pp.

Banks, Kate. *The Bunnysitters.* Random House, 1991, 63 pp.

Ben-Ezer, Ehud. *Hosni the Dreamer.* Farrar, Straus & Giroux, 1997, 28 pp.

Blume, Judy. *Blubber.* Dell, 1974, 153 pp.

Brown, Jeff. *Flat Stanley.* HarperCollins, 1964, 44 pp.

Butterworth, Oliver. *The Enormous Egg.* Little, Brown, 1956, 169 pp.

Choi, Yangsook. *The Name Jar.* Knopf, 2001, 30 pp.

Christopher, Matt. *The Dog That Pitched a No-Hitter.* Little, Brown, 1988, 32 pp.

Christopher, Matt. *Baseball Turnaround.* Little, Brown, 1997, 122 pp.

Clifford, Eth. *Help! I'm a Prisoner in the Library.* Scholastic, 1979, 96 pp.

Cooper, Floyd. *Coming Home: From the Life of Langston Hughes.* Philomel, 1994, 30 pp. **N**

Costain, Meredith, & Collins, Paul. *Welcome to China.* Chelsea House, 2002, 32 pp. **N**

Curtis, Gavin. *The Bat Boy and His Violin.* Simon & Schuster, 1998, 28 pp.

Dadey, Debbie, & Jones, Marcia Thornton. *Martians Don't Take Temperatures.* Scholastic, 1996, 67 pp.

Dean, Harvey. *Secret Elephant of Harlan Kooter.* Houghton Mifflin, 1992, 130 pp.

Donati, Annabelle. *Animal Record Holders.* Western, 1993, 32 pp. **N**

Earth Works Group. *50 Simple Things Kids Can Do to Save the Earth.* Andrews and McMeel, 1990, 156 pp. **N**

Engel, Trudie. *We'll Never Forget You, Roberto Clemente.* Scholastic, 1996, 106 pp. **N**

Facklam, Margery. *Creepy, Crawly Caterpillars.* Little, Brown, 1996, 32 pp. **N**

Flournoy, Valerie. *The Patchwork Quilt.* Dial, 1985, 29 pp.

Fritz, Jean. *The Cabin Faced West.* Puffin, 1958, 124 pp.

Fritz, Jean. *And Then What Happened, Paul Revere.* Coward, McCann & Geoghegan, 1973, 48 pp. **N**

Gardiner, John Reynolds. *Stone Fox.* HarperCollins, 1980, 71 pp.

Hopkinson, Deborah. *Birdie's Lighthouse.* Atheneum, 1997, 29 pp.

Hughes, Carol. *Toots and the Upside-Down House.* Random House, 1996, 143 pp.

Hurwitz, Johanna. *Aldo Applesauce.* Morrow, 1979, 127 pp.

James, Mary. *Shoebag Returns.* Scholastic, 1996, 144 pp.

Kimmel, Eric A. *Ten Suns, A Chinese Legend.* Holiday House, 1998, 30 pp.

Kramer, S. A. *Basketball's Greatest Players.* Random House, 1997, 48 pp. **N**

Kramer, S. A. *Wonder Women of Sports.* Grossett & Dunlap, 1997, 48 pp. **N**

Krumgold, Joseph. *And Now Miguel.* Crowell, 1953, 245 pp.

Krupinski, Loretta. *The Bluewater Journal, Voyage of the* Sea Tiger. HarperCollins, 1995, 26 pp.

Lauber, Patricia. *You're Aboard Spaceship Earth.* HarperCollins, 1996, 32 pp. **N**

Lindgren, Astrid. *Pippi Longstocking.* Puffin, 1950, 160 pp.

MacLachlan, Patricia. *Sarah, Plain and Tall.* HarperCollins, 1985, 58 pp.

Mead, Alice. *Junebug.* HarperCollins, 1995, 102 pp.

Minahan, John A. *Abigail's Drum.* Pippin, 1995, 64 pp.

O'Connor, Jim. *Jackie Robinson and the Story of All-Black Baseball.* Random House, 1989, 48 pp. **N**

Petty, Kate. *I Didn't Know That the Sun Is a Star and Other Amazing Facts about the Universe.* Copper Beech Books, 1997, 32 pp. **N**

Rylant, Cynthia. *The Van Gogh Cafe.* Harcourt, 1995, 53 pp.

Sachs, Marilyn. *The Bears' House.* Puffin Books, 1971, 67 pp.

Simon, Seymour. *Seymour Simon's Book of Trucks.* HarperCollins, 2000, 32 pp. **N**

Soto, Gary. *The Cat's Meow.* Scholastic, 1987, 78 pp.

Soto, Gary. *Chato and the Party Animals.* Putnam, 2000, 30 pp.

Spyri, Johanna. *Heidi* (retold by Loretta Krupinski). HarperCollins, 1996, 30 pp.

Taylor, Mildred D. *The Gold Cadillac.* Dial, 1987, 43 pp.

White, E. B. *Charlotte's Web.* HarperCollins, 1952, 184 pp.

Wilder, Laura Ingalls. *Little House in the Big Woods.* HarperCollins, 1932, 238 pp.

Woodruff, Elvira. *Awfully Short for the Fourth Grade.* Bantam Doubleday Dell, 1989, 142 pp.

Challenging Reading Level: Grade 5 (Interest Level: Grade 4)

Avi. *The Barn.* Orchard, 1994, 106 pp.

Bateman, Teresa. *The Ring of Truth.* Holiday House, 1997, 28 pp.

Baum, L. Frank. *The Wizard of Oz.* Puffin, 1900, 1988, 188 pp.

Dahl, Roald. *James and the Giant Peach.* Puffin, 1961, 126 pp.

Facklam, Margery. *The Big Bug Book.* Little, Brown, 1994, 32 pp. **N**

Fritz, Jean. *Why Don't You Get a Horse, Sam Adams?* Coward, McCann & Geoghegan, 1974, 48 pp. **N**

Gutman, Bill. *Becoming Your Dog's Best Friend.* Millbrook Press, 1996, 64 pp. **N**

Henry, Marguerite. *Benjamin West and His Cat Grimalkin.* Macmillan, 1947, 147pp.

Kipling, Rudyard. *The Jungle Book.* Weathervane Books, 1893, 1964, 213 pp.

Taylor, Mildred. *Roll of Thunder, Hear My Cry.* Puffin, 1976, 275 pp.

The World Almanac for Kids. World Almanac Books, 2007. **N**

Fifth-Grade Books

Easy Reading Level: Grade 3 (Interest Level: Grade 5)

Adler, David A. *Jeffrey's Ghost and the Fifth-Grade Dragon.* Holt, 1985, 52 pp.

Avi. *Silent Movie.* Atheneum, 2003, 44 pp. **N**

Blatchford, Claire H. *Going with the Flow*. Carolrhoda, 1998, 40 pp.

Bulla, Clyde Robert. *White Bird*. Random House, 1966, 1990, 63 pp.

Cole, Joanna, & Calmeson, Stephanie. *Yours Till Banana Splits*. Morrow, 1995, 64 pp. **N**

Giovanni, Nikki. *Spin a Soft Song (*Rev. ed.). Farrar, Straus & Giroux, 1985, 57 pp. **N**

Haas, Jessie. *Beware the Mare*. Greenwillow, 1993, 66 pp.

Hamilton, Virginia. *The People Could Fly*. Knopf, 1985, 173 pp.

Peck, Robert Newton. *Banjo*. Knopf, 1982, 80 pp.

Slote, Alfred. *Finding Buck McHenry*. HarperCollins, 1991, 250 pp.

Easy Reading Level: Grade 4 (Interest Level: Grade 5)

Bledsoe, Lucy Jane. *Tracks in the Snow*. Holiday House, 1997, 152 pp.

Boyd, Candy Dawson. *Chevrolet Saturdays*. Penguin, 1995, 176 pp.

Bryan, Ashley. *Ashley Bryan's ABC of African American Poetry*. Atheneum, 1997, 26 pp. **N**

Bunting, Eve. *The In-Between Days*. HarperCollins, 1994, 119 pp.

Byars, Betsy. *Cracker Jackson*. Puffin, 1985, 146 pp.

Cohen, Barbara. *Thank You, Jackie Robinson*. Lothrop, Lee & Shepard, 1974, 125 pp.

Coville, Bruce. *I Left My Sneakers in Dimension X*. Pocket Books, 1994, 180 pp.

DeClements, Barthe. *Nothing Is Fair in Fifth Grade*. Penguin, 1990, 137 pp.

Etra, Jonathan, & Spinner, Stephanie. *Aliens for Lunch*. Random House, 1991, 64 pp.

Gutman, Dan. *Honus & Me*. Avon, 1997, 138 pp.

Haas, Jessie. *Be Well, Beware*. Greenwillow, 1996, 66 pp.

Hamm, Diane Johnston. *Daughter of Suqua*. Whitman, 1997, 154 pp.

Hest, Amy. *Private Notebook of Katie Roberts, Age 11*. Candlewick Press, 1995, 75 pp.

Howe, James. *Bunnicula*. Avon, 1979, 98 pp.

Hurwitz, Johanna. *The Up and Down Spring*. Morrow, 1993, 103 pp.

Marschall, Ken. *Inside the* Titanic. Little, Brown, 1997, 31 pp. **N**

McSwigan, Marie. *Snow Treasure*. Scholastic, 1942, 156 pp.

Myers, Walter Dean. *Mop, Moondance, and the Nagasaki Knights*. Bantam Doubleday Dell, 1992, 150 pp.

Naylor, Phyllis Reynolds. *Shiloh*. Dell, 1991, 144 pp.

O'Dell, Scott. *Island of the Blue Dolphins*. Houghton Mifflin, 1960, 192 pp.

Oliver, Diana. *McCracken's Class, Tough Luck, Ronnie*. Random House, 1994, 124 pp.

Paulsen, Gary. *Mr. Tucket*. Delacorte, 1994, 166 pp.

Paulsen, Gary. *My Life in Dog Years*. Delacorte Press, 1998, 137 pp. **N**

Prelutsky, Jack. *A Pizza the Size of the Sun: Poems by Jack Prelutsky*. Greenwillow, 1996, 159 pp. **N**

Roop, Peter, & Roop, Connie. *Ahyoka and the Talking Leaves*. Lothrop, Lee & Shepard, 1992, 60 pp.

Sachar, Louis. *There's a Boy in the Girls' Bathroom*. Random House, 1987, 195 pp.

Simon, Seymour. *Animals Nobody Loves*. North South Books, 2001, 48 pp. **N**

Spinelli, Jerry. *Wringer*. HarperCollins, 1997, 229 pp.

Strasser, Todd. *Kidnap Kids*. Putnam, 1998, 166 pp.

Tamar, Erika. *The Junkyard Dog*. Knopf, 1995, 185 pp.

Average Reading Level: Grade 5 (Interest Level: Grade 5)

Anderson, William. *Laura Ingalls Wilder: A Biography*. HarperCollins, 1992, 240 pp. **N**

Armstrong, Jennifer. *Black-Eyed Susan*. Crown, 1995, 120 pp.

Arnosky, Jim. *Watching Water Birds*. National Geographic, 1997, 28 pp. **N**

Avi. *Poppy*. Camelot, 1995, 160 pp.

Banks, Lynne Reid. *The Indian in the Cupboard*. Doubleday, 1980, 181 pp.

Barrie, J. M. *Peter Pan*. Bantam, 1911, 168 pp.

Betancourt, Jeanne. *My Name is Brain Brian*. Scholastic, 1993, 128 pp.

Birdseye, Tom. *Just Call Me Stupid*. Holiday House, 1993, 181 pp.

Brink, Carol Ryrie. *Caddie Woodlawn*. Macmillan, 1933, 275 pp.

Bryan, Jenny. *Your Amazing Brain*. Joshua Morris Publishing, 1995, 17 pp. **N**

Byars, Betsy. *The TV Kid*. Puffin Books, 1976, 123 pp.

Byars, Betsy. *The Pinballs*. HarperCollins, 1977, 136 pp.

Choldenko, Gennifer. *Al Capone Does My Shirts*. Putnam, 2004, 225 pp.

Christopher, Matt. *Baseball Jokes and Riddles*. Little, Brown, 1996, 45 pp. **N**

Cleary, Beverly. *The Mouse and the Motorcycle*. Morrow, 1965, 160 pp.

Cleary, Beverly. *Dear Mr. Henshaw*. Morrow, 1983, 133 pp.

Conrad, Pam. *Pedro's Journal: A Voyage with Christopher Columbus, August 3, 1492–February 14, 1493*. Boyd's Mill, 1991, 81 pp.

Coville, Bruce. *Jennifer Murdley's Toad*. Harcourt Brace, 1992, 148 pp.

Dahl, Roald. *Charlie and the Chocolate Factory*. Penguin, 1964, 162 pp.

Fitzgerald, John D. *The Great Brain*. Bantam Doubleday Dell, 1967, 174 pp.

Fleschman, Sid. *The Whipping Boy*. Greenwillow, 1986, 89 pp.

Giff, Patricia Reilly. *Lily's Crossing*. Delacorte, 1997, 180 pp.

Horvath, Polly. *When the Circus Came to Town*. Farrar, Straus & Giroux, 1996, 138 pp.

King-Smith, Dick. *Babe the Gallant Pig*. Random House, 1983, 118 pp.

Knight, Eric. *Lassie Come Home*. Dell, 1940, 230 pp.

Konigsburg, E. L. *From the Mixed-Up Files of Mrs. Basil E. Frankweiler*. Atheneum, 1967, 162 pp.

Lester, Julius, & Pinkney, Jerry. *Black Cowboy, Wild Horses*. Dial, 1998, 38 pp.

Lisle, Janet Taylor. *The Gold Dust Letters*. Avon, 1994, 116 pp.

Lofting, Hugh. *Voyages of Doctor Dolittle*. Bantam Doubleday Dell, 1922, 311 pp.

Lord, Betty Bao. *In the Year of the Boar and Jackie Robinson*. HarperCollins, 1984, 169 pp.

Lowry, Lois. *Number the Stars*. Houghton Mifflin, 1989, 137 pp.

Markle, Sandra. *Outside and Inside Sharks*. Atheneum, 1996, 40 pp. **N**

McKissack, Patricia C. *Run Away Home*. Scholastic, 1997, 160 pp.

Myers, Jack. *Highlights Book of Science Questions That Children Ask*. Boyds Mill, 1995, 251 pp. **N**

Norton, Mary. *The Borrowers*. Harcourt Brace, 1953, 180 pp.

Polacco, Patricia. *Thank You, Mr. Falker*. Philomel, 1998, 36 pp. **N**

Rawls, Wilson. *Where the Red Fern Grows*. Doubleday, 1961, 212 pp.

Rosen, Michael. *Walking the Bridge of Your Nose: Wordplay Poems and Rhymes*. Kingfisher, 1995, 61 pp. **N**

Ryan, Pam Muñoz. *Becoming Naomi León*. Scholastic, 2004, 246 pp.

Sewell, Anna. *Black Beauty*. Scholastic, 1877, 245 pp.

Spyri, Johanna. *Heidi*. Scholastic, 1959, 234 pp.

Stengel, Joyce A. *Letting Go*. Poolbeg, 1997, 110 pp.

Stolz, Mary. *Stealing Home*. HarperCollins, 1992, 153 pp.

Travers, P. L. *Mary Poppins*. Harcourt, 1934, 206 pp.

Winthrop, Elizabeth. *Counting on Grace*. Random House, 2006, 240 pp.

Woodruff, Elvira. *The Summer I Shrank My Grandmother*. Bantam Doubleday Dell, 1990, 153 pp.

Challenging Reading Level: Grade 6 (Interest Level: Grade 5)

Christian, Mary Blount. *Sebastian (Super Sleuth) and the Copycat Crime*. Macmillan, 1993, 62 pp.

Darling, Kathy. *Komodo Dragon on Location*. Lothrop, Lee & Shepard, 1997, 40 pp. **N**

Erickson, Paul. *Daily Life in the Pilgrim Colony*. Clarion, 2001, 48 pp. **N**

Hall, Elizabeth. *Child of the Wolves*. Houghton Mifflin, 1996, 160 pp.

Lewis, C. S. *The Lion, the Witch, and the Wardrobe*. HarperCollins, 1950, 189 pp.

Spinelli, Jerry. *Knots in My Yo-yo String*. Knopf, 1998, 148 pp. **N**

Wallace, Barbara Brooks. *The Twin in the Tavern*. Aladdin, 1993, 177 pp.

Challenging Reading Level: Grade 7 (Interest Level: Grade 5)

Aiken, Joan. *The Wolves of Willoughby Chase.* Dell, 1962, 168 pp.

Burnett, Frances Hodgson. *The Secret Garden.* HarperCollins, 1912, 224 pp.

Collier, Christopher, & Collier, James Lincoln. *The American Revolution.* Marshall Cavendish, 1998, 95 pp. **N**

Kipling, Rudyard. *Just So Stories.* New American Library, 1912, 158 pp.

Sixth-Grade Books

Easy Reading Level: Grade 4 (Interest Level: Grade 6)

Bunting, Eve. *The Waiting Game.* Lippincott, 1981, 56 pp.

Byars, Betsy. *Summer of the Swans.* Viking, 1970, 142 pp.

Coerr, Eleanor. *Sadako and the Thousand Paper Cranes.* Bantam Doubleday Dell, 1977, 64 pp.

Coville, Bruce. *Aliens Ate My Homework.* Simon & Schuster, Avon, 1993, 179 pp.

Fitzhugh, Louise. *Harriet the Spy.* HarperCollins, 1964, 298 pp.

Gantos, Jack. *Heads or Tails: Stories from the Sixth Grade.* Farrar, Straus & Giroux, 1994, 151 pp.

MacLachlan, Patricia. *Journey.* Delacorte, 1991, 83 pp.

Mills, Claudia. *Losers, Inc.* HarperCollins, 1997, 150 pp.

Nobisso, Josephine. *In English, of Course.* Gingerbread House, 2002, 32 pp.

Paulsen, Gary. *Hatchet.* Simon & Schuster, 1987, 195 pp.

Spinelli, Jerry. *Crash.* Knopf, 1996, 162 pp.

Stolz, Mary. *Explorer of Barkham Street.* HarperCollins, 1985, 179 pp.

Strasser, Todd. *Help! I'm Trapped in the First Day of School.* Scholastic, 1994, 114 pp.

Easy Reading Level: Grade 5 (Interest Level: Grade 6)

Armstrong, William H. *Sounder.* HarperCollins, 1969, 116 pp.

Balgassi, Haemi. *Tae's Sonata.* Clarion, 1997, 123 pp.

Dygard, Thomas J. *Infield Hit.* Morrow, 1995, 149 pp.

Fleischman, Sid. *The Thirteenth Floor: A Ghost Story.* Greenwillow, 1995, 131 pp.

Fletcher, Ralph. *Spider Boy.* Houghton Mifflin, 1997, 180 pp.

George, Jean C. *My Side of the Mountain.* Dutton, 1959, 177 pp.

Gipson, Fred. *Old Yeller.* HarperCollins, 1956, 158 pp.

Haddix, Margaret Peterson. *Running Out of Time.* Simon & Schuster, 1995, 184 pp.

Harrison, Michael. *It's My Life.* Holiday House, 1997, 132 pp.

Hesse, Karen. *Out of the Dust.* Scholastic, 1997, 227 pp.

Hurwitz, Johanna. *The Down and Up Fall.* Morrow, 1996, 165 pp.

Kehret, Peg. *Small Steps: The Year I Got Polio.* Whitman, 1996, 179 pp. **N**

Lowry, Lois. *Anastasia, Absolutely.* Houghton Mifflin, 1995, 119 pp.

Merrill, Jean. *The Pushcart War.* Bantam Doubleday Dell, 1964, 223 pp.

Paulsen, Gary. *Woodsong.* Puffin, 1991, 132 pp. **N**

Slepian, Jan. *Back to Before.* Philomel, 1993, 170 pp.

Spinelli, Jerry. *Maniac Magee.* HarperCollins, 1990, 184 pp.

Taylor, Theodore. *The Cay.* Avon, 1969, 144 pp.

Average Reading Level: Grade 6 (Interest Level: Grade 6)

Alcott, Louisa May. *Little Women.* Viking, 1868, 1997, 285 pp.

Armstrong, Alan. *Whittington.* Random House, 2005, 191 pp.

Carroll, Lewis. *Alice's Adventures in Wonderland.* Holt, Rinehart & Winston, 1865, 122 pp.

Coville, Bruce. *Jeremy Thatcher, Dragon Hatcher.* Pocket Books, 1991, 148 pp.

Duffey, Betsy. *Fur-ever Yours, Booker Jones.* Viking, 2001, 100 pp.

Forbes, Esther. *Johnny Tremain.* Houghton Mifflin, 1943, 256 pp.

Fox, Paula. *One-Eyed Cat.* Bantam Doubleday Dell, 1984, 216 pp.

Freedman, Russell. *Out of Darkness.* Houghton Mifflin, 1997, 81 pp. **N**

Fritz, Jean. *Bully for You, Teddy Roosevelt.* Scholastic, 1991, 127 pp. **N**

George, Jean Craighead. *Julie of the Wolves.* HarperCollins, 1972, 170 pp.

Juster, Norton. *The Phantom Tollbooth.* Knopf, 1961, 256 pp.

L'Engle, Madeline. *A Wrinkle in Time.* Bantam Doubleday Dell, 1962, 190 pp.

Levine, Gail Carson. *Ella Enchanted.* HarperCollins, 1997, 232 pp.

O'Brien, Robert C. *Mrs. Frisby and the Rats of NIMH.* Aladdin, 1971, 233 pp.

Paterson, Katherine. *The Great Gilly Hopkins.* HarperCollins, 1978, 148 pp.

Paterson, Katherine. *Jacob Have I Loved.* HarperCollins, 1980, 244 pp.

Sachar, Louis. *Holes.* Farrar, Straus & Giroux, 1998, 233 pp.

St. George, Judith. *Sacagawea.* Putnam, 1997, 115 pp. **N**

Snyder, Zilpha Keatley. *Gib Rides Home.* Delacorte Press, 1998, 246 pp.

Stein, R. Conrad. *The Underground Railroad.* Children's Press, 1997, 32 pp. **N**

Challenging Reading Level: Grade 7 (Interest Level: Grade 6)

Blos, Joan W. *A Gathering of Days.* Aladdin, 1979, 144 pp.

Bonar, Samantha. *Comets.* Franklin Watts, 1998, 64 pp. **N**

Brook, Donna. *The Journey of English.* Clarion, 1998, 47 pp. **N**

Bumford, Sheila. *The Incredible Journey.* Bantam, 1961, 145 pp.

Cooper, Susan. *The Boggart.* Simon & Schuster, 1995, 196 pp.

Freedman, Russell. *Lincoln, A Photobiography.* Clarion, 1987, 150 pp. **N**

King, Martin Luther, Jr. *I Have a Dream.* Scholastic, 1997, 40 pp. **N**

Konigsburg, E. L. *The View from Saturday.* Atheneum, 1996, 163 pp.

Lowry, Lois. *The Giver.* Bantam Doubleday Dell, 1993, 180 pp.

Meigs, Cornelia. *Invincible Louisa.* Little, Brown, 1933, 195 pp. **N**

Sperry, Armstrong. *Call It Courage.* Macmillan, 1940, 95 pp.

Wiggin, Kate Douglas. *Rebecca of Sunnybrook Farm.* Bantam Doubleday Dell, 1903, 252 pp.

Seventh- & Eighth-Grade Books

Easy Reading Level: Grade 5 (Interest Level: Grades 7–8)

Ayers, Katherine. *North by Night: A Story of the Underground Railroad.* Delacorte, 1998, 176 pp. **N**

Byars, Betsy. *Disappearing Acts.* Viking, 1998, 120 pp.

Curtis, Christopher Paul. *Bud, Not Buddy.* Delacorte, 1999, 256 pp.

Duffey, Betsy. *Utterly Yours, Booker Jones.* Viking, 1995, 116 pp.

Easy Reading Level: Grade 6 (Interest Level: Grades 7–8)

Atkin, S. Beth. *Voices from the Fields: Children of Migrant Farm Workers Tell Their Stories.* Little, Brown, 1993, 96 pp. **N**

Collier, James L. *My Brother Sam Is Dead.* Scholastic, 1974, 216 pp.

Fleischman, Paul. *A Joyful Noise: Poems for Two Voices.* HarperCollins, 1993, 102 pp.

Fleischman, Paul. *Bull Run.* HarperCollins, 1995, 104 pp.

Peck, Richard. *A Year Down Yonder.* Dial Books, 2000, 230 pp.

Roop, Connie. *Girl of the Shining Mountains: Sacagawea's Story.* Hyperion, 1999, 178 pp. **N**

Average Reading Level: Grades 7–8 (Interest Level: Grades 7–8)

Armstrong, Jennifer. *Shipwreck at the Bottom of the World: The Extraordinary True Story of Shackleton and the* Endurance. Crown, 1998, 131 pp. **N**

Armstrong, Jennifer. *In My Hands: Memories of a Holocaust Rescuer.* Knopf, 1999, 276 pp. **N**

Bradbury, Ray. *Dandelion Wine.* Bantam, 1957, 239 pp.

De Angeli, Marguerite. *The Door in the Wall.* Scholastic, 1949, 121 pp.

DeAngelis, Gina. *Jackie Robinson.* Chelsea, 2001, 104 pp. **N**

Dingle, Derek T. *First in the Field: Baseball Hero Jackie Robinson.* Hyperion, 1998, 48 pp. **N**

Frank, Anne. *The Diary of a Young Girl.* Random, 1952, 285 pp. **N**

Freedman, Russell. *Kids at Work: Lewis Hine and the Crusade against Child Labor.* Clarion, 1994, 97 pp. **N**

Henry, O. *The Gift of the Magi and Other Stories.* Creative, 1986, 32 pp.

Herriot, James. *All Creatures Great and Small.* Bantam, 1989, 499 pp. **N**

Kadohata, Cynthia. *Kira-Kira.* Atheneum, 2004, 256 pp.

Kipling, Rudyard. *Captains Courageous.* Doubleday, 1896, 1964, 210 pp.

Mazer, Harry. *A Boy at War: A Novel of Pearl Harbor.* Simon & Schuster, 2001, 104 pp.

McKissack, Patricia C., & McKissack, Fredrick L. *Days of Jubilee, The End of Slavery in the United States.* Scholastic, 2003, 134 pp. **N**

Miller, Marilyn. *Words That Built a Nation.* Scholastic, 1999, 172 pp. **N**

Nicolson, Cynthia Pratt. *Hurricane!* Kids Can Press, 2002, 32 pp. **N**

Perkins, Lynne Rae. *Criss Cross.* Greenwillow, 2005, 352 pp.

Pinkney, Andrea Davis. *Let It Shine: Stories of Black Women Freedom Fighters.* Harcourt, 2000, 30 pp. **N**

Soto, Gary. *Jessie De La Cruz: A Portrait of a United Farm Worker.* Persea Books, 2000, 116 pp. **N**

Tolkien, J. R. R. *The Hobbit.* Balantine, 1938, 1979, 304 pp.

Wulffson, Don L. *The Kid Who Invented the Trampoline.* Dutton, 2001, 120 pp. **N**

Challenging Reading Level: Grade 9 (Interest Level: Grades 7–8)

London, Jack. *The Call of the Wild.* Viking, 1903, 1996, 126 pp.

McKissack, Patricia C. *Black Hands, White Sails: The Story of African American Whalers.* Scholastic, 1999, 152 pp. **N**

Rodriguez, Consuelo. *César Chavez.* Chelsea House, 1991, 106 pp. **N**

Sandburg, Carl. *Abe Lincoln Grows Up.* Harcourt, 1928, 222 pp. **N**

Informal Assessment of Word Building

Name _____   Total number correct _____

Date _____   Estimated level _____

Phonics Progress Monitoring Assessment

1. hat	_____	18. truck	_____	35. yawn	_____
2. man	_____	19. must	_____	36. growl	_____
3. sit	_____	20. black	_____	37. toy	_____
4. big	_____	21. make	_____	38. fault	_____
5. can	_____	22. ride	_____	39. noise	_____
6. top	_____	23. place	_____	40. could	_____
7. hen	_____	24. hope	_____	41. turn	_____
8. bug	_____	25. sheep	_____	42. girl	_____
9. hot	_____	26. use	_____	43. fair	_____
10. wet	_____	27. sail	_____	44. card	_____
11. sand	_____	28. play	_____	45. store	_____
12. back	_____	29. coat	_____	46. first	_____
13. pick	_____	30. night	_____	47. shirt	_____
14. drip	_____	31. brook	_____	48. smart	_____
15. fill	_____	32. blue	_____	49. clear	_____
16. sock	_____	33. broom	_____	50. morning	_____
17. step	_____	34. ground	_____		

Directions: Explain to the student that he or she will be asked to read a series of words. Say that some of the words might be difficult but that the student is expected to try her or his hardest. Put the words on cards or have them read from the list. Mark each response + or −, and write incorrect responses in the blanks as time allows. If the student doesn't respond within 5 seconds, supply the word. Stop when the student gets five words in a row wrong. The student's level is the highest one at which she or he gets 8 out of 10 words correct. Students should be instructed at a level if they get more than 2 out of 10 wrong. Each level has ten items: 1–10, short-vowel patterns; 11–20, short vowels with clusters; 21–30, long vowels; 31–40, other vowels; 41–50, *r* vowels. (See pp. 199–200.)

From T. Gunning (2007). *Teacher's Guide for Word Building* (Rev.). Honesdale, PA: Phoenix Learning Resources. Reprinted by permission of Galvin Publications.

Name _____   Total number correct _____

Date   _____   Estimated level _____

Syllable Survey

1. sunup	_____	18. distant	_____	35. creature	_____
2. inside	_____	19. prevent	_____	36. audience	_____
3. ago	_____	20. museum	_____	37. pleasant	_____
4. open	_____	21. several	_____	38. spaghetti	_____
5. under	_____	22. building	_____	39. information	_____
6. farmer	_____	23. probably	_____	40. voyage	_____
7. finish	_____	24. modern	_____	41. confusion	_____
8. mistake	_____	25. monument	_____	42. neighborhood	_____
9. thunder	_____	26. opposite	_____	43. studio	_____
10. morning	_____	27. message	_____	44. allowance	_____
11. reward	_____	28. success	_____	45. microphone	_____
12. famous	_____	29. struggle	_____	46. auditorium	_____
13. mumble	_____	30. repeat	_____	47. available	_____
14. spider	_____	31. recognize	_____	48. disappointment	_____
15. chicken	_____	32. survive	_____	49. bulletin	_____
16. rocket	_____	33. appreciate	_____	50. moisture	_____
17. magnet	_____	34. antelope	_____		

Directions: Give one copy of the survey to the student and keep one for marking. Mark each response + or −. Start with the first item for all pupils. Say to the student, "I am going to ask you to read a list of words. Some of the words may be hard for you, but read as many as you can." Stop when the student gets five in a row wrong. A score of 45 or above indicates that the student is able to decode multisyllabic words. A score between 40 and 44 indicates some weakness in decoding multisyllabic words. A score below 40 indicates a definite need for instruction and practice in decoding multisyllabic words. A score of 5 or below suggests that the student may be deficient in basic decoding skills.

From the *Teacher's Guide for Word Building, Book D*, by T. Gunning, 2007. Honesdale, PA: Phoenix Learning Resources. Reprinted by permission of Galvin Publications.

References

Professional

Achilles, C. M., Finn, J. D., & Bain, H. P. (1997–1998). Using class size to reduce the equity gap. *Educational Leadership, 54*(8), 40–43.

Adams, M. J. (1990). *Beginning to read: Thinking and learning about print: A summary.* Cambridge, MA: MIT Press.

Adams, M. J. (1994). Modeling the connections between word recognition and reading. In R. B. Ruddell, M. R. Ruddell, & H. Singer (Eds.), *Theoretical models and processes of reading* (4th ed.) (pp. 838–863). Newark, DE: International Reading Association.

Adams, M. J. (2005). The promise of automatic speech recognition for fostering literacy growth in children and adults. In M. McKenna, L. Labbo, R. Kieffer, & D. Reinking (Eds.), *Hand-book of literacy and technology* (Vol. 2). Hillsdale, NJ: Erlbaum.

Adams, M. J., & Higgins, A. W. F. (1985). The growth of children's sight vocabulary: A quick test with educational and theoretical implications. *Reading Research Quarterly, 20,* 262–281.

Adler, M., & Rougle, E. (2005). *Building literacy through classroom discussion: Research-based strategies for developing critical readers and thoughtful writers in middle school.* New York: Scholastic.

Afflerbach, P. (1990). The influence of prior knowledge on expert readers' main idea construction strategies. *Reading Research Quarterly, 25,* 31–46.

Afflerbach, P. P., & Johnston, P. H. (1986). What do expert readers do when the main idea is not explicit? In J. F. Baumann (Ed.), *Teaching main idea comprehension* (pp. 49–72). Newark, DE: International Reading Association.

Ahlmann, M. E. (1992). Children as evaluators. In K. S. Goodman, L. B. Bird, & Y. M. Goodman (Eds.), *The whole language catalog: Supplement on authentic assessment* (p. 95). Santa Rosa, CA: American School Publishers.

Akroyd, S. (1995). Forming a parent reading-writing class: Connecting cultures, one pen at a time. *The Reading Teacher, 48,* 580–584.

Allen, V. (1991). Teaching bilingual and ESL children. In J. Flood, J. M. Jensen, D. Lapp, & J. R. Squire (Eds.), *Handbook of research on teaching the English language arts* (pp. 356–364). New York: Macmillan.

Allen, V. G. (1994). Selecting materials for the reading instruction of ESL children. In K. Spangenberg-Urbschat, & R. Pritchard (Eds.), *Kids come in all languages: Reading instruction for all ESL students* (pp. 108–131). Newark, DE: International Reading Association.

Allington, R. L. (2006). Fluency: Still waiting after all these years. In S. J. Samuels & A. E. Farstrup (Eds.), *What research has to say about fluency instruction* (pp. 94–105). Newark, DE: International Reading Association.

Almasi, J. F., O'Flahavan, J. F., & Arya, P. (2001). A comparative analysis of student and teacher development in more and less proficient discussions of literature. *Reading Research Quarterly, 36,* 96–120.

Altwerger, B., Edelsky, C., & Flores, B. M. (1987). Whole language: What's new? *The Reading Teacher, 41,* 144–154.

Alvermann, D. E., & Phelps, S. F. (1994). *Content area reading and literacy: Succeeding in today's diverse classrooms.* Boston: Allyn & Bacon.

Alvermann, D. E., Young, J. P., Weaver, D., Hinchman, K. A., Moore, D. W., Phelps, S. F., Thrash, E. C., & Zaleewski, P. (1996). Middle and high school students' perceptions of how they experience text-based discussions: A multicase study. *Reading Research Quarterly, 31,* 244–267.

Anderson, E., & Guthrie, J. T. (1996). Teaching with CORI: Taking the big jump. *NRRC News, 3,* 1–3.

Anderson, G., Higgins, D., & Wurster, S. R. (1985). Differences in the free-reading books selected by high, average, and low achievers. *The Reading Teacher, 39,* 326–330.

Anderson, R. C. (1984). Role of the reader's schema in comprehension, learning, and memory. In R. C. Anderson, J. Osborn, & R. J. Tierney (Eds.), *Learning to read in American schools: Basal readers and content texts* (pp. 469–482). Hillsdale, NJ: Erlbaum.

Anderson, R. C. (2006). *Collaborative reasoning: An approach to literature discussion that promotes children's social and intellectual development.* Paper presented at the Reading Research Conference, Chicago.

Anderson, R. C., Hiebert, E. H., Scott, J. A., & Wilkinson, I. A. G. (1985). *Becoming a nation of readers: The report of the commission on reading.* Washington, DC: National Institute of Education.

Anderson, R. C., Wilson, P. T., & Fielding, L. G. (1988). Growth in reading and how children spend their time outside of school. *Reading Research Quarterly, 23,* 285–303.

Anderson, T. H., & Armbruster, B. B. (1984). Studying. In P. D. Pearson, R. Barr, M. L. Kamil, & P. Mosenthal (Eds.), *Handbook of reading research* (pp. 657–679). New York: Longman.

Andre, M. E. D. A., & Anderson, T. H. (1978–1979). The development and evaluation of a self-questioning study technique. *Reading Research Quarterly, 14,* 605–623.

Anthony, H. M., Pearson, P. D., & Raphael, T. E. (1989). *Reading comprehension research: A selected review* (Technical Report No. 448). Champaign: University of Illinois, Center for the Study of Reading.

Anthony, J. L., & Lonigan, C. J. (2004). The nature of phonological awareness: Converging evidence from four studies. *Journal of Educational Psychology, 96,* 43–55.

Appel, R., & Vermeer, A. (1996). Speeding up the acquisition of Dutch vocabulary by migrant children. Uitbreiding van de Nederlandse woordenschat van allochtone leerlingen in het basisonderwijs, *Pedagogische Studieen, 73,* 82–92.

Applebee, A. N., Langer, J. A., & Mullis, I. V. S. (1988). Who reads best? *Factors related to reading achievement in grades 3, 7, and 11.* Princeton, NJ: Educational Testing Service.

Applegate, M. D., Quinn, K. B., & Applegate, A. J. (2002). Levels of thinking required by comprehension questions in informal reading inventories. *The Reading Teacher, 56,* 174–180.

Arciero, J. (1998, October). *Strategies for shared text reading responses.* Paper presented at Connecticut Reading Association meeting, Waterbury.

Armbruster, B. B., & Anderson, T. H. (1981). *Content area textbooks* (Technical Report No. 23). Champaign: University of Illinois, Center for the Study of Reading.

Asch, S., & Nerlove, H. (1967). The development of double function terms in children: An exploratory investigation. In J. P. Cecco (Ed.), *The psychology of thought, language, and instruction* (pp. 283–291). New York: Holt.

Ashcraft, M. H. (1994). *Human memory and cognition.* New York: HarperCollins.

Athanases, S. Z. (2003). Thematic study of literature: Middle school teachers, professional development, and educational reform. *English Education, 35,* 107–121.

Atkinson, R. L., Atkinson, R. C., Smith, E. E., & Hilgard, E. R. (1987). *Introduction to psychology* (9th ed.). New York: Harcourt.

Atwell, N. (1987). *In the middle.* Portsmouth, NH: Boynton/Cook.

Atwell, N. (1990). *Coming to know: Writing to learn in the intermediate grades.* Portsmouth, NH: Heinemann.

Au, K. H. (1994). Portfolio assessment: Experiences at the Kamehameha elementary education program. In S. W. Valencia, E. H. Hiebert, & P. P. Afflerbach (Eds.), *Authentic reading assessment: Practices and possibilities* (pp. 103–126). Newark, DE: International Reading Association.

Au, K. H., & Mason, J. M. (1989). Elementary reading programs. In S. B. Wepner, J. T. Feeley, & D. S. Strickland (Eds.), *The administration and supervision of reading programs* (pp. 60–75). New York: Teachers College Press.

August, D., Calderón, M., & Carlo, M. (2001). *Transfer of skills from Spanish to English: A study of young learners, report for practitioners, parents, and policy makers.* Office of English Language Acquisition, Language Enhancement, and Academic Achieve-ment for Limited English Proficient Students (OELA), U.S. Department of Education. Available online at http://www.cal.org/pubs/articles/skillstransfer-nabe.html

Australian Ministry of Education. (1990). *Literacy profiles handbook.* Victoria, Australia: Author.

Ausubel, D. P. (1960). The use of advance organizers in the learning and retention of meaningful verbal material. *Journal of Educational Psychology, 51,* 267–272.

Badders, W., Bethel, L. J., Fu, V., Peck, D., Sumners, C., & Valentino, C. (1999). *Discovery works 6.* Parsippany, NJ: Silver Burdett Ginn.

Bader, L. A. (2002). *Reading and language inventory* (4th ed.). Upper Saddle River, NJ: Prentice Hall.

Bagge-Rynerson, B. (1994). Learning good lessons: Young readers respond to books. In T. Newkirk (Ed.), *Workshop 5: The writing process revisited* (pp. 90–100). Portsmouth, NH: Heinemann.

Baker, L., & Brown, A. L. (1984). Metacognitive skills and reading. In P. D. Pearson, R. Barr, M. L. Kamil, & P. Mosenthal (Eds.), *Handbook of reading research* (pp. 353–394). New York: Longman.

Baldwin, D. (2004). A guide to standardized writing assessment. *Educational Leadership, 62*(2), 72–75.

Bangert-Downs, R. L. (1993). The word processor as an instructional tool: A meta-analysis of word processing in writing instruction. *Review of Educational Research, 63,* 69–93.

Banks, J. A. (1994). *Introduction to multicultural education.* Boston: Allyn & Bacon.

Banks, J. A., & Banks, C. A. M. (1997). *Multicultural education* (2nd ed.). Boston: Allyn & Bacon.

Barr, R. (1974). Instructional pace differences and their effect on reading acquisition. *Reading Research Quarterly, 9,* 526–554.

Barr, R., & Dreeben, R. (1991). Grouping students for reading instruction. In R. Barr, M. L. Kamil, P. Mosenthal, & P. D. Pearson (Eds.), *Handbook of reading research* (Vol. II, pp. 885–910). New York: Longman.

Barron, R. R. (1969). Research for the classroom teacher: Recent developments on the structured overview as an advanced organizer. In H. L. Herber & J. D. Riley (Eds.), *Research in reading in the content areas: The first report* (pp. 28–47). Syracuse, NY: Syracuse University, Reading and Language Arts Center.

Bartlett, F. C. (1932). *Remembering.* Cambridge: Cambridge University Press.

Barton, J., & Sawyer, D. M. (2003). Our students are ready for this: Comprehension instruction in the elementary school. *The Reading Teacher, 57,* 322–333.

Bauer, G. F. (1995). *The poetry break.* New York: H. W. Wilson.

Bauman, G. A. (1990, March). *Writing tool selection and young children's writing.* Paper presented at the spring meeting of the National Conference of Teachers of English, Colorado Springs, CO.

Baumann, J. F. (1986). The direct instruction of main idea comprehension ability. In J. F. Baumann (Ed.), *Teaching main idea comprehension* (pp. 133–178). Newark, DE: International Reading Association.

Baumann, J. F., & Duffy, A. M. (1997). *Engaged reading for pleasure and learning: A report from the National Reading Research Center.* Athens, GA: National Reading Research Center.

Baumann, J. F., Hoffman, J. V., Duffy-Hester, A. M., & Ro, J. M. (2000). "The first R" yesterday and today: U.S. elementary reading instruction practices reported by teachers and administrators. *Reading Research Quarterly, 35,* 338–377.

Baumann, J. F., & Ivey, G. (1997). Delicate balances: Striving for curricular and instructional equilibrium in a second-grade, literature/strategy-based classroom. *Reading Research Quarterly, 32,* 244–275.

Baumann, J. F., Kame'enui, E. J., & Ash, G. (2003). Research on vocabulary instruction: Voltaire redux. In J. Flood, D. Lapp, J. Jensen, & J. R. Squire (Eds.), *Handbook of research on teaching the English language arts* (2nd ed.) (pp. 752–785). New York: Macmillan.

Baumann, J. F., & Serra, J. K. (1984). The frequency and placement of main ideas in children's social studies textbooks: A modified replication of Braddock's research on topic sentences. *Journal of Reading Behavior, 16,* 27–40.

Bear, D. (1995). *Word study: A developmental perspective based on spelling stages.* Paper presented at the annual meeting of the International Reading Association, Anaheim, CA.

Bear, D. R., & Templeton, S. (1998). Explorations in developmental spelling: Foundations for learning and teaching phonics, spelling, and vocabulary. *The Reading Teacher, 52,* 222–242.

Beck, I. L., & Juel, C. (1995). The role of decoding in learning to read. *American Educator, 9*(2), 8, 21–25, 39–42.

Beck, I. L., & McKeown, M. G. (1983). Learning words well—a program to enhance vocabulary and comprehension. *The Reading Teacher, 36,* 622–625.

Beck, I. L., & McKeown, M. (2006). *The three Cs of comprehension instruction.* Comprehension Forum. Pacific Resources for Education and Learning. Available online at http://www.prel.org/programs/rel/comprehensionforum/beck.pdf

Beck, I. L., McKeown, M. G., Hamilton, R. L., & Kucan, L. (1997). *Questioning the author: An approach for enhancing student engagement with text.* Newark, DE: International Reading Association.

Beck, I. L., & McKeown, M. G. (2001). Text talk: Capturing the benefits of read-aloud experiences for young children. *The Reading Teacher, 55,* 10–20.

Beck, I. L., McKeown, M. G., & Kucan, L. (2002). *Bringing words to life: Robust vocabulary instruction.* New York: Guilford.

Beck, I. L., McKeown, M. G., & Omanson, R. C. (1987). The effects and uses of diverse vocabulary instructional techniques. In M. G. McKeown & M. E. Curtis (Eds.), *The nature of vocabulary acquisition* (pp. 147–163). Hillsdale, NJ: Erlbaum.

Beck, I. L., Omanson, R. C., & McKeown, M. G. (1982). An instructional redesign of reading lessons: Effects on comprehension. *Reading Research Quarterly, 17*, 462–481.

Beers, K. (2003). *When kids can't read, what teachers can do: A guide for teachers 6–12*. Portsmouth, NH: Heinemann.

Benson, V., & Cummins, C. (2000). *The power of retelling: Developmental steps for building comprehension*. Bothell, WA: Wright Group/McGraw-Hill.

Benson-Castagna, V. (2005). *Reciprocal teaching, a workshop*. Houston, TX: Author.

Bereiter, C., & Scardamalia, M. (1982). From conversation to composition: The role of instruction in a developmental process. In R. Glass (Ed.), *Advances in instructional psychology* (Vol. 2, pp. 1–64). Hillsdale, NJ: Erlbaum.

Berk, L. E. (1997). *Child development* (4th ed.). Boston: Allyn & Bacon.

Berliner, D. C. (1981). Academic learning time and reading achievement. In J. T. Guthrie (Ed.), *Comprehension and teaching: Research reviews* (pp. 203–226). Newark, DE: International Reading Association.

Berliner, D. C. (1984). The half-full glass: A review of research on teaching. In P. Hosford (Ed.), *Using what we know about teaching*. Alexandria, VA: Association for Supervision and Curriculum Development.

Berliner, D. C. (1985). Effective classroom teaching: The necessary but not sufficient condition for developing exemplary schools. In G. R. Austin & H. Gartier (Eds.), *Research on exemplary schools* (pp. 211–234). New York: Academic.

Berne, J. I., & Clark, K. F. (2006, May). *Strategic literary discussion: Teachers and students test new ground for comprehension strategy use*. Paper presented at the International Reading Association convention, Chicago.

Bertrand, J. E. (2000). "I hate words": Bridging the gap with learning disabled fourth graders. In C. F. Stice & J. E. Bertrand (Eds.), *Teaching at-risk students in the K–4 classroom: Language, literacy, learning* (pp. 79–94). Norwood, MA: Christopher-Gordon.

Beyer, B. (2001). What research says about teaching thinking skills. In A. L. Costa (Ed.), *Developing minds: A resource book for teaching thinking* (3rd ed.) (pp. 275–282). Alexandria, VA: Association for Supervision and Curriculum Development.

Bielenberg, B., & Fillmore, L. W. (2004). The English they need for the test. *Educational Leadership, 62*(4), 45–49.

Biemiller, A. (1994). Some observations on acquiring and using reading skill in elementary schools. In C. K. Kinzer & D. J. Leu (Eds.), *Multidimensional aspects of literacy research, theory, and practice (43rd yearbook of the National Reading Conference)* (pp. 209–216). Chicago: National Reading Conference.

Biemiller, A. (2005). Size and sequence in vocabulary development: Implications for choosing words for primary vocabulary instruction. In E. Hiebert & M. Kamil (Eds.), *Teaching and learning vocabulary: Bringing research to practice* (pp. 223–242). Mahwah, NJ: Erlbaum.

Birnbaum, R. K. (1999). *NewPhonics*. Pittsford, NY: NewPhonics Literacy System.

Bissex, G. L. (1980). *GNYS AT WRK*. Cambridge, MA: Harvard University Press.

Bitter, G. G. (1999). *Using technology in the classroom* (4th ed.). Boston: Allyn & Bacon.

Bitter, G. G., & Pierson, M. E. (2002). *Using technology in the classroom* (5th ed.). Boston: Allyn & Bacon.

Bjorklund, B., Handler, N., Mitten, J., & Stockwell, G. (1998, October). *Literature circles: A tool for developing students as critical readers, writers, and thinkers*. Paper presented at the 47th annual conference of the Connecticut Reading Association, Waterbury.

Blachman, B. A., Tangel, D. M., Ball, E., Black, R., & McGraw, C. K. (1994). Kindergarten teachers develop phonological awareness and word recognition skills: A two-year intervention with low-income, inner-city children. *Reading and Writing: An Interdisciplinary Journal, 11*, 239–273.

Blachowicz, C. L. Z. (1977). Cloze activities for primary readers. *The Reading Teacher, 31*, 300–302.

Blachowicz, C. L. Z., & Fisher, P. (2000). Vocabulary instruction. In M. L. Kamil, P. B. Mosenthal, P. D. Pearson, & R. Barr (Eds.), *Handbook of reading research* (Vol. III, pp. 503–523). Mahwah, NJ: Erlbaum.

Black, P., & Wiliam, D. (1998). Inside the black box: Raising standards through classroom assessment. *Phi Delta Kappan, 80*(2), 139–148. Available online at http://www.pdkintl.org/kappan/kbla9810.htm

Block, C. C., & Israel, S. E. (2004). The ABCs of performing highly effective think-alouds. *The Reading Teacher, 58*, 154–167.

Bloodgood, J. W., & Pacifici, L. C. (2004). Bringing word study to intermediate classrooms. *The Reading Teacher, 58*, 250–263.

Bloom, B. (Ed.). (1957). *Taxonomy of educational objectives*. New York: McKay.

Blum, I. H., Koskinen, P. S., Tennant, S., Parker, E. M., Straub, M., & Curry, C. (1995). Using audiotaped books to extend classroom literacy instruction into the homes of second-language learners. *Journal of Reading Behavior, 27*, 535–564.

Boehm, A. E. (1971). *Boehm test of basic concepts manual*. New York: Psychological Corporation.

Bond, G. L., & Dykstra, R. (1967). The cooperative research program in first-grade reading instruction. *Reading Research Quarterly, 2*, 1–142.

Bond, G. L., & Dykstra, R. (1997). The cooperative research program in first-grade reading instruction. *Reading Research Quarterly, 32*, 348–427.

Boote, C. (2006). *Reading comprehension requires word meaning knowledge: A classroom model for teaching word meanings in primary grades*. Paper presented at the Reading Research Conference, Chicago.

Boothroyd, K. (2001, December). *Being literate in urban third-grade classrooms*. Paper presented at the annual meeting of the National Reading Conference, San Antonio, TX.

Borders, S., & Naylor, A. P. (1993). *Children talking about books*. Phoenix, AZ: Oryx.

Boyd, C. D., Gay, G., Geiger, R., Kracht, J. B., Pang, V. O., Risinger, F. C., & Sanchez, S. M. (2003). *Scott Foresman social studies: The United States*. Glenview, IL: Scott, Foresman.

Boyd-Batstone, P. (2004). Focused anecdotal records assessment: A tool for standards-based, authentic assessment. *The Reading Teacher, 58*, 230–239.

Boyle, C. (1996). *Efficacy of peer evaluation and effects of peer evaluation on persuasive writing*. Unpublished master's thesis, San Diego State University, San Diego, CA.

Boyles, N. (2004). *Constructing meaning*. Gainesville, FL: Maupin House.

Bransford, J. D. (1994). Schema activation and schema acquisition: Comments on Richard C. Anderson's remarks. In R. B. Ruddell, M. R. Ruddell, & H. Singer (Eds.), *Theoretical models and processes of reading* (4th ed.) (pp. 483–495). Newark, DE: International Reading Association.

Bransford, J. D., Stein, B. S., Shelton, T. S., & Owings, R. A. (1981). Cognition and adaptation: The importance of learning to learn. In J. Harvey (Ed.), *Cognition, social behavior, and the environment*. Hillsdale, NJ: Erlbaum.

Brewster, P. G. (Ed.). (1952). *Children's games and rhymes.* Durham, NC: Duke University Press.

Bridge, C. A., Winograd, P. N., & Haley, D. (1983). Using predictable materials vs. preprimers to teach beginning sight words. *The Reading Teacher, 36,* 884–891.

Bromley, K. D. (1998). *Language arts: Exploring connections* (3rd ed.). Boston: Allyn & Bacon.

Brophy, J. E., & Good, T. L. (1970). Teachers' communication of differential expectations for children's classroom performance: Some behavioral data. *Journal of Educational Psychology, 61,* 365–375.

Brophy, J. E., & Good, T. L. (1986). Teacher behavior and student achievement. In M. E. Wittrock (Ed.), *Handbook of research on teaching* (pp. 328–375). New York: Macmillan.

Brown, A. L. (1985). *Reciprocal teaching of comprehension strategies: A natural history of one program for enhancing learning* (Technical Report No. 334). Champaign: University of Illinois, Center for the Study of Reading.

Brown, A. L., & Day, J. D. (1983). Macrorules for summarizing text: The development of expertise. *Journal of Verbal Learning and Verbal Behavior, 22*(1), 1–14.

Brown, C. S., & Lytle, S. L. (1988). Merging assessment and instruction: Protocols in the classroom. In S. M. Glazer, L. W. Searfoss, & L. M. Gentile (Eds.), *Reexamining reading diagnosis: New trends and procedures* (pp. 94–102). Newark, DE: International Reading Association.

Brown, J. J. (1988). *High impact teaching: Strategies for educating minority youth.* Lanham, MD: University Press of America.

Brown, K. J. (2003). What do I say when they get stuck on a word? Aligning teachers' prompts with students' development. *The Reading Teacher, 56,* 720–733.

Bruce, B. (1980). Plans and social actions. In R. J. Spiro, B. C. Bruce, & W. F. Brewer (Eds.), *Theoretical issues in reading comprehension* (pp. 367–384). Hillsdale, NJ: Erlbaum.

Bruck, M. (1992). Persistence of dyslexics' phonological awareness deficits. *Developmental Psychology, 28,* 874–886.

Bruner, J. (1975). The ontogenesis of speech acts. *Journal of Child Languages, 2,* 1–40.

Bruner, J. (1986). *Actual minds, possible worlds.* Cambridge, MA: Harvard University Press.

Buettner, E. G. (2002). Sentence by sentence self-monitoring. *The Reading Teacher, 56,* 34–44.

Bunce, B. H. (1995). *Building a language-focused curriculum for the preschool classroom. Volume II: A planning guide.* Baltimore: Brookes.

Burns, J. M., & Richgels, D. S. (1989). An investigation of task requirements associated with the invented spelling of 4-year-olds with above average intelligence. *Journal of Reading Behavior, 21,* 1–14.

Bus, A. G., & van IJzendoorn, M. H. (1999). Phonological awareness and early reading: A meta-analysis of experiential training studies. *Journal of Educational Psychology, 91,* 403–414.

Bush, C., & Huebner, M. (1979). *Strategies for reading in the elementary school* (2nd ed.). New York: Macmillan.

Button, K., Johnson, M. J., & Ferguson, P. (1996). Interactive writing in a primary classroom. *The Reading Teacher, 49,* 446–454.

Byrne, B. (1992). Studies in the acquisition procedure for reading: Rationale, hypotheses, and data. In P. B. Gough, L. C. Ehri, & R. Treiman (Eds.), *Reading acquisition* (pp. 1–35). Hillsdale, NJ: Erlbaum.

Calder, L., & Carlson, S. (2002). *Using "think alouds" to evaluate deep understanding.* Policy Center on the First Year of College. Available online at http://www.brevard.edu/fyc/listserv/remarks/calderandcarlson.htm

Caldwell, J. H., Huitt, W. G., & Graeber, A. O. (1982). Time spent in learning: Implications from research. *Elementary School Journal, 82,* 471–480.

Calfee, R., & Hiebert, E. (1991). Classroom assessment of reading. In R. Barr, M. L. Kamil, P. Mosenthal, & P. D. Pearson (Eds.), *Handbook of reading research* (Vol. II, pp. 281–309). New York: Longman.

California Literature Project. (1992). *Meaning-making strategies for a literature-based curriculum.* Dominguez Hills: California State University.

Calkins, L. (1986). *The art of teaching writing.* Portsmouth, NH: Heinemann.

Calkins, L. (1994). *The art of teaching writing* (new ed.). Portsmouth, NH: Heinemann.

Calkins, L. (2001). *The art of teaching reading.* Portsmouth, NH: Heinemann.

Calkins, L. (2003). *Nuts and bolts of teaching writing.* Portsmouth, NH: Heinemann.

Calkins, L. (2006). *A guide to the writing workshop.* Portsmouth, NH: Heinemann.

Calkins, L., Hartman, A., White, Z., et al. (2003). *Units of study for primary writing: A yearlong curriculum (K–2).* Portsmouth, NH: Heinemann.

Calkins, L., & Harwayne, S. (1991). *Living between the lines.* Portsmouth, NH: Heinemann.

Calkins, L., & Martinelli, M. (2006). *Launching the writing workshop.* Portsmouth, NH: Heinemann.

Calkins, L., Martinelli, M., Kesler, T., Gillette, C., McEvoy, M., Chiarella, M., & Cruz, C. (2006). *Units of study for teaching writing, grades 3–5.* Portsmouth, NH: Heinemann.

Calkins, L., & Mermelstein, L. (2003). *Nonfiction writing: Procedures and reports. Units of study for primary writing: A yearlong program.* Portsmouth, NH: Heinemann.

Calkins, L., Montgomery, K., & Santman, D. (1998). *A teacher's guide to standardized reading tests.* Portsmouth, NH: Heinemann.

Campbell, R. (1998). Looking at literacy learning in preschool settings. In R. Campbell (Ed.), *Facilitating preschool literacy* (pp. 70–83). Newark, DE: International Reading Association.

Campbell, R. (2001). *Read-alouds with young children.* Newark, DE: International Reading Association.

Carbo, M. (1997). *What every principal should know about teaching reading: How to raise test scores and nurture a love of reading.* Syosset, NY: National Reading Styles Institute.

Carbo, M., Dunn, R., & Dunn, K. (1986, 1991). *Teaching students to read through their individual learning styles.* Boston: Allyn & Bacon.

Carlisle, J. F., & Stone, C. (2005). Exploring the role of morphemes in word reading. *Reading Research Quarterly, 40,* 428–449.

Carlson, N. R., & Buskist, W. (1997). *Psychology: The science of behavior* (5th ed.). Boston: Allyn & Bacon.

Carnine, D., Kame'enui, E. J., & Coyle, G. (1984). Utilization of contextual information in determining the meaning of unfamiliar words. *Reading Research Quarterly, 19,* 188–204.

Carnine, D., Silbert, J., & Kame'enui, E. J. (1990). *Direct instruction in reading.* Columbus, OH: Merrill.

Carr, E., Dewitz, P., & Patberg, J. P. (1989). Using cloze for inference training with expository text. *The Reading Teacher, 42,* 380–385.

Carr, K. S. (1983). The importance of inference skills in the primary grades. *The Reading Teacher, 36,* 518–522.

Cartwright, C. P., Cartwright, C. A., & Ward, M. E. (1989). *Educating special learners.* Belmont, CA: Wadsworth.

Caruso, C. (1997). Before you cite a site. *Educational Leadership, 55*(3), 24–25.

Castle, M. (1994). Helping children choose books. In E. H. Cramer & M. Castle (Eds.), *Fostering the love of reading: The affective domain in reading education* (pp. 145–168). Newark, DE: International Reading Association.

Cattagni, A., & Westnat, E. F. (2001). *Internet access in U.S. public schools and classrooms: 1994–2000.* Washington, DC:

U.S. Department of Education, National Center for Educational Statistics. Available online at http://nces.ed.gov/pubs2001/2001071.pdf

Caverly, D. C., & Orlando, V. P. (1991). Textbook study strategies. In D. C. Caverly & V. P. Orlando (Eds.), *Teaching reading and study strategies at the college level* (pp. 86–165). Newark, DE: International Reading Association.

Center for Education Policy. (2006). *From the capital to the classroom: Year 4 of the No Child Left Behind Act.* Available online at http://www.cep-dc.org/nclb/Year4/Press

Center for the Study of Reading. (1990). *Suggestions for the classroom: Teachers and independent reading.* Urbana: University of Illinois Press.

CHADD. (2006). *About AD/HD: Statistical prevalence.* Available online at http://www.help4adhd.org/en/about/statistics

Chall, J. S. (1967). *Learning to read: The great debate.* New York: McGraw-Hill.

Chall, J. S. (1983a). *Learning to read: The great debate* (rev. ed.). New York: McGraw-Hill.

Chall, J. S. (1983b). *Stages of reading development.* New York: McGraw-Hill.

Chall, J. S. (1996). *Stages of reading development* (2nd ed.). Fort Worth, TX: Harcourt.

Chall, J. S., Bissex, G. L., Conard, S. S., & Harris-Sharples, S. H. (1996). *Qualitative assessment of text difficulty: A practical guide for teachers and writers.* Cambridge, MA: Brookline.

Chall, J. S., & Dale, E. (1995). *The new Dale-Chall readability formula.* Cambridge, MA: Brookline.

Chall, J. S., Jacobs, V. A., & Baldwin, L. E. (1990). *The reading crisis: Why poor children fall behind.* Cambridge, MA: Harvard University Press.

Chamot, A. U., & O'Malley, J. M. (1994). Instructional approaches and teaching procedures. In K. Spangenberg-Urbschat & R. Pritchard (Eds.), *Kids come in all languages: Reading instruction for ESL students* (pp. 82–107). Newark, DE: International Reading Association.

Chapman, J. W., Tunmer, W. E., & Prochnow, J. E. (2001). Does success in the reading recovery program depend on developing proficiency in phonological-processing skills? A longitudinal study in a whole language instructional context. *Scientific Studies of Reading, 5,* 141–176.

Chard, N. (1990). How learning logs change teaching. In N. Atwell (Ed.), *Coming to know: Writing to learn in the intermediate grades* (pp. 61–68). Portsmouth, NH: Heinemann.

Charney, R. S. (2002). *Teaching children to care: Classroom management for ethical and academic growth, K–8.* Turners Falls, MA: Northeast Foundation for Children.

Chicago Public Schools. (2000). *Rubrics.* Available online at http://intranet.cps.k12.il.us/Assessments/Ideas_and_Rubrics.html

Children's books in print 2006. (Annual). New York: Bowker.

Christenbury, L., & Kelly, P. (1983). *Questioning: A path to critical thinking.* Urbana, IL: National Council of Teachers of English.

Christie, J. F. (1990). Dramatic play: A context for meaningful engagements. *The Reading Teacher, 43,* 542–545.

Clark, K. F., & Berne, J. (2005). *A microanalysis of intermediate grade students' comprehension strategy use during peer-led discussions of text: An initial inquiry.* Paper presented at the National Reading Conference, Miami.

Clark, K. F., & Berne, J. (2006). *Sentence starters.* Paper presented at the International Reading Association convention, Chicago.

Clarke, L. K. (1988). Invented vs. traditional spelling in first graders' writings: Effects on learning to spell and read. *Research in the Teaching of English, 22,* 281–309.

Clarkson, C. (2000). Discovering children and creating curriculum in one small-town third grade. In C. F. Stice & J. E.

Bertrand (Eds.), *Teaching at-risk students in the K–4 classroom: Language, literacy, learning.* Norwood, MA: Christopher-Gordon.

Clay, M. M. (1972). *Reading: The patterning of complex behavior.* Auckland, New Zealand: Heinemann.

Clay, M. M. (1975). *What did I write?* Auckland, New Zealand: Heinemann.

Clay, M. M. (1982). *Observing young readers.* Portsmouth, NH: Heinemann.

Clay, M. M. (1991). *Becoming literate: The construction of inner control.* Portsmouth, NH: Heinemann.

Clay, M. M. (1992). Introducing a new storybook to young readers. *The Reading Teacher, 45,* 264–272.

Clay, M. M. (1993a). *An observation survey of early literacy achievement.* Portsmouth, NH: Heinemann.

Clay, M. M. (1993b). *Reading Recovery: A guidebook for teachers in training.* Portsmouth, NH: Heinemann.

Clay, M. M. (2000). *Running records for classroom teachers.* Portsmouth, NH: Heinemann.

Clay, M. M. (2006). *An observation survey of early literacy achievement* (rev. 2nd ed.). Portsmouth, NH: Heinemann.

Cline, R. K. J., & Kretke, G. L. (1980). An evaluation of long-term SSR in the junior high school. *Journal of Reading, 23,* 503–506.

Cole, A. D. (1998). Beginner-oriented texts in literature-based classrooms: The segue for a few struggling readers. *The Reading Teacher, 51,* 488–501.

Collins, A., & Smith, E. (1980). *Teaching the process of reading comprehension* (Technical Report No. 182). Urbana: University of Illinois, Center for the Study of Reading.

Collins, J. L. (1998). *Strategies for struggling writers.* New York: Guilford.

Collins, M. F. (2005). ESL preschoolers' English vocabulary acquisition from storybook reading. *Reading Research Quarterly, 40,* 406–408.

Combs, M. (1987). Modeling the reading process with enlarged texts. *The Reading Teacher, 40,* 422–426.

Connor, C. M., Morrison, F. J., & Katch, L. E. (2004). Beyond the reading wars: Exploring the effect of child-instruction interactions on growth in early reading. *Scientific Studies of Reading, 8,* 305–336.

Constantino, M. (1999, May). *Reading and second language learners: Research report.* Olympia, WA: Evergreen State College. Available online at http://www.evergreen.edu/user/K-12/readingSecondLangLearners.htm

Cook, D. M. (1986). *A guide to curriculum planning in reading.* Madison: Wisconsin Department of Public Instruction.

Cook, M. (2006). *A journal for* Corduroy: *Responding to literature.* Read•Write•Think. Available online at http://www.readwritethink.org/lessons/lesson_view.asp?id=30

Cook, V. (2001). *Second language learning and language teaching* (3rd ed). New York: Oxford University Press.

Cooper, C. R., & Odell, L. (1977). *Evaluating writing: Describing, measuring, judging.* Urbana, IL: National Council of Teachers of English.

Cooper, H. (2003, May). *Summer learning loss: The problem and some solutions* (Eric Digest, EDO-PS-03-5). Available online at http://ericeece.org/pubs/digests/2003/cooper03.pdf

Cooper, P. D. (1996). *Intervention literacy instruction for hard-to-teach students in grades 3–6.* Paper presented at the annual meeting of the International Reading Association, New Orleans, LA.

Cooper, P. D. (1997). *Literacy: Helping children construct meaning* (3rd ed.). Boston: Houghton Mifflin.

Cooper, P. D., & Pikulski, J. J. (2005). *Houghton Mifflin reading.* Boston: Houghton Mifflin.

Cooter, K. S., & Cooter, R. B., Jr. (2004). One size doesn't fit all: Slow learners in the reading classroom. *The Reading Teacher, 57,* 680–684.

Cox, C., & Many, J. E. (1992). Towards an understanding of the aesthetic stance towards literature. *Language Arts, 66,* 287–294.

Cox, C., & Zarillo, J. (1993). *Teaching reading with children's literature.* New York: Merrill.

Crafton, L. K. (1991). *Whole language: Getting started . . . moving forward.* Katonah, NY: Richard C. Owen.

Craik, F. I. M., & Lockhart, R. S. (1972). Levels of processing. *Journal of Verbal Learning and Verbal Behavior, 11,* 671–684.

Crévola, C., & Vineis, M. (2004). *Building essential literacy with bookshop, a research-based reading program.* New York: Mondo.

Cronin, J., Kingsbury, C. G., McCall, M. S., & Bowe, B. (2005, April). *The impact of the No Child Left Behind Act on student achievement and growth: 2005 edition.* Lake Oswego, OR: Northwest Evaluation Association. Available online at http://www.nwea.org/assets/research/national/NCLBImpact_2005_Brief

Cummins, J. (1994). The acquisition of English as a second language. In K. Spangenberg-Urbschat & R. Pritchard (Eds.), *Kids come in all languages: Reading instruction for all ESL students* (pp. 36–62). Newark, DE: International Reading Association.

Cummins, J. (2001). Assessment and intervention with culturally and linguistically diverse learners. In S. R. Hollins & J. V. Tinajero (Eds.), *Literacy assessment of second language learners* (pp. 115–129). Boston: Allyn & Bacon.

Cunningham, A. E., & Stanovich, K. E. (1998). What reading does for the mind. *American Educator* (Spring/Summer), 1–8.

Cunningham, J. W., & Foster, E. O. (1978). The ivory tower connection: A case study. *The Reading Teacher, 31,* 365–369.

Cunningham, J. W., & Moore, D. W. (1986). The confused world of main idea. In J. F. Baumann (Ed.), *Teaching main idea comprehension* (pp. 1–17). Newark, DE: International Reading Association.

Cunningham, J. W., Spadorcia, S. A., Erickson, K. A., Koppenhaver, D. A., Sturm, J. M., & Yoder, D. E. (2005). Investigating the instructional supportiveness of leveled texts. *Reading Research Quarterly, 40,* 410–427.

Cunningham, P. M. (1978). Decoding polysyllabic words: An alternative strategy. *Journal of Reading, 21,* 608–614.

Cunningham, P. M. (1998). The multisyllabic word dilemma: Helping students build meaning, spell, and read "big" words. *Reading and Writing Quarterly: Overcoming Learning Disabilities, 14,* 189–218.

Cunningham, P. M., & Allington, R. L. (1999). *Classrooms that work: They can all read and write* (2nd ed.). New York: Longwood.

Cunningham, P. M., & Allington, R. L. (2003). *Classrooms that work: They can all read and write* (3rd ed.). Boston: Allyn & Bacon.

Cunningham, P. M., & Cunningham, J. W. (1992). Making words: Enhancing the invented spelling-decoding connection. *The Reading Teacher, 46,* 106–115.

Cunningham, P. M., & Hall, D. P. (1997). *Month-by-month phonics for first grade.* Greensboro, NC: Carson-Dellosa.

Cunningham, P. M., Yoder, D. E., & McKenna, M. C. (1999). Assessing decoding from an onset-rime perspective. *Journal of Literacy Research, 31,* 391–414.

Curtis, M. E. (1987). Vocabulary testing and vocabulary instruction. In M. G. McKeown & M. E. Curtis (Eds.), *The nature of vocabulary acquisition* (pp. 37–51). Hillsdale, NJ: Erlbaum.

Daane, M. C., Campbell, J. R., Grigg, W. S., Goodman, M. J., & Oranje, A. (2005). *Fourth-grade students reading aloud: NAEP 2002 special study of oral reading* (NCES 2006-469). Washington, DC: U.S. Department of Education, Institute of Education Sciences, National Center for Education Statistics.

Dahl, K. (1992). Kidwatching revisited. In K. S. Goodman, L. B. Bird, & Y. M. Goodman (Eds.), *The whole language catalog: Supplement on authentic instruction* (p. 50). Santa Rosa, CA: American School Publishers.

Dahl, K., & Farnan, N. (1998). *Children's writing: Perspectives from research.* Newark, DE: International Reading Association & National Reading Conference.

Dahl, K. & Freppon, P. (1995). A comparison of inner city children's interpretations of reading and writing instruction in the early grades in skills-based and whole language classrooms. *Reading Research Quarterly, 31,* 50–75.

Dale, E., & O'Rourke, J. (1971). *Techniques of teaching vocabulary.* Chicago: Field.

Daniels, H. (2002). *Literature circles: Voice and choice in book clubs and reading groups.* York, ME: Stenhouse.

D'Arcy, P. (1989). *Making sense, shaping meaning: Writing in the context of a capacity-based approach to learning.* Portsmouth, NH: Boynton/Cook.

Davis, F. B. (1968). Research on comprehension in reading. *Reading Research Quarterly, 3,* 449–545.

Davis, G., Jackson, J., & Johnson, S. (2000, May). *Guided writing: Leveling the balance.* Paper presented at the annual meeting of the International Reading Association, Indianapolis, IN.

Davis, Z. T., & McPherson, M. D. (1989). Story map instruction: A road map for reading comprehension. *The Reading Teacher, 43,* 232–240.

Day, J. P. (2001). How I became an exemplary teacher (although I'm really still learning just like anyone else). In M. Pressley, R. L. Allington, R. Wharton-McDonald, C. C. Block, & L. M. Morrow (Eds.), *Learning to read: Lessons from exemplary first-grade classrooms* (pp. 48–69). New York: Guilford.

DeFord, D. E. (1985). Validating the construct of theoretical orientation in reading instruction. *Reading Research Quarterly, 20,* 351–367.

Deighton, L. C. (1959). *Vocabulary development in the classroom.* New York: Columbia University Press.

Delpit, L. D. (1990). *A socio-cultural view of diversity and instruction.* Paper presented at the Annual Conference on Reading Research, Atlanta.

Dennis-Shaw, S. (2006). *Guided comprehension: Making connections using a double-entry journal.* Read•Write•Think. Available online at http://www.readwritethink.org/lessons/lesson_view.asp?id=228

Denton, C. A., Fletcher, J. M., & Ciancio, D. J. (2006). Validity, reliability, and utility of the observation survey of early literacy achievement. *Reading Research Quarterly, 41,* 8–34.

Denton, K., & West, J. (2002). *Children's reading and mathematics achievement in kindergarten and first grade.* Washington, DC: National Center for Educational Statistics. Available online at http://nces.ed.gov/pubs2002/kindergarten

Denton, K., West, J., & Walston, J. (2003). *Reading—young children's achievement and classroom experiences.* Washington, DC: National Center for Education Statistics. Available online at http://nces.ed.gov/programs/coe/2003/analysis/sa05.asp

Devine, T. G. (1986). *Teaching reading comprehension: From theory to practice.* Boston: Allyn & Bacon.

Dewitz, P., Carr, E. M., & Patberg, J. P. (1987). Effects of inference training on comprehension and comprehension monitoring. *Reading Research Quarterly, 22,* 99–121.

Dewitz, P., & Dewitz, P. K. (2003). They can read the words, but they can't understand: Refining comprehension assessment. *The Reading Teacher, 56,* 422–435.

Dias, P. (1990). A literary-response perspective on teaching reading comprehension. In D. Bogdan & S. B. Straw (Eds.), *Beyond communication: Reading comprehension and criticism* (pp. 283–299). Portsmouth, NH: Boynton/Cook.

Díaz-Rico, L. T. (2004). *Teaching English learners: Strategies and methods* (2nd ed.). Boston: Allyn & Bacon.

Dickinson, D. K., & Smith, M. W. (1994). Long-term effects of preschool teachers' book reading on low-income children's vocabulary and story comprehension. *Reading Research Quarterly, 29,* 104–122.

Dierking, C. (2006). *Growing up literate: Orchestrating speaking, writing, and reading.* Paper presented at the International Reading Association's Reading Research Conference, Chicago.

Dillon, J. T. (1983). *Teaching and the art of questioning.* Bloomington, IN: Phi Delta Kappa.

DiLuglio, P., Eaton, D., & de Tarnowsky, J. (1988). *Westward wagons.* North Scituate, RI: Scituate School Department.

Dodge, B. (2001). *FOCUS: Five rules for writing a great WebQuest.* Available online at http://www.iste.org/L&L/archive/vol28/no8/featuredarticle/dodge/index.html

Dole, J. S., Duffy, G. G., Roehler, L. R., & Pearson, P. D. (1991). Moving from the old to the new: Research on reading comprehension. *Review of Educational Research, 61,* 239–264.

Donahue, P. A., Voekl, K. E., Campbell, J. R., & Mazzeo, J. (1999). *NAEP 1998 report card for the nation and the states.* Washington, DC: U.S. Department of Education.

Donovan, C. A., &. Smolkin, L. B. (2001). Genre and other factors influencing teachers' book selection for science instruction. *Reading Research Quarterly, 36,* 421–440.

Dooling, D. J., & Lachman, R. (1971). Effects of comprehension on retention of prose. *Journal of Experimental Psychology, 88,* 216–222.

Dorion, R. (1994). Using nonfiction in a read-aloud program: Letting the facts speak for themselves. *The Reading Teacher, 47,* 616–624.

Dowhower, S. L. (1987). Effects of repeated reading on second-grade transitional readers' fluency and comprehension. *Reading Research Quarterly, 22,* 389–406.

Doyle, B., & Bramwell, W. (2006). Promoting emergent literacy and social-emotional learning through dialogic reading. *The Reading Teacher, 59,* 554–564.

Duffelmeyer, F. A. (1985). Main ideas in paragraphs. *The Reading Teacher, 38,* 484–486.

Duffy, G. G. (2002). The case for direct explanation of strategies. In C. C. Block & M. Pressley (Eds.), *Comprehension instruction: Research based best practices* (pp. 28–41). New York: Guilford.

Duffy, G. G., & Roehler, L. R. (1987). Improving reading instruction through the use of responsive elaboration. *The Reading Teacher, 40,* 514–520.

Duffy, R. (1994). It's just like talking to each other: Written conversation with five-year-old children. In N. Hall & A. Robinson (Eds.), *Keeping in touch: Using interactive writing with young children* (pp. 31–42). Portsmouth, NH: Heinemann.

Duke, N. K. (2003, July). *Comprehension difficulties.* Presentation at the CIERA Summer Institute, Ann Arbor, MI.

DuPaul, G. J., & Eckert, T. L. (1996). Academic interventions for students with attention-deficit/hyperactivity disorder: A review of the literature. *Reading and Writing Quarterly: Overcoming Learning Difficulties, 14,* 58–82.

Durgunoglu, A. Y., & Oney, B. (2000). *Literacy development in two languages: Cognitive and sociocultural dimensions of cross-language transfer. A research symposium on high standards in reading for students from diverse language groups: Research, practice & policy.* Washington, DC: U.S. Department of Education, Office of Bilingual Education and Minority Languages Affairs. Available online at http://www.ncbe.gwu.edu/ncbepubs/symposia/reading/reading3.html

Duthie, C. (1996). *True stories: Nonfiction literacy in the primary classroom.* York, ME: Stenhouse.

Dykstra, R. (1974). Phonics and beginning reading instruction. In C. C. Walcutt, J. Lamport, & G. McCracken (Eds.), *Teaching reading: A phonic/linguistic approach to developmental reading* (pp. 373–397). New York: Macmillan.

Dymock, S. (2005). Teaching expository text structure awareness. *The Reading Teacher, 59,* 177–181.

Dzaldov, B., & Peterson, S. (2005). Book leveling and readers. *The Reading Teacher, 59,* 222–229.

Early, M., & Sawyer, D. J. (1984). *Reading to learn in grades 5 to 12.* New York: Harcourt.

Echevarria, J. (1998). *Teaching language minority students in elementary schools.* Washington, DC, and Santa Cruz, CA: Center for Research in Education, Diversity & Excellence.

Echevarria, J., Vogt, M. E., & Short, D. (2000). *Making content comprehensible for English language learners: The SIOP model.* Boston: Allyn & Bacon.

Edelsky, C. (1994). Exercise isn't always healthy. In P. Shannon & K. Goodman (Eds.), *Basal readers: A second look* (pp. 19–34). Katonah, NY: Richard C. Owen.

Education Department of Western Australia. (1994). *Writing resource book.* Melbourne, Australia: Longman.

Education Trust. (2003). *Dispelling the myth—online.* Available online at http://64.224.125.0/dtm

Education Week. (2006). *Quality counts at 10: A decade of standards-based education.* Available online at http://www.edweek.org/ew/articles/2006/01/05/17execsum.h25.html

Edwards, L. (2000). "We taught ourselves." In C. F. Stice & J. E. Bertrand (Eds.), *Teaching at-risk students in the K–4 classroom: Language, literacy, learning* (pp. 1–18). Norwood, MA: Christopher-Gordon.

Eeds, M., & Wells, D. (1989). Grand conversations: An exploration of meaning construction in literature study groups. *Research in the Teaching of English, 23,* 4–29.

Ehri, L. C. (1991). Development of the ability to read words. In R. Barr, M. L. Kamil, P. Mosenthal, & P. D. Pearson (Eds.), *Handbook of reading research* (Vol. II, pp. 383–417). New York: Longman.

Ehri, L. C. (1994). Development of the ability to read words: Update. In R. B. Ruddell, M. R. Ruddell, & H. Singer (Eds.), *Theoretical models and processes of reading* (4th ed.) (pp. 323–358). Newark, DE: International Reading Association.

Ehri, L. C. (1998). Research on learning to read and spell: A personal-historical perspective. *Scientific Studies of Reading, 2,* 97–114.

Ehri, L. C., & McCormick, S. (1998). Phases of word learning: Implications for instruction with delayed and disabled readers. *Reading and Writing Quarterly: Overcoming Learning Disabilities, 14,* 135–163.

Ehri, L. C., Nunes, S. R., Willows, D. M., Schuster, B. V., Yaghoub-Zadeh, Z., & Shanahan, T. (2001). Phonemic awareness instruction helps children learn to read: Evidence from the National Reading Panel's meta-analysis. *Reading Research Quarterly, 36,* 250–287.

Elbow, P. (2002). The role of publication in the democratization of writing. In C. Weber (Ed.), *Publishing with students: A comprehensive guide (1–8).* Portsmouth, NH: Heinemann.

Elbow, P. (2004). Writing first! *Educational Leadership, 62*(2), 9–13.

Elbro, C., Bornstrom, I., & Petersen, D. K. (1998). Predicting dyslexia from kindergarten: The importance of the distinctiveness of phonological representations of lexical items. *Reading Research Quarterly, 33,* 36–60.

Elkonin, D. B. (1973). Reading in the USSR. In J. Downing (Ed.), *Comparative reading* (pp. 551–579). New York: Macmillan.

Elley, W. B. (1989). Vocabulary acquisition from listening to stories. *Reading Research Quarterly, 24,* 174–187.

Elley, W. B. (1992). *How in the world do students read?* The Netherlands: IEA.

Elliott, S. N. (1999). *A multi-year evaluation of the Responsive Classroom® approach: Its effectiveness and acceptability in promoting social and academic competence. Final report, 1996–1998.* Madison: University of Wisconsin–Madison.

Ellis, E. (2004). *Workshop resources. Think sheet presentations: Comparison frames.* Masterminds Publishing. Available online at http://graphicorganizers.com/resources.html

Emig, J. (1971). *The composing processes of twelfth-graders.* Urbana, IL: National Council of Teachers of English.

Engelmann, S. (1999). *Student-program alignment and teaching to mastery.* Paper presented at the 25th National Direct Instruction Conference, Eugene, OR.

Enz, B. (1989). *The 90 percent success solution.* Paper presented at the International Reading Association annual convention, New Orleans, LA.

Epstein, J. L., & Dauber, S. L. (1991). School programs and teacher practices of parent involvement in inner-city elementary and middle schools. *The Elementary School Journal, 91,* 290–305.

Ericson, L., & Juliebo, M. F. (1998). *The phonological awareness handbook for kindergarten and primary teachers.* Newark, DE: International Reading Association.

Estes, T. H., Mills, D. C., & Barron, R. F. (1969). Three methods of introducing students to a reading-learning task in two content subjects. In H. L. Herber & R. F. Barron (Eds.), *Research in reading in the content areas: First-year report* (pp. 40–48). Syracuse, NY: Syracuse University, Reading and Language Arts Center.

Evans, A. M., Fox, M., Cremaso, L., & McKinnon, L. (2004). Beginning reading: The views of parents and teachers of young children. *Journal of Educational Psychology, 96,* 130–141.

Evans, K. S. (2002). Fifth-grade students' perceptions of how they experience literature discussion groups. *Reading Research Quarterly, 37,* 46–69.

Farr, R. (1991). Current issues in alternative assessment. In C. P. Smith (Ed.), *Alternative assessment of performance in the language arts: Proceedings* (pp. 3–17). Bloomington, IN: ERIC Clearinghouse on Reading and Communication Skills & Phi Delta Kappa.

Farr, R. (2003). Appendix A: Purposeful reading. In W. J. Popham (Ed.), *Crafting curricular aims for instructionally supportive assessment* (pp. 19–29). Available online at http://www.education.unm.edu/NCEO/Presentations/CraftingCurricular.pdf

Farr, R. (2005). *Handout materials: Language—modeling, coached practice and reflection.* Available online at http://www.rogerfarr.com

Farr, R., & Carey, R. F. (1986). *Reading: What can be measured?* Newark, DE: International Reading Association.

Farr, R., & Farr, B. (1990). *Integrated assessment system.* San Antonio, TX: Psychological Corporation.

Farr, R., et al. (2006). *Trophies.* Orlando, FL: Harcourt.

Feitelson, D., Kita, B., & Goldstein, Z. (1986). Effects of reading series stories to first-graders on their comprehension and use of language. *Research in the Teaching of English, 20,* 339–356.

Ferreiro, E. (1986). The interplay between information and assimilation in beginning literacy. In W. H. Teale & E. Sulzby (Eds.), *Emergent literacy* (pp. 15–49). Norwood, NJ: Ablex.

Ferreiro, E., & Teberosky, A. (1982). *Literacy before schooling.* Portsmouth, NH: Heinemann.

Fielding, L. G., Wilson, P. T., & Anderson, R. C. (1986). A new focus on free reading: The role of trade books in reading instruction. In T. E. Raphael (Ed.), *The contexts of school-based literacy* (pp. 149–160). New York: Random House.

Fielding-Barnsley, R. (1997). Explicit instruction of decoding benefits children high in phonemic awareness and alphabet knowledge. *Scientific Studies of Reading, 1*(1), 85–98.

Fields, M. W., Spangler, K., & Lee, D. M. (1991). *Let's begin reading right: Developmentally appropriate beginning literacy* (2nd ed.). New York: Macmillan.

Fillmore, L. W., & Valdez, C. (1986). Teaching bilingual learners. In M. E. Wittrock (Ed.), *Handbook of research on teaching* (pp. 648–685). New York: Macmillan.

Fischbaugh, R. (2004). Using book talks to promote high-level questioning skills. *The Reading Teacher, 58,* 296–298.

Fisher, D., Flood, J., Lapp, D., & Frey, N. (2004). Interactive read-alouds: Is there a common set of implementation practices? *The Reading Teacher, 58,* 8–17.

Fitzgerald, J. (1989). Research on stories: Implications for teachers. In K. P. Muth (Ed.), *Children's comprehension of text: Research into practice* (pp. 2–36). Newark, DE: International Reading Association.

Flexner, S. B., & Hauck, L. C. (Eds.). (1994). *The Random House dictionary of the English language* (2nd ed., rev.). New York: Random House.

Flood, J., Medcaris, A., Hasbrouk, J. E., Paris, S., Hoffman, J., Stahl, S., Lapp, D., Tinejero, J. V., & Wood, K. (Eds.). (2001). *McGraw-Hill reading.* New York: McGraw-Hill.

Flynt, E., & Cooter, R. B., Jr. (2005). Improving middle-grade reading in urban schools: The Memphis comprehension framework. *The Reading Teacher, 58,* 774–780.

Fogg, B. J., Soohoo, C., Danielson, D. R., Marable, L., Stanford, J., & Tauber, E. R. (2003). *How do users evaluate the credibility of web sites? A study with over 2,500 participants.* New York: ACM Press. Available online at http://portal.acm.org/citation.cfm?id=997078.997097

Foorman, B. R., Fletcher, J. M., Francis, D. J., Schatschneider, C., & Mehta, P. (1998). The role of instruction in learning to read: Preventing reading failure in at-risk children. *Journal of Educational Psychology, 90,* 37–55.

Ford, M. P. (1994). *Keys to successful whole group instruction.* Paper presented at the annual conference of the Connecticut Reading Association, Waterbury.

Fountas, I. C. (1999). *Little readers for guided reading teacher's manual.* Boston: Houghton Mifflin.

Fountas, I. C., & Pinnell, G. S. (1996). *Guided reading: Good first teaching for all children.* Portsmouth, NH: Heinemann.

Fountas, I. C., & Pinnell, G. S. (1999a). *Matching books to readers: Using leveled books in guided reading, K–3.* Portsmouth, NH: Heinemann.

Fountas, I. C., & Pinnell, G. S. (Eds.). (1999b). *Voices in word matters.* Portsmouth, NH: Heinemann.

Fountas, I. C., & Pinnell, G. S. (2001a). *Guiding readers and writers, grades 3–6.* Portsmouth, NH: Heinemann.

Fountas, I. C., & Pinnell, G. S. (2001b). *The primary literacy video collection: Guided reading.* Portsmouth, NH: Heinemann.

Fountas, I. C., & Pinnell, G. S. (2001c). *Using guided reading to strengthen students' reading skills at the developing level grades 1–3.* Portsmouth, NH: Heinemann.

Fountas, I. C., & Pinnell, G. S. (2006). *Teaching for comprehending and fluency.* Portsmouth, NH: Heinemann.

Franklin, E. A. (1988). Reading and writing stories: Children creating meaning. *The Reading Teacher, 42,* 184–190.

Fredericks, A. D. (1986). Mental imagery activities to improve comprehension. *The Reading Teacher, 40,* 78–81.

Freeman, Y. S., & Freeman, D. E. (1998). Effective literacy practices for English learners. In C. Weaver (Ed.), *Practicing what we know: Informed reading instruction* (pp. 409–438). Urbana, IL: National Council of Teachers of English.

Fry, E. (1977a). *Elementary reading instruction.* New York: McGraw-Hill.

Fry, E. (1977b). Fry's readability graph: Clarifications, validity, and extension to level 17. *Journal of Reading, 21,* 242–252.

Fuchs, D., & Fuchs, L. S. (2006). Introduction to Response to Intervention: What, why, and how valid is it? *Reading Research Quarterly, 41,* 93–99.

Gage, F. C. (1990). *An introduction to reader-response issues: How to make students into more active readers.* Paper presented at the annual meeting of the Connecticut Reading Conference, Waterbury.

Gallagher, K. (2005). *Deeper reading, comprehending challenging texts, 4–12.* Portland, ME: Stenhouse.

Gallo, D. R. (1985). Teachers as reading researchers. In C. N. Hedley & A. N. Baratta (Eds.), *Contexts of reading* (pp. 185–199). Norwood, NJ: Ablex.

Gambrell, L. B. (1980). Think time: Implications for reading instruction. *The Reading Teacher, 34,* 143–146.

Gambrell, L. B. (2004). Shifts in the conversation: Teacher-led, peer-led and computer-mediated discussions. *The Reading Teacher, 58,* 212–215.

Gambrell, L. B., & Bales, R. J. (1986). Mental imagery and the comprehension monitoring performance of fourth- and fifth-grade poor readers. *Reading Research Quarterly, 21,* 454–464.

Gambrell, L. B., Codling, R. M., & Palmer, B. M. (1996). *Elementary students' motivation to read* (Reading Research Report No. 52). Athens, GA: National Reading Research Center.

Gambrell, L. B., Wilson, R. M., & Gantt, W. N. (1981). Classroom observations of good and poor readers. *Journal of Educational Research, 24,* 400–404.

Gandara, P. (2000). In the aftermath of the storm: English learners in the post-227 era. *Bilingual Research Journal, 24*(1–2), 1–13.

Gans, R. (1940). *Study of critical reading comprehension in intermediate grades: Teachers College contributions to education, No. 811.* New York: Bureau of Publications, Teachers College, Columbia University.

García, G. E. (1990). Response to "A socio-cultural view of diversity and instruction." Paper presented at the annual Conference on Reading Research, Atlanta.

García, G. E., Pearson, P. D., & Jiménez, R. T. (1994). *The at-risk situation: A synthesis of reading research.* Champaign, IL: University of Illinois, Center for the Study of Reading.

Garner, R., Hare, V. C., Alexander, P., Haynes, J., & Winograd, P. (1984). Inducing use of a text lookback strategy among unsuccessful readers. *American Educational Research Journal, 21,* 789–798.

Garner, R., MacCready, G. B., & Wagoner, S. (1984). Readers' acquisition of the components of the text lookback strategy. *Journal of Educational Psychology, 76,* 300–309.

Gaskins, I. W. (1998). *What research suggests are ingredients of a grades 1–6 literacy program for struggling readers.* Paper presented at International Reading Association Convention, Orlando, FL.

Gaskins, I. (2005). *Success with struggling readers: The Benchmark School approach.* New York: Guilford.

Gates, A. I. (1917). Recitation as a factor in memorizing. *Archives of Psychology, 40,* 65–104.

Gensemer, E. (1998). *Teaching strategies for taking charge of task, text, situation, and personal characteristics.* Paper presented at International Reading Association Convention, Orlando, FL.

Gibson, E. J., Gibson, J. J., Pick, A. D., & Osser, H. (1962). A developmental study of the discrimination of letter-like forms. *Journal of Comparative and Physiological Psychology, 55,* 897–906.

Gibson, E. J., & Levin, H. (1974). *The psychology of reading.* Cambridge, MA: MIT Press.

Gibson, E. J., Osser, H., & Pick, A. (1963). A study in the development of grapheme-phoneme correspondences. *Journal of Verbal Learning and Verbal Behavior, 2,* 142–146.

Gipe, J. P. (1980). Use of a relevant context helps kids learn. *The Reading Teacher, 33,* 398–402.

Glass, G. G. (1976). *Glass analysis for decoding only: Teacher's guide.* Garden City, NY: Easier to Learn.

Glenberg, A. M., Gutierrez, T., Levin, J. R., Japuntich, S., & Kaschak, M. P. (2004). Activity and imagined activity can enhance young children's reading comprehension. *Journal of Educational Psychology, 96,* 424–436.

Glynn, S. M. (1994). *Teaching science with analogies: A strategy for teachers and textbook authors* (Reading Research Report No. 15). Athens, GA: National Reading Research Center.

Gold, J., & Fleisher, L. S. (1986). Comprehension breakdown with inductively organized text: Differences between average and disabled readers. *Remedial and Special Education, 7,* 26–32.

Goldenberg, C. (1994). Promoting early literacy development among Spanish-speaking children: Lessons from two studies. In E. H. Hiebert & B. M. Taylor (Eds.), *Getting reading right from the start* (pp. 171–200). Boston: Allyn & Bacon.

Good, R. H., III, Kaminski, R. A., Smith, S. B., Simmons, D. C., Kame'enui, E., & Wallin, J. (2003). Reviewing outcomes: Using DIBELS to evaluate a school's core curriculum and system of additional intervention in kindergarten. In S. R. Vaughn & K. L. Briggs (Eds.), *Reading in the classroom: Systems for the observation of teaching and learning.* Baltimore: Brookes.

Goodman, K. S. (1974). Miscue analysis: Theory and reality in reading. In J. E. Merritt (Ed.), *New horizons in reading* (pp. 15–26). Newark, DE: International Reading Association.

Goodman, K. S. (1986). *What's whole in whole language?* Portsmouth, NH: Heinemann.

Goodman, K. S. (1994a). Forward: Lots of changes, but little gained. In P. Shannon & K. Goodman (Eds.), *Basal readers: A second look* (pp. xiii–xxvii). Katonah, NY: Richard C. Owen.

Goodman, K. S. (1994b). Reading, writing, and written texts: A transactional sociopsycholinguistic view. In R. B. Ruddell, M. R. Ruddell, & H. Singer (Eds.), *Theoretical models and processes of reading* (4th ed.) (pp. 1093–1130). Newark, DE: International Reading Association.

Goodman, K. S., & Goodman, Y. M. (1978). *Reading of American children whose language is a stable rural dialect of English or a language other than English.* Detroit: Wayne State University Press. (ERIC Document Reproduction Service No. ED 182 465)

Goodman, Y. M. (1985). Kidwatching: Observing children in the classroom. In A. Jagger & M. T. Smith-Burke (Eds.), *Observing the language learner* (pp. 9–18). Newark, DE: International Reading Association.

Gordon, C. J. (1985). Modeling inference awareness across the curriculum. *Journal of Reading, 28,* 444–447.

Gordon, C. J. (1989). Teaching narrative text structure: A process approach to reading and writing. In K. P. Muth (Ed.), *Children's comprehension of text: Research into practice* (pp. 79–102). Newark, DE: International Reading Association.

Gormley, W. T., Gayer, T., Phillips, D., & Dawson, B. (2005). The effects of universal pre-K cognitive development. *Developmental Psychology, 41,* 872–884.

Goswami, U. (2001). Early phonological development and acquisition of literacy. In S. B. Neuman & D. K. Dickinson (Eds.), *Handbook of early literacy research* (pp. 111–125). New York: Guilford.

Gough, P. B., & Hillinger, M. L. (1980). Learning to read: An unnatural act. *Bulletin of the Orton Society, 30,* 179–196.

Gough, P. B., Juel, C., & Griffith, P. L. (1992). Reading, spelling, and the orthographic cipher. In P. B. Gough, L. C. Ehri, & R. Treiman (Eds.), *Reading acquisition* (pp. 35–48). Hillsdale, NJ: Erlbaum.

Gough, P. B., Larson, K. C., & Yopp, H. (2001). *The structure of phonemic awareness.* Unpublished paper. Austin: University of Texas.

Graesser, A., Golding, J. M., & Long, D. L. (1991). Narrative representation and comprehension. In R. Barr, M. L. Kamil, P. Mosenthal, & P. D. Pearson (Eds.), *Handbook of reading research* (Vol. II, pp. 171–205). New York: Longman.

Graesser, A. C., & Bertus, E. L. (1998). The construction of causal inferences while reading expository texts on science and technology. *Scientific Studies of Reading, 2*(3), 247–269.

Graves, D. H. (1975). Examination of the writing processes of seven-year-old children. *Research in the Teaching of English, 9,* 221–241.

Graves, D. H. (1983). *Writing: Teachers and children at work.* Exeter, NH: Heinemann.

Graves, D. H. (1985). All children can write. *Focus, 1,* 5–10.

References

580

References

Graves, M. F. (1987). Roles of instruction in fostering vocabulary development. In M. G. McKeown & M. E. Curtis (Eds.), *The nature of vocabulary acquisition* (pp. 165–184). Hillsdale, NJ: Erlbaum.

Graves, M. F., & Dykstra, R. (1997). Contextualizing the first-grade studies: What is the best way to teach children to read? *Reading Research Quarterly, 32,* 342–344.

Graves, M. F., & Hammond, H. K. (1980). A validated procedure for teaching prefixes and its effect on students' ability to assign meaning to novel words. In M. Kamil & A. Moe (Eds.), *Perspectives of reading research and instruction* (pp. 184–188). Washington, DC: National Reading Conference.

Graves, M. F., Juel, C., & Graves, B. B. (2001). *Teaching reading in the 21st century* (2nd ed.). Boston: Allyn & Bacon.

Gray, W. S., & Holmes, E. (1938). *The development of meaning vocabulary in reading.* Chicago: University of Chicago.

Great Books Foundation. (1999). *An introduction to shared inquiry: A handbook for Junior Great Books leaders* (4th ed.). Chicago: Author.

Great Books Foundation. (2006). *Junior Great Books.* Chicago: Author.

Greenlaw, M. J. (1983). Reading interest research and children's choices. In N. Roser & M. Frith (Eds.), *Children's choices: Teaching with books children like* (pp. 90–92). Newark, DE: International Reading Association.

Griffith, P. L., & Olson, M. W. (1992). Phonemic awareness helps beginning readers break the code. *The Reading Teacher, 45,* 516–523.

Guastello, E., & Lenz, C. (2005). Student accountability: Guided reading kidstations. *The Reading Teacher, 59,* 144–156.

Gunning, T. (1975). *A comparison of word attack skills derived from a phonological analysis of frequently used words drawn from a juvenile corpus and an adult corpus.* Unpublished doctoral dissertation, Temple University, Philadelphia.

Gunning, T. (1982). Wrong level test: Wrong information. *The Reading Teacher, 35,* 902–905.

Gunning, T. (1994). *Word building book D.* New York: Phoenix Learning Systems.

Gunning, T. (1995). Word building: A strategic approach to the teaching of phonics. *The Reading Teacher, 48,* 484–488.

Gunning, T. (1996). *Choosing and using books for beginning readers.* Paper presented at the annual meeting of the Connecticut Reading Conference, Waterbury.

Gunning, T. (1998a). *Assessing and correcting reading and writing difficulties.* Boston: Allyn & Bacon.

Gunning, T. (1998b). *Best books for beginning readers.* Boston: Allyn & Bacon.

Gunning, T. (2000a). *Assessing the difficulty level of material in the primary grades: A study in progress.* Paper presented at the annual meeting of the National Reading Conference, Scottsdale, AZ.

Gunning, T. (2000b). *Best books for building literacy for elementary school children.* Boston: Allyn & Bacon.

Gunning, T. (2000c). *Phonological awareness and primary phonics.* Boston: Allyn & Bacon.

Gunning, T. (2001). *An analysis of second graders' attempts to read multisyllabic words.* Paper presented at the annual meeting of the National Reading Conference, San Antonio, TX.

Gunning, T. (2002). *Assessing and correcting reading and writing difficulties* (2nd ed.). Boston: Allyn & Bacon.

Gunning, T. (2003). *Building literacy in the content areas.* Boston: Allyn & Bacon.

Gunning, T. (2005, November). *Assessing the comprehension processes of good decoding but poor comprehending students.* Paper presented at the National Reading Conference, Miami, FL.

Gunning, T. (2006). *Closing the literacy gap.* Boston: Allyn & Bacon.

Gunning, T. (2007). *Reading, reasoning, responding, and reflecting: Developing higher-level literacy.* Boston: Allyn & Bacon.

Guthrie, J. T. (1980). Research views: Time in reading programs. *The Reading Teacher, 33,* 500–502.

Guthrie, J. T. (2002). Preparing students for high-stakes test taking in reading. In A. E. Farstrup & S. J. Samuels (Eds.), *What research has to say about reading instruction* (pp. 370–391). Newark, DE: International Reading Association.

Guthrie, J. T. (2004). Teaching for literacy engagement. *Journal of Literacy Research, 36,* 1–28.

Guthrie, J. T., & McCann, A. D. (1997). Characteristics of classrooms that provide motivations and strategies for learning. In J. Guthrie & A. Wigfield (Eds.), *Reading engagement: Motivating readers through integrated instruction* (pp. 128–148). Newark, DE: International Reading Association.

Guthrie, J. T., & Wigfield, A. (1997). Reading engagement: A rationale for theory and teaching. In J. Guthrie & A. Wigfield (Eds.), *Motivating readers through integrated instruction* (pp. 1–12). Newark, DE: International Reading Association.

Gutkin, R. J. (1990). Sustained reading. *Language Arts, 67,* 490–492.

Guzman-Johannessen, G. (2006, May). *Stages of second-language acquisition.* Paper presented at the International Reading Association conference, Chicago.

Hackett, J. K., Moyer, R. H., & Adams, D. K. (1989). *Merrill science 5.* Columbus, OH: Merrill.

Hagerty, P., Hiebert, E., & Owens, M. (1989). Students' comprehension, writing, and perceptions in two approaches to literacy instruction. In S. McCormick & J. Zutell (Eds.), *38th yearbook of the National Reading Conference* (pp. 453–459). Chicago: National Reading Conference.

Hague, S. A. (1989). Awareness of text structure: The question of transfer from L1 and L2. In S. McCormick & J. Zutell (Eds.), *Cognitive and social perspectives for literacy research and instruction* (pp. 55–64). Chicago: National Reading Conference.

Hall, D., & Ken, S. (2006). *Primary progress, secondary challenge: A state-by-state look at student achievement patterns.* Education Trust. Available online at http://www2.edtrust.org/ EdTrust/Product+Catalog/recentreports

Halstead, J. W. (1988). *Guiding gifted readers.* Columbus, OH: Ohio Psychology.

Hammond, D. W. (2001). *The essential nature of teacher talk and its effect on students' engagement with expository text.* Paper presented at the annual meeting of the International Reading Association, New Orleans, LA.

Hansen, J. (1981). The effects of inference training and practice on young children's reading comprehension. *Reading Research Quarterly, 16,* 391–417.

Hansen, J., & Pearson, P. D. (1980). *The effects of inference training and practice on young children's comprehension* (Technical Report No. 166). Urbana: University of Illinois, Center for the Study of Reading.

Hansen, J., & Pearson, P. D. (1982). *Improving the inferential comprehension of good and poor fourth-grade readers* (Report No. CSR-TR-235). Urbana: University of Illinois, Center for the Study of Reading. (ERIC Document Reproduction No. ED 215-312)

Hansen-Krening, N., Aoki, E. M., & Mizokawa, D. T. (Eds.). (2003). *Kaleidoscope: A multicultural booklist for grades K–8* (4th ed.). Urbana, IL: National Council of Teachers of English.

Harcourt Educational Measurement (2000). *Some things parents should know about testing: A series of questions and answers.* Available online at http://www.hbem.com/library/parents.htm

Hardman, M. L., Drew, C. J., Egan, M.W., & Wolf, B. (1993). *Human exceptionality* (4th ed.). Boston: Allyn & Bacon.

Hare, V. C., & Borchardt, K. M. (1984). Direct instruction of summarization skills. *Reading Research Quarterly, 20,* 62–78.

Harmon, J. M. (1998). Constructing word meanings: Strategies and perceptions of four middle school learners. *Journal of Literacy Research, 30,* 561–599.

Harper, L. (1997). The writer's toolbox: Five tools for active revision instruction. *Language Arts, 74,* 193–200.

Harris, A. J., & Jacobson, M. D. (1982). *Basic reading vocabularies*. New York: Macmillan.

Harris, A. J., & Sipay, E. R. (1990). *How to increase reading ability* (9th ed.). New York: Longman.

Harris, T. L., & Hodges, R. E. (1995). *The literacy dictionary, the vocabulary of reading and writing*. Newark, DE: International Reading Association.

Harste, J. C., Short, K. G., & Burke, C. (1988). *Creating classrooms for authors: The reading-writing connection*. Portsmouth, NH: Heinemann.

Harste, J. C., Woodward, V. A., & Burke, C. L. (1984). *Language stories and literacy lessons*. Portsmouth, NH: Heinemann.

Hart, B., & Risley, T. (1995). *Meaningful differences in the everyday experience of young American children*. Baltimore: Brookes.

Hartford Public Schools. (1983). *The writing handbook*. Hartford, CT: Author.

Hartman, D. K. (1994). The intertextual links of readers using multiple passages: A postmodern semiotic/cognitive view of meaning making. In R. B. Ruddell, M. R. Ruddell, & H. Singer (Eds.), *Theoretical models and processes of reading* (4th ed.) (pp. 616–636). Newark, DE: International Reading Association.

Hasbrouck, J., & Tindal, G. A. (2006). Oral reading fluency norms: A valuable assessment tool for reading teachers. *The Reading Teacher, 59*, 636–644.

Hayes, D. A., & Tierney, R. J. (1982). Developing readers' knowledge through analogy. *Reading Research Quarterly, 17*, 256–280.

Head, M. H., & Readence, J. E. (1986). Anticipation guides: Meaning through prediction. In E. K. Dishner, T. W. Bean, J. E. Readence, & D. W. Moore (Eds.), *Reading in the content areas* (2nd ed.) (pp. 229–234). Dubuque, IA: Kendall/Hunt.

Heath, S. B. (1991). The sense of being literate: Historical and cross-cultural features. In R. Barr, M. L. Kamil, P. Mosenthal, & P. D. Pearson (Eds.), *Handbook of reading research*, (Vol. II, pp. 3–25). New York: Longman.

Heimlich, J. E., & Pittelman, S. D. (1986). *Semantic mapping: Classroom applications*. Newark, DE: International Reading Association.

Helper, S. (1989). A literature program: Getting it together, keeping it going. In J. Hickman & B. Culliman (Eds.), *Children's literature in the classroom: Weaving* Charlotte's Web (pp. 209–220). Needham Heights, MA: Christopher-Gordon.

Henderson, E. H. (1990). *Teaching spelling*. Boston: Houghton Mifflin.

Henk, W. A., Marinak, B. A., Moore, J. C., & Mallette, M. H. (2003). The writing observation framework: A guide for refining and validating writing instruction. *The Reading Teacher, 57*, 322–333.

Henry, M. K. (1990). Reading instruction based on word structure and origin. In P. G. Aaron & R. M. Joshi (Eds.), *Reading and writing disorders in different orthographic systems* (pp. 25–49). Dordrecht, The Netherlands: Kluwer Academic.

Herman, P. A., Anderson, R. C., Pearson, P. D., & Nagy, W. E. (1987). Incidental acquisition of word meanings from expositions with varied text features. *Reading Research Quarterly, 22*, 263–284.

Hidi, S., & Anderson, V. (1986). Producing written summaries: Task demands, cognitive operations, and implications for instruction. *Review of Educational Research, 56*, 473–493.

Hiebert, E. H. (1983). An examination of ability grouping for reading instruction. *Reading Research Quarterly, 18*, 231–255.

Hiebert, E. H. (1994). A small-group literacy intervention with Chapter 1 students. In E. H. Hiebert & B. M. Taylor (Eds.), *Getting reading right from the start* (pp. 85–106). Boston: Allyn & Bacon.

Hiebert, E. H. (1999). Text matters in learning to read. *The Reading Teacher, 52*, 552–566.

Hiebert, E. H., Martin, L. A., & Menon, S. (2005). Are there alternatives in reading textbooks? An examination of three beginning reading programs. *Reading and Writing Quarterly, 21*, 7–32.

Hiebert, E. H., Pearson, P. D., Taylor, B. M., Richardson, V., & Paris, S. G. (1998). *Every child a reader*. Ann Arbor: University of Michigan School of Education, Center for the Improvement of Early Reading Achievement.

Hiebert, E. H., & Taylor, B. M. (2000). Beginning reading instruction: Research on early interventions. In M. L. Kamil, P. B. Mosenthal, P. D. Pearson, & R. Barr (Eds.), *Handbook of reading research* (Vol. III, pp. 455–482). Mahwah, NJ: Erlbaum.

Hiebert, E. H., Valencia, S. W., & Afflerbach, P. P. (1994). Definitions and perspectives. In S. W. Valencia, E. H. Hiebert, & P. P. Afflerbach (Eds.), *Authentic reading assessment: Practices and possibilities* (pp. 6–25). Newark, DE: International Reading Association.

Hildreth, G. (1936). Developmental sequences in name writing. *Child Development, 7*, 291–303.

Hildreth, G. (1950). *Readiness for school beginners*. New York: World.

Hirsch, E. D. (1987). *Cultural literacy: What every American needs to know*. Boston: Houghton Mifflin.

Hoffman, J., Roser, N., & Battle, J. (1993). Reading aloud in classrooms: From the modal to a model. *The Reading Teacher, 46*, 496–503.

Hoffman, J. V. (1991). Teacher and school effects in learning to read. In R. Barr, M. L. Kamil, P. Mosenthal, & P. D. Pearson (Eds.), *Handbook of reading research* (Vol. II, pp. 911–950). New York: Longman.

Hoffman, J. V., Sailors, M., & Patterson, E. U. (2003*). Decodable texts for beginning reading instruction: The year 2000 basals* (CIERA Report #1-016). Available online at http://www .ciera.org/library/reports/inquiry-1/1-016/1-016fm.html

Holdaway, D. (1979). *The foundations of literacy*. New York: Ashton Scholastic.

Homa, L. L. (2000). *The elementary school library collection: A guide to books and other media, phases 1-2-3* (22nd ed.). Williamsport, PA: Brodart.

Hoonan, B. (2006). *Using literature and providing access to books*. Paper presented at the International Reading Association Conference, Chicago.

Hornsby, P., Sukarna, P., & Parry, J. (1986). *Read on: A conference approach to reading*. Portsmouth, NH: Heinemann.

Hulit, L. M., & Howard, M. R. (2002). *Born to talk*. Boston: Allyn & Bacon.

Hyerle, D. (2001). Visual tools for mapping minds. In A. L. Costa (Ed.), *Developing minds: A resource book for teaching thinking* (3rd ed.) (pp. 401–407). Alexandria, VA: Association for Supervision and Curriculum Development.

Hyman, R. T. (1978). *Strategic questioning*. Englewood Cliffs, NJ: Prentice-Hall.

Hyson, M., Marion, C., & Hyson, M. C. (2003). *Emotional development of young children. Building an emotion-centered curriculum*. New York: Teachers College Press.

Idol, L., & Croll, V. (1985). Story mapping training as a means of improving reading comprehension. *Learning Disability Quarterly, 10*, 214–229.

Individuals with Disabilities Act Amendments of 1997. 20 U.S.C. 1400 *et seq.*

International Reading Association. (1988). *New directions in reading instruction*. Newark, DE: Author.

International Reading Association. (1998a). *Multiple methods of beginning reading instruction*. Newark, DE: Author. Available online at http://www.reading.org/positions/begin_reading.html

International Reading Association. (1998b). *Social promotion and grade retention*. Newark, DE: Author. Available online at http://www.reading.org/positions/social_promotion.html

International Reading Association. (1999a). *High stakes assessments in reading: A position statement of the International Reading Association.* Newark, DE: Author.

International Reading Association. (1999b). *Providing books and other print materials for classroom and school libraries.* Newark, DE: Author. Available online at http://www.reading.org/positions/media_center.html

International Reading Association. (1999c). *The role of phonics in reading instruction: A position statement of the International Reading Association.* Newark, DE: Author.

International Reading Association. (2001a). *Integrating literacy and technology in the curriculum.* Newark, DE: Author. Available online at http://www.reading.org/positions/technology.html

International Reading Association. (2001b). *Second-language literacy instruction.* Newark: DE: Author. Available online at http://www.reading.org/positions/second_language.html

International Reading Association. (2002a). *Family-school partnerships: Essential elements of reading instruction in the United States.* Newark, DE: Author. Available online at http://www.reading.org/positions/family-school.html

International Reading Association. (2002b). *What is evidence-based reading? A position statement of the International Reading Association.* Newark, DE: Author. Available online at http://www.reading.org/resources/issues/positions_evidence_based.html

International Reading Association & National Association for the Education of Young Children. (1998). Learning to read and write: Developmentally appropriate practices for young children. *The Reading Teacher, 52,* 193–216.

Invernizzi, M., & Hayes, L. (2004). Developmental-spelling research: A systematic imperative. *Reading Research Quarterly, 39,* 216–228.

Invernizzi, M., Meier, J. D., Swank, L., & Juel, C. (2001). *PALS-K, Phonological awareness literacy screening, 2000–2001.* Charlottesville: University of Virginia.

Irwin, P. A., & Mitchell, J. N. (1983). A procedure for assessing the richness of retellings. *Journal of Reading, 26,* 391–396.

Jenkins, J. R., Matlock, B., & Slocum, T. A. (1989). Approaches to vocabulary instruction. *Reading Research Quarterly, 24,* 215–235.

Jett-Simpson, M. (Ed.) (1990). *Toward an ecological assessment of reading progress.* Schofield: Wisconsin State Reading Association.

Jiganti, M. A., & Tindall, M. A. (1986). An interactive approach to teaching vocabulary. *The Reading Teacher, 39,* 444–448.

Jiménez, R. T. (1997). The strategic reading abilities and potential of five low-literacy Latina/o readers in middle school. *Reading Research Quarterly, 32,* 224–243.

Jiménez, R. T. (2004). More equitable literacy assessment for Latino students. *The Reading Teacher, 57,* 576–578.

Johns, J. L. (1997). *Basic reading inventory* (7th ed.). Dubuque, IA: Kendall/Hunt.

Johnson, D. D., Moe, A. J., & Baumann, J. F. (1983). *The Ginn word book for teachers: A basic lexicon.* Lexington, MA: Ginn.

Johnson, D. D., & Pearson, P. D. (1984). *Teaching reading vocabulary* (2nd ed.). New York: Holt.

Johnson, M. S., & Kress, R. A. (1965). *Developing basic thinking abilities.* Unpublished manuscript, Temple University, Philadelphia.

Johnson, M. S., Kress, R. A., & Pikulski, J. J. (1987). *Informal reading inventories* (2nd ed.). Newark, DE: International Reading Association.

Johnson, N. L. (1995). *The effect of portfolio design on student attitudes toward writing.* Unpublished master's thesis, San Diego State University, San Diego, CA.

Johnston, F. R. (1999). The timing and teaching of word families. *The Reading Teacher, 53,* 64–75.

Johnston, F. R. (2001). The utility of phonic generalizations: Let's take another look at Clymer's conclusions. *The Reading Teacher, 55,* 132–150.

Johnston, P. H. (2000). *Running records, a self-tutoring guide.* Portland, ME: Stenhouse.

Johnston, P. H., & Rogers, R. (2001). Early literacy development: The case for "informed assessment." In S. B. Neuman & D. K. Dickinson (Eds.), *Handbook of early literacy research* (pp. 377–389). New York: Guilford.

Joint Task Force on Assessment. (1994). *Standards for the assessment of reading and writing.* Newark, DE & Urbana, IL: International Reading Association & National Council of Teachers of English.

Jones, B. F., Palincsar, A. S., Ogle, D. S., &. Carr, E. G. (Eds.). (1986). *Strategic teaching and learning: Cognitive instruction in the content areas* (pp. 73–91). Alexandria, VA: Association for Supervision and Curriculum Development.

Jongsma, E. (1980). *Cloze instruction research: A second look.* Newark, DE: International Reading Association.

Juel, C. (1994). *Learning to read and write in one elementary school.* New York: Springer-Verlag.

Juel, C., & Minden-Cupp, C. (2000). Learning to read words: Linguistic units and instructional strategies. *Reading Research Quarterly, 35,* 458–492.

Juel, C., & Roper-Schneider, D. (1985). The influence of basal readers on first-grade reading. *Reading Research Quarterly, 20,* 134–152.

Jurek, D. (1995). *Teaching young children.* Torrance, CA: Good Apple.

Kaissen, J. (1987). SSR/Booktime: Kindergarten and first grade sustained silent reading. *The Reading Teacher, 40,* 532–536.

Kame'enui, E. J., Dixon, R. C., & Carnine, D. W. (1987). Issues in the design of vocabulary instruction. In M. E. McKeown & M. E. Curtis (Eds.), *The nature of vocabulary instruction* (pp. 129–145). Hillsdale, NJ: Erlbaum.

Kamhi, A. G., & Catts, H. W. (1999). Language and reading: Convergences and divergences. In H. W. Catts and A. G. Kamhi (Eds.), *Language and reading disabilities* (pp. 1–24). Boston: Allyn & Bacon.

Kamil, M. L., & Bernhardt, E. B. (2001). Reading instruction for English language learners. In M. F. Graves, C. Juel, & B. Graves, *Teaching reading in the 21st century* (pp. 460–503). Boston: Allyn & Bacon.

Karweit, N. (1985). Should we lengthen the school term? *Educational Researcher, 14,* 9–14.

Kawakami-Arakaki, A., Oshiro, M., & Farran, D. (1989). Research to practice: Integrating reading and writing in a kindergarten curriculum. In J. Mason (Ed.), *Reading and writing connections* (pp. 199–218). Boston: Allyn & Bacon.

Keene, E. O., & Zimmermann, S. (1997). *Mosaic of thought: Teaching reading comprehension in a reader's workshop.* Portsmouth, NH: Heinemann.

Kelly, P. R., Gomez-Valdez, C., Neal, J., & Klein, A. F. (1995, May). *Progress of first and second language learners in an early intervention program.* Paper presented at the annual meeting of the American Education Research Association, San Francisco. (ERIC Document Reproduction Service No. ED 394 296)

Kibby, M. W. (1989). Teaching sight vocabulary with and without context before silent reading: A field test of the "focus of attention" hypothesis. *Journal of Reading Behavior, 21,* 261–278.

Kibby, M. W., Rapaport, W. J., & Wieland, K. M. (2004). *Contextual vocabulary acquisition: From algorithm to curriculum.* Paper presented at the International Reading Association Convention, Reno, NV. Available online at http://www.cse.buffalo.edu/~rapaport/CVA/cvaslides.html

Kibby, M. W., Rapaport, W. J., Wieland, K. M., & Dechert, D. A. (2006). *CSI: Contextual semantic investigation for word meaning*. Available online at http://www.cse.buffalo.edu/~rapaport/CVA/CSI

Kimmel, S., & MacGinitie, W. H. (1984). Identifying children who use a perseverative text processing strategy. *Reading Research Quarterly, 19,* 162–172.

King-Sears, M. E., & Cummings, C. S. (1996). Inclusive practices of classroom teachers. *Remedial and Special Education, 17,* 217–225.

Klesius, J. P., & Griffith, P. L. (1996). Interactive storybook reading for at-risk learners. *The Reading Teacher, 49,* 552–560.

Kletzien, S. B. (1991). Strategy use by good and poor comprehenders reading expository text of differing levels. *Reading Research Quarterly, 26,* 67–86.

Knox, C. M. (2002). *Accelerated literacy for English language learners (ELLs): A field-tested, research-based model of training and learning.* Paper presented at the annual convention of the International Reading Association, San Francisco.

Koskinen, P. S., Gambrell, L. B., Kapinus, B. A., & Heathington, B. S. (1988). Retelling: A strategy for enhancing students' reading comprehension. *The Reading Teacher, 41,* 892–896.

Krashen, S. (1991). Sheltered subject matter teaching. *Cross Currents, 18,* 183–189.

Krashen, S. (1993). *The power of reading: Insights from the research.* Englewood, CO: Libraries Unlimited.

Krashen, S. (1997–1998). Bridging inequity with books. *Educational Leadership, 55*(4), 18–21.

Kucan, L., & Beck, I. L. (1996). Thinking aloud and reading comprehension research: Inquiry, instruction, and social interaction. *Review of Educational Research, 67,* 271–299.

Kucan, L., & Beck, I. L. (2003). Inviting students to talk about expository texts: A comparison of two discourse environments and their effects on comprehension. *Reading Research and Instruction, 42,* 1–29.

Kuhn, M. (2004). Helping students become accurate, expressive readers: Fluency instruction for small groups. *The Reading Teacher, 58,* 338–344.

Kuhn, M. R., & Stahl, S. A. (2000). Fluency: A review of developmental and remedial practices. *Journal of Educational Psychology, 95,* 3–21.

Kuhn, M. R., & Stahl, S. A. (2003). Fluency: A review of developmental and remedial practices. *Journal of Educational Psychology, 95,* 3–21.

Kulik, J. A. (1992). *An analysis of the research on ability grouping: Historical and contemporary perspectives.* Storrs: The National Research Center on the Gifted and Talented, University of Connecticut. (ERIC Document Reproduction Service No. ED350 777)

Laberge, D., & Samuels, S. J. (1974). Toward a theory of automatic information processing in reading. *Cognitive Psychology, 6,* 293–323.

Lake, J. H. (1973). *The influence of wait time on the verbal dimensions of student inquiry behavior.* Dissertations Abstracts International, 34, 6476A. (University Microfilms No. 74-08866)

Lalas, J., Solomon, M., & Johannessen, G. (2006). *Making adaptations in content area reading and writing: A gateway to academic language development for English language learners.* Paper presented at the International Reading Association convention, Chicago.

Lane, B. (1993). *After the end: Teaching and learning creative revision.* Portsmouth, NH: Heinemann.

Lane, B. (1998). *The reviser's toolbox.* Shoreham, VT: Discover Writing Press.

Langer, J. A. (1986). Reading, writing, and understanding: An analysis of the construction of meaning. *Written Communication, 3,* 219–266.

Langer, J. A. (1990). Understanding literature. *Language Arts, 67*(8), 817–823.

Langer, J. A., & Applebee, A. N. (1987). *How writing shapes thinking.* Urbana, IL: National Council of Teachers of English.

Langer, J. A., & Applebee, A. N. (2006, April). *The partnership for literacy: A study of professional development, instructional change and student growth.* Paper presented at the Reading Research Conference, Chicago.

Langer, J. A., Applebee, A. N., Mullis, I. V. S., & Foertsch, M. A. (1990). *Learning to read in our nation's schools: Instruction and achievement in 1988 at grades 4, 8, and 12.* Princeton, NJ: Educational Testing Service.

Language Enrichment Activities Program. (2004). *Teacher training overview.* Available online at http://www.leapsandbounds.org/trainingoverview.htm

Law, B., & Eckes, M. (2002). *The more than just surviving handbook: ESL for every classroom teacher.* Winnipeg, Canada: Portage & Main.

Learning Media. (1991). *Dancing with the pen: The learner as writer.* Wellington, New Zealand: Ministry of Education.

Learning Sciences Institute. (2003). *Take me to your readers: Project description.* Nashville, TN: Vanderbilt University. Available online at http://www.takemetoyourreaders.org/project_description.htm

Lee, J. (2006). *Tracking achievement gaps and assessing the impact of NCLB on the gaps: An in-depth look into national and state reading and math outcome trends.* Cambridge, MA: Civil Rights Project at Harvard University, Harvard Education Publishing Group. Available online at http://www.civilrightsproject.harvard.edu

Lehr, S., & Thompson, D. L. (2000). The dynamic nature of response: Children reading and responding to *Maniac Magee* and "The Friendship." *The Reading Teacher, 53,* 480–493.

Lensmire, T. (1994). *When children write: Critical re-visions of the writing workshop.* New York: Teachers College Press.

Leseman, P. P. M., & deJong, P. F. (1998). Home literacy: Opportunity, instruction, cooperation and social-emotional quality predicting early reading achievement. *Reading Research Quarterly, 33,* 294–318.

Leslie, L., & Caldwell, J. (2006). *Qualitative reading inventory—4.* Boston: Allyn & Bacon/Longman.

Leu, D. J., Jr. (2006). *The new literacies.* Paper presented at the International Reading Association's Reading Research Conference, Chicago.

Leung, C. B. (1992). Effects of word-related variables on vocabulary growth through repeated read-aloud events. In C. K. Kinzer & D. J. Leu (Eds.), *Literacy research, theory, and practice: Views from many perspectives* (pp. 491–498). Chicago: National Reading Conference.

Levin, M. (2002). Putting students in charge. In C. Weber (Ed.), *Publishing with students: A comprehensive guide* (pp. 31–37). Portsmouth, NH: Heinemann.

Liberman, I. Y., & Shankweiler, D. (1991). Phonology and beginning reading: A tutorial. In L. Rieben & C. A. Perfetti (Eds.), *Learning to read: Basic research and its implications* (pp. 3–18). Hillsdale, NJ: Erlbaum.

Lima, C. W., & Lima, J. A. (2006). *A to zoo subject access to children's picture books* (7th ed.). New Providence, NJ: Bowker.

Lindamood, P., & Lindamood, P. (1998). *The Lindamood phoneme sequencing program for reading, spelling, and speech: LIPS.* Austin, TX: Pro-Ed.

Linden, M., & Wittrock, M. C. (1981). The teaching of reading comprehension according to the model of generative learning. *Reading Research Quarterly, 17,* 44–57.

Linebarger, D. L. (2000). *Summative evaluation of* Between the Lions: *A final report to the WGBH Educational Foundation.* Kansas City: University of Kansas. Available online at http://pbskids.org/lions/about/report/BTL_Report

Linn, R. L., Baker, E. L., & Betebenner, D. W. (2002). *Accountability systems: Implications of requirements of the No*

Child Left Behind Act of 2001 (CSE Technical Report 567). Los Angeles: UCLA, National Center for Research on Evaluation. Available online at http://www.cse.ucla.edu/CRESST/pages/reports.htm

Lipson, M. Y. (1984). Some unexpected issues in prior knowledge and comprehension. *The Reading Teacher, 37,* 760–764.

Lipson, M. Y., Valencia, S. W., Wixson, K. K., & Peters, C. W. (1993). Integration and thematic teaching and learning. *Language Arts, 70,* 252–263.

Lipson, M. Y., & Wixson, K. K. (1997). *Assessment and instruction of reading disability: An interactive approach* (2nd ed.). New York: HarperCollins.

Long, T. W., & Gove, M. K. (2003–2004). How engagement strategies and literature circles promote critical response in a fourth-grade, urban classroom. *The Reading Teacher, 57,* 350–361.

Lubliner, S., & Smetana, L. (2005). The effects of comprehensive vocabulary instruction on Title 1 students' metacognitive word-learning skills and reading comprehension. *Journal of Literacy Research, 37,* 163–199.

Lyman, F. (1981). The responsive classroom discussion. In A. S. Anderson (Ed.), *Mainstreaming digest* (pp. 109–113). College Park: University of Maryland, College of Education.

Lyon, G. R. (2003). *The critical need for evidence-based comprehensive and effective early childhood programs.* Available online at http://olpa.od.nih.gov/hearings/108/session1/testimonies/headstart.asp

MacDonald, M. R., & Sturm, B. W. (2001). *The storyteller's source book: A subject, title, and motif index to folklore collections for children 1983–1999.* New York: Thomson Gale.

Maclean, M., Bryant, P., & Bradley, L. (1987). Rhymes, nursery rhymes, and reading in early childhood. *Merrill Palmer Quarterly, 33,* 255–281.

Maimon, E. P., & Nodine, B. F. (1979). Measuring syntactic growth: Errors and expectations in sentence-combining practice with college freshmen. *Research in the Teaching of English, 12,* 233–244.

Maldonado-Colon, E. (2003, September 19). *Literacy for English language learners. Where are we?* Paper presented at the STAR Conference, New Haven, CT.

Maloch, B. (2004). On the road to literature discussion groups: Teacher scaffolding during preparatory experiences. *Reading Research and Instruction, 44,* 1–20.

Mansell, J., Evans, M. A., & Hamilton-Hulak, L. (2005). Developmental changes in parents' use of miscue feedback during shared book reading. *Reading Research Quarterly, 40,* 294–317.

Many, J. E. (1990). The effect of reader stance on students' personal understanding of literature. In J. Zutell & S. McCormick (Eds.), *Literacy theory and research: Analyses from multiple paradigms* (39th yearbook of the National Reading Conference) (pp. 51–63). Chicago: National Reading Conference.

Many, J. E. (1991). The effects of stance and age level on children's literary responses. *Journal of Reading Behavior, 21,* 61–85.

Many, J., Fyfe, R., Lewis, G., & Mitchell, E. (1996). Traversing the topical landscape: Exploring students' self-directed reading-writing-research processes. *Reading Research Quarterly, 31,* 122–135.

Manzo, A. V. (1969). The ReQuest procedure. *Journal of Reading, 13,* 123–126.

Manzo, A. V., & Manzo, U. C. (1993). *Literacy disorders.* Fort Worth, TX: Harcourt.

Manzo, A. V., Manzo, U. C., & Albee, J. J. (2004). *Reading assessment for diagnostic-prescriptive teaching* (2nd ed.). Belmont, CA: Thomson Learning.

Maria, K. (1990). *Reading comprehension instruction: Issues and strategies.* Parkton, MD: York Press.

Maria, K., & MacGinitie, W. (1987). Learning from texts that refute the reader's prior knowledge. *Reading Research and Instruction, 26,* 222–238.

Marshall, J. C. (2002). *Are they really reading? Expanding SSR in the middle grades.* Portland, ME: Stenhouse.

Martin, M. (1995). *Spelling in the kindergarten.* Paper presented at the annual meeting of the International Reading Association, Anaheim, CA.

Martinez, E. (1998). *CyberGuide for* Caddie Woodlawn. San Diego, CA: San Diego County Office of Education. Available online at http://www.sdcoe.k12.ca.us/score/caddie/caddiesg3.html

Martinez, M., & Teale, W. H. (1987). The ins and outs of a kindergarten writing program. *The Reading Teacher, 40,* 444–451.

Marzano, R. J., & Marzano, J. S. (1988). *A cluster approach to elementary vocabulary instruction.* Newark, DE: International Reading Association.

Maslin, P. (2003). *Comparing basal programs.* Charlottesville: University of Virginia. Available online at http://readingfirst.virginia.edu/pdfs/Maslin_whitepaper

Mason, J. M., Peterman, C. L., & Kerr, B. M. (1988). *Fostering comprehension by reading books to kindergarten children* (Technical Report No. 426). Champaign: University of Illinois, Center for the Study of Reading.

Mathes, P. G., Denton, C. A., Fletcher, J. M., Anthony, J. L., Francis, D. J., & Schatschneider, C. (2005). The effects of theoretically different instruction and student characteristics on the skills of struggling readers. *Reading Research Quarterly, 40,* 148–182.

Mathes, P. G., & Fuchs, L. S. (1993). Peer-mediated reading instruction in special education resource rooms. *Learning Disabilities Research and Practice, 8,* 233–243.

McArthur, T. (Ed.). (1992). *The Oxford companion to the English language.* New York: Oxford University.

McClure, A. A., & Kristo, J. V. (Eds.). (1994). *Inviting children's responses to literature.* Urbana, IL: National Council of Teachers of English.

McCoach, D. B., O'Connell, A. A., Reis, S. M., & Levitt, H. A. (2006). Growing readers: A hierarchical linear model of children's reading growth during the first 2 years of school. *Journal of Educational Psychology, 98,* 14–28.

McCormick, S. (1992). Disabled readers' erroneous responses to inferential comprehension questions: Description and analysis. *Reading Research Quarterly, 27,* 55–77.

McCoy, K. M., & Pany, D. (1986). Summary and analysis of oral reading corrective feedback research. *The Reading Teacher, 39,* 548–554.

McCracken, R. A. (1991). *Spelling through phonics.* Grand Forks, ND: Pegasus.

McGee, L. M., & Tompkins, G. E. (1981). The videotape answer to independent reading comprehension activities. *The Reading Teacher, 34,* 427–433.

McGinley, W. J., & Denner, P. R. (1987). Story impressions: A prereading/writing activity. *Journal of Reading, 31,* 248–253.

McKenna, M. C., & Kerr, D. J. (1990). Measuring attitude toward reading: A new tool for teachers. *The Reading Teacher, 43,* 626–639.

McKenna, M.C., & Walpole, S. (2005). How well does assessment inform our reading instruction? *The Reading Teacher, 59,* 84–86.

McKeown, M. G. (1993). Creating effective definitions for young word learners. *Reading Research Quarterly, 28,* 16–32.

McKeown, M. G. (2006). *Understanding text: What does it mean, why is it hard, and how can we support students to do it?* Paper presented at the Reading Research conference, Chicago.

McKeown, M. G., Beck, I. L., & Sandora, C. A. (1996). Questioning the author: An approach to developing meaningful classroom discourse. In M. F. Graves, P. van den Broek, & B. M. Taylor (Eds.), *The first R, every child's right to read* (pp. 97–119). New York: Teachers College Press.

McLane, J. B., & McNamee, G. D. (1990). *Early literacy.* Cambridge, MA: Harvard University Press.

McLaughlin, B., August, D., Snow, C., Carlo, M., Dressier, C., White, C., Lively, T., & Lippman, D. (2000). *Vocabulary knowledge and reading comprehension in English language learners* (Final performance report). Washington, DC: Office of Educational Research and Improvement. Available online at http://www.ncela.gwu.edu/ncbepubs/symposia/reading/6august

McMackin, M. C., & Witherell, N. L. (2005). Different routes to the same destination: Drawing conclusions with tiered graphic organizers. *The Reading Teacher, 59,* 242–252.

McMaster, J. C. (1998). "Doing" literature: Using drama to build literacy. *The Reading Teacher, 51,* 574–584.

McNamara, T. P., Miller, D. L., & Bransford, J. D. (1991). Mental models and reading comprehension. In R. Barr, M. L. Kamil, P. Mosenthal, & P. D. Pearson (Eds.), *Handbook of reading research* (Vol. II, pp. 490–511). New York: Longman.

McNeil, J. D. (1987). *Reading comprehension: New directions for classroom practice* (2nd ed.). Glenview, IL: Scott, Foresman.

Medley, D. M. (1977). *Teacher competence and teacher effectiveness: A review of process-product research.* Washington, DC: American Association of Colleges for Teacher Education.

Mehigan, K. (2005). The strategy toolbox: A ladder to strategic teaching. *The Reading Teacher, 58,* 552–566.

Menke, P. J., & Pressley, M. (1994). Elaborative interrogation: Using "why" questions to enhance the learning from text. *Journal of Reading, 37,* 642–645.

Menon, S., & Hiebert, E. H. (2003, April). *A comparison of first graders' reading acquisition with little books and literature anthologies.* Paper presented at the annual meeting of the American Educational Research Association, Chicago.

Mesmer, H. A. (1999). Scaffolding a crucial transition using text with some decodability. *The Reading Teacher, 53,* 130–142.

Mesmer, H. A., & Griffith, P. L. (2005). Everybody's selling it—but just what is explicit, systematic phonics instruction? *The Reading Teacher, 59,* 366–376.

Metsala, J. L. (1999). The development of phonemic awareness in reading-disabled children. *Applied Psycholinguistics, 20,* 149–158.

Meyer, B. J. F., & Rice, G. E. (1984). The structure of text. In P. D. Pearson, R. Barr, M. L. Kamil, & P. Mosenthal (Eds.), *Handbook of reading research* (pp. 319–351). New York: Longman.

Meyers, K. L. (1988). Twenty (better) questions. *English Journal, 77*(1), 64–65.

Miller, K. (2000). Hoa means "flower": Language, learners, and culture in an ESL multi-age classroom. In C. F. Stice, & J. E. Bertrand (Eds.), *Teaching at-risk students in the K–4 classroom: Language, literacy, learning* (pp. 95–112). Norwood, MA: Christopher-Gordon.

Moats, L. C. (2000). *Speech to print: Language essentials for teachers.* Baltimore: Brookes.

Moats, L. C. (2004). *Language essentials for teachers of reading and spelling. Module 2: Phonetics, phonology, and phoneme awareness.* Longmont, CO: Sopris West.

Modiano, N. (1968). National or mother language in beginning reading: A comparative study. *Research in the Teaching of English, 2,* 32–43.

Moldofsky, P. B. (1983). Teaching students to determine the central story problem: A practical application of schema theory. *The Reading Teacher, 38,* 377–382.

Moll, L. C., Estrada, E., Diaz, E., & Lopez, L. (1980). The organization of bilingual lessons: Implications for schooling. *The Quarterly Newsletter of the Laboratory of Comparative Human Cognition, 2*(3), 53–58.

Moore, D. W., & Moore, S. A. (1986). Possible sentences. In E. K. Dishner, T. W. Bean, J. E. Readence, & D. W. Moore (Eds.), *Reading in the content areas: Improving classroom instruction* (2nd ed.) (pp. 174–179). Dubuque, IA: Kendall/Hunt.

Moore, D. W., Moore, S. A., Cunningham, P. M., & Cunningham, J. W. (1986). *Developing readers and writers in the content areas.* New York: Longman.

Morris, D., Bloodgood, J. R., Lomax, R. G., & Perney, J. (2003). Developmental steps in learning to read: A longitudinal study in kindergarten and first grade. *Reading Research Quarterly, 38,* 302–328.

Morrow, L. M. (1985). Reading and retelling stories: Strategies for emergent readers. *The Reading Teacher, 38,* 871–875.

Morrow, L. M. (1988). Young children's responses to one-to-one story readings in school settings. *Reading Research Quarterly, 23,* 89–107.

Morrow, L. M. (1997). *Literacy development in the early years: Helping children read and write* (3rd ed.). Boston: Allyn & Bacon.

Morrow, L. M. (2002). *The literacy center: Contexts for reading and writing.* Portland, ME: Stenhouse.

Morrow, L. M., & Asbury, E. B. (2001). Patricia Loden. In M. Pressley, R. L. Allington, R. Wharton-McDonald, C. C. Block, & L. M. Morrow (Eds.), *Learning to read: Lessons from exemplary first-grade classrooms* (pp. 184–202). New York: Guilford.

Mosenthal, J. H. (1990). Developing low-performing, fourth-grade, inner-city students' ability to comprehend narrative. In J. Zutell & S. McCormick (Eds.), *Literacy theory and research: Analyses from multiple paradigms* (39th yearbook of the National Reading Conference) (pp. 275–286). Chicago: National Reading Conference.

Moustafa, M. (1995). Children's productive phonological recoding. *Reading Research Quarterly, 30,* 464–476.

Moustafa, M., & Maldonado-Colon, E. (1999). Whole-to-part phonics instruction: Building on what children know to help them know more. *The Reading Teacher, 52,* 448–458.

Mullis, I. V. S., Campbell, J. R., & Farstrup, A. E. (1993). *Executive summary of the NAEP 1992 reading report card for the nation and the states.* Princeton, NJ: Educational Testing Service.

Mullis, I. V. S., Martin, M. O., Gonzalez, E. J., & Kennedy, A. M. (2003). *PIRLS 2001 international report: IEA's study of reading literacy achievement in primary schools in 35 countries.* Chestnut Hill, MA: Boston College.

Murphy, C. (1992). Study groups foster schoolwide learning. *Educational Leadership, 50*(3), 71–74.

Murphy, L. L., Plake, B. S., Impara, J. C., & Spies, R. A. (Eds.). (2003). *Tests in print VI.* Lincoln: University of Nebraska Press.

Murphy, P. K., & Edwards, M. E. (2005, April). *What the studies tell us: A meta-analysis of discussion approaches.* Paper presented at the meeting of American Educational Research Association, Montreal.

Murray, B. (1998). Gaining alphabetic insight: Is phoneme manipulation skill or identity knowledge causal? *Journal of Educational Psychology, 90,* 461–475.

Murray, B. (2006a). How to help beginners with oral reading. *The Reading Genie.* Available online at http://www.auburn.edu/academic/education/reading_genie/oralrdg.html

Murray, B. (2006b). Making friends with phonemes. *The Reading Genie.* Available online at http://www.auburn.edu/academic/education/reading_genie/phon.html

Murray, B. (2006c). Overview: How children learn to read words. *The Reading Genie.* Available online at http://www.auburn.edu/academic/education/reading_genie/overview.html

Murray, B. (2006d). Adopting a reading series? *The Reading Genie*. Available online at http://auburn.edu/academic/education/reading_genie

Murray, D. (1979). The listening eye: Reflections on the writing conference. *College English, 41*, 13–18.

Murray, D. M. (1989). *Expecting the unexpected: Teaching myself—and others—to read and write*. Portsmouth, NH: Boynton/Cook.

Muschla, G. R. (1993). *Writing workshop survival kit*. West Nyack, NY: Center for Applied Research in Education.

Muter, V., & Snowling, M. (1998). Concurrent and longitudinal predictors of reading: The role of metalinguistic and short-term memory skills. *Reading Research Quarterly, 33*, 320–337.

Muth, K. D. (1987). Teachers' connection questions: Prompting students to organize text ideas. *Journal of Reading, 31*, 254–259.

Nagy, W. E. (1988). *Teaching vocabulary to improve reading comprehension*. Newark, DE: International Reading Association.

Nagy, W. E., & Anderson, R. C. (1984). How many words are there in printed English? *Reading Research Quarterly, 19*, 304–330.

Nagy, W. E., Anderson, R. C., & Herman, P. A. (1987). Learning word meanings from context during normal reading. *American Educational Research Journal, 24*, 237–270.

Nagy, W. E., Berninger, V. W., & Abbott, R. D. (2006). Contributions of morphology beyond phonology to literacy outcomes of upper elementary and middle school students. *Journal of Educational Psychology, 98*, 134–147.

Nagy, W. E., & Herman, P. A. (1987). Breadth and depth of vocabulary knowledge: Implications for acquisition and instruction. In M. G. McKeown & M. E. Curtis (Eds.), *The nature of vocabulary acquisition* (pp. 19–35). Hillsdale, NJ: Erlbaum.

Nagy, W. E., & Scott, J. A. (2000). Vocabulary processes. In M. L. Kamil, P. B. Mosenthal, P. D. Pearson, & R. Barr (Eds.), *Handbook of reading research* (Vol. III, pp. 269–284). Mahwah, NJ: Erlbaum.

Nation, P. (2001). *Learning vocabulary in another language*. Cambridge, England: Cambridge University Press.

National Center on Education and the Economy & University of Pittsburgh. (1997). *Performance standards: Vol. 1, Elementary school*. Washington, DC: New Standards.

National Institute on Deafness and Other Communication Disorders. (2003). *Speech and language: Developmental milestones*. Available online at http://www.nidcd.nih.gov/health/voice/speechandlanguage.asp

National Reading Panel. (2000). *National Reading Panel report*. Washington, DC: U.S. Department of Education.

Nelson, J. S., Epstein, M. H., Bursuck, W. D., Jayanthi, M., & Sawyer, V. (1998). The preferences of middle school students for homework adaptations made by general education teachers. *Learning Disabilities Research and Practice, 13*, 109–117.

Nessel, D. (1987). The new face of comprehension instruction: A closer look at questions. *The Reading Teacher, 40*, 604–606.

Neubert, G. A., & Wilkins, E. A. (2004). *Putting it all together: The directed reading lesson in the secondary content classroom*. Boston: Pearson.

Neuman, S. B. (1997). *Getting books in children's hands: A study of access to literacy*. Paper presented at National Reading Conference, Scottsdale, AZ.

New Literacies Research Team. (2006). *Results summary reports 1–6 from the survey of Internet usage and online reading*. Storrs: University of Connecticut, Neag School of Education. Available online at http://www.newliteracies.uconn.edu/pubs.html

New Standards Primary Literacy Committee. (1999). *Reading and writing grade by grade: Primary literacy standards through third grade*. Washington, DC: National Center on Education and the Economy & University of Pittsburgh.

New Standards Speaking and Listening Committee. (2001a). *Reading and writing grade by grade: Primary literacy standards through third grade*. Washington, DC: National Center on Education and the Economy & University of Pittsburgh.

New Standards Speaking and Listening Committee. (2001b). *Speaking and listening for preschool through third grade*. Washington, DC: National Center on Education and the Economy & University of Pittsburgh.

NICHD Early Child Care Research Network. (2002). The relation of global first grade classroom environment to structural classroom features and teacher and student behaviors. *The Elementary School Journal, 102*, 367–387.

NICHD Early Child Care Research Network. (2005). Pathways to reading: The role of oral language in the transition to reading. *Developmental Psychology, 41*, 428–442.

Nicholson, T., & Whyte, B. (1992). Matthew effects in learning new words while listening to stories. In C. K. Kinzer & D. J. Leu (Eds.), *Literacy research, theory, and practice: Views from many perspectives* (pp. 499–501). Chicago: National Reading Conference.

Nisbet, J., & Shucksmith, J. (1986). *Learning strategies*. London: Routledge & Kegan Paul.

No Child Left Behind Act of 2001, Public Law PL 107-110, Sec. 1001.

Noe, K. L. S. (2002, May). *Literature circles: Fostering thinking and response*. Paper presented at the annual convention of the International Reading Association, San Francisco.

Noll, E., & Watkins, R. (2003–2004). The impact of homelessness on children's literacy experiences. *The Reading Teacher, 57*, 362–371.

Northwest Regional Educational Laboratory. (2003). *Overview of second language acquisition theory*. Available online at http://www.nwrel.org/request/2003may/overview.html

Norton, D. E. (1989). *Through the eyes of a child*. Columbus, OH: Merrill.

Noyce, R., & Christie, J. F. (1989). *Integrating reading and writing instruction in grades K–8*. Boston: Allyn & Bacon.

Oakhill, J., & Yuill, N. (1996). Higher-order factors in comprehension disability: Processes and remediation. In C. Cornoldi & J. Oakhill (Eds.), *Reading comprehension difficulties: Processes and intervention* (pp. 69–92). Mahwah, NJ: Erlbaum.

O'Brien, C. A. (1973). *Teaching the language-different child to read*. Columbus, OH: Merrill.

Oczkus, L. (2003). *Reciprocal teaching at work: Strategies for improving reading comprehension*. Newark, DE: International Reading Association.

Oczkus, L. (2005). *Reciprocal teaching strategies at work: Improving reading comprehension, grades 2–6* [Video recording]. Newark, DE: International Reading Association.

Office of English Language Acquisition (OELA). (2005). *The growing number of limited English proficient students: 1993/94–2003/04*. Available online at http://www.ncela.gwu.edu/stats/2_nation.htm

Office of Special Education and Rehabilitation. (2005). IDEA-reauthorized statute Individualized Education Program (IEP). Available online at http://www.ed.gov/about/offices/list/osers/index.html

Ogle, D., & Fogelberg, E. (2001). Expanding collaborative roles of reading specialists: Developing an intermediate reading support program. In V. J. Risko & K. Bromley (Eds.), *Collaboration for diverse learners: Viewpoints and practices*. Newark, DE: International Reading Association.

Ogle, D. M. (1989). The know, want to know, learn strategy. In K. D. Muth (Ed.), *Children's comprehension of text* (pp. 205–223). Newark, DE: International Reading Association.

Ogle, L., Sen, A., Pahlke, E., Jocelyn, L., Kastberg, D., Roey, S., & Williams, T. (2003). *International comparisons in fourth-grade reading literacy: Findings from the Progress in International Reading Literacy Study (PIRLS) of 2001* (NCES 2003–073). Washington, DC: U.S. Department of Education,

NCES. Available online at http://nces.ed.gov/pubs2004/pirlspub

Oken-Wright, P. (1998). Transition to writing: Drawing as a scaffold for emergent writers. *Young Children, 53*(2), 76–81.

Olson, J. L. (1987). Drawing to write. *School Arts, 87*(1), 25–27.

O'Rourke, J. P. (1974). *Toward a science of vocabulary development.* The Hague: Mouton.

Owens, R. E. (1992). *Language development: An introduction.* Boston: Allyn & Bacon.

Owens, R. E. (2001). *Language development* (5th ed.). Boston: Allyn & Bacon.

Palincsar, A. S., & Brown, A. L. (1986). Interactive teaching to promote independent learning from text. *The Reading Teacher, 39,* 771–777.

Palincsar, A. S., Winn, J., David, Y., Snyder, B., & Stevens, D. (1993). Approaches to strategic reading instruction reflecting different assumptions regarding teaching and learning. In L. J. Meltzer (Ed.), *Strategy assessment and instruction for students with learning disabilities: From theory to practice* (pp. 247–292). Austin, TX: Pro-Ed.

Paratore, J. R. (1995). Implementing an intergenerational literacy project: Lessons learned. In L. M. Morrow (Ed.), *Family literacy: Connections in schools and communities* (pp. 37–53). Newark, DE: International Reading Association.

Paris, S. G., & Carpenter, R. D. (2003). FAQs about IRIs. *The Reading Teacher, 56,* 578–580.

Paris, S. G., Wasik, B. A., & Turner, J. C. (1991). The development of strategic readers. In R. Barr, M. L. Kamil, P. Mosenthal, & P. D. Pearson (Eds.), *Handbook of reading research* (Vol. II, pp. 609–640). New York: Longman.

Parker, D. (2002). *Accelerated literacy for English language learners (ELLs): A field-tested, research-based model of training and learning.* Paper presented at the annual convention of the International Reading Association, San Francisco.

Parsons, L. (1990). *Response journals.* Portsmouth, NH: Heinemann.

Paterson, W. A., Henry, J. J., O'Quin, K., Ceprano, M. A., & Blue, E. V. (2003). Investigating the effectiveness of an integrated learning system on early emergent readers. *Reading Research Quarterly, 38,* 172–207.

Pauk, W. (1989). The new SQ3R. *Reading World, 23,* 386–387.

Paul, R., & Elder, L. (2001). *Critical thinking: Tools for taking charge of your learning and your life.* New York: Prentice Hall.

Pearson, P. D. (1985). Changing the face of reading comprehension instruction. *The Reading Teacher, 38,* 724–738.

Pearson, P. D. (2003, May). *Maintaining momentum: Getting inside the problem.* Paper presented at the annual convention of the International Reading Association, Orlando, FL.

Pearson, P. D., & Camperell, K. (1994). Comprehension of text structures. In R. B. Ruddell, M. R. Ruddell, & H. Singer (Eds.), *Theoretical models and processes of reading* (4th ed.) (pp. 448–568). Newark, DE: International Reading Association.

Pearson, P. D., & Gallagher, M. C. (1983). The instruction of reading comprehension. *Contemporary Educational Psychology, 8,* 317–345.

Pearson, P. D., & Johnson, D. D. (1978). *Teaching reading comprehension.* New York: Holt.

Perfetti, C. A. (1985). *Reading ability.* New York: Oxford University Press.

Perfetti, C. A. (1992). The representation problem in reading acquisition. In P. B. Gough, L. C. Ehri, & R. Treiman (Eds.), *Reading acquisition* (pp. 145–174). Hillsdale, NJ: Erlbaum.

Perie, M., Grigg, W., & Donahue, P. (2005). *The nation's report card: Reading 2005* (NCES 2006–451). Washington, DC: U.S. Department of Education, National Center for Education Statistics.

Persky, H., Daane, M, & Jin, Y. (2003). *The nation's report card: Writing 2002* (NCES 2003-529). Washington, DC: U.S. Department of Education, National Center for Education Statistics.

Peterson, P. L., & Swing, S. R. (1982). Beyond time on task: Students' reports of their thought processes during classroom instruction. *Elementary School Journal, 82,* 481–491.

Peterson, R. (1992). *Life in a crowded place: Making a learning community.* Portsmouth, NH: Heinemann.

Petty, W., Herold, C., & Stoll, E. (1968). *The state of the knowledge of the teaching of vocabulary* (Cooperative Research Project No. 3128). Champaign, IL: National Council of Teachers of English.

Pianta, R. C., & La Paro, K. (2003). Improving early school success. *Educational Leadership, 60*(7), 24–29.

Pike, K., Compain, R., & Mumper, J. (1994). *New connections: An integrated approach to literacy.* New York: HarperCollins.

Pikulski, J. J. (2006). Fluency: A developmental and language perspective. In S. J. Samuels & A. E. Farstrup (Eds.), *What research has to say about fluency instruction* (pp. 70–93). Newark, DE: International Reading Association.

Pincus, A. (2005). Teaching tips: What's a teacher to do? Navigating the worksheet curriculum. *The Reading Teacher, 59,* 75–79.

Pinnell, G. S., & Fountas, I. C. (1998). *Word matters.* Portsmouth, NH: Heinemann.

Pinnell, G. S., & Fountas, I. C. (2002). *Leveled books for readers grades 3–6.* Portsmouth, NH: Heinemann.

Pinnell, G. S., Pikulski, J. J., Wixson, K.K., Campbell, J. R., Gough, P. B., & Beatty, A. S. (1995). *Listening to children read aloud.* Washington, DC: U.S. Department of Education, National Center for Education Statistics.

Platt, P. (1978). Grapho-linguistics: Children's drawings in relation to reading and writing skills. *The Reading Teacher, 31,* 262–268.

Popham, W. J. (2000). *Modern educational measurement: Practical guidelines for educational leaders.* Boston: Allyn & Bacon.

Popham, W. J. (2004). "Teaching to the test": An expression to eliminate. *Educational Leadership, 62*(3), 82–83.

Prawat, R. S. (1989). Promoting access to knowledge, strategy, and disposition in students: A research synthesis. *Review of Educational Research, 59,* 1–41.

Pressley, M. (1994). *What makes sense in reading instruction according to research.* Paper presented at the annual meeting of the Connecticut Reading Association, Waterbury.

Pressley, M. (2001, December). *Teachers who motivate, students who learn to read and write.* Paper presented at the annual meeting of the National Reading Conference, San Antonio, TX.

Pressley, M. (2006, April 29). *What the future of reading research could be.* Paper presented at the Reading Research Conference, Chicago.

Pressley, M., Allington, R. L., Wharton-McDonald, R., Block, C. C., & Morrow, L. M. (2001). The nature of first-grade instruction that promotes literacy achievement. In M. Pressley, R. L. Allington, R. Wharton-McDonald, C. C. Block & L. M. Morrow (Eds.), *Learning to read: Lessons from exemplary first-grade classrooms* (pp. 48–69). New York: Guilford.

Pressley, M., Borkowski, J. G., Forrest-Pressley, D., Gaskins, I. W., & Wiley, D. (1993). Closing thoughts on strategy instruction for individuals with learning disabilities: The good information-processing perspective. In L. Meltzer (Ed.), *Strategy assessment and instruction for students with learning disabilities: From theory to practice* (pp. 355–377). Austin, TX: Pro-Ed.

Pressley, M., Gaskins, I. W., & Fingeret, L. (2006). Instruction and development of reading fluency in struggling readers. In S. J. Samuels & A. E. Farstrup (Eds.), *What research has to say about fluency instruction* (pp. 47–69). Newark, DE: International Reading Association.

Pressley, M., Johnson, C. J., Symons, S., McGoldrick, J. A., & Kurita, J. A. (1989). Strategies that improve children's memory and comprehension of what is read. *Elementary School Journal, 89,* 3–32.

Pressley, M., Wharton-McDonald, R., Mistretta-Hampston, J., & Echevarria, M. (1998). Literacy instruction in 10 fourth- and fifth-grade classrooms in upstate New York. *Scientific Studies of Reading, 2*, 159–194.

Princiotta, D., Flanagan, K. D., & Germino Hausken, E. (2006). *Fifth grade: Findings from the fifth-grade follow-up of the early childhood longitudinal study, kindergarten class of 1998–99* (NCES 2006-038). Washington, DC: U.S. Department of Education, National Center for Education.

Probst, R. (1988). Dialogue with a text. *English Journal, 77*(1), 32–38.

Prochaska, J. O., Norcross, J. C., & DiClemente, D. C. (1994). *Changing for the good.* New York: Avon.

Purcell-Gates, V. (1997). Stories, coupons, and the TV guide: Relationships between home literacy experiences and emergent literacy knowledge. *Reading Research Quarterly, 31*, 406–428.

QuanSing, J. (1995, May). *Developmental teaching and learning using developmental continua as maps of language and literacy development which link assessment to teaching.* Paper presented at the annual meeting of the International Reading Association, Anaheim, CA.

Radencich, M. C. (1995). *Administration and supervision of the reading/writing program.* Boston: Allyn & Bacon.

Raines, S., & Isbell, R. (1994). *Stories: Children's literature in early education.* Albany, NY: Delmar.

Rapaport, W. J. (2004). *What is "context" in contextual vocabulary acquisition? Lessons learned from artificial intelligence and verbal protocol of good readers when they encounter unknown words in context.* Paper presented at the International Reading Association convention, Reno, NV.

Raphael, T. E. (1984). Teaching learners about sources of information for answering questions. *The Reading Teacher, 28*, 303–311.

Raphael, T. E. (1986). Teaching question/answer relationships, revisited. *The Reading Teacher, 39*, 516–522.

Raphael, T. E., & Au, K. H. (2005). QAR: Enhancing comprehension and test taking across grades and content areas. *The Reading Teacher, 59*, 206–221.

Raphael, T. E., & Boyd, F. B. (1997). When readers write: The book club writing component. In S. I. McMachon & T. E. Raphael (Eds.), *The book club connection: Literacy learning and classroom talk* (pp. 69–88). New York: Teachers College Press.

Raphael, T. E., & Englert, C. S. (1990). Writing and reading: Partners in constructing meaning. *The Reading Teacher, 43*, 388–400.

Raphael, T. E., Englert, C. S., & Kirschner, B. W. (1989). Acquisition of expository writing skills. In J. M. Mason (Ed.), *Reading and writing connections* (pp. 261–290). Boston: Allyn & Bacon.

Rashotte, C. A., & Torgesen, J. K. (1985). Repeated reading and reading fluency in learning disabled children. *Reading Research Quarterly, 20*, 180–188.

Ray, K. W. (2004). When kids make books. *Educational Leadership, 62*(2), 9–13.

Read, C. (1971). Pre-school children's knowledge of English phonology. *Harvard Educational Review, 41*, 1–34.

Readence, J. E., Bean, T. W., & Baldwin, R. S. (1992). *Content area literacy: An integrated approach* (4th ed.). Dubuque, IA: Kendall/Hunt.

Reading Recovery Council of North America. (2006). *Reading Recovery facts and figures (1984–2005).* Available online at http://readingrecovery.org/sections/reading/facts.asp

Reading Recovery North American Trainers Group. (2002). *What evidence says about Reading Recovery.* Columbus, OH: Reading Recovery Council of North America. Available online at http://www.readingrecovery.org/sections/home/Evidence.asp

Reeves, D. (2003). *High performance in high poverty schools: 90/90/90 and beyond.* Available online at http://www.makingstandardswork.com/ResourceCtr/fullindex.htm

Resnick, L. B. (1999, June 16). Making America smarter. *Education Week on the Web, 18.* Available online at http://www.edweek.org/ew/vol18/40resnick.h18

Resnick, L. B., & Hall, M. W. (2001). *The principles of learning: Study tools for educators* [CD-ROM, version 2.0]. Pittsburgh, PA: University of Pittsburgh, Learning Research and Development Center, Institute for Learning.

Reutzel, D. R., & Cooter, R. B. (1991). Organizing for effective instruction: The reading workshop. *The Reading Teacher, 44*, 548–555.

Rhodes, L. K. (1990, March). *Anecdotal records: A powerful tool for ongoing literacy assessment.* Paper presented at the National Council of Teachers of English Conference, Colorado Springs, CO.

Rhodes, L. K., & Dudley-Marling, C. (1988). *Readers and writers with a difference: A holistic approach to teaching learning-disabled and remedial students.* Portsmouth, NH: Heinemann.

Richardson, J. S., & Morgan, R. F. (1994). *Reading to learn in the content areas* (2nd ed.). Belmont, CA: Wadsworth.

Richek, M. (2005). Words are wonderful: Interactive, time-efficient strategies to teach meaning vocabulary. *The Reading Teacher, 58*, 414–423.

Richgels, D. S., McGee, L. M., & Slaton, E. A. (1989). Teaching expository text structure in reading and writing. In K. D. Muth (Ed.), *Children's comprehension of text* (pp. 167–184). Newark, DE: International Reading Association.

Richgels, D. S., & Wold, L. S. (1998). Literacy on the road: Backpacking partnerships between school and home. *The Reading Teacher, 52*, 18–29.

Rickelman, R. J., & Henk, W. A. (1990). Reading technology: Children's literature and audio/visual technologies. *The Reading Teacher, 43*, 682–684.

Riddle Buly, M., & Valencia, S. W. (2002). Below the bar: Profiles of students who fail state reading assessment. *Educational Evaluation and Policy Analysis, 24*, 219–239.

Rief, L. (2003). *100 quickwrites.* New York: Scholastic.

Riley, J. (1996). *The teaching of reading.* London: Paul Chapman.

Rimer, S. (1990, June 19). Slow readers sparkling with a handful of words. *New York Times*, pp. B1, B5.

Rimm-Kaufman, S. E., Fan, X., Chiu, Y. I., & You, W. (2006, April). *The contribution of the Responsive Classroom® approach on children's academic achievement: Results from a three-year longitudinal study.* Paper presented at the American Education Research Association Conference, San Francisco.

Risley, T. (2003, May 5). *Meaningful differences in the everyday experiences of young American children.* Paper presented at the annual convention of the International Reading Association, Orlando, FL.

Rist, R. (1970). Student social class and teacher expectations. The self-fulfilling prophecy in ghetto education. *Harvard Educational Review, 40*, 411–451.

Ritchey, K. D. (2004). From letter names to word reading: The development of reading in kindergarten (IRA Outstanding Dissertation Award for 2004). *Reading Research Quarterly, 39*, 374–376.

Rittle-Johnson, B., & Siegler, R. S. (1999). Learning to spell: Variability, choice, and change in children's strategy use. *Child Development, 70*, 332–348.

Roberts, E. M. (2006). Join the club. *Scholastic Instructor.* Available online at http://teacher.scholastic.com/products/instructor/jointheclub.htm

Robinson, D. H. (1998). Graphic organizers as aids to text learning. *Reading Research and Instruction, 37*, 85–105.

Robinson, F. P. (1970). *Effective study* (4th ed.). New York: Harper.

Rose, M. C., Cundick, B. P., & Higbee, K. L. (1983). Verbal rehearsal and visual imagery: Mnemonic aids for learning disabled children. *Journal of Learning Disabilities, 16*, 352–354.

Rosenblatt, L. (1978). *The reader, the text, the poem.* Carbondale: Southern Illinois University Press.

Rosenblatt, L. (1991). Literature—S. O. S.! *Language Arts, 68*, 444–448.

Rosenblatt, L. M. (1994). The traditional theory of reading and writing. In R. B. Ruddell, M. R. Ruddell, & H. Singer (Eds.), *Theoretical models and processes of reading* (4th ed.) (pp. 1057–1092). Newark, DE: International Reading Association.

Rosenshine, B., & Meister, C. (1994). Reciprocal teaching: A review of the research. *Review of Educational Research, 64*, 479–530.

Rosenshine, B., Meister, C., & Chapman, S. (1996). Teaching students to generate questions: A review of the intervention studies. *Review of Educational Research, 66*, 181–221.

Rosenshine, B., & Stevens, R. (1984). Classroom instruction in reading. In P. D. Pearson, R. Barr, M. L. Kamil, & P. Mosenthal (Eds.), *Handbook of reading research* (Vol. II, pp. 745–798). New York: Longman.

Rosier, P. (1977). *A comparative study of two approaches introducing initial reading to Navajo children: The direct method and the native language method.* Unpublished doctoral dissertation, Northern Arizona University, Flagstaff.

Routman, R. (1991). *Invitations: Changing as teachers and learners K–12.* Portsmouth, NH: Heinemann.

Routman, R. (2000). *Conversations.* Portsmouth NH: Heinemann.

Rowe, D. (2005). Writing as an instructional factor in early literacy development. In C. M. Connor (Ed.), *International Reading Association–National Institute for Child Health and Human Development conference on early childhood literacy research: A summary of presentations and discussions.* Available online at http://reading.org/resources/issues/reports/ira-nichd_conference.html

Rowe, M. B. (1969). Science, silence, and sanctions. *Science for Children, 6*(6), 11–13.

Ruddell, M. R. (1992). Integrated content and long-term vocabulary learning with the vocabulary self-collection strategy. In E. K. Dishner, T. W. Bean, J. E. Readence, & D. W. Moore (Eds.), *Reading in the content areas: Improving classroom instruction* (3rd ed.) (pp. 190–196). Dubuque, IA: Kendall/Hunt.

Ruddell, R. B. (1995). Those influential literacy teachers: Meaning negotiators and motivators. *The Reading Teacher, 48*, 454–463.

Ruddell, R. B., & Boyle, O. F. (1989). A study of cognitive mapping as a means to improve summarization and comprehension of expository text. *Reading Research and Instruction, 29*(1), 12–22.

Ruddell, R. B., & Ruddell, M. R. (1995). *Teaching children to read and write: Becoming an influential teacher.* Boston: Allyn & Bacon.

Rumelhart, D. (1980). Schemata: The building blocks of cognition. In R. J. Spiro, B. C. Bruce, & W. F. Bruner (Eds.), *Theoretical issues in reading comprehension* (pp. 33–58). Hillsdale, NJ: Erlbaum.

Rumelhart, D. (1984). Understanding understanding. In J. Flood (Ed.), *Understanding reading comprehension* (pp. 1–20). Newark, DE: International Reading Association.

Rye, J. (1982). *Cloze procedure and the teaching of reading.* London: Heinemann.

Saddler, B., & Andrade, H. (2004). The writing rubric. *Educational Leadership, 62*(2), 48–52.

Sadow, M. K. (1982). The use of story grammar in the design of questions. *The Reading Teacher, 35*, 518–522.

Sadowski, M., & Paivio, A. (1994). A dual coding view of imagery and verbal processes in reading comprehension. In R. B. Ruddell, M. R. Ruddell, & H. Singer (Eds.), *Theoretical models and processes of reading* (4th ed.) (pp. 582–601). Newark, DE: International Reading Association.

Salinger, T. (2001). Assessing the literacy of young children: The case for multiple forms of evidence. In S. B. Neuman & D. K. Dickinson (Eds.), *Handbook of early literacy research* (pp. 390–418). New York: Guilford.

Samuels, S. J. (1979). *The method of repeated reading. The Reading Teacher, 32*, 403–408.

Samuels, S. J. (1988a). Characteristics of exemplary reading programs. In S. J. Samuels & P. D. Pearson (Eds.), *Changing school reading programs: Principles and case studies* (pp. 3–9). Newark, DE: International Reading Association.

Samuels, S. J. (1988b). Decoding and automaticity: Helping poor readers become automatic at word recognition. *The Reading Teacher, 41*, 756–760.

Samuels, S. J. (1994). Toward a theory of automatic information processing in reading revisited. In R. B. Ruddell, M. R. Ruddell, & H. Singer (Eds.), *Theoretical models and processes of reading* (4th ed.) (pp. 816–837). Newark, DE: International Reading Association.

Samuels, S. J. (2006). Fluency: Toward a model of reading fluency. In S. J. Samuels & A. E. Farstrup (Eds.), *What research has to say about fluency instruction* (pp. 24–46). Newark, DE: International Reading Association.

Santa, C. (1989). *Comprehension strategies across content areas.* Paper presented at the annual conference of the New England Reading Association, Newport, RI.

Santa, C. (1994, October). *Teaching reading in the content areas.* Paper presented at the International Reading Association's Southwest Regional Conference, Little Rock, AR.

Santa, C. M. (1988). *Reading opportunities in literature.* Unpublished manuscript.

Santa, C. M., & Høien, T. (1999). An assessment of Early Steps: A program for early intervention. *Reading Research Quarterly, 34*, 54–79.

Savin, H. B. (1972). What the child knows about speech when he starts to learn to read. In J. F. Kavanagh & I. G. Mattingly (Eds.), *Language by ear and by eye* (pp. 319–326). Cambridge, MA: MIT Press.

Scardamalia, M., & Bereiter, C. (1986). Research on written composition. In M. C. Wittrock (Ed.), *Handbook of research on teaching* (pp. 778–863). New York: Macmillan.

Scardamalia, M., Bereiter, C., & Goelman, H. (1982). The role of production factors in writing ability. In M. Nystrand (Ed.), *What writers know: The language, process, and structure of written discourse* (pp. 173–210). New York: Academic.

Schatz, E. K., & Baldwin, R. S. (1986). Context clues are unreliable predictors of word meanings. *Reading Research Quarterly, 21*, 439–453.

Schickedanz, J. A. (1999). *Much more than the ABCs: The early stages of reading and writing.* Washington, DC: National Association for the Education of Young Children.

Schnorr, J. A., & Atkinson, R. C. (1969). Repetition versus imagery instructions in the short- and long-term retention of paired associates. *Psychonomic Science, 15*, 183–184.

Schulz, J. B. (1993). Teaching students with disabilities in the regular classroom. In J. A. Banks & C. A. M. Banks (Eds.), *Multicultural education: Issues and perspectives* (2nd ed.) (pp. 262–278). Boston: Allyn & Bacon.

Schunk, D. H., & Rice, J. H. (1987). Enhancing comprehension skill and self-efficacy with strategy value information. *Journal of Reading Behavior, 19*, 285–302.

Schunk, D. H., & Zimmerman, B. J. (1997). Developing self-efficacious readers and writers: The role of social and self-regulatory processes. In J. T. Guthrie & A. Wigfield (Eds.), *Reading engagement: Motivating readers through integrated instruction* (pp. 34–50). Newark, DE: International Reading Association.

Schwanenflugel, P. J., Hamilton, A. M., Kuhn, M. R., Wisen-baker, J. M., & Stahl, S. A. (2004). Becoming a fluent reader: Reading skill and prosodic features in the oral reading of young readers. *Journal of Educational Psychology, 96,* 119–129.

Schwartz, R. M. (2005). Decisions, decisions: Responding to primary students during guided reading. *The Reading Teacher, 58,* 436–443.

Scott, T. (1998). *Using content area text to teach decoding and comprehension strategies.* Paper presented at the annual meeting of the International Reading Association, Orlando, FL.

Scruggs, T. E., Bennion, K., & Lifson, S. (1985). An analysis of children's strategy use on reading achievement tests. *Elementary School Journal, 85,* 479–484.

Scruggs, T. E., & Mastropieri, M. A. (1992). *Teaching test-taking skills.* Cambridge, MA: Brookline.

Searfoss, L. W., & Readence, J. E. (1994). *Helping children learn to read* (3rd ed.). Boston: Allyn & Bacon.

Shankweiler, D., Lundquist, E., Katz, L., Stuebing, K. K., Fletcher, J. M., Brady, S., Fowler, A., Dreyer, L. G., Marchione, K. E., Shaywitz, S. E., & Shaywitz, B. A. (1999). Comprehension and decoding: Patterns of association in children with reading difficulties. *Scientific Studies of Reading, 3,* 69–94.

Shany, M. T., & Biemiller, A. (1995). Assisted reading practice: Effects on performance for poor readers in grades 3 and 4. *Reading Research Quarterly, 30,* 382–395.

Shaywitz, S. (2003). *Overcoming dyslexia: A new and complete science-based program for overcoming reading problems at any level.* New York: Knopf.

Shearer, B. (1999). *The vocabulary self-collection strategy (VSS) in a middle school.* Paper presented at the 49th annual meeting of the National Reading Conference, Orlando, FL.

Shefelbine, J. (1990). A syllabic-unit approach to teaching decoding of polysyllabic words to fourth- and sixth-grade disabled readers. In J. Zutell & S. McCormick (Eds.), *Literacy theory and research: Analyses from multiple paradigms* (39th yearbook of the National Reading Conference) (pp. 223–229). Chicago: National Reading Conference.

Shefelbine, J. (1997). *Beginning Phonics Skills Test (BPST).* Sacramento, CA: Author.

Shefelbine, J., & Newman, K. K. (2000). *SIPPS (systematic instruction in phoneme awareness, phonics, and sight words): Challenge level.* Concord, CA: Developmental Studies Center.

Shuy, R. (1973). Nonstandard dialect problems: An overview. In J. L. Laffey & R. Shuy (Eds.), *Language differences: Do they interfere?* (pp. 3–16). Newark, DE: International Reading Association.

Silvaroli, N. J., & Wheelock, A. (2001). *Classroom reading inventory* (9th ed.). New York: McGraw-Hill.

Simmons, J. (1990). Portfolios as large-scale assessment. *Language Arts, 67,* 262–268.

Simmons, J. (1996). What writers know with time. *Language Arts, 73,* 602–605.

Sinatra, G. M., Brown, K. J., & Reynolds, R. E. (2002). Implications of cognitive resource allocation for comprehension strategies instruction. In C. C. Block & M. Pressley (Eds.), *Comprehension instruction: Research-based best practices* (pp. 62–76). New York: Guilford.

Sinatra, R. C., Stahl-Gemeke, J., & Berg, D. N. (1984). Improving reading comprehension of disabled readers through semantic mapping. *The Reading Teacher, 38,* 22–29.

Sinatra, R. C., Stahl-Gemeke, J., & Morgan, N. W. (1986). Using semantic mapping after reading to organize and write original discourse. *Journal of Reading, 30,* 4–13.

Singer, H., & Donlan, D. (1989). *Reading and learning from text* (2nd ed.). Hillsdale, NJ: Erlbaum.

Singleton, S. (1997). The creation of a basal program: A collaborative effort. In J. Flood, S. B. Heath, & D. Lapp (Eds.), *Handbook of research on teaching literacy through the communicative and visual arts* (pp. 869–871). New York: Simon & Schuster/Macmillan.

Skillings, M. J., & Ferrell, R. (2000). Student-generated rubrics: Bringing students into the assessment process. *The Reading Teacher, 53,* 452–455.

Skjelfjord, V. J. (1976). Teaching children to segment words as an aid to learning to read. *Journal of Learning Disabilities, 9,* 39–48.

Slater, W. H., & Graves, M. F. (1989). Research on expository text. Implications for teachers. In K. D. Muth (Ed.), *Children's comprehension of text* (pp. 140–166). Newark, DE: International Reading Association.

Slavin, R. E. (1987a). Ability grouping and student achievement in elementary schools: A best-evidence synthesis. *Review of Education Research, 57,* 293–336.

Slavin, R. E. (1987b). Cooperative learning and the cooperative school. *Educational Leadership, 45*(3), 7–13.

Slavin, R. E. (1997–1998). Can education reduce societal inequity? *Educational Leadership, 55*(4), 6–10.

Slavin, R. E, & Madden, N. A. (1998). *Longitudinal study of Success for All.* Baltimore, MD: Johns Hopkins University, Center for Research on the Education of Students Placed at Risk.

Slavin, R. E., Madden, N. A., Karweit, N. L., Dolan, L. J., & Wasik, B. A. (1994). Success for all: Getting reading right the first time. In E. H. Hiebert & B. M. Taylor (Eds.), *Getting reading right from the start* (pp. 125–148). Boston: Allyn & Bacon.

Sloan, G. D. (1984). *The child as critic* (2nd ed.). New York: Teachers College Press.

Smith, T. E., Polloway, E. A., Patton, J. R., & Dowdy, C. A. (1998). *Teaching students with special needs in inclusive settings* (2nd ed.). Needham Heights, MA: Allyn & Bacon.

Snider, M. A., Lima, S. S., & DeVito, P. J. (1994). Rhode Island's literacy portfolio assessment project. In S. Valencia, E. H. Hiebert, & P. P. Afflerbach (Eds.), *Authentic reading assessment: Practices and possibilities* (pp. 71–88). Newark, DE: International Reading Association.

Snow, C. E., Burns, M. S., & Griffin, P. (1998). *Preventing reading difficulties in young children.* Washington, DC: National Academy Press.

Spandel, V. (2001). *Creating writers through 6-trait writing assessment and instruction.* New York: Longman.

Spandel, V., & Stiggins, R. J. (1997). *Creating writers: Linking writing assessment and instruction* (2nd ed.). New York: Longman.

Spies, R. A., & Plake, B. S. (Eds.). (2005). *The sixteenth mental measurements yearbook.* Lincoln: University of Nebraska Press.

Spires, H. A., & Donley, J. (1998). Prior knowledge activation: Inducing engagement with informational texts. *Journal of Educational Psychology, 90,* 249–260.

Stahl, S. A. (1990). *Responding to children's needs, styles, and interests.* Paper presented at the 35th annual convention of the International Reading Association, Atlanta.

Stahl, S. A. (1998). Teaching children with reading problems to decode: Phonics and "not-phonics" instruction. *Reading and Writing Quarterly: Overcoming Learning Disabilities, 14,* 165–188.

Stahl, S. A., & Fairbanks, M. M. (1986). The effects of vocabulary instruction: A model-based meta-analysis. *Review of Educational Research, 56,* 72–110.

Stahl, S. A., Heubach, K., & Crammond, P. (1997). *Fluency-oriented reading Instruction* (Reading Research Report No. 79). Athens, GA: National Reading Research Center. (ERIC Document Reproduction Service No. ED 405 554)

Stahl, S. A., & McKenna, M. M. (2002). *The concurrent development of phonological awareness, word recognition, and spelling.* Atlanta: University of Georgia, Center for the Improvement of Early Reading Achievement. Available online at http://www.ciera.org/library/archive/2001–07/200107.htm

Stahl, S. A., Osborne, J., & Lehr, F. (1990). *Beginning to read: Thinking and learning about print: A summary*. Urbana-Champaign: University of Illinois, Center for the Study of Reading.

Stallman, A. C., Commeyras, M., Kerr, B., Reimer, K., Jiménez, R., & Hartman, D. K. (1990). Are "new" words really new? *Reading Research and Instruction, 29,* 12–29.

Stauffer, M. H. (1999). *Outline on literary elements*. Tampa: University of South Florida. Available online at http://www.cas.usf.edu/lis/lis6585/class/litelem.html

Stauffer, R. G. (1969). *Directing reading maturity as a cognitive process*. New York: Harper.

Stauffer, R. G. (1970). *Reading-thinking skills*. Paper presented at the annual reading conference at Temple University, Philadelphia.

Stecher, B. M., Barron, S., Kaganoff, T., & Goodwin, J. (1998). *The effects of standards-based assessment on classroom practices: Results of the 1996–97 RAND survey of Kentucky teachers of mathematics and writing* (CSE Technical Report 482). Los Angeles: University of California, Graduate School of Education & Information Studies, Center for the Study of Evaluation, National Center for Research on Evaluation, Standards and Student Testing (CRESST) & RAND Education.

Sternberg, R. J. (1987). Most vocabulary is learned from context. In M. G. McKeown & M. E. Curtis (Eds.), *The nature of vocabulary acquisition* (pp. 89–105). Hillsdale, NJ: Erlbaum.

Sticht, T. G., & James, J. H. (1984). Listening and reading. In P. D. Pearson, R. Barr, M. L. Kamil, & P. Mosenthal (Eds.), *Handbook of reading research* (pp. 293–317). New York: Longman.

Stien, D., & Beed, P. L. (2004). Bridging the gap between fiction and nonfiction in the literature circle setting. *The Reading Teacher, 57,* 510–518.

Stiggins, R. J. (2004). New assessment beliefs for a new school mission. *Phi Delta Kappan, 86*(1), 22–27.

Stotsky, S. (1983). Research of reading/writing relationships: A synthesis and suggested directions. *Language Arts, 60,* 568–580.

Strickland, D., & Shanahan, T. (2004). What research says about reading: Laying the groundwork for literacy. *Educational Leadership 61*(6), 74–77.

Strickland, D. S. (1998). Educating African American learners at risk: Finding a better way. In C. Weaver (Ed.), *Practicing what we know: Informed reading instruction* (pp. 394–408). Urbana, Il: National Council of Teachers of English.

Strickland, D. S., & Taylor, D. (1989). Family storybook reading: Implications for children, curriculum, and families. In D. S. Strickland & L. M. Morrow (Eds.), *Emerging literacy: Young children learn to read and write* (pp. 27–33). Newark, DE: International Reading Association.

Success for All Foundation. (2006). *Randomized research proves Success for All raises student achievement*. Baltimore: Author. Available online at http://www.successforall.net/press_Random_research_06.htm

Sulzby, E. (1989a). Appendix 2.1: Forms of writing and rereading from writing, example list. In J. M. Mason (Ed.), *Reading and writing connections* (pp. 51–63). Boston: Allyn & Bacon.

Sulzby, E. (1989b). Assessment of writing and of children's language while writing. In L. Morrow & J. Smith (Eds.), *The role of assessment and measurement in early literacy instruction* (pp. 83–109). Englewood Cliffs, NJ: Prentice-Hall.

Sulzby, E. (1992). Classification scheme for children's emergent reading of favorite storybooks. In J. W. Irwin & M. A. Doyle (Eds.), *Reading/writing connections, learning from research* (pp. 137–138). Newark, DE: International Reading Association.

Sulzby, E., & Barnhart, J. (1992). The development of academic competence: All our children emerge as writers and readers. In J. W. Irwin & M. A. Doyle (Eds.), *Reading/writing connections, learning from research* (pp. 120–144). Newark, DE: International Reading Association.

Sulzby, E., Barnhart, J., & Hieshima, J. A. (1989). Forms of writing and rereading from writing: A preliminary report. In J. M. Mason (Ed.), *Reading and writing connections* (pp. 31–50). Boston: Allyn & Bacon.

Sulzby, E., Teale, W., & Kamberelis, G. (1989). Emergent writing in the classroom: Home and school connections. In D. S. Strickland & L. M. Morrow (Eds.), *Emerging literacy: Young children learn to read and write* (pp. 63–79). Newark, DE: International Reading Association.

Sundbye, N. (1987). Text explicitness and inferential questioning: Effects on story understanding and recall. *Reading Research Quarterly, 22,* 82–98.

Sutherland, Z. (1997). *Children and books* (9th ed.). Glenview, IL: Scott, Foresman.

Sutton, C. (1989). Helping the nonnative English speaker with reading. *The Reading Teacher, 42,* 684–688.

Sweet, A. P. (1997). Teacher perceptions of student motivation and their relation to literacy learning. In K. Guthrie & A. Wigfield (Eds.), *Reading engagement: Motivating readers through integrated instruction* (pp. 86–101). Newark, DE: International Reading Association.

Taba, H. (1965). The teaching of thinking. *Elementary English, 42,* 534–542.

Tabors, P. O. (1997). *One child, two languages: A guide for preschool educators of children learning English as a second language*. Baltimore: Brookes.

Taylor, B. M., Pearson, P. D., Clark, K. F., & Walpole, S. (1999). *Beating the odds in teaching all students to read: Lessons from effective schools and accomplished teachers* (CIERA Report #2-006). Available online at http://www.ciera.org/library/reports/inquiry-2/2-006/2-006.html

Taylor, B. M., Strait, J., & Medo, M. A. (1994). Early intervention in reading: Supplemental instruction for groups of low-achieving students provided by first-grade teachers. In E. H. Hiebert & B. M. Taylor (Eds.), *Getting reading right from the start* (pp. 85–106). Boston: Allyn & Bacon.

Taylor, D., & Dorsey-Gaines, C. (1988). *Growing up literate: Learning from inner-city families*. Portsmouth, NH: Heinemann.

Taylor, H. H. (2001, March). Curriculum in Head Start. *Head Start Bulletin No. 67*, p. 2. Available online at http://www.headstartinfo.org/publications/hsbulletin67/hsb67_00.htm

Taylor, K. K. (1986). Summary writing by young children. *Reading Research Quarterly, 21,* 193–208.

Taylor, M. A. (1990, March). *Exploring mythology and folklore: The macrocosm and microcosm*. Paper presented at the National Council of Teachers of English Conference, Colorado Springs, CO.

Teale, W. H., & Sulzby, E. (1986). *Emergent literacy: Writing and reading*. Norwood, NJ: Ablex.

Temple, C., Martinez, M., Yokota, J., & Naylor, A. (1998). *Children's books in children's hands: An introduction to their literature*. Boston: Allyn & Bacon.

Temple, C., Nathan, R., Temple, F., & Burris, N. A. (1993). *The beginnings of writing* (3rd ed.). Boston: Allyn & Bacon.

Terman, L. M. (1954). The discovery and encouragement of exceptional talent. *American Psychologist, 9,* 221–230.

Terry, A. (1974). *Children's poetry preferences*. Urbana, IL: National Council of Teachers of English.

Texas Instrument Foundation, Head Start of Greater Dallas, & Southern Methodist University. (1996). *Leap into a brighter future*. Paper presented at Head Start's 3rd National Research Conference, Dallas. Available online at http://www.ti.com/corp/docs/company/citizen/foundation/leapsbounds/leap.pdf

Thames, D. G., & York, K. C. (2003). Disciplinary border crossing: Adopting broader, richer view of literacy. *The Reading Teacher, 56,* 602–610.

Thomas, E. L., & Robinson, H. A. (1972). *Improving reading in every class: A sourcebook for teachers.* Boston: Allyn & Bacon.

Thomas, P. (2004) The negative impact of testing writing skills. *Educational Leadership, 62*(2), 76–79.

Thompson, A. (1990). Thinking and writing in learning logs. In N. Atwell (Ed.), *Coming to know: Writing to learn in the intermediate schools* (pp. 35–51). Portsmouth, NH: Heinemann.

Thonis, E. (1983). *The English-Spanish connection: Excellence in English for Hispanic children through Spanish language and literacy development.* Compton, CA: Santillana.

Thorndike, R. L. (1973). Reading as reasoning. *Reading Research Quarterly, 9,* 135–147.

Thorndyke, P. (1977). Cognitive structures in comprehension and memory of narrative discourse. *Cognitive Psychology, 9,* 77–110.

Tiedt, P. M., & Tiedt, I. M. (2002). *Multicultural teaching: A handbook of activities, information, and resources* (6th ed.). Boston: Allyn & Bacon.

Tiedt, P. M., & Tiedt, I. M. (2006). *Multicultural teaching: A handbook of activities, information, and resources* (7th ed.). Boston: Allyn & Bacon.

Tierney, R. J., Carter, M. A., & Desai, L. E. (1991). *Portfolio assessment in the reading-writing classroom.* Norwood, MA: Christopher-Gordon.

Tierney, R. J., & Readence, J. E. (2000). *Reading strategies and practices: A compendium* (5th ed.). Boston: Allyn & Bacon.

Tierney, R. J., Readence, J. E., & Dishner, E. K. (1995). *Reading strategies and practices: A compendium* (4th ed.). Boston: Allyn & Bacon.

Tompkins, G. E., & Yaden, D. B. (1986). *Answering questions about words.* Urbana, IL: National Council of Teachers of English.

Topping, D., & McManus, R. (2002). *Real reading, real writing, content area strategies.* Portsmouth, NH: Heinemann.

Topping, K. (1987). Paired reading: A powerful technique for parent use. *The Reading Teacher, 40,* 608–609.

Topping, K. (1989). Peer tutoring and paired reading: Combining two powerful techniques. *The Reading Teacher, 42,* 488–494.

Topping, K. (1998). Effective tutoring in America Reads: A reply to Wasik. *The Reading Teacher, 52,* 42–50.

Topping, K. (2006). Building reading fluency: Cognitive, behavioral, and socioemotional factors and the role of peer-mediated learning. In S. J. Samuels & A. E. Farstrup (Eds.), *What research has to say about fluency instruction* (pp. 106–129). Newark, DE: International Reading Association.

Torgesen, J. K., Rashotte, C. A., Alexander, A., Alexander, J., & MacPhee, K. (2003). Progress towards understanding the instructional conditions necessary for remediating reading difficulties in older children. In B. Foorman (Ed.), *Preventing and remediating reading difficulties: Bringing science to scale* (pp. 275–298). Parkton, MD: York Press.

Torgesen, J. K., Wagner, R. K., Rashotte, C. A., Burgess, S. R., & Hecht, S. A. (1997). The contributions of phonological awareness and rapid automatic naming ability to the growth of word reading skills in second to fifth grade children. *Scientific Studies of Reading, 1,* 161–185.

Touchstone Applied Science Associates. (1994). *DRP handbook.* Brewster, NY: Author.

Touchstone Applied Science Associates. (1997). *Text sense, summary writing: Teacher's resource manual.* Brewster, NY: Author.

Touchstone Applied Science Associates. (2006). The DRP model of reading. *TASA Talk.* Available online at http://www.tasaliteracy.com/tasatalk/tasatalk-main.html

Trabasso, T., & Magliano, J. P. (1996). How do children understand what they read and what can we do to help them? In M.

F. Graves, P. van den Broek, & B. M. Taylor (Eds.), *The first R, every child's right to read* (pp. 160–188). New York: Teachers College Press & International Reading Association.

Trelease, J. (2001). *The new read-aloud handbook* (5th ed.). New York: Penguin.

Trelease, J. (2006). *The new read-aloud handbook* (6th ed.). New York: Penguin.

Trussell-Cullen, A. (1994). *Celebrating the real strategies for developing non-fiction reading and writing.* Paper presented at the annual meeting of the Connecticut Reading Association, Waterbury.

Tunnell, M. O., & Jacobs, J. S. (1989). Using "real" books: Research findings on literature-based reading instruction. *The Reading Teacher, 42,* 470–477.

Tyson, E. S., & Mountain, L. (1982). A riddle or pun makes learning words fun. *The Reading Teacher, 36,* 170–173.

U.S. Census Bureau. (2005). Age and sex of all people, family members and unrelated individuals iterated by income-to-poverty ratio and race. *Annual demographic survey, March supplement* (POV01). Available online at http://pubdb3.census.gov/macro/032005/pov/new01_100.htm

U.S. Department of Education. (1991, September 16). *Memorandum: Clarification of policy to address the needs of children with attention deficit disorders with general and/or special education.* Washington, DC: Author.

U.S. Department of Education. (2002a). *Early Reading First: Frequently asked questions.* Available online at http://www.ed.gov/offices/OESE/earlyreading/faq.html

U.S. Department of Education. (2002b). *Guidance for the Reading First program.* Washington, DC: Author.

U.S. Department of Education. (2002c). *Head Start regulations, Part 1304.21.* Available online at http://www.acf.hhs.gov/programs/hsb/peformance/index.htm

U.S. Department of Education. (2002d). *Reading First criteria for review of state applications.* Available online at http://www.ed.gov/offices/OESE/readingfirst/grant.html

U.S. Department of Education. (2002e). *The No Child Left Behind Act of 2001.* Available online at http://www.ed.gov/legislation/ESEA02

U.S. Department of Education, Office of Bilingual Education and Minority Languages Affairs. (1998). *Facts about limited English proficient students.* Available online at http://www.ed.gov/offices/OBEMLA/index.html

U.S. Department of Education, Office of Special Education and Rehabilitative Services. (2003). *Twenty-fifth annual report to Congress on the implementation of the Individuals with Disabilities Education Act.* Washington, DC: Government Printing Office.

Vacca, R. T., & Vacca, J. L. (1986). *Content area reading* (2nd ed.). Boston: Little, Brown.

Valdes, G. (1996). *Con respeto—bridging the distances between culturally diverse families and schools: An ethnographic portrait.* New York: Teachers College Press.

Valencia, S. (2001). *Integrated theme tests, Levels 2.1–2.2.* Houghton Mifflin Reading. Boston: Houghton Mifflin.

Valencia, S. W., & Place, N. A. (1994). Literacy portfolios for teaching, learning, and accountability: The Bellevue literacy assessment project. In S. W. Valencia, E. H. Hiebert, & P. P. Afflerbach (Eds.), *Authentic reading assessment: Practices and possibilities* (pp. 134–156). Newark, DE: International Reading Association.

Valencia, S. W., & Riddle Buly, M. (2004). Behind test scores: What struggling readers really need. *The Reading Teacher, 57,* 520–531.

Van Bon, W. H. J., Bokesbeld, L. M., Font Freide, T. A., & Van den Hurk, A. J. (1991). A comparison of three methods of reading-while-listening. *Journal of Learning Disabilities, 24,* 471–477.

van den Broek, P., & Kremer, K. E. (2000). The mind in action: What it means to comprehend during reading. In B. Taylor,

M. F. Graves, & P. van den Broek (Eds.), *Reading for meaning: Fostering comprehension in the middle grades* (pp. 1–31). New York: Teachers College Press.

van den Broek, P., Lynch, J. S., Naslund, J., Ievers-Landis, C. E., & Verduin, K. (2003). The development of comprehension of main ideas in narratives: Evidence from the selection of titles. *Journal of Educational Psychology, 95,* 707–718.

Vandervelden, M. C., & Siegel, L. S. (1997). Phonological recoding and phoneme awareness in early literacy: A developmental approach. *Reading Research Quarterly, 30,* 854–876.

Vaughn, S. (2003, December). *How many tiers are needed within RTI to achieve acceptable prevention outcomes and to achieve acceptable patterns of LD identification?* Paper presented at NRCLD Symposium, Response to Intervention, Kansas City, MO. Available online at http://www.nrcld.org/symposium2003/index.html

Vaughn, S., Klinger, J., & Schumm, J. (n. d.). *Collaborative strategy instruction: A manual to assist with staff development.* Miami, FL: University of Miami.

Vellutino, F. R., & Scanlon, D. M. (2001). Emergent literacy skills. Early instruction and individual differences as determinants of difficulties in learning to read: The case for early intervention. In S. B. Neuman & D. K. Dickinson (Eds.), *Handbook of early literacy research* (pp. 295–321). New York: Guilford.

Vellutino, F. R., Scanlon, D. M., Sipay, E. R., Small, S. G., Pratt, R., Chen, R., & Denckla, M. B. (1996). Cognitive profiles of difficult-to-remediate and readily remediated poor readers: Early intervention as a vehicle for distinguishing between cognitive and experiential deficits as basic causes of specific reading disability. *Journal of Educational Psychology, 88,* 601–638.

Venezky, R. L. (1965). *A study of English spelling-to-sound correspondences on historical principles.* Unpublished doctoral dissertation, Stanford University, Stanford, CA.

Verhallen, M., & Schoonen, R. (1993). Vocabulary knowledge of monolingual and bilingual children. *Applied Linguistics, 14,* 344–363.

Vygotsky, L. S. (1962). *Mind and society: The development of higher psychological processes.* Cambridge, MA: MIT Press.

Vygotsky, L. S. (1978). *Thought and language.* Cambridge, MA: MIT Press.

Vygotsky, L. S. (1987). The development of scientific concepts in childhood. In R. F. Rieber & A. S. Carton (Eds.), *The collected works of L. S. Vygotsky* (N. Mnick, Trans.) (Vol. 1, pp. 167–241). New York: Plenum.

Walker, M. L. (1995). Help for the "fourth-grade slump"— SRQ2R plus instruction in text structure or main idea. *Reading Horizons, 36,* 38–58.

Wasik, B. A. (1999). Reading coaches: An alternative to reading tutors. *The Reading Teacher, 52,* 653–656.

Wasik, B. A., Bond, M. A., & Hindman, A. (2006). The effects of a language and literacy intervention on Head Start children and teachers. *Journal of Educational Psychology, 98,* 63–74.

Watkins, C. (1985). *The American Heritage dictionary of Indo-European roots.* Boston: Houghton Mifflin.

Watson, A. J. (1984). Cognitive development and units of print in early reading. In J. Downing & R. Valten (Eds.), *Language awareness and learning to read* (pp. 93–118). New York: Springer-Verlag.

Weaver, C. (1994). Understanding and educating students with attention deficit hyperactivity disorders: Toward a system-theory and whole language perspective. In C. Weaver (Ed.), *Success at last: Helping students with AD(H)D achieve their potential.* Portsmouth, NH: Heinemann.

Webb, N. L. (1999). *Alignment of science and mathematics standards and assessments in four states* (Research Monograph No. 18). Madison: University of Wisconsin–Madison, National Institute for Science Education.

Weber, E., Nelson, B., & Woods, R. (2000). *Into the millennium: Profiles in writing.* Clinton Township, MI: Macomb Intermediate School District.

Weber, R. M., & Longhi-Chirlin, T. (2001). Beginning in English: The growth of linguistic and literate abilities in Spanish-speaking first graders. *Reading Research and Instruction, 41,* 19–50.

Weinstein, C., & Mayer, R. (1986). The teaching of learning strategies. In M. C. Wittrock (Ed.), *Handbook of research on teaching* (pp. 315–327). New York: Macmillan.

Wells, G. (1986). *The meaning makers: Children learning language and using language to learn.* Portsmouth, NH: Heinemann.

West, J., Denton, K., & Germino-Hausken, E. (2000). *Early childhood longitudinal study: Kindergarten class of 1998–99.* Washington, DC: National Center for Educational Statistics. Available online at http://nces.ed.gov/pubsearch/pubsinfo.asp?pubid=2000070

Westby, C. E. (1999). Assessing and facilitating text comprehension problems. In H. W. Catts & A. G. Kamhi (Eds.), *Language and reading disabilities* (pp. 154–223). Boston: Allyn & Bacon.

Wharton-McDonald, R. (2001). Teaching writing in first grade: Instruction, scaffolds and expectations. In M. Pressley, R. L. Allington, R. Wharton-McDonald, C. C. Block, & L. M. Morrow (Eds.), *Learning to read: Lessons from exemplary first-grade classrooms* (pp. 70–91). New York: Guilford.

White, T. G. (2005). Effects of systematic and strategic analogy-based phonics on grade 2 students' word reading and reading comprehension. *Reading Research Quarterly, 40,* 234–255.

White, T. G., Power, M. A., & White, S. (1989). Morphological analysis: Implications for teaching and understanding vocabulary growth. *Reading Research Quarterly, 24,* 283–304.

White, T. G., Sowell, J., & Yanagihara, A. (1989). Teaching elementary students to use word-part clues. *The Reading Teacher, 42,* 302–308.

Wigfield, A. (1997). Children's motivations for reading and writing engagement. In J. Guthrie & A. Wigfield (Eds.), *Motivating readers through integrated instruction* (pp. 14–33). Newark, DE: International Reading Association.

Wigfield, A., & Asher, S. R. (1984). Social and motivational influences on reading. In P. D. Pearson, R. Barr, M. L. Kamil, & P. Mosenthal (Eds.), *Handbook of reading research* (pp. 423–452). New York: Longman.

Wilde, S. (1995). *Twenty-five years of inventive spelling: Where are we now?* Paper presented at the annual meeting of the International Reading Association, Anaheim, CA.

Williams, J. P. (1986a). Identifying main ideas: A basic aspect of reading comprehension. *Topics in Language Disorders, 8,* 1–13.

Williams, J. P. (1986b). Research and instructional development on main idea skills. In J. F. Baumann (Ed.), *Teaching main idea comprehension* (pp. 73–95). Newark, DE: International Reading Association.

Wilson, J. (1960). *Language and the pursuit of truth.* London: Cambridge University Press.

Wilson, P. (1986). *Voluntary reading.* Paper presented at the annual convention of the International Reading Association, Philadelphia.

Wilson, P. (1992). Among nonreaders: Voluntary reading, reading achievement, and the development of reading habits. In C. Temple & P. Collins (Eds.), *Stories and readers: New perspectives on literature in the elementary classroom* (pp. 157–169). Norwood, MA: Christopher-Gordon.

Wilson, P., Martens, P., & Arya, P. (2005). Accountability for reading and readers: What the numbers don't tell. *The Reading Teacher, 58,* 622–631.

Winne, R. H., Graham L., & Prock, L. (1993). A model of poor readers' text-based inferencing: Effects of explanatory feedback. *Reading Research Quarterly, 28,* 536–566.

Wittrock, M. C. (1991). Generative teaching of comprehension. *Elementary School Journal, 92,* 169–180.

Wixson, K. K. (1983). Questions about a text: What you ask about is what children learn. *The Reading Teacher, 37,* 287–293.

Wolf, M., & Katzir-Cohen, T. (2001). Reading fluency and its intervention. *Scientific Studies of Reading, 5,* 211–238.

Worthy, J., & Broaddus, K. (2001). Fluency beyond the primary grades: From group performance to silent, independent reading. *The Reading Teacher, 55,* 334–343.

Wright, G., Sherman, R., & Jones, T. B. (2004). Are silent reading behaviors of first graders really silent? *The Reading Teacher, 57,* 546–553.

Wutz, J., & Wedwick, L. (2005). Bookmatch: Scaffolding book selection for independent reading. *The Reading Teacher, 59,* 16–32.

Yaden, D. B., Tam, A., Madrigal, P., Brassell, D., Massa, J., Altamirano, S., & Armendariz, J. (2001). Ear literacy for inner-city children: The effects of reading and writing interventions in English and Spanish during the preschool years. (CIERA Article #00-04). Available online at http://www.ciera.org/ciera/publications/report-series/

Yopp, H. K. (1988). The validity and reliability of phonemic awareness tests. *Reading Research Quarterly, 23,* 159–199.

Yopp, R. H., & Yopp, H. K. (2000). *Literature-based reading activities* (3rd ed.). Boston: Allyn & Bacon.

Yuill, N., & Oakhill, J. (1991). *Children's problems in text comprehension: An experimental investigation* (Cambridge Monographs & Texts in Applied Psycholinguistics). New York: Cambridge University Press.

Zarnowski, M. (1990). *Learning about biographies: A reading-and-writing approach for children.* Urbana, IL: National Council of Teachers of English.

Zeno, S. M., Ivens, S. H., Millard, R. T., & Duvvuri, R. (1995). *The educator's word frequency guide.* Brewster, NY: Touchstone Applied Science Associates.

Zevenbergen, A. A., & Whitehurst, G. J. (2003). Dialogic reading: A shared picture book reading intervention for preschoolers. In A. van Kleeck, S. A. Stahl, & E. B. Bauer (Eds.), *On reading books to children: Parents and teachers* (pp. 177–200). Mahwah, NJ: Erlbaum.

Zill, N., Resnick, G., Kim, K., O'Donnell, K., Sorongon, A., Ziv, Y., Alva, S., McKey, R. H., Pai-Samant, S., Clark, C., O'Brien, R., & D'Elio, M. A. (2006). Head Start Performance Measures Center family and child experiences survey (FACES 2000) [Technical report]. Washington, DC: U.S. Department of Health and Human Services, Administration for Children and Families. Available online at http://www.acf.hhs.gov/programs/opre/hs/faces/reports/technical_2000_rpt/tech2k_title.html

Zimmermann, S., & Hutchins, C. (2003). *7 Keys to Comprehension: How to help your kids read it and get it!* New York: Prima Lifestyles.

Zinsser, W. (1988). *Writing to learn.* New York: Harper.

Zorfass, J., Corley, P., & Remy, A. (1994). Helping students with disabilities become writers. *Educational Leadership, 51*(7), 62–66.

Zutell, J. (1998). Word sorting: A developmental spelling approach to word study for delayed readers. *Reading and Writing Quarterly: Overcoming Learning Difficulties, 14,* 219–238.

Zwaan, R. A., & Graesser, A. C. (1998). Introduction to special issue of SSR: Constructing meaning during reading. *Scientific Studies of Reading, 2*(3), 195–198.

Children's

Aardema, V. (1975). *Why mosquitoes buzz in people's ears: A West African folk tale.* New York: Dial.

Ada, A. F. (1999). *The kite.* Miami, FL: Santillana.

Aiken, J. (1962). *Wolves of Willoughby Chase.* New York: Dell.

Albee, S. (1997). *I can do it.* New York: Random House.

Alexander, A. (1961). *Boats and ships from A to Z.* New York: Rand McNally.

Arnold, C. (2001). *Did you hear that?* Watertown, MA: Charlesbridge.

Atwater, R., & Atwater, F. (1938). *Mr. Popper's penguins.* Boston: Little, Brown.

Avi. (1994). *The barn.* New York: Orchard.

Baldwin, D., & Lister, C. (1984). *Your five senses.* Chicago: Children's Press.

Barracca, S. (1990). *The adventures of taxi dog.* New York: Dial.

Barton, B. (1982). *Airport.* New York: Crowell.

Bauer, C. (1984). *Too many books.* New York: Viking.

Berger, M., & Berger, G. (1995). *What do animals do in winter?* Nashville, TN: Ideals Children's Books.

Blos, J. W. (1979). *A gathering of days: A New England girl's journal.* New York: Scribner's.

Bonsall, C. (1974). *And I mean it, Stanley.* New York: Harper.

Bridwell, N. (1972). *Clifford the small red puppy.* New York: Scholastic.

Brink, C. (1935). *Caddie Woodlawn.* New York: Macmillan.

Brown, A. (2001). *Hoot and holler.* New York: Knopf.

Brown, C. M. (1991). *My barn.* New York: Greenwillow.

Brown, J. G. (1976). *Alphabet dreams.* Englewood Cliffs, NJ: Prentice-Hall.

Burnford, S. (1961). *Incredible journey.* New York: Bantam.

Burningham, J. (1986). *Colors.* New York: Crown.

Burton, L. L. (1942). *The little house.* Boston: Houghton Mifflin.

Byars, B. (1970). *Summer of the swans.* New York: Viking.

Byars, B. (1977). *The pinballs.* New York: Harper.

Cameron, A. (1994). *The cat sat on the mat.* Boston: Houghton Mifflin.

Carle, E. (1969). *The very hungry caterpillar.* New York: Philomel.

Carle, E. (1973). *Have you seen my cat?* New York: Watts.

Carle, E. (1987). *Papa, please get the moon for me.* New York: Simon & Schuster.

Carlson, N. (1996). *Sit still.* New York: Viking Penguin.

Carroll, L. (2000). *Alice's adventures in Wonderland.* New York: Signet Classics.

Choi, Y. (2001). *The name jar.* New York: Knopf.

Cleary, B. (1975). *Ramona the brave.* New York: Morrow.

Cleary, B. (1981). *Ramona Quimby, age 8.* New York: Morrow.

Cleary, B. (1983). *Dear Mr. Henshaw.* New York: Morrow.

Clifford, E. (1979). *Flatfoot Fox and the case of the bashful beaver.* Boston: Houghton Mifflin.

Clifford, E. (1997). *Help! I'm a prisoner in the library!* New York: Scholastic.

Cohen, B. (2005). *Molly's pilgrim.* New York: Harper.

Cole, H. (1995). *Jack's garden.* New York: Greenwillow.

Cole, J. (1992). *The magic school bus on the ocean floor.* New York: Scholastic.

Cole, J. (1997). *The magic school bus and the electric field trip.* New York: Scholastic.

Cole, J., & Calmenson, S. (1993). *Six sick sheep: 101 tongue twisters.* New York: Morrow.

Coxe, M. (1996). *Cat traps.* New York: Random House.

Crews, D. (1984). *Schoolbus.* New York: Greenwillow.

Curtis, F. (1977). *The little book of big tongue twisters.* New York: Harvey House.

Dalgliesh, S. (1954). *Courage of Sarah Noble.* New York: Scribner's.

Degen, B. (1983). *Jamberry.* New York: Harper.

dePaola, T. (1973). *Andy: That's my name.* Englewood Cliffs, NJ: Prentice-Hall.

Douglas, B. (1982). *Good as new.* New York: Lothrop.

Eastman, P. D. (1960). *Are you my mother?* New York: Random House.

Eastman, P. D. (1962). *Go, dog, go!* New York: Random House.

Ehlert, L. (2001). *Waiting for wings.* San Diego, CA: Harcourt.

Ellwand, D. (1996). *Emma's elephant & other favorite animal friends.* New York: Dutton.

Emberley, E. (1987). *Cars, boats, planes.* New York: Little, Brown.

Everitt, B. (1998). *Up the ladder, down the slide.* New York: Harcourt.

Fitzgerald, J. D. (2000). *The great brain.* New York: Dial.

Fleschman, S. (1986). *The whipping boy.* New York: Greenwillow.

Fletcher, R. J. (1997). *Spider boy.* New York: Clarion.

Folsom, M., & Folsom, M. (1986). *Easy as pie.* New York: Clarion.

Freeman, D. (1978). *A pocket for Corduroy.* New York: Viking.

Gág, W. (1928). *Millions of cats.* New York: Coward.

Galdone, P. (1975). *The gingerbread boy.* New York: Clarion.

Gantos, J. (1994). *Heads or tails: Stories from the sixth grade.* New York: Harper.

Garten, J. (1964). *The alphabet tale.* New York: Random House.

Geisel, T. S. (Dr. Seuss). (1957). *The cat in the hat.* New York: Random House.

Geisel, T. S. (Dr. Seuss). (1961). *The cat in the hat comes back.* New York: Random House.

Geisel, T. S. (Dr. Seuss). (1974). *There's a wocket in my pocket.* New York: Beginner.

Geisel, T. S. (Dr. Seuss). (1996). *The foot book.* New York: Random House.

George, J. C. (2000). *My side of the mountain.* New York: Puffin.

Gershator, D., & Gershator, P. (1997). *Palampam Day.* New York: Marshall Cavendish.

Gibbons, G. (1992). *Recycle! A handbook for kids.* Boston: Little, Brown.

Grahame, K. (1966). *The reluctant dragon.* New York: Holiday House.

Greydanus, R. (1988). *Let's get a pet.* New York: Troll.

Gwynne, F. (1987). *The king who rained.* Englewood Cliffs, NJ: Prentice-Hall.

Gwynne, F. (1988a). *A chocolate moose for dinner.* New York: Aladdin.

Gwynne, F. (1988b). *A little pigeon toad.* New York: Simon & Schuster.

Hamilton, V. (1971). *The planet of Junior Brown.* New York: Simon & Schuster.

Hamilton, V. (1985). *The people could fly.* New York: Knopf.

Hausherr, R. (1994). *What food is this?* New York: Scholastic.

Heling, K., & Hembrook, D. (2003). *Mouse's hide-and-seek words.* New York: Random House.

Henry, M. (1947). *Misty of Chincoteague.* New York: Rand McNally.

Hill, E. (1980). *Where's Spot?* New York: Putnam.

Hoban, L. (1981). *Arthur's funny money.* New York: Harper.

Hoban, R. (1964). *Bread and jam for Frances.* New York: Harper.

Hope, A. (1894/1994). *Prisoner of Zenda.* New York: Geddes & Grosset.

Hutchins, P. (1976). *Don't forget the bacon!* New York: Mulberry.

Hutchins, P. (1987). *Rosie's walk.* New York: Simon & Schuster.

Juster, N. (1961). *The phantom tollbooth.* New York: Knopf.

Keats, E. J. (1962). *The snowy day.* New York: Viking.

Keats, E. J. (1964). *Whistle for Willie.* New York: Viking.

Kipling, R. (1992). *The jungle book.* New York: Tor Books.

Komori, A. (1983). *Animal mothers.* New York: Philomel.

Krauss, R. (1945). *The carrot seed.* New York: Harper.

Kremetz, J. (1986). *Jamie goes on an airplane.* New York: Random House.

L'Engle, M. (1962). *A wrinkle in time.* New York: Farrar.

Lessem, D. (1997). *Supergiants: The biggest dinosaurs.* Boston: Little, Brown.

Lewis, C. S. (1950). *The lion, the witch, and the wardrobe.* New York: Macmillan.

Lewison, W. C. (1992). *Buzz said the bee.* New York: Scholastic.

Lionni, L. (1963). *Swimmy.* New York: Knopf.

Lobel, A. (1972). *Frog and Toad together.* New York: Harper.

Lowry, L. (1989). *Number the stars.* Boston: Houghton Mifflin.

MacLachan, P. (1985). *Sarah, plain and tall.* New York: Harper.

Maitland, B. (2000). *Moo in the morning.* New York: Farrar.

Malam, J. (1998). *Leonardo DaVinci.* Minneapolis, MN: Carolrhoda.

Martin, B., Jr. (1983). *Brown bear, brown bear, what do you see?* New York: Holt.

Martin, B., Jr., & Archambault, J. (1989). *Chicka chicka boom boom.* New York: Simon & Schuster.

Mazer, H. (2001). *A boy at war: A novel of Pearl Harbor.* New York: Simon & Schuster.

McCloskey, R. (1941). *Make way for ducklings.* New York: Viking.

McGovern, A. (1968). *Stone soup.* New York: Scholastic.

McKissack, P., & McKissack, F. (1988). *Bugs.* Chicago: Children's Press.

Meddaugh, S. (1997). *Cinderella's rat.* Boston: Houghton Mifflin.

Minarik, E. H. (1961). *Little Bear's visit.* New York: HarperCollins.

Modesitt, J. (1990). *The story of z.* Saxonville, MA: Picture Book Studio.

Most, B. (1991). *A dinosaur named after me.* Orlando, FL: Harcourt.

Naylor, P. (1991). *Shiloh.* New York: Atheneum.

Naylor, P. (1996). *Fear Place.* New York: Alladin.

Naylor, P. (1997). *Ducks disappearing.* New York: Atheneum.

Nedobeck, D. (1981). *Nedobeck's alphabet book.* Chicago: Children's Press.

Nobisso, J. (2002). *In English, of course.* Westhampton Beach, NY: Gingerbread House.

Noble, T. H. (1980). *The day Jimmy's boa ate the wash.* New York: Dial.

Nodset, J. L. (1963). *Who took the farmer's hat?* New York: Harper.

Parish, P. (1964). *Thank you, Amelia Bedelia.* New York: Harper.

Petrie, C. (1983). *Joshua James likes trucks.* Chicago: Children's Press.

Phillips, L. (1997). *Ask me anything about dinosaurs.* New York: Avon.

Pomerantz, C. (1984). *Where's the bear?* New York: Greenwillow.

Potter, B. (1908). *The tale of Peter Rabbit.* London: Warne.

Richards, J. (2002). *Howling hurricanes.* Broomall, PA: Chelsea House.

Rockwell, A. (1984). *Cars.* New York: Dutton.

Rolfer, G. (1990). Game day. *Sports Illustrated for Kids, 2*(8), 25.

Rylant, C. (1985). *The relatives came.* New York: Bradbury.

Rylant, C. (1987). *Henry and Mudge, the first book.* New York: Scholastic.

Segal, L. (1973). *All the way home.* New York: Farrar.

Sendak, M. (1963). *Where the wild things are.* New York: Harper.

Shaw, N. (1986). *Sheep in a jeep.* Boston: Houghton Mifflin.

Shaw, N. (1992). *Sheep on a ship.* Boston: Houghton Mifflin.

Shaw, N. (1996). *Sheep in a shop.* Boston: Houghton Mifflin.

Shuter, J. (1997). *The ancient Greeks.* Des Plaines, IL: Heinemann.

Slepian, J., & Seidler, A. (1992). *The hungry thing goes to a restaurant.* New York: Scholastic.

Snow, P. (1984). *A pet for Pat.* Chicago: Children's Press.

Sobol, D. (1961). *The Wright brothers at Kitty Hawk.* New York: Dutton.

Soto, G. (1998). *Big, bushy mustache.* New York: Knopf.

Souza, D. M. (1998). *Fish that play tricks.* Minneapolis: Carolrhoda.

Speare, E. (1958). *The witch of Blackbird Pond.* Boston: Houghton Mifflin.

Stevenson, R. L. (1967). *Treasure island.* Feltham, England: Hamlyn.

Stevenson, R. L. (1985). *A child's garden of verses*. London: Longman.

Stone, L. M. (1985). *Antarctica*. Chicago: Children's Press.

Stone, L. M. (1998). *Brown bears*. Minneapolis: Lerner.

Taylor, M. D. (1987). *The friendship*. New York: Dial.

Thompson, S. E. (1998). *Built for speed: The extraordinary, enigmatic cheetah*. Minneapolis: Lerner.

Tolkien, J. R. R. (2002). *The hobbit*. New York: Houghton Mifflin.

White, E. B. (1952). *Charlotte's web*. New York: Harper.

Whitebird, M. (2001). *Ta-Na-E-Ka*. In J. Flood et al. (Eds.), *McGraw-Hill reading*. New York: McGraw-Hill.

Wilder, L. I. (1932). *Little house in the big woods*. New York: Harper.

Wilder. L. I. (1941). *Little house on the prairie*. New York: Harper.

Wildsmith, B. (1982). *Cat on the mat*. New York: Oxford University Press.

Wildsmith, B. (1988). *Squirrels*. New York: Oxford University Press.

Williams, M. (1926). *The velveteen rabbit*. New York: Doubleday.

Winthrop, E. (2006). *Counting on Grace*. New York: Random House.

Withers, C. (Ed.). (1948). *A rocket in my pocket: The rhymes and chants of young Americans*. New York: Holt.

Yashima, T. (1955). *Crow boy*. New York: Viking.

Yep, L. (1975). *Dragonwings*. New York: Harper.

Yep, L. (1991). *The star fisher*. New York: Morrow.

Ziefert, H. (1984). *Sleepy dog*. New York: Random House.

Ziefert, H. (1993). *Jason's bus ride*. New York: Puffin.

Ziefert, H. (1998). *I swapped my dog*. Boston: Houghton Mifflin.

Zion, G. (1956). *Harry the dirty dog*. New York: Harper.

Photo Credits

Index

Page numbers followed by *f* or *t* indicate figures or tables, respectively.